THE
ALL ENGLAND
LAW REPORTS

1973
VOLUME I

CONSULTING EDITOR
Paul H Niekirk MA
of Gray's Inn, Barrister

EDITOR
R N G Harrison BA
of Lincoln's Inn, Barrister

ASSISTANT EDITOR
Christine Ivamy MA
of Gray's Inn, Barrister

LONDON
BUTTERWORTHS

ENGLAND: Butterworth & Co (Publishers) Ltd
                London: 88 Kingsway, WC2B 6AB

AUSTRALIA: Butterworths Pty Ltd
                Sydney: 586 Pacific Highway, Chatswood, NSW 2067
                Melbourne: 343 Little Collins Street, 3000
                Brisbane: 240 Queen Street, 4000

CANADA: Butterworth & Co (Canada) Ltd
                Toronto: 14 Curity Avenue, 374

NEW ZEALAND: Butterworths of New Zealand Ltd
                Wellington: 26-28 Waring Taylor Street, 1

SOUTH AFRICA: Butterworth & Co (South Africa) (Pty) Ltd
                Durban: 152-154 Gale Street

ISBN 0 406 85105 0

Printed in Great Britain by R J Acford Ltd, Industrial Estate, Chichester, Sussex.

REPORTERS

House of Lords
S A Hatteea Esq Barrister

Privy Council
S A Hatteea Esq Barrister

Court of Appeal, Civil Division
F A Amies Esq Barrister

Wendy Shockett Barrister

L J Kovats Esq Barrister

Mary Rose Plummer Barrister

Ilyas Khan Esq Barrister

Court of Appeal, Criminal Division
N P Metcalfe Esq Barrister

Courts-Martial Appeals
N P Metcalfe Esq Barrister

Chancery Division
Jacqueline Metcalfe Barrister

R W Farrin Esq Barrister

Susan Corbett Barrister

Queen's Bench Division
Jacqueline Charles Barrister

M Denise Chorlton Barrister

J M Collins Esq Barrister

Janet Harding Barrister

D Morgan Hughes Esq Barrister

E H Hunter Esq Barrister

Gwynedd Lewis Barrister

Deirdre McKinney Barrister

Family Division
R C T Habesch Esq Barrister

National Industrial Relations Court
Gordon H Scott Esq Barrister

Rating Cases
F A Amies Esq Barrister

Admiralty
N P Metcalfe Esq Barrister

Revenue Cases
F A Amies Esq Barrister

Rengan Krishnan Esq Barrister

MANAGER
John W Wilkes Esq

House of Lords

The Lord High Chancellor: Lord Hailsham of Saint Marylebone

Lords of Appeal in Ordinary

Lord Reid	Lord Diplock
Lord Morris of Borth-y-Gest	Lord Simon of Glaisdale
Viscount Dilhorne	Lord Cross of Chelsea
Lord Wilberforce	Lord Kilbrandon
Lord Pearson	Lord Salmon

Court of Appeal

The Lord High Chancellor

The Lord Chief Justice of England: Lord Widgery

The Master of the Rolls: Lord Denning

The President of the Family Division: Sir George Gillespie Baker

Lords Justices of Appeal

Sir William Arthian Davies	Sir David Arnold Scott Cairns
Sir Charles Ritchie Russell	Sir Edward Blanshard Stamp
Sir Eric Sachs	Sir John Frederick Eustace Stephenson
(retired 10th January 1973)	Sir Alan Stewart Orr
Sir Herbert Edmund Davies	Sir Eustace Wentworth Roskill
Sir Henry Josceline Phillimore	Sir Frederick Horace Lawton
Sir Seymour Edward Karminski	Sir Leslie George Scarman
(retired 10th January 1973)	(appointed 11th January 1973)
Sir John Megaw	Sir Arthur Evan James
Sir Denys Burton Buckley	(appointed 11th January 1973)

Chancery Division

The Lord High Chancellor
The Vice-Chancellor: Sir John Pennycuick

Sir John Anthony Plowman
Sir Reginald William Goff
Sir Robert Edgar Megarry
Sir John Patrick Graham
Sir Peter Harry Batson Woodroffe Foster
Sir John Norman Keates Whitford

Sir John Anson Brightman
Sir Ernest Irvine Goulding
Sir Sydney William Templeman
Sir Raymond Henry Walton
    (appointed 11th January 1973)

Queen's Bench Division

The Lord Chief Justice of England

Sir John Percy Ashworth
Sir George Raymond Hinchcliffe
Sir Aubrey Melford Steed Stevenson
Sir Gerald Alfred Thesiger
Sir Basil Nield
Sir Bernard Joseph Maxwell MacKenna
Sir Alan Abraham Mocatta
Sir John Thompson
Sir Daniel James Brabin
Sir Helenus Patrick Joseph Milmo
Sir Joseph Donaldson Cantley
Sir Patrick Reginald Evelyn Browne
Sir George Stanley Waller
Sir Arthur Evan James
    (appointed Lord Justice of Appeal, 11th
    January 1973)
Sir Hugh Eames Park
    (transferred from Family Division, 11th
    January 1973)
Sir Ralph Vincent Cusack
Sir Stephen Chapman
Sir John Ramsay Willis
Sir Graham Russell Swanwick
Sir John Francis Donaldson
Sir Geoffrey Dawson Lane
Sir Patrick McCarthy O'Connor

Sir John Robertson Dunn Crichton
Sir Samuel Burgess Ridgway Cooke
    (appointed Chairman of the Law Com-
    mission, 11th January 1973)
Sir Bernard Caulfield
Sir Nigel Cyprian Bridge
Sir Sebag Shaw
Sir Hilary Gwynne Talbot
Sir Edward Walter Eveleigh
Sir William Lloyd Mars-Jones
Sir George Joseph Bean
Sir Ralph Kilner Brown
Sir Phillip Wien
Sir Peter Henry Rowley Bristow
Sir Hugh Harry Valentine Forbes
Sir Desmond James Conrad Ackner
Sir William Hugh Griffiths
Sir Robert Hugh Mais
Sir Neil Lawson
Sir David Powell Croom-Johnson
Sir John Raymond Phillips
Sir Leslie Kenneth Edward Boreham
Sir John Douglas May
Sir Michael Robert Emanuel Kerr
Sir Alfred William Michael Davies
    (appointed 11th January 1973)

Family Division

The President of the Family Division

Sir Geoffrey Walter Wrangham
    (retired 10th January 1973)
Sir Roger Fray Greenwood Ormrod
Sir Charles William Stanley Rees
Sir Reginald Withers Payne
Sir Neville Major Ginner Faulks
Sir Robert James Lindsay Stirling
Sir James Roualeyn Hovell-Thurlow
    Cumming-Bruce
Sir John Brinsmead Latey
Sir Hugh Eames Park
    (transferred to Queen's Bench Division,
    11th January 1973)

Dame Elizabeth Kathleen Lane
Sir Henry Vivian Brandon
Sir Robin Horace Walford Dunn
Sir William Arthur Bagnall
Sir Alfred Kenneth Hollings
Sir Tasker Watkins VC
Sir John Lewis Arnold
Sir Charles Trevor Reeve
    (appointed 11th January 1973)
Sir Morris Finer
    (appointed 11th January 1973)

CITATION

These reports are cited thus:

[1973] 1 All ER

REFERENCES

These reports contain references, which follow after the headnotes, to the following major works of legal reference described in the manner indicated below—

Halsbury's Laws of England, Simonds Edition

The reference 2 Halsbury's Laws (3rd Edn) 20, para 48, refers to paragraph 48 on page 20 of volume 2 of the third edition of Halsbury's Laws of England, of which the late Viscount Simonds was Editor-in-Chief.

Halsbury's Statutes of England

The reference 5 Halsbury's Statutes (3rd Edn) 302 refers to page 302 of volume 5 of the third edition of Halsbury's Statutes of England.

English and Empire Digest

References are to the replacement volumes (including reissue volumes) of the Digest, and to the continuation volumes of the replacement volumes.

The reference 31 Digest (Repl) 244, 3794, refers to case number 3794 on page 244 of Digest Replacement Volume 31.

The reference Digest (Cont Vol B) 287, 7540b, refers to case number 7540b on page 287 of Digest Continuation Volume B.

The reference 28 (1) Digest (Reissue) 167, 507, refers to case number 507 on page 167 of Digest Replacement Volume 28 (1) Reissue.

Halsbury's Statutory Instruments

The reference 12 Halsbury's Statutory Instruments (Second Re-issue) 124, refers to page 124 of the second re-issue of volume 12 of Halsbury's Statutory Instruments; references to subsequent re-issues are similar.

Encyclopaedia of Forms and Precedents

The reference 7 Ency Forms & Precedents (4th Edn) 247, Form 12, refers to Form 12 on page 247 of volume 7 of the fourth edition, of the Encyclopaedia of Forms and Precedents.

Cases reported in volume 1

Index

Cases noted

Statutes, etc, noted

Words and Phrases

Corrigenda

[1972] 3 All ER

  p 1084.   **T Wright & Son (Hull) Ltd v Westoby (Saffman & Co, garnishees).** Line b 2: solicitors for the judgment creditors: read *'Lucien A Isaacs & Co,* agents for *Gosschalk, Austin & Wheldon,* Hull.'

[1973] 1 All ER

  p 2.   **R v Hall (PB).** Line h 4: for '11th May 1971' read '11th May 1972'.

R v Hall (P B)

COURT OF APPEAL, CRIMINAL DIVISION
KARMINSKI LJ, O'CONNOR AND FORBES JJ
10th, 20th OCTOBER 1972

c

Criminal law – Evidence – Admissibility – Hearsay – Evidence of witness given at earlier trial – Transcript of evidence – Death of witness – Discretion to admit transcript evidence – Authentication of transcript – New trial ordered after jury disagreeing – Death of witness before second trial – Transcript of witness's evidence at first trial admissible at second trial – Method of authenticating transcript – Exercise of discretion whether to admit evidence.

d

The appellant was charged with uttering forged dollar notes. His defence was that R had given him the notes to change for him. At the trial R was called by the Crown and denied that he had given any notes to the appellant. R was an unsatisfactory witness, however, and his evidence contained contradictions on one or two matters. The jury failed to agree on their verdict and a new trial was ordered. Before the

e

second trial R died and at that trial the defence sought to put in the transcript of R's evidence at the earlier trial to show that R had been an evasive and unreliable witness, and that the appellant had not made up his story after R's death. The trial judge ruled, however, that the transcript was inadmissible under the rule against hearsay evidence. The appellant was convicted and appealed.

f

Held – (i) The transcript of a witness's evidence given at a previous trial was admissible at common law in criminal cases if the witness was dead, provided that the transcript was authenticated in some appropriate way, e g by calling the shorthand writer who had taken the original note. The judge had a discretion, however, to exclude such evidence if he considered that it would be unfair to the accused to admit it (see p 7 b to d, post).

g

(ii) It followed that the judge was wrong in holding that he had no discretion to admit the transcript of R's evidence. Since it was impossible to say that the jury would without doubt have convicted the appellant if the transcript had been admitted, the appeal would be allowed and the conviction quashed (see p 7 e and f, post).

R v Radbourne (1787) 1 Leach 457, *R v Smith* (1817) Holt NP 614 and *R v Beeston* (1854) Dears CC 405 applied.

h

Per Curiam. It may be that the absence of opportunity to observe the demeanour of the witness would be a powerful factor to be taken into account in considering whether to exercise the discretion to admit a transcript of the witness's evidence given in the earlier trial (see p 7 d, post).

Notes

j

For admissibility of evidence in criminal cases, see 15 Halsbury's Laws (3rd Edn) 263, 264, para 481; for judge's discretion as to admissibility, see ibid, 274, para 499; and for cases on the subject, see 14 Digest (Repl) 313, 314, 2993-3001.

Cases referred to in judgment

Customs and Excise Comrs v Harz [1967] 1 All ER 177, [1967] 1 AC 760, [1967] 2 WLR 297, 131 JP 146, 51 Cr App Rep 123, HL, Digest (Cont Vol C), 211, 4507a.

R v Beeston (1854) Dears CC 405, 24 LJMC 5, 24 LTOS 100, 18 JP 728, 6 Cox CC 425, *a*
   169 ER 782, CCR, 14 Digest (Repl) 314, *2996*.
R v Christie [1914] AC 545, [1914-15] All ER Rep 63; sub nom *Public Prosecutions Director*
   v Christie 83 LJKB 1097, 111 LT 220, 78 JP 321, 24 Cox CC 249, 10 Cr App Rep 141,
   HL, 14 Digest (Repl) 405, *3962*.
R v Edmunds (1909) 2 Cr App Rep 257, CCA, 14 Digest (Repl) 314, *3000*.
R v Ledbetter, Jenkins, Brain & Goode (1850) 3 Car & Kir 108, 175 ER 483, 14 Digest *b*
   (Repl) 313, *2993*.
R v Lee (1864) 4 F & F 63, 176 ER 468, 14 Digest (Repl) 308, *2938*.
R v Radbourne (1787) 1 Leach 457, 168 ER 330, CCR.
R v Smith (1817) Russ & Ry 339, Holt NP 614, 2 Stark 208, 171 ER 357, CCR, 14 Digest
   (Repl) 313, *2994*.
Selvey v Director of Public Prosecutions [1968] 2 All ER 497, [1970] AC 304, [1968] 2 WLR *c*
   1494, 132 JP 430, 52 Cr App Rep 443, HL, Digest (Cont Vol C) 217, *5016b*.
Wright v Doe d Tatham (1834) 1 Ad & El 3, 110 ER 1108; *subsequent proceedings*
   (1838) 4 Bing NC 489, 7 LJEx 363; sub nom *Wright v Tatham* (1838) 5 Cl & Fin 670,
   2 Jur 461, 7 ER 559, HL, 22 Digest (Repl) 364, *3928*.

Cases and authorities also cited   *d*
Doncaster (Corpn) v Day (1810) 3 Taunt 262, 128 ER 104.
Forest Lake, The, Steamer Janet Quinn (owners) v Motor Tanker Forest Lake (owners) [1966]
   3 All ER 833, [1968] P 270.
Llanover v Homfray, Phillips v Llanover (1881) 19 Ch D 224, CA.
Ratten v Reginam [1971] 3 All ER 801, [1972] AC 378, PC.
R v Cooper [1969] 1 All ER 32, [1969] 1 QB 267, CA.   *e*
R v Noakes [1917] 1 KB 581, CCA.
Archbold's Criminal Pleading, Evidence and Practice (37th Edn, 1969), pp 316-318,
   paras 891-893.
Cross on Evidence (3rd Edn, 1967), pp 293, 381.
Phipson on Evidence (11th Edn, 1970), p 277, para 647.

                                                                       f

Appeal
On 11th May 1972 at Middlesex Crown Court before Judge Olsen and a jury the
appellant, Peter Barnabas Hall, was convicted at a retrial on counts 1 and 3 of uttering
forged documents, on count 2 of obtaining money on a forged instrument and on
count 4 of attempting to obtain money on a forged instrument. He was sentenced
to concurrent terms of nine months' imprisonment on counts 1, 2 and 3, and to six *g*
months' imprisonment, also concurrent, on count 4 making nine months' imprisonment in all. He appealed against his convictions with leave of Cusack J. The facts are
set out in the judgment of the court.

A J Brigden for the appellant.   *h*
D C J Paget for the Crown.

                                                          Cur adv vult

20th October. **FORBES J** read the judgment of the court at the invitation of
Karminski LJ. On 11th May 1971 at Middlesex Crown Court the appellant was *j*
convicted on two counts of uttering forged documents, on one count of obtaining
money on a forged instrument and on another of attempting to obtain money by a
forged instrument—four counts in all. He was sentenced to nine months' imprisonment on the first three counts, and six months' imprisonment on the fourth count.
   The appellant was a customs officer at material times on duty at Heathrow Airport.
There was evidence that there is always one bank open day and night, and banks

a take it in turn to provide that facility. It was common ground that on 16th April 1971 the appellant, dressed in his uniform as customs officer, went to Lloyds Bank at Heathrow at 10.00 a m, and obtained from the bank a little over £81 by producing two United States 100 dollar notes which were in fact forged. He signed a receipt in which he gave his correct name and address. On the next day he went to Midland Bank at Heathrow at 1.00 a m and attempted to cash two further similar forged *b* notes. They were detected by the cashier who called the police.

The appellant's story, in which he persisted at all times after his initial prevarication, was that he had got the notes from a Mr Reeve. Mr Reeve was the publican at the public house which, the appellant said, he frequented. He and Mr Reeve, it was said, were on very good terms as evidenced by invitations to dinner extended by Mr Reeve, the fact that Mr Reeve was in the habit of cashing cheques for him and certain *c* other matters. Mr Reeve told him a story about changing the notes for a man called Ron, who had something to do with a fairground and who came to the public house occasionally. The appellant went into a considerable amount of detail about what he was told by Mr Reeve and about the way in which the notes were handed over. Mr Reeve was a man of 70, in poor health who was at the time confined to a wheelchair which made it difficult for him to go to a bank himself.

d When the matter first came to trial, the Crown called Mr Reeve. He denied entirely that he had given the notes to the appellant. When cross-examined, he contradicted himself on one or two matters, the questions which he answered being designed to show that he and the appellant were on very friendly terms. The transcript of his evidence shows these discrepancies, and also gives the impression that he was perhaps a testy and cantankerous witness. Counsel for the Crown in this court *e* (who was not counsel who appeared at either of the trials) told us that he was instructed that both counsel for the Crown at the first trial and the police officer in charge of the case, regarded Mr Reeve as an unsatisfactory witness. In the event, despite being told about the possibility of a majority verdict, the jury failed to agree, and a new trial was ordered.

Before the new trial came on, Mr Reeve died. Solicitors for the prosecution wrote *f* to the defence solicitors saying that although they proposed to proceed with the case without his evidence, they would not oppose an application by the defence that the transcript of Mr Reeve's evidence or his depositions should be put before the jury. When the new trial began, counsel for the Crown (who was not counsel in the first trial nor counsel before this court), while making it clear he was not opposing the application, pointed out that s 13 of the Criminal Justice Act 1925 only applied to depositions before justices, and not to transcripts of evidence at a previous trial, *g* and that although the Criminal Appeal Act 1968, Sch 2, para 1, allows the reading of a transcript of evidence given at the original trial, that referred only to retrials ordered by the Court of Appeal. Neither of these matters pertained in this second trial. Counsel for the appellant then made an application to the trial judge for the transcript of Mr Reeve's evidence to be put in or alternatively the shorthand writer *h* called to give evidence that he had heard Mr Reeve give that evidence and had transcribed the questions and answers. Counsel made it clear that the reason he wanted this evidence in was twofold: first, because he hoped to persuade the jury, by reference to the transcript, that Mr Reeve was at least an evasive, if not a lying, witness, and secondly, because it was important to establish both that Mr Reeve was dead and that the appellant had not just made up this story on the spur of the moment after *j* Mr Reeve had died, but had made the allegations at a time when Mr Reeve would have had a chance to rebut them.

The trial judge overruled defence counsel's submission, and apparently took the view that although Mr Reeve's deposition was admissible under the Criminal Justice Act 1925, the transcript of his evidence was not and that any evidence of what he had said at the previous trial was inadmissible under the hearsay rule. The trial therefore proceeded without Mr Reeve's evidence, although the judge did refer in his summing-up to the fact that Mr Reeve had died and in previous proceedings these matters were put to him.

We have heard argument from counsel on both sides for which we are greatly indebted. Counsel for the appellant relied, inter alia, on certain passages from the well-known American textbook, Wigmore's Treatise on the Anglo-American System of Evidence. Despite our regard for that learned work, this court thinks that the matter can be looked at in the light of the English authorities.

It seems plain that a transcript of evidence given in previous proceedings, at least where the evidence was on oath, was in a suit between the same parties, and where the evidence was open to cross-examination by the opposing party, was at common law admissible in civil proceedings. In *Wright v Doe d Tatham*[1] Tindal CJ had this to say:

> 'Now, if the former trial had taken place in a suit between Mr. Wright and Mr. Tatham, and those persons alone, no doubt could have been raised that, after the death of this witness, the evidence which he gave upon the former trial would have been admissible upon the second. For, in that case, it would have been evidence given in a suit between the very same parties, upon the same subject-matter, at a trial on which Mr. Tatham had the right to object to the competency of the witness, to cross-examine him at the trial, and to contradict him by other testimony. Upon such a state of facts, therefore, it is unnecessary to cite cases to the point, that the evidence of this witness, given on the former occasion, would, after his death, be admissible at the second trial.'

In other words, Tindal CJ regarded it as trite law in 1834 that in these circumstances evidence given at the earlier trial would be admissible in the later, but these of course were civil proceedings. No case has been cited to us, and we have been able to find none, where it has been held that the evidence given at a previous criminal trial was admissible in a subsequent criminal trial, but counsel for the appellant has argued that there is and should be no difference between the laws of evidence applicable to civil and criminal suits. He said that such evidence could only be excluded because it was hearsay, and the rationale of the hearsay rule is that such testimony suffers from the four defects traditionally said to apply to it, that it is not on oath, that it is not cross-examined, that there is no opportunity of observing the demeanour of the witness, and that there may be a danger of inaccuracy through repetition; he then argued that none of these defects applies to the transcript of evidence in previous proceedings, except that the demeanour of the witness cannot necessarily be gleaned from perusing the transcript.

These arguments apply, of course, equally to evidence in civil as in criminal matters. Although there is no direct authority relating to the admissibility of evidence given at a previous criminal trial, it is possible, we think, to extract a principle from a consideration of some of the other cases.

It is convenient to refer at the outset to a note in Stephen's Digest of the Law of Evidence[2]. The note concerns evidence in former proceedings:

> 'In reference to this subject it has been asked whether this principle applies indiscriminately to all kinds of evidence in all cases. Suppose a man were to be tried twice upon the same facts—e.g. for robbery after an acquittal for murder—and suppose that in the interval between the two trials an important witness who had not been called before the magistrates were to die, might his evidence be read on the second trial from a reporter's shorthand notes? This case might easily have occurred if Orton had been put on his trial for forgery as well as for perjury. I should be disposed to think on principle that

---

1 (1834) 1 Ad & El 3 at 18, 19
2 12th Edn (1936), pp 199, 200, note to art 33

a   such evidence would be admissible, though I cannot cite any authority on
     the subject. The common law principle on which depositions taken before
     magistrates and in Chancery proceedings were admitted seems to cover the
     case.'

     The common law principle to which that learned judge referred can be deduced
     from a number of cases of which the earliest appears to be R v Radbourne[1]. In that
b   case a lady called Mrs Morgan was severely wounded by her servant, the accused
     In view of her serious condition her deposition was taken, in the presence of the
     accused, before two justices in accordance with the statutes of Philip and Mary[2].
     These statutes provided machinery for the taking of such depositions but did not
     themselves provide for reception in evidence of the depositions so taken.   Some
     time after the taking of the depositions Mrs Morgan died and Henrietta Radbourne
c   was charged with petty treason and murder. She was acquitted of the former offence
     but convicted of murder. Much of the argument in the case turned on whether the
     acquittal for the petty treason necessarily involved an acquittal for the murder also.
     But one of the important pieces of evidence at the trial had been Mrs Morgan's
     deposition which prosecuting counsel had contended was admissible, either as a dying
     declaration or an information taken on oath before a regular magistrate under the
d   statutes of Philip and Mary. The court of trial had admitted the deposition and the
     question of its admissibility was one of the matters referred for the consideration
     of the 12 judges. Their decision was recorded thus[3]:

        'Mr. Recorder, on the first day of the December Session following, reported,
        that it was the unanimous opinion of eleven Judges, Lord Mansfield being absent,
e   that the learned Judge did right in admitting the information of Hannah Morgan
        to be received in evidence, and that the prisoner was legally convicted of murder
        on the indictment and inquisition for petit treason.'

     It is not clear, of course, whether it was held admissible as a dying declaration or an
     information on oath, but this matter is referred to in later cases which I shall deal
f   with in a moment.
        The next case is R v Smith[4]. Here again a deposition was taken from the deceased
     before he died, although at that time the defendant was only charged with assault.
     The main argument put forward in objecting to its admission was that it was taken
     on another charge. It appears to have been conceded by counsel for the defence that
     it would have been admissible on the same charge. Again the matter was referred
g   for consideration of the judges, whose opinion is recorded thus[5]:

        'In Michaelmas term, 1817, eleven of THE JUDGES met, and considered this
        case, (GIBBS C.J., being absent). Ten of the learned JUDGES thought the conviction
        right; and that the deposition had been properly received in evidence. ABBOTT J.,
        thought the evidence ought not to have been received. DALLAS J., GRAHAM B.,
        RICHARDS C.B., and LORD ELLENBOROUGH, stated that they should have doubted
h   of the admissibility of the evidence, but for the case of Rex v. Radbourne[1] . . .'

     Following that there is the important case of R v Beeston[6]. Here again a deposition
     was taken from the victim of a violent assault in the presence of the accused who was
     at that time charged with wounding with intent. On the death of the victim the

j   1   (1787) 1 Leach 457
     2   1 & 2 Ph & M c 13 (1554) and 2 & 3 Ph & M c 10 (1555), both repealed by 7 Geo 4 c 64, s 32
         (1826)
     3   (1787) 1 Leach at 462
     4   (1817) Russ & Ry 339, Holt NP 614
     5   (1817) Russ & Ry at 341
     6   (1854) Dears CC 405

accused was charged with murder and counsel for the prosecution offered in evidence   *a*
the deposition. Despite objection, the deposition was admitted and the accused was
convicted. The matter was referred for the opinion of the Court of Crown Cases
Reserved. The argument for rejection of the evidence was in part again that of
deposition was taken on a different charge, but defence counsel also argued that
the deposition was not admissible independently of the statute. That statute was
s 17 of the Indictable Offences Act 1848 (which was replaced by s 13 of the Criminal   *b*
Justice Act 1925) and provided in terms for the admission of depositions at a
subsequent trial if the deponent was, inter alia, dead. Jervis CJ had this to say[1]:

> 'We are unanimously of opinion that this deposition was under the circums-
> tances admissible in evidence against the prisoner. Notwithstanding the decision
> in *Reg.* v. *Ledbetter*[2], it is quite clear that before the passing of the 11 & 12 Vict.
> c. 42 [i e the Indictable Offences Act 1848], the deposition would have been admis-   *c*
> sible, and on this point the cases are all one way. In *Rex* v. *Radbourne*[3], the
> deposition of a deceased person was read on a trial for the murder of that person,
> and the decision in that case was acted upon in *Rex* v. *Smith*[4]. There, upon a
> trial for murder, the deposition of the deceased before a magistrate on a charge
> of assault against the prisoner was received in evidence, and upon a question
> submitted for the consideration of the Judges, ten of the eleven Judges who met   *d*
> and considered the case held that the deposition had been properly received in
> evidence. It is true, that in that case some of the Judges seem at first to have
> doubted as to the admissibility of the evidence; but they might well have done so
> without reference to the question now under discussion, for it is quite possible
> they might have thought that the prisoner had not in that case had sufficient
> means of cross-examination; but be this as it may, the Judges at all events held   *e*
> themselves bound by the previous decision in *Rex* v. *Radbourne*[3], and there is
> no reason why we, fortified as we are by a second decision, should depart from
> the convenient rule of abiding by decided cases; therefore, independently of the
> statute, we think that the deposition in this case would have been admissible . . .'

Martin B and Crowder J in their judgments[5] both expressly say that the deposition   *f*
was clearly admissible at common law. In that case the fact that the decision in
R v Ledbetter[2] did not indicate whether the deposition was held admissible as a
dying declaration or as an information on oath was referred to by counsel in argument,
and by founding themselves on *R v Radbourne*[3] the judges must be taken to have
rejected the former possibility. In *R v Lee*[6] where the victim's deposition was taken
on a charge of robbery and subsequently, after his death the two accused were   *g*
charged with murder, it was objected that the depositions were taken on the charge
of robbery and not murder. Pollock CB said[7]:

> 'Robbery with violence to the person. The deceased afterwards dying, the
> deposition is admissible on the charge of murder, not indeed as a dying deposi-
> tion, but as made in the presence of both prisoners with full opportunity of
> cross-examination.'   *h*

In a more modern case, *R v Edmunds*[8], both *R v Beeston*[9] and *R v Lee*[6] were cited
with approval by Lord Alverstone CJ.

---

1 (1854) Dears CC at 411, 412
2 (1850) 3 Car & Kir 108
3 (1787) 1 Leach 457   *j*
4 (1817) Russ & Ry 339, Holt NP 614
5 (1854) Dears CC at 414
6 (1864) 4 F & F 63
7 (1864) 4 F & F at 64, 65
8 (1909) 2 Cr App Rep 257 at 258
9 (1854) Dears CC 405

a From this line of authorities, we think it plain that a deposition properly taken before a magistrate on oath in the presence of the accused and where the accused has had the opportunity of cross-examination was always admissible at common law in criminal cases if the original deponent was dead, despite the absence of opportunity to observe the demeanour of the witness. The only difference between such a deposition and the transcript of evidence given at a previous trial is that the transcript is not signed by the witness. Provided it is authenticated in some appropriate way,
b as by calling the shorthand writer who took the original note, there seems no reason to think that such a transcript should not be equally receivable in evidence.

This is not to say that transcripts of previous testimony, because of this rule, are always to be received. The judge in a criminal trial still has a discretion to exclude such evidence if he considers it would be unfair to the prisoner (although not to the prosecution) to admit it. We do not desire to deal in detail with the principles affect-
c ing the use of this discretion. Its extent and the principles on which it is applied are conveniently set out in the well-known passage in the speech of Lord Moulton in *R v Christie*[1]. This passage was cited with approval in the recent case of *Selvey v Director of Public Prosecutions*[2]. I do not intend to quote the passage. It may be that the absence of opportunity to observe the demeanour of the witness could be a
d powerful factor to be taken into account in considering the exercise of such discretion.

The true position, therefore, as we see it is that the transcript of Mr Reeve's evidence was admissible, but the judge could have refused to receive it in evidence in his discretion if he thought its reception might prejudice the accused. In fact the judge considered that he had no discretion and ruled that in law the evidence was not admissible. No question of a wrongful exercise of discretion therefore arises and the ruling was, in our view, wrong.
e We have considered whether we should apply the proviso[3]. We bear in mind what was said by Lord Morris of Borth-y-Gest in *Customs and Excise Comrs v Harz*[4] on the subject of the disagreement of a jury at the first trial. We have only to note the fact of that disagreement in considering the effect which the admission of this evidence might have had on a reasonable jury properly directed. Doing so, and taking
f into consideration all the other circumstances, we have come to the conclusion that we could not say that such a jury would without doubt have convicted the appellant. The conviction will accordingly be quashed.

Appeal allowed. Conviction quashed.

Solicitors: *Registrar of Criminal Appeals* (for the appellant); *Director of Public*
g *Prosecutions.*

N P Metcalfe Esq Barrister.

---

1 [1914] AC 545 at 559, [1914-15] All ER Rep 63 at 69
h 2 [1968] 2 All ER 497, [1970] AC 304
3 I e to s 2 (1) of the Criminal Appeal Act 1968
4 [1967] 1 All ER 177 at 186, [1967] 1 AC 760 at 823

a

Heather (Inspector of Taxes) v P-E Consulting Group Ltd

COURT OF APPEAL, CIVIL DIVISION   b
LORD DENNING MR, BUCKLEY AND ORR LJJ
12th, 13th, 14th JULY 1972

*Income tax – Deduction in computing profits – Capital expenditure – Payments to trust fund
– Trust to enable employees to purchase shares in taxpayer company – Taxpayer company's
business dependent on highly qualified staff promoting business free from outside control –
Annual payments to trust fund related to taxpayer company's profits – Aggregate amount of* c
*payments unpredictable – Object of scheme to enable employees to acquire stake in taxpayer
company and to remove possibility of outside interference in business – Whether payments
to trust fund capital or revenue expenditure.*

*Income tax – Deduction in computing profits – Expenses – Payments wholly and exclusively
for purposes of trade – Payments to trust fund – Trust to enable employees to purchase* d
*shares in taxpayer company – Taxpayer company's business dependent on highly qualified
staff promoting business free from outside control – Object of scheme to enable employees to
acquire stake in taxpayer company and to remove possibility of outside interference in business
– Whether payments to trust fund wholly and exclusively for purposes of trade – Income
Tax Act 1952, s 137 (a).*

e

*Income tax – Computation of profit – Application of principles of commercial accountancy –
Evidence – Weight of evidence – Issue whether expenditure of a capital or revenue nature –
Issue a question of law for court to determine – Weight to be given to evidence as to practice
of commercial accountants – Evidence not binding on court.*

f

The shares in the taxpayer company were owned by a holding company. The shares
in the holding company were owned as to 41 per cent by the group's pension fund
and as to 59 per cent by outside shareholders. The taxpayer company carried on a
management consultancy business and had a professional staff of 310, all of whom
held university degrees or professional qualifications. The outside shareholders had
no professional qualifications. Following drastic changes in management made on
two occasions by the outside shareholders which upset the senior professional staff,   g
a scheme was introduced in accordance with s 54 (1) (b) of the Companies Act 1948 to
enable the employees to obtain control of the taxpayer company. A trust fund was
set up to purchase shares in the taxpayer company or the holding company to be
held by or for the benefit of employees of the taxpayer company. Under the scheme
the taxpayer company was to make annual payments to the trustees of the fund   h
amounting to 10 per cent of the consolidated profits of the group with a minimum of
£5,000 a year. The trustees were to use the fund to acquire shares in the taxpayer
company and the holding company so as to gain control. They were to hold them
for the benefit of the employees to whom they would offer them for sale, with
arrangements for them to be bought back by the trustees or other employees on the
death or retirement of an employee. If the trust came to an end the fund was to be   j
divided among the employees. The commissioners found that the objects of the
scheme were (a) to give staff an opportunity to purchase a stake in the taxpayer
company and (b) to remove the possibility of outside interference with the business
of the taxpayer company. In successive years the taxpayer company paid sums of
£5,000, £5,000, £16,412, £25,119 and £23,426 to the trustees. They claimed to deduct
those sums in computing their income for income tax purposes as being revenue

Dicta of LORD DENNING MR and
ORR LJ at 13, 19 applied in ECC
QUARRIES v WATKIS [1975] 3 All
ER 843

a expenditure constituting expenses incurred wholly exclusively in the course of their trade under s 137 (a)[a] of the Income Tax Act 1952.

Held – The payments were deductible in computing the taxpayer company's profits for the following reasons—
(i) the payments to the trust were revenue and not capital expenditure because (a) the object of the scheme was to enable the taxpayer company's business to be b carried on more efficiently, for the conduct of its business depended on the high qualifications and expertise of its staff and their efforts in promoting the taxpayer company's business free from outside interference; and (b) the expenditure consisted, not of a single payment on which the scheme depended, but of a series of annual payments, the aggregate of which was unpredictable, and none of which was in itself sufficient to achieve the object of the scheme (see p 13 b to e, p 15 j to p 16 b and c d to g, p 17 g to p 18 a and p 19 b to d, post); *Inland Revenue Comrs v Carron Co* (1968) 45 Tax Cas 18 applied; *British Insulated and Helsby Cables Ltd v Atherton* [1925] All ER Rep 623 explained and distinguished;
(ii) the payments had been incurred wholly and exclusively for the purposes of the taxpayer company's trade in that the taxpayer company was dependent on the qualifications and experience of its employees and the object of the scheme was to d retain their goodwill and to secure that control remained in their hands (see p 14 b, p 18 b and p 19 e, post); dictum of Lord Reid in *Morgan (Inspector of Taxes) v Tate & Lyle Ltd* [1954] 2 All ER at 429 distinguished.
Per Curiam. Although the evidence of accountants as to accountancy practice should be given due weight in determining whether expenditure is of a capital or revenue nature, the question is one of law for the court alone to determine and the e court is not bound by the evidence of accountants (see p 13 g and h, p 14 f and g and p 19 g and h, post).
Decision of Goulding J [1972] 2 All ER 107 affirmed.

Notes
For the deduction of trade expenses in computing profits for income tax purposes, f see 20 Halsbury's Laws (3rd Edn) 158-170, paras 277-292, and for cases on the subject, see 28 (1) Digest (Reissue) 141-158, 421-505.
For items ranking as capital expenditure, see 20 Halsbury's Laws (3rd Edn) 162-164, para 281, and for cases on the subject, see 28 (1) Digest (Reissue) 182-196, 544-608.
For the application of accountancy principles in computing profits, see 20 Halsbury's Laws (3rd Edn) 139, para 247.
g For the Companies Act 1948, s 54, see 5 Halsbury's Statutes (3rd Edn) 163.
For the Income Tax Act 1952, s 137, see 31 Halsbury's Statutes (2nd Edn) 134.
For the year 1970-71 and subsequent years of assessment, s 137 of the 1952 Act has been replaced by s 130 of the Income and Corporation Taxes Act 1970.

Cases referred to in judgments
Anglo-Persian Oil Co Ltd v Dale [1932] 1 KB 124, [1931] All ER Rep 725, 100 LJKB 504, h 145 LT 529, 16 Tax Cas 253, CA, 28 (1) Digest (Reissue) 185, 563.
Associated Portland Cement Manufacturers Ltd v Inland Revenue Comrs, Associated Portland Cement Manufacturers Ltd v Kerr (Inspector of Taxes) [1946] 1 All ER 68, 27 Tax Cas 103, CA, 28 (1) Digest (Reissue) 189, 582.
BP Australia Ltd v Comr of Taxation of the Commonwealth of Australia [1965] 3 All ER 209, [1966] AC 224, [1965] 3 WLR 608, [1966] ALR 274, PC, 28 (1) Digest (Reissue) 196, *598.
j *British Insulated and Helsby Cables Ltd v Atherton (Inspector of Taxes)* [1926] AC 205, [1925] All ER Rep 623, 95 LJKB 336, 134 LT 289, HL; *affg* CA sub nom *Atherton*

---

a Section 137 (a), so far as material, provides: '... in computing the amount of the profits or gains to be charged under Case I or Case II of Schedule D, no sum shall be deducted in respect of—(a) any disbursements or expenses, not being money wholly and exclusively laid out or expended for the purposes of the trade ...'

(*Inspector of Taxes*) *v British Insulated and Helsby Cables Ltd* [1925] 1 KB 421, 10 Tax   a
Cas 155, 28 (1) Digest (Reissue) 211, 627.
Comr of Taxes v Nchanga Consolidated Copper Mines Ltd [1964] 1 All ER 208, [1964]
AC 948, [1964] 2 WLR 339, PC, 28 (1) Digest (Reissue) 204, *677.
Inland Revenue Comrs v Carron Co (1968) 45 Tax Cas 18, 47 ATC 192, 1968 SC (HL) 47,
HL, 28 (1) Digest (Reissue) 196, 608.
Law Shipping Co Ltd v Inland Revenue Comrs 1924 SC 74, (1923) 12 Tax Cas 621, 28 (1)   b
Digest (Reissue) 599, *1480.
Mallett v Staveley Coal & Iron Co Ltd [1928] 2 KB 405, [1928] All ER Rep 644, 97 LJKB
475, 139 LT 241, 13 Tax Cas 772, CA, 28 (1) Digest (Reissue) 184, 557.
Morgan (*Inspector of Taxes*) *v Tate & Lyle Ltd* [1954] 2 All ER 413, [1955] AC 21, [1954]
3 WLR 85, 35 Tax Cas 367, HL, 28 (1) Digest (Reissue) 145, 437.
Odeon Associated Theatres Ltd v Jones (*Inspector of Taxes*) [1971] 2 All ER 407, [1971] 1   c
WLR 442; *affd* CA [1972] 1 All ER 681, [1972] 2 WLR 331, 28 (1) Digest (Reissue)
170, 517.
Regent Oil Co Ltd v Strick (*Inspector of Taxes*), *Regent Oil Co Ltd v Inland Revenue Comrs*
[1965] 3 All ER 174, [1966] AC 295, [1965] 3 WLR 636, HL; *affg* CA sub nom *Strick v
Regent Oil Co Ltd, Inland Revenue Comrs v Regent Oil Co Ltd* [1964] 3 All ER 23, [1964]
1 WLR 1166, 43 Tax Cas 1, 28 (1) Digest (Reissue) 183, 552.
   d
Van den Berghs Ltd v Clark [1935] AC 431, [1935] All ER Rep 874, 104 LJKB 345, 153
LT 171, 19 Tax Cas 390, HL, 28 (1) Digest (Reissue) 185, 564.

Appeal

P-E Consulting Group Ltd ('the taxpayer company') was incorporated in 1955 and had
an authorised share capital of £20,000 divided into 20,000 ordinary shares of £1 each,
of which 100 shares were issued and fully paid up. Almost all the issued shares in   e
the taxpayer company were held by P-E Holding Ltd ('the holding company'). A
third company, Barmel Investment Co Ltd ('Barmel'), which had been incorporated
for the investment of the group's pension fund, had by 1962 acquired 41 per cent of
the equity in the holding company. By 1962 the taxpayer company had become the
main trading company in the group, which provided services in managerial and
industrial consultancy. Its professional staff numbered 310, all of whom held univer-   f
sity degrees or professional qualifications. Following the death of the founder of
the business in 1957 senior professional staff became concerned at the prospect of
control of the holding company being exercised by outside shareholders with no
professional qualifications, and in 1962 a scheme was devised in accordance with
s 54 (1) (*b*) of the Companies Act 1948 to enable employees to purchase shares in the
taxpayer company and in the holding company. In July 1962 a first payment of   g
£5,000 was made by the taxpayer company to Barmel, which acted as temporary
bankers pending the formal setting up of a trust pursuant to s 54 (1) (*b*). In 1963 a
trust deed was entered into between the taxpayer company and trustees with a view
to enabling the trustees to acquire shares in the taxpayer company and the holding
company at a fair value (as defined) for the benefit of employees other than directors   h
and trustees. Under the deed the taxpayer company was to pay to the trustees 10
per cent of the consolidated gross profits of the taxpayer company (but not less
than £5,000) for each financial year for a period of 21 years commencing with 1962
(the first payment having already been made to Barmel) or until the trustees should
have acquired 40 per cent in nominal value of the shares of the holding company,
whichever should be the earlier. The taxpayer company could, however, discontinue,   j
suspend, reduce or increase those payments. The trustees had power at any time to
transfer to or for the benefit of a beneficiary under the trust any ordinary share of
the holding company or the taxpayer company on payment of the fair value by the
beneficiary to the trustees. The following payments were made by the taxpayer
company to the trustees: 1962 (via Barmel), £5,000; 1963, £5,000; 1964, £16,412;
1965, £25,119; 1966, £23,426. By 1966 the value per share in the holding company

a had risen to £20, and at the hearing of the appeals stood at £40. By 31st December 1966 no shares had been transferred to employees by the trustees but by the date of the hearing some 150 employees of the taxpayer company had acquired about 30-40 per cent of the shares in the holding company through the trust. The Special Commissioners held that the payments made by the taxpayer company to the trustees were allowable deductions in computing the taxpayer company's liability for income tax, profits tax and corporation tax. The commissioners accepted the evidence of an

b accountant that 'the cost to a company in securing and retaining the services of employees was usually treated as revenue expenditure' and that it was normal practice to write off expenditure for that purpose since it was impossible to evaluate 'employee goodwill'. The commissioners found that the objects of the scheme were broadly (a) to provide an incentive to greater effort on the part of the staff, and (b)

c 'to remove the possibility of outside interference with the business of the company'. The Crown required the commissioners to state a case for the opinion of the High Court[1]. By an order dated 10th December 1972 and reported at [1972] 2 All ER 107 Goulding J affirmed the commissioners' decision. The Crown appealed against the order of Goulding J on the following grounds: (i) that he was wrong in law in holding that the disputed payments made by the taxpayer company to the trust were revenue

d payments and properly deductible in computing the taxpayer company's taxable profits; (ii) that the true and only reasonable conclusion to be drawn from the facts found by the commissioners was that the taxpayer company had made the disputed payments for the purpose of bringing into existence an asset or advantage for the enduring benefit of the taxpayer company's trade and, therefore, the payments were properly to be regarded as capital payments and were not deductible in computing

e the taxpayer company's taxable profits; (iii) that the judge was wrong in law in holding that because of the evidence given by an accountant his decision should be governed by the decision of the Court of Appeal in *Odeon Associated Theatres Ltd v Jones (Inspector of Taxes)*[2]; (iv) that, if the judge was right in holding that the decision of the Court of Appeal in *Odeon Associated Theatres Ltd v Jones*[2] governed his decision, that case had been wrongly decided; (v) that, in any event, the judge was wrong in

f law in holding that the disputed payments were disbursements or expenses wholly and exclusively laid out for the purposes of the taxpayer company's trade and that the true and only reasonable conclusion to be drawn from the facts found by the commissioners was that the disputed payments were not made wholly and exclusively for the purposes of the taxpayer company's trade and, therefore, by virtue of s 137 (*a*) of the Income Tax Act 1952, the payments were not deductible in computing the taxpayer company's profits. The Crown also appealed against an order of Goulding J

g on a separate case stated relating to assessments to profits tax. The material facts and the grounds of appeal were the same in both appeals.

M P Nolan QC and *Patrick Medd* for the Crown.
S T Bates QC and *A R Thornhill* for the taxpayer company.

h **LORD DENNING MR.** The facts of this case are fully set out in the report of the court below[3]. I need therefore only set out the salient points. The taxpayer company, P-E Consulting Group Ltd, are management consultants. In 1962 they had a professional staff of 310, all of whom held university degrees or professional qualifications. The shares in the taxpayer company were all owned by a holding company, P-E Holdings Ltd. The shares in the holding company were owned in

j 1962 as to 41 per cent by the group's pension fund and as to 59 per cent by outside shareholders with no professional qualifications. On two occasions drastic changes in management had been made by the outside shareholders. This upset the senior

---

1 The case stated by the commissioners is set out at [1972] 2 All ER 109-115
2 [1972] 1 All ER 681, [1972] 2 WLR 331
3 [1972] 2 All ER 107, [1972] 2 WLR 918

professional staff. In consequence a scheme was introduced to enable the employees
to obtain control. The scheme was designed to take advantage of s 54 (1) (*b*) of the
Companies Act 1948. This enables a company to provide moneys for a trust fund
under which the trustees can purchase the company's own shares, or the shares of
a holding company—provided always that the shares are held by or for the benefit
of employees of the company. Under the scheme the taxpayer company was to pay
to the trustees 10 per cent of the consolidated profits of the group (with a minimum
of £5,000 a year). The trustees were to use that fund to acquire shares in the taxpayer
company and the holding company so as to gain control. The trustees were to hold
the shares for the benefit of the employees. They would offer them for sale to the
employees; but arrangements were made whereby, on death or retirement, the
shares were bought back by the trustees or other employees. If the trust came to an
end, the whole fund would be divided amongst the employees.

The commissioners found that the objects of the scheme were broadly (a) to give
staff an opportunity to purchase a stake in the taxpayer company, and (b) to remove
the possibility of outside interference with the business of the company. In pursuance
of the scheme, the taxpayer company paid these sums to the trustees: £5,000 for
the year 1962; £5,000 for 1963; £16,412 for 1964; £25,119 for 1965; £23,426 for 1966.

The taxpayer company contended that these payments were revenue expenditure
and were proper deductions to be made in computing the company's tax. The Crown
contended that they were instalments of capital and could not be deducted. The
commissioners held they were revenue expenditure and the judge[1] upheld them.
The Crown appeals.

The question—revenue expenditure or capital expenditure—is a question which
is being repeatedly asked by men of business, by accountants and by lawyers. In
many cases the answer is easy; but in others it is difficult. The difficulty arises
because of the nature of the question. It assumes that all expenditure can be put
correctly into one category or the other; but this is simply not possible. Some cases
lie on the border between the two; and this border is not a line clearly marked out;
it is a blurred and undefined area in which anyone can get lost. Different minds
may come to different conclusions with equal propriety. It is like the border between
day and night, or between red and orange. Everyone can tell the difference except
in the marginal cases; and then everyone is in doubt. Each can come down either
way. When these marginal cases arise, then the practitioners—be they accountants
or lawyers—must of necessity put them into one category or the other; and then,
by custom or by law, by practice or by precept, the border is staked out with more
certainty. In this area, at least, where no decision can be said to be right or wrong,
the only safe rule is to go by precedent. So the thing to do is search through the cases
and see whether the instant problem has come up before. If so, go by it. If not,
go by the nearest you can find.

One of the nearest cases to this one is *British Insulated and Helsby Cables Ltd v Atherton
(Inspector of Taxes)*[2] where a large sum was provided by a company to form the
nucleus of a pension fund for employees. Each year thereafter the company made
annual contributions to the fund. That was a marginal case. Different minds could,
and did, come to different conclusions with equal propriety. The reasoning in the
House of Lords shows it. The majority (three to two) held that this large initial
contribution was capital and not revenue expenditure; but all agreed that the annual
contribution thereafter was revenue expenditure. Viscount Cave LC for the
majority used a sentence which has been repeatedly quoted since[3]:

  ' . . . when an expenditure is made, not only once and for all, but with a view
  to bringing into existence an asset or an advantage for the enduring benefit of
  a trade, I think that there is very good reason (in the absence of special

---

1   [1972] 2 All ER 107, [1972] 2 WLR 918
2   [1926] AC 205, [1925] All ER Rep 623
3   [1926] AC at 213, 214, [1925] All ER Rep at 629

a   circumstances leading to an opposite conclusion) for treating such an expenditure as properly attributable not to revenue but to capital.'

In applying that case to the present, there are different views. Each can be held with equal propriety. The commissioners thought that this case did not fall within the *Atherton* decision[1]; but the judge thought it did, or at any rate that it fell within the language of Lord Cave LC. I must say that I agree with the commissioners.
b   It seems to me that the purpose of these payments was to provide an incentive for the staff, to make them more contented and ready to remain in the service of the taxpayer company, and also to help in the recruitment of new staff—they were annual payments too—all of which makes them more like the annual payments in *Atherton's* case[1] than the nucleus fund. They were like the taxpayer company's contributions to a cash profit sharing scheme and to the pension fund. They were all regarded by the
c   taxpayer company as rewards to staff for the profits they had helped to make.

There is this difference, however, from *Atherton's* case[1]. One of the objects here was to remove the possibility of outside interference with the business of the taxpayer company. Does this alter the nature of the payments? I think not. Here we have guidance from another case in the House of Lords, but it was not cited to the judge. It is *Inland Revenue Comrs v Carron Co*[2]. It came from Scotland. A company had a
d   charter and constitution which was out of date, so much so that it was inimical to the good running of the company. They could not get good managers or staff. The company paid considerable sums to amend the charter and to get rid of dissentient shareholders. Those payments were held to be revenue expenditure and not capital expenditure.

On the cases, therefore, it seems to me that the payments to the trust were revenue
e   and not capital expenditure. In addition, I have no doubt that the commissioners were influenced considerably by the evidence of a distinguished accountant, Mr Bailey of Messrs Price Waterhouse:

'Mr Bailey gave evidence (which we accepted) to the effect that the cost to a company in securing and retaining the services of employees was usually treated as revenue expenditure, and that as it was impossible to evaluate "employee
f   goodwill" it was the normal practice to write off expenditure for that purpose.'

The commissioners were entitled to give weight to that evidence of Mr Bailey, but the judge went further[3]. He seems to have thought that, as a result of the decision of this court in *Odeon Associated Theatres Ltd v Jones (Inspector of Taxes)*[4] the evidence of accountants should be treated as conclusive and that all the commis-
g   sioners or the court would have to do would be to evaluate their evidence. And counsel for the taxpayer company submitted to us that the *Odeon* case[4] had upgraded the evidence of accountants so that the commissioners and the courts were bound by their evidence to a greater degree than they had been in the past. I cannot agree with that for a moment. It seems to me that that case does not add to or detract from the value of accountancy evidence. The courts have always been assisted
h   greatly by the evidence of accountants. Their practice should be given due weight; but the courts have never regarded themselves as being bound by it. It would be wrong to do so. The question of what is capital and what is revenue is a question of law for the courts. They are not to be deflected from their true course by the evidence of accountants, however eminent. However in the end the judge agreed with the commissioners—as I agree with them—that the payments here were revenue and
j   not capital expenditure.

The other question is whether these payments were 'wholly and exclusively . . . for the purposes of the [taxpayer company's] trade' within s 137 (*a*) of the Income

1   [1926] AC 205, [1925] All ER Rep 623
2   (1968) 45 Tax Cas 18
3   [1972] 2 All ER at 121, [1972] 2 WLR at 934
4   [1972] 1 All ER 681, [1972] 2 WLR 331

Tax Act 1952. The Crown relied particularly on an observation by Lord Reid in
Morgan (Inspector of Taxes) v Tate & Lyle Ltd[1], in which he said:

> '... a change of shareholders does not interest the company as a trader, and
> expenditure to prevent a change of shareholders can hardly be expenditure for
> the purposes of the trade.'

That may in some circumstances be correct; but not in this case. This company is
dependent on a large number of graduates and professional men. The object of
the scheme is to keep their goodwill and to secure that the control will remain in
their hands. Both the commissioners and the judge found that the moneys were
wholly and exclusively for the purposes of the taxpayer company's trade. I think the
decisions of the commissioners and the judge were right and I would accordingly
dismiss the appeal.

BUCKLEY LJ. The question with which we are concerned in this case is whether
the payments which were made by the taxpayer company under cl 3 of the trust deed[2],
which is set out in extenso in the case stated, are deductible in calculating the profits
of the taxpayer company in the several years in which those payments were made
for tax purposes. The Crown submits that the question should be answered in the
negative, on two grounds. First, because the expenditure was not, it is submitted,
revenue expenditure but was expenditure of a capital nature. Secondly, because
the expenditure was not, it is submitted, made wholly and exclusively for the purposes of the taxpayer company's trade: s 137 (a) of the Income Tax Act 1952.
    It is common ground that the first of these questions is a question of law. In this
connection there has been a good deal of discussion about the effect of the evidence
of Mr Bailey to which Lord Denning MR has already referred. The judge was much
affected by this, as he says in the passage in his judgment[3] to which again Lord
Denning MR has already referred. I think that, if that passage is read in its literal
sense, it puts the effect of an expert accountant's evidence on such a matter too high.
It must be axiomatic that the evidence of no witness can be conclusive on a question
of law. It is well established that the question whether a particular payment is a
payment of a capital nature or of a revenue nature must be answered in accordance
with sound accountancy principles. Skilled accountants may well be much better
qualified than most judges to formulate and explain such principles; but nevertheless in every case of this kind it is the judge and not the witness who must decide
whether a witness's evidence in fact exemplifies sound accountancy principles. A
judge may, as Lord Wilberforce did in *Regent Oil Co Ltd v Strick (Inspector of Taxes)*[4]
reject the accountant's evidence, or he may accept it. I endeavoured to state this
position in *Odeon Associated Theatres Ltd v Jones*[5], and this I think precisely accords
with what was said by Pennycuick V-C in that case at first instance[6]. It also, I
think, accords with what was said by Salmon LJ in the Court of Appeal, where he
said this[7]:

> 'Where, however, there is evidence which is accepted by the court as establish-
> ing a sound commercial accounting practice conflicting with no Act, that normally
> is the end of the matter. The court adopts the practice, applies it and decides
> the case accordingly.'

1   [1954] 2 All ER 413 at 429, [1955] AC 21 at 55
2   See [1972] 2 All ER at 117, [1972] 2 WLR at 930
3   [1972] 2 All ER at 121, [1972] 2 WLR at 934
4   [1965] 3 All ER 174 at 206, [1966] AC 295 at 355, 356
5   [1972] 1 All ER 681 at 694, [1972] 2 WLR 331 at 340
6   [1971] 2 All ER 407 at 413, [1971] 1 WLR 442 at 454
7   [1972] 1 All ER at 691, [1972] 2 WLR at 337

a I emphasise the words 'which is accepted by the court as establishing a sound commercial accounting practice'. If Goulding J in the present case meant to attribute any more binding character than this to Mr Bailey's evidence, I would respectfully think that he went too far; but I doubt if he really intended to do so. I think he may well have meant no more than that in the state of the evidence in this case, he saw no reason to reject Mr Bailey's evidence, which consequently should be accepted as exemplifying sound principles of commercial accountancy.

b The Crown has claimed in the present case that it is governed by the decision in *Atherton's* case[1]. It has been emphasised in many cases of high authority that cases concerned with this particular problem must be considered in the light of their particular facts. I would refer to *Comr of Taxes v Nchanga Consolidated Copper Mines Ltd*[2], *BP Australia Ltd v Comr of Taxation of the Commonwealth of Australia*[3] per Lord Pearce and *Regent Oil Co Ltd v Strick*[4] per Lord Reid. The decision in *Atherton's*

c case[1] must have turned on the character of the payments there in question as being the nucleus of a new pension fund. The annual contributions which the company was thereafter to make under the pensions fund scheme were conceded to be deductible. I confess to sympathy with the views expressed by Lord Blanesburgh, who dissented in that case. He could see no difference in principle between the initial

d payment and the annual payments. The majority of the House of Lords, however, thought that there was such a difference, although I do not find it very easy to put a finger on any passage in any of the speeches which clearly states what the difference was. The fact that the payment was a single payment and not one of a series of recurrent payments is no doubt a circumstance to be taken into account, but cannot have been conclusive, any more than the circumstance that a payment is made by instalments or is a periodic payment of some other kind as the price of a capital

e asset could establish that those payments were not properly to be regarded as capital expenditure. It seems to me that the majority view in the House of Lords in *Atherton's* case[1] must have been founded on some such consideration as this: the company was anxious to establish a contributory pension scheme for its employees to which the company would itself contribute in circumstances which would allow a deduc-

f tion of its own contribution for tax purposes. It could not, however, establish such a scheme which would be solvent in respect of its existing senior employees unless a fund were initially provided to cover actuarial liabilities in respect of these employees. The establishment of such a fund was a condition precedent to the establishment of the contributory scheme. In order to open the way to the establishment of the scheme, the company itself provided the fund. That is what is called the

g nucleus fund. As an expenditure distinct from the company's subsequent contributions, it was a once-for-all expenditure, which made it possible for the company to embark on a scheme which would benefit its commercial activity. It might perhaps in fanciful language be said to have prepared the ground or provided the site on which the scheme itself should be erected. Seen in this light, the initial payment can perhaps justifiably be viewed as having a different character and being made with a

h different object from the company's subsequent annual contributions. In any case, I think it is worthy of note that judicial views differed as to what was the right interpretation of the position in *Atherton's* case[1]; the decision was a majority decision.

In the present case it seems to me that the payments with which we are concerned are different in their character in several respects, which may be material, from the sort of payment which was under consideration in *Atherton's* case[1]. In the first

j place, whereas the payment in question in *Atherton's* case[1] was a single payment, we are here concerned with a series of payments being made annually under the covenant contained in the trust deed. No one of those payments was in itself sufficient

1 [1926] AC 205, [1925] All ER Rep 623
2 [1964] 1 All ER 208, [1964] AC 948
3 [1965] 3 All ER 209 at 217, [1966] AC 224 at 263
4 [1965] 3 All ER at 179, [1966] AC at 313

to achieve the object of the scheme incorporated in the trust deed. The aggregate *a*
of those payments was unpredictable. The payments year by year were to be
calculated by reference to the fair value for the time being of the shares in the taxpayer company, which might vary year by year, and so it would be impossible at
any stage to say what moneys would have to be contributed by the taxpayer company in the future in order to achieve the objective of buying 40 per cent of the shares
of the taxpayer company at their fair value. Moreover, the taxpayer company *b*
could under the trust deed at any time have discontinued these contributions
or brought the whole scheme to an end. It is not a case in which the payments
can be regarded as instalments of a specified purchase price. The purposes for
which the scheme was established must I think be taken to have been those which
the commissioners found in the case stated to have been its purposes. They say:

> 'The objects of the scheme were broadly to be: (a) to give staff an opportunity *c*
> to purchase a stake in the [taxpayer] company, thereby providing an incentive
> to greater effort on their part; and (b) to remove the possibility of outside
> interference with the business of the [taxpayer] company.'

The first of those two objectives is one intimately connected with the day-to-day
operation of the taxpayer company's business, for the goodwill of the staff was some- *d*
thing which might change or fluctuate from day to day. The advantage to be obtained
by giving the staff an incentive to greater effort is one which would depend on the
state of the taxpayer company's business from time to time and the state of the
employer-employee relationship between the taxpayer company and its employees
from time to time. It was also an objective directly related to the profitability of the
taxpayer company's business from time to time. The taxpayer company was one *e*
which in its character depended for the efficient conduct of its trade on the high qualifications and expertise of its employees. The taxpayer company's business was that of
business management and industrial consultants, and the value of the services which
it provided depended to a very great extent on the quality and expertise of those
whom it employed and, as I think it right to infer, on these employees being permitted
to carry out their functions as management and industrial consultants uninterfered *f*
with or uninhibited by interference by any persons who were not as well qualified
to deal with the problems which had to be dealt with as they were themselves.
It was therefore a case in which the independence as well as the qualifications of
the staff—independence, I mean, from inhibiting superior supervision—were very
important to the welfare of the trade of the taxpayer company, and in that respect
it appears to me that the second objective which the commissioners found to obtain *g*
in this case was one directly related to the conduct of the taxpayer company's trade.
It seems to me that the present case comes much closer in its nature to *Inland
Revenue Comrs v Carron Co*[1] than it does to *Atherton's* case[2]. In the *Carron* case[1] the
company which was there under consideration had been established by a charter
in 1773 which had become archaic; so that the company was not able to operate
within the terms of its charter advantageously in the field of its trade, and the company *h*
therefore sought a new charter. Costs were incurred in obtaining the new charter,
but there was also a faction in the company among the shareholders which was
anxious to resist this reform in the company's constitution; and eventually a settlement of litigation between the company and this minority faction was compromised
on terms which involved a payment by the company to the minority who objected
to the reform. The House of Lords in that case came to the conclusion that the *j*
expenditure on obtaining the new charter and the expenditure on getting rid of
the opposition to the charter was a revenue expenditure. I think the passages which

---

1 (1968) 45 Tax Cas 18
2 [1926] AC 205, [1925] All ER Rep 623

a are perhaps most helpful to refer to are passages in the speech of Lord Wilberforce[1]. He had said[2] that he thought that the case then under consideration, the *Carron* case[3], was closer to a decision in *Anglo-Persian Oil Co Ltd v Dale*[4] than to another case, *Van den Berghs Ltd v Clark*[5]. Lord Wilberforce then said this[6]:

> b 'By contrast, in *Van den Bergh's* case[5] the payment was made in consideration of the recipient company cancelling an agreement which regulated the division of trading activity as between it and the paying company. It was in this context that Lord Macmillan used the words invoked by the Solicitor-General—"the whole structure of the appellant's profit-making apparatus"—and it is obvious that he used them in a sense quite different from any sense in which the Carron Company's "profit-making apparatus" may be said to have been affected here.
> c In *Van den Bergh's* case[5] the two companies traded in quite a different manner after the agreement from that in which they had traded before; the Carron Company's business was unaffected: it provided itself merely with the means of organising itself more effectively to trade more profitably.'

Lord Wilberforce then went on to comment on a submission which had been made by the Solicitor-General to the effect that, for expenditure to take on the d character of capital expenditure, it was not necessary for it to produce any recognisable capital asset. Lord Wilberforce pointed out that there must be something which can be pointed to as in the nature of a permanent advantage to the company if it is to be treated as expenditure on a capital asset. And then he said[1]:

> e 'Again, as was pointed out by Lord Morris of Borth-y-Gest in *Strick v. Regent Oil Co. Ltd.*[7], an asset may be of a capital nature whether it is of a tangible or of an intangible nature. I respectfully agree, but this does not assist the Solicitor-General's argument. Finally, the Solicitor-General relied for support in his contention upon *Mallett v. Staveley Coal & Iron Co. Ltd.*[8], but this only shows that the disposition of a source of liability may be equivalent to the acquisition of a source of profit—an extension perhaps, but not an exception, to the principle
> f that in some sense or other an asset of a capital nature, tangible or intangible, positive or negative, must be shown to be acquired. If this is correct—and until a case arises which constitutes a true exception I shall continue to think that it is—the present expenditure cannot be brought within the capital class. It procured indeed an advantage—important and not of a transitory nature— but one essentially of a revenue character in that it enabled the management and
> g conduct of the Company's business to be carried on more efficiently.'

Now, I for my part would say that in the present case the objects of this scheme were to enable the taxpayer company's business to be carried on more efficiently; they were directed to improving and maintaining the trading potential of the taxpayer company and facilitating its trading to advantage. I would myself think that h the present case fell much nearer to the *Carron* case[3] than to *Atherton's* case[9]; but once again I would say the case must be considered on its own facts and not, I think, be decided by reference to other cases with similar but not identical facts as binding

---

j 1 (1968) 45 Tax Cas at 75
2 (1968) 45 Tax Cas at 74
3 (1968) 45 Tax Cas 18
4 [1932] 1 KB 124, [1931] All ER Rep 725
5 [1935] AC 431, [1935] All ER Rep 874
6 (1968) 45 Tax Cas at 74, 75
7 [1965] 3 All ER at 189, [1966] AC at 329
8 [1928] 2 KB 405, [1928] All ER Rep 644
9 [1926] AC 205, [1925] All ER Rep 623

authority. On the facts of this particular case I have reached the conclusion that the learned judge was right in upholding the commissioners in the view that this *a* was an expenditure of a revenue nature.

Finally, as regards s 137 (*a*) of the Income Tax Act 1952, I would say that, having regard to the particular character of the taxpayer company and of its business and of the relation to that business of the qualifications and experience of the taxpayer company's employees, the expenditure here ought to be regarded as being expenditure incurred wholly and exclusively for the purposes of the taxpayer company's *b* trade.

For these reasons I agree that this appeal should be dismissed.

ORR LJ. In *British Insulated and Helsby Cables Ltd v Atherton (Inspector of Taxes)*[1] the respondent company established a pension fund by way of a trust deed for the *c* benefit of its salaried staff and contributed to that fund first a payment of some £31,000, calculated actuarially as the amount required in order that past years of service of the existing staff should rank for pension, and thereafter made successive yearly payments sufficient to raise the income from investment of the fund to a net 4 per cent. It was common ground that the latter payments were properly deductible in computing the profits and gains of the company for income tax purposes; *d* and the issue which arose was only as to the payment of £31,000 which was described in the trust deed as being made in order to form a nucleus of the pension fund. It was held by a majority of the House of Lords that that payment was in the nature of capital expenditure and not admissible as a deduction for tax purposes, and it was with reference to that payment that Viscount Cave LC made the statement which Lord Denning MR has quoted as to the characteristics of a capital expenditure. *e* Lord Carson and Lord Blanesburgh, dissenting, found it difficult to see how the object with which the payment of £31,000 was made differed in any way from the object of the succeeding payments; but in my judgment the basis of the majority decision was that the £31,000 was a sum which had to be expended before the scheme could begin to operate, and that the subsequent payments, on the other hand, merely represented annual servicing of the scheme after it had begun to operate. *f*

In the present case we are concerned with the establishment by the taxpayer company of a trust fund designed, like the pension fund in the *Atherton* case[1], to retain and attract employees and to improve the quality of their services, but in this case not by means of a pension fund but by enabling them to acquire shares in the taxpayer company. The means by which the scheme was to operate were that the taxpayer company would annually make payments to the trustees so as to enable *g* them, in accordance with directives given from time to time by the taxpayer company, to acquire shares in the taxpayer company or in the holding company which they would then sell to employees on terms that after the employee's death or on his leaving the taxpayer company or wishing to sell his shares, the taxpayer company would have a right to sell them as his agent and would offer them either to the trustees of one of its schemes or to some other employee. The taxpayer company contracted *h* to make these payments until the trustees should have acquired shares amounting to 40 per cent of the shares of the holding company or until the expiry of a period of 21 years, whichever should be the earlier, but the taxpayer company also retained the right on six months' notice to discontinue or suspend or reduce the payments.

It is not contended that any one of these payments differed at all in character from the others, the taxpayer company claiming that all of them were on revenue account, *j* and the Crown that they were all on capital account, for tax purposes. It has been common ground that if in law they represent a capital expenditure, that expenditure would not be deprived of its capital character by being paid in instalments,

---

1   [1926] AC 205, [1925] All ER Rep 623

a but that the fact that what is in question is a series of payments and not a single payment is a consideration to be taken into account in determining their character. The main issue in the case is whether these payments in their total represent a capital expenditure comparable to that involved in the payment of £31,000 in the *Atherton* case[1]. The argument for the Crown is that they did, on the basis that it was essential for the operation of the scheme that this expenditure should be incurred and that the object of it was to produce, if not an asset, at least an advantage for the

b enduring benefit of the trade.

There are, however, in my judgment, important differences between the facts of the *Atherton* case[1] and those of the present case. In the *Atherton* case[1] the scheme could not begin to operate until the expenditure was incurred; whereas in the present case it could begin to operate as soon as the taxpayer company's first contribution

c was made, inasmuch as that contribution could be applied at once in the acquisition of shares and so on from year to year. The total of the contributions to be made was indeterminate for the reasons given by Buckley LJ and also because the taxpayer company could at any time by six months' notice discontinue its contributions, and the payments were from the outset to be made by annual contribution. I have not found the case at all an easy one and have not reached a conclusion without some

d degree of doubt, but the conclusion I have come to is that the factors I have mentioned do materially differentiate this case from the *Atherton* case[1], and that the expenditure in question was for tax purposes incurred on revenue account. I also agree with the view expressed by both Lord Denning MR and Buckley LJ that the case is closer in all the circumstances to those of *Inland Revenue Comrs v Carron Co*[2] than to those of the *Atherton* case[1].

e As to the second issue, whether the expenditure was incurred wholly and exclusively for the purposes of the trade, I agree with the views expressed by Lord Denning MR and Buckley LJ and do not wish to add anything.

I would add, because I was a party to the decision in the recent *Odeon Associated Theatres Ltd v Jones (Inspector of Taxes)*[3], a few words with regard to the place of accountancy evidence in cases of this kind. The main issue in the *Odeon* case[3] was

f whether it was governed by the earlier decision in *Law Shipping Co Ltd v Inland Revenue Comrs*[4], and this court found a number of differences between the two cases of which only one was that accountancy evidence had been called in the *Odeon* case[3] but not in the *Law Shipping* case[4]. Nothing in any of the judgments in the *Odeon* case[3] throws any doubt on the proposition, which was common ground in this appeal and is supported by a long line of authority, that the question whether an

g expenditure is for tax purposes on revenue or on capital account is ultimately a question of law. Accountancy evidence may be helpful in a case of this kind insofar as it discloses in what manner accountants dealt in practice with a particular item; but it is for the court to decide whether what is done in practice is in accordance with sound accountancy practices; and, further, what is in other respects properly done in practice may not, for the reasons given by Lord Greene MR in *Associated Portland*

h *Cement Manufacturers Ltd v Inland Revenue Comrs*[5] accurately reflect the difference between income and capital expenditure for the purposes of income tax.

I agree that this appeal should be dismissed.

Appeal dismissed. Leave to appeal to the House of Lords.

Solicitors: *Solicitor of Inland Revenue; Waltons & Co* (for the taxpayer company).

j F A Amies Esq Barrister.

1 [1926] AC 205, [1925] All ER Rep 623
2 (1968) 45 Tax Cas 18
3 [1972] 1 All ER 681, [1972] 2 WLR 331
4 1924 SC 74
5 [1946] 1 All ER 68 at 70

Bellingham v Dhillon and another

QUEEN'S BENCH DIVISION

FORBES J

12th, 15th, 30th MAY 1972

Damages – Personal injury – Measure of damages – Loss of profits – Mitigation of loss – Same principle applicable in contract and tort – Plaintiff owner and manager of a business – Plaintiff injured as result of defendants' negligence – Plaintiff unable to complete negotiations for purchase of important piece of equipment for business – Plaintiff able to buy equipment at much reduced price 3½ years later – Plaintiff claiming loss of profits which would have accrued during 3½ years later if he had had equipment – Whether account to be taken of fact that breakdown of negotiations enabled plaintiff to acquire equipment at great saving of expense 3½ years later.

The plaintiff was the owner and manager of a driving school. In December 1965 he was injured in a motor accident as a result of the defendants' negligence. In 1967, in the course of his business, the plaintiff began negotiations for the acquisition of a simulator, an electronic device which enabled driving tuition to be given in a lecture room. The price was some £7,000. However, at a critical stage of the negotiations, the plaintiff suffered an onset of backache, a consequence of his injury, and had to receive medical treatment. As a result the transaction fell through. Thereafter he was unable to acquire a simulator until the autumn of 1971 when he bought a secondhand simulator at a total cost of £2,160. In an action by the plaintiff against the defendants, the plaintiff claimed a sum of £4,816, the loss of profits which would have been earned by the simulator between February 1968 and the autumn of 1971. It was common ground that, because the breakdown of negotiations in 1967 had enabled the plaintiff to acquire a simulator for only £2,160, his actual loss was nothing. The plaintiff contended, however, that in assessing damages in an action in tort, the court could not take account of an advantage which had come to him as a result of the accident but which would not have come to him but for the accident.

Held – Where a plaintiff's claim for damages was based on loss of profits of his business the damages were to be calculated in the same way whether the claim was in contract or tort, i e by taking the profits which the business would have earned but for the wrong which the plaintiff had suffered at the hands of the defendant and subtracting from that figure the profits which had in fact been earned after the wrong had been suffered. In making that calculation the court was bound to take into account any steps which the plaintiff, as a reasonable and prudent man of business, had taken to mitigate his loss. It followed that, as the plaintiff had suffered no loss on the simulator venture, he was not entitled to recover damages in respect thereof (see p 24 h to p 25 c, post).

British Westinghouse Electric and Manufacturing Co Ltd v Underground Electric Railways Co of London Ltd [1911-13] All ER Rep 63 applied.

Parry v Cleaver [1969] 1 All ER 555 distinguished.

Notes

For the duty of a plaintiff to mitigate loss, see 11 Halsbury's Laws (3rd Edn) 289-293, paras 476-481, and for cases on the subject, see 17 Digest (Repl) 106-112, 208-259.

For collateral liabilities and benefits in assessing the measure of damages, see 11 Halsbury's Laws (3rd Edn) 240, para 408, and for cases on the subject, see 17 Digest (Repl) 80, 81, 27-38.

a
Cases referred to in judgment

British Transport Commission v Gourley [1955] 3 All ER 796, [1956] AC 185, [1956] 2 WLR
   41, 220 LT 354, [1955] 2 Lloyd's Rep 475, HL, Digest (Cont Vol A) 462, 28a.

*British Westinghouse Electric and Manufacturing Co Ltd v Underground Electric Railways
   Co of London Ltd* [1912] AC 673, [1911-13] All ER Rep 63, 81 LJKB 1132, 107 LT 325,
   HL, 17 Digest (Repl) 108, 226.

b
Dunkirk Colliery Co v Lever (1878) 9 Ch D 20, CA, 17 Digest (Repl) 108, 225.

Parry v Cleaver [1969] 1 All ER 555, [1970] AC 1, [1969] 2 WLR 821, [1969] 1 Lloyd's
   Rep 183, HL, Digest (Cont Vol C) 750, 1061e.

Redpath v Belfast & County Down Railway [1947] N I 167, 18 Digest (Repl) 177, *902.

Staniforth v Lyall (1830) 7 Bing 169, 4 Moo & P 829, 9 LJOSCP 23, 131 ER 65, 41 Digest
   (Repl) 350, 1439.

c
Action

This was an action by the plaintiff, Anthony David Bellingham, against the defendants, Majit Singh Dhillon and Devinder Singh Bains, for damages for personal
injuries sustained in a motor accident on 25th December 1965. The defendants
admitted liability but contested the action on the amount of damages, in particular
d the amount of special damages to be awarded for the loss of profits suffered by the
plaintiff in his business as a result of his injuries. The facts are set out in the judgment.

G M Hamilton for the plaintiff.
Michael Wright for the defendants.

e
                                                            Cur adv vult

30th May. **FORBES J** read the following judgment. This case arises out of an
accident which took place on Christmas Day 1965. The plaintiff was at the wheel of
his stationary motor car when he was run into from behind by a vehicle driven by
the defendants or for which they were responsible. Liability is admitted and the sole
f question is one of damages. Although the accident happened some 6½ years ago, no
one suggests this delay was due to any dilatoriness on the part of either party, but
nevertheless it is unfortunate that it should have taken so long to come to trial. As
liability is not in issue, one of the major difficulties which sometimes arises does not
of course arise in this case. I will deal first with the injuries and the question of
general damages. [His Lordship then considered the plaintiff's injuries and the
medical evidence, which showed that, in consequence of the accident, the plaintiff
g had suffered from increasingly severe backaches, and continued:] The plaintiff runs
a driving school. In the nature of things, because he is in charge of it, he devotes
much of his time towards the administration of that school. The effect of his backache on his work is that he is no longer able to give driving tuition for more than an
hour at a time. [His Lordship then assessed the general damages at £2,500 and
continued:] The more difficult problem is, however, the question of special damages.
h The plaintiff owns 500 out of 501 shares in a company which carries on the business
of the driving school; the remaining share is held by the wife. He is the managing
director. Both parties agree that the company's loss is his loss for the purpose of
this action. I may say at once that I found him a most impressive witness and I
have not the least doubt that in business he is a man of immense drive and acumen.
It is also clear that he has a profound knowledge of the business of running a driving
j school. Because of his injury, his work at the driving school was affected. Originally
in the amended statement of claim special damage was claimed on the basis of loss
of profits of the business, but at the trial a rather more sophisticated calculation was
advanced. I accept the plaintiff's explanation as to the manner in which this alteration of emphasis arose and although to some extent it came late in the day for the
defendants, I am satisfied that they were not unduly prejudiced.

The way the plaintiff now puts his claim is this. There were three particular *a* enterprises on which his company was engaged or would have been engaged which were affected by his incapacity. These have been conveniently referred to as the Strood, Meopham and Simulator enterprises respectively. I can best explain the point by referring briefly to the history of the plaintiff's business. The plaintiff started with one car part-time from his home in Rochester. The business expanded. In 1961 he had two cars; in 1963, and in 1965 when the company was formed, he *b* had seven cars. [His Lordship related that the plaintiff had established branches of the business at Strood and Meopham. The plaintiff claimed that because of his injury he was not able to devote his energies to expanding the Strood branch as quickly as it should have expanded. After considering the evidence his Lordship awarded the plaintiff £1,019 damages, after allowing for the incidence of tax, in respect of that venture. The plaintiff had been forced to close down the Meopham *c* branch in April 1967 and his Lordship awarded the plaintiff £340 damages in respect of that venture after deduction of tax.]

Lastly the Simulator venture. The plaintiff became interested at an early stage in an electronic device which enables driving tuition to be given in a lecture room rather than in a car on the road. There were American equipments marketed in this country by a company called Indoor Driving Trainers Ltd ('IDT'). He was of *d* some assistance to this company and in 1967 was seriously considering the purchase of an equipment from them. The cost was £7,000 and capital was needed. At the first attempt he was turned down by a finance house but IDT were so keen to see their product in operation that they were prepared to guarantee a leasing arrangement from the finance house. Unfortunately at the critical stage in the negotiations the plaintiff had a serious attack of backache and was eventually forced to have the *e* first of his laminectomy operations. By the time he came out of hospital IDT had changed its policy and proposed to make an agreement with another company, Indoor Driving Centres ('IDC'), whereby the latter company would take the entire production of simulators for installation in establishments operated by that company. The plaintiff claims under this head the sum of £4,816, the loss of profits which would have been earned by the simulator over a period of three years and five *f* months from February 1968 to the autumn of 1971. In the autumn of 1971 the plaintiff installed a simulator. He bought it from the liquidator of IDC which had by then gone out of business. He bought a ten seat simulator for a price of £1,900. It was secondhand, having had a year's use. The plaintiff used it as a six seater employing the remainder of the equipment for the purpose of 'cannibalising' for spares. The hire purchase charges amounted to £250 making the total cost £2,160. *g* Had the plaintiff been able to arrange the agreement which he was negotiating in 1967, he would not have been in a position to buy that equipment at that price; he would have been paying £1,824 a year for five years and thereafter £71 a year. It is on this latter basis that his claim is calculated. But in fact because this agreement was thwarted he is now the owner of an equipment which has only cost him £2,160. It is agreed by counsel for both parties that if this windfall, as it was called, were not *h* to be taken into account, the plaintiff's loss is a figure of £2,774 net. If the defendants are entitled to take advantage of it, the loss is nil, subject to one point. The plaintiff's abortive agreement would have put him in a favourable posisition vis-à-vis his competitors in that he would have been the first driving school in the area to operate a simulator. I should say at once that in my view any additional loss due to this factor has already been taken into account by basing the income from the *j* simulator on intake over the whole period of 40 pupils per month and I would add nothing more for the hypothetical advantage of being the first in the field.

On the main issue counsel for the defendants has referred me to McGregor on Damages[1] and to *British Westinghouse Electric and Manufacturing Co Ltd v Underground*

---

1   13th Edn (1972), pp 176, 177, para 246

a   *Electric Railways Co of London Ltd*[1] and in particular to the opinion of Viscount Haldane LC[2]. He argues that although that case arose in contract the principle must apply in an action for personal injuries at any rate where the claim arises out of calculations of business loss. Counsel for the plaintiff on the other hand regards the acquisition of this equipment in 1971 as a collateral matter, res inter alios acta, and he referred me to *Parry v Cleaver*[3] and in particular to the speech of Lord Reid[4].

b   The editor of McGregor puts it in this way[5]:

c   'Actions taken after breach by the plaintiff himself are directly within the principles laid down in *British Westinghouse Co. v. Underground Ry*[1]: It is here that is found the core of the problem. The matter is not well worked out in the authorities and all that can be done is to sketch what the law probably is. Some applications of the rule are admittedly simple and are so straightforward as generally to be taken for granted. Thus where the plaintiff has recovered damages from a third party who is also liable, as by being a joint tortfeasor for instance, he cannot recover damages over again from the defendant for the same loss. Again, where a plaintiff has accepted the return of his goods which the defendant had converted, he cannot sue the defendant for their value. The difficult cases generally concern contracts of sale of goods, where on the *d*   defendant's default the plaintiff takes steps to remedy his situation by acquiring substitutes or by disposing of the goods to a third party. It is suggested [and this is the important sentence] that the basic rule is that the benefit to the plaintiff, if it is to be taken into account in mitigation of damage, must arise out of the act of mitigation itself.'

e   The principles referred to in that passage are conveniently to be collected from the speech of Lord Haldane LC in the *British Westinghouse* case[6]. He said this:

f   '... I think that there are certain broad principles which are quite well settled. The first is that, as far as possible, he who has proved a breach of a bargain to supply what he contracted to get is to be placed, as far as money can do it, in as good a situation as if the contract had been performed. The fundamental basis is thus compensation for pecuniary loss naturally flowing from the breach; but this first principle is qualified by a second, which imposes on a plaintiff the duty of taking all reasonable steps to mitigate the loss consequent on the breach, and debars him from claiming any part of the damage which is due to his neglect to take such steps.'

g   After quoting a passage from *Dunkirk Colliery Co v Lever*[7], he went on[6]:

h   '... this second principle does not impose on the plaintiff an obligation to take any step which a reasonable and prudent man would not ordinarily take in the course of the business. But when in the course of his business he has taken action arising out of the transaction, which action has diminished his loss, the effect in actual diminution of the loss he has suffered may be taken into account even though there was no duty on him to act.'

After referring to *Staniforth v Lyall*[8] Lord Haldane LC went on[9]:

1   [1912] AC 673, [1911-13] All ER Rep 63
2   [1912] AC at 688, 689, [1911-13] All ER Rep at 69
j   3   [1969] 1 All ER 555, [1970] AC 1
4   [1969] 1 All ER at 557, [1970] AC at 13
5   13th Edn (1972), pp 176, 177, para 246
6   [1912] AC at 689, [1911-13] All ER Rep at 69
7   (1878) 9 Ch D 20 at 25
8   (1830) 7 Bing 169
9   [1912] AC at 690, [1911-13] All ER Rep at 70

'I think that this decision illustrates a principle which has been recognized in other cases, that, provided the course taken to protect himself by the plaintiff in such an action was one which a reasonable and prudent person might in the ordinary conduct of business properly have taken, and in fact did take whether bound to or not, a jury or an arbitrator may properly look at the whole of the facts and ascertain the result in estimating the quantum of damage.'

If this were a case arising in contract there would be no difficulty in applying these principles to this case. The plaintiff was only doing what a prudent and reasonable businessman would do in buying so cheaply this equipment when it came on the market. In doing so, he would have been discharging his duty to mitigate his damages and I have no doubt that in contract this profitable purchase would have resulted in the award of merely nominal damages for breach. But can these principles be carried over into the field of tortious liability? Counsel for the plaintiff argued they could not and referred me, as I have said, to *Parry v Cleaver*[1]. That case was concerned with a question of whether a contributory police pension payable to the plaintiff on his disablement in a motor car accident was to be taken into account in assessing damages for personal injury. Lord Reid said[2]:

'Before *Gourley's* case[3] it was well established that there was no universal rule with regard to sums which came to the plaintiff as a result of the accident but which would not have come to him but for the accident. In two large classes of case such sums were disregarded—the proceeds of insurance and sums coming to him by reason of benevolence.'

Then dealing with those two classes he continued[4]:

'So I must enquire what are the real reasons, disregarding technicalities, why these two classes of receipts are not brought into account. I take first the case of benevolence. [After quoting a passage from *Redpath v Belfast and County Down Railway*[5], Lord Reid went on:] It would be revolting to the ordinary man's sense of justice, and therefore contrary to public policy, that the sufferer should have his damages reduced so that he would gain nothing from the benevolence of his friends or relations or of the public at large, and that the only gainer would be the wrongdoer ... As regards moneys coming to the plaintiff under a contract of insurance, I think that the real and substantial reason for disregarding them is that the plaintiff has bought them and it would be unjust and unreasonable to hold that the money which he prudently spent on premiums and the benefit from it should enure to the benefit of the tortfeasor. Here again I think that the explanation that this is too remote is artificial and unreal.'

There are other passages in the speeches of others of their Lordships which indicated that their Lordships are not very much in favour of the explanation arising from the argument on remoteness or res inter alios acta. Here, however, we have no question of benevolence or insurance. The action of the plaintiff was that of a reasonable and prudent man of business. It was his duty to mitigate his damage by buying his equipment just as much when that damage arose in tort as if it had arisen in contract. It seems to me that when the plaintiff's claim for damages is based on loss in his business so that a detailed examination has to be made of his accounts and methods of trading, there should be no difference on this point between actions in contract and tort. The damages in either case are arrived at by a calculation in essence of

---

1   [1969] 1 All ER 555, [1970] AC 1
2   [1969] 1 All ER at 557, [1970] AC at 13
3   I e *British Transport Commission v Gourley* [1955] 3 All ER 796, [1956] AC 185
4   [1969] 1 All ER at 557, 558, [1970] AC at 14
5   [1947] NI 167 at 170

a extreme simplicity. Take the profits which the business would have earned on
the hypothesis that the defendants' wrong had not reduced them, and subtract
from that figure the profits which the business in fact earned after the wrong had
been suffered. The first of these mathematical terms must be hypothetical. The
second should be actual and real. It seems to me artificial in the extreme to say
that in calculating the actual profits earned, one must shut one's eyes to a profitable

b transaction if the wrong was a tortious one but look at the realities and take them
into account if the wrong amounted to breach of contract. In my view the principles
enunciated in the *British Westinghouse* case[1] apply in this particular case and should
be followed. Fortunately it would be unnecessary to go through the figures of
profits because both counsel agreed that if I were to decide the issue of principle by
applying this reasoning in *British Westinghouse*[1] no loss arose on the simulator venture.

c The result is that in my view the plaintiff is entitled to recover £2,500 by way of
general damages and the sums of £1,019 and £340, a total of £1,359 by way of special
damage, this last figure having taken into account the incidence of taxation as laid
down in *British Transport Commission v Gourley*[2].

Judgment for the plaintiff for £2,500 general damages and £1,359 special damages.

d Solicitors: *Milners, Curry & Gaskell* (for the plaintiff); *Joynson-Hicks & Co*, Croydon
(for the defendants).

Janet Harding Barrister.

e

Practice Direction

f QUEEN'S BENCH DIVISION

*Practice – Chambers – Queen's Bench Division – Chambers applications – Hearing before
judges in chambers – Sittings in chambers at trial centres outside London.*

1. Pursuant to para 1 of the Practice Direction of 10th December 1971[3], it is
notified that, to the extent that the business of the courts permits and subject to
the terms of that direction, all business which may be dealt with by a judge of

g the Queen's Bench Division in chambers may be dealt with by such a judge sitting
at a specified trial centre out of London except as may be notified.

2. Liverpool and Newcastle are additionally specified as trial centres for the
foregoing purposes.

11th December 1972   WIDGERY CJ

h _____

1 [1912] AC 673, [1911-13] All ER Rep 63
2 [1955] 3 All ER 796, [1956] AC 185
3 [1972] 1 All ER 286, [1972] 1 WLR 4

Mount v Oldham Corporation

COURT OF APPEAL, CIVIL DIVISION

LORD DENNING MR, EDMUND DAVIES AND STEPHENSON LJJ

11th OCTOBER 1972

Contract – Frustration – Contract for personal services – Temporary enforced inability to perform services – Education – Special school – Contract between headmaster and local authority for education of maladjusted child – Headmaster charged with indecency – Enforced absence from school for six months in consequence of charges – Running of school continued by staff – Local authority withdrawing child from school without notice – Headmaster returning to school after dismissal of charges – Whether contract frustrated – Whether local authority liable to pay a term's fee in lieu of notice.

Contract – Implied term – Notice – Breach – Remedy – Education – Contract between parent and headmaster for education of child – Notice by parents of intention to withdraw child from school – Payment in lieu of notice – Usage of profession – Payment of term's fee in lieu of notice – Term implied into contract – Claim by headmaster against parent – Claim for term's fees rather than damages.

The plaintiff was the proprietor and headmaster of a school for maladjusted children to which the defendants, a local authority, sent pupils under their statutory duty to provide for such children. In July 1970 two boys absconded from the school and, when they were found by the police, made charges against the plaintiff of indecency. The plaintiff was arrested and later released on bail on condition that he did not reside at the school and that he had no contact with the children. The staff at the school informed the defendants of what had happened. They stated that the school would continue as usual and that the next term would start, as planned, on 28th July. The defendants however decided to withdraw their pupils from the school. On 31st December the plaintiff was cleared of the charges and his character vindicated. He returned and the defendants sent their pupils back to the school which thereafter continued to run as successfully as before. The defendants however refused to pay the fees for the term commencing on 28th July and, in an action by the plaintiff, denied that they were liable therefor.

Held – The plaintiff was entitled to claim a term's fees against the defendants for the following reasons—

(i) it was a well-established usage in the educational world that, if a parent wished to withdraw his child from school, he was bound to give a term's notice, or to pay a term's fees in lieu of notice; since the plaintiff was not in breach of contract the defendants were only entitled to refuse to pay the fees if the contract had been frustrated by the plaintiff's absence (see p 28 j, p 29 b c and g and p 30 b, post);

(ii) although in certain special schools the services of the headmaster might be so personal and so important to the running of the school that his enforced absence would result in the contract with a parent being frustrated, the plaintiff's school did not fall into that category; the staff were able to carry on the school in the plaintiff's absence which was not, in any event, likely to be for long; accordingly the contract had not been frustrated (see p 29 d e and j to p 30 b, post);

(iii) the plaintiff's claim was properly made for a term's fees, rather than for damages, since that was the understanding of his profession (see p 29 f and p 30 a to c, post); *Denman v Winstanley* (1887) 4 TLR 127 doubted.

Notes

For provisions as to fees in contracts to educate, see 13 Halsbury's Laws (3rd Edn) 590, 591, para 1243, and for cases on the subject, see 19 Digest (Repl) 593, 594, 13-22.

For the application of the doctrine of frustration to contracts for personal services, see 8 Halsbury's Laws (3rd Edn) 188-191, para 322.

Case referred to in judgments

a *Denman v Winstanley* (1887) 4 TLR 127, DC, 19 Digest (Repl) 593, 17.

Tamplin (FA) SS Co Ltd v Anglo-Mexican Petroleum Co Ltd [1916] 2 AC 397, [1916-17] All ER Rep 104, 85 LJKB 1389; sub nom *Re Tamplin (FA) SS Co Ltd & Anglo-Mexican Petroleum Products Co Ltd* 115 LT 315, 13 Asp MLC 467, HL, 12 Digest (Repl) 442, 3361.

b **Appeal**

This was an appeal by the plaintiff, Jack Mount, against the judgment of his Honour Judge Burrell QC in the Ludlow County Court given on 13th January 1972 whereby he dismissed the plaintiff's claim against the defendants, Oldham Corporation, for fees payable to the plaintiff as proprietor of Brookside School, Culmington Manor, Craven Arms, by the defendants. The facts are set out in the judgment of Lord

c Denning MR.

N W Budgen for the plaintiff.
Donald Hart for the defendants.

LORD DENNING MR. In Shropshire there is a school for maladjusted children.

d It is Brookside School, Culmington Manor, Craven Arms. It is an independent school owned by the headmaster, Mr Jack Mount. There were only 38 children at the school. They were all maladjusted; they were all sent there by their local authorities and paid for by them; because local authorities are under a statutory duty to provide for maladjusted children.

The corporation of Oldham sent four boys to the school. The first boy they sent

e was Michael Aspin. He was ten years of age when he was sent there in 1968. He was maladjusted and had been rejected by his family. For the first two years everything was satisfactory. Then a most unfortunate thing happened. Two of the other boys absconded from the school. When the police found them, they made charges against Mr Mount, the headmaster, of indecency. On 16th July 1970 the police arrested Mr Mount. He remained in custody for six days. Then he was allowed

f out on bail on terms that he did not reside at the school and had no contact with the children. That put the school in great difficulty, as I will show. But I will first say what happened to Mr Mount. The case took six months to come on for hearing. Then on 31st December 1970 it came before the justices at Ludlow. They dismissed the charges against Mr Mount altogether. He was acquitted and returned to the school. His character was vindicated. In the course of the judgment in this very

g sad case, the judge said:

> '... I would like here to express my admiration for the plaintiff's [Mr Mount's] dedication to his calling, his evident sincerity, and the complete lack of bitterness following the tragic experience he underwent at the hand of some of his charges. I do not doubt his belief in anything he told me in evidence.'

h Now I must return to the school and tell what happened after Mr Mount's arrest on 17th July 1970. The second master, Mr Trickett, and the matron, Miss Foster, sought to carry on the school. On the very next day they wrote letters to the local authorities (who had boys at the school) telling them what had happened. This is the letter they wrote to Mr Pritchett, the Director of Education at Oldham, on 18th July 1970:

j > 'Dear Mr. Pritchett, We are writing to inform you that the Principal of this School Mr. J. Mount has had to relinquish his position as Principal. We sincerely hope that this is purely temporary and that he will soon be back with us.
> 'In the meantime however, we wish to assure you that not only will the School remain open but will be conducted along the same sound lines which have proved so successful in the past.

'The staff, both domestic and tutorial have assured us that they are very happy to continue serving the School and to continue giving us their full support.   *a*
'May we remind you that the new term commences on July 28th.'

Meanwhile, however, Mr Pritchett had heard from the police. They asked him that none of the Oldham boys should return to the school. Mr Pritchett had a conversation with the Ministry of Education and decided not to send any of the four boys back. On 24th July 1970 he wrote to the school: *b*

'I write to inform you that it will not be possible for these four boys to return to school for the term beginning Tuesday 28th July.'

The boys did not return to the school that term or the next. Nearly all the local authorities did the same. They took the boys away. Only three boys were left   *c*
at the school. But the headmaster was cleared on 31st December 1970 and returned to the school. The Director of Education did then send the four Oldham boys back. So did the other local authorities. All sent the boys back. All is going well with the school now. We are told it is doing better now than it did before.

The only question that remains is as to the fees for the term which started on 28th July 1970, but during which the boys did not attend. Most of the local authorities   *d*
have paid the fees for that term, but Oldham Corporation refused to do so. Mr Mount sued the corporation for the fees. The corporation put in a defence saying that on receiving the letter about Mr Mount they 'thereupon resolved that it was no longer expedient for the relevant treatment to be provided at the Plaintiff's special school'; and they denied liability for the fees.

In the course of the case some questions arose as to the date when the term com-   *e*
menced and so forth; but these were resolved. It was held that the term was to commence on 28th July 1970; and that the corporation withdrew the boys without giving any notice. In the ordinary way, they could not do so without paying a term's fees in lieu of notice. But the judge found that the corporation were not liable to pay a term's fees. He held that on Mr Mount's arrest the contract was frustrated. He said: *f*

'In my view the change, the instability and insecurity of environment at the school as a result of the plaintiff's arrest, his physical absence, and the police enquiries was (and see Treitel[1]) an " occurrence . . . of a character and extent so sweeping that the foundation of what the parties are deemed to have had in contemplation has disappeared, and the contract itself has vanished with that foundation." I come to that conclusion despite the deepest sympathy that any-   *g*
body concerned with this case must feel for the plaintiff . . . I have come quite firmly to the conclusion that in the light of his knowledge and acting as a res- ponsible parent would have acted . . . Mr Pritchett [the Director of Education] was fully justified in removing the boy Aspin on first hearing of the plaintiff's unfortunate plight.'

h

Now, I quite agree that the Director of Education acted entirely reasonably in withdrawing the boys from the school. But it does not follow that the corporation of Oldham are to be excused from paying the fees. It is an understood thing in all schools that if a parent wishes to withdraw a boy, he can do so; but if he does so he has either to give a term's notice or to pay a term's fee in lieu of notice. That is a usage well known throughout the educational world. So well known that we can   *j*
take notice of it ourselves. If the parent wishes to avoid this liability, he must show that the school has been guilty of a breach going to the root of the contract, such as

1   Law of Contract (3rd Edn, 1970), p 781, quoting Lord Haldane in *F A Tamplin SS Co Ltd v Anglo-Mexican Petroleum Products Co Ltd* [1916] 2 AC 397 at 406, 407, [1916-17] All ER Rep 104 at 109

a   to entitle the parent to treat himself as discharged from any further obligation. It is similar to the employment of a domestic servant. You may not get on with him, or you may suspect that he has been guilty of misconduct which you cannot prove. If so, you can discharge him; but if you do not give him notice, you must pay his wages in lieu of notice. Your conduct may be entirely reasonable, but at common law you are bound to pay him his wages in lieu of notice. Likewise with

b   a school. After a boy goes to school, he may be very unhappy. The school may not suit him. Other boys may be unkind to him. The staff may change for the worse, and so forth. The parent may be quite reasonable in withdrawing the boy; but he must still give a term's notice or pay a term's fees in lieu of notice.

There was no breach by the headmaster of the contract. If Mr Mount had been found guilty of the charges, he would, of course, have been guilty of a breach going to the root of the contract and he could not have recovered any fees; but he was not

c   found guilty. He was acquitted. He was the victim of misfortune, not the cause of it. Does it entitle the corporation to refuse to pay the fees? The only point on which it could do so would be if it amounted to a frustration of the contract. I can well understand that in some special schools the services of the headmaster may be so personal and his presence so important that if he were to die or have a prolonged illness, or any other misfortune causing prolonged absence, the contract might be

d   frustrated. But this school is not in that category. First, the position of the head-master was not so very personal. Everything would not come to an end if he died or had a long illness or was absent for a term or two. The staff here could and did carry on the school. Secondly, he was not likely to be absent for very long. It was only as if he had been taken ill with a serious illness from which he should recover in six months. I do not think this contract was frustrated by what happened.

e   The net result is that the corporation acted quite reasonably in withdrawing the boys, but they were only entitled to do so on a term's notice or a term's fee in lieu. It was suggested that the claim should lie for damages and not a term's fees. *Denman v Winstanley*[1] was cited for that proposition. But I do not think that is correct. The claim can properly be made for fees in lieu of notice, because that is the understanding in the profession.

f   I would allow the appeal and enter judgment for Mr Mount for the sum of £280, the fees for one term.

EDMUND DAVIES LJ. At this late hour, I confine myself to two short points in expressing my concurrence with Lord Denning MR. First of all, it was conceded

g   before the learned county court judge that a term's notice was to be expected in the existing circumstances, in the absence of any express provisions to the contrary. Therefore, on the face of it there was clearly a breach of contract by the local authority, they having given no notice before withdrawing the four pupils they had sent to the plaintiff's school. Secondly, if it was intended to rely on the defence of frustration, it was necessary to plead it expressly and with particularity; furthermore it needed

h   to be established clearly by the party raising it. In the present case, neither of those requirements was fulfilled. Frustration was never pleaded. Instead, after relating in the defence the sending by the school matron of the letter of 18th July already quoted by Lord Denning MR, the defence pleads this and this only:

> 'The Defendants thereupon resolved that it was no longer *expedient* for the relevant treatment to be provided at the Plaintiff's special school ...'

j   That is nothing like a plea of frustration. Nor when the evidence was called was there established any special and significant relationship between pupil and head-master, the continuation of which went to the root of the contract.

In my view, on the exiguous evidence presented, no proper foundation was laid

---

1   (1887) 4 TLR 127

for a finding that frustration of the contract had been established by the defendants, *a*
on whom lay the burden. Accordingly, also concurring with Lord Denning MR
that the proper remedy in the circumstances of the case was a claim for a term's fees
and not for unliquidated damages, I agree in holding that this appeal should be
allowed.

STEPHENSON LJ. I also agree, for the reasons which Lord Denning MR and *b*
Edmund Davies LJ have given. I would only add that I am not sure that I understand the reasoning which led the Divisional Court in *Denman v Winstanley*[1], on which
counsel for the defendants relied, to reduce the county court judge's award, of what
seems to have been the full amount of fees in lieu of notice to half that amount as
damages for loss of profits. I agree that at this time of day it is quite clear that if
notice is required by such a contract to educate as this, so fees in lieu of notice are also *c*
required and payable under the contract.

Appeal allowed.

Solicitors: *Kenneth Brown, Baker, Baker*, agents for *G H Morgan & Sons*, Ludlow (for
the plaintiff); *Sharpe, Pritchard & Co*, agents for *S Mottram*, Borough Solicitor, Oldham
(for the defendants).
d

L J Kovats Esq Barrister.

Practice Direction

e

CHANCERY DIVISION

*Practice – Chancery Division – Lists – Witness list – Part I – Procedure for fixing date for
trial.*

1. It is not generally understood that when a case is set down for hearing in *f*
Part I of the Witness List and counsels' certificate as to length of hearing has been
lodged it is necessary to apply to the Vice-Chancellor's clerk for the fixing of a date
for trial.

2. It is the duty of the plaintiff's solicitor to arrange for application to be made to
the Vice-Chancellor's clerk promptly after counsels' certificate has been lodged.

3. The plaintiff's solicitor may if he so wishes make the application himself after
notice to the solicitors for the other parties. But the normal and convenient procedure *g*
is for dates to be fixed in consultation between the Vice-Chancellor's clerk and the
clerks to counsel for the respective parties, and when the plaintiff's solicitor wishes
to follow this procedure he should notify his counsel accordingly in order that that
counsel's clerk may make the necessary application to the Vice-Chancellor's clerk
in consultation with the clerks to the other counsel.

4. If the plaintiff's solicitor omits to make the application within one month *h*
after counsels' certificate has been lodged the solicitor for any of the defendants may
make the application and the foregoing paragraph shall apply with the appropriate
modifications.

5. If the plaintiff appears in person he should apply to the cause clerk at room 136,
who will notify the Vice-Chancellor's clerk. Where a defendant appears in person *j*
the foregoing paragraphs shall apply with the appropriate modifications.

By the direction of the Vice-Chancellor.

R E BALL
Chief Master

24th November 1972

---

1 (1887) 4 TLR 127

a

Stewart v Stewart

FAMILY DIVISION
SIR GEORGE BAKER P
4th OCTOBER 1972

b

Husband and wife – Property – Matrimonial home – Decree absolute – After decree husband undertaking to vacate matrimonial home – Breach of undertaking – Court's jurisdiction to commit husband for contempt.

Where the welfare of the children is in jeopardy the court has jurisdiction to commit
c a spouse to prison for contempt for breach of an undertaking to leave the matrimonial home, even though the undertaking was given after the grant of a decree absolute of divorce.

  Montgomery v Montgomery [1964] 2 All ER 22, *Gurasz v Gurasz* [1969] 3 All ER 822
and *Adams v Adams* (1965) 109 Sol Jo 899 followed.

d **Notes**
For committal for breach of an undertaking, see 8 Halsbury's Laws (3rd Edn) 29,
30, paras 54, 55, and for cases on the subject, see 16 Digest (Repl) 56, 57, *520-535*.

Cases referred to in judgment
Adams v Adams (1965) 109 Sol Jo 899, Digest (Cont Vol B) 380, *6528b*.
e *Gurasz v Gurasz* [1969] 3 All ER 822, [1970] P 11, [1969] 3 WLR 482, CA, Digest (Cont
  Vol C) 427, *621gga*.
Montgomery v Montgomery [1964] 2 All ER 22, [1965] P 46, [1964] 2 WLR 1036, Digest
(Cont Vol B) 380, *6527d*.

Case also cited
Jones v Jones [1971] 2 All ER 737, [1971] 1 WLR 396, CA.
f

Application for committal
This was an application by the wife for an order that the husband be committed to
prison for breach of an undertaking given by him to the court on 11th September 1972
that he would, before 12 noon on 18th September 1972, vacate the matrimonial
home at 86 Shell Road, London SE 13, which the wife and the two children occupied.
g The facts are set out in the judgment,

Eleanor Platt for the wife.
H M Morgan for the husband.

SIR GEORGE BAKER P. On 11th September the husband gave an undertaking
h to the court to vacate the matrimonial home at 86 Shell Road, London SE 13, on
or before 12 noon on 18th September 1972. This is now 4th October and he has not
yet left. I am satisfied from the evidence before me and the information that I have
been given that he is in fact living in a part of what was the matrimonial home,
although the whole house which is owned by him or, at least, is in his name, is let
in parts to various tenants. There is, I find, a clear breach of his undertaking to the
court. Counsel for the husband has argued that the court cannot or, at any rate,
j should not, commit this man to prison because the undertaking which he gave was
to do something which the court could not order him to do. The basis of the submission is that as long ago as March 1971 the decree was made absolute in this suit
and, says counsel for the husband, the proceedings are at an end and the court has
no jurisdiction in the divorce matter. I do not think that is correct because there still
remains to be decided in these proceedings a question concerning the Matrimonial

Homes Act 1967 under which a caution has been registered; also there are proceedings under s 17 of the Married Women's Property Act 1882 and, perhaps, most important, there is an application under s 4 of the Matrimonial Proceedings and Property Act 1970.

But, be that as it may, the fact is that this is the matrimonial home in which the wife and the two children aged 11 and five lived and have continued to live. The husband was away from the matrimonial home for a considerable time living, I gather, with another lady and with a gentleman called Mr Stirling. Difficulties arose and he returned to the matrimonial home in April 1972 in circumstances which are in dispute. He says he was asked back but the wife does not accept that. It certainly would be surprising, having regard to the lengthy history of this case which it is unnecessary to recount, if the wife did ask him to come back. But I find that this court has jurisdiction, not necessarily because the proceedings are still in being; not necessarily because this woman is a wife and mother who has always been in possession, but because there are the two young children who have to have a roof over their heads. In my view, their interests are such that this court ought to protect them and has jurisdiction to do so. Ormrod J said so in *Montgomery v Montgomery*[1]:

'Similarly, if the welfare of the children was in jeopardy, different considerations would apply. In such cases the court has wide powers to intervene for their protection.'

So too Lord Denning MR in *Gurasz v Gurasz*[2], where he said:

'Some features of family life are elemental in our society. One is that it is the husband's duty to provide his wife with a roof over her head; and the children too.'

And in 1965, in *Adams v Adams*[3] which was surprisingly reported only in the Solicitors' Journal, I held that I had jurisdiction to make an injunction against a mistress because of the need to protect the interests of the children. For that reason alone I consider that the court could grant an injunction if necessary in this case and that in any event the undertaking given by the father is a binding undertaking on him and can be enforced and should be enforced.

Now he says, although I am not at all impressed with the evidence he has put before me, that he has been trying very hard to obtain some alternative accommodation, and he has failed. He will have to try somewhat harder. It does not seem to me that there is any good end to be achieved by committing him to prison today because when he comes out of prison the same situation will exist and it may be expected that he will turn up at the matrimonial home and somehow or other get himself into the house.

The order that I propose to make and that I now make is that there will be a committal order but it is not to be issued for a period of 14 days, that is to say, it is not to be issued before 12 noon on Thursday, 19th October, that is a fortnight tomorrow, so it gives a full 14 days because it is now 2.40 p m. So the husband has to be out of the house by 12 noon on 19th October otherwise the committal order will issue. The normal procedure will apply: if he is not out, then on an affidavit by the wife and/or the solicitors the order will be issued.

Order accordingly.

Solicitors: *Good, Good & Co* (for the wife); *J B Wheatley & Co* (for the husband).

R C T Habesch Esq   Barrister.

---

1 [1964] 2 All ER 22 at 24, [1965] P 46 at 51
2 [1969] 3 All ER 822 at 823, [1970] P 11 at 16
3 (1965) 109 Sol Jo 899

a

Lyndale Fashion Manufacturers v Rich

COURT OF APPEAL, CIVIL DIVISION
DAVIES, STAMP AND ORR LJJ
18th OCTOBER, 9th NOVEMBER 1972

b

Damages – Measure of damages – Loss of future earnings – Tax – Deduction from award – Calculation of tax payable on lost earnings – Method of calculation – Deduction of tax paid on actual earnings from tax payable on total assumed income – Deduction of difference from award of damages – Allowance for expenses and earned income relief exclusively referable to assumed additional income.

c The employee was engaged by the employers as a travelling salesman on a commission basis and taxed under Sch D on his profits. His employment was terminated and he was held to be entitled to damages for wrongful dismissal. In the tax year in which the dismissal occurred the employee's total earnings amounted to £1,343. He was awarded damages of £495 less tax against the employers in respect of loss of earnings. The employee contended that the tax to be deducted was to be *d* calculated by dividing the tax that would be payable on his total assumed income rateably between the amount actually earned and the assumed additional income of £495.

Held – (i) The employee's method was incorrect. The amount of tax to be deducted from the damages was the difference between the actual tax paid on the employee's *e* earnings and the tax which he would have paid on the assumed total income (see p 37 g, post); *West Suffolk County Council v W Rought Ltd* [1956] 3 All ER 216 applied; dictum of Wynn-Parry J in *Re Houghton Main Colliery Co Ltd* [1956] 3 All ER at 304 doubted.

(ii) Any expenses which might have been incurred in earning the additional income and the earned income relief exclusively referable to the assumed additional income *f* should be set against that assumed income only and not against the total income (see p 38 a, post).

Note

For effect of income tax on assessing damages, see 11 Halsbury's Laws (3rd Edn) 240, para 408.

g **Cases referred to in judgment**

British Transport Commission v Gourley [1955] 3 All ER 796, [1956] AC 185, [1956] 2 WLR 41, 220 LT 354, [1955] 2 Lloyd's Rep 475, 34 ATC 305, 49 R & IT 11, HL, Digest (Cont Vol A) 462, *28a*.

Houghton Main Colliery Co Ltd, Re [1956] 3 All ER 300, [1956] 1 WLR 1219, 35 ATC 320, 50 R & IT 189, Digest (Cont Vol A) 196, *7339.*

h *West Suffolk County Council v W Rought Ltd* [1956] 3 All ER 216, [1957] AC 403, [1956] 3 WLR 589, 120 JP 522, HL, Digest (Cont Vol A) 209, *190a.*

Appeal

In an action commenced by the plaintiffs, Lyndale Fashion Manufacturers, to recover certain loans made to the defendant, Max Rich, the defendant counterclaimed by *j* way of set-off damages for wrongful dismissal. It was held that the defendant was entitled to recover from the plaintiffs the sum of £495 less tax to be agreed between the parties or failing that to be decided by the court. The parties failed to agree. On 23rd February 1972 at Bloomsbury and Marylebone County Court his Honour Judge Leslie held that the amount to be deducted from the award of £495 was £42·97. The plaintiffs appealed. The facts are set out in the judgment of Orr LJ.

Roderick Adams for the plaintiffs.   *a*
Aron Owen for the defendant.

Cur adv vult

9th November. **ORR LJ** read the following judgment at the invitation of Davies
LJ. This is an appeal by the plaintiffs in a county court action against a judgment
given by his Honour Judge Leslie in the Bloomsbury and Marylebone County Court   *b*
on 23rd February 1972. Before referring at all to the terms of the judgment it is
necessary to recount the course which the case had previously taken for it is only
against that background that either the judgment itself or the criticisms made against
it can be understood.

In 1969, in an action commenced in the High Court but later transferred to the
county court, the plaintiff firm claimed from the defendant sums totalling £459 9s 3d   *c*
alleged to be due in respect of a loan and also of commission overpaid to the
defendant. By his defence the defendant admitted his liability in the total amount
claimed but alleged by way of set-off and counterclaim that the plaintiffs were
liable to him in damages for wrongful termination, in September 1967, of a contract
whereby he was employed by the plaintiffs as a travelling salesman on a commission
basis.   *d*

On 30th October 1969, in the Bloomsbury County Court, judgment was entered for
the plaintiffs in the admitted sum to which I have referred and it was also adjudged
that the defendant should recover on his counterclaim the sum found to be due
after enquiry and report by the registrar and that there should be a set-off of
these two sums, the question of costs being reserved.

On 4th February 1971, following a report by the registrar, to the terms of which   *e*
I shall later refer, the matter came again before the county court and it was ordered
that the defendant should recover on the counterclaim the sum of £495 less tax to
be agreed between the parties or decided by the court in default of agreement and
that there should be a set-off of the resulting sum against the judgment previously
entered in favour of the plaintiffs. The reason for the reference to tax was that it
was common ground between the parties that in accordance with the principle   *f*
laid down in *British Transport Commission v Gourley*[1] the incidence of tax fell to be
taken into account in arriving at the defendant's true loss for which he was being
compensated by damages. The court had therefore determined, without reference
to the incidence of tax, a sum by way of damages which was to be reduced by whatever amount should be agreed or determined as the appropriate deduction to be made
in respect of income tax which would have been payable in respect of the £495   *g*
if it had been received by the defendant by way of additional commission and not
by way of an award of damages.

In the event, the parties were unable to agree this figure and the matter therefore
came again before the judge on 23rd February 1972, when, having heard the evidence
of an accountant for the defendant and the argument of counsel on both sides, he
held that the amount to be deducted in respect of tax was £42·97 and also ordered   *h*
that three-quarters of the defendant's taxed costs of that hearing should be paid
by the plaintiffs. It is against that order that the plaintiffs now appeal claiming that
the appropriate deduction was not £42·97 but £152·81 or alternatively £137·30 and
that the defendant should pay to the plaintiffs the whole of their costs of the hearing
on 23rd February.

The relevant facts of the case are largely common ground. The defendant was   *j*
a travelling salesman remunerated by commission and taxed under Sch D on his
profits of that business. In the year in question, 1967-68, he received by way of commission from the plaintiffs prior to his dismissal by them £873, and after his dismissal,
in an endeavour to mitigate his loss, £470 from a new employer; making a total

1   [1955] 3 All ER 796, [1956] AC 185

a of £1,343 without taking into account the award of £495 by way of damages which
is agreed not to have been in itself a taxable subject-matter.

In the circumstances the principle laid down in *Gourley's* case[1] plainly applies and
the effect of that principle is that in assessing the damages the figure of £495 falls
to be reduced by the additional tax which the defendant would have been liable
to pay if he had received that sum by way of additional remuneration, for other-
b wise he would be receiving by way of damages a compensation in excess of his true
loss. For this purpose, in my judgment, two calculations fall to be made, the first
as to the tax which the defendant was liable to pay in respect of his actual income
of the year in question, and the second as to the tax which he would have been liable
to pay if he had earned by way of additional commission the sum of £495 in the
same year; and the difference between these two liabilities will be the amount to
c be deducted in making the award. This proposition, in my judgment, clearly emerges
from the following passage in the speech of Lord Morton of Henryton in *West
Suffolk County Council v W Rought Ltd*[2], a case concerned with compensation for
disturbance:

> 'It is for the respondents to prove the loss which they have suffered. Their
> trading year ends on Aug. 31. They have proved to the satisfaction of the
d > tribunal that they have lost £11,600 profits which they would have made during
> the trading year ending Aug. 31, 1953, but it is still incumbent on them to prove
> their loss after taking into account the incidence of taxation. This they could
> do by submitting to the tribunal (a) a statement of the tax liability which they
> actually incurred in respect of their trading during the year in question, and
> (b) an estimate of the tax liability which they would have incurred in respect
e > of their trading during the same year if they had made this profit of £11,600.
> These figures would, of course, be open to criticism by the appellants. When
> the tribunal had decided what are the right figures under (a) and (b), the net
> loss to the respondents by disturbance would be £11,600 less the amount by
> which (b) exceeds (a). In saying this, I am not attempting to lay down any general
> rule as to how the relevant figure is to be ascertained; nor do I say that the
f > procedure which I have outlined is the only possible procedure in the present
> case.'

To the same effect, as it appears to me, is the passage in the speech of Lord Goddard
in the *Gourley* case[3] itself where he said:

> 'But, in considering special damage in these cases, the rate of tax to be taken
g > must, as it seems to me, be the effective rate of income tax and, if necessary,
> surtax, which would have been applicable to the sums in question if they had
> been earned. That rate depends on the combination of a number of factors
> that may vary with each case—allowances, reduced rates, surtax rates, other
> income of the claimant or his wife, charges or reliefs. The task of determining
> it may not always be an easy one, but, in complicated cases, it is to be
h > hoped that the parties, with the help of accountants, will be able to agree figures.
> If not, the court must do its best to arrive at a reasonable figure, even though
> it cannot be said to be an exact one.'

Before turning to the rival theories advanced before the judge as to the tax calculation to be made in the present case it is necessary to refer to two further matters.
j The first is that the sum of £495 damages was arrived at without making any
deduction for expenses, additional to those in fact incurred, which would have been

---

1 [1955] 3 All ER 796, [1956] AC 185
2 [1956] 3 All ER 216 at 221, [1957] AC 403 at 413, 414
3 [1955] 3 All ER at 805, 806, [1956] AC at 208

incurred if the £495 had been earned as additional commission. There can be no doubt, in my judgment, that if there were any such expenses they should have been deducted in assessing the defendant's loss, before application of the *Gourley* principle[1]; for that loss would be the additional commission which he would have received if the contract had not been broken, less any additional expenses which he would have incurred in earning it. The registrar in his report made no reference to any such expenses but assessed the damages on the basis of the comparable commission which the defendant's successor earned in the relevant period, less certain deductions, including the £470 obtained by the defendant in mitigation of his damage, that is to say, in lieu of the amount which he would have received from the plaintiffs in addition to the £495 if the contract had been performed. The plaintiffs on reference of the report to the judge gave notice of various reductions which they sought to have made in the registrar's figure, some of which were accepted by the judge at the hearing on 4th February 1971, but they did not claim that any expenses fell to be deducted from the registrar's figure thus reduced. It would clearly have been against the defendant's interest to seek such a deduction and no such argument was advanced on his behalf. When, however, the matter came back to the judge on 23rd February 1972 to determine the further deduction, if any, to be made under the *Gourley* principle[1], it appears to have been argued for the defendant that, in computing the defendant's net taxable income on the assumption that he had received the £495 by way of additional commission, that sum should be treated as reduced for tax purposes by an amount representing additional expenses which would have been incurred in earning it. This argument was in my view misconceived, for any such additional expenses should, as I have already pointed out, have been deducted in assessing the £495 on 4th February 1971, but in any case the argument was clearly rejected by the learned judge, who said that there was nothing before him to show that the expenses were any less when the defendant was mitigating his damage than when he had been earning commission from the plaintiffs before his dismissal. He went on to hold, however, that the expenses allowable in 1967-68 would in any event have been less for that year than for the preceding year in the sum of £100 for capital allowances (since the judge considered that these would be less for a subsequent than for a previous year) and also in a further sum of £20 for incidental expenses. We are not concerned with the basis for this reasoning since the figures are accepted in the plaintiffs' calculation. But these reductions made by the judge do not, in my judgment, assist the defendant since they were not attributed by the judge to any saving in expenses due to the £495 not having been earned as additional commission.

The second matter to be referred to is that the defendant disclosed to the plaintiffs before the hearing on 23rd February 1972 his income tax assessment for the year 1967-68, but this was not the relevant year of assessment for the present purposes since the defendant's profits of 1967-68 would have been assessable under Sch D in the following year, 1968-69. He did not produce, although pressed by the plaintiffs to do so, his assessment for 1968-69 until after the hearing on 23rd February. It was, however, disclosed to the plaintiffs after that hearing and has been shown, at our request, to us. It reveals that the defendant's capital allowances for that year were in fact reduced by £30, and if we were to work on the figures disclosed by this assessment it would result in the deduction from the £495 to be made in accordance with the *Gourley* principle[1] being reduced by a pound or two. We do not, however, consider it right to work on the basis of this assessment since it was not before the learned judge and neither party sought an adjournment of the hearing for the purposes of its being produced.

On this appeal the first argument advanced for the plaintiffs was that the deduction to be made from the £495 should be £158·81, on the basis that the defendant,

1   [1955] 3 All ER 796, [1956] AC 185

a having failed to produce his relevant income tax assessment (i e for 1968-69) at the hearing, should be deemed in the absence of evidence to the contrary to have been liable to income tax at the standard rate on the whole of the £495. But in the event counsel for the plaintiffs, in my view wisely, did not press this argument. The answer to it is, in my judgment, that neither party sought an adjournment for the actual assessment to be produced, and that on the available figures it was clear from the computations made on both sides that the whole of the £495, treated as additional

b commission, would not have attracted income tax at the standard rate. To assume that it would have done so is therefore entirely unreal and in my judgment this ground of appeal has no substance.

The alternative and in the event main argument for the plaintiffs was that the sum to be deducted should be £137·30, and the question which it raises is whether the

c proper calculation to be made in order to apply the *Gourley* principle[1] is the plaintiffs' calculation (adjusted to take into account the judge's findings on expenses) or the defendant's calculation which was accepted in principle by the judge and when adjusted for the lower expenses allowed by him produces the deduction of £42·97 under appeal.

The difference between these two calculations is that the plaintiffs treat the £495 as

d the top part of the assumed income and having, after deducting expenses, reliefs (including earned income relief) and allowances, arrived at a net taxable income of £494, calculate the tax payable on that sum by applying the appropriate rates, thus arriving at an assumed tax bill of £160 from which the actual tax bill of £22·70 is then deducted, leaving a balance of £137·30 which it is claimed is the amount by which the award should be reduced. The defendant's calculation, on the other hand, after arriving in a similar manner at a net taxable income and calculating the tax

e on it, divides the tax bill rateably between the assumed and the actual income, thus applying an average rate of tax between the £495 and the other income. This computation was supported by the defendant's accountant, who apparently gave evidence that it was in his view the fairer computation in all the circumstances, and whose approach to the matter the judge preferred to that of the plaintiffs.

f These rival calculations raise, in my judgment, three questions. The first is whether, having arrived at a net taxable income, it is proper to divide the total tax bill rateably between the £495 and the other income, or whether the £495 falls to be treated as the top part of the income and as thus attracting to itself the higher rates of tax applicable in the assumed assessment.

In my judgment, the question which, on the authorities, has to be posed, namely,

g how much larger would the tax bill have been if the £495 had been received as additional commission, admits of only one answer, for if a comparison is to be made between a given income and that income with something added, the addition must be treated as the top part of the income. To treat it otherwise would not produce the true amount of the additional tax, since it is the increase in income which attracts the higher rates of tax; and insofar as the passage cited to us from the judgment of Wynn-Parry J in *Re Houghton Main Colliery Co Ltd*[2] indicates a contrary view I would

h not, with respect, accept it as correct, at all events in the circumstances of the present case.

The remaining questions are whether in arriving at the net taxable income for the purposes of the *Gourley* calculation[1] there should be attributed to the assumed additional income any expenses and earned income relief referable to it. As to

j expenses I would accept that if there were any which were not in fact incurred but would have been incurred in earning the additional income they should be treated in the calculation as wholly referable to that income; but, for the reasons I have already given, it must be taken that there were no such expenses in the present case.

---

1 [1955] 3 All ER 796, [1956] AC 185
2 [1956] 3 All ER 300 at 304, [1956] 1 WLR 1219 at 1225

As to earned income relief, however, it is clear that a proportion of the total of that *a*
relief (£246) brought into the plaintiffs' calculations was exclusively referable to the
additional assumed income of £495, and in my judgment that proportion of the
relief should be set against the £495 and not against the total income. This can be
achieved by deducting personal allowances and life insurance relief from the figure
of £1,108 and treating the resulting figure of £740 as divided into £495, representing
the assumed additional income, and £245 representing other income. The £495 *b*
would thus be reduced by its own earnéd income relief of £110 and the £245 by
the balance of the earned income relief of £136. The appropriate tax rates would
then be applied to the resulting figures, the figure for other income being treated as
attracting the lowest rate. On a rough calculation I estimate that the effect would be
that the deduction of £137.30 claimed by the plaintiffs would be reduced by some
£20, but the correct figure can be calculated and agreed. *c*

Subject to this adjustment, the plaintiffs' computation is in my view correct, and
the approach of the defendant's accountant was wrong in law in that it did not provide
a true answer to the question to be posed.

To the extent I have indicated I would allow the appeal, and I would hear consequential argument as to the proper order to be made with reference to the costs
of the hearing before the judge. *d*

DAVIES LJ. I entirely agree, and wish to add nothing.

STAMP LJ. I also agree, and have nothing to add.

*Appeal allowed accordingly. Order of county court judge varied by substituting figures to
be agreed between the parties.* *e*

Solicitors: *Parker, Thomas & Co* (for the plaintiffs); *H Fishman & Co* (for the
defendant).

Ilyas Khan Esq Barrister.

f

Brannan v Brannan

FAMILY DIVISION

SIR GEORGE BAKER P, PAYNE AND LANE JJ

10th, 11th JULY, 10th OCTOBER 1972 *g*

*Husband and wife – Maintenance – Wilful neglect to maintain – Meaning of 'wilful' –
Wilfulness connoting deliberate conduct with knowledge of facts – Husband suffering
from psychotic delusion that wife was going to kill or injure him – Husband leaving
wife – Justices finding that husband had no animus deserendi because of delusion – Evidence
that husband knowing of circumstances of wife and of his legal duty to maintain her – Husband failing to pay maintenance to wife – Whether wilfulness connoting an element of malice *h*
or wickedness – Whether in spite of delusion husband's conduct 'wilful'.*

The husband and wife were married in 1962. Soon after the marriage the husband
showed signs of mental illness and in July 1970 spent a fortnight in hospital undergoing treatment. The day following his release from hospital, he left the matrimonial home and never returned. He was subsequently readmitted to hospital
for a longer period of treatment. The husband had a fixed, irrational belief that his *j*
wife was going to injure or kill him. Apart from that delusion, he appeared
perfectly normal and knew how to conduct himself in public and in private, except
with regard to his wife. In 1971 the husband returned to his job. The wife remained
at the matrimonial home and was in receipt of social security benefits. In June
1971 the wife, at the instigation of the Department of Health and Social Security,

a complained to the justices that her husband had deserted her and issued a further complaint of wilful neglect to maintain. In September 1971 the justices dismissed the complaint of desertion on the ground that the husband, by reason of his delusion, was unable to form an intention to end cohabitation and that the separation was one of necessity. At the hearing of the complaint of wilful neglect in December, the justices ordered the husband to pay the wife £6 a week. The husband appealed.

b He admitted that he was under a legal duty to maintain his wife but contended that for the same reason that he could not be guilty of desertion, so too, he could not be guilty of wilful neglect to maintain, since the word 'wilful' connoted an element of wrongdoing or blame which did not exist in his case because of the delusion.

Held – The appeal would be dismissed for the following reasons—

c (i) the complaints of desertion and wilful neglect to maintain did not automatically stand or fall together; accordingly, the fact that the husband had no animus deserendi did not afford him a good defence to the complaint of wilful neglect to maintain (see p 44 b, post); dicta of Asquith LJ in *Chapman v Chapman* (4th April 1951) unreported, and of Lord Merriman P in *Stringer v Stringer* [1952] 1 All ER at 377 applied;

d (ii) the word 'wilful' did not connote any malice or wickedness on the part of the husband; the husband's neglect was wilful if, with the knowledge of the relevant facts, he deliberately failed to pay to the wife such sums as, in the opinion of the court, were in all the circumstances sufficient for her reasonable maintenance and support; despite his psychotic delusion, the evidence showed that at all material times the husband had that degree of knowledge and appreciation of the facts which sufficed to support a finding that his neglect to pay maintenance was 'wilful' (see

e p 45 f and p 47 f, post); *Tulip v Tulip* [1951] 2 All ER 91, *Dowell v Dowell* [1952] 2 All ER 141 and dicta of Lord Goddard CJ in *National Assistance Board v Prisk* [1954] 1 All ER at 401, 402 and of Hodson LJ in *Lilley v Lilley* [1959] 3 All ER at 289 applied.

Notes

f For the meaning of wilful neglect to maintain, see 12 Halsbury's Laws (3rd Edn) 482-485, paras 1077-1080 and for cases on the subject, see 27 (2) Digest (Reissue) 966-971, 7785-7816.

Cases referred to in judgment

Biggs v Burridge (1924) 89 JP 75, 22 LGR 55, DC, 14 Digest (Repl) 39, 93.
Chapman v Chapman (4th April 1951) unreported.
g *Chilton v Chilton* [1952] 1 All ER 1322, [1952] P 196, 116 JP 313, DC, Digest (Cont Vol A) 827, 6807a.
Clark v Clark (1931) 145 LT 487, 95 JP 170, 29 Cox CC 339, DC, 27 Digest (Repl) 702, 6718.
Dowell v Dowell [1952] 2 All ER 141, 116 JP 350, DC, Digest (Cont Vol A) 819, 6720a.
h *Everitt v Everitt* [1949] 1 All ER 908, [1949] P 374, 113 JP 279, CA, 27 Digest (Repl) 348, 2881.
Glenister v Glenister [1945] 1 All ER 513, [1945] P 30, 114 LJP 69, 172 LT 250, 109 JP 194, 27 Digest (Repl) 367, 3040.
Jones v Jones [1924] P 203, 93 LJP 94, 132 LT 63, DC, 27 Digest (Repl) 722, 6905.
Kaczmarz v Kaczmarz [1967] 1 All ER 416, [1967] 1 WLR 317, Digest (Cont Vol C) 442, 2791b.
j *Lilley v Lilley* [1959] 3 All ER 283, [1960] P 158, [1959] 3 WLR 306, 123 JP 525, CA, Digest (Cont Vol A) 667, 619ba.
Markovitch v Markovitch (1934) 151 LT 139, 98 JP 282, 30 Cox CC 115, DC, 27 Digest (Repl) 702, 6713.
Morton v Morton [1942] 1 All ER 273, 111 LJP 33, 166 LT 164, 106 JP 139, 27 Digest (Repl) 706, 6750.

Morton v Morton (No 2) [1954] 2 All ER 248, [1954] 1 WLR 737, CA, Digest (Cont Vol A)　*a*
677, 636k.

National Assistance Board v Prisk [1954] 1 All ER 400, [1954] 1 WLR 443, 118 JP 194, DC,
Digest (Cont Vol A) 667, 619a.

National Assistance Board v Wilkinson [1952] 2 All ER 255, [1952] 2 QB 648, 116 JP 428,
DC, Digest (Cont Vol A) 673, 630a.

Papadopoulos v Papadopoulos [1930] P 55, 99 LJP 1, 142 LT 237, 94 JP 39, 11 Digest　*b*
(Repl) 486, 1107.

Perry v Perry [1963] 3 All ER 766, [1964] 1 WLR 91, Digest (Cont Vol A) 720, 2791a.

Roberts v Regnart (1921) 86 JP 77, 126 LT 667, 27 Cox CC 198, DC.

Spence v Spence [1964] 3 All ER 61, [1965] P 140, [1964] 3 WLR 1115, Digest (Cont
Vol B) 346, 636f.

Stringer v Stringer [1952] 1 All ER 373, [1952] P 171, 116 JP 102, DC, Digest (Cont Vol A)　*c*
674, 636b.

Tulip v Tulip [1951] 2 All ER 91, [1951] P 378, CA, 27 Digest (Repl) 85, 635.

Weatherley v Weatherley (1929) 142 LT 163, 94 JP 38, 29 Cox CC 22, DC, 27 Digest
(Repl) 706, 6748.

West v West [1954] 2 All ER 505, [1954] P 444, [1954] 3 WLR 163, CA, Digest (Cont
Vol A) 677, 636m.　　　　　　　　　　　　　　　　　　　　　　　　　　　　　　　　　*d*

Whittaker v Whittaker [1939] 3 All ER 833, 55 TLR 1070, DC, 27 Digest (Repl) 713,
6805.

Cases also cited

Barker v Barker [1950] 1 All ER 812, CA.

Cox v Cox [1958] 1 All ER 569, [1958] 1 WLR 340.

Diggins v Diggins [1927] P 88, [1926] All ER Rep 268, DC.　　　　　　　　　　　　　　　*e*

G v G [1964] 1 All ER 129, [1964] P 133, DC.

Jones (A) v Jones (D L) (1929) 142 LT 167, [1929] All ER Rep 424, DC.

Morris v Edmonds (1897) 77 LT 56, [1895-99] All ER Rep 1089, DC.

Price v Price [1951] 2 All ER 580, [1951] P 413, CA.

Read v Legard (1851) 6 Exch 636.

Tickle v Tickle [1968] 2 All ER 154, [1968] 1 WLR 937, DC.　　　　　　　　　　　　　　*f*

Appeal

This was an appeal by the husband, Patrick Michael Brannan, against an order of
the Bromfield justices sitting at Wrexham dated 3rd December 1971, on a complaint by the wife, Ann Christine Brannan, that the husband had wilfully neglected
to maintain her. The facts are set out in the judgment of the court.　　　　　　　*g*

Martin Thomas for the husband.
A C Carlile for the wife.

　　　　　　　　　　　　　　　　　　　　　　　　　　　　　　　Cur adv vult

10th October. **SIR GEORGE BAKER P** read the following judgment of the　*h*
court. This appeal by the husband is against the decision of the justices of the petty
sessional division of Bromfield, sitting at Wrexham on 3rd December 1971, that he
wilfully neglected to provide reasonable maintenance for the wife from July 1970.
They ordered him to pay £6 a week. The amount is not in dispute.

　The parties were married on 23rd June 1962. The husband soon began to show
signs of mental illness; he had blackouts or 'collapses'; was in hospital on two or
three occasions and showed hostility to the wife. On 28th July 1970 he was admitted　*j*
to Wrexham War Memorial Hospital, where he remained for a fortnight in the care
of Dr Philip Evans. The wife visited him every night, but was told by the husband
and his mother to keep away. He then returned to the matrimonial home at
2 Nelson Terrace, Southsea, in the company of his mother and brother, but refused
to let his wife make a meal for him, he would not go to bed, and he left early next

a morning without telling his wife, who eventually discovered that he had gone to his sister. He never returned. On 2nd September he was admitted to a hospital in Wrexham, and from 23rd September 1970 to 21st January 1971 he was in the North Wales Hospital, Denbigh, in the care of Dr Powell, a consultant psychiatrist, who said of him:

b 'He appears to have a fixed, apparently irrational and, as far as I can discover, unreasonable belief that his wife is going to kill or injure him. She does not seem able to support this contention with any evidence or understandable reason why he should be acting in this fashion. Furthermore if pressed he says he cannot understand this idea himself. Nevertheless it is very real to him, causing him great apprehension and concern.'

c Although the exact diagnosis was doubtful, Dr Powell believed he had a psychotic illness, probably schizophrenia.

The wife remained in the matrimonial home on social security. In 1971 the husband returned to his employment (as second driver of a diesel engine) with British Railways. On 3rd June 1971 the wife, at the instigation of the social security authorities, issued a complaint that the husband had deserted her on 28th July 1970.

d That was heard by the justices on 17th September and dismissed. On the same day, but before the hearing, the wife issued the further complaint of wilful neglect to maintain. Counsel for the wife and the solicitor for the husband applied for the complaints to be heard separately but by the same bench. The justices agreed. The delay between the hearings was unavoidable.

The justices having found that the husband had left the matrimonial home on or e about 12th August 1970 and had not returned, say in their reasons:

'We found that the [husband], on account of his delusion was unable to form any intention to bring cohabitation permanently to an end and that the separation was one of necessity. Accordingly we dismissed the complaint for desertion.'

f Subsequently the wife appealed against the dismissal of the complaint of desertion, but her counsel withdrew that appeal at the hearing before us. We have, however, been referred to the evidence given to the justices on the issue of desertion as well as to the evidence given at the later hearing on the issue of wilful neglect to maintain. All the evidence is recorded verbatim.

At the first hearing Dr Powell, called for the husband, was asked:

g 'Is it right that there are times when he does go through periods of what might be called lucidity? Periods of just being a normal individual?'

He answered:

h 'I would say that to all outward observation, apart from being a somewhat silent and uncommunicative person, as perhaps you will have seen in court, he does appear, you know, a perfectly normal person. That is he knows who he is, how to conduct himself in public and at home and in every respect except with regard to his wife.'

On the second hearing, at which the husband did not give evidence, Dr Powell, called this time for the wife, having agreed that the husband would pass well within j the bounds of normality but that in a discussion about the relationship with his wife the husband's views would be coloured by his delusion and that he appeared or had appeared 'to be in mortal dread', was asked in cross-examination:

'But nothing in his behaviour leads you to believe that he is different now to what he was when you came to the conclusion that he was suffering from those delusions?'

He replied: *a*

'I am afraid there seems to be very little change in his condition. I think
that he is capable of understanding ideas such as maintenance and what people
should and shouldn't do.'

In their reasons for finding proved the complaint of wilful neglect to maintain
the justices, having considered a submission that they had no jurisdiction to hear   *b*
the complaint because of their earlier dismissal of the charge of desertion (this
ground of appeal was not argued before us), continued:

'We found that since leaving the matrimonial home on or about the 12th day
of August, 1970, the [husband] had not paid any maintenance to his wife. He
had been working, and we were of the opinion that his mental condition did
not prevent him from knowing that his wife was in need of money. We were   *c*
of the opinion that, although his delusion justified him in living apart from his
wife, he had no delusion that harm might befall him as a result of sending his
wife money or that there was any other good reason why he should not do so.
Accordingly we found his failure to maintain his wife to be wilful, and, therefore,
we found the complaint proved.'
                                                                                     d
The husband's two remaining grounds of appeal against this decision are:

'2. The Justices having previously held that the [husband] had not deserted
the [wife] and was not under a duty to cohabit with the [wife], it was not open
to the Justices to find that the [husband] had wilfully neglected to provide
reasonable maintenance for the [wife], the duty to maintain being co-extensive   *e*
with the duty to cohabit.
'3. The Justices were wrong in law in holding that the [husband's] neglect
to maintain was wilful, the evidence being that his conduct was the result of, or
alternatively was substantially induced by insane delusions which, if true, would
justify the [husband's] neglect to maintain the [wife].'

Counsel for the husband has presented a clear, lucid and not unattractive argument *f*
which can be summarised thus. (1) The husband is and has at all material times
been under a duty to maintain the wife. This duty arises from the common law
and now has the statutory authority of s 22 of the Ministry of Social Security
Act 1966. (2) In the circumstances of this case the husband, although he has left his
wife and brought cohabitation to an end, is not guilty of desertion because he has not
the necessary animus deserendi. (3) The delusion found as a fact by the justices   *g*
was of such a kind that, if the facts which he believed to exist were true, the husband
would be justified in refusing to live with his wife. The husband cannot therefore
be held to have the necessary intention to desert his wife. (4) The same reasoning
must be applied to the allegation that the husband is guilty of wilfully neglecting to
provide reasonable maintenance for his wife. Although his legal obligation to   *h*
maintain his wife may continue in spite of the intervention or continuance of his
insane delusions, his failure to pay maintenance was not 'wilful' and was not a matrimonial offence in the light of his mental condition. (5) The word 'wilful' connotes
an element of wrongdoing or blame which does not exist, or has not been proved,
in this case because of the husband's delusion. (6) A distinction must be drawn
between 'liability to maintain' and 'wilful neglect to maintain'.

This argument, in our view, contains fallacies but it deserves careful consideration *j*
not least because the questions arising in this case are of general interest and importance. A husband's duty to maintain his wife has long existed under the common
law. An interesting review of the history of this obligation is contained in the judgment of Lord Goddard CJ in *National Assistance Board v Wilkinson*[1] and it is unnecessary

---

1   [1952] 2 All ER 255, [1952] 2 QB 648

a to repeat it in this judgment. The duty to provide reasonable maintenance for a wife and children can now be enforced by proceedings in the High Court or in a divorce county court under s 6 of the Matrimonial Proceedings and Property Act 1970 or in the magistrates' courts under the Matrimonial Proceedings (Magistrates' Courts) Act 1960, ss 1 and 2. In the present case the court is concerned with the wife's allegation that the husband has wilfully neglected to provide reasonable maintenance

b for her and the defence raised by the husband that by reason of his delusion his neglect to pay maintenance for his wife is not wilful. There appears to be no direct authority precisely covering this defence.

In support of his argument, counsel for the husband first invited our consideration of *Perry v Perry*[1], which he relied on as authority for the proposition that a husband who suffers from such a delusion that he believes himself to be justified in leaving his wife does not have the necessary animus deserendi. One must take the facts as

c he genuinely believes them to be and he is exculpated in respect of his conduct in bringing cohabitation to an end. He is not therefore guilty of desertion. In *Perry's* case[1] the husband was petitioning for divorce on the grounds of the wife's desertion. This was defended by the wife, on whose behalf it was contended that at all material times she was suffering from paranoid psychosis and, although when she left home she knew what she was doing, she was under a delusion as to her husband's violent

d intentions towards her and was incapable of forming an intention to desert him. It was held that the rights of the parties in relation to the charge of desertion were to be adjudicated as if the wife's belief were true, and accordingly the husband had not shown that the wife had the mental capacity to form an intention to desert him.

Counsel then asked us to extend this reasoning to a case of wilful neglect to maintain and drew our attention to *Glenister v Glenister*[2] and *Chilton v Chilton*[3]. In *Glenister's*

e case[2], where a finding of desertion had been made by the justices against the husband, the Divisional Court allowed his appeal on the grounds that on the evidence relating to his wife's conduct the husband had reasonable cause for supposing that the wife had committed adultery and should not therefore be held to have left her without reasonable cause. *Glenister's* case[2] is, therefore, one of those cases in which the wife by her conduct forfeited her right to an order for maintenance in the magis-

f trates' court. The reasoning in *Glenister's* case[2] was applied in *Chilton's* case[3] to a situation in which the husband turned his wife out of the matrimonial home relying on a bona fide belief induced by the wife that she had committed adultery with another man. The court held that this, being based on the wife's conduct, afforded a defence not only to a charge of desertion but also to a charge of wilful neglect to maintain. *Chilton's* case[3], therefore, is also one in which the wife forfeited her right

g to relief by reason of her own misconduct, notwithstanding that the evidence fell short of proof of the full offence of adultery.

Kaczmarz v Kaczmarz[4], to which we were also referred, is distinguishable from *Perry's* case[1] in that the evidence in *Kaczmarz's* case[4] did not establish that the wife was suffering at the material time from such delusions as rendered her incapable of forming the necessary intention to desert. She was found to have deserted her

h husband.

In approaching counsel's submission two matters must not be overlooked. The first is that summonses for desertion and wilful neglect to maintain do not necessarily stand or fall together. In *Stringer v Stringer*[5], Lord Merriman P quotes from an unreported judgment of Asquith LJ in *Chapman v Chapman*[6]:

j

---

1   [1963] 3 All ER 766, [1964] 1 WLR 91
2   [1945] 1 All ER 513, [1945] P 30
3   [1952] 1 All ER 1322, [1952] P 196
4   [1967] 1 All ER 416, [1967] 1 WLR 317
5   [1952] 1 All ER 373 at 377, [1952] P 171 at 179
6   4th April 1951

' "Often two such summonses do so [i e fall together], and if the wife fails on
desertion she automatically fails on wilful neglect to maintain, but that is not   *a*
necessarily or inevitably so. Sometimes, where, for instance the evidence is
that the separation was consensual she may fail on desertion and win on maintenance; in cases, that is, where the consensus impliedly includes a term that the
wife should be entitled to some support from the husband." '

So in this case the fact that the husband has a good defence to desertion does not   *b*
necessarily or inevitably mean that he has an answer to wilful neglect to maintain.

Secondly, as we have seen in *Glenister's* case[1] and *Chilton's* case[2], a wife by her
own conduct or misconduct can forfeit her right to be maintained by her husband.
This statement must be qualified by recognition of the fact that a wife in a divorce
suit, both before and after the recent changes in the law, might recover some maintenance notwithstanding her adultery or other failure to fulfil her duties as a wife;   *c*
but the old traditional and discretionary bars to relief may still obtain if a wife is
seeking to establish wilful neglect to maintain, whether in the High Court, a divorce
county court or a magistrates' court. She may be barred from her remedy if, for
example, she has committed adultery (Summary Jurisdiction (Married Women) Act
1895, s 6, now the Matrimonial Proceedings (Magistrates' Courts) Act 1960, s 2 (3) (*b*)),
or has been guilty of conduct giving rise to a reasonable suspicion of adultery   *d*
(*Glenister's* case[1], *Chilton's* case[2], *Everitt v Everitt*[3] and *West v West*[4]), or has deserted
her husband, of has refused to perform or has without just cause renounced her wifely
duties (*Clark v Clark*[5] and *Weatherley v Weatherley*[6], but see also *Spence v Spence*[7]).
There are many cases of this kind, but they throw little or no light on the problem
before the court, because in this case there is no ground for attacking the character
or conduct of the wife, and she has not forfeited or prejudiced her right to be   *e*
maintained.

The crucial question is whether the ratio decidendi of *Perry's* case[8] in its application to desertion can properly be applied to any case of wilful neglect to maintain,
and in particular to this case. The reason why the insane delusion of the husband
in *Perry's* case[8] afforded a defence to desertion was that he had not the capacity
to form the intent which was a necessary ingredient and had not, therefore, the   *f*
essential state of mind, the animus deserendi. Whether this defence can succeed
in the present case depends on the meaning to be given to the word 'wilful'. In
Stone's Justices' Manual[9] it is stated:

'The phrase "wilful neglect to provide reasonable maintenance" ... imports
some element of matrimonial misconduct, ... The wrongdoing may however   *g*
consist of the very fact of a failure to maintain: there need be no other matrimonial offence imputed to the husband.'

The authority for the first part of this text is *Morton v Morton*[10] in which Lord
Merriman P said:

'It is unnecessary to attempt, as other judges have consistently refused to do,   *h*
to give an exhaustive definition of "wilful neglect to provide reasonable maintenance". I am not satisfied that cases dealing solely with the meaning of the

1 [1945] 1 All ER 513, [1945] P 30
2 [1952] 1 All ER 1322, [1952] P 196
3 [1949] 1 All ER 908, [1949] P 374
4 [1954] 2 All ER 505, [1954] P 444   *j*
5 (1931) 145 LT 487
6 (1929) 142 LT 163
7 [1964] 3 All ER 61, [1965] P 140
8 [1963] 3 All ER 766, [1964] 1 WLR 91
9 104th Edn (1972), vol 1, pp 1411, 1412
10 [1942] 1 All ER 273 at 273, 274

a word "wilful," or cases dealing solely with the meaning of the word "neglect," are of very great assistance. Justices have to be satisfied affirmatively that the husband has been guilty of the subject-matter of the complaint . . . "wilful neglect to provide reasonable maintenance." The phrase must be considered as a whole, and, as I have already indicated in *Whittaker* v. *Whittaker*[1], I agree with the view of LORD MERRIVALE, P., expressed in *Jones* v. *Jones*[2], that the phrase b imports some element of matrimonial misconduct. Further than that, for the purposes of this case, it seems to me to be unnecessary to go.'

It must be appreciated that in *Morton's* case[3] the husband was held to be not guilty of misconduct and the court did not, therefore, have to consider what kind or amount of misconduct would have to be proved to establish 'wilful' neglect.

c There are two lines of cases in which wives have alleged that their husbands have been guilty of wilful neglect to provide reasonable maintenance although they have previously entered into agreements, whether by deed or otherwise, under which the amount of maintenance has been fixed. One line establishes that, where a husband is paying reasonable maintenance under an agreement, he cannot be found guilty of wilful neglect to provide reasonable maintenance because he and his wife have already decided what they regard as reasonable and the husband has fulfilled d his part of the agreement. Such a case is *Morton* v *Morton (No 2)*[4]. On the other side there are cases to the effect that, if, owing to a change in the value of money or other changes in the circumstances, the maintenance payable under an agreement is not adequate provision for the wife, she can apply to the court for an order on the grounds of wilful neglect to provide reasonable maintenance. The observance of the agreement does not absolve the husband because the amount of maintenance e is insufficient in the changed circumstances which have arisen. Two such cases are *Tulip* v *Tulip*[5] and *Dowell* v *Dowell*[6]. It is also clear on the authorities that the husband will not be held guilty of wilful neglect owing to changed circumstances unless the changes have been brought to his notice by some communication from the wife or her solicitors or otherwise.

f These cases suggest that 'wilfulness' in this context does not connote any malice or wickedness but that the misconduct, if it is appropriate to use that word, consists only in the failure to pay to the wife sums which, in the opinion of the court, are in all the circumstances sufficient for her reasonable maintenance and support. The wilfulness amounts to nothing more than this, that the husband knows what he is doing and intends to do what he is doing.

This is not a new approach to the problem. In two earlier cases, *Roberts* v *Regnart*[7] g and *Biggs* v *Burridge*[8], the husband was charged under the Vagrancy Act 1824 with wilfully refusing and neglecting to maintain his wife, or wife and family. In each case the husband genuinely believed that he was not legally liable to maintain his wife, and she became chargeable to the union. It was held, in the first case sending the case back to the justices for conviction, and in the second upholding the conviction of the husband, that 'mens rea' was immaterial and that the husband's error was a h mistake of law and not of fact. In *Biggs* v *Burridge*[9] Lord Hewart CJ, sitting with Roche and Branson JJ, who concurred in the judgment, said:

1 [1939] 3 All ER 833
2 [1924] P 203
i 3 [1942] 1 All ER 273
4 [1954] 2 All ER 248, [1954] 1 WLR 737
5 [1951] 2 All ER 91, [1951] P 378
6 [1952] 2 All ER 141
7 (1921) 86 JP 77
8 (1924) 89 JP 75
9 (1924) 89 JP at 76

'. . . the contention of the appellant really came to this, that although he was
legally bound, there was no *mens rea* on his part, and he ought not to be con-   *a*
victed because he obstinately persisted in the error about his legal position.'

In *Papadopoulos v Papadopoulos*[1] and *Markovitch v Markovitch*[2] the court treated
'wilfully' as meaning no more than 'knowingly'.

There are more recent authorities. In *National Assistance Board v Prisk*[3] Lord
Goddard CJ, referring to earlier proceedings before the justices, said: *b*

'The wife took proceedings before the justices in December, 1952, alleging
wilful neglect to maintain. At first sight it looks rather odd that a husband
should be said to be wilfully neglecting to maintain his wife if he is paying money
due under a deed, but it is too late to argue that now. "Wilful" means, in the
Summary Jurisdiction (Separation and Maintenance) Acts, 1895 to 1949, "de-   *c*
liberate", that is to say, deliberately refusing to pay, with no excuse except the
deed.'

After referring to *Tulip v Tulip*[4] and *Dowell v Dowell*[5], Lord Goddard CJ said[6]:

'If one analyses those cases, the reason why the deed cannot be set up as an
answer is that the respondent still remains liable to maintain his wife unless,   *d*
of course, she has committed a matrimonial offence. He remains liable to
maintain his wife because of the common law relationship of husband and wife.
It may be shown that the fact that he has covenanted to pay her £1 a week does
not provide her with adequate maintenance and, of course, one object of these
orders that are made against husbands in respect of their wives is to prevent
the wives becoming a charge on public funds.'   *e*

An important case which assists towards the solution of the questions which arise
in the present case is *Lilley v Lilley*[7]. In that case at the relevant time the wife suffered
from a neurosis which produced an acute revulsion to any physical contact with the
husband. Medical evidence showed that, if she returned to him, there would be a
serious breakdown in her health. The Court of Appeal accepted the justices'
finding that, in the circumstances of that case, the wife was guilty of desertion, but in   *f*
his judgment Hodson LJ considered the wife's allegation of wilful neglect to provide
reasonable maintenance apart from the finding of desertion. The judgment contains
the following passages[8]:

'The authorities, in our opinion, are consistent only with the view of the law
repeatedly enunciated by [Lord Merriman P] and his predecessor LORD MERRI-   *g*
VALE—that whatever may be the position as against the public authority, nevertheless, as between the husband and the wife he cannot be found guilty of wilful
neglect to maintain her unless he is a wrongdoer. The wrongdoing may, however, consist of the very fact of a failure to maintain. There need be no other
matrimonial offence imputed to the husband . . . There is in this case no agreement to live apart, but there is a de facto separation which is explained by the   *h*
wife's state of neurosis, because of which, as the learned stipendiary found, the
wife would be risking grave consequences to her mental health if she returned
to her husband at the present time. She maintains that in the circumstances

---

1   [1930] P 55
2   (1934) 151 LT 139   *j*
3   [1954] 1 All ER 400 at 401, [1954] 1 WLR 443 at 444
4   [1951] 2 All ER 91, [1951] P 378
5   [1952] 2 All ER 141
6   [1954] 1 All ER at 402, [1954] 1 WLR at 445
7   [1959] 3 All ER 283, [1960] P 158
8   [1959] 3 All ER at 289, [1960] P at 179-181

a if he does not maintain her apart from him he is guilty of wilful neglect to maintain just as much as if she were separated from him by necessity. Examples of separation by necessity come readily to mind where the occupation of the husband makes it necessary for him to spend long periods apart from his wife by reason of his absence at sea or otherwise away from his home. The changes and chances of life may often, where there is a separation of necessity, put on the husband the obligation to support his wife when she is separated from him, and *b* if he does not do so he will be guilty of the offence with which he is charged. This duty must surely subsist if separation is forced on the parties by illness which compels residence in hospital, and this would be the same whatever the nature of the illness, even if it be mental disorder, provided always that the intention of the absent spouse to return to the other continues . . . We see no reason why the obligation to maintain which exists when the husband and wife *c* are living together should be affected by an enforced separation. If the husband does not maintain his wife while in the home he is clearly in default under the statutes, and an enforced separation of itself can make no difference.'

This reasoning seems to us exactly to cover the facts of the present case. The husband by reason of his psychotic illness, probably a form of schizophrenia, has been impelled *d* to leave his wife and has so produced an enforced separation. He remains legally liable to maintain his wife—and his counsel does not argue otherwise. He knows that the Department of Health and Social Security is supporting his wife and that he is not. He does not criticise his wife for pursuing these proceedings because he understands that they are brought under the advice or at the request of the department. In those circumstances we are wholly satisfied that he has, and at all material times *e* has had, that degree of knowledge and appreciation of the facts which suffices to support a finding that his neglect to pay maintenance to his wife is 'wilful'. The husband's delusion may well have provided him with a moral excuse, satisfactory to him, for not paying regular maintenance to his wife, but he knows that he is not paying it and does not intend to pay it. His delusion does not give rise to any legal justification for failing to maintain his wife. The state of mind which is an ingredient *f* of 'wilful' neglect to maintain is distinguishable, therefore, from that state of mind which has to be proved in order to establish a complaint of desertion. In our opinion the husband's appeal must be dismissed.

In the course of argument at the Bar the question arose whether in the event of a claim by the department for contribution from a husband towards maintenance paid to a wife the same or similar defences were open to him as would be available *g* where a wife claimed maintenance on the grounds of wilful neglect to maintain. This important problem must receive consideration in depth sooner or later, but it does not arise in this case and should therefore be deferred until the court can hear full argument on it.

Appeal dismissed.

h

Solicitors: *Amery-Parkes & Co*, agents for *Gwilym Hughes & Partners*, Wrexham (for the husband); *Manches & Co*, agents for *Cyril Jones & Co*, Wrexham (for the wife).

R C T Habesch Esq Barrister.

a

Sullivan v Henderson

CHANCERY DIVISION
MEGARRY J
4th, 5th, 6th OCTOBER 1972

b

Specific performance – Agreement for sale of shares in company – Vendor and purchaser entering into contract before commencement of winding up of company – Vendor claiming specific performance of contract after winding-up order made – Whether contract enforceable – Companies Act 1948, s 227.

Specific performance – Summary procedure – Leave to defend – Order for examination on oath – Circumstances in which such an order should be made – RSC Ord 86.

c

After the commencement of the winding up of a company the court will not order the specific performance of a contract previously made for the sale of shares in it, for to do so would be to force on the transferee a transfer which, although valid as between him and the transferor, would be void under s 227ᵃ of the Companies Act 1948 as against the company (see p 50 h to p 51 a, post).

On the hearing of an application for summary judgment under RSC Ord 86, the court should not give leave for a defendant to be cross-examined on his affidavit unless the circumstances are very exceptional. Although there may be cases in which it is right to give leave to cross-examine, perhaps limited to a single point, such cases are likely to be comparatively rare (see p 51 h and j and p 52 b, post).

d

Notes

e

For application of specific performance to sale of shares and the effect of winding up, see 36 Halsbury's Laws (3rd Edn) 276, para 381.

For proceedings for summary judgment for specific performance, see 36 Halsbury's Laws (3rd Edn) 333, para 490.

Cases referred to in judgment

f

Millard v Baddeley [1884] WN 96, Bitt Rep in Ch 125; *affd* CA (1884) 28 Sol Jo 427, 50 Digest (Repl) 423, *1290*.

Onward Building Society, Re [1891] 2 QB 463, 60 LJQB 752, 65 LT 516, 56 JP 260, CA, 7 Digest (Repl) 532, *343*.

Summons

g

By this summons the plaintiff, William Patrick Sullivan, applied under RSC Ord 86 for summary judgment in an action in which he claimed against the defendant, James Joseph Henderson, (i) specific performance of an oral contract alleged to have been made in or about October 1968, whereby the defendant agreed to purchase certain shares in a company from the plaintiff for £1,000; alternatively, (ii) damages for breach of contract. The facts are set out in the judgment.

h

Neil Butter for the plaintiff.
The defendant appeared in person.

MEGARRY J. This case has become encrusted with a variety of procedural and other points, at least one of which is of some general importance; but in the end, when these points have been disposed of, the real issue lies within a narrow compass. By a writ issued on 22nd June 1971 the plaintiff claims against the defendant specific performance of an oral contract alleged to have been made in or about October 1968, whereby the defendant agreed to purchase certain shares from the plaintiff for £1,000, with an alternative claim for damages for breach of contract. Mr Butter

j

---

a   Section 227 is set out at p 50 f, post

a has appeared for the plaintiff and the defendant has appeared in person; he has, if I may say so, conducted his case with considerable skill.

Two companies are involved in this case; one is Thornhill & Co (Developments) Ltd, to which I shall refer as 'the Developments company'; the other is Thornhill (Drawing & Tracing) Co Ltd, which I shall call 'the Drawing company'. Both companies have now come to grief; a winding-up order was made in the case of

b the Drawing company in about March 1970, and in the case of the Developments company, after there had been a resolution for a voluntary winding-up in about August 1971, a winding-up order was made on 11th January 1972. The defendant was managing director of both companies and for all practical purposes he was in control of both companies at all material times. The Developments company was, I understand, mainly a holding company, whereas the Drawing company prepared,

c drawings, tracings, electrical circuits and so on.

The plaintiff met the defendant in about January 1968; the plaintiff was seeking employment. In the end, the plaintiff entered the employment of the Drawing company and on 29th February 1968 a typewritten agreement, drafted by solicitors, was entered into between the two companies, the plaintiff and the defendant. I shall call this the 'February contract'. The agreement was a contract for the Draw-

d ing company to employ the plaintiff as a director, and among the various clauses of that contract there was cl 7. This provided that on the signing of the agreement the plaintiff was to pay to the Drawing company the sum of £1,000 as the issue price for the allotment to him of 200 ordinary shares of £1 each in the company, unissued at the date of the agreement; and it provided that on receipt of the £1,000 the Drawing company was to allot and issue these shares to the plaintiff. There was

e also cl 8, whereby the plaintiff was given an option, exercisable within three months of the signing of the agreement, to purchase from the defendant 1,000 ordinary shares of £1 each in the Developments company for the sum of £4,000. It is common ground that this option was a mere option for the plaintiff which he never in fact exercised. Nevertheless, despite its terms, the defendant seems to have regarded this option, set in the context of discussions between the plaintiff and the defendant,

f as imposing some obligation on the plaintiff to invest £4,000 in addition to the £1,000 under cl 7.

On the evidence before me, the 200 shares in the Drawing company were never in fact issued to the plaintiff, although from time to time he pressed the defendant for them. Instead, on 1st July 1968, a certificate for 1,000 £1 shares in the Developments company was issued to the plaintiff; and on the defendant's evidence these were his shares, which he transferred to the plaintiff. What the plaintiff originally

g alleged is that in or about October 1968 the defendant orally agreed to purchase the shares in the Developments company from the plaintiff for £1,000, although by an amendment, made at a late stage, the agreement is in the alternative related to the 200 shares in the Drawing company that were never in fact issued to the plaintiff. I shall call this oral agreement 'the October agreement'. I observe from the

h February contract that the option to purchase the 1,000 shares in the Developments company was at a price of £4,000, so that, depending on which shares the October agreement related to, the defendant was to purchase them at either the full price to be found in the February contract or at one-quarter of that price.

The defendant does not in effect deny that he agreed to buy some shares from the plaintiff for £1,000. What he contends is that the agreement was subject to a condition that was never fulfilled, namely (and I put it briefly), that he was to pay

j the £1,000 only when the companies were doing well enough to provide him with the necessary money, a position which was never in fact achieved. The plaintiff, I may say, left the employment of the Drawing company at about the time of the October agreement, on obtaining a better job, and it was in relation to his impending departure that the October agreement was made. He remained a director of the company for a few months after his employment ceased.

Procedurally the matter comes before me as a summons under RSC Ord 86, *a*
seeking only specific performance of the October agreement in relation to the shares
in the Developments company, or, by the amendment made late in the hearing,
alternatively the shares in the Drawing company. However, again by amendment
during the hearing, a claim for damages was added to the summons in the alternative. The summons differs from the usual run of such summonses in relation to
the evidence. On 22nd March 1972 the Master made an order giving the plaintiff *b*
unrestricted liberty to cross-examine the defendant on his affidavit; and I was told
that a previous order of the Master, made on 15th December 1971, gave the plaintiff
leave to adduce oral evidence in reply on giving written notice, which notice was
duly given. The result of these orders, coupled with the fact that the defendant
appeared in person, has led to the adduction of full and detailed oral evidence about
all aspects of the disputed transaction, and much else besides. What in theory was *c*
to be a hearing to decide whether in effect leave to defend should be given, or
whether summary judgment should be entered for the plaintiff for specific performance, became in fact a virtual trial of the action. This is not what RSC Ord 86, as
I understand it, is intended for; nor is the case in a very satisfactory state, because,
having been brought under the summons, there has been no discovery of documents, and no pleadings, apart from the short statement of claim endorsed on *d*
the writ. Further, no notices to produce have been given, and none of the documents
relating to the companies, which are presumably in the hands of the liquidator, is
before the court. Even so, I think that with the aid of the parties I have got to the
bottom of the essentials of the dispute, and if in the event some saving of time and
money can be effected, I propose to attempt to do this. Certainly, to direct a trial
of the action now would be to require the parties to go again over ground which *e*
has already occupied the court for the best part of the last two days.

One question that arises is whether there is a case for specific performance at all.
What is sought is a decree of specific performance of a contract for the sale of shares
in a company (whichever company it is) that was made before the commencement
of the compulsory winding-up of the company, but is being enforced after that
winding-up has commenced. The Companies Act 1948, s 227, reads as follows: *f*

'In a winding up by the court, any disposition of the property of the company,
including things in action, and any transfer of shares, or alteration in the status
of the members of the company, made after the commencement of the winding
up, shall, unless the court otherwise orders, be void.'

It may thus be said that the plaintiff is seeking specific performance of a contract *g*
which statute has declared to be void unless the court (that is, the Companies Court)
otherwise orders. Without canvassing the question of whether a judge of the
Chancery Division, when not sitting for the purpose of exercising the court's company
winding-up jurisdiction, could make an order under the section, or whether this is
a fit case for such an order, counsel for the plaintiff contended that *Re Onward
Building Society*[1] showed that the word 'void' in the section merely meant void quoad *h*
the company and not void as between vendor and purchaser. He accepted, however,
that even on this footing there may be grave reasons why no order for specific performance should be made in such a case. If before any question of a winding-up
has arisen, V contracts to sell shares in a company to P, and then, after a winding-
up order has been made, V sues P for specific performance, I think that any court
would be most reluctant to force upon P, who had agreed to take a fully effective *j*
transfer of the shares, a transfer that, although valid as between him and the vendor,
would be void as against the company. Counsel for the plaintiff was not able to
contend for any contrary view; and in my judgment it would require remarkable

---

1 [1891] 2 QB 463, especially at 475

a circumstances to support making a decree in such a case. This plainly is not such a case, and in my judgment the claim for specific performance must fail.

The plaintiff's real claim is to get his money back; and under this head the real question is whether or not the defendant ever effectually agreed to pay the money back in return for some shares, either unconditionally or on conditions that have been satisfied. [His Lordship, having considered the evidence, continued:] It follows

b that in my judgment the plaintiff has established that the defendant orally contracted, in or about October 1968, to purchase from the plaintiff the shares in the Drawing company to which the plaintiff was entitled under the February contract, and that this contract was not conditional upon the prosperity of the companies or on anything else.

RSC Ord 86, r 1, applies to proceedings in which the writ is endorsed with a

c claim for specific performance of an agreement, or in the alternative for damages. The writ in this case satisfies this requirement. The defendant has not satisfied me, within r 4, that 'there is an issue or question in dispute which ought to be tried or that there ought for some other reason to be a trial of the action'. Accordingly, under the rule I may give judgment for the plaintiff in this action. For the reasons I have given, it seems right for me to do this, and accordingly I give judgment for

d the plaintiff for damages to be assessed by the Master, unless the parties prefer some other mode of assessment. I do not think I can avoid ordering the damages to be assessed, for although the claim is primarily for £1,000, it may be that the 200 unissued shares in the Drawing company to which the plaintiff was entitled under the February contract will prove to have had some value which ought to be deducted from the £1,000. Whether this is so must presumably await the con-clusion of the winding-up, although it may be possible to resolve the matter sooner.

e I may add that in addition to feeling some sympathy for the plaintiff, I also feel some sympathy for the defendant, who seems to have tried to behave honourably towards the plaintiff in agreeing to buy back the shares at their cost price, and to have lost much of his time and money in the collapse of his companies. If they had prospered, this action would never have been brought. But my duty is to

f decide the rights of the parties according to law, and that I have endeavoured to do.

There is one further point that I should mention for guidance in future cases. The present case seems to me to illustrate the difficulties that may arise if leave to cross-examine a witness on his affidavit is given in cases under RSC Ord 86. The summary process under RSC Ord 86 is one thing, and the trial of an action is another: a hearing under RSC Ord 86 with oral evidence is liable to become neither one nor the other, and to share the disadvantages of each. The hearing ceases to be summary,

g and the absence of pleadings and discovery, for example, prevents the hearing from achieving the exhaustiveness of a trial. The court may be put in the position, at the end of a two day hearing, of saying that there ought to be a trial of the action, in which case there will then be the repetition of much that has occupied the court and the parties during the hearing under RSC Ord 86. I observe that r 5 (3) (b) of

h the order, which authorises the making of an order for the defendant to attend and be examined on oath, qualifies the power by the words 'if it appears to the court that there are special circumstances which make it desirable that he should do so.' These are weighty qualifications, and I would subscribe to the cautionary words of Field J in *Millard v Baddeley*[1], uttered in relation to the corresponding procedure under RSC Ord 14. There may be cases where it is right to give leave to cross-

j examine, perhaps limited to a single point, although this has its own problems both for counsel and for litigants who are bursting to reveal all; and in any case I would expect cases in which it would be desirable for such leave to be given to be of comparatively rare occurrence.

I am conscious that there are difficulties in a case which, like this, has been subs-tantially reshaped by amendments at a late stage of the hearing; but after I had

1 [1884] WN 96; *affd* (1884) 28 Sol Jo 427

done my best to explain to the defendant the differing effects of giving leave to *a*
amend and of refusing it, he very sensibly agreed to the amendments being made
in the cause of economy and of the avoidance of further delay. If I have erred in
continuing with the case, I have erred in the same cause. At least this case may serve
as a warning to others that proceedings under RSC Ord 86 are intended to be summary, and that serious procedural difficulties are likely to arise if oral evidence be
admitted, save in truly exceptional cases, and with proper restrictions.   *b*

[On the defendant agreeing to waive any claim to have the possible value of the
200 unissued shares deducted, his Lordship gave judgment for the plaintiff for
£1,000, the defendant to pay half the plaintiff's costs.]

Judgment for the plaintiff.

Solicitors: *Waterhouse & Co*, agents for *T G Baynes & Sons*, Bexleyheath (for the *c*
plaintiff).

Ilyas Khan Esq Barrister.

Practice Direction   *d*

SUPREME COURT TAXING OFFICE

*Costs – Taxation – Bill of costs – Lodging of bill when reference taken – Procedure – RSC
Ord 62, rr 21, 23.*

1.   To assist solicitors to bring in their bills of costs at the same time as they take *e*
a reference, for the purpose of giving them time to decide whether it is possible to
agree their costs with the opposing party without taking a reference and in order
to simplify the work in each chambers of the Supreme Court Taxing Office, RSC
Ord 62, rr 21 and 23, have been amended with effect from 1st January 1973, as
follows: (a) The time for taking a reference is extended to three months from the
date of judgment or order etc, except in the case of a taxation under the Solicitors *f*
Act 1957 where it will remain seven days. (b) There will be separate ballots for
masters and principal clerks. (c) Unless the solicitor satisfies the rota clerk it is
impracticable to do so, the bill and full supporting papers must be lodged at the
same time as the reference is taken.

2.   The statement of parties must contain the telephone number and office
reference of every solicitor concerned whether as principal or agent, and of every *g*
party acting in person, and must be lodged when the reference is taken.

3.   Where the bill is not lodged at the same time as the reference is taken, the
solicitors must state whether or not the bill is likely to be within the principal clerk's
limit to enable the reference to be ballotted correctly.

4.   In cases where more than one bill has to be taxed and the solicitors having
carriage of the order fail to take a reference within the time limited by RSC Ord 62, *h*
r 21 (3), any other party having a bill may apply for leave to refer his bill on production
of an office copy of the order to tax, whereupon he shall comply with the rules as
if he were the party having carriage of the order.

5.   Where there has been a previous reference, the order will be referred to the
master or the principal clerk in the chambers concerned.

6.   Where, for any reason, a reference has been ballotted on the basis of wrong *j*
information, application should be made to the chambers concerned for leave to
take a fresh reference.

7.   The existing procedure as to r 30 cases will continue.

GRAHAM J GRAHAM-GREEN
Chief Taxing Master

30th November 1972

a

Pegler v Abell (Inspector of Taxes)

CHANCERY DIVISION
GOFF J
13th, 14th NOVEMBER 1972

b

Income tax – Income – Earned income – Meaning – Income immediately derived from carrying on of exercise of trade, profession or vocation – Immediately derived – Partnership – Accountants – Retirement of partner – Agreement with continuing partners – Payment of 'retirement allowance' – Allowance computed as a percentage of the profits of the firm – Whether the allowance 'immediately derived' by retired partner from carrying on of his profession
c *as a partner – Income Tax Act 1952, s 525 (1) (c).*

The taxpayer was a full-time partner in a firm of chartered accountants. Under the deed of partnership the taxpayer was entitled to receive by way of retirement allowance from the date of his retirement, such half-yearly sum, after deduction of tax at the standard rate for the time being in force, as was equivalent to 3 per cent
d of the net profits of the business calculated in accordance with the terms of the partnership deed. On 27th January 1967 the taxpayer entered into an agreement with his co-partners, which varied the deed of partnership by providing, inter alia, for his retirement on 31st January 1967 and by increasing his retirement allowance to 5 per cent of the net profits of the business until the end of the half year in which his 60th birthday occurred. The taxpayer duly retired from the partnership on
e 31st January 1967 and pursuant to the agreement received the sum of £5,158 after deduction of tax as his allowance for the year 1967-68. He claimed earned income relief in respect of that sum, contending that, since the allowance was income charged under Sch D and immediately derived by him from the carrying on of his profession as a partner in the partnership, it was 'earned income' within the meaning of s 525 (1) (c)[a] of the Income Tax Act 1952.
f

Held – The allowance paid to the taxpayer was not derived, immediately or otherwise, from the past carrying on of his profession, but from the contractual liability of the continuing partners under the partnership deed as amended by the agreement; the words 'income ... immediately derived by the individual from the carrying on or exercise by him of his trade, profession or vocation' in s 525 (1) (c) referred to money
g received as a reward for or as the emoluments of some present activity; even if it were true to say that the allowance was derived from the carrying on of a profession at all, it was from the carrying on of their profession by the existing partners after the taxpayer's retirement and not from the carrying on by the taxpayer of his profession; accordingly the allowance was not earned income within the meaning of s 525 (1) (c) (see p 58 j, p 60 h and p 61 b, post).
h   Dictum of Pennycuick J in *Bucks v Bowers (Inspector of Taxes)* [1970] 2 All ER at 208 applied.
   Hale v Shea (Inspector of Taxes) [1965] 1 All ER 155 and *Peay (Inspector of Taxes) v Newton* [1971] 2 All ER 172 distinguished.

Notes
j For earned income relief, see 20 Halsbury's Laws (3rd Edn) 438-440, paras 818, 819, and for cases on the subject see 28 (1) Digest (Reissue) 450-452, *1611-1620*.
   For the Income Tax Act 1952, s 525, see 31 Halsbury's Statutes (2nd Edn) 488.
   In relation to tax for the year 1970-71 and subsequent years of assessment, the

---

a Section 525 (1) is set out at p 58 f and j, post

Income Tax Act 1952, s 525, has been replaced by the Income and Corporation Taxes   a
Act 1970, s 530.

Cases referred to in judgment

Bucks v Bowers (Inspector of Taxes) [1970] 2 All ER 202, [1970] Ch 431, [1970] 2 WLR
    676, 46 Tax Cas 267, [1969] TR 559, 48 ATC 588, 28 (1) Digest (Reissue) 451, *1619*.

Dale v Inland Revenue Comrs [1953] 2 All ER 671, [1954] AC 11, [1953] 3 WLR 448,   b
    34 Tax Cas 468, [1953] TR 269, 32 ATC 294, 46 R & IT 513, HL, 28 (1) Digest (Re-
    issue) 583, *2163*.

Hale v Shea (Inspector of Taxes) [1965] 1 All ER 155, [1965] 1 WLR 290, 42 Tax Cas 260,
    [1964] TR 413, 43 ATC 448, 28 (1) Digest (Reissue) 450, *1615*.

Inland Revenue Comrs v Butterley Co Ltd [1956] 2 All ER 197, [1957] AC 32, [1956] 2
    WLR 1101, 36 Tax Cas 411, [1956] TR 103, 35 ATC 66, 49 R & IT 303, HL, 28 (1)   c
    Digest (Reissue) 532, *1943*.

Inland Revenue Comrs v Parkhouse Collieries Ltd (1956) 36 Tax Cas 675; sub nom *Park-
    house Collieries Ltd v Inland Revenue Comrs* [1956] TR 223, 49 R & IT 667, 32 ATC 157,
    CA, 28 (1) Digest (Reissue) 402, *1472*.

M'Dougall v Smith (Surveyor of Taxes) 1919 SC 86, 56 SLR 90, 7 Tax Cas 134, 28 (1) Digest
    (Reissue) 418, *1155*.   d

Peay (Inspector of Taxes) v Newton [1971] 2 All ER 172, [1971] 1 WLR 133, 46 Tax Cas
    653, [1970] TR 313, 28 (1) Digest (Reissue) 452, *1620*.

Cases also cited

FPH Finance Trust Ltd v Inland Revenue Comrs [1944] 1 All ER 653, [1944] AC 285, HL.

Fry (Surveyor of Taxes) v Shiels' Trustees 1915 SC 159, 6 Tax Cas 583.

Waterloo Main Colliery Co Ltd v Inland Revenue Comrs (1954) 35 Tax Cas 454, [1954]   e
    TR 355.

Case stated

At a meeting of the Commissioners for the General Purposes of the Income Tax for the
division of Godley in the county of Surrey held on 29th July 1971 for the purpose   f
of hearing appeals, Richard Graham Pegler ('the taxpayer'), Fellow of the Institute
of Chartered Accountants, of Costards, West Lavington, Midhurst, in the county of
Sussex, appealed against the refusal by the inspector of taxes of a claim under s 211 (1)
of the Income Tax Act 1952 for earned income relief in respect of income tax for
the year 1967-68 on the sum of £5,158 ('the allowance') received by him in the circumstances appearing below. The point for the determination of the commissioners
was whether the allowance was, in relation to the taxpayer, 'earned income' within   g
the definition contained in s 525 (1) (c) of the 1952 Act.

The following facts were admitted or proved. (a) Up to 31st January 1967 the
taxpayer was an active full-time partner in the firm of Spicer & Pegler, chartered
accountants ('the partnership'). The terms on which the partnership was conducted
at the material time were contained in a deed dated 31st October 1966[1]. (b) As a
result of the taxpayer's ill-health following a motor accident in 1965, he agreed   h
to retire from the partnership on 31st January 1967 in accordance with the terms of
an agreement ('the agreement') contained in a letter[2] addressed to him by all
the other partners therein dated 26th January 1967 which he accepted and signed
the next day. (c) The terms of the agreement were duly performed by the taxpayer and in the year 1967-68 the taxpayer was paid the allowance thereunder by   j
the partnership under deduction of income tax at the then standard rate.

It was agreed between the parties: (a) that to qualify as earned income the payment would have to fall within s 525 (1) (c) of the 1952 Act, as being income which

---

1   The provisions of the deed, so far as material, are set out at p 56 a to p 57 e, post
2   See p 57 g to p 58 c, post

a had been charged under Sch D and which was immediately derived by the individual from the carrying on or exercise by him of his profession, in the case of the partnership, as a partner personally acting therein; (b) that the allowance was indeed income charged on the taxpayer for the year 1967-68 under Sch D, Case III, being an annuity or other annual payment paid by virtue of a contract, namely, the deed of partnership as amended by the agreement.

b (a) The taxpayer contended that the allowance fell within s 525 (1) (c) of the 1952 Act in that it was income charged under Sch D, and income immediately derived by the taxpayer from the carrying on by him of his profession as a partner acting in the partnership. (b) His claim that the income was 'immediately derived' by him from the carrying on by him in the manner required by s 525 (1) (c) was based on a dictionary definition of the words 'immediately' and 'derived'. Those words being c nowhere defined in the Income Tax Acts, they should be given their ordinary meaning. If there be any doubt then the doubt should be exercised in favour of the taxpayer. (c) The taxpayer referred to *Peay (Inspector of Taxes) v Newton*[1] as establishing that a sum received under an agreement for the disposal of a business was nonetheless immediately derived from the carrying on of the business. In his case although the sum was payable under the deed of partnership as amended by the d agreement it was nonetheless immediately derived from and was exclusively attributable to his personal endeavours in the partnership which latter were the sole source of the income to him. That, notwithstanding that, as expressed in the deed of partnership the income was to be calculated as an amount equivalent to a percentage of profits taxed under Case II of Sch D on the remaining partners after the taxpayer ceased to be a partner. (d) The taxpayer contended that the income in respect of e which relief was claimed was therefore earned income within the meaning of s 211 of the Act.

The Crown contended: (a) that the allowance was not derived from the carrying on or exercise in 1967-68 by the taxpayer of his profession of chartered accountant, as a partner personally acting in the partnership for the reasons that on 31st January 1967 he had ceased to be a partner, and therefore to act as a partner, and had as of f that date ceased to have any interest in any of the assets of the partnership (including the goodwill, if any); alternatively (b) that the source from which the allowance was derived was the profits, not of the partnership of which he was a partner, but of the partnership as constituted after his retirement; and (c) that the allowance was 'immediately derived' from the agreement and did not commence until the taxpayer had given up his interest in the partnership and ceased to act on its behalf; g (d) that *Peay (Inspector of Taxes) v Newton*[1] was irrelevant.

In the absence of judicial authority, the Crown referred to the debate in Parliament on the report stage of the Finance Bill (1962)[2] which concerned the treatment of pensions as earned income.

The commissioners found that on the evidence before them, the retirement allowance paid under the deed of partnership as modified by the agreement was h not earned income within the definition of s 525 (1) (c) of the 1952 Act and that the claim for deduction under s 211 (1) of the 1952 Act failed. The taxpayer immediately after the determination of the appeal expressed his dissatisfaction therewith as being erroneous in point of law, and in due course required the commissioners to state a case for the opinion of the High Court pursuant to s 56 of the Taxes Management Act 1970.

j *S J L Oliver* for the taxpayer.
Patrick Medd for the Crown.

---

1 [1971] 2 All ER 172, [1972] 1 WLR 133
2 Hansard, Parliamentary Debates, HC, vol 62, cols 410-418

GOFF J. The taxpayer in this case is a chartered accountant who is a member *a*
of a large firm of considerable standing. They were operating under a deed of
partnership dated 31st October 1966 which contained, among other provisions,
the following. In cl 5:

'ALL the assets of the partnership including the goodwill (if any) shall be held
by the partners as joint tenants and upon the retirement or death of one of the
partners his interest in them shall cease entirely and all his interest shall become *b*
vested entirely in the continuing or surviving partners or partner the partner
so retired or the heirs or personal representatives of the deceased partner having
no claim whatsoever to any part thereof either on the ground of the said assets
having been part of his private estate or on the ground that they were part
of the property of the firm.'

c

Clause 6 provided for the division of profits and the way in which they were to be
calculated. Clause 13 contained provision for the retirement of partners, and it
reads as follows:

'(a) EACH partner may retire from the partnership with effect from any
Thirtieth day of April or any Thirty first day of October after he shall have *d*
attained the age of Sixty years subject to not less than six months' notice given
so as to expire on any such day. (b) Each partner shall retire on the Thirtieth
day of April or Thirty first day of October (as the case may be) immediately
following the day on which he shall have attained the age of Sixty five years
unless he agrees to a Seventy five per cent. majority decision of the other partners
requesting him to continue as a partner for a specified period after his attain- *e*
ment of that age. (c) Subject to the agreement of a Seventy five per cent.
majority decision of the other partners any partner may retire from the partnership before attaining the age of Sixty years on account of illness or of some other
reason approved by such decision. Provided that [the taxpayer] shall be at
liberty to retire on any Thirtieth day of April or Thirty first day of October
before attaining the age of Sixty years if he shall have given not less than six *f*
months' notice of his desire so to do.'

Thus he had a special power enabling him to retire when he saw fit.
    Then, in cl 15 there were restrictive covenants to be observed by retiring partners.
Clause 16 provided:

'(i) THE provisions of this Clause apply solely to the respective cases of Adriaan *g*
Evan Spicer and [the taxpayer], each being in this Clause referred to as "the
partner". (ii) The partner shall (whether his retirement occurs pursuant to
Clause 13 or 14 hereof) be entitled to receive by way of retirement allowance
from the date on which he retires (in this Clause called "the Commencement
Date") such half-yearly sum (less income tax thereon at the standard rate for *h*
the time being in force) as is equivalent to the under-mentioned percentage set
opposite his name of the net profits of the business calculated in accordance
with the provisions of Clause 18 hereof:—[Then it prescribed for the taxpayer
3 per cent.] (iii) If the partner shall die within Ten years after the Commencement Date survived by his wife an amount at the rate of two-thirds of
the retirement allowance which the deceased would have received but for his
death shall be paid to his widow for whichever shall be the shorter of the follow- *j*
ing periods:—(a) the balance of the period of Ten years from the Commencement Date; and (b) the remainder of her life. (iv) If the partner shall die
before retirement there shall be paid to the person or persons and for the period
applicable to the particular case an amount at the rate of two-thirds of the
retirement allowance to which the deceased would have been entitled in

a

accordance with paragraph (ii) of this Clause if he had retired on the date of death . . . '

Clause 18 provided:

b

'(i) THE partners MUTUALLY UNDERTAKE that if they admit any new partner to the partnership or if they enter into an arrangement whereby the partnership is re-constituted they will do so on terms that such new partner or such other person or persons forming with themselves or any of them such reconstituted partnership shall be responsible in like manner as themselves for payment of the allowances mentioned in Clauses 16 and 17 hereof. (ii) Where an allowance is payable for any period which does not coincide with the half-yearly accounting period of the firm it shall be deemed to accrue from day to day and shall be calculated accordingly and for the purpose of arriving at the net profits of the business for division between the partners the above-mentioned allowances shall be outgoings of the business of the accounting periods in respect of each year in respect of part of which they are payable.'

c

Clause 19 provided:

d

'(i) FOR the purposes of Clauses 16 and 17 hereof the "net profits of the business" shall be the same as in Clause 6 hereof [that being the clause which defined net profits for the purposes of division of profits] but before charging the allowances payable to Henry Ernest Spry Frank Anthony Sibley the children of Brian Runciman Pollott and any other allowances payable to retired or deceased partners their spouses or dependants . . . '

e

Unfortunately, the taxpayer met with a serious motor car accident which so impaired his health that it was necessary for him to retire from the partnership. He might, of course, have exercised the special power given to him which I have mentioned, but in fact a special agreement was negotiated with his partners. All the other partners signed a letter dated 26th January 1967, setting out the terms as they understood them, and in fact correctly, and asking him, if he approved them, to sign in token thereof, which he did. That letter reads as follows:

f

'Dear Mr. Pegler, We write this letter to record the terms agreed between us for your retirement from the partnership. If you agree that the terms set out below correctly record the agreement will you please sign the acknowledgment at the bottom of this letter and return it to us. We enclose a copy of this letter signed by all the partners for you to keep for your own records and attached to it for reference is a copy of the partnership deed of the 31st October 1966. The terms are as follows: (1) You will retire from the partnership with effect from the 31st January 1967 "the date of retirement" [which, be it observed, was not a retirement date under the provisions of the partnership deed]. (2) You will be entitled to a retirement allowance for the rest of your life in accordance with the provisions in Clauses 16, 18 and 19 of the partnership deed but the rates shall be as follows: (a) from the date of retirement till the end of the half year (i.e. 31st October or 30th April as the case may be) in which your 60th birthday occurs the rate will be 5% of the "net profits" of the business calculated in accordance with the provisions of Clause 18. (b) from the end of the half year in which your 60th birthday occurs the rate will be 3% of the "net profits". (3) After your death a pension at the rate of 2% of the "net profits" will be payable to your widow for the shorter of (a) a period ending 10 years from the end of the half year following your 60th birthday or (b) her life. (4) You will retire from the trusteeship of all trusts with which the firm is connected. (5) You will offer your resignation to the Boards of all the client companies of which you are a director. Should you remain or become a director after your retirement you

g

h

j

will be entitled to retain the whole of the fees notwithstanding Clause 20 of the partnership deed. (6) All the provisions of the partnership deed applicable to retirement shall apply to your retirement except in so far as they have been expressly varied by this letter. (7) There are three further points: (a) To assist in the assimilation of your work by other partners we should like to retain you as a Consultant for a year and in view of your health we suggest this should be from 1st April 1967. Your salary will be £5,000 for the year and your duties will be to make yourself available to be consulted by the firm, particularly with regard to clients who have been your responsibility. [Sub-paragraph (b) dealt with the balance standing to the credit of his provision for surtax.] (c) Bearing in mind that the present partnership determines in 1974 it is suggested we all agree that in Clause 6 (iv) of the partnership deed there should be inserted immediately after the words "the business" where those words first occur the words 'which expression shall for the purpose of this deed be deemed to include any business carried on in succession to or in continuation of the said business".'

It will be seen that there are at least three variations in that agreement from the provisions of the partnership articles: first, the retirement date; secondly, the rate at which he was to be paid; and, thirdly, a variation of cl 20 concerning directors' fees.

The taxpayer duly retired pursuant to the agreement so made, and in the year 1967-68 he was paid the allowance thereunder by the partnership under deduction of income tax at the then standard rate, the amount being a sum of £5,158. He claimed earned income allowance in respect of that sum under s 211 of the Income Tax Act 1952. That being refused, he appealed to the General Commissioners, who upheld the inspector's refusal, and the taxpayer now appeals to me against that decision.

The only part of the Income Tax Act 1952 which I think it is necessary for me to read is s 525, which contains the definition of 'earned income'. Subsection (1) provides:

'Subject to the provisions of subsection (2) of this section, in this Act, "earned income" means, in relation to any individual—(a) any income arising in respect of any remuneration from any office or employment of profit held by the individual, or in respect of any pension, superannuation or other allowance, deferred pay or compensation for loss of office, given in respect of the past services of the individual or of the husband or parent of the individual in any office or employment of profit, or given to the individual in respect of the past services of any deceased person, whether the individual or husband or parent of the individual shall have contributed to such pension, superannuation allowance or deferred pay or not; and (b) any income from any property which is attached to or forms part of the emoluments of any office or employment of profit held by the individual; and (c) any income which is charged under Schedule B or Schedule D and is immediately derived by the individual from the carrying on or exercise by him of his trade, profession or vocation, either as an individual or, in the case of a partnership, as a partner personally acting therein. In cases where the income of a wife is deemed to be income of the husband, any reference in this subsection to the individual includes either the husband or the wife.'

The allowance in question, it is agreed, falls within Sch D, and the portion of s 525 directly relevant is sub-s (1) (c), although, of course, the whole section must be regarded as a matter of context.

Looking at the matter, first, apart from any authority, the words in para (c) seem to me to refer to money received as a reward for or as the emoluments of some present activity, and not one which has ceased, particularly when one compares para (c) with the dichotomy in para (a), where provision is expressly made for pensions of certain types.

a   So far as authority goes, there is no case directly in point but a number of cases
have been cited to me, and some are helpful in construing the section. Counsel for
the taxpayer says that one must distinguish source, which is cl 16 of the deed, and
quality; that is, how the money looks as a receipt in the taxpayer's hands. The
allowance, he says, must have been derived, and derived immediately, from his
activities while a partner. The source is the totality of the contract between the
b   parties, but the quality is his earnings, that which he contracted for and earned by
his work before he retired and by discharging in full his duties as a partner under
the deed; and counsel for the taxpayer stresses that what is received is not a share
of the profits of the new partnership but a sum equivalent thereto which is
the personal liability of the continuing partners.
       Counsel for the taxpayer relied strongly on *Dale v Inland Revenue Comrs*[1], where
c   Lord Normand said[2]: 'The source of the sum and its character as a receipt in the
hands of the trustee are two separate and unconnected things.' Counsel for the
taxpayer also cited, from Lord Cohen, these words[3]:

> 'I would add that a decision that the source of a payment is the bounty of the
> testator seems to me of little relevance to the question which arises between
> the trustee and the Inland Revenue as to its character as a receipt in the hands
d   > of the trustee.'

But there the question was whether the income was the fruits of an office of profit or
was the bounty or legacy of the testator, and that directed one to consider not the
source but the quality. That is quite different, as I see it, from the problem here,
where the words of the section appear to direct one to the source.
       In *Inland Revenue Comrs v Parkhouse Collieries Ltd*[4], Romer LJ[5] also stresses the
e   difference between reason, source and qualification. There, the relevant factor was
source, and in the particular case that defeated the taxpayer. But that was one of
the coal compensation cases which the court was at pains to point out are really
sui generis.
       Counsel for the Crown submits that s 525 (1) (c) in its terms directs one to the
source, and that source is not the taxpayer's earnings but the earnings of a new
f   partnership. He submits further that in any case this is not exclusively remuneration earned by his past services but a return for all his obligations under the contract,
including giving up the right he would otherwise have had to a share in the partnership
assets after his retirement. In reply, counsel for the taxpayer said that that was
given up ab initio and is really beside the point. Indeed, he says that the taxpayer
earned the allowance by performing all his obligations under the contract, one of
g   which was the term, to which he bound himself, foregoing a share of the assets after
retirement.
       As I have said, there is no case directly in point, but there are passages which I
find helpful. First, I derive assistance from the way in which the Lord President
(Lord Strathclyde) put it in *M'Dougall v Smith (Surveyor of Taxes)*[6]. The facts and the
problem were quite different. There, a business was carried on on behalf of a
h   lunatic, and the question really was whether the income was the income of the
patient's business or of his curator's. But the Lord President said[7]:

> 'The terms of that section seem to me to be very plain. The object is to exempt
> from a larger scale of tax all those who earn profits by their own personal exer-
> tions, care, skill, and work. In every instance it appears to me to be a question

j   1   [1953] 2 All ER 671, [1954] AC 11
       2   [1953] 2 All ER at 674, 675, [1954] AC at 28
       3   [1953] 2 All ER at 678, [1954] AC at 34
       4   (1956) 36 Tax Cas 675
       5   (1965) 36 Tax Cas at 709
       6   1919 SC 86
       7   1919 SC at 88

of fact whether or not the person whose profits are sought to be assessed did
manage his own business—did, by the exercise by him of his own profession,
trade, or vocation, earn those profits. In the present case it is common ground
that the person who is incapable of managing his own affairs did not earn the
profits, and was not engaged in business in any way.'

The coal compensation cases, being sui generis, are not a very reliable guide, but
I find further assistance in the analysis made by Lord Radcliffe in *Inland Revenue Comrs
v Butterley Co Ltd*[1], where he pointed out that the compensation could not be
said to arise from a business which had ceased. I quote this brief passage[2]:

'They cannot arise from the colliery trade, for, as the Case finds, that trade
ceased entirely on Jan. 1, 1947; and, short of special enactment, taxable income
cannot arise in one year from a source that ceased to exist in a previous year.'

Hale v Shea (Inspector of Taxes)[3], to which I was referred, is in my judgment distinguishable because that was a dissolution agreement under which the outgoing
partner assigned his share and also undertook consultancy duties, and he was unable
to say that the fee paid to him was not in fact consideration for the assignment.
Peay (Inspector of Taxes) v Newton[4] is also distinguishable. That was a case of capital
gains tax, and the capital gain had notionally to be treated as income. The question
then was how that gain was derived, and it was held that it was from the taxpayer's
work. But there was there a concession that the goodwill that was sold had been
entirely built up by her.

On the other hand, I find that *Bucks v Bowers (Inspector of Taxes)*[5] does support
the Crown's submissions. There, merchant bankers had investments and received
income under deduction, and that was held not to be earned income because it was
not derived, or not immediately derived, from the trade. Pennycuick J said[6]:

'Quite apart from authority, I do not think that, in the context of an income
tax statute, one would naturally treat income received under deduction by
a trader in the carrying on of his trade as "derived", still less "immediately
derived" from the carrying on of that trade. It is certainly derived by him
in the course of that trade; but the word "from" [and this is the significant part]
suggests that the trade must be the source of the income, and that is not so in
the case of income charged by deduction. The source of interest is not the trade
but the loan obligations from which the interest springs. Equally, the source
of the income from foreign investments is not the trade, but the foreign investments. Again, the word "immediately" rather suggests that the trade must be
the direct source, so as to exclude income derived from a different source itself
owned by a trader in the carrying on of his trade.'

In the present case it seems to me that the allowance was not derived, and certainly not immediately derived, from the past carrying on by the taxpayer of his
profession, but from the contractual liability of the partners to the retired partner.
But if it be derived from the carrying on of a profession at all, it seems to me that it
was derived from the carrying on by the continuing or any new partners of the
partnership after the retirement, and not from the carrying on by the taxpayer of
his profession. It must be borne in mind also that the parties made the special
agreement to which I have referred, which certainly gave the taxpayer advantages

---

1 [1956] 2 All ER 197, [1957] AC 32
2 [1956] 2 All ER at 205, [1957] AC at 58
3 [1965] 1 All ER 155, [1965] 1 WLR 290
4 [1971] 2 All ER 172, [1971] 1 WLR 133
5 [1970] 2 All ER 202, [1970] Ch 431
6 [1970] 2 All ER at 208, [1970] Ch at 440

a to which he was not entitled under the terms of the partnership deed, and which could not therefore in any sense be said to have been earned by the performance by him prior to his retirement of his contractual duties.

The extra 2 per cent cannot, it seems to me, on any showing, be within para (*c*), and this is not, I think, a case for severance but emphasises the conclusion I have reached, that the allowance in toto was not derived, or not immediately derived—
b and the two points do, I think, overlap—from the taxpayer's past activities, but from the contract which his co-partners made initially in the partnership deed to cover retirement pursuant to the deed, and then specially to meet this particular case. In my judgment, therefore, the commissioners were right and the appeal fails.

I should add that, if I were wrong, then, in any event, it would seem to me that only 3 per cent would be entitled to the benefit of the allowance in respect of earned income.
c

Appeal dismissed.

Solicitors: *Freshfields* (for the taxpayer); *Solicitor of Inland Revenue.*

d   Rengan Krishnan Esq Barrister.

Practice Direction

FAMILY DIVISION

e *Husband and wife – Maintenance – Wife or child – Husband's whereabouts unknown – Disclosure of husband's address by government departments – Disclosure at request of registrar – Particulars to be certified in request – Information to be supplied to registrar by solicitors prior to request.*

f *Ward of court – Disappearance of ward – Address of ward or of person with whom ward believed to be – Disclosure by government departments at request of registrar – Particulars to be certified in request – Information to be supplied by solicitors prior to request.*

Arrangements have been made whereby the court may request the address of a husband from the records of the Department of Health and Social Security, Passport
g Office or Ministry of Defence for the assistance of a wife seeking to obtain or enforce an order for maintenance for herself or the children. Similar arrangements exist in wardship proceedings for attempting to trace the whereabouts of a missing ward or the person with whom a missing ward is said to be. Requests for such information will be made officially by the registrar. The request, in addition to stating (or enclosing) the information mentioned below, should certify: (A) IN MAINTENANCE
h PROCEEDINGS either (a) that an order is in existence but cannot be enforced because the husband cannot be traced; or (b) that the wife has filed or issued a notice, petition or originating summons containing an application for maintenance which cannot be served because the husband cannot be traced. (Note: The expression 'maintenance' is used to include all forms of periodical payment.) (B) IN WARDSHIP PROCEEDINGS that the minor is the subject of wardship proceedings and cannot be traced
j [and is believed to be with the person whose address is sought].

(1) *Department of Health and Social Security.*

The department most likely to be able to assist is the Department of Health and Social Security, whose records are the most comprehensive and complete. The possibility of identifying one person amongst so many will depend on the particulars given. An address will not be supplied by the department unless it is satisfied from

the particulars given that the record of the person has been reliably identified. *a*
The solicitor should therefore be asked to supply as much as possible of the
following information about the person sought: (i) national insurance number;
(ii) surname; (iii) Christian (or fore-) names in full; (iv) date of birth (or, if not known,
approximate age); (v) last known address, with date when living there; (vi) any
other known address(es) with dates; (vii) if the person sought is a war pensioner,
his war pension and service particulars (if known); and in maintenance proceedings *b*
(viii) the exact date of the marriage and the wife's Christian name or forenames.

The department will be prepared to search if given full particulars of the person's
name and date of birth, but the chances of accurate identification are increased by
the provision of more identifying information.

Second requests for records to be searched, provided that a reasonable interval
is allowed to elapse, will be met by the Department of Health and Social Security. *c*
The most common method whereby a change of address is reported is by the exchange of a national insurance contribution card which occurs once a year, the time
of exchange depending upon the suffix letter of the national insurance number A, B,
C, or D. Cards with these letters are exchanged respectively in March, June,
September and December, normally in the first week. As, however, it takes some
little time to sort these cards, records are not likely to show any new address until *d*
four to six weeks later.

National Health Service—These records are in respect of persons registered for
general medical service in the National Health Service and show the address at the
time the person concerned last registered for such medical service. It has to be
remembered, however, that one may move and yet keep the same doctor, so that
the records may vary considerably in their reliability as a source of a recent address. *e*

When application is to be made for the disclosure of an address from these records,
the solicitors should supply as much as possible of the following information about
the person sought: (i) surname and full Christian (or fore-) names; (ii) exact
date of birth, or if not known, approximate age; (iii) National Health Service number
(if known); (iv) home address as it was in 1939; (v) any subsequent known address,
with dates. *f*

Supplementary Benefits Commission—Where, in the case of maintenance proceedings,
the wife is in receipt of supplementary benefit, it would be advisable in the first
instance to make enquiries of the manager of the local Social Security (Supplementary
Benefits) Office for the area in which she resides in order to avoid possible duplication
of enquiries.

g

(2) *Passport Office*
If all reasonable enquiries including the aforesaid methods have failed to reveal
an address, or if there are strong grounds for believing that the person sought may
have made a recent application for a passport, enquiries may be made to the Passport
Office. The solicitors should provide as much of the following information about
the person as possible: (i) surname and full Christian (or fore-) names; (ii) exact *h*
date of birth, or, if not known, approximate age; (iii) place of birth; (iv) occupation;
(v) whether known to have travelled abroad, and, if so, the destination and dates;
(vi) last known address, with date living there; (vii) any other known address, with
dates.

They must also undertake in writing that information given in response to the
enquiry will be used solely for the purpose for which it was requested, i e to assist
in tracing the husband in connection with the enforcement of a maintenance order *j*
or in tracing a missing ward, as the case may be.

(3) *Ministry of Defence*
In cases where the person sought is known to be serving or to have recently served
in the Royal Navy, Army or Royal Air Force, the solicitor representing the applicant

a should be advised that he may obtain the address for maintenance or wardship proceedings direct from the appropriate service department. The solicitor's request should be accompanied by a written undertaking that the address will be used by him solely for the service of process and will not be disclosed to the applicant or any other person except in the normal course of proceedings. Alternatively, if the solicitor wishes to serve process on the person's commanding officer under the rules

b set out in s 101 of the Naval Discipline Act 1957, s 153 of the Army Act 1955 and s 153 of the Air Force Act 1955 (all of which as amended by s 62 of the Armed Forces Act 1971), he may obtain that officer's address in the same way.

Where the applicant is acting in person the appropriate service department is prepared to disclose the address of the person sought, or that of his Commanding Officer, to a registrar on receipt of an assurance that the applicant has given an under-

c taking that the information will be used solely for the purpose of serving process in the proceedings.

As much of the following information as possible should be provided: (i) the person's surname and full Christian (or fore-) names; (ii) his service number; (iii) his date of birth, or, if not known, his age; (iv) his rank and, in the case of a soldier, regiment or corps; (v) his date of entry into the service and, if no longer

d serving, date of discharge; (vi) any other information, such as his last known address.

General Notes

Records held by other departments are less likely to be of use, either because of their limited scope or because individual records cannot readily be identified. If, however, the circumstances suggest that the address may be known to another

e department, application may be made to it by the registrar, all relevant particulars available being given.

When any department is able to supply the address of the person sought to the registrar, it will be passed on by him to the applicant's solicitor (or, in proper cases, direct to the applicant if acting in person) on an undertaking to use it only for the purpose of the proceedings.

f Nothing in this practice note affects the service in matrimonial causes of petitions which do not contain any applications for maintenance, etc. The existing arrangements whereby the Department of Health and Social Security will at the request of the solicitor forward a letter by ordinary post to a party's last known address remain in force in such cases.

Issued with the concurrence of the Lord Chancellor.

g

D NEWTON

Senior Registrar

28th November 1972

a

Practice Direction

FAMILY DIVISION

Adoption – Practice – Application for adoption order – Appeal from magistrates' court to Divisional Court of Family Division – Procedure – Adoption Act 1958, s 10 – RSC Ord 90, rr 9 (2), 16.

b

Under RSC Ord 90, r 9 (2), Ord 90 r 16 applies, with the necessary modifications, to appeals under s 10[1] of the Adoption Act 1958.

In view of the special nature of adoption applications the following is the modified procedure for such appeals.

1. The appeal shall be entered by lodging three copies of the notice of motion

c

in the principal registry of the Family Division.

2. Notice of motion must be served by the appellant on: (a) the clerk to the justices whose order is appealed from; (b) the guardian ad litem appointed by the magistrates' court.

3. The appellant must also lodge with the clerk to the justices a sufficient number of copies of the notice of motion to enable service to be effected on all other parties

d

affected by the appeal, including: (a) the proposed adopter(s) (not being the appellant(s)); (b) every person whose consent is required by s 4 (1)[2] of the Adoption Act 1958 (not being the appellant); and (c) any other person or body made a respondent to the application under r 12[3] of the Adoption (Juvenile Court) Rules 1959[4] and 1965[5]; and shall request the clerk to the justices to serve such persons and bodies with the notice of motion.

e

4. Notice of motion must be served and the appeal entered, within six weeks after the date of the order or determination appealed against. Service of notice of motion need not be personal service.

5. On entering the appeal, or as soon as possible afterwards, the appellant must lodge three certified copies of: (a) the clerk's notes of evidence taken in the magistrates' court; and (b) the justices' reasons for their decision, and a certificate of service

f

of notice of motion on the clerk to the justices and the guardian ad litem.

The appellant must also request the clerk to the justices to forward to the Principal Clerk of the Contentious Department, Principal Registry of the Family Division, a certified copy of: (a) the adoption application and any documents exhibited thereto; (b) the notice of determination or of the making of the adoption order served under r 25[6] of the aforesaid Rules of 1959 and 1965; (c) the report by the guardian ad litem

g

and any other reports from welfare agencies; (d) any other exhibits used at the hearing; and a certificate of service of notice of appeal on the parties referred to in para 3 above, specifying the persons and bodies to whom the clerk to the justices has sent the notice of appeal.

6. If the appellant seeks leave to appeal out of time he must also lodge a certificate, and a copy thereof, by the appellant's solicitor (or by the appellant if he is acting

h

in person) setting out the reasons for the delay and the relevant dates.

D NEWTON
Senior Registrar

7th December 1972

j

1   See 17 Halsbury's Statutes (3rd Edn) 648
2   See ibid p 640
3   See 11 Halsbury's Statutory Instruments (Second Reissue) 222
4   SI 1959 No 504
5   SI 1965 No 2072
6   See 11 Halsbury's Statutory Instruments (Second Reissue) 224

Pagebar Properties Ltd v Derby Investment Holdings Ltd

CHANCERY DIVISION

GOULDING J

28th SEPTEMBER 1972

Sale of land – Contract – Completion – Notice to complete – Validity – Party giving notice ready and willing to fulfil own outstanding obligations – Notice by vendor – Sale of freehold property – Duty of vendor to make available to purchaser particulars of leases – Purchaser's solicitors discovering existence of undisclosed lease on final date stipulated by notice to complete – Solicitor refusing to complete without further instructions – Contract providing that errors, omissions etc not having effect of annulling sale or entitling party to compensation unless materially affecting value of property – Purchaser subsequently agreeing to complete at agreed price – Vendor purporting to call off sale and forfeit deposit – Whether entitled to give notice to complete – National Conditions of Sale (18th Edn), conditions 17, 18, 22.

By an agreement dated 7th June 1972 the plaintiff agreed to buy from the defendant certain freehold property and paid 10 per cent of the purchase price by way of deposit. Clause 8 of the contract, which incorporated the National Conditions of Sale (18th Edn), provided that the property was sold subject to and with the benefit of leases and tenancies particulars of which were set out in a schedule to the contract. The schedule included particulars relating to Flat 2 on the second floor of the property. The particulars referred to a seven year lease from 1st April 1964 in respect of which the tenant was stated to be holding over. Under general condition 17 of the National Conditions no error mis-statement or omission in any preliminary answer or the special conditions would annul the sale and compensation was only allowable where the error etc materially affected the value of the property. By general condition 18, abstracts or copies of the leases or agreements under which tenants held 'having been made available' the plaintiff was deemed to have notice of and take subject to the terms of existing tenancies. General condition 22, as modified by the special conditions, provided that at any time on or after the completion date 'either party, being ready and willing to fulfil his own outstanding obligations' could give notice to complete within 14 days, with a provision for forfeiture of the deposit if the plaintiff failed to complete within the time stipulated by the notice. On 28th July, the completion date having passed, the defendant served a notice on the plaintiff under general condition 22 requiring completion by Friday, 11th August. On that day the managing clerk to the plaintiff's solicitors, who had attended the defendant's solicitors' office to effect completion, discovered that Flat 2 was subject to an unexpired three year lease which had not been mentioned in the schedule. He decided to take instructions over the weekend. Having done so, he informed the defendant's solicitors that the plaintiff was prepared to complete at the original price despite the existence of the undisclosed lease. The defendant, however, refused, on the ground that the time allowed by the notice had not been complied with, and purported to forfeit the deposit. On the plaintiff's summons for specific performance by way of summary judgment under RSC Ord 86 the defendant contended (i) that, under general condition 18, the plaintiff was bound to take subject to existing tenancies, (ii) that, by the terms of general condition 17, the existence and discovery of the error did not annul the sale or, in the circumstances, give rise to a claim for compensation, (iii) that the defendant was, as required by general condition 22, ready to fulfil his own obligations when he served the notice to complete, and (iv) that the plaintiff having failed to complete within the time stipulated by the notice, the deposit had been forfeited and the bargain lost.

D

Held – The plaintiff was entitled to specific performance for the following reasons—
 (i) the requirement in general condition 18 that the plaintiff should take subject to   *a*
existing tenancies applied in terms only to those tenancies in relation to which
'abstracts or copies of the leases or agreements' had been 'made available to' the
plaintiff (see p 69 e and f, post);
 (ii) the defendant was not entitled to serve the notice to complete on 28th July
under general condition 22, since he was himself in breach of an obligation which   *b*
ought to have been performed by that date, i e the obligation to disclose all existing
tenancies; it was immaterial that, by virtue of general condition 17, that breach did
not have the effect of annulling the sale or entitle the plaintiff to compensation (see
p 68 e and h and p 69 j to p 70 c, post);
 (iii) alternatively, the plaintiff, having at the last moment and through no fault of
his own, discovered the existence of a new lease on the last day allowed for completion, was entitled to have a reasonable opportunity to consider the document   *c*
as it might have materially affected the value of the property thus enabling him to
make a deduction from the balance of the purchase money under general condition
17 (see p 70 c to e, post).

Notes   *d*
For the duty to disclose existing tenancies, see 34 Halsbury's Laws (3rd Edn) 220,
para 365, and for cases on the subject, see 40 Digest (Repl) 52, *329, 332, 135, 1043.*

Case referred to in judgment
*Englefield Holdings Ltd and Sinclair's Contract, Re, Rosslyn & Lorimer Estates Ltd v Engle-
 field Holdings Ltd* [1962] 3 All ER 503, [1962] 1 WLR 1119, Digest (Cont Vol A) 1310,   *e*
 1072a.

Cases also cited
Courcier and Harrold's Contract, Re [1923] 1 Ch 565, [1923] All ER Rep 497.
Flight v Booth (1834) 1 Bing NC 370, [1824-34] All ER Rep 43, 131 ER 1160.   *f*

Summons
By a summons dated 17th August 1972 the plaintiff, Pagebar Properties Ltd, sought
against the defendant, Derby Investment Holdings Ltd, an order, by way of summary
judgment under RSC Ord 86, for the specific performance of a contract dated 7th
June 1972 for the sale of freehold property known as 127 Mitcham Lane, London,
SW16, and registered under title number LN 5682. The facts are set out in the   *g*
judgment.

Leolin Price QC and *D M Levy* for the plaintiff.
N C H Browne-Wilkinson QC and *G C Raffety* for the defendant.

GOULDING J. In this case a purchaser seeks specific performance of a contract   *h*
for the sale of a freehold property in London, known as 127 Mitcham Lane, whereof
different parts are occupied by a number of tenants.
 The plaintiff purchaser seeks summary judgment under RSC Ord 86. The plaintiff and the defendant are both companies which, from their names, look as though
they are traders or investors in immoveable property. The contract between them   *j*
is dated 7th June 1972, and made between the defendant as vendor, and the plaintiff as purchaser. I need not read a great deal of the contract; it provided for payment of a purchase price of £30,000 with the usual 10 per cent payable on the signing
of the contract by way of deposit. The completion date was on or before 19th July
1972.
 Clause 8 of the contract is important:

a 'THE property is sold subject to and with the benefit of the Leases or tenancies short particulars of which are set out in the Second Schedule hereto and the Counterparts or other written evidence of tenancies having been made available for the Purchaser's inspection the Purchaser shall be deemed to purchase with full knowledge of the contents of the same and no representation is made as to the above matters'.

b The second schedule contains particulars of six leases relating to different parts of the property. The lease which it is material to notice for present purposes is the fifth in the list. The particulars read as follows:

'Flat 2, second floor; tenant, J. R. Morton Esq.; lease, seven years from April 1, 1964; rent £275 per annum exclusive; reversion 1971; remarks: tenant holding over.'

c I should also mention that by cl 2 of the contract it was expressed to incorporate the National Conditions of Sale (18th Edn) so far as the latter are not inconsistent with the special conditions set out in the contract itself. I shall have to refer to the national conditions later.

As stated in cl 8 of the contract, counterparts of the tenancy agreements or leases d were made available for the plaintiff's inspection and the plaintiff did in fact inspect them, so it was informed of the details of all the leases set out in the second schedule. Having bought the property on 7th June, the plaintiff on the same date agreed to sell it at a somewhat higher price to yet another company. The date for completion of that sale was 25th August 1972, more than a month later than the completion date under the first contract.

e The plaintiff seems to have been a dilatory and inactive purchaser. It is suggested by the defendant (and I will assume for the purposes of my judgment that the suggestion is justified) that the plaintiff was seeking to spin out time in order that the sub-sale should be completed on the same date as the principal sale. The defendant was not prepared to allow matters to drift, and served a notice on 28th July under general condition 22 of the National Conditions of Sale, incorporated into the f contract. That condition, so far as material, is as follows:

'(1) At any time on or after the completion date, either party, being ready and willing to fulfil his own outstanding obligations under the contract, may (without prejudice to any other right or remedy available to him) give to the other party or his solicitor notice in writing requiring completion of the contract in conformity with this condition.

g '(2) Upon service of such notice as aforesaid it shall become and be a term of the contract, in respect of which time shall be of the essence thereof, that the party to whom the notice is given shall complete the contract within twenty-eight days after service of the notice (exclusive of the day of service): but this condition shall operate without prejudice to any right of either party to rescind the contract in the meantime.

h '(3) In case the purchaser refuses or fails to complete in conformity with this condition, then (without prejudice to any other right or remedy available to the vendor) the purchaser's deposit may be forfeited (unless the court otherwise directs) . . .'

And then there are various provisions enabling the vendor to recover any loss on resale.

i The period of 28 days established by general condition 22 had been reduced by one of the special conditions, condition 3, to 14 days. Accordingly, a notice having been served on 28th July, it would expire on 11th August. The notice does not appear to have itself galvanised the plaintiff into activity. However, on 10th August there was a telephone conversation between the managing clerks of the respective solicitors of the plaintiff and the defendant, so that the plaintiff's solicitors were made aware, if they were not aware before then, that the notice had very nearly expired. On 10th August the representative of the defendant's solicitors said over the telephone *a* that completion must be by 5.30 p m on Friday, 11th August, otherwise the deposit of £3,000 would be forfeited.

The managing clerk of the plaintiff's solicitors accordingly attended at the defendant's solicitors' offices at 2.15 p m on 11th August with an engrossed transfer of the property and a bankers' draft for £27,000, the balance of the purchase money, plus *b* a small sum in respect of interest. When the documents of title relating to the property were produced on behalf of the defendant, it came at once to the notice of the managing clerk on the other side that there had been an error in the particulars of a tenancy contained in the second schedule to the contract. In fact, on the date of the contract, and still on 11th August, the existing lease affecting the second floor flat was not that of which particulars had been given, and of which a copy had been produced and inspected, but a later lease dated 16th September 1971, whereby the *c* flat was let to a Mr Mitchell for three years from 8th September 1971 at a rent of £350.

That created a difficult situation for the clerk representing the interests of the plaintiff. He said that he would obtain instructions. He did, over the weekend, obtain instructions, and on Monday, 14th August, he informed the defendant's solicitors that the plaintiff was prepared to complete at the original price, despite *d* the existence of a lease other than that disclosed. However, the defendant was not prepared to go ahead, and insisted that the deposit was forfeited, since completion had not taken place by the date required by the notice served on 28th July. The question which I have to decide—which in my judgment can and ought to be decided on the affidavit evidence and on the application for summary judgment—is whether *e* the defendant was entitled to take that attitude or not.

A vendor of land is under a duty to disclose the tenancies, if any, affecting the property. In *Re Englefield Holdings Ltd and Sinclair's Contract*[1] Pennycuick J cited a passage from Halsbury's Laws of England[2] which succinctly puts the matter thus:

'*Existing tenancies.* In the absence of an intimation to the contrary, a purchaser is entitled to assume that property offered for sale is in hand, so that he *f* will obtain possession of the property on completion; consequently any existing lease or tenancy must be mentioned in the particulars or referred to in the agreement for sale. The information as to past or existing tenancies must not be misleading; for example, by stating the rent paid by the last tenant and implying, contrary to the fact, that a similar rent can be obtained at the time of the sale, or stating the existing tenancies without mentioning that the tenants *g* have given notice to quit . . .'

The contract in the present case does not, in my judgment, relieve the vendor, i e the defendant, from that duty of disclosure, but it does, by the incorporated general conditions, modify the consequences of a failure to perform such duty. The argument before me has been directed for the most part to the effect of general *h* conditions 17 and 18. They read as follows:

'17. *Immaterial errors* (1) Without prejudice to any express right of either party, or to any right of the purchaser in reliance on section 24 of the Law of Property Act 1969, to rescind the contract before completion, no error, misstatement or omission in any preliminary answer concerning the property, or in *i* the sale plan or the Special Conditions, shall annul the sale, nor (save where the error, mis-statement or omission relates to a matter materially affecting the

---

1 [1962] 3 All ER 503 at 505, [1962] 1 WLR 1119 at 1122
2 3rd Edn, vol 34, pp 220, 221, para 365

a description or value of the property) shall any damages be payable, or compensation allowed by either party, in respect thereof. [Then there is a definition of 'preliminary answer' which I need not read.]

'18. *Leases and tenancies* (1) Abstracts or copies of the leases or agreements (if in writing) under which the tenants hold having been made available, the purchaser (whether he has inspected the same or not) shall be deemed to have

b notice of and shall take subject to the terms of all the existing tenancies and the rights of the tenants, whether arising during the continuance or after the expiration thereof, and such notice shall not be affected by any partial or incomplete statement in the Special Conditions with reference to the tenancies, and no objection shall be taken on account of there not being an agreement in writing with any tenant.'

c I need not read the other sub-paragraph of condition 18, but I ought to read the definition of the 'Special Conditions' in general condition 1:

'In these conditions, where the context admits . . . References to the "Special Conditions" include references to the particulars of sale and to the provisions of the contract which is made by reference to these conditions'.

d I will deal first with condition 18. Counsel for the defendant submits that the effect of condition 18 is that a purchaser is bound to take the land subject to all existing tenancies, whatever they may be, qualified only by the effect of the preceding general condition 17, and by any rules of the general law which are not displaced by the contract.

e In my judgment, sub-para (i) of general condition 18 cannot bear so wide a construction. When the condition says that the purchaser shall take subject to the terms of all the existing tenancies, and that his notice of the tenants' rights shall not be affected by any partial or incomplete statement in the special conditions, it is in my view operating within the framework of the opening words 'abstracts or copies of the leases or agreements (if in writing) under which the tenants hold, having been

f made available . . .' It would, in the context, to my mind, be a false and unfair construction of condition 18 to treat that condition as imposing on the purchaser a tenancy quite different from any of those of which abstracts or copies had been supplied.

Condition 17 is more difficult. It falls into two parts; one is that any error, misstatement or omission in the special conditions, as defined by the general conditions, shall not annul the sale; and then, secondly, there is a provision that no damages or

g compensation are payable or allowed in respect of any such error, mis-statement or omission, except in the case where it relates to a matter materially affecting the description or value of the property. In the last case, compensation is, by implication, allowable, although the sale is not annulled.

I approach this matter on the footing that, so far as the evidence shows, the error,

h i e the non-disclosure of the 1971 lease, does not materially affect the value of the property now in question. Accordingly, whether or not it materially affects the description of the property, no compensation could be claimable.

Counsel for the defendant puts his case in this way. When the notice to complete was served under general condition 22, on 28th July, the defendant was, as required by that condition, ready and willing to fulfil all its own obligations under the contract.

j Accordingly, time became of the essence, and 11th August was the latest permissible completion date. The existence and discovery of the error, by the very terms of general condition 17, did not annul the sale, nor, in the circumstances, did it give rise to a claim for compensation. The plaintiff did not in fact complete within the time allowed by the notice, and therefore the deposit is forfeited and the bargain lost.

The answer made by counsel for the plaintiff really falls under two alternative heads. First of all, he says, the defendant was not entitled to serve a notice making

time of the essence on 28th July, because the defendant itself was in breach of an
obligation that ought to have been performed by that date; namely, the obligation   *a*
to disclose all existing tenancies. In my judgment that contention is sound. In
terms condition 22 merely speaks of a party giving notice being ready and willing
to fulfil all his outstanding obligations under the contract. However, in the context
of these conditions and the ordinary framework of a contract of sale and purchase
of land, it is in my judgment clearly intended that the procedure allowed by general   *b*
condition 22 is only available to a party who is not in default; and just as the vendor
who had not delivered a complete abstract of title could not serve a notice under
condition 22, so in my judgment a vendor who has not yet disclosed existing tenancies
cannot serve a valid notice. The fact that, at the end of the day, general condition 17
might prevent the purchaser from obtaining any relief in respect of the non-disclosure
does not, in my judgment, affect that point.   *c*
    Counsel for the plaintiff's alternative argument assumed that the notice was a
valid notice making time of the essence. Nonetheless, he said, if, without any fault
on the part of the plaintiff, it only found out about the existence of a lease on the last
day allowed for completion, and at the moment of attempted completion, then the
framework of the conditions or the principles of equity demand that the plaintiff
must have a reasonable opportunity to consider the document newly disclosed; for   *d*
example, without consideration it would not be possible for a purchaser to know
whether or not the newly disclosed lease materially affected the description or value
of the property in a manner which, under general condition 17, would enable the
purchaser to make a deduction from the outstanding balance of the purchase money.
That contention also, to my mind, is well founded if the first contention is wrong,
but I would for myself prefer to rely on the first point, that the vendor, not having   *e*
disclosed the existing tenancy, was not in a position to give a notice under general
condition 22.
    I would add one word on the procedural aspect of this matter. I cannot criticise
counsel for having brought the matter before the Vacation Court in view of the
statement in the Supreme Court Practice 1970[1] that among those classes of application
treated as vacation business in the Chancery Division are applications for summary   *f*
judgment under RSC Ord 86. I would use this opportunity to suggest to those
responsible that possibly the item might be qualified by the same parenthesis as
applies to the two preceding heads in the list, possession applications, and payment
applications in mortgage cases, namely, 'if urgency shown'. I very much doubt,
although the matter has not been fully gone into, whether there is any urgency that
merits treating the present case as vacation business, and on a future revision of the
Supreme Court Practice the matter may perhaps be reconsidered. In the result,   *g*
the plaintiff is entitled to judgment for specific performance.

Order accordingly.

Solicitors: *David Lewis & Co* (for the plaintiff); *Burton & Ramsden* (for the defendant).   *h*

                                                R C T Habesch Esq Barrister.

1 Vol 1, p 977, para 64/4/2   *j*

a

Jarvis v Swans Tours Ltd

COURT OF APPEAL, CIVIL DIVISION
LORD DENNING MR, EDMUND DAVIES AND STEPHENSON LJJ
17th, 18th OCTOBER 1972

b

Contract – Breach – Damages – Measure – Mental distress and inconvenience – Vexation and disappointment – Contract to provide holiday – Brochure representing facilities available on holiday – Facilities lacking – Plaintiff entitled to compensation for loss of entertainment and enjoyment – Damages not restricted to physical inconvenience – Vexation and disappointment relevant considerations in assessing compensation – Holiday costing £63 –
c *Plaintiff entitled to an award of £125 damages.*

The defendants, a firm of travel agents, issued a brochure of winter sports holidays for 1969-70 in which one of the holidays was described as a 'Houseparty in Morlialp', Switzerland, with 'special resident host'. The brochure stated that the price of the holiday included the following houseparty arrangements: 'Welcome party on arrival. Afternoon tea and cake...Swiss Dinner by candlelight. Fondue-party.
d Yodler evening...farewell party'. It also stated that there was a wide variety of ski runs at Morlialp; that ski-packs, i e skis, sticks and boots, could be hired there; that the houseparty hotel was chosen by the defendants because of the 'Gemutlichkeit', i e geniality, comfort and cosiness, that the hotel owner spoke English, and that the hotel bar would be open several evenings a week. The brochure added, '...you will be in for a great time, when you book this houseparty holiday'. The plaintiff,
e a solicitor aged about 35, who was employed by a local authority, preferred to take his annual fortnight's holiday in the winter. He looked forward to his holidays and booked them far ahead. In August 1969, on the faith of the representations in the defendants' brochure, he booked with the defendants a 15 day houseparty holiday at Morlialp, with ski-pack, from 20th December 1969 to 3rd January 1970. The
f total cost of the holiday was £63·45. The plaintiff went on the holiday but he was very disappointed. In the first week the houseparty consisted of only 13 people, and for the whole of the second week the plaintiff was the only person there. There was no welcome party. The ski-runs were some distance away and no full length skis were available except on two days in the second week. The hotel owner did not speak English and in the second week there was no one to whom the plaintiff could talk. The cake for tea was only potato crisps and dry nutcake. There was
g not much entertainment at night; the yodler evening consisted of a local man in his working clothes singing a few songs very quickly, and the hotel bar was an unoccupied annexe open only on one evening. During the second week there was no representative at the hotel. Therefore, although the plaintiff was conveyed to Switzerland and back and had meals and bed provided in the hotel, the holiday was largely inferior to what he was led to expect by the representations in the brochure. On
h a claim by the plaintiff against the defendants for breach of the contract to provide the holiday promised, the trial judge held that the plaintiff was entitled to damages. He took as the measure of damages the difference between what the plaintiff had paid for the holiday and what he had got, and on that basis he awarded the plaintiff damages of £31·72, i e half the amount paid for the holiday. The plaintiff appealed

j **Held** – In a proper case damages for mental distress could be recovered in an action for breach of contract; the plaintiff was not necessarily restricted to recovery of damages for physical inconvenience suffered by the breach. A proper case in which to award damages for mental distress, or inconvenience, was for breach of a contract to provide a holiday or entertainment and enjoyment, for (per Stephenson LJ) in such a contract the parties contemplated that on breach there might be mental

inconvenience, e g frustration, annoyance, disappointment, and damages could be a
awarded for such inconvenience. The correct measure of the damages to which the
plaintiff was entitled was not restricted by the sum which he had paid for the holiday
but was the sum required to compensate him for the loss of entertainment and enjoyment which he had been promised and did not get, his vexation and disappointment
in the holiday being relevant considerations in arriving at that sum. Looking at
the case broadly, the plaintiff was entitled to an award of £125 and the appeal would b
be allowed accordingly (see p 74 f, p 75 a, p 76 a b and f and p 77 b c and f, post).

Dictum of Mellor J in *Hobbs v London & South Western Railway Co* [1874-80] All ER
Rep at 463 disapproved.

Notes

For damages for breach of contract affecting convenience, see 11 Halsbury's Laws c
(3rd Edn) 285, 286, para 472.

For remoteness of damage generally in contract, see ibid, 268-273, paras 445-450
and for cases on the subject, see 17 Digest (Repl) 114-121, 268-324.

Cases referred to in judgments

Bailey v Bullock [1950] 2 All ER 1167, 66 (pt 2) TLR 791, 17 Digest (Repl) 121, 321. d
Bruen v Bruce [1959] 2 All ER 375, [1959] 1 WLR 684, CA, Digest (Cont Vol A) 326,
1065a.
Feldman v Allways Travel Services [1957] CLY 934.
Griffiths v Evans [1953] 2 All ER 1364, [1953] 1 WLR 1424, CA, 43 Digest (Repl) 116,
1050.
Hamlin v Great Northern Railway Co (1856) 1 H & N 408, 26 LJEx 20, 28 LTOS 104, e
156 ER 1261, 17 Digest (Repl) 103, 175.
Hobbs v London & South Western Railway Co (1875) LR 10 QB 111, [1874-80] All ER
Rep 458, 44 LJQB 49, 32 LT 252, 39 JP 693, 17 Digest (Repl) 115, 274.
Stedman v Swan's Tours (1951) 95 Sol Jo 727, CA, 17 Digest (Repl) 121, 322.

Cases also cited   f

Farnworth Finance Facilities Ltd v Attryde [1970] 2 All ER 774, [1970] 1 WLR 1053, CA.
Pearce v Lunn-Poly [1968] CLY 528.

Appeal

The plaintiff, James Walter John Jarvis, appealed against the judgment of his Honour
Judge Corley at Ilford County Court, given on 2nd March 1972, awarding the plaintiff g
damages of £31·72 on the trial of his claim against the defendants, Swans Tours Ltd,
in respect of breach of a contract to provide the plaintiff with the holiday facilities
represented in the defendants' brochure, in which the plaintiff claimed special damages of £63·45 for the cost of the holiday and £93·27 for two weeks' salary, and general
damages for inconvenience and loss of benefit. The facts are set out in the judgment
of Lord Denning MR.   h

S N Parrish for the plaintiff.
Peter K J Thompson for the defendants.

LORD DENNING MR. The plaintiff, Mr Jarvis, is a solicitor employed by a local j
authority at Barking. In 1969 he was minded to go for Christmas to Switzerland. He
was looking forward to a ski-ing holiday. It is his one fortnight's holiday in the year.
He prefers it in the winter rather than in the summer.

Mr Jarvis read a brochure issued by Swans Tours Ltd. He was much attracted by
the description of Morlialp, Giswil, Central Switzerland. I will not read the whole of
it, but just pick out some of the principal attractions:

a   'HOUSE PARTY CENTRE with special resident host . . . MÖRLIALP is a most
     wonderful little resort on a sunny plateau . . . Up there you will find yourself
     in the midst of beautiful alpine scenery, which in winter becomes a wonderland
     of sun, snow and ice, with a wide variety of fine ski-runs, a skating-rink and an
     exhilarating toboggan run . . . Why did we choose the Hotel Krone . . .
     mainly and most of all, because of the "GEMUTLICHKEIT" and friendly welcome
b   you will receive from Herr and Frau Weibel . . . The Hotel Krone has its own
     Alphütte Bar which will be open several evenings a week . . . No doubt you
     will be in for a great time, when you book this houseparty holiday . . . Mr.
     Weibel, the charming owner, speaks English.'

On the same page, in a special yellow box, it was said:

c   'SWANS HOUSEPARTY IN MORLIALP. *All these Houseparty arrangements are included
     in the price of your holiday.* Welcome party on arrival. Afternoon tea and cake
     for 7 days. Swiss Dinner by candlelight. Fondue-party. Yodler evening. Chali
     farewell party in the "Alphutte Bar". Service of representative.'

Alongside on the same page there was a special note about ski-packs: 'Hire of Skis,
d   Sticks and Boots . . . 12 days £11·10.'
     In August 1969, on the faith of that brochure, Mr Jarvis booked a 15 day holiday,
with ski-pack. The total charge was £63·45, including Christmas supplement. He
was to fly from Gatwick to Zurich on 20th December 1969 and return on 3rd January
1970.
     The plaintiff went on the holiday, but he was very disappointed. He was a man of
e   about 35 and he expected to be one of a houseparty of some 30 or so people. Instead,
he found there were only 13 during the first week. In the second week there was no
houseparty at all. He was the only person there. Mr Weibel could not speak English.
So there was Mr Jarvis, in the second week, in this hotel with no houseparty at all,
and no one could speak English, except himself. He was very disappointed, too, with
the ski-ing. It was some distance away at Giswil. There were no ordinary length skis.
f   There were only mini-skis, about 3 ft long. So he did not get his ski-ing as he wanted
to. In the second week he did get some longer skis for a couple of days, but then, because of the boots, his feet got rubbed and he could not continue even with the long
skis. So his ski-ing holiday, from his point of view, was pretty well ruined.
     There were many other matters, too. They appear trivial when they are set down
in writing, but I have no doubt they loomed large in Mr Jarvis's mind, when coupled
g   with the other disappointments. He did not have the nice Swiss cakes which he was
hoping for. The only cakes for tea were potato crisps and little dry nutcakes. The
yodler evening consisted of one man from the locality who came in his working
clothes for a little while, and sang four or five songs very quickly. The 'Alphütte
Bar' was an unoccupied annexe which was only open one evening. There was a
representative, Mrs Storr, there during the first week, but she was not there during
h   the second week. The matter was summed up by the learned judge:

     '. . . during the first week he got a holiday in Switzerland which was to some
     extent inferior . . . and, as to the second week he got a holiday which was very
     largely inferior [to what he was led to expect].'

j   What is the legal position? I think that the statements in the brochure were representations or warranties. The breaches of them give Mr Jarvis a right to damages.
It is not necessary to decide whether they were representations or warranties;
because, since the Misrepresentation Act 1967, there is a remedy in damages for
misrepresentation as well as for breach of warranty.
     The one question in the case is: what is the amount of damages? The judge seems
to have taken the difference in value between what he paid for and what he got.

He said that he intended to give 'the difference between the two values and no other   *a*
damages' under any other head. He thought that Mr Jarvis had got half of what he
paid for. So the judge gave him half the amount which he had paid, namely, £31·72.
Mr Jarvis appeals to this court. He says that the damages ought to have been much
more.

There is one point I must mention first. Counsel together made a very good note
of the judge's judgment. They agreed it. It is very clear and intelligible. It shows   *b*
plainly enough the ground of the judge's decision; but, by an oversight, it was not
submitted to the judge, as it should have been: see *Bruen v Bruce*[1]. In some circumstances we should send it back to the judge for his comments. But I do not think we
need do so here. The judge received the notice of appeal and made notes for our
consideration. I do not think he would have wished to add to them. We will, therefore, decide the case on the material before us.

What is the right way of assessing damages? It has often been said that on a breach   *c*
of contract damages cannot be given for mental distress. Thus in *Hamlin v Great
Northern Railway Co*[2] Pollock CB said that damages cannot be given 'for the disappointment of mind occasioned by the breach of contract'. And in *Hobbs v London & South
Western Railway Co*[3] Mellor J said that—

> '. . . for the mere inconvenience, such as annoyance and loss of temper, or   *d*
> vexation, or for being disappointed in a particular thing which you have set your
> mind upon, without real physical inconvenience resulting, you cannot recover
> damages.'

The courts in those days only allowed the plaintiff to recover damages if he suffered
physical inconvenience, such as, having to walk five miles home, as in *Hobbs's* case[4];   *e*
or to live in an overcrowded house: see *Bailey v Bullock*[5].

I think that those limitations are out of date. In a proper case damages for mental
distress can be recovered in contract, just as damages for shock can be recovered in
tort. One such case is a contract for a holiday, or any other contract to provide entertainment and enjoyment. If the contracting party breaks his contract, damages can
be given for the disappointment, the distress, the upset and frustration caused by the   *f*
breach. I know that it is difficult to assess in terms of money, but it is no more difficult
than the assessment which the courts have to make every day in personal injury
cases for loss of amenities. Take the present case. Mr Jarvis has only a fortnight's
holiday in the year. He books it far ahead, and looks forward to it all that time.
He ought to be compensated for the loss of it.

A good illustration was given by Edmund Davies LJ in the course of the argument.   *g*
He put the case of a man who has taken a ticket for Glyndbourne. It is the only night
on which he can get there. He hires a car to take him. The car does not turn up.
His damages are not limited to the mere cost of the ticket. He is entitled to general
damages for the disappointment he has suffered and the loss of the entertainment
which he should have had. Here, Mr Jarvis's fortnight's winter holiday has been a
grave disappointment. It is true that he was conveyed to Switzerland and back and   *h*
had meals and bed in the hotel. But that is not what he went for. He went to enjoy
himself with all the facilities which the defendants said he would have. He is entitled
to damages for the lack of those facilities, and for his loss of enjoyment.

A similar case occurred in 1951. It was *Stedman v Swan's Tours*[6]. A holiday-maker
was awarded damages because he did not get the bedroom and the accommodation

j

---

1 [1959] 2 All ER 375, [1959] 1 WLR 684
2 (1856) 1 H & N 408 at 411
3 (1875) LR 10 QB 111 at 122, [1874-80] All ER Rep 458 at 463
4 (1875) LR 10 QB 111, [1874-80] All ER Rep 458
5 [1950] 2 All ER 1167
6 (1951) 95 Sol Jo 727

a
which he was promised. The county court judge awarded him £13 15s. This court increased it to £50.

I think the judge was in error in taking the sum paid for the holiday, £63·45, and halving it. The right measure of damages is to compensate him for the loss of entertainment and enjoyment which he was promised, and which he did not get. Looking at the matter quite broadly, I think the damages in this case should be the sum of
b
£125. I would allow the appeal accordingly.

EDMUND DAVIES LJ.   Some of the observations of Mellor J in the 100 year old case of *Hobbs v London & South Western Railway Co*[1] call today for reconsideration. I must not be taken to accept that, under modern conditions and having regard to the developments which have taken place in the law of contract since that decision
c
was given, it is right to say, as the learned judge did[2], that—

> '. . . for the mere inconvenience, such as annoyance and loss of temper, or vexation, or for being disappointed in a particular thing which you have set your mind upon, without real physical inconvenience resulting, you cannot recover damages. That is purely sentimental, and not a case where the word
d
> inconvenience, as I here use it, would apply.'

On the contrary, there is authority for saying that even inconvenience that is not strictly physical may be a proper element in the assessment of damages. In *Griffiths v Evans*[3], in the course of a dissenting judgment where a solicitor was being sued for negligence in wrongly advising a plaintiff as to his right to sue his employers at common law, Denning LJ[4] said that the damages should be assessed—
e
> 'by taking into account the inconvenience and expense to which [the plaintiff] will be put in suing the employers and the risk of failure.'

Be that as it may, Mellor J was dealing with a contract of carriage and the undertaking of the railway company was entirely different from that of the defendants in the present case. These travel agents made clear by their lavishly illustrated brochure
f
with its ecstatic text that what they were contracting to provide was not merely air travel, hotel accommodation and meals of a certain standard. To quote the assurance which they gave regarding the Morlialp House Party Centre, 'No doubt you will be in for a great time, when you book this houseparty holiday'. The result was that they did *not* limit themselves to the obligation to ensure that an air passage was booked, that hotel accommodation was reserved, that food was provided and that
g
these items would measure up to the standards they themselves set up. They went further than that. They assured and undertook to provide a holiday of a certain quality, with 'Gemutlichkeit' (that is to say, geniality, comfort and cosiness) as its overall characteristics, and 'a great time', the enjoyable outcome which would surely result to all but the most determined misanthrope.

If in such circumstances travel agents fail to provide a holiday of the contracted
h
quality, they are liable in damages. In assessing those damages the court is not, in my judgment, restricted by the £63·45 paid by the client for his holiday. Nor is it confined to matters of phyiscal inconvenience and discomfort, or even to quantifying the difference between such items as the expected delicious Swiss cakes and the depressingly desiccated biscuits and crisps provided for tea, between the ski-pack ordered and the miniature skis supplied, nor between the 'Very good . . . House-
j
party arrangements' assured and the lone-wolf second week of the unfortunate

---

1   (1875) LR 10 QB 111, [1874-80] All ER Rep 458
2   (1875) LR 10 QB at 122, [1874-80] All ER Rep at 463
3   [1953] 2 All ER 1364, [1953] 1 WLR 1424
4   [1953] 2 All ER at 1371, [1953] 1 WLR at 1432

plaintiff's stay. The court is entitled, and indeed bound, to contrast the overall   *a*
quality of the holiday so enticingly promised with that which the defendants in fact
provided.

In determining what would be proper compensation for the defendants' marked
failure to fulfil their undertaking I am of the opinion that, again to use Mellor J's
terms, 'vexation' and 'being disappointed in a particular thing which you have set
your mind upon' *are* relevant considerations which afford the court a guide in arriving   *b*
at a proper figure.

When a man has paid for and properly expects an invigorating and amusing
holiday and, through no fault of his, returns home dejected because his expectations
have been largely unfulfilled, in my judgment it would be quite wrong to say that
his disappointment must find no reflection in the damages to be awarded. And it is
right to add that, in the course of his helpful submissions, counsel for the defendants   *c*
did not go so far as to submit anything of the kind. Judge Alun Pugh took that view
in *Feldman v Allways Travel Services*[1]. That, too, was a holiday case. The highly
experienced senior county court judge there held that the correct measure of damages
was the difference between the price paid and the value of the holiday in fact
furnished, 'taking into account the plaintiff's feelings of annoyance and frustration'.

The learned trial judge clearly failed to approach his task in this way, which in my   *d*
judgment is the proper way to be adopted in the present case. He said:

> 'There is no evidence of inconvenience or discomfort, other than that arising
> out of the breach of contract and covered by my award. [There was] no evidence
> of physical discomfort, e.g. bedroom not up to standard.'

His failure is manifested, not only by these words, but also by the extremely small   *e*
damages he awarded, calculated, be it noted, as one half of the cost of the holiday.
Instead of 'a great time', the plaintiff's reasonable and proper hopes were largely and
lamentably unfulfilled. To arrive at a proper compensation for the defendants'
failure is no easy matter. But in my judgment we should not be compensating the
plaintiff excessively were we to award him the £125 damages proposed by Lord
Denning MR. I therefore concur in allowing this appeal.   *f*

STEPHENSON LJ. I agree. What damage has the plaintiff suffered for the loss
to him which has resulted from the defendants' breaches of this winter sports holiday
contract and was within the reasonable contemplation of the parties to this contract
as a likely result of its being so broken? This seems to me to be the question raised
by this interesting case.   *g*

The judge has, as I understand his judgment, held that the value of the plaintiff's
loss was what he paid under the contract for his holiday; that as a result of the
defendants' breaches of contract he has lost not the whole of what he has paid for,
but broadly speaking a half of it; and what he has lost and what reduces its value by
about one half includes such inconvenience as the plaintiff suffered from the holiday
he got not being, by reason of the defendants' breaches, as valuable as the holiday he   *h*
paid for.

I approach the judge's judgment bearing in mind the unfortunate fact that
counsel's note of it has not been submitted to him for his approval in accordance
with what has been said by this court about the rule which is now RSC Ord 59, r 19 (4).
I agree with the judge that the breaches were not fundamental, that the consideration
for the plaintiff's payment to the defendants did not wholly fail and that, although   *j*
the plaintiff was frustrated, the contract was not. In my judgment, however, the
judge seems to have undervalued the loss to the plaintiff from the breaches which he
found: no welcome party; no suitable cakes for afternoon tea; no yodler evening in

---

1   [1957] CLY 934

a the true sense of the words; the Alphütte Bar not open several evenings of the week; no service of the representative in the second week and no houseparty arrangements for the second week; no English spoken by Mr Weibel, the owner; no full length skis until the second week; not much fun at night and no tobogganing or bowling by day or by night.

b The learned judge in assessing the loss also underestimated the inconvenience to the plaintiff, perhaps because he followed the distinction drawn by Mellor J in *Hobbs's* case[1] and disallowed any inconvenience or discomfort that was not physical, insofar as that can be defined. I agree that, as suggested in McGregor on Damages[2], there may be contracts in which the parties contemplate inconvenience on breach which may be described as mental: frustration, annoyance, disappointment; and, as counsel for the defendants concedes that this is such a contract, the damages for breach of it should take such wider inconvenience or discomfort into account.

c I further agree with Lord Denning MR and Edmund Davies LJ that the judge was wrong in taking, as I think he must have taken, the amount which the plaintiff paid the defendants for his holiday as the value of the holiday which they agreed to provide. They ought to have contemplated, and no doubt did contemplate, that he was accepting their offer of this holiday as an offer of something which would benefit him d and which he would enjoy, and that if they broke their contract and provided him with a holiday lacking in some of the things which they contracted to include in it, they would thereby reduce his enjoyment of the holiday and the benefit he would derive from it.

These considerations lead me to agree with Lord Denning MR and Edmund Davies LJ that the judge was wrong in applying to this contract to provide a winter sports holiday the method of measuring damages for breach of warranty set out in s 53 (3) e of the Sale of Goods Act 1893, as it was applied in *Feldman v Allways Travel Services*[3] and that rather than try to put a value on the subject-matter of this contract, first as promised and then as performed, and to include the inconvenience to the plaintiff in the process, we should award the plaintiff a sum of general damages for all the breaches of contract at the figure suggested by Lord Denning MR.

f I would add that I think the judge was right in rejecting the plaintiffs' ingenious claim, however it is put, for a fortnight's salary. I agree that the appeal should be allowed and the plaintiff be awarded £125 damages.

Appeal allowed; damages of £125 awarded.

g Solicitors: *Maples, Teesdale & Co* (for the plaintiff); *Paisner & Co* (for the defendants).

Wendy Shockett Barrister.

h 1 (1875) LR 10 QB 111 at 122, [1874-80] All ER Rep 458 at 463
   2 13th Edn (1972), p 45, para 68
   3 [1957] CLY 934

R v Taylor (Vincent)

COURT OF APPEAL, CRIMINAL DIVISION
KARMINSKI LJ, O'CONNOR AND FORBES JJ
5th, 6th, 9th OCTOBER 1972

Criminal law – Affray – Unlawful fighting – Only one person fighting unlawfully – Whether proper to convict one person alone of offence.

Two police officers went to a social club for the purpose of arresting the appellant on a charge of burglary. The appellant was at the club drinking with his brothers, D and M. The police officers began questioning the appellant. Within a very short time a fight broke out in which the appellant, his brothers and the police were all involved. Tables were overturned and other people in the club were plainly frightened. The appellant and his brothers were charged with affray. M was acquitted but the jury failed to agree with respect to the appellant and D. At the retrial the defence alleged that the fight had been started by the police officers and that the appellant and D were acting in self-defence. The appellant was convicted and D was acquitted. On appeal the appellant contended that in order to constitute an affray there had to be at least two people fighting unlawfully and that the appellant could not, therefore, be guilty of the offence on his own.

Held – The appeal would be dismissed. Where only one person was fighting unlawfully in circumstances where all the ingredients of an affray were present, he could properly be charged with and convicted of an affray on his own; where two persons were charged with affray and one acquitted on the ground that he was not fighting unlawfully, it was perfectly proper to convict the other (see p 88 d and h, post).

R v Scarrow (1968) 52 Cr App Rep 591 followed.

R v Sharp, R v Johnson [1957] 1 All ER 577 not followed.

Button v Director of Public Prosecutions [1965] 3 All ER 587 considered.

Semble. Where the affray is alleged to have taken place on private premises there must be people actually present in contrast to an affray in a public place where the law is satisfied if there may be people present who, although reasonably stout-hearted, would be put in fear by what they see and hear (see p 86 f, post).

Notes

For affray, see 10 Halsbury's Laws (3rd Edn) 584, para 1086, and for a case on the subject, see 15 Digest (Repl) 785, 7360.

Cases referred to in judgment

Button v Director of Public Prosecutions, Swain v Director of Public Prosecutions [1965] 3 All ER 587, [1966] AC 591, [1965] 3 WLR 1131, 130 JP 48, 50 Cr App Rep 36, HL; *affg* CCA, sub nom *R v Button and Swain* [1965] 1 All ER 964, [1965] 2 WLR 992, Digest (Cont Vol B) 189, 7360f.

R v Scarrow, R v Brown, R v Attlesey (1968) 52 Cr App Rep 591, CA, Digest (Cont Vol C) 244, 7360ea.

R v Sharp, R v Johnson [1957] 1 All ER 577, [1957] 1 QB 552, [1957] 2 WLR 472, 121 JP 227, 41 Cr App Rep 86, CCA, Digest (Cont Vol A) 410, 7360a.

R v Summers [1972] Crim LR 635, CA.

Cases and authorities also cited

R v Allan [1963] 2 All ER 897, [1965] 1 QB 130, CCA.

R v Khan and Rakhman [1963] Crim LR 562, CCA.

R v Meade (1903) 19 TLR 540.

R v Woodrow (1959) 43 Cr App Rep 105, CCA.

a
State of New Jersey v Jordon (1965) A 2d 563.
State of New Jersey v Scaduto (1907) 65 A 908.
Archbold's Pleading and Evidence in Criminal Cases (1st Edn, 1822), p 337.
Blount's Law Dictionary (3rd Edn, 1717) 'Affray'.
Burn's Justice of the Peace (23rd Edn, 1820), vol 1, pp 25, 28.
Cowell's Law Dictionary or the Interpreter of Words and Terms (1708 Edn) 'Affray'.
b
Dalton's Country Justice (1635 Edn), pp 33-35.
Fitzherbert's L'Office et Auctoritie de Justices de Peace (1617 Edn), pp 146, 147.
10 Halsbury's Laws of England (3rd Edn), p 584, para 1086.
Nelson's The Office and Authority of a Justice of Peace (6th Edn, 1718), pp 9-11.
Russell on Crime (1st Edn, 1819), vol 1, p 388, (12th Edn, 1964), vol 1, p 265.
Stephen's Digest of the Criminal Law (9th Edn, 1950), p 74.

c
Appeal and application

On 21st March 1972 at Nottingham Crown Court before Phillips J and a jury, the appellant, Vincent Taylor, was convicted on a majority verdict (10 to 2) of affray. He was sentenced to three years' imprisonment. He appealed against conviction by certificate of the trial judge under s 1 (2) of the Criminal Appeal Act 1968. The

d
appellant also applied for leave to appeal against sentence. The facts are set out in the judgment of the court.

Basil Wigoder QC and *W H Joss* for the appellant.
Charles McCullough QC and *J B M Milmo* for the Crown.

e
O'CONNOR J delivered the judgment of the court at the invitation of Karminski LJ. On 21st March 1972 at Nottingham Crown Court before Phillips J and a jury the appellant was convicted of affray by a majority verdict of 10 to 2. He was sentenced to three years' imprisonment. He appeals against that conviction on a certificate of the trial judge and applies for leave to appeal against sentence. The certificate reads:

f
'The appellant, Vincent Taylor, was convicted of affray and his co-accused, David Reginald Lowndes, was acquitted. The allegation was that they fought police officers who were questioning the appellant about another offence. It was not alleged that any other persons fought the police officers. The question is whether, Lowndes having been acquitted, the appellant could properly be convicted of affray.'

g
The matter arose out of an incident which occurred on 21st August 1971. On that day two police officers in plain clothes, Det Con Flowers and Det Con Everitt, went to the Strelley Social Club for the purpose of arresting the appellant on a charge of burglary. He was in the club with his two brothers, David and Michael Lowndes, and not surprisingly they were drinking beer. When the police officers arrived it

h
appears that the appellant was minded to go quietly but that his brother David Lowndes stepped in between him and the police officers, handed him back his pint of beer and told him not to go with them. In a very short time a mêlée broke out in which the two police officers, the appellant, his brothers David and Michael Lowndes, were all fighting. Tables were overturned and beer was thrown all over the place. There was evidence that the other people in the club were screaming and plainly frightened—in the ordinary course of events all the ingredients of affray now that the

j
question whether it has to be in a public place or can occur on private premises has been resolved by the House of Lords in *Button v Director of Public Prosecutions*[1], to which I will refer in due course.

1 [1965] 3 All ER 587, [1966] AC 591

A little further history is necessary. In the first instance all three brothers were *a*
charged with affray and the trial came on at an earlier date before Caulfield J and a
jury. At that trial the jury acquitted Michael Lowndes of that offence and they could
not agree in respect of David Lowndes and the appellant; thus it was a retrial with
which we are concerned on this occasion.

Broadly the prosecution case was that the fight had started at the instigation of
David Lowndes and that the police officers were only carrying out their lawful duty *b*
as best they might, namely, to arrest the appellant. The defence case was that the
two police officers had barged into the club in a forceful manner and had for practical
purposes started the fight and that insofar as the appellant and David Lowndes participated it was only in self-defence. Those matters were left quite unexceptionably by
the trial judge to the jury.

He dealt with the law as far as affray is concerned perhaps too favourably to the *c*
appellant, but it matters not for the purpose of this appeal. He said:

'What it [affray] means is this: it is where persons fight together in the presence
of other persons so that those persons are put in fear. Therefore the essence of it is
this, which the [Crown] have to prove, a fight, the presence of other people and
that those other people are put in fear. [On the authorities the latter part of that
proposition is not strictly necessary.] ... I must say a word about the meaning *d*
of "fought" because it can be different things in different connections. We all
in a general way know what fighting is but it can have shades of meaning. What
it really means here is that the person alleged to have fought must be shown to
have engaged in violence of some kind against others, and it must be shown, and
when I say "shown" I mean shown by the [Crown], that the violence in which
they engaged was not in reasonable self-defence. It must be shown not to have *e*
been justified in some other way, as, for example, trying to peaceably settle other
people or something like that. What you are looking for is to see it is proved that
those men fought in the sense that they engaged in violent activities against
others without justification.'

Once again that is a wholly unexceptionable direction on unlawful fighting. Lastly *f*
on this topic the judge concluded his direction in these words:

'So, as I have told you, you have to consider each separately. You could have
these results, you could be satisfied about both of them and find them both
guilty. You could be satisfied about one or the other and find him guilty. You
could be satisfied about neither and find them both not guilty. So all those
opinions are open to you, but basically the [Crown] must satisfy you so you *g*
are sure they, putting it in a sentence, attacked the police and fought them in the
way which I have indicated before.'

It is that part of the direction which is raised in the certificate and is the question of
law for decision by this court.

The offence of affray is a very old one in our law. The number of decided cases is *h*
comparatively few and the early learning on the topic is found in the textbook writers
in the 15th, 16th, 17th and 18th centuries. We are indebted to counsel for both the
appellant and the Crown for the extremely thorough and full review of the authorities placed before us in argument. For reasons which will become apparent in a short
while it is not necessary for the purposes of this judgment to go in great detail through
all the textbook writers. A very full and convenient summary of the topic can be *j*
found in the report of *Button v Director of Public Prosecutions*[1]. There the ruling of
MacKenna J is set out in full in the course of the judgment of the Court of Criminal
Appeal given by Marshall J[2], and in the argument before the House of Lords and in

1   [1965] 3 All ER 587, [1966] AC 591
2   [1965] 1 All ER 964 at 967-972, [1966] AC at 600-607

a the speech of Lord Gardiner LC the authorities are fully reviewed[1]. Suffice it to say that the offence of affray from textbook writers has an essential ingredient, namely, that it is an offence against public order, it is an offence against the peace, and the necessary element is that persons—they are always referred to as Her Majesty's subjects by the textbook writers—are put in fear. The offence was designed to provide protection against violent disturbance of the peace.

b The violence, the authorities show, may be of two kinds. It could arise by fighting in the ordinary sense and that means the actual preparation for the delivery of blows and the delivering of blows; taunting by words was never sufficient. At the same time, as exemplified by the Statute of Northampton 1328[2], going armed in an unusual and terrifying fashion, particularly into the market place or fairgrounds, was also an example of affray. So we find as we look at the textbook writers, starting with Lambard's Eirenarcha[3] and going down through the various writers, through Coke[4], c Hawkins[5] and Hale[6], that the offence is well established in these forms.

One looks to see at once whether one person could be guilty of affray in those circumstances because it is obvious that in the ordinary course of events fighting involves two people being engaged at least. I can start with Hawkins and I do that because it was with Hawkins that the error which was corrected in *Button v Director of Public Prosecutions*[7] originated. It will be found that the true origin was in Hawkins's d description of affray[8]:

'In treating of affrays, I shall consider, 1. What shall be said to be an affray. 2. How far it may be suppressed by a private person. 3. How far by a constable. 4. How far by a justice of peace. 5. In what manner the several kinds of affrays may be punished.'

e In dealing with the first point he has this to say[8]:

'*Sect. 1.* It is said, that the word "affray" is derived from the French word *effraier*, to terrify, and that, in a legal sense, it is taken for a public offence to the terror of the people. From this definition it seems clearly to follow, that there may be an assault which will not amount to an affray; as where it happens in a f private place, out of the hearing or seeing of any, except the parties concerned; in which case it cannot be said to be to the terror of the people; and for this cause such a private assault seems not to be inquirable in a court leet, as all affrays certainly are, as being common nuisances. *Sect. 2.* Also it is said, that no quarrelsome or threatening words whatsoever shall amount to an affray; and that no one can justify laying his hands on those who shall barely quarrel with angry g words, without coming to blows; yet it seemeth, that the constable may, at the request of the party threatened, carry the person, who threatens to beat him, before a justice, in order to find sureties.'

He deals with certain special kinds of affray with which we are not concerned, such as quarrelling in a churchyard which in those days was regarded as an extremely grave offence. But in dealing with how far an affray may be suppressed by a h constable Hawkins has this to say[9]:

'*Sect. 14.* And it is said, that if a constable see persons either actually engaged in an affray, as striking, or offering to strike, or drawing their weapons, &c. or

1 See [1965] 3 All ER at 589-591, [1966] AC at 612-627
2 2 Edw 3, c 3
j 3 1614 Edn, pp 125, 126
4 3 Institutes (1817 Edn) Pt III, ch 72, pp 157, 159
5 Pleas of the Crown (1716 Edn) vol 1, ch 63, pp 134, **135**, 138, 139
6 Pleas of the Crown (1685 Edn) pp 134, 135
7 [1965] 3 All ER 587, [1966] AC 591
8 Pleas of the Crown (8th Edn, 1824), vol 1, ch. 28, p 487
9 Pleas of the Crown (8th Edn, 1824), vol 1, ch 28, p 490

upon the very point of entering upon an affray, as where one shall threaten to
kill, wound, or beat another, he may either carry the offender before a justice   *a*
of the peace, to the end that such justice may compel him to find sureties for the
peace . . .'

Hawkins plainly envisages what in modern terminology would be that one unlawful assailant can be apprehended on a charge of affray and brought before the
justices. So too when I turn to Blackstone[1]:   *b*

'AFFRAYS . . . are the fighting of two or more persons in some public place,
to the terror of his majesty's subjects: for, if the fighting be in private, it is no
affray but an *assault*. Affrays may be suppressed by any private person present,
who is justifiable in endeavouring to part the combatants, whatever consequence
may ensue.'   *c*

He deals with various forms of aggravation of affrays, and he also deals, of course,
with the unlawful carrying of arms. In the notes of that edition it will be found[2]:

'It seems certain, that in some cases there may be an affray where there is no
actual violence; as where a man arms himself with dangerous and unusual   *d*
weapons, in such a manner as will naturally cause a terror to the people,'

and Hawkins[3] is cited as the authority.
    It will be seen in Blackstone's definition[1] that there was a requirement that the
affray should be in a public place and thereafter that requirement stood in our law
for about 100 years until it was demonstrated to be erroneous in *Button v Director*   *e*
of Public Prosecutions[4].
    Counsel for the appellant has submitted that affrays may be of different natures.
He accepts that the type of affray where the offender was unusually armed could be
carried out by a single individual. He has submitted that that is no longer the law
today because the Statute of Northampton 1328 has been repealed by the Criminal
Law Act 1967[5].   *f*
    The authorities show that affray was a common law misdemeanour alongside the
statute at all times, and it is unnecessary for the purposes of this case to decide whether
the definition of affray given in *Button v Director of Public Prosecutions*[4] has had the
effect of limiting the modern offence to fighting as opposed to the other forms of
affray of which the textbook writers speak.
    It will be seen that in Blackstone[1] we have two or more people fighting unlaw-   *g*
fully. I point out that in the earlier authorities there is no reference to two people as
such. The first reference to any numbers at all is to be found in Rastell's Les Termes
de la Ley[6] where it is 'many people fighting together', but that disappears from the
books and we are left with the modern definition of 'two or more people fighting
together'.
    I should turn for this definition at once to *Button v Director of Public Prosecutions*[4] *h*
and see what was said. In that case the two appellants who were convicted went into
a dance hall where a dance was being given by a darts club and they fought and
made an affray. The real question was whether it was a public place and whether
that was a necessary ingredient of the offence. Nevertheless when the Court of
Criminal Appeal certified the matter to the House of Lords the House was asked to

j

---

1 Commentaries on the Laws of England (16th Edn, 1825), bk IV, ch XI, p 145
2 16th Edn, bk IV, ch XI, p 145, note (6)
3 Pleas of the Crown (1716 Edn), bk I, ch 63, para 4
4 [1965] 3 All ER 587, [1966] AC 591
5 Section 10, Sch 3, Pt I
6 1721 Edn, p 28

a   rule that a point of law of general public importance was involved in affray itself, namely, as to the true ingredients of the offence of affray. Nevertheless the whole of the argument and indeed the review of the authorities turned on the question whether the affray must take place in a public place, and so when we come to the matter in the speech of Lord Gardiner LC he said[1]: 'The essence of the offence is that two or more fight together to the terror of the Queen's subjects.'

b   Counsel for the appellant relies on that and says that the House of Lords had declared what the essence of the offence is and it requires that two or more fight together and that that must mean that two or more fight unlawfully. He is supported in that contention by the decision of the Court of Criminal Appeal in *R v Sharp, R v Johnson*[2]. It will be remembered that at that time there was the requirement of a public place. No problem arose because the fight between the two appellants took place in the street. The facts of that case were again straightforward. Sharp

c was a cripple armed with a razor; he met Johnson and a fight à l'outrance took place. Johnson was badly cut. He disarmed Sharp of his razor and either cut off or bit off his ear before the police broke it up. When the matter was tried at the Central Criminal Court the recorder refused to allow self-defence to be put on behalf of either of the appellants. Each had contended that he only fought in self-defence.

d That was the point which came before the Court of Criminal Appeal constituted by Lord Goddard CJ, Cassels and Hinchcliffe JJ. In the result the court held that self-defence was a defence to the charge of affray and had to be left to the jury and in the result both convictions were quashed. However, it is necessary to examine the case in a little bit more detail. The concession made by counsel for the Crown in that case with regard to self-defence was[3]:

e   '. . . it is conceded that this could be a good defence. It would mean there was no fight; but it could not arise on the facts of the present case.'

In *R v Sharp, R v Johnson*[4] Lord Goddard CJ, after making a short review of the authorities, said:

f   'We must now turn to the second ground of appeal. It will be remembered that the appellant Sharp contended that he only acted in self-defence after he had been set on by the other appellant, and, apparently attempted to excuse the use of a razor because he was handicapped by his crippled condition. The appellant Johnson also seems to have endeavoured to justify his conduct in biting off his opponent's ear by the fact that he was attacked with a razor. Now as the recorder said, and we see no reason why he should not, one object in charging the

g   appellants with an affray which is of necessity a joint offence, is that, in this class of case, each prisoner throws the blame on the other and there is a danger that, perhaps being disgusted with both and thinking each only got his deserts, a jury will acquit both if the charges are of the one wounding the other.'

It will be seen that in that passage Lord Goddard CJ was clearly of the opinion
h that affray was a joint offence, namely, that this kind of affray at all events—fighting— could not be committed by one person. Later he said[4]:

    'The appellant Sharp's case was that he was attacked by the appellant Johnson and that, as a partial cripple, he used the razor to protect himself. The jury might well have rejected this as extravagant, but we do not feel able to say that they must have done so on a proper direction. The facts are such that the court is
j   strongly inclined to apply the proviso[5], but we think on the whole that were

---

1 [1965] 3 All ER at 590, [1966] AC at 625
2 [1957] 1 All ER 577, [1957] 1 QB 552
3 (1957) 41 Cr App Rep 86 at 89
4 [1957] 1 All ER at 580, [1957] 1 QB at 561
5 I e the proviso to s 4 of the Criminal Appeal Act 1907

we to do so we should be going further than we ought, and it is obvious that
one cannot be convicted and the other acquitted. We reluctantly, therefore,
quash the convictions.'

Counsel for the appellant has submitted that a fair reading of that shows that
Lord Goddard CJ and the court thought that one person in such circumstances could
not be found guilty of affray; that there must be at least two unlawful fighters.
On that, for the purposes of the case, it was quite plain that each defendant had raised
self-defence and what was sauce for the goose must be also sauce for the gander,
and if Sharp had his conviction quashed on that ground it seems to this court that it
must follow that so too Johnson is entitled to have his conviction quashed. However,
it is quite plain that Lord Goddard CJ put the matter in terms that it was a joint
offence and that, if there were only two people charged in a fight where they fought
together in that fashion, if one was acquitted the other ought to be acquitted too.

That that was a fair reading of it is shown by numerous references in the textbook
writers. It was certainly Professor Smith's view (see his up-to-date note in the
Criminal Law Review on *R v Summers*[1] to which I will refer shortly).

There the matter stood in 1957. In 1965 *Button v Director of Public Prosecutions*[2] was
decided in the House of Lords, and in 1968 came *R v Scarrow*[3]. In that case three
persons were charged with affray—Scarrow, Brown and Attlesey. The indictment
contained nine counts. Counts 1 to 4 related to an incident which occurred at the
Carlton Hotel, Newmarket, and counts 5 to 9 at the Snug Cafe in Red Lodge. Count 1
alleged an affray and, therefore, it is limited to what took place at the Carlton Hotel
in Newmarket. The three appellants went into the Carlton Hotel and they set about
the people inside. The manageress said[4]:

'They got back into the main bar before I did and by the time I got there
fighting had broken out. The others were not so aggressive as these three. They
were fighting everyone, young and old, punching, kicking and no one retaliated.
Brown kicked a young man.'

The point in *R v Scarrow*[3] taken before this court was that although these three
people could have been said to have acted unlawfully in various places that they had
not committed an affray. It was submitted that it was a necessary ingredient of the
offence that there should be fighting and that involved reciprocal violence, namely,
a fight between two people actually exchanging blows. It was said, therefore, that if
three people moved into a public house and each set about victims who did not resist
that that was not fighting, and *R v Sharp*[5] where a concession had been made that
if there was only one unlawful fighter there was no fight for the purposes of the
affray was prayed in aid.

Lord Parker CJ, presiding over the division of this court in *R v Scarrow*[6] said:

'The second and more difficult point possibly is, as Mr. Martin puts it, that
fighting, for the purpose of constituting an affray, means a true combat in which
there is a reciprocity, as he puts it, of violence. On the evidence here, he says,
those who were attacked did not retaliate and accordingly there was no reciprocity of violence, and, while each of the appellants might be guilty of an assault in
some form, it cannot be said that they are guilty of an affray. It is clear, as Mr.
Martin says, that there is no direct authority on this matter whatsoever and he
invites this Court to hold that unless there is a true fight in which there is reciprocity of violence there can be no affray. The Court can see no ground whatever

---

1 [1972] Crim LR 635
2 [1965] 3 All ER 587, [1966] AC 591
3 (1968) 52 Cr App Rep 591
4 (1968) 52 Cr App Rep at 593
5 [1957] 1 All ER 577, [1957] 1 QB 552
6 (1968) 52 Cr App Rep at 594, 595

a for limiting the nature of the offence in that way. As the learned Chairman said in ruling against the appellants in this matter: "It is argued that if a number of people or members of two gangs fight one against another an offence is committed, but that when they set upon members of the public no offence of affray is committed; but my common sense rebels against it and I propose to overrule this submission and leave this count to the jury." This court entirely

b agrees with the learned Chairman when one bears in mind, as I have already pointed out, that many forms of conduct other than actual fighting may constitute an affray and in SHARP AND JOHNSON[1] Lord Goddard C.J. referred to passages in *Blackstone*[2] and *Hawkins*[3] which show that there may be an affray where there is no actual violence, as where a man arms himself with dangerous and unusual weapons in such a manner as will naturally cause a terror to the

c people.'

Lord Goddard CJ then dealt with the Statute of Northampton 1328. Lord Parker CJ continued[4]:

'Bearing that in mind, the court asks itself whether there is any need to give fighting, where fighting is alleged as the disturbance, the narrow meaning of

d two people each exerting violence on the other, or whether the more apt meaning in this connection is a perfectly general one; fighting in the colloquial sense; fighting in the sense that Mrs. Keatley in her evidence described and called fighting. This court is quite satisfied that there is no ground whatever for giving "fighting" the limited meaning of two people using violence the one on the other and that in the present case the attack that was made by these men on

e other people in the Carlton Hotel, who for one reason or another did not or were unable to retaliate, constitutes fighting sufficient to constitute an affray. Mr. Martin's main ground for supporting his argument was words used by Lord Goddard C.J. in the case of SHARP AND JOHNSON[5]. It is to be observed that in that case the Recorder of London (Sir Gerald Dodson), refused to leave self-defence as a defence to affray. Indeed he went further and said that self-defence

f is quite irrelevant and that when two people were fighting together the man who was acting in self-defence was just as guilty of the affray as the one who had attacked him, and the court in holding that that was a misdirection said this[5]: "If two men are found fighting in a street, one must be able to say the other attacked him and he was only defending himself. If he was only defending himself and not attacking, that is not a fight, and consequently, not an affray." And

g accordingly the court in that case, on an appeal by both the men concerned, quashed the convictions. Mr. Martin very naturally emphasises here that on the strict words used by Lord Goddard C.J. there is no fight at all if one is defending himself, so he would say there could be no fight at all if one did not even defend himself but just did not retaliate. It is important to note, however, that those words were merely adopting a concession which had been made by Mr. Morton,

h counsel for the Crown, in that case. He said, "With regard to self-defence, it is conceded that this could be a good defence. It would mean there was no fight." This court is not able to accept that concession in the way in which it is put. It may well be that if two people fight and one is acting in self-defence that man cannot be said to be guilty of an affray, but it would appear to this court that there is no reason why his attacker, whether acting alone or jointly with another

j attacker, should not be held guilty of the affray.'

---

1   [1957] 1 All ER at 578, 579, [1957] 1 QB at 559
2   Commentaries on the Laws of England (16th Edn, 1825), bk IV, ch XI, p 145
3   Pleas of the Crown (8th Edn, 1824), vol 1, ch 28, p 487
4   (1968) 52 Cr App Rep at 595, 596
5   [1957] 1 All ER at 580, [1957] 1 QB at 561

Counsel for the appellant submits that that part of the judgment is obiter—not necessary to the matter in hand in R v Scarrow[1] for this reason. He submits that the requirement, as he submits the law should be, that there must be two or more people fighting unlawfully is satisfied if the attackers can be found to be fighting unlawfully or attacking unlawfully, and that in R v Scarrow[1] the activities of the three appellants when they broke into the hotel satisfied the requirement that there were two or more fighting unlawfully. He accepts that R v Scarrow[1] is an authority that those who do not retaliate may still be involved in fighting for the purposes of affray.

In our judgment, that is not a correct appreciation of the decision in R v Scarrow[1]. The realities were that the Court of Appeal, when looking at the words used by Lord Goddard CJ in R v Sharp, R v Johnson[2], were seeking to say that insofar as Lord Goddard CJ had declared that affray was a joint offence and that one person could not be convicted of it where only two persons were involved, that that simply is not the law. It is sufficient for our purposes when faced with these two authorities to choose between them.

In fact, R v Scarrow[1] has been followed in this court in the recent case of R v Summers[3] of which a transcript of the judgment of this court was made available to us and cited to us in argument. It is unnecessary to deal in very great detail with the case.

What happened in R v Summers[3] was that the appellant Summers had a grudge against a man named Manning whom he thought was responsible for cutting and scarring his wife. He engaged the service of the other two appellants, Burns and Bond, who were two long-term prisoners on licence, to go and do his dirty work for him. He drove them to Manning's address where Manning was in his flat upstairs with his housekeeper and four children. The two men Burns and Bond broke in, one armed with a knife. Manning did not fight at all. He retreated; no retaliation. Someone grabbed the housekeeper's arm. The brave woman bashed her fist through the window and yelled for the police and the two men ran away.

Now it was submitted that this could not be an affray on the grounds that no fight had occurred, although it might have been terrifying to the children, namely, the other people who were, in fact, present. Where the affray is laid on private premises it may be—it is unnecessary to decide it for the purposes of this judgment —that there must be people actually present as opposed to an affray in a public place where it is clear that the law is satisfied if there may be people present who reasonably stoutheartedly would be put in fear by what they see and hear.

Edmund Davies LJ dealt with the matter in this way. He said:

'Affray is indeed a crime in relation to which ideas have developed, and certain misconceptions eradicated. It is necessary to refer to two cases in this context. In order of dates they are, first, R v Scarrow[1] and Button v Director of Public Prosecutions[4]',

and he then dealt with R v Scarrow[1] and set out the facts to which I have referred and referred to the part of the judgment of Lord Parker CJ[5] which I have already read. Edmund Davies LJ continued:

'In the light of that authority[6], in the present case the learned trial judge directed the jury that if they accepted Manning's and Mrs Summers' account of

1   (1968) 52 Cr App Rep 591
2   [1957] 1 All ER at 578, 579, [1957] 1 QB at 559
3   [1972] Crim LR 635
4   [1965] 3 All ER 587, [1966] AC 591
5   (1968) 52 Cr App Rep at 594-596
6   I e R v Scarrow (1968) 52 Cr App Rep 591

a
what had happened in the Manning flat that night, it was open to them to find that a fight had in fact taken place, a fight between Burns and Bond on the one hand and Manning and Mrs Summers on the other, notwithstanding that Manning had not raised a hand against either of the two intruders, and that all Mrs Summers had done was, having received rough treatment, to break the window and scream for the police. [Counsel for the appellant Summers] says

b
that was a misdirection. He has sought—if he will allow me to say so, manfully —to quarrel with the decision in the *Scarrow*[1] case. We have to say that we think, despite his valour, he has failed in that regard. Let me illustrate, if he will forgive the word, the absurdity of accepting his submission. He concedes, albeit with reluctance, that if, on the open blade being pointed at his stomach, Manning instead of retreating—as was perhaps the discreet thing to do—had made a

c
grab at Burns's hand and twisted it in an effort to wrest the weapon from him, there would thereby have arisen a situation which was properly capable of being described as a "fight" for the purposes of the crime of affray. The direction of the learned judge, accurately based as it was on the direction of Lord Parker CJ in *Scarrow*[1], finds respectful acceptance by this court and we hold that there was no misdirection by the learned judge in that regard.'

d
He then went on to deal with *Button v Director of Public Prosecutions*[2]. This was the private place situation and it is unnecessary to recite that part of the judgment.

It is to be noted that in *R v Summers*[3] Edmund Davies LJ said:

'The question therefore arises as to what exactly is meant by an "affray". We respectfully approve of and adopt a passage which appears in Smith and Hogan's

e
Criminal Law[4]. It is in these terms "Affray is a common law misdemeanour which, after a long period of desuetude, has not only been brought back into regular use, but greatly expanded in scope by judicial decision. [Then follows the definition proper:] Its elements are (1) fighting by one or more persons: or a display of force by one or more persons without actual violence; (2) in such a manner that reasonable people might be frightened or intimidated." '

f
So we have an approval of that passage from Smith and Hogan's Criminal Law[4] in *R v Summers*[3] in this court. In the passage quoted there is an oversight in the definition probably because Professors Smith and Hogan thought it too obvious to need stating; fighting by one or more persons has to be qualified: 'unlawful fighting by one or more persons'.

g
Counsel for the appellant has submitted that both the textbook writers and this court in *R v Scarrow*[1], and again in *R v Summers*[3], were in error in accepting that unlawful fighting by one person could amount to affray.

It is perfectly right to say that there is no case where that has occurred before the present one. There has always got to be a first time. As I have said, he has submitted that either there must be unlawful fighting by the two people actually engaged in the

h
fight, or, alternatively, unlawful fighting by two or more on the same side even if the opposition run away and do not fight in the colloquial sense. Just as 'this court in *R v Scarrow*[1] was unable to see why the offence should be limited in that fashion, so too we are unable to see why it should be limited in that fashion. If one takes as an example *R v Sharp, R v Johnson*[5], and uses the facts from that case for the purposes of analysis let us see where it leads to. Here you have two men fighting in the street

j

1   (1968) 52 Cr App Rep 591
2   [1965] 3 All ER 587, [1966] AC 591
3   [1972] Crim LR 635
4   2nd Edn (1969), p 539
5   [1957] 1 All ER 577, [1957] 1 QB 552

with a crowd of onlookers and, as I have already said, fighting à l'outrance, armed
with a razor, kicking and biting with blood flowing, a scene in ordinary English which
would be one which would be likely to frighten stouthearted members of the public
who might be passing by. If the result be that one person only is fighting unlawfully
because the Crown do not negative the possibility of self-defence in the other, it is
said that that is not an affray.

Let me examine that situation for one moment as was done by Forbes J during the
course of the argument in this case. If it be right that one person is fighting only in
self-defence, then it is submitted there is no affray, there is only an assault by the
unlawful fighter. So the story starts off with one person fighting in self-defence, but
he then oversteps the mark, as may well have happened in *R v Sharp, R v Johnson*[1],
namely, when Johnson seized the razor. Thereafter the same fight, which has been
undoubtedly frightening as far as the public was concerned, has turned into an affray
because the person has now lost his shield of self-defence and is an unlawful fighter
because he has used too great force. I draw that example because indeed it is what
happened in the instant case because it has been conceded on behalf of the Crown that
the appellant's conviction must be looked on on the basis that he fought unlawfully
in that he overdid defending himself against the assault by the police officers.

That situation seems to this court to be a wholly unreal one. We can see no reason,
when all the ingredients of affray, namely, the spectacle of fighting to the terror of
other persons who may be present or are present, are taking place and there is only
one unlawful fighter, why that person should not be properly charged and found
guilty of the offence of affray.

It leads to further difficulties if counsel for the appellant's submission were to be
accepted. Take the case of people who mill out of a dance hall or club late at night
into the street and fighting breaks out. This a very common form of affray unfortunately in this country and to have to find that if, shall we say, two people fighting
in different parts of the street could not be convicted of making an affray unless the
Crown could prove that they were acting in concert, namely, that there was a preconceived plan to fight, or, alternatively, that the proper inference was that they
joined in the same fight—that is sometimes an extremely difficult thing to do when
this class of case is before the courts—but it would be impossible to convict them of
the offence of affray unless one could find that they were acting in concert. That is
not a situation which should arise, and this court can see no grounds for saying that
the law requires that kind of direction before two such persons could be found guilty
of affray. I am assuming, of course, for that example that it was not possible to find
that they had unlawfully each fought with another person who was also fighting
unlawfully, namely, a third defendant or a person who could properly be described
as fighting unlawfully. These are practical reasons for examining the possibilities
which may arise if counsel for the appellant's careful submission were adopted by
this court. It is sufficient to say that for the reasons given by Lord Parker CJ in *R v
Scarrow*[2] this court is clearly of the opinion that one unlawful fighter in circumstances such as this can properly be charged with and convicted of affray and that
where two people are charged, as was done in the present case, and one is acquitted,
it is perfectly proper to convict the other. The judge's direction to the jury, therefore,
was the correct direction to give and there was no misdirection. The appeal, therefore, against conviction must be dismissed.

Last Friday this court gave the appellant leave to appeal against his sentence and
varied the sentence of three years' imprisonment to a term such as would allow for
his release on Saturday last. It is necessary for me to shortly give our reasons for
interfering with the sentence. The appellant is 27 years old and he has a very long
criminal record. He has been before the courts starting as a juvenile and I can take

---

1   [1957] 1 All ER 577, [1957] 1 QB 552
2   (1968) 52 Cr App Rep 591

a up the story in 1964 when he was sent to prison for housebreaking for three years. There were five concurrent sentences for five cases. In 1968 he received 18 months for burglary and, again in 1968, 12 months consecutive for another case of housebreaking and larceny and taking and driving away. In August 1968, again for another case of assault occasioning actual bodily harm, he received six months consecutive to his previous sentences. In 1969 for theft and in 1971 for dishonest handling

b he was sentenced to a total of 12 months' imprisonment. He was, therefore, a man who in the ordinary course of events, one would say, if he resisted arrest for a charge of burglary with violence and against men whom he knew to be police officers richly deserved a sentence such as that imposed by the trial judge.

There were, however, factors in this case which, in the judgment of this court, make the sentence too severe. It must not be thought that we are in any way suggest-

c ing that persons who attack police officers in the lawful execution of their duty must not expect to be severely punished. Far be it from us to say that. But in the present case the facts establish that the turmoil in the public house really broke out at the instigation of the two brothers, both of whom were acquitted at their respective trials, and secondly in this court counsel for the Crown has very fairly made a concession for the Crown, and this makes a difference to the position before

d the trial judge, for although the submission was made to him, it is quite different where the Crown makes the concession, that we should approach this conviction, as I have already said in an earlier part of this judgment, as on the basis that the jury found that the appellant had fought too vigorously in defending himself against an assault by the police officers. Once that concession is made, then, in the judgment of this court, a sentence of three years' imprisonment, even on a hardened criminal,

e for assaulting the police in this fashion is too severe and it is for those reasons that we came to the conclusion that a sentence of about nine months' imprisonment, which is what our order involved, would be a correct punishment for this man.

Appeal against conviction dismissed. Application for leave to appeal against sentence granted; appeal allowed; sentence varied.

f *The court certified under s 33 (2) of the Criminal Appeal Act 1968 that a point of law of general public importance was involved, namely, whether a person commits the offence of affray if he alone is fighting to the terror of other persons, but refused leave to appeal.*

5th December 1972. The appeal committee gave leave to appeal to the House of Lords.

g Solicitors: *Freeth, Cartwright & Sketchley,* Nottingham (for the appellant); D W *Ritchie,* Nottingham (for the Crown).

N P Metcalfe Esq Barrister.

Shiloh Spinners Ltd v Harding

HOUSE OF LORDS
LORD WILBERFORCE, VISCOUNT DILHORNE, LORD PEARSON, LORD SIMON OF GLAISDALE AND
LORD KILBRANDON
11th, 12th, 13th, 16th, 17th, 18th, 19th, 23rd, 24th OCTOBER, 13th DECEMBER 1972

*Land charge – Registration – Option to purchase, right of pre-emption or 'other like right' –
Equitable easement – Right or privilege over or affecting land being an equitable interest –
Right of re-entry – Re-entry on breach of covenant – Assignment of leasehold interest in part
of premises – Covenant to perform and observe stipulations for benefit of retained premises –
Covenant by purchaser that successors in title would observe stipulations –Whether right of
re-entry void against successor in title to purchaser for want of registration – Land Charges
Act 1925, s 10 (1), class C (iv), class D (iii).*

*Sale of land – Leasehold interest – Right of re-entry – Assignment of leasehold interest in part
of premises – Covenant to perform and observe stipulations for benefit of retained premises –
Right of re-entry on breach of covenant – Covenant by purchaser that successors in title
would observe stipulations – Purchaser relieved from liability for non-performance of covenant
after parting with interest – Covenant not directly enforceable against successor in title –
Failure by successor in title to perform or observe stipulations – Whether right of re-entry
effective although no one liable to be sued for breach of covenant.*

*Equity – Forfeiture – Relief – Breach of covenant – Jurisdiction to grant relief – Covenant
other than for payment of money – Circumstances in which relief will be granted – Assignment of leasehold interest in part of premises – Covenant for benefit of retained premises –
Right of re-entry for breach of covenant – Covenant as to maintenance of boundary fence and
support of retained building – Jurisdiction to grant relief – Exercise of jurisdiction.*

*Land – Estates or interests capable of subsisting at law – Rights of entry exercisable over or
in respect of a legal term of years absolute – Right of entry on breach of covenant – Assignment of leasehold interest in part of premises – Assignment reserving to assignor right of
entry on breach of covenant – Right of entry limited to perpetuity period – Whether right of
entry a legal interest – Law of Property Act 1925, s 1 (2).*

The appellants were the lessees of certain property. In 1961 they assigned their
interest in part of the property to T Ltd retaining the rest. The assignment contained
a covenant by T Ltd that they and their successors in title would observe certain
stipulations. The stipulations related, inter alia, to (a) fencing of boundaries, (b)
keeping in repair a tower so as to give support and protection to buildings on the
retained premises, (c) bricking up openings into a retained roadway, and (d) not
diminishing support and protection of the retained premises. The assignment contained a right to re-enter or retake the assigned premises, during a period defined
by reference to the rule against perpetuities, in the event of failure to perform or
observe the stipulations. There was a proviso by which T Ltd were exonerated from
liability under any of the covenants after parting with their interest in the assigned
premises. In 1965 T Ltd for consideration assigned their interest to the respondent, a
demolition contractor, who had actual knowledge of the terms of the 1961 assignment. The respondent proceeded to demolish the greater part of the buildings on his
premises and in doing so, and generally, committed breaches of the stipulations
contained in the 1961 assignment. It was common ground that the stipulations as
such were not enforceable against the respondent. The appellants claimed possession
of the assigned premises; the respondent disputed their right of re-entry and alternatively sought relief against forfeiture. The trial judge gave judgment for the

a appellants but the Court of Appeal*a* allowed the respondent's appeal holding that the right of re-entry was unenforceable since it had not been registered as a class D (iii) charge under s 10*b* of the Land Charges Act 1925. On appeal, it was contended, inter alia, by the appellants that the right of entry was a legal interest, being a right of entry 'exercisable over or in respect of a legal term of years absolute' within s 1 (2) (e)*c* of the Law of Property Act 1925 and as such did not require to be registered.

b **Held** – (i) The right of entry had been validly reserved by the appellants as assignors even though they retained no reversion. Furthermore the right of entry was capable of subsisting at law in respect of non-compliance with the covenants by the assignees, even though those covenants were not, as such, enforceable after 1965 (see p 96 c to f, p 103 e to h and p 105 h, post); *Doe d Freeman v Bateman* (1818) 2 B & Ald 168 and *Hyde v Warden* (1877) 3 Ex D 72 approved; *Stevens v Copp* (1868) LR 4 Exch 20 and

c *Horsey Estate Ltd v Steiger* [1895-99] All ER Rep 515 distinguished.

(ii) The right of entry was not a legal interest within s 1 (2) of the Law of Property Act 1925. The effect of the right of entry was to cause a legal term of years to be divested from one person to another on an event which might occur over a perpetuity period. Since the scheme of the 1925 Act was to require the limiting and vesting of legal estates and interests by reference to a fee simple or term of years absolute, the

d right of entry could not be allowed to rank as a legal interest (see p 97 f, p 103 e to h and p 105 h, post).

(iii) Although an equitable interest, the right of entry was not, however, unenforceable for want of registration under the Land Charges Act 1925, s 10, since it did not fall within any of the classes of charge specified in that section. In particular (a) it was not registrable as a class C (iv) charge because, being penal in character and in-

e volving the revesting of the lease, in the event of default, in a previous owner, it bore no relevant likeness to an option or right of pre-emption; (b) neither was it registrable as a class D (iii) charge since, on its prima facie meaning the word 'right', in the phrase 'easement, right or privilege over or affecting land' in class D (iii), did not have a meaning so different in quality from easement and privilege as to include a right of entry; furthermore, no conclusive or compelling reason could be drawn from the

f overreaching provisions of s 2 of the Law of Property Act 1925 why rights of entry should be included in class D (iii) for, although a right of entry was not suitable for overreaching, it was not the case that an equitable claim affecting land which was incapable of being overreached must necessarily be registrable under the Land Charges Act 1925 (see p 97 j, p 98 d f h and j, p 99 e and g, p 103 e to h and p 105 h, post); *E R Ives Investments Ltd v High* [1967] 1 All ER 504 applied.

g (iv) Although the case was one which fell within the class of case in which a court of equity could intervene and grant relief against forfeiture, in the circumstances relief should not be granted since the evidence established a case of clear and wilful breaches of more than one covenant, a case of continuous disregard by the respondent of the appellants' right over a period of time coupled with a lack of evidence as to the respondent's ability speedily and easily to make good the consequences of his default,

h and a failure to show any such disproportion between the expenditure required and the value of the interest involved as to amount to a case of hardship (see p 102 h, p 103 c to h and p 105 f to h, post); *Sanders v Pope* (1806) 12 Ves 282, *Hill v Barclay* [1803-13] All ER Rep 379 and *Barrow v Isaacs & Son* [1891] 1 QB 417 explained and applied.

Per Curiam. Although equity expects men to carry out their bargains and will not

j let them buy their way out by uncovenanted payment, courts of equity have the right in appropriate and limited cases to relieve against forfeiture for breach of covenant or condition where the primary object of the bargain is to secure a stated result which can effectively be attained when the matter comes before the court and

a [1971] 2 All ER 307
b Section 10, so far as material, is set out at p 97 h and p 98 a, post
c Section 1 is set out at p 97 b to d, post

where the forfeiture provision is added by way of security for the production of that
result. The word 'appropriate' involves consideration of the conduct of the applicant
for relief, in particular whether his default is wilful, of the gravity of the breaches,
and of the disparity between the value of the property of which forfeiture is claimed
as compared with the damage caused by the breach (see p 101 f and g, p 103 e to h,
p 104 c to f and p 105 h, post).

Decision of the Court of Appeal [1971] 2 All ER 307 reversed.

Notes

For class C and D land charges, see 23 Halsbury's Laws (3rd Edn) 72-75, paras 145-153,
and for the effect of omission to register a land charge, see ibid 77, paras 159, 160.

For right of re-entry on breach of covenant in landlord and tenant cases, see 23
Halsbury's Laws (3rd Edn) 665-670, paras 1389-1395, and for cases on the subject, see
31 Digest (Repl) 514-520, 6377-6427.

For relief against forfeiture in landlord and tenant cases, see 23 Halsbury's Laws
(3rd Edn) 674-683, paras 1400-1411, and for cases on the subject, see 31 Digest (Repl)
534-536, 6592-6608.

For legal estates and equitable interests, see 32 Halsbury's Laws (3rd Edn) 230, 231,
paras 317-319.

For the Land Charges Act 1925, s 10, see 27 Halsbury's Statutes (3rd Edn) 696, and
for the Law of Property Act 1925, ss 1, 2, see ibid 346, 350.

Cases referred to in opinions

Bargent v Thomson (1864) 4 Giff 473, 9 LT 365, 28 JP 4, 9 Jur NS 1192, 66 ER 792, 31
Digest (Repl) 542, *6653*.

Barrow v Isaacs & Son [1891] 1 QB 417, 60 LJQB 179, 64 LT 686, 55 JP 517, CA, 31 Digest
(Repl) 547, *6696*.

Blunt v Blunt [1943] 2 All ER 76, [1943] AC 517, 112 LJP 58, 169 LT 33, HL, 27 (1) Digest
(Reissue) 565, *4119*.

Bracebridge v Buckley (1816) 2 Price 200, 146 ER 68, 20 Digest (Repl) 549, *2574*.

Doe d Freeman v Bateman (1818) 2 B & Ald 168, 106 ER 328, 31 Digest (Repl) 527, *6497*.

Herrington v British Railways Board [1971] 1 All ER 897, [1971] 2 QB 107, [1971] 2 WLR
477, CA.

Hill v Barclay (1811) 18 Ves 56, [1803-13] All ER Rep 379, 34 ER 238, 30 Digest (Repl)
428, *712*.

Horsey Estate Ltd v Steiger [1899] 2 QB 79, [1895-99] All ER Rep 515, 68 LJQB 743, 80
LT 857, CA, 31 Digest (Repl) 413, *5422*.

Hughes v Metropolitan Railway Co (1877) 2 App Cas 439, [1874-80] All ER Rep 187,
46 LJQB 583, 36 LT 932, HL, 31 Digest (Repl) 556, *6757*.

Hyde v Warden (1877) 3 Ex D 72, 47 LJQB 121, 37 LT 567, CA, 31 Digest (Repl) 124,
2630.

Ives (E R) Investments Ltd v High [1967] 1 All ER 504, [1967] 2 QB 379, [1967] 2 WLR
789, CA, Digest (Cont Vol C) 339, *1222a*.

Kara v Kara and Holman [1948] 2 All ER 16, [1948] P 287, [1948] LJR 1741, CA, 27 (2)
Digest (Reissue) 690, *5274*.

Nash v Earl of Derby (1705) 2 Vern 537, 23 ER 948, 2 Digest (Repl) 95, *599*.

National Provincial Bank Ltd v Ainsworth [1965] 2 All ER 472, [1965] AC 75, [1965] 3
WLR 1, HL, Digest (Cont Vol B) 619, *933a*.

Osenton (Charles) & Co v Johnston [1941] 2 All ER 245, [1942] AC 130, 110 LJKB 420,
165 LT 235, HL, 51 Digest (Repl) 681, *2840*.

Peachy v Duke of Somerset (1721) 1 Stra 447, Prec Ch 568, 93 ER 626, 20 Digest (Repl)
547, *2549*.

Reynolds v Pitt (1812) 19 Ves 134, 2 Price 212n, 34 ER 468, 31 Digest (Repl) 405, *5346*.

Sanders v Pope (1806) 12 Ves 282, 33 ER 108, 20 Digest (Repl) 549, *2572*.

Stevens v Copp (1868) LR 4 Exch 20, 38 LJEx 31, 19 LT 454, 33 JP 87, 25 Digest (Repl)
380, *100*.

a   *Wadman v Calcraft* (1804) 10 Ves 67, 32 ER 768, 31 Digest (Repl) 535, 6595.
    Webber v Smith (1689) 2 Vern 103, 23 ER 676, 31 Digest (Repl) 551, 6714.

Appeal

By a writ issued on 15th January 1969, the appellants, Shiloh Spinners Ltd, claimed against the respondent, Joseph James Harding, (1) a declaration that the appellants
b were entitled to re-enter into property situate at Holdenfold Road in the county of Lancaster and known as Shiloh No 2 Mill comprised in an assignment dated 31st October 1961 and made between the appellants of the one part and Thornber Brothers Ltd of the other part and to hold the property for their own absolute use and benefit as if the assignment had not been made; and (2) possession of the property.

c   On 9th February 1970, in the Chancery of the County Palatine of Lancaster, Burgess V-C delivered judgment and found the following facts. The land in question was comprised in two leases, one dated 20th January 1876 and the other dated 8th October 1904; both were for terms of 999 years, subject to a rentcharge. In 1961 both the leases were vested in the appellants and the premises comprised therein were used by them for the purpose of their textile business, the greater part of the land
d being covered by two cotton mills, with the customary ancillary buildings and reservoirs.

On 31st October 1961 the appellants assigned to Thornber Brothers Ltd certain land, part of which was comprised in one of the principal leases and part in the other, which was in effect the site of the mill known as 'Shiloh No 2 Mill'. In addition, the assignment included the second, third and fourth floors of what was called 'the
e lavatory block', and also the ash hopper. Those buildings were situate over and above certain land over which the parties were to have common rights of way, which passed in a tunnel under the lavatory tower and the ash hopper. The tunnel divided Shiloh No 2 Mill from a warehouse and other property retained by the appellants. The assignment was for the respective terms of years comprised in the original leases. The burden of the rentcharge under the 1904 principal lease was to be borne
f by the assignee. The consideration was £25,000. By cl 2 the purchasers covenanted, inter alia, to perform and observe all the covenants on the part of the lessee in the principal leases so far as they related to the premises thereby assigned. Clause 5 provided:

g   'FOR the benefit and protection of the premises comprised in the [principal leases] (other than the premises hereby assigned) and so as to bind so far as may be the premises hereby assigned into whosoever hands the same may come the purchaser hereby covenants with the [appellants] that the purchaser and the persons deriving title under it will at all times hereafter observe and perform the stipulations set out in the first part of the Third Schedule hereto but so that the purchaser shall not be liable for a breach of this covenant occurring on or in
h   respect of the premises hereby assigned after it shall have parted with all interests therein.'

Clause 7 (a), the terms of which are set out at p 95, post, reserved a right to re-enter the property in the event of any failure to perform or observe the covenants. The third schedule to the assignment contained certain stipulations, some positive and
j some negative, four of which were in issue in the proceedings. Shortly stated, they were: (1) a fencing covenant; (2) a covenant to keep in repair the second, third and fourth storeys of the lavatory block so as to protect and support the appellants' adjoining property; (3) a covenant to brick up to the satisfaction of the appellants the openings leading from the assigned premises to the retained premises; and (4) a covenant not to lessen or diminish the support or protection then given or afforded by all parts of the assigned premises to the retained premises.

On 5th March 1965 Thornber Brothers Ltd assigned to the respondent the property *a* comprised in the 1961 assignment in consideration of a sum of £8,000. Thornber Brothers Ltd had never in fact made any real use of the property which they had acquired from the appellants, and the sale on their interest was not known to the appellants until in about June 1965 the respondent began to demolish the former Shiloh No 2 Mill. Demolition continued until March 1966, when there was a pause after about two-thirds of the former mill had been demolished. The work was later *b* resumed. Since the summer of 1968 the premises had remained in the same state of demolition; the whole of the old mill, save that part of the wall adjoining the tunnel, had been demolished; but the lavatory block (second, third and fourth floors) remained open to the elements.

It was conceded that the stipulations in the third schedule to the 1961 assignment were not directly enforceable against the respondent, first because, insofar as they *c* were positive, an action such as specific performance would not lie; secondly, insofar as they were negative, an action for breach would not lie because the covenants had never been registered under the Land Charges Act 1925.

As a result of the demolition efforts of the respondent the site was in an appalling mess, particularly the lavatory block and the former wall of the mill where it adjoined the roadway under the tunnel and leading into which there are at least two *d* doorways. From the start the appellants, through their solicitors, were concerned with the manner in which the Shiloh No 2 Mill was being demolished and as to the future intentions of the respondent as regards the ultimate demolition. They asked on many occasions for assurances and also for the production of an insurance policy that the respondent had to protect himself and others in the course of his work. To those requests, by the appellants' solicitors, no reply was ever received from the *e* respondent, nor were insurance policies ever produced until the hearing when the respondent produced certain policies that he had been able to locate, and which were far from satisfactory. The anxiety of the appellants was increased by the fact that, when the old mill tower was being demolished, considerable damage was done to their office block on part of the retained land. The damage, which was the result of work done by independent contractors, was such as to justify the anxiety of the *f* appellants then and for the future. The reason given by the respondent in his evidence for the non-reply to letters and the non-production of insurance cover was that it was his land on which he was doing work and that the appellants had no concern with it.

Burgess V-C found that meetings between Mr Gartside, the chairman and managing director of the appellants, and the respondent would have had no chance of success in leading to any sort of mutual agreement in view of the likely clash of *g* personalities between the two men and the general attitude of the respondent in his disregard for any rights of the retained land. The vice-chancellor was satisfied that at no time had the respondent ever attempted to keep his property fenced off or in any other way to perform the covenants. He found as facts (i) that the covenant to fence and maintain had not been performed by the respondent; (ii) that doorways *h* in the wall on the mill side of the tunnel had not been bricked up in accordance with the covenant to brick up openings; and (iii) that, although the support of the appellants' premises might not yet have been affected, there was no doubt that the protection which they formerly enjoyed had unquestionably been lessened.

Burgess V-C held that the right of re-entry was one which did not require to be registered under s 10 of the Land Charges Act 1925 and was therefore exercisable *i* against the respondent. He further held that the conduct and attitude of the respondent throughout the case and in the matters leading up to it has been such that it would not be proper in the court's discretion to grant him relief since he had chosen to stand throughout on what he considered were his strict legal rights, and there was no reason or exceptional circumstances why in equity the court should relieve him from the result of clear breaches of the covenants of which he was fully aware. Accordingly *a* Burgess V-C granted the declaration sought and ordered that the respondent give to the appellants possession of the property.

The respondent appealed against that order. By its judgment dated 10th February 1971, and reported at [1971] 2 All ER 307, the Court of Appeal (Russell, Sachs and Buckley LJJ) allowed the appeal holding (Sachs LJ dissenting) that the right of re-entry reserved by the 1961 assignment was unenforceable for want of registration as a class *b* D (iii) land charge. The appellants appealed to the House of Lords.

John Vinelott QC and *Andrew Morritt* for the appellants.
A J Balcombe QC and *P B Keenan* for the respondent.

Their Lordships took time for consideration.

13th December. The following opinions were delivered.

c

LORD WILBERFORCE. My Lords, the present dispute, one of a commonplace character between neighbours, was tried in the County Palatine Court of Lancaster by Burgess V-C who, after a full hearing and in a careful judgment, allowed the appellants' claim. It has attracted in its subsequent progress a number of points of law, more or less substantial, which may have wider influence. I can state the facts *d* briefly. The appellants were the assignees of two long leases of adjoining properties on which there stood, inter alia, a mill called Shiloh No 2 Mill. On 31st October 1961 the appellants assigned their interest in a part of the properties, including Shiloh No 2 Mill, to Thornber Brothers Ltd retaining the rest. There were contained in the assignment to Thornber Brothers Ltd a number of covenants, positive and negative, relating (inter alia) to (a) fencing of boundaries (b) keeping in repair a tower (the 'lavatory tower') so as to provide support and protection to retained buildings (c) *e* bricking up openings into a retained roadway (d) not diminishing support and protection given to the retained premises. There was reserved in the assignment a right to re-enter or retake the assigned property in the following terms:

> '7. (a) If at any time during the lifetime of the last survivor of the descendants now living of His Late Majesty King George V and twenty one years after the *f* death of such last survivor or during such further period (if any) as shall not infringe the law against perpetuities there shall be any failure to perform or observe any of the covenants herein contained implied or referred to on the part of the Purchaser then and in every such case and notwithstanding the waiver of any previous default it shall be lawful for the Vendor or the owner or owners for the time being of the premises comprised in the First Lease and the Second Lease *g* not hereby assigned at any time or times during the periods aforesaid into and upon the premises hereby assigned or any part thereof in the name of the whole to re-enter and to hold the same for their own absolute use and benefit as if this deed had not been made but without prejudice to any right of action or remedy in respect of any antecedent breach of any of the covenants by the Purchasers herein contained implied or referred to'.

h There was a proviso by which Thornber Brothers Ltd were exonerated from liability under any of the stipulations after they had parted with their interest in the assigned premises.

On 5th March 1965 Thornber Brothers Ltd for consideration assigned their interest to the respondent, a demolition contractor: he had actual knowledge of the terms of *j* the 1961 assignment. He has demolished the greater part of the buildings on his premises and in doing so, and generally, has committed breaches of the covenants above referred to. The present action was brought by the appellants claiming possession of the premises comprised in the assignment of 1961: the respondent disputed the appellants' right of re-entry and alternatively sought relief against forfeiture. He failed before Burgess V-C but succeeded in the Court of Appeal[1].

---

1 [1971] 2 All ER 307, [1972] Ch 326

The questions which arise may be logically arranged in the following order: (1) **a**
Whether a right of entry can be validly reserved on an assignment of leasehold property when the assignor retains no reversion. (2) Whether a right of entry can subsist
in law in respect of non-compliance with covenants if those covenants, as such, are not
enforceable. (3) As a matter of construction of the assignment whether the right of
entry is exercisable in the circumstances of the case. (4) Whether the right of entry is
exercisable against the respondent, a purchaser for value, not having been registered **b**
under the Land Charges Act 1925. (5) Whether this is a case where a court of equity
may grant relief against exercise of the right of entry. (6) Whether relief should be
granted to the respondent in the circumstances.

My Lords, I can deal briefly with the first three questions. The question of law raised
by the first was answered in the affirmative in 1818 by the King's Bench, following
older authorities, in *Doe d Freeman v Bateman*[1]. In 1877 this case was approved by the **c**
Court of Appeal in *Hyde v Warden*[2] and it has never been criticised. No intelligible
objection in point of principle was formulated against the proposition so stated, which
would merely apply to leaseholds a similar rule as, indisputably, applies to freeholds.
In my opinion this House should leave it undisturbed.

As regards the second question, there is again, no convincing reason for giving other
than a positive answer. The purpose of the right of entry was to provide a remedy to **d**
the lessor in the event—clearly foreseeable since some of the covenants are positive
in character—that the covenants themselves could not be enforced against assignees.
The only support in law for a negative answer was sought to be drawn from two
cases between landlord and tenant: *Stevens v Copp*[3] and *Horsey Estate Ltd v Steiger*[4].
Neither of these cases give me satisfaction but it is not necessary to disagree with them
since they do not apply directly. Moreover the principle accepted in *Doe d Freeman v* **e**
Bateman[1], that the validity of the right of entry does not depend on annexation to a
reversion, removes any reason for their application here by analogy. I can see no
reason for applying technical rules which since the 16th century have confused the
law of landlord and tenant to a different relationship, namely, one which is, or at least
closely resembles, that of restrictive covenants.

On the third question, the respondent sought to invoke the words 'failure to per- **f**
form and observe' and 'default' appearing in the re-entry clause in order to found an
argument that this clause became inoperative when the covenants themselves became
unenforceable. The argument, though forcefully put, failed to persuade me that the
construction it sought to place on the clause was otherwise than strained. Since this is
an issue which does not extend beyond the present litigation I am content to express
my entire satisfaction with the disposal of it by Russell LJ[5], any addition to whose **g**
words would be repetitive.

The next question is of a substantial character. The right of entry, it is said, is
unenforceable against the respondent, although he took with actual notice of it,
because it was not registered as a charge under the Land Charges Act 1925. There is
no doubt that if it was capable of registration under that Act, it is unenforceable if
not registered: the appellants deny that it was so capable either (i) because it was a **h**
legal right not an equitable right or (ii) because, if equitable, it does not fall within
any of the classes or descriptions of charges registration of which is required.

I consider first whether the right of entry is legal in character or equitable, using
these adjectives in the technical sense in which they are used in the 1925 property
legislation. The question is purely one of statutory definition, the ingredients of
which are found in ss 1 and 205 (1) (x) of the Law of Property Act 1925. The contention
that the right is legal was not accepted by Burgess V-C, or advanced in the Court of **j**

1 (1818) 2 B & Ald 168
2 (1877) 3 Ex D 72
3 (1868) LR 4 Exch 20
4 [1899] 2 QB 79, [1895-99] All ER Rep 515
5 [1971] 2 All ER at 317, [1972] Ch at 346

a   Appeal[1], nor was it contained in the printed case signed by eminent counsel, though
     if it were upheld it would be decisive of the case. The appellants were however
     permitted to lodge an amended case raising the point. I set out for convenience
     s 1 (1), (2) and (3) of the Act. The definition section, s 205 (1) (x), uses the same verbiage
     and adds nothing to the argument.

b   '(1) The only estates in land which are capable of subsisting or of being conveyed
     or created at law are—(a) An estate in fee simple absolute in possession; (b) A
     term of years absolute.
         '(2) The only interests or charges in or over land which are capable of subsisting
     or of being conveyed or created at law are—(a) An easement, right, or privilege
     in or over land for an interest equivalent to an estate in fee simple absolute in
     possession or a term of years absolute; (b) A rentcharge in possession issuing out
c   of or charged on land being either perpetual or for a term of years absolute;
     (c) A charge by way of legal mortgage; (d) Land tax, tithe rentcharge[2], and any
     other similar charge on land which is not created by an instrument; (e) Rights of
     entry exercisable over or in respect of a legal term of years absolute, or annexed,
     for any purpose, to a legal rentcharge.
         '(3) All other estates, interests, and charges in or over land take effect as
d   equitable interests.'

     The right of entry in this case is not contained in a lease, so as to be annexed to a
     reversion, nor is it exercisable for a term of years, or (comparably with a fee simple)
     indefinitely. Its duration is limited by a perpetuity period. Whether it can be said to be
     'exercisable over or in respect of a legal term of years absolute' appears obscure. It
e   is not exercisable for a legal term of years (whether that granted by the lease or any
     other term): it is not so exercisable as to determine a legal term of years. To say that
     a right of entry is exercisable in respect of a legal term of years appears to me, with
     respect, to be without discernible meaning. The effect of this right of entry is to
     cause a legal term of years to be divested from one person to another on an event
     which may occur over a perpetuity period. It would I think be contrary to the whole
f   scheme of the Act, which requires the limiting and vesting of legal estates and interests
     to be by reference to a fee simple or a term of years absolute, to allow this to rank
     as a legal interest. In my opinion it is clearly equitable.
         So I pass, as did the Court of Appeal[1], to the Land Charges Act 1925. The original
     contention of the respondent was that the equitable right of entry was capable of
     registration under class D (iii) of the Act. In the Court of Appeal[1] an alternative
g   contention was raised, apparently at the court's suggestion, that it might come within
     class C (iv). In my opinion this is unmaintainable. Class C (iv) embraces:

         'Any contract by an estate owner or by a person entitled at the date of the
         contract to have a legal estate conveyed to him to convey or create a legal estate,
         including a contract conferring either expressly or by statutory implication a
h   valid option of purchase, a right of pre-emption or any other like right (in this
         Act referred to as "an estate contract").

     The only words capable of including a right of entry are 'any other like right', but in
     my opinion no relevant likeness can be found. An option or right of pre-emption
     eventuates in a contract for sale at a price; this is inherent in 'purchase' and 'pre-
j   emption'; the right of entry is penal in character and involves the revesting of the
     lease, in the event of default, in a previous owner. There is no similarity in law or
     fact between these situations.

---

1   [1971] 2 All ER 307, [1972] Ch 326
2   The words in italics were repealed by the Finance Act 1963, s 73 (8) (b), Sch 14, Part IV
    and the Tithe Act 1936, s 48 (3), Sch 9

Class D (iii) reads:

> 'A charge or obligation affecting land of any of the following kinds, namely:—
> . . . (iii) Any easement right or privilege over or affecting land created or arising
> after the commencement of this Act, and being merely an equitable interest (in
> this Act referred to as an "equitable easement").'

The argument for inclusion in this class falls into two parts. First it is said that a
right of entry falls fairly within the description, or at least that if the words do not
appear to include it they are sufficiently open in meaning to admit it. Secondly it is
said that the provisions of the Law of Property Act 1925 as to 'overreaching' compel the
conclusion that a right of entry must fall under some class or sub-class of the Land
Charges Act 1925, and since this is the only one whose words can admit it, they should
be so interpreted as to do so. Thus the argument depends for its success on a combination of ambiguity, or openness of class D (iii) with compelling consideration brought
about by the overreaching provision. In my opinion it fails under both limbs: class
D (iii) cannot be interpreted so as to admit equitable rights of entry, and no conclusive,
compelling, or even clear conclusions can be drawn from the overreaching provisions
which can influence the interpretation of class D (iii).

Dealing with class D (iii) I reject at once the suggestion that any help (by way of
enlarging the content of this class) can be derived either from the introductory words,
for they limit themselves to the 'following kinds', or from the words 'and being
merely an equitable interest' for these are limiting, not enlarging, words. I leave out
of account the label at the end—though I should think it surprising if so expert a
draftsman had attached that particular label if the class included a right of entry.
To include a right of entry in the description of 'equitable easement' offends a sense
both of elegance and accuracy. That leaves 'easement right or privilege over or affecting land'. If this were the only place where the expression occurred in this legislation, I should find it difficult to attribute to 'right' a meaning so different in quality
from easement and privilege as to include a right of entry. The difference between a
right to use, or draw profit from another man's land, and a right to take his land altogether away, is one of quality, not of degree. But the words are plentifully used both
in the Law of Property Act 1925 and elsewhere in the 1925 legislation, so are the words
'rights of entry', and I find it impossible to believe that in this one context the one
includes the other. The two expressions are even used by way of what seems deliberate contrast in two contexts: first, in s 1 of the Law of Property Act 1925, where sub-s
(2) (*a*) mentions 'An easement, right, or privilege in or over land', and para (*e*) of the
same subsection 'Rights of entry'; secondly, in s 162 (1) (*d*) which mentions both.
An argument, unattractive but perhaps just palatable, can be devised why it might
have been necessary in s 1 of the Law of Property Act 1925 to mention both easements, rights or privileges and the particular rights of entry described in sub-s (2) (*e*),
but no explanation can be given why, if the latter are capable of being included in
the former, they should be mentioned with such a degree of separation. I do not
further elaborate this point because a reading of their judgments leaves little doubt
that the Lords Justices[1] would themselves have read class D (iii) as I can only read it
but for the influence of the overreaching argument.

So I turn to the latter. This, in my opinion, only becomes compelling if one first
accepts the conclusion that all equitable claims relating to land are either registrable
under the Land Charges Act 1925, or capable of being overreached under s 2 of the
Law of Property Act 1925, i e are capable by use of the appropriate mechanism of
being transferred to the proceeds of sale of the land they affect. If this dilemma
could be made good, then there could be an argument for forcing, within the limits
of the possible, an equitable right of entry into one of the registrable classes, since it is
obviously not suitable for overreaching. But the dilemma cannot be made good.

---

1   [1971] 2 All ER 307, [1972] Ch 326

a What may be overreached is 'any equitable interest or power affecting that estate': yet 'equitable interest' (for powers do not enter into the debate) is a word of most uncertain content. The searcher after a definition has to be satisfied with s 1 (8) 'Estates, interests, and charges in or over land which are not legal estates are in this Act referred to as "equitable interests" '—a tautology rather than a definition. There is certainly nothing exhaustive about the expression 'equitable interests'—just as certainly it has no clear boundaries. The debate whether such rights as equity, over **b** the centuries, has conferred against the holder of the legal estate are truly proprietary in character, or merely rights in personam, or a hybrid between the two, may have lost some of its vitality in the statutory context but the question inevitably rises to mind whether the 'curtain' or 'overreaching' provisions of the 1925 legislation extend to what are still conveniently called 'equities' or 'mere equities', such as rights to rectification, or to set aside a conveyance. There is good authority, which I do not **c** presume to doubt, for a sharp distinction between the two—I instance Lord Upjohn in *National Provincial Bank Ltd v Ainsworth*[1] and Snell[2]. I am impressed by the decision in *E R Ives Investments Ltd v High*[3] in which the Court of Appeal held that a right by estoppel—producing an effect similar to an easement—was not registrable under class D (iii). Lord Denning MR[4] referred to the right as subsisting only in equity. Danck-werts LJ[5] thought it was an equity created by estoppel or a proprietary estoppel: **d** plainly this was not an equitable interest capable of being overreached, yet no member of the court considered that the right—so like an easement—could be brought within class D (iii). The conclusion followed, and the court accepted it, that whether it was binding on a purchaser depended on notice. All this seems to show that there may well be rights, of an equitable character, outside the provisions as to registration and which are incapable of being overreached.

e That equitable rights of entry should be among them is not in principle unaccept-able. First, rights of entry, before 1925, were not considered to confer an interest in the land. They were described[6] as bare possibilities so that it is not anomalous that equitable rights of entry should not be treated as equitable interests. Secondly, it is important that s 10 of the Land Charges Act 1925 should be given a plain and ordinary interpretation. It is a section which involves day to day operation by solicitiors doing **f** conveyancing work: they should be able to take decisions and advise their clients on a straightforward interpretation of the registration classes, not on one depending on a sophisticated, not to say disputable, analysis of other statutes. Thirdly, the conse-quence of equitable rights of entry not being registrable is that they are subject to the doctrine of notice, preserved by s 199 of the Law of Property Act 1925. This may not give complete protection, but neither is it demonstrable that it is likely to be less **g** effective than the present system of registration against names. I am therefore of opinion that class D (iii) should be given its plain prima facie meaning and that so read it does not comprise equitable rights of entry. It follows that non-registration does not make the appellants' right unenforceable in this case.

The consequence is that the appellants' claim to re-enter must succeed unless the respondent can and should be relieved in equity against the appellants' legal right. **h** This involves two questions: first, in law, whether a court exercising equity juris-diction does relieve against forfeiture in a case such as the present, viz in a case of breaches of condition as to fencing, support, or blocking of openings, and bearing in mind the relationship of the parties; secondly, the question whether the court ought to relieve the respondent in the circumstances.

j

1   [1965] 2 All ER 472 at 488, [1965] AC 1175 at 1238
2   Principles of Equity (26th Edn, 1966), p 28
3   [1967] 1 All ER 504, [1967] 2 QB 379
4   [1967] 1 All ER at 508, [1967] 2 QB at 395
5   [1967] 1 All ER at 511, [1967] 2 QB at 400
6   Challis's Law of Real Property (3rd Edn, 1911), p 76

There cannot be any doubt that from the earliest times courts of equity have a asserted the right to relieve against the forfeiture of property. The jurisdiction has not been confined to any particular type of case. The commonest instances concerned mortgages, giving rise to the equity of redemption, and leases, which commonly contained re-entry clauses; but other instances are found in relation to copyholds, or where the forfeiture was in the nature of a penalty. Although the principle is well established, there has undoubtedly been some fluctuation of authority as to the self- b limitation to be imposed or accepted on this power. There has not been much diffi- culty as regards two heads of jurisdiction. First, where it is possible to state that the object of the transaction and of the insertion of the right to forfeit is essentially to secure the payment of money, equity has been willing to relieve on terms that the payment is made with interest, if appropriate, and also costs (*Peachy v Duke of Somer- set*[1] and cases there cited). Yet even this head of relief has not been uncontested: c Lord Eldon LC in his well known judgment in *Hill v Barclay*[2] expressed his sus- picion of it as a valid principle, pointing out, in an argument which surely has much force, that there may be cases where to oblige acceptance of a stipulated sum of money even with interest, at a date when receipt had lost its usefulness, might represent an unjust variation of what had been contracted for (see also *Reynolds v Pitt*[3]). Secondly there were the heads of fraud, accident, mistake or surprise always a ground for d equity's intervention, the inclusion of which entailed the exclusion of mere inadvertence and a fortiori of wilful defaults.

Outside of these there remained a debatable area in which were included obliga- tions in leases such as to repair and analogous obligations concerning the condition of property, and covenants to insure or not to assign. As to covenants to repair and cases of waste, cases can be quoted before the 19th century in which relief was granted e (see *Webber v Smith*[4] and *Nash v Earl of Derby*[5]). There were hostile pronouncements. In *Wadman v Calcraft*[6] both Sir William Grant MR and Lord Eldon LC are found stating it to be clear that relief cannot be given against the breach of other covenants —i e than covenants to pay rent.

It was soon after that the critical divide or supposed divide occurred, between the liberal view of Lord Erskine LC in *Sanders v Pope*[7] and the strict view of Lord Eldon f LC in *Hill v Barclay*[2]. The latter case came to be followed as the true canon; the former was poorly regarded in Lincoln's Inn, but it is important to observe where the difference lay. This was not, as I understand it, in any disagreement as to the field in which relief might be granted, for both cases seem to have accepted that, in principle, relief from forfeiture might be granted when the covenant was to lay out a sum of money on property: but rather on whether equity would relieve against a wilful breach. The breach in *Sanders v Pope*[7] was of this kind but Lord Erskine LC g said[8]:

'If the covenant is broken with the consciousness, that it is broken, that is, if it is wilful, not by surprise, accident, or ignorance, still if it is a case, where full com- pensation can be made, these authorities say, not that it is imperative upon the Court to give the relief, but that there is a discretion.' h

To this Lord Eldon LC answers[9]:

---

1   (1721) 1 Stra 447
2   (1811) 18 Ves 56, [1803-13] All ER Rep 379
3   (1812) 19 Ves 134
4   (1689) 2 Vern 103
5   (1705) 2 Vern 537
6   (1804) 10 Ves 67
7   (1806) 12 Ves 282
8   (1806) 12 Ves at 293
9   In *Hill v Barclay* (1811) 18 Ves at 63

j

a   '. . . with regard to other cases [sc waste or omitting repairs], the doctrine I have
repeatedly stated is all wrong, if it is to be taken, that relief is to be given in
case of a wilful breach of covenant.'

The emphasis here, and the root of disagreement, clearly relates to wilful breaches,
and on this it is still Lord Eldon's view which holds the field.

The suggestion that relief could not be granted against forfeiture for breach of other
b   covenants was not one that followed from either case: relief was so granted in *Bargent
v Thomson*[1]. Equally in *Barrow v Isaacs & Son*[2], a case of a covenant against under-
letting without consent, a high water mark of the strict doctrine, the emphasis is not
so much on the nature of the breach which may or may not be relieved against, but
on the argument that it is enough to show that compensation can be given[3]:

c   '. . . it was soon recognised that there would be great difficulty in estimating
the proper amount of compensation; and, since the decision of Lord Eldon in
Hill v. *Barclay*[4], it has always been held that equity would not relieve, merely on
the ground that *it could give compensation*, upon breach of any covenant in a lease
except the covenant for payment of rent.'

We are not bound by these decisions, certainly not by every shade of opinion they
d   may reflect, but I am entirely willing to follow them in their main lines.

As regards the present appeal it is possible to disengage the following considerations.
In the first place there should be put on one side cases where the court has been asked
to relieve against conditions contained in wills or gifts inter vivos. These raise considerations of a different kind from those relevant to contractual stipulations.
Secondly, no decision in the present case involves the establishment or recognition
directly or by implication of any general power—that is to say, apart from the special
e   heads of fraud, accident, mistake or surprise—in courts exercising equitable jurisdiction to relieve against men's bargains. Lord Eldon LC's firm denial of any such
power in *Hill v Barclay*[4] does not call for any revision or review in this case. Equally
there is no need to qualify Kay LJ's proposition in *Barrow v Isaacs*[2]. I would fully
endorse this: it remains true today that equity expects men to carry out their bargains
and will not let them buy their way out by uncovenanted payment. But it is con-
f   sistent with these principles that we should reaffirm the right of courts of equity in
appropriate and limited cases to relieve against forfeiture for breach of covenant or
condition where the primary object of the bargain is to secure a stated result which
can effectively be attained when the matter comes before the court, and where the
forfeiture provision is added by way of security for the production of that result.
The word 'appropriate' involves consideration of the conduct of the applicant for
g   relief, in particular whether his default was wilful, of the gravity of the breaches, and
of the disparity between the value of the property of which forfeiture is claimed as
compared with the damage caused by the breach.

Both as a matter of history and by the nature of things, different considerations
apply to different covenants. As regards covenants to pay rent, in spite of Lord
Eldon LC's reservations, the matter has, subject to qualifications which need not be
h   discussed, been taken over by statute, first by 4 Geo 2 c 28[5], then by later Acts leading
up to the Law of Property Act 1925. The same is true of covenants to insure and other
covenants in leases. I shall consider shortly the implications of the legislation as
regards other covenants than those expressly mentioned. As regards covenants to
repair and analogous covenants concerning the condition of property, other than
i   those now dealt with by Act of Parliament, it is not necessary to overrule *Hill v
Barclay*[4] any more than it was necessary for Lord Eldon LC to do more than to

1   (1864) 4 Giff 473
2   [1891] 1 QB 417
3   [1891] 1 QB at 425, per Kay LJ
4   (1811) 18 Ves 56, [1803-13] All ER Rep 379
5   Landlord and Tenant Act 1730

distinguish *Sanders v Pope*[1].   Lord Eldon LC's decision was in fact based partly on the
circumstance that he was concerned with a wilful default and partly on the impossi-   *a*
bility of speculating whether the later doing of the repairs would compensate the
landlord: such considerations remain relevant.   Where it is necessary, and in my
opinion right, to move away from some 19th century authorities, is to reject as a
reason against granting relief, the impossibility for the courts to supervise the doing
of work.   The fact is a reality, no doubt, and explains why specific performance   *b*
cannot be granted of agreements to this effect but in the present context it can now
be seen (as it was seen by Lord Erskine LC in *Sanders v Pope*[1]) to be an irrelevance:
for what the court has to do is to satisfy itself, ex post facto, that the covenanted
work has been done, and it has ample machinery, through certificates, or by enquiry,
to do precisely this.   This removes much of the support from one of the more
formidable authorities, viz the majority judgment in *Bracebridge v Buckley*[2].
There remain two other arguments which cannot be passed over.   First it is said   *c*
that the strict view (that there should be no relief except under the two classical
headings) has been endorsed in this House in *Hughes v Metropolitan Railway Co*[3].
There is no substance in this.   The basis of decision in this House was that the landlord's notice was suspended in operation by acquiescence, so that there was no effective breach.   The opinion invoked is that of Lord Cairns LC, in which there appears   *d*
this portion of a sentence[4]: '. . . it could not be argued, that there was any right of
a Court of Equity . . . to give relief in cases of this kind, by way of mercy, or by way
merely of saving property from forfeiture . . .'—words which have only to be re-read
to show that they are no sort of denial of the jurisdiction now invoked.
Secondly, a point of more difficulty arises from the intervention of Parliament in
providing specific machinery for the granting of relief against forfeiture of leases   *e*
(see Law of Property Amendment Act 1859, Common Law Procedure Act 1852,
Law of Property Act 1925, Leasehold Property (Repairs) Act 1938 and other statutes).
This, it is said, negatives an intention that any corresponding jurisdiction should
exist outside the cases of leases.   I do not accept this argument.   In my opinion
where the courts have established a general principle of law or equity, and the legislature steps in with particular legislation in a particular area, it must, unless showing   *f*
a contrary intention, be taken to have left cases outside that area where they were
under the influence of the general law.   To suppose otherwise involves the conclusion that an existing jurisdiction has been cut down by implication, by an enactment moreover which is positive in character (for it amplifies the jurisdiction in
cases of leases) rather than negative.   That legislation did not have this effect was
the view of Kay LJ in *Barrow v Isaacs & Son*[5] when he held that covenants against
assigning—excluded from the Conveyancing Act 1881—were left to be dealt with   *g*
according to the ordinary law.   The Occupiers' Liability Act 1957 gave rise to a
similar problem since it legislated as to one part of a larger total field; I may perhaps
refer to what I said in *Herrington v British Railways Board*[6].
The present case, in my opinion, falls within the class of case in which it would
be possible for a court of equity to intervene.   When the appellants assigned a   *h*
portion of their leased property, retaining the rest, which adjoined and was supported by the portion assigned, they had an essential interest in securing adequate
protection for their buildings, in having the entire site fenced, in preventing unauthorised access through the assigned property.   The covenants were drafted
accordingly.   The power of re-entry was inserted by way of reinforcement of the

j

1   (1806) 12 Ves 282
2   (1816) 2 Price 200
3   (1877) 2 App Cas 439, [1874-80] All ER Rep 187
4   (1877) 2 App Cas at 448, [1874-80] All ER Rep at 191
5   [1891] 1 QB at 430
6   [1971] 1 All ER 897, [1971] 2 QB 107

a contractual obligation which it must have been perceived might cease to be enforceable as such. Failures to observe the covenants having occurred, it would be right to consider whether the assignor should be allowed to exercise his legal rights if the essentials of the bargain could be secured and if it was fair and just to prevent him from doing so. It would be necessary, as stated above, to consider the conduct of the assignee, the nature and gravity of the breach, and its relation to the value of

b the property which might be forfeited. Established and in my opinion sound principle requires that wilful breaches should not, or at least should only in exceptional cases, be relieved against, if only for the reason that the assignor should not be compelled to remain in a relation of neighbourhood with a person in deliberate breach of his obligations.

In this light should relief have been granted? The respondent's difficulty is

c that Burgess V-C, who heard the witnesses, and went into all the facts, clearly took the view that the case was not one for relief. I should be reluctant, in any event, except on clear conviction to substitute a different view of my own. But I have examined in detail the evidence given, the correspondence over a period of four years, the photographs and plans of the site. All this material establishes a case of clear and wilful breaches of more than one covenant which, if individually not serious, were certainly substantial: a case of continuous disregard by the respondent

d of the appellants' rights over a period of time, coupled with a total lack of evidence as to the respondent's ability speedily and adequately to make good the consequences of his default, and finally a failure to show any such disproportion between the expenditure required and the value of the interest involved as to amount to a case of hardship. In my opinion the case is not, on established principles, one for relief.

e For all these reasons I would allow the appeal.

VISCOUNT DILHORNE. My Lords, I have had the advantage of reading my noble and learned friend Lord Wilberforce's speech. I agree with all he says and that the appeal should be allowed. I only desire to add that the cases in which it is right to give relief against forfeiture where there has been a wilful breach of covenant are likely to be few in number and where the conduct of the person seeking

f to secure the forfeiture has been wholly unreasonable and of a rapacious and unconscionable character.

LORD PEARSON. My Lords, I have had the advantage of reading the opinion of my noble and learned friend, Lord Wilberforce, and I agree with it and have nothing to add.

g Accordingly I would allow the appeal.

LORD SIMON OF GLAISDALE. My Lords, I have had the advantage of reading in draft the speech prepared by my noble and learned friend, Lord Wilberforce. As I am in general agreeement with it what follows is by way of marginal comment.

h In setting himself to answer the fourth main question which he poses, my noble and learned friend deals with the issue whether the right of re-entry is legal or equitable. My agreement with his conclusion that the right is equitable does not imply that I think that if the right of re-entry had been for a defined or indefinite term— not merely limited by reference to the uncertain perpetuity period—the right would have been legal and not equitable.

j With reference to the fifth question—whether this is a case where a court of equity might grant relief against exercise of the right of entry—I agree that *Sanders v Pope*[1] and *Hill v Barclay*[2] are not in themselves inconsistent authorities; nevertheless, they seem to me to be the respective culminations of a more liberal and a stricter

1 (1806) 12 Ves 282
2 (1811) 18 Ves 56, [1803-13] All ER Rep 379

attitude towards equity's jurisdiction to relieve against forfeiture. Lord Eldon LC's **a** inclination, with its emphasis on strict respect for contractual rights and obligations, was more congenial to the following age, and came to be followed. *Barrow v Isaacs & Son*[1] was a natural consequence; and I am bound to say that it seems to me to demonstrate an abnegation of equity, and to show that the trail from *Hill v Barclay*[2] leads into a juristic desert. Since what was said by Lord Cairns LC in *Hughes v Metropolitan Railway Co*[3] was obiter, and merely reflects the acceptance then generally current, **b** none of the authorities binds your Lordships. The last 100 years have seen many examples of relaxation of the stance of regarding contractual rights and obligations as sacrosanct and exclusive of other considerations: although these examples do not compel equity to follow—certainly not to the extent of overturning established authorities—they do at least invite a more liberal and extensively based attitude on the part of courts which are not bound by those authorities. I would therefore **c** myself hold that equity has an unlimited and unfettered jurisdiction to relieve against contractual forfeitures and penalties. What have sometimes been regarded as fetters to the jurisdiction are, in my view, more properly to be seen as considerations which the court will weigh in deciding how to exercise an unfettered jurisdiction (cf *Blunt v Blunt*[4] and *Kara v Kara and Holman*[5]). Prominent but not exclusive among such considerations is the desirability that contractual promises should be observed and **d** contractual rights respected, and even more the undesirability of the law appearing to condone flagrant and contemptuous disregard of obligations. Other such considerations are how far it is reasonable to require a party who is prima facie entitled to invoke a forfeiture or penalty clause to accept alternative relief (e g money payment or re-instatement of premises) and how far vindication of contractual rights would be grossly excessive and harsh having regard to the damage done to the **e** promisee and the moral culpability of the promisor. (I do not intend this as an exhaustive list.) It is these internal considerations which may limit the cases where courts of equity will relieve against forfeiture, rather than any external confine on jurisdiction.

Lastly there being, in my judgment, jurisdiction to relieve against re-entry in the present case, how should it be exercised? Burgess V-C, himself holding that he **f** had jurisdiction to relieve, addressed himself to the question whether it would be right to exercise it in favour of the instant respondent, and held that it would not be. This is a discretionary jurisdiction. The proper attitude o fan appellate court in the review of a discretionary jurisdiction has frequently been stated. Perhaps the locus classicus is the speech of Viscount Simon LC in *Blunt v Blunt*[6], in which the rest of the House concurred. He was speaking of the exercise of the divorce court's **g** discretion under s 4 of the Matrimonial Causes Act 1937; but his invocation of a widely different discretionary jurisdiction shows that his observations were of general application. He said:

'This brings me to a consideration of the circumstances in which an appeal may be successfully brought against the exercise of the Divorce Court' discretion. If it can be shown that the court acted under a misapprehension of **h** fact in that it either gave weight to irrelevant or unproved matters or omitted to take into account matters that are relevant, there would, in my opinion, be ground for an appeal. In such a case the exercise of discretion might be impeached, because the court's discretion will have been excercised on wrong or inadequate materials. But, as was recently pointed out in this House in another

j

1 [1891] 1 QB 417
2 (1811) 18 Ves 56, [1803-13] All ER Rep 379
3 (1877) 2 App Cas 439 at 443, [1874-80] All ER Rep 187 at 188
4 [1943] 2 All ER 76, [1943] AC 517
5 [1948] 2 All ER 16 at 18, 19, [1948] P 287 at 292
6 [1943] 2 All ER at 79, [1943] AC at 526, 527

connection in *Charles Osenton & Co. v. Johnston*[1]: "The appellate tribunal is not at liberty merely to substitute its own exercise of discretion for the discretion already exercised by the judge. In other words, appellate authorities ought not to reverse the order merely because they would themselves have exercised the original discretion, had it attached to them, in a different way. But if the appellate tribunal reaches the clear conclusion that there has been a wrongful exercise of discretion in that no weight, or no sufficient weight, has been given to relevant considerations ... then the reversal of the order on appeal may be justified." *Osenton's* case[2] was one in which the discretion being exercised was that of deciding whether an action should be tried by an official referee, and the material for forming a conclusion was entirely documentary and was thus equally available to the appellate court. The reason for not interfering, save in the most extreme cases, with the judge's decision under the Matrimonial Causes Act, 1937, s. 4, is of a far stronger character, for the proper exercise of the discretion in such a matter largely depends on the observation of witnesses and on a deduction as to matrimonial relations and future prospects which can best be made at the trial.'

Viscount Simon LC did not, in my view, intend in any way to suggest that it was enough to justify an appellate court in interfering with the exercise of a discretion that the appellate court would give different weight to the various considerations which the court exercising the jurisdiction must have had in mind; that would be to substitute the appellate court's discretion for that of the court charged with the exercise of the discretion, since it is generally of the essence of a discretionary jurisdiction that there are conflicting considerations to be weighed, to which different minds could reasonably attach different weight. It is only if there has been misdirection (in fact or in law) or if the exercise of the discretion is 'plainly wrong' (which means, I think, that no reasonable tribunal could exercise the discretion in such a way) that the appellate court is entitled to interfere.

In the instant case Burgess V-C had the advantage, denied to your Lordships, of observing the witnesses; and the impression he formed was obviously influential in his discretionary decision. He had to judge of future prospects, notably the likelihood of the respondent being good for the cost of remedying the defects and the relationship between neighbours if discretion were exercised to relieve against re-entry. Such observations and judgment are, as Viscount Simon LC said[3], best made at the trial. Burgess V-C in no way misdirected himself and there was abundant material to justify him in exercising his discretion in the way he did.

I therefore agree that the appeal should be allowed.

LORD KILBRANDON. My Lords, I have had the advantage of seeing in writing the speech which my noble and learned friend, Lord Wilberforce, has delivered. I entirely agree with it, and cannot usefully add anything.

I would allow the appeal.

Appeal allowed.

Solicitors: *Gregory, Rowcliffe & Co*, agents for *John Taylor & Co*, Manchester (for the appellants); *Collyer-Bristow & Co*, agents for *Frederick Howarth, Son & Maitland*, Bury (for the respondent).

S A Hatteea Esq   Barrister.

---

1   [1941] 2 All ER 245 at 250, [1942] AC 130 at 138
2   [1941] 2 All ER 245, [1942] AC 130
3   [1943] 2 All ER at 79, [1943] AC at 527

R v Holah

COURT OF APPEAL, CRIMINAL DIVISION

ROSKILL LJ, BRISTOW AND FORBES JJ

24th, 25th OCTOBER, 3rd NOVEMBER 1972

*Road traffic – Driving with blood-alcohol proportion above prescribed limit – Evidence–
Provision of specimen – Breath test – Administration of test – Inflation of bag in requisite
manner – Provision of specimen of breath in sufficient quantity to enable test to be carried
out – Failure to inflate bag fully – Sufficient quantity of breath to produce positive reading –
Whether failure to provide specimen of breath – Road Safety Act 1967, ss 2 (5), 7 (3).*

*Road traffic – Driving with blood-alcohol proportion above prescribed limit – Evidence –
Provision of specimen – Specimen for laboratory test – Conditions precedent to request for
specimen – Arrest – Lawful arrest – Necessity of informing driver of reason for arrest –
Driver giving specimen of breath sufficient to give positive reading – Driver informed that
arrest for failing to provide specimen of breath – Whether arrest lawful – Road Safety Act
1967, s 2 (4), (5).*

While driving his car the appellant was stopped by police officers and required to
take a breath test under the provisions of the Road Safety Act 1967. The appellant
breathed into the breathalyser equipment but failed to inflate the bag fully. The
officers observed that the reading was positive but, taking the view that the appellant
had failed to take the test properly, they informed him that he was being arrested
under s 2 (5)[a] of the 1967 Act for failure to provide a specimen of breath. At no
time was the arrest effected in purported pursuance of s 2 (4)[b] of the 1967 Act on
the ground that the test had proved positive. A subsequent laboratory test showed
that the appellant had a blood-alcohol content exceeding the prescribed limit.
The appellant was accordingly charged with an offence under s 1 (1) of the 1967 Act
and convicted. On appeal,

Held – The appeal would be allowed and the conviction quashed for the following
reasons—
    (i) where a person who was required to give a specimen of breath for a breath
test gave one in sufficient quantity to produce a positive reading on the breathalyser
he was 'providing a specimen [of breath] in sufficient quantity to enable the test to
be carried out' within the meaning of s 7 (3)[c] of the 1967 Act and therefore could not
be said to have failed to provide a specimen within s 2 (5); the police officers therefore had no power to arrest the appellant under s 2 (5) but should instead have
arrested him under s 2 (4) (see p 110 b e and f, post);
    (ii) in order to make a valid arrest under the provisions of s 2 (4) or (5) of the 1967
Act, a police officer was bound to make clear to the motorist what it was that he
was being arrested for; it followed that, as the appellant should have been arrested
on the ground that the breath test had proved positive, he should have been informed
that that was the reason for his arrest; since he had not been so informed it followed

---

a   Section 2 (5), so far as material, provides: 'If a person required by a constable ... to
    provide a specimen of breath for a breath test fails to do so and the constable has reason-
    able cause to suspect him of having alcohol in his body, the constable may arrest him
    without warrant ...'

b   Section 2 (4), so far as material, provides: 'If it appears to a constable in consequence of
    a breath test carried out by him on any person ... that the device by means of which
    the test is carried out indicates that the proportion of alcohol in that person's blood
    exceeds the prescribed limit, the constable may arrest that person without warrant ...'

c   Section 7 (3) is set out at p 110 a, post

a   that his arrest was unlawful and, in consequence, the result of the analysis of the laboratory specimen inadmissible (see p 111 j to p 112 a d and e, post).

Notes

For the power to require a breath test and powers of arrest, see Supplement to 33 Halsbury's Laws (3rd Edn) para 1061A, 3-6.

b   For the Road Safety Act 1967, ss 1, 2, 7, see 28 Halsbury's Statutes (3rd Edn) 459, 462, 471.

As from 1st July 1972, ss 1, 2 and 7 of the 1967 Act have been replaced by ss 6, 8 and 12 respectively of the Road Traffic Act 1972.

Cases referred to in judgment

Campbell v Tormey [1969] 1 All ER 961, [1969] 1 WLR 189, 133 JP 267, 53 Cr App Rep
c   99, DC, Digest (Cont Vol C) 931, *322kb.*
Christie v Leachinsky [1947] 1 All ER 567, [1947] AC 573, [1947] LJR 757, 170 LT 443, 111 JP 224, HL, 14 Digest (Repl) 204, *1691.*
Director of Public Prosecutions v Carey [1969] 3 All ER 1662, [1970] AC 1072, [1969]
3 WLR 1169, 54 Cr App Rep 119, [1970] RTR 14, HL, Digest (Cont Vol C) 936, *322aa.*
R v Gordon (1969) 53 Cr App Rep 614, [1970] RTR 125, CA, Digest (Cont Vol C) 933,
d   *3220a.*
R v Kulynycz [1970] 3 All ER 881, [1971] 1 QB 367, [1970] 3 WLR 1029, 135 JP 82, 55 Cr App Rep 34, CA, Digest (Cont Vol C) 189, *1252Aa.*
R v Wall [1969] 1 All ER 968, [1969] 1 WLR 400, 153 JP 310, 53 Cr App Rep 283, CA, Digest (Cont Vol C) 933, *3220.*
Rendell v Hooper [1970] 2 All ER 72, [1970] 1 WLR 747, 134 JP 441, [1970] RTR 252,
e   DC, Digest (Cont Vol C) 937, *322bb.*
Sakhuja v Allen [1972] 2 All ER 311, [1972] 2 WLR 1116, 56 Cr App Rep 464, [1972] RTR 315, HL.
Scott v Baker [1968] 2 All ER 993, [1969] 1 QB 659, [1968] 3 WLR 796, 132 JP 422, 52 Cr App Rep 566, DC, Digest (Cont Vol C) 928, *322c.*

f ## Cases also cited

Dumbell v Roberts [1944] 1 All ER 326, CA.
R v Bove [1970] 2 All ER 20, [1970] 1 WLR 949, DC.
R v Chapman [1969] 2 All ER 321, [1969] 2 QB 436, CA.
R v Hyams [1972] 3 All ER 651, CA.
R v Mackenzie [1971] 1 All ER 729.

g ## Appeal

This was an appeal by John William Patrick Holah against his conviction at Croydon Crown Court on 6th January 1972 before his Honour Judge Grieves and a jury on a charge of driving with a blood-alcohol content above the prescribed limit contrary to s 1 (1) of the Road Safety Act 1967. The appellant was found guilty, fined £100
h   and disqualified from driving for three years. He appealed against conviction, the trial judge having certified that the case was a fit case for appeal. The facts are set out in the judgment of the court.

William Denny for the appellant.
Ann Goddard for the Crown.

Cur adv vult

j

3rd November. **ROSKILL LJ** read the following judgment of the court. At the beginning of his speech in *Sakhuja v Allen*[1], the latest of the appeals under the Road Safety Act 1967 to reach the House of Lords, Lord Hailsham of St Marylebone

---

1   [1972] 2 All ER 311, [1972] 2 WLR 1116

LC observed[1] that 'like many appeals under the Road Safety Act 1967, this appeal   **a**
is wholly without merits'; that observation is especially pertinent to the present
appeal.

The appellant was arrested by two police officers in the early hours of the morning
of Monday, 22nd March 1971. They had observed a Rolls-Royce car being driven
in Church Road, Upper Norwood, in South London, in a highly erratic and indeed
dangerous manner. After the Rolls-Royce car stopped, a man, later identified as   **b**
the appellant, staggered towards the officers. One officer, Sgt Turner, asked the
appellant if he had been drinking. The appellant replied truthfully in the affirmative adding that he had last drunk about five minutes before. The two police officers
then fetched the Alcotest equipment and the appellant agreed to take the test after
20 minutes had elapsed from his last drink.

The appellant and the police officers compared their watches and waited. At   **c**
1.59 a m, by which time Sgt Turner had told the appellant how to provide the sample,
the appellant was given the equipment. He began to breathe into it but failed fully
to inflate the bag. The officers observed that the reading was positive but Sgt
Turner nevertheless considered that the appellant had failed to take the test properly.
The sergeant arrested the appellant for failure to provide a specimen of breath.
There was no question but that both police officers acted in complete good faith   **d**
at all times.

It was common ground at the trial that the intention of the police officers was to
arrest the appellant for failure to comply with s 2 (5) of the 1967 Act in purported
pursuance of the power to arrest without warrant which that subsection confers.
It was not disputed that the arresting officer had ample reasonable cause to suspect
the appellant of having alcohol in his body. At no time was the arrest effected in   **e**
purported pursuance either of s 2 (4) of the 1967 Act or s 6 (4) of the Road Traffic Act
1960. When a sample of the appellant's urine was taken it showed a concentration
of 257 milligrammes of alcohol in 100 millilitres of urine.

The appellant was tried at Croydon Crown Court on 5th and 6th January 1972
before his Honour Judge Grieves and a jury. The primary facts outlined above
were not in dispute. The appellant did not give evidence. At the close of the case   **f**
for the Crown a number of submissions were made by counsel on behalf of the
appellant. Certain of those submissions have been overtaken by subsequent events,
notably the decision of the House of Lords in *Sakhuja v Allen*[2] already referred to.
These were not repeated in this court.

Counsel for the appellant made other submissions to the learned judge which
were repeated by him in this court, principally that on those facts the judge ought
to have withdrawn the case from the jury and directed a verdict of 'not guilty'   **g**
to be entered. Stated in summary form his submissions were as follows: 1. The
appellant was only obliged to give a specimen of blood or urine pursuant to s 3 (1)
of the 1967 Act if he had previously been lawfully arrested without warrant either
under s 2 (4) or (5) of that Act. 2. Unless the appellant had been lawfully arrested,
the result of the analysis of that specimen could not properly be adduced in evidence   **h**
against him: see *Scott v Baker*[3] per Lord Parker CJ, *Director of Public Prosecutions v Carey*[4] per Lord Diplock and *Sakhuja v Allen*[5] per Lord Hailsham of St
Marylebone LC. 3. The only ground given and intended to be given for the appellant's arrest was that the appellant had failed to supply a specimen of breath for
a breath test contrary to s 2 (5) of the 1967 Act. 4. The appellant had manifestly

1   [1972] 2 All ER at 313, [1972] 2 WLR at 1118
2   [1972] 2 All ER 311, [1972] 2 WLR 1116
3   [1968] 2 All ER 993 at 998, [1969] 1 QB 659 at 671
4   [1969] 3 All ER 1662 at 1677, [1970] AC 1072 at 1094
5   [1972] 2 All ER at 315, [1972] 2 WLR at 1120

not so failed since the specimen of breath in fact supplied by him sufficed to give a positive reading on the breathalyser. 5. The appellant could have been lawfully arrested pursuant to s 2 (4) of the 1967 Act since in truth and in fact it appeared to the arresting officer that the breathalyser indicated that the proportion of alcohol in the appellant's blood exceeded the prescribed limit but the appellant was not so arrested. 6. The arrest having been unlawfully effected pursuant to s 2 (5) it was not now open to the Crown to justify the arrest retrospectively on the ground that the appellant might have been lawfully arrested under s 2 (4). 7. The analysis of the sample taken pursuant to s 3 (1) was therefore inadmissible since the conditions precedent to its admissibility had not been complied with. 8. The trial judge was wrong in leaving to the jury the issue whether the appellant had failed to supply a specimen of breath pursuant to s 2 (5), even though the judge gave a strong indication that the jury should conclude that the appellant had not so failed since there was no evidence on which a jury properly directed could find that he had so failed. 9. The trial judge was also wrong in directing the jury that even if they found that there was no such failure to take the breath test, it was enough to justify the arrest and thus make the analysis of the sample of urine admissible, if the appellant had been told the substance of the offence for which he was being arrested.

The jury convicted the appellant. As already stated the appellant did not give evidence. He was fined £100 and disqualified for three years. On 10th January 1972 the learned judge granted a certificate in the following terms:

> 'Whether I was right in telling the jury that it was open to them on the evidence in the case to find that the arrest was valid and that the defendant was sufficiently informed of the substance of the matter for which he was arrested.'

Although leave to appeal was sought from this court on other grounds, the argument in this court on the hearing of the appeal was limited to the subject-matter of that certificate.

If it be admissible to look at the true facts of this case, the appellant, who, this court was told, had a previous conviction for an offence against the Road Safety Act 1967, was driving a Rolls-Royce car when he was clearly unfit to do so by reason of the amount of alcohol which he had consumed and when the analysis of the sample of his urine showed him to be in very grave breach indeed of the law. Nonetheless he seeks to avoid conviction on the ground that his arrest was unlawful because the arresting officer, honestly believing that because the appellant had not fully inflated the bag, he had failed to provide a specimen of breath (despite the positive result shown on the breathalyser), wrongly arrested him under s 2 (5) when he could and should have arrested him under s 2 (4).

The difficulties of police officers in enforcing the 1967 Act are notorious and the argument for the appellant, if it must succeed, must place further difficulties in the way of the enforcement of the law. But sympathy with the difficulties of enforcing the Act cannot deflect this court from its overriding duty to ensure freedom of the individual from unlawful arrest. An arrest of the subject without warrant pursuant to the provisions of, and for the limited purposes allowed by, the 1967 Act—albeit only for a short period—is just as much a serious deprivation of personal liberty as is an arrest of the subject with a view to his immediately being charged with an even more serious criminal offence. The arresting authority must always be able to justify the arrest as lawful. If an arrest for the limited purposes of the 1967 Act cannot be justified by the provisions of that Act and is thus unlawful, one resulting sanction is the exclusion of the evidence obtained pursuant to s 3 (1) of the Act.

We were told by counsel for the Crown that the view taken by the arresting officer that the appellant had failed to provide the specimen of breath required notwithstanding that the breathalyser gave a positive reading was based on established police practice. Such practice, if it exists, would seem perhaps to be founded on certain of the earlier decisions under the 1967 Act now laid to rest by the House of Lords in *Director of Public Prosecutions v Carey*[1]. Furthermore this view would seem to ignore the provisions of s 7 (3) of the Act which provides:

'References in this Part of this Act to providing a specimen of breath for a breath test are references to providing a specimen thereof in sufficient quantity to enable that test to be carried out.'

If s 7 (3) is read with s 2 (5) it seems to this court clear that a person who is required to give a specimen of breath for a breath test and who gives one sufficient to produce a positive reading on the breathalyser, albeit without fully inflating the bag, is 'providing a specimen [of breath] in sufficient quantity to enable that test to be carried out' and accordingly cannot be said to have failed to provide the specimen asked for.

The argument for the Crown in the present case that there can be a failure under s 2 (5) even if the crystals go green if in the opinion of the arresting officer the instructions accompanying the breathalyser have not been properly complied with fails for three reasons. First, it ignores the effect of s 7 (3) on the true construction of s 2 (5); secondly, it introduces the concept of the need for compliance with the instructions accompanying the breathalyser contrary to the principles underlying the decision in *Director of Public Prosecutions v Carey*[1]; see also *Rendell v Hooper*[2]; thirdly, it introduces the subjective opinion of the arresting officer for which no room is to be found in s 2 (5), the provisions of which are in this respect to be contrasted with the opening words of s 2 (4).

In the view of this court a breath test which is both positive and a failure is a contradiction in terms. If sufficient breath is supplied to produce a positive reading it cannot be said that there has been a failure to supply a specimen of breath in sufficient quantity to enable the test to be carried out. In other words the dichotomy between s 2 (4) and (5), of the 1967 Act is complete and this court finds it difficult to suppose that Parliament intended otherwise.

It follows that the judge ought to have withdrawn the issue of failure to provide a specimen of breath from the jury and ought to have told them (if the case were to be left to them at all) that they must proceed on the assumption that the appellant had not failed to provide a specimen. But in view of the strong indication which the judge gave to the jury how they should determine that issue which he left to them as one of fact, this court would not regard the judge's direction on this issue as of itself sufficient to justify quashing the appellant's conviction if the judge's direction on the validity of the arrest can be supported.

The question of what an officer arresting a motorist pursuant to the powers conferred by s 2 (4) or (5) of the 1967 Act must tell the motorist has been touched on in a number of cases but seems never to have arisen for precise decision. It was touched on by Lord Parker CJ in *Campbell v Tormey*[3] and in *R v Wall*[4] (both decisions recently criticised in *Sakhuja v Allen*[5]) and again by Salmon LJ in *R v Gordon*[6] where he said:

'This Court is certain that nothing that was said in CAMPBELL v. TORMEY[7], as explained in WALL[8], in relation to the obligation upon the police to make plain to a man whom they are arresting the offence for which he is being arrested

1 [1969] 3 All ER 1662, [1970] AC 1072
2 [1970] 2 All ER 72, [1970] 1 WLR 747
3 [1969] 1 All ER 961 at 967, [1969] 1 WLR 189 at 196, 197
4 [1969] 1 All ER 968, [1969] 1 WLR 400 at 402, 403
5 [1972] 2 All ER 311, [1972] 2 WLR 1116
6 (1969) 53 Cr App Rep 614 at 618
7 [1969] 1 All ER 961, [1969] 1 WLR 189
8 [1969] 1 All ER 968, [1969] 1 WLR 400

a at the time of his arrest was intended to be read other than in the light of the observations of the House of Lords in CHRISTIE v. LEACHINSKY.[1]'

Thus Salmon LJ thought it axiomatic that what was there laid down by the House of Lords equally applied to arrests under s 2 (4) or (5) of the 1967 Act or under s 6 (4) of the 1960 Act.

b Counsel for the Crown in argument before this court did not seek, to use her own words 'to escape from *Christie*[1]' but said that the present case came within the exceptions referred to in the speeches in that case. It is not necessary to refer to the facts of that case. Viscount Simon stated the law in the form of five propositions[2]:

c '1. If a policeman arrests without warrant on reasonable suspicion of felony, or of other crime of a sort which does not require a warrant, he must in ordinary circumstances inform the person arrested of the true ground of arrest. He is not entitled to keep the reason to himself or to give a reason which is not the true reason. In other words a citizen is entitled to know on what charge or on suspicion of what crime he is seized. 2. If the citizen is not so informed, but is nevertheless seized, the policeman, apart from certain exceptions, is liable for false imprisonment. 3. The requirement that the person arrested should be informed *d* of the reason why he is seized naturally does not exist if the circumstances are such that he must know the general nature of the alleged offence for which he is detained. 4. The requirement that he should be so informed does not mean that technical or precise language need be used. The matter is a matter of substance, and turns on the elementary proposition that in this country a person is, *prima facie*, entitled to his freedom and is only required to submit to restraint on *e* his freedom if he knows in substance the reason why it is claimed that this restraint should be imposed. 5. The person arrested cannot complain that he has not been supplied with the above information as and when he should be, if he himself produces a situation which makes it practically impossible to inform him, *e.g.*, by immediate counter-attack or by running away. There may well be other exceptions to the general rule in addition to those I have indicated, *f* and the above propositions are not intended to constitute a formal or complete code, but to indicate the general principles of our law on a very important matter.'

Lord Simonds said[3]:

g 'These and similar considerations lead me to the view that it is not an essential condition of lawful arrest that the constable should at the time of arrest formulate any charge at all, much less the charge which may ultimately be found in the indictment, but this, and this only, is the qualification which I would impose on the general proposition. It leaves untouched the principle, which lies at the heart of the matter, that the arrested man is entitled to be told what is the act for which he is arrested. The "charge" ultimately made will depend on the view *h* taken by the law of his act. In ninety-nine cases out of a hundred the same words may be used to define the charge or describe the act, nor is any technical precision necessary . . .'

Lord du Parcq used language to the same effect[4].

There can be no doubt since the appellant was perfectly fit to be informed for what *j* he was being arrested, that he was being arrested because it appeared to the arresting

---

1 [1947] 1 All ER 567, [1947] AC 573
2 [1947] 1 All ER at 572, 573, [1947] AC at 587, 588
3 [1947] 1 All ER at 575, 576, [1947] AC at 593
4 [1947] 1 All ER at 579, 580, [1947] AC at 599, 600

officer in consequence of the breath test that the breathalyser indicated that the a
proportion of alcohol in his blood exceeded the prescribed limit or to put the matter
more shortly rather than in the formal language of the subsection, that the breathalyser appeared to the officer to be positive. The appellant was not so informed. On
the contrary he was told that he was being arrested for failing to supply a specimen
of breath for the test.

It is now sought to be said that to tell him what he was in fact told was in sub- b
stance to tell him the opposite, namely, what he ought to have been told. No doubt
there is no precise formula which has to be used. Cases will vary infinitely. But it is
not and should not be difficult to make clear what it is for which a motorist is being
arrested. In fact, the appellant was told what was the contrary of the true facts,
albeit in complete good faith, and this court is unable to see how in counsel for the
appellant's pungent phrase 'the contrary of the facts can be the generality of the c
truth'.

Counsel for the Crown relied on *R v Kulynycz*[1], but this court is unable to find
anything in that decision which assists in the determination of the present problem.
It is not enough to say, as counsel sought to say, that the appellant knew that he was
being taken to the police station for further investigation whether or not he had more
than the prescribed quantity of alcohol in his blood. On the authorities it would d
plainly be wrong for him to have been told nothing. If a wrong reason can be given
it is difficult to see why he need be given any reason at all. Yet the authorities require
him to be given the reason unless the case is one which falls within well recognised
exceptions. Furthermore a motorist arrested pursuant to s 2 (4) or (5) has certain
rights accorded to him under other provisions of the statute and it may well be in
certain cases that a motorist would wish to determine on his course of action after e
arrest in the light of the information given to him at the time of his arrest as to the
reason for that arrest. There is a plain duty on the arresting officer to give information and the information given must in substance be the correct information and
not its reverse.

This court has great sympathy with the police officers concerned but it has reluctantly reached the conclusion that the answer to the question raised in the certificate f
from the trial judge must be 'No' and that the appellant's conviction must be
quashed.

Appeal allowed.

Solicitors: *H C L Hanne, Crawley & Co* (for the appellant); *Solicitor, Metropolitan* g
Police.

Jacqueline Charles Barrister.

---

1 [1970] 3 All ER 881, [1971] 1 QB 367

a

Wachtel v Wachtel and another

FAMILY DIVISION

ORMROD J

25th, 26th JULY, 3rd OCTOBER 1972

b

Divorce – Financial provision – Matters to be considered by court when making order –
Policy – Shift of emphasis from maintenance to redistribution of assets – Re-allocation of
property rights so as to do broad justice between parties – Relevance of contributions to welfare
of the family – Matrimonial Proceedings and Property Act 1970, ss 4 (a), 5 (1).

c *Divorce – Financial provision – Conduct of parties – Weight to be given to conduct – Conduct*
not to be equated with share of responsibility for breakdown – Conduct as a factor which
may modify result after consideration of other factors – Conduct only a marginal issue unless
obvious and gross – Matrimonial Proceedings and Property Act 1970, s 5 (1).

In 1956 the husband and wife purchased the matrimonial home in the husband's
d name with a 100 per cent mortgage. Two children were born to them, a boy and a
girl. In 1972 the husband and wife were granted cross-decrees of divorce, each
party having established a case under s 2 (1) (b) of the Divorce Reform Act 1969.
Custody of the son, a boarder at a public school, was granted to the father and
custody of the daughter, aged 11, to the mother. The husband was a dentist earning
a reasonably good income. The parties had no capital assets other than the matri-
e monial home which was estimated to have a market value of £20,000 to £22,000
with a balance of some £2,000 outstanding on mortgage. The judge found that,
judging the parties' conduct in terms of responsibility for the breakdown of the
marriage, each spouse was roughly equally responsible. The wife applied under
s 2 of the Matrimonial Proceedings and Property Act 1970 for periodical payments
for herself and the daughter, secured provision and a lump sum or sums, and, under
f s 4 of the 1970 Act, for a settlement, transfer of property or variation of settlement
order.

Held – Taking account of the matters specified in s 5 (1)[a] of the 1970 Act, and in
particular having regard, in accordance with s 5 (1) (f), to the contribution which the
wife had made to the welfare of the family in looking after the home and caring for
g the family for 18 years, and having regard also to the fact that each of the parties
had the responsibility of looking after one of the children, it was essential that each

<hr>

a Section 5 (1) provides: 'It shall be the duty of the court in deciding whether to exercise
its powers under section 2 or 4 of this Act in relation to a party to the marriage and, if so,
in what manner, to have regard to all the circumstances of the case including the following
matters, that is to say—(a) the income, earning capacity, property and other financial
h resources which each of the parties to the marriage has or is likely to have in the foreseeable
future; (b) the financial needs, obligations and responsibilities which each of the parties to
the marriage has or is likely to have in the foreseeable future; (c) the standard of living
enjoyed by the family before the breakdown of the marriage; (d) the age of each party to
the marriage and the duration of the marriage; (e) any physical or mental disability of
either of the parties to the marriage; (f) the contributions made by each of the parties to
the welfare of the family, including any contribution made by looking after the home or
j caring for the family; (g) in the case of proceedings for divorce or nullity of marriage, the
value to either of the parties to the marriage of any benefit (for example, a pension) which,
by reason of the dissolution or annulment of the marriage, that party will lose the chance
of acquiring; and so to exercise those powers as to place the parties, so far as it is practicable
and, having regard to their conduct, just to do so, in the financial position in which they
would have been if the marriage had not broken down and each had properly discharged
his or her financial obligations and responsibilities towards the other.'

of them should have a home, and therefore that capital should be made available   *a*
to the party leaving the home, i e the wife. In the circumstances the only fair solution
was to divide the only capital asset more or less equally between them and to order
that a sum of £10,000 or half the net value of the house, whichever was the less,
should be transferred to the wife (see p 119 g to j, post).

Per Ormrod J. (i) Section 4 (*a*) of the 1970 Act, read in conjunction with s 5 (1),
suggests that Parliament has intended to bring about a shift of emphasis from the   *b*
old concept of 'maintenance' of the wife and children by the husband, to one of
redistribution of assets and 'purchasing power'. The indications are that the court
should, in appropriate cases, use its powers to re-allocate property rights in such a
way as to do broad justice between the spouses after dissolution and to reflect in this
their real contributions to the welfare of the family (see p 116 h and j and p 117 c to e,
post).

(ii) There is no statutory authority for the view that 'conduct' in the context of   *c*
s 5 (1) of the 1970 Act means conduct which has contributed to the breakdown of the
marriage, with the consequence that financial provision for the wife should be discounted in proportion to her share of the responsibility for the breakdown. The
analogy with contributory negligence is misleading. Conduct is to be taken into
account as a factor which may modify the result after consideration of all the other
factors specified in s 5 (1). In practice conduct usually proves to be a marginal issue   *d*
which exerts little effect on the ultimate result unless it is both obvious and gross
(see p 118 e to g and p 119 a to c, post).

Notes
For financial provision on granting a decree of divorce and the matters to be considered by the court in exercising its powers, see Supplement to 12 Halsbury's Laws   *e*
(3rd Edn) para 987A, 1-4.

For the Matrimonial Proceedings and Property Act 1970, ss 2, 4, 5, see 40 Halsbury's
Statutes (3rd Edn) 800, 802, 803.

Cases referred to in judgment
Ackerman v Ackerman [1972] 2 All ER 420, [1972] Fam 225, [1972] 2 WLR 1253, CA;   *f*
   varying [1971] 3 All ER 721, [1972] Fam 1, [1971] 3 WLR 725.
Iverson v Iverson [1966] 1 All ER 258, [1967] P 134, [1966] 2 WLR 1168, 27 (2) Digest
   (Reissue) 823, *6593*.
Jones v Jones [1971] 3 All ER 1201, CA, 27 (2) Digest (Reissue) 844, *6720*.
Leslie v Leslie [1911] P 203, 80 LJP 139; sub nom *L v L* 104 LT 462, 27 (2) Digest (Reissue)
   808, *6481*.
Millward v Millward [1971] 3 All ER 526, [1971] 1 WLR 1432, CA, 27 (2) Digest (Reissue)   *g*
   852, *6788*.
Pettitt v Pettitt [1969] 2 All ER 385, [1970] AC 777, [1969] 2 WLR 966, HL, 27 (1) Digest
   (Reissue) 102, *707*.
Porter v Porter [1969] 3 All ER 640, [1969] 1 WLR 1155, CA, 27 (2) Digest (Reissue)
   823, *6594*.
Sydenham v Sydenham [1949] 2 All ER 196, [1949] LJR 1424, CA, 27 (2) Digest (Reissue)   *h*
   824, *6596*.
Trestain v Trestain [1950] 1 All ER 618, [1950] P 198, CA, 27 (2) Digest (Reissue) 827,
   6612.
White v White (1972) The Times, 10th March, CA.
Wood v Wood [1891] P 272, [1891-94] All ER Rep 506, 60 LJP 66, 64 LT 686, CA, 27 (2)   *j*
   Digest (Reissue) 848, *6747*.

Cases also cited
Davis v Davis [1967] 1 All ER 123, [1967] P 185, CA.
Hakluytt v Hakluytt [1968] 2 All ER 868, [1968] 1 WLR 1145, CA.
Von Mehren v Von Mehren [1970] 1 All ER 153, [1970] 1 WLR 56, CA.

a
Petition and cross-petition

By a petition dated 18th April 1972 the husband sought the dissolution of his marriage and by her answer, dated 9th May 1972, the wife cross-petitioned for a decree and sought, inter alia, (i) an order that the husband pay by way of periodical payments, secured periodical payments and lump sum or sums, such sums as might be just, and (ii) such orders by way of settlement of property and/or transfer of property and/or variation of settlement as might be just.   On 21st July 1972 Ormrod J granted each party a decree nisi and awarded custody of the son to the father and of the daughter to the mother.   The hearing of the wife's application for financial relief was in chambers and adjourned into open court for judgment.   The facts are set out in the judgment.

Roger Gray QC and *E S Cazalet* for the wife.
A B Ewbank QC for the husband.

Cur adv vult

3rd October.   **ORMROD J** read the following judgment.   This case has now reached the stage when the court is called on to decide various matters relating to property and financial provision, following on the dissolution of the marriage by a decree nisi which I granted on 21st July 1972.   At the same time I made an order as to custody of the two children.   In the divorce proceedings each party established a case under s 2 (1) (*b*) of the Divorce Reform Act 1969, and, therefore, each obtained a decree nisi.   In the unfortunate circumstances of this case the custody of the children had to be divided; custody of the boy, who is a boarder at Epsom College, going to the father; custody of the daughter, now aged 11, going to the mother.   My judgment in the suit contains my detailed findings of fact which cover the entire matrimonial history.   From these findings can be drawn any conclusions as to conduct which may be relevant to the present proceedings.   I have also had the advantage of hearing the present applications myself with the assistance of leading counsel on both sides which has involved a very thorough investigation into the financial position of both parties.   In this way I have obtained an unusually detailed picture of this family.

The applications (all by the wife) which must now be considered are as follows: under s 2 of the Matrimonial Proceeedings and Property Act 1970 for periodical payments for the wife and the daughter, secured provision, and a lump sum or sums and, under s 4 of the 1970 Act for settlement or transfer of property or variation of settlements.   There is also a summons by the wife under the Married Women's Property Act 1882, s 17, in relation to the former matrimonial home, 37 Pollards Hill North, Streatham.   Counsel for the wife, while not abandoning this summons, has preferred to rest his case on the discretionary powers of the court under s 4, using the evidence filed in the summons as part of his case under this section.   A number of questions, therefore, arise on the scope of the discretionary powers of the court under the Matrimonial Proceedings and Property Act 1970 and the principles to be applied in the exercise of them.

Counsel for the husband has submitted that the principles remain more or less as they were under the old legislation.   Counsel for the wife has contended for a new approach to these problems of property and financial provision after dissolution of marriage.   There is at present very little authoritative guidance about the exercise of these discretionary powers which are of great importance to all who are involved in divorce proceedings and to those who are called on to advise on or make decisions in such situations.   In the circumstances I have decided to give that part of the judgment which deals with general matters in open court but to go into chambers when I come to the particular facts of this case.

Counsel for the husband has referred me to four cases in the Court of Appeal on which he relies in support of his general proposition. These are *White v White*[1], *Millward v Millward*[2], *Jones v Jones*[3] and *Ackerman v Ackerman*[4]. All these judgments are concerned with the particular facts of each case and contain little or no general guidance, although in *Ackerman's* case[5] Phillimore LJ observed that s 5 of the 1970 Act 'was obviously intended to codify the existing law and practice'. In that case, however, the court was concerned with the relatively narrow question whether the trial judge ought to attempt to quantify conduct in percentage terms for the assistance of those who have subsequently to make discretionary orders. I do not think that Phillimore LJ intended to say anything more than that most of the phrases in s 5 are to be found in various leading judgments under the old law, because the new law undoubtedly contains several important provisions relating to the discretionary powers of the court which were not to be found in the old law and which must influence the manner in which these powers are exercised in the future.

The 1970 Act itself contains specific directions for the exercise of the much enlarged powers which it has conferred on the court. These are to be found in s 5. Section 5 (1) specifies seven matters which the court is required to take into consideration in addition to 'all the circumstances of the case'. With one exception, these are much the same as those laid down by Lindley LJ in *Wood v Wood*[6] although the phraseology is slightly different. The exception, which is important, is para (*f*) which requires the court to have regard to—

'the contributions made by each of the parties to the welfare of the family, including any contribution made by looking after the home or caring for the family'.

Having taken these matters into consideration the subsection goes on to instruct the court—

'so to exercise [its] powers as to place the parties . . . in the financial position in which they would have been if the marriage had not broken down and each had properly discharged his or her financial obligations and responsibilities towards the other.'

This instruction is qualified by the words 'so far as it is practicable and, having regard to their conduct, just to do so'. Two difficulties immediately arise on this part of the subsection. In all but a very small percentage of cases the practical difficulties of achieving the result envisaged by the Act will be insuperable, so that only a very rough approximation to it will be possible. Moreover, it poses the fundamental difficulty of comparing two wholly unlike situations, a united family, with two individuals living separately, with or without children. The other qualification, the conduct of the parties, poses two problems, assessment or evaluation of the conduct and its translation into financial terms.

A careful reading of this subsection together with s 4, which gives the court very wide new powers to interfere with proprietary rights, suggests that Parliament has intended to bring about a shift of emphasis from the old concept of 'maintenance' of the wife and children by the husband to one of redistribution of assets and, what might be called, 'purchasing power'. A parallel shift of emphasis has been brought about, much more clearly, by the Divorce Reform Act 1969 which has changed the

---

1　(1972) The Times, 10th March
2　[1971] 3 All ER 526, [1971] 1 WLR 1432
3　[1971] 3 All ER 1201
4　[1972] 2 All ER 420, [1972] Fam 225
5　[1972] 2 All ER at 424, [1972] Fam at 232
6　[1891] P 272, [1891-94] All ER Rep 506

conceptual basis of divorce from matrimonial fault or offence, to irretrievable break-down of the relationship of marriage, retaining some elements of the old fault concept but using them essentially as evidence of irretrievable breakdown.

These two Acts, which are clearly intended to be read together, form the new code of family law. In my judgment it is the duty of the court when exercising its discretionary powers under the 1970 Act to give effect to the new approach to these family problems which is explicit in the 1969 Act and implicit in the 1970 Act. It is no longer appropriate, if indeed it ever was, to talk about an 'innocent' or a 'guilty' wife in this context. These phrases still survive in conventional advocacy in these cases in spite of repeated disapproval by the Court of Appeal and at first instance: see *Trestain v Trestain*[1], *Porter v Porter*[2] and *Iverson v Iverson*[3]. Counsel for the husband at one point in his argument asked me to remember that the wife was 'not an innocent wife'! Conduct of the parties, however, continues to be a matter for consideration and I shall return to this question later.

Apart from the general tenor of the new code, there are three specific changes in the new law which must modify the approach to these problems. The first of these is s 4 (*a*) which gives the court the new power to order property to be transferred from one spouse to the other. This is a most important innovation and there is little guidance as to how it should be exercised. Taken in conjunction, however, with the second major change, to which I have already referred, namely, para (*f*) of s 5 (1), the indications are that the court should, in appropriate cases, use this power to re-allocate property rights in such a way as to do broad justice between the spouses after dissolution and to reflect in this their real contributions to the welfare of the family. These provisions obviate the difficulties arising from *Pettitt v Pettitt*[4] and enable the court to achieve all and more than Lord Denning MR, Lord Diplock and others sought unsuccessfully to do by extending the scope of s 17 of the Married Women's Property Act 1882. The third important change is in s 7 (2) which provides for the automatic cessation of periodical payments for the wife on remarriage. This must affect the attitude of the court to lump sum payments because the former wife of a man with a substantial income but only a small amount of capital will be adversely affected if she marries a man of small or modest means. Unless some lump sum provision, even quite a small one, has been made for her she will, in some cases, suffer a substantial injustice, and the order will fail to achieve the objective set out by s 5 (1) by an unnecessarily wide margin.

Before coming to the facts of this particular case, an attempt must be made to determine the effect of the words in s 5 (1) which refer to conduct of the parties. For obvious reasons this is a source of great anxiety to the parties and to their legal advisers in many cases. Ever since the original Matrimonial Causes Act 1857, conduct has been one of the matters which the court is required to take into account in deciding property and financial questions arising after divorce, yet there is surprisingly little authority on it. Moreover, practice seems to have been more or less immune to such authority as there is on the subject. The notion that a 'guilty' wife is virtually disqualified from obtaining an order for maintenance has persisted in the face of strong authority to the contrary. In the past this has led to bitterly contested divorce cases in which the only real issue has been maintenance and which party should get the decree. There are some signs that the same thing is happening, although to a lesser extent, under the new Act. This attitude has little or no support in the authorities. On the contrary, in the days of divorce by Act of Parliament the practice was to include financial provision for the adulterous wife; a wife judicially separated on the ground of cruelty was entitled to apply for permanent alimony (see *Leslie v Leslie*[5])

1 [1950] 1 All ER 618, [1950] P 198
2 [1969] 3 All ER 640, [1969] 1 WLR 1155
3 [1966] 1 All ER 258, [1967] P 134
4 [1969] 2 All ER 385, [1970] AC 777
5 [1911] P 203

and such phrases as 'compassionate allowance' have been judicially condemned on   *a*
many occasions (see *Sydenham v Sydenham*[1], *Trestain v Trestain*[2] and others).

But, faced with the problems set by each successive Matrimonial Causes Act of
taking conduct into account, there has been a tendency in practice to fall back on an
'all or nothing' rule. A wife who had a decree could expect to obtain a 'normal'
order for maintenance whereas a wife against whom a decree has been made had an
uphill struggle to get anything. A successful wife who had to ask for discretion in   *b*
respect of her own adultery quickly came to be treated as an 'innocent wife'. When
joint decrees became fashionable the same thing happened, although some marginal
reduction might be made in the amount of the order. This tendency may reflect
the difficulty which registrars and judges have experienced in evolving a satisfactory
way of evaluating conduct and of relating it to financial issues. The all or nothing
approach evades these problems.   *c*

The prevailing view at present seems to be that conduct in this context means
conduct which has contributed to the breakdown of the marriage, with the consequence that financial provision for the wife should be discounted in proportion to her
share of responsibility for the breakdown. This suggestion first appeared, I think
in Denning LJ's judgment in *Sydenham v Sydenham*[1]. It occurs also in *Trestain v
Trestain*[2] and in the judgment of Sachs LJ in *Porter v Porter*[3] in which the word   *d*
'discount' appears. In his judgment in *Ackerman v Ackerman*[4] Sir George Baker P
followed this line of authority to its logical conclusion by assessing the wife's share
of responsibility for the breakdown at 25 per cent which was to be the discount figure
in subsequent maintenance proceedings. The Court of Appeal[5], however, overruled
his decision holding that there was nothing in the 1970 Act or any other Act which
justified this approach or which gave the court power to make a declaratory judgment   *e*
of this kind.

There is, in fact, no statutory authority for this view of conduct at all. The 1970
Act refers simply to 'conduct' whereas nothing would have been easier than to include
an additional paragraph in s 5 (1) to the effect that the court should have regard to
'the extent to which the wife by her conduct contributed to the breakdown'. The
analogy with contributory negligence is attractive but misleading. The fact is that   *f*
the forensic process is reasonably well adapted to determining in broad terms the
share of responsibility of each party for an accident on the road or at work because
the issues are relatively confined in scope, but it is much too clumsy a tool for dissecting
the complex interactions which go on all the time in a family. Shares in responsibility for breakdown cannot be properly assessed without a meticulous examination
and understanding of the characters and personalities of the spouses concerned, and
the more thorough the investigation the more the shares will, in most cases, approach   *g*
equality. There are, of course, cases in which the contribution of one party seems to
be either very marginal or quite clear, yet a more subtle approach will reveal how
much the other has in fact contributed to the ultimate result. The present case
illustrates this very clearly. On the face of it, the principal cause of the breakdown of
this marriage was the wife's sudden decision to leave home and go to Dr Fyvie, yet, as   *h*
the history of the marriage unfolded, it became increasingly clear that the real cause
of the breakdown lay in the personalities of the spouses and their behaviour to each
other over the years. The Dr Fyvie episode was, in fact, no more than a symptom,
a conclusion which might have been guessed from the fact that the marriage had
lasted 18 years. This case is yet another illustration of Vaisey J's favourite dictum in
ward of court cases—'it takes three to commit adultery'.   *j*

1 [1949] 2 All ER 196
2 [1950] 1 All ER 618, [1950] P 198
3 [1969] 3 All ER 640, [1969] 1 WLR 1155
4 [1971] 3 All ER 721, [1972] Fam 1
5 [1972] 2 All ER 420, [1972] Fam 225

a But the problem remains, because conduct must still be taken into account. In my judgment the Act itself indicates the answer. As s 5 stands, conduct is to be taken into account as a factor which may modify the result which is arrived at after consideration of all the other factors specified in the section. The court can only approach this issue in a broad way. It should bear in mind the new basis of divorce which recognises that, generally speaking, the causes of breakdown are complex and rarely

b to be found wholly or mainly on one side, and that the forensic process is not well-adapted to fine assessments or evaluations of behaviour, and that it is not only conduct in relation to the breakdown which may have to be considered. Conduct subsequent to the separation by either spouse may affect the discretion of the court in many ways, e g the appearance of signs of financial recklessness in the husband or of some form of socially unacceptable behaviour by the wife which would suggest to a reasonable person that in justice some modification to the order ought to be made. In my

c experience, however, conduct in these cases usually proves to be a marginal issue which exerts little effect on the ultimate result unless it is both obvious and gross.

There are two important issues in this case. The first is the future of the matrimonial home and the second is the amount of the periodical payments for the wife and the daughter. This is a typical middle-class professional family with virtually

d no capital assets other than the home which is being bought on mortgage but with an above average earning capacity. Due largely to inflation the house has greatly increased in value and the balance outstanding on mortgage, about £2,000, is small in relation to its current value, which is said to be about £20,000 to £22,000 but it is, in fact, only a modest suburban house. The husband is a dentist carrying on practice in the Streatham/Tooting area and earning a reasonably good income. The family

e have hitherto enjoyed a reasonably comfortable standard of living and there is nothing to suggest that there has been any real shortage of money. I shall have to examine the income position in more detail later.

So far as the house is concerned, it was bought in the husband's name in 1956, with the assistance of a 100 per cent mortgage, but about £1,000 was spent on repairs and redecoration. There was an issue in the Married Women's Property Act 1882 pro-

f ceedings about the contribution alleged to have been made to its purchase by the wife. On any view this was relatively small but it might have been an important issue in those proceedings as the law now stands. So far as the discretionary powers under s 4 of the Matrimonial Proceedings and Property Act 1970 are concerned it is of little importance compared with the fact that like so many couples since the last war the husband and the wife set about building up a home together by their joint efforts. This house represents an investment for each of them of 18 years of their

g adult lives. Applying s 5 (1) (f) and taking into account the contribution which the wife has made to the welfare of this family in looking after the home and caring for the family, I am quite satisfied that hers has been a very substantial contribution over these 18 years.

To put these two people into a position which even approximates to their position

h before the dissolution of the marriage it is essential that each of them should have a home. Since each has to care for one of the two children, their needs in this respect are clearly similar. In these days the difficulty of finding accommodation to rent and the cost of such accommodation if it can be found is so great that it is almost essential to make provision, if it can be done, for some capital to be available to the party, in this case the wife, who has left the matrimonial home. Taking all the circumstances

j into account the only fair way of dealing with these two people, in my judgment, is to divide the only capital asset more or less equally between them. I think that a sum of £10,000 or half the net value of the house whichever is the less should be transferred to the wife. Whether this is to be done by transferring to her a half interest in the house or by way of a lump sum payment is a matter of arrangement to be decided by them and their legal advisers. I think that it is a practicable arrangement although inconvenient for the husband and that in the light of the whole

history of their conduct as spouses and as parents and as members of a family it is the
just result. If I had to assess conduct in terms of responsibility for breakdown I
would, with some doubts, regard each spouse as roughly equally responsible. My
doubts are double-edged; in some ways the husband could be regarded as primarily
to blame, in others the wife. At that point I shall go into chambers.

*Order that the husband pay the wife £10,000 or one half the value of the matrimonial home,
whichever is the less; that the husband pay the wife periodical payments at the rate of
£1,500 per annum, less tax; that the husband pay the daughter periodical payments
at the rate of £9·50 per week.*

Solicitors: *Cowles & Co* (for the wife); *Malcolm Fraser & Co* (for the husband).

R C T Habesch Esq Barrister.

Beckett v Cohen

QUEEN'S BENCH DIVISION
LORD WIDGERY CJ, MELFORD STEVENSON AND BRABIN JJ
30th OCTOBER 1972

*Trade description – False or misleading statement – Provision of services – Promise in
regard to future – Building of garage – Statements made before building started – Statement
as to the date on which garage would be completed – Statement incapable of being true or
false at time when made – Trade Descriptions Act 1968, s 14 (1).*

The defendant, a builder, agreed to build a garage for a customer. During the course
of the negotiations the defendant undertook to complete the work within ten days.
The garage was not completed within ten days. The respondent was charged
under s 14 (1)[a] of the Trade Descriptions Act 1968 with recklessly making a statement in the course of trade which was false as to the time at which a service, i e
the building of a garage, would be provided.

Held – The defendant had no case to answer since s 14 (1) of the 1968 Act did not apply
to a statement which amounted to a promise as to what a person would do in the
future and which could not therefore, at the time when it was made, have the
character of being either true or false (see p 121 g and j to p 122 c, post).

Semble. A builder who erects a building for another provides a service within
the meaning of s 14 (1) of the 1968 Act (see p 121 g and p 122 c, post).

Notes
For false or misleading statements as to services under the Trade Descriptions Act
1968, see Supplement to 10 Halsbury's Laws (3rd Edn) para 1314c, 3.

For the Trade Descriptions Act 1968, s 14, see 37 Halsbury's Statutes (3rd Edn) 959.

Case stated
This was an appeal by way of case stated by justices for the county of Essex acting
in and for the petty sessional division of Rochford, in respect of their adjudication
as a magistrates' court sitting at Southend-on-Sea on 15th March 1972, whereby
they held that the respondent, Ben Cohen, alias Ben Conn, had no case to answer
on an information laid by the appellant, B W Beckett, alleging the commission by
the respondent of two offences contrary to s 14 (1) of the Trade Descriptions Act
1968. The facts are set out in the judgment of Lord Widgery CJ.

A F B Scrivener for the appellant.
A B Baillie for the respondent.

a Section 14 (1), so far as material, is set out at p 121 h, post

LORD WIDGERY CJ. This is another case in which prosecuting authorities appear to me to be pressing the ambit of the Trade Descriptions Act 1968 to a wholly unacceptable degree.

This is an appeal by case stated from justices for the county of Essex sitting as a magistrates' court at Southend, who on 15th March 1972 dismissed, under an application of no case, two charges brought by the appellant against the respondent under s 14 (1) of the Trade Descriptions Act 1968. Counsel for the appellant today accepts that the justices' action in regard to the first charge was probably correct, and only seeks to pursue the appeal on the second, but it is convenient to mention both charges.

The first alleged that the respondent in the course of trade as a builder recklessly made an oral statement, namely 'complete the work within about ten days' which was false as to the time at which a service, namely the building of a garage, would be provided, contrary to s 14 (1) of the Trade Descriptions Act 1968. The second charge was that in the course of trade as a builder recklessly made a written statement in an estimate namely 'build garage as the existing' which statement was false as to the manner in which a service would be provided.

The only facts found are that the respondent had not completed the work within ten days and that the garage was not identical in construction or appearance with the existing garage. To make any sense out of this case at all, one has to look at the evidence, because the findings of fact are wholly deficient. What seems to have happened is that the respondent agreed for a customer, Mr Bailey, that he would build Mr Bailey a garage within ten days, and that it would be, to use the words of the agreement 'as the existing', which meant similar to another garage already erected by Mr Bailey's neighbour against which this garage was to stand. Again picking one's way through the evidence, and in the absence of any finding of fact, it seems that the respondent set about building this garage with a will, but he ran out of money before he finished it, so in fact he did not complete it within ten days and it was not exactly like the other garage. Then the weights and measures inspector was called; he brought a lecturer in building to view the site and take photographs with a polaroid camera, photographs which have not been shown to us. In the end, the respondent was charged with the two offences to which I have referred. The justices listened to an argument whether the work of a builder in these circumstances was the work of providing a service. It may be that this is a matter which may have to be more fully argued another day, and I do not find it necessary to decide the point at the moment, although I think it right to say that I would have thought at first impression that it was providing a service, and would be surprised if a different conclusion is ultimately produced, but the argument for the respondent which the justices adopted, and which to my mind answers the whole case for the appellant, is that s 14 (1), under which the offence is charged, has no application to statements which amount to a promise in regard to the future, and which therefore at the time when they are made cannot have the character of being either true or false. The section, so far as material, reads as follows:

'It shall be an offence for any person in the course of any trade or business— (a) to make a statement which he knows to be false; or (b) recklessly to make a statement which is false; as to any of the following matters, that is to say,— (i) the provision in the course of any trade or business of any services, accommodation or facilities ... (iii) the time at which, manner in which or persons by whom any services, accommodation or facilities are so provided ...'

This section matches earlier provisions in the Act dealing with the sale of goods. The purpose of the earlier sections is to prevent persons when selling goods from attaching a false description to the goods, and in the same way s 14 is concerned as I see it, when services are performed under a contract, to make it an offence if the person providing the service recklessly makes a false statement as to what he has

done. The section specifically refers to the reckless making of a statement which ͢a
is false. That means that if at the end of the contract a person giving the service
recklessly makes a false statement as to what he has done, the matter may well fall
within s 14, but if before the contract has been worked out, the person who provides
the service makes a promise as to what he will do, and that promise does not relate
to an existing fact, nobody can say at the date when that statement is made that it
is either true or false. In my judgment Parliament never intended or contemplated ͢b
for a moment that the Act should be used in this way, to make a criminal offence
out of what is really a breach of warranty.

There are many other defects in the case which would have made it difficult
for us to continue the consideration of the point raised in any way, but I am quite
satisfied on the one short point to which I have referred that the justices were right.
I would dismiss the appeal.   ͢c

MELFORD STEVENSON J. I agree.

BRABIN J. I agree.

Appeal dismissed.   ͢d

Solicitors: *Sharpe, Pritchard & Co*, agents for *T Hambrey Jones*, Chelmsford (for the
appellant); *Bates, Son & Braby*, Southend-on-Sea (for the respondent).

Ilyas Khan Esq   Barrister.   ͢e

R v Singh (Amar Jit), R v Meeuwsen

COURT OF APPEAL, CRIMINAL DIVISION
LAWTON LJ, CHAPMAN AND WIEN JJ
12th, 20th OCTOBER 1972

*Alien – Immigration – Illegal immigrant – Entry into United Kingdom – Assisting entry –
Knowingly carrying out arrangements for facilitating entry of anyone known or believed* ͢g
*to be an illegal entrant – Arrangements carried out after entrant having entered United
Kingdom – Whether an offence – Immigration Act 1971, s 25 (1).*

Twelve Asians who did not have leave to enter the United Kingdom were concealed
in boilers in Rotterdam. The boilers were shipped to the United Kingdom on a ͢h
ferry and disembarked at Felixstowe. The trailer on which they were loaded passed
through the customs and parked in a trailer park. The park was outside that part
of the port which was under the control of the immigration authorities. Next day
some of the Asians were seen crouching under the trailer and were taken into custody
as illegal entrants. That night the appellant M arrived at the dock gatehouse,
carrying a heavy spanner. He was arrested and found to have on him a torch and
large wrench. He admitted that he had been told to open the boilers and let out the ͢j
Asians concealed there. The appellant S was arrested at the same time and admitted
to the police that he had gone to Felixstowe knowing that his brother was coming
to the United Kingdom in circumstances which were such that he must have known
that the brother's entry would be illegal. The appellants were charged with being
knowingly concerned in carrying out arrangements for facilitating entry into the

a United Kingdom of illegal entrants, contrary to s 25 (1)*a* of the Immigration Act 1971. They were convicted and appealed contending, inter alia, that once the illegal entrants had left that part of the port which was subject to the control of the immigration authorities they were no longer deemed under s 11 (1)*b* of the 1971 Act not to have entered the United Kingdom, so that anything done after they had entered the United Kingdom by leaving that part of the port could not in law be deemed to have been
b done for the purpose of securing or facilitating entry into the United Kingdom.

Held – The appeal would be dismissed. Effective arrangements for securing or facilitating the entry into the United Kingdom of anyone would be likely to include plans for getting the entrant away as quickly as possible from the point of disembarkation. Those who made or carried out such plans would be 'facilitating . . . entry into the United Kingdom' within the meaning of s 25 (1) of the 1971 Act; s 11 (1) had no bearing
c on s 25 (1) (see p 125 j to p 126 b, post).

Notes
For offences connected with illegal entry of immigrants into the United Kingdom, see Supplement to 5 Halsbury's Laws (3rd Edn) para 1515.
    For the Immigration Act 1971, ss 11, 25, see 41 Halsbury's Statutes (3rd Edn) 32, 45.

d **Cases cited in argument**
R v Chapman [1931] 2 KB 606, CA.
R v Hurley and Murray [1967] VR 526.

Appeals
These were appeals by Amar Jit Singh and Johannes Hendrikus Petres Meeuwsen
e against their convictions on 28th March 1972 at Ipswich Crown Court before his Honour Judge Richards and a jury. The appellant Singh was convicted of carrying out arrangements for securing or facilitating the entry into the United Kingdom of illegal entrants, contrary to s 25 (1) of the Immigration Act 1971 (count 2), and the appellant Meeuwsen of conspiracy to facilitate the entry into the United Kingdom of illegal entrants (count 1) and of carrying out arrangements for securing or facili-
f tating the entry into the United Kingdom of illegal entrants, contrary to s 25 (1) of the 1971 Act (count 3). The appellant Singh was sentenced to six months' imprisonment suspended for 18 months and fined £100, and the appellant Meeuwsen was sentenced to 12 months' imprisonment concurrent on each count and fined £500. They both appealed pursuant to a certificate of the trial judge under s 2 (1) of the Criminal Appeal Act 1968, which, so far as material, was in the following terms:
g   '1. Whether I was right in holding that the offence created by s 25 (1) of the
    Immigration Act 1971 of being knowingly concerned in making or carrying out
    arrangements for securing or facilitating the entry into the United Kingdom
    of anyone whom he knows or has reasonable cause of believing to be an illegal
    entrant may be committed by actions of the accused performed either prior to
    or subsequently to the time and place of disembarkation of illegal entrants as
h   defined by s 11 (1) of the 1971 Act . . .'

The facts are set out in the judgment of the court.

Sir Dingle Foot QC and *S T D Rafique* for the appellant Singh.
J F F Platts-Mills QC and *S Kadri* for the appellant Meeuwsen.
J C C Blofeld for the Crown.

j   *Cur adv vult*

---

a Section 25 (1), so far as material, provides: "Any person knowingly concerned in making or carrying out arrangements for securing or facilitating the entry to the United Kingdom of anyone whom he knows or has reasonable cause for believing to be an illegal entrant shall be guilty of an offence . . .'
b Section 11 (1) is set out at p 125 e and f, post

20th October. **LAWTON LJ** read the following judgment of the court. These *a*
appellants, Amar Jit Singh and Johannes Hendrikus Petres Meeuwsen, on 28th
March 1972, after a trial before his Honour Judge Richards and a jury, were convicted
as follows: the appellant Singh of carrying out arrangements for securing or facilitating the entry into the United Kingdom of illegal entrants, contrary to s 25 (1) of
the Immigration Act 1971; the appellant Meeuwsen of a similar offence and of conspiring to carry out arrangements to facilitate the entry into the United Kingdom of *b*
illegal entrants. The appellant Singh had been charged with but acquitted of conspiracy. He was sentenced to six months' imprisonment suspended for 18 months
and fined £100. The appellant Meeuwsen was sentenced to 12 months' imprisonment and fined £500. Both appeal against conviction on the certificate of the trial
judge. They also apply for leave to appeal against sentence but these applications
were ineffective as no grounds were given.

Both appellants submitted that the judge misconstrued s 25 (1) of the Immigration *c*
Act 1971 in holding and directing the jury that an offence of being knowingly concerned in carrying out arrangements for securing or facilitating entry into the United
Kingdom of anyone whom the accused knows or has reasonable cause for believing to
be an illegal entrant may be committed if he does acts either prior to or subsequently
to the time and place of disembarkation of illegal entrants as defined by s 11 (1) *d*
of the same Act. Put in more simple terms, both appellants submitted that on the
true construction of the Act they ought not to have been found guilty because what
was alleged against them had been done after the illegal entrants had landed and
passed beyond the part of the port of Felixstowe which was under the control of the
immigration and customs authorities, in other words after they had entered into
the United Kingdom. In addition both appellants sought to rely on alleged matters
of misdirection which were not mentioned in the judge's certificate. *e*

The evidence which was put before the court established the following facts.
One or more persons in Holland arranged for 12 Asians, who had no leave to enter
the United Kingdom, to be hidden in two empty boilers which were being shipped
from Rotterdam to Felixstowe on a ferry. The plot was put into operation and the
ferry docked at Felixstowe at about 8 am on 3rd December 1971. The trailer on which *f*
the boilers had been carried was driven off the ferry; it passed through the customs
not later than about 12 noon and was parked in an enclosed trailer park to await
collection before being delivered forward. It was accepted by the Crown that this
trailer park was not a part of the port which was under the control of the immigration
authorities. The next day between 5 and 6 pm a number of Asians were seen crouching under the trailer. They, together with a few who had moved away from the
trailer, were taken into custody as illegal entrants. Later that night the appellant *g*
Meeuwsen came to the dock gatehouse. He was carrying a heavy spanner in his
pocket. He told a security officer there that he was looking for a ship to take him to
Holland. About two hours later he was arrested and was found to be in possession of
a torch and a large wrench. At about the same time the appellant Singh and another
man, who was tried on the same charge as the appellant Singh but acquitted, were
arrested in Ipswich. Both appellants made statements to the police and in them they *h*
each admitted that they had travelled to Felixstowe on 4th December 1971 in a convoy
of three motor cars. In both his statement and his evidence the appellant Singh
admitted that he knew that his brother was going to come to the United Kingdom
and the circumstances in which he came to know this, as he recounted them, were
such that he must have known that his brother's entry into the United Kingdom
was going to be illegal. His explanation for going to Felixstowe on 4th December *j*
1971 was that a man named Mohnder Singh, who had been active in arranging for
his brother to come to the United Kingdom illegally, had threatened that if he did
not pay him £200 his brother would be killed. Under this threat and in fear for his
brother's life he had paid money and done as he was told by Mohnder Singh. His
account of what had happened was the basis for the defence of duress which had to

a be dealt with by the judge in his summing-up and it was submitted that he had mis-directed the jury about it. The appellant Meeuwsen's defence was that he was the innocent victim of a blackmailer called Scheier. According to both his statement and his evidence, he was blackmailed in Holland because of some marital infidelity into doing what he was asked by Scheier; and what Scheier asked him to do was to go to England to collect a motor car and bring it back to Holland. He was given

b some money and Mohnder Singh's address in Southall. He did as he was told. He met Mohnder Singh and went with him and others to Felixstowe. He thought he was going there to collect a motor car; but when he got there he was given a torch, a spanner and a piece of paper showing where the trailer with its load of boilers was to be found. Then, and for the first time, he was told that he was to open the boilers and let the people in them out. He refused, so he said, to do anything of the kind

c and left Mohnder Singh and the others. When arrested he was waiting for a ship to take him back to Holland.

There was ample evidence before the jury to justify their finding (as they clearly did) that these appellants had gone to Felixstowe together for the purpose of helping on their way Asians who had been hidden in the boilers. It was, however, the con-tention of the appellants that once the illegal entrants had crossed the 'state line', to

d adopt words used by counsel for the appellant Meeuwsen, they had effected entry into the United Kingdom so that anything arranged to be done on the inland side of that line could not in law be deemed to have been done for the purpose of securing or facilitating entry. This resulted, so it was submitted, from s 11 (1) of the Immigration Act 1971 which is in these terms:

e   'A person arriving in the United Kingdom by ship or aircraft shall for the purposes of this Act be deemed not to enter the United Kingdom unless and until he disembarks, and on disembarkation at a port shall further be deemed not to enter the United Kingdom so long as he remains in such area (if any) at the port as may be approved for this purpose by an immigration officer; and a person who has not otherwise entered the United Kingdom shall be deemed

f   not to do so as long as he is detained, or temporarily admitted or released while liable to detention, under the powers conferred by Schedule 2 to this Act.'

We do not agree.

The Immigration Act 1971 is in four parts. Part I is concerned with the regulation of entry into and stay in the United Kingdom; Part II with appeals by those refused leave to enter the United Kingdom and those who have been made the subject of

g either deportation orders or removal directions; Part IV with various supplementary matters; and Part III, which is in question in this case, with criminal proceedings against those who commit the offences created by the Act for the purposes of safe-guarding the regulation and control system set up by, and under, Part I. Section 24 defines the offences which can be committed by any one entering the United King-dom illegally; s 25 defines the offences which can be committed by those who help

h illegal entrants. The help may come in two ways: the illegal entrant may be given help to get into the United Kingdom or he may be helped after he has arrived here. Section 25 (1) was intended to deal with the first kind of help; s 25 (2) with the second; but they are not mutually exclusive. The help to get in may be, and often is, con-tinued without any break long after the illegal entry has been effected. There may be no dividing line between helping to effect entry and helping by way of harbouring.

j This seems to have been recognised by the words with which s 25 (2) starts, i e 'Without prejudice to subsection (1) above...' The offence created by s 25 (1) is defined in wide terms and the words used are in common use. The words 'the entry into the United Kingdom' must be construed in their context and not by them-selves. Now those who are minded to enter the United Kingdom illegally have no wish to be discovered as soon as they disembark. Effective arrangements for an illegal entry would be likely to include plans for getting the entrant away as quickly *a* as possible from the point of disembarkation. Those who made or carried out such plans would be facilitating entry into the United Kingdom. In this case there was evidence that both appellants were doing just this. In our judgment the trial judge was right to direct the jury as he did. Further, s 11 (1), which comes in the regulating part of the Act, has no bearing on s 25 (1). It is concerned with what is deemed *not* to be entry; and one of its objects may well have been to take out of *b* the administrative ambit of Part I of the Act that section of the travelling public which is in transit to some other country.

We turn now to the other alleged misdirections. Counsel on behalf of the appellant Singh submitted first that the trial judge had misdirected the jury as to what was entailed in duress, secondly that he had suggested that some words used by the appellant Singh could bear a meaning which they could not and, thirdly, that the appellant Singh had had an opportunity of averting the threat to kill which he had not had. *c* In our judgment there is nothing in any of these points. The trial judge directed the jury fully and correctly as to what constitutes duress. He pointed out that the essence of duress was the making of a threat either to kill or to do grievous bodily harm, and that if there was no threat, merely a gloomy prediction, or the threat had been rendered ineffective by some other action (reporting a threat to the police is an *d* obvious way of making it ineffective) then no question of duress arose. We can see nothing wrong in what he said.

The submission on duress which counsel for the appellant Meeuwsen made was bold but wrong. He asked us to say that a man who commits a crime at the request of a blackmailer whom he fears can plead duress. He cannot. Duress arises from threats of violence, not exposure.

There was no misdirection on any material point. For these reasons the appeals *e* were dismissed.

Appeals dismissed. The court certified under s 33 (2) of the Criminal Appeal Act 1968 that a point of law of public general importance was involved, namely, whether the offence created by s 25 (1) of the Immigration Act 1971 of being knowingly concerned in carrying out arrangements for facilitating entry into the United Kingdom of anyone whom he knows or has reasonable cause for believing to be an illegal entrant may be committed by actions of the accused performed after the time of disembarkation of an illegal entrant, but refused leave to appeal to the House of Lords.

5th December 1972. The appeal committee refused leave to appeal to the House of Lords.

Solicitors: *S A Rafique*, Southall (for the appellant Singh); *Michael Sears & Co* (for the appellant Meeuwsen); *Director of Public Prosecutions*.

N P Metcalfe Esq   Barrister.

Saint and another v Jenner and others

COURT OF APPEAL, CIVIL DIVISION
RUSSELL, EDMUND DAVIES AND STAMP LJJ
25th, 26th JULY, 31st OCTOBER 1972

Easement – Disturbance – Remedy – Undertaking by servient tenant – Enforcement against servient tenant's successor – Adoption of disturbance – Action for nuisance – Right of way – Servient tenant placing ramps on way to slow down vehicles – Potholes developing at end of ramps resulting in interference with plaintiff's right of way – Undertaking by servient tenant to remake and maintain way and ramps so as to protect plaintiff's enjoyment of right of way – Adequacy of undertaking – Enforcement against servient tenant's successor – Failure of successor to comply with undertaking amounting to adoption of nuisance.

The plaintiff was the lessee of a farm where he carried on business as a nurseryman. The defendants owned the adjoining property where they had a house and riding school. The plaintiff had a right of way along a lane which led from the public highway over the defendants' land. The lane served as access both to the plaintiff's farm and to the defendants' premises. When the defendants purchased their property in 1963 the lane was nothing more than a cart track with ruts and was overgrown. In 1964 the defendants metalled the roadway and put up a five mile an hour sign at the entrance to the roadway. From then onwards they had to complain about the speed at which vehicles went along the road. When the defendants established their riding stables in 1966 the road became more dangerous because of the horses emerging from the defendants' premises and using the road. In 1968 the defendants constructed four ramps on the roadway to slow down the speed of the vehicles. In time the condition of the road changed and potholes developed at the end of some of the ramps, with the result that the height of the ramps in relation to the bottom of the potholes had become so great as to make the ramps a substantial interference with the enjoyment of the right of way of the plaintiff. The plaintiff therefore sought an order for the removal of the ramps. The county court judge refused the order on the defendants' undertaking to remake and maintain the roadway and the ramps thereon. The plaintiff appealed contending that once the defendants had sold their property the plaintiff would not be able to enforce the undertaking against the defendants' successors in title, since a servient successor could not be made liable in law for maintaining on his land a ramp which because of the decline (by potholing or otherwise) of the adjacent roadway, had become a substantial interference with the dominant owner's right of way.

Held – The appeal would be dismissed. There was no difference in point of remedy between an ordinary case of nuisance and disturbance of an easement. If the defendants' successor allowed the ramps, by a decline of the road surface, to become a disturbance of the plaintiff's right of way, he would be liable to the plaintiff since, by keeping ramps for his own benefit and convenience but failing to maintain the road surface, he would be adopting the disturbance. It followed that, since the plaintiff would have an adequate remedy against the defendants' successors, the county court judge was entitled not to order the removal of the ramps (see p 131 f to h, post).

Notes
For liability for private nuisance and continuance or adoption of nuisance, see 28 Halsbury's Laws (3rd Edn) 155-157, paras 217, 218, and for cases on the subject, see 36 Digest (Repl) 314-317, 606-633.

For interference with easements generally, see 12 Halsbury's Laws (3rd Edn) 615, para 1336.

Case referred to in judgment
Sedleigh-Denfield v O'Callagan [1940] 3 All ER 349, [1940] AC 880, 164 LT 72; sub nom

Sedleigh-Denfield v St Joseph's Society for Foreign Missions, 109 LJKB 893, HL, 36 Digest (Repl) 316, 629.

Appeal

This was an appeal by the first plaintiff, Stanley Oliver Saint, against that part of the order of his Honour Judge Granville-Smith given at Edmonton County Court on 25th January 1972 refusing to grant the first plaintiff and the second plaintiff, William Derek Beech, an injunction for the removal of certain ramps placed on a roadway over which the plaintiffs had a right of way, on the defendants, Ronald Victor Jenner, Rene Gertrude Elsie Jenner and Woodlands Stables Ltd, undertaking to remake and maintain the driveway and ramps thereon. The second plaintiff did not appeal.

At all material times the first plaintiff was the tenant and the second plaintiff the freeholder of the farm and premises at Sewardstone Road, Chingford, Essex, known as Woodlands Farm, together with a right of way for the owners thereof and all persons authorised by them with or without vehicles and for all purposes and at all times to pass and repass over and along a 200 yards driveway leading from the farm to the public highway, Sewardstone Road. The first plaintiff carried on the trade or business of nurseryman at the farm. In 1953 the first two defendants, Mr and Mrs Jenner, purchased the driveway and the property adjoining the plaintiffs' farm known as Woodlands, Sewardstone Road. At that time the lane was nothing more than a cart track with ruts and was overgrown. In 1963 Mr and Mrs Jenner built a house on their land. In 1964 they metalled the driveway at a cost of £1,500 and put up a five mile an hour sign. From then onwards they had to complain of the speed at which vehicles went along the land. In 1966 they built a stable block. In 1968 they caused four concrete ramps to be placed on the driveway. On or about 23rd April 1970 they conveyed part of the driveway together with certain other land to the third defendant, a company which they owned and controlled. The driveway served as access both to the plaintiffs' farm and to the defendants' house and riding school. The plaintiffs claimed that the ramps constituted an obstruction of the driveway and interfered with the exercise by them of their right of way and that as a result of the obstruction they had suffered damage and tradesmen and customers had been deterred from using the driveway and the first plaintiff's trade and business had suffered accordingly. They therefore claimed (1) an order that the defendants remove the ramps; (2) an injunction restraining the defendants by themselves their servants or agents or otherwise howsoever from obstructing the driveway or interfering with the exercise by the plaintiffs and each of them of the right of way, and (3) damages for nuisance. The county court judge ordered that there be no order for an injunction on all the defendants undertaking within three months (i) to remake and thereafter to maintain the lane surface to a maximum of ten feet from the centre of the first three ramps so as to secure that the level of the surface as remade and maintained was not more than four inches below the highest point of each ramp; (ii) thereafter to maintain the three ramps at a height of not more than four inches above the lane surface at a minimum overall breadth of five feet six inches. It was further ordered that the defendants should pay the first plaintiff £75 damages.

By his notice of appeal the first plaintiff sought an order that the part of the judge's order whereby it was ordered, inter alia, that there be no order for an injunction be set aside and so much of the judgment as adjudged that the ramps as originally constructed did not constitute a substantial interference with the plaintiffs' right of way over the driveway, be reversed and that it be ordered (i) that the defendants remove from the driveway the first three ramps; and (ii) that the defendants be restrained whether by themselves their servants or agents or otherwise howsoever from placing or constructing on the driveway any ramps or other obstacles so as to cause any substantial interference with the plaintiffs' right of way over the

a driveway. The grounds of appeal were as follows: (i) on the question whether the ramps as originally constructed constituted a substantial interference with the right of way the judge misdirected himself in law in taking into account (a) the motives of the defendants in constructing the ramps and (b) whether the defendants acted reasonably in so doing; (ii) the judge, having found as a fact that two of the ramps were causing substantial interference with the right of way, had no

b evidence before him to justify his finding that the ramps as originally constructed would not have caused substantial interference therewith; (iii) the judge ought to have found that the ramps at a distance of 30 yards apart or thereabouts were excessive in number and constituted a substantial interference with the right of way; (iv) the judge ought to have found on the evidence before him of damage caused by the ramps to vehicles being driven thereover and of grounding by vehicles on the

c top of the ramps while being driven thereover that the ramps as originally constructed caused substantial interference with the right of way; (v) the undertakings extracted by the judge from the defendants did not adequately protect the plaintiffs in that (a) the undertakings would not bind any successors in title of the defendants to the driveway; (b) the issue whether the ramps as originally constructed, or re-made and maintained in accordance with the undertakings, constituted an actionable

d nuisance would be res judicata and could not be raised by the plaintiffs against such successors in title; and (c) no obligation could be placed on such successors in title to maintain the ramps or any part of the driveway; and accordingly the judge, having found that the second and third ramps constituted a substantial interference with the right of way ought to have granted an injunction restraining the defendants from interfering by the ramps or otherwise with the right of way and to have made

e an order that the ramps be removed from the driveway or orders to a like effect; (vi) the judge ought, on the evidence before him, to have made the mandatory order and granted the injunction sought.

Richard Scott for the first plaintiff.
T W Preston for the defendants.

Cur adv vult

f 31st October. **STAMP LJ** read the following judgment of the court at the invitation of Russell LJ. This is an appeal by the first plaintiff from an order of his Honour Judge Granville-Smith made on 25th January 1972 in the Edmonton County Court. In the action the plaintiffs, who are respectively the lessee and freeholder of a certain farm, sought an order for the removal of some ramps which the defendants had

g placed on a roadway over which the plaintiffs have a right of way, and damages. By the order under appeal, the learned county court judge awarded the first plaintiff £75 damages, but, on the defendants giving certain undertakings referred to hereafter, refused an order for the removal of the ramps. It is against this refusal that the first plaintiff appeals.

The action is concerned with a lane in the parish of Waltham Holy Cross, in Essex,

h leading from the public highway, Sewardstone Road, over and along the edge of the defendant company's land known as The Woodlands to the farm known as Woodlands Farm. The lane is about 200 yards long and serves as access as well to Woodlands Farm, where the first plaintiff, who is its tenant, carries on business as a nurseryman, as to the defendant company's premises where they have a house and riding school. The lane has a bend and, because it is bounded on the defendants' side by a wall

j with several gaps in it through which vehicles, horses and people emerge, it is common ground that it is dangerous for vehicles to go along it otherwise than very slowly.

The second plaintiff owns the freehold of the farm, and it is common ground that he and his tenants have a right of way for all purposes, in common with the owners of Woodlands and all persons authorised by them, over the lane. The lane was formerly nothing more than a cart track. It had ruts and was overgrown. So bad

was the surface that in very wet weather vehicles were in general left at the entrance   a
of the lane and not taken up it. Then in 1964 the first defendant, Mr Jenner, who, together with Mrs Jenner, owns and controls the defendant company, metalled the
road at a cost of some £1,500. At the same time he put up a five mile an hour sign
at the entrance to the road. From then onwards Mr and Mrs Jenner had to complain
at the speed at which vehicles went along the lane. A Mr Mortimer who kept horses
at the farm was, according to the evidence of Mr Jenner, a particular offender in this   b
regard. At the time he metalled the road, Mr Jenner had not got the establishment
of riding stables in mind; but in 1966 he built a stable yard on the defendant company's premises. With horses emerging from the defendants' premises and using
the road, it became more dangerous. There was an episode when Mr Jenner and
three others were riding and, according to Mr Jenner's evidence, the first
plaintiff came along the lane on his moped at an excessive speed and Mr Jenner was   c
thrown from his frightened horse. Mrs Jenner, whose evidence the learned county
court judge accepted, was on another occasion leading a horse into the lane from the
stable yard when a car driven at some 30 mph went across her path. She sustained
fright and was poorly for several days and, although the driver of the car apologised,
one of the plaintiffs who was present when she complained merely grinned.

In the circumstances, Mr Jenner—and we know not what other steps, except the   d
digging out of gullies, one can take to prevent vehicles being driven along a private
road at excessive speed—determined to construct ramps on the roadway. They were
placed at four points and were designed to secure that the speed of vehicles at the
points of particular danger was reduced almost to a walking pace. Conspicuous
warning notices of the existence of each ramp were put up on each side of each ramp
and the position of each ramp was marked by a post at the side of the road. The   e
learned county court judge, after hearing the evidence and inspecting the roadway,
came to the clear conclusion that it was reasonable to have ramps and that there
should be something to diminish the speed of cars. We are unable to conclude
that there was not evidence on which he could properly so find.

Now, of course, if ramps are to achieve their purpose, they must be so constructed
as to induce in the mind of the driver of a vehicle the fear that if he drives over them   f
too fast, there will be a scraping of, and perhaps damage to, the bottom of the vehicle;
and there was evidence before the judge of some such scraping and damage. The
first time the first plaintiff went over the ramps he fell off his moped.

There was, it appears, some mistake on the part of the foreman when the ramps
were first constructed, but this was remedied and the learned judge found that as
originally planned and laid down the ramps were not a substantial interference with   g
the right of way. In this connection it is to be observed that in deciding what is a
substantial interference with the dominant owner's reasonable user of a right of way,
all the circumstances must be considered, including the rights of other persons
entitled to use the way: here the rights of the defendants in connection with their
property and riding activities; and there was, in our judgment, evidence on which the
judge could properly hold, as he did, that the ramps as originally planned and   h
constructed did not constitute a substantial interference.

By the time the proceedings were launched, the situation had, however, changed.
The condition of the road had changed and potholes had developed at the ends of
some of the ramps, with the result that the height of the ramps in relation to the
bottom of the potholes had, as the learned judge in effect found, become so great
as to make these ramps a substantial interference with the enjoyment of the right of   j
way by the plaintiffs. Indeed, Mr Jenner conceded that the ramps needed rectification and asserted that this would have been done by the time the case was heard but
for the advice which he had received. Coming to the conclusion that the first plaintiff had suffered damage to his business because customers had been deterred from
coming up the lane, the judge awarded him £75 damages. He, however, refused
the plaintiffs an injunction on the defendants' undertakings, in relation to the three

a   ramps which were causing the trouble, first to remake and maintain the lane surface up to a maximum of ten feet from the centre of each ramp so that the lane surface was not more than four inches below the highest point of each ramp, and second to maintain the ramps at a height of not more than four inches above lane surface at a minimum overall breadth of five feet six inches. He no doubt took the view that by the effect of compliance with these undertakings a situation would be reached in

b   which the existence of the ramps would cease to constitute a substantial interference with the plaintiffs' right of way and, in our judgment, he was, on the evidence to which we have been referred, fully entitled to come to that conclusion.

It is the first plaintiff's submission on this appeal that even if the judge was correct in his finding—a finding which, in our judgment, cannot be successfully challenged— that the ramps as originally planned (and after compliance with the undertakings) would not be a substantial interference with the plaintiffs' right of way in common

c   with the defendant company and their assigns and all other persons authorised by them, yet a mandatory order ought to have been granted. In support of this submission it was urged that it has been demonstrated that in due course the forma- tion of potholes or other lowering of the road surface will lead to a situation in which the ramps will again constitute a substantial interference with the plaintiffs' rights;

d   and although, so that argument runs, the defendants, while they retained the land, could be required by the effect of their undertakings to remedy the situation so arising, the plaintiffs would have no remedy on the undertakings against a successor in title of the defendant company. It was common ground in this connection that ordinarily a servient owner cannot be required to carry out work necessary to make a road fit for the use of the owner of the dominant tenement, and it was submitted

e   that if the ramps were not now altogether removed the plaintiffs, if that situa- tion arose after the defendant company had parted with the servient tenement, would have no remedy at all.

Basic to these arguments is the submission that a servient successor could not be made liable in law for maintaining on his land a ramp which, because of the decline (by potholing or otherwise) of the adjacent roadway, had become a substantial

f   interference with the dominant owner's right of way; that is to say, that that suc- cessor could not be required to remove the ramp if he was not prepared to readapt the height relationship between the top of the ramp and the adjacent road level. We do not think that this submission is well founded. We see no reason in principle why there should be any relevant distinction in point of remedy between an ordinary case of nuisance and disturbance of an easement, frequently referred to as a nuisance:

g   see the general statement in Gale on Easements[1]. If in the occupation of a servient successor that which had not been a disturbance (i e the ramps) became a disturbance (by decline of the road surface), surely by taking no steps but by keeping the ramps for his own benefit and convenience, the servient successor is squarely within *Sedleigh- Denfield v O'Callagan*[2], as adopting the nuisance or disturbance.

Consequently, since the judge was, in our judgment, correct in concluding that

h   the disturbance would be cured by the methods suggested, there was no obligation on him to order the removal of the ramps; and we accordingly dismiss the appeal.

Appeal dismissed.

Solicitors: *H B Wedlake, Saint & Co* (for the first plaintiff); *Lewis, Foskett & Co* (for the

j   defendants.

Mary Rose Plummer   Barrister.

---

1   14th Edn (1972), p 351
2   [1940] 3 All ER 349, [1940] AC 880

Re Colebrook's Conveyances
Taylor v Taylor and another

CHANCERY DIVISION
GRAHAM J
10th MAY 1972

Deed – Rectification – Conveyance – Land conveyed to father and son as joint tenants – Death of son – Father as surviving joint tenant accountable for estate duty in respect of son's share of land – Evidence that parties had intended father and son should take as tenants in common – Whether court should order rectification of conveyance – Whether possible tax advantage bar to relief.

By three conveyances made in 1954 and 1955 farmland was conveyed to the plaintiff and his son as joint tenants. In 1962 the son died and the land devolved on the plaintiff as the surviving joint tenant. He thereupon became accountable to the Revenue for estate duty in respect of his son's share in the land. The plaintiff contended however that the conveyances did not accurately represent the agreement of the parties at the date when they were executed and he asked the court to rectify the three conveyances to give effect to the true intention of the parties by substituting the words 'tenants in common' for the words 'joint tenants'.

Held – The court would order the rectification of the conveyances in the manner sought because (i) on the evidence it was clear that the parties had intended that the farmland should be conveyed to the plaintiff and his son as tenants in common, so that each half share of the land would pass on death to their respective estates and the right of survivorship would not apply (see p 133 f, post); and (ii) in such circumstances it was no bar to relief that rectification would, or might, incidentally give one of the parties a tax advantage (see p 134 b, post).

Whiteside v Whiteside [1949] 2 All ER 913 distinguished.

Notes

For rectification, see 26 Halsbury's Laws (3rd Edn) 914-921, paras 1698-1710, and for cases on the subject, see 35 Digest (Repl) 135-145, *291-362.*

Case referred to in judgment

Whiteside v Whiteside [1949] 2 All ER 913, [1950] Ch 65, 66 (pt 1) TLR 126, CA; *affg* [1949] 1 All ER 755, [1949] Ch 448, 27 (2) Digest (Reissue) 846, 6736.

Ajourned summons

By this summons dated 30th September 1970 the plaintiff, David Taylor, sought rectification of three conveyances dated respectively 2nd July 1954, 22nd April 1955 and 22nd April 1955, all made between Harold John Colebrook of the one part and the plaintiff, David Taylor, and his son, Henry Alfred Taylor, of the other part, whereby farmland near Chalfont St Giles, Buckinghamshire, was conveyed to the plaintiff and his son as joint tenants. The son died in December 1962 and the land devolved on the plaintiff by right of survivorship. The plaintiff asked the court to rectify the three conveyances by substituting the words 'tenants in common' for the words 'joint tenants' in the conveyances. The son's personal representatives, Winifred Margaret Taylor and David George Evans, were made defendants. The facts are set out in the judgment.

James Leckie for the plaintiff.
J L Jopling for the defendants.

a **GRAHAM J.** By this summons the plaintiff asks for rectification of three conveyances of farmland near Chalfont St Giles. The conveyances were made between a vendor, Harold John Colebrook, of the one part and the plaintiff and his son, Henry Alfred Taylor, of the other part. The conveyances are dated some 18 years ago and conveyed the land to the plaintiff and his son as joint tenants. The son died in December 1962 and on his death the effect of the conveyances was, therefore, that the

b land devolved on the plaintiff by the right of survivorship.

The plaintiff asks the court to rectify the three conveyances by substituting the words 'tenants in common' for the words 'joint tenants' in the conveyances, so that the effect of the conveyances will be that the plaintiff and his son were always tenants in common of the land in question. This would have the effect that the plaintiff, in the events which have happened, never became the owner of his son's half share

c of the land and would result in the plaintiff not being, as he now is, with the conveyances in their present form, the person accountable to the Revenue for estate duty in respect of his son's share in the land. Furthermore, if the plaintiff never became the owner of his son's half share of the land, there would be no question of any need, if he felt so inclined, for the plaintiff to make a gift to his son's estate with consequent possible liability to duty if the plaintiff, now over 80, died within seven years of the

d gift. There seem to me to be several questions which I have to decide.

First, does the evidence show that the intention was that the conveyances should have conveyed the land to the purchasers as tenants in common rather than as joint tenants, and in considering this question ought the court to hear oral evidence or is it sufficient to try the matter on affidavit? As to this, I do not think, having read the evidence carefully, that it would be advanced at all by cross-examination. It is,

e in my judgment, clear that the parties, now some 18 years after the event, only have a vague recollection as to what actually happened when the conveyances were drafted and signed, and cross-examination on this aspect of the matter would be unlikely to elucidate the position at all. On the other hand, it seems quite clear, and I so find, that the plaintiff and his son intended that each half share of the land in question should pass on death to their respective estates and that the right of survivorship

f should not apply. On the evidence, therefore, the conveyances here do not accurately represent the agreement of the parties at the date when they were executed, and in this respect, in my judgment, the evidence is quite strong enough to discharge the heavy burden of proof which is required in such cases. In the words of Mr Wolfe in *Whiteside v Whiteside*[1], modified by Sir Raymond Evershed MR, each party here (ie the plaintiff and his son) had the right against the other to have the document reformed in such a way that it would place each in the same position vis-à-vis each

g other as they intended.

Prima facie, therefore, it seems to me that this is a case where the court should grant an order for rectification unless it is prevented from doing so by, for example, such considerations as were held to be present in the *Whiteside*[2] case. It was strongly argued by counsel for the plaintiff, an argument concurred in by counsel for the defendants, that the present case is clearly distinguishable from

h *Whiteside*[2]. Amongst other things in the *Whiteside* case[2] the husband had executed a supplemental deed which put an end to all possible dispute between the parties even if the plaintiff ever had had a cause of action against his wife. It was argued in that case that the only effect of refusing rectification would be to deprive the plaintiff of a benefit from the point of view of payment of surtax, but, as Cohen LJ pointed out[3], there was no evidence that it was the common intention to secure him

j that benefit. In fact, the evidence showed that the plaintiff himself had by his solicitors altered the original draft agreement, which, by its then wording, would have

1 [1949] 2 All ER 913 at 917, 918, [1950] Ch 65 at 75, 76
2 [1949] 2 All ER 913, [1950] Ch 65
3 [1949] 2 All ER at 918, [1950] Ch at 77

given him a surtax benefit, to the form ultimately adopted which deprived him of such benefit.

As I read the *Whiteside* case[1], it may well be an authority for saying that if the only result of the rectification of an error which was due to the plaintiff himself, will be to give the plaintiff a tax advantage, then that may well be a good reason for refusing to exercise the equitable jurisdiction.   Where, on the other hand, the document is found not to carry out the true intention of the parties and rectification, whilst enabling that intention to be carried out, incidentally gives, or may give, one of the parties a tax advantage, the case is not an authority for saying that such presence, or possibility of such tax advantage, is a bar to relief.

The present case falls, to my mind, in the second category and not the first. Here, in fact, the plaintiff, contrary to his intention, has, by the conveyances, become owner of the whole of the land in question and is also, in consequence, under a larger liability for duty than he otherwise would have been. Except by rectification, he cannot divest himself of such liability. In fact, as I understand it, duty has been paid out of the son's estate in respect of his half share in the land and his estate has in fact received half of the rents of the property since his death. That, of course, does not accord with the position of the parties as joint tenants. There is here, says counsel for the defendants, a position in which the conveyances have caused a muddle which has the result that there are clearly left issues between the parties which can only be resolved by a rectification order. This is quite different, he says, from the position in the *Whiteside* case[1].   Both the plaintiff and defendants are, therefore, here contending that a rectification order should be made.

It should be stated that, by a letter dated 12th July 1971, the Inland Revenue Estate Duty Office informed the parties' solicitors as follows:

'I am instructed to inform you that the Board do not wish to be joined in the rectification proceedings, and that they will regard themselves as bound by the decision of the court provided that its attention is properly drawn to *Whiteside v Whiteside*[2] and the court considers that there is a real issue before it on which a decision is given.'

It is right that I should say that the duty of bringing the *Whiteside* case[1] to the attention of the court has been fully and faithfully discharged by counsel for the plaintiff. I need only add that, for the reasons I have given, in my judgment the *Whiteside* case[1] does not cover the position in the present case and does not prevent the court here making the order for rectification asked for. This I, therefore, propose to do.

Order accordingly.

Solicitors: *Walter C Hetherington & Co*, Gerrards Cross (for all parties).

Mary Rose Plummer   Barrister.

1 [1949] 2 All ER 913, [1950] Ch 65
2 [1949] 1 All ER 755, [1949] Ch 448; *on appeal* [1949] 2 All ER 913, [1950] Ch 65

Re NFU Development Trust Ltd

CHANCERY DIVISION
BRIGHTMAN J
17th, 18th, 28th JULY 1972

Company – Scheme of arrangement – Compromise with creditors or members – Compromise or arrangement – Meaning – Element of accommodation on both sides – Company limited by guarantee having no share capital – Large membership – Members having very limited rights – Scheme whereby vast majority of members deprived of membership – Whether scheme qualifying as a 'compromise or arrangement' – Companies Act 1948, s 206 (1), (2).

Company – Scheme of arrangement – Compromise with creditors or members – Meeting – Majority in number representing three-fourths in value of creditors or members present and voting – Company limited by guarantee having no share capital – Members liable to contribute 5p if assets deficient – Board having power to distribute assets among members in such proportions as they might determine – Right of membership non-transferable and ceasing on death – Calculation of majority of three-fourths in value of members – Companies Act 1948, s 206 (2).

The NFU Development Trust Ltd was a company limited by guarantee without a share capital, its objects being generally to further, encourage and assist the farming community and in particular farmers engaged in the production of fatstock. The NFU Development Co Ltd was a member of the company. In addition there were about 94,000 other members all of whom were farmers, farming companies or retired farmers. The company's assets exceeded £3 million and its liabilities were less than £25,000. Members were elected by the board. Their only obligation was to pay an entrance fee of 25p and to contribute 5p should the company's assets be deficient. The articles provided that no dividends should be paid to members but that, on a winding-up, surplus assets would be divided among members in such proportion as the board might determine and in default of such determination equally between the members. Members had the right to elect members of nine area 'electoral colleges' each of which appointed a member of the board, other members of the board being appointed by the NFU Development Co Ltd and the farmers' unions. Every member had a right to vote at a general meeting of the company save that on a resolution to alter the memorandum or articles, to wind up the company or to remove or appoint a director, the NFU Development Co Ltd had three times the number of votes cast by all other members who voted. In order to reduce the expenses of administration the board proposed a scheme reducing the membership of the company to seven, one of the seven being the NFU Development Co Ltd, and depriving all other members of their membership. At the meeting directed by the court 1,439 votes were cast, seven in person and the remainder by proxy. 1,211 votes were cast in favour of the scheme and 228 against, a majority of almost 85 per cent. On a petition to sanction the scheme under s 206[a] of the

---

a Section 206, so far as material, provides:
   '(1) Where a compromise or arrangement is proposed between a company and its creditors or any class of them or between the company and its members or any class of them, the court may, on the application in a summary way of the company or of any creditor or member of the company . . . order a meeting of the creditors or class of creditors, or of the members of the company or class of members, as the case may be, to be summoned in such manner as the court directs.
   '(2) If a majority in number representing three fourths in value of the creditors or class of creditors or members or class of members, as the case may be, present and voting either in person or by proxy at the meeting, agree to any compromise or arrangement, the compromise or arrangement shall, if sanctioned by the court, be binding on all the creditors or the class of creditors, or on the members or class of members, as the case may be, and also on the company or . . .'

Companies Act 1948 the objectors contended, inter alia, that, as the company had
no share capital and the right of membership was non-transferable and ceased on
death, it was impossible to ascertain whether a particular majority represented
three-fourths in value of those present and voting as required by s 206 (2) of the 1948
Act.

Held – (i) In a case such as the present where each member had precisely the same
financial stake in the company, every member had in law an identical stake. The
position was therefore the same as if each member owned a single share in the company, with the result that a three-fourths majority of members present and voting
satisfied the requirements of s 206 (2) (see p 139 c and d, post); *Re Albert Life
Assurance Co* (1871) 6 Ch App 381 distinguished.

    (ii) However the scheme would not be sanctioned because the terms of the scheme
were such that it did not qualify as a 'compromise or arrangement' between the
company and its members within s 206 of the 1948 Act. The words 'compromise'
and 'arrangement' implied some element of accommodation on each side and were
not apt to describe a total surrender of the rights of one side. Since the rights of
members were being expropriated without any compensating advantage, it could
not be said that they were entering into a compromise or arrangement with the
company (see p 139 e and p 140 f and g, post); dictum of Bowen LJ in *Re Alabama,
New Orleans, Texas and Pacific Junction Railway Co* [1891] 1 Ch at 243 applied.

Notes
For the sanctioning of compromises and arrangements, see 6 Halsbury's Laws (3rd
Edn) 764, 765, para 1548, and for cases on the subject, see 10 Digest (Repl) 1126-1130,
1133, 1134, 7841-7869, 7884-7895.
    For the Companies Act 1948, s 206, see 5 Halsbury's Statutes (3rd Edn) 274.

Cases referred to in judgment
Alabama, New Orleans, Texas and Pacific Junction Railway Co, Re [1891] 1 Ch 213, 60
    LJCh 221, 64 LT 127, 10 Digest (Repl) 803, 5213.
Albert Life Assurance Co, Re (1871) 6 Ch App 381, 40 LJCh 505, 24 LT 768, 10 Digest
    (Repl) 1139, 7930.

Petition
The NFU Development Trust Ltd ('the company') sought the sanction of the court
to a scheme of arrangement under s 206 of the Companies Act 1948 between the
company and (1) its members other than the National Farmers' Union Development
Co Ltd ('the NFU Development Co') and (2) the NFU Development Co. The scheme
was opposed by five members of the company, R H Mason, J A Forbes, W Elliot, E G
Johnson and R H Wheelock ('the objectors'). The facts are set out in the judgment.

Peter Curry and *E A Davidson* for the company.
D G Rice for the objectors other than Mr Wheelock.
Mr Wheelock appeared in person.

Cur adv vult

28th July. **BRIGHTMAN J** read the following judgment. This is an application
by the NFU Development Trust Ltd for the sanction of the court to a scheme of
arrangement under s 206 of the Companies Act 1948.
    The NFU Development Trust Ltd, which I will call 'the company', was formed
in 1954 under the name of the Fatstock Marketing Corporation Ltd. It is a company
limited by guarantee. It has no share capital. In the event of a winding-up, a
member of the company is liable to contribute 5p should the company's assets be
deficient. Originally the principal object of the company was to buy and sell fatstock. The company was to be a means whereby farmers could keep the wholesale

a   marketing of fatstock in their own hands.   The intention was that the company should purchase livestock from farmers, should undertake the slaughtering, and should then market the meat.   The members of the company were the National Farmers' Union Development Co Ltd, which I will call 'the NFU Development Co', the other six subscribers to the memorandum, and all persons elected to membership by the board of directors.   It was envisaged that the members should be farmers

b   who would sell their fatstock to the company.   The board of directors were entitled to cancel the membership of a farmer whose transactions were small or infrequent. A member paid an entrance fee of 5s but nothing further.   An elected member had no right to vote.   The directors were appointed by the NFU Development Co, the National Farmers' Union (of England and Wales), the National Farmers' Union of Scotland and the Ulster Farmers' Union.   Article 52 provided in effect that no

c   dividends should be paid to members of the company but that the company's money should be applied solely towards its objects, save that on a winding-up the surplus assets of the company should be divided among the members (other than the NFU Development Co) in such proportions as the board should determine, and in default of such determination equally between such members (less 1s for the NFU Development Co).

d   In 1959 new articles of association were adopted.   The main effect was to broaden the basis on which the board of the company were appointed and to give members limited voting rights which they did not previously possess.   The first effect was achieved by dividing England, Wales, Scotland and Northern Ireland into nine areas, establishing an electing body (called an electoral college) for each area, and providing that each electoral college should appoint one director.   The number of directors

e   to be appointed by the three farmers' unions was reduced.   Pig and poultry farming representation was introduced.   There was also introduced a provision that at a general meeting every member should have one vote, save that on a resolution to alter the memorandum or articles or to wind up the company or to remove or appoint a director, the NFU Development Co after seeking the advice of the councils of the three farmers' unions should have three times the number of votes cast by

f   all the other members who voted.
        In 1962 the company ceased trading.   The marketing business of the company was transferred to FMC (Meat) Ltd.   The company acquired shares in a new public company, FMC Ltd, which was a holding company for shares in FMC (Meat) Ltd and in Marsh & Baxter Ltd.   The company changed its name to that which it now bears. It also changed its memorandum of association.   Its first two objects became and are

g   now:

   '(A) To further, encourage and assist the interests and efforts of farmers engaged in the production of fatstock and other live stock of every description and also the farming community and the agricultural industry in general; and to do so by any lawful means including the provision of technical and general education, the establishment of scholarship grants and rewards, the promotion of physical

h   and mental welfare, the diffusion of information and the promotion of research.
   '(B) To establish, administer and contribute to any charitable or benevolent fund from which may be made donations or advances to or for the benefit of individual farmers; and to contribute to or otherwise assist any charitable or benevolent object, institution or undertaking connected with or in the opinion of the Company calculated to benefit farmers or the farming community or the

j   agricultural industry.'

The company adopted new articles, but the constitution of the board of directors and the definition of voting rights were not significantly changed.
    The evidence is that there are about 94,000 members of the company, all of whom (leaving aside the NFU Development Co) are farmers or farming companies or retired farmers.   The company is now wealthy.   It owns more than 35 per cent of

the issued share capital of FMC Ltd. As at April 1972 the value of its shareholding
exceeded £3,000,000. Its liabilities are stated to have been under £25,000. According
to the latest accounts in evidence, its annual income for 1970-71, after deduction of
taxation, was £42,490. It is relevant to see exactly where this income went. In
round figures, £4,000 was expended on directors' fees, and £8,000 on other administrative expenses. Only £8,000 was spent on furthering the objects of the company,
namely, £4,000 to the Pig Health Control Association, £2,700 to the British Farm
Produce Council and £1,400 on marketing research projects. No less than £22,000
was carried forward, and added to the £94,000 brought forward from the previous
year.

The proposed scheme takes the following form. (1) The only members of the
company are to be the NFU Development Co and six persons who are called 'the
New Members'. Five of them are existing directors of the company, according to
the list of directors at the head of the explanatory statement. It is apparent from
the proposed new articles that the so-called new members are and will continue to be
the several nominees of the Council of the National Farmers' Union (of England and
Wales), the Council of the National Farmers' Union of Scotland and the Council of
the Ulster Farmers' Union. (2) All other existing members are to be deprived of
their membership. They forfeit all rights of every description. (3) New articles
are to be adopted.

Under the new articles, the board of the company will consist only of nominees
of the board of the NFU Development Co, and of the councils of the three farmers'
unions. On a winding-up, surplus assets may be distributed to any other similar
body, or will go to charity.

I will deal subsequently with the reasons given by the board of directors of the
company for recommending the approval of this root and branch scheme. Broadly,
the reason is to reduce administrative expenses.

The meeting directed by the court was held on 19th May 1972. 1,439 votes were
cast, seven in person and the remainder by proxy. 1,211 votes were cast in favour
of the scheme, and 228 against. That is a majority in favour of almost 85 per cent.

The petition to sanction the scheme is opposed by five persons. Four of the opposers
are represented by counsel. Three of them are in fact directors of the company,
namely, Mr Mason, Mr Forbes and Mr Elliott, so that this is a scheme on which
the board is divided. The fourth is Mr Johnson, a member but not a director of
the company. The other opposer appeared before me in person. He is Mr
Wheelock, also a member but not a director. Counsel for the objectors made three
submissions. The first two submissions went to jurisdiction, the third to the general
merits of the scheme.

Section 206 of the Companies Act 1948 empowers the court to sanction a scheme of
arrangement proposed between a company and its members if the scheme is agreed
by a majority in number representing three-fourths in value of the members present
and voting in person or by proxy. Counsel's first submission was that as the company
has no share capital, and the right of membership is non-transferable and ceases on
death, it is impossible to ascertain whether a particular majority does or does not
represent three-fourths in value of the members present and voting. Membership
confers no right to receive anything from the company while it is a going concern.
A member receives financial value when and only when the company is placed in
liquidation. The value of each person's membership is impossible to ascertain. It
depends on many imponderables, including in particular the expectation of life
of the member; for a youthful member has more chance of surviving to the date
of liquidation (if any) than an older member; further, on a liquidation the directors
have a power of selection, so that the chance of a particular member receiving anything is incapable of assessment. Such was the argument in support of counsel's
first submission. He referred me to Re Albert Life Assurance Co[1]. In that case the

1 (1871) 6 Ch App 381

a sanction of the court was sought to a scheme for the reconstruction of the Albert Life Assurance Co under the Joint Stock Companies Arrangement Act 1870. That Act enabled the court to bind the creditors of a company in liquidation to an arrangement or compromise agreed by a majority in number representing three-fourths in value of the creditors present at a meeting convened for the purpose. The petition was dismissed, the court holding that it was impossible on the evidence to place an

b ascertained value on the individual claims of the various policy holders as creditors of the company.

I reject counsel's first submission. It appears to me that s 206 (2) of the Companies Act 1948, in referring to 'three fourths in value of the . . . members or class of members' is directing attention to the size of the stake which each member has in the company. The purpose is to prevent a numerical majority with a small stake voting

c a minority with a large stake, e g to prevent 51 members with one share each outvoting 49 members with ten shares each. In a case such as the present where each member has precisely the same financial stake in the company, namely, a right if he survives the liquidation of the company to be considered for a payment at the discretion of the board, and a right to an aliquot share of any assets not distributed pursuant to such discretion, every member has in law an identical stake. The

d position therefore is the same as if each member owned a single share in the company, with the result that a three-quarter majority of votes satisfies the statutory requirements. *Re Albert Life Assurance Co*[1] was quite a different case. The policyholders were creditors of the company for amounts which varied not only by the amounts assured but also by reference to other factors such as the nearness of maturity date and whether the policy was or was not a participating policy. The evidence in

e the case did not establish the values.

Counsel's second submission was that the terms of the scheme were such that it did not qualify as an arrangement within the meaning of s 206. The effect of the scheme would be that all the members of the company, except the NFU Development Co and such of the so-called new members as were not already members of the company, would be stripped of all their rights and receive in exchange no com-

f pensating benefit of any description, except the theoretical extinction of their contingent liability to contribute 5p in case of a winding-up; theoretical, because it is de minimis and has no significance in the context of a non-trading company with assets of £3,000,000 and liabilities which do not exceed £25,000. A member loses his right to attend the annual general meetings and other meetings of the company; his right to make his voice heard at meetings; his right to receive the board's annual

g report and the company's accounts; his right to question the use which the board makes or omits to make of the company's considerable financial resources; the right to vote on the remuneration of directors; the right to put himself forward for appointment to an area electoral college and thus acquire a say in the election of a director. Admittedly the rights of a member are very limited, and so it may be said that a member does not lose much under the scheme because he has not much

h to lose. Nor did he pay much for his membership rights in the first place—merely an entrance fee of 5s. Be that as it may, the company has become prosperous, no doubt as a result of the support which members gave to the company's marketing undertaking during the period that it traded, and the profit thereby made by the company. However little a member originally paid for his membership, and however small his effective stake in the company and his opportunity to control its

j operations, nevertheless he has rights and under the scheme he loses all. Counsel referred me to what was said in *Re Alabama, New Orleans, Texas and Pacific Junction Railway Co*[2]. In that case debenture holders objected to a scheme which diminished their rights. The scheme was sanctioned by North J and his decision was upheld on appeal. In the course of his judgment Bowen LJ said[3]:

---

1 (1871) 6 Ch App 381   3 [1891] 1 Ch at 243
2 [1891] 1 Ch 213

'Then comes the more serious point, whether this is a compromise or arrange- *a*
ment which is within either the words of the section or within the true spirit
of the legislation; that is to say, whether the Court has either jurisdiction to
sanction it, or ought to sanction it. I do not think myself that the point of jurisdiction is worth discussing at much length, because everybody will agree that a
compromise or agreement which has to be sanctioned by the Court must be
reasonable, and that no arrangement or compromise can be said to be reasonable *b*
in which you can get nothing and give up everything. A reasonable compromise
must be a compromise which can, by reasonable people conversant with the
subject, be regarded as beneficial to those on both sides who are making it.
Now, I have no doubt at all that it would be improper for the Court to allow
an arrangement to be forced on any class of creditors, if the arrangement cannot
reasonably be supposed by sensible business people to be for the benefit of that *c*
class as such, otherwise the sanction of the Court would be a sanction to what
would be a scheme of confiscation. The object of this section is not confiscation.'

Perhaps these observations go to merits more than to jurisdiction.

Counsel for the company submitted that any transaction affecting the rights of
persons in their capacity as members of a company is an arrangement between
the company and its members, even if the transaction takes the form of total for- *d*
feiture of membership rights. In the case of a commercial company it is difficult to
envisage an arrangement involving uncompensated forfeiture of the rights of fully
paid-up shareholders which would be reasonable. The company in the present case
however, is not a commercial undertaking and it does not now exist for the benefit of
its members. It was submitted that in the case of such a company, if it could be shown
that the existence of membership impeded the execution of the objects of the com- *e*
pany, a scheme extinguishing membership was reasonable. Counsel were not,
however, able to refer me to any reported case, or (drawing on their personal ex-
periences) to recall any case, where a scheme was sanctioned that involved the total
uncompensated forfeiture of the rights of the members of a company.

In my judgment the submission of counsel for the objectors on this issue is correct.
Section 206 is dealing with what is described as a 'compromise or arrangement . . . *f*
between a company and its creditors . . . or between the company and its members'.
The word 'compromise' implies some element of accommodation on each side.
It is not apt to describe total surrender. A claimant who abandons his claim is not
compromising it. Similarly, I think that the word 'arrangement' in this section
implies some element of give and take. Confiscation is not my idea of an arrangement. A member whose rights are expropriated without any compensating advan- *g*
tage is not, in my view, having his rights rearranged in any legitimate sense of that
expression.

That conclusion is sufficient to dispose of the matter. Nevertheless, in case my
conclusion is wrong, I think I ought to deal with counsel for the objectors' third
submission. This was, that the scheme was unreasonable, that is to say, not an
arrangement which an intelligent and honest man, considering the interests of the *h*
class of which he forms part, might reasonably approve. By way of comment on the
large proportion of favourable votes, counsel said that there is inevitably a momen-
tum that follows the lead of the establishment. The turn-out of voters was only
2 per cent. Against that small turn-out of voters, counsel submitted that the high
percentage of favourable voters has little significance. He also submitted that the
explanatory statement did not give a sufficient exposition to members of what they *j*
were being asked to give up.

In the *Alabama* case[1], Bowen LJ said, admittedly obiter, that no arrangement or
compromise can be said to be reasonable in which you get nothing and give up everything. I appreciate that it is exceptional for the court to refuse its sanction to a scheme
which has been approved by the requisite majority. Nevertheless I do not feel that

1 [1891] 1 Ch at 243

a I can disregard what was said in the *Alabama* case[1]. It was urged that Bowen LJ probably had in mind commercial companies rather than the sort of company that I am considering in the present case. I am not convinced that his observations should be treated as qualified in that way. Money is not everything. Many persons would value, for example, their right to be a member of and vote at meetings of a charitable corporation although they received no financial advantage from their membership.

b I was also addressed by Mr Wheelock in person. He told me that he went to the meeting hoping that he would be allowed to suggest amendments. Another member asked the chairman: 'Are we allowed to put forward modifications which would be of some help?' The chairman's reply was, 'No, you are not'. I am not concerned whether the chairman's answer was correct or incorrect in law. I merely wish to explain Mr Wheelock's approach. He says, and the notes of the meeting bear this out, that he did not get an opportunity to ask questions and to make suggestions.

c He therefore appeared before me to make his comments in this court. He disregarded his theoretical loss of his right to share in surplus assets on a liquidation. This was a remote contingency which he regarded as irrelevant. What did concern him was the loss of his right to speak and vote at meetings of the company. He did not consider it satisfactory that in future the voice of an ex-member of the company should only be heard at long range through the medium of the National Farmers'

d Union (of England and Wales) which owned and controlled the NFU Development Co and under the proposed articles would henceforth control the company. He agreed with the effort to save administrative expense. He felt that this object could be at least partially achieved by some method other than the cancellation of the existing membership.

e What reasons do the directors put forward in the explanatory statement for recommending the scheme? I will take each in turn.

Reason (1): 'The administrative costs of maintaining the register of 94,000 members, printing and posting accounts to members and the expenses of a large board of Directors and two committees exceeds £11,000 per annum'. There is no evidence as to how much, if anything, is spent on maintaining the register. It

f does not appear from the evidence that the company makes a practice of taking any positive steps to ensure that the register is kept up-to-date; for, according to the company's evidence, the chairman said in answer to a question at the meeting, 'If people do not notify us of a change of address it is not our fault'. The cost of printing and posting in the exhibited accounts was £3,693, a relatively small proportion of the company's spendable income of £42,490. The expense of maintaining a large board of directors and two committees, if truly this is wasted money, can

g surely be avoided by reducing the number of directors and abolishing the committees.

Reason (2): 'The rights and privileges of farmer members are of little practical value'. There then follow five comments, '(a) So long as the [company] continues in being members can receive no monies from it in respect of their membership'. Absence of personal financial profit does not seem to me an adequate reason for depriving a person of membership of a company, e g of his right to vote. '(b)

h The [NFU Development Co] has a controlling vote on several important resolutions including a resolution to wind up'. This does not seem to me a valid reason for depriving a member of such voice as he may have. '(c) The Directors have been informed by the [NFU Development Co] that there is no foreseeable prospect of a winding up of the [company]'. This merely means that membership holds out no prospect of financial gain. It prompts the same reply as I make to reason (2) (a).

j '(d) It is not necessary to be a member of the [company] in order to trade with F.M.C. (Meat) Limited, Marsh and Baxter Limited or other subsidiaries of F.M.C. Limited'. This does not appear to me to be a justification for cancelling the membership of the company. '(e) The rights and privileges of membership are not transferable and cease on resignation or death.' This does not seem to me an adequate

---

1 [1891] 1 Ch at 243

reason for determining the rights and privileges of membership prior to resignation   *a*
or death.

Reason (3): 'The administrative costs of retaining a very large membership are not
justified by the practical value of the rights and privileges accruing to members.'
As I have indicated, according to the evidence the only unavoidable administrative
cost of retaining a very large membership was, in 1970-71, £3,693. The balance of
the £11,000 which is mentioned in reason (a) does not appear from the evidence   *b*
before me to be due to the size of the membership, but (inter alia) to the size and
expenses of the board of directors and the committees.

Reason (4): 'The [company] does not and cannot trade and its main object is to
benefit the agricultural industry in general and not the members as such.' That
does not seem to me a valid reason for depriving members of their right to vote.

Reason (5): 'Membership is not terminated when a member ceases to farm, and it   *c*
is thought that some members are no longer engaged in farming.' That may be a
reason for making some alteration to the articles of association or for inviting non-
farming members to resign, but it cannot be a valid reason for expelling farmers and
non-farmers alike.

Reason (6): 'The income of the [company] available for application towards its
objects will be increased by the substantial saving in administrative costs mentioned   *d*
above.' This, of course, is basically correct. But the saving achieved by the cancellation of membership will, on the evidence, only be a small part of the £11,000—
namely £3,693. The remainder of the administrative costs which make up the
£11,000, so far as they can be saved at all, would equally be saved by reducing the
size of the board and abolishing the committees, which can be done by special resolution altering the articles. In any event, how important is it to save the £3,693 spent   *e*
on maintaining the membership, having regard to the fact that, according to the
exhibited accounts, the company only spent one-fifth of its net income on furthering
its objects and leaves unapplied a balance for the year of £22,136 which is added to
the £94,328 tucked away from previous years?

There is obviously a case for altering the articles of association if the directors are
correct that money is being wasted on too large a board and on needless committees.   *f*
There is also a case for inviting members to resign who do not want to be bothered
with accounts and notices of meetings. There may be a case for spending more of
the company's available income on the furthering of its objects instead of carrying the
major part of its income to reserves. All this can be done without abolishing the
existing membership. On the evidence before me I cannot discern among the board's
own reasons for recommending the scheme, any which justifies depriving a member of   *g*
his right to continue to be a member. It may be that some members said to themselves: 'I have no interest in the company; I do not want to be encumbered with
accounts and notices of meetings; I am glad to vote in favour of the scheme so as to
lose my membership. If this has the effect of increasing the company's spendable
income, so much the better.' Such a person, though acting reasonably, intelligently
and honestly in a subjective sense, is not purporting to assess the reasonableness of   *h*
the scheme from the point of view of the membership as a whole. On the facts before
me, I am driven to the conclusion that this is a scheme which, properly examined,
no member voting in the interests of members as a whole could reasonably approve.

Although, therefore, this scheme has been devised in the sincere belief that it could
properly be recommended by the board of directors to members for their approval,
I do not think that, even if I considered that I had jurisdiction, I would have been   *j*
justified in sanctioning it.

I accordingly dismiss the petition.

Petition dismissed.

Solicitors: *Slaughter & May* (for the company); *Sydney Morse & Co* (for the objectors
other than Mr Wheelock).

Gillian Whitear   Barrister.

Practice Direction

FAMILY DIVISION

Husband and wife – Property – Real or leasehold property – Application to determine ownership – Application for transfer of such property – Procedure – Married Women's Property Act 1882, s 17 – Matrimonial Proceedings and Property Act 1970, s 4.

1.   On any application under s 17 of the Married Women's Property Act 1882 or under s 4 of the Matrimonial Proceedings and Property Act 1970 in which the ownership of, or transfer of, real or leasehold peoperty is in question the affidavit in support of the application should state whether the title to the property is registered or unregistered and, if the former, should quote the Land Registry title number. Where necessary, in order to obtain this information the applicant should apply to the appropriate district land registry for a search of the public index map.

2.   Where the title to the property is registered the applicant should, when filing the affidavit or as soon as possible thereafter, and in any case by the time of the first hearing before the registrar, lodge an up-to-date office copy of the register.   Such an office copy is normally issued only to, or on the written authority of, the registered proprietor.

3.   If such authority is not forthcoming, the court has power to make an order that the applicant be allowed to inspect the register of title, but, pending the making of rules giving jurisdiction to the county courts to make such orders, it may be necessary to transfer county court proceedings in which such an order is sought to the High Court before the order is made.

4.   The order should direct that the applicant be allowed to inspect the register of title no   , which will automatically allow him to obtain an office copy.

This Practice Direction is issued with the concurrence of the Lord Chancellor.

D NEWTON
Senior Registrar

14th December 1972

Practice Direction

FAMILY DIVISION

Ward of court – Application to make minor ward of court – Originating summons – Contents – Notice to defendant – Form of notice – RSC Ord 90, r 3 (4)-(7).

1. RSC Ord 90, r 3 (4) (added with effect from 1st January 1973 by the Rules of the Supreme Court (Amendment No 3) 1972[1]) requires that, unless the court otherwise directs, every originating summons by which application is made to make a minor a ward of court shall state the whereabouts of the minor or, as the case may be, that the plaintiff is unaware of his whereabouts.

2. In accordance with Ord 90, r 3 (7) (added as above) every such originating summons must contain a notice to the defendant in the following form:

To THE DEFENDANT(S) (other than the minor)

TAKE NOTICE that, pursuant to RSC Ord 90, r 3 (5) and (6): (1) You must forthwith after being served with this summons, lodge in the above-mentioned registry a notice stating your address and the whereabouts of the minor (or, if it be the case, that you are unaware of the minor's whereabouts), and unless the court otherwise directs, you must serve a copy of such notice on the plaintiff; and (2) If you subsequently change your address or become aware of any change in the minor's whereabouts, you must, unless the court otherwise directs lodge in the above-mentioned Registry notice of your new address or of the new whereabouts of the minor, as the case may be, and serve a copy of such notice on the plaintiff.

Any notice required to be lodged in the above-mentioned registry shall be sent or delivered to [the Principal Clerk (CD) Principal Registry of the Family Division, Somerset House, Strand, London WC2R 1LP] [or as the case may be].

D NEWTON
18th December 1972   Senior Registrar

---

1   SI 1972 No 1898

a

Earl v Slater & Wheeler (Airlyne) Ltd

NATIONAL INDUSTRIAL RELATIONS COURT
SIR JOHN DONALDSON P, MR R BOYFIELD AND MR R DAVIES
18th, 27th OCTOBER 1972

b *Industrial relations – Unfair dismissal – Fair and unfair dismissal – Determination whether dismissal fair or unfair – Unfair procedure – Right of employee to put his case before or at time of dismissal – Employee summarily dismissed with no opportunity of putting his case before or at time of dismissal – Employee having no valid answer to employers' complaints regarding his work – Employers not knowing whether employee had explanation of conduct – Whether tribunal entitled to make finding of unfair dismissal where unfair procedure leads*
c *to no injustice to employee – Whether employee entitled to compensation where unfair procedure the only matter rendering dismissal unfair – Industrial Relations Act 1971, s 24.*

Industrial relations – Unfair dismissal – Fair and unfair dismissal – Question to be determined 'in accordance with equity and the substantial merits of the case' – Meaning – Industrial Relations Act 1971, s 24 (6).

d
An employee had received several verbal complaints from his employers regarding work. While the employee was absent from work due to sickness, his employers made certain discoveries which showed that the employee was not carrying out his work in a satisfactory manner. On his return to work the employers handed the employee a letter of immediate dismissal. The letter set out reasons relating to
e the employee's conduct or capability which the employers considered as justifying them in dismissing the employee. The employee had no opportunity to state his case either before or at the time of his dismissal, nor was there at the employers' place of work a disciplinary procedure whereby an employee could state his case and be accompanied by an employee representative. The employee had no valid answer to his employers' complaints but the employers did not know that when
f they dismissed him, nor had they taken any steps to find out. An industrial tribunal dismissed the employee's claim for unfair dismissal, holding that it was not open to them to find under s 24 (6)[a] of the Industrial Relations Act 1971 that the employee had been unfairly dismissed solely because the procedure adopted by the employers had been unfair, when that procedure had led to no injustice to the employee. The employee appealed.

g
Held – (i) The tribunal had erred in holding that an unfair procedure which led to no injustice was incapable of rendering unfair a dismissal which would otherwise be fair; the employers at the moment of dismissal could not and did not know whether the employee could explain the matters which had been discovered during his absence; they had dismissed the employee for a reason which might or might
h not be sufficient according to whether the employee could or could not offer an adequate explanation; thus the tribunal should have found that the employee had been unfairly dismissed (see p 150 h to p 151 b, post).

(ii) The employee was not, however, entitled to compensation. The only matter rendering his dismissal unfair had been his lack of an opportunity to explain matters which had been discovered during his absence from work, and on the accepted facts
j he had no valid explanation to offer respecting those matters. Consequently the employers' failure to give the employee an opportunity to offer an explanation had caused the employee no loss (see p 151 f and g, post).

Per Curiam. In considering whether a dismissal is fair or unfair, the words 'shall be determined in accordance with equity and the substantial merits of the case' in

---

a Section 24 (6) is set out at p 149 h, post

s 24 (6) of the 1971 Act do not mean that the principles of equity (as contrasted with common law) are applicable as such; those words should be taken to mean that in considering whether an employer has acted reasonably or unreasonably a tribunal should adopt a broad approach of common sense and common fairness, eschewing all legal or other technicality (see p 150 b, post).

Notes
For fair and unfair dismissal, see Supplement to 38 Halsbury's Laws (3rd Edn) para 677B, 20.
For the Industrial Relations Act 1971, s 24, see 41 Halsbury's Statutes (3rd Edn) 2090.

Case referred to in judgment
Ridge v Baldwin [1963] 2 All ER 66, [1964] AC 40, [1963] 2 WLR 935, 127 JP 295, HL, 37 Digest (Repl) 195, 32.

Cases also cited
Disher v Disher [1963] 3 All ER 933, [1965] P 31, DC.
Fisher v Jackson [1891] 2 Ch 84.
Malloch v Aberdeen Corpn [1971] 2 All ER 1278, [1971] 1 WLR 1578, HL.

Appeal
This was an appeal by Maurice Earl against the decision of an industrial tribunal (chairman H C Easton Esq) sitting at Colwyn Bay, dated 21st June 1972, that the appellant had not been unfairly dismissed by the respondents, Slater & Wheeler (Airlyne) Ltd. The facts are set out in the judgment of the court.

Jeffrey Burke for the appellant.
Caroline Alton for the respondents.

Cur adv vult

27th October. **SIR JOHN DONALDSON P** read the following judgment of the court. The appellant was dismissed from his position as an estimating and planning engineer in March 1972. With the support of his union, the Association of Scientific, Technical and Managerial Staffs, he applied to the industrial tribunal at Colwyn Bay for compensation for unfair dismissal. His application was dismissed and, again supported by his union, he has appealed to this court.

Before the tribunal the reasons for the dismissal were in issue, but before this court, and solely for the purposes of arguing the appeal, the appellant accepted the findings of the tribunal. That left a substantial issue as to the construction of s 24 of the Industrial Relations Act 1971 and as to the relevance of the fact that the appellant was given no opportunity of making representations before the decision to dismiss him was taken.

The tribunal found that the appellant had been employed by the respondents from June 1966 until March 1972. Originally a toolmaker and later a tool room foreman, he became an estimating and planning engineer during the last two years of his employment. As such, his work included certain matters relating to training and problem liaison or 'trouble shooting'. The appellant regarded the change as promotion, but Mr Budge (the managing director) and Mr Marsland (the works director) both said that in fact he was given this job as being one where his deficiencies as a foreman would be less important. This result was not wholly achieved and during the year before the dismissal the appellant was on several occasions told that he must 'buck his ideas up'.

The appellant was taken ill in early March 1972 and during his absence Mr Marsland discovered certain matters which led him to the decision to dismiss the appellant.

a   A drawing which was missing was found at the appellant's home, certain contracts were found to be behind time and one which should have been completed had not been started by the appellant's department. Further, although the appellant had told Mr Marsland that the foreman had been fully instructed in another matter, it emerged that he knew nothing about it although the contract concerned was a matter of some urgency. Mr Marsland and Mr Budge concluded that the appellant

b   was unsatisfactory and was not carrying out his job in a sufficiently energetic or competent manner. Accordingly they decided to dismiss him and replace him by another man.

   This brings us to the method of the appellant's dismissal which was strongly and rightly criticised by the tribunal. The appellant had notified the company that he would be returning to work on Monday, March 27th 1972. On the preceding

c   Friday (March 24th), the appellant was asked to go to the office on the Saturday morning to see Mr Marsland. This he did. On arrival he was confronted by Mr Marsland and Mr Budge and without more ado handed a letter of immediate dismissal in the following terms:

'Dear Mr. Earl,

d   'The following reasons are considered, without prejudice, by this Company to be sufficient to warrant the termination of your employment forthwith and that you are entitled to one month's salary in lieu of notice plus holiday pay due to date:—
   A. Considerable decline in work rate over the past twelve months.
   B. No improvement in the foregoing in spite of several warnings from two of the Directors.

e   C. Either an unwillingness or inability to cope with pressure of work at peak demand.
   D. Serious embarrassment caused in Customer relationship due to orders not being processed for Production in good time.
   E. Unreliability of word and action due to increasing absentmindedness, this

f   has promoted many instances of other members of Management being unable to properly carry out their duties caused by:—
       (a) Loss of Drawings and information
       (b) Lack of proper information
       (c) Delay in passing of Information
   F. Complete lack of confidence has now developed among all members of

g   Management in that they feel their efforts to make progress are being considerably nullified by your shortcomings.
   'A replacement has been appointed to the post you have hitherto occupied.
                    Yours faithfully
                    R. J. Marsland, Works Director
                    J. S. Budge, Director.'

h   Whilst the appellant could in fact have made representations, he rightly appreciated that the decision had already been made and that there was no point in doing so. In reality, therefore, he had no opportunity of saying anything in his own defence. Counsel for the appellant submits that the tribunal should have found that the appellant was unfairly dismissed because: (i) no dismissal is fair unless the employer has an opportunity to state his case before or at the time of his dismissal; (ii) as

j   is admitted, no such opportunity was given to the appellant; (iii) no tribunal could reasonably hold that the employer had satisfied the onus of proving that he had acted reasonably in dismissing the employee, unless the employee had had an opportunity of stating his case. His arguments in support of these submissions fall into two categories, namely, those based on the concept of natural justice and those based on public policy as summarised in s 1 of the Industrial Relations Act 1971, and on the Industrial Relations Code of Practice[1] and the construction of s 24 of the Act. *a*

Counsel for the appellant conceded that prior to the 1971 Act the principle of audi alteram partem had no general application to the case of master and servant, but he relied on *Ridge v Baldwin*[2] where Lord Reid, after stating the position in relation to 'a pure case of master and servant', said[3]:

'But this kind of case can resemble dismissal from an office where the body employing the man is under some statutory or other restriction as to ... the *b* grounds on which it can dismiss them.'

Counsel for the appellant went on to submit that s 22 of the 1971 Act imposed such a restriction on dismissal as to import this principle. The difficulty about this submission, as counsel for the appellant very fairly admitted, is that it logically leads to the conclusion that the appellant was not effectively dismissed, although dismissal *c* is of the essence of his claim. Suffice it to say that we have to deal with this appeal on the basis of an effective dismissal. However, counsel for the appellant can and does rely on the speech of Lord Morris of Borth-y-Gest in *Ridge v Baldwin*[4] for the proposition that 'natural justice is only fair play in action'. This brings us to his arguments based on s 1 of the 1971 Act, the code of practice and s 24.

Section 1 of the 1971 Act contains the guiding principles which both the industrial *d* tribunals and this court are required to apply. Counsel for the appellant relied in particular on the principle of developing and maintaining orderly procedures in industry and submitted that this was fundamentally inconsistent with summary dismissal. We do not agree. The principle requires orderly procedures but does not exclude procedures which, in exceptional cases, provide for or permit of summary dismissal. *e*

The code of practice is much more relevant. Paragraphs 130-133 are concerned with disciplinary procedure. Paragraph 130 provides that 'there should be a formal procedure except in very small establishments where there is close personal contact between employer and his employees'. The respondent company's establishment is certainly not large. We were told that there were between 40 and 50 shop floor and between 15 and 27 management employees—but it hardly ranks as 'very small'. *f* However, whether or not it is 'very small', the principles of conduct should be the same, size being only relevant to the need for formality. Accordingly, the appellant is fully entitled to rely on para 132 which provides that the disciplinary procedure should 'give the employee the opportunity to state his case and the right to be accompanied by his employee representative'. So far as representation is concerned, the respondents neither knew nor had any reason to know that the appellant had recently *g* become a member of a trade union, but the procedure which they operated contravened the code of practice in that, in the circumstances of the appellant's case, it did not give the employee the opportunity to state his case.

But quite apart from the code of practice, good industrial relations depend on management not only acting fairly but being manifestly seen to act fairly. This did not happen in the case of the appellant. Granted that his work had been unsatis- *h* factory over a long period and that he had been told that it must improve, the fact remains that the decisive matters leading to his dismissal were all discovered whilst the appellant was absent due to sickness. The appellant was unable to satisfy the tribunal that he had any answer to these complaints, but the employers did not know this when they dismissed him and they took no steps to find out. Whilst we do not say that in all circumstances the employee must be given an opportunity of *j*

---

1 The Code of Practice was brought into operation on 28th February 1972 by the Industrial Relations (Code of Practice) Order 1972 (SI 1972 No 179)
2 [1963] 2 All ER 66, [1964] AC 40
3 [1963] 2 All ER at 71, [1964] AC at 65
4 [1963] 2 All ER at 102, [1964] AC at 113

a stating his case, the only exception can be the case where there *can* be no explanation which *could* cause the employers to refrain from dismissing the employee. This must be a very rare situation. The appellant's case was far removed from this. The manner of his dismissal cannot possibly be justified, notwithstanding the fact that if a proper procedure had been adopted he would still have been dismissed and would then have been fairly dismissed.

b It is against this background that it is necessary to apply s 24 of the Act in order to determine whether the appellant's dismissal was 'fair' or 'unfair'. It operates in two stages. In the first stage it is for the employer to show what was the principal or only reason for the dismissal and that it was a potentially valid reason, that is to say a reason falling within s 1 (*b*) 'or some other substantial reason of a kind such as to justify the dismissal of an employee holding the position which that employee held'.

c If the employer fails to discharge this burden, the tribunal must find that the dismissal was unfair. In the present case the respondents proved that the principal reason for the dismissal related to the capability or conduct of the appellant. The tribunal therefore quite rightly proceeded to the second stage which consists of determining whether the dismissal was fair or unfair in accordance with the provisions of sub-ss (4), (5) and (6) of s 24. Only sub-s (6) is relevant to the appellant's claim, but

d since doubts have been expressed as to incidence of the burden of proof, it may be useful if we consider that aspect in relation to all three subsections.

Section 24 (4)—Subsection (4) deals with the situation in which it has already been proved that the principal or only reason for the dismissal was that the employee had exercised or indicated an intention of exercising his rights under s 5 (1) of the 1971 Act, which relates to membership of a trade union. No question of burden of proof therefore arises and the only effect of the subsection is to declare such a dismissal to

e be unfair. At the earlier stage at which the tribunal is concerned to ascertain the reason for the dismissal, the employer will presumably have been seeking to prove some other reason for the dismissal and the employee will have been seeking to rebut this and to set up the s 5 reason. To this extent, but no further, the burden of proof will have been on the employee.

f *Section 24 (5)*—Subsection (5) provides that in a redundancy situation the selection of the complainant for dismissal rather than some other employee may in certain circumstances render the dismissal unfair. The burden of proving such circumstances, which relate to the exercise by him of rights relating to union membership and breaches of customary or agreed redundancy procedures, undoubtedly lies on the complainant employee.

g *Section 24 (6)*—Subsection (6) requires closer analysis, both in relation to the burden of proof, which is not relevant to the present appeal, and in relation to the facts of the appellant's case. It is in the following terms:

h 'Subject to subsections (4) and (5) of this section, the determination of the question whether the dismissal was fair or unfair, having regard to the reason shown by the employer, shall depend on whether in the circumstances he acted reasonably or unreasonably in treating it as a sufficient reason for dismissing the employee; and that question shall be determined in accordance with equity and the substantial merits of the case.'

j It will be seen that there is no presumption one way or the other whether a dismissal is fair or unfair or whether the employer acted reasonably or unreasonably. Furthermore, the subsection only operates after the employer has proved the reason for the dismissal. The only additional matters which may have to be proved are particular 'circumstances' affecting the reasonableness or otherwise of the employer's action. Most of these will probably have emerged in the process of the employer seeking to prove the reason for the dismissal, but insofar as further matters are relevant the burden of proof lies on the party alleging that the circumstances existed.

The subsection provides for the determination of the question 'whether the dismissal was fair or unfair, having regard to the reason shown by the employer' by, in effect, substituting another question, namely, 'whether in the circumstances he acted reasonably or unreasonably in treating it as a sufficient reason for dismissing the employee'. It is therefore simpler to concentrate on this latter question. The subsection goes on to provide that this question 'shall be determined in accordance with equity and the substantial merits of the case'. This does not, in our judgment, mean that the principles of 'equity' as contrasted with the 'common law' are applicable as such, but rather that in considering whether the employer acted reasonably or unreasonably the tribunal should adopt a broad approach of common sense and common fairness, eschewing all legal or other technicality. In other words they should constitute themselves an industrial 'special jury'. Provided that they do so, that they ask themselves the right question and that the evidence is such that they could properly reach their conclusion, this court will have neither the wish nor the right to vary their decision even if, exceptionally, it may doubt whether it would have reached the same conclusion.

The tribunal's direction to itself and its verdict are contained in para 8 of the reasons which reads as follows:

'Whilst we accept that Management in this case must be held to have fallen far short of the standard procedure which is to be expected, and do not at the hearing appear to have implemented any proper grievance procedure even since the Act came into force, we feel that what we have got to decide is not whether they acted in accordance with natural justice, or with the procedure advised in the code of practice, but whether the result was in all respects fair in accordance with the definition or directions contained in section 24 (6) of the Act. We do not think that we have the same power, as the High Court undoubtedly has under its inherent jurisdiction, to declare a decision reached in this way wholly inoperative, or to set it aside, still less to award compensation. The Tribunal has no inherent jurisdiction, but is confined to the jurisdiction conferred upon us by the Statute. That jurisdiction is confined to deciding whether a dismissal was fair or unfair, not according to whether the procedure adopted was fair, but according to whether in all the circumstances it is properly found by us that the employers acted reasonably or unreasonably in treating the allegations made and accepted by us as a sufficient reason for dismissal. If we are right in that view, reading the subsection in question, then we do not think it is open to us to hold that this was an unfair dismissal merely because of the procedure adopted. If that procedure had in fact led to any conceivable injustice, then it would be inequitable to dismiss the claim, but although the procedure was such that it is wide open to criticism, we do not think that in all the circumstances it led to injustice.'

With respect to the tribunal, we think that it erred in holding that an unfair procedure which led to no injustice is incapable of rendering unfair a dismissal which would otherwise be fair. The question in every case is whether the employer acted reasonably or unreasonably in treating the reason as sufficient for dismissing the employee and it has to be answered with reference to the circumstances known to the employer at the moment of dismissal.

If an employer thinks that his accountant may be taking the firm's money, but has no real grounds for so thinking and dismisses him for this reason, he acts wholly unreasonably and commits the unfair industrial practice of unfair dismissal, notwithstanding that it is later proved that the accountant had in fact been guilty of embezzlement. Proof of the embezzlement affects the amount of the compensation but not the issue of fair or unfair dismissal.

In the present case, which is, of course, quite different from the example which we have just given, the respondents at the moment of dismissal could not and did not *a* know whether the appellant could explain the various matters which had been discovered during his absence. They thus acted on the basis of a reason which, so far as they then knew, might or might not be sufficient, according to whether the appellant could or could not offer an adequate explanation. Such action was unreasonable at the time and does not retrospectively acquire a different character because of what was proved before the tribunal, but was then unknown to the employers. It follows that in our judgment the tribunal should have found that the appellant was unfairly

b dismissed.

This brings us to whether the appellant is entitled to any compensation and, if so, how much. Compensation falls to be assessed in accordance with the general principles set out in s 116 of the 1971 Act. Section 116 (1) provides that the compensation shall be—

c 'such amount as the Court or tribunal considers just and equitable in all the circumstances, having regard to the loss sustained by the aggrieved party in consequence of the matters to which the complaint relates, in so far as that loss was attributable to action taken by or on behalf of the party in default.'

Section 116 (3) provides:

d 'Where the Industrial Court or industrial tribunal finds that the matters to which the complaint relates were to any extent caused or contributed to by any action of the aggrieved party in connection with those matters . . . the Court or tribunal shall reduce its assessment of his loss to such extent as, having regard to that finding, the Court or tribunal considers just and equitable.'

e 'The matters to which the complaint relates' is the conduct of the respondent employers in dismissing the appellant unfairly, contrary to his rights under s 22 of the 1971 Act. It was the appellant's own conduct or lack of capability which led to his dismissal, but he in no way caused or contributed to its unfair character which is the essence of his complaint. There are, therefore, no grounds for reducing the assessment of compensation under s 116 (3). But what alone rendered the dismissal unfair

f was that the appellant was not given any opportunity to explain the various matters which had come to light during his absence. On the findings of the tribunal that he had in fact no valid explanation to offer, the unfairness of the dismissal, i e the failure to give him an opportunity of attempting to do so, appears to have caused him no loss. We do not think that there is any room in this field for the award of nominal compensation and in the light of the tribunal's finding that the appellant suffered 'no

g conceivable injustice' they must, even if they had found unfair dismissal, have assessed the compensation at 'nil'.

It follows that for reasons which differ slightly from those given by the tribunal, we consider that the appellant's claim for compensation was rightly dismissed. The appeal will therefore also be dismissed.

h *Appeal dismissed.*

Solicitors: *W H Thompson* (for the appellant); *Osborn, Bennison & Hughes*, Colwyn Bay (for the respondents).

Gordon H Scott Esq Barrister.

Edwards v Reginam   *a*

PRIVY COUNCIL
LORD WILBERFORCE, LORD PEARSON, LORD SALMON, SIR EDWARD MCTIERNAN AND SIR RICHARD WILD
26th, 27th JUNE, 16th OCTOBER 1972

Criminal law – Murder – Provocation – Provocation itself provoked by accused's conduct – *b*
Availability to accused of plea of provocation – Accused blackmailing victim – Victim attacking accused with knife – Accused wresting knife from victim and killing him – Accused pleading provocation – Circumstances in which plea of provocation available to blackmailer.

In the course of a struggle between the appellant and C in an hotel bedroom in Hong Kong, the appellant inflicted on C many knife wounds, which caused C's death. *c* The appellant, who also sustained several knife wounds in the struggle, was charged with murder. At his trial he pleaded self-defence but mainly contended for a verdict of manslaughter on the ground of provocation. He admitted that he had followed C to Hong Kong from Australia with the deliberate intention of blackmailing him and had gone to see him in his hotel bedroom for that purpose, but he claimed that when he there pressed C for payment of the sum that he was demanding, C *d* swore at him, attacked him with a knife and inflicted several wounds and that he, the appellant, then wrested the knife from C and stabbed him in a fit of 'white hot' passion. The prosecution alleged that the appellant had gone to Hong Kong with the deliberate intention of killing C and that his motive for so doing was financial in that he was in league with C's wife, who would, it was claimed, receive a superannuation payment of some A\$100,000 as a result of her husband's death. In his summing-up the *e* trial judge, inter alia, directed the jury that the plea of provocation was not available to the appellant in view of his own evidence that he was attempting to blackmail C. The appellant was convicted of murder and appealed. The Full Court of the Supreme Court of Hong Kong held that the trial judge's direction was erroneous in law but, applying the proviso to s 81 (2)[a] of the Criminal Procedure Ordinance (of Hong Kong), dismissed the appeal on the ground that no substantial miscarriage of justice *f* had actually occurred. The appellant appealed to the Privy Council.

Held – The appeal would be allowed and a conviction for manslaughter would be substituted for the conviction of murder for the following reasons—
(i) the trial judge was guilty of an error in law in withdrawing the defence of provocation from the jury for, although a blackmailer could not generally rely on the *g* predictable results of his own blackmailing conduct as constituting provocation sufficient to reduce his killing of the victim from murder to manslaughter, if the hostile reaction by the person sought to be blackmailed went to extreme lengths it might constitute sufficient provocation, and, as C had, according to the appellant, gone to extreme lengths by violently attacking him, wounding him and putting his life in danger, there was some evidence of provocation fit for consideration by the *h* jury (see p 158 g to p 159 a, post);
(ii) the alleged motive for the killing relied on by the prosecution had not been proved (see p 156 g, post);
(iii) in the circumstances the case was not a proper one for the application of the proviso to s 81 (2) of the Criminal Procedure Ordinance because (a) if the question of provocation had been put to the jury they might have found the plea of provocation *j* more plausible than the plea of self-defence and (b) they might have taken a different view of the case generally if it had been appreciated that the alleged motive was unproved (see p 159 e and f, post).
Bullard v R [1961] 3 All ER 470 n applied.

***

a The provision to s 81 (2) is set out at p 159 b, post

Notes

For provocation reducing a charge of murder to manslaughter, see 10 Halsbury's Laws (3rd Edn) 710, para 1362, and for cases on the subject, see 15 Digest (Repl) 938, 8980-8993.

Cases referred to in opinion

Bullard v R [1961] 3 All ER 470 n, [1957] AC 635, [1957] 3 WLR 656, 121 JP 576, 42 Cr App Rep 1, PC, Digest (Cont Vol A) 400, 6685a.

De Freitas v R (1960) 2 WIR 523.

Palmer v R [1971] 1 All ER 1077, [1971] AC 814, [1971] 2 WLR 831, 55 Cr App Rep 223, PC.

Parker v R [1964] 2 All ER 641, [1964] AC 1369, [1964] 3 WLR 70, [1964-65] NSWR 361, PC, Digest (Cont Vol B) 196, *5758a.

R v Howe (1958) 100 CLR 448, 32 ALJR 212, [1958] ALR 753, Digest (Cont Vol A) 432, *6009a.

Appeal

This was an appeal by Graham Edwards alias David Christopher Murray against a judgment of the Supreme Court of Hong Kong in its appellate jurisdiction (Blair-Kerr, Huggins and Pickering JJ) dated 1st June 1971 dismissing the appellant's appeal against his conviction by the Supreme Court in its criminal jurisdiction (Rigby CJ and a jury) on 24th March 1971 for the offence of murder, in respect of which he was sentenced to death. The facts are set out in the opinion of the Board.

M Stuart-Smith QC and P A Twigg for the appellant.

J G Le Quesne QC and A P Duckett (of the Victoria Bar) for the Crown.

LORD PEARSON. The appellant was tried before the Chief Justice of Hong Kong (Rigby CJ) and a jury and was convicted of murder, and on appeal to the Full Court the conviction was upheld. Having heard the present appeal, their Lordships have humbly advised Her Majesty that the conviction for murder should be reduced to a conviction for manslaughter. The reasons will now be given.

In the course of a struggle which took place in the early hours of Tuesday, 1st December 1970, in a hotel bedroom in Hong Kong, the appellant inflicted on the deceased, Dr Coombe, many knife wounds, from which he died, and the appellant himself sustained several knife wounds.

Some facts were not in dispute at the trial. The deceased and his wife, Mrs Coombe, and their two children lived in Perth, Western Australia, and so did the appellant, who was a young man of 19 years of age. There were divorce proceedings between Dr Coombe and Mrs Coombe. The first petition was presented by Dr Coombe, alleging adultery between Mrs Coombe and the appellant. The second petition was presented by Mrs Coombe alleging that Dr Coombe had cohabited and committed adultery with another woman. Dr Coombe did not wish to defend Mrs Coombe's petition and certain terms were arranged between them. On or about Thursday, 26th November 1970, Dr Coombe travelled from Perth to Hong Kong on the first stage of an intended world trip, and he stayed in room 1223 of the Hong Kong Hotel at Kowloon. The appellant followed him on the next day, Friday, 27th November, and stayed in the Sun Ya Hotel.

An important question of fact at the trial was, why did the appellant follow Dr Coombe in this way? The theory of the prosecution was that the appellant went to Hong Kong with the deliberate intention of killing Dr Coombe, and that he carried out that intention by taking a knife to Dr Coombe's bedroom in the early hours of 1st December 1970 and stabbing him to death. The alleged motive was that on the death of Dr Coombe a superannuation payment of about A$100,000 would be payable to his estate and would go to his wife, and the appellant was in league with Mrs Coombe.

On the other hand, the appellant's explanation at the trial was that he went to Hong Kong with the intention of blackmailing Dr Coombe, and that when they met in Dr Coombe's bedroom in the early hours of 1st December and the appellant pressed for payment of the sum previously demanded Dr Coombe swore at him and attacked him with a knife and inflicted several wounds, but the appellant wrested the knife from Dr Coombe and was in a blind rage, a 'white-hot' passion, and must have stabbed Dr Coombe so that he was fatally wounded. The contention on behalf of the appellant was that he acted in self-defence or under the influence of such provocation as would reduce the crime to manslaughter.

As to what happened in Australia, the Hong Kong police made enquiries of the Western Australian police, but the only direct evidence was that of the appellant. His evidence, by no means necessarily reliable, was to this effect: he had been staying at Mrs Coombe's house as a lodger and committing adultery with her and carrying on a 'call-girl business' in conjunction with her 'escort business', and was planning to go on a trip to the United Kingdom with her, but was not intending to marry her, although he had said jokingly that he would do so; he was indignant that Dr Coombe had reduced from A$5,000 to A$3,500 the cash payment to be made by him to Mrs Coombe as part of the terms arranged in respect of the divorce; the appellant decided to blackmail Dr Coombe, having learnt from Mrs Coombe that Dr Coombe engaged in perverted sexual practices and kept a collection of indecent photographs in his flat; the appellant and another man broke into that flat, and the appellant found the collection of indecent photographs and took out one showing Dr Coombe in a highly indecent situation; the other man photographed this photograph for the appellant and returned it to him but kept the negative so that copies could be made from it; the appellant stole the passport of a friend of his named David Christopher Murray and assumed that name for his journey to Hong Kong, and wore a dark brown wig over his own very blond hair; the appellant was provided with A$600 by Mrs Coombe to pay his fare to Hong Kong and back to Australia; the appellant inserted the stolen photograph of Dr Coombe in a photograph album, which he took with him in a suitcase to Hong Kong. There was independent evidence that the appellant did use the name of David Christopher Murray in Hong Kong, and that he did wear a dark brown wig, and that there was in his suitcase in his room in the Sun Ya Hotel a photograph album.

As to what happened between 27th November and 1st December, there was evidence from the staff of the Hong Kong Hotel. At 9.00 p m on 27th November the appellant came to the room attendant on the 12th floor of the Hong Kong Hotel and asked where room 1223 was and if the occupant was in the room, and on being invited to go and knock on the door himself said 'Don't bother, I don't wish to trouble him' and then went down in the lift. At about 6.00 p m on 28th November the appellant came to the no 1 room boy on the 12th floor and asked where room 1223 was and went to the door and knocked but got no answer and went to the lift to go down. On 29th November at 4.30 p m the no 1 room boy on the 12th floor went into room 1223 and found the appellant there, and he telephoned to the manager, and the manager came and took the appellant down to the office; the appellant gave the name of David Christopher Murray and his address at the Sun Ya Hotel; he went to the toilet under guard of Securicor men, and he was wearing a dark brown wig, but he emerged from the toilet without his wig, showing his blond hair; at 6.30 p m Dr Coombe came in and recognised and spoke to the appellant, and both Dr Coombe and the appellant apologised to the manager for the trouble caused.

The appellant said in evidence that he had spoken to Dr Coombe on the telephone on the previous day (28th November) and told him he had some property taken from Dr Coombe's flat which Dr Coombe might wish to buy and otherwise copies of it would be sent to his friends and associates; and that on 29th November at about 4.30 p m when he was found in room 1223 he left his brief case containing the photograph in the bathroom, lest he might be questioned about it; and that after a Dr Coombe had come to the hotel at about 6.30 p m on that day (29th November) they went up to room 1223 and the appellant retrieved his brief case and showed the photograph to Dr Coombe and said 'If you do not wish this to be sent around to all your friends and wish it back, it will cost you $3,000 in cash within 24 hours'. There was doubt whether the appellant's evidence of this visit with Dr Coombe to room 1223 was consistent with the manager's recollection of the appellant's and Dr Coombe's movements, but as the manager was not present in the hotel lobby all the time the visit might have occurred in his absence.

b Then on the following day (Monday 30th November) at about 10.40 p m both the no 1 room boy and the room attendant on the 12th floor saw the appellant go along the corridor in the direction of room 1223 carrying a brief case and afterwards return without the brief case. The appellant said in his evidence that after knocking on the

c door of no 1223 and receiving no answer he went to the fire escape and hid the brief case containing the photograph behind some material that was there, because he was afraid that Dr Coombe might have informed the police of the attempted blackmail and he did not wish to have the brief case in his possession if he was stopped by the police. The prosecution theory was that the brief case contained the knife with which the appellant intended to kill Dr Coombe.

d The appellant said that after hiding the brief case and returning to the ground floor of the hotel he went back to the Sun Ya Hotel and packed his bags, meaning to leave Hong Kong on the following morning, and that he made telephone calls at intervals of 20 to 30 minutes to Dr Coombe's room and eventually received an answer at about 12.30 a m and proposed to come to the lobby of the Hong Kong Hotel and receive the money there but Dr Coombe said 'Come up and get it'. The appel-

e lant said he then went to the Hong Kong Hotel, went to the fire escape, found the brief case, took out the photograph and put it in the waistband of his trousers, and then waited a considerable time to see if there were any police in the corridor. Eventually he knocked on the door and Dr Coombe opened it. As to what happened in room 1223 after that, the only evidence, apart from that of the appellant, was that of hotel staff and a hotel guest saying what they heard from outside, and medical

f evidence of the wounds inflicted on the two men.

At about 2.30 a m on Tuesday, 1st December, the room attendant on duty on the 12th floor of the Hong Kong Hotel heard a commotion in room 1223 and rushed to the door. It was very noisy inside, and what he heard sounded like some object hitting the drawer. He also heard a noise of what sounded like a struggle. So he went to his counter and telephoned to the office. He then went back to the door of room 1223, and there were still noises there. He telephoned again and returned

g to the door of room 1223. There were still noises from the inside but when he knocked on the door and said 'What is happening?' the noises stopped. Somebody came up from the office, but as the noises had stopped and there was a 'Do not disturb' notice on the door, no entry was made until about 8.50 a m when there was no answer to a telephone call.

h A hotel guest occupying a room on the 14th floor was awakened at about 2.30 a m on 1st December by loud screaming with a shout of 'Help me, help me'. He looked out of the window and saw nothing, but he went again a little later and saw someone walking on a cement ledge along the outside of the bedroom windows of the hotel and disappearing round the far end of the building. The person whom he saw was in fact the appellant.

j The medical evidence with regard to the body of Dr Coombe was that he had been stabbed 27 times, and that the stabs were on the face, neck, arms, left hand, thighs and chest, and three of the chest wounds, penetrating to the lungs were fatal, and that there were areas of abrasion near the right eye region. The medical evidence with regard to the appellant was that he had cut wounds on the ring finger and little finger of his left hand and an abrasion on his left arm and two cut wounds above his left knee. The cut wounds on the fingers affected the tendons, and the knee wounds cut part of the muscle as well as the skin.

The appellant's version of the events inside room 1223 was that there was an angry   *a*
and vituperative altercation and then, he said:

> 'All this happened in a very short time, a few seconds. Dr Coombe then came
> towards me with a knife which I assumed was at that time in his hand. He
> was still cursing and swearing at me during this time, and his wife. Instinctively
> I went into the defence against an underarm thrust . . . What happened after that
> I can only say was I felt an extremely searing pain in my left hand. I then imme-   *b*
> diately forgot all of the unarmed combat I had learned, and resorted to brawling
> tactics. I have a very quick temper. What happened after this is very con-
> fusing. All can say is I remember seizing Dr Coombe's arm with the knife in it
> with both my hands and attempting to wrest the knife from him. From the
> evidence at hand it can be seen that I succeeded, and in fact did use this knife
> on Dr Coombe.'   *c*

He was asked 'By that time, what was the state of your temper?' and he replied
'White hot, sir'. The appellant added:

> 'I will say this, that during the whole course of the fight . . . witnesses say that
> it took from 10 to 15 minutes. My own conscious recollection of this fight
> would place the time factor at between 10 and 15 seconds. I quite realise that   *d*
> this is impossible. This is in my own mind, in my own opinion, how long the
> fight took place, for me. I was not at any time conscious that I had the knife
> in my hand.'

The appellant climbed out of the window and made his way perilously, leaving a
trail of blood from his wounds, along the cement ledge past the windows, climbing   *e*
from the 12th to the 17th floor, and then through a bathroom window and
up the stairs to the roof, and then down scaffolding on the side of the building
to the ground. After that he was anxious to avoid the police but in need of hospital
treatment and eventually he received hospital treatment but was questioned by the
police. He told a number of different stories to account for his movements. First, he
said 'This will teach me not to get involved in a fight when playing cards'. Secondly,   *f*
he said he had gone to a bar with a Chinese and while there had a fight with four
Europeans and was injured. Thirdly, he told a story of a fight over contraband
goods. Fourthly, he said that Dr Coombe had made a homosexual attack on him,
and he the appellant had picked up a knife and struck at Dr Coombe. Fifthly, he
told the story of attempted blackmail, of which he afterwards gave evidence at the
trial.   *g*
As to the motive alleged by the prosecution—that on Dr Coombe's death there
would be a superannuation payment of about A$100,000 owing to Dr Coombe's
estate and this would come to Mrs Coombe and the appellant was in league with
Mrs Coombe—there was no satisfactory evidence. The Hong Kong police had made
enquiries in Australia, but there was no witness from Australia nor were any Australian documents produced. At an interview on 9th December Senior Superintendent   *h*
Harris in the presence of Senior Inspector Gravener put to the appellant certain points
arising from the information received in or from Australia. Then by 14th December
the appellant had composed a 'statement listing 5 reasons why the death of Ronald
Alan Coombe cannot be construed as a result of a [pre-meditated] Murder Plot by
his wife and myself'. In the course of the statement he set out from memory the
terms of the divorce settlement between Dr Coombe and Mrs Coombe. The terms   *j*
set out included among others a cash settlement of A$3,500 and weekly maintenance
and '(c) Transfer of Certain Insurance Policies (Details Unknown)'. Later in the
statement he calculated that from the maintenance Mrs Coombe stood to make in
30 years in the vicinity of A$150,000 tax free. Then he said:

> 'By her husband's death she would receive, if my information is correct,

a $A100,000 less probate, currently at 25% the estate and other taxes. Her total gain would be in the vicinity of $A60,000.'

At the trial Senior Superintendent Harris was asked in cross-examination 'In that interview did you suggest the motive of insurance?' and he said 'Yes'. Senior Inspector Gravener was asked in re-examination with regard to the sum of A$100,000 referred to in the appellant's statement. He said:

b

'Yes. There was a sum, approximately A$95,000, which was part of a super-annuation scheme of the West Australian Institute of Technology. This scheme was part of the conditions of service of the deceased and on his death the sum, as I say, in the region of A$95,000 would be due to his estate.'

c   The appellant gave evidence on this point in cross-examination as follows:

'Q I suggest it was the 90,000 Australian Dollars that you and Mrs. Coombe had in mind when you planned this expedition to Hong Kong. A That is quite incorrect, sir.

'Q You did know that on the death of Dr. Coombe, his Estate would benefit by about 100,000 Australian Dollars, didn't you? A I did not, sir, not until I was informed by Mr Harris.

d

'Q That was the first time you knew anything about it? A That is correct, sir.'

Thus the only evidence about the A$100,000 was hearsay. Senior Inspector Gravener was only repeating what he had been told in or from Australia, and the appellant was or may have been only repeating what he had been told by somebody, who may *e* well have been Senior Superintendent Harris. The defect in the evidence is not merely technical. There was no evidence to show that the superannuation payment, if it existed and if it belonged to Dr Coombe's estate, would come to Mrs Coombe. Dr Coombe might have made a will leaving his residuary estate, or at any rate the capital, to his children, or if he was intestate the law of Western Australia (of which there was no evidence) might give the children an interest in it. There was no *f* evidence to show that, if the sum existed and if it would come to Mrs Coombe, the appellant could expect any substantial benefit from it. There was no evidence that the appellant knew of this sum until the police told him of it.

Counsel for the prosecution in his closing speech repeatedly and emphatically relied on the alleged motive. For instance he said:

g

'... it is, of course, the prosecution case that he came here not to blackmail Dr Coombe but in order to kill him so that Dr Coombe's estate would benefit by approximately A$100,000. He came here as part of a conspiracy with the deceased's wife.'

Counsel for the defence maintained the plea of self-defence, but mainly contended *h* for a verdict of manslaughter on the ground of provocation.

Rigby CJ in summing up to the jury reviewed the main body of the evidence in considerable detail and with great accuracy, but in reminding the jury of the case for the prosecution he did not point out the inadequacy of the evidence relating to motive. His review of the evidence brought out very clearly the sequence of five different stories which had been told by the appellant. Plainly it was open to the jury to find that his fifth and final story, the possibly rather melodramatic story *j* involving attempted blackmail, was no less fictitious than the four previous stories which had been told, and then abandoned by the appellant. On the other hand Rigby CJ's review of the evidence also brought out a number of points in favour of the defence, namely (1) the fact that both the men had knife wounds tended to show that the knife changed hands, (2) the evidence from the hotel staff showed that there had been a protracted struggle, (3) if the appellant intended to murder Dr Coombe

it would be surprising that he should pay several visits to the Hong Kong Hotel and
speak to the hotel staff and especially that he should first wear a disguising wig and
then take it off at the hotel, (4) if the appellant intended to murder Dr Coombe it
would be surprising that he should do it so inefficiently, (5) the attempted blackmail
would be in itself a serious offence and the appellant might seek to conceal it by
telling other stories to account for his wounds. Although Rigby CJ duly left the
question to be decided by the jury, he indicated or strongly hinted that in his opinion
a verdict of manslaughter would be appropriate. The jury unanimously found the
appellant guilty of murder.

On appeal the Full Court held that there were two errors in law in the directions
given by Rigby CJ to the jury, but that there had been no miscarriage of justice and
so 'the proviso' was to be applied and the conviction for murder should be upheld.
Their Lordships agree as to the two errors of law but not as to the applicability of
'the proviso' in this case.

The first error in law was in directing the jury that, if the appellant acted in self-
defence but used more force than was necessary, the proper verdict would be not a
conviction of murder but a conviction of manslaughter. As there was no argument
on this question in the present appeal, it is enough to say that the direction was not in
accordance with the decision of their Lordships in *Palmer v R*[1] preferring the West
Indian decision in *De Freitas v R*[2] to the Australian decision in *R v Howe*[3]. The error
is understandable because the judgment in *Palmer v R*[1] was given on 15th February
1971 and Rigby CJ was summing up on 24th March 1971 and *Palmer v R*[1] was
apparently not cited.

The second error in law was in directing the jury to the effect that the plea of
provocation reducing the crime from murder to manslaughter was not available to
the appellant in this case because according to his own evidence he was attempting
to blackmail Dr Coombe. Rigby CJ said to the jury:

> '. . . in my view the defence of provocation cannot be of any avail to the accused
> in this case. Provocation . . . is undoubtedly a valid legal defence in certain
> circumstances, but you may well think that it ill befits the accused in this case,
> having gone there with the deliberate purpose of blackmailing this man—you
> may well think that it ill befits him to say out of his own mouth that he was
> provoked by any attack. In my view the defence of provocation is not one which
> you need consider in this case.'

That direction was held by the Full Court to be erroneous in relation to the facts of
this case, and their Lordships agree with the Full Court. No authority has been
cited with regard to what may be called 'self-induced provocation'. On principle
it seems reasonable to say that (1) a blackmailer cannot rely on the predictable
results of his own blackmailing conduct as constituting provocation sufficient to
reduce his killing of the victim from murder to manslaughter, and the predictable
results may include a considerable degree of hostile reaction by the person sought to
be blackmailed, for instance vituperative words and even some hostile action such as
blows with a fist; (2) but if the hostile reaction by the person sought to be blackmailed goes to extreme lengths it might constitute sufficient provocation even for
the blackmailer; (3) there would in many cases be a question of degree to be decided
by the jury.

In the present case, if the appellant's version of the facts be assumed to be correct,
Dr Coombe, the person sought to be blackmailed, did go to extreme lengths, in that
he made a violent attack on the appellant with a knife, inflicting painful wounds
and putting the appellant's life in danger. There was evidence of provocation and

---

1 [1971] 1 All ER 1077, [1971] AC 814
2 (1960) 2 WIR 523
3 (1958) 100 CLR 448

a it was fit for consideration by the jury: see *Parker v R*[1]. The burden of proof would be on the prosecution to satisfy the jury that the killing was unprovoked. If the evidence raised in their minds a reasonable doubt whether it was provoked or not, the proper verdict would be a conviction for manslaughter: see *Bullard v R*[2]. The Full Court however held that this was a proper case for the application of the proviso to s 81 (2) of the Criminal Procedure Ordinance, which is:

b 'Provided that the Full Court may, notwithstanding that it is of the opinion that the point raised in the appeal might be decided in favour of the appellant, dismiss the appeal if it considers that no substantial miscarriage of justice has actually occurred.'

The Full Court's reason for applying the proviso was that—

c 'By their verdict the jury necessarily rejected the possibility that the Deceased attacked the Appellant in this way ... In our view the verdict of murder which was returned shows that the jury was satisfied that the Deceased did not attack the Appellant first.'

The argument is that if the jury had thought that the appellant might have been
d acting in self-defence but used excessive force, they would in accordance with the direction given to them (although it was erroneous) have returned a verdict of manslaughter, and therefore their verdict of murder shows that they rejected the appellant's version of the struggle in room 1223. There is however a difficulty in 'delving into the minds of the jury' and speculating as to what the exact mental processes of the jury in fact were and what they would have been if a different question had
e been presented to them for decision: see *Bullard v R*[3]. They might have found the plea of provocation more plausible than the plea of self-defence, when the appellant had stabbed Dr Coombe 27 times and on his own showing had done so after he had wrested the knife away from Dr Coombe. There is the further point that the jury might have taken a different view of the case generally, if it had been appreciated that the alleged motive relied on by the prosecution was unproved. In their Lord-
f ships' opinion this was not a proper case for the application of the proviso.

When the proviso is not applied, the case is one of unlawful killing which has not been proved to be murder, because there was some evidence of provocation fit for the consideration of the jury and the question of provocation was wrongly withdrawn from the jury. Accordingly a conviction for manslaughter should be substituted for the conviction of murder, as in *Bullard v R*[2].

g
Appeal allowed. Conviction of murder reduced to manslaughter.

Solicitors: *Stephenson, Harwood & Tatham* (for the appellant); *Charles Russell & Co* (for the Crown).

                 S A Hatteea Esq Barrister.

h ────────────────────────────────

1 [1964] 2 All ER 641 at 652, [1964] AC 1369 at 1392
2 [1961] 3 All ER 470, [1957] AC 635
3 [1957] AC at 643, 644

George Hensher Ltd v Restawile Upholstery (Lancs) Ltd

CHANCERY DIVISION

GRAHAM J

16th, 17th, 18th, 19th, 20th, 23rd, 24th, 31st OCTOBER 1972

Copyright – Artistic work – Work of artistic craftsmanship – Authorship – Collaboration in conception and execution of work – Work made by craftsmen having distinctive characteristics of shape, form and finish – Furniture suite – Collaboration between plaintiffs' managing director and two craftsmen employed by plaintiffs – Managing director largely responsible for general conception – All three taking part in working out and embodiment of conception in prototype models – Whether suite work of artistic craftsmanship – Copyright Act 1956, s 3 (1) (c).

The plaintiff company manufactured upholstered furniture and in particular three-piece drawing room suites. In 1966 their managing director, H, decided that one of their suites, which they sold under the name 'Denver', should be made more attractive. H and two of his colleagues, S and B, who were craftsmen and employees of the plaintiffs, collaborated as a team in a new design for a three-piece suite, incorporating some of the features of the Denver suite. H was largely responsible for the general conception of the new design but all three of them took part in the working out and embodiment of that conception by the building and upholstering of the prototype models. The new suite, which was called the Bronx, was completed and shown publicly in January 1967. The defendants, who also manufactured upholstered furniture, produced a three-piece suite known as the Amazon. The plaintiffs brought an action against the defendants claiming damages and injunctions, inter alia, on the ground that the defendants had infringed the plaintiffs' copyright in the Bronx suite by direct copying of it in the Amazon suite. The defendants contended, inter alia, that the Bronx chairs and settees could not be the subject of copyright as they were not 'works of artistic craftsmanship' within the meaning of s 3 (1) (c)[a] of the Copyright Act 1956 in that the idea had originated in H but S and B, as craftsmen, had put the idea into execution.

Held – Since, on the evidence, there had been collaboration between H, S and B and all three had taken part in the conception, embodiment and completion of the finished chairs and settees, and since those articles had distinctive characteristics of shape, form and finish which rendered them more than purely utilitarian, they were 'works of artistic craftsmanship' within s 3 (1) (see p 164 b to j, post).

Burke & Margot Burke Ltd v Spicers Dress Designs [1936] 1 All ER 99 distinguished.

Notes

For copyright in artistic works, see 8 Halsbury's Laws (3rd Edn) 378-381, paras 695, 696, and for cases on the subject, see 13 Digest (Repl) 65, 66, 117-127.

For the Copyright Act 1956, s 3, see 7 Halsbury's Statutes (3rd Edn) 135.

Cases referred to in judgment

Burke & Margot Burke Ltd v Spicers Dress Designs [1936] 1 All ER 99, [1936] Ch 400, 105 LJCh 157, 154 LT 561, 13 Digest (Repl) 65, 124.

---

a   Section 3 (1) provides: 'In this Act "artistic work" means a work of any of the following descriptions, that is to say,—(a) the following, irrespective of artistic quality, namely paintings, sculptures, drawings, engravings and photographs; (b) works of architecture, being either buildings or models for buildings; (c) works of artistic craftsmanship, not falling within either of the preceding paragraphs.'

a   *Ladbroke (Football) Ltd v William Hill (Football) Ltd* [1964] 1 All ER 465, [1964] 1 WLR
    273, HL; *affg sub nom William Hill (Football) Ltd v Ladbroke (Football) Ltd* (1962)
    107 Sol Jo 34, CA, Digest (Cont Vol B) 145, 98b.

    Cases also cited
    Amp Incorporated v Utilux Proprietary Ltd [1970] RPC 397, CA, *rvsd* [1972] RPC 103, HL.
b   *Benchairs Ltd v Chair Centre Ltd* [1972] FSR 397.
    Cuisenaire v Reed [1963] VR 719.
    Dunlop Rubber Co Ltd v Golf Ball Developments Ltd (1931) 48 RPC 268.
    Francis Day & Hunter Ltd v Bron (trading as Delmar Publishing Co) [1963] 2 All ER 16,
        [1963] Ch 587, CA.
    Hecla Foundry Co v Walker, Hunter and Co (1889), 6 RPC 554, HL.
    King Features Syndicate (Incorporated) v O & M Kleeman Ltd [1941] 2 All ER 403, [1941]
c   AC 417, HL.
    Sifam Electrical Instrument Co Ltd v Sangamo Weston Ltd [1971] 2 All ER 1074.
    Tate v Thomas [1921] 1 Ch 503.
    Walter v Lane [1900] AC 539, HL.

d   **Action**
    By a writ issued on 23rd April 1971, the plaintiffs, George Hensher Ltd, brought
    an action against the defendants, Restawile Upholstery (Lancs) Ltd, claiming,
    inter alia, injunctions restraining the defendants from infringing the plaintiffs 'copy-
    right in certain chairs and settees comprised within the drawing room suites design-
    ated by the plaintiffs as the 'Bronx', 'Continental', 'Manhattan', 'Atlantic', 'Florida'
    and 'Denver' suites and from selling etc chairs or settees similar in appearance to
e   those of the plaintiffs so as to cause confusion and deception and to lead to the defen-
    dants' goods being passed off as and for goods of the plaintiffs.   The facts are set
    out in the judgment.

    A Kynric Lewis and *Hugh Laddie* for the plaintiffs.
    Lord Cawley for the defendants.
f   *Cur adv vult*

    31st October.   **GRAHAM J** read the following judgment.   The plaintiffs and
    defendants in this case are both manufacturers of upholstered furniture and in
    particular of three-piece drawing-room suites consisting of two chairs and a settee.
    The plaintiffs have designed and sold a number of such suites under the names
g   'Florida', 'Denver', 'Bronx', 'Continental', 'Manhattan', and 'Atlantic'.   The dates
    when these were first sold or offered for sale in the United Kingdom are set out in
    the statement of claim and are from January 1964 in the case of the 'Denver' and
    'Florida' to February 1969 when the 'Continental' was introduced.   The defendants'
    suite is known as the 'Amazon' and there is a conflict between the parties as to the
    date when this was first designed and introduced to the market by the defendants.
h   The various chairs and settees are conveniently shown in the photograph exhibits
    P4 (a) to (h), exhibits P4 (a) to (f) being the various plaintiffs' suites, P4 (g) being the
    'Rufford' suite made by a company called Relaxatease Ltd, who originally infringed
    but after challenge became licensees of the plaintiffs, and P4 (h) is a photograph of
    the 'Amazon' suite of the defendants.   P16 (a) and P16 (b) are respectively the plain-
    tiffs' 'Bronx' chair and settee, P17 is the plaintiffs' 'Manhattan' chair, P15 is the Relax-
j   atease 'Rufford' chair and P18 (a) and (b) are the defendants' 'Amazon' chair and
    settee respectively.
        The material allegations in the statement of claim disclose two independent
    causes of action, namely infringement of copyright and passing off.   It is alleged
    by the plaintiffs that the defendants have infringed the plaintiffs' copyright in the
    drawing exhibits P5, P8 and P9, having, as is alleged, indirectly reproduced those

    H

drawings by copying the plaintiffs' suites in the design of their 'Amazon' suite.
Secondly, the plaintiffs say that there has been infringement of their copyright in
one or more 'works of artistic craftsmanship', within the meaning of s 3 (1) (c) of
the Copyright Act 1956, namely the plaintiffs' suites, by direct copying of those suites.
The passing off issue has somewhat unusual features in that the only false representation by the defendants which can be relied on by the plaintiffs, is the copying
of the shape of the plaintiffs' articles. There is no question here of a trade name
having been imitated or of representations having been made by travellers or sales-
men as so frequently happens in passing off cases. What is said is that the shape
of the plaintiffs' suites is distinctive of their manufacture and that merely by copying
that shape the defendants have represented that their 'Amazon' suite is a product
of the plaintiffs' manufacture.

In the statement of claim it was also alleged that the plaintiffs had copyright in
their catalogues and in the photographs of their suites already referred to. These
particular separate heads of copyright were not however pursued, the burden of
the plaintiffs' case being confined to copying of the drawings and of the settees themselves. It is not clear how far it could have been successfully contended that there
was infringement of the copyright in the photographs or catalogues in contrast
with infringement of the copyright in the articles themselves which are there illustrated but in any event, in view of the way the case was confined and presented and
of my conclusions, it is I think unnecessary to say any more on these two heads of
copyright.

The defendants have a number of answers to the plaintiffs' case. First of all, they
say that in fact they were making their 'Amazon' suite before the plaintiffs made
the drawings in question and before they placed any of the suites, except the 'Denver'
and 'Florida' on the market. In regard to the two latter suites the defendants say,
in any event, the 'Amazon' is not a copy of either the 'Denver' or the 'Florida' and
does not infringe any copyright that the plaintiffs may have in those articles or in
any drawings relating to them. They further say that, in any event, the plaintiffs'
suites are not 'works of artistic craftsmanship' within s 3 (1) (c) of the Copyright Act
1956. Even if they are wrong on this point they say that the 'Amazon' is so different
from any of the plaintiffs' suites that it cannot be said to be an infringement. With
regard to the drawings they also specifically say that they have a defence in accordance
with the provisions of s 9 (8) of the Act which enacts:

'The making of an object of any description which is in three dimensions
shall not be taken to infringe the copyright in an artistic work in two dimensions,
if the object would not appear, to persons who are not experts in relation to
objects of that description, to be a reproduction of the artistic work.'

In this case they say that the drawings in which copyright is alleged to exist would
not be thought by the non-expert to be reproduced by the defendants' 'Amazon'
suite.

[His Lordship then dealt with the passing off action and continued:]   The matter
must of course be one of fact and degree, but, giving the matter here the best consideration I can and after reviewing the only evidence which was called on behalf
of the plaintiffs, I do not think it would be right to hold here that the plaintiffs have
established sufficient reputation in the shape alone of their goods to enable them to
found their action of passing off.

I turn then to the question of infringement of copyright and must, as the case
has developed, deal with this under a number of heads. As already stated, the most
important part of the plaintiffs' case on copyright was based on s 3 (1) (c) of the 1956
Act. It was alleged that the plaintiffs' chairs were 'works of artistic craftsmanship'
within that section and therefore that copyright subsisted in them. It was not
disputed that, if they were 'works of artistic craftsmanship', the plaintiff company
was the owner of that copyright.

The matter arises in this way. The evidence given by the plaintiffs was that the authorship of these chairs resided in three people: Mr Arthur George Hensher, the managing director of the plaintiff company, Mr Tudah Sutton, the works director of the plaintiff company, and Mr John Charles Batchelor, the upholstery manager of the plaintiff company. What is said is that the 'Denver' and 'Florida' suites had been selling since about 1963 or 1964, but in 1966 sales of these suites started to fall off. The plaintiff company therefore decided that they must introduce new models, and the three gentlemen in question got together and as a team designed the first of the new models, namely the 'Bronx'. Mr Hensher was largely responsible for the general conception but all three of them took part in the working out and embodiment of that conception by the building and upholstering of the necessary 'nailed up' and prototype models. It is quite clear to my mind, and I find as a fact, that all three of them did co-operate in the way I have stated. As Mr Hensher said:

'... I decided that we would endeavour to make the Denver more attractive by bringing it down to the ground, and, at the same time, in so doing, incorporate various selling points. It was with that end in view that we worked for quite a considerable time to produce the Bronx design.'

He then went on to describe the various features which they incorporated, and in particular the addition of the plinth to the 'Denver' so as to turn it into the 'Bronx', thereby giving it a 'floating' effect. When asked whose idea it was to provide the plinth, he said that 'It was my idea originally, and then in consultation with my colleagues'. In answer to my question: 'You mean it was developed in consultation, do you? Is that what you mean?', he said 'Yes'. It apparently took them something of the order of six weeks to complete the prototype and the date of completion is firmly fixed because there was a discussion between the three of them and a Mr Cecil Bright, who at that time was managing director of the plaintiffs' associated company, Superest Ltd, of South Wales. That discussion took place at the London factory at Wallis Road, E9, on the day when the Aberfan disaster occurred and that firmly fixed the date in everybody's memory. The disaster was in fact in October 1966. The 'Bronx' was completed and was shown publicly at the Earls Court Exhibition in January 1967. It was also shown in March 1967 at the Ideal Home Exhibition on the stand of the Times Furnishing Co.

Counsel for the defendants, on the authority of *Burke & Margot Burke Ltd v Spicers Dress Designs*[1] submitted that the plaintiffs' chairs could not be 'works of artistic craftsmanship' for the following reasons. He said that the *Burke* case[1] showed that where the work in question was the result of one person supplying the ideas and another person or a number of people merely working out those ideas and applying the craftsmanship necessary to produce the finished article, these latter, who merely worked out the ideas, could not claim to have any copyright in the completed work. In that case the plaintiff was the company which employed the workpeople who actually made the dress and Clauson J said[2]:

'The first difficulty in their way is that all their workwomen have done is to do certain acts of craftsmanship and thus produce a work of craftsmanship. It is said that, having regard to the beauty of this frock when completed, it is not only a work of craftsmanship but a work of artistic craftsmanship. For the moment, though I am not satisfied that this is correct, I will assume that it is. But where did the artistic element which has become connected with this work of craftsmanship originate? It certainly did not originate in the workpeople. All they did was by purely mechanical processes to produce the article; they are craftswomen, but they were not "artistic" craftswomen; they borrowed the artistic qualities of the article from the inspiration of Mrs. Burke in her sketch

---

1 [1936] 1 All ER 99, [1936] Ch 400
2 [1936] Ch at 407, 408, cf [1936] 1 All ER at 101

and accordingly, although I can well understand that it might be said that the *a*
frock was an original work of craftsmanship, the craftsmanship being original,
it is not, in my view, an original work of artistic craftsmanship, because the
artistic element did not originate in those who made the work.'

So here it is said that the chairs and settees cannot be 'works of artistic craftsmanship'
because the ideas all originated in Mr Hensher and he did nothing to complete the
work with his own hands as a craftsman. *b*

It seems to me that the case of *Burke*[1] is quite a different one from the present
case where, as I have found, there was quite clearly collaboration between Mr
Hensher, Mr Sutton and Mr Batchelor, and where they all took part in the conception, embodiment and completion of the finished article. I do not therefore think
that the *Burke* case[1] is an authority which governs the present.

My conclusion on this part of the case is therefore that these chairs and settees are *c*
'works of artistic craftsmanship' in that they have, whether one admires them or not,
distinctive characteristics of shape, form and finish, which were conceived and executed
by Mr Hensher and those working with him so as to result in articles which are
much more than purely utilitarian. They exhibit in my judgment distinctive
features of design and skill in workmanship which the words of definition 'artistic
craftsmanship' on their proper construction in their context connote. *d*

Mr Carter, a design consultant, gave evidence on behalf of the plaintiffs. He was
quite independent of the plaintiffs and, although he did not admire the plaintiffs'
design, was clearly of opinion that it had appeal to the public and was a good commercial design. He said he thought that the general character of the upturned ends
and the sort of flared base had a quite distinctive individuality. It was those features
which he thought constituted the significant part of the whole concept. In his view, *e*
'artistic' as applied to furniture meant a design concept or a concept of form, the form
being either completely decorative or completely functional, but in his view a design
could properly be said to be artistic in respect of furniture if it had features which gave
it individual character and his view was that the 'Bronx' chair did have strong individual character. In making the last few observations I am paraphrasing his evidence
as I understand it. *f*

Now, although the matter is of course one of construction and is not one for the
witness, I agree, as will be clear from what I have already said, that the proper
construction of the phrase 'works of artistic craftsmanship' in the section in question
does denote a work which, while it is the subject of craftsmanship, that is to say made
or designed by craftsmen, at the same time has individual characteristics which
distinguish it from a mere utilitarian work of craftsmanship which has no distinctive *g*
features of design. The matter is not a particularly easy one to put into words, but
if one compares an ordinary plain kitchen chair of no artistic merit with, for example,
a chair produced in the factory of Mr Chippendale, one can readily appreciate that,
whilst the latter will clearly be regarded as a work 'of artistic craftsmanship', the
former may well not be, although it may be very well made and could properly be
described as a work of craftsmanship. *h*

In view of what I have said the plaintiffs are, I think, entitled to claim that in the
'Bronx' chair and the developments of it they have made 'works of artistic craftsmanship' which give them copyright in accordance with the section. There is no dispute
that the three gentlemen responsible for the design and production of the prototypes
were all under contracts of service with the plaintiff company and therefore any
copyright which they may have created and of which they were the authors passes *j*
automatically to the company itself who employs them. I should add that both
Mr Sutton and Mr Batchelor gave evidence that they personally were craftsmen.

There remains the question of infringement which in my judgment can be dealt
with quite shortly. The test for infringement has been laid down many times and

1   [1936] 1 All ER 99, [1936] Ch 400

the plaintiffs have to show that there has been a reproduction by the defendants of the whole or a substantial part of the plaintiffs' work in which their copyright subsists. Furthermore it has been frequently said that it is quality rather than quantity which is the important matter. The words of Lord Reid in *Ladbroke (Football) Ltd v William Hill (Football) Ltd*[1] are well known, and are as follows:

'If he does copy, the question whether he has copied a substantial part depends much more on the quality than on the quantity of what he has taken.'

[His Lordship then considered the evidence and held that the 'Amazon' suite was an infringement of the plaintiffs' copyright in the 'Bronx' suite. He rejected the defendants' claim that they had made the 'Amazon' before they knew of the 'Bronx', finding that on the evidence it was impossible not to draw the inference that the former must in some way have been copied from the latter. On the plaintiffs' claim for infringement of copyright in the drawings, his Lordship found, applying the test in s 9 (8) of the Copyright Act 1956, that an ordinary member of the public would not consider that the 'Amazon' suite was a reproduction of the drawings, and concluded:] The upshot of the whole matter is therefore that the plaintiffs, in my judgment, fail on the issue of passing off; they fail on the issue of infringement of their copyright in drawings, but they do succeed on the issue of the copying of their chairs as 'works of artistic craftsmanship' in which copyright can exist in accordance with the provisions of s 3 (1) (c) of the Copyright Act 1956.

Judgment accordingly.

Solicitors: *Simmonds, Church, Rackham* (for the plaintiffs); *Simpson, Silvertown & Co*, agents for *Donn & Co*, Manchester (for the defendants).

Susan Corbett   Barrister.

East African Airways Corporation v Secretary of State for Social Services

QUEEN'S BENCH DIVISION
BROWNE J
1st, 2nd NOVEMBER 1972

National insurance – Employed person – Absence abroad – Payment of contributions in respect of periods abroad – Employment outside Great Britain – Employment in continuation of employed contributor's employment in Great Britain – 'In continuation of' – Period of non-employment intervening between termination of employment in Great Britain and subsequent employment outside Great Britain – Whether subsequent employment must be continuous in point of time with employment in Great Britain – National Insurance (Residence and Persons Abroad) Regulations 1948 (SI 1948 No 1275), reg 3 (1).

In 1965 L was ordinarily resident in Great Britain. He was employed by British Overseas Airways Corporation ('BOAC') and contributions were paid in respect of him under the national insurance scheme at the employed person's rate. His employment with BOAC terminated on 31st December 1965. In January 1966 L was offered, and accepted, employment with East African Airways Corporation ('EAAC'). From 7th February, when he joined EAAC, L remained at all material times continuously in their employment. He was based in East Africa and his flying duties were world wide, including flights to the United Kingdom. His duties were performed substantially outside Great Britain, but he remained ordinarily resident in Great

---

1   [1964] 1 All ER 465 at 469, [1964] 1 WLR 273 at 276

Britain.   At all material times EAAC had a place of business in London.   EAAC a
appealed under s 65 (3)^a of the National Insurance Act 1965 against a decision by
the Secretary of State that they were liable, by virtue of reg 3 (1)^b of the National
Insurance (Residence and Persons Abroad) Regulations 1948, to pay national insurance
contributions in respect of L.   EAAC contended that employment outside Great
Britain was not, within reg 3 (1), 'in continuation of' the employment in Great Britain
unless the employment abroad was not only of the same nature and quality as that b
in Great Britain, but also continuous with it in point of time.

Held – The words 'in continuation of' in reg 3 (1) meant only that the person had
to continue outside Great Britain to be employed by an employer, i e to be employed in what would be class (a) employment, within s 1 (2)^c of the 1965 Act, if
he was in Great Britain, as opposed to being self-employed.   Although in certain
circumstances a period of non-employment intervening between the employment c
in Great Britain and the subsequent employment abroad might be such as to prevent
the subsequent employment being 'in continuation of' the employment in Great
Britain, it was impossible to say that the Secretary of State had been wrong in law
in concluding that L's employment with EAAC was in continuation of his previous
employment with BOAC.   Accordingly the appeal would be dismissed (see p 171
e and h and p 172 b, post). d
   Per Browne J.   If a period of self-employment intervenes between the class (a)
employment in Great Britain and the employment abroad, the latter is not, within
reg 3 (1) of the 1948 regulations, 'in continuation of' the former (see p 171 f, post).

Notes
For the meaning of 'employed persons' for the purposes of national insurance, see e
27 Halsbury's Laws (3rd Edn) 711, 712, para 1295.
   For the National Insurance Act 1965, ss 1, 65, see 23 Halsbury's Statutes (3rd Edn)
254, 332.

Appeal
By notice of motion dated 19th October 1971 the appellant, East African Airways
Corporation, moved, inter alia, for an order that the decision of the respondent, f
the Secretary of State for Social Services, as stated in the case stated by the respondent
dated 17th June 1971, be reversed.   The facts are set out in the judgment.

D H Farquharson QC and *P Rouch* for the appellant.
Gordon Slynn for the Secretary of State.

                                                                                                      g
BROWNE J.   This is an appeal by the East African Airways Corporation under
s 65 (3) of the National Insurance Act 1965 from a decision of the Secretary of State
for Social Services given under s 64 (1) of that Act.   I do not think I need read s 64 (1)
but I think I should read s 65 (3) which provides:

   'Any person aggrieved by the decision of the Minister on any question of law h
   such as is mentioned in subsection (1) of this section . . . may appeal from that
   decision to the High Court.'

Accordingly, my powers on this appeal are limited in the familiar way applicable
where the appeal is only on a question of law.
   The facts are set out in para 5 of the case stated, which is as follows:

   'On consideration of information available from the files which information i
   in so far as it was relevant was disclosed to the Appellant the Secretary of State

---

a Section 65 (3), so far as material, is set out at h, supra
b Regulation 3 (1) is set out at p 169 b and c, post
c Section 1 (2) is set out at p 168 d, post

a   found the following facts:—(i) the Appellant was incorporated at Nairobi, Kenya in 1963. The business of the Appellant is civil air transport in East Africa and elsewhere; (ii) at all relevant times the Appellant had a place of business in London, up to about March 1967 at Grand Buildings, Trafalgar Square, WC2, and thereafter at 29 New Bond Street, W1; (iii) Mr Arthur Gerald Lacy was born on 21 August 1919. In 1965 he was ordinarily resident in Great Britain and was insured under the National Insurance Scheme ... Up to 31 December

b   1965 he was employed by the Flight Operations Department of the British Overseas Airways Corporation, London Airport, Heathrow and contributions were paid in respect of him at the employed person's rate; (iv) in or about the month of January 1966 Mr Lacy was interviewed in London by a representative of the Appellant who had travelled from East Africa for the purpose. As a result of that interview Mr Lacy was offered and accepted employment with

c   the Appellant as a Navigating Officer on their aircraft based in East Africa; (v) Mr Lacy's employment with the Appellant commenced in East Africa on 7 February 1966 and he remained continuously full time in the Appellant's employ up to at least 10 February 1969'.

d   Pausing there, the relevance of that date, 10th February 1969, appears from para 1 of the case, because that was the date on which the appellant applied to the Secretary of State for a decision under s 64 (1) of the Act. Sub-paragraph (v) continues:

'Mr Lacy was based in East Africa and his flying duties were world wide, including flights to the United Kingdom, but were performed substantially outside Great Britain; (vi) Mr Henry Hesketh was born on 26 October 1916.

e   In the earlier part of 1968 he was ordinarily resident in Great Britain and insured under the National Insurance Scheme ... Up to 20 June 1968 he was employed by Cambrian Airways, Rhoose Airport, Glamorgan, and contributions were paid in respect of him at the employed person's rate'.

Pausing there, it is common ground that his employment by Cambrian Airways

f   was as an aircraft engineer. Going back to the case:

'(vii) in or about the month of June 1968 Mr Hesketh was interviewed in London by a representative of the Appellant who had travelled from East Africa for the purpose. As a result of that interview he was offered and accepted employment with the Appellant in East Africa as an aircraft engineer; (viii)

g   Mr Hesketh's employment with the Appellant commenced in East Africa on 2 July 1968. Thereafter he remained in the Appellant's employ in East Africa, engaged full time on aircraft maintenance and repair work up to at least 10 February 1969'.

Just to repeat the relevant dates because they could be important in this case, Mr

h   Lacy's employment with BOAC ended on 31st December 1965, his interview with a representative of the appellant was in January 1966, and his employment with the appellant began on 7th February 1966. Mr Hesketh was employed by Cambrian Airways until 20th June 1968, his interview with the appellant was in June 1968, it is not clear from the case whether before or after 20th June, and his employment with the appellant began on 2nd July 1968. Going back again to the findings of

j   fact, sub-para (ix) reads:

'while in the employ of the Appellant both Mr Lacy and Mr Hesketh were controlled by the Appellant as to the method of performance of their work through departmental heads or other designated senior officials and required to observe the Appellant's Staff Regulations. They were both remunerated by an annual salary paid monthly and notice of termination was required on either side.'

The decision of the Secretary of State from which this appeal is brought was that the appellant was liable to pay national insurance contributions in respect of the two men mentioned, Mr Lacy and Mr Hesketh.

I refer now to the relevant provisions of the National Insurance Act 1965, and the regulations. By s 1 (1) of the Act:

'Subject to the provisions of this Act—(a) every person who—(i) immediately before the date of commencement of this Act was insured under the Act of 1946 [that of course was the National Insurance Act 1946]; or (ii) on or after the said date, being over school leaving age and under pensionable age, is in Great Britain, and fulfils such conditions as may be prescribed as to residence in Great Britain, shall be insured under this Act; and (b) any person who at the said date is, or who subsequently becomes, insured under this Act shall thereafter continue throughout his life to be so insured.'

I pause there to say that the National Insurance Act 1965 was a consolidation Act. By s 1 (2):

'For the purposes of this Act, insured persons shall be divided into the following three classes, namely—(a) employed persons, that is to say, persons gainfully occupied in employment in Great Britain, being employment under a contract of service; (b) self-employed persons, that is to say, persons gainfully occupied in employment in Great Britain who are not employed persons; (c) non-employed persons, that is to say, persons who are neither employed nor self-employed persons.'

The expression 'contract of service' is defined in s 114 (1) of the Act:

' "contract of service" means any contract of service or apprenticeship, whether written or oral and whether express or implied'.

The 1965 Act continues in s 1 (3):

'Provision may be made by regulations for modifying the classification aforesaid in relation to cases where it appears to the Minister desirable by reason of the nature or circumstances of a person's employment or otherwise, and such regulations may in particular provide—(a) for treating as an employed contributor's employment—(i) employment under a public or local authority constituted in Great Britain notwithstanding that it is not employment under a contract of service; (ii) [and this is the relevant one for present purposes] employment outside Great Britain in continuation of any employed contributor's employment . . .'

'Employed contributor's employment' is defined in s 114 (1): ' "employed contributor's employment" means any employment by virtue of which an insured person is an employed person.' The words 'employed person' in that definition throw one back to s 1 (2) (a), and it is common ground that 'an employed contributor's employment' means, and means only, employment of people falling within class (a) of s 1 (2) and does not include self-employed people or non-employed people.

Counsel for the Secretary of State very helpfully referred me to various other provisions of the Act to show me its general scheme. I do not think I need refer to them in detail, but they were s 3, dealing with the contributions payable by each of the three classes laid down by s 1 (2); s 8 (1), which provides:

'Subject to the provisions of this Act and of any regulations, no person shall be entitled to pay any contribution under this Act other than a contribution which he is liable to pay . . .'

Section 19 and Sch 2, which deal with unemployment and sickness benefits and contribution conditions for those benefits, as to which he also referred me to the National

Insurance (Classifications) Regulations 1972, Sch 2[1], and the National Insurance (Unemployment and Sickness Benefit) Regulations 1967, regs 2 and 13[2].

The National Insurance (Residence and Persons Abroad) Regulations 1948[3], which are the vital ones in this case, were made under the 1946 Act but were continued under the 1965 Act. The relevant provision in this case is reg 3 (1). The appellant originally contended that part of this regulation was ultra vires, but before me counsel for the appellant abandoned this contention. Regulation 3 is as follows:

'(1) Where a person employed in an employed contributor's employment ceases to be so employed in Great Britain but is employed (whether by the same or a different employer) outside Great Britain in continuation of an employed contributor's employment, that employment outside Great Britain shall be treated as an employed contributor's employment for the period for which contributions are payable in respect of it under sub-paragraph (a) of paragraph (2) of this regulation, provided the employer has a place of business in Great Britain, and the person concerned is ordinarily resident therein.

'(2) Where under the preceding paragraph employment outside Great Britain is treated as an employed contributor's employment, the following provisions shall apply with respect to the payment of contributions under the Act:—(a) Weekly contributions at the appropriate rates specified in Part I and Part II of the First Schedule to the Act (which Parts respectively specify the contributions payable by employed persons and the employers of such persons) shall be payable in respect of such employment during the period of twelve months from the commencement thereof. (b) After the completion of the period for which contributions are payable under the preceding sub-paragraph, the insured person shall, for any week thereafter during the whole of which he is outside Great Britain [be entitled in various circumstances to pay a contribution as a non-employed person].'

The Secretary of State's decision as set out in the case is contained in para 6:

'. . . The Secretary of State concluded as follows:—(i) the Appellant had a place of business in Great Britain and both Mr Lacy and Mr Hesketh were ordinarily resident in Great Britain; (ii) the employment of Mr Lacy in Great Britain prior to 31 December 1965 was employed contributor's employment and his employment by the Appellant outside Great Britain was in continuation of that employment; (iii) the employment of Mr Hesketh in Great Britain prior to 20 June 1968 was employed contributor's employment and his employment by the Appellant outside Great Britain was in continuation of that employment; (iv) the employment of Mr Lacy and Mr Hesketh by the Appellant outside Great Britain was employed contributor's employment; (v) the Appellant was liable as employer to pay contributions under section 3 of the National Insurance Act 1965 and Regulation 3 (2) of the said Regulations in respect of Mr Arthur Gerald Lacy from 7 February 1966 to 6 February 1967 and in respect of Mr Henry Hesketh from 2 July 1968 to 10 February 1969.'

The appellant's contentions all relate to the phrase 'in continuation of an employed contributor's employment' in reg 3 (1). I am satisfied that all the other requirements of reg 3 (1) were fulfilled in this case: (1) while in this country both Mr Lacy and Mr Hesketh were employed in employed contributor's employment; (2) they ceased to be so employed in Great Britain; (3) they were then employed outside Great Britain, although by a different employer; (4) both conditions of the proviso are satisfied: (a) the appellant had a place of business in Great Britain; the fact that

---

1 SI 1972 No 555
2 SI 1967 No 330
3 SI 1948 No 1275

this was only a place where the appellant sold tickets and had no other connection
with the work done by Mr Lacy and Mr Hesketh seems to me irrelevant, and I get
no help from the reference to the employer's *principal* place of business in reg 2 (i) (*b*)
of the National Insurance (Airmen) Regulations 1948[1]; I agree with counsel for the
Secretary of State that the obvious reason for the inclusion of this condition is that it
would be futile to provide that an overseas employer should pay contributions unless
he had a place of business here from which the contributions could be collected;
(*b*) it is admitted that Mr Lacy and Mr Hesketh were at all material times ordinarily
resident in Great Britain. The whole question is: was the employment of Mr Lacy
and Mr Hesketh by the appellant 'in continuation of' an employed contributor's
employment in Great Britain, or rather, was the Secretary of State wrong in law in
deciding that it was.

Counsel for the appellant submits that employment outside Great Britain is not
'in continuation of' employment in Great Britain unless there is a nexus between the
two employments by the fulfilment of three conditions, or at least by the fulfilment
of the second and third of his suggested conditions. The conditions he suggested were
(1) the employment abroad must be under the same contract as the employment
in Great Britain, or at least by the same employer, or at the very least by an associated
company in the same group as the employer in Great Britain; (2) the employment
abroad must be continuous in time with the employment in Great Britain; there
must be no break beyond what can be ignored under the de minimis principle;
(3) the employment abroad must be of the same nature and quality as the employment in Great Britain; he admits that in this particular case this condition is fulfilled,
because both in Great Britain and abroad Mr Lacy was employed as air-crew and
Mr Hesketh as an aircraft engineer.

Counsel for the Secretary of State submits that 'in continuation' only means that the
employment abroad which would be class (*a*) employment if it was in the United
Kingdom (i e employment by someone else as opposed to self-employment) must
follow the class (*a*) employment in Great Britain without the intervention of any
employment which is not class (*a*) employment, that is, without any intervening
period of self-employment, either in Great Britain or abroad; he says that a period
of non-employment would not prevent subsequent employment abroad from
being 'in continuation', but says, alternatively, that on the facts of these particular
cases the Secretary of State was not wrong in law in deciding that any intervening period
of non-employment of Mr Lacy and Mr Hesketh did not prevent their subsequent
employment by the appellant from being in continuation of their previous
employment.

In my judgment the effect of the words 'in continuation of' in reg 3 (1) is not
limited to cases fulfilling the three conditions, or the second and third of the conditions, suggested by counsel for the appellant. The provision that the employment
outside Great Britain may be either by the same or a different employer, which is
not now argued to be ultra vires, seems to me to rule out counsel's first condition.
I cannot see how a 'different employer' abroad can be limited to an associated
company of the employer in Great Britain. What reg 3 requires is that persons should
be employed abroad in continuation of *an* employed contributor's employment in
Great Britain, not of *the* employment in Great Britain. I think this conclusion is
supported by the reference to *any* employed contributor's employment in s 1 (3) (*a*)
(ii) of the Act. There is no express provision that there must be no break between
the employment in Great Britain and the employment outside Great Britain, and
the Oxford Dictionary definitions of 'continuation' include under heading 5 'resump-
tion after an interruption'. I think there is force in the contrast of counsel for the
Secretary of State 'in continuation of' in reg 3 with 'continuous with' in reg 4 and continuous period' in reg 5 (2) (*b*) (i). I think that 'in continuation' is wider than 'continuous', which can only mean uninterrupted (again see the Oxford Dictionary).

1 SI 1948 No 1466

a   There is no express provision that the employment outside Great Britain must be the same as or of a similar nature to the employment in Great Britain. I again stress that the requirement is that the foreign employment must be in continuation of *an* employed contributor's employment in Great Britain, not *the* employed contributor's employment in Great Britain. What is relevant to qualification under class (*a*) is the *fact* of employment, not the *nature* of the employment.

b   Counsel for the Secretary of State relied on the contrast with the wording of reg 2, proviso (*c*), (i) and (ii), but the context is so different that I do not find this of any help.

   If I reject the submissions of counsel for the appellant about what conditions must be fulfilled before a foreign employment is 'in continuation of' an employment in Great Britain, as I do, what does 'in continuation of' mean? I confess I find it difficult

c   to know what it is intended to mean, but no other meaning has been suggested except that of counsel for the appellant. People in Great Britain have to fulfil two conditions to be in class (*a*) of insured persons; they must be gainfully employed in Great Britain and that employment must be under a contract of service. If they fulfil the first condition but not the second they are in class (*b*), self-employed (see s 1 (2) (*a*) and (*b*) of the Act). Regulation 3 requires that people should have been in class (*a*)

d   employment in Great Britain and that in continuation of an employed contributor's employment in Great Britain they should be employed by an employer outside Great Britain, that is, that their foreign employment should be of the nature of class (*a*) employment and not of the nature of class (*b*) employment. For people abroad, reg 3 removes the requirement of s 1 (2) (*a*) that they should be employed in Great Britain, but preserves the requirement that they shall be employed under a contract of service.

e   In my view, 'in continuation of' means only that the person must continue outside Great Britain to be employed by an employer, that is, to be employed in what would be class (*a*) employment if he was in Great Britain, as opposed to being self-employed.

   I find it difficult to know what 'in continuation of employment in Great Britain' means in reg 4, but that regulation does not contain the words 'whether by the same

f   or a different employer' and therefore does not necessarily mean the same thing as in reg 3.

   I agree with counsel for the Secretary of State that if there was an intervening period of self-employment between the class (*a*) employment in Great Britain and the employment abroad the latter would not be in continuation of the former. I think the effect of an intervening period of non-employment is more difficult. I am inclined to

g   think that if the nature (for example, retirement) or the duration of the non-employment was such as to show an intention at the time when the first employment ceased never to take up employment again, an eventual new employment might not be in continuation of the old, but it is not necessary to decide that point in this case. Assuming that in those sort of circumstances non-employment can be such as to prevent the new employment from being in continuation of the old, the question

h   whether it is or not must be a question of fact and degree in each particular case. From this point of view I cannot possibly say that the Secretary of State was wrong in law in saying that in these cases the new employment was in continuation of the old; on the contrary, I think he was in fact clearly right.

   It is clear that the purpose of reg 3 is to preserve, fully for the first 12 months and then partially, the rights under the Act of people who in Great Britain were in

j   employment which made them class (*a*) employed persons. If they had stayed in Great Britain and were in class (*a*) employment they would continue to qualify for class (*a*) even though their employment was under a different contract or by a different employer, or in a different sort of work or there was a break between employments. In my view, the effect of reg 3 is to put them in these respects for a limited period in the same position if they go abroad. It is true that in one respect they are worse off if they go abroad. As I understand it, a period of self-employment in Great Britain would not bar a subsequent claim for unemployment or sickness benefit if the person later returned to class (a) employment, although it might make it impossible for him to fulfil (or fully to fulfil) the contribution conditions, whereas on the argument of counsel for the respondent the period of self-employment would be a complete bar if the person goes abroad. I confess that I do not understand the reason for this limitation, but it does not seem to me any ground for holding that reg 3 imposes other limitations.

The result is that in my judgment the decision of the Secretary of State was right in law, substantially for the reasons submitted by counsel for the respondent. Accordingly in my judgment the appeal fails and this motion must be dismissed.

Appeal dismissed.

Solicitors: *Peacock & Goddard* (for the appellant); *Solicitor, Department of Health and Social Security.*

E H Hunter Esq Barrister.

Middlemiss & Gould (a firm) v Hartlepool Corporation

COURT OF APPEAL, CIVIL DIVISION
LORD DENNING MR, EDMUND DAVIES AND STEPHENSON LJJ
12th OCTOBER 1972

Arbitration – Award – Enforcement – Leave of High Court – Refusal – Circumstances in which leave may be refused – Doubt as to validity of award – Point specifically referred to arbitrator by respondents – Award not expressly dealing with point – Award in favour of claimants – Point to be taken as decided by implication – No application to set aside award within six week time limit – Award final and binding – Wrong decision on point of law by arbitrator not invalidating award – Claimants entitled to leave to enforce award as a judgment – Arbitration Act 1950, s 26.

A contract was made between the claimants, who where building contractors, and a local authority ('the corporation'), incorporating the RIBA form, for the erection of 85 houses and 27 bungalows. The contract contained provisions for interim certificates. The contractors began work but differences arose as to the way in which the interim certificates were to be calculated. The contractors in accordance with the contract referred the dispute to arbitration. The arbitrator held a preliminary meeting at which directions were given regarding the proceedings before him. On the following day, however, the corporation gave notice to the contractors alleging that they were in default in that they had not proceeded regularly and diligently with the works. Subsequently, alleging that the default had continued for 14 days, the corporation determined the employment of the contractors. The arbitration went ahead and points of claim and counterclaim were delivered. The corporation in their defence did not confine themselves to setting out their contentions as to the way in which the interim certificates were to be calculated. Relying on the terms of the contract the corporation pleaded that they had paid all money due to the contractors on the ground that, because of the termination of the agreement, no further payments were due by virtue of cl 25 (4) (d) of the contract which provided that, in the event of the contractors' employment being determined, the corporation were not bound to make any further payment to the contractors until completion of the works. The arbitrator did not expressly deal with that point raised by the corporation, but upheld the contractors' contentions on the method of calculating the interim certificates. Accordingly he made his award directing that the corporation 'shall *a*   pay to the [contractors] the sum of £7,957·74p ... within 14 days'. On his own initiative the arbitrator gave his reasons in the form of a special case as he was authorised to do by s 21[a] of the Arbitration Act 1950. The corporation did not, however, challenge the award within six weeks, with the result that it became a final and a binding determination of the matters between the parties. The contractors applied under s 26[b] of the 1950 Act to enforce the award, but the judge

b   refused leave on the ground that the corporation had an arguable point of law in that they might be entitled to rely on cl 25 (4) (*d*) of the contract. The contractors appealed.

Held – The appeal would be allowed for the following reasons—

(i) although the arbitrator had not expressly dealt with the point on cl 25 (4) (d), it had been distinctly raised by the corporation; in consequence the arbitrator must

c   be taken to have fully considered and rejected their contention which was therefore res judicata (see p 176 b to d and g and p 177 d to g, post);

(ii) once an award had been made and the time limit for challenging it had expired the award became final and binding; it should therefore be entered as a judgment and enforced accordingly; leave to enforce an award should only be refused where there was a real ground for doubting the validity of an award; even if it were the

d   case that the arbitrator had wrongly decided a point of law, that did not make the award invalid; the point should have been brought up by way of case stated; as it had not been the award was final and binding (see p 175 f and j to p 176 b and e and p 177 g, post); dictum of Diplock J in *Margulies Brothers Ltd v Dafnis Thomaides & Co (UK) Ltd* [1958] 1 All ER at 782 applied; dictum of Scrutton LJ in *Re Boks & Co and Peters, Rushton & Co Ltd* [1918-19] All ER Rep at 771 disapproved.

e

Notes

For enforcement of an award as a judgment, see 2 Halsbury's Laws (3rd Edn) 50, 51, paras 110, 111, and for cases on the subject, see 2 Digest (Repl) 702, 703, 2146-2159.

For the Arbitration Act 1950, ss 21, 26, see 2 Halsbury's Statutes (3rd Edn) 450, 456.

f   **Cases referred to in judgments**

Birks v Trippet (1666) 1 Saund 28, 1 Sid 303, 85 ER 32, 2 Digest (Repl) 709, 2211.

Boks & Co and Peters, Rushton & Co Ltd, Re [1919] 1 KB 491, [1918-19] All ER Rep 767, 88 LJKB 351, 120 LT 516, CA, 2 Digest (Repl) 701, 2133.

Fidelitas Shipping Co Ltd v V/O Exportchleb [1965] 2 All ER 4, [1966] 1 QB 630, [1965] 2 WLR 1059, [1965] 1 Lloyd's Rep 223, CA, Digest (Cont Vol B) 27, 1147a.

g   *Harrison v Creswick* (1853) 13 CB 399, 21 LJCP 113, 16 Jur 315, 138 ER 1254, 2 Digest (Repl) 631, 1553.

Henderson v Henderson (1843) 3 Hare 100, [1843-60] All ER Rep 378, 1 LTOS 410, 67 ER 313, 21 Digest (Repl) 244, 306.

Margulies Brothers Ltd v Dafnis Thomaides & Co (UK) Ltd [1958] 1 All ER 777, [1958] 1 WLR 398, [1958] 1 Lloyd's Rep 250, Digest (Cont Vol A) 39, 1236a.

h   *Wood v Griffith* (1818) 1 Swan 43, [1814-23] All ER Rep 294, 1 Wils Ch 34, 36 ER 291, 2 Digest (Repl) 717, 2315.

Appeal

By a summons dated 22nd December 1971 the claimants, Middlemiss & Gould (a firm), applied to the district registrar at Hartlepool for an order pursuant to s 26

j   *a*   Section 21, so far as material, provides: '(1) An arbitrator or umpire may ... state—(*a*) any question of law arising in the course of the reference; or (*b*) an award or any part of an award, in the form of a special case for the decision of the High Court ...'

    b   Section 26 provides: 'An award on an arbitration agreement may, by leave of the High Court or a judge thereof, be enforced in the same manner as a judgment or order to the same effect, and where leave is so given, judgment may be entered in terms of the award.'

of the Arbitration Act 1950 that the claimants be at liberty to enforce the award
dated 21st September 1971 of William Mills, the arbitrator duly appointed in the
arbitration between the claimants and the respondents, Hartlepool Corporation
('the corporation'), in the same manner as a judgment or order to the same effect.
By an order dated 23rd February 1972 the district registrar dismissed the application.
On 21st March 1972 Cumming-Bruce J at Leeds dismissed the claimants' appeal
but gave leave to appeal to the Court of Appeal. The facts are set out in the judgment
of Lord Denning MR.

D G Wright for the claimants.
P N Garland QC and *A T K May* for the corporation.

LORD DENNING MR. In 1969 the claimants, Middlemiss & Gould ('the contractors') entered into a contract to build 85 houses and 27 bungalows on an estate
at Hartlepool for the corporation. The contract incorporated the RIBA form.
It contained provisions for interim certificates. The total price was some £300,000.
The contractors started the work. By the middle of 1970 they had done about one-
third of it, which they valued at about £100,000. Differences arose as to the way
in which the interim certificates were to be calculated. Seeing that the dispute was
whether the certificate was in accordance with the conditions, it could be referred
to arbitration whilst the work was proceeding. On 24th July 1970 the contractors
asked the President of the Royal Institute of British Architects to appoint an arbitrator.
On 24th September 1970 he appointed Mr William Mills of Sutton Coldfield. On
7th October the arbitrator held a preliminary meeting at which directions were
given for pleadings and so forth. But on the very next day, 8th October, the corporation gave notice to the contractors, alleging that they were in default in that they had
not proceeded regularly and diligently with the works. On 26th October the corporation alleged that the default had continued for 14 days, and on that ground
determined the employment of the contractors.

Notwithstanding that termination, the arbitration went forward. Points of claim
and points of defence were delivered. In the points of claim the contractors set
out their contentions as to the way in which interim certificates were to be calculated
and claimed to be paid a sum of £9,209 on that basis. In the points of defence the
corporation set out their contentions about the calculations. But they did not confine
themselves to the calculation. They said that the contract had been terminated on
26th October, and that on that account no sums were payable to the contractors.
These are the material paragraphs in the defence:

'8 ... The second £3,000 has not been paid because the work did not progress
as promised by the [contractors] and the said Agreement for the building of
the houses and bungalows was determined on the 26th of October, 1970 by
notice given by the [corporation] to the [contractors] under the provisions of
clause 25 of the said Agreement.

11. The [corporation] therefore repudiate the claim ... (c) Because of the
termination of the Agreement no further payments are due to the [contractors]
at the present time (see clause 25 (d) of the Agreement).'

So on the pleadings the first issue was: what was the amount properly payable
to the contractors? The second issue was: in any event, seeing that the employment
had been terminated, was any sum payable at all to the contractors?

The arbitrator, Mr Mills, did not have a hearing. He did not have witnesses, nor
lawyers arguing before him. He considered the matter on the papers submitted
to him. He is very well qualified. He is a chartered architect and quantity surveyor
and a Fellow of the Institute of Arbitrators. Mr Mills gave a written award in which
he dealt with the matter fully and carefully. He decided in favour of the contractors.
In his award he said that the interim certificates should be calculated in a way which

a   was that which the contractors had urged and not as the corporation wanted. Further, he made this very definite award: 'I ... DO HEREBY award and direct that the [corporation] shall pay to the [contractors] the sum of £7957·74p ... within fourteen days'. He also awarded interest and costs to the contractors.

The arbitrator gave his reasons in the form of a special case. He did so on his own initiative, as the Arbitration Act 1950, s 21, authorised him to do. That means that

b   either party, if they wish to take it up to the High Court, could do so. The arbitrator set out the contentions of the parties, including the corporation's claim that 'they have paid all moneys due to the contractors'. He must have decided that point against the corporation, because he awarded, as I have said, a sum of £7,957·74 to be due with interest. The total came to £9,046·53 and costs. If the corporation wished to challenge that award, they should have brought it up to the High Court within

c   six weeks[1]. They did not do so. So it became and was a final and binding determination of the matters between them.

The contractors, wishing to be paid, applied to the court under s 26 of the Arbitration Act 1950 for leave to enforce this award in the same manner as a judgment to the same effect in the High Court. The district registrar refused. So did the judge. The judge found it a difficult point. He had to decide it hurriedly on circuit.

d   He refused leave because he thought that the corporation might be able to rely on cl 25 (4) (d) of the RIBA form[2]. Clause 25 (4) provides:

'In the event of the employment of the Contractor being determined as aforesaid ... (a) The Employer may employ and pay other persons to carry out and complete the Works ... (d) ... Until the completion of the Works under paragraph (a) of this sub-clause the Employer shall not be bound by

e   any provision of this Contract to make any further payment to the Contractor...'

The judge thought that, by reason of cl 25 (4) (d), the corporation might not be bound to pay, despite the fact that the award had been made by the arbitrator. Regarding it as an arguable point, he refused leave to enforce the award. Now there is an appeal by the contractors to this court.

f   I am afraid that I cannot agree with the judge. Once an award has been made— and not challenged in the court—it should be entered as a judgment and given effect accordingly. It should not be held up because the losing party says he wants to argue some point or other or wants to set up a counterclaim or anything of that sort. He would not be allowed to do so in the case of a judgment not appealed from. Nor should do so in the case of an award that he has not challenged. I am in agree-

g   ment with what Diplock J said in *Margulies Brothers Ltd v Dafnis Thomaides & Co (UK) Ltd*[3]:

'It would be contrary to the purpose of s. 26 of the Arbitration Act, 1950, if, in a case where the validity of the award and the right to proceed on it is beyond doubt, it should be given less effect than a judgment.'

h   In this case the judge was impressed by *Re Boks & Co and Peters, Rushton & Co Ltd*[4]. But in that case the validity of the award was doubtful—very doubtful I would say because of the illegality of the whole transaction. Naturally enough, no leave was given. But I think that Scrutton LJ went a good deal too far. He said[5] that 'this summary method of enforcing awards is only to be used in reasonably clear cases'. I would put it just the opposite. I would say that it is to be used in

j   nearly all cases. Leave should be given to enforce the award as a judgment unless there is real ground for doubting the validity of the award.

---

1   See RSC Ord 73, r 5 (1)
2   Local Authorities Edition with Quantities, 1963 Edn (December 1967 issue)
3   [1958] 1 All ER 777 at 782, [1958] 1 WLR 398 at 404
4   [1919] 1 KB 491, [1918-19] All ER Rep 767
5   [1919] 1 KB at 497, [1918-19] All ER Rep at 771

In this case there is no possible ground for doubting the validity of this award. The corporation thinks that there is a point of law which has been wrongly decided. But that does not make the award invalid. If a point of law has been wrongly decided, the corporation should have brought it up to the High Court on a case stated. As it has not been brought up, the award is final and binding. It should be enforced.

But counsel for the corporation then suggested that the arbitrator had not decided the point under cl 25 (4) (d) at all. He contended that the arbitrator had only decided the way in which the certificates should be calculated. It is true that the arbitrator did not expressly say anything about cl 25 (4) (d) in his award. But the point was distinctly raised by the corporation in para 11 of their defence. By implication the arbitrator rejected their contention. He held that the money was payable despite cl 25 (4) (d). It is therefore res judicata. It falls within the principles stated in many cases from *Henderson v Henderson*[1] to *Fidelitas Shipping Co Ltd v V/O Exportchleb*[2]. If a point is raised for decision and by implication has been decided, that is final. The parties cannot be allowed thereafter to re-open it. This has been applied to arbitrations. It is stated in Russell on the Law of Arbitration[3]:

'The award will be sustained even though the arbitrator has omitted to notice some claim put forward by a party, if, according to the fair interpretation of the award, it is to be presumed that the claim has been taken into consideration.'

So here. The arbitrator had cl 25 (4) (d) before him, but nevertheless, he ordered that this sum was to be paid by the corporation. It should be enforced as a judgment. Leave should be given.

I would allow the appeal.

EDMUND DAVIES LJ. I desire to concur respectfully with Lord Denning MR as to the ambit of s 26 of the Arbitration Act 1950, and I would not circumscribe it, as Scrutton LJ did, the corresponding statutory provision in *Re Boks & Co and Peters, Rushton & Co Ltd*[4]. When parties to a dispute submit to having it decided by an arbitrator, two consequences flow from the making of his award. First, unless there is an express contrary provision in the arbitration submission or unless it is only an interim award, it operates as a final and conclusive judgment. This has long been and remains the position at common law: see the cases cited in Russell on the Law of Arbitration[5]. The matter is now also dealt with by s 16 of the Arbitration Act 1950. The second consequence, and for present purposes the more directly relevant one, is that the award constitutes a final judgment on *all* matters referred to the arbitrator. There is ample authority, both old and new, for this proposition. I propose to refer briefly to only two decisions which have stood for many years. In *Wood v Griffith*[6] Lord Eldon LC said:

'It is extremely clear that every award must be certain and final; but it has, particularly in more modern times, been considered the duty of the Court, in construing an award, to find that it is certain and final; and instead of leaning to a construction, which in effect would destroy nine-tenths of the awards made, if possible to put one consistent sense on all the terms.'

And in *Harrison v Creswick*[7] Parke B said:

1   (1843) 3 Hare 100, [1843-60] All ER Rep 378
2   [1965] 2 All ER 4, [1966] 1 QB 630
3   18th Edn (1970), p 277
4   [1919] 1 KB 491 at 497, [1918-19] All ER Rep 767 at 771
5   18th Edn (1970), p 312
6   (1818) 1 Swan 43 at 52, [1814-23] All ER Rep 294 at 298
7   (1853) 13 CB 399 at 415, 416

'... the only question, therefore, is whether the arbitrator has not by his award impliedly, if not in express terms, finally disposed of the matter. The rule as laid down in the notes to *Birks* v. *Trippet*[1], is, that, where an award professes to be made de praemissis, "Even where there is no award of general releases, the silence of the award as to some of the matters submitted and brought before the arbitrator, does not per se prevent it from being a sufficient exercise of the authority vested in him by the submission. An award is good, notwithstanding the arbitrator has not made a distinct adjudication on each or any of the several distinct matters submitted to him, provided that it does not appear that he has excluded any."'

Parke B then cited a number of reported decisions supporting that approach, and concluded[2]:

'Where an award is made de praemissis, the presumption is, that the arbitrator intended to dispose finally of all the matters in difference; and his award will be held final, if by any intendment it can be made so.'

In the present case it is unchallenged that the operation and impact of cl 25 (4) (d) of the building contract was one of the issues referred to the arbitrator, being expressly raised by the corporation in their points of defence as a ground for their assertion that no further payments were due to the claimants. It is to be observed that the arbitrator virtually adopted the language used by the corporation themselves in his summary of their contentions under two heads, saying: 'The [corporation] claim (1) that they have paid all moneys due to the claimants.' But, contrary to such contention, he made an award that in point of fact £7,957 was due from them. In my judgment, it would be bordering on the mischievous if in circumstances such as are here present this award could now be impeached on the ground that this arbitrator of high qualifications and I have no doubt great experience failed to bear in mind the matter which had thus been expressly raised and referred to him. In line with the authorities, I prefer to make the assumption that he fully considered cl 25 (4) (d) of the building contract in coming to his conclusion.

I accordingly agree with Lord Denning MR in holding that this appeal should be allowed.

STEPHENSON LJ. I agree with both judgments. Once it is accepted, as I understand it was accepted by counsel for the corporation, that the corporation have to show that the arbitrator did not decide the point raised by para 11 (c) of their points of defence, this appeal must, I agree, succeed. The arbitrator can only be shown to have failed to decide the point by necessary inference from his silence, and I am not satisfied that such an inference is necessary or that his silence is pregnant with any such negative. The corporation have only themselves to blame if we are wrong in refusing to draw that inference, because they agreed to arbitration and that this point should be included in the arbitration and decided on the documents without hearing or argument. If we do not draw that inference, we must give the claimants leave to enforce the award, as Edmund Davies LJ has said.

Appeal allowed; leave under s 26 of the Arbitration Act 1950 to enforce the award as if it were a judgment of the court.

Solicitors: *Warren, Murton & Co*, agents for *Atha, Denison, Suddards & Co*, York (for the claimants); *Lewin, Gregory, Mead & Sons*, agents for *E J Waggott*, Town Clerk, Hartlepool (for the corporation).

L J Kovats Esq   Barrister.

---

1 (1666) 1 Saund 28 at 33, note (a)
2 (1853) 13 CB at 416

R v Mutch   a

COURT OF APPEAL, CRIMINAL DIVISION
LAWTON LJ, CHAPMAN AND WIEN JJ
20th OCTOBER, 7th NOVEMBER 1972

Jury – Direction to jury – Comment by judge on failure of accused to give evidence – Form
of comment.   b

The accused was arrested and charged with robbery in a grocer's shop. The accused
denied the charge claiming that he was not in the shop at the time of the incident.
He was released on bail. No formal identification parade was held by the police
as it was alleged by the prosecution that, whilst on bail and for the purpose of confusing anyone attending an identification parade of which he was the suspect member, c
the accused tried to alter his appearance by tinting his hair and moustache and by
reshaping the latter. At his trial, a girl assistant in the shop at the time of the incident
identified the accused but he elected not to give evidence. He did however call
two witnesses to prove that he had not altered his appearance as alleged. The trial
judge, in summing up, told the jury, inter alia, that they were entitled to draw
inferences unfavourable to the accused where he was not called to establish an d
innocent explanation of facts proved by the prosecution which, without such an
explanation, told for his guilt. The accused was convicted and he appealed.

Held – The appeal would be allowed and the conviction quashed; in the circumstances it was unsafe and unsatisfactory to allow it to stand as the form of words
used by the trial judge was inappropriate in a case where the sole issue was whether e
the identification was correct and where the accused had admitted nothing (see
p 180 c, p 181 a f and g and p 182 c, post).

Per Curiam. The words used by the trial judge might have been permissible
if the evidence had established a situation calling for 'confession and avoidance'
(see p 189 g, post).

Dicta of Lord Oaksey in *Waugh v R* [1950] AC at 211, and of Lord Parker CJ in *R v* f
Bathurst [1968] 1 All ER at 1178, 1179 approved and applied.

R v Corrie (1904) 68 JP 294 distinguished.

Notes
For contents of summing-up in criminal cases, see 10 Halsbury's Laws (3rd Edn)
424, 425, para 780, and for cases on comment by judges on failure of accused to give g
evidence, see 14 Digest (Repl) 341, *3313-3317*.

Cases referred to in judgment
Bessela v Stern (1877) 2 CPD 265, 46 LJCP 467, 37 LT 88, 42 JP 197, CA, 27 (1) Digest
   (Reissue) 20, *58.*
R v Bathurst [1968] 1 All ER 1175, [1968] 2 QB 99, [1968] 2 WLR 1092, 52 Cr App Rep h
   251, CA, Digest (Cont Vol C) 183, *239bbb.*
R v Bernard (1908) 1 Cr App Rep 218, CCA, 14 Digest (Repl) 75, *355.*
R v Corrie, R v Watson (1904) 68 JP 294, 20 TLR 365, CCR, 8 Digest (Repl) 675, *157.*
R v Sullivan (1966) 51 Cr App Rep 102, CA.
Waugh v R [1950] AC 203, 66 (pt 1) TLR 554, PC, 15 Digest (Repl) 973, *5961.*

Case also cited   j
R v Pratt [1971] Crim LR 234, CA.

Appeal
The appellant, Kenneth Mutch, was charged with robbing Mary Scahill of £104·81
on 17th May 1971 in a shop in Liverpool. He denied that he was on the premises

a at the time of the incident. On 15th November 1971 he was convicted of the offence
at the Crown Court at Liverpool before his Honour Judge Trotter and a jury and
on 16th November he was sentenced to two years' imprisonment. He appealed
against his conviction. The facts are set out in the judgment of the court.

Andrew Mattison for the appellant.
b *V A Saunders* for the Crown.

Cur adv vult

7th November. **LAWTON LJ.** Chapman and Wien JJ are both absent today.
They have both seen the judgment which I propose to read and they have authorised
me to say that they agree with its terms.
c   This is an appeal by Kenneth Mutch against his conviction for robbery at Liverpool Crown Court on 15th November 1971 after a trial before his Honour Judge Trotter
and a jury. He was sentenced to two years' imprisonment. The appeal raises the
question whether the trial judge was justified in telling the jury that they were
entitled to draw inferences unfavourable to the appellant because of his absence
from the witness box.
d   The Crown's case against the appellant was that on 17th May 1971 he had gone
with another man to a grocer's shop in Liverpool. This man had put his arm round
a young female assistant's throat whilst the appellant had taken £104·81 from the
till. Both then ran away. At the trial the assaulted girl and another female assistant
had identified the appellant as one of the robbers; but there were features about
the former's identification which weakened it somewhat. A young male assistant,
e who chased the robbers, saw one of them disappear into one of a block of houses
where the appellant's father lived.
The appellant was arrested on 16th July 1971 and, when told why, he made comments which amounted to a denial. He was released on bail and it was alleged
against him by the Crown that, whilst on bail and for the purpose of confusing any
one attending an identification parade of which he was the suspect member, he had
f tried to alter his appearance by tinting his hair and moustache and by reshaping the
latter. As a result of these suspicions on the part of the police, no formal identification
parade was held.
At his trial there was clearly a case for him to answer. He elected not to give
evidence. He called two witnesses to prove that he had not altered his appearance
as alleged. The trial judge, when summing up, commented on the appellant's
g absence from the witness box in these terms:

'In this case there is another matter about which I have to give you a direction
and it is this: as you are aware, the [appellant] himself has not given evidence.
That is an attitude that he is perfectly entitled to adopt. He has called evidence
which, of course, you must consider with the rest of the evidence in the case.
He has not gone into the witness box himself and he is perfectly entitled to take
h up that attitude. He is entitled to sit back in the dock where he is and say to
the prosecution, "Now you prove it", and that is what he does say apart, of course,
from the two witnesses relative to his appearance that he has called. But, at
the same time, members of the jury, you must not think that in not giving
evidence he is not doing what he is perfectly entitled to do. He is entitled to
sit where he is as he has done and please do not think that the onus of proof is
j in any way shifting, it isn't. It remains fairly and squarely upon the shoulders
of the prosecution but, at the same time, I have to tell you this: the jury are
entitled to draw inferences unfavourable to the prisoner where he is not called
to establish an innocent explanation of facts proved by the prosecution which,
without such explanation, tell for his guilt. I will give you that again because it
is extremely important: the jury are entitled to draw inferences unfavourable

to the prisoner where he is not called to establish an innocent explanation of   *a*
facts proved by the prosecution which, without such explanation, tell for his
guilt. He is entitled not to give evidence and the burden of proof does not
shift in the slightest, but you are entitled to have in mind that passage that I
have just read to you when you come to make your assessment as to where the
proof of this matter lies.'

It was submitted that the judge was wrong to tell the jury that they were entitled   *b*
to draw inferences unfavourable to the appellant because of his absence from the
witness box and that he had made his error worse by repeating what he had said.
There is nothing in the complaint about repetition. In repeating what he had said the
judge was doing nothing more than helping the jury to understand what he thought,
and rightly thought, was a somewhat complicated and involved legal formula. The
legal concept underlying the formula is one which is founded on authorities over   *c*
60 years old. The problem is whether it was applicable in a case such as this where the
sole issue was whether an identification was correct. If it is applicable, accused persons
faced with evidence of identity, however weak it may be, will be doing themselves
no good but positive harm by not giving evidence because the unfavourable inferences to be drawn from their silence may be regarded as strengthening the
prosecution's weak evidence to such an extent as to warrant a conviction.   *d*

The reference to reading in the passage complained of shows what the judge had
done; he had read to the jury the last sentence in para 1308 of the current edition of
Archbold's Criminal Pleading, Evidence and Practice[1]. In the current edition the
editors quote two cases to support the proposition set out, namely, *R v Corrie, R v*
Watson[2], a decision of the Court of Crown Cases Reserved, and *R v Bernard*[3].

In *R v Corrie*[2] the question to be decided was whether there was any evidence to go   *e*
to the jury of the offences charged which were keeping a common gaming house and
under statutes relating to gambling. The police had gone to some premises used as a
club and had found the accused seated at a table with a racing card in front of them.
There was a tape machine recording the names of runners and prices on one side and a
telephone on the other. The accused did not give evidence and as far as can be judged
from the report[4] the facts testified to by the police witnesses were not in issue. The   *f*
deputy recorder had taken a special verdict from the jury and on getting their answers
to his questions he had directed them to find a verdict of guilty. On its facts this case
seems to be a long way from the present one but it has no doubt been quoted as an
authority by the editors of Archbold because of the following passage in the judgment
of Lord Alverstone CJ[5]:   *g*

'No inference should be drawn in support of a weak case from the fact that the
defendants were not called; but when transactions were capable of an innocent
explanation, then, if the defendants could have given it, it was not improper,
once a *prima facie* case had been established, for the jury to draw a conclusion
from their not being called.'

In our judgment on the facts of *Corrie's* case[2] Lord Alverstone CJ's reference to the   *h*
accused not being called was but one way of stating that an inference can be drawn
from uncontested or clearly established facts which point so strongly to guilt as to
call for an explanation; if no explanation is given when the circumstances are such
that an innocent man would be expected either to give an explanation or deny the

1   37th Edn (1969), p 500. The sentence reads: 'But the jury are entitled to draw inferences   *j*
    unfavourable to the prisoner where he is not called to establish an innocent explanation
    of facts proved by the prosecution, which, without such explanation, tell for his guilt.'
2   (1904) 68 JP 294, 20 TLR 365
3   (1908) 1 Cr App Rep 218
4   (1904) 20 TLR at 365, cf 68 JP at 296, 297
5   (1904) 20 TLR at 365, cf 68 JP at 297

a   basic facts, this is a factor which can be taken into consideration: see *Bessela v Stern*[1]. As Professor Cross has pointed out in his book on Evidence[2] whether guilt should be inferred from silence in this kind of case must depend on the facts. The facts of this case were very different from those in *R v Corrie*[3]. Nothing here was admitted or had been at any stage of the police investigation.

b   *R v Bernard*[4] provided another illustration of the principle applied in *R v Corrie*[3]. The accused, who had been convicted with another man of conspiracy to defraud, had signed letters containing untrue statements and had been a party to a fraudulent conveyance. The defence put forward at the trial had been that this accused had been nothing more than a paid servant and that there was no evidence that he knew of any fraudulent design. The trial judge, who was Lord Alverstone CJ, when summing up, had referred to the absence of the accused from the witness box and had told the jury they must draw their own conclusions from the absence of his explanation.

c   Darling J, giving the judgment of the court in *R v Bernard*[5], said:

> 'It is right that the jury should know, and if necessary, be told to draw their own conclusions from the absence of explanation by the prisoner. Here he failed to given any explanation of the circumstances in which he signed letters containing false statements ... There was abundant evidence of his guilt, and the jury were
d   satisfied, in the absence of explanation by him, in convicting him.'

Since the first decade of this century, there have been many cases in which this court and its predecessor have had to rule whether comments about an accused's absence from the witness box or a failure to disclose a defence when questioned by the police were permissible, and as Salmon LJ pointed out in *R v Sullivan*[6]:

e
> 'The line dividing what may be said and what may not be said is a very fine one, and it is perhaps doubtful whether in a case like the present it would be even perceptible to the members of any ordinary jury.'

Nevertheless, as long as the law recognises the so called right to silence, judges must keep their comments on the correct side of the line even though the differences between what is permissible and what is not may have little significance for many
f   jurors. In the circumstances of this case there would be no point in reviewing the cases, some of which are not easy to reconcile, as we are firmly of the opinion that the trial judge used a form of words which was inappropriate to the case and the evidence which he was summing up. The words he used might have been permissible if the evidence had established a situation calling for 'confession and avoidance'; they were not proper for one of flat denial as this case was. The court is of the opinion that
g   the trial judge was led into error by the passage in Archbold[7] to which we have already referred. The concept there set out has a limited application and it would be helpful to both judges and practitioners if this was made clear.

Judges who are minded to comment on an accused's absence from the witness box should remember, first, Lord Oaksey's comment in *Waugh v R*[8]:

h
> 'It is true that it is a matter for the judge's discretion whether he shall comment on the fact that a prisoner has not given evidence; but the very fact that the prosecution are not permitted to comment on that fact shows how careful a judge should be in making such comment';

---

j
1   (1877) 2 CPD 265
2   3rd Edn (1967), p 168
3   (1904) 68 JP 294, 20 TLR 365
4   (1908) 1 Cr App Rep 218
5   (1908) 1 Cr App Rep at 219
6   (1966) 51 Cr App Rep 102 at 105
7   37th Edn (1969), p 500, para 1308
8   [1950] AC 203 at 211

and, secondly, that in nearly all cases in which a comment is thought necessary (the *R v Corrie*[1] and *R v Bernard*[2] type of cases being rare exceptions) the form of comment should be that which Lord Parker CJ described in *R v Bathurst*[3], as the accepted form, namely, that—

> 'the accused is not bound to give evidence, that he can sit back and see if the prosecution have proved their case, and that, while the jury have been deprived of the opportunity of hearing his story tested in cross-examination, the one thing that they must not do is to assume that he is guilty because he has not gone into the witness box.'

The trial judge in this case went very near to encouraging this assumption.

For these reasons the court allowed the appeal and quashed the conviction because we adjudged that it was unsafe and unsatisfactory to allow it to stand.

Appeal allowed. Conviction quashed.

Solicitors: *Registrar of Criminal Appeals* (for the appellant); *Stanley Holmes, Town Clerk, Liverpool* (for the Crown).

N P Metcalfe Esq Barrister.

Practice Direction

Crown Court – Distribution of court business – Committals for sentence or to be dealt with – Procedure.

With the concurrence of the Lord Chancellor and pursuant to s 4 (5) of the Courts Act 1971, I direct that the following amendments shall be made to the directions[4] on the distribution of Crown Court business given by me on 14th October 1971:

1. For para 5 there shall be substituted:

> '5. Where (1) a probation order or order for conditional discharge has been made, and the offender is committed to be dealt with for the original offence; or (2) a suspended sentence has been passed and the offender is committed to be dealt with in respect of the suspended sentence; or (3) a community service order has been made and the offender is committed (a) to be dealt with for failure to comply with any of the requirements of s 16 of the Criminal Justice Act 1972 or (b) because it appears to the magistrates' court specified in the order that the order should be revoked or that the offender should be dealt with in some other manner for the offence in respect of which the order was made; the offender shall be committed in accordance with paras 6 to 9 of these directions.'

2. In para 12 (iv) after the words 'care order' there shall be added the words 'community service order'.

1st January 1973   WIDGERY CJ

---

1 (1904) 68 JP 294, 20 TLR 365
2 (1908) 1 Cr App Rep 218
3 [1968] 1 All ER 1175 at 1178, 1179, [1968] 2 QB 99 at 107, 108
4 See *Practice Note* [1971] 3 All ER 829, [1971] 1 WLR 1535

Norton Tool Co Ltd v Tewson

NATIONAL INDUSTRIAL RELATIONS COURT

SIR JOHN DONALDSON P, MR R BOYFIELD AND MR R E GRIFFITHS

12th, 30th OCTOBER 1972

Industrial relations – Unfair industrial practice – Compensation – Assessment – General principles applicable – Amount which is just and equitable having regard to the loss sustained by the aggrieved party – Discretion of court or tribunal – Discretion to be exercised judicially and on basis of principle – Duty of court or tribunal to indicate in sufficient detail principles on which assessment made – Industrial Relations Act 1971, s 116.

Industrial relations – Unfair industrial practice – Compensation – Assessment – Unfair dismissal – Common law principles relating to wrongful dismissal irrelevant – Heads of loss – Immediate loss of wages – Manner of dismissal – Future loss of wages – Loss of future statutory protection in respect of unfair dismissal or dismissal by reason of redundancy – Industrial Relations Act 1971, s 116.

An employee aged 50, who had been continuously employed for 11 years, was summarily dismissed following a heated exchange of words between him and one of the employers' directors. Although the employee would normally have been entitled to six weeks' notice or six weeks' wages in lieu, he in fact received neither. The employee's net weekly wage had been £25·60. The employee was out of work for four weeks before he obtained other employment where he received wages slightly higher than those he had received from his former employers. An industrial tribunal found that the employee had been unfairly dismissed and awarded him the sum of £250 compensation. The tribunal, in its reasons, merely stated that, in taking into account the circumstances of the employee's dismissal, it had had regard to the fact that a sacking without notice involved a degree of stigma and the employee had lost the benefit of 11 years' service with the employers. The employers appealed against the tribunal's assessment of compensation, contending (a) that, notwithstanding s 116[a] of the Industrial Relations Act 1971, the common law rules relating to damages for wrongful dismissal applied in relation to compensation for unfair dismissal, and (b) that in the context of s 116 of the 1971 Act the burden lay on the employee to offer strict proof of every item of his loss.

---

[a] Section 116, so far as material, provides: '(1) Where in any proceedings on a complaint under this Act the Industrial Court or an industrial tribunal makes an award of compensation to be paid by a party to the proceedings (in this section referred to as "the party in default") to another party (in this section referred to as "the aggrieved party"), the amount of the compensation shall, subject to the following provisions of this Part of this Act, be such amount as the Court or tribunal considers just and equitable in all the circumstances, having regard to the loss sustained by the aggrieved party in consequence of the matters to which the complaint relates, in so far as that loss was attributable to action taken by or on behalf of the party in default.

'(2) The loss sustained by the aggrieved party, as mentioned in the preceding subsection, shall be taken to include—(a) any expenses reasonably incurred by him in consequence of the matters to which the complaint relates, and (b) loss of any benefit which he might reasonably be expected to have had but for those matters, subject, however, to the application of the same rule concerning the duty of a person to mitigate his loss as applies in relation to damages recoverable under the common law of England and Wales or of Scotland, as the case may be.

'(3) Where the Industrial Court or industrial tribunal finds that the matters to which the complaint relates were to any extent caused or contributed to by any action of the aggrieved party in connection with those matters (whether that action constituted an unfair industrial practice on his part or not), the Court or tribunal shall reduce its assessment of his loss to such extent as, having regard to that finding, the Court or tribunal considers just and equitable . . .'

Held – (i) The common law rules and authorities on wrongful dismissal were irrelevant in relation to unfair dismissal which was an entirely new cause of action created by the 1971 Act. Nonetheless, in assessing compensation for unfair dismissal, courts and tribunals had a discretion which was to be exercised judicially and on the basis of principle. The tribunal had erred in law by not setting out their reasoning in sufficient detail to make entirely clear the principles on which it had acted in assessing the employee's compensation (see p 186 h and j and p 187 g, post).

(ii) The employee's loss fell to be considered under the following heads: (a) his immediate loss of wages, (b) the manner of his dismissal, (c) his future loss of wages and (d) his loss of protection in respect of unfair dismissal or dismissal by reason of redundancy. On that basis the compensation to which the employee was entitled was to be calculated as follows:

(a) as he was entitled to six weeks' notice or six weeks' wages in lieu, his immediate loss of wages was to be assessed at £153·60, i e six weeks at £25·60 per week; it was immaterial that the employee had obtained other work within the six week period since good industrial practice required an employer to give either the appropriate notice or six weeks' wages in lieu and, if he had received six weeks' wages in lieu, the employee would not have had to make any repayment if he had obtained further work within the notice period (see p 188 a to d, post);

(b) no account was to be taken of the manner of the employee's dismissal; 'loss', in the context of s 116, did not include injury to pride or feelings; as the employee had secured employment within four weeks of dismissal it was only necessary to consider whether the manner of his dismissal had made him less acceptable to potential employers or exceptionally liable to selection for dismissal; there was however no evidence that the employee had suffered any such disability (see p 188 f, post);

(c) since there was no evidence that the employee's present employment was less secure than his former employment, no account could be taken of possible future loss (see p 188 g, post);

(d) the employee had enjoyed statutory protection against unfair dismissal while he worked with his former employers and would not acquire a similar right until he had worked for two years for his new employers; although it was impossible to quantify the employee's loss respecting protection against unfair dismissal, the sum of £20 would be included under that head; the employee's loss of rights under the Redundancy Payments Act 1965 were more serious since, if he had been dismissed on account of redundancy, he would have been entitled to payment of £380; in his new employment he could never build up to the statutory maximum of 20 years' service; accordingly it was just and equitable that his compensation under that head be based on one-half of his accrued redundancy protection in his former employment, the sum being assessed at £200 (see p 188 h to p 189 c, post).

(iii) As the total under those heads amounted to £373·60 that sum, rounded to £375, would be substituted for the sum of £250 awarded by the tribunal (see p 189 d, post).

Notes

For general principles as to assessment of compensation on a complaint to the Industrial Court or an industrial tribunal, see Supplement to 38 Halsbury's Laws (3rd Edn) para 677F, 20.

For the Industrial Relations Act 1971, s 116, see 41 Halsbury's Statutes (3rd Edn) 2143.

Case referred to in judgment

Addis v Gramophone Co Ltd [1909] AC 488, [1908-10] All ER Rep 1, 78 LJKB 1122, 101 LT 466, HL, 34 Digest (Repl) 131, 891.

a
Cases also cited

Edwards v Society of Graphical and Allied Trades [1970] 3 All ER 689, [1971] Ch 354, CA.
National Dock Labour Board v John Bland & Co Ltd [1971] 2 All ER 779, [1972] AC 222, HL.

Appeal and cross-appeal

Norton Tool Co Ltd appealed against the decision of an industrial tribunal (chairman
b B R Miles Esq) sitting in London, dated 8th June 1972, that the respondent, Norman
John Tewson, be awarded £250 by way of compensation for unfair dismissal, on the
ground that the tribunal had misdirected itself in law in assessing the amount of
compensation payable to the respondent. The respondent cross-appealed. The
facts are set out in the judgment of the court.

Stephen Silber for the appellants.
c *Roderick Adams* for the respondent.

Cur adv vult

30th October. **SIR JOHN DONALDSON P** read the following judgment
of the court. The industrial tribunal, sitting in London, unanimously decided that the
d respondent was unfairly dismissed and that he should be awarded £250 by way of
compensation. There is no appeal from the finding of unfair dismissal, but the employers have appealed against the assessment of compensation on the grounds that if
the tribunal had directed itself correctly in law it would have been lower, whilst
the respondent has cross-appealed on similar grounds, save that he says that the award
should have been higher. Both parties have asked that if either appeal or cross-appeal
e succeeds we should ourselves substitute some other figure rather than send the claim
back to the tribunal for further consideration. This request involves no disrespect to
the tribunal and reflects only a common desire to avoid increasing the costs of the
proceedings. As this is the first appeal on the amount of an award for compensation
for unfair dismissal, and as a number of points of principle have been argued—and
very well argued—by counsel for the appellants and by counsel for the respondent,
f we thought it right to reserve our judgment.

The passage in the tribunal's reasons dealing with compensation is short:

'With regard to the [respondent's] loss of wages, he was paid 64p per hour for a
40 hour week which works out at a weekly wage of £25·60. He was out of work
for 4 weeks so that he has lost 4 weeks wages. In addition we are entitled to take
g into account the circumstances of his dismissal: the fact that it was abrupt, that
a sacking without notice involves a degree of stigma and that furthermore the
[respondent] had 11 years' service with the [appellants] and he has lost the benefit
of that.'

Section 116 of the 1971 Act sets out the general principles to be applied in the assessment of compensation. Those principles are not solely applicable to cases of unfair
h dismissal, but apply to all awards of compensation in respect of unfair industrial
practices of which unfair dismissal is only one. The guiding principle is set out in
sub-s (1) in these terms:

'... the amount of the compensation shall ... be such amount as the Court or
tribunal considers just and equitable in all the circumstances, having regard to
j the loss sustained by the aggrieved party in consequence of the matters to which
the complaint relates, in so far as that loss was attributable to action taken by or
on behalf of the party in default.'

This guiding principle is then elaborated and modified in the following subsections as
follows. Subsection (2) makes it clear that the relevant loss includes expenses reasonably incurred as a result of the matters complained of and the loss of any benefit

which, but for those matters, the complainant could reasonably have expected. However, the subsection goes on to bring in the common law rules concerning the duty of a
complainant to take reasonable steps to mitigate his own loss. Accordingly if he could,
acting reasonably, have avoided suffering the loss, incurring the expenses or losing the
benefit, the amount of the compensation will be reduced to the extent that the loss,
expense or loss of benefit was avoidable. Subsection (3) introduces the further modification that the assessment of the complainant's loss, and thus the amount of the compensation, falls to be reduced having regard to the extent to which the complainant caused
or contributed to the occurrence of the matters of which he complains. This is a concept
which is akin to, but not necessarily precisely the same as, that contained in the Law
Reform (Contributory Negligence) Act 1945, which forms part of the statute law of all
parts of Great Britain. It can apply in relation to a claim for compensation for unfair
dismissal but is not relied on in the present appeal. Subsection (4) (*a*) makes special
provision for the circumstance in which a complainant has refused an offer of employment made in accordance with a recommendation of the court or a tribunal and
sub-s (4) (*b*) for that in which the employer refuses to implement such a recommendation. Subsection (5) relates to the assessment of compensation in the case where the
employer dismisses, penalises or discriminates against an employee as a result of
pressure by a third party designed to achieve this result. Subsections (4) and (5) are
not material to the present appeal and are mentioned solely for completeness.

    Counsel for the appellants has submitted that it is well-established that at common
law in any action for wrongful dismissal, no account can be taken of injury to the plaintiff's feelings by the manner of the dismissal or, with the possible exception of the case
of an actor, of the effect of the dismissal on prospects of future employment: see
Addis v Gramophone Co Ltd[1]. The measure of damage in such a case is what the plaintiff
would have earned during the period of notice, less anything which he in fact earned
or, in accordance with the duty to mitigate his loss, he could have earned in that
period. In counsel's submission, much clearer words than are contained in s 116 are
required to vary the common law and, accordingly, the common law rules apply in
relation to compensation for unfair dismissal. Alternatively, counsel for the appellants
further submits that, in the context of s 116, 'loss' can only refer to financial loss and the
burden is on the complainant to offer strict proof of every new penny of loss which is
alleged.

    Counsel for the respondent, on the other hand, has relied on the fact that s 116 (1)
requires the court or tribunal to award such amount as it considers just and equitable
in all the circumstances, the only relevance of 'loss', whether financial or otherwise,
being that this is one factor to which regard must be had. Accordingly, in his submission, the court or tribunal has a virtually unfettered discretion and one which is
open to review on appeal only in extreme cases.

    In our judgment, the common law rules and authorities on wrongful dismissal
are irrelevant. That cause of action is quite unaffected by the 1971 Act which has
created an entirely new cause of action, namely the 'unfair industrial practice' of
unfair dismissal. The measure of compensation for that statutory wrong is itself the
creature of statute and is to be found in the 1971 Act and nowhere else. But we do not
consider that Parliament intended the court or tribunal to dispense compensation
arbitrarily. On the other hand, the amount has a discretionary element and is not to be
assessed by adopting the approach of a conscientious and skilled cost accountant or
actuary. Nevertheless, that discretion is to be exercised judicially and on the basis
of principle.

    The court or tribunal is enjoined to assess compensation in an amount which is
just and equitable in all the circumstances, and there is neither justice nor equity
in a failure to act in accordance with principle. The principles to be adopted emerge
from the section. First, the object is to compensate, and compensate fully, but

a   not to award a bonus, save possibly in the special case of a refusal by an employer to make an offer of employment in accordance with the recommendation of the court or a tribunal. Second, the amount to be awarded is that which is just and equitable in all the circumstances having regard to the loss sustained by the complainant. 'Loss', in the context of the section, does not include injury to pride or feelings. In its natural meaning the word is to be so construed, and that this meaning is intended

b   seems to us to be clear from the elaboration contained in sub-s (2). The discretionary element is introduced by the words 'having regard to the loss'. This does not mean that the court or tribunal can have regard to other matters, but rather that the amount of the compensation is not precisely and arithmetically related to the proved loss. Such a provision will be seen to be natural and possibly essential, that the amount of compensation is not precisely and arithmetically related to the

c   proved loss. Such a provision will be seen to be natural and possibly essential, when it is remembered that the claims with which the court and tribunals are concerned are more often than not presented by claimants in person and in conditions of informality. It is not therefore to be expected that precise and detailed proof of every item of loss will be presented, although, after making due allowance for the skills of the persons presenting the claims, the statutory requirement for informality

d   of procedure and the undesirability of burdening the parties with the expense of adducing evidence of an elaboration which is disproportionate to the sums in issue, the burden of proof lies squarely on the complainant.

Let us now consider the decision under appeal. Our jurisdiction is limited to a consideration of questions of law. Accordingly, it is not sufficient for an appellant to satisfy this court that, within the range of discretion conferred on the tribunal, it

e   might or even would have reached a different conclusion. If an appellant is to succeed, he must satisfy this court that the tribunal has erred in principle. But it is a corollary of the discretion conferred on the tribunals that it is their duty to set out their reasoning in sufficient detail to show the principles on which they have proceeded. A similar obligation lies on this court, when sitting as a court of first instance from which appeal lies to the Court of Appeal on questions of law alone. Were it

f   otherwise, the parties would in effect be deprived of their right of appeal on questions of law. No great elaboration is required and the task should not constitute a burden. Indeed, the need to give reasons may well assist in the process of properly making the discretionary assessment of damages.

In the present case the tribunal has not made entirely clear the principles on which it has acted and to that extent has erred in law. We know that the tribunal was

g   aware that the respondent had lost four weeks' wages at £25·60 per week and it is therefore probable, but not certain, that about £100 out of the £250 awarded is referable to this factor. As to the balance it must be attributable to the circumstances of the dismissal and the loss of the benefit of 11 years' service. The latter consideration is highly relevant, but the circumstances of the dismissal were only relevant if they were such as to cause or be likely to cause future loss. Injury to

h   the respondent's pride or feelings is not loss and is irrelevant. But this faces us with the problem of not knowing how much of the compensation is attributable to the circumstances of the dismissal and whether the tribunal based itself on future financial loss or on injury to self-esteem.

In these circumstances, and in the light of the request of the parties to which we have already referred, we shall substitute our own award. In our judgment the

j   respondent is entitled to compensation in the sum of £375. This sum we regard as just and equitable in all the circumstances having regard to the loss sustained by the respondent. That loss falls to be considered under the following heads.

(a) Immediate loss of wages

The Contracts of Employment Act 1963, as amended by the Industrial Relations Act 1971, entitles a worker with more than ten years' continuous employment to

not less than six weeks' notice to terminate his employment. Good industrial *a*
practice requires the employer either to give this notice or pay six weeks' wages in
lieu. The respondent was given neither. In an action for damages for wrongful,
as opposed to 'unfair', dismissal he could have claimed this six weeks' wages, but
would have had to give credit for anything which he earned or could have earned
during the notice period. In the event he would have had to give credit for what he
earned in the last two weeks, thus reducing his claim to about four weeks' wages. *b*
But, if he had been paid the wages in lieu of notice at the time of his dismissal, he
would not have had to make any repayment on obtaining further employment
during the notice period. In the context of compensation for unfair dismissal we
think that it is appropriate and in accordance with the intentions of Parliament that
we should treat an employee as having suffered a loss insofar as he receives less than
he would have received in accordance with good industrial practice. Accordingly, *c*
no deduction has been made for his earnings during the notice period.

We have no information as to whether the £25·60 per week is a gross or a 'take-
home' figure. The relevant figure is the 'take-home' pay since this and not the gross
pay is what he should have received from his employer. However, neither party
took this point and we have based our assessment of this head of loss on six weeks at
£25·60 per week or £153·60. *d*

The respondent drew £3 unemployment benefit for a short period, but we were
not asked to make any deduction for this and have not done so. Finally, we have
taken no account of the extent to which the respondent's income tax liability may be
reduced by his period of unemployment, since we consider that the sums involved
will be small and that such a calculation is inappropriate to the broad common
sense assessment of compensation which Parliament contemplated in the case of *e*
unfair dismissal of a man earning the respondent's level of wages.

(b) Manner of dismissal

As the respondent secured employment within four weeks of his dismissal and we
have taken full account of his loss during this period, we need only consider whether
the manner and circumstances of his dismissal could give rise to any risk of financial
loss at a later stage by, for example, making him less acceptable to potential employers *f*
or exceptionally liable to selection for dismissal. There is no evidence of any such
disability and accordingly our assessment of the compensation takes no account of
the manner of his dismissal. This took place during a heated exchange of words
between him and one of the directors.

(c) Future loss of wages

There is no evidence to suggest that the respondent's present employment is any *g*
less secure than his former employment, and we have therefore taken no account
of possible future losses due to short time working, lay-off or unemployment, apart
from loss of rights in respect of redundancy and unfair dismissal which are considered
separately at (d) below.

(d) Loss of protection in respect of unfair dismissal or dismissal by reason of redundancy

These losses may be more serious. So long as the respondent remained in the *h*
employ of the appellants he was entitled to protection in respect of unfair dismissal.
He will acquire no such rights against his new employers until he has worked for
them for two years (see s 28 (a) of the 1971 Act). Accordingly, if he is unfairly dismissed during that period his remedy will be limited to claiming damages for wrongful dismissal which are unlikely to exceed six weeks' wages and may be less. Further- *j*
more, on obtaining further employment he will be faced with starting a fresh two
year period. This process could be repeated indefinitely so that he was never again
protected in respect of unfair dismissal. Whilst it is impossible for us to quantify
this loss, which must be much affected by local conditions, we think that we shall do
the respondent no injustice if we include £20 in our assessment on account of it.

a   The loss of rights under the Redundancy Payments Act 1965 is much more serious. The claimant is aged 50 and had been continuously employed for 11 years. Accordingly, if he had been dismissed on account of redundancy he would have received about £380. In other words, he had a 'paid up insurance policy' against dismissal by reason of redundancy which was worth this amount and would have increased in value at the rate of about £38 per annum, until it reached a maximum of perhaps

b   £800. In his new job, the respondent will receive no compensation if he is dismissed on account of redundancy within the first two years and, since he is now within 15 years of his 65th birthday, can never build up to the maximum which is based on 20 years' service. We have no evidence as to whether the respondent is more or less likely to be made redundant in his new employment, but, if a redundancy situation does arise, he is clearly more likely to be selected for dismissal on the normal

c   practice of 'last in, first out'. Nor have we any evidence as to the likelihood that if he had not been dismissed by the appellants when he was, he might thereafter have been dismissed by reason of redundancy. In all the circumstances, we think it just and equitable to base our award of compensation on approximately one-half of his accrued protection in respect of redundancy—say, £200.

   The arithmetical sum of these sub-heads is £373·60, which we have rounded off

d   at £375, which in our judgment represents compensation which is just and equitable in all the circumstances.

   In conclusion, we wish to emphasise that it is only because the parties so requested that we have substituted our own figure for that of the tribunal. But for that request we should have remitted the matter and, so long as the correct principles were applied and shown to have been applied, would not have interfered if they had

e   awarded a different figure which might have been higher or lower.

Appeal dismissed. Cross-appeal allowed. Award of £375 compensation substituted.

Solicitors: *Clintons* (for the appellants); *Garber & Co*, Coulsdon (for the respondent).

f
                                                           Gordon H Scott Esq Barrister.

R v Stafford, R v Luvaglio

COURT OF APPEAL, CRIMINAL DIVISION
LORD WIDGERY CJ, MELFORD STEVENSON AND BRABIN JJ
14th NOVEMBER 1972

Criminal law – Appeal – Court of Appeal – Examination of witnesses – Examination before person appointed by court – Procedure – Criminal Appeal Act 1968, s 23 (4) – Criminal Appeal Rules 1968 (SI 1968 No 1262), r 9 (2).

On its true construction, r 9 (2)[a] of the Criminal Appeal Rules 1968 requires the examination of witnesses before a person appointed by the Court of Appeal, under s 23 (4)[b] of the Criminal Appeal Act 1968, to be conducted in public unless the court thinks that the ends of justice would not be served if the sitting were in open court. In a vast number of cases, however, the ends of justice will not be served by a sitting in open court (see p 191 h and p 192 c, post).

Notes

For examination of witnesses by order of the Court of Appeal, see 10 Halsbury's Laws (3rd Edn) 532, 533, para 978.

For the Criminal Appeal Act 1968, s 23, see 8 Halsbury's Statutes (3rd Edn) 706.

For the Criminal Appeal Rules 1968, r 9, see 6 Halsbury's Statutory Instruments (Second Re-issue) 60.

Reference of examiner's decision

On 15th March 1967 at Newcastle Assizes the appellants, Dennis Stafford and Michael Luvaglio, were convicted of murder. The appellants applied to the Court of Appeal for leave to appeal against their convictions but the court dismissed their applications on 26th July 1968. On 3rd March 1972 the Home Secretary referred their cases to the Court of Appeal under s 17 of the Criminal Appeal Act 1968. The court, in pursuance of s 23 (4) of the Act, appointed Croom-Johnson J to conduct an examination of witnesses whose attendance might be required. He refused an application in chambers by the appellants for the examination to be held in open court. That decision was referred to the court.

Lewis Hawser QC and B H Anns for the appellant Stafford.
J B R Hazan QC, J C Mathew and D A Jeffreys for the appellant Luvaglio.
J F S Cobb QC, Rudolph Castle-Miller and P J M Kennedy as amici curiae.

LORD WIDGERY CJ. The question for us to decide is whether certain proceedings about to start before Croom-Johnson J should be held in public or private. The learned judge has been appointed by the court under s 23 of the Criminal Appeal Act 1968 to conduct an examination of witnesses whose attendance before the court might be required under s 23 and for the examination of whom by, inter alia, a judge, provision is made in the section.

The first thing which we think must be clearly understood is that the proceedings in question are not the proceedings of a court. There is no question of Croom-Johnson J having to reach a decision. His functions are not judicial in that respect and there is, therefore, no particular reason why we should approach this question on the footing that the well-known principles applicable to strictly judicial proceedings necessarily apply. We approach this question first of all by looking to see what the Acts and the rules say about it. A provision similar to that in s 23 was contained in the Criminal

---

a   Rule 9 (2) is set out at p 191 f, post
b   Section 23 (4), so far as material, provides: '. . . the Court of Appeal may . . . order the examination of any witness whose attendance might be required . . . to be conducted, in manner provided by rules of court, before any judge or officer of the Court or other person appointed by the Court for the purpose . . .'

a Appeal Act 1907, and rules were made under that Act to deal with the manner in which the examination of the witnesses should take place. The rules relevant from 1908 until 1968, a period of 60 years, are contained in r 40 (g) of the Criminal Appeal Rules 1908[1]. What that said was:

b 'The examination of every such witness shall be taken in the form of a deposition in the same manner as is prescribed by Section 17 of The Indictable Offences Act, 1848 . . . and unless otherwise ordered shall be taken in private . . .'

There is no doubt whatever that was the rule governing this kind of proceeding at any rate up to the 1968 Act.

The rule associated this kind of proceeding with proceedings before examining justices and provided that the manner in which they be conducted should be assimilated to that under the Indictable Offences Act 1848 and certainly from 1952 onwards *c* it was abundantly clear that examining justices had the power to sit in private if they wished. That was the provision of s 4 (2) of the Magistrates' Courts Act 1952, and as far as we know no difficulty of the present kind arose during the succeeding years following the passing of that statute. However, in 1967, a significant change was made because under s 6 (1) of the Criminal Justice Act 1967 the following *d* provisions are to be found:

'Examining justices shall sit in open court except where any enactment contains an express provision to the contrary and except where it appears to them as respects the whole or any part of committal proceedings that the ends of justice would not be served by their sitting in open court.'

e So we have a significant change directed in our opinion by other changes then brought into force by the 1967 Act, in particular the right of an accused person to, as it is said, opt for privacy in committal proceedings. Section 6 is not to be regarded in isolation. It is clearly associated with other reforms which the same Act was bringing in at that time. The rules were not immediately changed in 1967, but the modern version presently applicable is to be found in r 9 of the Criminal Appeal Rules 1968[2]. Rule *f* 9 (2) says:

'The evidence of a witness taken before an examiner shall be taken in like manner as depositions are taken in proceedings before a magistrates' court acting as examining justices.'

Again, one finds the association between the manner in which an examination is to be conducted and the manner in which magistrates act when sitting as examining *g* justices. This time it is to be observed, the provision that examination shall take place in private is perhaps significantly omitted.

What then is the position in law at the present time? In my judgment (whether or not the rules should be amended to deal with problems which have arisen in this case), we ought to treat the examination of a witness under s 23 as being in manner controlled by s 6 (1) of the Criminal Justice Act 1967. In other words, as the rules *h* presently stand the examination should be in open court unless the court thinks that the ends of justice would not be served by sitting in open court. We would say without hesitation, we think in a vast number of cases of this kind, the ends of justice would not be served by sitting in open court. One has to remember among other things, that these procedures cover the taking of evidence from a witness who is critically ill in a hospital bed. There are many circumstances of that kind where the *j* giving of publicity at this stage is not necessarily in the interests of justice and where arguments based on strictly judicial proceedings do not outweigh that consideration. In principle we have come to the conclusion that the court has a discretion to hear these matters in private. The discretion is to be exercised where the ends of justice

1 SR & O 1908 No 227
2 SI 1968 No 1262

would not be served by the examiner sitting in open court and we would expect in a very large number of cases that the conclusion reached in exercise of that discretion would be that the proceedings should be in private. So much for the principle.

The question is, what manner of exercising our discretion is appropriate in the circumstances of this case. We have been told on many occasions that this case is a very unusual one, if not a unique one. It has been forcibly pointed out to us this morning that all the parties, including the prosecution, are with one degree of emphasis or another, favourable to the idea that in this case that there should be publicity. We have had argument from both counsel for the appellants that, in certain aspects, publicity might actually be beneficial to their clients. Without impinging on the general principles, we have come to the conclusion in this case proceedings should be in public and will order accordingly.

MELFORD STEVENSON J. I agree.

BRABIN J. I agree.

Order accordingly.

Solicitors: *L S de Meza, Jonas & Partners* (for the appellant Stafford); *Kingsley, Napley & Co* (for the appellant Luvaglio); *Director of Public Prosecutions.*

Ilyas Khan Esq   Barrister.

Practice Direction

FAMILY DIVISION

Divorce – Ancillary relief – Application – Affidavit of means – Standard form.

The registrars of the Divorce Registry (in consultation with the Law Society and other interested bodies) have prepared a suggested form of affidavit of means including a questionnaire designed to provide the information which seems likely to be required on the hearing of most applications for ancillary relief. The form is appended[1]. Clearly such a questionnaire cannot include every relevant question in every case without being unduly long, and it may require alterations and additions in particular cases. Nevertheless, it is thought that there are advantages both to practitioners and to the court in a uniform presentation of the facts in ordinary cases and that the questionnaire may be useful as an aide-memoire so that necessary information will not be omitted through mere inadvertence. It is hoped, therefore, that practitioners will find it convenient to use the form in most cases, modifying it and adding to it as may be necessary. In particular, there will be cases in which an applicant desires to proceed in default of evidence from a respondent, where an additional section may have to be added giving evidence of the respondent's means including a statement of the source of knowledge, and other cases where the respondent wishes to allege misconduct by the applicant material to the application.

Where, instead of using the suggested form, an affidavit is drawn in the conventional narrative style, it will be convenient if information is presented in the order in which the questions appear in the form.

Issued with the concurrence of the Lord Chancellor.

D NEWTON
Senior Registrar

22nd December 1972

---

1   It is not reproduced here but it is Form D635 issued by the Principal Registry of the Family Division

a

Gillespie Brothers & Co Ltd v Roy Bowles Transport Ltd and another

COURT OF APPEAL, CIVIL DIVISION

b LORD DENNING MR, BUCKLEY AND ORR LJJ
24th, 25th, 26th, 27th JULY, 24th OCTOBER 1972

Indemnity – Negligence – Contract – Contract of carriage – Contract between trader and carrier – Trader to keep carrier indemnified against 'all claims or demands whatsoever' – Van and driver hired to trader by carrier – Trader having exclusive use of van and driver – Loss of goods belonging to trader's customer whilst in van – Loss due to driver's negligence –
c *Customer recovering damages from carrier – Whether indemnity extending to claims which succeed on ground of carrier's negligence – Road Haulage Association Conditions of Carriage (1967 revision), cl 3 (4).*

A firm of forwarding agents entered into a contract with carriers for the hire of a driver and van on a month-to-month basis, the forwarding agents making use of the
d van for the purposes of their business. The contract incorporated the Conditions of Carriage (1967) of the Road Haulage Association, which included a clause (cl 3 (4)) whereby the forwarding agents agreed to keep the carriers 'indemnified against all claims or demands whatsoever by whomsoever made in excess of the liability' of the carriers, which, by cl 12, was limited in respect of a whole consignment at the rate of £800 per ton with a proviso that it should not be limited below £10 in respect
e of any one consignment. Subject thereto, and to certain immaterial exceptions, the carriers were, by cl 11, liable 'for any loss, or misdelivery of or damage to goods occasioned during transit'. In the course of his duties the driver was instructed by the forwarding agents to collect a parcel containing three gold watches from a bonded warehouse at London Airport. Owing to the negligence of the driver the parcel was stolen from the van. The owners of the watches recovered damages in respect
f of the loss against the carriers as the driver's employers. The carriers claimed indemnity against the forwarding agents under cl 3 (4) but the claim was dismissed on the ground that cl 3 (4) did not extend to claims against the carriers which had succeeded on the ground of their own or their servants' negligence. The carriers appealed.

g **Held** – The appeal would be allowed for the following reasons—
(i) (per Buckley and Orr LJJ) on its true construction the provision of cl 3 (4) that the forwarding agents should keep the carriers indemnified against 'all claims or demands whatsoever' constituted an agreement in express terms to indemnify the carriers against all claims or demands without exception and including therefore those arising from the negligence of the carriers or their servants (see p 205 a to c and f and j,
h post); furthermore (per Buckley LJ) there were no grounds on which cl 3 (4), read together with cll 11 and 12, could be rejected as being incurably irreconcilable with the context and tenor of the contract as a whole (see p 202 g and p 203 e, post);
(ii) (per Lord Denning MR) the words of an indemnity clause, an exemption clause or a limitation clause were to be construed in the same way as any other clause; the clause was to be given its ordinary meaning, i e the meaning which the parties understood by it, and was to be given effect to according to that meaning provided
j always that it was reasonable as between the parties and was applied reasonably in the circumstances of the particular case; cl 3 (4), in its ordinary meaning, was wide enough to cover the negligence of the carriers and, when given that meaning, was reasonable as between the parties for it gave effect to the provisions limiting the carriers' liability which were based on the understanding that it was the duty of the owners of the goods or the forwarding agents to insure the goods for any sum in

I

excess of the carriers' liability (see p 198 h, p 201 a to c and g and p 202 b and c, post); *Hinton v Dibbin* (1842) 2 QB 646 and dicta of Lord Blackburn in *Peek v North Stafford-* *a* *shire Railway Co* (1863) 10 HL Cas at 499, 500, and in *Manchester, Sheffield & Lincolnshire Railway Co v Brown* (1883) 8 App Cas at 709, 710 applied.

Dictum of Lord Morton of Henryton in *Canada Steamship Lines Ltd v R* [1952] 1 All ER at 310 considered.

Per Lord Denning MR. Where the words of an exemption clause are clearly unreasonable the courts are not bound to give effect to it. The common law will not *b* allow a party to exempt himself from his liability at common law when it would be quite unconscionable for him to do so (see p 200 h, post).

Per Buckley LJ. It is not the function of a court of construction to fashion a contract in such a way as to produce a result which the court considers that it would have been fair or reasonable for the parties to have intended (see p 205 d, post).

c

Notes

For construction of a clause in a contract exempting from liability for negligence, see 8 Halsbury's Laws (3rd Edn) 83, para 144, and for cases on the modification of the carrier's contract for liability for negligence or conversion, see 8 Digest (Repl) 43-45, 256-272.

For common carriers' liability for loss or damage, see 4 Halsbury's Laws (3rd Edn) *d* 141-150, paras 382-398.

Cases referred to in judgments

Alderslade v Hendon Laundry Ltd [1945] 1 All ER 244, [1945] KB 189, 114 LJKB 196, 172 LT 153, CA, 3 Digest (Repl) 102, 286.

AMF International Ltd v Magnet Bowling Ltd [1968] 2 All ER 789, [1968] 1 WLR 1028, Digest (Cont Vol C) 63, 548Aa. *e*

Canada Steamship Lines Ltd v R [1952] 1 All ER 305, [1952] AC 192, PC, 11 Digest (Repl) 594, *165*.

Gibaud v Great Eastern Railway Co [1921] 2 KB 426, [1921] All ER Rep 35, 90 LJKB 535, 125 LT 76, CA, 8 Digest (Repl) 141, 906.

Glengoil Steamship Co v Pilkington, Glengoil Steamship Co v Ferguson (1897) 28 SCR 146, *f* 41 Digest (Repl) 361, *293*.

Great Western Railway Co v James Durnford & Sons Ltd [1928] All ER Rep 89, 139 LT 145, 44 TLR 415, 33 Com Cas 251, HL, 26 Digest (Repl) 244, 1866.

Harris (L) (Harella) Ltd v Continental Express Ltd [1961] 1 Lloyd's Rep 251, Digest (Cont Vol B) 71, 53b.

Hinton v Dibbin (1842) 2 QB 646, 2 Gal & Dav 36, 11 LJQB 113, 114 ER 253, 8 Digest *g* (Repl) 51, 318.

Hollier v Rambler Motors (AMC) Ltd [1972] 1 All ER 399, [1972] 2 QB 71, [1972] 2 WLR 401, [1972] RTR 190, CA.

Jones v European & General Express Co (1920) 25 Com Cas 296, 90 LJKB 159, 124 LT 276, 15 Asp MLC 138, 8 Digest (Repl) 11, 52.

Lee Cooper Ltd v C H Jeakins & Sons Ltd [1965] 1 All ER 280, [1967] 2 QB 1, [1965] *h* 3 WLR 753, [1964] 1 Lloyd's Rep 300, Digest (Cont Vol B) 43, 417a.

Lee (John) & Son (Grantham) Ltd v Railway Executive [1949] 2 All ER 581, 65 TLR 604, CA, 38 Digest (Repl) 402, 624.

Manchester, Sheffield & Lincolnshire Railway Co v Brown (1883) 8 App Cas 703, 53 LJQB 124, 50 LT 281, 48 JP 388, HL, 8 Digest (Repl) 66, 441.

Marston Excelsior Ltd v Arbuckle, Smith & Co Ltd [1971] 2 Lloyd's Rep 306, CA.

Mersey Docks and Harbour Board v Coggins & Griffiths (Liverpool) Ltd [1946] 2 All ER 345, *j* [1947] AC 1, 115 LJKB 465, 175 LT 270, HL, 34 Digest (Repl) 180, 1279.

Morris v C W Martin & Sons Ltd [1965] 2 All ER 725, [1966] 1 QB 716, [1965] 3 WLR 276, [1965] 2 Lloyd's Rep 63, CA, Digest (Cont Vol B) 30, 151a.

Peek v North Staffordshire Railway Co (1863) 10 HL Cas 473, 3 New Rep 1, 32 LJQB 241, 8 LT 768, 11 ER 1109, HL, 8 Digest (Repl) 60, 394.

a   *Reynolds v Boston Deep Sea Fishing & Ice Co Ltd* (1922) 38 TLR 429, CA, 3 Digest (Repl) 78, 160.

Rutter v Palmer [1922] 2 KB 87, [1922] All ER Rep 367, 91 LJKB 657, 127 LT 419, CA, 3 Digest (Repl) 78, 159.

Satterthwaite (A N) & Co Ltd v New Zealand Shipping Co Ltd, The Eurymedon [1972] 2 Lloyd's Rep 544, CA.

b   *Scruttons Ltd v Midland Silicones Ltd* [1962] 1 All ER 1, [1962] AC 446, [1962] 2 WLR 186; sub nom *Midland Silicones Ltd v Scruttons Ltd* [1961] 2 Lloyd's Rep 365, HL, Digest (Cont Vol A) 271, 261a.

Suisse Atlantique Société d'Armement Maritime SA v NV Rotterdamsche Kolen Centrale [1966] 2 All ER 61, [1967] 1 AC 361, [1966] 2 WLR 944, [1966] 1 Lloyd's Rep 529, HL, Digest (Cont Vol B) 652, 2413a.

c   *Travers (Joseph) & Sons Ltd v Cooper* [1915] 1 KB 73, [1914-15] All ER Rep 104, 83 LJKB 1787, 111 LT 1088, 12 Asp MLC 561, CA, 3 Digest (Repl) 78, 158.

UGS Finance Ltd v National Mortgage Bank of Greece and National Bank of Greece SA [1964] 1 Lloyd's Rep 446, CA.

Walters v Whessoe Ltd and Shell Refining Co Ltd [1968] 2 All ER 816n, CA.

Wyld v Pickford (1841) 8 M & W 443, 10 LJEx 382, 151 ER 1113, 8 Digest (Repl) 15, 73.

d   **Appeal**

By a writ issued on 22nd December 1969 the plaintiffs, Gillespie Brothers & Co Ltd, claimed against the defendants, Roy Bowles Transport Ltd, damages for breach of duty and/or negligence and/or detinue and/or conversion of the plaintiffs' goods arising out of the failure of the defendants their servants or agents to deliver the plain-
e   tiffs' goods on 7th March 1969. By a third party notice dated 24th February 1970 the defendants claimed against the third party, Rennie Hogg Ltd, in the event of their being found liable to the plaintiffs, to be indemnified by the third party under the terms of a contract between the defendants and the third party made on 8th August 1968 incorporating the Conditions of Carriage (1967 revision) of the Road Haulage Association Ltd on the ground that by cl 3 (4) of those conditions it was provided that
f   the third party should save harmless and keep the defendants indemnified against all claims or demands whatsoever by whomsoever made in excess of the defendants' liability under those conditions. On 13th October 1971 Browne J held that the defend-ants were liable to the plaintiffs in negligence and awarded the plaintiffs £853·20 damages with £155·43 interest thereon. On 2nd November 1971 Browne J held that the indemnity given by cl 3 (4) of the Conditions of Carriage did not extend to claims or demands which had succeeded against the defendants on the ground of their own
g   or their servants' negligence and accordingly dismissed the defendants' claim against the third party. The defendants appealed against that decision. The facts are set out in the judgment of Lord Denning MR.

Raymond Kidwell QC and *N F Irvine* for the defendants.
h   *Robert Alexander* for the third party.

Cur adv vult

24th October. The following judgments were read.

j   **LORD DENNING MR.** On 7th March 1969 a small parcel containing three gold watches was stolen at London Airport, at Heathrow. Who is to bear the loss? It may fall on one or other of three persons. Either (a) the owners of the watches; or (b) the forwarding agents; or (c) the carriers. I will describe them in turn.

(a) The *owners* of the watches were the plaintiffs, Gillespie Brothers & Co Ltd, who carry on business in the City of London. They ordered the watches from Swiss manufacturers. The watches were for resale to buyers in Jamaica. The parcel

containing the watches was sent by air from Basle to London Airport. It was to be   *a*
sent on to Jamaica. It arrived at Heathrow on 26th February 1969. It was placed
in the customs warehouse in bond. Customs duty would not be payable—provided
that a trans-shipment bond was given to the customs.

(b) The *forwarding agents* were the third party, Rennie Hogg Ltd. As soon as the
parcel arrived at Heathrow, the owners asked the forwarding agents to arrange
for the trans-shipment and to put the parcel on the first flight to Jamaica. On 6th   *b*
March 1969 the forwarding agents gave to the customs authorities a trans-shipment
bond in their own name. They filled in a trans-shipment shipping bill. They named
themselves as exporters and also as the firm conveying the goods to the export
flight. The customs passed it as sufficient. They taped and sealed the parcel ready
for collection. It was the duty of the *forwarding agents* to collect the parcel from the
bonded warehouse and take it to their office, which was only a mile away; and thence   *c*
to take it to the export shed for the flight to Jamaica.

(c) The *carriers* were the defendants, Roy Bowles Transport Ltd. The forwarding
agents did not have their own vans and drivers. They hired them from the carriers.
This particular van and driver was hired on a monthly basis. During the period of
hire it was exclusively at the disposal of the forwarding agents. On the morning
of 7th March 1969 the driver drove the van to the import shed of the bonded ware-   *d*
house. He went to an office and got from a pigeon-hole the Rennie Hogg papers,
that is, the cleared papers relating to the various goods being dealt with by the
forwarding agents. Amongst them were the papers for the parcel of three watches.
The parcel was of such high value that it was in a security cage. The warehousemen
got it out and handed it to the driver. He put the parcel in the back of his van and
covered it up. He went back to sign the book. He signed it, came back, closed the   *e*
van and drove to the office of the forwarding agents a mile away. When he got
there, he looked for the parcel and found it was missing. It had been stolen whilst
he was signing the book.

The judge held that the driver had been at fault. He ought to have locked up the
van before going back to sign. Although the driver was engaged in work for the
forwarding agents, nevertheless the driver remained the servant of the carriers: see   *f*
Mersey Docks and Harbour Board v Coggins & Griffiths (Liverpool) Ltd[1]. It was the carriers
who, by their servant, had taken the parcel into their charge, and they were under a
duty to take reasonable care of it: see *Morris v C W Martin & Sons Ltd*[2]. There were
two contracts underlying these transactions.

1. *The contract between the owners and the forwarding agents*

First, there was the contract between the owners of the goods and the forwarding   *g*
agents. It was made by correspondence on 27th February 1969. The owners asked
the forwarding agents to arrange the trans-shipment.

The position of a forwarding agent was described by Rowlatt J in *Jones v European
& General Express Co*[3], applied by this court in *Marston Excelsior Ltd v Arbuckle, Smith &
Co Ltd*[4]. They usually act as agents for the owners of the goods in arranging transport. But in this case there was one activity which they conducted as principals.   *h*
They themselves were, by the usage of the trade, responsible for the trans-shipment
of the goods from the customs warehouse to their office, and thence to the export
shed for Jamaica. They employed the carriers as sub-contractors to execute this
activity.

The correspondence shows that the forwarding agents, in their contract with the
owners, made this stipulation: *j*

'All goods carried or business undertaken is subject to the Standard Terms and

1 [1946] 2 All ER 345, [1947] AC 1
2 [1965] 2 All ER 725 at 732, [1966] 1 QB 716 at 728
3 (1920) 25 Com Cas 296, 90 LJKB 159
4 [1971] 2 Lloyd's Rep 306

a   Conditions of the Institute of Shipping and Forwarding Agents obtainable on application.'

Among those conditions were conditions to the effect that all goods were carried *subject to the conditions stipulated by carriers into whose possession or custody the goods may pass*; that the forwarding agents were not liable for loss or damage to goods unless it happened whilst the goods were in their actual custody; and that in no case should
b   the liability of the forwarding agents exceed a sum of £50 per ton. In view of those conditions, the owners did not sue the forwarding agents. They preferred to sue the carriers in tort, having a precedent in *Lee Cooper Ltd v C H Jeakins & Sons Ltd*[1].

2.   *The contract between the forwarding agents and the carriers*
There was the contract between the forwarding agents and the carriers. This was
c   made by a telephone conversation on 8th August 1968. The forwarding agents hired a three ton van, with a driver, from the carriers on a month-to-month basis. The forwarding agents used this van and driver much as if it was their own, telling him where to go, what to collect, and so forth. It was in pursuance of this contract that the driver of the van collected the parcel in this case. The correspondence shows that the carriers made their contract with the forwarding agents 'subject to
d   the conditions of the Road Haulage Association'. They sent copies of this to the forwarding agents from time to time.
Under the conditions of the Road Haulage Association, the carriers were liable for loss or damage to goods in terms equivalent to the liability of a common carrier. Condition 11 says:

e   'Subject to these Conditions the Carrier shall be liable for any loss, or misdelivery of or damage to goods occasioned during transit unless the Carrier shall prove that such loss, misdelivery or damage has arisen from ...'

There follow in (a) to (j) several exceptions, such as, act of God, act of foreign enemy, act or omission of consignor, inherent vice, insufficient packing, nearly all of which are defences available to a common carrier.
f   But the conditions go on to stipulate for a limitation of liability. Condition 12 says:

'Subject to these Conditions, the liability of the Carrier in respect of any one consignment shall in any case be limited: (1) where the loss or damage however sustained is in respect of the whole of the consignment to a sum at the rate of £800 per ton ... Provided that: (a) nothing in this clause shall limit the Carrier's
g   liability below the sum of £10 in respect of any one consignment .. '

3.   *Can the limitation be avoided?*
If the carrier were sued by the customer who contracted with him, he would, no doubt, rely on the limitation; but in this case he is sued not by the contracting party, but by the owners of the goods. As against an owner, the carrier has difficulty in
h   setting up the limitation, because of *Scruttons Ltd v Midland Silicones Ltd*[2]. That case proceeds on the broad proposition that, on a contract of carriage, the conditions only apply as between the two parties to the contract. If an injured person can frame an action in tort—not between those two parties—the conditions, it is said, do not apply. That proposition is fair enough when it is a contract for the carriage of passengers, who do not usually insure their own safety by land or sea. But it has been the source
j   of much trouble when applied to the carriage of goods. It has been the common practice of carriers—by land, sea or air—to make conditions limiting their liability to specific sums; and to leave the goods owner to insure if he wants greater cover

---

1   [1965] 1 All ER 280, [1967] 2 QB 1
2   [1962] 1 All ER 1, [1962] AC 446

Carriers base their charges, and the insurers calculate their premiums, on the footing
that the limitation is valid and effective between all concerned. The law should
support this course of trade and uphold the limitation. But it has not done so. The
effectiveness of the conditions was seriously undermined by *Scruttons Ltd v Midland
Silicones Ltd*[1]. So in consequence many efforts have been made to get round the
decision. One way is by inserting a clause expressly to protect persons who handle
the goods (such as stevedores) saying that the carrier is their agent. Such a clause
has, however, been held ineffective by the Court of Appeal in New Zealand in *A N
Satterthwaite & Co Ltd v New Zealand Shipping Co Ltd, The Eurymedon*[2]. Another way
is by holding that the owner of the goods (if he is not a party to the contract) is bound
by the conditions if he impliedly consented to them as being in the usual form:
see *Morris v C W Martin & Sons Ltd*[3]. Yet another way is by way of international
convention, which is made law by statute. Thus, in the schedule to the Carriage of
Goods by Sea Act 1971, it is provided (art IV bis, para 1):

> 'The defences and limits of liability provided for in these Rules shall apply
> in any action against the carrier in respect of loss or damage to goods covered by
> a contract of carriage whether the action be founded in contract or in tort.'

Finally, there is the way to be found in the conditions of the Road Haulage Association,
which we have before us today. To these conditions I now turn.

4. *The road haulage conditions*

'1. *Definitions*
'In these Conditions the following expressions shall have the meanings hereby
respectively assigned to them, that is to say:—"*Trader*" shall mean the customer
who contracts for the services of the Carrier. [It means, therefore, in this case,
the forwarding agent.] . . .
'3. *Parties and Sub-Contracting*
'(1) Where the Trader is not the owner of some or all of the goods in any
consignment he shall be deemed for all purposes to be the agent of the owner
or owners.
'(2) The Carrier may employ the services of any other carrier for the purposes
of fulfilling the Contract . . .
'(3) The Carrier enters into the Contract for and on behalf of himself and his
servants, agents, and sub-contractors and his sub-contractors servants, agents,
and sub-contractors; all of whom shall be entitled to the benefit of the Contract
and shall be under no liability whatsoever to the Trader or anyone claiming
through him in respect of the goods in addition to or separately from that of the
Carrier under the Contract.
'(4) The Trader shall save harmless and keep the Carrier indemnified against
all claims or demands whatsoever by whomsoever made in excess of the liability
of the Carrier under these conditions.'

That indemnity at cl 3 (4) is the one here relied on by the carrier. It is designed to
enable the carrier (when he is sued by the owner of the goods) to come down on the
trader, i e the forwarding agents, for indemnity. If the words of cl 3 (4) are given their
ordinary meaning, they clearly cover this case. The words 'all claims or demands
whatsoever' are certainly wide enough.

5. *The ruling in Canada Steamship Lines Ltd v R*[4]
But the forwarding agents deny that the carriers can pray in aid the indemnity
clause. They say that the carriers were by their servants guilty of negligence; and

---

1   [1962] 1 All ER 1, [1962] AC 446
2   [1972] 2 Lloyd's Rep 544
3   [1965] 2 All ER at 733, [1966] 1 QB at 729, 730
4   [1952] 1 All ER 305, [1952] AC 192

a that they cannot get indemnity for their own negligence.   They say that an indemnity clause is to be treated in the same way as an exemption clause.   They rely on the ruling, numbered (iii), of the Privy Council in *Canada Steamship Lines Ltd v R*[1]:

> 'If the words used are wide enough [in their ordinary meaning, to cover negligence on the part of the servants of the proferens] . . . the existence of a possible head of damage other than that of negligence is fatal to the *proferens* . . .'

b
Taking that ruling literally, the forwarding agents explored the possibility of other heads of damage.   They put forward five possible heads of damage other than that of negligence.   (1) The carriers might, without negligence, be faced with a claim for conversion.   There might be two rival claimants to the goods.   If the carriers handed them to one, they might be held liable to the other in conversion.   (2) The carriers c might have got a sub-contractor to carry the goods for them.   The carriers might, without negligence on their part, be liable for the negligence of the sub-contractor. (3) The goods might be liquids which leaked and caused damage to the vehicle of a sub-contractor; and the carriers might be liable to the sub-contractor.   (4) The carriers might have a claim brought against them for negligence and resist it successfully—and get an order for costs against the claimant—and must be able to recover d them because the claimant had no money to pay them.   (5) The carriers might be called on to pay customs duty or air hire charges.

The judge considered those five possible heads.   He held that those numbered 1, 2, 4 and 5 were possible heads of damage, other than negligence and that, applying the Privy Council ruling, the existence of them was 'fatal' to the claim for indemnity.

I can well see that the judge felt obliged to explore all those five heads.   He had e before him the explicit words of the Privy Council in the *Canada Steamship* case[2], which had been applied by Slade J in *Walters v Whessoe Ltd and Shell Refining Co Ltd*[3] and by Mocatta J in *AMF International Ltd v Magnet Bowling Ltd*[4].   So explicit were the words of the Privy Council that I felt myself, at first, that we ought to explore all those five heads.   I considered the many authorities cited by counsel, and I actually went so far as to prepare a judgment differing from the judge on them.   But it f proved so long and so tedious that I have discarded it.   And I am glad to find that Buckley and Orr LJJ have not now discussed those five heads either.

In justification of this course, I would make this comment on the Privy Council ruling.   It was based in terms on the words of Lord Greene MR in *Alderslade v Hendon Laundry Ltd*[5].   But those words have recently come under review in *Hollier v Rambler Motors (AMC) Ltd*[6]; and this court there issued a warning against taking Lord g Greene MR's words au pied de la lettre.   It actually overruled two of the cases on which he relied.   I would issue a like warning about the Privy Council ruling.   Taken at its face value, it assumes that the words of an exempting clause are wide enough, in their ordinary meaning, to cover negligence; but then lays down an artificial rule by which the court is compelled to depart from their ordinary meaning.   It says: 'The existence of a possible head of damage other than that of negligence h is fatal.'   Such compulsion is not a rule of construction.   It is a rule of law.   I would quote against it the words of Salmon LJ in *Hollier v Rambler Motors (AMC) Ltd*[7]:

> 'If it were so extended, it would make the law entirely artificial by ignoring that rules of construction are merely our guides and not our masters; in the end you are driven back to construing the clause in question to see what it means.'

j 1 [1952] 1 All ER at 310, [1952] AC at 208
2 [1952] 1 All ER 305, [1952] AC 192
3 See [1968] 2 All ER 816 n
4 [1968] 2 All ER 789 at 811, [1968] 1 WLR 1028 at 1055
5 [1945] 1 All ER 244 at 245, [1945] KB 189 at 192
6 [1972] 1 All ER 399 at 406, [1972] 2 QB 71 at 80
7 [1972] 1 All ER at 406, [1972] 2 QB at 80

I would suggest, therefore, that we should not apply the Privy Council ruling in
its full force. We should not explore in depth 'other possible heads'. The correct
proposition, as I have always understood it, is this: even though the words of a
clause are wide enough in their ordinary meaning to exclude liability for negligence,
nevertheless if it is apparent that sufficient content can be given to them without
doing so (as in the case of a common carrier), then they will be given that content
only. They will not be held to cover negligence. So stated, however, the forwarding
agents may still rely on it. Condition 11 puts a liability on the carrier equivalent
to a common carrier. So they may still say that the indemnity clause should not be
held to cover the negligence of the carrier himself.

6. What is the justification?

But, even so, I say to myself: this indemnity clause, in its ordinary meaning, is
wide enough to cover the negligence of the carrier himself. Why should not effect
be given to it? What is the justification for the courts, in this or any other case,
departing from the ordinary meaning of the words? If you examine all the cases,
you will, I think, find that at bottom it is because the clause (relieving a man from
his own negligence) is unreasonable, or is being applied unreasonably in the circumstances of the particular case. The judges have, then, time after time, sanctioned a
departure from the ordinary meaning. They have done it under the guise of
'construing' the clause. They assume that the party cannot have intended anything
so unreasonable. So they construe the clause 'strictly'. They cut down the ordinary
meaning of the words and reduce them to reasonable proportions. They use all
their skill and art to this end. Thus they have repeatedly held that words do not
exempt a man from negligence unless it is made clear beyond doubt; nor entitle
a man to indemnity from the consequences of his own negligence: see *Great Western
Railway Co v James Durnford & Sons Ltd*[1] and *John Lee & Son (Grantham) Ltd v Railway
Executive*[2]. Even when the words are clear enough to ordinary mortals, they have
made fine distinctions between the *kind* of loss and the *cause* of loss; so that, if a
clause exempts from 'any loss' it is not sufficient, but if the magic words 'however
caused' are added, it is: see *Joseph Travers & Sons Ltd v Cooper*[3], *Gibaud v Great
Eastern Railway Co*[4] and *Rutter v Palmer*[5]. Likewise, they have regularly disallowed
exemption clauses where sufficient content can be given to them without exempting
negligence: see *Hollier v Rambler Motors (AMC) Ltd*[6]. Nor will the words of an exemption clause normally be held to apply to a situation created by a fundamental breach
of contract: see *UGS Finance Ltd v National Mortgage Bank of Greece and National Bank
of Greece SA*[7], per Pearson LJ, which was approved by the House of Lords in
Suisse Atlantique Société d'Armement Maritime SA v NV Rotterdamsche Kolen Centrale[8].
The time may come when this process of 'construing' the contract can be pursued
no further. The words are too clear to permit of it. Are the courts then powerless?
Are they to permit the party to enforce his unreasonable clause, even when it is so
unreasonable, or applied so unreasonably, as to be unconscionable? When it gets
to this point, I would say, as I said many years ago, '... there is the vigilance of the
common law which, while allowing freedom of contract, watches to see that it is
not abused': see *John Lee & Son (Grantham) Ltd v Railway Executive*[9]. It will not
allow a party to exempt himself from his liability at common law when it would be
quite unconscionable for him to do so.

1   [1928] All ER Rep 89, 139 LT 145
2   [1949] 2 All ER 581
3   [1915] 1 KB 73 at 101, [1914-15] All ER Rep 104 at 115
4   [1921] 2 KB 426 at 437, [1921] All ER Rep 35 at 40
5   [1922] 2 KB 87 at 94, [1922] All ER Rep 367 at 371
6   [1972] 1 All ER 399, [1972] 2 QB 71
7   [1964] 1 Lloyd's Rep 446 at 453
8   [1966] 2 All ER 61, [1967] 1 AC 361
9   [1949] 2 All ER at 584

7. *Reasonableness*

But none of that applies to the present case, because this clause, as I see it, when given its ordinary meaning, is perfectly fair and reasonable. When a clause is reasonable, and is reasonably applied, it should be given effect according to its terms. I know that the judges hitherto have never confessed openly to the test of reasonableness. But it has been the driving force behind many of the decisions. And now it has the backing of the Law Commissions[1] of England and Wales, and of Scotland. I venture to suggest that the words of such a clause (be it an exemption clause, or a limitation clause, or an indemnity clause) should be construed in the same way as any other clause. It should be given its ordinary meaning, that is, the meaning which the parties understood by the clause and must be presumed to have intended. The courts should give effect to the clause according to that meaning, provided always (and this is new) that it is reasonable as between the parties and is applied reasonably in the circumstances of the particular case.

There is a line of authority which supports that proposition. It was common in the last century for a carrier or a warehouseman to give notice that he 'will not be responsible for loss or damage' to goods worth more than £10, or, as the case might be, unless the value was declared and an increased charge paid. Such clauses did not contain the magic words 'however caused' or any similar words. On such a clause in 1841 the Court of Exchequer held that those words did not exempt the carrier from liability for the negligence of his servants: see *Wyld v Pickford*[2]. But in the following year (1842) under a statute[3] which said that no common carrier 'shall be liable for the loss of or injury' to property above the value of £10 unless the value was declared and an increased charge paid, the Court of Queen's Bench held that those words were valid and effective to exempt the carrier from liability for the negligence of his servants: see *Hinton v Dibbin*[4]. The view of the Queen's Bench judges prevailed. Since that time it has been always accepted that such a stipulation in a contract, or a statute, must be given its ordinary meaning, namely, that unless the value is declared and an increased charge paid, the carrier is exempt from liability for loss or damage, even though it is caused by the negligence of his servants. That is made clear by the celebrated opinion of Lord Blackburn in *Peek v North Staffordshire Railway Co*[5], and his speech in *Manchester, Sheffield & Lincolnshire Railway Co v Brown*[6].

What then is the justification for upholding such a clause? It does not include the magic words 'however caused', or their equivalent. The only justification, as I see it, is that such a clause, when given its ordinary meaning, is in the words of Scrutton LJ 'an eminently reasonable clause': see *Gibaud v Great Eastern Railway Co*[7]. When such a clause is *agreed on*, and is *reasonable*, it should be given effect according to its terms. No one surely can dispute that proposition.

Conclusion

Apply this first to the limitation clause (cl 12) in the Road Haulage Conditions. It says '... the liability of the Carrier in respect of any one consignment shall in any case be limited' to £10. That limitation applies, even though it does not say 'however caused'. So with many limitation clauses in carriage by land, sea and air, often contained in contracts, and sometimes in statutes. They are all valid. They apply even though the carrier, by his servants, is negligent. This is because they are reasonable.

---

1 See Working Paper No 39, paras 57-65
2 (1841) 8 M & W 443
3 I e 11 G 4 & 1 W 4, c 68
4 (1842) 2 QB 646
5 (1863) 10 HL Cas 473 at 499, 500
6 (1883) 8 App Cas 703 at 709, 710
7 [1921] 2 KB at 436, [1921] All ER Rep at 39

Apply it next to the indemnity clause (cl 3 (4)) in the road haulage conditions. It gives the carriers an indemnity against 'all claims or demands whatsoever by whomsoever made in excess of the liability of the Carrier under these conditions'. Those words, in their ordinary meaning—especially the word 'whatsoever'—are wide enough to cover negligence. I next ask: is this indemnity clause, when given that meaning, reasonable as between the parties? The answer is: yes, it is. Under the road haulage conditions, the carrier stipulates that his liability shall be limited to £10 in respect of any one consignment, leaving the owner of the goods to insure for any excess above that sum. The indemnity clause is inserted so as to make that limitation effective. It is perfectly fair to put the responsibility on to the forwarding agents. They have been employed by the owner of the goods to make the necessary arrangements for him. They should see that the owner of the goods has insured the goods (as he probably has) or they themselves should take out an insurance to cover the goods. But all we have to decide is whether the indemnity clause avails the carriers against the forwarding agents. I think it does. I am glad to find that in 1961 in *L Harris (Harella) Ltd v Continental Express Ltd*[1] Paull J held such a clause to be good. I agree with him. I would allow the appeal accordingly.

BUCKLEY LJ. The decision of this case depends, in my opinion, on the proper interpretation to be given to one word, 'whatsoever'. The learned judge found as a fact that the Road Haulage Association's Conditions of Carriage were expressly incorporated orally in the contract with which we are concerned, namely the contract made on or about 8th August 1968, for the hire by the third party from the defendants of the vehicle from which the watches were stolen. This he was clearly entitled to do on the evidence before him.

It was contended before Browne J as well as in this court that, nevertheless, the conditions of carriage should be treated as of no effect, because their terms were so inconsistent with the nature and terms of the contract as to be in their entirety repugnant to it. Although this is a conclusion to which a court may be impelled where no other conclusion is possible, it is one which a court should reach only with the greatest reluctance and as a last resort, for it renders part of the contract nugatory and makes the express incorporation of the imported material inoperative in contradiction of the clear intention of the parties. The learned judge, in my opinion, rightly considered that the contract must be construed as a whole as if all its terms, including the road haulage conditions, were contained in one document. Those terms must be reconciled so far as possible, only those, if any, being rejected which, due regard being had to the language used, the context and the circumstances, are incurably irreconcilable with the context and tenor of the whole.

The condition with which we are primarily concerned in this case is that contained in cl 3 (4) of the road haulage conditions:

> 'The Trader shall save harmless and keep the Carrier indemnified against all claims or demands whatsoever by whomsoever made in excess of the liability of the Carrier under these conditions.'

Of the expressions used in this sub-clause 'the Carrier' is defined in the opening words of the conditions as meaning the defendants, 'the Trader' is defined in cl 1 as meaning 'the customer who contracts for the services of the Carrier' and 'the liability of the Carrier' is dealt with in cll 11 and 12.

The contract in the present case was not a contract of carriage in an accurate sense. It was in terms a contract for the hire of a lorry, but I think that counsel for the defendants was right in saying that it was to be distinguished from the earlier hiring agreements dated 9th May and 8th August 1966, between the third party and the defendants in this respect, that whereas each of those agreements related to a specific

---

1　[1961] 1 Lloyd's Rep 251

a vehicle, the contract in the present case did not relate in terms to any particular vehicle. The defendants could, I think, have discharged their obligation under the contract by making different three ton lorries available to the third party from time to time during the course of the 'hiring'. The contract may consequently be said to be more in the nature of a contract for a service than a contract of hiring, but the service to be provided was the provision of a vehicle rather than the carrying of goods.

b In these circumstances there seems to me to be nothing inappropriate in reading the definition of 'the Trader' as applying in this case to the third person. It is true that 'Contract' (as a substantive) is defined in cl 1 of the conditions as meaning 'the contract of carriage between the Trader and the Carrier' which clearly infers that the word 'contract' (as a verb) in the definition of 'Trader' relates to a contract of carriage. But I find no difficulty in reading this language as applicable to the contract presently under consideration. As Browne J observed, the whole purpose of that contract was c that the vehicle to be provided by the defendants should be used by the third party for the carriage of goods.

The liability of the defendants as carriers for loss or damage is dealt with in cl 11 of the conditions under which, subject to the conditions, the carriers are declared to be 'liable for any loss, or misdelivery of or damage to goods occasioned during transit' d subject to certain stated exceptions, none of which is applicable in the present case. This clause is expressed in terms wide enough to cover the loss of the stolen watches.

The extent of the defendants' liability is, however, limited by cl 12. This limitation is related to each 'consignment'. In this contract I think that the term 'consignment' is capable of being read as referring to such goods as the driver of the lorry (who, as Browne J observed, is accepted as having remained the servant of the defendants), should be instructed by the third party to carry from one destination to e another. Accordingly I find nothing in any of these clauses which makes them inappropriate to the nature of the contract. There is, in my judgment, no ground for rejecting cl 3 (4) of the conditions as an operative term of the contract.

The question, therefore, arises: what are its extent and effect? It is clearly settled that liability for negligence can be effectively excluded by contract or (which has the f same effect) the risk of such damage may be thrown by contract exclusively on the party damaged, provided that the language or the circumstances are such as to make it perfectly clear that this was the intention of the parties: see Chitty on Contracts[1]. It is, however, a fundamental consideration in the construction of contracts of this kind that it is inherently improbable that one party to the contract should intend to absolve the other party from the consequences of the latter's own negligence. The intention to do so must therefore be made perfectly clear, for otherwise the court g will conclude that the exempted party was only intended to be free from liability in respect of damage occasioned by causes other than negligence for which he is answerable.

The principles of construction applicable to such clauses have been lucidly stated by Lord Morton of Henryton in *Canada Steamship Lines Ltd v R*[2], a Canadian appeal h to the Privy Council. The fact that Lord Morton here only speaks of the negligence of the party's servants and not of his own negligence is of no significance. Lord Morton said[3]:

> 'Their Lordships think that the duty of a court in approaching the consideration of such clauses may be summarised as follows: (i) If the clause contains language which expressly exempts the person in whose favour it is made (hereafter called "the *proferens*") from the consequence of the negligence of his own j servants, effect must be given to that provision. Any doubts which existed as to

---

1   23rd Edn (1968) vol 1, pp 327-329, paras 728-730
2   [1952] 1 All ER 305, [1952] AC 192
3   [1952] 1 All ER at 310, [1952] AC at 208

whether this was the law in the Province of Quebec were removed by the decision
of the Supreme Court of Canada in *Glengoil S.S. Co.* v. *Pilkington*[1]. (ii) If there is *a*
no express reference to negligence, the court must consider whether the words
used are wide enough, in their ordinary meaning, to cover negligence on the part
of the servants of the *proferens*. If a doubt arises at this point, it must be resolved
against the *proferens* in accordance with art. 1019 of the Civil Code of Lower Canada; "In cases of doubt, the contract is interpreted against him who has stipulated
and in favour of him who has contracted the obligation." (iii) If the words used *b*
are wide enough for the above purpose, the court must then consider whether
"the head of damage may be based on some ground other than that of negligence"
to quote again LORD GREENE, M.R., in the *Alderslade* case[2]. The "other ground"
must not be so fanciful or remote that the *proferens* cannot be supposed to have
desired protection against it, but, subject to this qualification, which is, no doubt,
to be implied from LORD GREENE's words, the existence of a possible head of *c*
damage other than that of negligence is fatal to the *proferens* even if the words
used are, *prima facie*, wide enough to cover negligence on the part of his servants.'

English law is, in my judgment, in these respects the same as Canadian law.
    Precisely the same reasoning must, in my opinion, apply to a clause of indemnity
as to an exemption clause. The one is in essence the correlative of the other. Indeed *d*
in contracts under which one party is expressly exempted from liability to the other
party in some specified respect or to some specified extent it is not unusual to find a
complementary provision by which the latter agrees to indemnify the former against
liability of the same extent. An exactly parallel inherent improbability arises in
respect of an indemnity as in respect of an exemption.
    We must therefore consider first whether cl 3 (4) contains an express agreement to *e*
the effect that the trader shall indemnify the carrier against claims arising by reason
of the negligence of the latter's own servants. If on the true interpretation of the
language this is not the case, we must next consider whether the language is nevertheless wide enough in its ordinary meaning to cover negligence on the part of the carrier's
servants. If this is so, we must finally enquire whether the circumstances are such that
the indemnity may reasonably be supposed to have been intended to apply to claims *f*
of any kind other than claims for negligence. If the first question is answered affirmatively, or if the first question is answered in the negative, the second in the affirmative
and the third in the negative, this appeal will succeed. Otherwise it must fail.
    Chitty on Contracts[3] contains several forms of expression which have been held
to amount to clear indications that clauses of exemption were intended to compre-
hend claims arising from negligence, including 'however arising' and 'from any cause *g*
whatsoever'. In the present case the indemnity is in respect of 'all claims or demands
whatsoever by whomsoever made in excess of the liability of the Carrier under these
conditions'. The contention of the third party has been that these words relate to the
nature of the claim, not to its cause, and so are insufficient to demonstrate that the
indemnity is to extend to claims howsoever caused. I cannot accept this distinction.
Where the expression used is 'any loss' or 'all claims and demands', it is legitimate *h*
and, having regard to the inherent improbability which I have mentioned, rational to
construe it as subject to a silent and implied exception of losses claims or demands due
to the negligence of the party occasioning the loss claim or demand; but if the word
'whatsoever' be added the proper interpretation may very well be different. 'Whatsoever' is a word which is prima facie inconsistent with any exception from the class of
objects referred to. It is true that one might say colloquially 'any claim whatsoever *j*

1   (1897) 28 SCR 146
2   [1945] 1 All ER 244 at 245, [1945] KB 189 at 192
3   23rd Edn (1968), vol 1, pp 327, 328, para 728

a except one due to negligence', but here the use of 'whatsoever' would be tautologous, for it adds nothing to the meaning of 'any claim except one due to negligence'. One must suppose that the word 'whatsoever' was inserted in cl 3 (4) for some purpose and it should, if reasonably possible, be given some effect. In my judgment, it signifies that the indemnity is intended to extend to all claims and demands of whatsoever kind, that is to say without exception, in excess of the liability accepted by the defendant company under cll 11 and 12. The nature of any claim is essentially linked with

b and dependent on the cause from which it arises, and any indemnity extending in express terms to all claims and demands of whatsoever kind must, in my opinion, extend to all claims and demands however caused, including claims for negligence. The expression is one which cannot sensibly be construed as subject to an implied qualification.

c I accordingly reach the conclusion that on its true construction cl 3 (4) does contain an agreement in express terms that the trader, i e the third party, shall indemnify the carriers against all claims and demands including any arising from the negligence of the carriers or their servants. So the second and third questions do not, in my opinion, arise. For these reasons I reach the same conclusion as Lord Denning MR but partly, it seems, by a different route. It is not in my view the function of a court of

d construction to fashion a contract in such a way as to produce a result which the court considers that it would have been fair or reasonable for the parties to have intended. The court must attempt to discover what they did in fact intend. In choosing between two or more equally available interpretations of the language used it is of course right that the court should consider which will be likely to produce the more reasonable result, for the parties are more likely to have intended this than a less reasonable

e result. This seems to me to be precisely the reasoning followed in Lord Morton's formulation in *Canada Steamship Lines Ltd v R*[1], cited earlier, which does not, in my opinion and with deference to Lord Denning MR, enunciate a rule of law but an approach to the problem of interpretation.

I would allow this appeal.

f **ORR LJ.** I agree that this appeal should be allowed on the ground that the words 'all claims or demands whatsoever' constitute, for the purposes of the first test laid down by Lord Morton of Henryton in *Canada Steamship Lines Ltd v R*[2], an agreement in express terms to indemnify the carriers against all claims or demands without exception and therefore including those arising from the negligence of the carrier or his servants.

g The distinction between the two lines of cases with which we have been concerned, rightly described as a fine one, has been said (per Phillimore LJ in *Joseph Travers & Sons Ltd v Cooper*[3]) to be that if you say 'any loss' you are directing attention to the kinds of losses and not to their cause or origin and therefore you have not brought it home to the person entrusted with the goods that you are not going to be responsible for your servants exercising due care for them, but if you direct attention to the causes

h of any loss you give sufficient warning and it is not necessary to say in express terms 'whether or not caused by my servants' negligence'.

For my part I do not find it possible to apply this reasoning where, as in the present case, a word is used ('whatsoever') which is itself plainly inconsistent with any exception or qualification, and on this part of the case I am in entire agreement with the reasoning of Buckley LJ. It must equally follow, in my judgment, that *Reynolds*

j *v Boston Deep Sea Fishing & Ice Co Ltd*[4], which was much discussed in argument

---

1   [1952] 1 All ER at 310, [1952] AC at 208
2   [1952] 1 All ER 305 at 310, [1952] AC 192 at 208
3   [1915] 1 KB 73 at 101, [1914-15] All ER Rep 104 at 115
4   (1922) 38 TLR 429

before us and where the wording used was 'no liability whatever', satisfied the first *a*
as well as the second and third tests in the *Canada Steamship* case[1].

Appeal allowed. Leave to appeal to the House of Lords refused.

Solicitors: *Herbert Smith & Co* (for the defendants); *Richards, Butler & Co* (for the third
party).

L J Kovats Esq   Barrister. *b*

c

King v Victor Parsons & Co (a firm)

COURT OF APPEAL, CIVIL DIVISION
LORD DENNING MR, MEGAW LJ AND BRABIN J
25th, 26th, 27th OCTOBER, 16th NOVEMBER 1972

d

*Limitation of action – Postponement of limitation period – Concealment of right of action by
fraud – Equitable fraud – Conduct such as to hide from plaintiff existence of right of action –
Knowledge on part of defendants of facts giving plaintiff right of action – Building contract –
Contract for sale of land and erection of house thereon – Implied term that foundations reasonably fit for house – House built on site of old chalk pit – Pit having been filled in in haphazard
fashion and in part with organic matter – Failure of defendants as vendors to warn plaintiff* *e*
*of nature of site and risk of building thereon – Knowledge of defendants that house not having
properly reinforced foundations – Subsidence after lapse of years – Whether failure to warn
plaintiff of nature of site and risk amounting to concealment of right of action by fraud –
Limitation Act 1939, s 26 (b).*

In 1961 the defendants, a firm of estate agents, acquired a plot of land. Before doing *f*
so they surveyed the site and discovered that it was on the location of an old chalk pit
which had been filled in in 1954. They were advised by architects that, before building,
it would be necessary to have a reinforced concrete raft or a series of piles driven into
the ground connected by concrete ground beams. The defendants employed M to
build a house on the site. They gave him a plan which made no provision for a concrete raft or for piles. On making enquiries M discovered that the site had been used *g*
as a tip and that the ground was unsuitable for building. With the defendants' approval, M put some makeshift reinforcement into the concrete flooring. M subsequently got into financial difficulties and the defendants engaged one of their own men
to complete the building. In late 1961 the plaintiff inspected the site, on which the
foundations had already been laid and the floors covered with concrete. In December, by a written agreement, the plaintiff agreed to buy the site and the defendants *h*
agreed to erect the house to the reasonable satisfaction of the plaintiff. The house
was completed and the plaintiff went into occupation in March 1962. In July 1968
large cracks appeared in the walls of the house. The plaintiff then discovered that
the house had been built on the site of the chalk pit and also that the pit had been
filled in, between 1945 and 1947, with organic matter, afterwards covered with chalk
and hard matter. In consequence the house was so unsafe that it would have to be *j*
pulled down. In an action by the plaintiff the trial judge found that the defendants
were in breach of an implied term that the work which constituted the foundations
was proper and workmanlike and that the foundations were reasonably fit for the

1   [1952] 1 All ER 305, [1952] AC 192

a dwelling. The judge further held that the defendants ought to have known that the house was to be built on the site of a chalk pit which had been used as a rubbish tip and filled in before the erection of the house and therefore ought to have known of the risk of subsidence. Accordingly he held that, by failing to disclose those facts to the plaintiff, they had 'concealed by fraud' the plaintiff's right of action, within s 26 (*b*)[a] of the Limitation Act 1939, with the result that the plaintiff's claim was not statute-

b barred. He awarded the plaintiff damages limited to the value of the house in 1968 but without interest since the plaintiff had remained in occupation since 1968. The defendants appealed, and the plaintiff cross-appealed against the quantum of damages awarded.

Held – (i) On the facts found by the judge the only proper inference was, not that the
c defendants ought to have known, but that they had actual knowledge, at the time that the contract was made, that the site had been used for a rubbish tip, that it was unsuitable for building on without proper foundations and that, in consequence, there was a risk of subsidence. Accordingly, by failing to disclose the facts to the plaintiff they had concealed from him by fraud, within s 26 (*b*) of the 1939 Act, his right of action for breach of their implied warranty that the foundations were reasonably fit
d for their purpose. In any event (per Megaw LJ and Brabin J) M, as the defendants' building contractor, was their 'agent' within the meaning of s 26 (*b*), and his knowledge that the site was unsuitable for building was therefore to be imputed to the defendants. The appeal would therefore be dismissed (see p 210 h and j, p 212 c, p 213 a to c and f and p 217 b to d, post).

(ii) Although there might be circumstances in which a plaintiff who reasonably
e continued to reside in ruinous or defective premises would be entitled to an increased award or some interest on an award representing the value of the house at the time when the defects were discovered, the plaintiff had neither pleaded nor made out a case for such an increased award. Accordingly the cross-appeal would be dismissed (see p 211 b, p 214 c, and p 217 f and g, post).

Archer v Moss [1971] 1 All ER 747 followed.
f Per Megaw LJ. As a general principle the fact that a defendant ought to know, but does not know, of facts that would give the plaintiff a right of action is not sufficient to establish concealment by fraud within s 26 of the 1939 Act (see p 212 a and b, post).

Decision of Thesiger J [1972] 2 All ER 625 affirmed on other grounds.

Notes
g For fraudulent concealment of the cause of action, see 24 Halsbury's Laws (3rd Edn) 316-319, paras 628-631, and for cases on the subject, see 32 Digest (Repl) 605-607, 1891-1900.

For the measure of damages in contract, see 11 Halsbury's Laws (3rd Edn) 241, 242, para 409, and for cases on the subject, see 17 Digest (Repl) 91-99, 99-154.

For the Limitation Act 1939, s 26, see 19 Halsbury's Statutes (3rd Edn) 86.

Cases referred to in judgments
Archer v Moss, Applegate v Moss [1971] 1 All ER 747, [1971] 1 QB 406, [1971] 2 WLR 541, CA.
Beaman v ARTS Ltd [1949] 1 All ER 465, [1949] 1 KB 550, CA, 32 Digest (Repl) 605, 1889.
Bulli Coal Mining Co v Osborne [1899] AC 351, [1895-99] All ER Rep 506, 68 LJPC 49, 8
j LT 430, PC, 32 Digest (Repl) 603, 1872.
Clark v Woor [1965] 2 All ER 353, [1965] 1 WLR 650, Digest (Cont Vol B) 500, 1900a.
Hancock v B W Brazier (Anerley) Ltd [1966] 2 All ER 901, [1966] 1 WLR 1317, CA, Digest (Cont Vol B) 64, 41a.
Heron II, The, Koufos v C Czarnikow Ltd [1967] 3 All ER 686, [1969] 1 AC 350, [1967]

---

a Section 26 (*b*), so far as material, is set out at p 209 e, post

3 WLR 1491; sub nom *C Czarnikow Ltd v Koufos* [1967] 2 Lloyd's Rep 457, HL,
Digest (Cont Vol C) 882, 1754a.
Kitchen v Royal Air Forces Association [1958] 2 All ER 241, [1958] 1 WLR 563, CA, 32
Digest (Repl) 607, 1900.

Appeal
This was an appeal by the defendants, Victor Parsons & Co, a firm, against the judgment of Thesiger J given at the trial of the action on 21st December 1971 and reported
at [1972] 2 All ER 625, whereby it was adjudged that the plaintiff, Douglas King,
should recover from the defendants the sum of £7,250 damages for breach of contract in writing for the sale of land and erection of a dwelling-house. The plaintiff
cross-appealed on the quantum of damages. The plaintiff had also claimed against
A Thompson, a builder, but that claim was dismissed for want of prosecution by order
of Master Bickford-Smith on 4th February 1971. The facts are set out in the judgment
of Lord Denning MR.

Simon Goldblatt QC and *I T R Davidson* for the defendants.
Anthony Cripps QC and *K T Simpson* for the plaintiff.

Cur adv vult

16th November. The following judgments were read.

LORD DENNING MR. In December 1961 Mr King agreed to buy a plot of land
from Victor Parsons & Co for £3,500. At that time the plot had on it the foundations
for a house. There was a layer of concrete on the site and two courses of brickwork.
A written agreement was made on 6th December 1961. By it Victor Parsons agreed
that they would—

'before the 30th day of March 1962 procure the completion of the erection on
the [plot] of a semi-detached dwellinghouse to the reasonable satisfaction of [Mr
King] in accordance with the plan and specification approved by [Mr King]'.

The house was completed. In March 1962 Mr King went into occupation. In 1964
the house was conveyed to him.
In July 1968, when Mr King and his wife were asleep in bed, they were awakened
by a loud crack. It was the wall giving way. Later on more cracks appeared. Experts
came and dug a trial hole. They found that the house had been built on an old chalk
pit which had been filled with vegetable matter from a nearby nursery; and had afterwards been covered with chalk and hard matter, so that it seemed firm on top, but
was soft and slushy underneath. The house is so unsafe that it will have to be pulled
down. It might be underpinned but that would be more expensive than pulling it
down.
On 3rd April 1969 Mr King brought an action for damages against Victor Parsons.
Thesiger J[1] found that it was an implied term of the contract of sale that the work
which constituted the foundations was proper and workmanlike and that the
foundations were reasonably fit for the dwelling. He relied on *Hancock v B W Brazier
(Anerley) Ltd*[2]. Victor Parsons admit now that there was such an implied term.
The judge also found that there was a breach of this implied term. He found that
the subsidence was caused by the fact that the foundations of the dwelling were not
suitable, having regard to the nature of the in-filling of the chalk pit.
The point at issue is the application of the Statute of Limitations. Victor Parsons
said that the cause of action arose either in December 1961 (when the contract was
signed) or in March 1962 (when Mr King went into occupation). So more than six

1   [1972] 2 All ER 625, [1972] 1 WLR 801
2   [1966] 2 All ER 901, [1966] 1 WLR 1317

a years had elapsed before the writ was issued on 3rd April 1969. Mr King sought to overcome that plea on the ground that his cause of action was concealed by the fraud of Victor Parsons. He gave these particulars which the judge found to be proved subject to the omission of the words in round brackets:

b 'At all material times [Victor Parsons], who were estate agents, valuers, and surveyors practising in the district, (knew or) ought to have known that the ... dwelling house was to be built upon the site of a chalk pit or quarry, which had been used for many years as a (rubbish) dump and had been filled in shortly (at some period such as 1954) before the erection of the said dwelling house. In the premises [Victor Parsons] (knew or) ought to have known the risk of subsidence of the said dwelling house.'

c So the judge's finding of fact was not that Victor Parsons knew, but that they *ought* to have known, of the risk of subsidence. The judge held that that was enough, on the cases, to make them guilty of concealed fraud. So they could not rely on the statute. But, on the hearing of the appeal, Mr King found some difficulty in supporting the judge's reasoning. So Mr King applied for leave to serve a counter-notice in order to allege that Victor Parsons 'did know'. We gave leave. This means d that we have had to examine the evidence; but, before doing so, I will try to summarise the law.

The law

By s 26 (*b*) of the Limitation Act 1939, when—

e 'the right of action is concealed by the fraud of [the defendant, or his agent] ... the period of limitation shall not begin to run until the plaintiff has discovered the fraud ... or could with reasonable diligence have discovered it ...'

By s 31 (7) 'right of action' includes 'cause of action'.

The word 'fraud' here is not used in the common law sense. It is used in the equitable sense to denote conduct by the defendant or his agent such that it would be f 'against conscience' for him to avail himself of the lapse of time. The cases show that, if a man *knowingly* commits a wrong (such as digging underground another man's coal); or a breach of contract (such as putting in bad foundations to a house), in such circumstances that it is unlikely to be found out for many a long day, he cannot rely on the Statute of Limitations as a bar to the claim: see *Bullli Coal Mining Co v Osborne*[1] and *Archer v Moss*[2]. In order to show that he 'concealed' the right of action g 'by fraud', it is not necessary to show that he took active steps to conceal his wrongdoing or his breach of contract. It is sufficient that he *knowingly* committed it and did not tell the owner anything about it. He did the wrong or committed the breach secretly. By saying nothing he keeps it secret. He conceals the right of action. He conceals it by 'fraud' as those words have been interpreted in the cases. To this word 'knowingly' there must be added 'recklessly': see *Beaman v ARTS Ltd*[3]. h Like the man who turns a blind eye. He is aware that what he is doing may well be a wrong, or a breach of contract, but he takes the risk of it being so. He refrains from further enquiry lest it should prove to be correct; and says nothing about it. The court will not allow him to get away with conduct of that kind. It may be that he has no dishonest motive; but that does not matter. He has kept the plaintiff out of the knowledge of his right of action; and that is enough: see *Kitchen v Royal* j *Air Forces Association*[4]. If the defendant was, however, quite unaware that he was committing a wrong or a breach of contract, it would be different. So if, by an honest

1 [1899] AC 351, [1895-99] All ER Rep 506
2 [1971] 1 All ER 747, [1971] 1 QB 406
3 [1949] 1 All ER 465 at 469, 470, [1949] 1 KB 550 at 565, 566
4 [1958] 2 All ER 241, [1958] 1 WLR 563

K

blunder, he unwittingly commits a wrong (by digging another man's coal), or a *a*
breach of contract (by putting in an insufficient foundation) then he could avail
himself of the Statute of Limitations.

In all these instances when I speak of the defendant, I include, of course, his agent
for the statute expressly mentions him. If a defendant employs a contractor to do
something for him—and one or other knows that it may well be a wrong or a breach
of contract—and keeps quiet about it, then the right of action is concealed by fraud *b*
and the defendant cannot avail himself of the statute. The time does not begin to
run until the plaintiff knows of the right of action or could with reasonable diligence
have discovered it.

Facts

This brings me to the facts of this case. Early in 1961 Victor Parsons themselves
surveyed the site. They discovered that it was on the location of an old chalk pit *c*
which had been filled in in 1954. They took advice of an architect about its suitability. The architect told them that, if they were to build on the made-up part of
the site, it would be necessary to have a reinforced concrete raft which was properly
designed for the site; or, alternatively, there would have to be a series of piles driven
into the ground and connected by reinforced concrete ground beams.

Victor Parsons did not act on that advice. They employed a builder, Mr Moore, *d*
to do the work. They gave him a plan. It provided only for concrete to be spread
over the site as an underlay for the floor, but not as part of the foundations. It did
not provide for a reinforced concrete raft, nor for piles driven into the ground.
Mr Moore inspected the site and made enquiries of local people. They told him that
the old chalk pit had been used as a tip. He realised that it was most unsuitable
ground to build on. He approached Victor Parsons and told them it was unsuitable. *e*
Mr Moore suggested to them that some reinforcement should be put in. With
their approval, Mr Moore did put some makeshift reinforcement into the concrete
flooring; but he did not make a concrete raft. Victor Parsons knew what he was
doing. Their Colonel Parsons made periodic inspections. Later on, however,
Mr Moore got into financial difficulties and gave up the work. Then Victor Parsons
employed one of their men, a Mr Thompson, to complete the building, and he did *f*
so.

Mr King did not see the site until the foundations had been laid. The floors were
already covered with concrete. He assumed, quite reasonably, that the foundations
were sound and sufficient. He first became aware of their insufficiency in July
1968 when the big cracks appeared. He could not, with reasonable diligence, have
discovered it earlier. By that time more than six years had elapsed. If the Statute *g*
of Limitations applies, it means that he had lost his cause of action before he knew of
its existence.

On those facts, I think the judge put it too low when he said that Victor Parsons
'ought to have known' there was a risk of subsidence. The correct finding would
have been that Victor Parsons *knew* there was a risk of subsidence (because the
proper precautions had not been taken), and nevertheless they took their chance *h*
on it. They did not say a word to Mr King about it. They let him think that the
foundations were properly constructed and sufficient for the purpose. I call that a
reckless disregard of their obligations. It is unconscionable conduct such as to disentitle them from relying on the statute. They concealed the right of action by
'fraud' in the sense in which 'fraud' is used in the section. On this ground I would
dismiss the appeal. *j*

There remains the question of damages. It was found that the cost of under-
pinning the house was more than it was worth. It would have to be pulled down.
The judge followed *Archer v Moss*[1]. He awarded Mr King the value in 1968 when
the breaches were discovered. That was £7,000. He awarded also £250 for cost of

---

1 [1971] 1 All ER 747, [1971] 1 QB 406

a removal. Mr King says the damages are too little. He raised three points. (i) After he went into the house, he spent £1,000 on an extension. This expenditure was wasted, because this extension will have to be pulled down, too. I fear, however, that Mr King cannot recover it. At the time of the contract, it was not in the contemplation of the parties that the extension would be built, or that such a loss would be incurred in the event of a breach. (ii) He said that he should not be limited

b to the 1968 value. He ought to be awarded either the 1971 value (when the case was decided), or the 1968 value with interest from that time. As against that claim, it must be remembered that he has remained in occupation from 1968 onwards and had that benefit. I can understand that, in some circumstances, the benefit of the occupation might be small; and it might be legitimate to award him some interest. But, I do not think any such case was made out. In the absence of it, I

c think we should follow the lead given in this respect by *Archer v Moss*[1]. The benefit of occupation cancels out the award of interest. (iii) Mr King said that, on the evidence, the cost of removal should be £500. But the judge said he did not consider that more than £250 was justified. I do not think we can disturb that figure.

In the result, I think the appeal and cross-appeal should be dismissed. I would affirm the order of Thesiger J.

d **MEGAW LJ.** There is no dispute between the parties that the contract between the plaintiff and the defendants made on 6th December 1961 included an implied warranty. Counsel for the defendants said that he did not complain of Thesiger J's formulation of that implied warranty. Thesiger J said[2]:

e   'I hold that I can and should imply a term, condition or warranty that the work that constituted the foundations of this dwelling on this site was proper and workmanlike, and that the foundations were reasonably fit for the dwelling in the circumstances that prevailed at that site.'

There is no dispute that that warranty was broken.

However, the plaintiff, through no fault of his own, as Thesiger J has found, did
f not discover that the warranty had been broken until more than six years after the right of action had arisen. The warranty was broken, and the right of action arose, on the very date that the contract was made, for by that date the foundations of the house, such as they were, had already been constructed. It was not until 1968 that cracks began to appear in the walls of the house, leading to the discovery of the facts which constituted the breach of warranty.

g The question therefore is whether the plaintiff is defeated by the plea of limitation raised by the defendants, or whether he can overcome that plea by reliance on s 26 of the Limitation Act 1939. Was the plaintiff's right of action for breach of warranty concealed by the fraud of the defendants?

The defendants did not seek to challenge the authority of *Archer v Moss*[1]. Accordingly, they concede that if, at the date when the contract was made and the warranty
h was given and simultaneously broken, they knew that the foundations were defective and that there was therefore a substantial or real risk that the house would subside, the plea of limitation could not avail them. So much is conceded. However, the defendants stress that Thesiger J has not held that the defendants knew all the facts from which the inference could be drawn that they knew that the house was liable to subside because of defects in its construction. He has held that
j they ought to have known such facts. But, say the defendants, there is one relevant fact which the judge, at least by implication, held that the defendants did not actually know, although he held that they ought to have known it.

Thesiger J was prepared to hold that 'ought to know' was sufficient to establish

1   [1971] 1 All ER 747, [1971] 1 QB 406
2   [1972] 2 All ER 625 at 633, [1972] 1 WLR 801 at 809, 810

concealment by fraud, within the meaning given to that phrase by past decisions of
the courts for the purpose of s 26 of the 1939 Act. Accordingly he rejected the
defence of limitation and gave judgment for the plaintiff. The defendants say
that 'ought to know' is not enough. I do not think that the cases go so far; or that,
at least as a general principle and in the absence of very special circumstances, the
meaning of 'concealed by fraud' should be extended to cover a case where the
defendant, whether by himself or by persons whose knowledge should be treated
as his knowledge, did not know the fact or facts which constituted the cause of action
against him.

Nevertheless, I have reached the conclusion that on the true view of the facts as
they emerged in evidence the defendants, through one or other, if not through both,
of the partners of the defendant firm who were concerned with the matter, did know,
at the time when the contract was made and the warranty was given, all relevant
facts as a result of which they knew that the warranty was untrue.

This is how Thesiger J stated his finding[1]:

'Let me state now quite clearly my finding of fact based on the particulars in
para 7 of the statement of claim, although I have in fact already read them. It
is that the defendants ought to have known that the dwelling-house was to be
built on the site of a chalk-pit or quarry which had been used as a dump and
had been filled in shortly before the erection of the said dwelling-house, and
"shortly before" means "at some period such as 1954". From that, I think I can
infer that the defendants ought to have known that there was a risk of subsidence
of the dwelling-house.'

It seems to me beyond dispute, and counsel for the defendants did not seek
to contend the contrary, that Thesiger J is not in that passage seeking to say that
the defendants did not know *any* of the matters therein referred to; he is not seeking
to say that 'ought to have known' applied to them all. For there was a clear and
undisputed admission in the correspondence, that the defendants knew—actually
knew—that the house was to be built on the site of a chalk pit which had been filled
in in 1954. That is shown by the defendants' own letter, quoted by Thesiger J[2].
Thus the judge's finding of fact must be intended to be that the defendants actually
knew each of the facts with the single exception of the fact that the chalk pit had been
'used as a dump'. It must be to that item alone that the judge's finding of 'ought to
have known', in contrast with 'knew', must be intended to apply. As I see it, if the
judge had held that the defendants knew that the chalk pit 'had been used as a
dump', he would have held that the defendants knew (not merely 'ought to have
known') that the warranty was broken. I do not think that counsel for the defendants
disputes the conclusion, if the hypothesis were to be established. He does, however,
contend that the judge's finding, which he says is essentially a finding of fact, ought
not to be disturbed.

With great respect to Thesiger J, I find myself driven to the conclusion that he must
have misunderstood or forgotten a part of the evidence which was unchallenged and
uncontradicted; evidence which was given by a witness, Mr Moore, whom the judge
found[3] reliable and convincing. Mr Moore said this:

'When I realised from the local people that there had been a tip there, I realised
that this was most unsuitable ground to build on, and I approached Victor
Parsons with a suggestion that we should put reinforcement in it.'

It is to my mind inconceivable that if, as Mr Moore says, he approached the defendants (Mr Barnes or another partner, Colonel Parsons, or both) with a suggestion

1 [1972] 2 All ER at 634, 635, [1972] 1 WLR at 811, 812
2 [1972] 2 All ER at 630, [1972] 1 WLR at 806
3 [1972] 2 All ER at 629, [1972] 1 WLR at 806

a   for putting reinforcement in the ground, he would not have made known to them
why he was making the suggestion for additional work and expense. The fair
inference therefore is that Mr Moore told the defendants that the ground on which
he had been asked to build was most unsuitable, and it was most unsuitable because
'there had been a tip there'. I do not think that it could be suggested that there is,
for this purpose, any material distinction between 'a dump' and 'a tip'.

b   I would add that the judgments of two members of the court in *Archer v Moss*[1]
indicate that, in law, the knowledge of the contractor (in this case Mr Moore) may be
treated as the knowledge of the building-owner vendor (in this case the defendants)
for the purposes of consideration of the question of concealment by fraud in a case
such as this. On that basis, it would not matter whether or not Mr Moore had
actually told Mr Barnes or Colonel Parsons, or both, that this building site had been
c   used as a tip and was therefore unsuitable. Mr Moore's own knowledge would be
enough.

    Thesiger J does not appear to have given consideration to a further question of fact
which arose on the evidence. At least, he does not discuss it or make any findings
with regard to it. I think it must be a material matter for consideration, if the
judge's conclusion were correct as to the absence of actual knowledge by the defen-
d   dants of the fact that the chalk pit had been used as a dump or tip. I think that this
court is, in the circumstances, entitled to draw its own inference of fact from the
unchallenged evidence, bearing in mind, again, the judge's assessment of the credibility of the witnesses. The further question is this: did the knowledge which the
defendants must, on the evidence, have had as to the nature of the foundations which
had been laid mean that they must have known, when they gave the warranty as to
e   safety of the foundations, that the foundations were not safe; not safe, that is, even when
the assumption is made in the defendants' favour that they did not know that the chalk
pit had been used as a dump or tip in the process of being filled? In my judgment,
the uncontradicted evidence leads to the conclusion that the defendants knew that
the foundations which had been put in were not the foundations which they had been
advised must be used if the building was to be reasonably safe from settlement and
f   damage. The architects whom the defendants consulted had told them that it
would be necessary to have either a reinforced concrete raft or pile foundations.
In fact, there was neither. There was something which was not a raft. So the
plaintiff's expert witness, Mr Butler, said. Thesiger J found Mr Butler a convincing
witness, and said[2] that his evidence was not really contradicted by the defendants'
witnesses. Did the defendants know that the work which they had been advised
was necessary had not been done? The judge, as I have said, does not appear to have
g   made findings on that question of fact. Mr Barnes, a partner in the defendant firm,
said in cross-examination that it was the function of another partner, Colonel Parsons,
to see that the raft was properly constructed; that Colonel Parsons had quite a
lot of knowledge of this sort of thing; that 'he [Colonel Parsons] had a lot to do with
the actual construction of that raft'; and that he made periodic inspections of it.
h   There was no suggestion that Colonel Parsons was not alive and able to give evidence.
He was not called. Surely the inference is hard to escape? When the contract
was made, with the warranty as to the foundations, Colonel Parsons knew that the
foundations which had been put in were not safe, or, at least, that they did not conform with what the expert whom they had consulted had said was necessary for
safety. He knew, as Mr Barnes admitted he knew, that 'if the foundations were
j   not properly laid, the whole thing might give way or sink'; and this, irrespective of
any question whether the chalk pit had been used as a tip or dump.

    In my judgment, no question of law as to the meaning of s 26 of the 1939 Act arises,

1   [1971] 1 All ER 747, [1971] 1 QB 406
2   [1972] 2 All ER at 629, [1972] 1 WLR at 806

beyond what was decided in *Archer v Moss*[1], a decision which counsel for the defendants does not challenge. It is one of those cases in which the evidence, as it appears in the transcript, can be considered by this court in the light of the judge's express and clear statement as to his views on the reliability and the relative credibility of witnesses.

As regards the cross-notice raising three points[2] on the assessment of damages, I do not think that Thesiger J's decision as to damages is susceptible of legitimate criticism. As to the first point, I do not think that the building of the extension by the plaintiff falls within any of the formulae put forward by their Lordships in *The Heron II, Koufos v C Czarnikow Ltd*[3]. As to the second point, I agree that in certain cases an element of increase of damages may be permissible where a plaintiff reasonably continues to reside in a ruinous or defective house as the plaintiff and his wife did in this case. *Archer v Moss*[1], as I understand it, did not intend, or purport, to lay down any principle excluding the possibility of such damages being recovered. But I do not think that this possible element of damages was pleaded or proved in this case. On the third point, I do not see any valid ground for criticising Thesiger J's assessment of the amount of damages.

I would dismiss the appeal and the cross-appeal.

BRABIN J. The trial judge made certain specific findings of fact. Much of the evidence was unchallenged and in certain vital aspects not contradicted, and, therefore, without tabulating other findings, the judge having seen and heard the witnesses and judged their credibility, was content to say which were acceptable and which were not. The plaintiff's witnesses were believed. This court therefore has at least the same and in practice probably a fuller record of the accepted evidence than the trial judge would have had. From the judge's general and specific findings coupled with the agreed documents and admissions a sure factual history emerges.

The site on which the two semi-detached dwellings were built was formerly a chalk pit dug out so that it was 30 feet deep. Until 1938 it had been filled with garbage from many places. During the war it was less used. In 1945 and until 1947, nursery refuse was deposited there. This has been termed the organic matter. In 1947 there remained about five to six feet unfilled. This was filled in by 1954. Originally a Mr Griffiths intended to build on the site. He then asked the defendants to sell the land; they bought it in what was described as a package deal of land plans and specification. According to Mr Barnes both he and Colonel Parsons looked at that specification. It called for concreting as these described 'to form concrete raft'. These two men with a third described as a sleeping partner started their estate agency business in November 1959. Mr Barnes was then an insurance broker. His working partner Colonel Parsons was described as having considerable experience in survey work gained in the Royal Engineers.

Before they bought the site, as their letter of 10th January 1961 shows, as a result of what was learned from a survey made the previous day, the defendants were made aware that the site was that of an old chalk pit. The current ordnance survey maps would also have shown this. Mr Barnes said that their knowledge came from a man who lived in the area.

Within a short time the defendants sought advice from architects about the foundations which would be necessary for the proposed bungalows. The architects made it clear that one of two alternative methods of building them was necessary, either a reinforced concrete raft or pile foundations. A later letter of further enquiry wrongly stated that the plans passed by the council had established that a concrete raft would be necessary.

In April a small company, which was in effect Mr Moore, agreed to build. The

1   [1971] 1 All ER 747, [1971] 1 QB 406
2   See p 211 a to c, ante
3   [1967] 3 All ER 686, [1969] 1 AC 350

a defendants drew comfort from the fact that at that time he intended to live in one of the bungalows. Mr Moore had heard that the site was formerly a chalk pit; he also heard that it had been used as a tip. He considered that this ground was unsuitable for building. He spoke to one of the two working partners, seemingly Mr Barnes, suggesting a reinforcement of the foundations. Mr Moore stated that whereas it would have been safe to build on a chalk pit, he did not like the idea of *b* doing so, although he was willing to do so for what he called the adventure of it. But building on a chalk pit used as a tip was something he would not recommend, as such land is not suitable for building.

On 29th April Mr Moore was asked for what was referred to as his raft building contract. It is not clear whether this was the sole occasion when Mr Moore had a specification supplied to him. For he possessed it for a few days only in order to *c* give a quotation. At all times he worked from a plan with certain jottings on it.

It is clear that in acting thus the defendants took no steps to ensure proper compliance with the information they had sought and obtained from the architects; for Mr Barnes agreed that he had taken little notice of what the architects had said and that no design for a properly designed raft was ever obtained. The grillage, as it was found to be, which was laid was decided on, he said, after discussion with Mr *d* Moore, who had earlier seen someone from the council. In effect Mr Moore was left to decide the type of structure required, although Mr Barnes accepts that Colonel Parsons, being qualified to do so, supervised its construction. The evidence does not show that Mr Moore knew what Mr Barnes and presumably Colonel Parsons did about the type of reinforced raft which was required. The grillage was not even reinforced as Mr Timpson sought to say, with a reinforcement mat.

e Mr Moore had been dissatisfied with and had spoken to Mr Barnes about the need for more effective drainage, but he left the site after doing some four to six weeks work because his company could not find the small amount of further finance required for extra outlays. The work was taken over by Mr Timpson who, unlike Mr Moore, was supplied with what has been called the long specification. In September 1961 the plaintiff saw the site. The work done had the appearance of a concrete *f* raft with two courses of brick already laid.

The foundations were covered and would not have been capable of visual examination by him had he wished to see them. On the site Mr Timpson showed him a copy of the plan. Neither the estate agents nor the defendants nor Mr Timpson said a word about the history of the site which had caused others to be concerned about it earlier on. Had he been told the plaintiff said that he would have wanted to know details of the foundations. The plaintiff's evidence was accepted.

g Later the plaintiff received a specification. The trial judge rightly pointed out the confusion which existed and still does over the specifications, of which there were three. The muddle is not really resolved, as the specifications are referred to without identification. The judge found that the plaintiff received what is called the short specification, but did not notice the letters R S J contained in it. This called for a *h* concrete raft. Mr Barnes said that he had never seen the short specification until the trial in December 1971. This is strange in view of the use of the word specification in the letter of 3rd January 1962 written by the defendants' solicitors, which only becomes intelligible by the insertion of the missing words 'long' or 'short' at the appropriate places. Someone must have instructed the solicitors about the relevance of the respective specifications to the matters being reviewed.

j The reason given by Mr Barnes for not telling the plaintiff that which was then known by the defendants about the site was that, having received an assurance about the construction of the raft, a different situation had now arisen, as the defendants then felt that they were providing the right kind of foundations. They had, he claimed, moved from the stage when the chalk pit was discovered to the point when, so he said, they felt that they were taking adequate precautions.

Mr Butler, a civil engineer whose evidence was not contradicted, described the grillage as being rather homespun. He pointed out why such a structure with *a* rolled steel joists overlapping to give extra length as Mr Moore had described was unlikely to be successful. He explained that where vegetable matter or large voids existed it cannot be known where to reinforce to sustain the critical point of failure. The method adopted was in this expert's opinion such that it was pretty unlikely to succeed in any circumstances. An all-embracing condemnation. He further indicated that too few rails were used. Mr Butler stated that not only was the foundation *b* structure unsatisfactory but it never was a raft as that term was used in the specification. The word 'raft' when so used implies a reinforced structure, which this was not. The architects in their letters of 16th and 21st February had likewise described one of the alternative prerequisites as a reinforced concrete raft and a properly designed raft.

It is not disputed that a warranty in the terms pleaded was given and broken. The *c* plaintiff first noticed cracks in 1966 but it was in July 1968 that a loud crack heard in the night disclosed the inadequacy and instability of the foundations and that the warranty had been broken. What is said by the defendants is that it was discovered too late to permit a claim to succeed.

In order to succeed the plaintiff must bring his claim within s 26 (*b*) of the Limitation Act 1939. The judge found, I think rightly, on the evidence, that the plaintiff could *d* not with due diligence have discovered that he had a cause of action earlier. The plaintiff was therefore required to prove that the right of action was concealed by the fraud of the defendants or their agent. Fraud in this context meaning equitable fraud was described by Lord Evershed MR in *Kitchen v Royal Air Forces Association*[1] as being:

> '... a matter which LORD HARDWICKE did not attempt to define two hundred *e* years ago, and I certainly shall not attempt to do so now, but it is, I think, clear that the phrase covers conduct which, having regard to some special relationship between the two parties concerned, is an unconscionable thing for the one to do towards the other.'

In view of the decision in *Archer v Moss*[2] and *Clark v Woor*[3], there can be no doubt *f* that such a relationship can and did exist between this purchaser and the vendor agreeing to procure the completion of a dwelling house. Thesiger J made findings on this matter[4] to which reference has already been made.

The plaintiff sought and was granted leave to amend the notice of appeal claiming that for the findings by the trial judge of constructive knowledge in the defendants there should be substituted findings of actual knowledge.

I consider that the judge's findings of what the defendants ought to have known are *g* all matters in respect of which the evidence accepted by the judge shows that the defendants did know and took action upon the knowledge acquired. The finding that the site was an old chalk pit appears in the defendants' own letters; hence their enquiries of the architects. That it had been used as a dump is clear from the evidence of Mr Moore that he told Mr Barnes about this. That the defendants knew that *h* there was a risk of subsidence was the obvious and only reason for their letters of enquiry to the architects even before knowledge of tipping was obtained. Their knowledge of the site was the only reason for departing from the plan and ordering and supervising the construction of the homespun grillage raft. What the defendants did not know, for they took no steps to find out, was the precise nature of the infilling, and in particular that the erstwhile pit contained the organic matter which *j* had come from the nurseries and which in time had putrefied. There is a finding

1 [1958] 2 All ER 241 at 249, [1958] 1 WLR 563 at 572
2 [1971] 1 All ER 747, [1971] 1 QB 406
3 [1965] 2 All ER 353, [1965] 1 WLR 650
4 [1972] 2 All ER 625 at 632, 634, 635, [1972] 1 WLR 801 at 808, 811, 812

which cannot be challenged that they had neither actual nor constructive knowledge that the infilling contained rubbish. Mr Barnes did not contradict the evidence that Mr Moore had told him that the site had been a tip. Further, when it was suggested to Mr Barnes that if the foundations were not properly laid the defendants would know that the whole thing might give way or sink, he said: 'Of course we did.'

I consider that on the evidence, to all of which I find it unnecessary to refer, the defendants themselves had actual knowledge of all the matters of which it was found they had but constructive knowledge. When, however, it is further remembered that in *Archer v Moss*[1] the word 'agent' was so interpreted as to cover a person such as Mr Moore in this case, it follows that all he knew about this site and the foundations was the knowledge of the defendants.

No specific finding on this matter appears to have been made. I think that on any full review of the evidence the finding of constructive knowledge only is fundamentally wrong. It is I consider the irresistible conclusion from the evidence that actual knowledge was proved to exist in the defendants and in their agent. Their conduct was in my judgment unconscionable and reckless. It is not necessary to consider what the result would have been had the finding been otherwise. I therefore find without difficulty that, in view of the state of the defendants' knowledge, the right of action was concealed by fraud within the term of s 26 (b). I would dismiss the appeal.

Turning to the cross-appeal on damages; the claim as argued was not the claim as pleaded. The three main ways damages are claimed might have succeeded if sufficiently cogent evidence had been put before the judge. The burden of proof being on the plaintiff, I think that the judge was right not to conjecture in respect of the extension to the bungalow and to disallow the claim under this head.

I do not think the judge can be criticised when presented merely with two figures in respect of removal or disturbance for selecting one of them as the more acceptable

I do not accept that in respect of the refusal to allow interest on the damages during the period of occupation of the property the judge was following a strict principle laid down in *Archer v Moss*[1]. I do not think that the case laid down any such fixed principle, nor do I think that the judge thought that it did. He followed what seemed to him to be a sensible and fair course which had been followed in that case. Had the plaintiff mounted this damage claim differently, showing the burdens, inconveniences and shortcomings of their occupation, the judge may well have come to a different conclusion. On the evidence adduced I think that the criticisms fail; that the damages as and for the reasons given should stand and that the cross-appeal should be dismissed.

Appeal dismissed; cross-appeal dismissed. Leave to appeal refused.

Solicitors: *Mackrell & Co for Hatten, Wyatt & Co*, Gravesend (for the defendants); *James R White & Co* (for the plaintiff).

L J Kovats Esq Barrister.

---

1 [1971] 1 All ER 747, [1971] 1 QB 406

a

Chapman and others v Goonvean &
Rostowrack China Clay Co Ltd

NATIONAL INDUSTRIAL RELATIONS COURT
SIR JOHN DONALDSON P, MR J H ARKELL AND MR R DAVIES
9th OCTOBER, 9th NOVEMBER 1972

b

Employment – Redundancy – Dismissal by reason of redundancy – Diminution of require-
ments of business for employees to carry out work of a particular kind – Redundancy situation
involving dismissal of certain employees – Subsequent withdrawal of free bus service to and
from work for certain retained employees in order to cut costs – Alternative transport un-
available to those employees – Notice by them to terminate employment – Whether employees
dismissed by reason of redundancy – Whether tribunal bound to consider what would have
happened if employees had been retained on existing terms and conditions of employment –
Redundancy Payments Act 1965, s 1 (2)((b).

c

Judgment – Judicial decision as authority – National Industrial Relations Court – Whether
decision of the Queen's Bench Divisional Court binding on Industrial Court – Whether
Industrial Court bound by its own decisions.

d

Industrial relations – Practice – Position where doubt whether employee's dismissal on account
of redundancy or an unfair dismissal.

The employers had provided a free bus service to take ten of their employees to
and from work. The employers were obliged to dismiss three of those employees
because of redundancy. The employers decided that it was uneconomic to continue
the bus service for the seven other employees and informed them that it would
be withdrawn. There was no alternative method of transport to and from work for
those seven employees and so they gave notice to terminate their employment.
They claimed that they were entitled to redundancy payments under the Redundancy Payments Act 1965 on the ground that the employers' conduct in withdrawing
the free bus service was a breach of the employees' contracts of employment of a kind
that enabled them to regard themselves as having been dismissed by the employers
and that the dismissal was by reason of redundancy. An industrial tribunal found
that the seven employees had been dismissed but that their dismissal had not been
by reason of redundancy. The employees appealed contending (a) that the industrial
tribunal should, in accordance with the decision of the Divisional Court in *Dutton*
v C H Bailey Ltd[a], have enquired what in all the circumstances would have happened
if the employees had been retained on the old terms of their contracts of employment and (b) that had the tribunal done so it would have found that the employers'
business would have become less competitive, so that their requirements for employees to carry out work of the kind done by the seven employees would have
further diminished for the purposes of s 1 (2) (b)[b] of the 1965 Act.

e

f

g

h

Held – The appeal would be dismissed for the following reasons—
   (i) the test applied in *Dutton v C H Bailey Ltd[a]* involved reading s 1 (2) (b) as if the
words 'the fact that the requirements of that business for employees to carry out
work of a particular kind' were immediately followed by the words 'on the existing
terms and conditions of employment' and on its true construction those words could
not be read into s 1 (2) (b); the court was not required to follow *Dutton v C H Bailey Ltd[a]*
because decisions of the Divisional Court, while requiring most careful consideration,

j

---

a (1968) 3 ITR 355
b Section 1 (2) is set out at p 221 e and f, post

a were not binding on the National Industrial Relations Court (see p 222 g and h, p 223 g and p 224 f, post); *Dutton v C H Bailey Ltd* (1968) 3 ITR 355 not followed;

(ii) there was no evidence whatever of any actual or expected reduction in the requirements of the business for the employees to carry out work of a kind in which they had been engaged; nor was there evidence that the loss of free transport reduced the employees' remuneration to an unrealistic level (see p 223 e and f, post).

b Per Curiam.   (i) The National Industrial Relations Court, while treating its own former decisions as normally binding, is free to depart from them when it appears right to do so (see p 225 e, post).

(ii) If there is doubt whether an applicant's claim is or should be for a redundancy payment or for compensation for unfair dismissal or for both, the applicant should put forward or maintain both such claims until all the facts are known (see p 226 a, post).

c

Notes

For dismissal of an employee by reason of redundancy, see Supplement to 38 Halsbury's Laws (3rd Edn) para 808c, 1.

For the binding effect of decisions of the Court of Appeal and Divisional Courts,
d see 22 Halsbury's Laws (3rd Edn) 799–801, para 1687.

For the Redundancy Payments Act 1965, s 1, see 12 Halsbury's Statutes (3rd Edn) 238.

Cases referred to in judgment

Dutton v C H Bailey Ltd (1968) 3 ITR 355, [1968] 2 Lloyd's Rep 122, DC.

Line v C E White & Co (1969) 4 ITR 336, DC.
e
Palmer v Johnson (1884) 13 QBD 351, [1881–85] All ER Rep 719, 53 LJQB 348, 51 LT 211, CA, 30 Digest (Repl) 218, 611.

Secretary of State for Employment v Atkins Auto Laundries Ltd [1972] 1 All ER 987, [1972] 1 WLR 507, [1972] ICR 76, NIRC.

Vera Cruz, The (No 2) (1884) 9 PD 96, 53 LJP 33, 51 LT 104, 5 Asp MLC 270, CA, 30
f Digest (Repl) 226, 706.

Young v Bristol Aeroplane Co Ltd [1944] 2 All ER 293, [1944] KB 718, 113 LJKB 513, 171 LT 113, CA; *affd* HL [1946] 1 All ER 98, [1946] AC 163, 30 Digest (Repl) 225, 691.

Appeal

g This was an appeal by William Francis Chapman, Christopher George Hallett, Francis Henry Ford, Arthur William Chadband, Robert William Melhuish, John Henry Ford and Thomas John Avery against a decision of an industrial tribunal (chairman John Shaw Esq QC) sitting at Truro, dated 15th June 1972, that the appellants were not entitled to a redundancy payment under the Redundancy Payments Act 1965 from the respondents, Goonvean & Rostowrack China Clay Co Ltd.   The
h facts are set out in the judgment of the court.

Marcus Edwards for the appellants.
The respondents did not appear and were not represented.

Cur adv vult

j 9th November.   **SIR JOHN DONALDSON P** read the following judgment of the court.   This is an appeal from the unanimous decision of the industrial tribunal sitting in Truro that the seven appellants' claims for redundancy payments be refused.

The appellants all live in Port Isaac, on the north coast of Cornwall, and worked in the respondents' china clay works at St Stephen, which is about 30 miles from Port Isaac.   Prior to March 1972 the appellants and three other men, making a party of ten in all, were taken to and from their work each day in a bus paid for by the respondents, their employers. This service cost the respondents £20 per week.

The respondents employed 220 men and at the beginning of the year they felt obliged to reduce their labour force by 12 men. The choice of the men to be dismissed was made in consultation with the union and included three of the Port Isaac party. This left the respondents with a party of seven to be carried to work in the bus at their expense and, whilst they were prepared to spend £1,000 a year to obtain the services of ten men, they considered that such expenditure was uneconomic in relation to a party of seven. They therefore notified the seven appellants that as from 24th March the bus would be withdrawn. This left the appellants with a considerable problem, for there was no public transport which they could use for their journey to work. Two of them owned cars and the respondents suggested that the others might travel with them. However, the tribunal has found that the cars were old and unsuitable and that the insurers declined to give cover for passengers. In the circumstances the problem proved insoluble and the appellants gave notice to terminate their employment.

The first issue before the tribunal was whether the respondents' conduct in withdrawing the free bus service was such a breach of contract as entitled the appellants to treat themselves as having been dismissed by the respondents. It was decided by the tribunal in favour of the appellants and the respondents have not sought to challenge this conclusion. Indeed, they have not appeared on the hearing of the appeal. The second issue was whether the appellants were dismissed by reason of redundancy and it was on this issue that they failed. The relevant findings are in para 13 of the reasons which reads as follows:

'The respondents employed 220 men. They required to dismiss 12 of them and the personnel officer entered into discussions with the shop stewards as to who those 12 should be. The names and records of all the employees were examined and 12 were selected on the basis of age and length of service. Nine of them were picked because they were already over age and due for retirement, or because of ill health; and that left 3. Those 3 were the employees with the shortest service and all happened to be men from Port Isaac. The names and the reasons for their selection were put up to Mr Grose, the district officer of the union. Being satisfied that the men had been selected on this basis of age and length of service and therefore in accordance with union principles, Mr Grose agreed to these 12 men being dismissed. He did not then know that 3 of them came from Port Isaac. The [respondents] now found that the number of men travelling from Port Isaac was reduced to 7 and they did not consider it economic to run the bus at the cost of £20 a week to bring in 7 men. They decided, therefore, to stop running the bus in order to save £20 a week and that was their reason for the decision. When the 7 [appellants] said they could not get into work and left on 24 March, much to the regret of the respondents, they set about finding replacements, and Mr Grose conceded that 7 replacements had in fact been engaged. In these circumstances, although the dismissals were a repercussion of the redundancy of the 3 Port Isaac men, the 7 [appellants] were not dismissed because the respondents' requirements for them to carry out work of the particular kind they were employed to do had ceased or diminished. The respondents required that they should continue to work for them, but they were not prepared to pay £20 a week for a bus to transport them to St Stephen. We therefore find that the respondents have discharged the burden of proof which rests on them of satisfying us that the dismissals were not by reason of redundancy.'

Counsel for the appellants submits first that the tribunal attached insufficient significance to the fact that the seven men engaged to replace the appellants involved the respondents in less expenditure than did the appellants because no free bus

^a service was needed. Insofar as this point involves a question of law, it is bound up with counsel's second submission. This is summarised in the notice of appeal as follows:

'(3) That the Industrial Tribunal should have addressed itself to the question: What in all the circumstances would have happened if the Appellants had been retained upon the terms (as found by the Industrial Tribunal) of their contracts of employment (*Dutton v. C. H. Bailey Limited*[1] and *Line v. C. E. White & Co.*[2]).

'(4) That had the Industrial Tribunal addressed itself to the aforesaid question (bearing in mind the undisputed fact that the Respondents had at the material time dismissed 12 other men by reason of a diminution of the Respondents' business requirements), the Industrial Tribunal must have found that the answer was that the Respondents' business would have become less competitive and, accordingly, their requirements for employees to carry out work of the kind done by the Appellants would have further diminished.'

Both *Dutton v C H Bailey Ltd*[1] and *Line v C E White & Co*[2] were cases in which the employers sought to impose new terms of employment which would have saved them money. In each case the industrial tribunal found that the dismissal was wholly or mainly attributable to the desire for economy rather than redundancy. In each case the same Divisional Court (Lord Parker CJ, Melford Stevenson and Bridge JJ) reluctantly remitted the matter to the industrial tribunal to reconsider its findings on the basis that 'the proper approach is to say what in all the circumstances would have happened if these men had been retained on the old terms'.

The relevant provisions of the Redundancy Payments Act 1965 are contained in ss 1 (2) and 25 (3). Section 1 (2) is in the following terms:

'For the purposes of this Act an employee who is dismissed shall be taken to be dismissed by reason of redundancy if the dismissal is attributable wholly or mainly to—(a) the fact that his employer has ceased, or intends to cease to carry on the business for the purposes of which the employee was employed by him, or has ceased, or intends to cease, to carry on that business in the place where the employee was so employed, or (b) the fact that the requirements of that business for employees to carry out work of a particular kind, or for employees to carry out work of a particular kind in the place where he was so employed, have ceased or diminished or are expected to cease or diminish.'

Section 25 (3) provides as follows:

'In this Part of this Act "cease" means cease either permanently or temporarily and from whatsoever cause, and "diminish" has a corresponding meaning.'

The decision in *Line v C E White & Co*[2] followed that in *Dutton v C H Bailey Ltd*[1] and added nothing to it. It is, therefore, sufficient to consider *Dutton's* case[1]. In seeking to impose the new terms of employment the employers had written that the new terms represented 'the only conditions under which by providing a competitive service to our customers we can hope to provide employment and operate profitably and happily in the future'. But the tribunal has found as a fact that:

'There is no evidence at all that ... the employers had no work or had less work, or expected to have less work for boilermakers ... We find that the reason for the employers' termination of the old contract is that they wished—wisely or unwisely—to impose or to attempt to impose new terms upon their work force. It is not because of any existing or expected reduction in the need for boilermakers'.

---

1   (1968) 3 ITR 355
2   (1969) 4 ITR 336

The leading judgment, with which both Melford Stevenson and Bridge JJ agreed, was delivered by Lord Parker CJ. Having referred to the relevant statutory provisions as the tribunal's reasons he said[1]:

'In my judgment, however, the tribunal approached this in the wrong way. It seems to me that the proper approach is to say what in all the circumstances would have happened if these men had been retained on the old terms. To that there is only one answer as it seems to me, and that is that the requirements for boilermakers would diminish and possibly cease in that the employers would no longer be able, as they themselves said, to offer a competitive service. In other words, this was a case where, if instead of saying: unless you enter into new terms you will be dismissed, they at first dismissed these men and later on sought to negotiate new terms, it would then as it seems to me be perfectly clear that the dismissal was one on account of the expected diminution or cessation in the work for boilermakers. It is in my judgment *nihil ad rem* to look to the future and say what would have happened if this man had accepted these new terms. It may be then that the employers would have had so much work that they would even want more boilermakers. The test, as it seems to me, is what would have happened if termination of the contract had not been effected. Finally, I would like to say that I come to this decision with reluctance because it seems to me there should be every inducement to employers to make themselves more competitive, and every reason for employees to do away with their restrictive practices and the like. But as it seems to me those matters will arise at the second stage, namely on the basis that there has been a dismissal by reason of redundancy, when the terms of sub-section (3) and sub-section (4) of section 2 will fall to be considered to see whether, nevertheless the employee is not entitled to a redundancy payment. I would allow this appeal and send this case back to the tribunal in default of agreement to ascertain the position under section 2 of the Act.'

Decisions of the Divisional Court are on any view of the greatest persuasive authority and we will not lightly differ from them. *Dutton's* case[2] seems to us to be directly in point in the present appeal and we have therefore considered whether there is any compelling reason why we should not take a similar course. If we did so, we should remit the appellants' claims to the tribunal with a direction that the proper approach is to say what in all the circumstances would have happened if these men had been retained on terms that they would continue to be taken to work each day free of charge. But is this right? Lord Parker CJ in *Dutton's* case[2] held that if a business was becoming uncompetitive and the requirements of the business for employees to carry out work of a particular kind at the existing rates of pay had diminished or was expected to diminish, a redundancy situation had arisen, even if there was an increased requirement for such employees at a lower rate of pay. With the greatest respect to him and the other two judges who agreed with him, this seems to us to involve reading s 1 (2) (*b*) as 'the fact that the requirements of that business for employees to carry out work of a particular kind *on the existing terms and conditions of employment* . . .' although the italicised words are neither expressed nor necessarily to be implied.

An employer may seek to negotiate new terms and conditions of employment in two quite different situations. In the first situation, the business is being forced to reduce its output of a particular product because of competition from a rival product made in a different way or of different materials. Thus, for example, the need for glass workers may be reduced by the competition from the plastics industry which involves different skills. The employer may be loath to disband

1   (1968) 3 ITR at 357, 358
2   (1968) 3 ITR 355

a his team of skilled glass workers and may seek to introduce a measure of work sharing or short time working at a reduced level of wages. In the second situation, the business can maintain its output provided that it can reduce costs to the point at which it is competitive with other manufacturers or importers of a similar product. Taking the same example, large imports of cheap foreign glass may render the British manufacturer's product uncompetitive unless he can achieve a reduction in

b all costs, including labour costs; but if costs were reduced, his need for glass workers would not only be maintained, but actually increase. The employer therefore seeks to reduce the cost per unit, including labour costs, but, if successful, expects to keep his existing labour force fully employed. The first is a redundancy situation, because the requirement for employees to carry out work of a particular kind, i e glass workers, has diminished. The second is not a redundancy situation, because this

c requirement has not diminished. Glass workers are still needed as much as before, but the employer cannot afford to pay as much per unit for their work. Furthermore, the requirement remains even if the employees will not accept the proposed new terms and conditions. In each case, if employees are dismissed, it is for the employer to rebut the presumption of redundancy. But, as we have sought to show, the issue is not necessarily resolved by asking the question: what in all the circum-

d stances would have happened if these men had been retained on the old terms? For the avoidance of doubt, we should make it clear that an employer does not rebut the presumption of redundancy by proving that he has work for all if only they would work at unrealistic wages.

In the present case there is no evidence whatever of any actual or expected reduction in the requirements of the business for employees to carry out work of the particular kind carried out by the appellants once the 12 had been dismissed. The

e accident that three of the 12 came from Port Isaac increased the cost per man of employing the remaining seven Port Isaac men and rendered their further employment uneconomic. But even if the cost per man had remained the same and the employers had come to the conclusion that Port Isaac labour was too expensive, there would, subject to the effect of *Dutton's* case[1], have been no redundancy situation

f so long as there remained the same work for seven other less expensive men to do. There is no evidence that the loss of the benefit of free transport reduced the men's remuneration to an unrealistic level.

As we have said on more than one occasion, we are a court of law. As such, it is our duty to apply all the relevant law whether we agree with it or not. That law consists not only of Acts of Parliament but also of decisions of other courts on the meaning of those Acts insofar as those decisions are binding on this court. For the

g reasons which we have already given, we respectfully disagree with the decision of the Divisional Court in *Dutton's* case[1]; but if it is binding on us and therefore forms part of the law which it is our duty to apply, we shall loyally apply it notwithstanding our disagreement. In *Secretary of State for Employment v Atkins Auto Laundries Ltd*[2] it was unnecessary to decide whether we were bound by decisions of the Divisional Court, but we expressed some doubt whether we were. In the present appeal it

h is essential that we decide this issue but our decision is, of course, open to review by the Court of Appeal.

Before 1st December 1971, when this court was created by the Industrial Relations Act 1971, appeals from industrial tribunals in relation to claims under the Redundancy Payments Act 1965 lay to the Queen's Bench Divisional Court in the case of decisions by tribunals sitting in England or Wales, and to the Inner House of the

j Court of Session in the case of tribunals sitting in Scotland. All industrial tribunals were bound by the same statute; but whereas the Scottish tribunals were bound by decisions of the Inner House of the Court of Session and not by decisions of the Queen's

---

1   (1968) 3 ITR 355
2   [1972] 1 All ER 987 at 992, [1972] 1 WLR 507 at 512

Bench Divisional Court or of the Court of Appeal, these being only of high persuasive **a**
authority, the position was reversed in relation to English and Welsh industrial
tribunals which were bound by decisions of the Divisional Court and the Court of
Appeal but not by those of the Inner House.

Since 1st December 1971 all appeals, whether from Scottish, Welsh or English
industrial tribunals, have been to this court, which is not part of either the High Court
or the Court of Session but is a separate British court of comparable status. Appeals **b**
from this court lie to the Court of Appeal in the case of proceedings in England and
Wales, and to the Inner House of the Court of Session in the case of proceedings in
Scotland. Whether the proceedings of this court are in England, Wales or Scotland
depends on the convenience of the parties and is not affected by whether the decision
appealed from was that of an English or Welsh or of a Scottish tribunal. For example,
proceedings in a matter originating in Cumberland are being carried on in Glasgow **c**
at this time.

Bearing in mind the undivided character of this court's jurisdiction throughout
Great Britain, the Industrial Relations Act 1971 might well have provided that appeals
from this court would have been to a British Court of Industrial Appeals formed of
Lords Justices and judges of the Inner House of the Court of Session with a further
appeal to the House of Lords. Whatever the reason for Parliament not adopting **d**
this course, we consider that wherever this court may be sitting it must be bound both
by decisions of the Court of Appeal and by those of the Inner House just as it would
if these two courts had formed a composite industrial appellate court. The problem
of a conflict between their decisions can await the occurrence of such an event, but
whatever course is then adopted must apply throughout Great Britain. But the
proposition that the decisions of a part of the High Court having no equivalent in
Scotland should also bind this court is very different. In the context of our appellate **e**
jurisdiction, we think that the Queen's Bench Divisional Court is to be regarded as a
court of co-ordinate jurisdiction. There is no rule of statute or common law which
requires such courts to follow each other's decisions (see *The Vera Cruz (No 2)*[1]),
although it is the practice to do so as a matter of judicial comity where both are
parts of the same judicial system (see *Palmer v Johnson*[2]). Judicial comity certainly **f**
requires us to give most careful consideration to a decision of a Queen's Bench Divisional Court and we shall always do so, but we do not consider that it extends further
than this. Accordingly, we have reached the conclusion that we are not bound by
Dutton's case[3] and that, in the circumstances of this appeal, we should not follow it.

Although the point does not arise in the present appeal, it may be convenient to
mention the problem of whether this court is to regard itself as bound by its own **g**
decisions. Insofar as it is a court of first instance, no one would expect it to be so
bound and it will not be. Decisions given on appeal under s 114 of the Act are in a
different category. Subject to certain exceptions, the Court of Appeal regards itself
as bound by its own decisions (see *Young v Bristol Aeroplane Co Ltd*[4]) and a somewhat
similar approach is adopted by the Inner House of the Court of Session. The extent
to which a court regards itself as bound by its own decisions is probably a matter of **h**
procedure and, under para 18 (4) of Sch 3 to the Industrial Relations Act 1971, this
court has power to regulate its own procedure, subject only to the effect of any rules
made by the Lord Chancellor pursuant to para 18 (2). However, the desirability
of certainty would incline this court to treat itself as bound by its own decisions, but
or two important countervailing considerations. The first is that this is a court
which is concerned in part with a wholly new and developing system of law and **i**
many of the matters which come before it will be argued by those who have no

---

1   (1884) 9 PD 96 at 98 per Sir Baliol Brett MR
2   (1884) 13 QBD 351 at 355, [1881-85] All ER Rep 719 at 721, per Sir Baliol Brett MR
3   (1968) 3 ITR 355
4   [1944] 2 All ER 293, [1944] KB 718

a legal training. It is therefore peculiarly liable to err in law. In the case of manifest
error, it would be unfortunate if the parties to subsequent cases had to go to a higher
court to obtain a correction and that until they did so this court should be bound to
perpetuate its own error. The second, which may be related to the first, is that
r 68 of the Industrial Court Rules 1971[1], made by the Lord Chancellor under para 18
(2) of Sch 3 to the 1971 Act, has empowered this court to review its own decisions of
its own motion in a number of circumstances including that 'the interests of justice
b require such review'. It would, we think, be very odd that we should be bound
by a decision which we could ourselves set aside, albeit at the very undesirable price
of varying the settled rights of the parties to the earlier decision.

In our judgment, the interests of justice will best be served if this court retains a
measure of flexibility. Whilst expressly disavowing any pretentions to the status of
the House of Lords, we can think of no better way of stating the extent to which this
c court will treat itself as being bound by its own decisions than respectfully to adopt
and adapt the words of the declaration delivered by Lord Gardiner LC in 1966[2].
Accordingly, we wish to say that this court regards the use of precedent as an indis-
pensable foundation on which to decide what is the law and its application to individual cases. It provides at least some degree of certainty on which individuals can
rely in the conduct of their affairs, as well as a basis for orderly development of legal
d rules in the field of industrial relations. The court nevertheless recognises that too
rigid adherence to precedent may lead to injustice in a particular case and also unduly
restrict the proper development of industrial law. The court therefore, whilst
treating its own former decisions as normally binding, will consider itself free to depart from them when it appears right to do so. In this connection the court will
bear in mind the danger of disturbing retrospectively decisions which have formed
e the general basis of industrial relations agreements and practices.

Before concluding this judgment we should like to draw attention to a procedural
matter which has caused some concern both to the tribunal and to this court. Six of
the seven appellants claimed only under the Redundancy Payments Act 1965. The
seventh failed initially to make it clear whether his claim was under that Act or for
f unfair dismissal contrary to s 22 of the Industrial Relations Act 1971. Subsequently
he withdrew any claim for unfair dismissal. As the tribunal pointed out, cases can
arise in which there is real doubt as to whether the dismissal was on account of redundancy, was an unfair dismissal as defined in the 1971 Act, was both on account of
redundancy and also unfair, or was a justifiable dismissal. In such circumstances the
applicant should claim both for compensation for unfair dismissal and for a redundancy payment, leaving it to the tribunal to decide whether both or either is justified.
g The applicant will thereby avoid the injustice of, for example, pursuing a claim for a
redundancy payment only to find that the tribunal regards the case as one of unfair
dismissal and that he is out of time to make a complaint on this latter basis.

However, industrial tribunals, and this court, must and do recognise that many
of those who appear before them are without the benefit of advice from lawyers, trade
union officials or others who are familiar with the problems of redundancy payments
h and compensation for unfair dismissal. Furthermore, there is an additional complication in that it appears that some trade unions carry their opposition to the Industrial
Relations Act 1971 to the point of refusing assistance to those of their members who
wish to claim compensation for unfair dismissal which involves relying on the Act,
whilst freely granting assistance to those who seek redundancy payments under the
Redundancy Payments Act 1965.
j It is not for industrial tribunals or this court to approve or disapprove of any particular Act of Parliament or to give preference to one right created by Parliament in
preference to another similarly created. On the other hand, both have to take account

---

1 SI 1971 No 1777
2 See *Note* [1966] 3 All ER 77, [1966] 1 WLR 1234

of any circumstance which could lead to injustice and to do all in their power to prevent this result. Accordingly, if there is the slightest doubt whether an applicant's claim is or should be for a redundancy payment or for compensation for unfair dismissal, or for both (see s 24 (5) of the 1971 Act), the applicant should be encouraged to put forward or maintain both such claims until all the facts are known. The adoption of this course will not usually increase the time or expense involved as all or most of the evidence will be common to both claims. Even when the full facts are known and a decision has been made as to the true basis of claim, if there is any chance of this court taking a different view on appeal, the claim which is considered inappropriate should be dismissed rather than withdrawn, thus allowing this court to restore it if necessary. In all circumstances industrial tribunals should make the widest use of their powers to allow amendment of claims and to extend time limits in order to ensure that justice is done not only to the applicant, but to the respondent, who must always be granted any adjournment necessary to enable him to answer a new basis of claim which emerges at a late stage.

For the reasons which we have given, the appeals fail and will be dismissed.

Appeals dismissed.

Solicitors: *Pattinson & Brewer* (for the appellants).

Gordon H Scott Esq   Barrister.

Wilkes and others v Gee

CHANCERY DIVISION
PLOWMAN J
21st NOVEMBER 1972

Commons – Registration – Disputed claims – Jurisdiction – Commons Commissioner – Residual jurisdiction of High Court – Circumstances in which residual jurisdiction exercisable – Cases of emergency.

The defendant registered the plaintiffs' land as common land under the provisions of the Commons Registration Act 1965. The plaintiffs moved the High Court for an order that the defendant 'do forthwith procure or concur in the removal' of the land from the commons register. The evidence adduced by the defendant in support of his claim that that land was common land was of the most tenuous nature. Evidence was filed on behalf of the plaintiffs that, although Commons Commissioners had been appointed to hear objections, it would be at least a year if not longer before the plaintiffs' objection to the registration could be heard; that the plaintiffs were dealing with the local authority, who wished to purchase the land, and that as long as it was provisionally registered as common land it would be unsafe and improper for the parties to complete their negotiations.

Held – Prima facie, having regard to the provisions of the 1965 Act, the proper tribunal to decide such disputes was the Commons Commissioner. Even if the High Court had a residual jurisdiction, it would only be exercisable in special circumstances e g in a case of emergency where it was vital for the matter to be dealt with immediately. On the evidence no case of special emergency had been made out and the motion would be dismissed (see p 229 b c f and g, post).

Note
For effect of registration of rights of common, see Supplement to 5 Halsbury's Laws (3rd Edn) para 982A.

Cases cited

A-G v Chaudry [1971] 3 All ER 938, [1971] 1 WLR 1614, CA.
Booker v James (1968) 19 P & CR 525.
Cooke v Amey Gravel Co Ltd [1972] 3 All ER 579, [1972] 1 WLR 1310.
Thorne Rural District Council v Bunting [1972] 1 All ER 439, [1972] Ch 470.
Thorne Rural District Council v Bunting (No 2) [1972] 3 All ER 657 affd [1972] 3 All ER 1084, CA.
Trafford v Ashby (1969) 21 P & CR 293.

Motion

By notice of motion dated 7th November 1972, Michael Bruce Wilkes, Adrian Nicholas Wilkes, Colin Richard Burridge and Anthony John Burridge, the plaintiffs in an action against the defendant, Ernest Howard Valentine Gee, sought an order that the defendant forthwith procure or concur in the removal from the Commons Register kept by the Dorset County Council pursuant to the Commons Registration Act 1965, land of the plaintiffs at Sandford Pottery, Gorehill, Sandford, Wareham in the county of Dorset which was registered thereon as common land pursuant to an application made by the defendant under Unit No 721 and entry No CL309. The facts are set out in the judgment.

Ian McCulloch for the plaintiffs.
Norman Primost for the defendant.

PLOWMAN J. The plaintiffs own land at Gorehill, Sandford, Wareham, in the county of Dorset, which is known as Sandford Pottery. Formerly there was a factory in operation on the site which manufactured pottery, the factory being known as the Sandford Works. The factory site is partly enclosed by fences on certain parts and by hedges on others, and evidence has been filed, on behalf of the plaintiffs, to the effect that, for the last 50 years, no claim in respect of rights of common, pasture way or sporting rights over such land or any part thereof has been made and that, during that period, the land has been in full and free and undisturbed possession of the company which formerly owned it.

The defendant, who spends a good deal of his time in London, but who has a house in the country not far away from the land with which I am concerned, has registered that land as common land, as have certain other people. The defendant's house is not adjacent to the plaintiffs' land and the defendant claims no commonable rights over it, but, as I say, he, with others, has registered the land as common land.

By the notice of motion which is before me, the plaintiffs are asking for an order—

'that the Defendant do forthwith procure or concur in the removal of the land of the Plaintiffs mentioned in the Writ of Summons herein from the Commons Register kept by the Dorset County Council pursuant to the Commons Registration Act 1965 which is now registered thereon as common land pursuant to an application made by the Defendant under Unit No. 721 and entry No. CL309.'

The plaintiffs say that the defendant has produced no evidence at all in support of his assertion that this land is common land and they suggest that the defendant's motive in procuring this registration has been simply to prevent this land from being developed. Counsel for the defendant disputes the assertion that the defendant has put forward no evidence to suggest that he bona fide believes this land to be common land, but I am bound to say that the evidence which counsel points to as indicating that this land is or may be common land, is of the most tenuous nature.

The submission which is made on behalf of the defendant is that the proper tribunal to determine this dispute is not this court at all but the Commons Commissioner, established by the Commons Registration Act 1965, and counsel submits that that is so even if, which he does not admit, this court has a residual jurisdiction to deal with the matter.

I have been referred to a number of cases on the question whether there is a juris- *a* diction in this court. A number were decided before the Commons Commissioners under the Act had been appointed and others decided after that time. Without going into the cases, I will assume, for the purposes of this judgment, that there is some residual jurisdiction in this court. I am not deciding that there is, but I am assuming there is for the purposes of this application. The question then is, what as a matter of discretion ought I to do?

At this point I want to refer to one or two sections of the 1965 Act. Section 5 (6) *b* provides:

'Where such an objection is made [i e an objection to registration], then, unless the objection is withdrawn or the registration cancelled before the end of such period as may be prescribed, the registration authority shall refer the matter to a Commons Commissioner.' *c*

Section 6 (1) provides:

'The Commons Commissioner to whom any matter has been referred under section 5 of this Act shall inquire into it and shall either confirm the registration, with or without modifications, or refuse to confirm it; and the registration shall, if it is confirmed, become final, and, if the confirmation is refused, become void,— *d* (a) if no appeal is brought against the confirmation or refusal, at the end of the period during which such an appeal could have been brought; (b) if such an appeal is brought, when it is finally disposed of.'

Then s 14 gives the High Court a limited power of rectification of the register maintained under the Act. What it says is this: *e*

'The High Court may order a register maintained under this Act to be amended if—(a) the registration under this Act of any land or rights of common has become final and the court is satisfied that any person was induced by fraud to withdraw an objection to the registration or to refrain from making such an objection; or (b) the register has been amended in pursuance of section 13 of this Act and it appears to the court that no amendment or a different amend- *f* ment ought to have been made and that the error cannot be corrected in pur- suance of regulations made under this Act; and, in either case, the court deems it just to rectify the register.'

Then s 18 provides:

'(1) Any person aggrieved by the decision of a Commons Commissioner as *g* being erroneous in point of law may, within such time as may be limited by rules of court, require the Commissioner to state a case for the decision of the High Court.

'(2) So much of section 63 (1) of the Supreme Court of Judicature (Consolidation) Act 1925 as requires appeals to the High Court to be heard and determined by a Divisional Court shall not apply to an appeal by way of case stated under this *h* section, but no appeal to the Court of Appeal shall be brought against the decision of the High Court in such a case except with the leave of that Court or the Court of Appeal.'

I should, I think, have noticed s 17 (4), to which counsel for the defendant referred; that subsection provides: *j*

'A Commons Commissioner may order any party to any proceedings before him to pay to any other party to the proceedings any costs incurred by that party in respect of the proceedings; and any costs so awarded shall be taxed in the county court according to such of the scales prescribed by county court rules for proceedings in the county court as may be directed by the order, but subject *a*   to any modifications specified in the direction, or, if the order gives no direction, by the county court, and shall be recoverable in like manner as costs awarded in the county court.'

Counsel for the defendant referred to that as pointing out that the intention of Parliament is that these matters of dispute should be decided before a tribunal where the costs would be low compared with costs in the High Court.

b   This much I think must be clear, that prima facie, having regard to the provisions of the Act to which I have referred, the proper tribunal to decide disputes of this sort with which I am concerned is the Commons Commissioner, even if the court has a residual jurisdiction. And if there is such a jurisdiction, it follows, I think, that it would only be exercised in special circumstances, for example, in the case of some emergency in which it may be vital for the matter to be dealt with immediately.

c   And so, I ask myself what, if any, are the special circumstances in this case?

The evidence about this is to be found in paras 11 and 13 of the affidavit of Mr Cake, the plaintiffs' solicitor, sworn on behalf of the plaintiffs. He says:

> 'I have made full inquiries and I am informed that even although Commons Commissioners have been appointed to hear objections it will be at least a year
> *d*   if not longer before the objection of the Plaintiffs to the said Registration could be heard . . . The Plaintiffs are at present dealing with Dorset County Council who wish to purchase Sandford Pottery and build a school on the site. As long as the land is provisionally registered as common land it would be thoroughly unsafe and indeed improper for the dealing parties to complete their negotiations.'

e   So far as that last paragraph is concerned, it does not seem to me that any case of special urgency is made out there at all. So far as para 11 is concerned, in which Mr Cake says '. . . it will be at least a year if not longer before the objection of the Plaintiffs to the said Registration could be heard', it seems to me that it would be quite wrong to treat this court, as it were, as an overflow court for the Commons Commissioner and say that merely because it will be some time before this dispute can be brought before the Commons Commissioner, therefore it is right that the High Court *f*   should deal with it.

I am not satisfied that any case has been made out here for saying that this matter ought not to be dealt with by the tribunal which prima facie is the proper tribunal for dealing with it and, in those circumstances, I am not prepared to make the order which I am asked to make by the notice of motion which is before me.

g   *Motion dismissed.*

Solicitors: *Church, Adams, Tatham & Co,* agents for *Dickinson, Manser & Co,* Poole (for the plaintiffs); *Ellis & Fairbairn* (for the defendant).

Jacqueline Metcalfe   Barrister.

Brindle v H W Smith (Cabinets) Ltd   *a*

COURT OF APPEAL, CIVIL DIVISION
LORD DENNING MR, MEGAW LJ AND SIR GORDON WILLMER
6th, 7th NOVEMBER 1972

Industrial relations – Unfair dismissal – Date of dismissal – Notice by employer terminating **b**
contract – Whether employee dismissed when notice given or when period of notice expires –
Industrial Relations Act 1971, s 23 (2).

In 1946 B started work with S Ltd. In October 1971 S Ltd was taken over by M, who,
on Monday, 21st February 1972, gave B a month's notice. B's period of notice expired
on 24th March. She claimed compensation for unfair dismissal under the relevant   **c**
provisions of the Industrial Relations Act 1971, which came into force on 28th February
1972. S Ltd contended that B was not entitled to do so as she had been dismissed,
within the meaning of s 23 (2)[a] of the 1971 Act, on the date that she had been given
notice, i e before the 1971 Act came into operation.

Held – On the true construction of s 23 (2) an employee was 'taken to be dismissed' **d**
on the date that his contract was terminated, which was the date when his period of
notice expired or was due to expire; it followed that as B's period of notice expired
after the relevant part of the 1971 Act had come into force, she was entitled to claim
compensation (see p 232 d g and h, p 234 d and p 235 h, post).

Notes
For dismissal within the meaning of the Industrial Relations Act 1971, see Supplement **e**
to 38 Halsbury's Laws (3rd Edn) 677B, 19.
    For the Industrial Relations Act 1971, s 23, see 41 Halsbury's Statutes (3rd Edn) 2088.

Cases referred to in judgment
Haydon v South Eastern District of the Workers' Education Association (1972) 7 ITR 318, IT.
Henderson v Derek Crouch (Contractors) Ltd (25th April 1972) unreported, IT.   **f**
Johnson v John Thompson Water Tube Boilers Ltd (1966) 1 ITR 261, 1 KIR 111, IT.
Master Ladies Tailors Organisation v Minister of Labour and National Service [1950] 2 All
    ER 525, 66 (pt 2) TLR 728, 94 Sol Jo 552, 44 Digest (Repl) 383, *2223*.
Porter v Aga (UK) Ltd (14th April 1972) unreported, IT.
R v St Mary, Whitechapel (Inhabitants) (1848) 12 QB 120, 3 New Sess Cas 262, 17 LJMC
    172, 11 LTOS 473, 116 ER 811; sub nom *R v St Mary, Whitechapel (Inhabitants),* **g**
    R v St Pancras (Inhabitants) 12 Jur 792, 44 Digest (Repl) 285, *1144*.
Stokes v Sun Life Assurance Co of Canada (1972) The Times, 12th October, NIRC, *affg*
    7 ITR 256, IT.
Taylor's Cater Inns Ltd v Minister of Labour (1966) 1 ITR 242, 1 KIR 106, IT.

Appeal   **h**
This was an appeal by Iris Brindle against the judgment of the National Industrial
Relations Court (Sir John Donaldson P, Mr T L Johnson and Mr R E Griffiths) dated
25th October 1972, whereby an appeal by the respondents, H W Smith (Cabinets) Ltd,
against the decision of an industrial tribunal sitting at Reading on 19th June 1972,
awarding the appellant £3,000 compensation for unfair dismissal, was allowed and
the award of the industrial tribunal set aside. The facts are set out in the judgment **j**
of Lord Denning MR.

C W F Newman for the appellant.
Andrew J Bateson QC and *H P D Bennett* for the respondents.

---

a Section 23, so far as material, is set out at p 232 b and e and p 234 f, post

LORD DENNING MR. In 1946 the appellant, Miss Iris Brindle, then a girl of
20, started work as a secretary for a furniture firm at High Wycombe. She did well.
She got to know a lot about the furniture trade. She became a director and secretary
of the respondent company, H W Smith (Cabinets) Ltd. In October 1971 the company was taken over by a Mr Mainwaring. He was a merchant banker. He acquired
the shares in the company, including a few shares which Miss Brindle had. He took
control. He had had no experience in the furniture trade. Miss Brindle did all she
could to help Mr Mainwaring. Her salary was £2,400 a year. But three months after
the take-over, on Monday, 21st February 1972, Mr Mainwaring said to her: 'First
of all, I am reducing your salary to £1,300 a year [that is by nearly half] and, secondly,
I am giving you one month's notice.' Counting from Friday, that notice would have
expired on Friday, 24th March. But then on the evening of Friday, 25th February,
as she was leaving the office in the evening, Mr Mainwaring said to her: 'You are
going for a holiday this evening.' She said 'No'. She preferred to work her full
notice. He said: 'Some people will just not take a hint.' She said to him: 'Are
you telling me not to come to work?' He said 'Yes, I am'. She asked: 'Can I come
in on Monday morning to collect my things and return the keys?' He said 'Yes,
you can'. So, on Monday, 28th February, she went to the office. She collected her
things. She handed the keys to Mr Mainwaring. He checked them as correct.
That was the end. So she left the firm which she had served so well for 26 years.
Later on the employers stamped her insurance card for the full period of notice
which they calculated expired on 24th March.

On 27th March 1972 Miss Brindle applied to the industrial tribunal for compensation for unfair dismissal. The tribunal awarded her compensation in the sum of
£3,000. The company wish to challenge that figure. But meanwhile an important
point has arisen. The notice of dismissal 'straddled' the date when the Industrial
Relations Act 1971 came into force. The relevant provisions came into operation on
28th February 1972. She was given notice on 21st February *before* the Act came into
operation. But the notice expired on 24th March *after* the Act came into operation.
The question is whether she can avail herself of the compensation provisions, seeing
that the notice was given before the Act came into operation and it expired afterwards.

The relevant sections were brought into operation by statutory instrument[1]. It was
made on 17th January 1972, laid before Parliament on 27th January and came into
operation on 28th February. It set out (amongst others) ss 22 and 23, dealing with
unfair dismissal. It brought them into operation on 28th February 1972. But
before I read the sections, I would state the common law.

At common law Miss Brindle could have been dismissed on reasonable notice.
I should have thought she would have been entitled to three months' notice. She
would not have been entitled to any compensation for her long service, or for loss of
office. Just three months' notice. No more. Now the 1971 Act makes a great
difference. An employer is not allowed to dismiss a servant unfairly without compensation. The Act gives an employee a right in his job which is akin to a right
of property. The employer can no longer give the legal notice and say: 'Out you
go, without compensation.' The tribunal can enquire into the reasons for the dismissal. If the reasons are not sufficient to warrant it, the tribunal will hold it to be
an unfair dismissal. The employer will have to pay compensation. The amount
is very much in the discretion of the tribunal. It can award under s 116 an amount
which is just and equitable in all the circumstances of the case; subject to this: it
must not be more than two years' pay or £4,160, whichever is less: see s 118. The
tribunal awarded Miss Brindle £3,000.

The question is whether the Act applies when the notice 'straddles' 28th February
1972. The Act in s 170 (4) enables the Minister to make provision for transitional
cases. But he has not done so. So we must decide it on the interpretation of the

---

1 The Industrial Relations Act 1971 (Commencement No 4) Order 1972 (SI 1971 No 36)

Act. The important sections are these: s 22 (1) says that 'every employee shall have the right not to be unfairly dismissed by his employer'. Section 167 says that 'dismiss' and 'dismissal' have the meaning given to them in s 23. Section 23 (2) (omitting unnecessary words) says this:

'... an employee shall be taken to be dismissed by his employer if, but only if,
—(a) the contract under which he is employed by the employer is terminated by the employer, whether it is so terminated by notice or without notice ...'

Applying that subsection to this present case, when was Miss Brindle's contract terminated? She was given notice on 21st February 1972 to expire on 24th March 1972. Suppose Miss Brindle had worked out her notice so as to finish on 24th March. Her contract of employment would not have terminated until that date, that is, not until the expiry of the notice. She would be employed under the self-same contract until that date. So that date, 24th March, would be the date on which she would be 'taken to be dismissed'. That is clear from the subsection. But she did not in fact work out her notice. Mr Mainwaring turned her out on 25th February. Can that make any difference? I do not think so. Her employer should not be in any better position by turning her out before the notice expired. Nor should she be in a worse position.

So I hold that the date of dismissal is the date when the notice expires or is due to expire, and not when it is given. It follows that the dismissal of Miss Brindle took place after the Act came into operation, and she can claim the benefit of it.

I will not read s 23 (3) in detail, but it proceeds on the same footing as s 23 (2). Section 23 (5) is different. It contains a definition of the 'effective date of termination'. It does not apply in terms to the date of dismissal, but I think it has the same effect. It says:

'... "the effective date of termination"—(a) in relation to an employee whose contract of employment is terminated by notice, whether given by his employer or by the employee, means the date on which that notice expires ...'

In contrast to those subsections, it is significant that when the Act means the dismissal to take effect when the notice is given, it says so. It does so in s 26 (4).

So I am of opinion that on the true interpretation of s 23, the dismissal takes place when the contract is terminated, and that termination takes place at the date when the notice expires or is due to expire, and not when the notice is given.

I would add at this point that I do not think the Act can be got round by wrongfully dismissing a person summarily or by giving him a notice that is too short. No person should be able to take advantage of his own wrong in that way. If an employer should try to escape the Act by giving no notice at all or a notice that was too short, I should have thought that the tribunal, by means of a claim for wrongful dismissal (see s 113 of the Act), or by some such way, would see that the employee would get the same compensation as he would have done if he had been given notice of a proper length.

I must, however, deal with a serious argument which was put forward by counsel for the respondents. He suggested that, on the interpretation which I have given, we should be giving the Act a retrospective application. He took this illustration: an employer on 8th December 1971 gives an employee notice to expire on 8th March 1972. As the law stood on 8th December 1971 the employer had an absolute right to dismiss the employee by such a notice. He would not have to consider whether he had good reason for dismissal or not. He would not be liable to pay the employee any compensation. Why should he be adversely affected by the Act which only came into force on 28th February 1972? For a time I was troubled by this illustration, but, on reflection, it seems to me that on 28th February 1972 the Act would operate prospectively. It would operate on the dismissal which would take place on 8th March 1972. The Act is not to be condemned as 'retrospective' simply because a some of the facts are drawn from the time before it came into operation. In 1848 in *R v St Mary, Whitechapel (Inhabitants)*[1], Lord Denman CJ said[2]: '. . . it is not properly called a retrospective statute because a part of the requisites for its action is drawn from time antecedent to its passing.' That observation was applied by Somervell LJ in *Master Ladies Tailors Organisation v Minister of Labour and National Service*[3].

b I hold therefore that this statute applies to notices which 'straddle' the Act—notices which are given before but due to expire after 28th February 1972. This view is borne out by the way in which the tribunals have interpreted the same words about dismissal in s 3 of the Redundancy Payments Act 1965. In *Taylor's Cater Inns Ltd v Minister of Labour*[4] and in *Johnson v John Thompson Water Tube Boilers Ltd*[5], the President, Sir Diarmaid Conroy, was of opinion that a notice which 'straddled' 6th December 1965 (when that Act came into operation) amounted to a dismissal so as to give a

c right to redundancy payment. So similarly under the present Act. We are told that industrial tribunals in London in *Porter v Aga (UK) Ltd*[6], and in Newcastle in *Henderson v Derek Crouch (Contractors) Ltd*[7] and at Ashford, in *Haydon v South Eastern District of the Workers' Education Association*[8], have been expressing the view (sometimes obiter, sometimes relying on s 23 (5)) that these straddling notices are good; and that compensation can be awarded when a notice is given before but expires after the

d Act. The tribunals were all of one mind until *Stokes v Sun Life Assurance Co of Canada*[9]. It was decided the other way in Manchester on 17th May 1972. It came before the National Industrial Relations Court on 11th October 1972, presided over by Sir John Brightman. The court held that these straddling notices were bad; and that if a notice was given before the Act and expired afterwards, the employee could not get compensation in regard to it. The present case came a fortnight later before

e a court presided over by Sir John Donaldson P. That court had misgivings about the decision in *Stokes*.[9] They did not think that they could depart from it. But, holding the point to be 'highly arguable', they sought the guidance of this court about it.

In the result, on the interpretation of this statute, I am of opinion that a notice given before 28th February 1972 to expire after that date is a notice of dismissal. It

f is a dismissal which takes effect at the date when the notice expires or is due to expire. It entitles an employee, if he has a proper case, to compensation for unfair dismissal. In order to rebut his claim it is for the employer to bring himself within one of the reasons given in s 24 of the Act, such as that the employee was incapable or his conduct was bad. In the absence of good reason, the employee is entitled to compensation. It is then for the tribunal to fix the amount according to what is just and equitable.

g I would allow the appeal accordingly.

MEGAW LJ. Although the questions which are involved in this appeal are in my view far from easy, I think that, for the reasons which have been stated by Lord Denning MR, and which are emphasised in what was said by the President of the National Industrial Relations Court, it is desirable that we should give judgment

h in this matter at the earliest possible moment.

The main issue which has arisen is a question of the construction of s 23 of the Industrial Relations Act 1971, and, in particular, sub-s (2) of that section. The reason why that is important is this: the respondents, through counsel, contend that on the

1 (1848) 12 QB 120
2 (1848) 12 QB at 127
3 [1950] 2 All ER 525 at 527
4 (1966) 1 ITR 242
5 (1966) 1 ITR 261
6 (14th April 1972) unreported
7 (25th April 1972) unreported
8 (1972) 7 ITR 318
9 (1972) The Times, 12th October, *affg* 7 ITR 256

true construction of that subsection the date of dismissal has to be taken as being *a*
the date when the employer gave the notice to the employee. The appellant, Miss
Brindle, through counsel, contends, on the other hand, that on the true construction
of s 23 (2) the date of dismissal is the date when the notice given by the employer
expires. In the present case the notice was given a few days before the relevant
sections of the Act came into force; but the notice expired many days after those
sections came into force. Now, Parliament in enacting s 23 (2) has not expressly *b*
stated what is to be taken as being the date of dismissal. As it has become relevant,
and vitally relevant, for the purpose of this case and similar cases where the period
of notice straddles the date of coming into force of this part of the Act, it is necessary
for the court to construe s 23 (2) with a view to deciding what is the date of dismissal
on the true meaning of that subsection. So far as relevant, the subsection reads:

> '. . . an employee shall be taken to be dismissed by his employer if . . . (*a*) the *c*
> contract under which he is employed by the employer is terminated by the
> employer, whether it is so terminated by notice or without notice . . .'

That is the definition of 'dismissal' for this purpose. Counsel for the respondents
says that when one looks at the date to be deduced from those words, the date has
to be taken as being the date when notice was given. In my view, that, as a matter *d*
of construction, is wrong. The contract is terminated on the date when the legal
relationship between the two parties to the contract ceases to have effect. That
date is the date when the notice expires and not the date when the notice is given.
If there were doubt of that construction, to my mind it is resolved by the terms of
s 23 (3). I think it would be most remarkable if a different meaning had to be given
to the concept of 'termination of the contract' in sub-s (2) from that which appears *e*
in sub-s (3). Subsection (3) reads:

> 'Where an employer gives notice to an employee to terminate his contract of
> employment and, at a time within the obligatory period of that notice, the
> employee gives notice in writing to the employer to terminate the contract of
> employment on a date earlier than the date on which the employer's notice
> is due to expire, the employee shall for the purposes of this Act be taken to be *f*
> dismissed by his employer, and the reasons for the dismissal shall be taken to
> be the reasons for which the employer's notice is given.'

It seems clear that Parliament is there treating the phrase 'terminate a contract' as
meaning that the 'termination' takes place on the date on which the notice is due to
expire, and not the date when the notice is given. That in my view is equally
the meaning and effect of the words 'the contract is terminated by notice', where *g*
those words appear in sub-s (2) (*a*). Accordingly, as I see it, Parliament has provided,
with reference to the facts of the present case, that the dismissal of the appellant is to
be taken as having occurred on the date when the notice expired, which was after
the coming into force of the Act. Therefore an argument that the Act is not applicable
in my view is wrong.

However, a strong submission was made by counsel for the respondents that *h*
the words ought to be interpreted differently, because, if they were to be interpreted
in the way in which I have indicated, it would mean that Parliament had made a
retrospective provision; and one ought to do one's best to construe an Act of Parliament to avoid its having a retrospective effect, which would operate on (as counsel
put it) accrued rights. It is to be observed that this Act, in other aspects, has what *j*
might be called retrospective effect.

Let me give one example of that. It is a part of the provisions of this Act that where
there is a contract for a fixed period of time (subject to certain exceptions which are
expressly provided in the Act, such as, for example, by s 30) it is to be treated as
being a dismissal of the employee by the employer if he fails to renew that contract
on the date of its expiry. Now, that, as I say, is something which gives the Act, in

a one sense, retrospective effect. A contract has been made before the enactment of the Act, or before it has come into force. That contract provides, say, that the period of employment shall be for one year only and shall terminate on 1st April 1972. The parties, the employer and the employee, by their own perfectly lawful agreement have so provided. Apart from the Act, the employer is not bound to continue to employ the employee after 1st April 1972, and the employee has no right
b to require to continue to be employed after that date. But the Act says 'Never mind what the parties have agreed or what their legal rights were under the contract the day before the Act came into force: from the day that the Act operates the pre-existing contractual obligations, if they are still alive on that day, shall be altered: the employer shall be bound to continue the employment of the employee indefinitely beyond 1st April, and if he fails to do so he may be liable for unfairly dismissing the employee'. The Act operates in that way because the pre-existing contract is
c still in force on 28th February 1972. I do not see how, from the point of view of being retrospective, there is a material difference between such a case and the present case. Because the contract is still alive on 28th February 1972, and the Act operates to change its terms on that day. Where the Act provides as it clearly does, for a retrospective change in the terms of a contract of employment for a fixed term, it
d does not startle me to find that Parliament should have provided—if that be the true construction of s 23—that the relevant date of a dismissal, for the purpose of deciding whether the Act applies, should also be the date when the contract comes to an end according to its terms.

However that may be, in my judgment the words of s 23 with reference to the facts of the case which have arisen here are clear and unambiguous; and the retrospective effect, such as it is, of that interpretation cannot successfully be invoked to give to
e the words a different interpretation from that which they naturally and properly bear.

The other argument put forward by counsel on behalf of the respondents was, as I understand it, that this court, on the facts which have been put before it, ought to hold that the appellant had been dismissed before the date on which the Act came
f into force, either without notice or with notice which had expired before the Act came into force. He contended that in those circumstances the Act could have no operation whatever other remedy might be open to the appellant. For myself, I should wish to reserve consideration as to the position in law if such facts did arise; that is to say, if before 28th February 1972 an employer had purported to dismiss an employee without notice when that employee was lawfully entitled to notice running beyond 28th February 1972. But so far as the present case is concerned,
g the finding of the facts is a matter for the tribunal; and I should certainly not be prepared to say on the facts as they have emerged in this court that such a case has been made out on the facts.

I agree that this appeal should be allowed.

h **SIR GORDON WILLMER.** I have reached the same conclusion. As I fully agree with everything that has been said by Lord Denning MR and Megaw LJ in the two judgments which have just been delivered, I do not think it necessary or desirable for me to add anything further.

Appeal allowed. Case remitted to the National Industrial Relations Court. Leave to appeal
i *to the House of Lords refused.*

Solicitors: *Cripps, Harries, Willis & Carter*, agents for *Winter-Taylor, Woodward & Webb*, HighWycombe (for the appellant); *Bircham & Co* (for the respondents).

L J Kovats Esq Barrister.

Portsmouth Corporation v Nishar Ali

QUEEN'S BENCH DIVISION

LORD WIDGERY CJ, MELFORD STEVENSON AND BRABIN JJ

3rd NOVEMBER 1972

Licensing – Offence – Failure to comply with a condition of a late night refreshment house licence – Licensee owning restaurant – Licensee holding late night refreshment house licence for premises – Licence subject to a condition – Licensee also holding justices' on-licence under Part IV of the Licensing Act 1964 for same premises – Licensee acting in breach of condition of late night refreshment house licence – Whether possession of justices' on-licence exempting him from liability – Late Night Refreshment Houses Act 1969, ss 1, 7 (2).

N owned a restaurant in respect of which he was granted (i) a justices' on-licence under Part IV of the Licensing Act 1964 and (ii) a late night refreshment house licence under the Late Night Refreshment Houses Act 1969. It was a condition of the late night refreshment house licence that the premises would not be open between 1.00 am and 5.00 am for public refreshment. The premises were found to be open at 1.45 am one morning. One customer was eating a meal and four others were studying the menu. N was charged with failing to comply with a condition of the late night refreshment house licence, contrary to s 7 (2)[a] of the 1969 Act. He was acquitted by the justices and the prosecutor appealed.

Held – The appeal would be dismissed. The fact that N held a justices' on-licence in respect of the premises meant that they were 'licensed for the sale of beer, cider, wine or spirits' within the meaning of s 1[b] of the 1969 Act and thus excepted from the definition of a late night refreshment house in that section. Accordingly he was not liable to take out a licence under the 1969 Act (see p 238 j to p 239 c and p 240 b and c, post).

Notes

For refreshment house licences, see 22 Halsbury's Laws (3rd Edn) 622, 623, para 1303; and for cases on the subject, see 30 Digest (Repl) 11, 12, 40-44.

For the Late Night Refreshment Houses Act 1969, ss 1, 7, see 17 Halsbury's Statutes (3rd Edn) 1266, 1268.

Cases and authority cited

Munn v Southall (1862) 7 LT 356, DC.

Rous de Horsey v Rignell [1963] 1 All ER 38, [1963] 1 QB 914, DC.

Paterson's Licensing Acts (80th Edn, 1972) 981, note.

Case stated

This was an appeal by way of case stated by justices for the petty sessional division of the city of Portsmouth in respect of their adjudication as a magistrates' court sitting at Portsmouth on 28th April 1972.

On 13th March 1972 an information was preferred by the appellants, Portsmouth Corporation, against the respondent, Nishar Ali, that he, on 6th February 1972, did fail to comply with the condition of a late night refreshment house licence granted to him by the Portsmouth City Council prohibiting the opening of the refreshment house at 61 Albert Road between 1.00 am and 5.00 am for public refreshment resort or entertainment, contrary to s 7 (2) of the Late Night Refreshment Houses Act 1969.

---

a Section 7 (2) provides: 'In the event of a contravention of a condition imposed by the licensing authority under this section, the licensee of the refreshment house shall be guilty of an offence.'

b Section 1 is set out at p 238 h, post

a   The justices found the following facts which were not disputed by the respondent. At 1.45 a m on 6th February 1972 the 'open' sign was exhibited on the front door of the premises in question which was unlocked. In the restaurant at the premises one customer was eating a meal and four others were studying menus. The respondent was the proprietor of the premises and the restaurant business carried on there. It was agreed by the appellants that the respondent held a restaurant licence under
b   Part IV of the Licensing Act 1964 in respect of the premises.

  It was contended by the appellants that the definition 'late night refreshment house' in s 1 of the 1969 Act was not materially different from the definition of 'refreshment house' in s 1 of the Refreshment Houses Act 1860. The 1860 Act provided for refreshment house licensees also holding wine licences, and *Munn v Southall*[1] was authority for the proposition that the same premises could have a beer licence, a wine
c   licence and a licence under the 1860 Act. Sections 100 and 101 of the Licensing Act 1964 and s 11 of the 1969 Act read in conjunction contemplated the same premises being licensed under Part IV of the 1964 Act and under the 1969 Act concurrently. The intention of s 7 of the 1969 Act would be frustrated if it were held that the 1969 Act did not apply merely by reason of the existence of a restaurant licence under Part IV of the 1964 Act. The decision of Portsmouth City Quarter Sessions dated
d   27th September 1971 to the effect that the 1969 Act did apply to the premises notwithstanding that they were licensed under Part IV of the 1964 Act was binding on the justices and ought to be followed by them.

  On a preliminary submission of law it was contended by the respondent that because the premises had a restaurant licence under Part IV of the 1964 Act they could not by law be licensed under the 1969 Act as s 1 of the 1969 Act expressly excluded therefrom premises licensed for the sale of beer, cider, wines or spirits.
e   The licence granted to the respondent by the appellants under the 1969 Act and the conditions attached by them thereto were therefore nullities. The definition in s 1 of the 1969 Act was unambiguous and there was therefore no cause in this case to go outside the Act to interpret it. The 1969 Act was a consolidating Act and should properly be interpreted without reference to the legislation which it consolidated.
f   In the 1860 Act the words of exclusion were different from those in the 1969 Act, but nevertheless likewise excluded such premises licensed for the sale of intoxicating liquor, other than those licensed for certain sales of intoxicating liquor under the 1860 Act. The decision of Portsmouth City Quarter Sessions dated 27th September 1971 should not be followed. In the event of the relevant law being found to be ambiguous ss 1 and 7 of the 1969 Act being a penal provision should be construed strictly and in favour of the respondent. The respondent had found no reported
g   cases which suggested that refreshment houses licensed under the 1860 Act sold intoxicating liquor. The refreshment house legislation was intended to supplement the intoxicating liquor legislation by bringing under its control certain premises not licensed for the sale of intoxicating liquor in respect of which latter there already existed adequate control.

h   The justices were of the opinion that the 1969 Act did not apply to premises licensed for the sale of alcohol whatever the original intention of the legislators might have been; that because of radical changes in the law between 1860 and the present time they ought not to take into account cases relating to the issue of wine licences under the 1860 Act; that ss 100 and 101 of the 1964 Act did not contemplate the simultaneous holding of licences under both Part IV of the 1964 Act and under the 1969 Act in respect of the same premises or of any part of the same premises. Accordingly they
j   dismissed the information.

  The question for the opinion of the High Court was whether the respondent being the keeper of premises kept open for public refreshment resort and entertainment between the hours of 10.00 p m and 5.00 a m and in respect of which he held a

---

1   (1862) 7 LT 356

restaurant licence under Part IV of the Licensing Act 1964 was by reason of holding
such licence not liable or able to take out a licence under the provisions of the Late
Night Refreshment Houses Act 1969.

P B Creightmore for the appellants.
A M Abbas for the respondent.

LORD WIDGERY CJ. This is an appeal by case stated by justices for the city of
Portsmouth in respect of their adjudication as a magistrates' court in Portsmouth on
28th April 1972. On that occasion they had before them an information laid by the
appellants against the respondent that the respondent on 6th February 1972 did fail
to comply with the condition of a late night refreshment house licence granted to him
by the Portsmouth City Council prohibiting the opening of the refreshment house at
61 Albert Road, between 1.00 a m and 5.00 a m for public refreshment resort or
entertainment, contrary to s 7 (2) of the Late Night Refreshment Houses Act 1969.

The facts found were that the respondent was in possession, consequent on his own
application, of a late night refreshment house licence for the premises in question, and
that on the day of the alleged offence it had been observed that at 1.45 a m the 'open'
sign was exhibited on the front door of the premises; the front door was unlocked,
in the restaurant one customer was eating a meal and four others were studying menus
and the proprietor was present. It is also found, and it is very material to the argument addressed to us, that in addition to having a late night refreshment house
licence for this place, the respondent also held a restaurant licence under Part IV of
the Licensing Act 1964 for the same premises. It is clear enough from those facts
that the condition imposed on the refreshment house licence had been breached
because that forbade opening between 1.00 a m and 5.00 a m, and the premises were
as open as could be at 1.45 a m. The defence put forward before the court, which
prevailed in the view of the justices, was that in fact there was no need for this man
to have a late night refreshment house licence at all, and consequently the grant
of such a licence to him and the conditions which it contained were both nullities.
Accordingly it was said that he had committed no offence by ignoring that condition.
For myself I am by no means satisfied that a man who obtains a licence on his own
application subject to conditions, and thereupon breaches the conditions, can of
necessity excuse himself by saying that he need never have taken out the licence,
but that point was not argued below and no attempt is made to argue it before us
today. Therefore the issue which we have to resolve is whether it be true in law
that the fact that the respondent held a restaurant licence under the Licensing Act
1964 excused him from the obligation to take out a late night refreshment house
licence. I go straight to the relevant section, which is s 1 of the Late Night Refreshment Houses Act 1969. That section provides that:

> 'For the purposes of this Act, a "late night refreshment house" is a house,
> room, shop or building kept open for public refreshment, resort and entertain-
> ment at any time between the hours of 10 o'clock at night and 5 o'clock of the
> following morning, other than a house, room, shop or building which is licensed
> for the sale of beer, cider, wine, or spirits.'

Thus this was clearly a late night refreshment house within the first part of the
definition. Was it nevertheless excluded by reason of the fact that the proprietor
held a licence under the Licensing Act 1964? For my part as a matter of construction
and looking at the words of the section, I would be of the opinion that the possession
of a restaurant licence in these circumstances caused these premises to be premises
licensed for the sale of beer, cider, wine or spirits, and thus excepted them from the
definition of a late night refreshment house. I say that because if premises are
the subject of a justices' on-licence, then in the ordinary use of language in this subject
they are described as 'licensed premises'. Indeed, s 200 (1) of the Licensing Act
1964 defines 'licensed premises' in these terms:

a   'Any reference in this Act to licensed premises shall, unless the context otherwise requires, be construed as a reference to premises for which a justices' licence
[is in force].'

If we go back to Part IV of the Act to see what the substance of the so-called restaurant licence is, we find in s 94 (1) of the 1964 Act that it is a Part IV licence, that is
to say a justices' on-licence granted under special terms for premises in which meals
b   are regularly served.   I fully accept that the definition of licensed premises in s 200
of the Licensing Act 1964 does not necessarily apply to the use of this phrase in the
1969 Act.   But the two Acts are dealing with closely related subjects.   The phrase
is so well known in my judgment as representing premises to which a justices' on-
licence is attached that I would, as a matter of construction without very much
hesitation say that the existence of the restaurant licence means that the premises
c   are excepted from s 1 of the Late Night Refreshment Houses Act 1969.   If that be
so, the justices' decision on the point argued before us was right, and it would follow
that the appeal would have to be dismissed.

The argument to the contrary is really an argument based on absurdity, that is to
say an argument suggesting that the preliminary conclusion to which I have referred
is absurd.   The argument goes thus: under s 7 (1) of the 1969 Act there is power for
d   the licensing authority when granting a late night refreshment house licence to
impose conditions on the hours at which the premises may be kept open, in particular
as in this case the authority can restrict the hours in the early morning when activity
on the premises is undertaken.

Counsel for the appellants argues that it really would be absurd if the authority's
power to control premises in this way were taken away simply because there was a
e   justices' licence which allowed the service of liquor at some other and possibly quite
different part of the 24 hours.   More particularly he submitted that premises might
have a justices' licence to serve drinks with lunch-time meals and at no other time,
and he asks rhetorically: what relationship can that fact have to the need or otherwise
for the local authority to control the late night opening of the same premises?

I follow the form of the argument and for some time I was somewhat impressed
f   by it, but in the end I have come to the conclusion that that is wrong, and I think
that it is misleading to suppose, as the argument really does suppose, that the main
substance of the 1969 Act is concerned with opening in the early hours of the morning.
Reference to the Act itself shows that it deals with many other matters and in particular that it requires the payment of an annual duty on the grant of a licence under
that Act.   It seems to me to be very good sense for the legislature to have said: if
g   you have premises licensed under the 1964 Act and attracting the licence duty appropriate to a liquor licence, that there need be no obligation on the occupier to take
out another licence and pay another fee under the 1969 Act.   That itself would justify
the view that all licensed premises are excluded from the Late Night Refreshment
Houses Act 1969.   Furthermore I think it quite possible that Parliament took the
view that licensed houses, meaning houses possessing a justices' on-licence, are already
h   subject to adequate control from the point of view of the behaviour of persons resorting to them, and the manner in which the business is conducted under the general
licensing laws, and that it was not necessary to impose an additional and separate
code on them under the 1969 Act.   Accordingly as it seems to me nothing in the
points raised by counsel for the appellants to which I have so far referred should
displace the initial view which I took on the construction of this section and
j   its meaning.

We have, however, listened to considerable argument based on the earlier statute
to which the 1969 Act is lineal successor, that is the Refreshment Houses Act
1860.   I confess to my surprise I found when this argument was opened, that as long
ago as 1860 legislation provided for the taking out of refreshment house licences in
circumstances very similar to those which prevail under the 1969 Act and counsel

for the appellants has sought to persuade us that under the 1860 Act it was necessary
to have a refreshment house licence as well as the justices' liquor licence in circumstances such as the present.   For my part I am wholly unpersuaded by that argument.
I do not propose to go in detail into the terms of the 1860 Act, but my reading of
it does not support the view for which counsel for the appellants contends, and no
authority has been cited to us in the 100 years since that Act was passed to suggest
that his view of the Act is the right one.

Accordingly, at the end of the day I come back to my initial approach to this case,
and I would give s 1 what I regard as its obvious meaning, namely that if there is a
justices' on-licence in effect in respect of the premises, the premises are not a late
night refreshment house.   I therefore agree with the conclusion of the justices and I
would dismiss the appeal.

MELFORD STEVENSON J.   So would I.

BRABIN J.   I agree.

Appeal dismissed.

Solicitors: *Norton, Rose, Botterell & Roche*, agents for *J R Haslegrave*, Portsmouth (for
the appellants); *S W Arnold*, Portsmouth (for the respondent).

N P Metcalfe Esq   Barrister.

Practice Note

QUEEN'S BENCH DIVISION
LORD WIDGERY CJ, JAMES LJ AND DAVIES J
12th JANUARY 1973

Jury – Juror – Excuse – Grounds on which juror may be excused.

Note
For the grounds on which a juror may be excused, see 23 Halsbury's Laws (3rd Edn)
14, 15, para 17.

LORD WIDGERY CJ read the following direction at the sitting of the court:
I have to make a practice direction which is made after consultation with the judges
of the Queen's Bench and Family Divisions.   A jury consists of 12 individuals
chosen at random from the appropriate panel.   A juror should be excused if he is
personally concerned in the facts of the particular case, or closely connected with a
party to the proceedings or with a prospective witness.   He may also be excused at
the discretion of the judge on grounds of personal hardship or conscientious objection to jury service.   It is contrary to established practice for jurors to be excused on
more general grounds such as race, religion, or political beliefs or occupation.

N P Metcalfe Esq   Barrister.

a

Beloff v Pressdram Ltd and another

CHANCERY DIVISION

UNGOED-THOMAS J

6th, 7th, 11th, 12th, 13th, 14th, 17th, 18th JULY, 18th OCTOBER 1972

b
Copyright – Ownership – Work made in course of author's employment under a contract of service – Contract of service – Test whether employment a contract of service or for services – Whether employee employed as part of business and work an integral part of business – Journalist employed by newspaper – Journalist political and lobby correspondent of paper – No written contract of employment – Journalist also writing articles for other papers and broadcasting – Journalist active member of editorial staff in effect working full-time for paper and receiving substantial salary – Whether employed under a contract of service –
c
Copyright Act 1956, s 4 (4).

Copyright – Infringement – Defence – Public interest in publication – Scope of public interest – Defence not extending beyond misdeeds of a serious nature clearly recognisable as such.

Copyright – Infringement – Defence – Fair dealing – Fairness – Unpublished literary work –
d *Internal office memorandum – Memorandum not intended for publication – Memorandum written by plaintiff in course of employment by newspaper – Contents of memorandum leaked by member of staff to contributor of another journal – Memorandum published in other journal for purposes of criticism – Memorandum known to have been leaked – Leak constituting a 'dealing' with memorandum – Whether dealing 'fair' – Copyright Act 1956, s 6.*

e
Copyright – Infringement – Damages – Additional damages – Statutory provision for additional damages precluding claim for aggravated or punitive damages – Circumstances in which additional damages may be awarded – Effective relief available in another cause of action – Copyright Act 1956, s 17 (3).

f In 1947 the plaintiff was appointed to the staff of the Observer newspaper, which was owned by O Ltd. In 1964 she was appointed political and lobby correspondent of the newspaper. As such she occupied an important and regular position in the Observer organisation in that she held, on behalf of the newspaper, the advantages of special access to the House of Commons and arrangements available only to the group of lobby correspondents. She was a very active member of the general editorial staff, and shared in the editorial responsibility of the newspaper. Apart
g from letters of appointment from the editor in 1947 and 1948, the plaintiff had no written contract of employment with O Ltd. Like other journalists, she broadcasted and appeared on television, had written for other papers and had had leave from the Observer to write books. However she worked in effect full-time for the Observer, receiving a substantial salary from which deductions were made for PAYE and a pensions scheme. Her duties included the writing of a weekly article
h and the reporting of Parliamentary activities. She had the resources of the Observer organisation at her disposal and her remuneration was not affected by the financial success or otherwise of the newspaper.

F was a regular contributor to Private Eye, a fortnightly magazine, described by F as being in the tradition of the lampoon. For some time prior to February 1971 F had been concerned about the relationship which at one time had existed between
j M, a prominent member of the government, and H and various companies with which H had been associated. H had subsequently been sentenced in the United States to a term of imprisonment on fraud charges. In consequence F wrote a series of articles in Private Eye attacking M.

On 17th February 1971 the plaintiff wrote a memorandum to the editor of the Observer with copies to other members of the editorial staff, stating that she had had

L

a conversation with a named member of the government in which he had said that, if the Prime Minister were to run under a bus, he had no doubt that M would take over as Prime Minister. In her memorandum the plaintiff proposed that she should write a study of M, investigate the allegations made against him by Private Eye, and 'put it into the wider context of his political personality and morality'. In consequence, on 28th February, the Observer published a very prominent article by the plaintiff making a slashing attack on Private Eye's attitude to M, accusing it in effect of smearing M and, amongst other things, 'pure fabrication'. In the meantime the contents of the plaintiff's memorandum of 17th February had been communicated to F by telephone by a member of the Observer's staff. On 12th March Private Eye published an article in reply written by F. The article attacked the plaintiff personally in insulting terms and incorporated, verbatim and in full, the plaintiff's memorandum of 17th February. On 26th March the editor of the Observer 'for and on behalf of' O Ltd, purported to assign the copyright of O Ltd in the memorandum 'together with any accrued rights of action therein' to the plaintiff. The editor had never before executed an assignment of copyright on behalf of O Ltd, although he had on occasions given permission for the reproduction of copyright material. The editor had no express authority to execute the assignment but before doing so he had sought the views of certain directors of O Ltd on the matter. The plaintiff brought an action against the defendants, the publishers of Private Eye, for infringement of copyright in the memorandum, claiming, inter alia, statutory and aggravated and exemplary damages.

Held – (1) The plaintiff's claim failed for the following reasons—

(i) the plaintiff was employed by O Ltd under a 'contract of service', within s 4 (4)[a] of the Copyright Act 1956, because, on the evidence, the plaintiff was employed as part of the business of the Observer and her work was an integral part of that business; it followed that the copyright in the memorandum originally vested in O Ltd and not in the plaintiff (see p 250 g and p 253 g, post); dicta of Denning LJ in *Stevenson Jordan and Harrison Ltd v Macdonald and Evans* [1952] 1 TLR at 111 and of Cooke J in *Market Investigations Ltd v Minister of Social Security* [1968] 3 All ER at 737 applied;

(ii) on the evidence the plaintiff had failed to establish that the editor had authority to execute the assignment of copyright on behalf of O Ltd (see p 255 h, post);

(iii) furthermore, as the editor had no authority to assign, he could not bind O Ltd by any representation by him that he had such authority; in any event, the plaintiff had failed to establish that, if any representation had been made, the plaintiff had been induced by it to enter into the assignment or to take any relevant step (see p 256 g, post); dictum of Diplock LJ in *Freeman and Lockyer (a firm) v Buckhurst Park Properties (Mangal) Ltd* [1964] 1 All ER at 646 applied.

(2) The defendants would have had no valid defence to the claim on the ground that publication was in the public interest. That defence only justified disclosure of matters carried out or contemplated in breach of the country's security, or in breach of law, including statutory duty, fraud or matters otherwise destructive of the country or its people, including matters medically dangerous to the public, and other misdeeds of similar gravity. The defence did not extend beyond misdeeds of a serious nature, clearly recognisable as such. The publication by the defendants of the plaintiff's memorandum failed to disclose any iniquity or misdeed of that kind (see p 250 g and h and p 261 d, post); dicta of Lord Denning MR and Salmon LJ in *Initial Services Ltd v Putterill* [1967] 3 All ER at 148, 151 applied.

(3) The defendants would have had no defence to the claim, under s 6 (2)[b] of the 1956 Act, on the ground of 'fair dealing' for the purposes of criticism or review. The leak of the memorandum to the defendants was a 'dealing' with the work in which

---

a   Section 4, so far as material, is set out at p 246 j, post
b   Section 6 (2), so far as material, is set out at p 261 f, post

copyright subsisted at the time of the leak. Publication of information known to have been leaked, and which, without the leak, could not have been published, was unjustifiable for the authorised purposes of criticism or review and constituted dealing which was not 'fair' within s 6 (2) (see p 264 f to h, post).

(4) If her claim had succeeded, the plaintiff would not have been entitled to claim aggravated or punitive damages at common law because the provision of s 17 (3)^c of the 1956 Act giving the court power to award additional damages left no place outside its ambit for the award of aggravated or punitive damages. The plaintiff would, however, have been entitled to additional damages under s 17 (3), if she had proved original ownership of the copyright in the memorandum, in view of the insulting terms of the defendants' article and the personal distress caused to her, subject to consideration of her own conduct in attacking the defendants' veracity in her own article (see p 265 g and h, p 266 b, p 268 g and h, p 269 h and p 272 g and j, post).

Per Ungoed-Thomas J. If effective relief is available to a plaintiff in respect of another cause of action, relief cannot be given by way of additional damages for infringement of copyright under s 17 (3) of the 1956 Act (see p 267 b and d, post).

Notes

For the ownership of copyright where the author is in employment, see 8 Halsbury's Laws (3rd Edn) 406, 407, para 740, and for cases on the subject, see 13 Digest (Repl) 79-83, *230-267*.

For the defence of fair dealing, see 8 Halsbury's Laws (3rd Edn) 435, 436, para 788.

For the defence of public policy, see 8 Halsbury's Laws (3rd Edn) 375, 376, para 689, and for cases on the subject, see 13 Digest (Repl) 57, *65-71*.

For damages for infringement of copyright, see 8 Halsbury's Laws (3rd Edn) 447, 448, para 812, and for cases on the subject, see 13 Digest (Repl) 128, 129, *675-687*.

For the Copyright Act 1956, ss 4, 6, 17, see 7 Halsbury's Statutes (3rd Edn) 137, 141, 163.

Cases referred to in judgment

Addis v Gramophone Co Ltd [1909] AC 488, [1908-10] All ER Rep 1, 78 LJKB 1122, 101 LT 466, HL, 17 Digest (Repl) 74, *1*.

Annesley v Earl of Anglesea (1743) 17 State Tr 1139, 22 Digest (Repl) 403, *4326*.

Ashley & Smith Ltd, Re, Ashley v Ashley & Smith Ltd [1918] 2 Ch 378, [1918-19] All ER Rep 753, [1917-23] Mac CC 54, 88 LJCh 7, 119 LT 674, 34 Digest (Repl) 18, *19*.

Bagnall v Levinstein Ltd [1907] 1 KB 531, 76 LJKB 234, 96 LT 184, CA, 34 Digest (Repl) 349, *2660*.

British Oxygen Co Ltd v Liquid Air Ltd [1925] Ch 383, 95 LJCh 81, 133 LT 282, 13 Digest (Repl) 55, *55*.

Broome v Cassell & Co Ltd [1972] 1 All ER 801, [1972] AC 1027, [1972] 2 WLR 645, HL.

Cassidy v Ministry of Health [1951] 1 All ER 574, [1951] 2 KB 343, CA, 33 Digest (Repl) 534, *112*.

Collins v Hertfordshire County Council [1947] 1 All ER 633, [1947] KB 598, [1947] LJR 789, 176 LT 456, 111 JP 272, 33 Digest (Repl) 534, *111*.

Fraser v Evans [1969] 1 All ER 8, [1969] 1 QB 349, [1968] 3 WLR 1172, CA, 28 (2) Digest (Reissue) 1090, *917*.

Freeman and Lockyer (a firm) v Buckhurst Park Properties (Mangal) Ltd [1964] 1 All ER 630, [1964] 2 QB 480, [1964] 2 WLR 618, CA, Digest (Cont Vol B) 101, *3701a*.

Hubbard v Vosper [1972] 1 All ER 1023, [1972] 2 QB 84, [1972] 2 WLR 389, CA.

Initial Services Ltd v Putterill [1967] 3 All ER 145, [1968] 1 QB 396, [1967] 3 WLR 1032, CA, Digest (Cont Vol C) 564, *873h*.

Market Investigations Ltd v Minister of Social Security [1968] 3 All ER 732, [1969] 2 QB 173, [1969] 2 WLR 1, Digest (Cont Vol C) 701, *2636b*.

---

c Section 17 (3) is set out at p 265 b and c, post

Morren v Swinton and Pendlebury Borough Council [1965] 2 All ER 349, [1965] 1 WLR 576,   *a*
63 LGR 288, DC, Digest (Cont Vol B) 533, 64*b*.
Rookes v Barnard [1964] 1 All ER 367, [1964] AC 1129, [1964] 2 WLR 269, [1964] 1 Lloyd's
Rep 28, HL, Digest (Cont Vol B) 217, 13*a*.
Simmons v Heath Laundry Co [1910] 1 KB 543, 79 LJKB 395, 102 LT 210, CA, 34 Digest
(Repl) 587, 4015.
Stevenson Jordan and Harrison Ltd v Macdonald and Evans [1952] 1 TLR 101, 69 RPC 10,   *b*
CA, 28 (2) Digest (Reissue) 1086, 906.
Sutherland Publishing Co Ltd v Caxton Publishing Co Ltd [1936] 1 All ER 177, [1936]
Ch 323, 105 LJCh 150, 154 LT 367, CA; *affd* HL [1938] 4 All ER 389, 13 Digest (Repl)
128, 677.
Walker v Crystal Palace Football Club Ltd [1910] 1 KB 87, 79 LJKB 229, 101 LT 645, CA,
34 Digest (Repl) 340, 2613.   *c*
Weld-Blundell v Stephens [1919] 1 KB 520, 88 LJKB 689, 120 LT 494, CA; *affd* HL [1920]
AC 956, [1920] All ER Rep 32, 88 LJKB 705, 123 LT 593, 32 Digest (Repl) 93, 1156.
Whittaker v Minister of Pensions and National Insurance [1966] 3 All ER 531, [1967]
1 QB 156, [1966] 3 WLR 1090, Digest (Cont Vol B) 539, 2636*a*.
Williams v Settle [1960] 2 All ER 806, [1960] 1 WLR 1072, CA, Digest (Cont Vol A)
313, 685*a*.   *d*
Yorkshire Railway Wagon Co v Maclure (1882) 21 Ch D 309, 51 LJCh 857, 47 LT 290,
CA, 10 Digest (Repl) 756, 4917.

Cases also cited

Ash v Hutchinson & Co (Publishers) Ltd [1936] 2 All ER 1496, [1936] Ch 489, CA.
Bradbury v Hotten (1872) LR 8 Exch 1.
Compania Colombiana De Seguros v Pacific Steam Navigation Co [1964] 1 All ER 216,   *e*
[1965] 1 QB 101.
Dawson v Great Northern and City Railway Co [1905] 1 KB 260, [1904-7] 1 All ER Rep
913, CA.
Fector v Beacon (1839) 5 Bing 302, 132 ER 1121.
Johnstone v Bernard Jones Publications Ltd [1938] 2 All ER 37, [1938] Ch 599.
Mafo v Adams [1969] 3 All ER 1404, [1970] 1 QB 548, CA.   *f*
Moriarty v Regent's Garage and Engineering Co Ltd [1921] 2 KB 766, CA.
Performing Right Society Ltd v Mitchell & Booker (Palais de Danse) Ltd [1924] 1 KB 762.
Ready Mixed Concrete (South East) Ltd v Minister of Pensions and National Insurance [1968]
1 All ER 433, [1968] 2 QB 497.
Savory (E W) Ltd v World of Golf Ltd [1914] 2 Ch 566, CA.
Seager v Copydex Ltd [1967] 2 All ER 415, [1967] 1 WLR 923, CA.   *g*
University of London Press Ltd v University Tutorial Press Ltd [1916] 2 Ch 601.
Weatherby & Sons v International Horse Agency and Exchange Ltd [1910] 2 Ch 297.
Williams v Atlantic Assurance Co Ltd [1933] 1 KB 81, [1932] All ER Rep 32, CA.

Action

This was an action commenced by writ issued on 31st March 1971 by the plaintiff,   *h*
Nora Beloff, against the defendants (1) Pressdram Ltd and (2) Leo Thorpe Ltd,
respectively the publishers and printers of the magazine Private Eye. By para 1
of her statement of claim the plaintiff alleged that she was the author of and the
owner of the copyright in a memorandum dated 17th February 1971 entitled 'Maudling' either by reason of being the author thereof or by reason of an assignment
in writing of such copyright and accrued causes of action made on 26th March 1971   *j*
between The Observer Ltd of the one part and the plaintiff of the other part. By
para 3 she alleged that, without the licence of The Observer Ltd or of the plaintiff,
the first defendant had authorised the second defendant to print and the second
defendant had accordingly printed in the issue of the magazine for 12th March 1971
('the defendants' work') an article entitled 'The Ballsoff Memorandum' which reproduced the plaintiff's work or a substantial part thereof, thereby infringing the

plaintiff's copyright. Further, by para 4, she alleged that without the licence of The
Observer Ltd or of the plaintiff, the first defendant had authorised the second defendant to print and the second defendant had accordingly printed a large number of
copies of the defendants' work, and the first defendant had published, sold and distributed or authorised the publication, sale and distribution of such copies of the
defendants' work, thereby infringing the plaintiff's copyright. By para 5 the plaintiff
alleged that all copies of the defendants' work were infringing copies of the plaintiff's
work and that the first defendant, by publishing, selling and distributing it and by
authorising such publication, sale and distribution, had converted it to its own use. By
para 6 the plaintiff alleged that each of the defendants would, unless restrained, continue the acts of infringement. The plaintiff sought the following relief: as against
both defendants, an injunction against future infringement and damages for breach
of copyright, and against the first defendant alone, statutory, aggravated and exemplary damages, damages for conversion and delivery up of infringing material. By
their amended defence, the defendants, inter alia, denied each and every allegation
contained in para 1 of the statement of claim. Further, or alternatively they alleged
that the memorandum was not capable of forming the subject of copyright. Alternatively they alleged that the copyright, if any, in the memorandum was owned by
The Observer Ltd as the plaintiff's employers, the memorandum having been made,
if at all, by the plaintiff in the course of and for the purpose of her employment by
The Observer Ltd. They further denied that the copyright, if any, in the memorandum was assigned to the plaintiff as alleged, or at all. Alternatively, they alleged
that the alleged assignment had been purported to be made by Mr David Astor,
the editor of the Observer, who had no authority to make it on behalf of The Observer
Ltd; and further or alternatively they alleged that the assignment had been made
gratuitously and no notice given to them and that the plaintiff had no title to bring
the proceedings without joining The Observer Ltd as a party. The defendants
admitted causing to be printed and printing, inter alia, a text which substantially
conformed with the text of the memorandum dated 17th February 1971, and respectively causing to be printed and printing a large number of copies of the issue of the
magazine and publishing and authorising the publication, sale and distribution of
it with no express licence from The Observer Ltd or the plaintiff to print it, but
otherwise they denied paras 3, 4 and 5 of the statement of claim. Further or alternatively they alleged that the memorandum had been published to members of the
Observer's staff and contained matter of general public concern and interest and
constituted an item of news of public concern; and that the plaintiff and The Observer
Ltd had impliedly licensed the publication of the memorandum. Further or alternatively they alleged that the printing of the text was a fair dealing with the work for
the purposes of reporting current events in a newspaper, magazine or similar periodical and for purposes of criticism and review and was accompanied by a sufficient
acknowledgment, and alleged that they had printed and published the text as part
of an article in reply to the plaintiff's article in the Observer for 28th February 1971
attacking and criticising them, by way of reply to and information concerning the
plaintiff's article. The facts are set out in the judgment.

D H Mervyn Davies QC and *E P Skone James* for the plaintiff.
Michael Kempster QC and *Peter Bowsher* for the defendants.

Cur adv vult

18th October. **UNGOED-THOMAS J** read the following judgment. This
is an action for infringement of copyright. The plaintiff is political and lobby correspondent of the Observer newspaper, which is owned by The Observer Ltd. The first
defendant, Pressdram Ltd, is the publisher and the second defendant, Leo Thorpe Ltd,
is the printer of Private Eye magazine. The infringement alleged is by the reproduction
in an article in Private Eye of an internal Observer office memorandum written
by the plaintiff. The alleged infringement is in the case of the first defendant by

publishing and in the case of the second defendant by printing. There is also a
subsidiary claim against the first defendant for conversion in respect of copies of
the article infringing the plaintiff's alleged copyright. The relief as claimed before
me is, as against both defendants, for an injunction against future infringement and
damages for breach of copyright, together with, in the case of the first defendant
only, statutory and aggravated and exemplary damages, damages for conversion
and delivery up of infringing material.

It is common ground that (1) copyright subsists in the memorandum, and if the
plaintiff is entitled to sue for the alleged infringement of such copyright: (2) damages
for such infringement are nominal (apart from statutory, aggravated or exemplary
damages), (3) there is by the first defendant such conversion as is alleged for which
damages would (as I agree) be most conveniently assessed by enquiry, and (4) there
should be the usual order for delivery up by the first defendant of infringing material.

The main issues as they emerged before me are: (1) whether the plaintiff is the
owner of the copyright in the memorandum and, if so, whether she is entitled to
sue in respect of the alleged infringement; (2) whether the defendants establish their
statutory defence under s 6 of the Copyright Act 1956 (which I shall refer to as the
defence of fair dealing) or their defence of publication in the public interest, which
in the argument in this case has been interwoven with the defence of fair dealing;
(3) if the answer to (1) is Yes and (2) is No, whether the plaintiff is entitled to statutory,
aggravated or exemplary damages in respect of the infringement.

IS THE PLAINTIFF THE OWNER OF THE COPYRIGHT IN THE MEMORANDUM AND IS SHE
ENTITLED TO SUE FOR THE ALLEGED INFRINGEMENT?

This question raises five subsidiary issues. (1) Was the copyright originally vested
in The Observer Ltd or the plaintiff? If it was so vested in The Observer Ltd, (2) was
a duly proved purported assignment by the editor of the Observer on behalf of The
Observer Ltd of the copyright, together with any accrued rights of action therein, to
the plaintiff before the commencement of these proceedings made with the authority
of The Observer Ltd? Or, if not, (3) would such assignment nevertheless be valid on
the ground that the editor of the Observer represented to the plaintiff that he was
authorised to make the assignment on behalf of The Observer Ltd and that the plaintiff relied on such representation? (4) Was the assignment ineffective on the ground
that it was not a bona fide assignment of copyright? (5) Is the plaintiff incapable for
lack of notice to the defendants in accordance with s 136 of the Law of Property Act
1925 of suing, in this action as constituted, in respect of the alleged infringement?

These five issues turn partly on law and partly on fact, but insofar as any of them
turns on fact, the issue of fact falls within a small and separate ambit. It will therefore be convenient to deal with this main question separately from the other two
main questions which have substantial issues of fact in common.

(1) *Was the copyright originally vested in The Observer Ltd or the plaintiff?*

I will deal first with the law. The copyright subsisted in the memorandum as an
unpublished literary work and both the plaintiff and The Observer Ltd were qualified
to own the copyright in it: see Copyright Act 1956, ss 1 (1), (5) (*a*), 2 (1), (5), 49 (2),
(3) (*a*).

The original ownership of the copyright in this case is governed by s 4 (1) and (4).
These subsections read:

'(1) Subject to the provisions of this section, the author of a work shall be
entitled to any copyright subsisting in the work by virtue of this Part of this
Act.'

'(4) Where . . . a work is made in the course of the author's employment by
another person under a contract of service or apprenticeship, that other person
shall be entitled to any copyright subsisting in the work by virtue of this Part of
this Act.'

So if this case falls within sub-s (4) the original copyright was in The Observer Ltd. Otherwise it was in the plaintiff.

The memorandum was clearly made in the course of the plaintiff's employment by The Observer Ltd; nor was this disputed. The only question is whether the plaintiff's employment was under a contract of service. If yes, the copyright originally vested in The Observer Ltd; if no, it vested in the plaintiff.

The distinction, familiar to lawyers, is between contract of service and contract for services. In applying this distinction there appears to have been a tendency in the past towards considering, and therefore describing, contracts of service in terms of occupations of a lowly character—not surprisingly, because it was in such occupations that contracts of service were most apt to occur. This tendency may well have been accentuated by the concern with such occupations of statutes in whose setting contracts of service were from time to time considered. Thus *Simmons v Heath Laundry Co*[1] provides judicial quotations familiar in textbooks and in the courts on judicia of contracts of service. But that was a case under the Workmen's Compensation Act 1906 which was providing compensation for workmen. The material words in s 13 of the 1906 Act were:

> ' "Workman" . . . means any person who has entered into or works under a contract of service or apprenticeship with an employer, whether by way of manual labour, clerical work, or otherwise . . .'

And the distinguished members of the Court of Appeal who decided that case made it clear that the contract of service with which they were dealing was a contract of service 'under the Act'. In *Re Ashley & Smith Ltd*[2] a contract of service was considered in the context of provision of preferential payments for 'any clerk or servant', and 'any workman or labourer' on the winding up of a company under the Companies (Consolidation) Act 1908. In *Simmons v Heath Laundry Co*[3] Fletcher Moulton LJ said:

> 'These facts, although very simple, raise a question of law of considerable importance and difficulty. It turns substantially on the scope which is to be given to the phrase 'contract of service' in the Act. It is true that as a matter of law it is not every contract of service that constitutes a person a workman under the Act, since under the definition clause it must be "a contract of service or apprenticeship with an employer whether by way of manual labour, clerical work, or otherwise". But I do not feel called upon to limit the generality of the word "otherwise" in such a way as to exclude all contracts in respect of teaching . . . The greater the amount of direct control exercised over the person rendering the services by the person contracting for them the stronger the grounds for holding it to be a contract of service, and similarly the greater the degree of independence of such control the greater the probability that the services rendered are of the nature of professional services and that the contract is not one of service. The place where the services are rendered, i.e., whether at the residence of the person rendering the services or not, will also be an element in deciding the case, but is not in my opinion decisive . . .'

And Buckley LJ said[4]:

> 'A person employed to exercise his skill may or may not be a servant. The football player in *Walker v. Crystal Palace Football Club*[5] was held to be a workman, that is, to be employed under a contract of service, notwithstanding that

1 [1910] 1 KB 543
2 [1918] 2 Ch 378, [1918-19] All ER Rep 753
3 [1910] 1 KB at 549, 550
4 [1910] 1 KB at 552, 553
5 [1910] 1 KB 87

in certain respects it was his duty to exercise his own judgment uncontrolled by anybody. On the other hand in *Bagnall* v. *Levinstein, Ld.*[1] a skilled chemist was held not to be a workman notwithstanding that his employment involved manual labour . . . The question to be answered is, Was he employed as a workman or was he employed as a skilled adviser? I do not know whether it is possible to approach more closely to an answer to the question as to what is a contract of service under this Act than to say that in each case the question to be asked is what was the man employed to do; was he employed upon the terms that he should within the scope of his employment obey his master's orders, or was he employed to exercise his skill and achieve an indicated result in such manner as in his judgment was most likely to ensure success? Was his contract a contract of service within the meaning which an ordinary person would give to the words? Was it a contract under which he would be appropriately described as the servant of the employer?'

Parts of these passages are quoted in Copinger and Skone Jones[2] under the heading 'What is a contract of service?'. These passages bring out the way in which the test of control and contracts of service of a lowly nature have been associated with each other, as contrasted with contracts for professional or similarly skilled services. So counsel's original submission for the plaintiff was that 'a contract of service means a contract for domestic, manual or clerical service whose execution is superintended by some higher official or employee'.

But nowadays professional and similarly skilled persons are widely engaged under what are recognised as contracts of service. So I come to recent authorities which are rich in statements of principle and of relevant factors and in references to employment which, in the circumstances of particular cases, have been held to be, or not to be, under contracts of service.

In *Stevenson Jordan and Harrison Ltd v Macdonald and Evans*[3], it was held that some work done by an accountant was within a contract of service and some work done by him was outside it. Denning LJ said[4]:

'The test usually applied is whether the employer has the right to control the manner of doing the work. Thus in *Collins v. Herts County Council*[5], Mr. Justice Hilbery said: "The distinction between a contract for services and a contract of service can be summarized in this way: In the one case the master can order or require what is to be done, while in the other case he can not only order or require what is to be done but how it shall be done." But in *Cassidy v. Ministry of Health*[6], Lord Justice Somervell pointed out that that test is not universally correct. There are many contracts of service where the master cannot control the manner in which the work is to be done, as in the case of a captain of a ship. Lord Justice Somervell went on to say[7]: "One perhaps cannot get much beyond this 'Was the contract a contract of service within the meaning which an ordinary person would give to the words?'" I respectfully agree. As [Sir Raymond Evershed MR] has said, it is almost impossible to give a precise definition of the distinction. It is often easy to recognize a contract of service when you see it, but difficult to say wherein the difference lies. A ship's master, a chauffeur, and a reporter on the staff of a newspaper are all employed

1   [1907] 1 KB 531
2   Copyright (11th Edn, 1971), pp 145, 146, para 326
3   [1952] 1 TLR 101
4   [1952] 1 TLR at 110, 111
5   [1947] KB 598 at 615, cf [1947] 1 All ER 633 at 638
6   [1951] 1 All ER 574 at 579, [1951] 2 KB 343 at 352
7   [1951] 1 All ER at 579, [1951] 2 KB at 352, 353. Somervell LJ was quoting Buckley LJ in *Simmons v Heath Laundry Co* [1910] 1 KB at 553

under a contract of service; but a ship's pilot, a taxi-man, and a newspaper contributor are employed under a contract for services.'

Then Denning LJ goes to the test which he indicates[1]:

'One feature which seems to run through the instances is that, under a contract of service, a man is employed as part of the business, and his work is done as an integral part of the business; whereas, under a contract for services, his work, although done for the business, is not integrated into it but is only accessory to it.'

In *Morren v Swinton and Pendlebury Borough Council*[2] Lord Parker CJ held that an engineer was employed under a contract of service.   Lord Parker CJ observed[3]:

'The cases have over and over again stressed the importance of the factor of superintendence and control, but that it is not the determining test is quite clear. In *Cassidy* v. *Minister of Health*[4], Somervell, L.J., referred to this matter, and instanced, as did Denning, L.J., in the later case of *Stevenson, Jordan & Harrison, Ltd.* v. *MacDonald & Evans*[5], that clearly superintendence and control cannot be the decisive test when one is dealing with a professional man, or a man of some particular skill and experience.   Instances of that have been given in the form of the master of a ship, an engine driver, a professional architect or, as in this case, a consulting engineer.   In such cases there can be no question of the employer telling him how to do work; therefore, the absence of control and direction in that sense can be of little, if any, use as a test.   In my judgment, here all the other considerations point to a contract of service.   [Then I omit some lines, and he continues with reference to the engineer in that case:] he was appointed by the respondents, they had the right to dismiss him, he was paid such matters as subsistence allowance and for holidays, national insurance contributions were paid in regard to him, and, in addition, there was provision for one month's notice.   Pausing there, it seems to me that, looked at on those facts, the only possible inference is that he was engaged under a contract of service.   How different is the contract with Mr. Kaufman, who is not paid a subsistence allowance; nor is national insurance contribution provided in regard to him; and he is not entitled to holidays.   Further, there is no provision for termination of his services or service by notice.'

In *Whittaker v Minister of Pensions and National Insurance*[6] it was held that a trapeze artiste, who also undertook to help in moving the circus from place to place and to act as usherette, was employed under the one contract of service.   Mocatta J said[7]:

'It seems clear, therefore, from the more recent cases that persons possessed of a high degree of professional skill and expertise, such as surgeons and civil engineers, may nevertheless be employed as servants under contracts of service, notwithstanding that their employers can, in the nature of things, exercise extremely little, if any, control over the way in which such skill is used.   The test of control is, therefore, not as determinative as used to be thought to be the case, though no doubt it is still of value in that the greater the degree of control exerciseable by the employer, the more likely it is that the contract is one of service.'

---

1   [1952] 1 TLR at 111
2   [1965] 2 All ER 349, [1965] 1 WLR 576
3   [1965] 2 All ER at 351, 352, [1965] 1 WLR at 581, 582
4   [1951] 1 All ER 574, [1951] 2 KB 343
5   [1952] 1 TLR 101
6   [1966] 3 All ER 531, [1967] 1 QB 156
7   [1966] 3 All ER at 537, [1967] 1 QB at 167

In *Market Investigations Ltd v Minister of Social Security*[1] it was held that a part-time interviewer engaged by a market research company was under a contract of service. Cooke J observed[2]:

'The observations of LORD WRIGHT, of DENNING, L.J., and of the judges of the Supreme Court in the U.S.A. suggest that the fundamental test to be applied is this: "Is the person who has engaged himself to perform these services performing them as a person in business on his own account?". If the answer to that question is "yes", then the contract is a contract for services. If the answer is "no" then the contract is a contract of service. No exhaustive list has been compiled and perhaps no exhaustive list can be compiled of considerations which are relevant in determining that question, nor can strict rules be laid down as to the relative weight which the various considerations should carry in particular cases. The most that can be said is that control will no doubt always have to be considered, although it can no longer be regarded as the sole determining factor; and that factors, which may be of importance, are such matters as whether the man performing the services provides his own equipment, whether he hires his own helpers, what degree of financial risk he takes, what degree of responsibility for investment and management he has, and whether and how far he has an opportunity of profiting from sound management in the performance of his task.'

Cooke J continued[3]:

'The opportunity to deploy individual skill and personality is frequently present in what is undoubtedly a contract of service. I have already said that the right to work for others is not inconsistent with the existence of a contract of service. Mrs. Irving did not provide her own tools or risk her own capital, nor did her opportunity of profit depend in any significant degree on the way she managed her work.'

It thus appears, and rightly in my respectful view, that, the greater the skill required for an employee's work, the less significant is control in determining whether the employee is under a contract of service. Control is just one of many factors whose influence varies according to circumstances. In such highly skilled work as that of the plaintiff it seems of no substantial significance. The test which emerges from the authorities seems to me, as Denning LJ said[4], whether on the one hand the employee is employed as part of the business and his work is an integral part of the business, or whether his work is not integrated into the business but is only accessory to it, or, as Cooke J expressed it[5], the work is done by him in business on his own account.

The only documents produced relating to the nature of the plaintiff's employment were two letters of 1947 and 1948 and two statements by The Observer Ltd directed to the plaintiff under the Contracts of Employment Act 1963 and the Industrial Relations Act 1971.

The first letter, dated 19th September 1947, was from the editor of the Observer to the plaintiff confirming her appointment as Paris correspondent with a yearly salary and expenses. It reads:

'We are very pleased to hear that you are willing to become Paris correspondent for THE OBSERVER and THE OBSERVER Foreign News Service. You have

---

1   [1968] 3 All ER 732, [1969] 2 QB 173
2   [1968] 3 All ER 737, 738, [1969] 2 QB at 184
3   [1968] 3 All ER at 740, [1969] 2 QB at 188
4   In *Stevenson Jordan and Harrison Ltd v Macdonald and Evans* [1952] 1 TLR at 111
5   In *Market Investigations Ltd v Minister of Social Security* [1968] 3 All ER at 737, [1969] 2 QB at 184

a done excellent work for us on the Paris Conference, and I am happy to confirm your appointment, as from November 2nd, 1947, and for an initial period of six months, at the rate of £750 a year, plus expenses incurred on our behalf. We hope it will be possible, as you indicate, to keep the expenses within reasonable limits. In addition to full week-end coverage for THE OBSERVER, and the occasional provision of Profile, obituary and Notebook material as the needs arise,

b we shall require a minimum of one article a week, by mail or telephone, for SERVOB. (Hitherto we have stipulated two SERVOB articles weekly from our correspondents, but in practice one is usually sufficient. We should, however, like to be able to call on you for additional SERVOB articles in special circumstances, which would include occasions like the Paris Conference.) Your name will be used on all SERVOB contributions; for THE OBSERVER our customary rule

c is that correspondents' names are used on major pieces (leader-page articles, Notebooks, important and exclusive news stories), but not necessarily on all items of straight-forward reporting; and we shall prefer to apply this rather flexible rule to you, too. I understand you will be in London next month; we shall be happy to see you then to discuss any further aspects of your appointment.'

d The second letter is dated 15th October 1948 and made a different appointment on different terms. It appointed the plaintiff to the staff of the Observer, first in London and then in Washington for some years, on a full-time basis at a yearly salary of £1,200 in London and a salary with living allowance elsewhere. As far as it is material it reads:

'This is to inform you officially that we would like you to come back to London

e at the end of November and to join our staff on a whole-time basis. We would want you to leave for Washington at the end of December and to remain there for at least one year and more probably for several years. I suggested to you that we should ensure your future by giving you a contract for five years. I am quite confident that you can be an asset to this paper for much longer than that, but would like to ask you if a three year promise of employment would

f satisfy you. The reason for asking this is simply that five years is much longer than we promise any of the other members of the staff and might therefore cause some indignation amongst them. The promise of employment would be subject to your being willing to write whenever the paper might need you most and not necessarily in Washington all the time. The financial terms of our offer are a combined salary-cum-living-allowance while in Washington of £2,000

g per annum; when elsewhere your salary would be at £1,200 with an additional living allowance if outside Britain. We will, of course, have to talk over details of office accommodation, travel expenses, etcetera with you before you go to Washington.'

The two statutory statements came after the plaintiff's appointment as political and lobby correspondent of the Observer. The first is addressed to the plaintiff

h under the Contracts of Employment Act 1963, and states that the Act requires The Observer Ltd to state certain of the main terms and conditions on which it employs 'you Nora Leah Beloff as at August 1, 1964'. It states the commencement of employment as 1947, the rate of remuneration as £3,000 per year, the normal hours of work 'subject to day to day circumstances', as 10·00 a m to 6·00 p m Tuesday to Friday, 'and as required by the Head of your Department on Saturday'. 'Your

i employment is subject to six months' notice on either side' and 'Your paid holiday entitlement is four weeks per calendar year' with bank holidays, with the provision that, 'All holiday dates are to be settled by agreement with the Head of your Department/the Manager'; and that sickness payments are considered individually.

The second statement is described as a supplementary statement and is headed by reference to the 1963 Act as amended by the Industrial Relations Act 1971. It is addressed to the plaintiff and includes a statement that she is entitled to receive, and *a* required to give notice of termination of employment under her contract, or national agreements entered into by her trade union or in accordance with the above Acts.

The plaintiff said that she assumed that she was in the Observer as a result of the 1947 letter, but that she did not remember signing it. She was in Washington for the Observer from 1949 to 1950 as contemplated by the 1948 letter, and I have no doubt that those letters stated the terms under which she immediately thereafter *b* entered on her work for the Observer.

She said, however, that she must have received the statutory statements but that she did not think that she read them. It is of course clear that her work was not regulated by any specified hours; that she worked late hours, and had more than four weeks' holiday. It was submitted for the plaintiff that the statements were documents issued by The Observer Ltd and that she was not bound by them. But she *c* recognised that she must have received them, although she might not have read them; and it does at any rate seem that even after the coming into force of the Industrial Relations Act 1971 her employers did not contemplate her as being outside the Act. But I do not rely on these statements in deciding whether or not the plaintiff was under a contract of service.

The editor of the Observer said in evidence in answer to a question whether he *d* could direct the plaintiff to New York or elsewhere, that it was for him to allocate jobs; and since 1948, before her appointment as political and lobby correspondent, she was directed not only to Washington and to Moscow, but to cover Common Market negotiations, and since that appointment she has also done some foreign assignments for the Observer.

Like many journalists, such as Mr Howard, editor of the New Statesman, who gave *e* evidence, she has broadcast and appeared on television. And she has written on occasions for certain other papers such as the Atlantic Monthly and Punch, and she has had leaves from the Observer to write books. But these incidents do not appear to have affected the permanent basis of her salaried employment with the Observer, and appear to have been, in the case of leaves for writing books at any rate, with the consent of the Observer. Indeed, leave itself tends to indicate a permanent full-time *f* job on the staff.

In 1964 the plaintiff was appointed political and lobby correspondent of the Observer, and she has since done that job interspersed with the foreign assignments for the Observer as I have mentioned. As the accredited lobby correspondent for the Observer she holds a very important and regular position in the Observer organisation, and, so far as I know, she is the only person in the Observer organisation who *g* holds such a position. It means that she has on behalf of the Observer the advantages essential to a great national newspaper, of special access to the House of Commons, of arrangements available to the group of lobby correspondents, including various forms of help and briefings which are important, not only for writing informed articles but also for obtaining news items earlier than would otherwise be available for the Observer. This means, of course, that it is essential for the Observer that she *h* keeps in constant touch with Parliament at all hours when any such advantages are likely to be gained by doing so. Her work as lobby correspondent, as she explained, is not just the production of an article but also the reporting of political news. This work includes news and other coverage of Parliamentary occurrences for the Observer, including in particular briefings, news and other advantages which, as I have indicated, the lobby correspondent is appointed by his paper to obtain and supply. *j* The job of political and lobby correspondent for the Observer is essential for and woven into its political coverage. Such a paper as the Observer without its accredited lobby correspondent is hardly conceivable.

The plaintiff writes for the Observer a weekly article headed 'Politics—Nora Beloff': it is usually on one theme. She also write profiles, and on the major speeches of politicians, and she even writes leaders. The editor described her as 'a very active *a* member of the general editorial staff' and said that she shared in the editorial responsibility of the newspaper. She is a regular attendant at weekly and ad hoc editorial meetings presided over by the editor and whose wide scope is indicated by the functions of those who attend—deputy and assistant editors, chief reporters, the business editor, the leader writer, the news editor, and others as advisable from time to time. The plaintiff said its purpose was to plan the paper for the next issue to look ahead

b and to have a general discussion and exchange ideas. She said that her article for the following issue was very often discussed. The editor said that she tells him what she is going to write and that discussion only arises if it overlaps with something else. The editor has certainly some strong-minded persons attending these meetings and, as might be expected from his experience and wisdom, he said that 'my government is as a rule consensual'. The plaintiff said that she was free to decline to write on a suggested topic. Of course, she could not be forced to do so, nor can I imagine Mr

c Astor attempting to force her. The editorial meetings are for discussion, without power of decision; that rests solely with the editor, and not the less so, although as a rule consensually exercised by him.

I come to other recognised indications of contract of service, in addition to her substantial regular salary for her full-time job and her holidays. Apart from an

d electric typewriter, which the plaintiff has at home, the plaintiff does not provide any equipment of her own which she uses for her work. All the Observer's resources are available to her to carry out her job. She has an office in the Observer building, and a secretary who is provided by the Observer. She does not use her own capital for the job, nor is her remuneration affected by the financial success or otherwise of the Observer. In addition to PAYE deductions, deduction for the pension scheme to which she belongs is also made by the Observer from her salary. All these indica-

e tions are in favour of her contract being a contract of service.

The submission relied on for a contrary conclusion was, as I have indicated, that such contracts were limited to contracts to do lowly tasks under supervision. But this became clearly unsustainable, and at a later stage it was submitted that the overriding consideration was whether the plaintiff produced an article every week or worked

f full-time for the Observer or, as it was put, whether she was a contributor and not a reporter. But this submission clearly fails on the facts which I have stated—her job was full-time and was far from being limited to a weekly article and in fact included reporting Parliamentary events. Nor (in accordance with, e g *Market Investigations Ltd v Minister of Social Security*[1]) does a full-time contract of service exclude some television and broadcasting appearances and the writing of such articles as she wrote for Punch and Atlantic Monthly.

g I have increasingly in the course of this case, as the relevant facts came to be deployed, inclined to the conclusion which I now firmly hold that the plaintiff's job is 'an integral part of the business' of the Observer and its organisation and that the plaintiff's contract with The Observer Ltd is a contract of service. My conclusion, therefore, is that the copyright in the memorandum originally vested in The Observer Ltd and not in the plaintiff.

h (2) *Was the purported assignment made without authority?*

The purported assignment is in these terms:

'I DAVID ASTOR, for and on behalf of The Observer Limited of 160 Queen Victoria Street in Greater London, Editor of The Observer, Hereby assign the copyright of The Observer Limited in a Memorandum dated 17th February 1971

i entitled "Maudling" written by Miss Nora Beloff in so far as the Observer Limited may be entitled thereto to Miss Nora Beloff of 25 Walsingham Street, St John's Wood Park, NW 8, together with any accrued rights of action therein. Dated this 26th day of March 1971. Signed by the said DAVID ASTOR for and on behalf of The Observer Limited [and then Mr Astor's signature].'

1 [1968] 3 All ER at 735, [1969] 2 QB at 176

Assignment of copyright is, so far as is relevant for present purposes, governed by
s 36 (1) and (3) of the 1956 Act. They read, so far as is material:

> '(1) Subject to the provisions of this section, copyright shall be transmissible
> by assignment . . . as personal or moveable property.
> '(3) No assignment of copyright . . . shall have effect unless it is in writing signed
> by or on behalf of the assignor.'

It is, of course, common ground that an assignment cannot be assigned on behalf of an
assignor without his authority. Hence this issue.

The articles of association of The Observer Ltd provide as follows so far as they
might conceivably be thought to have any bearing on this question: by art 89 that the
directors may entrust to and confer on a managing director any of the powers
exercisable by them; by art 90, in the usual way, that the business of the company
shall be managed by the directors; by art 94 which deals with the 'Editor of the
Observer newspaper' and with 'General Manager', and which provides:

> 'Every appointment of an Editor or General Manager shall be upon such terms
> and conditions as the Trustees shall prescribe, and if there shall be any vacancy
> in either of those offices the Directors shall appoint such person to fill the vacancy
> as shall be nominated in writing by the Trustees';

by art 108 that the directors may delegate any of their powers to committees consisting
of a member or members of their body; by art 112 that directors shall cause proper
minutes to be made of proceedings of all meetings of directors and committees and
all business transacted thereat; by art 113 that a resolution in writing signed by all
the directors shall be as effective as a resolution passed at a meeting of directors.

The crucial evidence on this aspect of the case is that of the editor. He said in his
evidence-in-chief that he executed the assignment and was authorised by The
Observer Ltd to do so and that it was within the scope of his authority to execute 'such
documents' on behalf of the Observer. But the transcript of his cross-examination on
this evidence reads:

> 'Q I can, I think, ask you this. Do you often effect assignments of copyrights?
> A No, I do not.
> 'Q Have you ever assigned a copyright before? A I suppose I probably have
> because people's articles are reproduced in book form and I suppose I would have
> assigned copyright in those cases.
> 'Q What do you do if that happens—do they write and ask you for permission?
> A Yes.
> 'Q And then you write back and say, "Yes, you may"? A In effect, yes.
> 'Q So you give them a licence to publish? A Yes, presumably.
> 'Q I repeat my question: Have you ever signed any such document as this
> before, which I gather you will take from me *prima facie* constitutes an assignment
> of copyright? A I do not think I have.
> 'Q When you told Mr Mervyn Davies that you were authorised by the Observer
> to execute this document, what did you mean? A How do you mean?
> 'Q They are your words, and I am asking you to say what you meant when you
> gave an affirmative answer. A I consulted my colleagues, my directorial
> colleagues and managerial colleagues, as to whether there was any reason why
> this should not be done. I assumed in fact as editor I had the right to do it, but
> in case it required any support from the management I asked my colleagues on
> the management and they agreed that I have this right.
> 'Q Was there any meeting of the Board of the Observer? A No, not with this.
> 'Q Do you as editor have any directive from the Board rather as if a General
> is sent to the Middle East and he is told, "Your mandate is to re-take Tobruk",
> or something like that—are you given such a document? A No.'

a   It seemed to me clear beyond doubt that when the editor gave his evidence, and it so seems to me now, that the answers in cross-examination were by way of amplifying with the result of limiting and correcting the impression which might be obtained from reading his evidence-in-chief. His answers in cross-examination disclose that he had no specific or general authority from the board of directors to execute an assignment of copyright. Any colleagues whom he consulted clearly did not constitute *b*   a board or even all the directors signing a resolution within art 113, and clearly they did not even purport to make any decision at all. Nothing in writing or even oral was referred to as conferring the necessary authority on him. But, of course, it is proved that Mr Astor is editor of the Observer and thus this issue came to turn on whether or not his appointment as editor carried automatically with it authority to assign copyright. It is, of course, for the plaintiff to establish such authority, and so *c*   I come to the evidence of the scope of the editor's authority to assign copyright.

In 24 years as editor of the Observer he had never assigned copyright. What he had done or purported to do was by correspondence to agree to the reproduction in a particular book of a particular Observer article, i e to give a limited licence, limited to production in a particular book, a particular work already published in the paper of which he was editor. But such licence is, of course, very different from assignment, *d*   the out and out parting with all rights in a work for all time, the transfer of the property of The Observer Ltd. And in this case the work whose copyright was assigned was not an article or any other work which had appeared in his newspaper; it had not been published at all. It was purported to be assigned not even for publication but to further an action contemplated by the assignee, an action which would inevitably involve the Observer without the Observer being a party to it. These consid- *e*   erations tell against the editor automatically having by virtue of his appointment authority to assign copyright and, a fortiori, against authority to assign such copyright as is the subject of this action.

It is clear from the first part of the transcript of evidence which I have quoted that Mr Astor did not often even write permitting the reproduction of an Observer article; he was in some confusion about licences and assignments; and even contemplated such licences as 'assignments'. It was in this state of confusion that he 'assumed in *f*   fact as editor I had the right to do it', that is execute the assignment. But it appears that he was in sufficient doubt about it to consult colleagues, 'my directorial and managerial colleagues', 'my colleagues in the management', from which I gather he meant managers and executive directors at hand, possibly in the Observer office. But whatever their number or function, they were not, as I have said, conferring authority or making any decision. They were, at its highest, expressing or concurring *g*   with a view. We do not know precisely the circumstances, the questions or the answers, and not one of them has appeared in court to express or substantiate his view with reference to the authority of an editor to assign copyright in general, or in such a work as the memorandum in particular, and to be cross-examined, as Mr Astor was, on his evidence-in-chief. Nor has anyone else been called, as might be *h*   expected, to establish that it is in general by custom or practice or otherwise within the ambit of an editor's authority to assign copyright, much less the copyright of such a work as this memorandum.

So my conclusion on the evidence as a whole is that it has not been established that Mr Astor had authority to execute this assignment on behalf of The Observer Ltd.

j   (3) *Was the assignment validated on the grounds that the editor of the Observer represented to the plaintiff that he was authorised to make this assignment on behalf of The Observer Ltd and that the plaintiff relied on such representation?*

This issue was not raised until the speech of counsel for the plaintiff in reply, but an amendment to cover this issue has now been made. It alleges that if Mr Astor had no authority to make the assignment, then the plaintiff would rely on the following facts for its validity: (i) Mr Astor 'as Editor . . . represented to the Plaintiff that he was

authorised to make the assignment on behalf of Observer Ltd'; (ii) the plaintiff relied
on such representation, and (iii) the contents of the memorandum and articles of   *a*
The Observer Ltd. Palmer's Company Law[1] and Gower's Modern Company Law[2],
which were relied on by counsel for the plaintiff, mention four conditions which must
be fulfilled to entitle a party to a transaction to enforce it against a company whose
agent entered into it on behalf of the company without actual authority. These
conditions are taken from Diplock LJ's comprehensive judgment in *Freeman and*   *b*
Lockyer (a firm) v Buckhurst Park Properties (Mangal) Ltd[3], where he said:

> 'It must be shown: (a) that a representation that the agent had authority to
> enter on behalf of the company into a contract of the kind sought to be enforced
> was made to the contractor; (b) that such representation was made by a person
> or persons who had "actual" authority to manage the business of the company
> either generally or in respect of those matters to which the contract relates;   *c*
> (c) that he (the contractor) was induced by such representation to enter into the
> contract, i.e., that he in fact relied on it; and (d) that under its memorandum
> or articles of association the company was not deprived of the capacity either to
> enter into a contract of the kind sought to be enforced or to delegate authority
> to enter into a contract of that kind to the agent.'

With regard to condition (2), Diplock LJ said[4]:   *d*

> '. . . where the agent on whose "apparent" authority the contractor relies has
> no "actual" authority from the corporation to enter into a particular kind of
> contract with the contractor on behalf of the corporation, the contractor cannot
> rely on the agent's own representation as to his actual authority. He can rely only
> on a representation by a person or persons who have actual authority to manage   *e*
> or conduct that part of the business of the corporation to which the contract
> relates.'

And he reiterates this immediately after stating the four conditions: he said[5]:

> 'The confusion which, I venture to think, has sometimes crept into the cases is,
> in my view, due to a failure to distinguish between these four separate conditions,   *f*
> and in particular to keep steadfastly in mind (first) that the only "actual" authority
> which is relevant is that of the persons making the representation relied on . . .'

and I need not quote further.

If Mr Astor had actual authority to assign, this issue does not arise at all—it only
arises on the footing that he had none. And as he had no authority to assign he could
not bind the company by any representation by him that he had such authority.   *g*
Condition (3) also has difficulties for the plaintiff. I am not satisfied that, assuming
the alleged representation, the plaintiff was induced by it to enter into the assignment
or to take any relevant step.

(4) *Is the assignment invalid on the ground that it is not a bona fide assignment?*

On the supposition that the assignment was otherwise valid, it was submitted that   *h*
the assignment was not bona fide on the ground that it was in substance not an
assignment of property with a right of action incidental to it but an assignment of a
right of action. But this confuses substance with purpose. On the evidence, the
purpose clearly was to enable or assist the plaintiff to bring this action. But the
assignment was an assignment intended to take effect in all respects out and out as an
assignment, as contrasted with a bogus assignment, an assignment in form to take   *j*

---

1   21st Edn (1968), p 247
2   3rd Edn (1969), pp 156-158
3   [1964] 1 All ER 630 at 646, [1964] 2 QB 480 at 505, 506
4   [1964] 1 All ER at 645, [1964] 2 QB at 505
5   [1964] 1 All ER at 646, [1964] 2 QB at 506

a effect otherwise than as an assignment in substance and reality. Of course the court will always look behind the form into the reality of a transaction. But the reality of the document here is assignment. (See *Yorkshire Railway Wagon Co v Maclure*[1].)

(5) *Is the plaintiff incapable, for lack of notice to the directors in accordance with s 136 of the Law of Property Act 1925, of suing in this action, as constituted, in respect of the alleged*
b *infringement?*

As, according to my conclusion, the plaintiff was never entitled to the copyright, this issue does not arise; for the assignment of bare accrued rights of action without the assignment of copyright would indisputably be insupportable on grounds of maintenance and champerty.

Nor does this issue involve any matter of fact in which a trial judge could be of
c substantial assistance. It turns entirely on questions of law including questions of construction. Those questions raise considerable difficulties which would require lengthy consideration, unnecessary to my decision in this case. I therefore do not propose to add such lengthy obiter dicta to the length of this judgment.

So my overall conclusion on the first of the three main issues, which I indicated, is that the defendants succeed on it; and that means that they succeed in the action.

d
FAIR DEALING AND PUBLIC INTEREST AND DAMAGES

I must, however, add further observations on these three matters, particularly having regard to the advantages which inevitably arise from hearing the witnesses. This will involve not only matters of evidence and of fact but also of law, in order to realise the relevance and significance of evidence of fact to decisions dependent on
e them. I come first to the distasteful but necessary task of assessing the reliability of the evidence given.

The witnesses called for the plaintiff were the plaintiff and Mr Astor, and for the defendants, Mr Ingrams, the editor of Private Eye, Mr Paul Foot, who wrote the Private Eye article incorporating the memorandum, Mr Anthony Howard, who formerly wrote for the Observer and is now editor of the New Statesman, and Mr
f Bambridge, who is now and has been for the last six years the editor of the Observer Business News, which is a regular part of the Observer newspaper. All the witnesses were, as would be expected, highly intelligent and anxious to assist the court. So the evidence throughout was generally of a remarkably high standard.

The plaintiff has an exceptionally quick mind and fluent speech, is sensitive to all around her and is very adaptable. She is also forceful. She seemed conscious of being
g very much involved in this action and it might have been this that, understandably, affected her evidence.

Mr Astor was clearly experienced, wise and most kindly, with the qualities to get strong-minded persons to work together and produce the happy atmosphere which the evidence shows generally prevails amongst the Observer staff. He has the virtue of great loyalty to his staff and this came through in his evidence but without ever
h affecting in the least the accuracy of his evidence on factual occurrences—the basic and primary facts.

Mr Ingrams and Mr Foot were of a younger generation, very able and serious-minded, impatient with what they regarded as stuffiness or pomposity, sincere and truthful. Except on one or two rare occasions of no great significance, when dealing with matters of opinion or when their loyalty was involved, they were forthright and unrestrainedly outspoken, without hesitation even when they must inevitably have
j realised perfectly well that what they were saying was to their own disadvantage. There was nothing devious or muffled about them, and any criticism of them must be of very opposite qualities. They were excellent witnesses.

Mr Howard and Mr Bambridge were objective, reliable and most helpful. I accept

---

1 (1882) 21 Ch D 309 at 317

their evidence on fact without qualification and their opinions deserve the highest
respect.

The Observer is so well known that I merely record that it is a national Sunday
newspaper of the highest repute and that much of it is devoted to political and public
affairs. Private Eye is a fortnightly periodical or magazine started some ten years ago
and with an increasing circulation which now stands at about 98,000 and whose takings
are now at the rate of some £5,000 a week. Mr Foot described it as being in the
tradition of the lampoon. Mr Ingrams said:

> 'I'm sincerely concerned about the public interest. Private Eye is not merely a
> collection of jests. Jests can often be in the public interest.'

I accept this evidence of Mr Ingrams.

So in this case we have involved on the one side a long-established and highly
reputable paper and on the other side a comparatively new magazine, apparently run
largely by the comparatively young and doubtless largely for the comparatively
young. They reflect different generations in their staff, their attitudes and their
language. In such circumstances there is the danger of predilections. So I trust I
will be forgiven for emphasising the obvious—that what we are concerned with here
is the administration of the law and that that must be free of predilections; that this
court is not concerned with taste, morals, or even public interest except as recognised
by the law; that it is not a roving enquiry and cannot make its decisions on vague
information. This court is concerned only with deciding specific issues according to the
law on evidence that is admissible and advanced in this court. It is essential to bear
constantly in mind that what we are concerned with in this case is not the conduct
of Private Eye in general but only with the claims for breach of copyright by publishing
the memorandum in an article by Mr Foot, and to that this judgment is exclusively
directed.

I come now to the events leading immediately to this action. Mr Foot had for some
time been concerned about Mr Maudling's relations with Mr Hoffman and his Real
Estate Company of America, of which he was chairman or president. Private Eye had
published articles on this subject, and it appears that Mr Foot was the person in Private
Eye who dealt with the matter and that he wrote the 'Footnotes' articles whose description indicated that they were by him. Mr Hoffman was, I understand, sentenced
this year to two years' imprisonment and fined £400 in the United States of America
on fraud charges.

On 28th February 1971 the Observer published a very prominent article by the
plaintiff making a slashing attack on Private Eye's attitude towards Mr Maudling
and accusing Private Eye in effect of smearing Mr Maudling and amongst other things
of 'pure fabrication'. On 12th March 1971 Mr Foot replied by the Private Eye article
in which the memorandum is incorporated. The memorandum and the article contain matters of whose publication the plaintiff complains, and I shall come to consider
them later in some detail. The memorandum reads: 'From: Nora Beloff. 17th
February, 1971. To: David Astor, Editor'—and copies to Donald Trelford, Deputy
Editor, John Silverlight, Assistant Editor, Laurence Marks, Chief Reporter, Tony
Bambridge, Business Editor, Ivan Yates, Leader Writer, and John Lucas, News Editor.
It is headed 'Maudling', and the body of it reads:

> 'I had an interesting talk today with William Whitelaw, who drove me back
> from the Carlton Club to the House of Commons. I told him that the young Tory,
> that I had been lunching with, and I, had been speculating about who would
> take over if the P.M. ran under a bus. He said instantly there was no doubt at all
> it would be Reggie Maudling. He said this was not true when they were in
> opposition and when Reggie would hardly have been in the running, but it was
> overwhelmingly the fact that he had far more government experience and
> general confidence than anyone else in the Cabinet. He said that he talked the

matter over recently with Robert Carr and they had agreed that neither of them would agree to support anyone else or would, themselves, stand against Maudling. He didn't know what other members of the Cabinet thought, but without boasting he felt that if he and Carr stood together that might have some weight. I told him that the young Tory I had been speaking to thought Whitelaw himself would be a better choice and he said that in the present state he would never agree to oppose Maudling. I asked him about the "Private Eye" campaign and he conceded that in Maudling's place he probably already would have sued and he was sure that if it went on Maudling would have to. He did not, however, think the campaign had damaged Maudling as he thought "Private Eye" had over-reached itself and lied on so many subjects about which everybody knew. White-law's remarks were, I thought, particularly interesting as a sidelight on just how little the Conservative Party leaders have really moved towards the Radical Right, and the move away from consensus politics, which is what Maudling really represents. What I would like to suggest is that I do a study of Maudling instead of my usual political notebook, at some point soon when the Home Office is in the news, e.g. after the publication of the Immigration Bill, or some new development in Northern Ireland. If you agree I will very carefully look at the evidence accumulated against Maudling by the "Private Eye" people on the business side, and confront him frankly with the case to hear what he has to say. I still have to deal with it obviously within the restrictions imposed by the libel lawyer, but I will try also to put it into the wider context of his political personality and morality.'

Information is not the subject of copyright, but only 'the literary form in which the information is dressed' (*Fraser v Evans*[1], per Lord Denning MR).   But the nub of this case is not the verbal quotation of the memorandum at all. As the plaintiff's counsel made quite clear in his reply, it is not even that the names of Mr Whitelaw and Mr Carr were revealed in the memorandum as the two Cabinet Ministers referred to in the plaintiff's article as supporting Mr Maudling as the successor to Mr Heath in the event of his ceasing to be Prime Minister; but the disclosure by the memorandum of Mr Whitelaw as the source of the plaintiff's information. If it were not for that disclosure I am completely satisfied that this action would never have been brought. In that sense it is an action for breach of confidence under the guise of an action for infringement of copyright—an action springing from breach of confidence but framed in breach of copyright.

Public interest and fair dealing

In the course of this case, the defence of public interest has been interwoven with fair dealing. They are, however, separate defences and have rightly been separately pleaded. They are governed by separate considerations. Fair dealing is a statutory defence limited to infringement of copyright only. But public interest is a defence outside and independent of statutes, is not limited to copyright cases and is based on a general principle of common law. I will deal first with public interest and then with fair dealing.

Public interest

The most important recent cases referred to were the Court of Appeal cases, *Initial Services Ltd v Putterill*[2] and *Hubbard v Vosper*[3] (where the claims were for infringement of copyright and also for breach of confidence).

The *Initial Services* case[2] was on appeal to strike out certain provisions in the defence relying, in justification of disclosure of confidential information, on its exposure first

---

1 [1969] 1 All ER 8 at 12, [1969] 1 QB 349 at 362
2 [1967] 3 All ER 145, [1968] 1 QB 396
3 [1972] 1 All ER 1023, [1972] 2 QB 84

of breach of statutory duty to register a restrictive trade agreement and secondly   *a*
that a circular issued by the plaintiffs to their customers attributing increases in their
charges to the selective employment tax was misleading to the public. Lord Denning
MR said[1] that the exception to the obligation not to disclose confidential
information—

> 'extends to any misconduct of such a nature that it ought in the public interest
> to be disclosed to others. WOOD, V.-C., put it in a vivid phrase[2]: "There is no   *b*
> confidence as to the disclosure of iniquity." In *Weld-Blundell* v. *Stephens*[3] BANKES,
> L.J., rather suggested that the exception was limited to the proposed or contem-
> plated commission of a crime or a civil wrong; but I should have thought that
> that was too limited. The exception should extend to crimes, frauds and mis-
> deeds, both those actually committed as well as those in contemplation, provided
> always—and this is essential—that the disclosure is justified in the public interest.   *c*
> The reason is because "no private obligations can dispense with that universal
> one which lies on every member of the society to discover every design which
> may be formed, contrary to the laws of the society, to destroy the public welfare."
> See *Annesley* v. *Earl of Anglesea*[4].'

And Salmon LJ said[5]:   *d*

> 'I do not think that the law would lend assistance to anyone who is proposing
> to commit and to continue to commit a clear breach of a statutory duty imposed
> in the public interest.'

In that case publication, justifiable in the public interest, was considered to extend
beyond exposure of what appears, at first blush, to have been meant by 'contrary to   *e*
the laws of the society' as stated in *Annesley v Earl of Anglesea*[6], although not, as I
see it, beyond 'disclosure of iniquity' in Wood V-C's phrase[7].

In *Hubbard v Vosper*[8] Lord Denning MR treated material on scientology published
in breach of confidence as susceptible to a defence of public interest on the ground
that it was dangerous material, namely medical quackeries 'dangerous in untrained
hands'.   *f*

The defence of public interest clearly covers and, in the authorities does not extend
beyond, disclosure, which as Lord Denning MR emphasised must be disclosure justified in the public interest, of matters carried out or contemplated, in breach of the
country's security, or in breach of law, including statutory duty, fraud, or otherwise
destructive of the country or its people, including matters medically dangerous to
the public; and doubtless other misdeeds of similar gravity. Public interest, as a   *g*
defence in law, operates to override the rights of the individual (including copyright)
which would otherwise prevail and which the law is also concerned to protect. Such
public interest, as now recognised by the law, does not extend beyond misdeeds of a
serious nature and importance to the country and thus, in my view, clearly
recognisable as such.

Witnesses for the plaintiff and for the defendants alike gave evidence of their own   *h*
view of press practice and conceptions of what justified publications not normally
justifiable. They all involved 'public interest' as the justification. This public interest
was more permissive than is permissible as a defence in law. However, Mr Astor

---

1   [1967] 3 All ER at 148, [1968] 1 QB at 405
2   I e in *Gartside v Outram* (1856) 26 LJCh 113 at 114   *j*
3   [1919] 1 KB 520 at 527
4   (1743) 17 State Tr 1139 at 1223-1246
5   [1967] 3 All ER at 151, [1968] 1 QB at 410
6   (1743) 17 State Tr 1139
7   (1856) 26 LJCh at 114
8   [1972] 1 All ER 1023, [1972] 2 QB 84

and the plaintiff emphasised the seriousness of the national interest required. Nevertheless, the plaintiff's counsel in reply submitted that public interest as a defence in law should be given a wide meaning. Its meaning differed from witness to witness and, on occasion, even in different parts of the evidence of the same witness. All the witnesses considered that it was for the editor to decide on balance whether publication was justifiable, although counsel for the plaintiff in reply recognised that the press must, in this, be subject to the law.

The defendants submitted that the publication of the memorandum was in the public interest on such grounds as that the public should know what senior Minister had provided the plaintiff with the information appearing in the memorandum and in her article, what two key Ministers supported Mr Maudling as Mr Heath's successor, how the lobby correspondents obtained their information and how their system worked. On the other hand, the plaintiff maintained that, subject to narrow exceptions, it was not in the public interest in general, and indeed contrary to it, that press sources of information should be disclosed, as otherwise the sources of information that should be available to the public would soon dry up. On the other hand, it might be thought that informants, particularly if public representatives or public officials speaking on public affairs, should not be concealed by anonymity. These considerations are, of course, all of public importance; but what has to be decided here is whether public interest, in the sense in which it is recognised as a defence in such a case as this, is established. The publication of the memorandum did not disclose any 'iniquity' or 'misdeed'. It follows from the scope of public interest which I have ventured to indicate that the defence of public interest fails.

Fair dealing
(1) The meaning of statutory 'fair dealing'
The defence of fair dealing is governed by s 6 of the Copyright Act 1956 and so far as is relevant to this case by sub-ss (2), (3) and (10). Subsection (2) reads:

'No fair dealing with a literary . . . work shall constitute an infringement of the copyright in the work if it is for purposes of criticism or review, whether of that work or of another work, and is accompanied by a sufficient acknowledgment.'

Subsection (3) reads:

'No fair dealing with a literary . . . work shall constitute an infringement of the copyright in the work if it is for the purpose of reporting current events—(a) in a newspaper, magazine or similar periodical [I need not read (b)] and, in a case falling within paragraph (a) of this subsection, is accompanied by a sufficient acknowledgment.'

'Sufficient acknowledgment' is defined by sub-s (10), for present purposes, as 'an acknowledgment identifying the work in question by its title or other description and . . . also identifying the author'.

The defendants thus have to establish (1) fair dealing with the memorandum, (2) for purposes of criticism or review of the memorandum or of another work or for the purpose of reporting current events in a newspaper, magazine or similar periodical, and (3) sufficient identification of the work in question (i e the memorandum) by its title or other description and identifying the author. I will deal with these three matters in reverse order.

It seems to me that 'the work' and the plaintiff as its author are so clearly identified that I will not pause to give reasons for this conclusion.

Counsel for the defendants rightly submitted—and it was not disputed—that witnesses substantially agreed on what were the constituent elements of review and criticism of an article, namely, dealing with the article's literary merits, its truth, relevance, sources (including, as Mr Foot expressed it, how the research has been done) and how it came to be written. Mr Foot's evidence dealt with the question of

whether his article was for such purposes. He said that the plaintiff's article was *a*
written four days after a Mr Clarke had visited him on behalf of the Business Observer
(not on behalf of the plaintiff as the plaintiff originally stated in her evidence which
she returned to the box the next day to correct). This, he said, indicated that there
had been no substantial enquiry into the matter. My notes of evidence (from which
my quotations of evidence come throughout this judgment unless otherwise stated)
are: *b*

> 'Plaintiff's article doesn't go into it in any depth—states nothing not available
> to anyone who looks into it for a moment—appeared just whitewash without
> dealing with revelations that had been made at all.'

On the question whether Mr Foot's article was for the purpose of reporting current
events, the plaintiff was asked whether the fact that she had written her article in the *c*
Observer was news. She replied:

> 'It is news in the sense that everything I write is news. The fact of my writing
> this article is news; and of my writing any other article in the Observer is news.'

Mr Foot said:
                                                                                  d
> 'It was a very significant development that the political correspondent had
> written a large article on this. The Washington Post and the New York Times
> are constantly dealing with such matters. It was crucial that the Observer was
> doing so and in my view wrongly and shabbily, and had to be answered in sharp
> terms. Such an article is not far off editorial comment and is therefore very
> important.'   *e*

And Mr Howard likewise emphasised the importance of such a newspaper as the
Observer 'taking up the Maudling-Hoffman affair'.
    In his closing speech counsel for the plaintiff, rightly in the light of the evidence,
conceded that Mr Foot's article was for the purposes of criticism and review and
reporting current events within s 6.   *f*
    I come now to the requirement, which I specified, of fair dealing with this memor-
andum. Fair dealing is not defined by the Act, although subject to the requirements
which I have already stated including the purpose of criticism or review or reporting
current events. The references to purposes, which I have just read, differ in their
wording from the reference to purposes in s 6 (1), which reads:

> 'No fair dealing with a literary . . . work for purposes of research or private *g*
> study shall constitute an infringement of the copyright in the work.'

Thus 'for the purpose' in sub-s (1) and 'if it is for the purpose' in the other subsections
fundamentally have the same meaning and effect; and the difference in wording is
explained by the inclusion in sub-ss (2) and (3) of additional provisions and requirements without parallel in sub-s (1). It would, indeed, be whimsical if the relationship *h*
between fair dealing and the approved purposes were given a different significance
in sub-ss (2) and (3) from sub-s (1), in the absence of obvious reasons for making such a
difference. The relevant fair dealing is thus fair dealing with the memorandum for
the approved purposes. It is fair dealing directed to and consequently limited to and
to be judged in relation to the approved purposes. It is dealing which is fair for the
approved purposes and not dealing which might be fair for some other purpose or
fair in general. Mere dealing with the work for that purpose is not enough; it must *j*
also be dealing which is fair for that purpose; whose fairness, as I have indicated, must
be judged in relation to that purpose.
    Thus public interest as such is outside the purpose of the section and of fair dealing.
It is not of itself justification for infringement of copyright, except insofar as recognised
by common law as a separate defence irrespective of the section, as already mentioned.

a   (2) Factors in the defence of fair dealing

I come now to the relevant factors in determining fair dealing. A number of authorities were cited, but for present purposes, at any rate, the law is most conveniently stated in *Hubbard v Vosper*[1] by Lord Denning MR[2] and by Megaw LJ[3]. To summarise the statements: fair dealing is a question of fact and of impression, to which factors that are relevant include the extent of the quotation and its proportion to comment (which may be justifiable although the quotation is of the whole work);

b   whether the work is unpublished; and the extent to which the work has been circularised, although not published to the public within the meaning of the Copyright Act 1956.

In our case the memorandum was unpublished. Romer J in *British Oxygen Co Ltd v Liquid Air Ltd*[4], in dealing with a company's letter to a trade customer as a 'literary

c   work', said that publication without the author's consent would be 'manifestly unfair' as it is not a 'fair dealing' with the work. Romer J's observations were made when the relevant statute was s 2 of the Copyright Act 1911, the precursor of s 6 of the 1956 Act. It was in wide terms into which limitations were introduced by s 6, but the differences are not material for present purposes. However, unpublished as well as published works are within the fair dealing provisions of both Acts; and what would

d   otherwise be infringement cannot of itself, without regard to any other circumstances, be outside the exception to infringement made by those sections, as that would be to exclude from the sections what the sections in terms include. So I doubt if Romer J ever intended that his words should be read in the sense that an unpublished work should be automatically outside the provisions of the fair dealing defence rather than a factor, although doubtless an important factor, which with other factors have

e   to be taken into consideration in considering fair dealing. And such a conclusion seems to me to be in accordance with the decision and observations of the Court of Appeal in *Hubbard v Vosper*[1].

(3) Was the publication of the memorandum fair dealing within s 6 of the Copyright Act 1956?

The publication was of the whole memorandum. In extent it formed a quarter of

f   the article which was published. But that article was throughout dealing with the relationship of Mr Maudling and Mr Hoffman and his companies; how the plaintiff's article came to be written; replying to the plaintiff's criticisms of Private Eye's attitude towards Mr Maudling; criticising the plaintiff's article on fact and on attitude; and in the course of doing so reflecting adversely on the plaintiff in the context of these matters.

g   The plaintiff submitted that Mr Foot's article was not fair dealing, on the ground that it made a personal attack on her and disclosed a competitor's confidential source of information. Whilst not lacking in respect for those submissions as for all the submissions made by the plaintiff's counsel, I will come immediately to what appears to me to be the greatest and simplest difficulty which the defendants have to face on fair dealing.

h   The memorandum was unpublished and indeed it was never intended to be published. This is therefore not just a case of quoting excessively from a work which had already been made available to the public generally. The law by bestowing a right of copyright on an unpublished work bestows a right to prevent its being published at all; and even though an unpublished work is not automatically excluded from the defence of fair dealing, it is yet a much more substantial breach of copyright than

j   publication of a published work. And in our case all the contents of the memorandum were obtained and used without the author's consent in the correct conviction that, if consent had been sought, it would have been refused.

---

1   [1972] 1 All ER 1023, [1972] 2 QB 84
2   [1972] 1 All ER at 1027, 1028, [1972] 2 QB at 94, 95
3   [1972] 1 All ER at 1031, [1972] 2 QB at 98
4   [1925] Ch 383 at 393

But receiving and using leaked information, in the sense of confidential information *a* which someone who has it gives to someone not entitled to it appears to be common practice in the press, and occurs in such a reputable paper as the Observer itself. An instance was even given in evidence of the publication by the plaintiff of such a leak. Distinctions were sought to be drawn by or on behalf of the plaintiff between different ways in which leaks occur. It was sought to distinguish between a leak by theft as contrasted with breach of confidence, and it was strongly maintained, particu- *b* larly by the plaintiff in the early stages of the hearing, that the memorandum was stolen from the Observer's offices by someone from Private Eye; but Mr Foot, who knew, said that the contents of the memorandum were disclosed by someone in the Observer who wanted the memorandum published; and I have no hesitation in accepting the evidence of Mr Foot. A distinction was also sought to be drawn between, on the one hand, receiving and using a leak of a rival's confidential informa- *c* tion (for example, by Private Eye of the confidential information of another news- paper) and, on the other hand, receiving and using confidential information of some other body not a rival (e g by Private Eye from a government department, an in- dustrial company or a private firm). Mr Foot disagreed and so do I. A distinction was also suggested between a leak of information never intended by its owner to be published and a pre-empting leak in anticipation of authorised publication. The *d* pre-empting leak might well be substantially prejudicial; and although the later such a leak takes place before authorised publication the less is apt to be the ill conse- quence, yet the less too is it apt to be in the public interest, which was mostly alone relied on to justify the publication of leaked information. On all these distinctions there may well be differences of responsible views sincerely held; but for my part I am unable to make any decisive distinction between the unsought voluntary leak in *e* this case by a person who wanted the leaked information published and other press publications of leaks which were referred to in evidence.

Is then the publication of what was thus obtained by Private Eye by the leak to it fair dealing or compatible with fair dealing within s 6?

Counsel for the defendants suggested that as the leak occurred before any infringe- ment by publication it did not affect the fair dealing defence to such infringement *f* and was outside the section. But the leak was clearly a dealing with the work in which copyright existed at the time of the leak, and the leak was given and accepted for the purpose of unauthorised publication. And, further, the publication itself was not just a publication in vacuo but a publication of information known to be leaked, which could not without the leak have been so published. The vice of the leak and publica- tion in this case was, to my mind, clearly unjustifiable for the authorised purposes of *g* criticism, review and news, and clearly in my view constituted dealing which was not fair within the statute. And this unfair dealing goes to the root of the publication— without it there would be no publication at all. This ground is ample to defeat the defence of fair dealing, and it is on this ground that I base my decision against the defendants on this issue.

h

Damages

(1) Damages for infringement of copyright

In infringement of copyright 'the measurement of damages is the depreciation caused by the infringement to the value of the copyright, as a chose in action' (*Suther- land Publishing Co Ltd v Caxton Publishing Co Ltd*[1] per Lord Wright MR). It is common ground that those damages in this case are nominal.

j

(2) Statutory additional and exemplary and aggravated damages

The difficulties arise over these damages.

Section 17 (1) provides in general terms for the kind of relief available, namely:

---

1   [1936] 1 All ER 177 at 180, [1936] Ch 323 at 336

'. . . all such relief, by way of damages, injunction, accounts or otherwise, shall be available to the plaintiff as is available in any corresponding proceedings in respect of infringements of other proprietary rights.'

Apart from the definition subsections, i e sub-ss (5) and (6), the other subsections, namely sub-ss (2), (3) and (4), make special provisions affecting the scope of the specifically mentioned kinds of relief, namely damages, injunction or accounts.

Section 17 (3) deals with 'additional damages'. It provides:

'Where in an action under this section an infringement of copyright is proved or admitted, and the court, having regard (in addition to all other material considerations) to—(a) the flagrancy of the infringement, and (b) any benefit shown to have accrued to the defendant by reason of the infringement, is satisfied that effective relief would not otherwise be available to the plaintiff, the court, in assessing damages for the infringement, shall have power to award such additional damages by virtue of this subsection as the court may consider appropriate in the circumstances.'

The subsection is directed to providing 'effective relief' for the plaintiff. It is thus directed to purely compensatory damages, so that exemplary or punitive damages are outside its ambit as the plaintiff conceded (in accordance with the opinion of Lord Kilbrandon in *Broome v Cassell & Co Ltd*[1]; *Williams v Settle*[2], where damages for breach of copyright were referred to as 'exemplary', occurred before the distinction was clearly drawn between exemplary and compensatory damages in *Rookes v Barnard*[3], and was the subject of criticism by Lord Devlin in that case).

However, para (b) of s 17 (3), to which the court must have regard in awarding additional damages, recalls Lord Devlin's second category of exemplary damages stated in *Rookes v Barnard*[4], namely cases in which—

'the defendant's conduct has been calculated by him to make a profit for himself which may well exceed the compensation payable to the plaintiff.'

But, although the common factor in para (b) and this second category is the advantage obtained by the defendant from the infringement, it is, in the second category, damages as punishment for the defendant's conduct, but in para (b) compensation as effective relief to the plaintiff in respect of the benefit obtained by the defendant out of the plaintiff's property. The mere fact of benefit, apart from calculated conduct to benefit, is enough to satisfy para (b).

In my view s 17 (3) leaves no place outside its ambit for the award of compensatory or aggravated damages nor for the award of punitive damages for reasons which may be summarised as follows: (a) special provisions are made in sub-ss (2), (3) and (4) with regard to the application of copyright of ordinary forms of relief; (b) sub-s (3) provides for 'additional' damages without reference to any other description of damages and in particular without any distinction in nomenclature between exemplary or punitive damages on the one hand and compensatory or aggravated damages on the other hand; (c) sub-s (3) (b) provides, in the circumstances already mentioned, for the advantage obtained by the defendants from the plaintiff's property being an element to be regarded in awarding the additional damages; (d) sub-s (3) substantially, if not completely, covers what could be awarded by aggravated damages; (e) the precondition that the court has to be satisfied that effective relief would not otherwise be available to the plaintiff applies to the award of 'additional' damages including any aggravated damages covered by additional damages; and it would be nugatory

1   [1972] 1 All ER 801 at 877, [1972] AC 1027 at 1134
2   [1960] 2 All ER 806, [1960] 1 WLR 1072
3   [1964] 1 All ER 367, [1964] AC 1129
4   [1964] 1 All ER at 410, [1964] AC at 1226

and senseless to limit 'additional' damages by the precondition but at the same time permit aggravated damages, which would be their equivalent, free from the precondition; (f) copyright is now exclusively a creature of statute and governed by statute; and it seems to me that s 17 (3) is a code for damages which are 'additional' without providing a place for additional exemplary and aggravated damages outside the subsection. The substantial result is that the subsection excludes exemplary damages for infringement of copyright and replaces any aggravated damages that might otherwise have been obtainable for infringement of copyright.

(3) The precondition that effective relief would not otherwise be available

I come now to the effect of the words of the precondition, namely, that 'the court . . . is satisfied that effective relief would not otherwise be available to the plaintiff'.

These words, considered in isolation, are words of general application without limit and are wide enough to cover compensatory damages recoverable for a different cause of action; and different causes of action can, of course, generally be combined in the same action. If the words are considered in their context amongst the other subsections it appears that the section is concerned to relate relief in copyright actions to relief in other actions. Thus, s 17 (1) provides for relief in copyright action by reference to relief available with regard to corresponding proceedings in respect of other proprietary rights, although subject to the particular provisions of the other subsections including sub-ss (3) and (4). And sub-s (4) excludes certain relief from copyright actions, although obtainable for other comparable causes of action. It was objected that, in general, damages are obtainable for one cause of action although another cause of action arises out of the same circumstances. But what we are concerned with here is not ordinary damages for the cause of action relied on (namely, for infringement of copyright, for which the damages are nominal) but with additional damages made available by statute and governed by the provisions laid down by that statute—in this case of the precondition 'that effective relief would not otherwise be available'.

The relief otherwise available is necessarily, of course, by its very meaning, a relief alternative to the additional damages obtainable in the infringement action. So if the alternative relief is given, then (to the extent to which it applies) there is no room for giving additional damages too—the alternative relief would already have provided the relief. If the alternative relief were a relief in the same action for the same injury, the reference to relief not being otherwise available would be a rigid and strange direction to insert in a statute, rather than leaving it in the ordinary way to the experienced practice of the court. But if it refers to an alternative remedy available in another action or for another cause of action then its insertion is readily understandable.

Judicial comments have been made on the undesirability of giving relief by way of compensatory or by way of punitive damages in addition to ordinary damages on grounds for which relief is available through another cause of action. In *Addis v Gramophone Co Ltd*[1] the decision was that aggravated damages could not be obtained for breach of contract, apparently because damages for breach of contract were necessarily limited to the loss of what the plaintiff would have received if there had been no breach. But Lord Atkinson observed[2]:

'I can conceive nothing more objectionable and embarrassing in litigation than trying in effect an action of libel or slander as a matter of aggravation in an action for illegal dismissal, the defendant being permitted, as he must in justice be permitted, to traverse the defamatory sense, rely on privilege, or raise every point which he could raise in an independent action brought for the alleged libel or slander itself.'

These observations would apply as forcefully whether the action sounded in contract

1 [1909] AC 488, [1908-10] All ER Rep 1
2 [1909] AC at 496, [1908-10] All ER Rep at 5

(if aggravated damages applied to it) or in tort. And these observations on aggravated damages are in accordance with the observations of Lord Devlin in *Rookes v Barnard*[1] stating limits to the categories to which exemplary damages applied.   He said[1]:

> 'I do not care for the idea that in matters criminal an aggrieved party should be given an option to inflict for his own benefit punishment by a method which denies to the offender the protection of the criminal law.'

(This limitation was further explained by Lord Reid (who had been a member of the House in that case) in *Broome v Cassell & Co Ltd*[2].)

My conclusion is that, if effective relief is available to the plaintiff in respect of another cause of action, relief cannot be given for it by way of additional damages for infringement of copyright.

(4) Additional damages in relation to this case

The two such relevant causes of action in our case are, first, for libel and, secondly, for breach of confidence. The passage relied on as libel states that the plaintiff's article 'took the form of an obsequious public relations job on behalf of Mr Maudling', although later it was stated that the plaintiff 'meant every word she wrote. She really does believe that Mr Maudling has been wronged by Private Eye'. Objections were powerfully developed in detail by counsel for the defendants to relief by way of additional damages being given in this case with regard to these two causes of action; but the nature of the objections have been sufficiently indicated by the quotations already made from the speeches in the House of Lords. Thus, in my view, additional damages cannot be given in this action in respect of these two causes of action.

This leaves additional damages on other matters which are material. Flagrancy of the infringement and its benefit to the defendants are of course expressly mentioned as material; but 'in addition to all other material considerations'. These include such matters as the defendants' conduct with regard to the infringement and motive for it, injury to the plaintiff's feeling for suffering insults, indignities and the like; and also the plaintiff's own corresponding behaviour. The damages go largely to compensation for the plaintiff's suffering from injured feelings and distress and strain (for a convenient and succinct reference to aggravated or compensatory damages replaced in our case by 'additional' damages, see *Broome v Cassell & Co Ltd*[3] per Lord Reid[4] and Lord Diplock[5]).

(5) The defendants' conduct

It is convenient to consider additional damages in this case with reference first to the defendants' conduct in its following aspects in particular:

(i) The memorandum was not a published work openly obtained but its unpublished contents were obtained by someone engaged in the Observer office voluntarily telephoning them to Mr Foot. (This goes to the way in which the subject of copyright was received for publication independent of any claim for breach of confidence.)

(ii) The memorandum's contents were published in the realisation that publication would not be consented to and indeed would be strongly resented.

These first two factors come within 'flagrancy' in s 17 (3) (*a*) of the 1956 Act.

(iii) The publication of the memorandum gave authority and weight to the defendants' article to the benefit of the defendants. I agree that, as the plaintiff complains, the verbatim quotation of the memorandum brought home to the reader that Private Eye had inside information and gave credibility to the rest of the article, or, as

1   [1964] 1 All ER at 412, [1964] AC at 1230
2   [1972] 1 All ER at 836-838, [1972] AC at 1085-1087
3   [1972] 1 All ER 801, [1972] AC 1027
4   [1972] 1 All ER at 839, [1972] AC at 1089
5   [1972] 1 All ER at 869, [1972] AC at 1124

Mr Foot expressed it, it gave 'a lift to the whole article'. It is thus a benefit within   *a*
s 17 (3) (*b*). But this is a benefit of a general nature. It only gave justifiable cause for
the plaintiff's complaint with regard to particular matters (as contrasted with the
general 'lift') to the extent to which they were untrue and that depends on the truth
of the matters complained of, which I shall deal with later.

(iv) For the plaintiff it was submitted that the defendants boasted of actions against
them in accordance with a calculation that the benefit to them of such actions would   *b*
outweigh the disadvantages. Mr Ingrams agreed that over the last ten years the
defendants had paid nearly £50,000 to aggrieved parties but maintained that you could
go to almost any publication (by that I presume he meant a national newspaper or
similar periodical) over the last ten years and find a similar list of apologies, and
that 'We are not reckless of publishing whether actionable or not'; and he denied
any boasting. Such alleged boasting or policy was not, in the course of the plaintiff's   *c*
submission, specifically related to any article by Mr Foot or about Mr Maudling, and
I am satisfied that the matters alleged did not affect the article complained of in any
way. Indeed legal advice on the article was taken before publication followed,
although it overlooked the possibility of copyright proceedings. I am not satisfied
about Mr Ingrams's comparison with other publications, but, as I have said, he was a
truthful and forthright witness, and subject to this reservation I accept what he said.   *d*
However, the submission for the plaintiff was directed to exemplary damages, which
I have already concluded are not available to the plaintiff in this action.

(v) References to the plaintiff throughout the defendants' article under the nickname
of 'Ballsoff', including the article's heading in large print 'The Ballsoff Memorandum'.
The nickname is a concocted word of no clear meaning. To my mind, at any rate, it
conveys an insulting impression and is thoroughly objectionable. Counsel for the   *e*
plaintiff strongly attacked the nickname, although the plaintiff herself seemed to be
less concerned about it and did not take the obvious advantage of exaggerating or
emphasising her feeling about it. Mr Foot's observations on this were perhaps the
only part of his evidence where I had the impression that his words, as spoken,
inadequately expressed his views. He said:

> 'She has always been so called and the nickname was attached to her before I   *f*
> went to Private Eye. I didn't think it a kindly nickname. It is in the tradition of
> the lampoon in which Private Eye stands.'

Insulting behaviour is a well established ground for compensatory damages and, in
my view, for additional damages within the section.

(vi) Lack of regret for causing the plaintiff hurt and distress. Mr Ingrams said: *g*

> 'The dealing in Private Eye was fair dealing—tit for tat, [and] I didn't mind the
> harmful article with regard to the plaintiff—she had written a harmful article
> about Private Eye. I don't regret having caused her hurt and distress.'

There are two elements in these quotations, first lack of regret and secondly provocation. In assessing additional damages the first tells against the defendants and the   *h*
second against the plaintiff. How far these elements carry weight depends on the
overall appraisement of the rest of the defendants' conduct on the one hand and the
plaintiff's conduct on the other hand.

(vii) The publication of the memorandum has involved disclosure of carelessness in
guarding the secrecy of the confidential information given to the plaintiff by Mr
Whitelaw. (This, like the first factor, is not a claim against the defendants for breach   *j*
of confidence.) This factor requires detailed consideration because of its importance
and its difficulties. It is important as the exclusive basis of the plaintiff's claim for
additional damages for personal distress. She said:

> 'The publication of the memorandum damaged me because it reflected on my
> reliability as a lobby correspondent. That is a reflection on my reputation. The

a distress which the Private Eye article caused me arose from the reflection on my reputation.'

This is in keeping with the breach of confidence being in reality, although not in form, at the root of this action and is as near as this action gets to that reality. The plaintiff was not complaining that the general reader might think that there had been careless-ness. She said: 'The general reader would think it was stolen'. What she was
b concerned about was what her anonymous informants would think.

'My informant would be very worried about trusting information to me. He would assume I'd left around something that had been picked up.'

And the editor said:

c 'That the whole letter was published looks as though our correspondence was chucked on the floor.'

But leaks might occur in the most efficiently run organisations and they have, of course, in fact occurred in Ministers' departments. Anonymous informants would naturally be concerned about such a leak; but such informants as the plaintiff was concerned about are informed persons perfectly capable of objective consideration
d and they would hardly necessarily leap to the conclusion that the plaintiff or the Observer was so careless as to 'chuck' confidential memoranda on the floor rather than any other possibility that reflected less adversely on the plaintiff's or the Observer's care of such information. But this, in fact, was what was apt to occur in the Observer office. The plaintiff said:

e 'Copies of the memorandum went to people to whom it was addressed. The secretary types it and puts it in an envelope and distributes it to the people concerned. It didn't have 'private and confidential' on it and it might go into a series of in trays. I didn't put "private and confidential" on it because all internal communications are private and confidential . . . Each of the addressees would have a secretary or share one, and the secretaries would deal with the documents in the in tray . . . I don't think most of them would file it—different people would
f do different things about an office memorandum.'

She also said: 'There has been carelessness with documents and they have not been locked up and they have been left on people's desks.' And she said later that an in-formant 'would assume I'd left around something that had been picked up. I suppose I had left it in my office.' It seems to me that much of any damage from the publicity given to carelessness has not arisen from mere publication of the memorandum. No
g evidence other than hearsay or by inference was given of such damage or concern. There was no direct evidence that any informant had or would withhold information that would otherwise be forthcoming. The most direct evidence of an informant's reaction was of Mr Whitelaw's annoyance at seeing the memorandum published— evidence of what Mr Whitelaw told an associate who told the plaintiff who told the court, and that is not evidence at all, let alone direct evidence that information would
h be withheld. It seems to me that any damage arising out of an informant's inference of carelessness on the part of the plaintiff or the Observer from the mere publication of this memorandum or the plaintiff's reasonably justifiable fears of it is not such as to be a very substantial factor in the assessment of additional damages. The plaintiff is, therefore, in my view entitled to additional damages as indicated subject to considerations of the plaintiff's own conduct.

j (6) The plaintiff's conduct
  The plaintiff's article, as I have said, preceded the defendants' article of which complaint is made. The article started with the sentence:

'REGINALD MAUDLING, though Mr Heath's number two, is currently neither the Prime Minister's nor the Conservative Party's favourite man. [And it ended

with the sentence:] But if these policies [ie of the government] fail, he would be
the man who could best offer a genuine alternative Conservative policy. The *a*
country may need him.'

The article itself, despite some qualified concessions, reads as very strong advocacy
in defence of Mr Maudling and in support of his succession to the Conservative leader-
ship in certain circumstances. Of this, it seems to me, there can be no reasonable
doubt. Likewise the plaintiff's sincerity is not in doubt and is recognised in Mr Foot's *b*
own article. Now I come to more controversial aspects.

The plaintiff herself described the origin and purpose of her article in these terms:

'I happened to meet Mr. Whitelaw and had a conversation—and thought it
appropriate because of the smear campaign on Mr. Maudling—and thought it
bad for public life, and time for us to go in on it.' *c*

So before embarking on her article, making any investigation for it, or writing her
memorandum, she already had the purpose to counter what she called the smear
campaign against Mr Maudling. This is what she set out to do by her article. She
had a purpose to serve rather than a question to answer.

The article had in large print across the top of the page 'Make no mistake. If *d*
Ted Heath falls off his yacht, Reggie will become Prime Minister.' Underneath that
in large print across the first two columns appeared 'OPTIMIST IN THE WINGS by NORA
BELOFF'; and underneath a photograph of Mr Maudling across four columns there
appeared in thick, prominent but smaller type: 'Reginald Maudling. "Private Eye"
campaign began in protest against Dutschke's expulsion.' She said in the body of the
article: *e*

'It seems that it was primarily in protest against the decision to expel Dutschke
that the fortnightly political comic, *Private Eye*, began its anti-Maudling campaign,
which still goes on. Given Maudling's record, it would have been useless to try
to dub him a "fascist beast", but *Private Eye* latched on to his earlier involvement
with Mr Jerome Hoffman's investment business . . .' *f*

The campaign is referred to by her later as a smear campaign, i e a campaign whose
purpose is to vilify Mr Maudling. So the plaintiff's charge is that Private Eye began
and still carries on a campaign against Mr Maudling to vilify him and that they have
'latched on' to his relations with Mr Hoffman for that purpose, and all this primarily
in protest against his decision to expel Dutschke. I am satisfied that no part of these
charges is true. It is clear that Private Eye started its articles about Mr Maudling *g*
and Mr Hoffman before his decision to expel Dutschke was made. Indeed if Private
Eye and Mr Foot were genuinely concerned to avoid Dutschke's expulsion it might
seem that attacking Mr Maudling and his Hoffman associations was a nonsensical
way of setting about it. I am satisfied that Private Eye and, in particular, Mr Foot,
were genuinely and seriously concerned in the public interest (which I here use
widely without regard to its meaning as a legal defence) about his relations with *h*
Mr Hoffman—as were others including the editor of the Business Observer and indeed
the editor of the Observer himself, as was shown by his approval of a thorough
investigation of these relations by the Business Editor.

The plaintiff also in the article made accusations against the defendants in general
terms and, what is important, linked these general accusations with the defendants'
Maudling-Hoffman articles. She wrote (in the last column): *j*

'With their familiar mix of genuine revelations, half-truths and pure fabrica-
tions, strung together by damaging insinuations, *Private Eye* has tried to show that
even after his three-month chairmanship Maudling was still actively involved in
this business. What is true is that Maudling never publicly repudiated Hoffman.
Indeed, he went to the firm's 1969 Christmas party, while Hoffman's firm's

private journal *Fund Forum* tried to make out that Maudling still belonged actively with them. Maudling denies being aware of this.'

In an Observer article headed 'Private Eye and public interest' by Mr Roy Perrott, which throughout gives the impression of being commendably objective, a distinction is clearly made between Private Eye in general and Mr Foot's articles in particular. In the course of the article it is stated:

'At least half the time (the problem is, which half?) *Eye* is also very serious-minded, though the label would embarrass them. Paul Foot's researches into various kinds of skulduggery are probably as good as or better than anything Fleet Street can show in that line, in a section that has been virtually free of writs. Its coverage of such causes as the Ronan Point flats collapse, the D'Oliveira affair, the London phone directories mystery, and heart-transplanting has been quick off the mark and apparently thorough.'

When, in cross-examination on this passage and the article in general, the plaintiff was given the opportunity of criticising it, her only criticism was that she disagreed that Private Eye had 'expert news research' as stated earlier in the article.

I have already dealt with such references as were made to libels generally by Private Eye. But the only specifically alleged inaccuracies relied on by the plaintiff and investigated before me have been those in Mr Foot's article—of which there were three. The first related to the 'obsequious' observation which I have concluded is not properly a matter for additional damages. The second bears on the Christmas party mentioned in my last quotation from the plaintiff's article. Mr Foot's article complained that the plaintiff did not mention that Mr Maudling attended a sales conference of Mr Hoffman's in the following spring, eight months after resigning. The plaintiff never denied that he did so. Mr Foot confirmed that he did so, and counsel for the plaintiff in reply mentioned that the plaintiff could not give evidence on it. So this inaccuracy was not established. The third alleged inaccuracy relied on was that 'the memorandum was greeted with considerable scepticism and opposition in the Business Observer'. Mr Bambridge had been concerned by what had been published by Granada Television 'World in Action', the Daily Express and Private Eye, and by what he had heard from persons in the business office of the Daily Express. So the Observer's business editor, Mr Bambridge, had, before the plaintiff's memorandum, decided on an investigation into Mr Maudling's association with Mr Hoffman. It was to be an investigation, as Mr Bambridge described it, to find out 'whether Mr. Maudling was a greedy rogue or ill-advised in his business contacts'. It was to be an investigation of a different order altogether from that contemplated or carried out by the plaintiff, and was to include a thorough investigation in America. Mr Bambridge had started by inviting Mr Foot to lunch and arranging to have from Private Eye the materials on which their articles had been based. Mr Bambridge said that the project was still in hand when he got the memorandum. The editor, as a result of the memorandum, saw Mr Bambridge who advised him that a proper job on the subject could not be done in the time suggested by the memorandum, that it required a long and detailed examination, and that there was danger of coming up with the wrong judgment. The editor told Mr Bambridge that he contemplated that the plaintiff's article should come out in two weeks, and in fact it came out in less time. But the editor decided that the plaintiff should write the article. Mr Astor said that he so decided because 'the Business Editor's treatment had been overtaken by the plaintiff's memorandum and following that with suggestions of proceedings against Hoffman'; although he did not know what proceedings. None in fact took place in this country. Mr Bambridge said he voiced his misgivings but accepted the position quite happily. He also said that he was upset that Mr Astor had not taken his advice that there was not time to carry out a thorough investigation. He said he dropped the matter and that he stopped his investigations because the

plaintiff had in effect taken over the job. He said that when he read the plaintiff's
article he felt he would have preferred to have dug into the matter much more.
He said the plaintiff's article was not such an article as he contemplated producing
but a profile of Mr Maudling which took in as one incident his association with Mr
Hoffman. It is clear that Mr Bambridge's approach was far more thorough and robust
than that of the plaintiff. Mr Bambridge said that he would have thought the Private
Eye comment was 'an exaggeration' of the circumstances. My impression on hearing
the evidence and my conclusion since reading it (of course with the advantage of
having heard it) is that the comment is substantially correct.

In the earlier stages of the hearing there was also emphatic complaint of the
references in Private Eye's article to the plaintiff being 'sour' and having 'bile' at
inroads into her territory by others employed by the Observer, including Mr Howard.
She denied the truth of these references but spoke pretty depreciatingly and, so it
seemed to me, with some feeling of Mr Howard in comparison with the person whom
he had replaced. When Mr Howard came to give evidence, he said that he knew
the plaintiff well and that she had stayed with him in America, but that at the
Observer she would not speak to him and he did not know why. He was not cross-
examined on this. His evidence seemed to me quite inconsistent with the far more
objective attitude on the part of the plaintiff that her words in evidence might convey
to their reader. I am satisfied that Mr Foot's statement was substantially true and
this complaint by the plaintiff, although not withdrawn, very properly ceased to
be pursued.

The plaintiff also emphasised the charge that Private Eye obtained the memorandum by theft. She said: 'I am suggesting someone employed by the Defendants
stole the document from my office.' This seems to be as clear an allegation as could
be made that an employee of Private Eye stole the document itself. But under further
cross-examination the plaintiff said: 'I don't say he took the document away but
the contents.' And when asked, 'You suggest someone employed by the Defendants
entered your office and took a copy of the memorandum?', she answered, 'Yes'
and added particulars which I need not quote.

As I have already indicated, there may be degrees of reprehensibility in unjustifiable leaks and different views may be held about them, but it is clear that the plaintiff
placed the theft, which she alleged, at the bottom of the scale as of quite a different
order from other forms of leak. But her positive assertion of theft was clearly only
one of the possible means by which the contents of the memorandum might reach
the defendants. The plaintiff alleged what she considered the worst, and that charge
was not true.

All these charges, untrue or unestablished, include serious charges. The plaintiff
acknowledged in her evidence that in her article 'I attack the veracity of Private Eye'
and that 'in this action for breach of copyright I seek to attack the honesty of the
defendants'. She persisted in this attitude throughout and did not withdraw any
charge.

(7) Scope of damages if the plaintiff obtained the copyright by the assignment

If the plaintiff's ownership of the copyright was obtained by assignment from
The Observer Ltd, then as the assignment was after the infringement, the plaintiff's
claim to additional damages would admittedly be limited to what would be recoverable by The Observer Ltd. They would thus not include any damages for personal
suffering or distress.

(8) The assessment of damages

Against the aspect of the defendants' conduct relevant to the claim for additional
damages has to be set the relevant aspects of the plaintiff's conduct. But the process
of assessment is not by the meticulous quantification of individual items, as the
damages cannot, generally at any rate, be ascertained by an accounting operation.

a They are fixed by judgment, not by calculation, and judgment of the whole is likely to produce a less unsatisfactory result.

They are a matter of impression rather than scientific or mathematical calculation. The difficulty of assessing any additional damages that might be awarded and that such assessment might reasonably vary very widely have been repeatedly recognised, as, recently by the House of Lords in *Broome v Cassell & Co Ltd*[1]. And in this case

b the assessment of damages is further complicated by considerations of law on which different views are tenable. So, in these circumstances, as the assessment is not required for my determination of the case, I shall not, in this judgment, make any investigation of damages further than is necessary to analyse the relevant evidence, which I have now done.

The overall result is that the plaintiff fails in her claim.

That is the end of the judgment, but I wish to make one concluding observation.

c It has of course been impossible to hear or decide this case without references to Mr Maudling and Mr Whitelaw. But neither has been heard in this action. So I wish to make it unmistakably clear that nothing I have said must be taken as casting the slightest reflection on either of them by implication or in any other way. It would be most unjust and unjustifiable to do so—so clearly so that I would have considered this observation more embarrassing than helpful, were it not for recent experience.

d *Judgment for the defendants.*

Solicitors: *Oswald Hickson, Collier & Co* (for the plaintiff); *Lawford & Co* (for the defendants).

Jacqueline Metcalfe Barrister.

e
Re S (F G) (mental health patient)

CHANCERY DIVISION (COURT OF PROTECTION)
UNGOED-THOMAS J
15th, 23rd NOVEMBER 1972

f *Mental health – Court of Protection – Jurisdiction – Property and affairs of patient – Patient – Person incapable of managing property or affairs – Jurisdiction only extending to person of whose incapacity a judge is satisfied – Mental Health Act 1959, ss 101, 103 (1).*

The exclusive jurisdiction of the Court of Protection over the property and affairs of a patient extends only to a person who is a patient within s 101[a] of the Mental Health Act 1959, i e a person as to whom a judge is satisfied that he is incapable,

g by reason of mental disorder, of managing and administering his property and affairs; the jurisdiction does not therefore extend to every person so incapable, but only to those of whose incapacity a judge is satisfied. Accordingly, on an application for an order under s 103 (1)[b] of the 1959 Act in respect of a person's property or affairs, there must be adduced evidence sufficient to satisfy the judge of that person's incapacity unless he is already subject to the jurisdiction of the Court of Protection (see

h p 275 a and e to g, post).

Dictum of Ungoed-Thomas J in *Re W* [1970] 2 All ER at 511 explained.

Observations on the relationship of the jurisdiction of the Court of Protection to authorise legal proceedings in the name or on behalf of a patient under s 103 (1) (h) of the 1959 Act and the rules of court providing for the appointment of a next friend or guardian ad litem (see p 276 f to j, post).

j **Notes**

For powers of the judge in relation to the property and affairs of a patient, see 29 Halsbury's Laws (3rd Edn) 573, 574, 577, 578, paras 1051, 1056.

---

1 [1972] 1 All ER 801, [1972] AC 1027
a Section 101 is set out at p 274 j, post
b Section 103 (1), so far as material, is set out at p 274 f, post

M

For the Mental Health Act 1959, ss 101, 103, see 25 Halsbury's Statutes (3rd Edn) 130, 131.

Case referred to in judgment

W, Re, [1970] 2 All ER 502; sub nom Re W (E E M) [1971] Ch 123, [1970] 3 WLR 87, Digest (Cont Vol C) 678, 723a.

Case also cited

Leather v Kirby [1965] 3 All ER 927, [1965] 1 WLR 1489, HL.

Summons

This was an application by the Official Solicitor acting as next friend on behalf of S for leave to prosecute a nullity petition on behalf of S. The summons was heard, and judgment delivered, in open court. The facts are set out in the judgment.

Lionel Swift for the Official Solicitor.

Cur adv vult

23rd November.   **UNGOED-THOMAS J** read the following judgment. This is an application by the Official Solicitor to be authorised on behalf of S to prosecute a suit for S's marriage to be declared null and void.   The Official Solicitor was requested by solicitors to S's mother to consent to becoming S's next friend in the contemplated nullity proceedings, and the Official Solicitor replied that he was willing to be next friend subject, inter alia, to his being authorised in accordance with s 103 (1) (h) of the Mental Health Act 1959 to conduct such proceedings.   Accordingly he made this application under that section.

After s 102 of the Mental Health Act 1959 has provided for the 'judge' having jurisdiction for specified purposes to exercise his jurisdiction in accordance with specified considerations, s 103 (1) provides that the judge—

> 'may for those purposes make orders or give directions or authorities for [inter alia] (h) the conduct of legal proceedings in the name of the patient or on his behalf, so however that an order, direction or authority to present a petition in the name or on behalf of the patient for divorce or nullity of marriage, for presumption of death and dissolution of marriage, or for judicial separation shall be made or given only by the Lord Chancellor or a nominated judge . . .'

So this application comes before me as a nominated judge. These sections come within Part VIII of the Act which is the Part that provides for and is headed 'Management of Property and Affairs of Patients'.

Before this application the Court of Protection had in no way been involved with S or his affairs. Somebody, however, although not counsel, seems to have feared that my observations in Re W[1] might extend to every person 'incapable, by reason of mental disorder, of managing and administering his property and affairs'. My observations, so far as material, are summarised in my conclusion[2], that the Court of Protection 'has exclusive jurisdiction over all the property and all the affairs of the patient in all their aspects; but not to the management or care of the patient's person'.

Section 101 defines the patient with whom the Court of Protection is concerned as follows:

> 'The functions of the judge under this Part of this Act shall be exercisable where, after considering medical evidence, he is satisfied that a person is incapable, by reason of mental disorder, of managing and administering his property and affairs; and a person as to whom the judge is so satisfied is in this Part of this Act referred to as a patient.'

1   [1970] 2 All ER 502, [1971] Ch 123
2   [1970] 2 All ER at 511, [1971] Ch at 143

'Patient' in the 1959 Act is thus not a person who is merely 'incapable by reason of mental disorder of administering his property and affairs' but a person as to whom a judge, after considering medical evidence, is satisfied that he is so incapable. 'The judge' is defined in s 100 which, so far as material, reads:

'(1) The Lord Chancellor shall from time to time nominate one or more judges of the Supreme Court (hereinafter referred to as "nominated judges") to act for the purposes of this Part of this Act.

'(2) There shall continue to be an office of the Supreme Court, called the Court of Protection, for the protection and management, as provided by this Part of this Act, of the property of persons under disability; and there shall be a Master and a Deputy Master of the Court of Protection appointed by the Lord Chancellor.

'(3) The Lord Chancellor may nominate other officers of the Court of Protection to act for the purposes of this Part of this Act.

'(4) The functions expressed to be conferred by this Part of this Act on the judge shall be exercisable by the Lord Chancellor or by any nominated judge, and shall also be exercisable by the Master or Deputy Master of the Court of Protection or by any officer nominated under the foregoing subsection, but [and then follow some restrictions which I need not quote] and references in this Part of this Act to the judge shall be construed accordingly.'

Thus the definition does not extend to any judges or officials of any court other than those associated with the Court of Protection and mentioned in the section.

In the passage in *Re W*[1] leading up to the conclusion which I have mentioned, I quoted from the s 101 definition of 'patient' the requirement of the judge's satisfaction of incapacity; and, in accordance with the facts in that case, that the person about whom the Court was concerned was a 'patient' within the 1959 Act, I emphasised[2] that:

'It is essential to bear in mind throughout that, although the patient was discharged from a mental hospital . . . she remained subject to the statutory protection of the Court of Protection.'

I am satisfied, after considering the medical evidence before me, that S is a person incapable by reason of mental disorder of managing and administering his property and affairs. Thus now, for the first time, S becomes a patient within the definition of the Act. And, as s 101 provides that 'The functions of the judge under this Part of this Act shall be exercisable', when a 'judge' is so satisfied, S, also for the first time, becomes a person subject to the jurisdiction of a 'judge' as defined by s 100 (4), i e to the jurisdiction, in less exact language, of the Court of Protection.

So much for the meaning of my conclusion in *Re W*[1] and its application to S. However, in the course of the application the relationship of the jurisdiction of the Court of Protection to order and give directions for or authorise legal proceedings in the name or on behalf of the patient on the one hand, and the rules of court providing for the appointment of a next friend or guardian ad litem on the other hand, have been considered. The rules considered were the Matrimonial Causes Rules 1971[3], the Rules of the Supreme Court and the County Court Rules.

The Matrimonial Causes Rules 1971, r 105 (1) provides, so far as immediately material:

'In this rule—"patient" means a person who, by reason of mental disorder within the meaning of the Mental Health Act 1959, is incapable of managing and

---

1   [1970] 2 All ER 502, [1971] Ch 123
2   [1970] 2 All ER at 510, [1971] Ch at 142
3   SI 1971 No 953

administering his property and affairs; "person under disability" means a person who is a minor or a patient . . .'

RSC Ord 80, r 1, repeats the definitions just quoted from the Matrimonial Causes Rules 1971 with a couple of immaterial verbal alterations, and the County Court Rules simply refer in wide terms to persons 'under disability'.

Thus, 'patient' in the Matrimonial Causes Rules 1971, r 105 (1), and RSC Ord 80, r 1, does not have the same meaning as 'patient' in s 101 of the Mental Health Act 1959, and therefore in Part VIII of the 1959 Act. The reference in r 105 (1) of the 1971 rules and RSC Ord 80, r 1, to the 1959 Act is only for the purpose of ascertaining the meaning of mental disorder, whose definition in the 1959 Act appears in s 4 as 'mental illness, arrested or incomplete development of mind, psychopathic disorder, and any other disorder or disability of mind'. So the difference between the definition of 'patient' in these rules and in the 1959 Act is that the rules merely require such incapacity, whereas the 1959 Act also requires that the Court of Protection judge, as defined by the Act, after considering medical evidence, is satisfied of such incapacity. The definition in the rules is thus wider than in the 1959 Act; it includes patients within the meaning in the 1959 Act, but also others not within that meaning.

The Matrimonial Causes Rules 1971 and the Rules of the Supreme Court then provide for the appointment of next friend and guardian ad litem for 'persons under disability', meaning minors or infants and 'patients' within the wider meaning of the rules. The County Court Rules provide for such appointment simply for 'persons under disability'. Insofar as such 'patients' and 'persons under disability' are not within the narrower meaning of 'patient' in the Mental Health Act 1959, the functions of the judge under Part VIII of that Act are not exercisable and the Court of Protection is not involved (unless and until, of course, they are brought within that definition by the Court of Protection judge being satisfied as to their incapacity as specified in s 101 of the 1959 Act).

Insofar as 'patient' or 'person under disability' within the meaning of the rules applies to patients within the meaning of the 1959 Act, the rules make provision for the appointment as next friend or guardian ad litem of the person authorised under s 103 of the Mental Health Act 1959 to conduct the proceedings for the patient. It is arguable however that difficulties might arise because the Court of Protection might, under s 103, make orders or give directions or authorities for the conduct of legal proceedings by a person for a patient; and the court in which those proceedings take place might, under its rules and as master of its own procedure, recognise or appoint some other person to be next friend or guardian ad litem. Such suggested difficulties might arise in accordance with this argument, whether or not the jurisdiction entrusted to the Court of Protection with regard to a patient within the meaning of the 1959 Act be exclusive or not. I am not satisfied that there is on construction any discrepancy between the provisions of the 1959 Act and the rules. And it has to be borne in mind that, on construction and on practical application, the Court of Protection would be standing in the place of the patient to make good the patient's incapacity, whereas the court, the forum of the litigation, would be concerned with its own procedure; and the objects of both courts would be to ensure the proper and effective conduct of the litigation. So I would not anticipate any material difficulty arising from the co-existence of s 103 (1) (h) of the 1959 Act (providing for the Court of Protection to make such orders and give such directions and authorities as it thinks fit for the conduct of legal proceedings in the interests of the patient) on the one hand, and of the rules (providing for the appointment of a next friend or guardian ad litem) on the other hand.

Order that the Official Solicitor shall have authority for and on behalf of the patient to prosecute a nullity petition.

Solicitor: *Official Solicitor.*

Jacqueline Metcalfe   Barrister.

a

Sargent (Inspector of Taxes) v Eayrs

CHANCERY DIVISION
GOFF J
20th NOVEMBER 1972

b *Income tax – Trade – Farming – All farming to be treated as one trade – Farming operations outside United Kingdom – Taxpayer farming in United Kingdom – Visit to Australia with a view to buying a farm and emigrating – Expenses of visit – Expenses attributable to taxpayer's farming activities – Whether incurred for the purposes of trade within United Kingdom – Income Tax Act 1952, ss 124 (1), 152.*

Income tax – Deduction in computing profits – Capital expenditure – Expenditure for purpose
c *of initiating or extending a business – Expenditure abortive – Taxpayer a farmer – Visit to Australia with a view to buying a farm and emigrating – Taxpayer deciding not to emigrate – Expenses of visit – Whether capital or revenue in nature.*

The taxpayer carried on a farming business in the United Kingdom. On an assessment made on him under Case I of Sch D, for the year 1969-70, in respect of his farming
d profits, he claimed as a deduction the sum of £1,093, representing the expenses which he had incurred in visiting Australia to investigate farming conditions with a view to emigrating and buying a farm there. He did not in fact emigrate as he found the cost of property prohibitive. The taxpayer contended that the expenses were deductible as expenses of the carrying on of his trade of farming within s 124 (1)*ᵃ* of the Income Tax Act 1952 since they had been incurred for an extension of his farming activity and, under s 152*ᵇ* of the 1952 Act, all the farming carried on by him
e was to be treated as one trade.

Held – The taxpayer was not entitled to deduct the expenses in question for the following reasons—
(i) s 152 was to be treated as referring only to farming in the United Kingdom; its purpose was to pick up all the farming operations in the United Kingdom where
f there were more than one; accordingly the expenses could not be allowed, for they had not been wholly and exclusively laid out or expended for the purposes of the taxpayer's trade within the United Kingdom (see p 281 a b and e, post).
(ii) alternatively the expenditure was not revenue in character, but of a capital nature, being expenditure incurred for the purpose of initiating or extending a business; the fact that it had proved abortive did not affect the nature of the expendi-
g ture (see p 281 g and p 282 e, post); *British Insulated and Helsby Cables Ltd v Atherton* [1925] All ER Rep 623 and *Inland Revenue Comrs v Granite City Steamship Co Ltd* 1927 SC 705 followed.

Notes
For the assessment of farming as a trade, see 20 Halsbury's Laws (3rd Edn) 230,
h para 419.
For capital expenditure, see ibid, 161-164, paras 280, 281.
For the Income Tax Act 1952, ss 124 and 152, see 31 Halsbury's Statutes (2nd Edn) 121, 147.
For 1970-71 and subsequent years of assessment, ss 124 and 152 of the 1952 Act have been replaced by s 110 of the Income and Corporation Taxes Act 1970.

j **Cases referred to in judgment**
British Insulated and Helsby Cables Ltd v Atherton [1926] AC 205, 10 Tax Cas 155, [1925] All ER Rep 623, 95 LJKB 336, 134 LT 289, HL, 28 (1) Digest (Reissue) 211, 627.

---

a Section 124 (1), so far as material, is set out at p 280 h, post
b Section 152, so far as material, is set out at p 280 j, post

Hancock v General Reversionary & Investment Co Ltd [1919] 1 KB 25, 7 Tax Cas 358, 88
LJKB 248, 119 LT 737, 28 (1) Digest (Reissue) 207, *619.*

Inland Revenue Comrs v Granite City Steamship Co Ltd 1927 SC 705, 13 Tax Cas 1, 28
(1) Digest (Reissue) 202 *658.

Lothian Chemical Co Ltd v Rogers, Lothian Chemical Co Ltd v Inland Revenue Comrs (1926)
11 Tax Cas 508, 28 (1) Digest (Reissue) 202, *657.

Smith v Incorporated Council of Law Reporting for England and Wales [1914] 3 KB 674,
6 Tax Cas 477, 83 LJKB 1721, 111 LT 848, 28 (1) Digest (Reissue) 211, *624.*

Vallambrosa Rubber Co Ltd v Farmer 1910 SC 519, 5 Tax Cas 529, 28 (1) Digest (Reissue)
165, *506.

Case stated

The Commissioners for the General Purposes of Income Tax for the division of
Ford in the county of Gloucester stated a case for the opinion of the High Court
under s 56 of the Taxes Management Act 1970.

1. At a meeting of the commissioners held on 6th May 1971, Group Captain
Douglas Joyce Eayrs ('the taxpayer') appealed against an assessment made on him
under Case I of Sch D for the income tax year 1969-70 in the sum of £3,250, the source
of the income being described as 'Farming'.

2. The point at issue was whether foreign travelling expenses of £1,093 incurred
by the taxpayer during the year ended 31st March 1969 were allowable in computing
the farming profit assessable for the year 1969-70. The expenditure at issue represented the cost of a visit to Western Australia to investigate farming conditions
with a view to emigration and buying a farm there.

3. On the basis of the taxpayer's contention that the expenditure was wholly
allowable, the assessment should be reduced to £1,762, less capital allowances on
plant and machinery of £660, with relief of £236 under s 68 of the Capital Allowances
Act 1968.

4. On the basis of the Crown's contention that the expenditure was wholly disallowable, the assessment should be reduced to £2,855, less capital allowances on
plant and machinery of £660 with relief, under s 68 of the Capital Allowances Act
1968, of £236.

5. The taxpayer gave evidence before the commissioners.

6. The following facts were admitted or proved: (i) The taxpayer farmed land
near Winchcombe, Gloucestershire. (ii) He travelled some 5,000 miles in Australia
in three weeks for the purpose of investigating farming conditions, methods and
technique there, with a possible view to emigrating to that country to carry on
his farming activities. With that in mind he had consulted financial advisers about
raising the necessary capital should the trip lead to emigration to Australia. However,
he found the cost of property prohibitive. (iii) In general he accepted that the visit
had little of value to offer as far as farming in the United Kingdom was concerned
and the main purpose of the visit was to ascertain whether conditions and prices
in Australia were such that emigration would be attractive. (iv) The cost of such
journey (a package deal journey) was £1,093. (v) That cost included the expenses
incurred by both the taxpayer and his wife, who accompanied him on the journey
so that she might have an idea of conditions in Australia from the point of view
of moving home and taking up residence there.

[Paragraph 7 listed the documents produced and admitted before the
commissioners.]

8. Mr C D Anderson FCA, the taxpayer's accountant, referred the commissioners
to s 137 (a) of the Income Tax Act 1952 as repeated in s 130 (a) of the Income and
Corporation Taxes Act 1970 and s 152 of the 1952 Act, pointing out that it did not
mention the United Kingdom only (as repeated in s 110 (2) of the 1970 Act).

9. The taxpayer's accountant stated that to the taxpayer's knowledge allowances
had been made to three other applicants in similar circumstances, but he was

a unable to tell the commissioners how many similar applications had been refused.

10. The Crown contended: (i) that neither the whole nor any part of the expenses in question was wholly and exclusively laid out or expended for the purposes of the taxpayer's trade; (ii) that if the taxpayer farmed land outside the United Kingdom that could not either form part of or be regarded as a continuance of the trade carried on by him in the United Kingdom but would constitute a separate trade in respect

b of which the taxpayer (if still resident) would only be assessable to United Kingdom tax on any part of the profits thereof which was remitted to the United Kingdom.

[Paragraph 11 referred to a case[1] cited to the commissioners.]

12. After considering the matter very carefully, the commissioners came to the conclusion that the portion of the expenditure of £1,093 which related to the taxpayer should be allowable as an extension of farming activity but that the portion of the

c expenditure which related to the taxpayer's wife should be disallowable. The matter was adjourned until 26th August 1971.

13. At a further meeting of the commissioners held on 26th August 1971, on the decision of the commissioners that the expenses of the taxpayer incurred on his visit to Australia for the purpose of viewing farms and farming techniques in that country should be allowed but not the expenses relating to the taxpayer's wife,

d the taxpayer's accountant submitted the following figures:

	£	£
Profit		2,308
Less:		
Capital allowances	660	
Section 68 allowance	236	896
Balance		1,412

14. The Crown agreed the figures on the basis of the commissioners' findings on 6th May 1971.

f 15. The commissioners then formally confirmed the net figure as calculated above, £1,412.

16. Immediately after the determination of the appeal, the Crown declared dissatisfaction therewith as being erroneous in point of law and in due course required the commissioners to state a case for the opinion of the High Court.

On 24th October 1972 the Crown gave notice that if, at the hearing of the case

g stated, it was held that the taxpayer's farming activities (if any) in Australia formed part of his trade of farming assessable to income tax under Case I of Sch D, then the Crown would contend that the expenditure in question was not deductible in computing the taxable profits of the trade on the ground that the expenditure was of a capital nature, or alternatively, was precluded from being deducted by virtue of s 137 (*f*) of the 1952 Act.

h Patrick Medd for the Crown.
The taxpayer appeared in person.

GOFF J. This is an appeal by the Crown against a decision of the Commissioners for the General Purposes of Income Tax for the division of Ford in the county of

j Gloucester. The taxpayer, who carries on a farming business in this country, was assessed to income tax on the profits, and he claimed as a deduction £1,093 which, as the case finds, 'represented the cost of a visit to Western Australia to investigate farming conditions with a view to emigration and buying a farm there'. It was further found that the cost—

---

1 *Strong & Co of Romsey Ltd v Woodifield* [1906] AC 448, 5 Tax Cas 215

'included the expenses incurred by both the [taxpayer] and his wife, who
accompanied him on the journey so that she might have an idea of conditions
in Australia from the point of view of moving home and taking up residence
there.'

The commissioners decided that, insofar as the expenditure related to the wife,
it was not allowable, but that, insofar as it was attributable to the taxpayer, it ought
to be allowed as, so they found, 'an extension of farming activity'. The Crown submit that no part should be allowed, and they put it in this way. They say that, for
the purposes of assessment to income tax, farming is a trade within the United Kingdom and a person who carries on trade in the United Kingdom is assessable to tax
on the profits, but that if profits arise from farming activities outside the United
Kingdom the matter is quite different and the assessment falls to be made under
Case V of Sch B on income from foreign possessions, and that tax is levied only on
income remitted to this country.

Prior to 1941, if a person occupied land for farming he could be assessed under
Sch B, not on profits but on value, and the farming was not regarded as a trade.
That was altered by s 10 (1) of the Finance Act 1941, which provided:

'. . . farming and market gardening shall be treated as trades for the purposes
of income tax and accordingly—(a) the profits or gains thereof shall be charged
under Case I of Schedule D; and (b) income tax shall not be charged under
Schedule B in respect of the occupation of any farm land or market garden
land . . .'

That subsection said nothing about territoriality, but sub-s (2) provided:

'For the purposes of this and the next succeeding section the following expressions have the meanings hereby respectively assigned to them, that is to
say, . . . "farm land" means land wholly or mainly occupied for the purposes
of husbandry, not being market garden land, and includes the farm house and
farm buildings, if any, and "farming" shall be construed accordingly; "land"
means land in the United Kingdom . . .'

So they say that 'land' means land in the United Kingdom; 'farm land' means land
in the United Kingdom; and 'farming', having to be construed accordingly, means
farming on land in the United Kingdom.

That conclusion on the 1941 Act is strengthened by the reference in sub-s (3) to
'the parishes in which any part of his or their farm land is situated'. That sub-s (3)
also provided: 'All the farming carried on by any particular person or partnership
or body of persons shall be treated as one trade'. It is, I think, important, having
regard to the taxpayer's argument, to observe that in that Act the subsection which
makes all the farming one trade is the subsection which refers to 'the profits or gains
thereof in any of the parishes in which any part of his or their farm land is situated'.

Those sections were replaced by sections in the 1952 Act, which are the sections
that govern this appeal. They are, in substance, the same, but in the 1952 Act they
are to be found in two separate sections. Section 124 (1) provides: 'All farming and
market gardening in the United Kingdom shall be treated as the carrying on of a
trade or, as the case may be, of a part of a trade', so that in the 1952 Act that provision specifically limits the subject-matter to farming in the United Kingdom. The
provision about one trade is to be found in s 152, which provides: 'All the farming
carried on byany particular person or partnership or body of persons shall be treated
as one trade'.

In his argument the taxpayer referred to the Income and Corporation Taxes Act
1970, but the relevant Act for the purposes of this appeal is the 1952 Act. However,
nothing turns on that, because the provisions are the same. His argument is that
s 152, the 'one trade' section, says nothing about the United Kingdom; and, therefore,

a if you have farming in the United Kingdom that is a trade under s 124, and if you have farming outside the United Kingdom as well that is part of the United Kingdom trade because s 152 makes it so and says nothing to limit the operation of that section to the United Kingdom. I cannot accept that construction. I think that, as a matter of construing the words in their context, and particularly when one reviews the history, as I have done, one must treat s 152 as referring to farming in the United Kingdom. It is merely a section which picks up all the farming operations where *b* there are more than one; not a section which widens the ambit of s 124.

If that be the right conclusion, as in my judgment it is, then it follows from the findings in the case stated that the allowance, even as restricted to the taxpayer himself, cannot be accepted, because there is the finding in para 6 (iii) of the case stated as follows:

c   'In general he [that is, the taxpayer] accepted that he found that the visit had little of value to offer as far as farming in the United Kingdom was concerned and the main purpose of the visit was to ascertain whether conditions and prices in Australia were such that emigration would be attractive.'

That is confirmed and strengthened by a letter from estate agents who organised *d* the tour which says this:

'We confirm that [the taxpayer] attended a Farm Inspection Tour arranged by this firm of properties for sale in Western Australia in the Autumn of 1968 and that the activities of this tour were confined solely to the inspection of properties for sale, meeting financial and agricultural advisers and others *e* concerned with the possible resettling of English farmers in Western Australia.'

If and so far as the commissioners found that the expenditure was wholly and exclusively laid out or expended for the purposes of the taxpayer's trade, they could not, in my judgment, have so found properly directing themselves as to the law, because if the construction I have put on the sections be right it is impossible, in the *f* face of their own findings, to reach the conclusion that this expenditure was wholly and exclusively laid out or expended for the purposes of the taxpayer's trade, that being ex hypothesi his trade in the United Kingdom.

That is sufficient to entitle the Crown to judgment on this appeal, but by a notice that they would support their appeal on a ground not raised before the commissioners they take an alternative point; that is, that even if the taxpayer be right in his contention that by virtue of s 152 of the 1952 Act the whole farming operation *g* must be looked at, as seems to be envisaged by the finding that 'the portion of the expenditure of £1,093. which related to the [taxpayer] should be allowable as an extension of farming activity', still the expenditure was not revenue in character but of a capital nature, being expenditure for the purpose of setting up a new or extended business. The taxpayer really had no answer to that way of putting the *h* matter, and in my judgment, even if the Crown were wrong (which, as I have said, in my view they are not) on the first ground, they would be entitled to succeed on the alternative ground.

The authorities which have been cited to me, although not by any means identical on the facts, establish the principle governing this case quite clearly. Thus, Viscount Cave LC, in *British Insulated and Helsby Cables Ltd v Atherton*[1], said:

j   'Now, in *Vallambrosa Rubber Co. v. Farmer*[2] Lord Dunedin, as Lord President of the Court of Session, expressed the opinion that "in a rough way" it was "not a bad criterion of what is capital expenditure—as against what is income

---

1 [1926] AC 205 at 213, 10 Tax Cas 188 at 192
2 1910 SC 519 at 525, 5 Tax Cas 529 at 536

expenditure—to say that capital expenditure is a thing that is going to be spent once and for all, and income expenditure is a thing that is going to recur every year''; and no doubt this is often a material consideration. But the criterion suggested is not, and was obviously not intended by Lord Dunedin to be, a decisive one in every case; for it is easy to imagine many cases in which a payment, though made "once and for all," would be properly chargeable against the receipts for the year. Instances of such payments may be found in the gratuity of 1500*l*. paid to a reporter on his retirement, which was the subject of the decision in *Smith* v. *Incorporated Council of Law Reporting for England and Wales*[1], and in the expenditure of 499*l*. in the purchase of an annuity for the benefit of an actuary who had retired, which, in *Hancock* v. *General Reversionary and Investment Co.*[2], was allowed, and I think rightly allowed, to be deducted from profits.'

Now comes the statement of principle[3]:

'But when an expenditure is made, not only once and for all, but with a view to bringing into existence an asset or an advantage for the enduring benefit of a trade, I think that there is very good reason (in the absence of special circumstances leading to an opposite conclusion) for treating such an expenditure as properly attributable not to revenue but to capital.'

In *Inland Revenue Comrs v Granite City Steamship Co Ltd*[4], Lord Sands said this[5]:

'Broadly speaking, outlay is deemed to be capital when it is made for the initiation of a business, for extension of a business, or for a substantial replacement of equipment.'

What the taxpayer did in this case appears to me, applying the principles so laid down, to have been something in which he incurred not revenue but capital expenditure. In the result, the business was not extended, because he found prices in Australia prohibitive, and therefore the expenditure was abortive. But *Lothian Chemical Co Ltd v Rogers*[6] shows, as one would expect, that that is an irrelevant consideration. The expenditure does not change its nature according to whether it be successful or unsuccessful.

Accordingly, the new point is sound in law also; and, whichever way one looks at it, this appeal succeeds.

Appeal allowed.

Solicitors: Solicitor of Inland Revenue.

Rengan Krishnan Esq   Barrister.

---

1   [1914] 3 KB 674
2   [1919] 1 KB 25
3   [1926] AC at 213, 214, 10 Tax Cas at 192, 193
4   1927 SC 705, 13 Tax Cas 1
5   1927 SC at 709, 710, 13 Tax Cas at 14
6   (1926) 11 Tax Cas 508

a   # Westwood and another v The Post Office

COURT OF APPEAL, CRIMINAL DIVISION
DAVIES, KARMINSKI AND LAWTON LJJ
2nd, 3rd, 23rd NOVEMBER 1972

b   *Master and servant – Liability of master – Offices, shops and railway premises – Safety of employees – Breach of statutory duty – Scope of statutory protection – Premises on which employee employed to work – Employee forbidden to enter room in building in which employed to work – Danger of injury from moving machinery in room – Room containing insecure trapdoor – Employer in breach of statutory duty in respect of trapdoor – Employee trespassing in room – Employee fatally injured by falling through trapdoor – Whether employer liable for breach of statutory duty – Offices, Shops and Railway Premises Act 1963,*
c   *s 16.*

The deceased was employed by the Post Office at a telephone exchange housed in a three-storeyed building with a flat roof. At one end of the roof was a lift motor room which contained the winding motor and apparatus for the lift serving the building. The door to that room was normally kept locked and the key kept behind
d   a conduit pipe near the door. There was a legend on the door which read: 'NOTICE Only the authorised attendant is permitted to enter.' The deceased was not the authorised attendant. Workmen were in the habit of going on to the roof of the building for short breaks. The Post Office knew of and accepted that practice. It was possible to go on to the roof by going through the lift motor room and climbing out of a casement window. There was a trapdoor in the floor of the lift motor room
e   which opened on to a landing below. The deceased went on to the roof through the lift motor room and whilst returning fell through the trapdoor and was fatally injured. In an action by the administrators of the deceased's estate the trial judge found that the Post Office knew and accepted that the lift motor room was being used by employees to gain access to the roof and, in consequence, held that the deceased was not, at the time of the accident, a trespasser. He also held that the
f   defendants were in breach of s 16[a] of the Offices, Shops and Railway Premises Act 1963 in that the trapdoor was not of sound construction. He therefore awarded damages against the Post Office. On appeal, it was contended by the plaintiffs that, even if the deceased was a trespasser at the material time, the Post Office were liable for breach of s 16 of the 1963 Act.

g   **Held** – The appeal would be allowed for the following reasons—
      (i) the evidence did not establish that the Post Office knew that workmen used the lift motor room to get on to the roof; accordingly by going on to a part of the premises which was forbidden to him, the deceased had become a trespasser (see p 286 g and h, post); *Hillen and Pettigrew v ICI (Alkali) Ltd* [1935] All ER Rep 555 applied;
      (ii) the plaintiffs could not rely on the 1963 Act because it only provided protection
h   for persons employed to work on the premises in question; although the deceased had been employed to work in the telephone exchange he had, to his knowledge, not been employed to work in the lift motor room since it had been put out of bounds to him; as a trespasser there he could not claim the protection of the 1963 Act (see p 288 g to p 289 a, post); *Napieralski v Curtis (Contractors) Ltd* [1959] 2 All ER 426 applied; *Uddin v Associated Portland Cement Manufacturers Ltd* [1965] 2 All ER 213 distinguished;
j   (iii) in any event the award of damages could not stand because the deceased had suffered injury as the result partly of his own 'fault', within the meaning of s 4[b] of

---

a   Section 16, as far as material, provides: '(1) All floors . . . comprised in premises to which this Act applies shall be of sound construction and properly maintained . . .'

b   Section 4, so far as material, provides: '. . . "fault" means negligence, breach of statutory duty or other act or omission which gives rise to a liability in tort or would, apart from this Act, give rise to the defence of contributory negligence.'

the Law Reform (Contributory Negligence) Act 1945, (i) by entering the lift motor
room as a trespasser, and (ii) by disregarding the express exclusion which should have   *a*
warned him of sources of danger in those premises, although the danger was not
of the kind he met (see p 289 b to d, post).

Notes

For the duty of employers to ensure that floors, passages and stairs are of sound
construction, see Supplement to 38 Halsbury's Laws (3rd Edn) para 679B, 12.   *b*

For an occupier's duty to trespassers, see 28 Halsbury's Laws (3rd Edn) 53, 54,
para 49, and for cases on the subject, see 36 Digest (Repl) 70, 71, *376-382*.

For the Offices, Shops and Railway Premises Act 1963, s 16, see 13 Halsbury's
Statutes (3rd Edn) 601.

For the Law Reform (Contributory Negligence) Act 1945, s 4, see 23 Halsbury's
Statutes (3rd Edn) 791.   *c*

Cases referred to in judgment

Davies v Swan Motor Co (Swansea) Ltd [1949] 1 All ER 620, [1949] 2 KB 291, CA, 36
    Digest (Repl) 171, *921*.
Herrington v British Railways Board [1972] 1 All ER 749, [1972] AC 877, [1972] 2 WLR
    537, HL.   *d*
Hillen and Pettigrew v ICI (Alkali) Ltd [1936] AC 65, [1935] All ER Rep 555, 104 LJKB 473,
    153 LT 403, HL, 36 Digest (Repl) 71, *377*.
Jones v Livox Quarries Ltd [1952] 2 QB 608, [1952] 1 TLR 1377, CA, 36 Digest (Repl) 185,
    996.
Napieralski v Curtis (Contractors) Ltd [1959] 2 All ER 426, [1959] 1 WLR 835, Digest
    (Cont Vol A) 584, *179a*.   *e*
Uddin v Associated Portland Cement Manufacturers Ltd [1965] 2 All ER 213, [1965] 2
    QB 582, [1965] 2 WLR 1183, CA, Digest (Cont Vol B) 301, *234a*.

Cases also cited

Allen v Aeroplane & Motor Aluminium Castings Ltd [1965] 3 All ER 377, [1965] 1 WLR
    1244, CA.
Leach v Standard Telephones & Cables Ltd [1966] 2 All ER 523, [1966] 1 WLR 1392.   *f*
Stevens v Woodward (1881) 6 QBD 318, DC.

Appeal

The plaintiffs, Hazel Mary Westwood and Roy Albert Batson (suing as administrators
of the estate of Norman Brian Westwood, deceased) brought an action for damages
against the deceased's employers, the Post Office, under the provisions of the Fatal   *g*
Accidents Acts 1846 to 1959 and the Law Reform (Miscellaneous Provisions) Act 1934.
On 24th March 1972 O'Connor J held the Post Office liable and entered judgment
for the plaintiffs in the agreed sum of £12,000. The Post Office appealed. The facts
are set out in the judgment of Lawton LJ.

Stephen Brown QC and *M A B Burke-Gaffney* for the Post Office.
C Fawcett QC and *G Rodway* for the plaintiffs.   *h*

Cur adv vult

LAWTON LJ read the following judgment at the invitation of Karminski LJ.
This is an appeal by the Post Office, who were the defendants at the trial, from
the judgment and order of O'Connor J, whereby he adjudged that the plaintiffs,   *j*
suing as the administrators of the estate of Norman Brian Westwood, deceased,
were entitled to an order for the payment by the Post Office of £12,000 agreed
damages together with £1,575 interest thereon. The action had been brought by
the plaintiffs under the provisions of the Fatal Accidents Acts 1846 to 1959, and the
Law Reform (Miscellaneous Provisions) Act 1934, and arose out of Mr Westwood's

death following an accident which he sustained at the Hackney telephone exchange
where he was employed by the Post Office as a technician.

The Post Office submitted before this court that, however much they may have
been to blame for the physical condition which was the immediate cause of the
accident, they were not liable to pay the plaintiffs damages because when the accident
happened the deceased was a trespasser. This submission has called for a detailed
examination of the evidence on which the trial judge had found that the deceased
had not been a trespasser. The Post Office conceded that if this finding was right,
the appeal failed. The plaintiffs' reply, broadly stated, was this: even if the trial
judge was wrong in adjudging that the deceased was not a trespasser, the plaintiffs
were entitled to the damages awarded because, first, the evidence established a
breach of statutory duty by the Post Office under the provisions of s 16 of the Offices,
Shops and Railway Premises Act 1963; secondly, that the deceased, being a person
employed to work in the telephone exchange, was one of the class of persons entitled
to the benefit of that Act; thirdly, that the breach of statutory duty was the
effective cause of the deceased's death; fourthly, that no deduction should be made
from the damages because the deceased's alleged trespass was not to be equated
with fault under the Law Reform (Contributory Negligence) Act 1945; and, fifthly,
that what he had done did not amount to contributory negligence for the purposes
of that Act.

When first made these submissions were startling; it seemed an odd kind of justice
which would require an occupier of premises to pay damages either in full or in a
reduced amount to an employee who was injured by going to a part of the premises
where he had no business to be and where he had been told in plain terms (as the
deceased had been) not to go. Counsel's lucid development of the plaintiffs' submissions soon revealed, however, that the problem presented by the appeal was a
complex one which was not covered by any authority directly in point.

Was the deceased trespassing when he sustained the accident which cause his death?
The Hackney telephone exchange was a three-storeyed building with a flat roof.
Standing proud of this roof at opposite ends were two structures containing
machinery. One was the fan room, with which this case is not concerned; the other
was the lift motor room, where the accident happened. This room contained the
winding motor and apparatus for the lift which served the building. When the lift
was working, the winding machinery would be in motion and whilst it was it could
be a source of danger to anyone who got too close to it. Probably because of this
possibility of danger, together, of course, with the need to discourage unauthorised
and unskilled interference with the machinery, the door to the lift motor room was
normally kept locked. On the outside of the door was a large, clear notice in these
terms: 'NOTICE Only the authorised attendant is permitted to enter'. One of the
agreed photographs showed the position of this notice on the outside of the door.
In my judgment, this notice would be understood by any intelligent person working
at the telephone exchange who knew what the room contained to mean that he was
to keep out because of some danger to be found therein. The deceased was intelligent
and he knew that the room contained winding machinery. The 'authorised attendant'
to whom the notice referred was one of the Post Office's maintenance staff who at
regular intervals greased and oiled the winding machinery and, as and when the
need arose, repaired it. He came from an engineering depot at the Walthamstow
telephone exchange. After each visit he normally locked the door and left the key
tucked behind an electric conduit pipe near the door.

For the convenience of those engaged on maintenance work, the floor of the
lift motor room had a trapdoor which opened on to a landing below; the object was,
no doubt, to enable heavy pieces of equipment to be hauled up rather than carried up.
The trial judge found that this trap door was not of sound construction. That finding
has not been challenged. One further descriptive fact about the lift motor room must
be stated. It had a casement window which opened on to the flat roof.

Access to the flat roof was by means of two staircases at opposite ends of the *a* premises. At the top of each staircase there were two doors: one led directly on to the roof, the other to the machinery rooms, which stood proud of the flat roof. The door giving access to the flat roof at the fan room end of the premises was normally kept unlocked; the similar door at the other end was sometimes locked and sometimes unlocked. The key to this door was normally kept in the supervisor's office. When the door was locked it was physically possible to get on to the flat *b* roof from the top of that staircase by unlocking the door of the lift motor room with the key left behind the electric conduit, passing round the winding machinery and climbing through the casement window.

The fatal accident to the deceased occurred at about 11 a m on 7th November 1969. Long before that date it had become the practice for some of the technicians to go on to the flat roof from time to time for a few minutes' break from work. This practice was known to, and accepted by, those in authority at the telephone *c* exchange. Shortly before 11 a m on 7th November 1969 at least five technicians went on to the flat roof for a break. Two got there by way of the staircase where the fan room was. The door at the top of that staircase was in its usual condition of being unlocked. The others—and the deceased was one of them—used the staircase by the lift motor room. When they got to the top they found the door leading on to the roof was locked but the door leading into the lift motor room was ajar. They all *d* entered the lift motor room and got out on to the roof through the casement window. After a few minutes on the roof about four of the men—and again the deceased was one of them—started to return to their work by passing through the lift motor room. Whilst the deceased was doing so he trod on the trapdoor; it gave way beneath him. He fell on to the landing below, whereby he sustained severe injuries *e* from which he died a fortnight later.

The trial judge made the following finding about the deceased's presence in the lift motor room: 'I have come to the conclusion', he said, 'that he was making a use of an unauthorised but accepted means of access to the roof. I hold that he was not a trespasser.' Earlier in his judgment, when reviewing the evidence, he said: 'I am also satisfied that the management in fact knew that it [the lift motor room] was being so used, and as nobody could see any harm in it a blind eye was turned to *f* it.'

Before this court the Post Office have submitted that there was no evidence to support the finding that the lift motor room was an accepted route. We were invited to look at all the evidence on this point and we have done so. [His Lordship reviewed the evidence and continued:] What the evidence, in my judgment, did establish was that the deceased had gone into a part of the premises which was forbidden to *g* him. This means that he was a trespasser there, and the trial judge should have so found. It is right to say that counsel for the plaintiffs, who did not appear for them in the court below, did not in the course of his powerful and sustained argument really contend that he could support the judge's finding that the means of access adopted by the deceased was known to and accepted by the management.

What consequences follow in law? Counsel for the defendants submitted that the *h* deceased, as a trespasser, went into the lift motor room at his own risk and the plaintiffs cannot base a claim on the fact that the trapdoor was unsafe. I agree that this is the position at common law. Counsel for the plaintiffs argued that the harshness of the common law rule had been mitigated in some measure by the decision of the House of Lords in *Herrington v British Railways Board*[1] in a way which would benefit the plaintiffs. The basis for his argument was the speech of Lord Reid[2], namely: *i*

'So the question whether an occupier is liable in respect of an accident to a trespasser on his land would depend on whether a conscientious humane man

---

1　[1972] 1 All ER 749, [1972] AC 877
2　[1972] 1 All ER at 758, [1972] AC at 899

with his knowledge, skill and resources could reasonably have been expected to have done or refrained from doing before the accident something which would have avoided it. If he knew before the accident that there was a substantial probability that trespassers would come, I think that most people would regard as culpable failure to give any thought to their safety.'

I cannot see how the plaintiffs can bring their case within this principle, because on the view of the evidence that I have taken the Post Office did not know before the accident that there was a substantial or any probability that the technicians would use the lift motor room for an unauthorised purpose and in disregard of a plainly-worded notice to keep out.

Counsel for the plaintiffs' main argument, however, was based on the operation of the Offices, Shops and Railways Premises Act 1963, which counsel for the Post Office conceded applied to most parts of the telephone exchange, being office premises for the purposes of the Act; but he submitted that it did not apply to the lift motor room. In my judgment it did. This room may not have been used for office purposes within the meaning of s 1 (2) (b) but it was a room 'occupied together with office premises for the purposes of the activities there carried on' and as such had to 'be treated as forming part of the office premises': see the concluding words of s 1 (2).

Counsel for the plaintiffs pointed out that the long title of the Act was in these terms: 'An Act to make fresh provision for securing the health, safety and welfare of persons employed to work in office or shop premises . . .' The deceased had been, he submitted, someone for whose benefit the Act had been passed. The fact of his employment gave him the protection set out in the Act. The Act in s 16 (1) imposed on the Post Office, as the deceased's employers, an absolute duty to ensure that all floors should be of sound construction and properly maintained. They had failed in their duty and had made themselves liable to penalties. The deceased, being a person entitled to the protection of the Act, had sustained injuries from which he had died as a result of this breach of duty. Unless there was some rule of law which either excluded or diminished their responsibility the Post Office were liable. There was, submitted counsel for the plaintiffs, nothing in the Act to limit its application to accidents 'arising in or out of employment'. Parliament, no doubt for good reason, had avoided the use of that notorious and troublesome phrase. The employee was to be protected whilst he was on his employer's premises: it was the duty of the employer to keep those premises safe. The only other rule of law which could operate, and then only to diminish responsibility, was that of contributory negligence. That could not apply because the deceased could not be said to have failed to use reasonable care for his own safety. He had had no reason for thinking that the trapdoor would give way under him.

To support his argument counsel for the plaintiffs invited our attention to *Uddin v Associated Portland Cement Manufacturers Ltd*[1]. In that case an Asian workman who had been in England four years and who was employed in the packing plant of the defendants' factory left his place of work and went to the dust-extracting plant where he had no business to be. His object in going there was to chase a pigeon. Whilst so engaged he caught his clothing in some unfenced machinery whereby he sustained severe injuries. Between the facts of that case and this there are what I consider to be two important differences: first, there was no physical barrier such as a door to bar his way; and secondly, he had not been told that the dust-extraction plant was out of bounds to him. The claim was for breach of statutory duty under the Factories Acts 1937 to 1959. On behalf of the employers it was argued that an employed person was protected under these Acts only so long as he was acting in the course of his employment. The court would have none of this. Lord Pearce summarised his view in these terms[2]:

---

1   [1965] 2 All ER 213, [1965] 2 QB 582
2   [1965] 2 All ER at 217, [1965] 2 QB at 594

'Once it [meaning the machinery] has been shown, however, to be dangerous
and to have needed fencing, it seems to be that he [the factory occupier] should,
under the general intention of the Act, be potentially liable to all employees
who suffer from that failure. There is nothing to justify the view that the Act of
1937 intended its protection for only the slightly stupid or slightly negligent
... Of course, when contributory negligence comes to be considered, the utterly
stupid or utterly negligent man may find that a large proportion (or even the
whole) of the fault is laid on his shoulders, so as to diminish or extinguish his
damages. It seems out of accord, however, with the general policy of the Act
of 1937 that he should be, at a certain stage of folly, outlawed from its protection
and denied a cause of action.'

Willmer LJ summarised his opinion on this point as follows[1]:

'In my judgment where, as here, there has been an admitted breach of s. 14 (1)
[of the Factories Act 1937] on the part of the employers, the behaviour of the
plaintiff is not relevant in considering the duty owed by the employers. It
becomes relevant (a) in relation to causation, i.e., in considering whether the
employer's breach was in fact the cause, or a cause, of the injury complained
of, and (b) in relation to apportionment of responsibility if it is found that the
employer's breach was in fact a contributory cause.'

For my part I would not wish to differ from, or qualify, the statement of the law
enunciated in Uddin's case[2]; but, as counsel for the Post Office pointed out, that case
was not concerned with the situation which arises when an employee is in a part of
factory or office premises to which he has been forbidden to go or when he is there
out of working hours.

There seems to be no authority dealing directly with the first of these situations
but there is one on the second, namely, Napieralski v Curtis (Contractors) Ltd[3]. In
that case the plaintiff had been injured on his employers' premises through their
failure to fence a circular saw in breach of s 14 of the Factories Act 1937, and reg 10 (c)
the Woodworking Machinery Regulations 1922[4]; but he was injured outside his working hours whilst doing, with his employer's permission, some work for himself. The
kind of argument which was put before this court by counsel for the plaintiffs was
put before the trial judge who was Havers J. He did not accept it; and the reason[5]
he gave was that at the time of the accident the plaintiff was not employed on manual
labour, he was voluntarily engaged in manual labour, and that if he could be said
to be working he was not working under an agreement with the defendants or under
any contract of service. This case was considered by this court when hearing the
appeal in Uddin's case[2] and distinguished. In my opinion, Havers J's judgment helps
to reveal the fallacy in the argument of counsel for the plaintiffs in this case. Although
the Offices, Shops and Railway Premises Act 1963 applied to the telephone exchange,
it did not provide protection for anybody who might go there; the protection was for
persons employed to work there: see the long title of the Act[6]. Now the deceased
was employed to work at the telephone exchange; but part of it, namely the lift
motor room, had been put out of bounds to him. He had never been employed to
work in the lift motor room—and he knew that he had not. When he was there he
was in the same position as the unsuccessful workman in Napieralski's case[3]; he was
there on his own account—and, unlike Napieralski, as a trespasser. It is the fact
of trespass, not mere conduct outside the scope of the deceased's employment, which

1 [1965] 2 All ER at 219, [1965] 2 QB at 597
2 [1965] 2 All ER 213, [1965] 2 QB 582
3 [1959] 2 All ER 426, [1959] 1 WLR 835
4 SR & O 1922 No 1196
5 [1959] 2 All ER at 432, [1959] 1 WLR at 841
6 The long title, so far as material, is set out at p 287 d, ante

a distinguishes this case from *Uddin's* case[1]. The line between trespass and conduct outside the scope of employment may not always be easy to see; but on the evidence in this case it is, in my judgment, clearly discernible. The concept of a man becoming a trespasser through going to parts of his place of work where he had no business to be is one which the law recognises: see *Hillen and Pettigrew v ICI (Alkali) Ltd*[2], in which members of a stevedores gang, who stood on hatch covers for the purpose of unloading

b when they knew they should not have done so, were adjudged to be trespassers.

This view of the law would dispose of the appeal; but there is another reason why the award made by the trial judge cannot stand. The deceased suffered his injuries as the result partly of his own fault and partly of the fault of the Post Office. His own fault arises under two heads both coming within the definition of 'fault' set out in s 4 of the Law Reform (Contributory Negligence) Act 1945. First, he entered

c the lift motor room as a trespasser; and secondly, he showed no regard for his own safety because he must have appreciated that the reason why the notice on the door told him to keep out was the existence in the room of sources of danger, albeit not of the kind which he did meet. By going into the room in disregard of the notice he deliberately exposed himself to such dangers as might be there. It is no answer for him to say that the danger he met was not one which either he or the Post Office

d had expected. Thus, in *Jones v Livox Quarries Ltd*[3] this court had to consider whether a workman who was riding on the towbar of a tracked vehicle in disobedience of his employers' orders not to do so and who was injured as a result of another of the employers' vehicles colliding with the back of the tracked vehicle had suffered 'damage as the result partly of his own fault'. The trial judge had found that the risk which the injured man had run in travelling on the tracked vehicle in the position he had was one of being thrown off and no other. It was argued unsuccessfully on his

e behalf that his disobedience of orders was not a cause of the accident—it was nihil ad rem. This court held that the injured man by his disobedience had exposed himself to danger and that his misconduct had contributed to the accident. What is relevant in this case is that the deceased man deliberately exposed himself to such dangers as existed in the lift motor room: in so doing he did not show proper regard

f for his own safety.

The ordinary plain common sense of the matter is that the deceased brought his death on himself by disregarding the notice; and if this should be thought to be an over-robust way of dealing with the finer points of counsel for the plaintiffs' argument as to causation and responsibility, I call in aid Bucknill LJ's judgment in *Davies v Swan Motor Co (Swansea) Ltd*[4] in which he used those very words; and his use of them

g was approved specifically by Singleton LJ in *Jones's* case[5]. Had an apportionment of responsibility been necessary I should have attributed 80 per cent to the deceased.

For these reasons I would allow the appeal.

KARMINSKI LJ. Davies LJ is unable to be here today but he has asked me to say on his behalf that he has read the judgment which has just been delivered by Lawton

h LJ and agrees with it. I also agree.

Appeal allowed. Leave to appeal to the House of Lords.

Solicitors: *William Charles Crocker* (for the plaintiffs); *Solicitor, Post Office.*

Ilyas Khan Esq   Barrister.

j
1   [1965] 2 All ER 213, [1965] 2 QB 582
2   [1936] AC 65, [1935] All ER Rep 555
3   [1952] 2 QB 608
4   [1949] 1 All ER 620 at 626, [1949] 2 KB 291 at 313
5   [1952] 2 QB at 613

Seyfang v G D Searle & Co and another

QUEEN'S BENCH DIVISION

COOKE J

27th, 28th NOVEMBER 1972

Evidence – Foreign tribunal – Examination of witness in relation to matters pending before foreign tribunal – Expert witness – Discretion of court to order evidence to be taken – Exercise of discretion – Expert witness having no connection with facts of case – Expert not wishing to testify – Evidence requiring considerable and careful preparation – Risk that giving of evidence would involve breach of confidence – Foreign Tribunals Evidence Act 1856, s 1.

The two appellants were medical experts. In 1966 they were appointed members of a sub-committee set up by the Medical Research Council to investigate whether birth control pills were or could be a cause of thrombo-embolic disease. The sub-committee's researches suggested that there could be a connection between certain types of thrombo-embolic disease and the use of oral contraceptives. The results of those researches were set out and discussed by the appellants in articles which they published in medical journals between 1967 and 1969. Subsequently the respondent brought proceedings in the courts of Ohio against two drug manufacturing companies alleging that she had suffered thrombo-phlebitis as a result of taking pills manufactured by those companies. Following the issue of letters rogatory by the Ohio court the respondent applied for an order under s 1[a] of the Foreign Tribunals Evidence Act 1856 that the appellants give oral testimony on oath in the Ohio proceedings and produce the working papers from which the articles in the medical journals had been prepared. The appellants were willing to do neither of those things. They pointed out that many of the papers in question had been returned to the authorities to whom their custody properly belonged and further that much of the information embodied in the records used for their research had been disclosed to them in confidence. On appeal against a decision of the master making the order sought, the appellants contended that there was no power under s 1 of the 1856 Act to order the examination on oath of an expert witness.

Held – (i) Under s 1 of the 1856 Act the court had power to order the examination on oath of an expert witness. However, although in the exercise of its discretion the court would generally oblige a witness of fact to testify to a fact which was in issue, it would not as a general rule require an expert to give expert evidence against his wishes in a case where he had no connection with the facts or the history of the matter in issue, particularly where the giving of evidence would involve breach of confidence and its preparation would require considerable time and study. Furthermore the court would

a   Section 1 provides: 'Where, upon an application for this purpose, it is made to appear to any court or judge having authority under this Act that any court or tribunal of competent jurisdiction in a foreign country, before which any civil or commercial matter is pending, is desirous of obtaining the testimony in relation to such matter of any witness or witnesses within the jurisdiction of such first-mentioned court, or of the court to which such judge belongs, or of such judge, it shall be lawful for such court or judge to order the examination upon oath, upon interrogatories or otherwise, before any person or persons named in such order, of such witness or witnesses accordingly; and it shall be lawful for the said court or judge, by the same order, or for such court or judge, or any other judge having authority under this Act, by any subsequent order to command the attendance of any person to be named in such order, for the purpose of being examined, or the production of any writings or other documents to be mentioned in such order, and to give all such directions as to the time, place, and manner of such examination, and all other matters connected therewith, as may appear reasonable and just; and any such order may be enforced in like manner as an order made by such court or judge in a cause depending in such court or before such judge.'

a not allow the procedure of the 1856 Act to be used as a means of obtaining discovery against a person not a party to the proceedings (see p 293 g to j, post).

(ii) In the circumstances it would be oppressive to allow the order to stand against the appellants, since neither could give the evidence required without considerable and careful preparation and neither could answer all the questions which might be put to him without serious risk of a breach of confidence. Further, insofar as the order *b* required the production of documents, it was so widely worded as to amount in effect to an order for discovery. Accordingly the appeals would be allowed (see p 294 a to c, post).

Notes

For the power to order evidence to be taken for use before foreign tribunals, see 15 Halsbury's Laws (3rd Edn) 473, 474, para 856, and for cases on the subject, see 22 Digest *c* (Repl) 603, 6940-6942.

For the Foreign Tribunals Evidence Act 1856, s 1, see 12 Halsbury's Statutes (3rd Edn) 826.

Cases referred to in judgment

d Burchard v Macfarlane, ex parte Tindall [1891] 2 QB 241, [1891-94] All ER Rep 137, 60 LJQB 587, 65 LT 282, 7 Asp MLC 93, CA, 18 Digest (Repl) 20, *141.*

McKinley v McKinley [1960] 1 All ER 476, [1960] 1 WLR 120, 124 JP 171, Digest (Cont Vol A) 533, *3058a.*

Webb v Page (1843) 6 Man & G 196, 1 Car & Kir 23, 6 Scott NR 951, 1 Dow & L 531, 12 LJCP 327, 134 ER 863, 8 Digest (Repl) 25, *147.*

e ### Appeals

Sir Richard Doll and Martin Paterson Vessey appealed against a decision of Master Ritchie given on 21st November 1972 whereby he refused to discharge an order made by him on 14th November ordering that the appellants attend before Basil John Bowen, the duly appointed examiner, on 21st November 1972 in order to submit to examination on oath or affirmation touching testimony required by the District Court *f* for the Southern District of Ohio, Western Division, United States of America, in proceedings between the respondent, Marvene A Seyfang as plaintiff and G D Searle & Co and Ortho Pharmaceutical Corpn as defendants, and to produce the working papers from which the appellants had prepared articles appearing in the British Medical Journal on 6th May 1967, 27th April 1968 and 14th June 1969 and in the issue of the American Heart Journal of February 1969 relating to oral contraception and *g* thrombo-embolic disease. The facts are set out in the judgment.

Thomas Bingham QC and *B Hargrove* for the appellants.
James Mitchell for the respondent.

COOKE J. These are appeals by Sir Richard Doll and Dr Martin Vessey against a *h* decision of Master Ritchie refusing to discharge an order made by him on 14th November 1972, under the Foreign Tribunals Evidence Act 1856. By that order each of the two appellants was required to submit to oral examination on oath and to produce certain documents.

Master Ritchie's order of 14th November was made ex parte on an affidavit of Mr Kimber, an English solicitor, following the issue of letters rogatory by the United *j* States District Court of the Southern District of Ohio. Those letters rogatory were issued in an action pending in that court in which the respondent is seeking to recover damages against two drug manufacturing companies alleging against them various forms of breach of duty in relation to birth control pills manufactured by them. Her case is that her physician prescribed first a drug manufactured by one of the defendant companies and then a drug manufactured by the other defendant company, that she took the drugs as prescribed and as a result developed thrombo-phlebitis and that most unfortunately it became necessary to treat the thrombo-phlebitis by surgery, as a result of which she ultimately lost the whole of her left leg below the hip.

Sir Richard Doll is the Regius Professor of Medicine in the University of Oxford. Dr Vessey is a lecturer in Sir Richard's department at the Radcliffe Infirmary.

An order similar to that made in the case of these two appellants has been made against Dr Inman, who is a senior medical officer in the Department of Health and Social Security. Dr Inman has been concerned with the work of the Committee on Safety of Medicines. The fate of the order against Dr Inman depends on the ultimate fate of the order against the two appellants whose appeals are now before me.

For some years medical circles in various parts of the world have been concerned with the question whether birth control pills are or can be a cause of thromboembolic disease. In 1966 the Medical Research Council in this country appointed a sub-committee to investigate the question and that sub-committee in turn appointed a working party. Among the members of the working party were Dr Doll, Dr Vessey and Dr Inman. The studies carried out by the working party included a study undertaken by Dr Doll and Dr Vessey of patients admitted to hospitals with a diagnosis of venous thrombosis or pulmonary embolism. A preliminary report on the findings of the sub-committee was published as an article in the British Medical Journal on 6th May 1967. The report was suggestive of a connection between certain types of thrombo-embolic disease and the use of oral contraceptives. Then there was an article in the British Medical Journal of 27th April 1968. That article was written by Dr Doll and Dr Vessey and embodied the final results of the study which they had carried out on patients admitted to hospitals. One of the conclusions of the article was that the risk of hospital admission for venous thrombo-embolism was greater in the case of women who used oral contraceptives. Then in February 1969 Dr Vessey published an article in the American Heart Journal dealing generally with the problem and setting out the results of the British research. In June 1969 Dr Doll and Dr Vessey published a further report on the same subject in the form of an article in the British Medical Journal.

Master Ritchie's order required Dr Doll and Dr Vessey to give oral testimony on oath and to produce the working papers from which the four articles which I have mentioned were prepared. The two doctors are willing to do neither of those things. Dr Doll objects that the description of the documents he is required to produce is too general. Further he says that many of those documents are no longer in his possession but have been returned to the authorities to whom their custody properly belongs. Further, both Dr Doll and Dr Vessey take the point that much of the information embodied in the records which they used for the purposes of their research was disclosed to them in confidence.

I have before me an affidavit of Mr Baggott, the attorney who represents the respondent in the action now proceeding in Ohio. Mr Baggott has also helpfully supplied a list of 105 questions which he would wish to be put to the two doctors in the course of examination-in-chief. Further it appears that Messrs Bieser, Greer & Landis, who are the attorneys for the first defendant in the action, have been considering how the two doctors should be cross-examined. They have written to Dr Vessey saying that it will be necessary for him to produce in connection with his testimony all the documents relevant to his studies.

Mr Baggott says in his affidavit that taking the testimony of the two doctors is the only way in which he can get the contents of the four articles into evidence in the action. While I accept this as a correct statement of Ohio law, in the absence of evidence to the contrary, I must confess that I find it surprising. The four articles now form part of the corpus of medical expertise on this particular subject. I apprehend that in England a medical expert witness with the proper qualifications would be allowed to refer to the articles as part of that corpus of expertise, even though he was not the author of the articles himself. It does appear to me with the greatest respect that a system which does not permit experts to refer in their expert evidence to *a* the publications of other experts in the same field is a system which puts peculiar difficulties in the way of proof of matters which depend on expert opinion.

Mr Baggott also says in his affidavit that there is no reason to fear that cross-examination will be wide ranging or require research since the rules of procedure of the Ohio court confine cross-examination to the area covered by examination-in-chief. While accepting Mr Baggott's uncontradicted evidence as to the rules of pro-

b cedure of the court I cannot accept his conclusion that there is no reason to believe that cross-examination would be wide-ranging. Some of the 105 questions which Mr Baggott proposes for examination-in-chief in effect ask the witness for his view on the whole subject-matter under discussion. It is surely to be anticipated that cross-examination would range equally widely, and the letter from the first defendant's attorneys to Dr Vessey certainly seems to support such an expectation.

c What are the principles to be applied in determining whether the court should allow the order applied for to stand in this case? Counsel for the appellants has submitted that s 1 of the Foreign Tribunals Evidence Act 1856 applies only to the testimony of witnesses of fact and not to the testimony of expert witnesses. He accordingly submits that there is no power under the section to order the examination on oath of an expert witness. That submission does not appear to me to accord with the true

d construction of the section. The word 'witness' is used perfectly generally in the section. I can find nothing in s 4 of the Act, on which counsel relied, which requires the word 'witness' in s 1 to be given a narrower meaning. Nor do I think that the decision in *Webb v Page*[1] leads to the conclusion that s 1 of the 1856 Act is concerned with witnesses of fact only. The distinction between a witness of fact and an expert witness is not an absolute distinction. A doctor, who has examined and treated a patient, is both an expert witness and a witness of fact and I see no reason why an order

e under s 1 should not in an appropriate case be made in the case of such a doctor. In my view s 1 confers a discretion on the court in the case of all witnesses, whether expert witnesses or witnesses of fact. The question is: what are the principles on which the discretion ought to be exercised?

I would venture to formulate the principles as follows: (1) Judicial and international

f comity requires that any request of a foreign court for evidence to be taken under the Act should be treated with sympathy and respect and complied with so far as the principles of English law permit. (2) The principles of English law to be applied in the case of an application under the Act are the same as those which the English courts apply to the calling and examination of witnesses in proceedings initiated in the courts of this country. (3) Following those principles the English courts will generally oblige a witness of fact to testify to a fact which is in issue. (4) On the other hand the

g English courts will not as a general rule require an expert to give expert evidence against his wishes in a case where he has had no connection with the facts or the history of the matter in issue. That principle will apply with particular force where the expert cannot give the evidence required of him without a breach of confidence, and where the preparation of the evidence required of him would require considerable time and study. This fourth principle, if it be correct, establishes a distinction

h between expert evidence and evidence as to matters of fact. The distinction is relevant in determining how the courts should exercise their discretion under s 1 of the 1856 Act. It would be equally relevant in determining whether the court should set aside a subpoena issued in proceedings in this country. The principle is not inconsistent with the decision of Wrangham J in *McKinley v McKinley*[2]. That case was concerned with a subpoena issued to a witness of fact. (5) Finally the English courts will not allow the

j procedure of the Foreign Tribunals Evidence Act 1856 to be used as a means of obtaining discovery against a person not a party to the proceedings. That is the familiar

---

1 (1843) 6 Man & G 196
2 [1960] 1 All ER 476, [1960] 1 WLR 120

principle laid down in *Burchard v Macfarlane, ex parte Tindall*[1] and applied in other   *a*
cases.

In my view the fourth and fifth principles are relevant here. Neither Dr Doll nor Dr Vessey has in any way been concerned with the facts of the respondent's case. Neither could give the expert evidence required of him without considerable and careful preparation. Neither could answer all the questions which might be put to him in cross-examination without serious risk of a breach of confidence. While   *b* Dr Doll and Dr Vessey were early researchers in this field, there is nothing to show, at any rate conclusively, that equally authoritative expert evidence might not be obtained on behalf of the respondent from witnesses in the United States. Indeed I should expect in a country where research generally is so advanced and so active such evidence to be available from United States citizens.

In those circumstances it would in my view be oppressive to allow the order to stand   *c* against the two appellants. Further, insofar as the order requires the production of documents, it is in my view so widely worded as to amount in effect to an order for discovery, thus contravening the well-known principle to which I have referred.

For those reasons I would allow the appeals and set aside the master's order.

Appeals allowed. Leave to appeal granted.

d

Solicitors: *Bircham & Co* and *Hempsons* (for the appellants); *P R Kimber* (for the respondent).

I D Turner Esq   Barrister.

Rider v Rider and another   *e*

COURT OF APPEAL, CIVIL DIVISION
SACHS, KARMINSKI AND LAWTON LJJ
20th, 21st, 22nd, 24th NOVEMBER 1972

*Highway – Maintenance – Statutory duty of highway authority – Breach of duty – Persons   *f* to whom duty owed – Test to be applied in determining whether actionable breach of duty – Highways Act 1959, s 44 (1).*

The plaintiff was injured when the car in which she was being driven by her husband swerved and collided with another vehicle. The collision occurred near a sharp bend in a winding lane, which served as a secondary through route from Romsey to Southampton and was regularly used by vehicles of all descriptions. The road   *g* was narrow and its edges, which were unsupported, were uneven with gaps just where the wheels of vehicles would pass. The edge was particularly bad by the bend at which the collision occurred. Southampton Corporation was the authority responsible for the maintenance of the road and the plaintiff brought an action for damages in respect of the personal injuries which she sustained against the driver of the car and the corporation alleging, inter alia, that a cause of the accident was the   *h* corporation's failure to keep the road in a proper state of repair in breach of its statutory duty under s 44 (1)[a] of the Highways Act 1959. The corporation denied liability contending that the state of the road would not have constituted a trap for an ordinary careful driver.

Held – (i) A highway authority's duty under s 44 (1) of the 1959 Act was reasonably to maintain and repair the highway so that it was free of danger to all users who used   *j* that highway in the way normally to be expected of them. In the performance of that duty, the authority had to provide not merely for the model motorist, who

1   [1891] 2 QB 241, [1891-94] All ER Rep 137
a   Section 44 (1), so far as material, provides: 'The . . . highway authority . . . shall be under a duty to maintain the highway.'

a   always used reasonable care, but for the normal run of drivers to be found on their highways, which included those who made the mistakes which experience and common sense taught were likely to occur (see p 299 e to p 300 a, p 301 j, p 302 g and p 303 d and e, post).

(ii) The test to be applied in determining whether a particular state of disrepair entailed danger to traffic being driven in the way normally expected on that highway *b*   was an objective one, i e whether the condition of the road was foreseeably dangerous to vehicles being driven in the way vehicles were normally driven on that road (see p 300 b, p 301 j and p 303 b, post).

(iii) In the circumstances the corporation were liable for damages because on the evidence the swerving of the car was due to the disrepair of the road which they failed to maintain and the condition of the road was such that it was foreseeably dangerous *c*   to the drivers who would normally be expected to be on it (see p 300 h, p 301 j and p 303 g, post).

Morton v Wheeler (1956) The Times, 1st February applied.

Dictum of Lord Denning MR in *Bright v Attorney-General* [1971] 2 Lloyd's Rep at 71 disapproved.

Per Curiam. The normal run of drivers does not include the drunk or the reckless *d*   and in most cases mere unevenness, undulations and minor potholes do not amount to proof of a danger for traffic through failure to maintain by a highway authority (see p 300 d, p 301 j, p 302 c and j and p 303 c, post).

Notes

For a highway authority's duty to maintain a highway, see 19 Halsbury's Laws (3rd Edn) 115, 116, para 173; for liability of highway authority in respect of damage result-*e*   ing from their failure to maintain the highway, see ibid 149-152, paras 227-229, and for cases on the subject, see 26 Digest (Repl) 418-422, 1278-1309.

For the Highways Act 1959, s 44, see 15 Halsbury's Statutes (3rd Edn) 195.

Cases referred to in judgments

Bright v Attorney-General [1971] 2 Lloyd's Rep 68; sub nom *Bright v Ministry of Transport* *f*   [1971] RTR 253, CA.

Burnside v Emerson [1968] 3 All ER 741, [1968] 1 WLR 1490, 133 JP 66, 67 LGR 46, CA, Digest (Cont Vol C) 410, 1309c.

Dymond v Pearce [1972] 1 All ER 1142, [1972] 1 QB 496, [1972] 2 WLR 633, [1972] RTR 169, CA.

Griffiths v Liverpool Corpn [1966] 2 All ER 1015, [1967] 1 QB 374, [1966] 3 WLR 467, 130 JP 376, CA, Digest (Cont Vol B) 329, 1278a.

g   *Levine v Morris* [1970] 1 All ER 144, [1970] 1 WLR 71, 134 JP 158, [1970] RTR 93, sub nom *Levine and Levine v Morris and Ministry of Transport* [1970] 1 Lloyd's Rep 7, CA, Digest (Cont Vol C) 916, 126b.

London Passenger Transport Board v Upson [1949] 1 All ER 60, [1949] AC 155, [1949] LJR 238, HL, 45 Digest (Repl) 21, 58.

Meggs v Liverpool Corpn [1968] 1 All ER 1137, [1968] 1 WLR 689, 132 JP 207, 65 LGR *h*   479, CA, Digest (Cont Vol C) 410, 1309b.

Morton v Wheeler (1956) The Times, 1st February, CA.

Case also cited

Summers (John) & Sons Ltd v Frost [1955] 1 All ER 870, [1955] AC 740, HL.

j   **Appeal**

The plaintiff, Susan Sylvia Rider, brought an action against Clive Raymond Rider and Southampton Corporation ('the corporation') for damages for negligence and/or breach of statutory duty, personal injury and consequential loss arising out of an accident in Rownhams Lane, Rownhams, Hants, on 27th November 1969, which she claimed was due to the negligent driving of the first defendant and/or the negligence and/or breach of statutory duty of the corporation. The corporation appealed against

that part of the decision of Stirling J given on the trial of the action at Winchester on
9th February whereby it was ordered that judgment be entered for the plaintiff   *a*
against the corporation in the sum of £8,000 and, in third party proceedings between
the first defendant and the corporation (with which Stirling J was not invited to deal
separately), for judgment to be entered for the first defendant against the corporation
in the sum of £5,332·67.   The facts are set out in the judgment.

Patrick Bennett QC and *A R Tyrrell* for the corporation.   *b*
Michael Turner for the first defendant.
The plaintiff did not appear and was not represented.

Cur adv vult

24th November.   The following judgments were delivered.

SACHS LJ.   This is an appeal from a judgment of Stirling J given at Winchester   *c*
Crown Court on 9th February 1972.   The action was one for personal injuries sustained on 27th November 1969 in a road accident which occurred in Rownhams Lane,
near Southampton.   The plaintiff, who lived at Rownhams, was a passenger in a
1100 Austin saloon being driven towards Southampton at 7.30 p m—when it was,
of course, dark.   The car was being driven by her husband, the first defendant, when   *d*
at a point about half a mile from home it came into collision with a Dormobile van
coming in the opposite direction.   The driver of the Dormobile van being in no way
to blame, the plaintiff started proceedings first against her husband, who remembered
nothing of the accident, and then, in view of the defence filed on his behalf, added
Southampton Corporation as second defendants, alleging that a cause of the accident
was that corporation's failure to keep Rownhams Lane in a proper state of repair.
    At the time when the action came to trial agreement had been reached between   *e*
all parties on certain points; first, that the damages suffered by the plaintiff should
be assessed at £8,500; next that the plaintiff was entitled to recover against one or
other of the two defendants; and thus that the real issue as to liability lay between
those two defendants.   It was further common ground that in those circumstances
the plaintiff need take no further part in the trial; and she did not.   At the conclusion   *f*
of a three day hearing the learned trial judge held both defendants liable, placing
two-thirds of the responsibility on the corporation and one-third on the first
defendant.
    The corporation now appeal, contending that they were under no liability at all,
and alternatively that the apportionment was erroneous, submitting that they were
the least blameworthy of the two parties.   In this court again the plaintiff has not
been represented.   *g*
    At the outset it is necessary to state the characteristics of Rownhams Lane, the
nature of the traffic which used it in November 1969, and the general state of its
repair.   Rownhams Lane went southwards from Rownhams towards Southampton,
which was only a few miles away.   It had originally been a truly country lane, winding its narrow way between villages.   As time went on, however, whilst it retained
its rural aspect, it became more and more used by motor traffic.   Responsibility   *h*
for its maintenance was taken over by the corporation in about 1964.   Well before
1969 it had become an escape route for those who found the A27 and A3057 roads
from Romsey to Southampton overfilled.   'A traffic jam avoider' it was called by a
police officer, and a 'secondary through route' by an officer of the corporation.   As
a result, it was regularly used by vehicles of all descriptions—cars, lorries, farm tractors and so forth.   At times the traffic was sufficiently heavy to be referred to as a   *j*
procession of vehicles.   All this was fully known to the corporation.   Yet this lane
remained not only winding, but narrow; the width of tarmac shown on the plan
put in evidence ranged from ten feet nine inches to 17 feet—it was less than 14 feet in
more than one place.   The edges led on to grass or mud verges, and these verges
were in places below the level of the tarmac—a fact that in the above circumstances

made adequate support essential for keeping the edges in repair. The road was, however, described by an officer of the corporation as having 'no real foundation'. In particular, it had no support at the edges. As it was necessary for vehicles passing each other to hug these unsupported edges, chunks were broken off. Up to 18 inches was at some spots bitten off the edges. In the result, they became uneven, with gaps just where the wheels of vehicles would pass. Moreover, they could vary in their state as lorries passed over them each day. In addition, there were some pot-holes more towards the centre of the road. The nearside edge going south, as the first defendant went, had the worst of the two edges, and that edge was particularly bad at a bend described as 'bad' and 'sharp' round which the first defendant went immediately before the accident.

This lane was described by more than one witness, including a police officer assessed as 'impressively experienced', as the worst conditioned lane in the area. No steps had been taken to bring its repair up to anything like the standard required for a secondary main route. On the contrary, during a number of months before the accident its condition had been allowed to grow, if anything, worse. In this behalf it is to be observed that some time before the accident, presumably towards the end of 1968, a decision had been taken to provide another road, to be known as Spine Road, to take through traffic from Romsey to Southampton, and when that was available to close Rownhams Lane so that it became in effect a cul de sac. One of the principal witnesses for the corporation said this as to what happened after the decision to provide another road had been taken:

> 'Well, since Rownhams Lane was only recently brought in to the City of Southampton boundary, or included in the City of Southampton, and since this area was only brought into Southampton to enable the development in this area to take place, and also it was known at that time that the Spine Road would be constructed, I would say that that was every reason why no work should have been carried out to Rownhams Lane in the form of improvement or widening.'

Not only was no improvement made, but it was shown that over the six months before the accident there is no record of any serious work of repair to the lane, although no doubt sometimes half an hour's casual patching may well have been done.

That then was the character and state of Rownhams Lane down which the first defendant was driving when on coming round this sharp bend his car went out of control and swung across into the path of the oncoming Dormobile van. Up to 40 feet before that happened the Austin car had been seen by the van driver to be coming 'quite correctly' towards him.

In that set of circumstances the learned trial judge proceeded in correct sequence to consider successively the four relevant issues. (i) Was the loss of control of the Austin car due to Rownham's Lane's state of disrepair? (ii) If so, was that state such as to constitute an actionable breach of the corporation's duty as a highway authority to maintain and repair the lane? (iii) If so, had the corporation established the statu-tory defence provided for highway authorities by s 1 (2) and (3) of the Highways (Miscellaneous Provisions) Act 1961? (iv) Had negligence on the part of the first defendant contributed to the accident?

As regards the first of those issues, the learned trial judge had to decide between two rival contentions put before him. For the corporation it was put that the way in which the Austin car swung across the road was simply due to an over-correction of a tail skid caused by the speed at which that car was being driven, and was not to any material degree caused by the disrepair. For the first defendant it was contended that the swing was of quite a different type, and in all probability caused by one of the nearside wheels going into an indentation in the edge of the lane, and that thus the swing was caused by the state of disrepair. In support of these contentions a considerable amount of evidence was tendered, aided by demonstrations with

models and by references to the ultimate position of two vehicles.   The learned trial
judge, after carefully sifting the material, found as a fact that the swing was due to
the disrepair.   In this court counsel for the corporation at one stage commenced to
challenge that finding, but later resiled from that course.   The learned judge's
finding was indeed in practice unassailable in this court.   So the first issue stands
resolved in favour of the first defendant.

I now turn to the second issue—whether the state of disrepair of the lane was such
as to constitute an actionable breach of the corporation's duty.   In the instant appeal
this has been the crucial issue, because counsel for the corporation felt unable to
contend that if that issue was resolved against the corporation they could then successfully resort to the statutory defence provided by s 1 (2) and (3) of the 1961 Act, where
the highway authority can prove it had taken appropriate care to secure that the
highway was not dangerous to traffic.

The duty of the corporation to road users was considered at first instance and in
this court on the basis that it arises under s 44 (1) of the Highways Act 1959.   This imposes on the highway authority 'a duty to maintain the highway'—a duty so defined
in s 295 (1) as to include a duty to keep in repair.   It is accordingly unnecessary in this
case to examine whether there is also a collateral duty at common law.   The origin
and nature of that statutory duty was examined in this court in *Griffiths v Liverpool
Corpn*[1].   It was there decided that had s 1 (1) of the 1961 Act (which abolished the rule
of law absolving highway authorities from liability for non-feasance) stood alone,

'a plaintiff who proved in a civil action against a highway authority the presence
of a danger in the highway which caused him to sustain damage would have
been entitled to succeed without proving that the existence of such danger was
due to any lack of care on the part of the highway authority.'

(see per Diplock LJ[2] and Salmon LJ[3]), but that s 1 (2) and (3) provided a defence if
the authority established the requisite facts.   Salmon LJ[3] referred to the highway
authority's liability in respect of anything dangerous as being 'absolutely and irrespective of any negligence on their part'—subject, of course, to a defence under the
above-mentioned two subsections.

In *Morton v Wheeler*[4] Denning LJ said, in a passage cited in *Dymond v Pearce*[5]:

'But how are we to determine whether a state of affairs in or near a highway is
a danger?   This depends, I think, on whether injury may reasonably be foreseen.   If you take all the cases in the books, you will find that if the state of
affairs is such that injury may reasonably be anticipated by persons using the
highway, it is a public nuisance.'

Then, after referring to need to take into account the chances of life relevant to the
facts of that case, he went on:

'If a reasonable man, taking such contingencies into account, and giving close
attention to the state of affairs, would say: "I think there is quite a chance that
someone going along the road may be injured if this stays as it is", then it is a
danger; but if the possibility of injury is so remote that he would dismiss it out
of hand, saying: "Of course, it is possible, but not in the least probable", then
it is not a danger.'

The learned trial judge, after examining a number of authorities, including *Meggs*

1   [1966] 2 All ER 1015, [1967] 1 QB 374
2   [1966] 2 All ER at 1022, [1967] 1 QB at 390
3   [1966] 2 All ER at 1024, [1967] 1 QB at 394
4   (1956) The Times, 1st February
5   [1972] 1 All ER 1142 at 1149, [1972] 1 QB 496 at 505

a *v Liverpool Corpn*[1], *Burnside v Emerson*[2] and *Bright v Attorney-General*[3] (although not *Griffiths v Liverpool Corpn*[4] or *Morton v Wheeler*[5], which were not cited to him) expressed his conclusions as follows:

> 'Applying what I hope are the correct principles to the present facts, I come to the conclusion that it is established that Rownhams Lane was because of its condition at the time foreseeably dangerous to reasonable users.   It was narrow,
b > had a tendency to break away and form holes at the edges.   It was used by vans and doubtless lorries which must frequently have had to travel on or even beyond the edge of the tarmac, and ruts tended to form.   The point of the accident was, I think, particularly bad, and it could and should have been foreseen by the highway authority that vehicles might well have to pass each other at night, and in consequence have to hug the edges.   Testing this position by
c > the innocent stranger driver, such a person could well have swung to his nearside when rounding the left hand bend at say, 30 m p h and encountered the sort of road condition which he should not reasonably expect.'

The question which was particularly canvassed in this court, as it was at first instance, has been in effect: 'To whom does the highway authority's duty extend—
d to whom must the danger be shown to be foreseeable?' The main burden of counsel for the corporation's submissions was that on the evidence a sufficiently careful driver would not have been put at risk by the state of the lane.   The duty, he maintained, only extended to such users, and accordingly there had been no breach of the highway authority's duty.

Putting on one side the fact that the bulk of the evidence on which he relied was
e found on analysis to refer to user by motorists aware that the lane was in a state of disrepair, the question still arises as to how far the above submission is correct. Ought the approach advocated by counsel for the corporation to be accepted, or does the duty of the highway authority extend rather further—adopting the common sense views of foreseeability of danger indicated both by Denning LJ in *Morton v Wheeler*[5] and by Phillimore LJ in *Bright v Attorney-General*[6]. The latter spoke
f (albeit in a negligence case) of the trial judge's approach to the creation of a danger in the highway in the following terms of approval:

> 'In his judgment, having considered those matters, he put to himself the proper test when he said "... Although an accident may not be inevitable in every case, if there is a real possibility of the state of the road producing an accident then that is something which ought to be guarded against; it is reason-
g > ably foreseeable in the circumstances like that, that an accident may occur ... well then steps must be taken in order to see that it does not occur."'

Having considered the authorities cited to the learned trial judge and in this court, it is in my judgment clear that the corporation's statutory duty under s 44 of the 1959 Act is reasonably to maintain and repair the highway so that it is free of danger to
h all users who use that highway in the way normally to be expected of them—taking account, of course, of the traffic reasonably to be expected on the particular highway. Motorists who thus use the highway, and to whom a duty is owed, are not to be expected by the authority all to be model drivers.   Drivers in general are liable to make mistakes, including some rated as negligent by the courts, without being merely for that reason stigmatised as unreasonable or abnormal drivers; some

j
---
1 [1968] 1 All ER 1137, [1968] 1 WLR 689
2 [1968] 3 All ER 741, [1968] 1 WLR 1490
3 [1971] 2 Lloyd's Rep 68
4 [1966] 2 All ER 1015, [1967] 1 QB 374
5 (1956) The Times, 1st February
6 [1971] 2 Lloyd's Rep at 72

drivers may be inexperienced; and some drivers may find themselves in difficulties   *a*
from which the more adept could escape.   The highway authority must provide
not merely for model drivers, but for the normal run of drivers to be found on their
highways, and that includes those who make the mistakes which experience and
common sense teaches are likely to occur.   In these days, when the number and speed
of vehicles on the roads is continually mounting and the potential results of accidents
due to disrepair are increasingly serious, any other rule would become more and   *b*
more contrary to the public interest.

In every case it is a question of fact and degree whether any particular state of
disrepair entails danger to traffic being driven in the way normally expected on that
highway.   The test is an objective one.   To define that degree by using words or
phrases suited to a particular case can end by putting an unwarranted gloss on the
duty.   In this behalf I would respectfully venture to doubt whether Lord Denning   *c*
MR in *Bright's* case[1] would, whether or not obiter, have used the word 'trap' or the
phraseology as to 'ordinary careful drivers' which he there adopted[2] had his attention
been called to his judgment in *Morton v Wheeler*[3].

It is perhaps as well, however, to emphasise my agreement with the manifestly
correct view that mere unevenness, undulations, and minor potholes do not normally
constitute a danger, and also to say that the normal run of drivers does not include   *d*
the drunk or the reckless.

Reverting now to the evidence in this case, the facts as to the character and conditions of Rownhams Lane have already been stated.   It is perhaps, however, as well
to stress that it had become 'a secondary through route' in the view of the corporation's principal witness—their assistant engineer responsible for the design of certain
roads.   Under effective cross-examination by counsel for the first defendant, he gave   *e*
the following answers:

'Q So does it come to this, that so far as you would be concerned, having regard
to the fact that Rownhams Lane carried this substantial volume of traffic on
the width of road surface that it did, unsupported in places, you would expect
from time to time and to a greater or lesser extent, the edges of the road in
certain sections to break away?   *A* I would, yes.   *f*

'Q Giving rise to a foreseeable risk that it might cause difficulty or damage or
danger to traffic using that road?   A It could, yes.

'Q All those three, difficulty, damage or danger?   A Yes.'

Then one finds in re-examination an answer to a question the relevant part of which
I will read:
                                                                                    g
'Q . . . what if you had something comparable at the edge of the road, even
though it might not be a complete circle, if you got an indentation perhaps nine
inches across and two or three inches deep?   *A* Yes, I would consider that would
constitute a danger, perhaps not to the same extent as the one in the centre of
the carriageway.'
                                                                                    h
In those circumstances there was ample evidence on which the learned trial judge
could properly find, as he did, that the condition of the lane was foreseeably dangerous
to reasonable drivers; indeed, it is difficult to see how he could have made any other
finding.

I would only add that in the recent case of *Levine v Morris*[4] this court in a negligence
action considered the duties of a highway authority engaged in the construction of a   *j*
new highway.   There Widgery LJ said[5]:

1   [1971] 2 Lloyd's Rep 68
2   [1971] 2 Lloyd's Rep at 70
3   (1956) The Times, 1st February
4   [1970] 1 All ER 144, [1970] 1 WLR 71
5   [1970] 1 All ER at 150, 151, [1970] 1 WLR at 79

a 'All motorists are guilty of errors of one kind or another on one occasion or another, and I think it would be quite unreal if roads were designed on the assumption that no driver would ever err. Indeed, as Lord du Parcq put it in *London Passenger Transport Board* v. *Upson*[1], "... a prudent man will guard against the possible negligence of others, when experience shows such negligence

b to be common." It seems to me that that phrase is entirely apt to dispose of the submission that no duty of care was owed to a motorist in the position of the driver in this case. Of course, the duty of the highway authority is limited by the fact that it is only required to do what is reasonable in order to avoid reasonably foreseeable accidents. The liability of the highway authority in damages may be limited in amount, or may be excluded entirely as between the authority and a negligent driver. But, subject to those limitations, the duty

c is owed to all motorists generally.'

That view of the duty of a highway authority to drivers who were not as careful as they should be accorded with those expressed by the other members of the court. It is unnecessary here to decide whether the above-quoted passage applies in full to the statutory duties of a highway authority to maintain an existing road, although it would obviously be unfortunate if there was a material difference between the

d standards of foresight to be applied to maintenance and construction respectively. It is sufficient to say that in the instant case the trial judge's finding as to the foreseeability of danger was well founded, and the second issue must be resolved adversely to the corporation.

For the reasons previously mentioned, it is unnecessary to consider in detail the third issue—whether the corporation established a defence under the provisions of

e s 1 (2) and (3) of the 1961 Act. The learned trial judge carefully examined the case sought to be made under these subsections and examined the facts relevant to paras (*a*) to (*e*) inclusive in sub-s (2). It is sufficient to say that, on the footing that the second issue in the instant case be resolved against the corporation, his conclusions on the third neither can be nor were challenged.

That leaves for consideration the corporation's contentions as regards the issue of

f contributory negligence. This is a defence specifically preserved to highway authorities by the terms of s 1 (2) of the 1961 Act. It is, incidentally, one that, having regard to the sliding scale of apportionment available to the court, provides to a considerable degree an answer to any suggestion that there might be some hardship in a rule that the authority must provide for those reasonable errors to which reference has been made.

g In the instant case there was no direct evidence of negligence. On the contrary, the driver of the Dormobile observed nothing wrong in Mr Rider's driving. The learned trial judge, however, came on the available material as a whole to the conclusion that he could not 'be absolved from all blame', and that has not been the subject of a cross-appeal. In substance, he based his finding of contributory negligence on the special knowledge this driver had of the relevant section of Rownhams Lane—

h holding that he had not been reckless, but nonetheless should have been going more slowly, and if so, he would not have been flung out of control to such an extent. In those circumstances, I am not prepared to differ from the apportionment of the learned trial judge, who after seeing the witnesses had carefully assessed the weight of the relevant evidence.

Accordingly, I would dismiss this appeal.

j **KARMINSKI LJ.** I agree with the judgment that has just been delivered by Sachs LJ and desire to add a few comments of my own on what was said by Lord Denning MR in *Bright v Attorney-General*[2]. In my view, what he said there was

1 [1949] 1 All ER 60 at 72, [1949] AC 155 at 176. Lord du Parcq was quoting his own words in *Grant v Sun Shipping Co Ltd* [1948] 2 All ER 238 at 247, [1948] AC 549 at 567
2 [1971] 2 Lloyd's Rep 68 at 70, 71

obiter, because it was unnecessary to his decision.   It is desirable that I should quote
what he is reported to have said:

> 'A highway is only to be considered dangerous when there is something which
> may be regarded as a trap into which an ordinary careful person may fall . . . A
> man or boy who comes off his bicycle and hurts himself must not think that
> he has a ready-made action against the highway authorities. No action lies unless
> the road is proved to be dangerous to persons using it with reasonable care:
> and then only if the highway authority has been negligent.'

My comment on that passage is this.   Highway drivers are of varying degrees of
competence, experience and carefulness; these attributes may change with, for
example, varying conditions of weather and with the driver's physical condition.
Leave out any question of drink.   A tired driver may drive less well than he usually
does through fatigue or anxiety.   Indeed, I do not think there is such an animal as
an ordinary careful driver.   In my view, in a case of this kind all the evidence must
be examined to discover the cause or causes of the accident.   Here the learned trial
judge did this, and I do not differ from his assessment of blame.   I too would dismiss
this appeal.

LAWTON LJ. I too agree that this appeal should be dismissed.   In my judgment,
the learned trial judge had to find answers to the following questions.   First, did the
highway authority perform their statutory duty under s 44 (1) of the Highways Act
1959?   As by the definition set out in that Act 'maintain' includes 'repair', the
evidence clearly establishes that they did not.   Secondly, did they so fail in the discharge of their statutory duty to maintain that at the part of Rownhams Lane where
the accident happened there was a danger for traffic?   The relevance of this question
follows from the terms of s 1 (2) of the Highways (Miscellaneous Provisions) Act 1961.
This subsection provides that it shall be a defence for the highway authority to prove
that they had—

> 'taken such care as in all the circumstances was reasonably required to secure
> that the part of the highway to which the action relates was not dangerous for
> traffic.'

It follows that they must maintain the roads for which they are responsible in such a
way as to secure that there are no dangers for traffic.   Most of the argument in this
case has centred round this question.   Thirdly, did such danger as there was cause the
accident wholly or in part?   Fourthly, did the highway authority establish a defence
under s 1 (2) of the 1961 Act?   Fifthly, did the driver of the motor car in which the
injured plaintiff was travelling cause the accident wholly or in part by his own
negligence?   As to the last three questions, I have nothing to add to what has already
been said.

As to the second question, whether part of a highway is a danger for traffic is a
question of fact; and the answer to the question will depend on the evaluation of
the evidence by the judge if he is sitting alone, or by a jury in the unlikely event
nowadays of there being one.   Be there judge or be there jury, the evidence must
be evaluated in a common sense way.   In most cases proof that there were bumps
or small holes in a road, or slight unevenness in flagstones on a pavement, will not
amount to proof of a danger for traffic through failure to maintain.   But it does not
follow that such conditions can never be a danger for traffic.   A stretch of uneven
paving outside a factory probably would not be a danger for traffic; but a similar
stretch outside an old people's home, and much used by the inmates to the knowledge
of the highway authority, might be.

The 1961 Act refers to traffic both in sub-ss (2) and (3) of s 1.   The danger to be
guarded against is one 'for traffic', and the traffic is that which is reasonably to be

expected to use the highway: see sub-s (3) of s 1. Now traffic can have many characteristics, arising from the number and types of vehicles and the abilities and competence of their drivers. A stretch of road with unusual features might not present any danger for police officers on an advanced driving course, but might for learner drivers under instruction. In each case it must be a question of fact what kinds and types of vehicles and what kinds of drivers were reasonably to be expected to use the highway. In this case the highway authority could reasonably have expected, lorries, vans, farm vehicles, motor cars, motor cycles and bicycles to use Rownhams Lane; but not huge container lorries or military tank transporters. They were likely to be driven or ridden by the ordinary citizen going to or from work or about his business. It is a matter of everyday experience for those of us who use the highways that driving abilities vary; but for the great majority within a certain range which can perhaps be described as normal driving. Such driving is impossible to define but easy to recognise on the highways. Some drivers keep a better look-out than others; some drive faster than is either prudent or the law allows; some are skilled at avoiding sudden emergencies; others are prone to make mistakes. Occasionally the reckless or drunken driver is to be seen on the roads; but such drivers are rare and their driving is not normal driving. In my judgment, highway authorities when performing their statutory duty to maintain their roads should keep in mind the driver who may take a corner too fast or who may be slow to notice changes in road conditions. Such drivers form part of the traffic on our roads and it would be unrealistic for highway authorities when deciding what standard of maintenance is necessary to forget their existence and to provide only for those who always use reasonable care—if any such paragons of driving virtue are to be found. Those drivers who do not use proper care for their own safety will pay for their carelessness by a reduction in the amount of such damages as may be awarded to them; and if their carelessness has been gross, it may well be on the facts the sole cause of the accident.

For those reasons, I am unable to accept the corporation's submission that as a matter of law a danger for traffic cannot exist unless the road conditions constituting it would be a trap for the careful driver. This submission was based on what I judge to be obiter dicta in the judgment of Lord Denning MR in *Bright v Attorney-General*[1]. If the correct evaluation of the evidence shows that there was nothing in the nature of a trap, and that what was alleged to be the danger could have been avoided without difficulty by the careful driver, then the correct inference to be drawn may well be that there was no danger for traffic. To say that there can only be a danger for traffic if the conditions would be a trap for the careful driver is, in my judgment, to turn an inference of fact into a rule of law.

For the reasons stated by Sachs LJ, I am satisfied that the part of the road where the accident happened was a danger for traffic in the sense that I have understood those words.

Appeal dismissed.

Solicitors: *J E Baring & Co*, agents for *Bernard Chill & Axtell*, Winchester (for the corporation); *Ward, Bowie & Co*, agents for *Woodford & Ackroyd*, Southampton (for the first defendant).

Mary Rose Plummer   Barrister.

1 [1971] 2 Lloyd's Rep 68 at 71

Note

Malloch v Aberdeen Corporation (No 2)

HOUSE OF LORDS

LORD REID, LORD SIMON OF GLAISDALE AND LORD KILBRANDON

6th NOVEMBER 1972

House of Lords – Costs – Taxation – Costs properly incurred – Appellant in person – Appeal successful – Costs incurred in preparing written case and in equipping appellant to appear and argue case in person – Solicitor assisting and advising appellant – Whether solicitor's charges and expenses properly included in bill of costs.

Note

For the award of costs on appeals to the House of Lords, see 36 Halsbury's Laws (3rd Edn) 122, para 161.

Petition for review of taxation of costs

On 29th June 1971 the House of Lords[1] allowed an appeal by the petitioner, John Strachan Malloch, against an interlocutor of the Second Division of the Court of Session dated 24th July 1970 in favour of the respondents, the Corporation of the City of Aberdeen. The petitioner conducted his appeal in person. By its order the House ordered, inter alia—

'... That the Respondents do pay, or cause to be paid, to the [petitioner] the Expenses incurred by him in respect of the Action in the Court of Session and also the Costs incurred by him in respect of the ... Appeal to this House, the amount of such last-mentioned Costs to be certified by the Clerk of the Parliaments ...'

The petitioner presented his bill of costs for taxation on 9th July 1971. The taxing officer disallowed certain items including (i) charges by Mrs Ewing, a Glasgow solicitor, amounting to £322·50 and (ii) her travelling expenses amounting to £12. The disallowances were subsequently confirmed by the Clerk of the Parliaments.

The petitioner thereupon prayed that the House review the taxation, submitting that the items disallowed were costs properly incurred in respect of the appeal. Mrs Ewing had assisted him in preparing the necessary documents and instructed him how to present his case when he appeared in person before the appellate committee.

LORD REID. Their Lordships are of opinion that the disputed items should be submitted for retaxation on the principle that the petitioner be allowed such sums as were reasonably necessary for him to spend in order to prepare his written case and equip himself to appear and argue his case in person.

S A Hatteea Esq   Barrister.

---

1   [1971] 2 All ER 1278, [1971] 1 WLR 1578

National Dock Labour Board v British Steel Corporation

HOUSE OF LORDS
LORD REID, LORD MORRIS OF BORTH-Y-GEST, LORD HODSON, LORD SIMON OF GLAISDALE
AND LORD CROSS OF CHELSEA
25th, 26th, 30th OCTOBER, 1st, 2nd NOVEMBER, 13th DECEMBER 1972

Employment – Regulation – Dock workers – Dock labour scheme – Application – Port – Port of Port Talbot – Meaning – 'All the Dock Estate' – New harbour and jetty built outside area of original dock estate – Whether part of the dock estate – Dock Workers (Regulation of Employment) (Amendment) Order 1967 (SI 1967 No 1252), Sch 2, App I.

Employment – Regulation – Dock workers – Dock labour scheme – Application – Dock work – Work ordinarily performed by dock workers of classes or description to which scheme applies – Work in connection with 'cargo' – Unloading of iron ore from ship's holds by crane on jetty – Ore deposited from cranes on to conveyor belt – Conveyor belt transporting ore from jetty direct to consignee's stock yard – What if any operations in connection with removal of ore from hold of ship to stock yard constituting 'dock work' – Dock Workers (Regulation of Employment) (Amendment) Order 1967 (SI 1967 No 1252), Sch 2, cll 1 (3), 2 (1).

The Dock Workers (Regulation of Employment) Scheme 1947[a] ('the 1947 scheme') was made under the Dock Workers (Regulation of Employment) Act 1946. It was replaced, with immaterial amendments, by the Dock Workers Employment Scheme 1967[b] ('the 1967 scheme') also made under the 1946 Act. One of the objects of the 1947 and 1967 schemes was that at certain specified ports in Great Britain work of a specified kind should only be performed by registered dock workers. The 1947 scheme was the first national scheme replacing earlier local schemes, relating to particular ports, which had been made under the[c] Essential Work (Dock Labour) Order 1941[c]. Under the provisions of Appendix I, the 1967 scheme applied to the port of Port Talbot. For that purpose 'Port Talbot' was defined by reference to the definition in the earlier local scheme, the Dock Labour Scheme for the South Wales Ports made in 1942 ('the 1942 scheme'): ' . . . the expression "Port" shall include the following places . . . (4) Port Talbot.—All the Dock Estate . . .' By cl 1 (3)[d] the 1967 scheme applied to dock workers 'employed or registered for employment in, or in the vicinity of, [Port Talbot] on work in connection with the loading, unloading, movement or storage of cargoes, or work in connection with the preparation of ships or other vessels for the receipt or discharge of cargoes or for leaving port'. By cl 2 (1)[e], incorporating the

---

a   Set out in the Schedule to the Dock Workers (Regulation of Employment) Order 1947 (SR & O 1947 No 1189)
b   Set out in Sch 2 to the Dock Workers (Regulation of Employment) (Amendment) Order 1967 (SI 1967 No 1252)
c   SR & O 1941 No 1440 made by the Minister of Labour and National Service under reg 58A of the Defence (General) Regulations 1939 (SR & O 1939 No 927)
d   Clause 1 (3), so far as material, is set out at p 312 d, post
e   Clause 2 (1), so far as material, provides: 'The following expressions have the meanings hereby respectively assigned to them unless the context otherwise requires:—"the Act" means the Dock Workers (Regulation of Employment) Act 1946 . . . "cargo" and "dock worker" have the meanings respectively assigned to them in the Act . . . "dock work" means operations at places or premises to which the Scheme relates, ordinarily performed by dock workers of the classes or descriptions to which the Scheme applies . . .'

N

definitions in s 6^f of the 1946 Act, 'cargo' included anything carried or to be carried in a ship and 'dock worker' meant a person employed or to be employed on the work described in cl 1(3). Further, cl 2(1) defined dock work as 'operations at [Port Talbot], ordinarily performed by dock workers of the classes or descriptions to which the Scheme applies'. The 'classes or descriptions' of dock work included in the 1967 scheme were defined by the 1942 scheme by reference to the port registration scheme, as amended^g, for Port Talbot. By that definition, it was provided, inter alia, that 'Dock Work' at the port of Port Talbot 'shall not include . . . Transporter grab driving at Margam Wharf except when employed discharging and/or loading vessels at Margam Wharf'.

Before 1970 the port of Port Talbot consisted of a complex of docks reached through an entrance lock a short distance up river from the mouth of the River Avon. At least 90 per cent of the cargo handled at the port was iron ore discharged at Margam Wharf and destined for the local steel works owned by the respondents. Margam Wharf itself was leased by the docks board to the respondents. Since the port was incapable of accommodating the increasingly large bulk iron ore carriers which were coming into use in the 1960s the local docks board obtained powers under a private Act of Parliament^h to develop and extend the harbour. This they did by building a large jetty in a dredged tidal harbour bounded by breakwaters to the east of the mouth of the River Avon and close to the entrance of the original port. Before the construction of the tidal harbour, when iron ore was unloaded at Margam Wharf, the men employed by the respondents to carry out the work of unloading actually in the ships were registered dock workers but those working on the wharf, including the drivers of the cranes used for unloading, were steel workers, i e employees of the respondents who were not registered dock workers. After the tidal harbour had been completed, deliveries to the new jetty harbour replaced those to Margam Wharf. At the new jetty the iron ore was lifted from the ships by 'grab unloaders', i e travelling cranes, which deposited the ore in the hoppers forming part of the unloaders. Once the ore had been weighed in the hopper it was deposited on a conveyor belt which transported it direct to the respondents' stock yard. The issue arose whether the respondents were required to employ registered dock workers to perform any, and if so which, of the operations required in the process of removing the ore from the ships' holds and transporting it to their stock yard, including operations in connection with the conveyor belt (e g picking up ore which fell to the ground or preventing the ore from 'jamming' up the belt). That issue raised two further questions: (1) whether the new harbour formed part of the port of Port Talbot for the purpose of the 1967 scheme, and (2) if so, what, if any, of the operations in question were 'dock work' for the purposes of the 1967 scheme.

Held – (i) For the purpose of the 1967 scheme the port of Port Talbot meant the particular area of land, or land covered by water which constituted the 'dock estate' at Port Talbot from time to time and was not limited to that area which constituted

---

f Section 6, so far as material, provides: 'In this Act the following expressions have the meanings hereby assigned to them respectively, that is to say:—"cargo" includes anything carried or to be carried in a ship or other vessel; "dock worker" means a person employed or to be employed in, or in the vicinity of, any port on work in connection with the loading, unloading, movement or storage of cargoes, or work in connection with the preparation of ships or other vessels for the receipt or discharge of cargoes or for leaving port . . .'

g The Port of Port Talbot Registration Amended Scheme (dated 5th April 1943) as amended in accordance with art 3 of the Essential Work (Dock Labour) Order 1941 (SR & O 1941 No 1440), approved by the Minister of Labour under the Dock Labour (Compulsory Registration) Order 1940 (SR & O 1940 No 1013), and subsequently amended with effect from 27th June 1947, by the substitution of a new definition of 'dock work'. That definition, so far as material, is set out at p 311 f to j, post

h The British Transport Docks Act 1964

the 'dock estate' in 1942. The word 'dock' in the phrase 'dock estate' was used adjectivally in a non-technical sense referring to the port or harbour area generally. 'Dock estate' therefore meant simply the land, or land covered by water, owned or controlled by the harbour authority which was from time to time used for harbour purposes. Accordingly the 1967 scheme applied to the new harbour (see p 309 e, p 310 g and h, p 311 a, p 315 h to p 316 a and d, p 318 a b and j and p 319 d to f, post).

(ii) (Lord Morris of Borth-y-Gest dissenting in part) To qualify as 'dock work' at Port Talbot for the purpose of the 1967 scheme the operations in question had to be (a) 'dock work' within the definition in the port registration scheme, (b) performed in connection with 'cargo', (c) being work which, at Port Talbot, had hitherto been 'ordinarily performed by dock workers' of the 'classes or descriptions' to which the 1967 scheme applied. Having regard to the limiting words 'of the classes or descriptions to which the scheme applies' and the fact that the 1967 scheme applied only to registered dock workers, to qualify as dock work for the purposes of the 1967 scheme it had to be shown that the operations in question had in fact been ordinarily performed at Port Talbot by *registered* dock workers (see p 309 e, p 315 c, p 316 d and p 320 h to p 321 c, post).

(iii) It followed therefore that—

(a) work done in the holds of ships at the new jetty could only be performed by registered dock workers since it was work in connection with cargo which had never been 'ordinarily performed' at Port Talbot by anyone other than registered dock workers (see p 309 e, p 315 c, p 316 d and p 321 c, post):

(b) (Lord Morris of Borth-y-Gest dissenting) the driving of 'grab unloaders' on the new jetty was not work which had to be performed by registered dock workers for, although it was work in connection with 'cargo', it was not work which had in fact been ordinarily performed at Port Talbot by registered dock workers since the unloading of iron ore at Margam Wharf, constituting 90 per cent of the cargoes coming to Port Talbot had been unloaded by crane drivers who were not registered dock workers; it was immaterial that, by virtue of the definition in the port registration scheme, that work should have been performed by registered dock workers (see p 309 e, p 315 c, p 316 d and p 322 c to e, post);

(c) (Lord Morris of Borth-y-Gest dissenting) work done as the ore passed along the conveyor to the stock yard was not work which had to be performed by registered dock workers since it was not work in connection with 'cargo'. The ore ceased to be 'cargo' when it fell out of the hopper on to the conveyor (see p 309 e, p 315 c, p 316 d and p 323 c, post).

Note

For dock labour schemes generally, see 38 Halsbury's Laws (3rd Edn) 455-463, paras 782-790.

Cases referred to in opinions

Bowers v Gloucester Corpn [1963] 1 All ER 437, [1963] 1 QB 881, [1963] 2 WLR 386, 127 JP 214, 61 LGR 209, DC, 45 Digest (Repl) 155, 614.

Director of Public Prosecutions v Ottewell [1968] 3 All ER 153, [1970] AC 642, [1968] 3 WLR 621, 132 JP 499, 52 Cr App Rep 679, HL, Digest (Cont Vol C) 224, 5364l.

Dyke v Elliott, The Gauntlet (1872) LR 4 PC 184, 8 Moo PCC NS 428, 26 LT 45, 1 Asp MLC 211, 17 ER 373, PC, 15 Digest (Repl) 877, 844f.

Liew Sai Wah v Public Prosecutor [1968] 2 All ER 738, [1969] 1 AC 295, [1968] 3 WLR 385, PC, Digest (Cont Vol C) 276, 598a.

London & North Eastern Railway Co v Berriman [1946] 1 All ER 255, [1946] AC 278, 115 LJKB 124, 174 LT 151, HL, 38 Digest (Repl) 297, 69.

National Dock Labour Board v John Bland & Co Ltd [1971] 2 All ER 779, [1972] AC 222, [1971] 2 WLR 1491, [1971] 2 Lloyd's Rep 20, HL.

Rugby Joint Water Board v Foottit [1972] 1 All ER 1057, [1972] 2 WLR 757, HL.

Appeal

The National Dock Labour Board appealed, by leave, against an order of the Court *a*
of Appeal (Sachs and Buckley LJJ, Salmon LJ dissenting in part) made on 29th July
1971 dismissing an appeal by the appellants and allowing an appeal by the respondents, the British Steel Corporation, against a judgment of the Divisional Court of the
Queen's Bench Division (Lord Parker CJ, Cooke and Bridge JJ) dated 8th June 1970
which reversed a decision on an industrial tribunal at Cardiff dated 17th March 1970 *b*
on a reference by the respondents for the determination of questions under s 51 of
the Docks and Harbours Act 1966 and the Industrial Tribunals (Dock Work)
Regulations 1967[1]. The questions referred to the tribunal were as follows:

'1. Which, if any, parts of the harbour and jetty recently constructed by British
Transport Docks Board at Port Talbot Glamorgan and the associated unloaders,
of the belt conveyor system to the stockyard of the Steel Works of the [respon- *c*
dents], and of such stockyard are places in the Port of Port Talbot to which
the [Dock Workers Employment Scheme 1967[2]] applies, and
'2. What, if any, work of the following work is dock work:—work done in the
holds of ships discharging at the jetty to piling in the steelworks stockyard,
including subsequent delivery to railway wagon or road vehicle or outward
vessel; driving the unloaders on the jetty, driving the mechanical trimming *d*
appliances in the holds; cleaning up deck spillage; attending the belts up to and
including piling in the stockyard, and all cleaning up connected therewith.'

The following facts are taken from the judgment of Salmon LJ in the Court of
Appeal. Before 1970 the port of Port Talbot consisted of a complex of docks reached
through the entrance lock lying a short distance up river and east of the mouth of the *e*
River Avon. At least 90 per cent of the cargo handled at Port Talbot was iron ore
discharged at Margam Wharf and destined for the Margam Steel Works and the
Abbey Steel Works, both adjacent to the port and both owned by the respondents.
The total annual amount of iron ore discharged at the port was about 3,250,000 tons
and was increasing. The docks board and their predecessors in title were the free-
holders of the land comprising the port, some of which, including Margam Wharf, *f*
was leased to the respondents and their predecessors in title. The port was incapable
of accommodating vessels of more than 10,000 tons and at neap tide even vessels of
that size were unable to reach Margam Wharf. Modern bulk ore carriers which
began to come into vogue in the early 1960s were very large vessels of up to 100,000
tons. Accordingly, the docks board obtained powers under a private Act of Parliament, the British Transport Docks Act 1964, to develop and extend the port of Port *g*
Talbot so that it might accommodate the large modern ore-carrying vessels. That
development and extension was completed early in 1970 and subsequently came
into use. It consisted of a large jetty lying in a dredged tidal harbour bounded by
breakwaters to the east of the mouth of the River Avon and close to the entrance of
the original port or harbour. The new jetty was to be leased by the docks board to
the respondents. The new tidal harbour together with its jetty was part of the port *h*
or harbour of Port Talbot, ss 3 and 28 (2) of the 1964 Act expressly so providing.
Port Talbot harbour was defined by s 3 as meaning 'the harbour of Port Talbot
transferred to and vested in the Board by the Transport Act, 1962'. Section 28 (2)
provided: 'Except as otherwise provided in this Act the tidal harbour shall for all
purposes form part of Port Talbot harbour.'

Once the bulk ore carriers had tied up at the new jetty the ore was unloaded and *i*
conveyed to the respondents' steelworks. For that purpose there were, on the jetty,
two semi-automatic grab unloaders which resembled large cranes. The unloader
moved under automatic power along the jetty. It was brought into position by its

1 SI 1967 No 313
2 Set out in Sch 2 to the Dock Workers (Regulation of Employment) (Amendment) Order
   1967 (SI 1967 No 1252)

driver with its boom projecting over the hatch to be unloaded. The grab automatically reached a predetermined distance from the hatch top and then came under the manual control of the driver. He lowered it into the hold where it was filled with ore. He then brought it back to the same point above the hatch top at which he had taken over manual control. From there the grab automatically slid back along the boom to a point above the hopper into which it discharged the ore and then returned to the predetermined point above the hatch top and the operation was repeated. When a pre-set weight of ore had been discharged into the hopper, the hopper automatically emptied its contents on to a plate feeder from which the ore was delivered on to a conveyor belt which took it off the jetty through a transfer station, where samples were taken to be tested in a sampling station, and thence towards and finally into the respondents' stock yard where a 'boomstacker' removed the ore from the conveyor and deposited it on one or other of 14 large stacks. The stock yard was an integral part of the steel works. The respondents owned the freehold of most of it and rented the rest from the board and it was there that their stores of raw material were kept.

P E Webster QC and *A E J Diamond* for the appellants.

R A MacCrindle QC and *Andrew Leggatt QC* for the respondents.

The Lordships took time for consideration.

13th December. The following opinions were delivered.

LORD REID. My Lords, I have had an opportunity of reading the speech of my noble and learned friend, Lord Cross of Chelsea. I agree with it and I would therefore make the order which he proposes.

LORD MORRIS OF BORTH-Y-GEST. My Lords, the Dock Workers (Regulation of Employment) Act 1946 enabled schemes to be made which (a) would ensure greater regularity of employment for dock workers and (b) would secure that an adequate number of dock workers would be available for the efficient performance of the work of dock workers. Broadly stated, the employment of dock workers was in certain places to be regulated by providing (i) that no employer could employ a dock worker unless he (the employer) was a registered employer and (ii) that a registered employer could only employ as a dock worker one who was a registered dock worker. The phrase 'dock worker' is one capable of being generally understood but it was given a statutory definition (see s 6). The definition is a wide one. It in turn picks up the definitions (see s 6) of 'cargo' and of 'port'. So a dock worker means a person (a) employed or (b) to be employed (c) in or (d) in the vicinity of (e) any place at which ships are loaded or unloaded (f) on work in connection with the loading or the unloading or the movement or the storage (g) of anything carried or to be carried in any ship or vessel or (h) on work in connection with the preparation of ships or other vessels for the receipt or discharge of anything carried or to be carried in any ship or vessel or (i) on work in connection with the preparation of ships or other vessels for leaving any place at which ships are loaded or unloaded.

If anyone went today to Port Talbot he would see large ships proceeding to a jetty in the tidal basin and he would learn that such ships carried iron ore and that such iron ore was to be taken from the holds of the ships and placed in a nearby storage area or stock yard so that from there it should later be taken away to blast furnaces. Anyone who had read the definition of a dock worker might be pardoned for thinking, if a scheme was applicable, that those employed in connection with the movement of the iron ore from the holds of the ships to the storage area were dock workers who could only be employed if they were registered dock workers. But such a person would have to be told that he must not reach conclusion until, with unfaltering step, he has picked his way successfully through the copious words of the Dock Labour

Scheme for the South Wales Ports which was made in 1942 under the Essential Work
(Dock Labour) Order 1941[1], and which for the meanings of some of its expressions   *a*
incorporated by reference the words of the Port of Port Talbot Registration Amended
Scheme as re-amended[2] and until he has mastered the wording of the amended
national scheme which is called the Dock Workers Employment Scheme 1967. If
he is told that in the long trail through the industrial tribunal and the the Divisional
Court[3] and then the Court of Appeal[4], different paths have been trodden and sometimes with a divergence between members of the same tribunal or court, he will   *b*
embark on his journey towards a conclusion with caution and with no little misgiving.

   The Dock Labour Scheme for the South Wales Ports was made in 1942; it was made
under the Essential Work (Dock Labour) Order 1941. The opening words of the 1942
scheme recite that 'The Ports and the Areas covered by this Scheme are set out in the
Appendix'. The appendix recites that for the purposes of the scheme 'the expression
"Port" shall include the following places'. Included in six 'places' was 'Port Talbot—   *c*
All the Dock Estate'. So 'All the Dock Estate' was included within the port or the
area covered by the scheme.   When in 1947 the first national scheme[5] was made
under the Dock Workers (Regulation of Employment) Act 1946, the scheme provided,
inter alia (see cl 1 (3)) that it should relate to the ports set out in Appendix 1. The
appendix included certain South Wales ports including 'Port Talbot'. It further laid
down in the appendix that port meant the area of that port as laid down by or under   *d*
any Act, order in council, provisional order or other statutory enactment passed or
made with reference to that port except where otherwise defined for the purposes of
any dock labour scheme in which case it should have the meaning set out in that dock
labour scheme. The 1942 scheme as set out above, covered 'Port Talbot—All the
Dock Estate'. So the national scheme related to 'Port Talbot—All the Dock Estate'.
The question which arises is whether the words 'All the Dock Estate' denote only the   *e*
exact confines of what might be called the docks at Port Talbot as they existed
in 1942 or whether the words denote what would rationally be referred to at any given
time and from time to time as the dock estate. It is said that until the recent developments ships had to pass through a dock gate or dock entrance in order to reach the
various wharves or bases or berths where ships were loaded or unloaded and that this
pointed to the view that the words 'All the Dock Estate' must be given the narrower   *f*
meaning. In my view, this is far too restricted and it puts too limited a construction
on the word 'dock'. It is to be remembered that the 1942 scheme is a dock labour
scheme for the South Wales ports. The words 'All the Dock Estate' are, in my view,
used to denote that all the areas devoted to the work of what might be called the port
of Port Talbot were places within the scheme. The scheme was concerned with port
transport workers who were doing 'port transport work' within the port of Port   *g*
Talbot. The use of the word 'dock' in the phrase 'All the Dock Estate' was not
designed to draw some sharp distinction in Port Talbot between the port of Port
Talbot and the docks in the port of Port Talbot. Rather does the phrase denote all
the area within which from time to time dock or port work is carried on at Port Talbot.
It is to be noted also that the 1942 scheme requires for the ascertainment of the
meaning of 'port transport work' a reference to the 'Port' Registration Scheme. The   *h*
words 'Dock' and 'Port' seem in some places to be interchangeable. The Dock
Workers (Registration of Employment) Act 1946 defines a 'dock' worker as one who
works in or in the vicinity of any 'port' and a 'port' as including any place at which
ships are loaded or unloaded. While the 1947 scheme (and the subsequent 1967
scheme) relate to the 'ports' as set out in Appendix I which in turn picks up the   *j*

---

1   SR & O 1941 No 1440
2   See footnote *g*, p 306, ante
3   [1970] 2 Lloyd's Rep 137
4   [1971] 2 Lloyd's Rep 439
5   SR & O 1947 No 1189

words 'Port Talbot—All the Dock Estate'; those latter words, in my view, mean the dock or port area as it is at any given time and from time to time.

For these reasons in agreement with the Divisional Court[1] I consider that the port of Port Talbot includes the whole area south and west of the continuous red line on the map used at the various hearings.

I pass then to consider the second question referred to the industrial tribunal and in particular whether the following work is dock work: (a) work done in the holds of ships discharging at the jetty; (b) driving the unloaders on the jetty; (c) driving the mechanical trimming appliances in the holds; (d) cleaning up deck spillage; (e) attending the belts up to and including piling in the stock yard and all cleaning up connected therewith. The tribunal did not consider whether the subsequent delivery from the stock yard (or ore storage area) to railway wagon or road vehicle or outward vessel would be dock work; so that question does not now arise.

One of the objects of the Dock Labour Scheme for the South Wales Ports which was made under the Essential Work (Dock Labour) Order 1941, and which I may refer to as 'the 1942 scheme' was (see cl 1) to regularise port transport work by the continuous employment of port transport workers; there was to be registration of port transport workers and of port transport employers. There was to be a port registration committee in each port and the committee were required (see cl 4) to set up a live register of port transport workers. Port transport workers (see cl 15) were those engaged in port transport work who were registered in the live register. In the terms of cl 7 an employer engaged in port transport work was required only to employ port transport workers. For the meaning of 'port transport work' reference had to be made to the port registration scheme. So the Port of Port Talbot Registration Amended Scheme as amended in accordance with art 3 of the Essential Work (Dock Labour) Order 1941 had to be consulted. That was a document of 5th April 1943. A revised definition of port transport work took effect as from 27th June 1947. In the result as at that date a port transport worker was a person who was registered in the live register and who was engaged in 'port transport work'. Such work, referring only to some of many paragraphs of descriptive definition, comprised:

'1. *Import Cargoes*
'(a) Discharging from ship, including unlashing and hatchminding, winch-driving and cranedriving, receiving to railway wagons, road vehicles, transit sheds, warehouses or coasting vessels, and assisting the reception of cargoes into Barges; also the work of discharging/loading Iron Ore or any other traffic ex/to Ship at Margam Wharf, and of Copper Ore or any other traffic ex/to Ship at Rio Tinto Wharf.
'(b) Storage of traffic in transit sheds or warehouses and subsequently delivering therefrom to railway wagons, road vehicles or to outward vessels.
'(c) Storage of traffic on open ground, whether direct from ship, railway wagon or road vehicle, and subsequently delivering to railway wagons, road vehicle or to outward vessels . . .'

But it did not include, inter alia—

'(ii) Wagon checking, storekeeping (including Gear Storing); Timber Pond Work; Weighing; Traffic, Marine and Coal Shipping operations; Policing, Engineering, (Mechanical, Electrical and Civil), Locomotive operations; Pilotages; Dockboatmen's duties and all Drydock operations . . .
'(iv) Transporter Grab Driving at Margam Wharf except when employed discharging and/or loading vessels at Margam Wharf . . .'

It seems clear from this that at what I may call the old Margam Wharf all discharging of iron ore from ships including discharging by transporter grab driving was port transport work; only if the transporter grab was later being used to move iron ore from the place on the quay where it had been put was the work not port transport work. I do not think that it is now being disputed that (save to the extent of the exception just mentioned) the work at the old Margam Wharf should have been done and should only have been done by registered port transport workers and that there was irregularity in that others were employed to perform the port transport work that was there done.

Immediately after the date of the revised definition of port transport work (for the purposes of the 1942 scheme and the port registration scheme) (i e 27th June 1947), a scheme under the Dock Workers (Regulation of Employment) Act 1946 came into effect. It came into effect on 28th June 1947. It was the Dock Workers (Regulation of Employment) Scheme 1947. That scheme was varied more than once and as amended became the Dock Workers Employment Scheme 1967. For present purposes it matters not whether the 1947 scheme or the 1967 scheme is looked at; for convenience I refer to the 1967 scheme. By cl 1 (3) it is provided that at each port to which the scheme relates—

> 'it shall apply to the same classes or descriptions of dock work and dock workers as, immediately before the coming into operation of the said Scheme of 1947, were included in any dock labour scheme or port registration scheme then in operation in respect of that port . . .'

So it becomes necessary to look back to the relevant pre-28th June 1947 dock labour scheme or port registration scheme. In this case, for the reason that in the 1942 scheme the words 'port transport work' had the meaning assigned to them in the port registration scheme—it is to that latter scheme that reference must be made in order to see what work was comprised within the words 'port transport work'. The circumstances that in the 1942 scheme the references are to 'port transport work' and to 'port transport worker' whereas in the 1947 and 1967 schemes the references are to 'dock work' and 'dock worker' suggest that the words 'dock' and 'port' were used somewhat interchangeably. Furthermore, as I have pointed out the 1946 Act is one dealing with 'dock workers' and the expression 'dock worker' is given a very wide meaning.

Before reverting to and considering the words of cl 1 (3) of the 1967 scheme which I have quoted above I should mention that there is a proviso. The effect of it seems to be that for the scheme to apply to a dock worker he must be one who is employed in or in the vicinity of the particular port in question. It reads:

> 'Provided that the Scheme shall not apply to a dock worker at any port unless he is employed or registered for employment in, or in the vicinity of, that port on work in connection with the loading, unloading, movement or storage of cargoes, or work in connection with the preparation of ships or other vessels for the receipt or discharge of cargoes or for leaving port.'

(Compare the definition in s 6 of the 1946 Act.)

At each port to which the scheme relates it applies to registered dock workers and registered employers. The provisions of cl 10 (1) of the scheme are emphatic:

> 'No person other than a registered employer and the [appellants] shall engage for employment or employ any worker on dock work nor save as hereafter in the Scheme provided shall a registered employer engage for employment or employ a worker on dock work unless that worker is a registered dock worker.'

If I am right in my view that the scheme does relate to the extended area of the port of Port Talbot as now in use then by cl 1 (3) of the scheme it applies (a) to the same classes or descriptions of dock work as before 28th June 1947 were 'included' in the then operating dock labour scheme or port registration scheme and (b) to the same classes or descriptions of dock workers as before 28th June 1947 were 'included' _a_ in the then operating dock labour scheme or port registration scheme. I will take these in turn.

What, then, were the classes or descriptions of dock work which were included in what I may call the pre-1947 schemes? The expression 'dock work' is defined in cl 2 of the 1967 scheme. The definition picks up the statutory definition of 'dock worker'. So dock work means operations at places or premises to which the scheme relates ordinarily performed by persons employed or to be employed in or in the vicinity _b_ of any place at which ships are loaded or unloaded on work in connection with the loading/unloading movement or storage of anything carried or to be carried in a ship or vessel or work in connection with the preparation of ships or other vessels for the receipt or discharge of anything carried or to be carried in any ship or vessel or for the preparation of ships or other vessels for leaving port such persons being of the class or descriptions of persons who were included in the pre-1947 schemes. It seems _c_ difficult to think that Parliament could have devised wider words. If a ship arrives at a berth in the port of Port Talbot which is a place within the words 'All the Dock Estate' and arrives with a cargo of iron ore and if it is desired to move the cargo from inside the ship and to move it to its first resting place (being a place within the dock estate) I would have little doubt that the operations to be performed would be such as would usually be performed by persons employed in the port on work in _d_ connection with the unloading or movement or storage of cargo. I think it would follow that only a registered employer could employ and only a registered worker could be employed. It would be quite immaterial whether or not the legal owner-ship in the cargo had passed to the consignee, or whether possession had passed, or whether he, the consignee, as a lessee, had control of the particular area of the port or dock estate at which the ship arrived, or whether he owned the cranes or grabs or _e_ belts which were in use, or whether direct labour was being employed. If the work being done is dock work then only a registered dock worker may by law do the work.

The contentions of the respondents have, however, been considerably founded on the word 'ordinarily'. In its context I would regard that word as merely meaning usually or normally. What is said, however, is that at the old Margam Wharf the _f_ work of unloading or moving cargo was performed by persons who were not regis-tered. Therefore it is said that at Port Talbot such work was 'ordinarily' performed by those who were not registered even though those doing the work were unlawfully employed. I regard this as a wholly unacceptable contention. The scheme is a national scheme which relates to a great many ports. It must be basic to it that at all ports to which it relates its objects should be uniformly attained. I see no trace of a provision designed to perpetuate irregularity. Nor do I think that the phrase _g_ 'ordinarily performed' would have been used if within the phrase it had been desired to embrace 'unlawfully performed'.

The words 'ordinarily performed by dock workers' occur in a definition of what is dock work. The meaning of the words must be considered as at 28th June 1947 when the Dock Workers (Regulation of Employment) Scheme 1947 first came into _h_ effect. The scheme provided (see cl 1 (4)) that at each port to which the scheme related it should apply to registered dock workers and registered employers. The scheme expressly provided (see cl 10) that only a registered employer could employ any worker on dock work and furthermore that such a registered employer could only employ a worker on dock work if such worker was a registered dock worker. So it became necessary to define 'dock work'. If I am right in my view that the words 'places or premises to which the Scheme relates' cover the extended area of _j_ the port of Port Talbot then the words of definition of what is dock work will read:

> ' "dock work" means operations [at the port of Port Talbot] ordinarily performed by dock workers of the classes or descriptions to which the Scheme applies.'

But the words 'dock workers' are also defined. The relevant words are as follows:

' "dock worker" means a person employed or to be employed in . . . [the port of Port Talbot] on work in connection with the loading, unloading, movement or storage of cargoes . . .'

Accordingly the definition of what is dock work is that it means operations at the port of Port Talbot ordinarily performed by persons employed or to be employed on work in connection with the loading, unloading, movement or storage of cargoes. This is a description of the nature of what is dock work. In its simplest form what is said is that dock work is work which is ordinarily performed by dock workers. The very purpose and object of the scheme is to ensure that that work which is in reality dock work and which is done by dock workers should only be done by registered dock workers. The work of discharging cargo at what I have called the old Margam Wharf was dock work and it was ordinarily performed by persons employed in connection with the unloading of cargo. The nature of the work did not change because, irregularly, unregistered people were employed to do it. The words of definition of 'dock work' show that dock work means operations of the kind which are ordinarily performed by dock workers. It seems to me to be a distortion to seek in effect to add to the definition words of exclusion providing that 'dock work' does not cover operations which in the past were performed by dock workers who should have been registered but in fact were not.

Passing to a consideration of 'the same classes or descriptions' of dock workers 'as before 28th June 1947 were included in' the then operating labour scheme or port registration scheme it seems to me that those who were doing port transport work and who under the schemes ought to have been registered in the live register were certainly classes or descriptions of dock workers and that they were 'included' in the schemes even though erroneously some who were doing the work were not on the live register. It is because such workers were 'included' in the schemes that they ought to have been on the live register.

For all these reasons I consider that those who were employed by the respondents to unload and move the iron ore and place it on the store yard were dock workers who were performing dock work and were within the scheme. There is a complication in that only a part of the store yard is within the 'Dock Estate'. But in practice no difficulty is here created. If the respondents must only employ registered workers (on what is dock work) within the dock estate they are in no way embarrassed by the fact that a part of the storage area is outside the 'Dock Estate'. When they come to move the ore from the storage area different questions arise. That operation would be comparable to the operation in *National Dock Labour Board v John Bland & Co Ltd*[1] of removing the timber from the rented areas to the yards of the respondents in that case. At that stage the timber was no longer regarded as cargo. So in the present case it may be that the iron ore would no longer fall to be described as cargo when it was being removed from its resting place at the storage area. But during the unloading of the iron ore from the ship and its movement to the storage area I consider that the iron ore would fairly and rationally be described as cargo. In the helpful words used by my noble and learned friend, Lord Cross, in *Bland's* case[2] what was then being done could fairly be regarded as ancillary to and in broad sense part of the carriage by sea. The work then being done would be the unloading, the moving and the storing of cargo. I regard it as wholly artificial to say that the unloading or discharging of the iron ore came to an end once it was deposited on to a moving conveyor belt. It do not find it necessary to say that there was one continuous process of discharging. What had to be achieved was the removal of the iron ore from the hold of a ship and the placing of it in a nearby storage area. The details of the transportation methods used seem to me to be of little account although had railway wagons been used to get the iron ore to its storage place it appears from the exceptions

---

1 [1971] 2 All ER 779, [1972] AC 222
2 [1971] 2 All ER at 790, [1972] AC at 238

a set out in the port registration scheme that those within the phrase 'Locomotive operations' would not be doing 'dock work'. Subject to that or to any comparable exception it seems to me that the work of getting the iron ore from the hold of a ship to the storage area was 'dock work' within the wording (and indeed the intention) of the pre-1947 schemes.

b No question arises for decision in this appeal concerning the subsequent delivery of the iron ore from the stock yard but, in my view, the other work described in the second question which was referred to the tribunal (under s 51 of the Docks and Harbours Act 1966) was dock work.

For the reasons which I have set out I would allow the appeal.

LORD HODSON. My Lords, I also have had the opportunity of reading the

c speech of my noble and learned friend, Lord Cross of Chelsea. I agree with it. I only wish to add a word on the geographical question on which there has been much difference of opinion in the courts below. The question is 'Which if any parts of the tidal harbour and jetty at Port Talbot, of the belt conveyor system and of the [respondents'] nearby stock yard are places in the port of Port Talbot to which the 1967 Scheme applies?'

d The answer is to be found in the wording of the scheme which applies to Port Talbot and defines the port by reference to an earlier dock labour scheme made in 1942 as for the purposes of the scheme including 'All the Dock Estate'.

The contention of the respondents which found favour with the industrial tribunal and also with the majority of the Court of Appeal[1] (where Salmon LJ dissented) but was rejected by the Divisional Court[2] was in effect that the manifest intention of

e the 1967 Act was, so to speak, to 'freeze' the geographical situation as it existed in 1942. The majority of the Court of Appeal accordingly held that the expression 'All the Dock Estate' referred to property answering the description in 1942.

It is on the wording of this expression that the argument has turned. Salmon LJ was of the opinion that the expression was apt to cover the whole area of the port or harbour at Port Talbot while excluding other parts of the town. He held that the

f new tidal harbour and jetty were not merely an adjunct of the steelworks but, as the respondents admitted, form part of the port of Port Talbot. He gave the expression a flexible interpretation which is on the face of it right so as to make the 1967 scheme include the tidal harbour and jetty and the ground on the landward side of the jetty over which the ore is conveyed to the steel works.

The argument forcibly presented to your Lordships against this view sought to

g limit the definition of a dock to something which can properly be described as a dock, that is to say an artificial enclosure converted into a harbour or river provided for the reception of vessels and generally shut off by gates regulating the flow of water. This ignores the use of the word 'estate' which indicates that the word 'dock' is used in an adjectival sense and does not have the effect of limiting the word 'estate' to something which can properly itself be described as a dock. I reject this argument

h which depends on the limited meaning of the word 'dock'.

A subsidiary argument was pressed based on the criminal penalties imposed by the Dock Workers (Regulation of Employment) Act 1946, s 1 (5), relying on the principle stated by Lord Simonds in *London & North Eastern Railway Co v Berriman*[3], where he said: 'A man is not to be put in peril upon an ambiguity, however much or little the purpose of the Act appeals to the predilection of the court.'

j It is sufficient for my purpose to say that with all respect to those who have construed the expression 'All the Dock Estate' so as to exclude the land and water under discussion I cannot agree that there is any ambiguity and I would unhesitatingly

---

1 [1971] 2 Lloyd's Rep 439
2 [1970] 2 Lloyd's Rep 137
3 [1946] 1 All ER 255 at 270, [1946] AC 278 at 313, 314

affirm the opinion of the Divisional Court[1] and that of Salmon LJ[2] that the expression
is to be construed not so as to freeze the subject-matter of the scheme at any particular   *a*
date but so as to allow the words 'All the Dock Estate' to be interpreted in a 'flexible'
or 'ambulatory' sense rather than so as to import a rigidity into the scheme which
might result in inconvenient and impractical results. In this connection I would
adopt the language of the Privy Council in a judgment delivered by James LJ in
Dyke v Elliott, The Gauntlet[3], of penal strictures: *b*

> 'But where the thing is brought within the words and within the spirit, there
> a penal enactment is to be construed, like any other instrument, according to the
> fair commonsense meaning of the language used, and the Court is not to find or
> make any doubt or ambiguity in the language of a penal statute, where such
> doubt or ambiguity would clearly not be found or made in the same language in
> any other instrument.'   *c*

On this point I would allow the appeal and agree to the order which my noble and
learned friend, Lord Cross of Chelsea, proposes.

LORD SIMON OF GLAISDALE.   My Lords, I have had the advantage of
reading the speech prepared by my noble and learned friend, Lord Cross of Chelsea.
My only reservation from complete concurrence is on a point which does not affect   *d*
his conclusions, with which I agree. This reservation is on the significance of the words
'discharge' (or 'unload') and 'cargo'—interrelated concepts. The meaning of such
words may sometimes be partly or wholly a matter of construction; for example, in
the instant case the revised definition of 'dock work', approved by the Minister by
letter dated 17th June 1947, shows that for the purpose of the scheme 'discharge' of
ship-borne goods is at an end when they are deposited in locomotive wagons, and   *e*
that they also then cease to be 'cargo'. But within such limits imposed by the construction of a particular instrument or enactment it is, in my view, a question of fact
when and where goods are to be regarded as finally unloaded or discharged, and when
and where they cease to be cargo. I agree with the general test proposed by my noble
and learned friend, Lord Cross of Chelsea, in *National Dock Labour Board v John Bland
& Co Ltd*[4]:   *f*

> ' . . . whether what has been done with them [the goods] up to the time when
> the question whether they are still cargo has to be answered can fairly be regarded
> as ancillary to and in a broad sense part of their carriage by sea.'

The tribunal of fact will take into account such matters as the distance the goods
have been moved from the ship's hold to the site in question, the method of transit,   *g*
whether such transit is a continuous process, in what circumstances and for how long
the goods come to rest in any particular place, how many separate mechanisms of
propulsion are involved, the ownership of the avenues of transit, and so on. In the
instant case the lay members of the industrial tribunal (constituting the majority)
concluded that the ore was not finally discharged until it had been deposited by the
primary boom stacker in the respondents' stock yard. The Divisional Court[5] agreed   *h*
with the industrial tribunal. This seems to me to be a conclusion to which a
tribunal could come, applying Lord Cross's general test; in other words, there
was no error in law. I do not think that any further appellate tribunal is justified in
interfering with such concurrent conclusions.
     My Lords, may I add a word on an aspect of what has been called 'the geographical
question'—the meaning of 'dock estate'? Counsel for the respondents cited case law   *j*

1   [1970] 2 Lloyd's Rep 137
2   [1971] 2 Lloyd's Rep 439
3   (1872) LR 4 PC 184 at 191
4   [1971] 2 All ER 779 at 790, [1972] AC 222 at 238
5   [1970] 2 Lloyd's Rep 137 at 141

a and dictionary definition to suggest that the primary meaning of 'dock' is an artificial basin within a harbour, enclosed by lock gates. Faced with the contention that in such famous ports as Liverpool, Southampton or the Lower Clyde what are known as 'the docks' largely consist of deep water quays where ships secure alongside, counsel for the respondents asserted that at least there was an ambiguity in the expression 'Dock Estate'; and that since the scheme with which your Lordships are

b concerned imposes penalties for employing unauthorised labour, the meaning should be adopted which favours the respondents.

The true rule as to the construction of penal provisions is, in my view, that set out in Halsbury's Laws of England[1], cited with approval by my noble and learned friend, Viscount Dilhorne, giving the opinion of the Judicial Committee of the Privy Council in *Liew Sai Wah v Public Prosecutor*[2]:

c 'It is a general rule that penal enactments are to be construed strictly, and not extended beyond their clear meaning. At the present day, this general rule means no more than that if, *after the ordinary rules of construction have first been applied, as they must be*, there remains any doubt or ambiguity, the person against whom the penalty is sought to be enforced is entitled to the benefit of the doubt.' (my italics.)

d In other words, the rule enjoining a restrictive construction of penal statutes is a secondary rule, to be applied only if the court is left in doubt as to the meaning—for example, where the Parliamentary intention is not clear, or there is a true residual ambiguity, or the rule of construction according to 'plain words' is not of primary force because in all probability the draftsman did not envisage the forensic situation

e with which the court is actually concerned (see *Rugby Joint Water Board v Foottit*[3]).

Moreover, it is not enough that the point of construction is a difficult one or one which respectable minds might answer differently; before applying any special rule relating to the construction of penal provisions, there must remain in the mind of the court of construction a genuine doubt as to the meaning intended by Parliament: see Lord Parker CJ in *Bowers v Gloucester Corpn*[4] and Lord Reid in *Director of*

f *Public Prosecutions v Ottewell*[5].

But in the instant case there can be no doubt at all about what Parliament intended. Its objects are explicitly stated in reg 1 (2) of the Dock Workers Employment Scheme 1967 (Sch 2 to the Dock Workers (Regulation of Employment) (Amendment) Order 1967):

g 'The objects of the Scheme are to ensure greater regularity of employment for dock workers and to secure that an adequate number of dock workers is available for the efficient performance of dock work.'

(The objects of the 1947 scheme were stated in precisely the same terms.) By 1967, if not a good decade before, it was well known that both dry cargo ships and tankers were being built of greatly increased tonnage; with the consequence that port instal-

h lations were moving down stream in tidal rivers, that new deep water quays and jetties were being built, and that the old enclosed docks upstream were in many cases being abandoned. On the respondents' interpretation less and less work would be reserved for registered dock workers. They would gradually be eased out of their secured employment. As Salmon LJ said[6], this 'would make no industrial sense'. Indeed, such an interpretation would be a formula for frustrating one of the

---

1   3rd Edn, vol 36, p 415, para 631
2   [1968] 2 All ER 738 at 741, [1969] 1 AC 295 at 301
3   [1972] 1 All ER 1057 at 1076, 1077, 1095, [1972] 2 WLR 757 at 778, 799
4   [1963] 1 All ER 437 at 439, 440, [1963] 1 QB 881 at 886, 887
5   [1968] 3 All ER 153 at 157, [1970] AC 642 at 649
6   [1971] 2 Lloyd's Rep 439 at 446

main objects of the scheme—to secure greater regularity of employment for dock   *a*
workers.

Although statutory interpretation must start by a consideration of the purpose
of the enactment in question, I would add that, insofar as linguistic considerations
are relevant, the word 'dock' in 'Dock Estate' seems to me to be used adjectivally
and not as a substantive; so that it is largely irrelevant if the primary dictionary
meaning of the substantive 'dock' is an artificial basin within a harbour, enclosed   *b*
by lock gates, or even if an ambiguity can be spelled out of the substantive.

I would also add that the special canon of construction of penal provisions is, in
my view, of differential potency according to the degree in which the provisions under
judicial scrutiny are generally or specifically penal in character, and according to
the gravity of the crime and the severity of the penalty. The penal provisions of
the scheme which is under your Lordships' consideration are a very minor incident   *c*
of it; the principal significance of the scheme is to secure industrial order and
regularity of employment practices; and those objectives are primarily to be vindicated by a declaration made by an industrial tribunal, rather than by the imposition
of penalties (see the Docks and Harbours Act 1966, s 51, especially sub-s (3)).

I therefore agree with the orders proposed by my noble and learned friend, Lord
Cross of Chelsea.
                                                                                      d

LORD CROSS OF CHELSEA. My Lords, the point at issue in this appeal is
whether any—and, if so, how much—of the work of moving iron ore from the holds
of ships lying at the jetty in the newly constructed harbour at Port Talbot, to the
neighbouring stock yard of the respondents, the British Steel Corporation, is work
which only registered dock workers can lawfully be employed to perform. This
involves the consideration of two separate questions. The first—which may be called   *e*
the 'geographical' question—is whether the new harbour is a place to which the Dock
Workers Employment Scheme 1967, made under the Dock Workers (Regulation
of Employment) Act 1946, applies. If the new harbour is such a place then one has
to decide how much of the work involved in moving this ore from ship's hold to
stock yard is 'dock work' as defined by the 1967 scheme. The facts of the case are
fully set out in the judgments of Salmon and Buckley LJJ in the Court of Appeal[1].   *f*
I will not set them out again but will proceed at once to consider the two questions
which arise for decision with only such reference to the facts as is essential to render
my views intelligible.

The geographical question

The 1967 scheme relates to many ports, including the port of Port Talbot, but to   *g*
find out what the port of Port Talbot means one is sent back to the long extinct
Dock Labour Scheme for the South Wales Ports made in 1942 under the Essential
Work (Dock Labour) Order 1941, the Appendix to which provided that for the purposes of that scheme 'the expression "Port" shall include the following places (1) . . .
(2) . . . (3) . . . (4) Port Talbot—All the Dock Estate . . .'. The basic problem in this part
of the case is whether the port of Port Talbot for the purpose of the 1967 scheme   *h*
means the particular area of land or of land covered by water which constituted
the 'Dock Estate' at Port Talbot in 1941 or whether it means the land or land covered
by water which constitutes the 'Dock Estate' at Port Talbot from time to time.
The industrial tribunal and Sachs and Buckley LJJ in the Court of Appeal[1] adopted
the former construction, while the judges in the Divisional Court[2] and Salmon LJ[1]
preferred the latter. For my part I have no doubt that the latter construction is the   *j*
right one. To treat the physical boundaries of the various ports as 'frozen' in 1942
and to take no notice of any changes whether by way of expansion or contraction which
might take place in them from time to time would, as Salmon LJ said, make no

1   [1971] 2 Lloyd's Rep 439
2   [1970] 2 Lloyd's Rep 137

a industrial sense'. As an argument against the ('ambulatory' construction reliance was placed on the fact that in the Appendix to the 1942 scheme some of the other ports are not defined by a general expression such as the 'dock estate' or the 'dock area' but by reference to specified wharves or docks. As in such cases a new wharf or dock would not become part of the port for the purpose of the scheme it would be odd—so it was said—if a new dock could become part of the port in cases where b it was defined by a general expression. I do not know why different ports were defined in different ways for the purposes of the scheme, but I can see no force in the argument based on this difference. Although at Newport, to take one example, an entirely new wharf would not form part of the port for the purposes of the scheme, it is surely obvious that anything which could fairly be said to be an extension of one of the named wharves would form part of the port and by parity of reasoning I c would have thought that any new dock which could fairly be said to be an extension of the 'Dock Estate' as it existed in 1941 would form part of the port of Port Talbot. Then it was argued that the new harbour could not be part of the 'Dock Estate' since it was not a 'dock' in the strict sense of the word—that is to say not, like the old part of the port, a basin entered through a lock—but a tidal harbour constituting an entirely new entity. I cannot accept that argument. Section 28 (2) of the British d Transport Docks Act 1964, under which the new harbour was constructed, says that except as otherwise provided in the Act the tidal harbour shall for all purposes form part of Port Talbot harbour. In the phrase 'the Dock Estate' the word 'dock' is not I think used in a technical sense. When one speaks of 'the docks' of a particular seaport one is referring to the port or harbour area generally and not simply to such part, if any, of it as consists of basins approached through locks, and I would construe the words 'Dock Estate' in the same sort of way. Finally, it was said that the new e harbour ought not to be considered as part of the 'Dock Estate' for the purpose of the scheme because it was simply an adjunct to the steel works and used exclusively by the respondents. It is, however, by no means unusual for particular wharves in ports to be used exclusively for the business of particular traders and in fact 90 per cent of the traffic passing through the old part of the port consisted of material going f to the steel works. In my judgment 'the Dock Estate' means simply the land or land covered by water owned or controlled by the harbour authority which is from time to time used for harbour purposes.

The 'dock work' point

Clause 1 (3) of the 1967 scheme provides that at Port Talbot the scheme shall apply to the same classes or descriptions of dock work and dock workers as im-
g mediately before the coming into force of the Dock Workers (Regulation of Employ-ment) Scheme 1947—which was the first 'national' scheme—were included in the local dock labour scheme for South Wales previously mentioned. Clause 1 (3) contains a proviso in the following terms:

h 'Provided that the Scheme shall not apply to a dock worker at any port unless he is employed or registered for employment in, or in the vicinity of, that port on work in connection with the loading, unloading, movement or storage of cargoes, or work in connection with the preparation of ships or other vessels for the receipt or discharge of cargoes or for leaving port.'

Clause 1 (4) of the 1967 scheme reads as follows: 'At each port to which the Scheme relates, it shall apply to registered dock workers and registered employers.' By
j cl 2 (1) of the scheme, read in conjunction with s 6 of the Dock Workers (Regulation of Employment) Act 1946, 'cargo' for the purposes of the scheme includes anything carried or to be carried in a ship, and 'dock worker' means a person employed or to be employed in or in the vicinity of any port on work in connection with the loading, unloading, movement or storage of cargoes or work in connection with the preparation of ships or other vessels for the receipt or discharge of cargoes or

for leaving port. Further by cl 2 (1) of the scheme 'dock work' is defined as 'operations at places or premises to which the Scheme relates, ordinarily performed by
dock workers of the classes or descriptions to which the Scheme applies' and 'registered dock worker' as a dock worker whose name is, for the time being, entered in
the register of dock workers. In the war-time schemes made before the passing of
corresponding phrases were 'port transport work' and 'port transport worker'. In
order, therefore, to discover what classes or descriptions of dock work and dock
workers were included in the Dock Labour Scheme for the South Wales Ports one
must turn to the definitions of 'Port Transport worker' and 'Port Transport work'
contained in it. They ran as follows: ' "port transport worker" means a person engaged in port transport work, who is registered in the live register'. ' "port transport
work" had the meaning assigned to it in the port registration scheme.' 'Port registration scheme' in its turn is defined as a scheme approved by the Minister under the
Dock Labour (Compulsory Registration) Order 1940[1], as amended in accordance with
the Essential Work (Dock Labour) Order 1941. There was such a scheme for Port
Talbot the definition of 'port transport work' in which was amended immediately
before the coming into force of the national scheme in 1947 and as amended contained
a definition of 'dock work' which so far as relevant ran as follows:

' "Dock Work" at the Port of Port Talbot shall comprise:

'1. *Import Cargoes*
'(a) Discharging from ship, including unlashing and hatchminding, winch-
driving and cranedriving, receiving to railway wagons, road vehicles, transit
sheds, warehouses or coasting vessels, and assisting the reception of cargoes into
Barges; also the work of discharging/loading Iron Ore or any other traffic ex/to
Ship at Margam Wharf, and of Copper Ore or any other traffic ex/to Ship at
Rio Tinto Wharf.
'(b) Storage of traffic in transit sheds or warehouses and subsequently delivering
therefrom to railway wagons, road vehicles or to outward vessels.
'(c) Storage of traffic on open ground, whether direct from ship, railway
wagon or road vehicle, and subsequently delivering to railway wagons, road
vehicle or to outward vessels . . .
' "Dock Work" shall not include: (i) . . . (ii) . . . Locomotive operations . . .
(iv) Transporter Grab Driving at Margam Wharf except when employed
discharging and/or loading vessels at Margam Wharf . . .'

It is by no means easy to find one's way through this maze of verbiage but, so far
as I can see, work at the port of Port Talbot is not 'dock work' for the purpose of the
1967 scheme unless it passes three tests. First, it must fall within the description of
'dock work' in the port registration scheme for Port Talbot. Secondly, having regard
to the definition of 'dock worker' in the 1967 scheme it must be work in connection
with 'cargo'. Thirdly, having regard to the definition of 'dock work' contained in
the 1967 scheme, it must be work which at Port Talbot was 'ordinarily performed
by dock workers' of the 'classes or descriptions to which the Scheme applies'. The
appellants made two submissions with regard to this definition of 'dock work' with
which I must deal. First, they submitted that in considering whether the operation
in question was ordinarily performed by dock workers one should not limit one's
attention to registered dock workers but should ask oneself whether it was ordinarily
performed by people who fall within the definition of 'dock worker' in the 1946 Act
whether registered or not. I cannot accept this submission which appears to me to
pay no regard to the limiting words 'of the classes or descriptions to which the scheme
applies' and the fact that the 1967 scheme only applies to registered dock workers
and that the war-time schemes only applied to port transport workers 'on the live

---

1 SR & O 1940 No 1013

a register'. One might perhaps have expected the draftsman to have used the phrase 'registered dock workers', of which he gives a definition, rather than the cumbrous phrase which he uses, but this scheme is not remarkable for the elegance, brevity or clarity of the language employed. The second submission was that the qualification that the work in question must have been ordinarily performed by dock workers did not apply to any work which was specified as 'dock work' in the port registration

b scheme but only to work which it was sought to bring in as incidental or ancillary to work so specified. To give effect to that submission, one would have to rewrite the definition. In the result, therefore, I think that even if the work in question is specified in the port registration scheme and is work on cargoes it will not qualify as 'dock work' for the purpose of the 1967 scheme as applied to Port Talbot unless it was ordinarily performed at Port Talbot by registered dock workers.

c The work involved in moving the ore from the hold of a ship lying at the jetty in the new harbour to the respondents' stock yard has to be considered under three heads (a) work done in the hold of the ship (b) the driving of the 'grab unloaders' stationed on the jetty by the operation of which the ore is lifted out of the ship and passes through the hoppers on to the conveyor belt and (c) work done as the ore passes along the conveyor to the stock yard (e g picking up ore which falls to the

d ground or preventing the ore from 'jamming' the belt) and the working of the 'primary boomstackers' in the stock yard by the operation of which the ore is taken off the conveyor and stacked in piles in the yard.

As to (a) there is no doubt that the work done in the hold of the ship is work on the unloading of cargo. Further, it is not suggested that such work was ever 'ordinarily performed' at Port Talbot by anyone other than registered dock workers. If there-

e fore the appellants succeed on the 'geographical' question—as in my judgment they do—it follows that the respondents must employ registered dock workers to do this work in the tidal harbour.

As to (b) the driving of the 'grab unloaders' on the new jetty is also clearly work on the unloading of cargo; but the question arises whether when the 1967 scheme took effect it was work 'ordinarily performed' at Port Talbot by registered dock

f workers. At that date—and indeed when this question was referred to the tribunal —the new tidal harbour was not yet in use, so what one has to ask oneself is whether the work of driving cranes or grabs on the wharves surrounding the old part of the harbour was 'ordinarily performed' by registered dock workers. The position in that regard was curious. Ninety per cent of the cargoes coming to the old part of the harbour consisted of iron ore to be unloaded at Margam Wharf which adjoined

g the steel works and was leased to the respondents. The cranes or grabs on that wharf were employed partly in taking the ore out of the holds of vessels tied up at the wharf and stacking it in the respondents' stock pile on the landward side of the wharf and partly—when, as often happened, there were no vessels at the wharf— in moving the ore from the stock pile and placing it on a conveyor belt on the landward side of the stock pile which took it into the steel works. The port registration

h scheme for Port Talbot recognised the distinction by providing expressly that 'transporter grab driving' at Margam Wharf should not be 'port transport work' or 'dock work' unless the grabs were being used in discharging and/or loading vessels at Margam Wharf. The crane or grab driving on the other wharves where the remaining 10 per cent of the cargoes were unloaded was performed by registered dock workers and according to the scheme dock workers should also have been doing the

j part of this work at Margam Wharf which consisted in the unloading or loading of vessels. In practice, however, in the years prior to the coming into force of the first 'national' scheme in 1947 the dockers allowed employees of the respondents who were not dock workers but members of another union to do that work as well as the work of driving the grabs or cranes when they were moving the iron ore from the stock pile to the conveyor—and these men went on doing all this work after the 1947 scheme came into force. So, notwithstanding the terms of the port transport

scheme—incorporated by reference into the national scheme—the work of unloading
cargoes of ore at Margam Wharf by means of cranes or grabs has, for many years
past, been performed by men who were not registered dock workers. In these circumstances the respondents say that the analogous work at the new jetty is not
'dock work' under the 1967 scheme. The industrial tribunal rejected that submission.
Their grounds for doing so were partly that it would be wrong to concentrate on
what had been happening at Margam Wharf to the exclusion of what was happening
in other parts of the port of Port Talbot or elsewhere in other ports and partly that
failure to enforce the provisions of a scheme could not deprive dock workers of a
right which they would otherwise possess.   The Divisional Court[1] upheld this view
of the matter but in the Court of Appeal[2] Salmon and Sachs LJJ held that the respondents were right.   Buckley LJ did not dissent from their view though he preferred
not to express a concluded opinion. For my part I agree with the Court of Appeal.
The definition of 'dock work' in cl 2 of the 1967 scheme, as I read it, directs one to
consider whether the operation at question is ordinarily performed by dock workers
at the place in question, i e in this case at Port Talbot. It may be right in this case
to take as the analogous operation the unloading of cargo by crane or grab and not
the unloading of iron ore by crane or grab but even so as 90 per cent of the cargoes
unloaded at Port Talbot were unloaded at Margam Wharf it is impossible to say that
the analogous operation was at Port Talbot ordinarily performed by registered
dock workers. It is no doubt curious that the schedule to the port registration scheme,
which was revised on the eve of the coming into force of the 1947 scheme, should
say that some work was 'dock work' at Port Talbot which for years had not ever
been performed by dock workers. But we must deal with the case as we find it.
The definition of 'dock work' in cl 2 is directed to preserving the 'status quo' and if
at any place or premises to which the scheme applies any operation was not as a
matter of fact being ordinarily performed by dock workers it will not be dock work
even though it would otherwise answer that description.

   As to (c): on this aspect of the case counsel for the respondents first submitted that
the work of discharging or unloading cargo is strictly speaking completed as soon
as the goods in question having been taken out of the ship are deposited on land.
The port registration scheme for Port Talbot says that 'discharging from ship' includes several activities, e g receiving to transit sheds or warehouses, which normally
take place after the goods have already been placed on land, but those, so the argument goes, are extensions which are not properly included in the meaning of 'discharging from ship'. Consequently one cannot include as part of the discharge of a cargo
for the purpose of the scheme any work such as, for example, moving the unloaded
goods along or across a jetty—which is not expressly mentioned in the scheme.
It is not, as I see it, necessary in this case to express a concluded opinion on this submission, but as at present advised I am not prepared to accept it. The process of
taking goods landed from a ship along the quay to a transit shed or warehouse might
well, in ordinary parlance, be spoken of as part of the unloading or discharge of the
cargo and the words following the word 'including' in 1 (a) of the definition of 'Dock
Work' in the port registration scheme might well be treated as instances of 'discharging' which are not necessarily exhaustive. Of course, if and so far as the work of
moving cargo along or across a quay involved 'locomotive' work it would not be
'dock' work because 'locomotive' work is expressly stated not to be 'dock' work.
But if the ore when it fell from the hopper on to the conveyor belt was taken by the
belt to some warehouse or transit shed there would I think be much to be said for
the view that the work of looking after the ore in its progress along the jetty was
'Dock Work' within the meaning of the port registration scheme. But this conveyor
does not take the ore to a warehouse or transit shed. It takes it to the respondents'

1   [1970] 2 Lloyd's Rep 137
2   [1971] 2 Lloyd's Rep 439

stock yard, the greater part of which is owned by the respondents and the remainder of which is leased to them by the appellants and is not being used for harbour purposes. So the question whether the work of looking after it on its way and of operating the 'primary boom stacker' is 'dock work' appears to be to depend on whether you regard the moving of the ore from ship's hold to stock yard as a single continuous operation—as though the grabs lifted the ore out of the hold and deposited it in the stock yard at one stroke, or whether you see no difference between the falling of the ore on to the moving conveyor and its falling into a series of railway wagons placed in turn under the hopper which are later all drawn away by an engine to the premises of a consignee outside the port. In the former case the ore might well be said to remain 'cargo' until it reached 'terra firma' in the stock yard; in the latter case it would, as I see it, cease to be 'cargo' when it fell into the wagons. This is eminently the sort of question which strikes different minds differently. The tribunal and the Divisional Court[1] regarded the movement of the ore from hold to stock yard as a continuous operation, whereas the Court of Appeal[2] thought that its movement involved several separate operations and that the ore ceased to be 'cargo' when it fell out of the hopper on to the conveyor. For my part I agree with the Court of Appeal on this point.

By its order the Court of Appeal declared:

'(1) that none of the land upon which the said jetty, belt conveyor system or stockyard is situated is within the port of Port Talbot to which the Dock Workers' Employment Scheme 1967 applies save for such parts of the said belt conveyor system and stockyard as are shown north and west of the green line on the agreed map;

'(2) that all work done in the holds of ships discharging at the said jetty would be dock work if performed in a place to which the said Scheme applies; and

'(3) that none of the following work is dock work (whether or not performed in a place to which the said Scheme applies), namely driving the unloaders on the jetty, attending the belt conveyor system and the piling of ore in the stockyard.'

I would be in favour of allowing the appeal to the extent of substituting for declarations (1) and (2) the following two declarations:

'(1) The land upon which the said jetty is situated and over which the said belt conveyor system runs up to the boundary of the respondents' stock yard is within the Port of Port Talbot to which the Dock Workers Employment Scheme, 1967, applies.

'(2) That all work done in the holds of ships discharging at the said jetty is dock work for the purposes of the said Scheme',

and of deleting the words in brackets in declaration (3).

Appeal allowed.

Solicitors: *Hill, Dickinson & Co* (for the appellants); *Lovell, White & King* (for the respondents).

S A Hatteea Esq Barrister.

---

1   [1970] 2 Lloyd's Rep 137
2   [1971] 2 Lloyd's Rep 439

R v Metropolitan Police Commissioner, ex parte Blackburn and another (No 3)

COURT OF APPEAL, CIVIL DIVISION

LORD DENNING MR, PHILLIMORE AND ROSKILL LJJ

16th, 17th, 27th NOVEMBER 1972

Mandamus – Chief officer of police – Enforcement of law – Obscene publications – Sale in shops of pornographic material – Police procedure to enforce law against sale of pornography ineffective – Policy of referring all prima facie cases for prosecution to the Director of Public Prosecutions for advice – Procedure of police in cautioning and taking 'disclaimers' of material seized not conforming with the law – Cause of ineffectiveness of police efforts largely due to difficulty of enforcing Obscene Publications Act 1959 – Whether mandamus would lie to Commissioner of Police of the Metropolis requiring him to enforce the law – Prosecution of Offences Regulations 1946 (SR & O 1946 No 1467), reg 6 (2) (d).

The Obscene Publications Act 1959, which was intended to strengthen the law concerning pornography, made it an offence for any person to publish, distribute or sell an obscene article or to have it in his possession or control for gain. The Act made the offence punishable, on summary conviction, with a fine not exceeding £100 or imprisonment not exceeding six months, and on indictment with a fine or imprisonment up to three years. In addition, the Act gave the police extensive powers (on obtaining a warrant for the purpose) of searching premises where there was ground for suspecting that obscene articles were kept there for publication for gain and of seizing and removing any articles found. The Act required that any articles seized should be brought before a magistrate who could then issue a summons to the occupier of the premises to show cause why the articles should not be forfeited. The Act was difficult to enforce effectively. The test of obscenity laid down was unsatisfactory, being too restrictive and not readily understandable by a jury; and the defence of 'public good' allowed by the Act enabled many pornographers to escape conviction. In several cases prosecuted by indictment acquittals were secured because of the uncertainty of the law. In summary proceedings the trivial nature of the fines imposed was not a deterrent having regard to the profits made from pornography, and under the existing law sentences of six months or less had had to be suspended. Further, there was uncertainty as to the powers and duties of the police when they seized articles.

In order to enforce the law under the 1959 Act the Metropolitan police had set up at Scotland Yard an obscene publications squad manned by 14 officers. Police divisions reported to the squad any case where it was thought obscene material was being sold in a shop and the squad sent one of its officers to investigate. If the officer thought the material on sale was obscene he obtained a warrant to search and seize the material. After seizure of the material it was the practice, in all cases, before any further steps were taken by the police, to consult the Director of Public Prosecutions by submitting the material to him. If the director thought the material was obscene he advised either a prosecution, which he undertook himself, or the lesser course of submitting the material to a magistrate for him to consider the issue of a summons for forfeiture against the occupier of the premises. If the lesser course was advised the director left it to the police to apply for the summons; but in many cases, contrary to the mandatory requirement of the Act that articles seized should be brought before a magistrate, the police merely cautioned the occupier and, invited him to sign a 'disclaimer' disclaiming any interest in the material seized; having obtained the disclaimer the police destroyed the material without reference to the courts. Although the procedure of caution and disclaimer was undesirable and possibly illegal, the police found it convenient and effective because of the unpredictable attitude of the courts to alleged obscenity and the time involved in referring cases to the courts. In the first ten months of 1972 the Metropolitan police made 166 searches in districts outside Soho and seized 871,468 items: but in Soho, during that period, searches were conducted only on 26 days throughout the period; of the 45 shops searched, 35 were searched once only and the results of the searches were meagre. The efforts of the police to prevent the sale of pornography were largely ineffective. In Soho 'hard pornography', i e extremely obscene material, was openly on sale in some 60 shops. In districts outside Soho 'soft pornography', i e moderately obscene publications, was openly on sale to anyone including young persons in very many shops, usually sweetshops and newsagents.

The applicants, being concerned about the sale of pornography in the metropolis, applied for an order of mandamus directed to the Metropolitan Police Commissioner requiring him to enforce the 1959 Act. The applicants asserted that the commissioner was not carrying out his duty of enforcing the law; they argued that he had adopted an erroneous view of the law in regarding himself as bound to take no action by way of prosecution or otherwise unless and until the Director of Public Prosecutions authorised such action; and that having regard to the obvious obscenity and continued availability of the publications in Soho and elsewhere in London the steps taken by the commissioner to enforce the law, in particular the search procedure and the procedure by way of caution and disclaimer, were ineffective and amounted to a total failure to enforce the law. The commissioner, on affidavit, stated that the practice of referring cases to the director was followed in reliance on reg 6 (2) (d)[a] of the Prosecution of Offences Regulations 1946, which provided that the chief officer of police 'shall report' to the director cases of obscene or indecent publications in which it appeared that there was a prima facie case for prosecution; that in view of the comparative absence of public complaint and the trivial penalties imposed by the courts pornography caused less public unease than other breaches of the law, and that there were enormous demands on the police force to enforce other breaches of the law. The commissioner had increased the number of the obscene publications squad to 18 officers and was reforming the squad and its administration.

Held – The application for mandamus would be dismissed. The court would interfere only in the extreme case where the commissioner was not carrying out his duty of enforcing the law; it would not interfere with the discretion which the commissioner had in carrying out that duty. Although the commissioner's practice, in accordance with reg 6 (2) (d) of the 1946 regulations, of referring cases to the Director of Public Prosecutions was open to question because the 1959 Act required the obscene article to be brought before the court, the evidence showed that the commissioner was doing what he could to enforce the law under the existing legal system and with the available manpower, and no more could reasonably be expected. The cause of the ineffectiveness of police efforts lay, largely, with the legal system and framework in which the police had to operate (see p 331 f and j to p 332 d, p 334 b, p 335 d, p 337 c to e and j to p 338 b, p 339 b and c and p 340 e and f, post).

R v Metropolitan Police Commissioner, ex parte Blackburn [1968] 1 All ER 763 considered.

Notes

For mandamus against public officers to enforce statutory duties, see 11 Halsbury's Laws (3rd Edn) 91-93, para 172, and for cases on the subject, see 16 Digest (Repl) 360, 1363-1370.

For the Commissioner of Police of the Metropolis, see 30 Halsbury's Laws (3rd

---

a   Regulation 6 (2), so far as material, provides: 'The chief officer of police shall ... report, as respect offences alleged to have been committed within his police district, to the Director of Public Prosecutions ... (d) cases of obscene or indecent libels, exhibitions or publications, in which it appears to the chief officer of police that there is a prima facie case for prosecution ...'

Edn) 63, 64, para 102, and for liaison with the Director of Public Prosecutions, see ibid 137, para 219.

For the Prosecution of Offences Regulations 1946, reg 6, see 6 Halsbury's Statutory Instruments (Second Re-issue) 5.

Cases referred to in judgments

Director of Public Prosecutions v Whyte [1972] 3 All ER 12, [1972] AC 849, [1972] 3 WLR 410, HL.

R v Anderson [1971] 3 All ER 1152, [1972] 1 QB 304, [1971] 3 WLR 939, CA.

R v Calder & Boyars Ltd [1968] 3 All ER 644, [1969] 1 QB 151, [1968] 3 WLR 974, 133 JP 20, 52 Cr App Rep 706, Digest (Cont Vol C) 249, 8631ba.

R v Gold (3rd November 1972) unreported, CCC.

R v Metropolitan Police Commissioner, ex parte Blackburn [1968] 1 All ER 763, [1968] 2 QB 118, [1968] 2 WLR 893, Digest (Cont Vol C) 279, 1113a.

Appeal

The applicants, Albert Raymond Blackburn and Tessa Marion Blackburn, appealed against the order of the Divisional Court (Lord Widgery CJ, Melford Stevenson and Brabin JJ) dated 30th October 1972, dismissing the applicants' motion for an order of mandamus directed to the respondent, the Commissioner of Police of the Metropolis, requiring him to enforce or secure the enforcement of the law against those who illegally published and sold pornographic material both by seizure thereof and by prosecution of the publishers and retailers; and requiring him to reverse the decision made under his authority or continued under his authority whereby no police officers could prosecute such offenders however obvious and scandalous the offence without obtaining the prior decision of the Director of Public Prosecutions; and requiring him to reverse his policy decision preventing the seizure of obviously pornographic material by officers of his force stationed outside New Scotland Yard. The facts are set out in the judgment of Lord Denning MR.

The applicants appeared in person.
D H Farquharson QC and *A B Hidden* for the respondent.
Gordon Slynn for the Attorney-General.

Cur adv vult

27th November. The following judgments were read.

LORD DENNING MR. Nearly five years ago Mr Blackburn came before us saying that the commissioner of police was not doing his duty in regard to gambling clubs: see *R v Metropolitan Police Commissioner, ex parte Blackburn*[1]. He comes again today; but this time it is in regard to obscene publications. He comes with his wife out of concern, he says, for their five children. He draws our attention to the shops in Soho which sell 'hard' pornography (that is, publications which are extremely obscene). There are about 60 of them. They usually have the one word 'Books' over the door or window, but no name of the proprietor. He also draws our attention to the many, very many, shops in other districts, usually sweetshops and newsagents, which sell 'soft' pornography (that is, publications which are moderately obscene). He says that all these publications, be they hard or soft, are plainly obscene. Yet they are openly on sale. Anyone can go into the shops and buy them without let or hinderance, if they are willing to pay the price. Mr Blackburn has done so himself: so has a solicitor. They went out during the course of the case and produced them to us. Whenever a point arose as to this shop or that, or as to this publication or that, he went and bought a copy.

---

1   [1968] 1 All ER 763, [1968] 2 QB 118

a Seeing that we have a law passed in 1959[1] which prohibits the publication of obscene matter, Mr Blackburn naturally says: 'Why have not the police done something about it? Why have they not seized these publications and destroyed them? Why have they not prosecuted the offenders?' Other people, I have no doubt, say the same. Mr Blackburn made such a case for enquiry that Lawton LJ and his colleagues called on the commissioner of police for an answer. The commissioner made answer which the Divisional Court thought sufficient. Mr Blackburn appeals to this court.

b His appeal raises so many questions that I will deal with them separately.

The social evil

Mr Blackburn condemned the evil in a telling phrase. Pornography, he said, is powerful propaganda for promiscuity. So it is for perversions. To those who come under its influence, it is altogether bad. We have been shown examples of it. The

c court below declined to look at them. We felt it our duty to do so, distasteful as it is. They are disgusting in the extreme. Prominent are the pictures. As examples of the art of coloured photography, they would earn the highest praise. As examples of the sordid side of life, they are deplorable. There are photographs showing young men and women, who appear to have worked themselves up into a state of extreme lust for the sake of the photographers. In their lust these young people have adopted

d positions natural, and positions unnatural; and have indulged in sexual relations and perversions, not only between themselves, but also between themselves and animals. The photographers have crouched close—inches close—to them and to their most private parts. They have photographed them apparently in the very act in the utmost detail. They have taken these photographs in bright colours. They have enlarged them. Then the printers have multiplied them in their thousands and

e hundreds of thousands. To add to it, there is letterpress. It tells of it all, gloatingly, without shame, as if to commend the readers to do likewise, or worse. To give the appearance of truth, letters are published, genuine or invented, describing the pleasures of perversions. Degrading as these publications are to the young people who participate, the prime evil-doers are those who promote them for money. The printers, the publishers, and the retailers. The 'hard' ones sell for as much as £5

f or £6 apiece. 'Soft' ones for 40p or 50p. Whereas clean publications of comparable size sell for 10p or 20p. The reason for the high prices is, of course, that the purveyors know that these publications are obscene. They know they are contrary to law. They run the risk that the police may come in to seize their whole stock and destroy it. Nay more, that they may be prosecuted to conviction, and be either fined or imprisoned. So they charge a high price to compensate them for the risk they run.

g Some may criticise the law and the way in which it is enforced. But, as to the evil itself, there can be no doubt. At any rate, Parliament has had no doubt about it. It has enacted laws with the express intention of stopping it. To these I now turn.

The law as to obscenity

The law of England has always condemned pornography and sought to suppress

h it. The history of it was given by Lord Birkett in the House of Lords[2] on the second reading of the Obscene Publications Bill on 2nd June 1959. To which I would add my few words there[3] and in The Road to Justice[4]. Lord Birkett spoke for all when he said[5]: '. . . while it is important that pornography should be struck at with vigour, and everybody would support such action, we ought to be extremely careful not to injure true literature.' Parliament heeded his words. When the Act was passed

j on 29th July 1959, its object was stated in the preamble to be: '. . . to provide for the protection of literature; and to strengthen the law concerning pornography.' In

1 I e the Obscene Publications Act 1959
2 See Hansard, Parliamentary Debates, HL, vol 216, cols 490-492
3 Ibid, cols 503 507
4 (1955) at pp 81-85
5 Hansard, Parliamentary Debates, HL, vol 216, col 495

1964 Parliament found that even that law was not strong enough. It passed another Act[1], the object of which was again 'to strengthen the law for preventing the publication for gain of obscene matter . . .'

The principal way in which Parliament strengthened the law against pornography was by giving the police extensive powers of search and seizure. The police could search the shops or stalls of retailers, the warehouses of wholesalers, the stores of printers and of publishers. They could seize all obscene material they found there' books, documents and articles of any kind which might be sold or kept for gain. Parliament was careful, however, to require safeguards against any abuse by the police of these powers. In order to search and seize, they had to obtain a warrant from a magistrate for the purpose; and, when they seized any articles, they had to bring them before the magistrate, who could then issue a summons against the occupier.

In addition to these powers of search and seizure, Parliament made a new statutory offence. Instead of the old common law misdemeanour, it made it an offence for any person to publish or distribute or sell an obscene article or even to have it in his possession or control with a view to gain. This statutory offence was punishable on summary conviction with a fine not exceeding £100, or imprisonment not exceeding six months; or on an indictment with a fine or imprisonment up to three years.

Unfortunately this legislation against pornography seems to have misfired—at any rate so far as prosecutions are concerned. Experience has shown that much material—which at first sight would appear to be pornographic in the extreme—has escaped the reach of the law. Thus, in the case of 'Last Exit to Brooklyn', the trial took nine days. Six expert witnesses for the prosecution. Thirty for the defence. The jury found the publishers guilty, but it was upset on appeal on the ground of misdirection: see *R v Calder & Boyars Ltd*[2]. In the case of 'Oz No 28 School Kids Issue', the trial took 27 days. Most of the time was taken up by expert evidence. The jury found that it was obscene contrary to the 1959 Act, but again this finding was upset on appeal on the ground of misdirection: see *R v Anderson*[3]. Then, in the case of the 'Dirty old men' the magistrates at Southampton, after two days, found that the books were not obscene because the only persons likely to read them were males of middle age and upwards. Their decision was upheld by two to one in the Divisional Court, but was reversed by three to two in the House of Lords: see *Director of Public Prosecutions v Whyte*[4]. Finally, we were shown some books which were the subject of a trial at the Old Bailey only three or four weeks ago: *R v Gold*[5]. It took seven days. Without any evidence, I should have pronounced them extremely obscene. But we are told that experts gave evidence that such material was very therapeutic for young people and would encourage them to sexual experiments without inhibition. The jury found the accused not guilty.

Those cases took an immense amount of time, manpower and money, not only of the police, but of witnesses and juries, of lawyers and of the accused persons themselves. Yet one may ask: to what avail? They have done nothing to stop pornography.

Apart from these cases, there have been several prosecutions in the magistrates' courts. The commissioner of police supplied us with a list of the results. There were several fines of £25 and £50, and a few of £100. These are obviously no deterrent. They are a mere trifle compared to the profits. Counsel for the commissioner of police told us: 'Fines of £5,000 or £10,000 would be nearer the mark. That is the sort of fine which would begin to pinch. Until the punishment really hurts, it is economically worth while to bring in more of this material.'

---

1 I e the Obscene Publications Act 1964
2 [1968] 3 All ER 644, [1969] 1 QB 151
3 [1971] 3 All ER 1152, [1972] 1 QB 304
4 [1972] 3 All ER 12, [1972] AC 849
5 (3rd November 1972) unreported

Why has the legislation misfired?

Why has the legislation misfired? I regret to say that it is in the wording of the statute and in the way the courts have applied it. In the first place, the test of obscenity is too restricted, or it has been interpreted too narrowly. It is defined as the tendency 'to deprave and corrupt persons who are likely ... to read' it. That test can be used skilfully to obtain an acquittal by this piece of sophistry: if the likely readers are those who are already depraved and corrupt, this item will not make them more so: but if the likely readers are just ordinary sort of folk, they will be so revolted that they will be turned away from it. This argument is called in the cases the 'aversion argument'. It is so plausible that the courts have held[1] that, when raised by the defence, it must be put to the jury. If it is not put, the conviction may be quashed.

In the second place, the 'defence of public good' has opened a door through which many a pornographer can escape. It says that publication can be justified, not only if it is in the interests of science, literature or art, but also if it is in the interests 'of other objects of general concern'. Under cover of this defence, experts have been allowed to come forward and say that it is good for young people to read these magazines because it removes their feelings of guilt. Such evidence is equal to saying that pornography itself is for the public good—which is quite contrary to what Parliament intended.

By way of contrast to this 1959 Act, I would draw attention to the Customs and the Post Office Acts. These prohibit the importation, or the sending by post of 'indecent or obscene articles': see s 42 of the Customs Consolidation Act 1876, and s 11 of the Post Office Act 1953. Those statutes do not attempt a definition of what is 'indecent or obscene', but the customs officers and the Post Office know pornography when they see it; and they act accordingly. Hardly ever are their decisions questioned. In 1968-1969 the customs authorities seized 1½ million magazines and books, and in no case was destruction contested. Juries also have no difficulty under those Acts. In the *Oz* case[1], the jury found the publishers guilty of sending 'obscene and indecent' articles by post. This conviction was upheld, although the conviction under the Obscene Publications Act 1959 was upset. Lord Widgery CJ pointedly observed that in the Post Office Act the word 'obscene' may have its ordinary meaning: see *R v Anderson*[2].

The procedure of the police

We were told of the procedure of the Metropolitan police to enforce the law under the 1959 Act. It is this. The police get to know—by their own inspection or by information from others—that pornographic material is on sale at a certain shop. They report it to the obscene publications squad at New Scotland Yard. They are 14 officers who are specially assigned to investigate obscenity. One of this squad goes to the shop. If he thinks the material is obscene, he goes to a magistrate and asks for a warrant. Armed with the warrant, he searches the shop and seizes all obscene material he finds there. Having seized it, he submits it to the Director of Public Prosecutions. The director then considers whether it is obscene or not. If he thinks it is obscene, he then gives his opinion, whether the occupier should be prosecuted, or not: or whether the lesser course should be taken of submitting it to the courts for a destruction order. If he advises a prosecution, the director himself undertakes the prosecution. If he advises the lesser course, he leaves it to the police to issue a summons and get the material destroyed. In many cases the police do not take the matter to the court. They caution the occupier and invite him to sign a 'disclaimer' disclaiming any interest in the material. They then destroy it. The commissioner has given figures to show the activities of the police under this procedure. He did so in a letter of 10th July 1972, and in the affidavit he put before the court. These figures are impressive. For instance, in the first 9½ months of 1972 the Metropolitan police made 166

---

1   *R v Anderson* [1971] 3 All ER 1152, [1972] 1 QB 304
2   [1971] 3 All ER at 1162, [1972] 1 QB at 317

searches and seized 871,468 items. Some of these were large-scale operators. At one address in Watford on 21st September 1972 the police seized 219,600 copies of 'Men Only' at an estimated value of £100,000. At other addresses large quantities of obscene material were seized of much value. But, impressive as those figures are, they seem to have made little impact on the trade. It remains very large. Next, the figures for Soho. They are not nearly so impressive. The commissioner gave them for the first 9½ months of 1972. In Soho the police searched 45 shops. In ten of them, they searched two, three or four times. But in the remaining 35, they searched once only in each shop. Out of these 35, eight shops gave a negative result, 27 resulted in a caution, four resulted in a prosecution. The remaining three await a decision, presumably by the director.

Mr Blackburn criticised the police severely on their search procedure. He gave evidence that he went to three shops where the police searches proved 'negative'. He found there obscene material readily on sale. He bought them and produced them to us. He also said that the procedure by way of caution or 'disclaimer' was quite ineffective; because the shops continued to sell their obscene material just the same. He asked us to infer that the police were not carrying out their duty of enforcing the law. Why were not the searches and seizures made every week, instead of once a year? That would, he suggested, bring the trade in hard pornography rapidly to a close. He also asked why the Director of Public Prosecutions should be consulted in every case? Many of these publications are obvious pornography. Why not proceed at once? Why should not the station commander himself take action? These are pertinent questions which require an answer. He submitted correspondence in which the commissioner acknowledges, quite frankly, that the practice was to consult the director, and go by his advice.

The legal position

Mr Blackburn's principal point was a legal one. He said that there was no legal justification for the police referring all cases to the director. It causes delay. They can and should act at once without his advice. I have, therefore, looked into the law; and I find that Mr Blackburn has a point worthy of serious consideration.

The powers of the police to search and seize are contained in s 3 of the Obscene Publications Act 1959, as amended by s 25 of the Criminal Justice Act 1967. Under it the police must first lay an information on oath before a magistrate and get a warrant to search and seize. If they find obscene articles and seize them, they must, as I read the Act, bring them before a magistrate and he can then order their destruction. But, instead of taking the articles before a magistrate, the police have adopted in many cases the practice of accepting disclaimers. I must describe this, because it goes back to a time before the Act was passed. It is described in the proceedings before the Select Committee on Obscene Publications in 1957. It was this. When the police searched premises and found articles which might be considered obscene, they submitted the articles to the Director of Public Prosecutions. In some cases the director would advise a prosecution. In other cases, he would instruct the officer to take steps to have the material destroyed. The officer would then go to the shopkeeper and ask him if he disputed the case. If he did not dispute it, the officer invited him to sign a disclaimer in this form: 'I do hereby disclaim ownership to the above items seized from my bookshop.' On getting that disclaimer, the officer destroyed the material. That practice was in use for many years before 1957. It had the advantage of saving time. No summons was issued. There was no hearing before a magistrate, and no examination of documents by a magistrate.

The Select Committee on Obscene Publications in 1957, however, regarded that practice as *undesirable*, and for this reason. It enabled the alleged obscene matter to be destroyed without reference to the courts[1]; whereas, the Select Committee thought it desirable that the material should be brought before the courts. When

---

1 See the Report from the Select Committee on Obscene Publications, HC Paper 123-1 Session 1957-58, para 30

a the Act was passed in 1959, it would appear that Parliament accepted the view of the Select Committee. It enacted that when the police, under the authority of a warrant, search premises and seize articles, they *must* bring the articles before a magistrate. As I read s 3 (3) it is mandatory. It says: 'Any articles seized . . . shall be brought before a justice of the peace . . .' The magistrate may then issue a summons to the occupier to show cause why the articles should not be forfeited.

b Notwithstanding that enactment, it appears that the police of the metropolis still continue the practice of accepting disclaimers. When the police search premises and seize articles, they do not submit them in the first instance to the courts. They submit them to the Director of Public Prosecutions. Then, after consultation with him and on his authority—I use the commissioner's own words—they do one of these things: (i) they may return the articles to the occupier; or (ii) they may caution him and accept a disclaimer to the property; or (iii) they may summons the occupier c before the court and seek a forfeiture order under s 3. That appears from the commissioner's affidavit.

I can see the practical advantages of the procedure adopted by the police. There is a great deal to be said for it. The attitude of the courts is so unpredictable, and the time and trouble so excessive, that the practice of accepting 'disclaimers' is far more convenient and effective. It is similar to the practice of the customs authorities who d can seize obscene or indecent articles, and destroy them, without reference to the courts, unless the owners contest the issue. But the customs authorities have wider powers than the police. There is no provision in the Customs Acts similar to s 3 (3) of the 1959 Act.

The commissioner of police, in justification of his practice, relies on the regulations relating to the prosecution of offenders[1]. These were made in 1946 long before the e 1959 Act. Regulation 6 (2) (*d*) says that the chief officer of police *shall* report to the Director of Public Prosecutions 'cases of obscene or indecent . . . publications, in which it appears to the chief officer of police that there is a prima facie case for prosecution'. I can see the reason for this regulation. It is because it is often difficult to know whether a book or magazine comes within the test of obscenity. It is also f desirable to apply a uniform standard throughout the country. So, whenever there is a prima facie case for prosecution, it should be reported to the director. So far so good. But I do not think the regulation is a complete answer to Mr Blackburn's point. Accepting that cases should be reported to the director, nevertheless, the police are not bound to hold their hand pending his advice. On the contrary, the 1959 Act, as I read it, requires the articles to be brought before the magistrate for him to g decide whether the occupier should be summoned, or not. Under the present practice, this is not done. In many cases, the articles are never brought before the magistrate. They are put before the director, and he advises whether the occupier should be summoned, or not. This may be a very convenient and sensible procedure; but I cannot forbear from asking the question: is it in accordance with the statute? And I would add: is it as effective as a summons issued by the court? A pornographic h trader might take little notice of a caution, but much of a summons for destruction, especially if it was coupled with a summons for an offence.

Conclusion

In *R v Metropolitan Police Commissioner, ex parte Blackburn*[2], we made it clear that, in the carrying out of their duty of enforcing the law, the police have a discretion with which the courts will not interfere. There might, however, be extreme cases in which j he was not carrying out his duty. And then we would. I do not think this is a case for our interference. In the past the commissioner has done what he could under the existing system and with the available manpower. The new commissioner is doing more. He is increasing the number of the obscene publications squad to 18

1 The Prosecution of Offences Regulations 1946 (SR & O 1946 No 1467)
2 [1968] 1 All ER at 769, [1968] 2 QB at 136

and he is reforming it and its administration. No more can reasonably be expected. *a*
  The plain fact is, however, that the efforts of the police have hitherto been largely
ineffective. Mr Blackburn amply demonstrated it by going out from this court
and buying these pornographic magazines—hard and soft—at shops all over the
place. I do not accede to the suggestion that the police turn a blind eye to pornography or that shops get a 'tip-off' before the police arrive. The cause of the ineffectiveness lies with the system, and the framework in which the police have to operate. *b*
The Obscene Publications Act 1959 does not provide a sound foundation. It fails to
provide a satisfactory test of obscenity; and it allows a defence of public good which
has got out of hand. There is also considerable uncertainty as to the powers and
duties of the police when they seize articles.
  If the people of this country want pornography to be stamped out, the legislature
must amend the Obscene Publications Act 1959 so as to make it strike unmistakably *c*
at pornography; and it must define the powers and duties of the police so as to
enable them to take effective measures for the purpose. The police may well say
to Parliament: 'Give us the tools and we will finish the job.' But, without efficient
tools, they cannot be expected to stamp it out. Mr Blackburn has served a useful
purpose in drawing the matter to our attention; but I do not think it is a case for
mandamus. I would, therefore, dismiss the appeal. *d*

PHILLIMORE LJ. Mr Blackburn is concerned about the sale of pornographic
booklets in the metropolis. He asserts that the commissioner is not trying to enforce
the Obscene Publications Act 1959 and (after refusal by the Divisional Court) appeals
to this court for an order of mandamus to require the commissioner so to do.
  His statement of the facts which I am prepared to accept as accurate is as follows.
There is a division between hard and soft pornographic material of this sort normally *e*
referred to as 'hard or soft porn'. 'Hard porn' is sold at a number of shops in Soho—
each shop bears the title 'Books' and there is never the name of a proprietor—the
man who runs the shop is merely a front for one of a small number of men who
control several such businesses. Altogether there are about 60 such shops in Soho.
(Counsel for the commissioner says that his client's figure is 45.) These shops are
open until 11.00 p m on most days and all day on Sunday. The principal merchandise *f*
is, of course, 'hard porn', namely booklets consisting of close up photographs of
acts of sexual intercourse normally involving several people interlocked, or if homosexual, two or more of the sex in question, whilst some depict various perversions
including acts of sexual intercourse between human beings and animals.
  These booklets sell at prices from £3 upwards but mostly for £5 each, and if
returned the purchaser may hope to be repaid half his initial stake for each of these *g*
valuable articles. Counsel for the commissioner and for the Attorney-General
rightly conceded that all booklets of the sort described were undoubtedly obscene and
their sale illegal.
  'Soft porn' on the other hand, is sold at sweet shops and other shops, where magazines can be bought, at innumerable places in London—there is one close to the offices
of Lord Longford in Piccadilly and others as far away as Hammersmith and Chiswick. *h*
These booklets show photographs of men and women in the nude but the photographs are not otherwise objectionable. The letterpress, however, is disgraceful
and an obvious encouragement to every form of sexual perversion. There are, for
example, accounts in revolting detail of a mother seducing her son after she has had
intercourse with another woman, tales of homosexuality between males, or females,
for example. The booklets often contain forms for completion and posting in order *j*
to obtain 'hard porn'.
  'Soft porn' booklets retail for 25p or a little more and of course are readily available
for purchase by young people. In my judgment they are in the long run likely to do
more damage than the 'hard porn', albeit not in the same class of obscenity. However,
the starting point in reform, if it is desired to stop this filthy traffic from which
enormous sums are undoubtedly being made, must be the 'hard porn'.

a   What has been done? Police orders have set up an obscene publications squad in Scotland Yard. If in any division it is thought that porn, and in particular 'hard porn', is being peddled in any shop, that division is required to inform the squad. An officer from the squad will then investigate and if he sees confirmation of the report when visiting the premises he will obtain a warrant authorising him to enter, search the premises and seize any material he thinks obscene.

b   It appears that thereafter he will either invite a disclaimer, by which the occupier states that he has no interest in the material, and if the disclaimer is signed the police proceed with the destruction of the material. As already described by Lord Denning MR, this is an undesirable and possibly illegal procedure and enables the shopkeeper to avoid any further proceeding. If he refuses the disclaimer (euphemistically described as a 'caution') a report will go to the Director of Public Prosecutions pursuant to reg 6 (2) (d) of the Prosecution of Offences Regulations 1946[1], with a view to his advice on whether the case merits prosecution.

c   Counsel for the commissioner produced a list of the searches made in Soho during the period of ten months from 1st January to 31st October 1972. Although on occasions several premises were searched on the same day, searches were only conducted on 26 days during the whole period of ten months with the most meagre results. It is to be observed that on 13th April, no less than nine shops were searched. In one case a prosecution was initiated but later adjourned sine die. In another the result is recorded as negative and in seven obscene literature was found and was later destroyed, a caution being recorded in each case. In none of those seven was any subsequent search made. It is also to be observed that in the case of two shops searched in October with negative results, Mr Blackburn was able to buy 'hard porn' in the course of the hearing by this court.

d   It is perhaps not surprising that counsel for the commissioner and for the Attorney-General should concede that the action taken against the shops in Soho has been relatively ineffective.

e   Now Mr Blackburn may not understand the legal problems but his instinct tells him that something is radically wrong. He asserts, and there is a lot to be said for his view, that the police are *not* really trying to enforce the law. During the hearing he and his friends have gone out again and again to premises where the police found nothing and have bought 'hard porn'. He points out that nobody can suggest or ever has suggested in the case of the 'hard porn' that the defence of the 'public good' afforded by s 4 of the Obscene Publications Act 1959 could be invoked with any real hope of success. I do not understand counsel for the commissioner or the Attorney-General to demur over this.

f   What is the commissioner's defence? I confess that originally I was inclined to think that (as was said in the Divisional Court) Mr Blackburn had not got within measurable distance of establishing his case; but having seen the material in question, which that court declined to do, and having seen the exhibits collected during the hearing, I do not think the problem entirely easy.

g   Perhaps the key is to be found in para 9 of the commissioner's affidavit where he says on oath:

h   '. . . The comparative absence of public complaint and the penalties imposed by the Courts suggest that pornography causes less public unease than most other breaches of the law. There is now produced and shown to me . . . a schedule of the results of the 44 most recent prosecutions under the Obscene Publications Act, 1959.'

j   No doubt the schedule shows great leniency by the courts, but the document does not disclose whether any of the fines varying between £20 and £100 concerned 'hard porn'. I assume that the few sentences of imprisonment did. As I understand it,

---

1   SR & O 1946 No 1467

the commissioner is saying public opinion is not interested, the penalties imposed by the courts are trivial and he has enormous other demands on his force and his time.

Ought an order of mandamus to go? I have hesitated, but there is force in the points the commissioner makes and he has already increased the squad from 14 to 18 and he has not long been in the saddle. I have come to the conclusion that it would be premature and unfair to say that the commissioner had—to adopt the words of Lord Widgery CJ—turned his back on his duties.

Nevertheless I have no doubt that it is high time that a major effort was made to deal with the 'hard porn' and to start to deal with the 'soft porn'. The responsibility does not rest solely with the police—it is in no small degree shared by Parliament which must give greater powers to the courts and by the press and public who must support the police in eradicating this filthy literature, most of which is coming here from overseas and from which a few rogues are making fortunes.

What are the real problems? The commissioner may be right when he says that at present pornography causes less public unease than most other breaches of the law. In my judgment, it is high time that its gravity was appreciated by the public. It cannot fail, especially in the light of the great volume of such material which is being put in circulation, to affect the morals and the moral outlook of many people, and, in particular, of the young and impressionable. It tends, of course, to encourage promiscuity and to weaken marriage.

The police have undoubtedly been greatly hampered in performing their duties by the provisions of the 1959 Act. In the first place the penalties, namely £100 or six months on summary conviction, and on indictment a fine or a maximum sentence of three years' imprisonment, are entirely inadequate, particularly in the case of summary proceedings, in that hitherto a sentence of six months or less has had to be suspended. Moreover, if they secure a conviction on indictment for conspiracy, which, of course, is the only count which can hit the men behind the scenes who are really making the money, there is no power to order destruction of the material. The actual sentences passed in the shape of trivial fines, as shown by the commissioner's schedule, no doubt explain why recourse has been had to the procedure by disclaimer, which is obviously undesirable if only because it does not rank as a conviction.

In several cases where the director has proceeded by indictment acquittals have been secured, often because the law is by no means clear or readily understandable by a jury. Ordinary people do not normally use the word 'obscene'; and the test under the Act, namely whether the material tends to deprave and corrupt, in the absence of proof that it has actually depraved or corrupted an individual is just the sort of test that a jury shrinks from applying. The short fact is that obscene means no more than indecent, a word which everybody understands and which any jury could readily apply, using the collective common sense of its members. Moreover, the defence of public good under s 4 has been the source of much confusion and difficulty. It defines the article in question as being 'for the public good' on the grounds that it is 'in the interests of science, literature, art or learning, or of other objects of general concern'. It is the final phrase which has really done the damage. Recently a jury acquitted[1], although the articles before it consisted at any rate partially of 'hard porn', having heard the evidence of a number of psychiatrists to the effect that the revolting material displayed might have therapeutic value in the case of some members of the public who were either unduly shy or unduly ignorant of sexual matters. I should have thought that it was high time that the phrase 'or of other objects of general concern' was eliminated from s 4.

I suggest that consideration should be given, whenever it is decided to strengthen the law, to any action which may hurt the real criminals as opposed to the front

---

1   *R v Gold* (3rd November 1972) unreported

men. One method worth consideration is whether the landlord, whether freeholder or lessee, should not be under a similar liability to that which applies to the owner of premises which are, to his knowledge, being used as a brothel. I doubt whether there are many landlords in Soho who do not know the use to which their premises are put.

It seems obvious, from the evidence before us, that the police searches have been far less effective than the activities of Mr Blackburn. It is not for a member of this court to tell the commissioner how to go about his duties, but I wonder how long it is before the identity of every member of the squad is well known in Soho. I suspect that if one of the squad is seen in that area, particularly coming out of one of these shops, any 'hard porn' on the premises is likely to be removed with some rapidity in order to anticipate the probable search.

In my judgment the evidence put before us amply justifies the view of Lawton LJ that the whole subject merits enquiry, and indeed, Mr Blackburn has done a public service in bringing the whole situation into the open.

Since I ventured to comment during the hearing on the absence of any affidavit from the Director of Public Prosecutions, it is only right that I should add that I fully understand why no such affidavit was thought to be necessary and that there is nothing in any of the material before us to justify any criticism of the way he has carried out his duties.

I agree in the result proposed by Lord Denning MR, namely, that this appeal fails.

ROSKILL LJ. The legal foundation for this application for an order of mandamus against the Commissioner of Police of the Metropolis is the decision of the court in *R v Metropolitan Police Commissioner, ex parte Blackburn*[1], a case in which the present applicant sought an order of mandamus against the previous commissioner, whose successor the present respondent is, in relation to the enforcement of the gaming laws of this country. This court held that the respondent owed a duty to the public to enforce the law which he could be compelled to perform and that while he had a discretion not to prosecute in particular cases, his discretion was not an absolute discretion, for as Salmon LJ said[2]: 'In the extremely unlikely event, however, of the police failing or refusing to carry out their duty, the court would not be powerless to intervene.' In their judgments in the present case the Divisional Court approached the questions which are now raised in the light of that decision and reached the conclusion that, whilst accepting the law as there stated, the applicant had failed to make out a case for an order requiring the present respondent in the terms of the present motion—

'to enforce or secure the enforcement of the law against those who illegally publish and sell pornographic material both by seizure thereof and by prosecution of the publishers and retailers: and requiring him to reverse the decision made under his authority or continued under his authority whereby no police officers can prosecute such offenders, however obvious and scandalous the offence, without obtaining the prior decision of the Director of Public Prosecutions; and requiring him to reverse his policy decision preventing the seizure of obviously pornographic material by officers of his force stationed outside New Scotland Yard ...'

The Divisional Court refused to make any order on the motion. The applicant now renews that motion in this court.

From the mass of affidavits that the applicant has placed before this court there emerge—ignoring as I do the not insubstantial amount of irrelevant and indeed inadmissible material which they contain—two points of substance, one of law and one of fact or possibly of mixed fact and law.

1 [1968] 1 All ER 763, [1968] 2 QB 118
2 [1968] 1 All ER at 771, [1968] 2 QB at 138

The question of law is this. It is argued that the respondent has adopted an
erroneous view of the law in that, being required to report cases of alleged infringement of the law relating to obscene publications to the Director of Public Prosecutions, he has regarded himself as bound to take no or no effective action whether
by way of prosecution of the alleged offenders or otherwise unless and until the
director either authorises such action or takes such action himself.

The second question, be it one of fact or of mixed fact and law, is that when this
court looks at the actual publications of the public availability of which, whether
within or without the Soho area of London, the applicant complains, and whether they
are what the applicant called 'hard porn' or 'sweet shop stuff', their obscenity is so
obvious and their continued availability so blatant and also so undisputed that
the steps which the respondent claims he has taken and does still take in pursuance
of his chosen policy in administering and enforcing this branch of the law to suppress the wide availability of these publications, are not only, almost by admission,
manifestly ineffective but amount to a total failure properly to enforce the law.
The applicant goes on to argue that a state of affairs has thus been reached in which
this court, in duty bound to enforce the rule of law, should and must interfere to
require the respondent to change his existing policy and effectively to enforce the
law by which he in common with all others is bound.

The Divisional Court declined to look at the many publications of which the
applicant complained, Lord Widgery CJ saying that the court had seen enough of
them in other cases. I respectfully sympathise with this view, for the Criminal
Division of this court has indeed seen more than enough of these and other publications like them on many occasions. But this court, at the applicant's urgent request,
has looked at the many publications which he says he has bought openly. It has also
looked, at the behest of counsel for the respondent, at a group of other publications,
the subject, we were told, of recent proceedings at the Central Criminal Court[1]
which resulted in an acquittal. I say no more about any of the publications produced
by the applicant than that at the lowest they are all prima facie obscene, and I can
readily understand and appreciate the applicant's view that they are so highly obscene
that no court and no jury could hold otherwise, save at the peril of being said to be
perverse. But the employment of pejorative adjectives does not assist to determine
the essential issues before this court.

I shall deal first with the question of law. The applicant's complaint arises in two
ways. First it is said that the respondent in the second paragraph of his letter to the
applicant dated 10th July 1972, stated the duty of the Metropolitan police in relation
to prosecutions for offences of the kind now in question, erroneously. The respondent
wrote:

'It is not for the police to decide whether a publication is in contravention of
the law. It is their task to bring publications which they think might be unlawful
to the notice of the Director of Public Prosecutions, who in every case will
decide whether to institute proceedings, or not.'

In his judgment in the Divisional Court, Lord Widgery CJ said:

'I am not in the least bit surprised if that sentence, perhaps hastily dictated in
a letter, has given rise to that impression, but I am entirely confident, having
read [the respondent's] affidavit, that it does not represent any deviation from
duty on his behalf.'

I confess that for myself I doubt, with all respect to Lord Widgery CJ, whether this
sentence can be regarded as a mere error in hurried dictation for the passage complained of appears in a long letter occupying three closely typed foolscap sheets of
paper, which bear all the marks of careful legal preparation before submission to

---

1   *R v Gold* (3rd November 1972) unreported

a   the respondent for his signature. But, however that may be, the sentence is to say the least elliptical to the point of being, no doubt quite inadvertently, inaccurate. Subsequently and in connection with these proceedings the respondent swore a long affidavit dated 26th October 1972—this is the affidavit to which Lord Widgery CJ referred in the passage I have just quoted. Paragraph 11 of this affidavit, which was sworn some three weeks after the applicant's notice of motion, sets out, so far as

b   now relevant, the inter-relationship between the Metropolitan police and the Director of Public Prosecutions, and to my mind implicitly if not explicitly corrects any misunderstanding which may have arisen from the passage in the second paragraph of the letter of 10th July. But there are passages in para 14 of this affidavit—and this is the second matter of which the applicant complains in this connection—which suggest that as a matter of law the police must not begin a prosecution unless and until a report has been made to the Director of Public Prosecutions and his advice

c   obtained. If this be what this part of this paragraph was intended to convey, I can only say that I disagree for reasons which I shall shortly explain. Indeed I understood counsel for the respondent and for the Attorney-General expressly to accept that as a matter of law the police are not bound to refrain from prosecuting until after the receipt of the director's advice whether or not to prosecute and whether or not he

d   intends to take over the prosecution himself. That it may be prudent for the police, having, as in duty bound, reported to the director, not to prosecute unless and until they have the director's advice is another matter. One can readily understand the respondent's apprehension of what might be said if the police had prosecuted without awaiting the director's advice and the director then offered no evidence in a prosecution previously launched by the police: see para 16 of the respondent's affidavit. I am solely concerned at this juncture with the strict position in point of law.

e   In order to appreciate the question of law involved, it is necessary to look at the Prosecution of Offences Regulations 1946[1], which were made by the then Attorney-General with the concurrence of the then Lord Chancellor and Secretary of State pursuant to the Prosecution of Offences Acts 1879-1908. I do not find it necessary to trace the history of the legislation which led to the authority possessed by the

f   Attorney-General to make regulations such as these. It will be found fully set out in the judgment of Lord Widgery CJ in the present case.

The duties of the director under these regulations are plain. In certain classes of case he is under a duty himself to prosecute. In other classes of case he may prosecute if the case appears to him to justify his intervention, even though such a case is not within the class where he has a positive duty himself to prosecute. He is also required to give advice in cases falling within reg 2. In addition to the duties, whether they be

g   mandatory or optional, imposed on the director under regs 1, 2 and 3, other and different duties are imposed on chief officers of police—this would of course include the respondent—to report both offences and cases falling within reg 6. For my part I think there is a certain overlap between reg 6 (1) and reg 6 (2), for example, between reg 6 (1) (b) and parts of reg 6 (2) (a); but that is immaterial for present purposes.

h   What is important for present purposes is that a chief officer of police is required by reg 6 (2) (d) to report to the director 'cases of obscene or indecent libels, exhibitions or publications, in which it appears to the chief officer of police that there is a prima facie case for prosecution'.

It is in pursuance of this provision that the respondent (as he has sworn) requires his officers to report such cases within the metropolis to the director. We were told that chief officers of police of forces outside the metropolis follow the same course.

j   But neither the Obscene Publications Act 1959, nor any other relevant statute makes the consent or advice of the director a condition precedent to prosecution by the police, if the police thought fit so to prosecute without awaiting the result of such a report. The applicant sought to argue that the regulations and in particular reg

1   SR & O 1946 No 1467

6 (2) (d) were ultra vires because in effect it imposed such a condition precedent on prosecution. In my judgment it clearly does not do so and the regulation equally clearly is not ultra vires. But it is only fair to the applicant to say that the passages in the correspondence and in the affidavit to which I have referred may have led him to think otherwise. It follows that the question of law on which the applicant sought to rest this part of his argument does not assist his case.

I now turn to the other branch of his argument. It is not I think necessary to consider the provisions of the Obscene Publications Act 1959 in detail. Section 2 creates the offence and prescribes the penalties. Section 3 accords rights of search and seizure. Section 4 creates the defence of public good as an answer to a charge under s 2. The gravamen of the applicant's complaints against the respondent rested perhaps more on alleged failure sufficiently to exercise the power of search and seizure under s 3 than on alleged failure to prosecute. The respondent has replied to these complaints with details of recent searches and seizures as well as of recent prosecutions and penalties imposed by the courts. The applicant has forcefully answered this reply of the respondent by pointing first to the comparatively small number of seizures and searches, to their comparative rarity and to their virtual ineffectiveness as demonstrated by the fact that he could and has bought obscene publications from premises already visited by the police. The applicant claims that he, without power of search and seizure, could bring this traffic to an end. He has launched and threatens further to launch private prosecutions to this end. How much more he claims could the police, possessed of this power of search and seizure, achieve even better results were they to use the power which Parliament has given them under s 3.

It is no part of the duty of this court to presume to tell the respondent how to conduct the affairs of the Metropolitan police, nor how to deploy his all too limited resources at a time of ever-increasing crime, especially of crimes of violence in London. The respondent has related in detail in his affidavit how the relevant work is done and the degree of centralisation which has been operated within the Metropolitan police district through the mechanism of the obscene publications squad and the office of the director. It is important in this connection to observe two things, first that searches and seizures by the obscene publications squad can be and are effected without the prior advice or consent of the director; and secondly, that individual divisional officers do not take and are by order precluded from taking action lest otherwise there be divergencies in practice and prosecution. The applicant rejoins that were this not so and were divisional officers permitted to search and seize on their own initiative and were there less centralisation than exists at present, the results would be far more effective. He claims this view to be supported by senior officers on division. This may be so. The respondent is envisaging changes being made (see paras 11 and 13 of his affidavit) which when brought into effect, one may be permitted to hope, go some way towards achieving the better results desired by the applicant than the existing arrangements have so far achieved.

If it be permissible to recall some past criticisms of the police in matters of prosecutions in connection with alleged obscene publications, one can sympathise with the wish of the respondent to secure centralisation in order to achieve a uniform standard by which to determine whether or not prosecutions should be launched in any particular case. The applicant took strong exception to this in his reply and said that uniformity of standard was a matter for the courts and not for the respondent or the director. I think with respect he misunderstood the argument of both counsel for the commissioner and for the Attorney-General in this respect. Although in any given case the question whether a particular publication offends or does not offend must depend in the last resort on the standard set by the courts in the case of summary proceedings or by the jury in the case of a trial on indictment. There can be no objection to a prosecuting authority seeking to achieve so far as possible a uniform practice or standard by which to judge whether or not a particular prosecution should be launched. So to do is not to refuse to enforce the law but to judge as a matter of the exercise of a proper executive discretion whether or not a particular prosecution should be launched, an exercise of judgment oft fraught with great difficulty and only to be taken after very many different and often conflicting factors have been considered.

I confess that like Lord Denning MR and Phillimore LJ I feel unhappy about the obvious and indeed admitted ineffectiveness of the measures thus far taken especially in the field of search and seizure. But I am not satisfied that this ineffectiveness can be wholly laid at the door of the respondent and his officers. It is notoriously difficult to prosecute the real offenders—too often if premises are raided it will be a 'front man' against whom alone proceedings can be taken. Whether the imposition of penalties on the owners of premises who knowingly permit their premises to be used for the sale of these publications, or whether the proposed new procedure of criminal bankruptcy could be widened to embrace offenders in this field perhaps merits consideration. But defects in the law cannot fairly be laid at the respondent's door.

The Obscene Publications Act 1959 has presented a host of difficulties to the courts as well as to the prosecuting authorities. The applicant referred us many times to the recent decision of the House of Lords in *Director of Public Prosecutions v Whyte*[1]. I do not find anything in the speeches in that case, whether of the majority or of the minority of their Lordships, which assists the applicant on this motion. But I would respectfully repeat and echo two passages in the speech of Lord Wilberforce in regard to the problems created by the Act. Lord Wilberforce said[2]:

'Both the policy and the language of the Act have been plentifully criticised: the former we cannot question, and with the latter we must do our best. One thing at least is clear from this verbiage, that the Act has adopted a relative conception of obscenity. An article cannot be considered as obscene in itself: it can only be so in relation to its likely readers. One reason for this was no doubt to exempt from prosecution scientific, medical or sociological treatises not likely to fall into the hands of laymen, but the section is drafted in terms wider than was necessary to give this exemption, and this gives the courts a difficult task.'

Later his Lordship said[3]:

'But the Act of 1959 changed all this. Instead of a presumed consequence of obscenity, a tendency to deprave and corrupt became the test of obscenity and became what had to be proved. One consequence appears to be that the section does not hit 'articles' which merely shock however many people. It can only have been the pressure of Parliamentary compromise which can have produced a test so difficult for the courts . . . I have serious doubts whether the Act will continue to be workable in this way, or whether it will produce tolerable results. The present is, or in any rational system ought to be, a simple case, yet the illogical and unscientific character of the Act has forced the justices into untenable positions.'

Where Lord Wilberforce has expressed serious doubts as to the workability of the Act in its present form, it seems harsh indeed to blame the respondent for the alleged ineffectiveness of the measures of his force. The blame might not unfairly be thought at least equally, and perhaps to a greater extent to rest on what Lord Wilberforce called 'pressure of Parliamentary compromise' revealed by the 1959 Act.

Nor I fear can the courts escape their share of the blame. The respondent has listed in an exhibit to his affidavit some of the penalties recently imposed by the courts. Without knowing the facts of each case it would be wrong to criticise those

---

1   [1972] 3 All ER 12, [1972] AC 849
2   [1972] 3 All ER at 17, [1972] AC at 859, 860
3   [1972] 3 All ER at 18, 19, [1972] AC 861, 862

penalties even in general terms. But having regard to the profits which on the applicant's own uncontradicted evidence must have been made in this trade, it is difficult to regard some at least of these penalties as other than almost derisory. It is only right to point out that the maximum penalty on summary conviction is a mere £100 fine or six months' imprisonment. The former maximum penalty seems, whether by oversight or design, to have escaped the general increase in maximum fines enacted in Sch 3 to the Criminal Justice Act 1967. The latter penalty of imprisonment must since that same Act, at least in the majority of cases, be suspended, although happily that position will not subsist much longer in the light of the provisions of the Criminal Justice Act 1972. Further, a possible defence of 'public good' under s 4 of the 1959 Act has always to be envisaged whether on summary trial or on trial on indictment, although it is perhaps more likely to be raised on a trial on indictment. I have already mentioned the recent acquittal at the Central Criminal Court[1] in a case the exhibits in which were shown to us. We were told that the s 4 defence was there raised. It is I hope permissible to say that the most casual glance at those exhibits makes one wonder how anyone could say that they were not obscene. But however that may be, this is a field in which differences of opinion are notorious and no prosecuting authority can afford to ignore the possibility of acquittals which may seem surprising to some and which, when they occur, neither encourage respect for the law as laid down by Parliament in 1959 nor facilitate the unenviable task of those responsible for its enforcement. Further repeated acquittals in this class of case by reason of a defence based on s 4 suggest that that section is now being used for purposes entirely different from that which its framers intended.

Although, like the Divisional Court, I think this motion must be refused on the ground that the applicant has failed to bring his case within the principles of law on which he must rely in order to succeed, this appeal will have served a useful purpose if it highlights: (1) the difficulties of enforcement of the 1959 Act; (2) the difficulties of obtaining a generally acceptable test of obscenity and of applying the test prescribed by the 1959 Act; (3) the inadequacy of the penalties for which that Act provides at least on summary conviction; (4) the problems to which s 4 gives rise; (5) the need for consideration whether more frequent and more effective searches and seizures pursuant to s 3 not only by the obscene publications squad but by officers on division who must be exceedingly familiar with the extent of the problem in their own divisions may not achieve better results than in the past.

I agree that the motion should be refused.

[Counsel for the commissioner applied for the costs of the appeal. In the Divisional Court an order for costs was made against the applicants.]

Appeal dismissed. No order for costs in the Court of Appeal or in the Divisional Court. Leave to appeal to the House of Lords refused.

18th December 1972. The appeal committee of the House of Lords gave leave to appeal.

Solicitors: *Solicitor, Metropolitan Police; Treasury Solicitor.*

Wendy Shockett Barrister.

---

1 *R v Gold* (3rd November 1972) unreported

R v Feely

COURT OF APPEAL, CRIMINAL DIVISION

PHILLIMORE, STEPHENSON, LAWTON LJJ, MELFORD STEVENSON AND BRABIN JJ

4th, 15th DECEMBER 1972

Criminal law – Theft – Dishonesty – Intention – Appropriation of money – Intention to repay – Ability to repay – Accused appropriating money from employer's safe – Accused acting contrary to express instructions of employer – Defence in law for accused to say that he intended to repay and believed on reasonable grounds that he would repay – 'Dishonestly' an ordinary word of English language – Jury requiring no direction on meaning – Whether accused acting dishonestly a question of fact for the jury – Theft Act 1968, s 1 (1).

The appellant was employed as a branch manager by a firm of bookmakers. The employers sent a circular to all their managers stating that the practice of borrowing from the employers' tills was to stop. A month after receiving the circular the appellant took £30 from his employers' safe to give to his father. Four days later he was transferred to another branch and the new manager discovered the loss. The appellant gave him an IOU to cover the deficiency. The matter subsequently came to the notice of the employers. In a written statement to the police the appellant said that he had borrowed £30 from 'the float' and had intended to pay it back, that he had given an IOU, and that his employers owed him £70 in wages and commission. He was charged with theft contrary to s 1 (1)[a] of the Theft Act 1968. At the trial a wages clerk gave evidence that the employers owed the appellant £43 for wages and £16 by way of bonus. The judge directed the jury that it was no defence for the appellant to say that he intended to repay the money and had the means to repay it, or that the employers owed him more than enough to cover what he had taken. At no stage did the judge direct the jury to decide whether the Crown had proved that the appellant had taken the money dishonestly, and he expressed his concept of dishonesty as follows: '... if someone does something deliberately knowing that his employers are not prepared to tolerate it, is that not dishonest?' The appellant was convicted and appealed.

Held – (i) It was a defence in law for a person charged with theft and proved to have appropriated money to say that the appropriation was not dishonest in that, when he took the money, he intended to repay it and had reasonable grounds for believing, and did believe, that he would be able to do so. Whether he had in fact appropriated the money dishonestly was a question for the jury. The word 'dishonestly', as used in s 1 (1) of the 1968 Act, was an ordinary word of the English language and a jury required no direction by the judge as to its meaning (see p 342 h, p 344 j to p 345c, p 347 c and p 348 d to f, post).

(ii) It followed that the jury should have been left to decide whether the appellant's taking of the money had been dishonest. Since they had not, the result was that a verdict of guilty had been returned without their having given thought to what was probably the most important issue in the case. Consequently the appeal would be allowed and the conviction quashed (see p 345 f and p 348 g, post).

Dictum of Lord Reid in *Brutus v Cozens* [1972] 2 All ER at 1299 applied.

Dictum of Lord Goddard CJ in *R v Williams* [1953] 1 All ER at 1070 explained.

Dictum of Winn LJ in *R v Cockburn* [1968] 1 All ER at 468, 469 disapproved.

Notes

For the meaning of theft and the element of dishonest appropriation, see Supplement to 10 Halsbury's Laws (3rd Edn) para 1475A, 1–3.

For the Theft Act 1968, s 1, see 8 Halsbury's Statutes (3rd Edn) 783.

---

a   Section 1 (1), so far as material, is set out at p 344 j, post

Cases referred to in judgment

Brutus v Cozens [1972] 2 All ER 1297, [1972] 3 WLR 521, HL; *rvsg* [1972] 2 All ER 1, [1972] 1 WLR 484, DC.

Halstead v Patel [1972] 2 All ER 147, [1972] 1 WLR 661, 56 Cr App Rep 334, DC.

R v Cockburn [1968] 1 All ER 466, [1968] 1 WLR 281, 132 JP 166, 52 Cr App Rep 134, CA, Digest (Cont Vol C) 263, 10,429a.

R v Holloway (1849) 2 Car & Kir 942, 1 Den 370, 3 New Sess Cas 410, 18 LJMC 60, 12 LTOS 382, 13 JP 54, 3 Cox CC 241, 175 ER 395, CCR, 15 Digest (Repl) 1060, 10,454.

R v Williams [1953] 1 All ER 1068, [1953] 1 QB 660, [1953] 2 WLR 937, 117 JP 251, 37 Cr App Rep 71, CCA 15 Digest (Repl) 1058, 10,429.

Cases and authority also cited

Kat v Diment [1950] 2 All ER 657, [1951] 1 KB 34, DC.

R v Mackinnon [1958] Crim LR 809, CCC.

R v Smith (Sidney) (1843) 1 Cox CC 10.

Smith, The Law of Theft (2nd Edn, 1972), pp 44, 45, para 116.

Appeal

On 20th March 1972 at the Crown Court at Liverpool before his Honour Judge Edward Jones and a jury, the appellant, David Feely, was convicted of theft, contrary to s 1 of the Theft Act 1968. He was sentenced to a fine of £50, ordered to pay the costs of the prosecution, the payment of his defence costs to be assessed, and he was also ordered to make a restitution in the sum of £29·89 to Ladbrokes (The Bookmakers) Ltd, less what was due to him. He appealed against both conviction and sentence by leave of the single judge. The case first came before the court (Phillimore, Cairns LJJ and Mars-Jones J) on 3rd November 1972 when it was adjourned to be heard before a full court of five judges. The facts are set out in the judgment of the court.

B A Hytner QC and *G H Wright* for the appellant.
R L Ward QC and *G M Clifton* for the Crown.

Cur adv vult

15th December. **LAWTON LJ** read the following judgment of the court. This appellant, David Feely, appeals by leave of the single judge against his conviction for theft at Liverpool Crown Court on 20th March 1972. He was fined £50 and ordered to make restitution in the sum of £29·89, the amount of the money said to have been stolen, to the losers, Ladbrokes (The Bookmakers) Ltd. He was also ordered to pay the costs of the prosecution and to make such contribution as was assessed to his legal aid costs.

The appeal raises an important point of law, namely, can it be a defence *in law* for a man charged with theft and proved to have taken money, to say that when he took the money he intended to repay it and had reasonable grounds for believing and did believe that he would be able to do so? The trial judge, his Honour Judge Edward Jones, adjudged that such a defence is not available. If the law recognises such a defence the question arises whether the decisions of this court in *R v Cockburn*[1] and of its predecessor the Court of Criminal Appeal in *R v Williams*[2] are applicable to a charge of theft under s 1 of the Theft Act 1968 and, if they are, whether those cases were correctly decided.

The court wishes at the outset to stress that the problem we have had to consider has been whether there can be such a defence *in law*. The experience of all of us has been that persons who take money from tills, safes or other receptacles, knowing full well that they have no right to do so, are usually and rightly convicted of theft. Nothing in this judgment should lead anyone, particularly those tempted to put their hands into other people's tills, to think that for the future the prospects of acquittal will be substantially improved.

---

1 [1968] 1 All ER 466, [1968] 1 WLR 281　　2 [1953] 1 All ER 1068, [1953] 1 QB 660

a   The relevant facts out of which this appeal arises can be stated shortly. At the beginning of October 1971 the appellant was employed by a firm of bookmakers as a manager of one of their branches in Liverpool. In mid-September 1971 his employers sent a circular to all their managers stating that the practice of borrowing from tills was to stop. After the receipt of that circular the appellant knew that he had no right of any kind to take money from a till or safe for his own purposes.

b   According to the story which the appellant first told in the witness box at his trial and which fitted with the facts known to the prosecution the appellant had taken about £30 out of the safe on 4th October 1971 and had handed it to his father who was out of work as the result of an accident. He did not then put into the safe an IOU or make any record in a book of account to show what he had done, or tell his employers.

c   On Friday, 8th October 1971, the appellant was transferred by his employers to another of their branches in Liverpool. A Mr Kiernan took over from him and checked the cash. He found that there was a shortage of £40. The appellant then gave him an IOU for this amount. Mr Kiernan did not report this deficiency but it was discovered the next day, when a Mr Connolly, a member of the security staff, carried out some checks. He asked the appellant why there had been a deficiency. He accounted for £10·92 of it by reference to some bets he had paid out; but as to the *d* balance of £29·89 he said that he had been 'stuck for cash', and that his father had been ill. Mr Connolly asked the appellant to go with him to the police station and he agreed to do so.

    At the police station the appellant made a written statement, the relevant parts of which are as follows:

e   'I was working as the manager of Ladbrokes in London Road for about six months. I borrowed about thirty pounds from the float and intended to pay it back. Yesterday morning I was transferred to another of the firms shops . . . and I had to hand over the cash to the fellow who was taking over. The cash was thirty pounds short, so I gave him an I.O.U. for forty pounds to cover the difference . . . I want to say that I would have paid the money back. The firm *f* owes me about £70 and I want them to take the money that's owing from that.'

    At the trial a wages clerk said that on 9th October 1971 the employers owed the appellant £43·32 for wages and £16·47 by way of bonus. The appellant was charged with theft and the indictment alleged that he had stolen £29·89 the property of his employers.

g   The facts known to the prosecution at the start of the trial were of a commonplace kind. Magistrates' courts and juries in all parts of England and Wales find themselves trying similar cases as part of their day-to-day work and they seldom have any difficulty at all in distinguishing the honest employee from the rogue. The honest employee who has to deal with an emergency for which cash is necessary there and then usually tells his employers either at the time or shortly afterwards what he has done, whereas the rogue says nothing until his taking is found out where- *h* upon he asserts his intention to repay and stresses his ability to do so. Had the jury in this case been left to decide whether the appellant had dishonestly taken the money, their task would have been an easy one, particularly as the trial took an unexpected course. After the appellant had given the evidence to which reference has already been made and witnesses had been called to prove that borrowing and taking of so called 'subs' from tills was an established practice amongst Ladbrokes' *j* employees, his father gave evidence. He refuted the evidence which the appellant had given about handing the money he had taken to him. What had happened, said the father, was that the appellant as Ladbrokes' manager had helped him to run his betting account and had paid out when he had won. This evidence brought the appellant back into the witness box. He resiled from what he had said when first giving evidence and stated that his father's evidence was true. He admitted that he had told an untrue story when first questioned by Mr Connolly. He felt, he said, *a* that he would have to keep to it at his trial.

Fortunately for the appellant some case law became entangled in this simple case. The trial judge had in mind the two cases mentioned earlier in this judgment, both of which bound him if applicable, and he directed the jury according to his understanding of them. He felt obliged to direct them that if the appellant had taken the money from either the safe or the till—and it was the Crown's case and the appel- *b* lant's own case to start with that he had taken it from the safe—it was no defence for him to say that he had intended to repay it and that his employers owed him more than enough to cover what he had taken.

The judge put his direction in stark terms. Early in his summing-up he said: 'If this man took the money he is guilty and if he did not take it he is not guilty.' A few sentences later he stated the law as follows: *c*

'It is clear in law that if someone takes money belonging to someone else and makes use of that money, even though he intends to return it, usually by other coins, that is permanently depriving that person of the money. Even in this case, if you come to the view that this man took out of the safe or the till a sum of money, that is in law stealing. This is a matter of law and I direct you as to it.'

The trial judge ended his summing-up with these words: *d*

'As a matter of law, members of the jury, I am bound to direct you, even if he were prepared to pay back the following day and even if he were a millionaire, it makes no defence in law to this offence. If he took the money; that is the essential matter you have to decide.'

At no stage of his summing-up did he leave the jury to decide whether the Crown *e* had proved that the appellant had taken the money dishonestly. This was because he seems to have thought that he had to decide as a matter of law what amounted to dishonesty and he expressed his concept of dishonesty as follows: '. . . if someone does something deliberately knowing that his employers are not prepared to tolerate it, is that not dishonest?'

Should the jury have been left to decide whether the appellant had acted dishonestly? *f* The search for an answer must start with the Theft Act 1968, under s 1 of which the appellant had been indicted. The long title of this Act starts with these words: 'An Act to revise the law of England and Wales as to theft and similar or associated offences . . .' The draftsman seems to have searched the statute book for all the statutes dealing with offences of dishonesty and it is probable that all the old enactments have been repealed so as to enable the Theft Act 1968 to deal comprehensively *g* with this branch of the law. The design of the new Act is clear; nearly all the old legal terms to describe offences of dishonesty have been left behind; larceny, embezzlement and fraudulent conversion have become theft; receiving stolen goods has become handling stolen goods; obtaining by false pretences has become obtaining pecuniary advantage by deception. Words in everyday use have replaced legal jargon in many parts of the Act. This is particularly noticeable in the series of sections (ss 1 *h* to 6) defining theft.

Theft itself is a word known and used by all and is defined, in what the marginal note to s 1 describes as the basic definition, as follows:

'(1) A person is guilty of theft if he dishonestly appropriates property belonging to another with the intention of permanently depriving the other of it . . .'

These words swept away all the learning which over the centuries had gathered *j* round the common law concept of larceny and in more modern times around the statutory definition of that offence, in s 1 (1) of the Larceny Act 1916.

In s 1 (1) of the Theft Act 1968 the word 'dishonestly' can only relate to the state of mind of the person who does the act which amounts to appropriation. Whether an accused person has a particular state of mind is a question of fact which has to be decided by the jury when there is a trial on indictment and by the justices when there are summary proceedings. The Crown did not dispute this proposition, but it was submitted that in some cases (and this, it was said, was such a one) it was necessary for the trial judge to define 'dishonestly' and when the facts fell within the definition he had a duty to tell the jury that if there had been an appropriation it must have been dishonestly done. We do not agree that judges should define what 'dishonestly' means.

This word is in common use whereas the word 'fraudulently', which was used in s 1 (1) of the Larceny Act 1916, had acquired as a result of case law a special meaning. Jurors, when deciding whether an appropriation was dishonest can be reasonably expected to, and should, apply the current standards of ordinary decent people. In their own lives they have to decide what is and what is not dishonest. We can see no reason why, when in a jury box, they should require the help of a judge to tell them what amounts to dishonesty. We are fortified in this opinion by a passage in the speech of Lord Reid in *Brutus v Cozens*[1], a case in which the words 'insulting behaviour' in s 5 of the Public Order Act 1936 had to be construed. The Divisional Court[2] had adjudged that the meaning of the word 'insulting' in this statutory context was a matter of law. Lord Reid's comment was as follows[3]:

'In my judgment that is not right. The meaning of an ordinary word of the English language is not a question of law. The proper construction of a statute is a question of law. If the context shows that a word is used in an unusual sense the court will determine in other words what that unusual sense is. But here there is in my opinion no question of the word "insulting" being used in any unusual sense . . . It is for the tribunal which decides the case to consider, not as law but as fact, whether in the whole circumstances the words of the statute do or do not as a matter of ordinary usage of the English language cover or apply to the facts which have been proved.'

When this trenchant statement of principle is applied to the word 'dishonestly' in s 1 (1) of the Theft Act 1968, and to the facts of this case it is clear in our judgment that the jury should have been left to decide whether the appellant's alleged taking of the money had been dishonest. They were not, with the result that a verdict of guilty was returned without their having given thought to what was probably the most important issue in the case.

This would suffice for the appeal were it not for the two decisions to which reference has already been made. In *R v Williams*[4] the two appellants, who were husband and wife, carried on a general shop, part of which was a sub-post office. The wife was the sub-postmistress. The business of the shop got into difficulties and in order to get out of them the wife, with the knowledge of her husband, took money from the post office till to discharge some of the debts of the business. In her evidence, which was supported by that of her husband, she said that she thought she would be able to repay the money out of her salary from the post office and from sales from the business. The husband said that he knew it was wrong to do what they had done, but he thought that it would all come right in the end. They were found guilty on a number of counts and in respect of two the jury added a rider that the appellants had intended to repay the money and honestly believed that they would be able to do so, but in respect of three counts, although they intended to repay, they had no honest belief that they would be able to do so. The main ground of the appeal was that the jury had been misdirected as to the word 'fraudulently' in s 1 (1) of the Larceny Act 1916.

1   [1972] 2 All ER 1297, [1972] 3 WLR 521
2   [1972] 2 All ER 1, [1972] 1 WLR 484
3   [1972] 2 All ER at 1299, [1972] 3 WLR at 525
4   [1953] 1 All ER 1068, [1953] 1 QB 660

The judgment of the Court of Criminal Appeal was delivered by Lord Goddard CJ. It is pertinent to point out that he considered that the appellants' own evidence had established fraudulent behaviour as they had admitted putting false accounts forward to disguise and conceal what they had been doing. The question in the case which is relevant for the purposes of this appeal was whether the facts found by the jury and recorded in their riders afforded any defence. This required the court to construe the words 'fraudulently and without a claim of right made in good faith' in s 1 (1) of the Larceny Act 1916 which, unlike the Theft Act 1968, was never intended to alter the law but to consolidate and simplify it (see its long title)[1].

Lord Goddard CJ rejected the opinion of Parke B in *R v Holloway*[2] that the word 'fraudulent' meant 'without a claim of right' and went on to say[3]:

> 'The court thinks that the word "fraudulently" does add, and is intended to add, something to the words "without a claim of right", and it means (though I am not saying that the words I am about to use will fit every case, but they certainly will fit this particular case) that the taking must be intentional and deliberate, that is to say, without mistake.'

Insofar as Lord Goddard CJ adjudged that a meaning had to be given to the word 'fraudulently' he was clearly right; and on the facts of the case with which he was dealing the rest of what he said was right; but if and insofar as he sought to lay down principles applicable in *all* cases we feel bound to say that we do not agree with him. For example, further on he said[4]:

> '. . . they knew they had no right to take the money which they knew was not theirs. The fact that they may have had a hope or expectation in the future of repaying that money is a matter which at most can go to mitigation. It does not amount to a defence.'

It is possible to imagine a case of taking by an employee in breach of instructions to which no one would, or could reasonably, attach moral obloquy; for example, that of a manager of a shop, who having been told that under no circumstances was he to take money from the till for his own purposes, took 40p from it, having no small change himself, to pay for a taxi hired by his wife who had arrived at the shop saying that she only had a £5 note which the cabby could not change. To hold that such a man was a thief and to say that his intention to put the money back in the till when he acquired some change was at the most a matter of mitigation would tend to bring the law into contempt. In our judgment a taking to which no moral obloquy can reasonably attach is not within the concept of stealing either at common law or under the Theft Act 1968.

There is some evidence that Lord Goddard CJ appreciated that his statement of principle in *R v Williams*[5] might not apply to every case. His judgment was not reserved and as delivered it is likely that it contained this passage[6]:

> 'It is one thing if a person with good credit and plenty of money uses somebody else's money which is in his possession—it having been entrusted to him or he having the opportunity of taking it—he merely intending to use those coins instead of some of his own which he has only to go to his room or to his bank to get. No jury would then say that there was any intent to defraud or any fraudu-

---

1   I e 'An Act to consolidate and simplify the Law relating to Larceny triable on Indictment and Kindred Offences'
2   (1849) 2 Car & Kir 942
3   [1953] 1 All ER at 1070, [1953] 1 QB at 666
4   [1953] 1 All ER at 1071, [1953] 1 QB at 668
5   [1953] 1 All ER 1068, [1953] 1 QB 660
6   [1953] 1 All ER at 1070, [1953] 2 WLR at 942

a lent taking, but it is quite another matter if the person who takes the money is not in a position to replace it at the time but only has a hope or expectation that he will be able to do so in the future . . .'

This passage is set out in the reports of *R v Williams* in the All England Law Reports and the Weekly Law Reports[1] but was omitted from the reports of that case in the Law Reports and the Criminal Appeal Reports[2]. The inference must be that when
b Lord Goddard CJ came to revise his judgment for the Law Reports he had second thoughts, perhaps as Winn LJ suggested in the later case of *R v Cockburn*[3], because he thought that it was 'an extremely dangerous and misleading statement'. We do not take this view; another explanation, and a more probable one, is that Lord Goddard CJ thought it unwise to express opinions on facts which were not before the court. But it matters little why Lord Goddard CJ revised his judgment as he did.
c What does matter is that he seems to have envisaged when delivering his judgment the possibility of an unauthorised taking which might not be fraudulent. Once this possibility exists it must be for the jury to decide whether the facts proved are within it.

If the law drifted off course in *R v Williams*[4] because of the strong inference of fraud arising on the facts of that case, it got on to the wrong tack in *R v Cockburn*[3] in which the manager of a shop took money from the till on a Saturday intending, so
d he said, to replace it with a cheque drawn by his daughter. Before he did so he was dismissed and when the deficiency of cash was discovered and he was asked by telephone about it he did not then put forward the explanation which was his defence to a charge of larceny as a servant. At his trial the jury were not directed that it would be a good defence to the charge if the accused were to satisfy them that he intended to replace the money with its currency equivalent. On the facts the accused
e had a lot to explain and such hope or expectation of repaying, if any, as he had probably could only have gone to mitigation, and this must be so in most cases of this kind. Winn LJ delivered the judgment of the court. After setting out the facts he said[5]:

f 'The point raised by counsel for the appellant is that it is a good defence in law to a charge of larceny of a sum of money if the defendant is able to satisfy the jury, or if it remains open in the minds of the jury as a reasonable possibility, that he intended to replace the money taken with its currency equivalent and had resources available to him which would enable him to make that replacement. The court is quite satisfied that that submission of counsel is founded on, and very ill-founded on, a passage in a report of *R. v. Williams*[6].'

g Winn LJ was referring to the passage to which reference has already been made. He went on to express the hope that it would for the future be entirely disregarded by the Bar—a hope which is now not likely to be fulfilled. He went on as follows[7]:

'The fact of the matter, however, is this: that whereas larceny may vary very greatly indeed to the extent, one might say, of the whole heavens between
h grave theft and a taking which, whilst technically larcenous, reveals no moral obloquy and does no harm at all, it is nevertheless quite essential always to remember what are the elements of larceny and what are the complete and total elements of larceny, that is to say, taking the property of another person against the will of that other person without any claim of right so to do, and

---

j 1 [1953] 1 All ER 1068, [1953] 2 WLR 937
2 [1953] 1 QB 660, 37 Cr App Rep 71
3 [1968] 1 All ER 466, [1968] 1 WLR 281
4 [1953] 1 All ER 1068, [1953] 1 QB 660
5 [1968] 1 All ER at 468, [1968] 1 WLR at 283
6 [1953] 1 All ER 1068, [1953] 1 QB 660
7 [1968] 1 All ER at 468, 469, [1968] 1 WLR at 284

a

with the intent at the time of taking it permanently to deprive the owner of it. If coins, half a crown, a 10s. note, a £5 note, whatever it may be, are taken in all the circumstances which I have already indicated with the intention of spending or putting away somewhere those particular coins or notes, albeit not only hoping but intending and expecting reasonably to be able to replace them with their equivalent, nevertheless larceny has been committed because with full appreciation of what is being done, the larcenous person, the person who commits the offence, has taken something which he was not entitled to take, had no claim of right to take, without the consent of the owner, and is in effect trying to force on the owner a substitution to which the owner has not consented.'

b

We find it impossible to accept that a conviction for stealing, whether it be called larceny or theft, can reveal no moral obloquy. A man so convicted would have difficulty in persuading his friends and neighbours that his reputation had not been gravely damaged. He would be bound to be lowered in the estimation of right thinking people. Further, no reference was made by Winn LJ to the factor of fraud which Lord Goddard CJ in *R v Williams*[1] had said had to be considered. It is this factor, whether it is labelled 'fraudulently' or 'dishonestly', which distinguishes a taking without consent from stealing.

c

d

If the principle enunciated in *R v Cockburn*[2] was right there would be a strange divergence between the position of a man who obtains cash by passing a cheque on an account which has no funds to meet it and one who takes money from a till. The man who passes the cheque is deemed in law not to act dishonestly if he genuinely believes on reasonable grounds that when it is presented to the paying bank there will be funds to meet it: see *Halstead v Patel*[3] per Lord Widgery CJ. But, according to the decision in *R v Cockburn*[2], the man who takes money from a till intending to put it back and genuinely believing on reasonable grounds that he will be able to do so (see per Winn LJ[4]) should be convicted of theft. Lawyers may be able to appreciate why one man should be adjudged to be a criminal and the other not; but we doubt whether anyone else would. People who take money from tills and the like without permission are usually thieves; but if they do not admit that they are by pleading guilty, it is for the jury, not the judge, to decide whether they have acted dishonestly.

e

f

We were not asked by the Crown to apply the proviso to s 2 (1) of the Criminal Appeal Act 1968, and, in consequence, we did not consider the matters which would have been relevant to that issue. For these reasons we allowed the appeal.

g

Appeal allowed. Conviction quashed.

Solicitors: *Garnetts*, Liverpool (for the appellant); *Stanley Holmes*, Town Clerk, Liverpool (for the Crown).

N P Metcalfe Esq Barrister.

h

1   [1953] 1 All ER 1068, [1953] 1 QB 660
2   [1968] 1 All ER 466, [1968] 1 WLR 281
3   [1972] 2 All ER 147 at 152, [1972] 1 WLR 661 at 666
4   [1968] 1 All ER at 469, [1968] 1 WLR at 284

D (J) v D (S)

FAMILY DIVISION
ORMROD J
6th NOVEMBER 1972

Divorce – Financial provision – Application – Practice and procedure – Death of applicant – Death before hearing of application – Whether application abating on death – Whether application a 'cause of action' surviving for benefit of applicant's estate – Law Reform (Miscellaneous Provisions) Act 1934, s 1.

The husband and wife were married in 1956. In 1965 certain property was purchased in their joint names. In March 1968 the husband obtained a decree of divorce on the ground of the wife's adultery and in August 1968 he married R. Later in the year, the husband, inter alia, took out a summons under s 17 of the Matrimonial Causes Act 1965 for the variation of the post-nuptial settlement in respect of the property. Before the matter could be heard the husband died and in November 1971 R, who was the administratrix of his estate, was given leave to proceed with the summons. At the hearing R contended that, despite the husband's death, s 1[a] of the Law Reform (Miscellaneous Provisions) Act 1934 kept alive the cause of action for the benefit of his estate thus enabling her to proceed with the application.

Held – The application would be dismissed; the court had no jurisdiction to entertain it for the following reasons—
(i) although the anomalous common law rule that causes of action did not survive the person in whom they were vested for the benefit of his estate had been abrogated by the 1934 Act, the court should be very cautious in extending the meaning of 'causes of action' under the 1934 Act to applications for financial relief in the Family Division which were essentially personal in nature, arising between parties to the marriage or children of the marriage, and deriving from the matrimonial legislation and from no other source (see p 352 f to h, post);
(ii) further, on a close examination of s 17 of the 1965 Act and its successor, s 4 of the Matrimonial Proceedings and Property Act 1970, it was clear that the survival of both parties to the marriage was envisaged by those statutes in proceedings for the variation of a settlement because the relative circumstances of either party might sway the court one way or another in the exercise of its discretion (see p 354 b c and g, post);
(iii) it followed that the husband's application abated by his death and could not be proceeded with by R (see p 354 g and h, post).
Thomson v Thomson and Rodschinka [1896] P 263, *Dipple v Dipple* [1942] 1 All ER 234 and *Sugden v Sugden* [1957] 1 All ER 300 followed.
Rysak v Rysak and Bugajaski [1966] 2 All ER 1036 distinguished.

Notes
For the effect of death on matrimonial causes, see 12 Halsbury's Laws (3rd Edn) 380, 454, paras 833, 1020, and for cases on the subject, see 27 (2) Digest (Reissue) 876, 898, 6992, 6993, 7189-7193.
For the Law Reform (Miscellaneous Provisions) Act 1934, s 1, see 13 Halsbury's Statutes (3rd Edn) 115.
For the Matrimonial Causes Act 1965, s 17, see 17 Halsbury's Statutes (3rd Edn) 185. Section 17 was repealed by the Matrimonial Proceedings and Property Act 1970, s 42 (2), Sch 3, and replaced by s 4 of the 1970 Act.
For the Matrimonial Proceedings and Property Act 1970, s 4, see 40 Halsbury's Statutes (3rd Edn) 802.

---

a   Section 1, so far as material, provides: '(1) ... on the death of any person after the commencement of this Act all causes of action subsisting against or vested in him shall survive against, or, as the case may be, for the benefit of, his estate ...'

Cases referred to in judgment

Dipple v Dipple [1942] 1 All ER 234, [1942] P 65, 111 LJP 18, 166 LT 120, 27 (2) Digest (Reissue) 817, *6569*.

Ling v Ling and Croker (1865) 4 Sw & Tr 99, 34 LJPM & A 52, 13 LT 251, 164 ER 1453, 27 (2) Digest (Reissue) 898, *7189*.

Rysak v Rysak and Bugajaski [1966] 2 All ER 1036, [1967] P 179, [1966] 3 WLR 455, 27 (2) Digest (Reissue) 743, *5844*.

Smithe v Smithe and Roupell (1868) LR 1 P & D 587, 27 (2) Digest (Reissue) 898, *7190*.

Sugden v Sugden [1957] 1 All ER 300, [1957] P 120, [1957] 2 WLR 210, 121 JP 121, CA; *rvsg* [1956] 3 All ER 874, [1956] 3 WLR 1010, 27 (2) Digest (Reissue) 817, *6570*.

Sykes v Sykes and Smith (1870) LR 2 P & D 163, 39 LJP & M 52, 23 LT 239, 27 (2) Digest (Reissue) 895, *7145*.

Thomson v Thomson and Rodschinka [1896] P 263, 65 LJP 80, 74 LT 801, CA, 27 (2) Digest (Reissue) 876, *6993*.

Summons

By a summons taken out in late 1968 against his divorced wife ('the former wife') the husband applied to the court for variation of a post-nuptial settlement of certain property which had been purchased in their joint names. The husband, having re-married, died in May 1970 before the summons could be heard. On 3rd November 1971 his widow, as administratrix of his estate, obtained leave of the registrar to proceed with the application. The facts are set out in the judgment.

A B Hollis QC and *M A Thorpe* for the widow.
T Ian Payne and *E V Paynter Reece* for the former wife.

ORMROD J. At the request of counsel, I have arranged to give this judgment in open court, but it is essentially a chambers matter, and I am sure that the press will not publish any names or otherwise enable the parties to be identified.

It is a series of applications. First of all, there is an application by the widow of the petitioner in the suit under s 17 of the Married Women's Property Act 1882 in relation to the house. There is a cross-application by the former wife of the husband in which she also asks for an order under s 17 in relation to that house. There is also an application for variation of two post-nuptial settlements made during the marriage of the husband to the former wife. The first post-nuptial settlement in question refers to the fact that the house was conveyed, when it was purchased in 1965, into the joint names of the husband and the former wife. The application there is to extin-guish all the former wife's interests in the property as if she were dead. The other post-nuptial settlement involved is an insurance policy effected under the Married Women's Property Act 1882, the value of which is now £1,661·81, but it has been agreed between the parties that that fund should be settled on the children of the husband and the former wife.

I will give a brief outline of the facts because the critical question I am now dealing with is a pure point of law which has been argued as a preliminary point. The basic facts of the case are these. The husband and the former wife were married on 26th December 1956. At that time the husband was 50 and the wife was 17. There are two children of that marriage, S, who was born on 19th May 1958 and C, who was born on 4th July 1960. That marriage came to an end by reason of the former wife's adultery, which began apparently in 1965, and was discovered, I am told by counsel, by the husband in 1966, and there was subsequent adultery with another man, with whom the former wife has been living ever since, and I am told has recently, within a matter of weeks, married.

I should say that C and S were both made wards of court. C, at her request, went to live with her mother and was de-warded; S is still a ward and at the moment is living with her stepmother, the widow.

The marriage was dissolved by decree nisi on 28th March 1968. The precise dates of the summonses are not very clear, but the s 17 summons, under the Married Women's Property Act 1882, was taken out, as far as I can make out, on 2nd August 1968 by the husband. The other summons was taken out some time later in 1968, probably December 1968, but none of the copies of the application are dated. In each case they were taken out during the lifetime of the husband and on his instructions, but it appears, for reasons into which I have not gone at all, that little further action was taken, although affidavits were sworn and filed, in 1968, 1969, and even up to, I think, 1971. The matter did not come before the court, and it has not come before the court until now.

On 10th May 1971 the husband died, and in due course the widow took out letters of administration and then she was given permission to carry on the two sets of proceedings, that is the s 17 summons under the Married Women's Property Act 1882 and the application to vary the settlement as his personal representative.

It is common ground, I think, between counsel that the Married Women's Property Act summonses, so far as the house is concerned, are in effect non-effective. It is quite clear that the former wife is entitled to an undivided half-share of the house as being one of the joint purchasers of it, and no problem arises on that. The other part of the s 17 summons relating to furniture I am not dealing with and say no more about.

Really the key question in this case, therefore, is the application to vary the post-nuptial settlement constituted by the conveyance of the house into the joint names of the husband and the former wife. After outlining the facts to me, counsel for the widow very fairly drew my attention to the fact that counsel for the former wife had what was in effect a preliminary point of law going to jurisdiction, and by consent of counsel that was argued before me and it is that which I am now dealing with.

The point taken by counsel for the former wife is a short one but quite difficult, and it is simply this: the husband having died before the hearing of the application, the application is barred and cannot be proceeded with by his administratrix or his widow.

There is very little direct authority on this, certainly in recent years, but the basic position is, I think, this, and I can take it quite shortly; counsel for the former wife relies on *Thomson v Thomson and Rodschinka*[1], which case seems to me to be exactly on all fours with the present case that I have to deal with. That was a case in which the husband, after having obtained a divorce from his wife, filed a petition to set aside a marriage settlement, and duly served it on his wife. In those days, of course, ancillary matters in this Division were dealt with by separate petitions, separate from the main suit. The matter came before Sir Francis Jeune P by which time the husband had died. So it is exactly analogous to the present case. In a long and careful judgment Sir Francis Jeune P rejected the application, holding that he had no jurisdiction to proceed with it, the husband having died; in other words, the application had abated by reason of the death of the husband.

The matter was taken to the Court of Appeal and the Court of Appeal dismissed the appeal and dealt with the matter very shortly, holding that under the existing legislation at that time, which was the Matrimonial Causes Act 1859, there was no jurisdiction to deal with it at all. The last sentence almost of the judgment contains the essential part of it, and it reads thus[2]:

'Both enactments are intended only to authorize the Court to act for the benefit of living persons. The present application seeks an order only for the benefit of the estate of a deceased person, and is not within those enactments.'

There have been a number of attempts to use the proceedings of the various Matrimonial Causes Acts after the death of one or other of the parties. I think the position is relatively clear in some respects. For example, in both *Ling v Ling and Croker*[3] and *Smithe v Smithe and Roupell*[4] it was established clearly that executors

1   [1896] P 263
2   [1896] P at 272, per Lindley LJ
3   (1865) 4 Sw & Tr 99
4   (1868) LR 1 P & D 587

could not petition for variation of post-nuptial settlements following on the death of the husband in each case, but on the other hand the guardian of the children could so petition.

The matter remained thus, Thomson[1] following on in 1896, until the Law Reform (Miscellaneous Provisions) Act 1934, which, by s 1, removed the old common law rule that actions, mostly in tort, did not survive the death of one of the parties. That Act was passed to remove or abolish that old common law rule.

Two cases have come before the court in which the question of the application of the 1934 Act to applications in this Division have been considered. The first one of those was Dipple v Dipple[2]. It is a decision of Hodson J. It was an attempt by a wife who had obtained a decree absolute of divorce to apply for secured maintenance against her husband's estate. It was held by the learned judge that that application was incompetent, the court having no jurisdiction to allow it. That was followed in a case in the Court of Appeal called Sugden v Sugden[3], in which once again an attempt was made to use the 1934 Act to keep alive rights in this Division. In that case an order had been made against the husband to pay maintenance for two children in the form of 'pay or cause to be paid' to the wife of the petitioner maintenance for each child, and the wife in that case attempted to enforce the arrears of maintenance accrued since the death of the husband against the husband's executrix. At first instance Karminski J[4] held that the claim did survive as a result of the 1934 Act, but the Court of Appeal reversed that decision, holding that there was no jurisdiction to make an order or enforce arrears which had accrued subsequent to the death of the father.

Counsel for the widow has submitted that the situation, when it comes to varying settlements, is different because there is a fund in existence on which the court can act, and that therefore there is or can be said to be something which could be described as a cause of action within s 1 of the 1934 Act which survives for the benefit of the estate of the husband and enables the administratrix to pursue the claim for variation.

It seems to me, first of all, in broad principle that the 1934 Act was passed to deal with a particular anomalous ruling or common law rule which had existed for centuries, and it was directed essentially to that. It seems to me that one must be extraordinarily cautious in extending or widening the meaning of the phrase 'cause of action', particularly when one is asked to extend it into a completely different section of the law.

In my judgment, the real answer to this application is this, that the whole of the matrimonial causes legislation, right back to 1857, is essentially a personal jurisdiction arising between parties to the marriage or the children of the marriage. The death of one or other of the parties to the litigation has nothing whatever to do with the old common law rule which was abrogated by the 1934 Act. The fact that these applications abate by death derives, in my judgment, from the legislation which created the rights, if they are rightly called 'rights', and from no other source. If that is right, then it is not necessary to examine very closely whether or not the administratrix in this case has something which could be called, by any stretch of imagination, a cause of action.

In one branch of the jurisdiction of this court there is a case in which a claim for damages against a co-respondent and a claim for costs against a co-respondent was held to survive the death of the co-respondent. The case is Rysak v Rysak and Bugajaski[5]. That was a case in which the damages had already been awarded during the lifetime of the co-respondent and it was simply a question of collecting them. I think that was clearly a case in which the cause of action, if one can call it so, to claim damages for adultery by the time the co-respondent died had, of course, merged into what was tantamount to a judgment debt. I say 'tantamount' because I appreciate

1   [1896] P 263
2   [1942] 1 All ER 234, [1942] P 65
3   [1957] 1 All ER 300, [1957] P 120
4   [1956] 3 All ER 874, [1957] P 120
5   [1966] 2 All ER 1036, [1967] P 179

a   that this court has always controlled the destination of damages, so it may not be strictly appropriate to refer to it as a judgment debt, but certainly it is so close to a judgment debt that it is not difficult to see why it should be enforceable against the estate of the co-respondent. But it seems to me that quite different considerations apply when one is dealing with matters like variation of settlements.

b   The only other aspect of the jurisdiction of this court which has been held to survive has been cases where an order to secure a given sum of money to a wife has already been made and the only matter outstanding has been the nature of the security to be provided. The court has enforced that sort of order against the estate of a deceased husband.

  But I think that the whole reasoning on which I would put my judgment is to be found not only from the ground that I have already given but in the detailed judgment of Sir Francis Jeune P in *Thomson v Thomson*[1]. He started by pointing out that
c   at that time there was no decision directly in point. He mentioned *Ling v Ling*[2] and *Smithe v Smithe*[3], which I have referred to, and also *Sykes v Sykes and Smith*[4], and quoted the judge ordinary in that case[5], saying[6]:

d   '"The object of the section is to enable the Court to divert the money to which a wife, who is proved to have been guilty of adultery, is entitled under settlement, from her, and to apply it for the benefit of her husband and children. It is plain that, when the husband and children are dead, the power of the Court is at an end."'

  Sir Francis Jeune P went on to say[7]: 'Notwithstanding this dictum, I confess I have had considerable doubt how this question should be decided.' He then considers
e   the position in some detail. He goes on later to say[8]:

  'But, on the whole, I do not think that such an intention [that is, the survival of the right to apply for variation of settlements] is to be gathered from the language of this section. It was the clear purpose of the enactment to limit the power of varying settlements within narrow boundaries specially defined, and the words, therefore, may well be confined within their narrowest significance,
f   and to the term "parents" be assigned the meaning of parents personally. It was clearly part of the intention of the enactment that, in the very common case of the funds for a marriage settlement being contributed by persons other than the parties to the marriage, such persons should not be allowed, on the dissolution of the marriage, to ask, as they otherwise inevitably would, for the return of those funds. But the intention of the Legislature seems to go further than this.
g   If, as is often, perhaps generally, the case, there is an interest in remainder, in default of issue, after the death of the parties to a marriage, the persons representing that interest are clearly prohibited from seeking to benefit at the expense of a guilty party to a dissolved marriage. If, for example, in this case, there had been a remainder in favour of the relatives of the husband after his death, those persons could not have asked to have the settlement varied for their benefit. It
h   seems to me impossible to suppose that the Legislature intended to grant to the representative of the husband what they denied to those persons whom the settlement itself named as the successors of his interest in it. It is obvious, also, that if once you let in representatives of a husband or wife to claim you may be raising questions as to conflicting rights very difficult to decide without further guidance than the section affords. For instance, the relative means of the husband and wife, and even their wishes, are material to be considered in varying
j   settlements; but such considerations as arise in these respects are supplanted

---

1   [1896] P 263
2   (1865) 4 Sw & Tr 99
3   (1868) LR 1 P & D 587
4   (1870) LR 2 P & D 163

5   (1870) LR 2 P & D at 164
6   [1896] P at 267, 268
7   [1896] P at 268
8   [1896] P at 268, 269

P

by others totally different when the representatives, or, it may be, the devisees, take the place of a party to a marriage. Certainly the difficulty of the problems that arise now, and are puzzling enough, would be intensified.'

He continues to expand that idea.

That reasoning appears to me, in my judgment, to be conclusive. At a very early stage of this case it seemed to me at once that if there were jurisdiction to entertain this application to vary the settlement, it would be a very difficult question to decide on what basis the court should proceed. Clearly the facts on which the court would have exercised its jurisdiction during the lifetime of the husband are now quite different and a decision which might be appropriate and fair during the lifetime of the husband might well be wholly inappropriate and unfair after his death. So I asked at what point in time had I to take the facts on which my discretion should be exercised. Counsel for the widow suggested that it should be the facts as subsisting immediately before the death of the husband; but again, as Sir Francis Jeune P[1] points out, even his wishes might swing or sway the court one way or the other in the exercise of such discretion. But for my part I would regard that as a wholly artificial situation, because the truth of the matter is that the case before me is a claim by the widow to all intents and purposes against the former wife and I could not do justice today, sitting here, between these two ladies without doing it on the basis of their rival claims, positions and rights, and so forth. It would be wholly artificial to do it on the basis of the situation subsisting during the husband's lifetime. One has only to postulate the situation where the husband was alive, a man of means, who chose, for reasons best known to himself, to leave the bulk of his money away from his widow, so that, for example, if just before his death, faced with this question of extinguishing the former wife's interest in the home, the court might have said there was no possible justification for depriving her of what was a substantial asset, whereas if one has to consider the rights and position vis-à-vis a widow left badly off and a former divorced wife, all kinds of other considerations come into the picture; and if the adminsitratrix can come in and ask for a variation of settlements, why not creditors? I cannot see any reason why a creditor should not in certain circumstances take out letters of administration and make the application, in which case, of course, the court would be faced with a quite impossible conundrum.

In my judgment, there is no jurisdiction to entertain the application in this case under s 17 of the Matrimonial Causes Act 1965 if that is the substantive section under which it is brought. I think I would only add this, that, whether one has to look to the terms of s 17 of the 1965 Act or s 4 of the Matrimonial Proceedings and Property Act 1970, the one thing that seems to me abundantly plain is that the statute contemplates both the parties to the marriage surviving, except insofar as the children, who are specifically named in all the relevant sections, have a right to apply for variation of the settlement, because they are personally one of the parties who are interested. But to my mind it is only the party who can apply and in whose favour orders of this kind can be made. I do not think the fact that a fund exists sufficiently distinguishes it from the other cases such as *Sugden*[2] and *Dipple*[3].

In those circumstances, therefore, I must hold as a matter of law, without having looked at the merits in any way, that the present application cannot be maintained.

Application refused.

Solicitors: *Cripps, Harries, Willis & Carter* (for the widow); *Horwich, Farrelly, Flacks & Co* (for the former wife).

R C T Habesch Esq Barrister.

---

1 [1896] P at 269
2 [1957] 1 All ER 300, [1957] P 120
3 [1942] 1 All ER 234, [1942] P 65

Prodexport State Company for Foreign Trade v E D & F Man Ltd

QUEEN'S BENCH DIVISION
MOCATTA J
3rd, 4th, 5th, 13th JULY 1972

Arbitration – Setting aside award – Jurisdiction – Award made without jurisdiction – Illegal contract – Contract legal at inception – Performance subsequently becoming illegal– English law proper law of contract – Contract to be performed in foreign country – Performance becoming illegal under foreign law after contract made – Arbitrator awarding damages for non-performance – Non-speaking award – Whether arbitrator having jurisdiction to award damages for breach of illegal obligation – Whether grounds for setting aside award – Arbitration Act 1950, s 23 (2).

Arbitration – Setting aside award – Application – Time limit – Extension – Application for leave to extend time – Practice – Notice of motion including both application for extension of time and application for substantive relief – RSC Ord 73, r 5.

In March 1970 the sellers, a Romanian state trading company, agreed to sell to the buyers, an English company, 10,000 metric tons of sugar at a price of £33 per ton, delivery to take place during the second half of September-October 1970 at Constanza. Under the terms of the contract all disputes arising out of it were to be submitted to the Council of the Sugar Association of London ('the association') for settlement in accordance with the arbitration rules of the association. The general rules of the association were incorporated in the contract. At the date of the contract there was nothing illegal about it either by its proper law, which was English, or by the lex loci solutionis, which was Romanian. In May 1970 the sellers informed the buyers that, in consequence of calamitous floods in Romania, they might not be able to fulfil the contract. Subsequently the contract was altered to provide for delivery in October-November 1970. At the end of October 5,000 tons of sugar were delivered. On 6th November, however, the Romanian government promulgated a decision prohibiting further exports of sugar. On 9th November the sellers informed the buyers that the remaining 5,000 tons could not be delivered, relying on the force majeure provisions of the association's rules. The matter then went to arbitration, the sellers relying on the decision of 6th November in their defence. On 29th March 1971 the council of the association made a non-speaking award merely recording that the council had decided that the sellers should pay the buyers £35,855. On 12th May 1972 the sellers, having applied for leave for an extension of time, moved for an order under s 23 (2)[a] of the Arbitration Act 1950 that the award be set aside on the grounds that the council had misconducted themselves or had acted in excess of their jurisdiction in awarding damages for the non-performance of an illegal obligation.

Held – (i) Where a contract was illegal at its inception it was open to the court to interfere with an award of arbitrators appointed under the contract on the ground of lack of jurisdiction in that, the contract having been void from the moment it was signed, no arbitrators or umpire appointed under the arbitration clause in the contract could ever have had jurisdiction. Where, however, the contract was originally valid, it could not be said that, because of some subsequent change in the law, particularly if it could only affect partial performance, the arbitrators appointed

---

a   Section 23 (2), so far as material, provides: 'Where an arbitrator ... has misconducted himself or the proceedings, or an arbitration or award has been improperly procured, the High Court may set the award aside.'

under the contract had no jurisdiction. That was so, a fortiori, when the change was one in foreign law, which was a question of fact. In such a case, interference with the decision of the arbitrators in a non-speaking final award on the basis that it enforced an obligation illegal by the lex loci solutionis, would infringe the principle that the arbitrators were sole judges of fact and law (see p 361 b to d and p 362 d, post).

(ii) On the facts of the case there was no ground for doubting the jurisdiction of the arbitrators. Romanian law and its application to the special circumstances of the case were matters of fact on which the arbitrators were the sole judges. Furthermore, as no special case had been requested, they were the sole judges of matters of English law. Accordingly the motion to set aside the award would be dismissed (see p 361 f and p 363 d e and g, post).

David Taylor & Son Ltd v Barnett [1953] 1 All ER 843 explained and distinguished.

Per Mocatta J. (i) It does not necessarily follow that, if English law changes during the life of a contract, the proper law of which is English and which can only be performed in England, so that performance or further performance has become illegal, a non-speaking award can be interfered with on the ground that it gives damages for failure to do something illegal (see p 362 h to 363 b, post).

(ii) Where an application for leave to extend the time within which to move to set aside an arbitrator's award after the expiry of six weeks allowed by RSC Ord 73, r 5, it is desirable for one notice of motion to be taken out asking both for leave to extend the time and for the substantive relief (see p 363 h, post).

Notes

For setting aside an arbitrator's award on the grounds of misconduct or improper procurement of award, see 2 Halsbury's Laws (3rd Edn) 57-60, paras 125, 126, and for cases on the subject, see 2 Digest (Repl) 678-683, *1929-1966*.

For the Arbitration Act 1950, s 23, see 2 Halsbury's Statutes (3rd Edn) 452.

Cases referred to in judgment

Giacomo Costa Fu Andrea v British Italian Trading Co Ltd [1962] 2 All ER 53, [1963] 1 QB 201, [1962] 3 WLR 512; sub nom *Andrea v British Italian Trading Co Ltd* [1962] 1 Lloyd's Rep 151, CA, Digest (Cont Vol A) 40, *1719a*.

Gillespie Brothers & Co v Thompson Brothers & Co (1922) 13 Lloyd LR 519.

Hartley (R S) Ltd v Provincial Insurance Co Ltd [1957] 1 Lloyd's Rep 121.

Heyman v Darwins Ltd [1942] 1 All ER 337, [1942] AC 356, 111 LJKB 241, 166 LT 306, 2 Digest (Repl) 492, *435*.

Kent v Elstob (1802) 3 East 18, [1775-1802] All ER Rep 637, 102 ER 502, 2 Digest (Repl) 650, *1714*.

Mackender v Feldia AG [1966] 3 All ER 847, [1967] 2 QB 590, [1967] 2 WLR 119, 50 Digest (Repl) 341, *689*.

Maritime National Fish Ltd v Ocean Trawlers Ltd [1935] AC 524, [1935] All ER Rep 86, 104 LJPC 88, 153 LT 425, 18 Asp MLC 551, PC, 12 Digest (Repl) 388, *3020*.

Miller (James) & Partners Ltd v Whitworth Street Estates (Manchester) Ltd [1970] 1 All ER 796, [1970] AC 583, [1970] 2 WLR 728, [1970] 1 Lloyd's Rep 269, HL; rvsg sub nom *Whitworth Street Estates (Manchester) Ltd v James Miller & Partners Ltd* [1969] 2 All ER 210, [1969] 1 WLR 377, CA, Digest (Cont Vol C) 141, *734d*.

Regazzoni v K C Sethia (1944) Ltd [1957] 3 All ER 286, [1958] AC 301, [1957] 3 WLR 752, [1957] 2 Lloyd's Rep 289, HL, Digest (Cont Vol A) 231, *838a*.

Smith, Coney & Barrett v Becker, Gray & Co [1916] 2 Ch 86, [1914-15] All ER Rep 398, 84 LJCh 865, 112 LT 914, CA, 2 Digest (Repl) 499, *473*.

Taylor (David) & Son Ltd v Barnett [1953] 1 All ER 843, [1953] 1 WLR 562, CA, 2 Digest (Repl) 697, *2102*.

Cases also cited

Ertel Bieber & Co v Rio Tinto Co Ltd [1918] AC 260, [1918-19] All ER Rep 127, HL.

Falkingham v Victorian Railways Commissioner [1900] AC 452, PC.
London Export Corpn Ltd v Jubilee Coffee Roasting Co Ltd [1958] 2 All ER 411, [1958] 1
    WLR 661, CA.
Ralli Brothers v Compania Naviera Sota y Aznar [1920] 2 KB 287, [1920] All ER Rep 427,
    CA.

Motion and summons

By notice of motion dated 8th July 1971 the plaintiffs, Prodexport State Company
for Foreign Trade, a Romanian state company for foreign trade carrying on business
in Bucharest, sought an order that, notwithstanding the time limited by RSC Ord 73,
r 5 (1), had expired, the plaintiffs be at liberty to apply to the court for an order
under s 23 (2) of the Arbitration Act 1950 that the award made in an arbitration between the plaintiffs and the defendants, E D & F Man Ltd (formerly Man (Brokers)
Ltd), by the Council of the Sugar Association of London ('the council') dated 29th
March 1971 be set aside. By a further notice dated 12th May 1972 the plaintiffs applied
for an order that the council's award might be set aside or declared to be void on
the grounds (1) that the council had misconducted themselves in awarding damages
for the non-performance of an illegal obligation, and (2) that the council had acted
in excess of their jurisdiction in awarding damages for the non-performance of an
illegal obligation. By an originating summons issued pursuant to an order of Master
Lubbock dated 30th November 1971, the defendants applied for an order that they
be at liberty to enforce the award made by the council in the same manner as a
judgment or order to the same effect pursuant to s 26 of the 1950 Act. The facts are
set out in the judgment.

C S Staughton QC and *A G S Pollock* for the sellers.
Andrew Leggatt QC and *A B R Hallgarten* for the buyers.

Cur adv vult

13th July. **MOCATTA J** read the following judgment. By a contract in writing
dated 4th March 1970, Prodexport State Company for Foreign Trade (whom I will call
'the sellers'), agreed to sell to Man (Brokers) Ltd (whom I will call 'the buyers'),
10,000 metric tons, 10 per cent more or less for chartering purposes only, of Romanian
raw beet sugar in bags. Delivery was to take place during the second half of September-October 1970 in buyers' option f o b Constanza. The price was £33 per
metric ton to be paid on first presentation of shipping documents in London. The
buyers had to declare the name of the vessel or vessels on which the sugar was to be
shipped and give not less than 14 days notice of expected readiness to load. The
buyers were entitled to call for delivery of the sugar between the first and last working
days inclusive of the period of delivery. All disputes arising out of the contract were
by its terms submitted to the Sugar Association of London for settlement in accordance with the arbitration rules of the association and the general rules of the association were also made applicable to the contract. The sellers are a state trading
organisation in Romania.

A dispute arose out of this contract which went to arbitration. As a result an
award of the Council of the Sugar Association was made dated 29th March 1971.
This was a non-speaking award. It recited the names of the parties, the date of the
contract and that a dispute had arisen in respect of 5,000 metric tons of raw sugar to
be shipped under the contract. The award merely recorded that the council had
decided that the sellers should pay the buyers £35,855, which sum included interest,
and that the fees and costs of £150 were to be paid by the sellers.

As the result of this award I have no fewer than two motions and one originating
summons before me. The first motion, taken out by the sellers, dated 8th July
1971, asked for liberty to apply for an order to set aside the award notwithstanding
that the statutory six weeks [1] from the date of publication of the award had elapsed.

---

1 See RSC Ord 73, r 5 (1)

The second motion, also by the sellers, dated 12th May 1972, was for an order that the award be set aside on the grounds that the council had misconducted themselves or had acted in excess of their jurisdiction in awarding damages for the non-performance of an illegal obligation. The originating summons, issued by Master Lubbock on 30th November 1971, had been held up owing to the need to serve a copy thereof on the sellers in Romania. It had been taken out by the buyers and asked for an order, under s 26 of the Arbitration Act 1950, to enforce the award as a judgment and sign final judgment in the terms of the award.

Although I considered there had been considerable delay on the part of the sellers in moving for an extension of time and to set aside the award, I decided in the exercise of my discretion that it was right to extend the time for the hearing of the substantive motion because so to do would not prejudice the buyers so far as replying to the motion was concerned, the sellers were a foreign state trading organisation and the matters arising on the motion were novel and of much importance. I will, however, say something more about the delays incurred and the procedure followed after I have dealt with the substantive motion on its merits.

At the date of the contract there was nothing illegal about it or its anticipated or intended performance either by its proper law, which was English, or by the lex loci solutionis, which was Romanian. However, there were very bad floods in the spring of 1970 in Romania affecting both sugar beet in the fields and the processing factories. In consequence on 25th May the sellers by telex informed the buyers they were not sure whether, owing to the calamity, they would be able to fulfil the contract.

Subsequently and, it would appear, because of the difficulties caused by the floods, alterations were made to the contract so that by 25th September the original terms had been altered by an increase of ¼ per cent in the price, changing the shipment period to the second half of October-November 1970 in buyers' option and providing for payment in advance on 30th September of the price for 5,000 tons against bank guarantee and warehouse receipt.

On 6th October the sellers by telex asked the buyers to nominate a vessel to carry 5,000 tons with ETA Constanza around 20th October. The buyers were asked not to charter a vessel for a larger quantity. On 12th October the buyers replied they were unable to find a 5,000 ton vessel and declared the vessel Hera to lift the 5,000 tons the sellers had confirmed ready from 20th October and a further quantity of 2,300 tons from 26th October onwards. They asked when it would be most suitable to put in a further vessel for the balance of the contract.

The subsequent story is not altogether clear from the affidavits. There was considerable argument and negotiation between the parties. However, what is clear is that the Hera was tendered, her notice of readiness was accepted on 22nd October, she began loading on 27th October and completed on 9th November. During that period, although it is uncertain on what dates therein, the sellers loaded 5,000 tons of raw sugar beet in bags and the buyers loaded 2,300 tons of white crystal sugar they had purchased aliunde in order to be able to fill the ship.

In the course of the negotiations by telephone and telex the sellers, inter alia, suggested the buyers should consider postponing delivery until the fourth quarter of the following year. They further, in a long telex to the buyers dated 20th October, in which amongst other matters they dealt with the details of a projected flight of a negotiator from Bucharest to London, said:

'Thanks for your comprehension We shall do our best in order to surpass these difficulties Please appreciate that instead to arise act of government for force majeure and cancelling the contract what should be more easy for us we are trying to find a friendly and reasonable settlement.'

I have purposely refrained from suggesting any punctuation in the last sentence lest such might affect its meaning.

a   On 6th November the Council of Ministers of the Socialist Republic of Romania promulgated a decision prohibiting sugar exports except quantities for which the equivalent value had by that date already been received. The sellers were officially informed of this on Monday, 9th November, and by telex of the same date to the buyers they declared that the remaining 5,000 tons could not be delivered relying on the force majeure provisions of r 218 of the Rules of the Sugar Association of

b   London. The matter then went to arbitration, the buyers and sellers in accordance with the rules stating their respective claim, defence and reply in writing. There was no challenge by the sellers in their defence to the jurisdiction of the arbitrators. An English translation of the decision of 6th November was before the arbitrators and the sellers relied on this in their defence. There was no oral argument. An affidavit in support of the motion of a Romanian lawyer was put in before me de-

c   posing that once the Council of Ministers had promulgated their decision of 6th November it would have been illegal for the sellers to have shipped the remaining 5,000 tons of sugar.

For the sellers it was submitted that (i) the court could and would set aside a non-speaking award on the ground of misconduct if it awarded damages for the non-performance of an act in England under a contract governed by English law, which

d   act, if performed, would have been illegal by that law as it prevailed at the date of the contract: see *David Taylor & Son Ltd v Barnett*[1]; (ii) the same result must in principle apply if the illegality by English law supervened after the date of the contract so as to make performance illegal; (iii) international comity required that the English courts would not enforce an award requiring the payment of damages for the non-performance of an act, which, by a change in the lex loci solutionis, had become

e   illegal since the date of the contract, and, would set aside such an award: see, for non-enforcement of a contract on grounds of international comity, *Regazzoni v K C Sethia (1944) Ltd*[2]; (iv) the court must form its own view on any evidence adduced before it, whether put before the arbitral tribunal or not, whether on the facts the award did in truth infringe the above principles; and (v) on the evidence before the court here, which was the same as the written evidence before the arbitrators,

f   the award would have to be remitted for the arbitrators to find whether there was on the facts any breach of contract by the sellers in not loading an additional 2,300 tons of raw sugar on the Hera before the prohibition came into effect; if there were, the damages awarded would probably require to be reconsidered; if there were not, then the tribunal should award in favour of the sellers and dismiss the buyers' claim.

For the buyers it was submitted that (i) the court would only interfere with or refuse to enforce a non-speaking award on the ground of illegality if it were established

g   that at the date of the relevant contract the current proper law was English and that law rendered performance of the contract illegal; (ii) on a true analysis of the authorities this principle and the decision in *David Taylor & Son Ltd v Barnett*[1] rested on lack of jurisdiction; (iii) only in cases of lack of jurisdiction or misconduct in the sense of unfairness in the procedural conduct of an arbitration would the court countenance

h   the receipt of evidence as to the facts or arguments advanced in an arbitration leading to a non-speaking award; (iv) if it were desired to raise matters of law before the court the right and only course to take was to ask for an award to be stated in the form of a special case; failing such a request the arbitrators were the sole judges of fact and law and the court would not look behind the award; and (v) no question of breach of international comity could arise in enforcing a non-speaking award when no special

j   case had been requested, since the court did not know and was not entitled to know what view had been taken by the arbitrators of the facts or the law of both of which they were the sole judges.

It is plain from the above recital of the main competing submissions that the issues

---

1   [1953] 1 All ER 843, [1953] 1 WLR 562
2   [1957] 3 All ER 286, [1958] AC 301

raised are of importance, not only because of considerations of international comity, *a*
but also because of another important matter, namely, maintaining the proper
distinction between the respective provinces of the courts and of arbitral tribunals.

Arbitration is a greatly used method of settling disputes in trade and commerce,
both as between parties resident in the same country and as between parties resident,
as here, in different countries and carrying on international trade. It is well known
that English law is nearly unique in the degree of interference it permits the courts in *b*
the conduct of arbitrations and the settlement of disputes thereby. Its provisions for
the statement of awards in the form of a special case for the decision of the court,
whether consultative or final, which may be mandatory, differ not only from the
law of most European countries, but, as is well known, even from the law of Scotland:
see e g *James Miller & Partners Ltd v Whitworth Street Estates (Manchester) Ltd*[1]. Its
provisions for setting aside a speaking award for error of law contained on its face, *c*
a development initiated in 1802 in *Kent v Elstob*[2], had often been regretted and have
led to highly technical and unsatisfactory refinements: see *Giacomo Costa Fu Andrea
v British Italian Trading Co Ltd*[3]. Unless principle or authority distinctly requires,
it would clearly be undesirable to blur still further the demarcation line between the
courts and arbitral tribunals and, incidentally, greatly increase the cost of arbitration
as a method of settling disputes. *d*

I think it important to bear in mind the following statement in Russell on
Arbitration[4]:

'It is not misconduct on the part of an arbitrator to come to an erroneous
decision, whether his error is one of fact or law, and whether or not his findings
of fact are supported by evidence.'

If authority for this be required, it is to be found in the following passage from the *e*
judgment of Atkin LJ in *Gillespie Brothers & Co v Thompson Brothers & Co*[5]:

'It is no ground for coming to a conclusion on an award that the facts are
wrongly found. The facts have got to be treated as found . . . Nor is it a ground
for setting aside an award that the conclusion is wrong in fact. Nor is it even a
ground for setting aside an award that there is no evidence on which the facts *f*
could be found, because that would be mere error in law, and it is not
misconduct to come to a wrong conclusion in law and would be no ground for
ruling aside the award unless the error in law appeared on the fact of it . . .'

See also per Lord Goddard CJ in *R S Hartley Ltd v Provincial Insurance Co Ltd*[6].

The foundation of the sellers' argument is the decision of the Court of Appeal in
David Taylor & Son Ltd v Barnett[7]. In that case a contract was entered into between *g*
the parties, who were wholesalers, whereby the defendants agreed to sell to the
plaintiffs 10,000 cases of Irish stewed steak at 2s 4d per lb. The contract contained
an arbitration clause. No deliveries were made by the defendants and the buyers
claimed damages in arbitration. The umpire awarded the buyers £11,000 and they
then began proceedings before a master for leave to enforce the award as a judgment.
The master adjourned the summons in order to give the sellers the opportunity of *h*
moving to set aside the award. This they sought by motion, which failed before
Lord Goddard CJ. The sellers appealed and were successful, the award being set aside.

At the date of the contract it was, by virtue of a statutory instrument[8], illegal

---

1 [1970] 1 All ER 796, [1970] AC 583
2 (1802) 3 East 18, [1775-1802] All ER Rep 637
3 [1962] 2 All ER 53 at 59, [1963] 1 QB 201 at 211
4 18th Edn (1970), p 391
5 (1922) 13 Lloyd LR 519 at 524, 525
6 [1957] 1 Lloyd's Rep 121
7 [1953] 1 All ER 843, [1953] 1 WLR 562
8 Meat Producers and Canned Meat (Control and Maximum Prices) Order 1948, SI 1948
   No 1509, as amended by SI 1951 No 1317

j

a to agree to buy or sell imported canned meat at a price in excess of 2s 0¼d per lb. Accordingly the contract was an illegal one. This point was admittedly made before the umpire and was not challenged on behalf of the buyers.

The problem raised by this authority in relation to the present case is whether the basis for that decision was on analysis, as the buyers submit, lack of jurisdiction or whether, as the sellers argue, it was a true case of misconduct and misconduct only.

b The relevance of the distinction is that on the facts in *David Taylor & Son Ltd v Barnett*[1] the contract can be said to have been void from the moment it was signed and therefore no arbitrators or umpire appointed under the arbitration clause in the contract could ever have had jurisdiction. If, on the other hand, there is during the life of a contract some change in the law, particularly if that can only affect partial performance of the contract, it is difficult if not impossible to say that arbitrators appointed

c under an arbitration clause in the contract have no jurisdiction. The position is, perhaps, a fortiori when the change is in foreign law, which in this country, whether it arises in court or in arbitration, is a question of fact. If then arbitrators have jurisdiction, interference with their decision in a non-speaking final award, on the basis that it enforced an obligation illegal by the lex loci solutionis, would infringe the principle that they are the sole judges of fact and law.

d This point can be illustrated strikingly by the facts here. I was referred to the written reply put in by the buyers before the arbitrators. It is clear from this—and I think also from the buyers' written claim—that the buyers were not relying or inviting the arbitrators to rely on lack of performance after 6th November 1970; they expressly took the point that the sellers were in default before that date. The arbitrators may well have decided as they did in favour of the buyers on the basis of this argument. In so deciding they may have taken what the court would

e consider wrong views on facts and law, but the court, if it were to interfere, would be substituting its own views on both matters for those of the arbitrators. Another, amongst other possibilities, is that the arbitrators took the view that the sellers could not rely on the decision of 6th November if they had themselves brought that about. In other words, if the change in the law frustrated the contract so far as further performance was concerned, the frustration was self-induced: see *Maritime National

f Fish Ltd v Ocean Trawlers Ltd*[2]. Even though such a view might be held by a court to be wrong in law, it is difficult to see why the arbitrators were not entitled so to decide and, as they were not asked to state a case, how it can be right to substitute the view of the court for what may have been their view.

It is true that there is frequent reference throughout the three judgments in *David Taylor & Son Ltd v Barnett*[1] to misconduct and, only once is there an express reference

g to jurisdiction, where Denning LJ said[3]: 'An arbitrator has no jurisdiction or authority to award damages on an illegal contract.' But Singleton LJ in the leading judgment said as follows[4]:

'In *Smith, Coney and Barrett* v. *Becker, Gray & Co.*[5] the plaintiffs attempted to obtain an injunction to restrain the other party to a contract going to

h arbitration on a dispute which had arisen, and one of the grounds being that the contract between the parties was illegal. The attempt to obtain the injunction failed because the court did not find that the contract was illegal. WARRINGTON, J., said[6], "I think that the plaintiffs in order to succeed must show that the contract for arbitration with the submission was invalid. For that purpose I think that I am bound to look at the date at which the contract was made, and

j

1 [1953] 1 All ER 843, [1953] 1 WLR 562
2 [1935] AC 524, [1935] All ER Rep 86
3 [1953] 1 All ER at 847, [1953] 1 WLR at 570
4 [1953] 1 All ER at 844, 845, [1953] 1 WLR at 566
5 [1916] 2 Ch 86, [1914-15] All ER Rep 398
6 (1915) 112 LT 914 at 916

to see whether at that date there is any reasonable ground for saying that the contract was invalid. Was that so? For that purpose it is necessary to turn to the contract and see what it really is." ... LORD COZENS-HARDY, M.R., in his judgment said[1]: "The plaintiffs in this action sought a declaration that the contract which I have just read was illegal by reason of the war. Of course, if it was illegal, then any question of arbitration under the contract would fall with it." '

These quotations clearly went to jurisdiction and were otherwise irrelevant. I was referred in this connection by counsel for the buyers to a very apt passage from the judgment of Diplock LJ in *Mackender v Feldia AG*[2]. The whole passage is too long to cite, but I quote one sentence:

'Where an agreement is wholly unenforceable because it is contrary to English law, it may, if the proper law of the agreement is itself English law, accurately be said to be void as a contract, that is, not to be a contract at all.'

In such a case it would follow, as in the passages quoted by Singleton LJ[3] from *Smith, Coney and Barrett v Becker, Gray & Co*[4], that the arbitration clause, the basis of any jurisdiction in the arbitral tribunal, would be as void in law as the rest of the document containing it.

In my judgment this is the true basis of the decision in *David Taylor & Son Ltd v Barnett*[5]. I notice that this is the view taken of the case in Chitty on Contracts[6], citing this case and *Heyman v Darwins Ltd*[7]. In Cheshire and Fifoot[8], the following appears:

'If the contract as made is expressly or implicitly forbidden by statute it is totally void. No action lies for its enforcement even though it is the defendant who has broken the law and who pleads his own illegality. Thus an award made by an arbitrator in respect of a prohibited contract will be set aside by the court.'

David Taylor & Son Ltd v Barnett[5] is cited as authority.

It is true that where a party seeks to avoid an ostensible award against him by establishing that there was no binding contract containing an arbitration clause to which he was a party, he usually today seeks his remedy, if he wishes to take the offensive rather than defend an application under s 26 of the Act to enforce the award as a judgment, by an action or an originating summons for a declaration rather than in a motion to set aside. There is some logical solecism in pursuing the statutory remedy to set aside an award under s 23 of the Act, when, ex hypothesi, nothing exists which the law regards as an award. This has, however, since 1965, been permitted by RSC Ord 73, r 2 (3), and the fact that the proceedings in *David Taylor & Sons Ltd v Barnett*[5] took the form of a motion to set aside is irrelevant to the legal basis of the decision of the Court of Appeal.

I do not think it necessarily follows from that decision that if the law of England changes during the life of a contract the proper law of which is English and which can only be performed in England so that it can be said that performance or further performance has become illegal, a non-speaking award can be interfered with by the courts on the ground that it gives damages for failure to do something illegal.

1   [1916] 2 Ch at 91, 92, [1914-15] All ER Rep at 399
2   [1966] 3 All ER 847 at 851, [1967] 2 QB 590 at 601
3   [1953] 1 All ER at 844, 845, [1953] 1 WLR at 566
4   [1916] 2 Ch 86, [1914-15] All ER Rep 398
5   [1953] 1 All ER 843, [1953] 1 WLR 562
6   23rd Edn (1968), vol 1, pp 352, 353, para 773
7   [1942] 1 All ER 337, [1942] AC 356
8   7th Edn (1969), p 303; cf 8th Edn (1972), p 335

a   In such a case the contract and its arbitration clause would not have been void ab initio and it is difficult to see on what ground the jurisdiction of the arbitral tribunal could be challenged. Indeed to deny the jurisdiction of the tribunal would be contrary to the decision in *Heyman v Darwins Ltd*[1]: see in particular per Viscount Simon LC[2]. The application of the altered law to the facts of the case would be peculiarly a matter for the tribunal and, prima facie, I would have thought that unless a special case were requested, the tribunal's award would be final. It is not, however,

b   necessary to express a concluded opinion on this matter and much might conceivably turn on the nature of the changed English law and the facts of the case.

When one turns to the position in the present case, however, one is dealing with a contract of which the proper law is English requiring performance in Romania. At the date of the contract it was undoubtedly valid by both systems of law. As the result of a change in Romanian law during the course of performance it is said that complet-

c   ion of performance by the sellers became impossible by reasons of supervening illegality and that accordingly the award of damages against the sellers must either be set aside or remitted because the court should make its own findings of fact and to them apply the relevant decision by the law of England. Unless this is done the court would not be acting in accordance with the principle of international comity expounded and applied in *Regazzoni v K C Sethia*[3].

d   I am, as must by now have become apparent, unable to accept this line of argument. The facts and situation here are vastly different from those in *David Taylor & Sons Ltd v Barnett*[4]. I can find no ground for doubting the jurisdiction of the arbitrators appointed under this widely drawn arbitration clause. Romanian law and its application to the special circumstances of the case were matters of fact on which the arbitrators were the sole judges. As no special case was requested, they were also the sole judges

e   of matters of English law arising. It would be pessimi exempli and uncalled for by any authority for the court to substitute its own views for those of the arbitrators on fact or law. No question of misconduct in the sense of procedural impropriety or the denial of natural justice arises. If the court refuses to set aside this award and orders its enforcement under s 26, it cannot with any show of reasons be said to be infringing any principle of international comity. By so doing the court expresses

f   no opinion on the issues of fact and law raised before the arbitrators or on the correctness in fact or law of the decision in the award. The latter gives no reasons and is of the utmost brevity as, in the absence of a request for an award in the form of a special case for the decision of the court, the arbitrators were entitled to express their decision.

For these reasons although I have acceded to the sellers' motion requesting an extension of time within which to move to set aside the award, I dismiss their sub-

g   stantive motion to set aside and make an order as asked by the buyers on their originating summons under s 26 of the Act.

I would add a few sentences about procedure. Now that a motion to set aside (or remit) an award must be made to a single judge (see RSC Ord 73, r 2) and, accordingly, by RSC Ord 3, r 5, leave to extend the time within which to move to set aside an award after the expiry of the six weeks from publication allowed by RSC Ord 73,

h   r 5, must also be made to a single judge, it is clearly desirable, in most cases, for one notice of motion to be taken out asking for both kinds of relief. The same affidavit or affidavits may support both and the suggested course is likely to effect substantial economies over the somewhat clumsy double-barrelled procedure adopted here.

However that may be it should be the practice, and in most cases is, for the party taking out a notice of motion, other than in the Commercial Court, to obtain from the

j   Crown Office a hearing date that can be inserted in the notice, which will then be

---

1   [1942] 1 All ER 337, [1942] AC 356
2   [1942] 1 All ER at 343, [1942] AC at 366
3   [1957] 3 All ER 286, [1958] AC 301
4   [1953] 1 All ER 843, [1953] 1 WLR 562

forthwith served on the other party. In default of such a date being allotted the motion will probably not find its way into any list until further action is taken by one of   *a*
the parties. In the present case no date was requested of the Crown Office and no
copy of the notice of motion for an extension of time dated 8th July 1971 was served
on the buyers until 12th May 1972. Had a date been obtained on 8th July 1971 these
matters would no doubt have come to a head with much greater expedition, probably
in the autumn of last year.

     b

*Leave to sellers to apply for order setting aside award granted. Application refused. Leave to
buyers to enforce award pursuant to s 26 of the Arbitration Act 1950 granted. Leave to appeal
granted.*

Solicitors: *Richards, Butler & Co* (for the sellers); *William A Crump & Son* (for the
buyers).   *c*

                                              E H Hunter Esq   Barrister.

R v Lawrence (Paul Antony)   *d*

COURT OF APPEAL, CRIMINAL DIVISION
LORD WIDGERY CJ, MEGAW LJ AND TALBOT J
29th NOVEMBER 1972

Road traffic – Drink or drugs – Person in charge of vehicle unfit to drive through drink or   *e*
*drugs – Defence – Circumstances such that no likelihood of driving while unfit – Condition of
vehicle – Relevance – Driver involved in collision – Vehicle damaged – Driver subsequently
consuming alcohol – Driver charged with being in charge while unfit through drink – Jury
directed to disregard fact that driver's vehicle might not have been capable of being driven
following accident – Whether a misdirection – Road Traffic Act 1960, s 6 (2)—Road Safety
Act 1967, s 1 (4).*   *f*

The appellant, while driving, collided with a parked car. Immediately following the
accident the appellant went to a nearby public house and fortified himself with
alcohol against the shock which he had suffered in the collision. Consequently, when
the police arrived, it was impossible for them to bring a charge in respect of driving
with an excessive blood-alcohol concentration. The appellant was arrested and in due   *g*
course charged on two counts: (i) being in charge of a motor car when unfit to drive
through drink, contrary to s 6 (2)[a] of the Road Traffic Act 1960, and (ii) being on the
same occasion in charge of the same motor car when the proportion of alcohol in his
blood exceeded the prescribed limit, contrary to s 1 (2)[b] of the Road Safety Act 1967.
The appellant contended that he was, by virtue of s 6 (2) of the 1960 Act and s 1 (3)[c]
of the 1967 Act, not liable to conviction on the ground that, following the accident,   *h*
the circumstances were such that there was no likelihood of driving the car so long
as he was unfit through drink or had an excess of alcohol in his blood. The trial
judge directed the jury that, in determining whether the circumstances were such
that there was no likelihood of the appellant driving the car in that condition, they
should disregard the fact that the appellant's car might be in such a state following the
accident that it could hardly be driven at all. The appellant was convicted on both   *j*
counts and appealed.

---

a   Section 6 (2), so far as material, is set out at p 367 c and d, post
b   Section 1 (2), so far as material, is set out at p 366 b, post
c   Section 1 (3) is set out at p 366 c, post

a **Held** – The trial judge's direction was perfectly proper in relation to the charge under s 1 (2) of the 1967 Act by virtue of the provisions of s 1 (4)^d of that Act. Section 6 of the 1960 Act, however, contained no provision corresponding to s 1 (4) of the 1967 Act and accordingly the judge had misdirected the jury in relation to the charge under s 6 (2) of the 1960 Act since, in determining whether the car was likely to be driven again while the appellant remained unfit through drink, the condition of the car was a *b* relevant factor. Accordingly the appeal against conviction under the 1967 Act would be dismissed and the appeal against conviction under the 1960 Act allowed (see p 367 a c e and f, post).

Notes
For the offence of being in charge of a vehicle when unfit through drink or drugs, see *c* 33 Halsbury's Laws (3rd Edn) 627, 628, para 1058, and for a case on the subject, see 45 Digest (Repl) 96, *330*.

For the Road Traffic Act 1960, s 6, see 28 Halsbury's Statutes (3rd Edn) 230, and for the Road Safety Act 1967, s 1, see ibid 459.

As from 1st July 1972 s 6 of the 1960 Act has been replaced by s 5 of the Road Traffic Act 1972 and s 1 of the 1967 Act has been replaced by s 6 of the 1972 Act.

d **Appeal**
This was an appeal by Paul Antony Lawrence against his conviction on 3rd February 1972 in the Crown Court at Sessions House, Newington Causeway, London, SE1, before his Honour Judge Abdela QC and a jury on two counts: (1) being in charge of a motor car when unfit to drive through drink, contrary to s 6 (2) of the Road Traffic *e* Act 1960, and (2) being on the same occasion in charge of the same motor car when the proportion of alcohol in his blood exceeded the prescribed limit, contrary to s 1 (2) of the Road Safety Act 1967. He was fined £30 on each count, his licence was endorsed and he was disqualified for one month on the first count and two months on the second. The facts are set out in the judgment of the court.

F E Wybrants for the appellant.
f *A J Arlidge* for the Crown.

LORD WIDGERY CJ delivered the judgment of the court. This appellant was convicted at the Inner London Crown Court in February 1972 on two counts, one of being in charge of a motor car when unfit to drive through drink, contrary to s 6 (2) *g* of the Road Traffic Act 1960, and one of being on the same occasion in charge of the same motor car when the proportion of alcohol in his blood exceeded the prescribed limit, contrary to s 1 (2) of the Road Safety Act 1967. He was fined £30 on each count; his licence was endorsed and he was disqualified for a short period, one month on the first count and two months on the second.

The case comes before this court on what is really a pure point of statutory con-*h* struction, and it arises in this way: the appellant had been driving his car on the North End Road about 11.00 pm on a January night and he turned a corner into a road called Barons Court Road and there collided with a car parked a few yards from the junction. It is not very clear how much damage was done to the two cars, but most of it was superficial, and there is at least some material in the papers to suggest that the appellant's car could have been driven away without too much trouble if a few *j* adjustments of the wing fouling the tyre and the like had been made. However, before it was driven away the police arrived, and the appellant was arrested; in due course he was charged with these two offences, it being found when he gave a sample of blood for a laboratory test that 151 milligrammes of alcohol per 100 millilitres of blood were present. I ought to add for completeness that according to the appellant's

---

d Section 1 (4) is set out at p 366 e, post

evidence, immediately following the accident he went to a nearby public house and fortified himself with alcohol against the shock he suffered in the collision, and that made it impossible for the police when they arrived to bring a charge in respect of driving with an excessive blood-alcohol concentration. In each case the prosecution had to rely on an allegation that the man was 'in charge'.

To take the Road Safety Act 1967 charge first of all, that Act provides in s 1 (1) for an offence of driving with excess alcohol in the blood, and in sub-s (2) the section goes on:

'Without prejudice to the foregoing subsection, if a person is in charge of a motor vehicle on a road or other public place having consumed alcohol as aforesaid, he shall be liable [and the penalty is prescribed].'

Then s 1 (3) provides:

'A person shall not be convicted under this section of being in charge of a motor vehicle if he proves that at the material time the circumstances were such that there was no likelihood of his driving it so long as there was any probability of his having alcohol in his blood in a proportion exceeding the prescribed limit.'

In other words a man in charge of a motor car if the alcohol content in his blood is excessive may still escape an allegation that he commits an offence under s 1 (2) if he can show there was no likelihood of his driving the car again whilst the alcohol content of his blood remained above the maximum legal limit. Then s 1 (4) contains this somewhat odd provision:

'In determining for the purposes of the last foregoing subsection the likelihood of a person's driving a motor vehicle when he is injured or the vehicle is damaged, the jury, in the case of proceedings on indictment, may be directed to disregard, and the court in any other case may disregard, the fact that he had been injured or that the vehicle had been damaged.'

For myself I find that a difficult subsection to understand in this sense, that its purpose escapes me. One would have thought that the concern of the draftsman was to ensure that a drunken man should not drive again until he ceased to be in that condition, and in deciding whether it was likely that he would drive again within the danger period, if one may so describe it, the condition of the car and the condition of himself in the sense of injury one would have thought at first sight would have been matters of considerable relevance. However, by s 1 (4) the court may direct the jury to disregard the injury to the person or the injury to the car in deciding whether there is or is not a likelihood of the accused driving before he had adequately recovered.

The direction given to the jury in this case, as far as we can see, entirely followed what the statute provides. In the summing-up we find that the learned judge is referring to the condition of the car, whether it could be driven again and the condition of the appellant, that is to say whether he suffered from shock as he alleged, and then he went on:

'You are entitled to disregard the fact altogether that there may have been some mechanical problem about the driving of the vehicle, when you come to consider the question as to [the appellant's] likelihood of driving it.'

That seems to be a perfectly proper interpretation of s 1 (4) which I have read. The judge continued:

'You are entitled, and indeed you should disregard that he himself may have been injured or the vehicle was damaged in some way or another. I mean, accidents happen and the vehicle may be in such a state that it could hardly be driven at all. Well that does not—and should be put on one side.'

a So that is a strong direction to the jury that they should disregard the physical condition of the appellant consequent on the accident and the condition of his car.

Complaint is made by counsel for the appellant that this is too strong a direction, but in our judgment it is entirely within the terms of the section. The section says that the judge may direct the jury to disregard these matters, and that is exactly what he did. He therefore cannot be said to have exceeded his statutory authority.

b Counsel for the appellant also argued, perhaps a little half-heartedly, that the effect of s 1 (4) of the 1967 Act is only to enable the jury to disregard personal injury or damage to the vehicle, and not both, where both occur. But that would be such a perverse result that we are not disposed to construe the section in that way, so that when all is said and done, as far as the offence under the 1967 Act is concerned, no fault is discernible in the summing-up, and there is no reason to suppose that the conviction is other than good.

c We come back to the conviction under the 1960 Act. Section 6 of the 1960 Act contains provisions not unlike those which I have already read from the 1967 Act. Section 6 (2) provides: '. . . a person who, when in charge of a motor vehicle which is on a road or other public place [but not driving the vehicle], is unfit to drive through drink or drugs' commits an offence. But the subsection goes on to say:

d   'A person shall be deemed for the purposes of this subsection not to have been in charge of a motor vehicle if he proves—(i) that at the material time the circumstances were such that there was no likelihood of his driving the vehicle so long as he remained unfit to drive through drink or drugs',

a provision which is on precisely the same lines as s 1 (2) and (3) of the 1967 Act. But, and this is where the difference comes in, there is nothing in the 1960 Act comparable
e to s 1 (4) of the 1967 Act. There is nothing, therefore, to say that the jury may be directed to disregard the condition of the vehicle or the condition of the driver, and in the absence of any such provision one must, in our opinion, come back to first principles, and according to them the condition of the vehicle or the condition of the driver might have some telling effect on the question of whether the vehicle
f was likely to be driven again that night by the particular man.

Accordingly, so far as the offence under the 1960 Act is concerned, there was a misdirection here and a misdirection which we think must result in the conviction being quashed. It is perhaps a matter which Parliament might consider in due course, because it seems wholly illogical that these different consequences flow from the two statutes, and it may be that it is an error, but as the law stands the conviction under the 1960 Act in our judgment is unsatisfactory, it will be quashed, and with it of
g course the attached penalty.

If and insofar as there is an application for leave to appeal against sentence, it has been abandoned.

Appeal allowed in part. Conviction on count (1) quashed.

h Solicitors: *Registrar of Criminal Appeals* (for the appellant); *Solicitor, Metropolitan Police.*

I D Turner Esq Barrister.

Fall (Inspector of Taxes) v Hitchen

CHANCERY DIVISION
PENNYCUICK V-C
29th, 30th NOVEMBER 1972

Income tax – Income – Emoluments from office or employment – Employment – Contract of service – Contract an incident in carrying on of profession – Professional dancer – Dancer entering into engagements in the carrying on of his profession – Engagement with theatrical company under standard form contract – Contract amounting to contract of service – Whether earnings from contract constituting emoluments from 'employment' – Income and Corporation Taxes Act 1970, s 181 (1) (Sch E).

The taxpayer, a professional ballet dancer, was engaged by Sadler's Wells Trust Ltd ('the company') under a standard form of contract for a minimum period of rehearsals plus 22 weeks and thereafter until the contract was determined by a fortnight's notice on either side. He was to work full time during specified hours for a regular salary. The contract provided that he should work exclusively for the company and should not undertake other work without its consent, which was not to be withheld unreasonably. The company provided the taxpayer with costumes for stage use. The taxpayer was assessed to income tax in respect of his earnings from the company for the year 1969-70 under Sch E in s 181^a of the Income and Corporation Taxes Act 1970. The general commissioners discharged the assessment holding, inter alia, that the taxpayer's employment constituted an 'incident' in the carrying on of his profession as a theatrical artiste and the assessment should therefore have been made under Sch D, Case II. The Crown appealed.

Held – The taxpayer, in respect of his engagement with the company, was not a person performing services in business on his own account; all the relevant factors pointed to the relation between the taxpayer and the company as being one of a contract of service. Once it had been established that the emoluments in question arose from a contract of service, it followed that they arose from an 'employment' within Sch E and it was immaterial that the taxpayer was at the same time carrying on his profession. Accordingly in respect of the income derived from his contract with the company, the taxpayer was assessable under Sch E and the appeal would be allowed (see p 373 h and j, p 374 b and c, p 376 g and p 378 g and h, post).

Davies v Braithwaite [1931] All ER Rep 792 distinguished.

Notes

For the charge to tax in respect of employments, see 20 Halsbury's Laws (3rd Edn) 307, 308, para 564, and for cases on emoluments from employment, see 28 (1) Digest (Reissue) 323-332, 1148-1195.

For the Income and Corporation Taxes Act 1970, s 181, see 33 Halsbury's Statutes (3rd Edn) 255.

Cases referred to in judgment

Davies v Braithwaite [1931] 2 KB 628, 18 Tax Cas 198, [1931] All ER Rep 792, 100 LJKB 619, 145 LT 693, 28 (1) Digest (Reissue) 241, 746.

Global Plant Ltd v Secretary of State for Social Services [1971] 3 All ER 385, [1972] 1 QB 139, [1971] 3 WLR 269.

Great Western Railway Co v Bater [1922] 2 AC 1, 8 Tax Cas 231, 1 ATC 104, 91 LJKB 472, 127 LT 170, HL; *rvsg* CA [1921] 2 KB 128, 90 LJKB 550, 125 LT 321; *affg* [1920] 3 KB 266, 90 LJKB 41, 124 LT 92, 28 (1) Digest (Reissue) 320, 1132.

Household v Grimshaw (Inspector of Taxes) [1953] 2 All ER 12, 34 Tax Cas 366, [1953]

---

a   Section 181, so far as material, is set out at p 369 h, post

1 WLR 710, 32 ATC 133, [1953] TR 147, 46 R & IT 347, 28 (1) Digest (Reissue) 338, 1227.

Inland Revenue Comrs v Brander & Cruickshank [1971] 1 All ER 36, 46 Tax Cas 574, [1971] 1 WLR 212, [1970] TR 353, HL, 28 (1) Digest (Reissue) 46, *193.*

Market Investigations Ltd v Minister of Social Security [1968] 3 All ER 732, [1969] 2 QB 173, [1969] 2 WLR 1, Digest (Cont Vol C) 701, *2636b.*

Mitchell and another (Inspectors of Taxes) v Ross [1961] 3 All ER 49, [1962] AC 813, 40 Tax Cas 11, [1961] 3 WLR 411, 40 ATC 199, [1961] TR 191, HL; *rvsg* CA [1960] 2 All ER 218, [1960] Ch 498, [1960] 2 WLR 766, 39 ATC 52, [1960] TR 79, 53 R & IT 347; *affg* [1959] 3 All ER 341, [1960] Ch 145, [1959] 3 WLR 550, 38 ATC 422, [1959] TR 225, 53 R & IT 75, 28 (1) Digest (Reissue) 321, *1138.*

Case stated

At a meeting of the Commissioners for the General Purposes of the Income Tax Acts for the division of St Martin's-in-the-Fields in the city of Westminster held on 7th January 1971, David Hitchen ('the taxpayer') appealed against an assessment to income tax made on him under Sch E in respect of his employment as a dancer by Sadler's Wells Trust Ltd. The commissioners allowed the appeal and discharged the assessment. The Crown immediately after the determination of the appeal declared its dissatisfaction therewith as being erroneous in point of law and in due course required the commissioners to state a case for the opinion of the High Court pursuant to the Taxes Management Act 1970, s 56. The case stated, so far as material, is set out in the judgment.

Leonard Bromley QC and *Patrick Medd* for the Crown.
Barry Pinson for the taxpayer.

PENNYCUICK V-C. I have before me an appeal by the Crown from a decision of the General Commissioners of Income Tax whereby they allowed an appeal by the taxpayer. The appeal relates to an assessment under Sch E for the year 1969-70 on the taxpayer in respect of his earnings as a dancer. The assessment was made under Sch E on the footing that the income in question was derived from an employment, that employment consisting of a service agreement between himself and Sadler's Wells Trust Ltd ('the company'). The taxpayer's contention, which prevailed before the commissioners, was that the income in question was derived not from that employment but from his profession as a dancer, and should accordingly have been assessed under Case II of Sch D. For the present purposes, nothing turns on the reasons why it was advantageous to him to be assessed under Sch D rather than Sch E.

The relevant head of charge is contained in s 181 of the Income and Corporation Taxes Act 1970 in these words:

> 'The Schedule referred to as Schedule E is as follows:—. . . 1. Tax under this Schedule shall be charged in respect of any office or employment on emoluments therefrom which fall under one, or more than one, of the following Cases . . .'

That head of charge reproduces a head of charge under the previously existing Act[1].

The taxpayer was employed by the company under a written agreement known as the Esher Standard Contract for Ballet. That is a standard form of contract which was no doubt adapted, with appropriate modifications, to suit particular cases. I think I should refer at once to the terms of the contract. It is made between the company of the one part, and the taxpayer of the other part. Clause 1: '[The company] engages the [taxpayer] . . . to rehearse, understudy, play and dance as and where required by the [company]'.

---

1 Ie the Income Tax Act 1952, s 156

Clause 2:

> 'The engagement shall be ... For a period of rehearsal and thereafter for a period of 22 weeks ... terminable at the end of such period or on any Saturday thereafter by either party giving to the other two weeks' prior notice in writing.'

Clause 3 provides for such period of rehearsal to commence on 7th July 1969. Clause 4:

> 'The [company] shall pay to the [taxpayer]:—(a) During the period of rehearsal such sums as the [taxpayer] shall be entitled to receive in accordance with the regulations set out in Schedule 1 hereto. (b) From the commencement of the tour or season the sum of £18.0.0 for every week as defined in the said regulations.'

Clause 5:

> 'In accordance with paragraph B (2) of Schedule 1 hereto the [taxpayer] agrees to give performances weekly for the salary stated in Clause 4 (b) hereof, such salary being more than £12 10s per week';

and then there is an arbitration clause.

Annexed to the agreement are three schedules, the first of which contains the detailed provisions regulating the taxpayer's engagement (to use a neutral term) with the company. Paragraph A: 'The following regulations shall apply to the period of rehearsal prior to the first performance of the [taxpayer].' Then there follow a number of details concerning pay and hours. Paragraph B: 'The following regulations shall govern payments, working time, etc., during production'. Again there follow a number of provisions relating to salary and hours. Paragraph C is concerned with dress fittings. Paragraph D: 'The salary provided in clause 4 (b) shall not be less than £12.' Paragraph E deals with closing of the theatre and suspension of engagement; para F with cancellation of bookings and force majeure; and para G with failure to produce. Paragraph H deals with the provision by the company of transport from place to place, and regulates the taxpayer's right to travel by any other means. Paragraph J:

> 'The [taxpayer] is engaged exclusively by the [company] and (save in the case where the [taxpayer] may be performing another engagement at a theatre in the same town during the first period of rehearsal) the [taxpayer] shall not during the engagement perform or otherwise exercise the [taxpayer's] talent for the benefit of any other company, institution or person without the written consent of the [company] first had and obtained which consent shall not be unreasonably withheld.'

Paragraph K is concerned with the illness of the taxpayer; para L with absence without cause; and para M provides that with one exception the company shall provide all the costumes and the like for stage use, and that the costumes and the like shall remain the property of the company. Then, under the head 'General provisions', para N contains certain requirements as to attendance at the theatre. Sub-paragraph (4) reads: 'The [taxpayer] shall comply with and conform to the rules of any theatre at which the Company may be rehearsing or performing and all rules made by [the company]'. Sub-paragraph (5):

> 'The [taxpayer] shall appear at all performances and perform the services required of [him] under this Agreement in a diligent and painstaking manner and shall not insert or omit any choreography except as may be approved by the [company] or [their] representative.'

I need not refer to Sch 2 or Sch 3.

I should mention that annexed to that agreement is a document in these terms:

'For the 1969/70 Season the following modifications of the Esher Standard Contract for Ballet have been agreed with British Actors' Equity Association: 1. Members of the group shall be required not only to dance but to act and mime as required. 2. Compulsory classes shall include two ballet classes, one character class, one modern class, one fencing class, and one combat class.'

I will next read the case stated, which is quite short. Paragraph 1 sets out the meeting at which the taxpayer appealed against an assessment made on him under Sch E of the 1970 Act for the year 1969-70 in the sum of £712 in respect of his earnings as a dancer. Paragraph 2:

'The question for our determination was whether the assessment was correctly made under Schedule "E", or whether, as the [taxpayer] contended, he should have been assessed under Schedule "D" Case II of the Income and Corporation Taxes Act, 1970.'

Paragraph 3:

'The [taxpayer] was represented by his accountant ... Oral evidence was given by the [taxpayer], Mr John William George Snape, Finance Director of [the company], and Miss Pauline Grant, Director of Sadler's Wells Opera Movement Group.'

Paragraph 4:

'The following facts were proved or admitted: (a) the [taxpayer] who is a professional dancer was at all material times employed by [the company], under a written Agreement known in the profession as the "Esher Standard Contract for Ballet" (hereinafter called "the Esher Contract"). It was accepted that the document produced to us dated the 14th June, 1969, contained the terms under which the [taxpayer] carried out his obligations as a dancer for [the company].'

In fact, his employment commenced, as appears from that paragraph, two months after the beginning of the fiscal year 1969-70, but nothing turns on that. The case continues:

'(b) the [taxpayer] regarded the sum of £18.0.0 per week paid to him under the Esher Contract as a fee and not as a salary. Throughout the period of the Esher Contract he communicated with agents and others with a view to obtaining film, television or theatre work as a dancer, singer or actor in which he had been trained, but by the date of the hearing had not succeeded in obtaining any such work. He had not registered with a Theatrical Agency until June, 1970. (c) the [taxpayer] did not intend to remain with [the company], as he could earn more money and further his artistic career in other spheres, for example participating in musical plays, and regarded his contract with [the company] as an interim measure to support himself while looking for more remunerative work. (d) during his first year with [the company], the [taxpayer] had one or two unsuccessful auditions with agents and others. He regarded the weekly payment by [the company] as steady income receivable whether or not he was called upon to perform or rehearse. (e) during the three-year period preceding his coming to London the [taxpayer] had about seventeen television engagements. At that time he was a student at the Manchester College of Music. (f) [the company] would not only allow but encouraged the [taxpayer] to carry on outside work provided he was not required by them on the relevant day or days. (g) the [taxpayer] was a member of the Sadler's Wells Movement Group which provided dancing and other activities, except singing, for particular productions. The scope of members of the group to act as individual creative artists was limited by the detailed requirements of the producer who had overall control of the production. (h) [The company] pay full National Health Insurance contributions for all artists under the Esher Contract as if they were employees and not self-employed. That has been theatrical practice for many years and is peculiar to the theatrical profession, possibly because actors are frequently off work and on the dole.'

Paragraphs 5-9:

   '5. It was contended on behalf of the [taxpayer] that: (i) the Esher Contract had been recognised by the Inland Revenue as a contract for services for upwards of 30 years. (ii) the [taxpayer] was carrying on the profession of a dancer and was not an employee or a consultant and should be assessed for tax under Schedule "D" and not under Schedule "E".
   '6. It was contended by the [Crown] that: (i) under the terms of his contract with [the company] the [taxpayer] held an office or employment within the meaning of Schedule "E" in Section 181 of the Income and Corporation Taxes Act, 1970. (ii) the emoluments from such office or employment were chargeable to tax under Schedule "E". (iii) the assessment should be confirmed.
   '7.   Reference was made to the cases of: *Davies v Braithwaite*[1], *Mitchell (Inspector of Taxes) v Ross*[2], *Inland Revenue Comrs v Brander & Cruickshank*[3].
   '8. We the Commissioners found that: (i) the [taxpayer's] employment by [the company] constituted an incident in the carrying on of his profession as a theatrical artiste. (ii) the Esher Contract was a contract for services, particularly as clause J thereof clearly envisaged the possibility of outside employment. (iii) the [company] not only permits outside employment but encourages its young artistes to further their career even if that meant their leaving Sadler's Wells. (iv) the fact that the National Health Stamp was paid on an employee basis was an anomaly which existed throughout the theatrical profession.
   '9.   We accordingly allowed the [taxpayer's] appeal and discharged the assessment.'

In para 10 the Crown expressed dissatisfaction. Paragraph 11: 'The question of law for the opinion of the Court is whether our determination was erroneous in point of law.'
   It is implicit in the findings of the commissioners that during the year of assessment the taxpayer was carrying on the profession of a theatrical artiste although so far he had been unsuccessful in finding any engagements in that profession. It is expressly held by the commissioners that the document dated 14th June 1969 (i e the contract to which I have referred) contained the terms under which the taxpayer carried out his obligations as a dancer for the company. The commissioners further found, so far as that is material, that the taxpayer did not intend to remain with the company as he could earn more money and further his career in other spheres, and that he regarded the contract as an interim measure. The fact that he regarded the sum of £18 a week paid under the contract as a fee and not as a salary is, I think, quite irrelevant.
   The first matter which falls to be considered is whether the relation created by the contract was that of a contract of service or a contract for services. I was taken by counsel for the Crown through a number of authorities dealing with this point. I do not propose to go into those at any length because, in the end, that was not the ground on which counsel for the taxpayer based his case. It will be sufficient for the present purpose to quote one paragraph from a very illuminating judgment of

1   [1931] 2 KB 628, [1931] All ER Rep 792, 18 Tax Cas 198
2   [1961] 3 All ER 49, [1962] AC 813, 40 Tax Cas 11
3   [1971] 1 All ER 36, [1971] 1 WLR 212, 46 Tax Cas 574

Cooke J in *Market Investigations Ltd v Minister of Social Security*[1]. As appears from that case, the National Insurance Act 1965, s 1 (2), provides:

'For the purposes of this Act, insured persons shall be divided into the following three classes, namely—(a) employed persons, that is to say, persons gainfully occupied in employment in Great Britain, being employment under a contract of service; (b) self-employed persons, that is to say, persons gainfully occupied in employment in Great Britain who are not employed persons; (c) non-employed persons . . .'

The question was whether a given individual was or was not engaged under a contract of service. Cooke J analysed some of the earlier law, and said this[2]:

'The observations of LORD WRIGHT, of DENNING, L.J., and of the judges of the Supreme Court in the U.S.A. suggest that the fundamental test to be applied is this: "Is the person who has engaged himself to perform these services performing them as a person in business on his own account?". If the answer to that question is "yes", then the contract is a contract for services. If the answer is "no" then the contract is a contract of service. No exhaustive list has been compiled and perhaps no exhaustive list can be compiled of considerations which are relevant in determining that question, nor can strict rules be laid down as to the relative weight which the various considerations should carry in particular cases. The most that can be said is that control will no doubt always have to be considered, although it can no longer be regarded as the sole determining factor; and that factors, which may be of importance, are such matters as whether the man performing the services provides his own equipment, whether he hires his own helpers, what degree of financial risk he takes, what degree of responsibility for investment and management he has, and whether and how far he has an opportunity of profiting from sound management in the performance of his task.'

That judgment was quoted with approval by Lord Widgery CJ in the recent case of *Global Plant Ltd v Secretary of State for Social Services*[3].

In the present case, it seems to me that virtually all the relevant factors point to this being a contract of service. The taxpayer is engaged to work for a minimum period of rehearsals plus 22 weeks, and thereafter until the contract is determined by a fortnight's notice on either side; he is engaged to work full-time during specified hours for a regular salary; the company has the first call on his services, and indeed the exclusive call subject only to this, that their consent to the taxpayer performing elsewhere shall not be unreasonably withheld; and then, again, the company provides and owns the gear used by the taxpayer, with one exception. All these indicia point to the conclusion that he is not a person who is performing those services in business on his own account; and there are really no indicia to the contrary.

I do not enlarge further on this point because at the outset of his argument counsel for the taxpayer very candidly accepted that if this were a case under the National Insurance Act 1965 he would have found it difficult to maintain a different contention. However, I would observe at this point that the expressions 'contract of service' and 'contract for services' are of general application, and, unless one finds in the context some limitation on the meaning of the words, those words must bear the same meaning in any other context as they do under the National Insurance Act 1965. I conclude, therefore, that this agreement is a contract of service within the ordinary meaning of those words.

---

1   [1968] 3 All ER 732, [1969] 2 QB 173
2   [1968] 3 All ER at 737, 738, [1969] 2 QB at 184, 185
3   [1971] 3 All ER 385 at 389, 390, [1972] 1 QB 139 at 150, 151

Once it is accepted that this is a contract of service, it seems to me to follow that it must equally represent an employment within the terms of Sch E. Indeed, unless some special limitation is to be put on the word 'employment' in any given context, the expression 'contract of service' appears to be coterminous with the expression 'employment'. I can find no such context in relation to Sch E. I do not see how it could be said that emoluments arising from a contract of service are not emoluments arising from an employment within the meaning of the charging words in Sch E.

The authorities in this connection are concerned with the particular facts of the cases before the court. I have not been referred to any general statement equating a contract of service with employment. It may be that this is too obvious to state; but there is certainly no authority to the contrary. I shall refer in a moment to the case on which counsel for the taxpayer primarily relied. And once it is accepted that the taxpayer's employment, being under a contract of service, represents an employment within the meaning of Sch E, then it follows conclusively on authority that the emoluments arising under that contract are chargeable under Sch E and not under Sch D.

Counsel relied on *Davies v Braithwaite*[1]. Indeed, he based his argument almost entirely on it. Broadly, his contention was that the word 'employment' in Sch E does not include engagements entered into by an actor as 'incident' to the carrying on of his profession, and he explained that by 'incident' he meant that which formed part of the fabric of the profession. That observation is derived from *Davies v Braithwaite*[1], the headnote in which is as follows[2]:

'The expression "employment" in Sch. E of the Income Tax Act, 1918, means something analogous to an office or a post. An actress earned her living by accepting and fulfilling engagements for which her professional qualifications fitted her. During the periods of assessment in question, she exercised her activities by (*a*) acting in various stage plays in England and one in the United States of America, under various contracts with theatrical producers; (*b*) performing for the films; (*c*) performing on the wireless for the British Broadcasting Corporation, and (*d*) performing for gramophone companies for reproduction on their records:—*Held*, that the actress was assessable under Sch. D of the Income Tax Act, 1918, in respect of the profits which she derived from her profession or vocation as an actress and not under Sch. E in respect of the profits of her employment.'

It should be observed that in that case the Crown was successfully contending that the assessment should be under Sch D.

Rowlatt J, in a characteristically short and lucid judgment, explained how employments other than public employment had come to be transferred from Sch D to Sch E, and analysed the meaning of the word 'employment' as it now stands in Sch E. I think I should read a considerable part of that judgment. He said[3]:

'The question of principle in this case is whether the respondent ought to be assessed under Sch. D of the Income Tax Act, 1918, as following her profession of an actress, or whether she ought to be assessed under Sch. E as exercising certain employments under the particular engagements which she makes. The question is a difficult one, mainly because of the want of precision in the meaning of the term "employment" as it comes into this controversy. The scheme of the Income Tax Acts used to be to include under Sch. D "profession, employment, or vocation." That was held to be a fairly comprehensive definition of the persons who carried on business on their own account. Under Sch. E

---

1 [1931] 2 KB 628, [1931] All ER Rep 792, 18 Tax Cas 198
2 [1931] 2 KB at 628
3 [1931] 2 KB at 633, [1931] All ER Rep at 794, 18 Tax Cas at 202, 203

were public offices. It was recognized that where a person was in a permanent situation it was much better to assess his salary as the salary of the situation than to go to him personally, and assess him in respect of his earnings. There were persons, like railway clerks, who were hired for an indefinite period. For the purposes of assessment to income tax they were treated as holders of offices. That was a very convenient method of assessment to income tax. Then a case arose (*Great Western Ry. Co.* v. *Bater*[1]), in which I pointed out that these railway clerks were not holders of offices at all. I said that my own view was that Parliament in using this language in 1842 meant by an office a substantive thing that existed apart from its holder. It was something which had an existence independent of the person who filled it. It was something which was held by tenure and title rather than by contract and which continued to exist, though the holders of it might change and it was filled in succession by successive holders. The House of Lords[2] decided that my view was right. It was therefore found convenient to put "employment" expressly in Sch. E. When the word "employment" is used in connection with a profession or vocation in Sch. D it means the way in which a man employs himself. But "employment" in Sch. E means something different. In that Schedule it means something analogous to an office and which is conveniently amenable to the scheme of taxation which is applied to offices as opposed to the earnings of a man who follows a profession or vocation. That unhappy word "employment" has now to be construed with reference to this case. The respondent is an actress, and, of course, the contract which an actor or actress, or any person whose livelihood is earned in that sort of way, has, is rather different from other contracts, as has been pointed out, because it involves that the employer under the contract is bound to let the actor or actress appear. But what is the criterion?'

He then dealt with and dismissed a contention advanced by the Solicitor-General. The learned judge proceeded[3]:

'It seems to me quite clear that a man can have both an employment and a profession at the same time, in different categories. A man may have the steadiest employment in the world by day and he may do something quite different in the evening and make some more money by the exercise of a profession or vocation. I cannot doubt that that would be so, and even if it were in the same sphere, I do not see why he should not have both an employment as well as a profession. For instance, a musician who holds an office or employment under a permanent engagement can at the same time follow his profession privately. I have to formulate some line of cleavage and it seems to me that what I must glean my inspiration from is the purpose of the change from Sch. D to Sch. E in the Finance Act, 1922, s. 18. I have to consider the effect of the change which was made in the different methods of raising income tax. It seems to me that when the Legislature took "employment" out of Sch. D, and put it into Sch. E, alongside "Offices," the Legislature had in mind employments which were something like offices, and I thought of the expression "posts" as conveying the idea required. When a person occupies a post resting on a contract, and if then that is employment as opposed to a mere engagement in the course of carrying on a profession, I do not think that is a very difficult term of distinction, though perhaps a little difficult to apply to all cases. But I would go further than that and say that it seems to me that where one finds a method of earning a livelihood which does not consist of the obtaining of a post and staying in it, but consists of a series of engagements and moving from one to the other—and in the case of an

---

1   [1920] 3 KB 266, 8 Tax Cas 231
2   [1922] 2 AC 1, 8 Tax Cas 231
3   [1931] 2 KB at 635, 636, [1931] All ER Rep at 794, 795, 18 Tax Cas at 203, 204

actor's or actress's life it certainly involves going from one to the other and not going on playing one part for the rest of his or her life, but in obtaining first one engagement, then another, and a whole series of them—then each of those engagements cannot be considered an employment, but is a mere engagement in the course of exercising a profession, and every profession and every trade does involve the making of successive engagements and successive contracts and, in one sense of the word, employments. In this case I think it is quite clear that the respondent must be assessed to income tax under Sch. D, because here she does not make a contract with a producer for a post. She makes a contract with a producer for the next thing that she is going to do, and then with another producer, and then a third producer, and at any time she may make a record for a gramophone company or act for a film. I think that whatever she does and whatever contracts she makes are nothing but incidents in the conduct of her professional career.'

In that judgment, Rowlatt J holds that the word 'employment' means a post, and distinguishes it from a succession of engagements made in the course of carrying on a profession. He then goes on to hold that, on the particular facts of that case, Miss Braithwaite did not hold any post and that none of her particular engagements could be treated as a post, but that on the contrary all her successive engagements must be treated as incidents in the conduct of her profession. The learned judge nowhere says that if an actor enters into a contract in such terms as to amount to what he calls a post, then that actor is not chargeable under Sch E but under Sch D. On the contrary, it is implicit in the whole of his judgment, it seems to me, that if a professional person, whether an actor or anybody else, enters into a contract involving what the learned judge calls a post, then that person will be chargeable in respect of the income arising from the post under Sch E notwithstanding that he is at the same time carrying on his profession, the income of which will be chargeable under Sch D. The instance of a musician puts that point very neatly.

I do not think most people today would use the word 'post', which does not seem very apt to cover the countless instances of employment in the sense of a contract of service; but every word of that judgment is applicable as between the carrying on of a profession and an engagement in the course of carrying on that profession, on the one hand, and a contract of employment, on the other hand. The fact that an actor normally undertakes a succession of engagements in the course of carrying on that profession in no way involves the result that if an actor enters an acting employment in the nature of a post, then he is not assessable under Sch E in respect of the income arising from that employment.

I think I need refer at any length to only one other decision, and that is *Mitchell (Inspector of Taxes) v Ross*[1]. The headnote reads[2]:

'Under the National Health Service Act, 1946, which, *inter alia*, required the Minister of Health to provide the services of specialists, the Respondents held part-time appointments as consultants with regional hospital boards. In addition to their hospital work, the Respondents under their terms of service paid visits to patients in their homes at the request of general practitioners; separate remuneration was paid for these "domiciliary visits". Certain of the Respondents also received payments for locum tenens work under the National Health Service. All the Respondents also had private practices. Assessments to Income Tax were made upon the Respondents under Schedules D and E on the footing that all payments received from regional hospital boards, including fees for domiciliary visits and locum tenens work, should be assessed under Schedule E; that income from private practice should be assessed under Schedule D; and that deductions *a* for expenses should be given in each assessment only so far as the expenses had been incurred in connection with the income assessed under the respective Schedule and were properly allowable under the Rules applicable thereto. On appeal to the Special Commissioners the Respondents contended that their activities as consultants constituted as a whole the carrying on of professions; that the holding of their part-time appointments was an incident of these profes-

b sions and the appointments were not offices or employments within the meaning of Schedule E; that if they were such offices or employments, any expenses in respect of them not allowable under the Rules applicable to Schedule E should be allowed in their Schedule D assessments; and that in any case the receipts attributable to domiciliary visits and locum tenens work should be assessed under Schedule D. The Special Commissioners found that the part-time appoint-

c ments were offices or "posts" and that the remuneration derived therefrom, together with the fees received in respect of domiciliary visits and locum tenens work, were profits of offices within the meaning of Schedule E. They also found, however, that at all material times the Respondents exercised the profession of consultant and that their part-time hospital appointments were necessary parts of the exercise of their profession. In these circumstances, the Commis-

d sioners considered that they were bound by the decisions in *Davies* v. *Braithwaite*[1] and *Household* v. *Grimshaw*[2] [that was an earlier decision by Upjohn J which was also relied on in that case], and held that the remuneration from the appointments fell to be assessed under Case II of Schedule D, as also did the fees for the domiciliary visits and the locum tenens work. *Held*, (1) in the Court of Appeal, that the part-time appointments were offices and that the remuneration from

e them, including payments in respect of the domiciliary visits and the locum tenens work, was assessable under Schedule E; and (2) in the House of Lords, that expenses attributable thereto could only be allowed so far as they satisfied the Rules applicable to Schedule E.'

That headnote is defective in that it does not mention that Upjohn J held that the part-time appointments were offices and reversed the decision of the commissioners.

f I think I should read a short passage from the judgment of Upjohn J. He referred to the history of the matter, which is the same, really, as was recited by Rowlatt J in *Davies v Braithwaite*[1]. He then cited authorities on the meaning of the word 'office', and went on[3]:

'On the question of employment a large number of authorities were cited to

g me. Many tests have been laid down to determine whether the relation of master and servant exists such as the degree of control exercised by the master, and so on. The relationship between a specialist and a board is so very special, however, that many of these cases, dealing either with entirely different types of engagements (to use a neutral word) or with the pre-Act relationship between hospitals and specialists, form no safe guide. The real question to be answered is this. Does a specialist who holds a part-time national health appointment

h (a) occupy an office, or (b) undertake an employment, or (c) does he merely render services in the course of the exercise or practice of his profession?'

He then went on to hold that alternative (a) was correct; i e that the specialist occupied an office. Having so held, obviously it was not necessary for him to decide whether he undertook an employment.

j In the House of Lords, it was not in dispute that the specialists in question were assessable under Sch E in respect of fees derived from that office, the question being

---

1 [1931] 2 KB 628, [1931] All ER Rep 792, 18 Tax Cas 198
2 [1953] 2 All ER 12, [1953] 1 WLR 710, 34 Tax Cas 366
3 [1959] 3 All ER 341 at 347, [1960] Ch 145 at 164, 165, 40 Tax Cas at 35

the allowance of the expenses. I think I should read one paragraph from the judgment of Lord Evershed MR in the Court of Appeal[1]:

'But it was the submission of counsel for the taxpayer that, because the taxpayer's engagement by the hospital board was a mere incident of his professional activity, therefore he should not be regarded as holding an office or employment at all; and counsel cited *Davies* v. *Braithwaite*[2] to support that argument. The cited case related to the professional activities as an actress of Miss Lilian Braithwaite, and it was proved that, in the ordinary course of those activities, Miss Braithwaite entered into contracts of "employment" with theatre managers and other persons. In that case the Crown (be it observed) was contending for the applicability not of Sch. E but of Sch. D; and the Crown's contention succeeded on the ground, putting it briefly but sufficiently, that such contracts which did not involve in any true sense the relation of master and servant were not in truth contracts of employment at all, or at least not "employments" within the purview of Sch. E. In my judgment, the case of *Davies* v. *Braithwaite*[2] is on its facts far removed from the present case. I agree, as I have already indicated, with UPJOHN, J., that the conclusion that the taxpayer's engagement with the Birmingham Regional Hospital Board constituted an "office" within the section is inescapable . . .'

I have read those passages partly because they contain an accurate exposition of what Rowlatt J really did decide in *Davies v Braithwaite*[2] and partly because they show that a person carrying on a profession may perfectly well hold an office and also, plainly, an employment in the same sphere as that in which he carries on his profession.

The only other cases to which I think I can usefully refer are, first, that of *Household v Grimshaw (Inspector of Taxes)*[3], in which Upjohn J upheld on the particular facts of that case a conclusion by the Special Commissioners that an author who bound himself to a film company for a minimum period of 12 weeks in each year was assessable in respect of the profits from that engagement under Sch D, and not as the holder of an office or employment under Sch E; and second that of *Inland Revenue Comrs v Brander & Cruickshank*[4], in which the House of Lords held, in one case with manifest reluctance, that a firm of lawyers who had entered into an engagement as professional registrars and had derived profits therefrom were assessable in respect of those profits under Sch E by reason of the fact that each of those engagements represented an office or employment within the meaning of Sch E. I say 'with manifest reluctance' because Lord Donovan considered that the distinction between Sch E and Sch D in this respect was an artificial one.

To return to the present case, it seems to me, as I have said, that the relation between the company and the taxpayer under their contract was that of a contract of service; that that contract of service represented an employment for the purpose of Sch E; and that the taxpayer is assessable under Sch E in respect of the income derived from that contract—and that nonetheless so by reason that at the same time he was carrying on, as found by the commissioners, the profession of an actor and would have been assessable under Sch D in respect of the profit of that profession if there had been any. I cannot see any reason why an actor should be in a different position in principle in this respect from that of any other professional man. It must depend on the particular facts whether or not he holds an employment within the meaning of Sch E.

Having reached that conclusion I turn back to the findings of the General Commissioners. It will be remembered that they found that—

1   [1960] 2 All ER 218 at 224, 225, [1960] Ch 498 at 520, 521, 40 Tax Cas at 43
2   [1931] 2 KB 628, [1931] All ER Rep 792, 18 Tax Cas 198
3   [1953] 2 All ER 12, [1953] 1 WLR 710, 34 Tax Cas 366
4   [1971] 1 All ER 36, [1971] 1 WLR 212, 46 Tax Cas 574

a   '(i) the [taxpayer's] employment ... constituted an incident in the carrying on of his profession as a theatrical artiste; (ii) the Esher Contract was a contract for services ... (iii) the [company] not only permits outside employment but encourages [it]'.

I think (iii) is merely one factor in deciding whether or not the contract is a contract for services or not. The question whether the contract is a contract for services or a
b   contract of service is for all practical purposes purely one of law. As the commissioners themselves said, 'the document ... contained the terms under which the [taxpayer] carried out his obligations as a dancer for [the company]'. Any other factors must be of trivial importance compared with that.

For the reasons I have given, I think the commissioners were wrong in holding that it was a contract for services. I think it was a contract of service. Once that con-
c   clusion has been reached, it seems to me that the first finding of the commissioners must equally be wrong in law; namely, that his employment constituted an incident in the carrying on of his profession. If their second finding had been right, that first finding would, I think, also be right. For the reasons which I have given, I propose to allow this appeal.

d   *Appeal allowed.*

Solicitors: *Solicitor of Inland Revenue; G B Croasdell* (for the taxpayer).

Rengan Krishnan Esq Barrister.

e
Hillman and others v Crystal Bowl Amusements Ltd and others

COURT OF APPEAL, CIVIL DIVISION
RUSSELL, CAIRNS AND STAMP LJJ
f   21st NOVEMBER 1972

Company – Meeting – Representation – Corporation – Representation of corporation at meeting of another company – Representative – Authority – Resolution of directors or other governing body – Other governing body – Liquidator – Parent company in course of creditor's voluntary winding-up – Meetings of subsidiary companies – Liquidator authorised to attend
g   *meetings as representative of parent company – Document authorising liquidator to attend as representative signed by liquidator he having caused parent company's seal to be affixed to it – No committee of inspection appointed – Liquidator having received no directions from creditors – Whether liquidator 'governing body' of parent company – Companies Act 1948, s 139 (1) (a).*

h   A parent company went into creditors' voluntary winding-up and C was appointed liquidator by the court. The company held the majority of shares in three subsidiary companies of which the plaintiffs, Mr and Mrs H and two others, were directors. C wished to call an extraordinary general meeting of each of the three subsidiary companies with a view to removing the plaintiffs as directors of those companies and substituting himself and his solicitor, X, with a view ultimately to winding up the whole group. Mr and Mrs H held 65 per cent of the capital in the holding
j   company as well as some shares in each of the subsidiary companies and against their opposition it was impracticable to call an extraordinary general meeting of any of those companies. Accordingly C obtained an order from the registrar directing that there should be an extraordinary general meeting of the three subsidiary companies to be convened by the liquidator. The order provided that X, who was not a share-holder, should take the chair at each of the meetings and that one member present

should constitute a quorum. No committee of inspection had been appointed in the winding-up of the parent company and, apart from the directions as to summoning the meetings, C had received no directions from the court and no directions from the body of creditors as to how he should conduct the affairs of the company. The meetings were attended by the chairman and C, a proxy appointed by Mr and Mrs H also being present at the first meeting. Resolutions removing the plaintiffs and the other directors and appointing C and X as directors were duly passed at each meeting. C was present at the meetings purportedly pursuant to a document bearing the seal of the parent company, signed by C as liquidator, he having caused the parent company's seal to be affixed to it. The document appointed C 'as our representative at the respective general meetings' of the three subsidiaries. Mr and Mrs H thereupon brought proceedings seeking, inter alia, a declaration that C and X had not been validly appointed directors and that the other directors had not been validly removed on the ground that there was no resolution of the parent company's 'directors or other governing body', within s 139 (1) (a)*a* of the Companies Act 1948, authorising C to act as the parent company's representative at the meetings of the subsidiaries.

Held – C as liquidator was the 'governing body' of the parent company, within s 139 (1) (a) of the 1948 Act, at the time when he executed the representational authority since he then had the effective management of the company and its affairs and was in no sense a servant of the company. Accordingly the resolutions dismissing the existing directors and appointing C and X in their place had been validly passed (see p 383 a to c and e and p 384 a b e and f, post).

Per Russell LJ. It may be that a case might arise when the situation of the liquidator was such that, having regard to the interferences by creditors or by court order, it would not be reasonable to describe him as the governing body of the company (see p 383 f, post).

Notes
For corporation representatives, see 6 Halsbury's Laws (3rd Edn) 344, para 672, and for a case on the subject, see 9 Digest (Repl) 609, 4044.

For the Companies Act 1948, s 139, see 5 Halsbury's Statutes (3rd Edn) 221.

Interlocutory appeals
These were three appeals by the plaintiffs, Raynor Hillman, Angel Greenberg, Hyman Alexander Hillman and Sol Gold in the first action, Isaac David Hillman, Raynor Hillman, Hyman Alexander Hillman and Sol Gold in the second and third actions, against a decision of Phillips J given on 13th September 1972 dismissing the plaintiffs' motions dated 7th September 1972 for an order that the second and third defendants in all three actions, Douglas Archibald Clarke and Derek Arthur Warren Hewson and each of them, be restrained pending the trial of the actions from acting on or giving effect directly or indirectly to the special resolutions purporting to have been passed at extraordinary general meetings of the defendant company in each of the actions on 5th September 1972. The defendant company in the first action was Crystal Bowl Amusements Ltd, in the second action, Ireton Properties Ltd, and in the third action, Calgary Development Co Ltd. The plaintiffs in each action by their writ sought a declaration that each of them was a director of the defendant company and an injunction restraining the second and third defendants and each of them from acting as or holding themselves out as being directors of the defendant company The facts are set out in the judgment of Russell LJ.

Dennis G Rice for the plaintiffs.
Richard Sykes for the second and third defendants.
The defendant companies were not represented.

---

a Section 139 (1), so far as material, is set out at p 382 b, post

RUSSELL LJ. This appeal from the decision of Phillips J on a motion in the vacation court raises a short point of construction of s 139 of the Companies Act 1948. The factual situation was this. There is a company called Calgary and Edmonton Land Co Ltd which has been in creditors' voluntary winding-up since some date before July 1970, which was the date when a Mr Clarke was appointed by the court the liquidator. That company is the parent company holding the majority of shares in three other companies, Crystal Bowl Amusements Ltd, Calgary Development Co Ltd and Ireton Properties Ltd. A Mr and Mrs Hillman and two others were, I think, directors of all three of those subsidiary companies. Mr and Mrs Hillman, who hold 65 per cent of the capital in the parent company, Calgary and Edmonton Land Co Ltd, also hold a few shares in each of the subsidiaries.

The liquidator of the parent company wished to call an extraordinary general meeting of the three subsidiary companies with a view to removing the existing directors of the subsidiary companies and substituting himself and a partner of his, a Mr Hewson (Mr Clarke and Mr Hewson being second and third defendants in each of these actions), as directors of those companies, I think with the view ultimately to the winding-up of the whole group. But of course it was impracticable against the opposition of the Hillmans to call an extraordinary general meeting of any of those three companies. Accordingly the liquidator of the parent company obtained an order on those grounds on 18th July 1972 from the registrar directing that there should be an extraordinary general meeting of those three companies to be convened by the liquidator, the order providing that a gentleman who in fact is a partner in the firm of solicitors acting for the liquidator, who is not a shareholder, should take the chair at each of those meetings, and providing that one member present should constitute a quorum, the purpose of that being that the Hillmans could no longer prevent an effective meeting being held. Notices of those meetings were in due course sent out.

On 5th September 1972 the meetings were held or purported to be held, and the resolutions which I have outlined were passed or purported to have been passed. Attending at the meeting of Crystal Bowl, in addition to the chairman, were Mr Clarke, the liquidator, and Mr Winch, who was present as proxy for the Hillmans. On a show of hands, Mr Winch voted against the resolution and Mr Clarke voted for the resolution. Mr Clarke then demanded a poll and naturally was successful on the poll. The other two meetings the Hillmans did not attend either personally or by proxy. Mr Clarke was there and the gentleman I have referred to as the chairman. The resolutions were accordingly put and passed on a show of Mr Clarke's hand alone.

Mr Clarke was present at each of those meetings purportedly pursuant to the following document which bore the seal of the parent company, dated 5th September 1972, signed by Mr Clarke as liquidator, he having caused the seal to be affixed to it, the document being in these terms:

> 'We, Calgary and Edmonton Land Company Limited, in liquidation, hereby appoint Douglas Archibald Clarke as our representative at the respective general meetings of the following companies [then the names of the three subsidiary companies appear] to be held on 5th September 1972. The seal of the company was affixed in the presence of:—Douglas A Clarke Liquidator.'

To continue the story, a writ was issued at the instance of the Hillmans on 6th September 1972 asking for a declaration that Mr Clarke and Mr Hewson had not been validly appointed directors, nor had the other directors been validly removed. On 7th September the notices of motion were launched seeking to restrain Mr Clarke and Mr Hewson from acting as directors in the three subsidiaries or from in any way giving effect to those three resolutions. Phillips J, sitting as vacation judge, found in favour of the defendants that the resolutions had been validly passed.

I turn now to s 139 of the Companies Act 1948, pursuant to which Mr Clarke purported to act, appear at the meetings, and vote both on a show of hands and on a

poll. That is a section which is concerned with the representation of corporations at
meetings of companies. So far as we are at present concerned, sub-s (1) reads as
follows:

> 'A corporation, whether a company within the meaning of this Act or not,
> may—(a) if it is a member of another corporation, being a company within the
> meaning of this Act, by resolution of its directors or other governing body
> authorise such person as it thinks fit to act as its representative at any meeting
> of the company or at any meeting of any class of members of the company';

and then it goes on to deal with the situation of a corporation being a creditor of
another company. Subsection (2) provides:

> 'A person authorised as aforesaid shall be entitled to exercise the same powers
> on behalf of the corporation which he represents as that corporation could
> exercise if it were an individual shareholder . . . of that other company.'

It will be seen from the nature of the document which I have read, signed by
Mr Clarke, that it purported to be an appointment of Mr Clarke 'by resolution of
its directors or other governing body' authorising Mr Clarke to act as such representative. The question is whether Mr Clarke, as liquidator of the parent company, is
within the scope of the phrase in s 139, 'or other governing body'.

I look first at the general purpose of s 139, which appears to me to be this. A corporation, because of its nature, cannot attend a meeting; it cannot per se vote; it
cannot show a hand; it cannot demand a poll; it cannot address the meeting and
speak its mind. It appears to me that the leading purpose of this section is that it
is designed to enable a corporation owning shares in a company to be in the same
situation for the purpose of meetings of that latter company and voting at such
meetings as would be the corporation if it were an individual. That appears to me to
be the distinct purpose as stated by s 139 (2). I begin by asking myself: if the section
provides for that whilst the shareholding corporation is a live corporation, that is to
say, if it has not taken any step on the road to winding-up or dissolution, why should
it be that the shareholding corporation, just because it has gone into winding-up,
particularly a creditors' winding-up, an event which in no way lessens the interest of
the shareholding corporation in the shares which it holds—why should it be intended
to deprive the shareholding company of the rights which were conferred on it whilst
it was still in every respect a live entity?

It is perfectly true to say that a company need not take advantage of s 139, and can
appoint a proxy to attend the meeting on its behalf. But if the company in which
the shares are held be a public company, the company cannot by its proxy exercise
what might be an important right, namely, the ability to address the meeting;
although that is not so, by force of statutory provision, if the company in which
the shares are held be, as indeed in fact each is here, a private company. So it is said
that, after the creditors' voluntary winding-up, the liquidator would have had power,
instead of purporting as governing body under s 139, to appoint a representative, to
nominate a proxy to attend the meeting on behalf of the company; and in fact that
proxy, the three subsidiary companies being private companies, could have not only
voted but could also have demanded a poll and, indeed, they being private companies,
he could have addressed the meeting.

Nevertheless I come back to the question whether on a fair construction of s 139,
as applied to the facts of this case, it is right to construe the phrase 'or other governing
body' as embracing the liquidator in this case. As I have said, the liquidator was
appointed by the court in July 1970. There has been no committee of inspection
appointed. The liquidator apart from the directions as to summoning these three
meetings, has received no directions from the court and no directions from the body
of creditors as to how he should conduct the affairs of the company. It seems to

a me, in the circumstances, that it is perfectly reasonable and fair to consider that the liquidator in the present case on 5th September, when he purported to act under s 139, was, within the description, the governing body of the parent company. Let me say at once it is perfectly plain there is no significance to be attached to the apparent plurality involved in 'other governing body', because it is conceded that in the case of a corporation in which there was only one person fulfilling the managing

b function of a board of directors, in, say, a foreign corporation, which is embraced in this section, the mere fact that there was only one person would not deprive that one person of the title of a 'governing body'. It seems to me that the liquidator in this particular case was the governing body at the time when he executed this representational authority. He was in the saddle and the only occupant of that saddle. He was in charge of the horse, although the horse might be described as being a little lame. I do not myself see why it is not an appropriate description of a person

c in the position that was occupied by the liquidator in this case, who at the relevant time had the effective management of the company and its affairs, and I do not see why he should not come within the phrase 'other governing body'. It must be borne in mind that the draftsman of this section is dealing not only with ordinary English limited companies, but by reason of the definition in s 455 (3) of a 'corporation' he is necessarily having to deal with all sorts and kinds of corporations, including foreign

d corporations.

It was suggested that, if it was intended to include in 'other governing body' the liquidator of any company in liquidation, it would have been very easy to say so; but I do not think it would have been easy to say so, because, once you start condescending to particulars in a section of that kind, you will find the usual argument for excluding other cases which otherwise would come within the phrase 'or other

e governing body'. Accordingly I accept the arguments that were advanced by counsel for the second and third defendants in support of the decision of the learned judge below that on a fair construction of s 139 Mr Clarke, as liquidator, was within the phrase 'other governing body'. On that ground I would dismiss the appeal.

Let me say that this decision relates to the particular situation of the particular

f liquidator in this particular case. It may be that a case might arise when the situation of the liquidator was such that, having regard to the interferences by creditors or by court order, it would not be reasonable to describe him as the man in the saddle. With that kind of case we are not concerned and we will deal with it as and when it arises.

An alternative point was put in support of the decision of the learned judge on

g which he did not give any final conclusion, based on the language of Table A, art 66, an article which applies to all three of the subsidiary companies. That article provides:

'No objection shall be raised to the qualification of any voter except at the meeting or adjourned meeting at which the vote objected to is given or tendered, and every vote not disallowed at such meeting shall be valid for all purposes.

h Any such objection made in due time shall be referred to the chairman of the meeting, whose decision shall be final and conclusive.'

As to the meetings which were only attended by Mr Clarke and the chairman, counsel for the second and third defendants finally conceded that, as an alternative, if he were wrong on the first point, he could not rely on art 66, since the objection was not to the voting, because if the point were right Mr Clarke would not be entitled

j to attend as a member or representative member, and the objection would be an objection that there was no quorum. There was an argument one way and an argument the other whether in the case of the Crystal Bowl meeting art 66 would in the alternative have availed counsel for the second and third defendants, if he had been wrong on the representation point, whether it was really an objection to the qualification of Mr Clarke as a voter, or whether the objection was outside art 66 because the real objection was that he had no right to demand a poll, and, therefore, the poll was not properly taken. I do not think it necessary or indeed desirable to express a concluded view on that point.

In the result it appears to me that the liquidator, not being in any sense a servant of the company, should be taken to be within the phrase in this case 'other governing body', and I would accordingly reject the appeals.

CAIRNS LJ. I agree.

STAMP LJ. I too agree. Section 139 is clearly designed to enable any corporation, other than a corporation sole, but including any foreign corporation (see s 455 (3) of the Companies Act 1948) to put itself, so far as may be, in the same position, as regards meetings of companies in which the corporation holds shares, as would be the case if the corporation was not a persona ficta but a natural person. This appears from sub-s (2) of s 139 itself. In relation to corporations having widely different constitutions, only general words describing how the appointment of a corporation's representative should be made and who was to make it could have achieved that result. The words 'or other governing body' must, therefore, in my judgment be taken to have been used in a general and not a technical sense, and to achieve the intended result so as to apply the words to widely differing circumstances and so give effect to the purposes of the section, the words ought to be construed, so far as possible, as all-embracing.

I cannot doubt that this particular liquidator was, within the meaning of the section so construed, the governing body at the relevant time of this particular corporation. Here there was no committee of inspection and the creditors had not, as they might have done under s 296, sanctioned the continuance of any of the powers of the directors. Whether if it had been otherwise it would have made any difference I express no opinion. It follows, however, that by the joint effect of ss 245 (1) (b) and 303 of the Act, this liquidator at the relevant time was responsible for carrying on the corporation's business and was the governing body for the purposes of s 139 (1). He, unlike a managing director or a headmaster of a school, was not the servant of the corporation, but governing it.

I would add this. In view of the necessity to use general words to cover widely differing circumstances I cannot accept the submission that the draftsman of s 139, because he did not specify corporations in liquidation, intended to exclude them. I agree with Russell LJ that, if the draftsman had specified liquidators of English companies, he might well have thrown doubt on the power of an equivalent or near equivalent of a liquidator in charge of the affairs of a foreign corporation to make the appointment contemplated by the section.

I would dismiss the appeals.

Appeals dismissed. Leave to appeal to the House of Lords refused.

Solicitors: *Michael Kramer & Co* (for the plaintiffs); *Frere, Cholmeley & Co* (for the second and third defendants).

Mary Rose Plummer   Barrister.

Grigsby v Melville and another

CHANCERY DIVISION
BRIGHTMAN J
26th, 27th, 28th APRIL 1972

Sale of land – Conveyance – Exception and reservation – Implied exception – General words of exception and reservation – Exception from conveyance of part of underlying structure of premises conveyed – Adjoining shop and cottage premises in common ownership – Cellar under cottage premises – Access to cellar only from shop – Sale of cottage – Conveyance excepting and reserving 'such rights and easements . . . as may be enjoyed in connection with' shop – Whether cellar excepted from conveyance – Whether fee simple in cellar reserved to vendor.

Easement – Storage – Right of unlimited storage in confined space – Whether capable of subsisting at law.

Two adjoining properties, a cottage and a shop, were both occupied by a butcher, who used the shop for the purposes of his business. Underneath the drawing-room of the cottage was a cellar. The only practical means of access to the cellar was by stairs leading from the shop. The butcher used the cellar to store brine. Subsequently the butcher's business ceased and, in February 1962, H, who then owned both properties, conveyed the cottage to the plaintiff's predecessor in title 'EXCEPT AND RESERVING unto the Vendor such rights and easements or quasi rights and quasi easements as may be enjoyed in connection with' the shop. In May 1962 H conveyed the shop to the defendant's wife and thereafter the defendant began to store various articles in the cellar. The plaintiff brought proceedings claiming an injunction to restrain the defendant from entering the cellar and from depositing articles therein. The defendant counterclaimed contending that, by reason of the general words of exception and reservation in the February 1962 conveyance, he was entitled to a declaration that the fee simple of the cellar was vested in his wife or, alternatively, a declaration that the shop enjoyed an easement of storage within the cellar.

Held – (i) When a vendor owned two adjoining houses and sold off one, and there was a void lying wholly beneath the house sold, that void would pass with the house sold unless the conveyance was clearly worded to the contrary. If the vendor intended to except part of the property from the conveyance it was his duty to include an express exception in the conveyance. Otherwise an exception would only be implied in a case of necessity. The general words of exception and reservation in the February 1962 conveyance did not preserve the freehold of the cellar for the vendor and his successors in title. A general clause of that sort was plainly intended to preserve, for the benefit of the grantor, quasi-rights and quasi-easements and the like, and not to withdraw by implication the freehold of part of the underlying structure of the house being conveyed. Furthermore there were no grounds on which an exception of the cellar could be implied; the cellar was inessential to the enjoyment of the shop and, although the only existing access to the cellar was from the shop, there would be no difficulty in creating a new means of access from the cottage (see p 389 c d and h, p 390 b and p 391 a to d and g, post).

Dictum of Thesiger LJ in *Wheeldon v Burrows* [1874-80] All ER Rep at 672 applied.

(ii) The general words of exception and reservation did not create an easement of storage for the benefit of the vendor and his successors in title. The cellar had been enjoyed in connection with the shop for the exclusive purpose of storing brine for the better conduct of the butcher's business then carried on in the shop. That

Q

business had ceased when the properties were divided and it was never contemplated that it would be resumed (see p 393 a to c, post).

Semble. An easement of unlimited storage within a confined space cannot exist in law (see p 392 h to p 393 a, post).

Copeland v Greenhalf [1952] 1 All ER 809 and *Wright v Macadam* [1949] 2 All ER 565 considered.

Notes

For exceptions and reservations, see 11 Halsbury's Laws (3rd Edn) 433-435, paras 696-698, and for cases on the subject, see 17 Digest (Repl) 388, 389, *1918-1935*.

For the creation of easements by implication, see 12 Halsbury's Laws (3rd Edn) 538-543, paras 1165-1175, and for cases on the subject, see 19 Digest (Repl) 40-46, *210-242*.

For the rights which can be created as legal easements, see 12 Halsbury's Laws (3rd Edn) 533, para 1157, and for cases on the subject, see 19 Digest (Repl) 22, 23, *89-94*.

Cases referred to in judgment

Copeland v Greenhalf [1952] 1 All ER 809, [1952] Ch 488, 19 Digest (Repl) 193, *1347*.

Eastwood v Ashton [1915] AC 900, 84 LJCh 671, 113 LT 562, HL, 40 Digest (Repl) 370, *2963*.

Laybourn v Gridley [1892] 2 Ch 53, 61 LJCh 352, 7 Digest (Repl) 267, *10*.

Truckell v Stock [1957] 1 All ER 74, [1957] 1 WLR 161, CA, Digest (Cont Vol A) 475, *1874a*.

Wheeldon v Burrows (1879) 12 Ch D 31, [1874-80] All ER Rep 669, 48 LJCh 853, 41 LT 327, CA, 19 Digest (Repl) 48, *269*.

Wright v Macadam [1949] 2 All ER 565, [1949] 2 KB 744, CA, 19 Digest (Repl) 39, *203*.

Cases also cited

Bulstrode v Lambert [1953] 2 All ER 728, [1953] 1 WLR 1064.

Corbett v Hill (1870) LR 9 Eq 671.

Cordell v Second Clanfield Properties Ltd [1968] 3 All ER 746, [1969] 2 Ch 9.

Hopgood v Brown [1955] 1 All ER 550, [1955] 1 WLR 213, CA.

Webb's Lease, Re, Sandom v Webb [1951] 2 All ER 131, [1951] Ch 808, CA.

Willson v Greene [1971] 1 All ER 1098, [1971] 1 WLR 635.

Action

The plaintiff, Anne Louise Grigsby, claimed, inter alia, an injunction to restrain the first defendant, Aubrey Vincent Melville—

'or his servants or agents henceforth from committing trespass in under or upon [certain] land and premises known as 3 Knockhundred Row Midhurst Sussex [of which the plaintiff was the freehold owner] and in particular to restrain the Defendant or his servants or agents henceforth from:—(a) entering upon the Plaintiff's cellar under the said premises; and (b) depositing any boxes, building materials or any other thing in the said cellar . . .'

The first defendant counterclaimed, inter alia, for (1) a declaration, inter alia, that the cellar formed part of and went with the fee simple estate in the premises adjoining 3 Knockhundred Row, known as 'Church Hill', then vested in the first defendant's wife, Joan Mary Melville, (2) alternatively a declaration that Church Hill was accommodated by an easement of storage within the cellar (equivalent to an estate in fee simple), and (3) an injunction to restrain the plaintiff by herself, her servants or agents or otherwise howsoever from entering the cellar or bricking up or obstructing in any other manner the entrance to the cellar from Church Hill. During the trial of the action, the first defendant's wife was joined as second defendant. The facts are set out in the judgment.

David Iwi for the plaintiff.

W D Ainger for the defendants.

BRIGHTMAN J. The plaintiff and the defendants are neighbours. The defendants claim the right to occupy a cellar beneath the plaintiff's drawing-room floor. That, put shortly, is what this action is about.

At the start of 1962, a builder by the name of Mr Holroyd was the owner of 3 Knockhundred Row at Midhurst in Sussex and also of certain adjoining premises known as 'Church Hill'. Shortly before, the two premises had been occupied as one. On 28th February 1962 Mr Holroyd conveyed no 3 on sale to a company known as Natinvil Builders Ltd ('Natinvil'), retaining Church Hill in his own possession. I will refer to that conveyance as the 'Natinvil conveyance'. There is a plan attached to the Natinvil conveyance. This plan depicts no 3 and Church Hill as follows. Each property is irregularly oblong in shape. To the east of the properties is the road from Haslemere to Chichester. The northern of the two properties is no 3. It contains a cottage which fronts the road. At the rear—that is to say to the west of the cottage—there is a yard followed by a small store house and then a garden. Church Hill is shown on the plan as consisting of a shop which fronts the road; according to the evidence, what is depicted on the plan as a shop was, in fact, divided into shop, office and hall. The division is unimportant and for simplicity I will refer to the whole as 'the shop'. To the rear of the shop there is a yard and to the rear of the yard there is a garden. The cottage of no 3 and the shop of Church Hill have a common wall for almost the whole of the south side of the cottage; that is to say the cottage and the shop are semi-detached. There is a narrow passageway which leads from the yard of no 3 along the west and south sides of the shop to the Haslemere/Chichester Road. The plan to the Natinvil conveyance contains the words 'party boundary' and arrows pointing to a line which is drawn between the two gardens and which continues so as to divide cottage from shop. No 3 as I have described it, is outlined on the plan in pink. The passageway is blue. The cottage of no 3 has three storeys. It has—or at any rate in 1962 it had—four bedrooms, three living-rooms, a kitchen and a bathroom. One of the living-rooms, used as a drawing-room, measured about 23 feet by 12 feet. Beneath a part of the drawing-room is the cellar in question.

Before I turn to the wording of the Natinvil conveyance it will be convenient to describe the cellar. I find as a fact that the cellar was of the following description at the time of the Natinvil conveyance, and that there is no significant difference today. It was rather a rough and dirty place with a floor partly of earth and partly of bricks. It had stone walls. The ceiling of the cellar was about five feet eight inches in height, consisting of the exposed joists and floor boards belonging to the drawing-room of no 3. The joists were underpinned by a number of posts or shores let into the floor of the cellar. It is not clear from the evidence whether these shores were in existence at the time of the Natinvil conveyance or were added very shortly afterwards. The ceiling of the cellar is at about the same level as the floor of the shop, as it then was. The only practical access to the cellar was from the shop.

The means of access calls for a little elucidation. It only became apparent as the evidence progressed. There is a small protuberance jutting out into the shop which looks like a cupboard. On the west wall of the protuberance there is a door. On opening the door, there are some stone steps leading in the first instance eastwards and then curving northwards—perhaps eight steps in all. At the bottom of the steps is the cellar. The first steps within, of course, the protuberance are to the south of the boundary line shown on the plan to the Natinvil conveyance. The last step or two are, I think, to the north of the boundary line, although their precise position is not exactly established by the evidence. There is also a small aperture at the top of the west wall of the cellar. Through this aperture an observer kneeling in the yard of no 3 can crane his neck and see inside the cellar. If he were slim and agile he might crawl through the aperture. The aperture was obviously meant only to light and ventilate the cellar. The cellar is not an exact rectangle. According to the plan annexed to the defence, which proved to be consistent with the evidence, the short sides of the cellar are about eight or ten feet and the long sides 15 or 16 feet. The cellar is, therefore, a bit smaller than the drawing-room above. The entirety of the cellar—leaving aside the steps—lies beneath the plaintiff's drawing-room. The cellar was empty at the time of the Natinvil conveyance. It served no purpose essential to Church Hill and was not reasonably necessary to its enjoyment. I have mentioned that there is no significant difference in the cellar today. The first defendant has however tacked some boarding to the joists beneath the drawing-room floor and he has also put up a few shelves to which I shall refer later.

I turn to the wording of the Natinvil conveyance. The parcels read as follows:

'ALL THAT dwellinghouse and premises situate on the west side of Church Hill or Knockhundred Row in the Parish of Midhurst in the County of Sussex as the same is for the purpose of identification only more particularly delineated on the plan annexed hereto and thereon edged with pink TOGETHER WITH all such rights and easements or quasi rights and quasi easements as may now be enjoyed in connection with the property hereby conveyed over the adjoining property to the south and edged with green on the said plan [The green colouring was by mistake omitted from the plan but there is no doubt that the words refer to 'Church Hill.] AND TOGETHER with a right of way on foot only over the passageway three feet in width coloured blue on the said plan leading from Church Hill or Knockhundred Row to the rear of the property hereby conveyed for the purpose only of removing and disposal of refuse by employees of the Midhurst Rural District Council and the delivery of fuel to the owner or occupier for the time being of the property hereby conveyed the Company [i e Natinvil] and its successors in title paying a fair and proper proportion of the expense of maintaining such passageway in good and sufficient repair EXCEPT AND RESERVING unto the Vendor such rights and easements or quasi rights and quasi easements as may be enjoyed in connection with the said adjoining property to the south and edged with green on the said plan over the property hereby conveyed'.

On 12th October 1962 Natinvil conveyed no 3 on sale to Mrs Butterfield who was then Mrs Sykes. On 16th July 1969 Mrs Butterfield conveyed no 3, by way of gift, to her daughter, Mrs Grigsby, the plaintiff in this action.

The first defendant is a veterinary surgeon. In 1962 his wife, the second defendant, bought Church Hill from Mr Holroyd. The property was conveyed to her by a conveyance dated 28th May 1962—that is to say three months after the conveyance on which the plaintiff relies. Thereafter, the first defendant converted what used to be a shop into a surgery and rooms connected therewith. He then began practising his profession from that address. He started, on my understanding of the evidence, to make use of the cellar for keeping a few things such as empty cartons, cat baskets, his larger bottles and the like. He put these things at that time at the foot of the stone steps. Although I do not think anything turns on this, I am satisfied that in terms of quantity of material the use which he made of the cellar at this time was fairly light. Later on he added three or four shelves to the walls at the head of the steps, more or less at surgery level. On those shelves he started to store bottles and one or two other things.

The plaintiff first became aware that the first defendant was making use of the cellar early in 1971 when she heard someone nailing boards to the underneath of the joists of her drawing-room floor. She then learnt for the first time that the first defendant claimed that the cellar was included in the conveyance to the second defendant. The plaintiff started proceedings. The writ was issued on 19th March 1971. The relief claimed, shortly stated, was an injunction to restrain the first defendant from entering the cellar and from depositing boxes and other things in the cellar. The first defendant served a defence and also a counterclaim. He counterclaimed for a declaration that the fee simple of the cellar was vested in the second defendant, and alternatively a declaration that Church Hill enjoyed an easement of storage within the cellar.

There are, therefore, three issues involved. First, did the Natinvil conveyance transfer the cellar to the purchaser of no 3, through whom the plaintiff claims? Secondly, and this is an issue not apparent on the pleadings but it arose by common consent during the progress of the case, did the Natinvil conveyance transfer the site of the cellar steps and the containing wall where they impinge on the site of Church Hill, or were they left in the ownership of Mr Holroyd? Thirdly, if the Natinvil conveyance did transfer the cellar, does Church Hill enjoy an easement of storage therein?

I deal first with the cellar, excluding the steps from consideration. I may say at once that where a vendor owns two adjoining dwelling-houses and sells off one, and there is a void lying wholly beneath the house sold and particularly a void which is not vaulted but has as its ceiling merely the joists and floor boards of the room above, I would need cogent authority or persuasive argument to convince me that the void does not pass with the house unless the conveyance is clearly so worded. A purchaser does not expect to find the vendor continuing to live mole-like beneath his drawing-room floor. I would expect the conveyance of a house to include all that lies beneath its roof. I think that is how a conveyance should be interpreted unless there is reason for construing it otherwise.

Counsel for the plaintiff read me a passage from *Wheeldon v Burrows*[1], which I think I should quote. It is from the judgment of Thesiger LJ[2]:

'We have had a considerable number of cases cited to us, and out of them I think that two propositions may be stated as what I may call the general rules governing cases of this kind. The first of these rules is, that on the grant by the owner of a tenement of part of that tenement as it is then used and enjoyed, there will pass to the grantee all those continuous and apparent easements (by which, of course, I mean *quasi* easements), or, in other words, all those easements which are necessary to the reasonable enjoyment of the property granted, and which have been and are at the time of the grant used by the owners of the entirety for the benefit of the part granted. The second proposition is that, if the grantor intends to reserve any right over the tenement granted, it is his duty to reserve it expressly in the grant. Those are the general rules governing cases of this kind, but the second of those rules is subject to certain exceptions. One of those exceptions is the well-known exception which attaches to cases of what are called ways of necessity; and I do not dispute for a moment that there may be, and probably are, certain other exceptions, to which I shall refer before I close my observations upon this case. Both of the general rules which I have mentioned are founded upon a maxim which is as well established by authority as it is consonant to reason and common sense, viz., that a grantor shall not derogate from his grant.'

That, of course, was a case dealing, in the second limb of the passage which I read, with the reservation of a right by implication to a grantor. It is equally applicable to the exception of part of the inheritance itself. By way of illustration of this principle in the context of overlapping structures, counsel for the plaintiff took me to *Laybourn v Gridley*[3]. An inn and a timber yard were in common ownership. There was a loft in the timber yard. A small part of this loft jutted over the inn. The inn was conveyed to the plaintiff, the property being defined by reference to a plan. Subsequently the timber yard was sold to the defendant's predecessor in title. The defendant became the owner of the timber yard and proceeded to raise the height of his loft including the part overhanging the inn. The plaintiff objected and claimed

1   (1879) 12 Ch D 31, [1874–80] All ER Rep 669
2   (1879) 12 Ch D at 49, [1874–80] All ER Rep at 672
3   [1892] 2 Ch 53

that the overhang had passed by his conveyance. His claim succeeded. *Laybourn v Gridley*[1] is a fairly extreme case. One is tempted to ask oneself whether perhaps it might be decided differently today. The learned judge laid great emphasis on the plan as decisive of the property conveyed. For my part I doubt whether the plaintiff's counsel needs to found himself on so extreme a case as *Laybourn v Gridley*[1]. But certainly it illustrates a principle on which he can rely. But it is to be noted that the case with which I am concerned is not one where part of a room belonging to Church Hill impinges on the airspace or structure of no 3. It is a much simpler case. Here there is a basement cellar, which I find inessential to the enjoyment of Church Hill, wholly contained within the structure of no 3.

Counsel for the defendants put his case in this way in relation to the cellar. First, he relied on the words of exception and reservation in the Natinvil conveyance: 'EXCEPT AND RESERVING unto the Vendor such rights and easements or quasi rights and quasi easements as may be enjoyed in connection with the said adjoining property to the south'. He submitted that the word 'rights' was wide enough to include the fee simple of the space occupied by the cellar and he submitted that that right, that fee simple, was something enjoyed in connection with Church Hill at the date of the Natinvil conveyance. If that argument were to fail, he submitted that there arose by necessary implication an exception of the fee simple of the airspace occupied by the cellar.

I deal first with his argument based on the express exception and reservation. He pointed out that the plan to the Natinvil conveyance was by force of the express words of the text of the conveyance 'for the purpose of identification only' and therefore not decisive of the precise boundaries. In any event, he said, the plan to the conveyance was merely a plan of the boundaries as they existed at ground level. In the result, he submitted, I ought not to treat the line which is described on the plan as 'party boundary', as indicative of the property conveyed so far as property below ground level was concerned. He conceded that if the plan had not been described as 'for the purpose of identification only' leaving unqualified the words 'more particularly delineated on the plan annexed hereto and thereon edged with pink', I would have been entitled to pay more attention to the line indicating the party boundary. He referred me to *Eastwood v Ashton*[2], and particularly to the speech of Lord Wrenbury[3].

He further submitted that even if the plan ought to be read as controlling the text of the conveyance, the defendants' claim to the cellar is not defeated merely because the cellar lies within the pink edging on the plan. As I have said, he submitted that the pink edging is a picture of the house only at ground level, and is not decisive at other levels. He referred me to *Truckell v Stock*[4]. In that case 44 and 45 East Street, Colchester, had been in common ownership. No 45 was conveyed to the plaintiff. The parcels referred to a plan and the plan was not described as 'solely for the purpose of identification' and therefore could play a leading part in the interpretation of the conveyance. Later, the common vendor sold no 44 to the defendant. A quarrel arose as to the ownership of the eaves and footings of no 45, which projected beyond the boundary line indicated on the plan attached to the conveyance of no 45. It was held that the plan was not decisive of the ownership of the projections that were not at ground level. Hodson LJ said[5]:

'... although the ground plan (as I understand it) would control the ownership of the air above, it does not in the least prevent the plaintiff owning the parts of his house which protrude over the line marked on the ground plan.'

So far as the cellar is concerned, exclusive of the steps and containing walls leading down to the cellar, I see no discrepancy whatever between the wording of the parcels

1   [1892] 2 Ch 53
2   [1915] AC 900
3   [1915] AC at 918
4   [1957] 1 All ER 74, [1957] 1 WLR 161
5   [1957] 1 All ER at 77, [1957] 1 WLR at 165

and the delineation on the plan. I find it, therefore, unnecessary to decide whether the parcels or the plan prevail because both, to my mind, point in precisely the same direction. So far as the text of the conveyance is concerned, the cellar is sited exclusively under no 3 and therefore, in my view, forms part of and passes with no 3. So far as the plan is concerned, the cellar lies wholly on no 3's side of the delineated party boundary. Both text and plan therefore, to my mind, speak the same message. I am quite unable to accept the submission that part of what would otherwise be the freehold of no 3 is drawn away from it by the general words of the exception and reservation. A general clause of that sort is plainly intended to preserve for the benefit of the grantor quasi-rights and quasi-easements and the like, and not to withdraw by implication the freehold of part of the underlying structure of the house which is being conveyed.

I turn to and deal shortly with the submission that there is an implied exception or reservation of the cellar in favour of Mr Holroyd and thus, now, in favour of the second defendant. In my view, it would be difficult to imagine a more perfect example of a derogation from a grant were such an implication to be made. Counsel for the defendants was constrained to base such an implication on the fact that access to the cellar at the date of the Natinvil conveyance was exclusively via Church Hill, which I accept, and that fact of course is also relevant to his argument based on the express exception and reservation. But it is to be noted that there was nothing whatever to prevent the grantee of no 3 enlarging the aperture on his land so as to gain easy access by that route to the cellar, if the grantee of no 3 were interested in using it. The fact of an existing access via Church Hill, viewed in the light of an easy future access via no 3, seems to me a slender basis for a decision against the grantee of no 3. A person might question why the opening was allowed to remain into Church Hill, why the steps and doorway were not blocked up. I think there was a fairly simple explanation. If that access had been blocked up, then without excavation nobody could easily have got down into the void under the plaintiff's drawing-room should an emergency arise. In fact, an emergency did once arise. A pipe belonging to Church Hill broke and flooded the cellar. Access to the cellar from Church Hill was of assistance in dealing with that emergency. No doubt it was a mistake, with hindsight, to have left the access there. But I think that there was a reasonable explanation.

In my judgment both the text and the plan of the conveyance and also the common sense of the situation are united against the claim of the second defendant to be the fee simple owner of the cellar. That claim accordingly fails.

Different considerations apply to the space occupied by the cellar steps lying within the structure of Church Hill. I see no reason in the text of the conveyance or in the plan for treating this space as passing to the plaintiff's predecessor in title. The space is not by definition within the structure of the plaintiff's house nor does it in any way serve the purposes of the plaintiff's house. In my judgment, this space did not pass under the Natinvil conveyance. Indeed, counsel for the plaintiff so conceded shortly after the point emerged during the course of the trial.

I am left with the defendants' claim to an easement of storage. This claim is again based on the words of exception and reservation in the conveyance. There was evidence that, when the two properties had been one, the occupier, who was a butcher had used the cellar to store brine. Therefore, it was submitted, a general right of storage was enjoyed in connection with Church Hill and that right was reserved to the vendor as an easement over no 3.

There are, I think, two issues here: first, whether an easement of unlimited storage within a confined or defined space is capable of existing as a matter of law. Secondly, if so, whether such an easement was reserved in the present case. Counsel for the plaintiff referred me to *Copeland v Greenhalf*[1]. I read from the headnote[2]:

---

1   [1952] 1 All ER 809, [1952] Ch 488
2   [1952] Ch at 488, 489

'The plaintiff was the owner of an orchard and an adjoining house. Access to   *a*
the orchard from the road was had by a strip of land, which was about 150 feet
long, with a width varying from 15 feet at the road entrance to 35 feet in the
middle, and then contracting towards the orchard end. The defendant was a
wheelwright, whose premises were opposite to the strip of land across the road,
owned by the plaintiff. The plaintiff brought an action against the defendant,
claiming to restrain him from placing and leaving vehicles on the strip. The   *b*
defendant claimed the right to do so, setting up a lost grant (which claim was not
persisted in at trial) and a prescriptive right. The defendant's claim, so far as
proved at the trial, was that for 50 years he and his father before him had, with
the knowledge of the plaintiff and of her predecessors in title, continuously
stored along the strip, except for a space left for access to the orchard, customers'
vehicles awaiting and undergoing repair, and awaiting collection after repair:—   *c*
Held, that the right exercised and claimed was too extensive to constitute an
easement in law, as it amounted practically to a claim to the whole beneficial
user of that part of the strip of land over which it had been exercised.'

The following passage occurs in the judgment of Upjohn J[1]:

'I think that the right claimed goes wholly outside any normal idea of an   *d*
easement, that is, the right of the owner or the occupier of a dominant tenement
over a servient tenement. This claim (to which no closely related authority
has been referred to me) really amounts to a claim to a joint user of the land by
the defendant. Practically, the defendant is claiming the whole beneficial user
of the strip of land on the south-east side of the track there; he can leave as
many or as few lorries there as he likes for as long as he likes; he may enter on   *e*
it by himself, his servants and agents to do repair work thereon. In my judgment,
that is not a claim which can be established as an easement. It is virtually a
claim to possession of the servient tenement, if necessary to the exclusion of the
owner; or, at any rate, to a joint user, and no authority has been cited to me which
would justify the conclusion that a right of this wide and undefined nature can be
the proper subject-matter of an easement. It seems to me that to succeed, this   *f*
claim must amount to a successful claim of possession by reason of long adverse
possession. I say nothing, of course, as to the creation of such rights by deeds or
by covenant; I am dealing solely with the question of a right arising by
prescription.'

Counsel for the defendants countered by observing that *Copeland v Greenhalf*[2] was   *g*
inconsistent with *Wright v Macadam*[3], an earlier decision of the Court of Appeal in
which it was held that the right of a tenant to store domestic coal in a shed on the
landlord's land could exist as an easement for the benefit of the demised premises.
I am not convinced that there is any real inconsistency between the two cases. The
point of the decision in *Copeland v Greenhalf*[2] was that the right asserted amounted
in effect to a claim to the whole beneficial user of the servient tenement and for that   *h*
reason could not exist as a mere easement. The precise facts in *Wright v Macadam*[3]
in this respect are not wholly clear from the report and it is a little difficult to know
whether the tenant had exclusive use of the coal shed or of any defined portion of it.
To some extent a problem of this sort may be one of degree.
   In the case before me, it is, I think, clear that the defendants' claim to an easement
would give, to all practical intents and purposes, an exclusive right of user over the

---

1   [1952] Ch at 498, [1952] 1 All ER at 812, 813
2   [1952] 1 All ER 809, [1952] Ch 488
3   [1949] 2 All ER 565, [1949] 2 KB 744

a whole of the confined space representing the servient tenement. I think I would be at liberty if necessary to follow *Copeland v Greenhalf*[1]. I doubt, however, whether I need express any concluded view on this aspect of the case. The cellar was, on the evidence, enjoyed in connection with Church Hill for the exclusive purpose of accommodating a brine bin for the better conduct of the butcher's business then carried on at Church Hill. When the properties were divided, that business ceased *b* and it was never contemplated that it would be resumed, because the two properties were divided for the purpose of making them into two private dwelling-houses. Consequently the function performed by the cellar for the benefit of Church Hill came to an end because there was no business, and it was never contemplated that there would thereafter be a business, which could be served by the cellar. In other words, the mode in which the occupant of Church Hill had used the cellar had *c* terminated for good and all prior to the Natinvil conveyance. For that reason I decide that the claim to an easement of storage fails.

I think it is right that I should say that the case has been argued throughout by counsel for the defendants with clarity and ability and I do not think that he has missed anything that might have been advocated in support of the defendants' claim. However, in the result I declare that the plaintiff is the owner of the cellar exclusive of the *d* space occupied by those steps leading down into the cellar that lie within the structure of Church Hill. I am prepared to grant an injunction to restrain trespass within the cellar. I will give the parties liberty to apply if it be necessary, to define more precisely the party boundary between the two properties. It only remains for me to add for the purposes of record that the first defendant's wife as the owner of the property has been joined as second defendant during the trial of the action and *e* accordingly is to be treated as associated with the first defendant in the counterclaim.

Judgment accordingly.

Solicitors: *Kingsford, Dorman & Co*, agents for *Johnson & Clarence*, Midhurst (for the plaintiff); *Lamport, Bassitt & Hiscock*, Southampton (for the defendants).

f

                                                Susan Corbett Barrister.

---

1 [1952] 1 All ER 809, [1952] Ch 488

Rother Iron Works Ltd v Canterbury Precision Engineers Ltd

COURT OF APPEAL, CIVIL DIVISION
RUSSELL, CAIRNS AND STAMP LJJ
23rd, 24th NOVEMBER, 8th DECEMBER 1972

Company – Charge – Floating charge – Crystallisation – Appointment of receiver by debenture holder – Assets of company – Claim for money due under contract of sale – Set-off – Claim subject to right of set-off – Debt owed by company to purchasers under previous contract – Right of purchasers to set off debt against sum due to company under contract of sale – Contract of sale made prior to crystallisation of charge – Goods delivered after crystallisation – Purchasers' obligation to pay arising after crystallisation – Whether purchasers entitled to set-off as against debenture holder.

In August 1971 the plaintiff company executed a mortgage debenture in favour of its bank which was in ordinary form containing a floating charge on all the assets and undertakings present and future of the company, and power to appoint a receiver and manager. At the relevant time the plaintiff company and the defendants traded with each other. On 4th October 1971 the plaintiff company owed the defendants £124 for goods sold and delivered. Between 4th and 18th October 1971 the plaintiff company contracted for the sale by the plaintiff company and purchase by the defendants of goods to the value of £159. On 21st October before the contract had been carried out the bank appointed a receiver and manager under its debenture, whereupon the floating charge crystallised. The goods ordered by the defendants were delivered to them on 3rd November. The receiver, suing in the name of the plaintiff company, claimed that the defendants were not entitled to set off the plaintiff company's debt of £124 since the defendants' debt, having arisen on delivery of the goods after crystallisation of the floating charge, was an asset of the company which thereby became subject to the bank's charge.

Held – The defendants were only liable to pay £35 to the receiver, being entitled to set off the £124 due to them under the earlier contract. The crystallisation of the floating charge on the appointment of the receiver operated to charge the plaintiff company's rights under the existing contract for the purchase by the defendants of goods from the plaintiff company. That was an equitable assignment (by way of charge) of those rights. Those rights were always subject to a right in the defendants to assert that since the plaintiff company owed £124 to the defendants a payment of £35 would settle the account; and the debenture holder as equitable assignee could not be in a different or better position in that regard than the plaintiff company (see p 396 c to e, post).

Notes

For set-off being confined to claims between same persons in same right, see 34 Halsbury's Laws (3rd Edn) 399, para 679, and for cases on the subject, see 40 Digest (Repl) 411, 412, 68-72.

For the effect of crystallisation of floating charge, see 6 Halsbury's Laws (3rd Edn) 476, para 920, and for cases on the subject, see 10 Digest (Repl) 783, 784, 5089-5094.

Cases referred to in judgment

Connolly Brothers Ltd (No 2), Re Wood v The Company [1912] 2 Ch 25, 81 LJCh 517, 106 LT 738, 19 Mans 259, CA, 10 Digest (Repl) 793, 5150.

Ince Hall Rolling Mills Co v Douglas Forge Co (1882) 8 QBD 179, 51 LJQB 238, 10 Digest (Repl) 991, 6818.

a   *Mersey Steel & Iron Co v Naylor, Benzon & Co* (1882) 9 QBD 648, 51 LJQB 576, 47 LT 369, CA; *on appeal* (1884) 9 App Cas 434, [1881-85] All ER Rep 365, 53 LJQB 497, 51 LT 637, HL, 44 Digest (Repl) 225, 422.

Robbie (N W) & Co Ltd v Witney Warehouse Co Ltd [1963] 3 All ER 613, [1963] 1 WLR 1324, CA, Digest (Cont Vol A) 1318, 72a.

Cases and authorities also cited

b   *Forster v Nixon's Navigation Co Ltd* (1906) 23 TLR 138.

Handley Page Ltd v Customs and Excise Comrs [1970] 2 Lloyd's Rep 459; *affd* [1971] 2 Lloyd's Rep 298, CA.

Parsons v Sovereign Bank of Canada [1913] AC 160, PC.

4 Halsbury's Laws (3rd Edn), pp 507, 508.

Kerr on Receivers (14th Edn, 1972), p 320.

c   Williams on Bankruptcy (18th Edn, 1968), p 218.

Appeal

This was an appeal by the plaintiff company, Rother Iron Works Ltd, against a decision of his Honour Judge Sumner QC given at Canterbury County Court on

d   8th June 1972 whereby he ordered that on the agreed statement of facts in the action the defendants, Canterbury Precision Engineers Ltd, were entitled to set off against their indebtedness to the plaintiffs a like sum due from the plaintiffs to the defendants. Originally the plaintiff was Eric George Barrett, the receiver and manager of Rother Iron Works Ltd, but with the judge's consent Rother Iron Works Ltd were substituted as plaintiffs. The facts are set out in the judgment of the court.

e   *R Potts* for the plaintiffs.
J H Vallat for the defendants.

Cur adv vult

f   8th December. **RUSSELL LJ** read the following judgment of the court. This appeal raises a question of a right of set-off. The plaintiff company in August 1971 executed a mortgage debenture in favour of its bank; it was in ordinary form containing a floating charge on all the assets and undertakings present and future of the company, and power to appoint a receiver and manager. The plaintiff company and the defendants traded with each other. On 4th October 1971 the plaintiff company owed the defendants £124 for goods sold and delivered. After 4th October 1971 the

g   plaintiff company and the defendants contracted for the sale by the plaintiff company and purchase by the defendants of goods to the value of £159. On 21st October before this contract had been carried out the bank appointed a receiver and manager under its debenture, whereupon the floating charge crystallised. The goods the subject of the contract were delivered to the defendants pursuant thereto on 3rd November 1971. The defendants maintain that it need only pay £35 to the receiver,

h   setting off the £124 due to the defendants under the previous contract. The receiver, suing of course in the name of the plaintiff company, says there is no right of set-off and appeals from the judge's decision against him.

The argument for the plaintiff company may be shortly stated. It proceeds thus. When the goods were delivered on 3rd November the obligation to pay first arose as an asset of the plaintiff company; simultaneously it became subject to the charge

j   in favour of the bank; the debt of £124 owed by the plaintiff company to the defendants was no concern of the debenture holder, whereas the debt of £159 owed by the defendants, being caught by the debenture charge, was every concern of the debenture holder. There was therefore lacking the quality of mutuality required for set-off.

The opposing contentions are these. The crystallisation of the floating charge on the appointment of the receiver operated to charge the plaintiff company's rights

under the existing contract for the purchase by the defendants of goods from the
plaintiff company. This was an equitable assignment (by way of charge) of those
rights. Those rights were always subject to a right in the defendants to assert that
since the plaintiff company owed £124 to the defendants a payment of £35 would
settle the account; and the debenture holder as equitable assignee could not be in
a different or better position in that regard than the plaintiff company.

Now we are not concerned in the present case with a situation in which the cross-
claim sought to be set off either arose or first came to the hands of the defendants
after the crystallisation of the charge. Nor are we concerned with a claim made by
a receiver against the defendants arising out of a contract made by the receiver
subsequent to his appointment; for it is clear that the delivery of the goods was
pursuant to the contract made by the plaintiff company before the appointment.
Nor are there here any special considerations that might arise from a winding-up
of the plaintiff company. The facts are simply as stated.

In our judgment the argument for the defendants is to be preferred. It is true
that the right of the plaintiff company to sue for the debt due from the defendant
company was embraced, when it arose, by the debenture charge. But if this was
because the chose in action consisting of the rights under the contract became subject
to the charge on the appointment of the receiver, then the debenture holder could
not be in a better position to assert those rights than had been the assignor plaintiff
company. And if the obligation of the defendant company to pay £159 be regarded
as a chose in action on its own it never in our view came into existence except subject
to a right to set off the £124 as in effect payment in advance. That which became
subject to the debenture charge was not £159, but the net claim sustainable by the
plaintiff company of £35. Some analogy may be found in *Re Connolly Brothers Ltd
(No 2), Wood v The Company*[1] in this court: there there was a floating charge with a
contract by the company not to charge its assets, which gave the debenture holder
an equity; the company bought land with money borrowed from X, the circumstances of completion being such that thereat X produced the money and took the
conveyance to the company by way of deposit to cover her loan, all by arrangement
with the company: it was held that the equitable rights of X had priority on the
ground that the company never acquired as an asset within the scope of the
debenture anything but the land subject to the charge to X.

Much dependence was put for the plaintiff company on the language used in this
court in *N W Robbie & Co Ltd v Witney Warehouse Co Ltd*[2] when referring to the
charge attaching to the debt due to the company 'as it arose'. But of course in that
case it was not necessary to consider the point here argued and the language cannot
be taken as directed to that point. Further, our attention was drawn to *Ince Hall
Rolling Mills Co v Douglas Forge Co*[3], which was a matter of the disallowance of set-off
in a liquidation, as producing (if set-off is available in the present case) an illogical
distinction between the case of a company in liquidation and a company under
receivership. We are not satisfied that the *Ince Hall* case[3] does necessarily show such
an illogical distinction: the liquidation produces a vital change in the status of a
company, and does not only operate as an equitable assignment by way of charge;
moreover, Lindley LJ in *Mersey Steel & Iron Co v Naylor, Benzon & Co*[4] said that *Ince
Hall*[3] was a case where the liquidator, after the winding-up had commenced, entered
into a new contract. Here there was certainly no new contract after the charge
crystallised. It was further argued that a receiver and manager could, if set-off were
available, never carry out such a contract as the present, for to do so would enable
an unsecured creditor (the defendants) to pay himself in effect out of assets of the

1   [1912] 2 Ch 25
2   [1963] 3 All ER 613, [1963] 1 WLR 1324
3   (1882) 8 QBD 179
4   (1882) 9 QBD 648 at 669

a company subject to the charge. But even if this were so in some instances, it does not follow by any means that commercial wisdom would not dictate completion of the contract.

The appeal is accordingly dismissed.

Appeal dismissed.

b Solicitors: *Ward, Bowie & Co*, agents for *Saffman & Co*, Leeds (for the plaintiffs); *Furley, Page, Fielding & Pembrook*, Canterbury (for the defendants).

Mary Rose Plummer Barrister.

c

Turner v Shearer

QUEEN'S BENCH DIVISION
d LORD WIDGERY CJ, SHAW AND WIEN JJ
9th MAY 1972

Police – Impersonation – Wearing articles of police uniform – Appearance so nearly resembling that of police officer as to be calculated to deceive – Calculated to deceive – Meaning – Whether requiring an intention to deceive – Police Act 1964, s 52 (2).

e On the true construction of s 52 (2)[a] of the Police Act 1964, which makes it an offence for a person to wear 'any article of police uniform in circumstances where it gives him an appearance so nearly resembling that of a member of a police force as to be calculated to deceive', the words 'calculated to deceive' mean 'likely to deceive'. Accordingly it is not a defence to a charge under s 52 (2) that the accused did not intend f to deceive (see p 399 e to j, post).

Notes
For the impersonation of police officers, see 30 Halsbury's Laws (3rd Edn) 143, para 232.

For the Police Act 1964, s 52, see 25 Halsbury's Statutes (3rd Edn) 365.

g **Case referred to in judgment**
McDowell v Standard Oil Co (New Jersey) [1927] AC 632, 96 LJCh 386, 137 LT 734; sub nom *Re McDowell's Application* 44 RPC 335, HL, 46 Digest (Repl) 59, *331*.

Case also cited
North Cheshire and Manchester Brewery Co v Manchester Brewery Co [1899] AC 83, HL.
h

Case stated
This was an appeal by way of case stated by the justices for the county of Essex acting in and for the petty sessional division of Southend in respect of their adjudication as a magistrates' court sitting at Southend on 5th October 1971.

1. The appellant, Ronald Charles Turner (a police inspector) preferred an in-
j formation against the respondent, Edward Henry Shearer, that he on 8th July 1971 at High Street, Southend-on-Sea, in the county of Essex, not being a constable, did wear articles of police uniform in circumstances where they gave him an appearance so nearly resembling that of a member of a police force as to be calculated to deceive, contrary to s 52 (2) of the Police Act 1964.

a Section 52, so far as material, is set out at p 399 b, post

2. The following facts were found. (a) On 8th July 1971 at 11.10 a m the appellant
saw the respondent in High Street, Southend-on-Sea, dressed in a black cap (similar
to those issued to the Essex constabulary save that in place of the appropriate badge,
the respondent wore a cloth badge on which there figured an eagle, and the sides of
the cap were rolled down so that when worn it bore little resemblance to a regulation
issue police cap), a blue shirt with rolled up sleeves (identical to an Essex constabulary
shirt) with a silver chain linked from one breast pocket to the other, black tie, black
shoes and black police trousers from which there hung a truncheon strap. (b) The cap,
shirt and trousers were ex-police uniform. (c) The respondent had purchased the
uniform legitimately from shops which advertised its sale. (d) At the material
time the respondent was representing himself as 'Thames Security Services' but was
standing near the central railway station, waiting for a friend. There was no reason
to disbelieve the respondent when he said that he was going to see someone that
afternoon regarding the possible employment of his firm. (e) There was a likelihood
that members of the public would be deceived into thinking that the respondent
was a police officer. (f) While a police officer was watching, a member of the public
did approach the respondent, and had a conversation with him. Whilst the respondent was speaking to the appellant (who was in uniform) another member of the
public approached the respondent and asked him to get a car moved that was alleged
to have been obstructing a run-in. (g) The respondent did not intend to pass himself
off as a police officer.

3. Being of the opinion that the words 'as to be calculated to deceive' were referable subjectively to the intentions of the respondent and being satisfied that the
respondent did not intend to pass himself off as a police officer the justices did not
decide whether or not members of the public were in fact deceived, but dismissed
the information.

B J Higgs for the appellant.
D Macrae for the respondent.

SHAW J delivered the first judgment at the invitation of Lord Widgery CJ.
This is an appeal by case stated by the Essex justices for the petty sessional division of
Southend who in October 1971 dismissed an information against the respondent which
alleged that, on a day in July 1971, he wore articles of police uniform in circumstances
where they gave him an appearance so clearly resembling that of a member of a
police force as to be calculated to deceive, contrary to s 52 (2) of the Police Act 1964.
The question raised by the case is what is the meaning to be attributed to the phrase:
'as to be calculated to deceive'. The justices imported into it the element of intention
on the part of the respondent to pass himself off as a police officer.

The facts found were that on 8th July 1971, in the middle of the morning, the
respondent was seen in the High Street, Southend-on-Sea, wearing a black cap with a
badge, and other articles some of which were part of police uniform, namely a
blue shirt and trousers. The justices found also that the respondent was wearing
them in an innocent connection, but that there was a likelihood that members of the
public would be deceived into thinking that the respondent was a police officer.
They, however, took the view that 'the words "as to be calculated to deceive" were
referable subjectively to the intentions of the respondent'. Being satisfied that the
respondent did not intend to pass himself off as a police officer they dismissed the
information.

If the words 'as to be calculated to deceive' mean no more than that there was a
likelihood that members of the public would be deceived, the questions whether or
not they were deceived, or whether or not the respondent intended that they should
be, would be immaterial. The whole issue here turns on what in the context of s 52
of the Police Act 1964 is meant by 'calculated to deceive'.

It is useful to begin by looking at s 52 (1) which makes it an offence for any person with intent to deceive to impersonate a member of a police force or to do anything or to say anything which is calculated falsely to suggest that he is a member of a police force. One sees that an essential ingredient of the offence created by that subsection is that there should be an intent to deceive, and the penalty for that offence may be six months' imprisonment or a fine of £100 or both. Section 52 (2), under which the information against the respondent was preferred, reads:

> 'Any person who, not being a constable, wears any article of police uniform in circumstances where it gives him an appearance so nearly resembling that of a member of a police force as to be calculated to deceive shall be guilty of an offence and liable on summary conviction to a fine not exceeding £100.'

It is quite clear that the Act is drawing a distinction between the offence created by s 52 (1), which is subject to penalties of imprisonment as well as fines, and where an intention to deceive is involved, and the kind of case where a person, perhaps with lack of forethought, or for some mistaken motive, perhaps failing to realise the impression he is creating, decks himself up in articles of clothing which in fact cause other people to think that he is a police officer because he is dressed like one.

The proper construction of the phrase 'as to be calculated to deceive' is not free from authority, for in a number of other contexts it has been held to mean 'likely to deceive or reasonably likely to deceive'. It does not involve that there should be an intention to deceive. In a case under the Trade Marks Acts, *McDowell v Standard Oil Co (New Jersey)*[1], where the suggestion made was that the trade mark which was used was calculated to deceive the public into thinking that they were buying the goods of the owner of a registered trade mark, Viscount Cave LC said[2]:

> '. . . it has been long ago decided, and is quite clear, that the words "calculated to deceive" which are found in s. 11 of the Trade Marks Act, 1905, do not mean "intended to deceive" but "likely (or reasonably likely) to deceive or mislead the trade or the public."'

The mischief, of course, under the Trade Marks Acts is deceiving or misleading the public, just as the mischief under s 52 (2) of the Police Act 1964 is deceiving or misleading the public.

For my part I see no reason to attach a different meaning to that phrase as used in the 1964 Act from that which was attributed to it by Lord Cave LC in *McDowell v Standard Oil Co (New Jersey)*[1] and in the many other cases where identical language was considered. If that is the right interpretation, and in my view it is, the finding in the case that there was a likelihood that members of the public would be deceived into thinking that the respondent was a police officer, concludes the matter. If the justices had applied the right construction to the subsection, they would have been bound to convict.

Accordingly, I would allow this appeal and remit the matter to the justices with a direction that the offence was proved.

WIEN J. I agree.

LORD WIDGERY CJ. I also agree.

Appeal allowed.

Solicitors: *Sharpe, Pritchard & Co*, agents for *T Hambrey Jones*, Chelmsford (for the appellant); *H Maxwell Lewis*, Southend-on-Sea (for the respondent).

Jacqueline Charles   Barrister.

---

1   [1927] AC 632
2   [1927] AC at 637

Furnell v Whangarei High Schools Board

PRIVY COUNCIL
LORD REID, LORD MORRIS OF BORTH-Y-GEST, VISCOUNT DILHORNE, LORD SIMON OF GLAISDALE
AND LORD KILBRANDON
19th, 20th, 24th, 25th JULY, 13th NOVEMBER 1972

Natural justice – Hearing – Duty to hear parties, etc – Preliminary investigation – Complaint against teacher – Complaint to school board – Board under statutory duty to appoint sub-committee to make preliminary investigation of complaint – Sub-committee reporting to board in accordance with statutory duty – Teacher knowing nothing of complaint and having no opportunity of making representations to sub-committee – Board suspending teacher following report – Charges referred to disciplinary committee for final determination – Teacher having right to a hearing before disciplinary committee – Whether teacher having right to be heard before decision to suspend taken – Education Act 1964 (New Zealand), s 158 – Secondary and Technical Institute Teachers Disciplinary Regulations 1969 (New Zealand), regs 4, 5.

The appellant was employed as a teacher at a high school in New Zealand and agreed to serve under the conditions laid down in the Secondary and Technical Institute Teachers Disciplinary Regulations 1969, made under s 161A[a] of the Education Act 1964. On 20th March 1970 he was notified by the chairman of the respondent school board that a complaint had been made about his conduct as a teacher at the school and that it had been investigated by a sub-committee set up under reg 4[b] of the 1969 regulations; that he was charged with certain disciplinary offences under s 158[c] of the 1964 Act and that by virtue of the occurrences listed he was guilty of conduct which showed his unfitness to remain in his position at the school and that he was suspended from his duties as from 20th March pending the determination of the charges. While suspended he was not entitled to any remuneration. The letter required him (pursuant to reg 5 (2)[d]) to state whether he admitted or denied the charges and to forward any explanation he might wish to give. In accordance with reg 5 (3) he was also informed that if he wished he might make a statement in person to the board. The appellant's solicitors wrote to the chairman of the board asking for detailed particulars of the charges. The chairman supplied them with those particulars on 6th April. On 20th April the appellant's solicitors sent a lengthy document to the chairman as the explanation of the appellant. He denied each and every offence. Pursuant to reg 5 (4) the board decided to refer the charges to the Director-General of Education, who in turn decided, under reg 5 (5) (c), to refer the charges to the Teachers' Disciplinary Board for hearing and determination. He notified the appellant to that effect by letter dated 29th May. The hearing was fixed for 30th June and the appellant was reminded that under reg 8 (2) he could either present his own case or be represented at the hearing by counsel or agent. The hearing never took place because the appellant brought proceedings against the school board and the members of the Teachers' Disciplinary Board. He claimed an injunction directed to the school board removing the suspension and reinstating him to teaching duties and, against the disciplinary board, a writ of prohibition prohibiting them from hearing and determining the charges. He also moved for a writ of certiorari to quash the decisions of the school board. He alleged that there had been a denial of natural justice in that, inter alia, he had not been told that his conduct was being investigated by the sub-committee under reg 4 and had not been given any opportunity of being heard

---

a Section 191A, as added by s 7 of the Education Amendment Act 1969, is set out at p 404 a to d post
b Regulation 4 is set out at p 404 j to p 405 a, post
c Section 158 is set out at p 403 b and c, post
d Regulation 5 is set out at p 405 f to 406 d, post

either by the sub-committee before they reported to the school board or by the school board before the decision to suspend him from his duties was taken. The trial judge granted the orders sought insofar as they related to the proceedings 'so far taken'. The school board appealed but before the hearing of the appeal came on the appellant resigned from the board's employment. The Court of Appeal of New Zealand allowed the school board's appeal. On appeal to the Privy Council the appellant sought the restoration of the issue of a writ of certiorari.

Held (Lord Reid and Viscount Dilhorne dissenting) – The appeal would be dismissed. The regulations had been faithfully followed and in the circumstances the court was not required to supplement their provisions. The procedure laid down in the regulations was not unfair; the principle of natural justice, that a person must be given a fair opportunity of correcting or contradicting what was said against him before he was condemned or criticised, had not been violated by the action of the sub-committee because under the scheme of procedure set out in the regulations they neither condemned nor criticised, and on the evidence there were no grounds for thinking that they had acted unfairly; nor were the school board required to give the appellant an opportunity of being heard before suspending him from his duties pending the determination of the charges against him; although suspension might involve hardship, it was not classified as a penalty either in the regulations or the Act; moreover reg 5, of which the appellant knew by the terms of his employment, clearly laid down that the written statement of a teacher (under reg 5 (2)) and the oral personal statement (under reg 5 (3)) would be made after any decision to suspend had been taken; in the appellant's case there were no grounds for thinking that the respondent board had acted unfairly in exercising their discretionary power to suspend him; they had to take into account the interests of the pupils and parents and of the public as well as those of a teacher and in the circumstances they had not acted irresponsibly or unfairly (see p 412 c f and g and p 414 c to p 415 d, post).

Dictum of Tucker LJ in *Russell v Duke of Norfolk* [1949] 1 All ER at 118 applied.
Re Pergamon Press Ltd [1970] 3 All ER 535 distinguished.

Notes

For observance of the rules of natural justice, see 30 Halsbury's Laws (3rd Edn) 718, 719, para 1368, and for cases on the subject, see 38 Digest (Repl) 102, 103, *731-736*.

Cases referred to in opinions

Brettingham-Moore v Municipality of St Leonards (1969) 121 CLR 509.
Cooper v Wandsworth Board of Works (1863) 14 CBNS 180, 2 New Rep 31, 32 LJCP 185, 8 LT 278, 9 Jur NS 1155, 143 ER 414, 26 Digest (Repl) 585, *2450*.
De Verteuil v Knaggs [1918] AC 557, 87 LJPC 128, PC, 8 Digest (Repl) 691, *38*.
K (H) (an infant), Re [1967] 1 All ER 226; sub nom *Re H K (infant)* [1967] 2 QB 617, [1967] 2 WLR 962, DC, Digest (Cont Vol C) 18, *157qa*.
Pearlberg v Varty (Inspector of Taxes) [1972] 2 All ER 6, [1972] 1 WLR 534, HL.
Pergamon Press Ltd, Re [1970] 3 All ER 535, [1971] Ch 388, [1970] 3 WLR 792, CA, Digest (Cont Vol C) 107, *4188c*.
R v Gaming Board for Great Britain, ex parte Benaim [1970] 2 All ER 528, [1970] 2 QB 417, [1970] 2 WLR 1009, 134 JP 513, CA, Digest (Cont Vol C) 397, *352Aa*.
Russell v Duke of Norfolk [1949] 1 All ER 109, 65 TLR 225, CA, 12 Digest (Repl) 693, *5321*.
Wiseman v Borneman [1969] 3 All ER 275, [1971] AC 297, [1969] 3 WLR 706, 45 Tax Cas 540, [1969] RTR 279, 48 ATC 278, HL, 28 (1) Digest (Repl) 493, *1760*.

Appeal

This was an appeal by Paul Wallis Furnell against the judgment of the Court of Appeal

of New Zealand (Wild CJ, North P and Turner J), given on 19th March 1971, allowing
an appeal by the respondents, the Whangarei High Schools Board, against the judgment of the Supreme Court of New Zealand (Speight J), given on 22nd October
1970, whereby it was ordered, inter alia, that a writ of certiorari issue removing certain decisions (including a decision to suspend the appellant) of the respondent
board into the Supreme Court and quashing those decisions. The facts are set out in
the majority opinion of the Board delivered by Lord Morris of Borth-y-Gest.

J D Gerard (of the New Zealand Bar) and *M E Goldsmith* for the appellant.
R C Savage QC (Solicitor-General, New Zealand) and *D L Mathieson* (of the New
    Zealand Bar) for the respondent board.

LORD MORRIS OF BORTH-Y-GEST. The Education Act 1964 (No 135) is
'An Act to consolidate and amend certain enactments of the General Assembly
relating to the education of the people of New Zealand'. It is an Act of over 200
sections. The undoubted public importance of the subject-matter is reflected in the
range and the precision of what the legislature has laid down. Part IV deals with the
enrolment and attendance of pupils. Part V (comprising ss 131 to 165) deals with the
appointment and employment of teachers. Part VI (comprising ss 166 to 182) deals
with the incorporation of societies of teachers and with appeals by teachers.
    Included in the sections dealing with the appointment and employment of teachers
are various sections which relate to offences. Section 157 concerns certain cases where
a criminal charge is brought against a teacher. It is provided that if a teacher is
charged with having committed any offence for which the maximum punishment is
not less than two years' imprisonment (whether on indictment or on summary
conviction) then he may be suspended by the school board employing him. The
board would exercise its discretion. In such cases the decision whether he had or had
not committed the alleged offence would of course be made in the appropriate
criminal court and not by the board. Likewise the board would not decide as to the
bringing of a charge. If the teacher were convicted, then (whether or not he had been
suspended) he might either be peremptorily dismissed by the board or if the board
so determined he might be deemed to have committed an offence under the Education Act 1964 and the board might impose on him one or more of certain prescribed
penalties. Further detailed provisions were made. The board is empowered to
transfer a teacher temporarily to other duties if of the opinion that pending the
hearing of the charge the teacher should be removed from his position but need not
be suspended (see s 157 (2)). A teacher may appeal to the Teachers Court of Appeal.
Section 157 (3) is as follows:

> 'Any teacher who is dismissed or otherwise punished, or who is suspended,
> by the Board under this section may appeal to the Teachers Court of Appeal in
> accordance with the provisions of Part VI of this Act against the decision of the
> Board.'

The subsection, as also does sub-s (4), makes it clear that suspension is not to be
regarded as a punishment. Subsection (4) is as follows:

> 'Where a teacher who is dismissed or otherwise punished or suspended under
> this section is subsequently acquitted of the charges made against him, he shall be
> reinstated in his position and shall receive his full salary in respect of the period
> for which he did not receive that salary; but, subject to any decision of the
> Teachers Court of Appeal, a teacher shall in no other case receive any salary or
> payment in respect of any period of suspension imposed under this section
> unless the Board otherwise directs.'

a   The next section (s 158) relates not to conduct which might constitute a serious criminal offence but to conduct which, within the framework of the Education Act, 1964, is to be regarded as constituting a disciplinary offence. The section is as follows:

b   '*Disciplinary offences.*—(1) Every teacher commits an offence against this section who—(a) By any act or omission fails to comply with the requirements of this Act: (b) In the course of his duties disobeys, disregards, or makes wilful default in carrying out any lawful order or instruction given by any person or Board having authority to give such order or instruction: (c) Is negligent, careless, or indolent in the discharge of his duties: (d) Is grossly inefficient or incompetent in the discharge of his professional duties: (e) Improperly uses property, stores, or equipment for the time being in his official custody or under his control or fails to take reasonable care of any such property or equipment: (f) Absents himself from his

c   duties without leave or valid excuse: (g) Is guilty of conduct in his capacity as a teacher or otherwise which is unbecoming to a member of the teaching service or shows his unfitness to remain in his present position or in the service.

'(2) A teacher who is alleged to have committed an offence under this section shall be dealt with in accordance with section 159 of this Act.'

d   The Act proceeds with precision and elaborate detail to prescribe the steps which are to be taken if it is alleged that an offence under s 158 has been committed. In that event (see s 159 (1)) the board 'shall forthwith advise the teacher in writing of the full details of the charge against him' and then the later provisions of the section 'shall apply'. By the next subsection the teacher concerned 'shall . . . be required to state in writing within a reasonable time to be specified in the notice whether he

e   admits or denies the truth of the charge'. Then if the board decide to proceed with the charge they may, pending its hearing and determination, either suspend or transfer the teacher. The charge is then referred for investigation to a committee. The committee consists of not more than three members appointed by the board and one member appointed by the teachers' organisation (as defined). Such committee is endowed with the powers and authority (to summon witnesses and receive

f   evidence) which are conferred by the Commissions of Inquiry Act 1908 on commissions of inquiry. At the investigation the teacher is entitled to be represented by counsel or agent. Then the committee, after hearing the case, reports to the board and sends notes of the evidence. The teacher is given a copy of the report and of the notes of evidence. Then the board after considering the reports relating to the charge, the reply or explanation of the teacher, and the report and notes of evidence of the

g   committee decide whether they are satisfied as to the truth of the charge. If they are then they may caution or reprimand the teacher and may in addition impose one of the following penalties: transfer to another position (even one involving a lower salary) or peremptory dismissal (see sub-s (5)). If a teacher has been suspended and if the charge made against him is sustained he is not entitled to receive any salary or payment in respect of the suspension period except with the express approval of

h   the board (see sub-s (8)). If charges are not proved a teacher is allowed legal costs (see sub-s (10)). A teacher who is aggrieved by any finding of the board or any penalty it imposes on him under s 159 may appeal to the Teachers' Court of Appeal.

The provisions thus described and summarised prescribed comprehensively the procedure which had to be followed in cases where an 'offence' under s 158 was alleged. The present litigation relates to such alleged offences but at the relevant

j   time other provisions even more comprehensive and detailed had in reference to certain teachers taken the place of those in s 159 above referred to. This came about as the result of s 7 of the Education Amendment Act 1969 (No 66). That section provides as follows:

'Procedure for alleged offences by certain teachers—The principal Act is hereby amended by inserting, after section 161, the following section:

"161A. On the advice of the Minister, given on the joint recommendation of the organisation of teachers representing the majority of the teachers employed in any class or classes of schools or in specified positions and of the association or associations representing the Boards employing the teachers in the schools or positions, the Governor-General may from time to time, by Order in Council, make regulations for all or any of the following purposes in respect of the teachers so employed: (a) Prescribing the procedure to be adopted for the investigation, hearing, and determination of the charge in any case where it is alleged that a teacher so employed has committed an offence against section 158 of this Act: (b) Prescribing the penalties which may be imposed and the rights of appeal against those penalties where, under the procedure so prescribed for the investigation, hearing, and determination of a charge against a teacher, the charge against a teacher so employed is held to have been proved: (c) Prescribing to what extent and with what modifications the provisions of Part VI of this Act relating to appeals by teachers shall apply in the case of any right of appeal by a teacher for which provision is made under paragraph (b) of this section: (d) Declaring that the provisions of section 159 of this Act shall not apply to any teacher so employed".'

Pursuant to the power so given the Secondary and Technical Institute Teachers Disciplinary Regulations 1969 were made on 15th December 1969. It is important to have in mind that they were made not only on the advice of the Minister but on the joint recommendation of those representing teachers and of those representing boards employing teachers. The regulations define (see reg 3) the teachers to whom they apply. It is not in doubt that the present appellant was one. By reg 12 it is provided that s 159 of the Education Act 1964 shall not apply to any teacher to whom the regulations apply.

It is clear therefore that these substituted regulations prescribe 'the procedure to be adopted for the investigation, hearing and determination' of any charge that the appellant committed an offence under s 158. It is reasonable to suppose that the new elaborate procedure which it became obligatory to adopt was that which was jointly evolved by the Minister and those representing teachers and boards as being procedure which for all concerned (the public, the employing boards and the teachers employed) was considered to be fair.

The new regulations lay down procedure which much differs from that laid down by s 159. Disciplinary action by the board is curtailed. Their powers are restricted. If a charge of an offence under s 158 is made and if it is dealt with by the board their powers are limited (see reg 6). In cases not dealt with by the board (with their limited powers) the charge is referred to a body called the Teachers' Disciplinary Board and that body is comprised as set out in reg 7. But before a matter can even be referred to this body (which alone can impose the severer penalties provided by reg 10) there must be the interposition of the Director-General of Education. But furthermore and apart from all this there is a provision for a preliminary investigation of a complaint. Whereas under s 159 (1) when it is alleged that any teacher has committed an offence against s 158 the board must forthwith advise the teacher in writing of the full details of the charge and require him to state in writing whether he admits or denies the truth of the charge, in the new regulations the procedure is different. The following provision is contained in reg 4:

'Preliminary investigation of complaint—(1) Where a Board receives a complaint against a teacher, it shall, before taking any action in accordance with regulation 5 of these regulations, either appoint a person (who may be a member of the Board or any other person except an employee of the Board) to investigate the complaint or set up a sub-committee (which shall include a representative of the teachers' organisation) for that purpose.

a   '(2) The person so appointed or the sub-committee set up for the purpose shall undertake the investigation of the complaint at such time and place as the Board may determine, and shall, on completing the investigation, forward a report in writing to the Board which shall include any recommendation which the person or the sub-committee, as the case may be, thinks fit to make.'

This provision operates in the interests of teachers and may be a valuable protec-
b   tion for them. A complaint may be found to lack substance, or to be the product of idle tittle-tattle, or to be unrelated to any possible charge of an 'offence' against s 158, or otherwise to be such as not to warrant any action being taken. In such cases the result would be that a complaint received by a board need not involve even the making of a charge. The board also is greatly assisted. They have a responsibility both to pupils and parents and they cannot afford lightly to ignore a complaint about
c   a teacher that they receive. They will however not wish to take any action if a complaint can be regarded as frivolous or trifling. Nor would they wish that such a complaint should come to the knowledge of the teacher concerned. The screening process may however lead to the view, which may be embodied in a report, that the teacher may have committed an offence under s 158, e g that he is grossly inefficient or incompetent as a teacher. But whatever view is taken of the value of the process
d   of having a preliminary investigation of a complaint, what is of great significance is that in the new regulations, which are lengthy and detailed and in which, as will be seen, there are precise provisions as to the times when and the way in which a teacher can deal with any matter raised, there is no provision requiring any communication to or enquiry of a teacher if a preliminary investigation of a complaint is being made. This fact of itself throws light on the nature of the preliminary investigation and
e   strongly suggests that the intention was that it should be the means of eliminating complaints which need never mature into charges.

Regulation 5 lays down the procedure which the board is to follow if after receiving what is called a 'report on a complaint' it thinks that a teacher 'may' have committed an offence. The regulation is in the following terms:

f   'Procedure for alleged offences—(1) Where a Board, after receiving a report on a complaint against a teacher in accordance with regulation 4 of these regulations, has reason to believe that the teacher may have committed an offence to which section 158 of the Act applies, the Board shall forthwith advise the teacher in writing of the full details of the alleged offence, and may then suspend the teacher pending the determination of the matter in accordance with the following provisions of these regulations.

g   '(2) The teacher concerned shall, by notice in writing given by the Board and delivered to the teacher or sent to him by post in a registered letter addressed to him at his usual or last known place of residence, be required, within a reasonable time to be specified in the notice, to state in writing whether he admits or denies the truth of the charge, and to forward any explanation which he wishes to give relating to the charge.

h   '(3) The Board shall, in any notice forwarded to a teacher in accordance with subclause (2) of this regulation, inform the teacher that, if he so wishes, he may make a statement in person to the Board concerning the alleged offence and that, on informing the Board accordingly, he shall be heard at a time to be specified by the Board.

j   '(4) The Board, after considering any statement or explanation supplied by the teacher in accordance with subclause (2) of this regulation and any statement made in person by him in accordance with subclause (3) of this regulation, shall do one of the following: (a) Decide that no further action is to be taken in relation to the charge, in which case the teacher shall, if he has been suspended, be reinstated in his position and receive his full salary for the period of suspension: (b) Decide that the offence with which the teacher is charged shall be dealt with under regulation 6 of these regulations, in which case the provisions of that *a* regulation shall apply accordingly: (c) Decide that the charge should be referred to the Director-General for consideration as to whether or not it should be referred to the Teachers' Disciplinary Board for hearing and determination, in which case the Board shall then forward to the Director-General all particulars relating to the charge.

'(5) The Director-General, on receiving the particulars of a charge against a *b* teacher, including the findings of any preliminary investigation undertaken in accordance with regulation 4 of these regulations, shall, after considering those particulars, do one of the following: (a) Direct that no further action is to be taken in relation to the charge, in which case the teacher shall, if he has been suspended, be reinstated in his position and receive his full salary for the period of suspension: (b) Require that the offence with which the teacher is charged *c* shall be dealt with under regulation 6 of these regulations, in which case the Board shall so deal with the matter and the provisions of that regulation shall apply accordingly: (c) Refer the matter to the Teachers' Disciplinary Board for hearing and determination.'

The scheme of the regulation is that if, following the receipt of a complaint, and *d* after there has been a preliminary look at it either by a single person or by a sub-committee who will report on it, the board think that a teacher 'may' have committed an offence they then write to the teacher and give him full details. The board then has a discretion whether to suspend the teacher. But if they do, that can only be 'pending the determination of the matter'. Such determination will be according to the procedure laid down. Before there is any such 'determination' a teacher will be heard. The regulations draw a distinction between a complaint and a charge. A *e* complaint may be stillborn, but once there is a charge the correct course of procedure is prescribed. After being notified of the charge of an alleged offence the teacher must do one thing and may do others. He must in writing say whether he admits or denies the charge. He may forward any explanation that he wishes to give. Furthermore he may appear personally before the board and make a statement. The board will then consider everything that the teacher has wished to say and will adopt one *f* of three courses. They may decide that no further action need be taken. If the teacher had not been suspended he would just continue his work, which would not have been interrupted. If the teacher had been suspended he would be reinstated and his salary would be paid him for the suspension period. Another course open to the board would be to deal with the matter themselves within the limited and restricted powers given them by reg 6. Under that regulation if they are 'satisfied' *g* that the alleged offence has been proved all that they can do is to caution the teacher or reprimand him or censure him and if the offence which is proved to their satisfaction is that the teacher absented himself from his duties without leave or valid excuse the board may order that he do not receive his salary for a part or all of the period during which he was so absent. Another course open to the board (a course that would probably be adopted in the more serious cases) is to refer the charge to the *h* Director-General for him to consider whether or not the charge should be referred to the Teachers' Disciplinary Board 'for hearing and determination'. Even if that course is adopted it does not follow that the charge will go to the Teachers' Disciplinary Board; the Director-General may direct that no further action be taken or he may require the board to deal with the matter under reg 6.

Regulations 7, 8, 9 and 10 deal in great detail with the hearing and determination *i* of a charge which is referred to the Teachers' Disciplinary Board. That board has as its chairman a barrister or solicitor of not less than seven years' practice. He is appointed by the Minister of Education. One member is appointed by a teachers' organisation. One member is appointed by the 'Boards' Association'. The Teachers' Disciplinary Board 'for the purposes of the investigation of any charge referred to it for hearing and determination' has the same powers and authority to summon witnesses and receive evidence as are conferred on commissions of inquiry by the Commissions of Inquiry Act 1908. The contrast is very marked between the preliminary investigation of a complaint and the investigation of a charge for the purposes of a hearing and determination.

Before the Teachers' Disciplinary Board the Director-General (or someone whom he appoints to act on his behalf) presents the case against a teacher. The teacher may present his own case or be represented by counsel or agent (reg 8 (2)). The procedure to be followed is laid down in great detail (see reg 8 (3)). The Teachers' Disciplinary Board hears the teacher or his counsel or agent and any evidence he may wish to adduce but in the first place the case against the teacher is heard and any evidence that may be adduced. Evidence in rebuttal may be adduced by either party. After the evidence the Director-General may sum up and the teacher or his counsel or agent may sum up after that. Then if the Teachers' Disciplinary Board 'is satisfied from the evidence adduced at that hearing that the charge has been proved' it may, subject to a right of appeal which the teacher is given by the regulations, impose one of certain prescribed penalties. These are set out in reg 10. There may be a caution or a reprimand or censure. There may be a deduction from salary to a limited extent. There may be one of the two penalties (a direction to transfer or peremptory dismissal) which under s 159 (but not under the substituted regulations) can be imposed by the board governing the school. There is a special provision relating to cases where the offence charged is one of having been absent from duty without leave or valid excuse. If the Teachers' Disciplinary Board holds that a charge has not been proved the teacher is reinstated in his position and gets his full salary for any period for which he did not receive it; the reasonable legal and other costs which he has incurred and as determined by the disciplinary board are paid to him by the board governing his school. In other cases (other than where it is held that the charge is not proved) a teacher does not receive salary or payment in respect of a suspension period unless the Teachers' Disciplinary Board expressly determines otherwise. But whenever a charge is referred to the Teachers' Disciplinary Board a teacher is paid the actual and reasonable expenses which he incurs in attending the hearing of the charge.

Whether a charge has been dealt with under reg 6 by the school board or whether the charge has been heard by the Teachers' Disciplinary Board a teacher has a right of appeal from any finding that an offence has been proved and furthermore a right of appeal from any penalty imposed on him by either body (see reg 11). The appeal is to the Teachers' Court of Appeal which is constituted as set out in the Act and which has a magistrate as its chairman. The appeal is by way of rehearing and the court must hear or rehear all evidence that either party wishes to present; an appellant may himself appear or be represented by some other person. Sections 174 to 182 contain provisions in reference to the appeals and by s 175 any teacher who has received a notice of dismissal, suspension, or transfer, or of any other decision in respect of which under the Act he is entitled to appeal may within a stated time appeal to the Teachers' Court of Appeal.

With this outline review of the multi-tiered and elaborate code which governs and protects the interests of teachers the facts may now be stated which have culminated in this appeal. At the relevant time the appellant was a school teacher at Kamo High School near Whangarei. He had been employed as a teacher at that school since 1968. After graduating in 1957 (he is a Master of Arts of Cambridge University) and after teaching in the United Kingdom for two years he went to New Zealand in 1960; he was engaged by the New Zealand government to teach. For three years he taught at Gisborne Boys High School; he advanced in his teacher gradings from grade I to grade II. Then for four years he taught at Waikohu College at Te Karaka near Gisborne; he advanced in grading to grade III. At Kamo High School his grading became B12. In the year 1969 certain difficulties arose. The headmaster considered that he was failing to keep order in school. The headmaster suggested to the appellant that he should make application for teaching positions elsewhere. The appellant did so but without success. In the following year (1970) complaint was made about the appellant's conduct and the procedure laid down in the regulations was followed. A sub-committee was set up under the regulations and the committee investigated the complaint. A letter was then sent to the appellant and he was advised in regard to his obligations and rights (see reg 5 (1), (2) and (3)). The letter was in the following terms:

'Whangerei High Schools Board
35 Bank Street,
Whangarei
20th March 1970.

'Dear Mr. Furnell,

'A complaint has been made about your conduct at Kamo High School and has been investigated by a Committee set up under the Secondary and Technical Institute Teachers' Disciplinary Regulations 1969. You are charged with various offences under Section 158 of the Education Act 1964 in that:—

'1. You have been grossly inefficient or incompetent in the discharge of your professional duties having:—(a) Failed consistently to maintain reasonable order and discipline in your classroom. (b) Struck children on several occasions. (c) Allowed a state of uproar to arise and continue in your classroom to such an extent that work in neighbouring classrooms has been disrupted.

'2. You have failed to take reasonable care of school equipment in that you have allowed the furniture and cupboards in your room to be grossly defaced.

'3. In the course of your duties you have disobeyed, disregarded or made wilful default in carrying out instructions given by a person having authority to give them, in that you have failed to carry out the following school administrative duties:—(a) In that your class attendance register was not marked from December 1st to 11th 1969. (b) You have not taken a normal part in teacher activity in that you did not enter the staffroom for long intervals to hear notices and instructions to staff.

'4. By virtue of the occurrences set out above you are guilty of conduct in your capacity as a teacher which shows your unfitness to remain in your present position.

'You are accordingly suspended from your duties at Kamo High School as from today's date March 20th 1970 pending further determination of these charges. You are required by not later than 4 p.m. on Wednesday April 8th to state in writing whether you admit or deny the truth of these charges and to forward by this date and time any explanation relative to these charges which you may wish to give. You may if you so wish in addition to any such written statement make a statement in person to the Board concerning the alleged offences. If you wish to make any such statement you must advise the Board Secretary by not later than 4 p.m. on April 8th of your wish, and an interview will be arranged for you. We recommend that you obtain legal assistance in this matter.

Yours faithfully,
C. A. Reed
Chairman'

The appellant consulted solicitors, who wrote to the chairman of the school board on 25th March 1970. In addition to a denial of the charges or of guilt of any offence under s 158 a number of points were taken. It was set out that the appellant had received no prior indication of any investigation or of any charge; that no investigation by the committee could properly take place without that committee at least obtaining some explanation from the appellant; that further particulars as requested should be provided and that without them explanation of the charges was not possible; that having lacked particularity the charges were null and void; that the *a* regulations were completely ultra vires with the consequence that the board could not validly proceed against the appellant pursuant to them; that there had been a denial of natural justice; and that all legal rights were reserved. It was also said that if, but only if, the appellant could be represented by counsel would he make a statement in person as laid down by reg 5 (3). Otherwise he would rely on a written explanation pursuant to reg 5 (2).

b There followed a lengthy letter in reply from the chairman of the school board (dated 6th April 1970) giving full details of the charges. The first part of the letter related to the charge that the appellant was grossly inefficient or incompetent in discharging his duties in that he had consistently failed to maintain order and discipline in his classroom. In relation to this charge some 15 items were set out (ranging in date from March 1969 to March 1970) alleging lack of order and control, alleging *c* various occasions when pupils complained that they were hampered in their work by the failure of the appellant to keep order, alleging occasions when the principal had to enter the appellant's class to restore order, alleging complaint that noise from the appellant's classroom was disturbing the teaching in other rooms, and alleging occasions when the principal had interviewed the appellant and suggested that he should leave. Other parts of the letter set out a number of items in relation to the *d* charges under paras 1 (*b*), 2, 3 and 4 contained in the letter of 20th March.

On 20th April 1970 the appellant's solicitors sent a lengthy document to the chairman as the explanation of the appellant pursuant to reg 5 (2) and the solicitors (while reserving all legal rights) stated that as the appellant was not allowed to make a statement through his solicitor before the board the appellant relied on the explanation. In general the appellant denied each and every offence, pointed out that fourth *e* formers were most difficult to control and contended that the various incidents set out in the letter of 6th April were of a comparatively trivial nature.

Pursuant to reg 5 (4) (*c*) the board decided to refer the charges to the Director-General of Education. He in turn decided under reg 5 (5) (*c*) to refer the charges to the Teachers' Disciplinary Board 'for hearing and determination'. He notified the appellant to that effect by letter dated 29th May 1970. The hearing was fixed for *f* 30th June 1970 and the appellant was reminded that pursuant to reg 8 (2) he could either present his own case or be represented at the hearing by counsel or agent.

If the hearing had taken place and if the charges had not been proved the appellant would have been reinstated and would have received arrears of salary and would have received his costs and expenses. But the hearing never took place. The appellant chose litigation rather than a hearing. First, he brought proceedings both against the *g* High Schools Board and the members of the Teachers' Disciplinary Board. He alleged that there was a denial of natural justice on the part of the investigating sub-committee that had been appointed and alleged that as a consequence his suspension by the board was unlawful. He claimed an injunction directed to the High Schools Board 'removing the suspension and reinstating him to teaching duties'. Against the members of the Teachers' Disciplinary Board he claimed a writ of prohibition to prohibit them from *h* hearing and determining the charges. Secondly, some two months later, i e on 2nd September 1970, he filed a motion for a writ of certiorari against the High Schools Board to remove the decisions of the board into the Supreme Court for the purpose of quashing them. Complaint was made that the appellant had not been given an opportunity to make an explanation to the investigating sub-committee and had not seen or had the opportunity of replying to or commenting on their report.

i Both sets of proceedings were heard together by Speight J on 15th September 1970. He delivered judgment on 22nd October. In the first he gave an injunction against the High Schools Board requiring them to remove the suspension and a writ against the Teachers' Disciplinary Board prohibiting them from hearing the charges. In the second he ordered that a writ of certiorari issue 'removing all decisions of the board subsequent to receiving the report of the investigating committee into this court and quashing the same'. Speight J stated that his orders only related to the proceedings 'so far taken', with the result that the original complaints were kept alive for such proper proceedings as the High Schools Board might desire to take.

The High Schools Board appealed. It was agreed that pending the hearing of the appeal the appellant should not return to the school but he was paid his salary from the date of the judgment of Speight J. It was so paid until 1st February 1971. The appeal came on for hearing on 10th and 11th February 1971 but before those dates, i e on 1st February 1971, the appellant resigned from the employment of the board. The Court of Appeal delivered judgment on 19th March 1971 and allowed the appeal. From that judgment the appellant now appeals.

Before considering the main issues which are raised two matters call for mention. First, from the recital of the facts it will have been seen that 'full details' were not set out in the letter of 20th March 1970 although they were set out in the letter of 6th April 1970. In the proceedings before Speight J this matter was relied on by the appellant as involving that the respondents had acted in breach of the regulations; but the contention was not pressed in the Court of Appeal, and is not raised in the appellant's printed case. Secondly, on the hearing of this appeal a point was raised to the effect that as the appellant had not known that a sub-committee had been set up under reg 4 it could not have included 'a representative of the teachers' organisation'. This point would involve partly some questions of fact and partly an issue as to the meaning in reg 2 of the words:

' "Teachers' organisation", in relation to any teacher, means the New Zealand Post-Primary Teachers' Association or the Association of Teachers in Technical Institutes, whichever the teacher may nominate.'

As this point had not previously been raised either before Speight J or in the Court of Appeal, and had not either as to fact or law been considered, it was clear that it could not now be entertained. The appeal proceeded on the assumption that the sub-committee was properly constituted and that therefore it included a representative of the 'Teachers' organisation'.

As the appellant resigned on 1st February 1971 it is necessary to state what order he now seeks. As he is no longer in the employment of the board it was said that the revival of the order of injunction was inappropriate and the writ of prohibition against the Teachers' Disciplinary Board was not sought; what is sought however is the restoration of the issue of a writ of certiorari so as to quash all decisions of the board subsequent to receiving the report of the sub-committee. It will be observed that the point originally taken in correspondence that the regulations were ultra vires was not thereafter pursued.

The main contention advanced on behalf of the appellant is that the so-called rules of natural justice were at some stage not observed. It becomes necessary to analyse this complaint in order to ascertain against whom it is made. In argument it was the sub-committee that was much criticised. But in the result it was the action of the board that was mainly criticised. The criticism related to the decision to suspend. If there had been no suspension it is not clear whether criticism of the procedure followed would have been made.

Speight J in his judgment pointed to the difference between the committee designated by s 159 to investigate a charge and the sub-committee which may be appointed under reg 4. He said (correctly as their Lordships think):

'Under the 1969 Regulations the situation is quite different. Presumably to provide additional protection for the teachers, the committee or the individual is required only to investigate the complaint and not to determine it. Presumably the purpose of such an investigation is to ensure that the complaint is not trivial, malicious or, in some other way, demonstrably ill founded.'

The main reasoning of Speight J was that the board ought not to have suspended the appellant before his point of view was ascertained; Speight J regarded suspension as a *a* punishment even though it might be one of only temporary duration. His view was that the board had a duty to satisfy themselves that they had ascertained both sides of the matter in a preliminary way before deciding on suspension. In one passage in his judgment he said that where it is contemplated that suspension will take place—

b 'this should not be done unless under reg 4, the "investigation of the complaint" has included some reference to the teacher of the nature of the allegations made against him and a statement from him giving his version of the event if he wishes.'

This suggests that the sub-committee in the present case erred in not interviewing the appellant. In a later passage the learned judge said:

c 'I wish to make it clear that in the present case invalidity only attaches to such proceedings as took place in accordance with the board's letter of 20th March 1970, and subsequent actions.'

d Even if there is some ambiguity whether the sub-committee (who were not parties and were not heard) were being condemned, the main conclusion was that if the board had not had the view of the appellant made known to them in a report of the sub-committee as a result of an interview of the appellant by the sub-committee they (the board) should not have suspended the appellant until they themselves had had his comments in regard to the charges.

e On behalf of the appellant it was contended that he had a right to be heard by the sub-committee; alternatively it was contended that if he was not heard by the sub-committee he should have been heard by the board if they contemplated suspending him; the submission was not developed that he had a right to be heard both by the sub-committee and by the board before any decision to suspend was made. The contentions as to the nature of his right to be heard by the sub-committee were somewhat imprecise; it was contended that he should have heard the evidence if any received by the sub-committee and should have been allowed to put questions inform-

f ally (without his questioning developing into a formal cross-examination) and been allowed to give his version of the matters of complaint and to call witnesses if he so wished.

In support of these claims the rules of natural justice were invoked. It becomes necessary therefore to consider whether the detailed and elaborate code which prescribes the procedure to be followed when there is a suggestion of an offence

g under s 158 is a code which gives scope for unfairness and whether in its operation the court in the interests of fairness must supplement the written provisions. In the present case do the well-known words of Byles J in *Cooper v Wandsworth Board of Works*[1] apply, viz, '. . . although there are no positive words in a statute requiring that the party shall be heard, yet the justice of the common law will supply the omission of the legislature'? Or is the code one that has been carefully and deliber-

h ately drafted so as to prescribe procedure which is fair and appropriate? In whatever way the status of the appellant as a teacher is in law to be defined he agreed to serve under the conditions laid down in the regulations and unless some provisions are to be read into them or are incorporated in them it is clear that they were faithfully followed. It is not lightly to be affirmed that a regulation that has the force of law is unfair when it has been made on the advice of the responsible Minister and on the

j joint recommendation of organisations representing teachers employed and those employing. Nor is it the function of the court to redraft the code. As was said in *Brettingham-Moore v Municipality of St Leonards*[2]:

---

1 (1863) 14 CNBS 180 at 194
2 (1969) 121 CLR 509 at 524

'The legislature has addressed itself to the very question and it is not for the
Court to amend the statute by engrafting upon it some provision which the
Court might think more consonant with a complete opportunity for an aggrieved
person to present his views and to support them by evidentiary material.'

It has often been pointed out that the conceptions which are indicated when natural
justice is invoked or referred to are not comprised within and are not to be confined
within certain hard and fast and rigid rules (see the speeches in *Wiseman v Borne-*
man[1]). Natural justice is but fairness writ large and juridically. It has been described
as 'fair play in action'. Nor is it a leaven to be associated only with judicial or quasi-
judicial occasions. But as was pointed out by Tucker LJ in *Russell v Duke of Norfolk*[2]
the requirements of natural justice must depend on the circumstances of each
particular case and the subject-matter under consideration.

The significance of what was said by Tucker LJ is illustrated when it is seen how
divergent have been the situations in certain reported cases and how different they
were from those in the present case. Thus *R v Gaming Board for Great Britain, ex parte*
Benaim[3] concerned the situation of a gaming board who have to make enquiries about
an intending applicant for a licence and who receive information from various sources.
A certificate of consent from the Gaming Board is necessary before there can be an
application to justices for a licence. What procedure therefore should the Gaming
Board follow to avoid the risk that a certificate of consent may be refused for reasons
which the would-be applicant could displace if he knew of them? The situation in
Re K (H) (an infant)[4] concerned the opportunity which should be given to an immi-
grant to satisfy the immigration officer of certain matters laid down by statute.
Re Pergamon Press Ltd[5] related to a Board of Trade investigation under the Companies
Act 1948 and to the duties of inspectors. Their role differed materially from that of the
sub-committee in the present case. Their function was inquisitorial and they could
if they thought fit make findings of fact. They were under a duty to report to the
Board of Trade and were obliged to send a copy of their report to the company
concerned. In the result the report might be made public and on the basis of it
proceedings against a director might be instituted. Lord Denning MR said[6]:

'The inspectors can obtain information in any way which they think best, but
before they condemn or criticise a man, they must give him a fair opportunity
for correcting or contradicting what is said against him.'

By comparison the sub-committee in cases such as the present one do not either condemn or criticise. They merely report in regard to a complaint and if at a later date
there follows a charge the code lays down specifically when and how the teacher has
opportunity to deal with the charge. While (bearing in mind what Tucker LJ said[7])
no complete or precise analogy with the situation in the present case is to be sought,
the words of Lord Reid in *Wiseman v Borneman*[8] are apposite:

'Every public officer who has to decide whether to prosecute or raise proceedings ought first to decide whether there is a prima facie case but no one supposes
that justice requires that he should first seek the comments of the accused or the
defendant on the material before him.'

---

1 [1969] 3 All ER 275, [1971] AC 297
2 [1949] 1 All ER 109 at 118
3 [1970] 2 All ER 528, [1970] 2 QB 417
4 [1967] 1 All ER 226, [1967] 2 QB 617
5 [1970] 3 All ER 535, [1971] Ch 388
6 [1970] 3 All ER at 539, [1971] Ch at 399, 400
7 In *Russell v Duke of Norfolk* [1949] 1 All ER at 118
8 [1969] 3 All ER at 277, 278, [1971] AC at 308

In *Pearlberg v Varty (Inspector of Taxes)*[1] there was an application to a general commissioner for leave to raise certain assessments and it was held, on a construction of s 6 of the Income Tax Management Act 1964, that the application for leave was intended to be ex parte and that the function of the commissioner in deciding whether or not to grant leave was an administrative one and that natural justice did not require that the taxpayer should have the right to be heard. In his speech Lord Hailsham of St Marylebone LC said[2]:

'It is true, of course, that the courts will lean heavily against any construction of a statute which would be manifestly unfair. But they have no power to amend or supplement the language of a statute merely because on one view of the matter a subject feels himself entitled to a larger degree of say in the making of a decision than the statute accords him. Still less is it the functioning of the courts to form first a judgment on the fairness of an Act of Parliament and then to amend or supplement it with new provisions so as to make it conform to that judgment.'

Viscount Dilhorne having cited what Lord Reid said in *Wiseman v Borneman*[3] said[4]:

'I would only emphasise that one should not start by assuming that what Parliament has done in the lengthy process of legislation is unfair. One should rather assume that what has been done is fair until the contrary is shown. And Parliament thought it fair that the person affected should have the right to be heard where leave was sought under s 51 of the Finance Act 1960 and have the right to make representations to the tribunal under s 28 of that Act. The omission so to provide in s 6 of the Income Tax Management Act 1964, cannot, as I have said, in my opinion be regarded as anything other than deliberate and, if deliberate, it should be assumed that Parliament did not think that the requirements of fairness made it advisable to provide any such rights for the person affected. If this was the view of Parliament, it would require a very strong case to justify the addition to the statute of requirements to meet one's own opinion of fairness.'

Lord Pearson in reference to the principles of natural justice said[5]:

'A tribunal to whom judicial or quasi-judicial functions are entrusted, is held to be required to apply those principles in performing those functions, unless there is a provision to the contrary. But where some person or body is entrusted by Parliament with administrative or executive functions, there is no presumption that compliance with the principles of natural justice is required, although, as "Parliament is not to be presumed to act unfairly", the courts may be able in suitable cases (perhaps always) to imply an obligation to act with fairness. Fairness, however, does not necessarily require a plurality of hearings or representations and counter-representations.'

The whole scheme of the regulations and of the provisions of the Education Act 1964 points to the conclusion that the task of the person or sub-committee appointed under reg 4 is to give consideration to a complaint with a view to presenting a report to the board (ie the governing body of the school in question). Their finding may be that the complaint could be ignored as being mischievous or irresponsible. Their finding on the other hand may be that the complaint might have substance and

---

1   [1972] 2 All ER 6, [1972] 1 WLR 534
2   [1972] 2 All ER at 11, [1972] 1 WLR at 540
3   [1969] 3 All ER at 277, [1971] AC at 308
4   [1972] 2 All ER at 15, 16, [1972] 1 WLR at 545
5   [1972] 2 All ER at 17, [1972] 1 WLR at 547

could not be ignored. The absence of any provision relating to making a communication to the teacher concerned must have been deliberate since the regulations proceed with great particularity to specify when and how communication should be made to him and when and how he should make response. The procedure for the preliminary investigation of a complaint before ever there is a charge is procedure which must have been devised as an additional safeguard for teachers. If those investigating a complaint thought in any particular circumstances that it would be desirable for them to ask a teacher to see them with a view to seeking his explanation of some matter it would be open to them to take that course. There might be some relatively straightforward issue capable of explanation or some situation which may have resulted from a misunderstanding. Those investigating in the exercise of their discretion would do what was reasonable. But if they thought that a complaint (as for example a complaint of sustained and continuing inefficiency) could not be so simply disposed of and could really only be dealt with under the subsequent procedure as laid down there would be nothing unfair in their reporting to such effect without communicating with the teacher concerned. Certainly in the present case there are no grounds for holding that the sub-committee acted unfairly. When the nature of the detailed and formulated charges in this case and of the lengthy and detailed comments of the appellant are considered it seems reasonably clear that matters could not possibly have been disposed of without some kind of inquiry extending very much beyond any form of preliminary investigation of complaints.

There is a marked contrast in the regulations between a complaint and a charge. So also is there a contrast between investigating a complaint before ever there is a charge and a 'determination of the matter' (see reg 5 (1)), which is the investigation of a charge. One of the principles of natural justice is that a man should not be condemned unheard. But the sub-committee do not condemn. Nor do they criticise.

In the present case the terms of the report of the sub-committee are not known. On behalf of the appellant it was first suggested and in his written case it is claimed that he had been entitled to see the report; that suggestion was not pursued. There is neither condemnation nor criticism of a person if it is found that there are matters calling for determination under a scheme of procedure which amply provides (1) that before there can be any adverse finding a person must know what charge is alleged and (2) must have opportunity to answer the charge and (3) that before those dealing with the charge can condemn to punish they must be satisfied of guilt and (4) that their decision is subject to an appeal by way of rehearing. In their Lordships' view the scheme of the procedure gives no scope for action which can properly be described as unfair and there are no grounds for thinking that the sub-committee acted unfairly.

It is next necessary to consider whether there was any unfairness on the part of the board, as was strongly suggested in the submissions made on behalf of the appellant. Although the board followed faithfully the directions of the regulations it is said that nevertheless they should give a teacher an opportunity of being heard before they decide to suspend. Neither in the regulations nor in the Act is suspension classified as a penalty. Section 157 (3) shows that it is not. It must however be recognised that suspension may involve hardship. During suspension salary is not paid and apart from this something of a temporary slur may be involved if a teacher is suspended. But the regulations (by reg 5) clearly contemplate or lay it down that the written statement of a teacher (under reg 5 (2)) and the oral personal statement (under reg 5 (3)) will be made after suspension if any has taken place. Suspension is discretionary. Decisions whether to suspend will often be difficult. Members of a board who are appointed or elected to act as the governing body of a school must in the exercise of their responsibilities have regard not only to the interests of teachers but to the interests of pupils and of parents and of the public. There may be occasions when having regard to the nature of a charge it will be wise, in the interests of all a concerned, that pending decision whether the charge is substantiated a teacher should be suspended from duty. In many cases it can be assumed that charges would be denied and that only after a full hearing could the true position be ascertained. It is not to be assumed that a board, constituted as it is, will wantonly exercise its discretion. Furthermore a teacher knows that under the terms governing his employment if charges are made and are to be investigated a suspension 'pending the determination of the matter' may take place. In the present case because of the course adopted by

b the appellant it cannot be known whether on 30th June 1970 the Teachers' Disciplinary Board would or would not have found the charges proved, but there is no warrant for supposing that the board (the governing body of the school) acted irresponsibly or unfairly in exercising their discretion to suspend in a case in which one matter for enquiry was whether a teacher was continuously failing to keep order and was allowing a state of uproar in his classrooms to continue. In their Lordships' view the

c procedure laid down in reg 5 is not unfair and there are no grounds for thinking that the board acted unfairly.

Their Lordships are in full agreement with the judgments delivered in the Court of Appeal. It becomes unnecessary to consider whether had the appellant been successful he would have been entitled to relief in the form that he sought.

d For the reasons set out above their Lordships will humbly advise Her Majesty that the appeal be dismissed.

Dissenting judgment of **VISCOUNT DILHORNE** *concurred in by* **LORD REID.**
By a letter dated 20th March 1970 the appellant, then employed by the respondent board and who had in 1960 been brought out to New Zealand as a teacher,

e was notified by the chairman of the respondent board that a complaint had been made about his conduct as a teacher at Kamo High School and that it had been investigated by a committee set up under the Secondary and Technical Institute Teachers Disciplinary Regulations 1969; that he was charged with three offences under s 158 of the Education Act 1964, namely (1) with having been grossly inefficient or incompetent in the discharge of his professional duties in that he had (a) failed con-

f sistently to maintain reasonable order and discipline in his classroom, (b) struck children on several occasions and (c) allowed a state of uproar to arise and continue in his classroom to such an extent that work in neighbouring classrooms had been disrupted; (2) with having failed to take reasonable care of school equipment in that he had allowed the furniture and cupboards in his room to be grossly defaced; and (3) that in the course of his duties he had disobeyed, disregarded or made wilful

g default in carrying out instructions in that he had failed to mark his class attendance register from 1st December to 11th December 1969 and had failed to take a normal part in teacher activity by not entering the staffroom for long intervals to 'hear notices and instructions to staff'.

The letter alleged that he had been guilty of conduct which showed his unfitness to remain in his position and stated that he was as from 20th March 1970 suspended

h from his duties. While suspended, he was not entitled to any remuneration. The letter required him to state whether he admitted or denied the charges and to forward any explanation he might wish to give by 8th April. He was also told that if he wished he might make a personal statement to the board. The letter ended by advising him to obtain legal assistance.

On 3rd October 1969 the appellant had been seen by the principal of the school

j and told that he was not teaching effectively and that he should resign. The appellant agreed to apply for positions elsewhere but had not by 20th March 1970 succeeded in obtaining one. The appellant, who was not told that his conduct was being investigated by a committee appointed under the disciplinary regulations, was not asked by the committee to appear before them and was given no opportunity by the committee of answering the allegations made against him. The committee made no attempt to find out what he had to say.

Apart from alleging failure to mark the class attendance register, the letter of 20th
March gave no indication of the dates and events on which the charges were based. *a*
On 25th March 1970 the appellant's solicitors asked for information as to them and
on 6th April the chairman of the board in a long letter gave details of numerous
incidents extending from 4th November 1968 to 2nd February 1970. That was the
first intimation that the appellant had of the occasions and events on which the
charges were based. Prior to the receipt of the letter of 6th April, he was consequently not in a position to offer any explanation, and he was required to furnish *b*
one by 8th April.

In the circumstances it is perhaps not surprising that the appellant should complain
that he was treated unfairly by the board and by the committee appointed by the
board in suspending him without pay and imposing on him the stigma which suspension brings, without having been told of the allegations made against him and
without being given any opportunity by the committee or by the board of answer- *c*
ing the case against him before he was suspended. Counsel for the respondent board
agreed that the investigating committee was under a duty to act fairly. The board
was also under a duty to do so.

In *Re Pergamon Press Ltd*[1] where two inspectors had been appointed under s 165 (*b*)
of the Companies Act 1948 to investigate the affairs of Pergamon Press Ltd and
report thereon, Lord Denning MR, after pointing out that their report might accuse *d*
some and condemn others, that it might ruin reputations and careers and might
lead to judicial proceedings, said[2]:

> 'Seeing that their work and their report may lead to such consequences, I
> am clearly of opinion that the inspectors must act fairly. This is a duty which
> rests on them, as on many other bodies, although they are not judicial, nor *e*
> quasi-judicial, but only administrative; see *R v Gaming Board for Great Britain,
> ex parte Benaim*[3]. The inspectors can obtain information in any way which
> they think best, but before they condemn or criticise a man, they must give him
> a fair opportunity for correcting or contradicting what is said against him. They
> need not quote chapter and verse. An outline of the charge will usually suffice.' *f*

I do not take Lord Denning MR's last sentence to mean that it will suffice to tell a
man what charges are being preferred against him, as in the letter of 20th March, but
as meaning that he must be given an outline of the case against him so that he knows
what is being said against him sufficiently to have a fair opportunity of correcting or
contradicting it.

In *De Verteuil v Knaggs*[4] where under an Immigration Ordinance the Governor *g*
of Trinidad had power 'on sufficient ground shown to his satisfaction' to transfer
the indentures of immigrants from one employer to another, it was held that this
power could not be properly exercised without inquiry and Lord Parmoor delivering
the judgment of the Board which consisted of Earl Loreburn, Lord Dunedin, Lord
Sumner and himself, said[5]:

h

> 'Their Lordships are of opinion that in making such an inquiry there is, apart
> from special circumstances, a duty of giving to any person against whom a
> complaint is made a fair opportunity to make any relevant statement which
> he may desire to bring forward and a fair opportunity to correct or controvert
> any relevant statement brought forward to his prejudice.'

j

---

1   [1970] 3 All ER 535, [1971] Ch 388
2   [1970] 3 All ER at 539, [1971] Ch at 399, 400
3   [1970] 2 All ER 528, [1970] 2 QB 417
4   [1918] AC 557
5   [1918] AC at 560

a He gave an instance of a special circumstance which might justify the governor taking action without giving the person affected such an opportunity, an emergency when promptitude was of importance.

Only after the board has received the report of the committee and if they have reason to believe that an offence against s 158 of the Education Act 1964 may have been committed, can they suspend a teacher to whom the disciplinary regulations

b apply. As the board suspended the appellant and charged him with offences against s 158 after receiving the committee's report, it can be assumed that that report was adverse to the appellant and accused him of committing the offences charged by the board. The committee may also have recommended his suspension.

In the light of Lord Denning MR's observations quoted above[1] and what was said in *De Verteuil v Knaggs*[2], in my opinion the investigating committee and the board acted unfairly and contrary to natural justice in not giving the appellant an

c opportunity of answering the case against him before he was suspended.

The proceedings of an investigating committee can be quite informal. If their investigation leads them to the conclusion that the complaints against a teacher are unjustified, and they propose so to report to the board, there is no need for them to communicate with the teacher before they report. If, however, they are minded

d to report adversely on the teacher, and a fortiori if they are thinking of recommending his suspension, the committee must before they report, to be fair, give the teacher an opportunity to put his case; and to enable him to do so, must tell him the case against him with sufficient particularity to enable him to counter it either in writing or orally. If they do not do so, the board will not get a proper picture of the case.

It must have been apparent to the board when they received the committee's report that the committee had not done so. There was no great urgency. Before

e suspending him the board could have given him an opportunity of stating his case or have remitted the matter to the committee for them to do so. In failing to take this course, the board in my opinion acted unfairly. Instead of doing so, the letter of 20th March was written. That letter gave him an opportunity after he had been suspended of tendering an explanation or of making an oral statement to the board

f but that letter did not tell him the case against him with sufficient particularity to enable him to answer it.

It was, however, contended by counsel for the respondent board that the disciplinary regulations did not provide for the giving of any such opportunity to an accused teacher; that the regulations formed a complete code and that consequently it was not right to import into them a duty on the part of the committee and of the board to furnish such an opportunity. In relation to this contention it is necessary to

g consider the regulations in some detail, and the background to them; to consider whether they do not, in fact, when properly construed, provide for the giving of such an opportunity by the committee; and, if they do not, whether the regulations clearly show an intention to exclude that which natural justice would otherwise require.

The Education Act 1964 itself contained a disciplinary code applying to teachers. If a teacher is charged with a criminal offence carrying a maximum punishment of

h not less than two years' imprisonment, the board which employs him may suspend him but if the board do not think that pending the hearing of the charge he should be suspended but that he should be removed from his position, they may transfer him to other duties (s 157). So even when a serious criminal charge is preferred, suspension is not automatic.

j Section 158 specifies conduct on the part of a teacher which constitutes 'an offence against this section' and s 159 prescribed the procedure that must be followed when it is alleged that an offence against s 158 has been committed. Presumably in the majority of, if not all, cases the allegation will be made by the board which employs

---

1   [1970] 3 All ER at 539, [1971] Ch at 399, 400
2   [1918] AC 557

the teacher. When such an allegation is made, the board must forthwith advise the teacher in writing of the 'full details of the charge against him' and require him to state within a specified time whether he admits or denies the truth of the charge. If the board decide to proceed with the charge, they must refer the matter to a committee of three, appointed by them, of whom one must be a representative of a teachers' organisation nominated by the teacher accused. That committee is given the powers and authority with regard to summoning witnesses and receiving evidence that are given to a commission of inquiry by the Commissions of Inquiry Act 1908. The committee 'after hearing the case' has to send its report to the board together with notes of the evidence received at the inquiry. Copies of the report and the notes of evidence have to be given to the accused teacher. Then if the board after considering the report of the committee and the notes of evidence and reports relating to the charge, and also 'the reply or explanation, if any, furnished by the teacher' (the section makes no express provision for such a reply or explanation), 'is satisfied as to the truth of the charge' they may caution or reprimand the teacher or transfer him to another post at an equivalent or lower salary or peremptorily dismiss him.

Section 159 (7) provides that any teacher against whom a charge is made under s 159 may, pending the hearing and determination of the charge, be suspended or transferred by the board and s 159 (8) provides that at any inquiry or investigation held under the section the teacher shall be entitled to be represented by counsel or agent.

Several matters are to be noted about this section: (1) a teacher may be suspended directly a charge is made and without any investigation before the charge is made; (2) the committee, which has the powers of a commission of inquiry, nevertheless exercises judicial or quasi-judicial functions; s 159 (3) refers to the hearing of the case and s 159 (7) to the hearing and determination of the charge; (3) although it is expressly provided that he may be represented at any inquiry or investigation, the section does not in terms provide that a teacher shall be entitled to give evidence or call witnesses or that the witnesses against him may be cross-examined; (4) after the committee has reported, the section does not provide for any further investigation by the board. If satisfied after considering the reports, the notes of evidence and the reply or explanation, if any, furnished by the teacher, of the truth of the charge the board can impose penalties; and (5) there is no provision for repayment of salary lost during suspension if the board is not satisfied of the truth of the charge although s 159 (8) provides that save with the express approval in writing of the board, he shall not receive any salary for that period 'if the charge made against him is sustained on inquiry or investigation as hereinbefore provided'.

In establishing this code of procedure in the Education Act 1964, the intention must have been to create a code that was fair. That one is entitled to assume. No one could regard a code as fair which did not allow an accused teacher proper opportunities of making his defence to the charge preferred against him and yet the section makes no express provision for that although it does for his representation.

Section 159 (3) commences with the words 'In any case where the Board decides to proceed with the charge it shall refer the matter for investigation . . .' What is meant in this context by investigation? Surely not just hearing the evidence in support of the charge, the evidence for the prosecution. If, as I think, investigation by the committee in the context means hearing both sides, allowing both sides to call witnesses and to cross-examine and allowing the teacher to give evidence if he wishes, then the section gives the accused teacher those rights which natural justice requires an accused person to have. But if I am wrong about this and investigation is not to be so interpreted, natural justice requires those rights to be imported.

As was said in *Wiseman v Borneman*[1]:

---

1   [1969] 3 All ER 275 at 277, [1971] AC 297 at 308, per Lord Reid

a
'Natural justice requires that the procedure before any tribunal which is acting judicially shall be fair in all the circumstances . . . For a long time the courts have, without objection from Parliament, supplemented procedure laid down in legislation where they have found that to be necessary for this purpose. But before this unusual kind of power is exercised it must be clear that the statutory procedure is insufficient to achieve justice and that to require additional steps would not frustrate the apparent purpose of the legislation.'

b
If I am wrong in giving this content to the word 'investigation', then it cannot be said that to import those rights for an accused person would frustrate the purpose of the Education Act 1964.

The appellant was not dealt with under s 159. He was proceeded against under the disciplinary regulations made on 15th December 1969 as he was a teacher to

c
whom they applied. The language of those regulations is clearly modelled on the provisions of the Act and if, as I think, the investigation by a committee appointed in accordance with the Act necessarily involves hearing both sides and the accused having the rights to which I have referred, it is unlikely that investigation by a committee under the regulations was intended to have a different meaning. Those regulations were made under s 161A of the Education Act 1964, a section inserted in that

d
Act by the Education Amendment Act 1969. That section gave the Governor-General power 'on the advice of the Minister, given on the joint recommendation of the organisation of teachers . . . and of the association or associations representing the Boards employing the teachers' to make regulations applying to teachers in any class or classes of schools prescribing the procedure to be adopted for 'the investigation, hearing and determination of' a charge under s 158 and declaring that s 159 should

e
not apply to those teachers.

On 15th December 1969 the Secondary and Technical Institute Teachers Disciplinary Regulations were made in the exercise of this power. They provided that s 159 should not apply in relation to teachers to whom the regulations applied. The procedure established by the regulations differed in a number of important respects from that under s 159. They provide that there must be a preliminary

f
investigation of a complaint against a teacher either by a person appointed by the board or by a sub-committee of the board; that that person or the sub-committee (as in this case it was a sub-committee, reference will only be made to a sub-committee) 'shall undertake the investigation of the complaint at such time and place as the Board may determine'; and that on completion of the investigation, the sub-committee has to report in writing to the board and that that report shall include

g
any recommendation which the sub-committee thinks fit to make (reg 4).

The provision that the board is to fix a time and place for the investigation indicates that there has to be a hearing. The sub-committee may recommend what action should be taken. They could if they thought fit recommend suspension and also peremptory dismissal. What their report contained in this case and what recommendation they made is not known for under the regulations a copy of the report

h
of the investigating committee is not required to be supplied to the teacher as it is under s 159.

If a board after receiving the report has reason to believe that an offence against s 158 may have been committed the board must forthwith advise the teacher in writing 'of the full details of the alleged offence'. They may then suspend the teacher pending the determination of the matter. The teacher is to be required to say

j
whether he admits or denies the truth of the charge and to put forward any explanation he wishes within a specified time and told that if he wishes he may make a personal statement to the board. Then, after considering any such statement or explanation, the board may decide to take no further action, or 'that the offence . . . shall be dealt with under Regulation 6', or to refer the charge to the Director-General for consideration as to whether or not it should be referred to the Teachers' Disciplinary Board 'for hearing and determination' (reg 5).

It is only after the teacher has received full details of the alleged offence, that any
express provision is made in the regulations for his giving an explanation or making
a statement and his suspension may precede that.

Merely telling the teacher what charges have been preferred, as did the letter
of 20th March, is not giving him full details of the alleged offences and not providing
him with sufficient information to enable him to have a fair opportunity of making
an explanation or statement about them. The appellant did not receive full details
of the alleged offences until he got the letter of 6th April. Although in the statement of claim the point was taken that his suspension was invalid as the condition
precedent to suspension, the furnishing of full details of the alleged offences, had not
been complied with, and was advanced in argument before Speight J who decided
in the appellant's favour on other grounds, it was not raised in the Court of Appeal
or in the appellant's printed case. Counsel for the respondent board contends that it is
now not open to the appellant and that in my opinion is the case. If it had been
open, it might have been necessary to consider whether an invalid suspension could
be validated by the giving of full details later, by the letter of 6th April.

If the case is referred to the Teachers' Disciplinary Board which 'for the purpose
of the investigation of any charge referred to it for hearing and determination' is
given the powers of a commission of inquiry conferred by the Commissions of Inquiry
Act 1908, detailed provisions for the hearing and determination of the charge are
made in reg 8. The teacher is entitled to present his own case or to be represented
at the hearing by counsel or agent. After hearing the case against the teacher,
the disciplinary board has then to hear the teacher charged or his counsel or agent
and any evidence he may wish to adduce. If he is found guilty, the disciplinary
board may impose penalties ranging from a caution, reprimand or censure to peremptory dismissal (reg 10). If the board decides that the case shall be dealt with
under reg 6, the board 'may (if satisfied that the alleged offence has been proved)
caution, reprimand, or censure the teacher'.

Unlike reg 8, reg 6 contains no provisions for the investigation, hearing and determination of the charge. It says that if the board is satisfied that the charge has been
proved, it may do certain things. This regulation appears to envisage that the board
may be so satisfied after considering the report of the sub-committee and any explanation or statement made by the teacher, and to reflect s 159 (5) which provides that a
board after considering the reports therein mentioned and the reply or explanation,
if any, of the teacher, may, if satisfied of the truth of the charge, do certain things.
If this is right, then it leads to an important conclusion. Where a charge is dealt
with under reg 6, the only investigation may be by the sub-committee under reg 4.
It is then an investigation preliminary to further action but not to a further investigation and hearing such as must take place if the case goes to the Teachers' Disciplinary
Board.

It must have been thought that the regulations improved the position of the teachers
to whom they applied. If, however, the contention of counsel for the respondent
board is right, their position was worse than it was under the Education Act 1964
for they can be reprimanded and censured by the board without having had an
opportunity of putting forward their defence and of calling witnesses. That result
cannot have been intended. That the disciplinary regulations contain a detailed disciplinary code is not disputable. That it is a complete code is. Regulation 8 does not
give an accused teacher the right to cross-examine. There is no provision for repayment to him of salary he has lost while suspended if the board decide to take no
further action although there is if he is acquitted by a Teachers' Disciplinary Board.

Merely to have had an opportunity of making a statement or giving an explanation
after he has been criticised or condemned by the sub-committee, criticism that may
lead to his immediate suspension and to his being censured by the board without any
further inquiry, is no substitute for an opportunity to put forward his defence and to
call witnesses. The opportunity to make a statement and to give an explanation

a   after condemnation by a sub-committee is, where the board deals with the case under reg 6, analogous to a prisoner being asked whether he has anything to say before he is sentenced.

As I have said, in my opinion s 159, when it speaks of an investigation by a committee, means that it is the duty of the committee to go into the matter thoroughly and to hear not just one side but both sides, if the teacher wants to be heard. A sub-committee appointed by a board, the teacher's employers under the regulations, *b*   is in my view under a similar duty. Investigation under s 159 and under reg 4 has the same meaning. The investigation by a Teachers' Disciplinary Board involves hearing both sides and resembles a trial. The investigation by a sub-committee is not the trial of the case where it is referred to a disciplinary board but it may be the only 'trial', if my construction of the regulations is right, that an accused teacher has if his case is dealt with under reg 6.

c   In my opinion the sub-committee failed to discharge the duty imposed on them by reg 4 by not giving the appellant an opportunity of being heard by them and so, in my opinion, this appeal should be allowed.

If, however, the reference to investigation in reg 4 does mean only that the case in support of the complaints is to be investigated and does not mean that the teacher's *d*   answer, if he wishes to put one forward, must also be investigated, and so that he must be given an opportunity of putting forward his answer, then in my opinion the appeal should also be allowed, for natural justice requires this duty to be read into the regulations. To do so would not frustrate their purpose. It would implement it. I see nothing in the regulations to suggest that what natural justice requires was deliberately excluded.

e   The function of a sub-committee, if it may lead to a board censuring a teacher without any further inquiry, although a further investigation must take place before he is censured by a Teachers' Disciplinary Board, is not comparable with the preparation of a case by the prosecution.

It is not in this case necessary to decide whether the function of the sub-committee is to be described as judicial, quasi-judicial or administrative. I am inclined to think *f*   that it is at least quasi-judicial, but if it be administrative, it was the duty of the sub-committee before they condemned or criticised the appellant 'to give him a fair opportunity of commenting or contradicting what is said against him'. That they did not do.

For these reasons in my opinion this appeal should be allowed.

g   *Appeal dismissed.*

Solicitors: *Slaughter & May* (for the appellant); *Allen & Overy* (for the respondent board).

S A Hatteea Esq   Barrister.

The News of the World Ltd v Friend

HOUSE OF LORDS

LORD HAILSHAM OF ST MARYLEBONE LC, LORD REID, LORD MORRIS OF BORTH-Y-GEST, LORD SIMON OF GLAISDALE AND LORD CROSS OF CHELSEA

29th, 30th NOVEMBER 1972, 31st JANUARY 1973

Gaming – Prize competition – Forecast of result of future event – Newspaper competition – Spot-the-Ball – Competitors marking position of football on photograph – Winning position selected by panel – Whether forecasts of result of future event involved – Betting, Gaming and Lotteries Act 1963, s 47 (1) (a) (i).

N Ltd conducted in their newspaper a competition called Spot-the-Ball, for which prizes were offered. The entry form in the newspaper contained a photograph taken during an actual football match, showing several players in action. The ball, which had appeared in the original of the photograph, was eliminated from the reproduction of it in the entry form. Competitors were instructed to use their skill and judgment to decide from all the information contained in the picture the spot where they thought the centre of the ball was most likely to be and to indicate that spot by marking a cross on the picture. They were informed that every entry would be examined carefully and that the newspaper's panel of football experts would select the entry in which, in their opinion, the centre of the cross, bearing in mind all the circumstances, most accurately represented the most logical position of the ball. N Ltd were charged with conducting in their newspaper a competition in which prizes were offered for 'forecasts of the result of a future event', contrary to s 47 (1) (a) (i)[a] of the Betting, Gaming and Lotteries Act 1963. The 'event', it was alleged by the prosecution, was the consideration of the entries by the panel of experts, 'the result of that event' the decision of the experts and the submission of entries by the competitors 'the forecasts of the result of that event'.

Held – (Lord Simon of Glaisdale dissenting)—No offence had been committed under s 47 (1) (a) (i) for (i) in the context of that subsection the words 'forecast', 'result' and 'event' had to be given their ordinary and natural meaning and not the artificial meaning attributed to them by the prosecution and (ii) on the evidence it was clear (a) that nothing was or was intended to be forecast by the entrants to the competition; all that an entrant was doing was to use his skill to arrive at the most logical result, and that did not mean that he was 'forecasting' the experts' decision simply because he arrived at the same result, and (b) the deliberations of the panel could not be described as an 'event' within the meaning of the subsection (see p 427 h and j, p 429 e, p 430 f, p 431 f and h, p 433 c to f, p 438 g to j and p 439 b, post).

Ladbroke (Football) Ltd v Perrett [1971] 1 All ER 129 overruled.

Semble. A 'Spot-the-Ball' competition in which the winning competitor is the one whose cross most accurately represents the actual position of the ball in the original photograph would not infringe s 47 (1) (a) (ii) of the 1963 Act (see p 426 d and e, p 429 f to h, p 431 j to p 432 a and p 439 c to e, post).

Notes

For competitions promoted through newspapers, see 18 Halsbury's Laws (3rd Edn) 199, para 391, and for cases on the subject, see 25 Digest (Repl) 510, 610-612.

---

[a] Section 47 (1) is set out at p 424 c and d, post

a For the Betting, Gaming and Lotteries Act 1963, s 47, see 14 Halsbury's Statutes (3rd Edn) 591.

Cases referred to in opinions

Barclay v Pearson [1893] 2 Ch 154, 62 LJCh 636, 3 R 388; sub nom *Barclay v Pearson, Oppler v Pearson* 68 LT 709, 25 Digest (Repl) 511, *614*.

b *Caminada v Hulton* (1891) 60 LJMC 116, 64 LT 572, 55 JP 727, 17 Cox CC 307, DC, 25 Digest (Repl) 509, *604*.

Challis v Warrender (1930) 144 LT 437, 95 JP 39, 29 LGR 109, 29 Cox CC 251, 25 Digest (Repl) 512, *618*.

Coles v Odhams Press Ltd [1936] 1 KB 416, [1935] All ER Rep 598, 105 LJKB 208, 154 LT 218, 100 JP 85, 34 LGR 34, 30 Cox CC 329, DC, 25 Digest (Repl) 489, *504*.

c *Hall v Cox* [1899] 1 QB 198, 18 LJQB 167, 79 LT 653, CA, 25 Digest (Repl) 513, *619*.

Hobbs v Ward (1929) 93 JP 163, 27 LGR 410, DC, 25 Digest (Repl) 512, *617*.

Ladbroke (Football) Ltd v Perrett [1971] 1 All ER 129, [1971] 1 WLR 110, 135 JP 181, DC.

Moore v Elphick [1945] 2 All ER 155, 110 JP 66, 43 LGR 142, DC, 25 Digest (Repl)
d 493, *512*.

Scott v Public Prosecutions Director [1914] 2 KB 868, [1914-15] All ER Rep 825, 83 LJKB 1025, 111 LT 59, 78 JP 267, 24 Cox CC 194, DC, 25 Digest (Repl) 513, *621*.

Stoddart v Sagar, Sagar v Stoddart [1895] 2 QB 474, 64 LJMC 234, 73 LT 215, 59 JP 598, 18 Cox CC 165, 15 R 579, DC, 25 Digest (Repl) 509, *605*.

Taylor v Smetten (1883) 11 QBD 207, 52 LJMC 101, 48 JP 36, DC, 25 Digest (Repl) 494,
e *521*.

Witty v World Service Ltd [1936] Ch 303, [1935] All ER Rep 243, 105 LJCh 63, 154 LT 491, 100 JP 68, 34 LGR 150, 30 Cox CC 375, 25 Digest (Repl) 513, *622*.

Appeal

f This was an appeal by The News of the World Ltd, by leave of the House of Lords, against an order of the Divisional Court of the Queen's Bench Division (Melford Stevenson, MacKenna and Forbes JJ) dated 11th February 1972, dismissing an appeal by way of case stated by the justices for the City of London against their adjudication as a magistrates' court sitting at the Mansion House Justice Room on 21st September 1971, whereby they convicted the appellants, on informations preferred by the respondent, Ronald Friend, of two offences: (i) on 29th November 1970 and (ii) on 4th
g April 1971, respectively conducting in the News of the World newspaper a competition called 'Spot-the-Ball' in which prizes were offered for forecasts of the result of a future event in each case, contrary to s 47 (1) (*a*) (i) of the Betting, Gaming and Lotteries Act 1963. The appellants were fined £25 for each offence. The facts are set out in the opinion of Lord Hailsham of St Marylebone LC.

h *J P Comyn QC* and *P C Bowsher* for the appellants.
Stephen Brown QC and *F E Beezley* for the respondent.

Their Lordships took time for consideration.

j 31st January. The following opinions were delivered.

LORD HAILSHAM OF ST MARYLEBONE LC.   In my opinion this appeal must be allowed, and I agree so entirely with the opinions to be expressed by my noble and learned friends, Lord Reid, Lord Morris of Borth-y-Gest and Lord Cross of Chelsea that I would not have added a separate opinion of my own were it not for the

fact that we are differing not merely from the Divisional Court and, regretfully, with *a*
my noble and learned friend, Lord Simon of Glaisdale in the instant case, but with the
reported judgments of Lord Parker CJ and of Ashworth J in *Ladbroke (Football) Ltd v
Perrett*[1] on which the judgment of the Divisional Court in the present case was largely
founded.

The proceedings originated in a case stated by the Guildhall justices after
the conviction of the appellants on two summonses under s 47 (1) (*a*) (i) of the *b*
Betting, Gaming and Lotteries Act 1963. This section reproduces with only
unimportant changes the wording of s 26 (1) of the Betting and Lotteries Act 1934.
Section 47 of the Betting, Gaming and Lotteries Act 1963, provides as follows:

> '*Restriction of certain prize competitions.*—(1) It shall be unlawful to conduct
> in or through any newspaper, or in connection with any trade or business or *c*
> the sale of any article to the public—(*a*) any competition in which prizes are
> offered for forecasts of the result either—(i) of a future event; or (ii) of a past
> event the result of which is not yet ascertained or not yet generally known;
> (*b*) any other competition success in which does not depend to a substantial
> degree upon the exercise of skill: Provided that nothing in this subsection with
> respect to the conducting of competitions in connection with a trade or business *d*
> shall apply in relation to sponsored pool betting or in relation to pool betting
> operations carried on by a person whose only trade or business is that of a
> bookmaker.
>
> '(2) Any person who contravenes the provisions of this section shall, without
> prejudice to any liability to be proceeded against under section 42 of this Act,
> be guilty of an offence.'   *e*

No summonses were issued by the respondent against the appellants in respect of
any offence alleged to have been committed under s 47 (1) (*b*) of the Act. The two
summonses issued related to two 'Spot-the-Ball' competitions conducted in the
appellants' newspaper respectively on 29th November 1970 and 4th April 1971.

Before I come to describe the actual competitions which gave rise to the present *f*
proceedings I think it will be helpful to describe the legal context in which the present
provisions first came to be enacted in 1934. Newspapers and other commercially
organised competitions in promotion of sales or to create 'brand loyalty' have been
the subject of controversy both in the courts and outside at least since 1892 when the
first newspaper competition appears to have been organised. By 1934 the position
which had been arrived at by the courts was, broadly speaking, as follows. Apart *g*
from any danger they might incur from the then current laws against cash and other
betting (irrelevant for this purpose) the only danger of prosecution the organisers
of such a competition really ran was that it might be held a lottery, which was then,
as (apart from irrelevant exceptions) it is now, illegal. But a lottery being a distribution of prizes by lot or chance, it came to be held that, even if a quite modest
degree of skill entered into the decisive test, the competition escaped. Thus, even *h*
competitions in which prizes were offered for forecasting the results of future events,
e g a horserace, could escape (*Caminada v Hulton*[2], *Stoddart v Sagar*[3]), and so could the
forecast of the result of an event contemporary or already in the past, but whose
result was not known (e g the number of births and deaths in London in a given
week: cf *Hall v Cox*)[4]. On the other hand, competitions, the final result of which
was determined by chance were lotteries and, therefore, illegal, even though a *j*

1 [1971] 1 All ER 129, [1971] 1 WLR 110
2 (1891) 60 LJMC 116
3 [1895] 2 QB 474
4 [1899] 1 QB 198

a degree of skill was required to winnow out all but the final competitors. Thus, a competition to determine the order of merit of the roles of Ellen Terry, to be decided by the vote of the competitors themselves, was a lottery (see *Challis v Warrender*[1]), and so was a competition, similarly decided, in which the prizes were offered for the correct order of merit of 13 named commodities (see *Hobbs v Ward*[2]). The same rule caught the missing word competition in *Barclay v Pearson*[3], and the crossword competition where several of the clues admitted of alternative solutions (*Coles v Odhams Press Ltd*[4] decided after the 1934 Act although on the old precedents). But if even a small degree of skill entered into the result the competition survived (see, for instance, *Scott v Public Prosecutions Director*[5]). A fortiori, where the degree of skill was substantial, e g a literary competition in a serious weekly, or a bridge or chess problem, it was never in question but that such competitions were permitted. In one case not wholly dissimilar from the present Eve J seems to have held that a puzzle picture came into this category (see *Witty v World Service Ltd*[6]) decided under the second limb of the section of the 1934 Act.

In these circumstances, Parliament passed the 1934 Act, following a Royal Commission in 1932. Incidentally, it is a salutary (and I hope cautionary) reflection for those who are eager to use Commission reports as a means of construing Acts of Parliament, to note that, although the 1934 Act followed the Royal Commission in time, it by no means enacted all the recommendations of the Commission, but departed from them in important respects.

Section 26 of the 1934 Act was contained in Part II of the Act which is headed 'Lotteries and Prize Competitions'. The scheme adopted by the Act was to continue to regard as illegal all lotteries with certain exemptions irrelevant for the present purpose (s 21 et seq) but to legislate specially for newspaper and commercially organised prize competitions (s 26). It made no attempt to redefine the word 'lottery' so as to bring within the definition competitions in which skill and chance are intermixed.

The remainder of the field of commercially organised prize competitions as defined was divided into two classes i e: (1) competitions in which prizes are offered for forecasts of the result of a future event, or of a past event, the result of which is not yet ascertained, or not yet generally known; these were prohibited absolutely (s 26 (1) (a)) however much, or however little, the skill involved and, it would seem, in theory at least, whether or not they be already illegal as lotteries; (2) any other competition; these were prohibited if success in them 'does not depend to a substantial degree upon the exercise of skill'.

Commercially organised competitions as defined in the opening words of the section can, therefore, be categorised in four classes, the last three of which at least and in practice probably all four, are mutually exclusive. These are: (1) lotteries: these are illegal under ss 21 and 22 as they always were; (2) forecasts of the results of future events or of events the result of which is either not yet ascertained or not yet generally known: these are illegal under s 26 (1) (a); (3) other competitions success in which does not involve a substantial degree of skill: these are prohibited under s 26 (1) (b); (4) Other competitions success in which *does* involve a substantial degree of skill: these are permitted, as they always have been.

In view of the case law in the context of which the law was passed and of the exhaustive character of the categories created, I see no reason to give a tortured or

j

1   (1930) 144 LT 437
2   (1929) 93 JP 163
3   [1893] 2 Ch 154
4   [1936] 1 KB 416, [1935] All ER Rep 598
5   [1914] 2 KB 868, [1914-15] All ER Rep 825
6   [1936] Ch 303, [1935] All ER Rep 243

extended meaning or 'forecast', 'event', or 'result' where they occur in s 26 (1) (a) of the 1934 Act or s 47 (1) (a) of the 1963 Act. On the contrary, they are most easily read in their ordinary sense. What is aimed at is the kind of competition depending on a correct forecast of the result of a race, as in *Stoddart v Sagar*[1], or, of an event such as was devised in *Hall v Cox*[2]. Other competitions depending on the solution of puzzles or other problems fall to be decided under s 26 (1) (b), and depend for their legality on the degree of skill found by the tribunal of fact to be involved.

It is these provisions which are re-enacted in the 1963 Act and with which this case is concerned. Since the only summonses related to s 47 (1) (a) I am not concerned to discuss into which category the relevant competitions may come other than category (2) above. It would be open to the authorities on some other occasion to argue that they come within (1) or (3), and so are prohibited by other provisions of the Act.

I come now to the competitions. We were told that 'Spot-the-Ball' competitions dated from 1935, that is, approximately from the commencement of the 1934 Act. All have one feature in common. A photograph is reproduced showing an actual incident in an actual football game. In the original the ball appears in the picture. In the reproduction the ball is eliminated. In its earliest, simplest, and most logical form the competition consisted in an attempt to replace the ball in its actual position. We were told that this was abandoned by the ingenious organisers of such schemes lest it be argued that this involved a 'forecast of a past event the result of which is not yet ascertained or not yet generally known'. For reasons which I will shortly elaborate, I think this fear was misplaced, but it is not, strictly speaking, essential for the decision of this appeal to decide the point. Whether the fear was misplaced or not the matter was never tested in court, at least until very recently. If it be tested I trust that those who have to decide the matter will take account of the opinions expressed in this case.

After the original form of the competition was abandoned, a series of variants on it was adopted. These all had the feature in common that instead of the prize being given to the competitor whose entry came closest to the real position of the ball, the competitors were asked to apply their skill and knowledge to the photograph and certain additional information and base their entries on their opinion of the spot where the ball ought logically to be expected to be. The merits of their entries were then judged by a panel of experts who went through the same process as the competitors, and the winning entry was that which approximated most closely to or coincided with the judgment of the experts which (as they were unaware of it) might or might not coincide with the true position of the ball. There were a number of variations on this theme, including the rather more sophisticated version which was the subject of the decision in *Ladbroke's* case[3], which both counsel admitted differed from the present on the facts and partook rather closely of some of the features of the ordinary football pool, in that success depended on a minimum of eight positions being selected out of a possible 40.

The particular variations adopted in the present instance were described in para 2 of the special case as follows:

'We heard the said informations on the 21st day of September 1971, and the following facts were proved:—(a) The Appellants on 29th November, 1970, and 4th April, 1971, conducted in the News of the World a competition for which prizes were offered called "Spot-the-Ball". '(b) The "News of the World" is a newspaper. (c) The Appellants conducted "Spot-the-Ball" competitions by means of entry forms published in the News of the World. The entry forms included a

---

1 [1895] 2 QB 474
2 [1899] 1 QB 198
3 [1971] 1 All ER 129, [1971] 1 WLR 110

photograph of an incident in a football match showing several players in action. The photographs were different each week but each photograph published portrayed a scene of vigorous movement and action. The image of the football had been removed from each photograph. The names of the teams playing were given above the photograph. (d) Below the entry form in the News of the World were published the instructions to competitors which included the following:—"Use your skill and judgment to decide from all the information contained in the picture the spot where you think the centre of the ball is most likely to be and indicate that spot by marking a cross in ink or ball-point pen on the picture. Every entry will be examined carefully, and our panel of football experts will select the entry in which, in their expert opinion, the centre of the cross, bearing in mind all the circumstances, most accurately represents the most logical position of the ball." A maximum of 40 attempts was allowed on each coupon. (e) The competitions for 29th November, 1970, and 4th April, 1971, were judged by a panel of experts who included Mr. Tom Finney (who was capped 76 times for England), Mr. Hepburn (the Appellants' Manchester Sports Editor) and Mr. Donald Evans, with the Appellants' Manchester Editor sitting as Chairman. The panel, in the course of judging the competitions, considered the information conveyed by the photograph including the postures of the players, the directions in which they appeared to be looking and moving, the markings on the field, the ground conditions, the position of the referee when he was shown, the teams involved, the identity and characteristics of individual players, and the apparent weather conditions.'

The case went on to describe the difference between the November and April competitions. I think this wholly immaterial. In each case the particular form depended on the fact that, before the final selection of the winners was made, a screening process took place, in which entries were bundled in accordance with the part of the photograph in which the ball was placed, and only that bundle corresponding with entries closest to the judgment of the experts was individually considered by the panel. In spite of the fact that MacKenna J appears to have been impressed by the fact that, in the event, the judges only considered some 200 to 250 individual entries which emerged from the screening process, I do not think anything turns on this. The entries which were not individually considered consisted of those which would have been discarded out of hand as too wide of the mark. The only other facts of which we were told which could have any bearing on the case were (i) that equally meritorious entries shared any prize to which they were entitled and (ii) that there were second and other prizes for the next most meritorious entries after that of the winner.

The question, and the only question, which arises is whether, in these circumstances, the prizes were being offered for a forecast of the result of a future event within the meaning of s 47 (1) (a). I agree myself wholeheartedly with the proposition submitted on behalf of the respondent that in these cases the court will look at the realities of the offer and the competition and will not allow itself to be deceived, whether innocently or otherwise, by delusive appearances or descriptions. But in this case I can see no difference between appearance and reality, and, with respect to the submission of counsel, none was suggested, that is, I cannot find anywhere any suggestion that the offer was intended to convey to the competitor anything other than what was said, or that the competitor did, or thought he was doing, anything other than what he was invited to do in the offer, or that the competition was in any way conducted or judged in a manner different from that which appeared on the surface.

The Divisional Court in this case, and in the earlier case of *Ladbroke*[1], arrived at

---

1   [1971] 1 All ER 129, [1971] 1 WLR 110

the conclusion they did by a process of reasoning which can best be summarised by the judgment of Lord Parker CJ in the latter case, where he said[1]:

'The second point that counsel for the newspaper companies took can be put in this form: even if I am wrong and there can truly be said here to have been an event and a result of that event, even so, the competitors here were not seeking or attempting to forecast the result, that is, the decision arrived at by the panel after an event, the meeting and the deliberation. They were doing what they were told to do by the small print in the advertisement, namely to decide in which eight squares the ball was most likely to be. He said with considerable force that not only is that what they were told to do, but what any competitor would naturally do. He would not, so it is said, attempt to ascertain what three other people might choose; he would concentrate on what he, using such football skill as he had, thought were the eight squares in which the ball was most likely to be. Counsel said that it may be true that the competitor's skill in choosing those eight squares may be judged in the end by the decision arrived at by the panel, yet that is only to confuse what is being attempted, namely to decide in which eight squares the ball is most likely to be, with what he calls the machinery of judging the skill so exercised. That is an attractive argument, but in my judgment it is wrong. True, and I accept it, the competitor is doing what he is told to do, to decide in which eight squares the ball is most likely to be; that is what he is directly putting his mind to, but at the same time, in the result he is in fact trying to forecast what the panel thinks by its decision are the eight squares in which the ball is most likely to be. Put I think in its simplest form, it is this: it is not what the competitor is directly attempting to do or thinks that he is doing but what in fact he is doing, that matters. In fact, whether he knows it or not, by reason of the panel being the judges, he is trying to arrive at a solution which will accord with the decision of the panel. On those short grounds, I would agree with the learned magistrate in this case that the first appellants had committed an offence and dismiss the appeal by them.'

The argument may be summarised as follows. Ex concessis, in order to fall within the terms of the section there must be (i) a forecast of (ii) the result of (iii) an event. According to Lord Parker CJ, and MacKenna J in the present case, the event was the competition itself, or rather the consideration of the entries by the panel, and the result of the event was their decision when they made it either in the future or in the past (although not generally known), and the entry to the competition was a forecast, because in the last resort, to quote from MacKenna J in the present case:

'Even if the entries shown to the judges had been the whole of those sent in by the public, I should still be convinced that there was an element of chance in the selection of the winning position. I do not believe that it would be possible to give a logical reason for preferring the pinpoint centre of a single cross as that most likely to be the position occupied by the ball. I should suppose that the judges could only give reasons for choosing a small area as distinct from a pinpoint as being most likely to have the ball within it, and that however small that area was, there would be room within it for the centre of more than one cross. The choice of the single winning position must therefore have been to some extent fortuitous. So far as their choice of that position was not governed by reason, it would be governed by chance. The competitors would be trying in effect to forecast this choice, which would, as I read Ladbroke's case[2], be the forecasting of the result of a future event.'

---

1 [1971] 1 All ER at 133, 134, [1971] 1 WLR at 115
2 [1971] 1 All ER 129, [1971] 1 WLR 110

I confess I cannot either follow the logic of this reasoning or reconcile it with the facts of the present case. I do not understand at all how, to use Lord Parker CJ's language, a man can be 'trying' to forecast the result of an event 'whether he knows it or not'. I find it particularly hard to understand when, as here, the competitor is being asked to apply his reasoning faculties to a puzzle picture in order to discover the most logical position of a hidden object, thinks he is doing it, and is in fact doing it. No doubt he hopes that by the exercise of his modest skill he may arrive at the same result as will a panel of experts indulging in the same process and seeking to obtain the same result by the same means. But since what the competitor is doing is to use his skill to arrive at the most logical result I cannot see that what he is doing is to forecast the judges' decision simply because the judges are doing the same thing as he. If I were to find myself driven to this (to my mind) quite unreasonable conclusion, I should also, I think, have to apply the same reasoning to bridge, chess, or literary competitions of the familiar kinds which are admittedly within the law.

I am not at all impressed by the fact, which I accept as accurate, that the exact pinpointing of the centre of the ball 'to the last millimetre', as it was put in argument, is, as MacKenna J said, to some extent a matter of chance, if, as I suppose, the most that skill and judgment can do is to estimate its approximate position. If what is attempted is the solution of a puzzle and not a forecast, if there be, as I think, no group of circumstances which can be described without misuse of language as an event, and no outcome which can properly be described as a result, the case cannot come within s 47 (1) (a). The element of chance may be so large, indeed, for aught I know in the present case may have been so large as to justify a prosecution under s 47 (1) (b), and, in another case, the element of skill might be wholly lacking so that the whole competition becomes a lottery. But in my opinion these are the real options open to the prosecuting authorities. Where what is offered to the competitors is a series of prizes for the solution of a puzzle picture containing a hidden object and professing to be capable of solution by skill, what the prizes are offered for is not a forecast, there is no future event, and no result of a future event on which success depends there is no offence committed under s 47 (1) (a). As I say, it is not necessary for this House to determine once and for all the legality under s 47 (1) (a) (ii) of the original and simpler form of the competition where the competitors were invited to discern the true position of the ball. I find it, however, difficult to discern what exactly is the event in the past the result of which is not yet known that is alleged to come within the terms of the section. The position of a moving ball in the air is hardly either a result or an event, and its cause, the kicking or heading of the ball, I find it difficult to describe naturally in terms of an event either, although I suppose it could be so described. It could of course also be alleged that the taking of the photograph is the event and the position of the ball on the plate its result. But this too seems a strangely artificial way of describing a puzzle picture. But even if this be the analysis, I am far from convinced that the competition entry could be described as a forecast. In view of what I have said, however, on any analysis I cannot find that an offence is committed under s 47 (1) (a) (i) in the particular circumstances described in the instant case whatever might be the results of a prosecution under s 47 (1) (b) or for an illegal lottery.

During the course of argument it was suggested that the existence of an option, for an additional entrance fee, of up to 40 tries as adumbrated in the case reinforced the contention of the respondent that the result of the competition was largely a matter of chance. By an ingenious riposte counsel for the appellants submitted that, on the contrary, the existence of the option enabled a competitor to reduce the element of chance if, as might be the case, he supposed that his skill enabled him to determine the approximate area where the ball might be expected to be, but not the precise pinpoint to be selected. I do not think either argument is relevant to this appeal. The result of this appeal depends on the existence of a forecast, an event, and a result. If these three elements were present the competition offends against s 47 (1) (*a*) no matter what the degree of skill involved in the forecast. If one or more of these elements is lacking (and a fortiori if all three are lacking) the competition escapes from this arm of the section no matter what the degree of chance in the ultimate choice, although, of course, the probability of it offending under s 47 (1) (*b*) or s 41 (which deals with lotteries) proportionately increases. That, in my view, is for another day, and will depend on the facts of each particular case.

For the above reasons, I would allow this appeal with costs here and in both courts below. The convictions must be quashed.

LORD REID. My Lords, the appellants conduct in their newspaper a competition called 'Spot-the-Ball'. They were prosecuted for infringement of s 47 (1) (*a*) (i) of the Betting, Gaming and Lotteries Act 1963. In *Ladbroke (Football) Ltd v Perrett*[1] the Divisional Court upheld a conviction in respect of a somewhat similar competition. It is necessary to consider whether that case was rightly decided.

Section 47 replaced an almost identical section in the Betting and Lotteries Act 1934. It deals with competitions in newspapers or in connection with trade, business or the sale of any article to the public. It makes all such competitions unlawful if success does not depend to a substantial degree on the exercise of skill. But in respect of one class of competition it goes farther and makes that class unlawful whether or not skill is involved in the competition. This class consists of all competitions in which prizes are offered for forecasts of the result of an event: the event may be a future event or a past event, the result of which is not yet ascertained or not yet generally known.

In the present case the competition is said to involve forecasting the result of a future event, but I think it necessary to consider the section as a whole. It deals with all competitions in newspapers whether they involve forecasting or not. The first question which must be determined is whether the particular competition is one in which prizes are given for forecasting the result of an event (future or past). In determining this question I see no reason for giving to the words 'forecast', 'event' or 'result' any other than their ordinary and natural meanings. The reason why competitions involving such forecasts are treated differently from other competitions is not apparent and I see nothing to require one to strive to widen the natural scope of the provisions dealing with such competitions. I do not see how anyone can be said to be forecasting the result of an event unless he knows what the event is. The typical case is a competition inviting forecasts of the result of some game or race, but there are many other kinds of event where there could be forecasts or predictions of the result.

The nature of the competition appears from the case stated by the justices. A photograph is taken during a game of football which portrays 'a scene of vigorous movement and action' and which shews the ball; then the photograph is printed in the newspaper after the ball has been erased from it and the following instructions are given to competitors:

'Use your skill and judgment to decide from all the information contained in the picture the spot where you think the centre of the ball is most likely to be and indicate that spot by marking a cross in ink or ball-point pen on the picture. Every entry will be examined carefully, and our panel of football experts will select the entry in which, in their expert opinion, the centre of the cross, bearing in mind all the circumstances, most accurately represents the most logical position of the ball.'

---

1   [1971] 1 All ER 129, [1971] 1 WLR 110

In some earlier competitions a simpler method of selecting the winner was used. The entries were compared with the original photograph and the winner was the competitor whose cross came nearest to the position of the centre of the ball in the original photograph.

In the competitions which are the subject of the present prosecution, the winner was determined in a rather different way. The photograph as published in the newspaper was studied by a panel of football experts and they decided the spot where, in their opinion, the ball was most likely to have been. It is, I think, a proper inference from the findings of fact in the case that their decision did depend on skill. And the instructions to competitors were clearly intended to represent to them that the winning position would be that determined by the expert skill of the panel. I do not think that anything turns on the precise way in which the panel set to work or the precise way in which the entries were examined. It would be very surprising if it did.

I can see no relevant difference between this competition and competitions which regularly appear in many newspapers inviting readers to send in entries giving their opinions as to the best solution of various problems. For instance, readers may be invited to say what they think would be the best bid on various bridge hands and to abide by the decisions of one or more experts. In each case what each competitor is invited to do and, in fact does, is to make up his own mind as to the best solution, and hope that the experts are of the same opinion so that he may get the prize.

But the explanation accepted by the Divisional Court is quite different. It is said that the consideration of the problems by the experts is an event, that their decisions are the result of that event and that the competitors in submitting their entries are forecasting the result of that event.

I reject that explanation on two grounds. In the first place, it is well settled that in this branch of the law the courts must look at realities and, in my opinion, no reasonable person would think that that is the real nature of these competitions. The reality, to my mind, is that competitors are invited to and do try their skill and that, as there is no absolute answer to such problems, judgment as to who has shewn the greatest skill must be a matter of opinion and experts are required to give that judgment. It might be different if there was really no skill involved. Suppose the reasonable inference from the whole facts to be that the so-called 'experts' were not really making a judgment but were only making a random selection. Then it might be said that the competitors could be doing no more than guessing what that random selection would be. But the facts in the case stated shew that that is not the case.

My second reason is that the facts of this case do not appear to me to come within the ordinary meaning of the words of the subsection. First, there must be a forecast; it requires too much ingenuity to find that anything was or was intended to be forecast by entrants to the competition. Then the forecast must be of the result of an event. Even if the competitors could be said to be forecasting the panel's decision, of what 'event' was that decision the result? The decision was no doubt the result of their deliberations, but it would be far-fetched to call their deliberations an event. That would be even clearer if, instead of a panel, there were only one judge. To call his making up his mind an event would indeed be a misuse of language, and it would be absurd to say that an offence is committed if there is a panel of judges but not if there is only one judge.

Then I think we should consider what the position would be if there were no panel of judges but the winner was found by comparing the entries sent in with the original photograph. Would the case then fall within s 47 (1) (a) (ii)? What would then be 'forecast' would be the position of the ball in the original photograph. Of what 'event' would that position be the result? Possibly the taking of the photograph, possibly the last kick before the photograph was taken; I can think of no other. But surely it would be utterly far-fetched to say that prizes were offered for forecasting the result of an unnoticed kick or of the taking of a photograph. It would

verge on the ridiculous to say that the original form of this competition was lawful   *a*
but that the intervention of a panel made it unlawful.

Now I must turn to *Ladbrokes'* case[1]. There the facts were different. The panel
had to find the eight most likely squares on a grid superimposed on the photograph
in which the ball might be. I find it difficult to see how any exercise of skill or judgment could do this. But we are not concerned with the question whether on the
facts there could have been an offence in that case. We are concerned with the   *b*
question whether the reasoning of the court can be upheld. I do not think it can.
There are, I think, two main steps in that argument. First, that the deliberations of
the panel and their result 'could quite fairly and squarely be said to come within the
words of the Act'[2]. I have already given my reasons for disagreeing with that.
And then it is said[2]:

> *c*
> 'True, and I accept it, the competitor is doing what he is told to do, to decide
> in which eight squares the ball is most likely to be; that is what he is directly
> putting his mind to, but at the same time, in the result he is in fact trying to
> forecast what the panel thinks by its decision are the eight squares in which the
> ball is most likely to be. Put I think in its simplest form, it is this: it is not what
> the competitor is directly attempting to do or thinks that he is doing but what in   *d*
> fact he is doing, that matters. In fact, whether he knows it or not, by reason of
> the panel being the judges, he is trying to arrive at a solution which will accord
> with the decision of the panel. On those short grounds, I would agree with the
> learned magistrate in this case that the first appellants had committed an offence
> and dismiss the appeal by them.'

e
I cannot agree that in fact the competitor is trying to forecast what the panel
think. In fact I doubt whether any single competitor ever tried to do that. I think
that that is neglecting the reality of what the competition was and was understood
to be and putting in its place a different kind of competition. One might argue from
the circumstances of the Ladbroke's competition that the competitors were making
their selection more at random than as a matter of skill and judgment, but I see no   *f*
ground for inferring that they were trying or were invited to try to forecast the
panel's decision.

I would therefore allow this appeal.

LORD MORRIS OF BORTH-Y-GEST. My Lords, the two offences of which   *g*
the appellants were convicted were that on two specified dates they had conducted
in their newspaper a competition in which prizes were offered for forecasts of the
result of a future event. The informations were laid in the terms of s 47 (1) (*a*) (i) of
the Betting, Gaming and Lotteries Act 1963. There was no doubt that the appellants
had conducted in their newspaper a competition in which prizes were offered. The
question is whether such prizes were offered for forecasts of the result of a future   *h*
event. The terms of the offer of prizes contain no hint or suggestion that the prizes
were offered for any such thing. The terms of the offer invited competitors to use
their skill and judgment to decide the spot where they thought that the centre of the
ball was most likely to be. They had so to decide on the basis of all the information
contained in the picture. The picture portrayed a scene of vigorous movement and
action in a game of football played between named teams. A competitor with a   *j*
lively and discerning interest in and knowledge of games of football might consider
himself equipped, by deploying his skill and his judgment in an examination of the

1 [1971] 1 All ER 129, [1971] 1 WLR 110
2 [1971] 1 All ER at 133, 134, [1971] 1 WLR at 115 per Lord Parker CJ

information given him on the picture, to decide where the ball was at the moment when the picture was taken. A competitor was invited to use his reasoning powers to decide where the ball was most likely to be or, stated otherwise, what would be its 'most logical position'. A competitor was also told that there would be a panel of experts and that they would exercise their expert opinion to decide which entry had the centre of a cross most accurately representing the position which would be the most logical position for the ball to be.

How, then, in these circumstances is it said that the prizes that were offered were offered for forecasts of the result of a future event? What forecast of the result of what future event? The answer given is that the future event was the meeting of the football experts; its result—their decision as to where, on a consideration of all the information shown on a photograph, the ball was most likely to be; and that what a competitor was doing was to make forecasts of what the result of that future event would be. Such a way of viewing or stating the matter seems to me to be artificial and to be wholly divorced from reality. If a competitor had been asked what he had been doing he would I think have said that he had been exercising his skill and judgment and that his conclusions were to be judged by a panel of experts. He would have been astonished if he were told that he had been engaged in forecasting what conclusions the expert judges would reach. The prizes were not offered for 'forecasts'. Nor would a competitor think he was making them.

It is said that whether a competitor appreciated it or not nevertheless he was in fact doing just that. I cannot agree. The facts in *Ladbroke (Football) Ltd v Perrett*[1] differ from those in the present case, but I cannot accept the reasoning which is contained in the judgments. Of course in any given case the court will not allow itself to be deluded by words which merely mask reality. But in the present case competitors were not either in form or in reality offered prizes for making forecasts of the result of a future event. They were doing just what they were invited to do and their efforts were to be judged by a panel of experts. There was no enquiry (for it was not in issue) whether success in the competition would or would not depend to a substantial degree on the exercise of skill and naturally I cannot express any opinion as to that matter.

I would allow the appeal and set aside the convictions.

LORD SIMON OF GLAISDALE. My Lords, the philosopher F H Bradley described metaphysics as the finding of bad reasons for what we believe on instinct. An opinion on a short point of construction is apt to be the rationalisation of a first impression; and I am all the more conscious of Bradley's jibe when I find myself differing from my noble and learned friends whose judgments I deeply respect.

The point of construction with which your Lordships are concerned is a very short one indeed: what is the meaning of 'forecasts of the result . . . of a future event' in s 47 (1) (a) of the Betting, Gaming and Lotteries Act 1963; and the outcome of this appeal depends on the application of that meaning to the simple facts as found by the justices. Section 47 (1) reads as follows:

'It shall be unlawful to conduct in or through any newspaper, or in connection with any trade or business or the sale of any article to the public—(a) any competition in which prizes are offered for forecasts of the result either—(i) of a future event; or (ii) of a past event the result of which is not yet ascertained or not yet generally known; (b) any other competition success in which does not depend to a substantial degree upon the exercise of skill . . .'

---

1 [1971] 1 All ER 129, [1971] 1 WLR 110

There is a proviso which is immaterial to the present appeal. The 1963 statute is a consolidation Act, but this is irrelevant to any matter of construction which arises in this appeal (s 47 of the 1963 Act reproduces s 26 of the Betting and Lotteries Act 1934). Section 47 appears in Part III of the 1963 Act, which deals, in significant combination, with both 'Lotteries and Prize Competitions'.

As always in statutory interpretation it is necessary to start by asking what was Parliament's general intention in the statute and particular intention in the provision to be construed. The general statutory intention was unquestionably to discourage gambling generally and otherwise to control it—presumably on the traditionally held grounds that gambling is personally demoralising, domestically degrading and economically stultifying (a reward being obtainable by chance rather than by effort which satisfies a social want). Thus, the leading provision of Part III of the Act is s 41 (reproducing s 21 of the 1934 Act), which, subject to the minor exceptions contained in the ensuing sections, declares that all lotteries are unlawful. A lottery is a scheme for distributing prizes by lot or chance (*Taylor v Smetten*[1], *Scott v Public Prosecutions Director*[2]), any element of skill being inconsistent with its being a lottery (*Caminada v Hulton*[3]; *Hall v Cox*[4]). Thus, the forecasting of the results of football matches for the purpose of football pools, not being entirely dependent on chance, but also requiring skill, is not a lottery (*Moore v Elphick*[5]). Common experience as well as a scrutiny of the cases can leave no doubt that, gambling being so alluring to many people and the reward for pandering to its taste being in consequence so rich, considerable ingenuity will be used to evade the parliamentary provisions for its discouragement and control.

It is in the light of this legal situation and these social and economic considerations that the interpretation of s 47 must be approached. Both in the 1934 and the 1963 Acts the statutory context suggests that the provisions relating to prize competitions were to prevent evasion of the law relating to lotteries. Section 47 goes farther than s 41, which makes lotteries unlawful; s 47 makes unlawful certain competitions even where there is some element of skill. It cannot be interpreted without ascertaining why Parliament so stipulated. It must have been because the offer of a reward dependent on a residual chance element (i e over and above any element of skill) offered through a newspaper (sometimes of mass circulation) would provide a considerable loophole in the general parliamentary provisions to discourage or control gambling and the particular parliamentary provisions relating to lotteries. This consideration would also apply to competitions conducted in connection with any trade or business or the sale of any article to the public, where the trade or business is a considerable one or the article sold one of general purchase. Moreover, the alluring prospect of chance reward would again lead to economic distortion, the customer buying the goods (and a brand of goods acquiring a value) not purely for their intrinsic worth in satisfying his needs for them, but for the opportunity they give him for surreptitious gambling contrary to the intention of Parliament.

Section 47 (1) is in two parts. Paragraph (b) deals with any competition (other than a competition falling within para (a)) in which there is no substantial element of skill. Paragraph (a) goes further and extends to competitions in which there is even a substantial element of skill, but where the competition involves the forecast of the result either of a future event or a past event the result of which is not yet ascertained or generally known. Again, it cannot be interpreted without recognising why Parliament made this particular provision. I think that there are likely to have been four

1 (1883) 11 QBD 207
2 [1914] 2 KB 868 at 875, 879, [1914-15] All ER Rep 825 at 831, 833
3 (1891) 60 LJMC 116
4 [1899] 1 QB 198
5 [1945] 2 All ER 155

reasons. First, forecasting the result of a future event or the unascertained result of a past event depends as often on conjecture as on informed judgment (this ambiguity is, indeed, implicit in the word 'forecast': see the Shorter Oxford English Dictionary). Secondly, it will often be difficult to evaluate in relation to an individual competitor how much of his effort is conjecture and how much informed judgment. Thirdly, some competitors may use conjecture and other competitors informed judgment. Fourthly, therefore, if Parliament did not make some such provision as in s 47 (1) (a) it would be presenting tribunals charged with adjudicating on offences against s 47 (1) (b) with virtually insoluble problems, and inviting widespread evasion of the statutory provisions to discourage and control gambling. (*Ladbroke (Football) Ltd v Perrett*[1] provides an example: the competition there struck Lord Parker CJ[2] as demanding 'a considerable element of skill'; whereas counsel for the appellants before your Lordships accepted that the chances against success were approximately the same enormously long odds as in a football pool where eight draws have to be forecast out of 40 given matches.) The foregoing, then, would, in my view, be the mischiefs which Parliament had in mind in enacting s 47 (1) (a), which should be construed accordingly. Certainly, if the competitions under your Lordships' scrutiny can escape its provisions, Parliament has been cleverly outwitted.

Not only do the instant competitions, in my judgment, fall squarely within the parliamentary intendment in s 47 (1) (a); they also fall fairly within its terminology. I find it helpful to approach this problem by considering earlier forms of 'Spot-the-Ball' competitions. I take these as set out in the appellants' own case. The original form is described as follows:

'A photograph of an incident in a football game is published, the image of the ball having been removed. Readers are invited to show by a cross the actual position of the ball in the photograph as originally taken.'

The promoters abandoned this easily understood form, with its obvious appeal to informed judgment in reconstructing a total situation from partial evidence, because they feared that it might offend against s 47 (1) (a) (ii). In my opinion, their fears were entirely justified. Was there an 'event'? Clearly, yes; since a primary meaning of 'event' is 'incident' (see the Shorter Oxford English Dictionary), which is the very word used by the appellants with entire terminological propriety. Was it a 'past event'? Again, clearly, yes; the incident in the football match had already taken place when the competition was published. Did the 'past event' have a 'result'? Once again, clearly, yes; the result of the incident in the football game was that the ball was in one particular position, which appeared in the photograph in its original development, and which the competitors had to reinstate in order to win the prize. Was that result 'not yet generally known'? Obviously, again, yes; even those who had been present at the match would not be able to recapitulate the precise incident photographed, still less the precisely resulting position of the ball; while those judging purely from the photograph with the ball removed would be in complete ignorance of its position. Was there, then, the 'forecast' of this resultant position? Since, 'forecast' embraces both pre-estimate and pre-conjecture it is unnecessary to attempt to determine how far skill and judgment, on the one hand, or chance, on the other, are factors in the pinpointing of the exact centre of the missing ball: one way or the other there was plainly a 'forecast' of 'a past event' (the incident in the football game) 'the result of which' (the position of the ball) was 'not yet generally known'. The competition in this form was thus, in my view, caught by s 47 (1) (a) (ii), and the promoters understandably devoted their ingenuity to devising a colourable alternative. (I may add, in respect of this form of the competition, that the same

1   [1971] 1 All ER 129, [1971] 1 WLR 110
2   [1971] 1 All ER at 133, [1971] 1 WLR at 114

conclusion obtains if the past event is conceived as the exposure of the photographic
plate and the result the image of the ball afterwards expunged; but, although equally
valid, this seems a more artificial way of adjudging the transaction.)

I pass over an intermediate variant which ingenuity contrived, and go to the variant
of the 'Spot-the-Ball' competition which was considered in *Ladbroke (Football) Ltd v
Perrett*[1]. It is thus described in the appellants' case:

> 'A photograph of an incident in a football game is published with the image
> of the ball removed and with a grid containing 40 squares imposed over a portion
> of the photograph. The readers are invited to select 8 out of the 40 squares as the
> positions where the ball is most likely to be. A panel of experts then meets and
> selects a combination of 8 out of the 40 squares where they think the ball is most
> likely to be. The entries are then scrutinized to see if any entries match that
> selection.'

There was the same solemn invocation of the skill and judgment of the competitor
as in the competitions under instant consideration, the same emphasis on the eminence
and expertise of the judges and their scrupulous deliberations. But I agree with my
noble and learned friend on the Woolsack that in these cases the court will look at
the realities of the offer and the competition and will not allow itself to be deceived
by delusive appearance or descriptions. And the reality in *Ladbroke's* case[1] was that
success depended on a minimum of eight positions chosen by the competitor
(selected out of a possible 40) coinciding with those independently chosen by the
judges—there being similar enormous odds against such coincidence as obtain in the
popular 'eight-draws' football pool. The fact that success depended predominantly
or finally on chance rather than on skill is not, of course, directly relevant to whether
the competition offends against s 47 (1) (*a*), nor is it any answer that success depends
to a substantial degree on the exercise of skill, as it would be to a charge under s 47
(1) (*b*). But the element of chance does help to determine whether there was a
relevant 'event' with a relevant 'result', and, if so, what these were. It seems to me
to be unquestionable that the 'result' (which won the prize) in *Ladbroke's* case[1] was
the coincidence of the eight squares chosen by the competitor with those independently chosen by the judges. The judges' choice of eight squares, coincidence with
which would win the prize, was the 'result' of the 'event' of the judges' meeting and
deliberation, and of nothing else. This meeting and deliberation took place after the
entries were submitted, and it was therefore a 'future event'. Was the resultant
choice of eight squares by the judges 'forecast' by the competitors? It matters not
whether it was pre-estimated or pre-conjectured by the competitor, or partly the
one partly the other, since the word 'forecast' embraces both pre-estimate and pre-
conjecture—one way or the other it was 'forecast'. It follows that I agree with the
decision in *Ladbroke's* case[1] and, with one reservation, with the reasoning.

My only reservation relates to a passage in the judgment of Lord Parker CJ[2]:

> ' . . . it is not what the competitor is directly attempting to do or thinks he
> is doing, but what in fact he is doing, that matters. In fact, whether he knows it
> or not, by reason of the panel being the judges, he is trying to arrive at a solution
> which will accord with the decision of the panel.'

I do not think that this is a necessary step towards Lord Parker CJ's conclusion: it is
merely an additional reason, with which I cannot, with all respect, agree. It would
apply to the ordinary bridge or chess or literary competition in a newspaper. These
are not within the mischief of the section—simply because the entrant for such

---

1   [1971] 1 All ER 129, [1971] 1 WLR 110
2   [1971] 1 All ER at 134, [1971] 1 WLR at 115

competition is not properly described as 'forecasting' anything at all in the ordinary sense of the word. The language which the draftsman has chosen is entirely appropriate to meet what I have ventured to discern as the intention of Parliament, while leaving the bridge, chess or literary competition, which it is inconceivable that Parliament would wish to declare unlawful, outside the ambit of the section.

I turn then, finally, to the two variants which were adopted after *Ladbroke's* case[1] and which are the subject of the instant appeal. The case stated is not entirely clear as to the detailed procedure, and it was supplemented by information given to your Lordships by counsel for the appellants. My noble and learned friend on the Woolsack has recounted the main features. In November 1970 all the entries were sorted by scrutineers according to the areas of the photograph in which the competitors had put their crosses. The judges then met and, without reference to the entries, selected an area within which the ball could reasonably be expected to be, having regard to the evidence supplied by the photograph. The judges then sent for all the entries (as sorted by the scrutineers) which fell within that area. (It does not appear, in relation to the November 1970 competition, how many competitors got as far as the successful area: if the April 1971 competition can be taken as a guide it would be some 200 to 250.) Having referred to the entries which fell within the selected area, the judges then picked one exact spot within the area as the most logical place for the ball to be. Entries which coincided with or approximated to the exact spot chosen by the judges won the substantial prizes.

The April 1971 competition differed in detail in its judging procedure. There was no longer a preliminary decision on the area within which the winning entry should be found. Instead, the judges called for the entries as sorted by the scrutineers into groups according to areas. Out of approximately ten groups of entries the judges selected one (consisting of some 200 to 250 entries). The judges then went, by direct reference to the entries within that group, to select one entry as actually the winner. That was used by assistants to find how many other entries either coincided or approximated. (The difference between the November 1970 and April 1971 competitions was, therefore, that in the latter the winning spot always coincided with at least one entry, whereas in the former it would not necessarily do so.)

The competitions under instant consideration differed, then, from that considered in *Ladbroke's* case[1] in that there was no pre-selection of the winning position by the judges, even in November 1970. I would, however, venture to draw attention to the following features: (1) an entry might pinpoint the actual position which the ball had occupied in the photograph but fail to win the prize because that was not the place the judges had selected; (2) the main difference between the original form of the competition and its subsequent variants was that in the former the prize was won by the choice of the actual position of the eliminated ball, while in the latter it was the choice of the position which the judges would or did pick; (3) a fair reading of the caption on the entry form is that the competitors were in fact being invited to select a particular spot in the picture which would coincide with the spot to be selected by the panel of judges; (4) skill and judgment and knowledge of football might enable the competitor to put his cross in approximately the right area (whether the area where the ball actually was or where the judges adjudged that it should be), but the final half millimetre which might make the difference between winning and losing must be purely a matter of chance.

As I ventured to submit earlier to your Lordships, although skill or chance are not directly relevant to s 47 (1) (*a*) (as they are to s 47 (1) (*b*)), they are indirectly relevant as indicating whether there was an 'event' with a 'result' within the meaning of the paragraph, and if so what they were. In my view, the four matters to which I ventured to draw attention show beyond question that prizes were offered for an entry which

---

1 [1971] 1 All ER 129, [1971] 1 WLR 110

would coincide with (or approximate to) the spot pinpointed by the judges, and for nothing else. The 'event' was therefore (as in *Ladbrokes'* case[1]) the meeting of the judges, and its 'result' was their pinpointing of a particular spot. Since the meeting of the judges which resulted in such pinpointing took place after the submission of the entries, it was 'a future event'. The 'resultant' pinpointing which determined who should win the prize was 'forecast' by the competitors—it being immaterial whether it was the subject of pre-estimate or pre-conjecture.

It follows that I think that the decision of the Divisional Court was correct in the instant case, too, and I would dismiss the appeal.

LORD CROSS OF CHELSEA. My Lords, the result of this appeal turns on the meaning of the words 'forecasts of the result . . . of a future event' in s 47 (1) (*a*) (i) of the Betting, Gaming and Lotteries Act 1963, which—so far as material—is in the following terms:

> 'It shall be unlawful to conduct in or through any newspaper, or in connection with any trade or business or the sale of any article to the public—(*a*) any competition in which prizes are offered for forecasts of the result either—(i) of a future event; or (ii) of a past event the result of which is not yet ascertained or not yet generally known; (*b*) any other competition success in which does not depend to a substantial degree upon the exercise of skill . . .'

In order to make a forecast of the result of a future event it is, as I see it, necessary for the forecaster to have in mind some event—such as a horserace—which he expects to take place in the future and which, if it takes place, will end in something which can be called its result and to predict what that result will be. A forecast may or may not involve the exercise of skill. One man's 'forecast' of the result of the Derby may be the outcome of a train of reasoning based on long experience of the 'turf' and a profound knowledge of 'form'. Another man's forecast may be avowedly a pure guess such as sticking a pin on the list of starters. If a competition does not involve 'forecasts' it will only be unlawful if it is caught by sub-s (1) (*b*) because it does not depend to a substantial degree on the exercise of skill. If, on the other hand, the competition involves the making of 'forecasts' it will be unlawful, however much skill is needed to make them successfully. The charge in this case was brought under sub-s (1) (*a*) (i) as was the charge in *Ladbroke (Football) Ltd v Perrett*[1] and in each case what was said by the prosecution was that the future event the result of which was the subject of the forecast was the deliberation of the judges and the result the decision at which they arrived. With all respect to those who have thought or think otherwise I cannot understand how it can be said that when in response to an invitation to take part in a competition a man sends in his answer to the problem posed he is, by sending in his answer, making a forecast of the result of the deliberations of the judges. Of course if, after sending his answer in, a competitor was bold enough to say to a friend, 'I predict that when they come to study the answers the judges will adjudge mine to be the best' that statement might be said to be a forecast of the result of the deliberations of the judges. But to say that simply to send in an answer is to make a forecast of the result of the deliberations of the judges is, to my mind, an abuse of language. The competitor may never think of the judges and their deliberations at all. Counsel for the respondent conceded, indeed, that if the composition of an answer or entry which had the least chance of winning and the process of judging between the various answers or entries involved the exercise of skill—as, for instance, in a bridge competition or a literary competition—the answers or entries sent in would not be forecasts of the result of the judges' deliberations. But he submitted that it was otherwise in a case such as this where, as he alleged, the competitor's decision to put his cross at a particular spot rather than at another spot a millimetre to the left or right must be the result of chance rather than skill and the decision of the panel to select as the winning cross one particular cross rather than another a millimetre away from it must also be the outcome of chance. But even if counsel was right in saying that in this competition there must be a good deal of 'guesswork' in the placing of the crosses and that the final decision of the judges must be something of a 'toss up'—(and on that point I express no view one way or the other)—I cannot see why those facts should prevent the entries from being regarded as attempts to solve a problem or puzzle and make them forecasts of the result at which the judges will arrive. It follows that, in my judgment, *Ladbroke's* case[1] was wrongly decided and that this present appeal should be allowed. I express, of course, no view on the question whether on their facts either case could have been brought under sub-s (1) (*b*). Although the point is not before us I would add that I must not be taken to accept that this competition in its original and natural form offended against sub-s (1) (*a*) (ii). The prosecution would presumably say that the 'result' which the competitor was being asked to state was the presence of the ball at the particular spot at which it was when the photograph was taken; but what would be the 'past event' of which that was the result? Even if one confines oneself to immediate causes the presence of the ball at that spot was the result of a number of contributory factors such as the direction and force of the immediately preceding kick or 'heading', the direction and force of the wind if the ball was in the air, and the state of the ground if it was travelling along the ground. It seems artificial to say the least, to treat these various factors as together making up a 'past event' to which the competitor must be taken to be directing his mind and of which he was stating the result.

Appeal allowed.

Solicitors: *Theodore Goddard & Co* (for the appellants); *Solicitor, Corporation of the City of London* (for the respondent).

                                        S A Hatteea Esq Barrister.

---

1 [1971]t All ER 129, [1971] 1 WLR 110

Director of Public Prosecutions v Kilbourne

HOUSE OF LORDS
LORD HAILSHAM OF ST MARYLEBONE LC, LORD REID, LORD MORRIS OF BORTH-Y-GEST,
LORD SIMON OF GLAISDALE AND LORD CROSS OF CHELSEA
13th, 14th, 15th NOVEMBER 1972, 31st JANUARY 1973

Criminal law – Evidence – Corroboration – Indecent assault – Child victim – Boy – Evidence of system – Mutual corroboration – Evidence of other boys alleging similar offences against themselves – Evidence of other boys admissible as proving system and negativing innocent association – Whether evidence of other boys capable of constituting corroboration of victim's evidence.

The accused was charged on an indictment containing seven counts, and convicted of one offence of buggery, one of attempted buggery and five of indecent assault. The counts fell into two groups. Counts 1 to 4 referred to offences alleged to have been committed in 1970 and involved four boys; counts 5 to 7 alleged offences committed a year later and involved two other boys. The boys were all between the ages of nine and 12 at the time of the alleged offences. All the boys were called for the prosecution and were allowed to give sworn evidence. The prosecution alleged that the accused encouraged the boys to come to his house by providing them with various inducements and having got them into his house he committed the acts charged in the indictment. The accused admitted that the boys had come to his house but claimed that his association with them had been entirely innocent. The judge directed the jury that, whereas the boys in each of the two groups knew each other well and could have collaborated in putting forward their stories, it was unlikely, if not impossible, for the two groups to have collaborated in that way and accordingly they were entitled to take the evidence of the boys in one group as corroborating the evidence of the boys in the other group. The Court of Appeal[a] quashed the convictions holding that, although the evidence of the boys of one group was admissible in relation to charges concerning boys of the other group as tending to show that the accused was a homosexual whose proclivities took a particular form and as tending to rebut the defence of innocent association, that evidence could not in law constitute corroboration of the evidence of boys of the other group. The prosecution appealed.

Held – The appeal would be allowed. The word 'corroboration' had no special technical meaning; by itself it meant no more than evidence tending to confirm other evidence. No distinction could, therefore, be drawn between evidence which could be used as corroboration and evidence which might help the jury to determine the truth of the matter. Since the evidence of one group of boys was admissible in relation to the charges concerning the other group as being relevant to matters in dispute and implicating the accused in the criminal conduct alleged, that evidence, if believed, constituted corroboration. It was immaterial that the evidence of boys of both groups was mutually corroborative, or that each boy was, technically, an accomplice in relation to the offence committed against him (see p 446 e and f, p 448 b d and e, p 453 a, p 454 h, p 455 c, p 456 b and g, p 457 d h and j and p 463 a and g to p 464 b e f and h, post).

Director of Public Prosecutions v Hester [1972] 3 All ER 1056 applied.

R v Sims [1946] 1 All ER 697 and dictum of Lord Goddard CJ in *R v Campbell* [1956] 2 All ER at 276 explained and disapproved in part.

Per Lord Hailsham of St Marylebone LC, Lord Morris of Borth-y-Gest and Lord Simon of Glaisdale. There is no general rule that no persons who come within the definition of 'accomplice' may be mutually corroborative. The rule does not neces-

---

a [1972] 3 All ER 545, [1972] 1 WLR 1365

sarily apply to all witnesses in the same case who may deserve to be categorised as 'accomplice'. In particular it does not necessarily apply to accomplices who give independent evidence of separate incidents as proving system and negativing accident, and where the circumstances are such as to exclude the danger of a jointly fabricated story (see p 454 e and f, p 457 j and p 463 e, post).

Decision of the Court of Appeal sub nom *R v Kilbourne* [1972] 3 All ER 545 reversed.

Notes

For corroboration, see 10 Halsbury's Laws (3rd Edn) 458-462, paras 843-850, and for cases on directions as to corroboration, see 14 Digest (Repl) 542-545, *5258-5304*.

Cases referred to in opinions

Arthurs v A-G for Northern Ireland (1970) 55 Cr App Rep 161, HL (NI).

Davies v Director of Public Prosecutions [1954] 1 All ER 507, [1954] AC 378, 118 JP 222, 38 Cr App Rep 11, HL, 14 Digest (Repl) 527, *5108*.

Director of Public Prosecutions v Hester [1972] 3 All ER 1056, [1972] 3 WLR 910, HL.

Harris v Director of Public Prosecutions [1952] 1 All ER 1044, [1952] AC 694, 116 JP 248, 36 Cr App Rep 39, HL, 14 Digest (Repl) 423, *4118*.

HM Advocate v AE 1937 JC 96, 15 Digest (Repl) 1025, **6338*.

HM Advocate v M'Donald 1928 JC 42.

Makin v A-G for New South Wales [1894] AC 57, 63 LJPC 41, 69 LT 778, 58 JP 148, 17 Cox CC 704, PC, 14 Digest (Repl) 420, *4094*.

Moorov v HM Advocate 1930 JC 68.

Ogg v HM Advocate 1938 JC 152.

People, The (at the suit of the Attorney-General) v Dominic Casey (No 2) [1963] IR 33.

R v Bailey [1924] 2 KB 300, [1924] All ER Rep 466, 93 LJKB 989, 132 LT 349, 88 JP 72, 27 Cox CC 692, 18 Cr App Rep 42, CCA, 14 Digest (Repl) 335, *3249*.

R v Ball [1911] AC 47, 75 JP 180; sub nom *Public Prosecutions Director v Ball (No 2)* 80 LJKB 691, 103 LT 738, 22 Cox CC 366, 6 Cr App Rep 31, HL, 14 Digest (Repl) 426, *4138*.

R v Baskerville [1916] 2 KB 658, [1916-17] All ER Rep 38, 86 LJKB 28, 115 LT 453, 80 JP 446, 25 Cox CC 524, 12 Cr App Rep 81, CCA, 14 Digest (Repl) 536, *5214*.

R v Campbell [1956] 2 All ER 272, [1956] 2 QB 432, [1956] 3 WLR 219, 120 JP 359, 40 Cr App Rep 95, CCA, Digest (Cont Vol A) 377, *5106a*.

R v Chandor [1959] 1 All ER 702, [1959] 1 QB 545, [1959] 2 WLR 522, 123 JP 131, 194, 43 Cr App Rep 74, CCA, Digest (Cont Vol A), 367, *4204a*.

R v Christie [1914] AC 545, [1914-15] All ER Rep 63; sub nom *Public Prosecutions Director v Christie* 83 LJKB 1097, 111 LT 220, 78 JP 321, 24 Cox CC 249, 10 Cr App Rep 141, HL, 14 Digest (Repl) 405, *3962*.

R v Cratchley (1913) 9 Cr App Rep 232, CCA, 14 Digest (Repl) 59, *228*.

R v Flack [1969] 2 All ER 784, [1969] 1 WLR 937, 133 JP 445, 53 Cr App Rep 166, CA, Digest (Cont Vol C) 195, *2238a*.

R v Gay (1909) 2 Cr App Rep 327, CCA, 14 Digest (Repl) 536, *5209*.

R v Smith (1915) 84 LJKB 2153, [1914-15] All ER Rep 262, 114 LT 239, 80 JP 31, 25 Cox CC 271, 11 Cr App Rep 229, CCA, 14 Digest (Repl) 341, *3312*.

R v Lillyman [1896] 2 QB 167, [1895-99] All ER Rep 586, 65 LJMC 195, 74 LT 730, 60 JP 536, 18 Cox CC 346, CCR, 14 Digest (Repl) 453, *4390*.

R v Manser (1934) 25 Cr App Rep 18, CCA, 14 Digest (Repl) 525, *5102*.

R v Noakes (1832) 5 C & P 326, 172 ER 996, 14 Digest (Repl) 536, *5199*.

R v Prater [1960] 1 All ER 298, [1960] 2 QB 464, [1960] 2 WLR 343, 124 JP 176, 44 Cr App Rep 83, CCA, Digest (Cont Vol A) 379, *5303a*.

R v Price [1968] 2 All ER 282, [1969] 1 QB 541, [1968] 2 WLR 1397, 132 JP 335, 52 Cr App Rep 295, CA, Digest (Cont Vol C) 258, *9881b*.

R v Robinson [1953] 2 All ER 334, 37 Cr App Rep 95; sub nom *Practice Note* [1953] 1 WLR 872, CCA, 14 Digest (Repl) 600, *5969*.

R v Russell (1968) 52 Cr App Rep 147, CA, Digest (Cont Vol C) 219, *5217a*.

R v Sims [1946] 1 All ER 697, [1946] KB 531, [1947] LJR 160, 175 LT 72, 31 Cr App Rep
    158, CCA, 14 Digest (Repl) 260, 2279.
Thompson v R [1918] AC 221; sub nom *Thompson v Public Prosecutions Director* 87 LJKB
    478, 118 LT 418, 82 JP 145, 26 Cox CC 189, 13 Cr App Rep 61, HL; *affg* sub nom
    R v Thompson [1917] 2 KB 630, CCA, 14 Digest (Repl) 682, 6966.
R v Williams (1956) Crim LR 833, CCA.
R v Whitehead [1929] 1 KB 99, [1928] All ER Rep 186, 98 LJKB 67, 139 LT 640, 92 JP 197,
    27 LGR 1, 28 Cox CC 547, 21 Cr App Rep 23, CCA, 15 Digest (Repl) 1018, *10,016*.

Appeal

The respondent, John Kilbourne, was charged on an indictment containing seven
counts.   On 19th April 1972 he was convicted in the Crown Court at Leeds before
Lawson J and a jury of buggery, attempted buggery and five offences of indecent
assault on boys aged between nine and 12 years.   He was sentenced to ten years'
imprisonment for buggery, seven years for attempted buggery and five years for
each of the offences of indecent assault.   Sentences on counts 1 to 4 and on counts
5 to 7 were to run concurrently.   The sentences totalled 15 years, all being certified
as extended sentences.   The respondent appealed against the convictions and sentences.   The Court of Appeal (Lawton LJ, MacKenna and Swanwick JJ) by their
judgment delivered on 31st July 1972 and reported at [1972] 3 All ER 545 quashed
the convictions.   The Crown appealed.   The facts are set out in the opinion of
Lord Hailsham of St Marylebone LC.

R A R Stroyan QC and *C J Holland* for the Crown.
G Baker QC and *E A Greenwood* for the respondent.

Their Lordships took time for consideration.

31st January.   The following opinions were delivered.

LORD HAILSHAM OF ST MARYLEBONE LC. My Lords, this is an appeal
by the Director of Public Prosecutions from a decision of the Court of Appeal,
Criminal Division[1] (Lawton LJ, MacKenna and Swanwick JJ) quashing convictions on
seven counts of an indictment on which the respondent was convicted at the Leeds
Crown Court (Lawson J and a jury) on 19th April 1972.   One of these convictions
(count 3 of the original indictment) no longer falls to be considered.   It was quashed
by the Court of Appeal on grounds extraneous to any important question of law,
and the Crown does not now seek to sustain it.

The remaining six convictions consisted, as to one count of buggery, as to the
remainder of indecent assault, one of which had originally been presented as a charge
of buggery.   The charges all related to offences alleged to have been committed
against young boys.   All the boys gave evidence and were sworn.   The first three
convictions still in question related to dates between October and November 1970,
and the boys concerned were John, Paul and Simon (the brother of Paul).   These
convictions are referred to in the judgment of the Court of Appeal[1], and hereafter,
as 'the first group'.   The third count relating to a boy, Mark, no longer falling to be
considered, also belonged to this group.   The fourth, fifth and sixth convictions
still outstanding (counts 5, 6 and 7 of the original indictment) related to two boys,
Gary and Kevin, and to offences alleged to have been committed against them in
October and November 1971, approximately one year after the first group.   These
three counts are referred to hereafter as 'the second group'.   Count 5 related to an
offence alleged to have been committed on 3rd October 1971.   The remaining two
convictions in the second group related to offences alleged to have been committed on
7th November 1971, one against each of the two boys, and led directly to the police
investigations which appear to have begun at least as early as the following day.

1   [1972] 3 All ER 545, [1972] 1 WLR 1365

On conviction, the respondent was sentenced to periods of imprisonment amounting to 15 years in all. These were described by the trial judge (Lawson J) as having been extended by virtue of s 37 of the Criminal Justice Act 1967 in view of a formidable list of previous convictions for similar offences and one of attempted murder, committed against the victim of a sexual offence. Pending his appeal to this House, the respondent was ordered by the Court of Appeal to be detained under s 37 of the Criminal Appeal Act 1968. If this appeal is allowed, the respondent's appeals against these sentences still fall to be adjudicated on by the Court of Appeal (Criminal Division).

The appeal relates to corroboration, and is the second of two appeals dealing with this subject which have reached this House in a matter of weeks. The other appeal was *Director of Public Prosecutions v Hester*[1]. The decision of this House in *Hester*[1] had not been given at the time when the present appeal was argued, but I have had the advantage of reading the opinions delivered in that case when they were in draft. There are two manifest distinctions to be drawn between the facts in *Hester*[1] and the present case. *Hester's* case[1] was concerned with the alleged mutual corroboration of two witnesses, one of whom (the victim of the alleged offence) was sworn, and one of whom was an unsworn child who gave her evidence pursuant to s 38 of the Children and Young Persons Act 1933. In the present case all the witnesses were sworn. Secondly, in *Hester's* case[1] both the witnesses whose evidence was in question gave evidence purporting to deal with the same incident, which each claimed to have witnessed. In the present case, of the five boys in question, only two pairs claimed actually to have seen the same incident, and in the way in which the trial judge's summing-up was framed, the corroboration in fact placed before the jury related to incidents similar in character to one another, but in respect of each of which the evidence alleged to be mutually corroborative was supported by witnesses from the other group.

Both the offences of the first and the second group were alleged to have been committed by the respondent at his home, where the respondent resided with a young man called 'Vic' who gave evidence on his behalf. It was conceded that all the boys concerned with the charges visited the respondent there, and partook there of various refreshments or amusements, comics, cards, a puppy to take on a walk and so forth. The reason why they visited the respondent's home was in dispute. The Crown alleged that what was set up was a 'baited trap'. The respondent's case, to which he testified in the box, was that the association was innocent. The boys' presence in his house served, he claimed, to help him in his business as a painter and decorator as they helped to make him known in the neighbourhood. Although a certain amount of physical contact was admitted, it was only 'skylarking', and the detailed and unequivocal acts of misconduct which were specifically alleged the respondent denied in the witness box. What he admitted, he alleged to have been innocent in intention and entirely devoid of any sexual character. In short, the respondent's defence was innocent association coupled with a denial of those features of the evidence which were wholly incapable of such a construction.

It has been common ground throughout the case that the evidence of the boys was of the class demanding the customary warning to the jury about corroboration. In the event the judge gave such a warning. There was indeed evidence which, if believed, was corroboration of the strongest possible kind. The police officers concerned in the case testified that, in relation to each group, the respondent had admitted to 'playing with the private parts' or 'playing with the penises' (sic) of all the boys of each group, and the Court of Appeal[2] said that, if they could have satisfied themselves that this evidence had been believed, they would have had no hesitation in applying the proviso to s 2 (1) of the Criminal Appeal Act 1968.

---

1 [1972] 3 All ER 1056, [1972] 3 WLR 910
2 [1972] 3 All ER 545 at 551, [1972] 1 WLR 1365 at 1372, 1373

Happily, or unhappily, counsel for the Crown felt unable to rest on the evidence of the police officers as corroboration of the boys, and—

'by way of safeguarding his case against the possibility that the jury might reject the police evidence, he submitted to the trial judge . . . that there was other evidence which was capable of corroborating some of the evidence of the boys.'[1]

If he had not taken this course the case would certainly never have reached the House of Lords, and, possibly, never have been the subject of a reported judgment in the Court of Appeal. On such small chances, legal history depends. Counsel's submission as to corroboration was in substance accepted by the trial judge, who, as the Court of Appeal held, although the construction of the summing-up is not quite clear, directed the jury that they could regard the evidence of either of the two boys of the second group, Gary and Kevin, as corroboration of the evidence of any of the boys of the first group, John, Paul, Simon and Mark (whose evidence related to the quashed count three) and conversely the evidence of any of the boys of the first group as corroboration of Gary or Kevin. On the other hand, the trial judge directed the jury that they must not use the evidence of any of the boys of either group to reinforce the evidence of any boy of the same group as that to which the witness belonged. He evidently had in mind that the boys of each group were respectively well known to one another and wished thereby to exclude the possibility that they might have put up within each group, but not between groups, a concocted tale.

The Court of Appeal whose judgment was given by Lawton LJ approached the matter in three stages. Lawton LJ said[2]:

'. . . we have had to decide whether the evidence of one group of boys was admissible at all on the counts in which the other group of boys were named. If it was not, there was a misdirection as to the admissibility of evidence; but if it was admissible, the second and third stages have to be considered. The question at the second stage is whether such evidence if it had involved neither victims nor children could have been capable of being corroboration; and the third stage is whether in the circumstances of this case in which child victims were involved, it was capable of being corroboration.'

The Court of Appeal then held on the authority of R v Sims[3], R v Chandor[4] and R v Flack[5] that the evidence was admissible and admissible because it was relevant to the matters in dispute and implicated the respondent in the criminal conduct alleged in the indictment. The nerve of their argument is contained in the following short passage in the judgment of the court[6]:

'In the present case, with the exception of the penis touching incident involving the boy Kevin, each accusation bears a resemblance to the other and shows not merely that the [respondent] was a homosexual (which would not have been enough to make the evidence admissible), but that he was one whose proclivities in that regard took a particular form. Further, the evidence of each boy went to rebut the defence of innocent association which the [respondent] put forward: this by itself made the similar fact evidence admissible (see R v Chandor[7] per Lord Parker CJ). We have no doubt that the evidence of one group of boys could properly be taken into account by the jury when considering the counts

---

1 [1972] 3 All ER at 547, [1972] 1 WLR at 1367, 1368
2 [1972] 3 All ER at 548, [1972] 1 WLR at 1369
3 [1946] 1 All ER 697, [1946] KB 531
4 [1959] 1 All ER 702, [1959] 1 QB 545
5 [1969] 2 All ER 784, [1969] 1 WLR 937
6 [1972] 3 All ER at 548, 549, [1972] 1 WLR at 1369, 1370
7 [1959] 1 All ER at 703, [1959] 1 QB at 548, 549

relating to the other group. But for what purpose since only relevant evidence is admissible? What, for example, did Gary's evidence prove in relation to John's on count 1? The answer must be that his evidence, having the striking features of the resemblance between the acts committed on him and those alleged to have been committed on John, makes it more likely that John was telling the truth when he said that the [respondent] had behaved in the same way to him.'

The court went on to quote the passage of the judgment of the Court of Criminal Appeal in R v Sims[1] when they say:

'The evidence of each man was that the accused invited him into the house and there committed the acts charged. The acts they describe bear a striking similarity. That is a special feature sufficient in itself to justify the admissibility of the evidence ... The probative force of all the acts together is much greater than one alone; for, whereas the jury might think that one man might be telling an untruth, three or four are hardly likely to tell the same untruth unless they were conspiring together. If there is nothing to suggest a conspiracy their evidence would seem to be overwhelming.'

In spite of this reasoning, the Court of Appeal[2] went on to say that nonetheless there was nothing mutually corroborative in testimony of this kind. They felt themselves constrained to come to this conclusion because of the later passage in R v Sims[3] which says:

'We do not think that the evidence of the men can be considered as corroborating one another, because each may be said to be an accomplice in the act to which he speaks and his evidence is to be viewed with caution.'

On this the Court of Appeal quoted with some relish, the comments of Professor Cross[4]:

'... it is difficult to see how admissible evidence of misconduct of the defendant or accused on other occasions could ever fail to corroborate the evidence relating to the question with which the court is concerned. If it is admissible at all on account of its relevance for some reason other than its tendency to show a propensity towards wrongdoing in general or wrongdoing of the kind into which the court is inquiring, the conduct must, it would seem, implicate the defendant or accused in a material particular in relation to the occasion into which the court is inquiring.'

In quashing all the convictions on this ground the Court of Appeal went on to rely on the authority of R v Campbell[5], where it is said:

'... we may perhaps endeavour to give some guidance to courts who have from time to time to deal with cases of sexual assaults on children where the evidence of each child deals only with the assault on him or her self. In such cases it is right to tell a jury that because A says that the accused assaulted him, it is no corroboration of his evidence that B says that he also was the victim of a similar assault though both say it on oath. At the same time we think a jury may be told that a succession of these cases may help them to determine the truth of the matter provided they are satisfied that there is no collaboration between the children to put up a false story. And if the defence is one of innocent association by the accused with the children, the case of R v. Sims[6], subse-

1 [1946] 1 All ER at 701, [1946] KB at 539, 540
2 [1972] 3 All ER at 550, [1972] 1 WLR at 1371
3 [1946] 1 All ER at 703, [1946] KB at 544
4 Evidence (3rd Edn, 1967), p 182
5 [1956] 2 All ER 272 at 276, [1956] 2 QB 432 at 438, 439
6 [1946] 1 All ER 697, [1946] KB 531

quently approved on this point by the House of Lords in *Harris* v. *Public Prosecutions Director*[1], shows that such evidence can be given to rebut the defence.'

On this particular passage the Court of Appeal comment[2]:

'Here Lord Goddard CJ is apparently distinguishing between evidence which can be used as corroboration and evidence which may help the jury in some way to determine the truth. A's evidence that the accused indecently assaulted him may not be used to corroborate B's evidence that B was indecently assaulted, but it may be used in some other way to help the jury to determine the truth, of B's evidence: see Cross on Evidence[3], where he cites *Sims'* case[4] as an authority for this difficult distinction.'

Basing themselves on this state of the authorities, the Court of Appeal decided that[5] 'Accordingly we must hold the direction to be defective, with whatever consequences may follow from this view.' The consequences, of course, involved the quashing of all the convictions.

We now have to determine at the invitation of the Court of Appeal how 'evidence which can be used as corroboration and evidence which may help the jury in some other way to determine the truth' can be validly distinguished, and the distinction explained to a jury. The question certified by the Court of Appeal in the present case as of general public importance is:

'Whether and in what circumstances the sworn evidence of a child victim as to an offence charged can be corroborated by the admissible but uncorroborated evidence of another child victim as to similar misconduct of the accused on a different occasion.'

I may say at once that I regard the passage in *R v Campbell*[6] which attempts to draw a distinction between evidence which helps the jury to arrive at a conclusion about evidence requiring corroboration and evidence which is confirmatory or corroborative of evidence requiring corroboration as a valiant, but wholly unsuccessful, attempt to reconcile the two quoted passages in *R v Sims*[7], the second of which I believe to be wholly inconsistent with the first. The second passage may be based on what I believe to be a false analogy with the use which can be made by the prosecution of complaints by the alleged victim of a rape as evidence of consistency, but not corroboration, since a witness requiring corroboration 'cannot corroborate herself'. It may also be based to some extent on the rule about joint accomplices stretching back to *R v Noakes*[8] per Littledale J. But this also, as I shall endeavour to show, is a false analogy.

In my view, there is no magic or artificiality about the rule of practice concerning corroboration at all. In Scottish law, it seems, some corroboration is necessary in every criminal case. In contrast, by the English common law, the evidence of one competent witness is enough to support a verdict whether in civil or criminal proceedings except in cases of perjury (cf Hawkins[9] and Foster[10]). This is still the general rule, but there are now two main classes of exception to it. In the first place, there are a number of statutory exceptions. The main statutory exceptions are contained in (i) Treason Act 1795[11], s 1 (compassing the death of the Sovereign etc); (ii) Perjury Act 1911, s 13 (re-enacting the common law exception); (iii) Children

---

1   [1952] 1 All ER 1044, [1952] AC 694
2   [1972] 3 All ER at 550, [1972] 1 WLR at 1371, 1372
3   3rd Edn (1967), pp 320, 321, footnote 7
4   [1946] 1 All ER 697, [1946] KB 531
5   [1972] 3 All ER at 551, [1972] 1 WLR at 1372
6   [1956] 2 All ER 272 at 276, [1956] 2 QB 432 at 438, 439
7   [1946] 1 All ER at 701, 703, [1946] KB at 539, 540, 544
8   (1832) 5 C & P 326 at 328
9   Pleas of the Crown (8th Edn, 1824), Bk 2, c 25, s 129, c 46, s 2, pp 351, 590
10   Crown Cases (3rd Edn, 1809), c 3, 58, p 233
11   36 Geo 3 c 7

and Young Persons Act 1933, s 38 (1), proviso (dealing with the unsworn evidence of young children and re-enacting a statute of 1908); (iv) Representation of the People Act 1949, s 146 (5) (personation at elections); (v) Sexual Offences Act 1956, ss 2 (2), 3 (2), 4 (2), 22 (2) and 23 (2) (procuration etc); (vi) Road Traffic Act 1960, s 4 (2) (speeding); (vii) Affiliation Proceedings Act 1957, s 4 (2) (complainant's evidence against putative father). In each of these cases the different, but closely similar, provisions of the different statutes override the common law. The other main statutory exception in civil proceedings, the evidence of a plaintiff in breach of promise case is, of course, now obsolete.

But side by side with the statutory exceptions is the rule of practice now under discussion by which judges have in fact warned juries in certain classes of case that it is dangerous to found a conviction on the evidence of particular witnesses or classes of witness unless that evidence is corroborated in a material particular implicating the accused, or confirming the disputed items in the case. The earliest of these classes to be recognised was probably the evidence of accomplices 'approving' for the Crown, no doubt, partly because at that time the accused could not give evidence on his own behalf and was therefore peculiarly vulnerable to invented allegations by persons guilty of the same offence. By now the recognised categories also include children who give evidence under oath, the alleged victims, whether adults or children, in cases of sexual assault, and persons of admittedly bad character. I do not regard these categories as closed. A judge is almost certainly wise to give a similar warning about the evidence of any principal witness for the Crown where the witness can reasonably be suggested to have some purpose of his own to serve in giving false evidence (cf *R v Prater*[1] and *R v Russell*[2]). The Supreme Court of the Republic of Ireland has apparently decided that at least in some cases of disputed identity a similar warning is necessary (*People v Dominic Casey (No 2)*[3]). This question may still be open here (cf *R v Williams*[4] and *Arthurs v A-G for Northern Ireland*[5]).

Since the institution of the Court of Criminal Appeal in 1907, the rule, which was originally discretionary in the trial judge, has acquired the force of a rule of law in the sense that a conviction after a direction to the jury which does not contain the warning will be quashed, unless the proviso is applied: see *R v Baskerville*[6] and *Davies v Director of Public Prosecutions*[7] per Lord Simonds LC.

However, it is open to a judge to discuss with the jury the nature of the danger to be apprehended in convicting without corroboration and the degree of such danger (cf *R v Price*[8]) and it is well established that a conviction after an appropriate warning may stand notwithstanding that the evidence is uncorroborated, unless, of course, the verdict is otherwise unsatisfactory (*R v Baskerville*[6]). There is, moreover, no magic formula to be used (*R v Price*[8]). I agree with the opinions expressed in this House in *Director of Public Prosecutions v Hester*[9] that it is wrong for a judge to confuse the jury with a general if learned disquisition on the law. His summing-up should be tailor-made to suit the circumstances of the particular case. The word 'corroboration' is not a technical term of art, but a dictionary word bearing its ordinary meaning; since it is slightly unusual in common speech the actual word need not be used, and in fact it may be better not to use it. Where it is used it needs to be explained.

The difficulty which has arisen in the present case was complicated by the fact that the witnesses requiring corroboration were said to be corroborated by witnesses not

1   [1960] 1 All ER 298, [1960] 2 QB 464
2   (1968) 52 Cr App Rep 147
3   [1963] IR 33 at 39, 40
4   (1956) Crim LR 833
5   (1970) 55 Cr App Rep 161 at 169
6   [1916] 2 KB 658, [1916-17] All ER Rep 38
7   [1954] 1 All ER 507 at 512, [1945] AC 378 at 398
8   [1968] 2 All ER 282 at 285, [1969] 1 QB 541 at 546
9   [1972] 3 All ER 1056, [1972] 3 WLR 910

of the same incident, but of incidents of a similar character themselves all of the class
requiring corroboration. A considerable part of the time taken up in argument was
devoted to a consideration whether such evidence of similar incidents could be used
against the respondent to establish his guilt at all, and we examined the authorities in
some depth from *Makin v A-G for New South Wales*[1], through Lord Sumner's observations in *Thompson v R*[2] to *Harris v Director of Public Prosecutions*[3]. I do not myself
feel that the point really arises in the present case. Counsel for the respondent was
in the end constrained to agree that all the evidence in this case was both admissible
and relevant, and that the Court of Appeal[4] was right to draw attention to the
'striking features of the resemblance' between the acts alleged to have been committed
in one count and those alleged to have been committed in the others, and to say
that this made it 'more likely that John was telling the truth when he said that the
[respondent] had behaved in the same way to him'. In my view, this was wholly
correct. With the exception of one incident[5]:

> '... each accusation bears a resemblance to the other and shows not merely
> that [the respondent] was a homosexual (which would not have been enough to
> make the evidence admissible), but that he was one whose proclivities in that
> regard took a particular form.'

I also agree with the Court of Appeal in saying that the evidence of each child went to
contradict any possibility of innocent association. As such it was admissible as part
of the prosecution case, and since, by the time the judge came to sum up, innocent
association was the foundation of the defence put forward by the respondent, the admissibility, relevance, and, indeed cogency of the evidence was beyond question. The
word 'corroboration' by itself means no more than evidence tending to confirm other
evidence. In my opinion, evidence which is (a) admissible and (b) relevant to the
evidence requiring corroboration, and, if believed, confirming it in the required
particulars, is capable of being corroboration of that evidence and, when believed,
is in fact such corroboration. As Professor Cross well says in his book on Evidence[6]:

> 'The ground of the admissibility of this type of evidence was succinctly stated
> by HALLETT, J., when delivering the judgment of the Court of Criminal Appeal
> [in *R v Robinson*[7]]: "If the jury are precluded by some rule of law from taking
> the view that something is a coincidence which is against all the probabilities if
> the accused person is innocent, then it would seem to be a doctrine of law which
> prevents a jury from using what looks like ordinary common sense."'

That this is so in the law of Scotland seems beyond dispute, and it would be astonishing if the law of England were different in this respect, since one would hope that
the same rules of logic and common sense are common to both. We were referred
to *Moorov v HM Advocate*[8] (an indecent assault case), *HM Advocate v AE*[9] (an incest
case) and *Ogg v HM Advocate*[10] (a case of indecent conduct with male persons).

I quote from these cases at length because they are not easily available in parts of
England. My only criticism of them in principle is that they seem to suggest in
places that cases of sexual misconduct are in some ways different from other cases.
I do not believe this is so. They are, I believe, particular applications of general

1   [1894] AC 57
2   [1918] AC 221
3   [1952] 1 All ER 1044, [1952] AC 694
4   [1972] 3 All ER 545 at 549, [1972] 1 WLR 1365 at 1370
5   [1932] 3 All ER at 548, 549, [1972] 1 WLR at 1369
6   3rd Edn (1967), p 316
7   (1953) 37 Cr App Rep 95 at 106
8   1930 JC 68
9   1937 JC 96
10   1938 JC 152

a principles which mutatis mutandis, can be applied elsewhere. In *Moorov v HM Advocate*[1] the Lord Justice-General (Lord Clyde) said[1]:

'In the present case there is direct evidence in support of the *factum probandum* as regards each charge which the jury found proved. But the evidence is that of a single credible witness only to each charge. Corroboration is sought from the circumstance that the charges thus supported are numerous and of
b the same kind, and the question is whether the case is one in which resort may legitimately be had to corroboration derived from this circumstance.

'It is beyond doubt, in the law of Scotland, that corroboration may be found in this way, provided that the similar charges are *sufficiently* connected with, or related to each other—Hume on Crimes[2]; Alison's Criminal Law[3]. But what is the test of *sufficiency*? The test I think is whether the evidence of the single
c witnesses as a whole—although each of them speaks to a different charge—leads by necessary inference to the establishment of some circumstance or state of fact underlying and connecting the several charges, which, if it had been independently established, would have afforded corroboration of the evidence given by the single witnesses in support of the separate charges. If such a circumstance or state of fact was actually established by independent evidence, it would not
d occur to anyone to doubt that it might be properly used to corroborate the evidence of each single witness. The case is the same, when such a circumstance is established by an inference necessarily arising on the evidence of the single witnesses, as a whole. The only difference is that the drawing of such an inference is apt to be a much more difficult and delicate affair than the consideration of independent evidence. No merely superficial connexion in time, character, and
e circumstance between the repeated acts—important as these factors are—will satisfy the test I have endeavoured to formulate. Before the evidence of single credible witnesses to separate acts can provide material for mutual corroboration, the connexion between the separate acts (indicated by their external relation in time, character, or circumstance) must be such as to exhibit them as subordinates in some particular and ascertained unity of intent, project, cam-
f paign, or adventure, which lies beyond or behind—but is related to—the separate acts. The existence of such an underlying unity, comprehending and governing the separate acts, provides the necessary connecting link between them, and becomes a circumstance in which corroboration of the evidence of the single witnesses in support of the separate acts may be found—whether the existence of such underlying unity is established by independent evidence, or by necessary
g inference from the evidence of the single witnesses themselves, regarded as a whole. It is just here, however, that the pinch comes, in such a case as the present. The Lord Advocate spoke as if it would be enough to show from the evidence of the single witnesses that the separate acts had occurred in what he called "a course of criminal conduct." Risk of confusion lurks behind a phrase of that kind; for it might correctly enough be applied to the everyday class of case in which a
h criminal recurs from time to time to the commission of the same kind of offence in similar circumstances. It might be justly said, in relation to the evidence in support of any indictment in which a number of such similar crimes committed over a period of (say) three years are charged together, that the accused had been following "a course of criminal conduct." If any of the crimes in the series had formed the subject of a former prosecution or prosecutions, and convictions had
j been obtained, neither the commission of such former crimes nor the previous convictions could afford any material for corroborating the evidence of a single witness in support of the last member of the series. And therefore—especially

---

1 1930 JC at 73, 74
2 Vol 2, p 384
3 Vol 2, p 552

in view of the growing practice of accumulating charges in one indictment—it
is of the utmost importance to the interests of justice that the "course of criminal   *a*
conduct" must be shown to be one which not only consists of a series of offences,
the same in kind, committed under similar circumstances, or in a common *locus*
—these are after all no more than external resemblances—but which owes its
source and development to some underlying circumstance or state of fact such
as I have endeavoured, though necessarily in very general terms, to define.'
                                                                                        b
The Lord Justice-Clerk (Lord Alness) in a similar passage said[1]:

   'The principle to be extracted from these passages may, I think, be expressed
   both negatively and positively. Negatively it may be expressed thus:—that where
   different acts of the same crime have no relation or connexion with each other,
   it is not competent to eke out and corroborate the evidence of one witness to
   one act by the evidence of another witness to another act. Positively the rule   *c*
   may be expressed thus:—that where, on the other hand, the crimes are related
   or connected with one another, where they form part of the same criminal
   conduct, the corroborative evidence tendered is competent. In that case, as
   Dickson[2] says:—"The unity of character in such cases makes it highly probable
   that they were all parts of one thieving expedition." The statement of the distinction is easy but its application is manifestly difficult. In every case, as it seems   *d*
   to me, the Court must put itself the question—Is there some sort of *nexus* which
   binds the alleged crimes together? Or, on the other hand, are they independent
   and unrelated?'

Lord Sands spoke to the same effect[3]:

   'In regard to the relevancy as corroboration of such evidence as is here in   *e*
   question, there is not, as in the case of previous convictions or of statements by a
   client to his agent, any clear-cut rule of law formulated in non-ambulatory terms.
   There are two extremes. On the one hand, it is not in dispute that, in the case of
   certain offences, such as indecent conduct towards young children, evidence of
   one offence is corroborative of the evidence of another alleged to have been
   committed at a near interval of time and under similar circumstances. On the   *f*
   other hand, it is not in dispute that, in the case of two thefts having no peculiar
   connexion the one with the other, evidence of the commission of the one is not
   corroboration of evidence of the commission of the other. Cases which fall clearly
   within the one class or the other present no difficulty. But between the two classes
   one seems to get into somewhat open country. This consideration leads me to
   fall back upon what I said at the outset about the function of evidence to ascer-   *g*
   tain the truth of the matter by fair and impartial inquiry. In that view it is
   admissible to take into account evidence in support of one charge as corroboration of the evidence in support of another, when the former, taken in connexion
   with the latter, is—to use a familiar old expression—relevant to infer that the
   panel committed the latter offence. It does not suffice merely that the evidence
   in support of the one charge makes it more comfortable to convict upon the   *h*
   other; it must be such evidence as helps to bring home the guilt of the accused
   to a reasonable and logical mind with sure conviction . . . The other landmark
   is what has been described as embarking on a course of conduct. Where the
   accused, about the time the alleged offence was committed, has embarked upon
   a certain peculiar course of conduct, the fact that he has done so is corroborative of evidence of a special act alleged to have been committed in pursuance   *j*
   of that course of conduct. I say "peculiar course," and I do so advisedly. Evidence
   of a general evil course will not suffice. There must be some peculiarity, or some

---

1 — 1930 JC at 80
2   Dickson on Evidence (Grierson's Edn), para 1810
3   1930 JC at 88, 89

a   special incidents, which stamp the offences charged as within the ambit of a
     course of conduct. This may be illustrated by the case I have already referred to
     of indecent offences against children. Evidence inferring a course of general
     immorality would not be admissible or corroborative of an indecent offence
     against an adult. But indecency against children is a rare and peculiar offence,
     and, accordingly, evidence inferring a course of conduct is admitted as relevant.'

b   Finally Lord Blackburn said[1]:

     'I agree with your Lordship in the chair that the greatest caution is necessary in
     applying the rule that the evidence of a single witness to a particular offence may
     be held to be corroborated by the evidence of another single witness to a similar
     offence. That such a rule may apply in certain cases admits of no doubt, but it is,
     I think, difficult, if not hopeless, to attempt to define within precise limits the
c   classes of cases, or the circumstances, in which it should be applied. I agree with
     your Lordship that there must be a close similarity between the nature of the
     two offences to each of which only one witness speaks, before the evidence of the
     one witness can be taken as corroborating the evidence of the other. I also agree
     that there must be some connexion between the two offences in the matter of
     time. I have already committed myself to the view that such corroboration is
d   competent in the case of offences against young girls—M'Donald[2]. That appears
     to me to be a class of case isolated from all others in one respect at any rate, viz.,
     that a child of tender age is not only liable to be easily influenced by an adult, but
     is herself in the eyes of the law incapable of giving any consent to, or encourage-
     ment of, the offence which is committed against her. If what the child says did
     happen, then a crime has been committed, and the fact that the child is telling
e   a true story may be corroborated by the proved truthfulness of the child on other
     incidental matters, and by the fact that another child, also proved to be truthful,
     has had a similar experience at the hands of the same man.'

     In HM Advocate v AE[3], a case at first instance, the Lord Justice-Clerk (Lord Aitchison)
     summed up to the jury as follows[4]:

f   'Now, I want finally to put before you one or two circumstances that you may
     think point in the direction of corroboration. First, I must give you a direction
     on this question—Can you take the evidence of the one girl as corroboration of
     the evidence of the other? Now, unless you believe both girls you need not
     consider whether you are going to take the evidence of the one as corroboration
     of the evidence of the other. If you believe J. and do not believe E., then, of course, E.'s evidence
g   would be no use in the case of J., because you do not believe what E. said. And
     J.'s evidence would be of no use in the case of E., for the same reason; but, if you
     believe both, I want you to consider anxiously whether you ought not to accept
     the evidence of the one as corroborating the evidence of the other. Now, it is a
     well-established rule in our criminal law that you do not prove one crime by
     proving another or by leading evidence tending to show that another crime has
h   been committed. That is a good general rule. But then, when you are dealing
     with this class of crime there is some relaxation of the rule, otherwise you might
     never be able to bring the crime home at all. Let me give you an illustration
     that is not at all unfamiliar—there are many cases of it, especially in our large
     cities—you get a degraded man who finds some little girl in the street, and he
     gives her a penny, and gets her to go up a close, and there he does something
j   immoral with her, and then he sends her away. Nobody sees what he has done;
     there is only the evidence of the child. And then the same thing happens with

---

1   1930 JC at 92, 93
2   1928 JC 42
3   1937 JC 96
4   1937 JC at 98-100

another child, and again nobody sees that; and then there is a third child, and
the same thing happens again. Well, of course, if you had to have two witnesses
to every one of these acts—they are all separate crimes—you would never prove
anything at all. But that is not the law. The law is this, that, when you find a
man doing the same kind of criminal thing in the same kind of way towards two
or more people, you may be entitled to say that the man is pursuing a course of
criminal conduct, and you may take the evidence on one charge as evidence on
another. That is a very sound rule, because a great many scoundrels would get
off altogether if we had not some such rule in our law. Now, I give you this
direction in law. If the conduct which is the subject of these charges is similar
in character and circumstances, and substantially coincident in time, and you
believe the evidence of both of these girls, then the evidence of the one may be
taken as corroboration of the evidence of the other. This is in substance what was
laid down in the High Court in the case of *Moorov v. H.M. Advocate*[1]. That was a
case where an employer in a Glasgow warehouse used to take one girl employee
at a time up to his private office, and there commit an act of indecency, and then
she was put out of the door. Nobody saw the act of indecency committed.
There was only the girl's word for it. And then he would get another girl to go
up, and the same thing would happen. Again nobody else was there, and there
was just the girl's word for it. Now, no doubt there were in that case a number
of these criminal assaults committed upon separate girls, whereas in this case
we are only dealing with two, but I do not hesitate to tell you—and I take the
responsibility of telling you—that if you believe the evidence of these two girls
whom you have seen in the witness-box, and accept it as the evidence of reliable
witnesses, you may take the one as corroborating the other, and, therefore, as
against the accused on each charge.'

In addition to the valuable direction to the jury, this summing-up appears to me to
contain a proposition which is central to the nature of corroboration, but which does
not appear to date to have been emphasised in any reported English decision until
the opinion delivered in *Director of Public Prosecutions v Hester*[2] by Lord Morris of
Borth-y-Gest although it is implicit in them all. Corroboration is only required or
afforded if the witness requiring corroboration or giving it is otherwise credible.
If his evidence is not credible, a witness's testimony should be rejected and the
accused acquitted, even if there could be found evidence capable of being corroboration in other testimony. Corroboration can only be afforded to or by a witness who
is otherwise to be believed. If a witness's testimony falls of its own inanition the
question of his needing, or being capable of giving, corroboration does not arise.
It is for this reason that evidence of complaint is acceptable in rape cases to defeat
any presumption of consent and to establish consistency of conduct, but not as
corroboration. The jury is entitled to examine any evidence of complaint, in order to
consider the question whether the witness is credible at all. It is not entitled to
treat that evidence as corroboration because a witness, although otherwise credible
'cannot corroborate himself'—i e the evidence is not 'independent testimony' to
satisfy the requirements of corroboration in *R v Baskerville*[3]. Of course, the moment
at which the jury must make up its mind is at the end of the case. They must look
at the evidence as a whole before asking themselves whether the evidence of a given
witness is credible in itself and whether, if otherwise credible, it is corroborated.
Nevertheless, corroboration is a doctrine applying to otherwise credible testimony
and not to testimony incredible in itself. In the present case Mark's evidence (count 3)
was corroborated. But it was not credible and the conviction founded on it was
rightly quashed.

---

1   1930 JC 68
2   [1972] 3 All ER 1056, [1972] 3 WLR 910
3   [1916] 2 KB at 667, [1916-17] All ER Rep at 43

a   It seems to me that the only way in which the doctrine on which the decision of the Court of Appeal[1] was founded can be supported, would be if there were some general rule of law to the effect that witnesses of a class requiring corroboration could not corroborate one another. For this rule of law counsel for the respondent expressly contended. I do not believe that such a rule of law exists. It is probably true that the testimony of one unsworn child cannot corroborate the testimony of

b   another unsworn child (see Cross[2]) but if so this is probably because this is expressly prohibited by statute (see *Director of Public Prosecutions v Hester*[3]). It is not 'other' testimony within the meaning of the proviso to the Children and Young Persons Act 1933, s 38 (1). This House has now decided in *Director of Public Prosecutions v Hester*[3] that the sworn testimony of a child can be corroborated by the unsworn testimony of another child and vice versa. In so doing the House disapproved the 'circular argument' doctrine first enunciated by Lord Hewart CJ in *R v Manser*[4] which was

c   at one time generally accepted, and which is probably the only real support for the general proposition contended for on behalf of the respondent. There Lord Hewart CJ said[5]:

> 'The argument for the prosecution is therefore an argument in a circle. Let it be granted that the evidence of Barbara [the elder child witness for the prosecution who may have been sworn or unsworn] has to be corroborated; it is corrob-
d   orated by the evidence of Doris [the younger child witness who was unsworn]. She, however, also needs to be corroborated. The answer is that she is corrobor-ated by the evidence of Barbara, and that is called "mutual corroboration." In truth and in fact the evidence of the girl Doris ought to have been obliterated altogether from the case, inasmuch as it was not corroborated.'

e   In *Director of Public Prosecutions v Hester*[3] this House has stigmatised this argument as fallacious. With respect, I wholly agree, and I hope no more will be heard of it.

The other ground on which the general proposition may be defended is the bald proposition that one accomplice cannot corroborate another. In support of this proposition were cited *R v Noakes*[6] per Littledale J, *R v Gay*[7], *R v Prater*[8] per Edmund Davies J, *R v Baskerville*[9] citing *R v Noakes*[6] and *R v Cratchley*[10]. I believe these
f   citations have been misunderstood. They all refer to fellow accomplices: see per Lord Diplock in *Director of Public Prosecutions v Hester*[11]. Obviously where two or more fellow accomplices give evidence against an accused their evidence is equally tainted. The reason why accomplice evidence requires corroboration is the danger of a concocted story designed to throw the blame on the accused. The danger is not less, but may be greater, in the case of fellow accomplices. Their joint evidence is not

g   'independent' in the sense required by *R v Baskerville*[12], and a jury must be warned not to treat it as a corroboration. But this illustrates the danger of mistaking the shadow for the substance. I feel quite sure that, for instance, where an unpopular officer in the army or the unpopular headmaster of a school could have been the victim of a conspiracy to give false evidence of this kind as the suggestion was in *R v Bailey*[13] a similar warning should be given. As Lord Hewart CJ said in that case[14] (which turned,
h   however, on a wholly different point):

1   [1972] 3 All ER 545, [1972] 1 WLR 1365
2   Evidence (3rd Edn, 1967), p 164
3   [1972] 3 All ER 1056, [1972] 3 WLR 910
4   (1934) 25 Cr App Rep 18
5   (1934) 25 Cr App Rep at 20
6   (1832) SC & P 326
7   (1909) 2 Cr App Rep 327
8   [1960] 1 All ER at 299, [1960] 2 QB at 465
9   [1916] 2 KB at 664, [1916-17] All ER Rep at 41
10 (1913) 9 Cr App Rep 232
11 [1972] 3 All ER at 1073, 1074, [1972] 3 WLR at 929, 930
12 [1916] 2 KB at 667, [1916-17] All ER Rep at 43
13 [1924] 2 KB 300, [1924] All ER Rep 466
14 [1924] 2 KB at 305, [1924] All ER Rep at 467

'The risk, the danger, the logical fallacy is indeed quite manifest to those who are in the habit of thinking about such matters. It is so easy to derive from a series of unsatisfactory accusations, if there are enough of them, an accusation which at least appears satisfactory. It is so easy to collect from a mass of ingredients, not one of which is sufficient, a totality which will appear to contain what is missing.'

On the other hand, where the so-called accomplices are of the third class listed by Lord Simonds LC in *Davies v Director of Public Prosecutions*[1] the danger is or may be nugatory. The real need is to warn the jury of the danger of a conspiracy to commit perjury in these cases, and, where there is the possibility of this, it is right to direct them not to treat as corroborative of one witness the evidence of another witness who may be part of the same conspiracy, but who cannot be an accomplice because if the evidence is untrue there has been no crime committed. This prompts me to point out that although the warning must be given in every appropriate case, the dangers to be guarded against may be quite different. Thus the evidence of accomplices is dangerous because it may be perjured. The evidence of Lady Wishfort complaining of rape may be dangerous because she may be indulging in undiluted sexual fantasy. A Mrs Frail making the same allegation may need corroboration because of the danger that she does not wish to admit the consensual intercourse of which she is ashamed. In another case the danger may be one of honestly mistaken identity as when the conviction of the accused depends on an identification by a single uncorroborated witness to whom he was previously unknown. These matters should, in suitable cases, be explored when the nature and degree of danger is being discussed, as suggested in *R v Price*[2]. I do not, therefore, believe that there is a general rule that no persons who come within the definition of accomplice may be mutually corroborative. It applies to those in the first and second of Lord Simonds LC's categories and to many other cases where witnesses are not or may not be accomplices. It does not necessarily apply to all witnesses in the same case who may deserve to be categorised as 'accomplice'. In particular it does not necessarily apply to accomplices of Lord Simonds LC's third class, where they give independent evidence of separate incidents, and where the circumstances are such as to exclude the danger of a jointly fabricated story.

Whatever else it is, the rule about fellow accomplices is not authority for the proposition that no witness who may himself require corroboration may afford corroboration for another to whom the same consideration applies, and this alone is what would help the respondent. When a small boy relates a sexual incident implicating a given man he may be indulging in fantasy. If another small boy relates such an incident it may be a coincidence if the detail is insufficient. If a large number of small boys relate similar incidents in enough detail about the same person, if it is not conspiracy it may well be that the stories are true. Once there is a sufficient nexus it must be for the jury to say what weight is given to the combined testimony of a number of witnesses.

These considerations lead inescapably to the conclusion that the appeal must be allowed. There is no dispute that the witnesses required corroboration, nor that the judge gave an adequate warning of the danger of convicting in the absence of corroboration. The witnesses of the several children were ex concessis admissible, and there were sufficient points of similarity in their several pieces of testimony to provide the underlying unity to make their evidence mutually probative within the meaning of the first passage from *R v Sims*[3] and the Scottish authorities quoted above. There is no general rule that witnesses of a class requiring corroboration cannot corroborate one another if otherwise admissible and relevant as probative. The distinc-

---

1　[1954] 1 All ER at 513, [1954] AC at 400
2　[1968] 2 All ER at 285, [1969] 1 QB at 546
3　[1946] 1 All ER at 701, [1946] KB at 539, 540

a tions adumbrated in *R v Sims*[1] and *R v Campbell*[2] on which the Court of Appeal[3] founded their decision is logically untenable, as is the 'circular argument' doctrine enunciated in *R v Manser*[4] and disapproved in *Director of Public Prosecutions v Hester*[5]. The rule regarding inability of fellow accomplices to corroborate one another does not apply in this case. A number of minor points criticising the summing-up were raised by counsel for the respondent. These were not raised on the grounds of appeal,

b nor before the Court of Appeal[3], and are not reflected in the question certified by the Court of Appeal. I do not believe they are now open to the respondent, and in any event, once the major question has been disposed of, I would not hesitate to apply the proviso.

To the question certified by the Court of Appeal as of general public interest, I would reply that the sworn evidence of a child victim can be corroborated by the

c evidence of another child victim of alleged similar misconduct where such evidence is otherwise admissible and, under the general law regarding relevance, is probative of the facts in dispute and indicative of the guilt of the accused, and if and when believed by the jury. I would observe that the adjective 'uncorroborated' in the third line of the question is inappropriate. Such evidence is not uncorroborated if itself corroborated in the above set of circumstances by the original testimony requir-

d ing corroboration. In my judgment the whole appeal illustrates the danger well stated in Cross on Evidence[1] where it is said in the context of Lord Hewart CJ's 'circular argument' doctrine in *R v Manser*[4]:

'The foregoing discussion reveals what may be a defect in the law relating to corroboration generally. There is a danger that the law will become enmeshed in technicalities concerning what does and does not amount to corroboration,

e whereas all that is required is the recognition that there are certain situations, including all cases in which material evidence is that of children, in which it is necessary for the tribunal of fact to proceed with caution.'

The law may not go quite so far as the last sentence. But as I have sought to show, artificiality is to be avoided and if this unhappy case serves to minimise it, it will have served a useful purpose.

f In my view, therefore, the appeal should be allowed, and the convictions restored, and the Court of Appeal should proceed to consider the appeals against sentence lodged in the case.

LORD REID. My Lords, the question in this case is whether the Court of Appeal[3] were right in quashing the conviction of the respondent on three counts alleging

g offences against s 12 (1) and four counts alleging offences against s 15 (1) of the Sexual Offences Act 1956. The Crown seeks restoration of the conviction on all counts except count 3.

The victims in all cases were boys between nine and 12 years of age. Each count charges an offence against a different boy. All the boys gave sworn evidence. On each count there was no direct evidence of the act charged under it beyond the

h evidence of the boy concerned. By what has now become a rule of law the trial judge was bound to warn the jury of the great danger of accepting the unsupported evidence of a boy of this age and to advise them that they should look for corroboration before convicting on any count. The learned judge did give a warning to the jury. But the Court of Appeal[3] held that he had misdirected them as to what they could regard as corroboration so they quashed the conviction.

i
1 [1946] 1 All ER 697, [1946] KB 537
2 [1956] 2 All ER 272, [1956] 2 QB 432
3 [1972] 3 All ER 545, [1972] 1 WLR 1365
4 (1934) 25 Cr App Rep 18
5 [1972] 3 All ER 1056, [1972] 3 WLR 910
6 3rd Edn (1967) p 166

Each count must of course be considered separately and in cases of this kind the first question must be whether evidence of acts charged under other counts can be taken into consideration. That is only permissible when the evidence as a whole discloses what has been loosely called a system. In the present case it has been admitted and I think that it is clearly established that that requirement is fulfilled. So as the question was not argued, I shall say no more than that this may often be a difficult question and that, in addition to the English authorities, valuable guidance may be obtained from the leading Scottish case of *Moorov v HM Advocate*[1].

The main difficulty in the case is caused by observations in *R v Manser*[2] to the effect that the evidence of one witness which required corroboration cannot be used as corroboration of that of another witness which also requires corroboration. For some unexplained reason it was held that there can be no mutual corroboration in such a case. I do not see why that should be so. There is nothing technical in the idea of corroboration. When in the ordinary affairs of life one is doubtful whether or not to believe a particular statement one naturally looks to see whether it fits in with other statements or circumstances relating to the particular matter; the better it fits in the more one is inclined to believe it. The doubted statement is corroborated to a greater or lesser extent by the other statements or circumstances with which it fits in.

In ordinary life we should be and in law we are required to be careful in applying this idea. We must be astute to see that the apparently corroborative statement is truly independent of the doubted statement. If there is any real chance that there has been collusion between the makers of the two statements we should not accept them as corroborative. And the law says that a witness cannot corroborate himself. In ordinary affairs we are often influenced by the fact that the maker of the doubted statement has consistently said the same thing ever since the event described happened. But the justification for the legal view must I think be that generally it would be too dangerous to take this into account and therefore it is best to have a universal rule.

So when we are considering whether there can be mutual corroboration between witnesses each of whom require corroboration the question must or at least ought to be whether it would be too dangerous to allow this. It might often be dangerous if there were only two children. But here we are dealing with cases where there is a 'system', and I do not think that only two instances would be enough to establish a 'system'. Where several children, between whom there can have been no collaboration in concocting a story, all tell similar stories it appears to me that the conclusion that each is telling the truth is likely to be inescapable and the corroboration is very strong. So I can see no ground at all for the law refusing to recognise the obvious. Once there are enough children to shew a 'system' I can see no ground for refusing to recognise that they can corroborate each other.

Many of the authorities cited deal with accomplices where the rule as to the need of warning that there should be corroboration is similar to the rule with regard to children. I do not think it useful to regard children as accomplices; the rule with regard to children applies whether or not they are accomplices. In most of the authorities the accomplices were accomplices to a single crime so the danger that they collaborated in concocting their story is obvious, and it is therefore quite right that there should be a general rule that accomplices cannot corroborate each other. Whether that should be a universal rule I greatly doubt, but I need not pursue that matter in this case. Then there are indications of a special rule for homosexual crimes. If there ever was a time for that, that time is past, and on the view which I take of the law any such special rule is quite unnecessary.

I must now turn to the authorities subsequent to the *Manser* case[2]. The most

1   1930 JC 68
2   (1934) 25 Cr App Rep 18

a important are *R v Sims*[1] and *R v Campbell*[2]. I am in general agreement with the greater part of the *Sims*[1] judgment but the last part appears to have been influenced by the *Manser*[3] doctrine and to that extent I think that it is erroneous. The present position of the law is set out in *R v Campbell*[4]:

'As we are endeavouring in this judgment to deal comprehensively with the evidence of children we may perhaps endeavour to give some guidance to courts who have from time to time to deal with cases of sexual assaults on children
b where the evidence of each child deals only with the assault on him or her self. In such cases it is right to tell a jury that because A says that the accused assaulted him, it is no corroboration of his evidence that B says that he also was the victim of a similar assault though both say it on oath. At the same time we think a jury may be told that a succession of these cases may help them to determine the truth of the matter provided they are satisfied that there is no collaboration
c between the children to put up a false story. And if the defence is one of innocent association by the accused with the children, the case of *R. v. Sims*[1], subsequently approved on this point by the House of Lords in *Harris* v. *Public Prosecutions Director*[5], shows that such evidence can be given to rebut the defence.'

I find this very difficult to understand. I do not see how evidence with regard to
d count B can help the jury to determine whether evidence with regard to count A is true unless it amounts to corroboration of that evidence. I can see no difference between saying that evidence corroborates other evidence, and saying that evidence helps one to determine the truth of the other evidence.

Any attempt to apply this distinction in practice must I think lead to confusion. How is the jury to be directed? Counsel were unable to suggest and I cannot suggest
e any better way than this. The judge must tell the jury to consider each count separately. He must then warn them of the danger of accepting the evidence of the child to whom count I relates unless it is corroborated. Then he must tell them that the evidence of the other children is not corroboration. Then he must tell them that they can act on the uncorroborated evidence of the first child if they feel sure that it is true and that in considering that matter they can obtain help by taking into
f consideration the evidence of the other children. I should be surprised if any jury understood such a direction: it could only confuse them.

The law cannot be left in such a state. In the present case the learned trial judge was obviously trying to make the passage which I have quoted from *R v Campbell*[4] intelligible to the jury, but the Court of Appeal[6] have held that he failed. I cannot blame the trial judge nor can I blame the Court of Appeal. And I would not blame
g the court which decided *Campbell's* case[2].

The trouble has arisen from the rule that the Court of Appeal is not permitted to reconsider an earlier judgment of that court. So in order to do justice they may have to invent a distinction without a difference. For a long time the court appear to have been reluctant to reach the logical result required by the *Manser*[3] doctrine. In my judgment this House should now set the matter at rest.

h I would therefore hold that there was no misdirection by the learned trial judge in the present case and restore the conviction of the respondent except as to count 3.

LORD MORRIS OF BORTH-Y-GEST. My Lords, I have had the advantage of reading in advance the speech prepared by my noble and learned friend, Lord Hailsham of St Marylebone LC. I am in agreement with it and accordingly I would allow the appeal.

j

---

1 [1946] 1 All ER 697, [1946] KB 531
2 [1956] 2 All ER 272, [1956] 2 QB 432
3 (1934) 15 Cr App Rep 18
4 [1956] 2 All ER at 276, [1956] 2 QB at 438, 439
5 [1952] 1 All ER 1044, [1952] AC 694
6 [1972] 3 All ER 545, [1972] 1 WLR 1365

LORD SIMON OF GLAISDALE. My Lords, the respondent, John Kilbourne, was convicted at Leeds Crown Court after a trial before Lawson J and a jury on the following counts of the indictment: 1. Buggery with John S, a male child of ten years. 2. Indecent assault on Paul G, a male child of ten years. 3. Attempted buggery of Mark G, a male child of nine years. 4. Indecent assault on Simon G, a male child of ten years. 5. Indecent assault on Gary W, a male child of ten years. 6. Indecent assault on Gary W, who had by the date of this assault attained the age of 11 years. 7. Indecent assault on Kevin E, a male child of 12 years.

The offences fell into two groups—counts 1 to 4 inclusive on the one hand (which I shall call 'the first group') and counts 5 to 7 inclusive (which I shall call 'the second group') on the other. The first group all took place in November 1970, the second all in October and November 1971. Moreover, to quote from the judgment of Lawton LJ in the Court of Appeal[1]:

> '. . . the boys in each group knew each other well and could have collaborated in putting forward their stories whereas it was unlikely, if not impossible, that the two groups could have got together to tell false stories or to embellish true stories with accusations of indecencies.'

The boy concerned in each count gave evidence on oath as to the offence concerning himself. The respondent admitted association with the boys, but averred that it was innocent, on the lines described by my noble and learned friend on the Woolsack. Apart from the police evidence of statements by the respondent, to which my noble and learned friend has also referred, there was no evidence which implicated the respondent except that of the boys.

The summing-up of the learned judge contained the following passages which I have conflated and have designated respectively '(A)', '(B)' and '(C)' for ease of reference later:

> (A) 'You are entitled to act on the sworn evidence of a boy . . . if you are thoroughly convinced that the boy is telling you the truth. On the other hand, . . . experience has indicated that it can be dangerous to convict solely upon the evidence of a child victim of a sexual offence, because children, as we all know, have fantasies, children as we all know do talk together about these sorts of things in certain circumstances, and it follows that children, being imaginative little creatures, can make up things and come into court, having made something up, and tell a story which is not true with a good deal of conviction. You must be very, very careful not to act on the sole evidence of a boy victim as to what happened to him, and what you should do, as the law suggests, is to see whether that boy victim's evidence is corroborated by some other piece of evidence which you have had before you. Corroboration means some independent evidence, some evidence coming from outside the boy himself, which leads you to the conclusion that it is safe to rely upon his sworn evidence . . . The fact that boy two says the same sort of thing was done to him as was done to boy one does not corroborate boy one's evidence. In other words, you cannot use the evidence on one charge to corroborate the evidence on another charge relating to a different boy . . . Remember that although you can, if you think it is safe and if you are certain about it, act on the uncorroborated sworn evidence of any one of those boys it is better and my advice to you would be that this is a case where you should particularly look for some corroborative evidence of what each small boy says.'

> (B) 'You would be entitled to take the evidence of [Kevin] and [Gary], or either of them, if you think their evidence is true as to what was done to them by the [respondent], and you would be entitled to take this view of it, "Well, we can use the evidence of [Kevin] and [Gary]", or either of them if you accept it as

a reliable, 'As supporting evidence given by the boys in the first group"'; but what you must not do is to use the evidence of [John] as to what was done to him to reinforce the evidence of another boy in the first group, [Paul] for example, as to what was done to him. You can use the evidence of the first group, if you accept it, in weighing up the evidence of [Gary] and [Kevin]. You can use the evidence of [Gary] and [Kevin], or either of them, if you accept it, in weighing up the evidence of the boys in the first group.'

b (C) 'His [the respondent's] case is, "Yes, they all came. They came a great deal but my association with these boys was an entirely innocent association, apart from a little bit of skylarking", and he gave you illustrations of one or two occasions of larking about with the boys in what he suggests, and you must consider it, was an entirely innocent way as far as sexual conduct was concerned

c . . . "I quite liked the small boys coming to my house; I thought it was good for my business" . . . the prosecution case is this, they submit to you that what was set up here by the [respondent] was, so to speak, a baited trap for small boys—comics, cards, mild refreshment from time to time, the puppy to be taken out for his walk, the van to be cleaned.'

I would point out four matters with regard to those passages. First, the learned
d judge's direction as to the meaning of corroboration did not include the requisite that it must implicate the respondent (unless this is irrelevant—e g when, on a charge of sexual assault, intercourse is admitted and the only issue is consent); but, in the context of this case, nothing turns on that, since the evidence of the other boys as to the offences committed against themselves, if corroborative at all, plainly implicated the accused. Secondly, the learned judge reminded the jury of the respondent's defence
e of 'innocent association": he did not, however, tell the jury that, in addition to treating the evidence of the other boys in the way set out in (B), they were in any case entitled to take it into account in deciding whether the respondent's defence of 'innocent association' might reasonably be true; as will appear, this was favourable to the respondent. Thirdly, the learned judge's reasons for treating the two groups separately as he did was because, as appears from the passage I have cited from the
f judgment of Lawton LJ[1], he had in mind a danger of collaboration within groups which could be disregarded as between groups. Fourthly, I have no doubt that in directing the jury the learned judge was seeking to apply the law as laid down in *R v Sims*[2] and *R v Campbell*[3]. I set out the relevant passages of these two judgments, dividing them by the signs '(a)', '(b)' and '(c)' to correspond with the passages from the summing-up which I have designated respectively '(A)', '(B)' and '(C)'.

g *R v Sims*[4]

(a) 'We do not think that the evidence of the men can be considered as corroborating one another, because each may be said to be an accomplice in the act to which he speaks . . .'

(b) 'Applying these principles, we are of opinion that on the trial of one of the
h counts in this case, the evidence on the others would be admissible. The evidence of each man was that the accused invited him into the house and there committed the acts charged [sodomy and gross indecency]. The acts they describe bear a striking similarity. That is a special feature sufficient in itself to justify the admissibility of the evidence; . . .'

(c) '. . . the visits of the men to the prisoner's house were either for a guilty
j or innocent purpose; that they all speak to the commission of the same class of acts upon them tends to show that in each case the visits were for the former and not the latter purpose. The same considerations would apply to a case where

---

1 [1972] 3 All ER at 548, [1972] 2 WLR at 1369
2 [1946] 1 All ER 697, [1946] KB 531
3 [1956] 2 All ER 272, [1956] 2 QB 432
4 [1946] 1 All ER at 703, 701, [1946] KB at 544, 540

a man is charged with a series of indecent offences against children, whether boys
or girls; that they all complain of the same sort of conduct shows that the interest
the prisoner was taking in them was not of a paternal or friendly nature but for
the purpose of satisfying lust.'

R v Campbell[1]

(a) 'As we are endeavouring in this judgment to deal comprehensively with
the evidence of children we may perhaps endeavour to give some guidance to
courts who have from time to time to deal with cases of sexual assaults on
children where the evidence of each child deals only with the assault on him or
her self. In such cases it is right to tell a jury that because A says that the accused
assaulted him, it is no corroboration of his evidence that B says that he also was
the victim of a similar assault though both say it on oath.'

(b) 'At the same time we think a jury may be told that a succession of these
cases may help them to determine the truth of the matter provided they are
satisfied that there is no collaboration between the children to put up a false
story.'

(c) 'And if the defence is one of innocent association by the accused with the
children, the case of *R. v. Sims*[2] ,subsequently approved on this point by the
House of Lords in *Harris v. Public Prosecutions Director*[3] shows that such evidence
can be given to rebut the defence.'

The Court of Appeal[4] set aside the instant convictions on the grounds of misdirection. They held that (B) in summing-up might, notwithstanding (A), have been
understood by the jury as a direction that evidence of a boy in the first group as to
an offence against him might be taken as corroboration of the evidence of a boy in the
second group as to an offence against himself, and vice versa; and that this would be
contrary to (a) in *R v Sims*[2] and *R v Campbell*[5] which the Court of Appeal felt that
they should follow. Before the Court of Appeal it was controverted on behalf of the
Crown that (B) could have been understood as going to corroboration; but
before your Lordships this contention was abandoned, and it was accepted that the
Court of Appeal were right on this point. But the fact that the learned trial judge
followed the authorities so closely in his summing-up, and yet was held to have fallen
into error, hardly suggests that the authorities are in a very satisfactory state as a
guidance to judge and jury. The Court of Appeal certified the following point of law
of general public importance as being involved:

'Whether and in what circumstances the sworn evidence of a child victim as
to an offence charged can be corroborated by the admissible but uncorroborated
sworn evidence of another child victim as to similar misconduct of the accused
on a different occasion.'

As will appear, the words 'but uncorroborated' beg the question whether there can
be 'mutual corroboration'. Also implicit in the point certified by the Court of Appeal
and in the appeal before your Lordships is the question whether the distinction
drawn in the authorities between, on the one hand, 'evidence which may help . . .
to determine the truth of the matter' (paraphrased in the summing-up as 'supporting
evidence' and as evidence which may be used in 'weighing up' other evidence) and,
on the other hand, 'corroboration' is a valid one.

Your Lordships have been concerned with four concepts in the law of evidence:
(i) relevance; (ii) admissibility; (iii) corroboration; (iv) weight. The first two terms
are frequently, and in many circumstances legitimately, used interchangeably; but

1   [1956] 2 All ER at 276, [1956] 2 QB at 438, 439
2   [1946] 1 All ER 697, [1946] KB 531
3   [1952] 1 All ER 1044, [1952] AC 694
4   [1972] 3 All ER 545, [1972] 1 WLR 1365
5   [1956] 2 All ER 272, [1956] 2 QB 432

a I think it makes for clarity if they are kept separate, since some relevant evidence is inadmissible and some admissible evidence is irrelevant (in the senses that I shall shortly submit). Evidence is relevant if it is logically probative or disprobative of some matter which requires proof. I do not pause to analyse what is involved in 'logical probativeness', except to note that the term does not of itself express the element of experience which is so significant of its operation in law, and possibly
b elsewhere. It is sufficient to say, even at the risk of etymological tautology, that relevant (i e logically probative or disprobative) evidence is evidence which makes the matter which requires proof more or less probable. To link logical probativeness with relevance rather than admissibility (as was done in *R v Sims*[1]) not only is, I hope, more appropriate conceptually, but also accords better with the explanation of *R v Sims*[1] given in *Harris v Director of Public Prosecutions*[2]. Evidence is admissible if it
c may be lawfully adduced at a trial. 'Weight' of evidence is the degree of probability (both intrinsically and inferentially) which is attached to it by the tribunal of fact once it is established to be relevant and admissible in law (though its relevance may exceptionally, as will appear, be dependent on its evaluation by the tribunal of fact).

Exceptionally evidence which is irrelevant to a fact which is in issue is admitted to lay the foundation for other, relevant, evidence (e g evidence of an unsuccessful search
d for a missing relevant document, in order to lay the foundation for secondary evidence of the document). Apart from such exceptional cases no evidence which is irrelevant to a fact in issue is admissible. But some relevant evidence is nevertheless inadmissible. To cite a famous passage from the opinion of Lord Herschell LC in *Makin v A-G for New South Wales*[3]:

e 'It is undoubtedly not competent for the prosecution to adduce evidence tending to show that the accused had been guilty of criminal acts other than those covered in the indictment, for the purpose of leading to the conclusion that the accused is a person likely from his criminal conduct or character to have committed the offence for which he is being tried. On the other hand, the mere fact that the evidence adduced tends to show the commission of other crimes does not render it inadmissible if it is relevant to an issue before the jury, and it may be
f so relevant if it bears upon the question whether the acts alleged to constitute the crime charged in the indictment were designed or accidental, or to rebut a defence which would otherwise be open to the accused.'

That what was declared to be inadmissible in the first sentence of this passage is nevertheless relevant (i e logically probative) can be seen from numerous studies of offences in which recidivists are matched against first offenders, and by considering
g that it has never been doubted that evidence of motive (which can be viewed as propensity to commit the particular offence charged, in contradistinction to propensity to commit offences generally of the type charged) is relevant. All relevant evidence is prima facie admissible. The reason why the type of evidence referred to by Lord Herschell LC in the first sentence of the passage is inadmissible is, not because it is irrelevant, but because its logically probative significance is considered to be
h grossly outweighed by its prejudice to the accused, so that a fair trial is endangered if it is admitted; the law therefore exceptionally excludes this relevant evidence; whereas in the circumstances referred to in the second sentence the logically probative significance of the evidence is markedly greater: see also Lord Moulton in *R v Christie*[4].

j Not all admissible evidence is universally relevant. Admissible evidence may be relevant to one count of an indictment and not to another. It may be admissible against one accused (or party) but not another. It may be admissible to rebut a

1 [1946] 1 All ER 697, [1946] KB 531
2 [1952] 1 All ER 1044, [1952] AC 694
3 [1894] AC 57 at 65
4 [1914] AC 545 at 559, 560, [1914-15] All ER Rep 63 at 69, 70

defence but inadmissible to reinforce the case for the prosecution. The summing-up
of Scrutton J in *R v Smith*[1] ('The Brides in the Bath' case) was a striking example—
the jury was directed to consider the drowning of other newly-wedded and well-
insured wives of the accused for the purpose only of rebutting a defence of accidental
death by drowning—but not otherwise for the purpose of positive proof of the murder
charged: see also Lord Atkinson, Lord Parker concurring, in *R v Christie*[2].

In the instant case it is not disputed that the evidence of the other boys with regard
to the offences committed against themselves was admissible on each count of the
indictment. It was plainly admissible to rebut the defence of innocent association
(*R v Sims*(c)[3], *R v Campbell*(c)[4], *R v Ball*[5]). But was it admissible for (i e relevant to,
logically probative of) any other matter in particular to reinforce the case for the
Crown? In view of *R v Sims*(b)[3] and *R v Campbell*(b)[4] counsel for the respondent
did not contend to the contrary; but it is necessary to examine the question, if only
as a step to considering the validity of *R v Sims*(a)[3] and *R v Campbell*(a)[4]. In *Moorov v
HM Advocate*[6] the accused was convicted of a series of assaults and indecent assaults
on various female employees. In respect of many of the charges the only direct
evidence against the accused was that of the woman against whom the particular
offence was alleged to have been committed. The evidence of each woman was,
however, held to have been corroborative of that of the others, which involved that
it was both admissible on and relevant to the other charges. The Lord Justice-
General (Lord Clyde) started his judgment[7]: 'The question in the present case
belongs to the department of circumstantial evidence. This consideration is vital
to the whole matter ...' Circumstantial evidence is evidence of facts from which,
taken with all the other evidence, a reasonable inference is a fact directly in issue.
It works by cumulatively, in geometrical progression, eliminating other possibilities.
Why should evidence of assault on the other women in *Moorov*[6] be evidence from
which it was a reasonable inference that the accused had committed that particular
assault? The answer was given in the passages cited by my noble and learned friend
on the Woolsack; there was such a striking similarity between the various offences
as to show an underlying unity, to provide a connecting link between them—so that
each confirmed another, rendered the other more probable. As it was put in *R v
Sims*[8]:

> 'The probative force of all the acts together is much greater than one alone;
> for, whereas the jury might think one man might be telling an untruth, three
> or four are hardly likely to tell the same untruth unless they were conspiring
> together. If there is nothing to suggest a conspiracy their evidence would seem
> to be overwhelming.'

(See also *R v Smith*[9].)

How, then, does this match with corroboration? The reason why corroboration
is required in some types of case, and the nature of corroboration, were recently
considered by your Lordships' House in *Director of Public Prosecutions v Hester*[10]. It
is required because experience has shown that there is a real risk that an innocent

---

1 See the report in The Trial of George Joseph Smith (Notable British Trials), pp 276–278;
   affd (1915) 84 LJKB 2153, [1914-15] All ER Rep 262
2 [1914] AC at 553, [1914-15] All ER Rep at 66
3 [1946] All ER 697, [1946] KB 531
4 [1956] 2 All ER 272, [1956] 2 QB 432
5 [1911] AC 47
6 1930 JC 68
7 1930 JC at 72
8 [1946] 1 All ER at 701, [1946] KB at 540
9 The Trial of George Joseph Smith (Notable British Trials), pp 277, 278; *affd* (1915) 84
   LJKB 2153, [1914-15] All ER Rep 262
10 [1972] 3 All ER 1056, [1972] 3 WLR 910

person may be convicted unless certain evidence against an accused (neatly called 'suspect evidence' by my noble and learned friend, Lord Diplock[1]) is confirmed by other evidence. Corroboration is therefore nothing other than evidence which 'confirms' or 'supports' or 'strengthens' other evidence (Lord Morris of Borth-y-Gest[2], Lord Pearson[3] and Lord Diplock[4]). It is, in short, evidence which renders other evidence more probable. If so, there is no essential difference between, on the one hand, corroboration and, on the other, 'supporting evidence' or 'evidence which helps to determine the truth of the matter'. Each is evidence which makes other evidence more probable. Once it is accepted that the direct evidence on one count is relevant to another by way of circumstantial evidence, it follows that it is available as corroboration if corroboration is required. Whether it operates as such depends on what weight the jury attaches to it, and what inferences the jury draws as to whether the offences demonstrate an underlying unity. For that purpose the jury will be directed in appropriate terms to take into account the proximity in time of the offences, their multiplicity, their similarity in detail and circumstance, whether such similarity has any unusual feature, what, if any, risk there is of collaboration in presenting a false case, and any other matter which tends to suggest or rebut an underlying unity—a system—something which would cause common sense to revolt at a hypothesis of mere coincidence.

I think that the contradistinction that was drawn in R v Sims[5] and R v Campbell[6] between corroboration and 'evidence which helps to determine the truth of the matter' was partly due to R v Manser[7], partly to such cases as R v Lillyman[8] and R v Whitehead[9]. So far as R v Manser[7] is concerned I agree with the criticisms made in Director of Public Prosecutions v Hester[10], particularly with the observation of my noble and learned friend, Lord Morris of Borth-y-Gest[11], that the concept of 'mutual corroboration' is not 'argument in a circle'—that would be to confuse relevance with weight of evidence. I also agree with what my noble and learned friend on the Woolsack has just said about accomplices corroborating each other. As for R v Lillyman[8] and R v Whitehead[9], they show that evidence of complaint immediately after a sexual assault is admissible and relevant to show consistency of conduct and negative consent, but does not amount to corroboration. But the only reason why this admissible and relevant evidence could not amount to corroboration was because it was not from an independent source—or, as it is sometimes put, 'a person cannot corroborate himself' or 'be his own corroborator' (Lord Atkinson in R v Christie[12]). The evidence was therefore admissible for and relevant to the limited purposes which I have stated: (see also R v Christie[13]—statement admissible as closely connected with an act of identification by the complainant, but not corroborative). But these types of case are no authority for the proposition that admissible and relevant evidence from an independent source (such as the other boys in the instant case) cannot amount to corroboration. In my view it can, if accepted by the jury, and if they discern such an underlying unity between the offences as to make coincidence an affront to common sense. I am reinforced in this view by the Scottish cases cited by my noble and learned friend on the Woolsack.

1   [1972] 3 All ER at 1072, [1972] 3 WLR at 928
2   [1972] 3 All ER at 1065, [1972] 3 WLR at 919, 920
3   [1972] 3 All ER at 1070, [1972] 3 WLR at 925
4   [1972] 3 All ER at 1071, 1073, [1972] 3 WLR at 927, 928
5   [1946] 1 All ER 697, [1946] KB 531
6   [1956] 2 All ER 272, [1956] 2 QB 432
7   (1934) 25 Cr App Rep 18
8   [1896] 2 QB 167, [1895-99] All ER Rep 586
9   [1929] 1 KB 99, [1928] All ER Rep 186
10 [1972] 3 All ER 1056, [1972] 3 WLR 910
11 [1972] 3 All ER at 1065, [1972] 3 WLR at 919
12 [1914] AC at 557, [1914-15] All ER Rep at 68
13 [1914] AC 545, [1914-15] All ER Rep 63

In the instant case Lawson J in (B) directed the jury as to the way they could approach the evidence of the other offences. Even if they understood it as a direction on corroboration, they must either have taken the police officers' evidence as corroboration (which would have involved believing it) or the evidence as to the other offences. For the reasons which I have given they were entitled so to treat the latter class of evidence; and there was no misdirection in this respect. Although Lawson J did not expressly invite the jury to consider whether there was an underlying unity encompassing the various offences, the jury must have accepted the boys' evidence in order to convict on each count; and there was here the same striking similarity between the offences charged as the Court of Justiciary discerned in *Moorov v HM Advocate*[1], and an even closer proximity in time. Collaboration between the boys in the different groups being excluded, common sense would be affronted by a hypothesis of coincidence. I would therefore apply the proviso and allow the appeal. I concur with the order proposed by my noble and learned friend on the Woolsack.

LORD CROSS OF CHELSEA. My Lords, the Court of Appeal[2] quashed these convictions because they thought that the summing-up might have led the jury to believe that when they were considering a count charging the respondent with an offence against a boy in the first group they could treat the evidence of boys in the second group as to what the respondent had done to them on other occasions as corroborating the evidence given by the boy in the first group. As I read his summing-up the judge was trying his best to direct the jury in accordance with the passage at the end of the judgment of the Court of Criminal Appeal in *R v Campbell*[3] which says that in a case of this sort the evidence of boys B, C and D as to similar incidents 'may help the jury to determine the truth of the matter' but cannot 'corroborate' the evidence of boy A who alleged the assault which is the subject of the count in question. I have no doubt that the judge failed completely to make this distinction clear to the jury for it is not, as the Court of Appeal calls it, a 'difficult' distinction; but a distinction which simply does not exist at all. Once the 'similar fact' evidence is admitted—and it was common ground that it was properly admitted in this case— then of necessity it 'corroborates'—i e strengthens or supports—the evidence given by the boy of an alleged offence against whom is the subject of the count under consideration. If one asks why it was that the court thought it necessary—as it did in *R v Sims*[4] and in the passage from *R v Campbell*[3] cited above—to try to draw this nonexistent distinction the answer, I think, is that each of the boys was, if his evidence was believed, technically an 'accomplice' of the respondent and that ever since the decision of the Court of Criminal Appeal in *R v Manser*[5] it had become generally accepted that 'mutual corroboration' was impossible—that is to say that the evidence of witness A in respect of which a warning as to the desirability of 'corroboration' had to be given could not be corroborated by the evidence of witness B whose evidence was of a similar character. If that is the law then obviously you get into difficulties if you admit 'similar fact' evidence from other accomplices. But in the recent case of *Director of Public Prosecutions v Hester*[6] this House has decided that there is no warrant for the doctrine laid down in *R v Manser*[5] and the supposed need to draw this nonexistent distinction has accordingly now disappeared. I would allow this appeal.

Appeal allowed.

Solicitors: *Director of Public Prosecutions*; *Ward, Bowie & Co* (for the respondent).

S A Hatteea Esq   Barrister.

1   1930 JC 68
2   [1972] 3 All ER 545, [1972] 1 WLR 1365
3   [1956] 2 All ER 272 at 276, [1956] 2 QB 432 at 438, 439
4   [1946] 1 All ER 697, [1946] KB 531
5   (1934) 25 Cr App Rep 18
6   [1972] 3 All ER 1056, [1972] 3 WLR 910

Stekel v Ellice

CHANCERY DIVISION
MEGARRY J
2nd, 3rd, 6th, 7th, 8th NOVEMBER 1972

Partnership – Nature – Relationship of partners – Salaried partnership – Two partners – One partner providing all capital and taking profits – Other partner paid a fixed salary – Other partner held out as partner – Circumstances in which relationship one of partnership rather than employment – Partnership Act 1890, ss 1 (1), 27 (1).

Partnership – Winding-up – Applicant – Persons who may apply – Salaried partner – Partnership having ceased in fact – Circumstances in which winding-up order may be refused.

The plaintiff and the defendant were chartered accountants. The defendant was in partnership with J under an oral partnership for life. In 1967 J died. In September 1967 the defendant met the plaintiff and it was agreed that the defendant would employ the plaintiff at a salary of £2,000 a year with a view to partnership. The defendant told the plaintiff that he would be expected to put £1,500 to £2,000 into the business when he became a partner but that the question of partnership would have to wait until it had been ascertained how much was owing to J's executors. In August 1968 the plaintiff raised the matter of his partnership again; he had potential clients who wanted him as a partner and not a mere employee. However, the figures for J's executors had not been finalised and, after some discussion, it was agreed that, as an interim arrangement, the plaintiff should become a salaried partner. A written agreement, dated 1st October, was drafted and signed by the parties. Clause 2 provided that the agreement would last until 5th April 1969 and that the parties would 'enter into a deed or agreement on or before the expiration whereby [the plaintiff] becomes a full Partner'. By cl 7 the plaintiff was to be paid a salary of £2,000 a year and, by cl 8, the capital of the partnership was to be 'provided by and shall solely belong to' the defendant, with an exception as to the plaintiff's furniture. Clause 18 provided for either partner to give notice determining the partnership on breach of certain terms of the agreement, etc. By cl 19, on the expiration of the partnership or determination under cl 18, the defendant was entitled to all capital (save the plaintiff's furniture) and to all clients save those introduced by the plaintiff; if either party died the other was entitled, without payment, to all clients of the deceased and if the defendant died the plaintiff was to have the practice, subject to paying to the defendant's executors by instalments the amount of the capital that the defendant had in the firm. After the 1968 agreement had been signed the parties continued as before save that the plaintiff was held out, e g by his name appearing on the firm's notepaper, as a partner; he also acted as a partner within the firm. Further, at the plaintiff's request, his salary was paid without deduction of tax. No further steps were taken however towards a full partnership agreement; 5th April 1969 passed without any such deed or agreement being entered into and in the event no such deed or agreement ever came into being. By June 1970 relations between the parties were breaking down. In August there were discussions on the footing that the partnership should cease. The defendant was to pay the plaintiff £2,000 but if a valuation of the firm was less than £10,000 the £2,000 was to be reduced pro rata; the plaintiff was to take a holiday; he was not to return to the firm and was to take with him the clients that he had introduced. Further, the partnership was to be deemed to have ceased after 5th April 1969 and thereafter the plaintiff was to receive one-fifth of the profits and bear one-fifth of the losses; the defendant alleged, and the plaintiff denied, that it had been agreed that the plaintiff was to repay the salary he had received since 5th April 1969. No final agreement was ever reached, but in August the plaintiff left, taking his clients with him. The plaintiff brought an action alleging that, since 6th April 1969, a partnership at will had existed between himself and the defendant to which, since no terms relating to the interests or duties of the partners had been agreed, s 24 of the Partnership Act 1890 applied. The plaintiff claimed, inter alia, an order that the affairs of the partnership be wound up and all necessary accounts and enquiries taken and made.

Held – (i) An agreement to enter into a partnership on certain terms might constitute a partnership forthwith, or from an agreed date, even though the agreement provided for some formal agreement which was never in fact executed. There was, however, prior to 6th April 1969, an existing relationship between the parties under the 1968 agreement. Accordingly when 5th April 1969 passed and no agreement had been entered into it was equally open to the parties to agree to the continuance of the existing relationship. The evidence indicated that after 5th April the parties continued as before, i e on the basis of the partnership established by the 1968 agreement. Accordingly no new partnership had arisen between the parties incorporating the terms of s 24 of the 1890 Act (see p 471 e to g, post).

(ii) The fact that a person was described as a salaried partner was not conclusive one way or the other of the question whether he was a partner in the true sense; the question whether there was a partnership depended on the true nature of the relationship and not on the label attached to it. Although the provisions for a salary and the ownership of capital were not those usually found in a partnership agreement, the 1968 agreement was very much more an agreement for a partnership than it was an agreement for employment; in particular the parties were 'carrying on a business in common with a view of profit' within s 1 (1)[a] of the 1890 Act. Furthermore the actual conduct of the parties after 1st October 1968 fully accorded with the concept of partnership. Accordingly there was a 'partnership entered into' for a fixed term for the purposes of s 27[b] of the 1890 Act, and that was continued after 6th April 1969 without any express new agreement. That partnership was determined by mutual agreement in August 1970 (see p 473 e f and h and p 474 f to j, post).

(iii) Under the terms of the 1968 agreement the plaintiff had no interest in the capital of the firm, or in the clients, save those he took with him, and further, although there was no express mention of goodwill, the intention of the agreement was to exclude the plaintiff from any proprietary interest in the partnership. Because a relationship was a partnership for the purposes of s 27 of the 1890 Act it did not necessarily follow that the court was obliged to make an order to wind up at the suit of a partner who lacked any such interest. The plaintiff had failed to show any grounds on which a winding-up order should be made and accordingly his action would be dismissed (see p 475 b and f to j, post).

Notes

For the meaning and nature of partnership, see 28 Halsbury's Laws (3rd Edn) 483, 484, paras 925, 926, for consideration affecting the question whether a partnership exists, see ibid 485-493, paras 930-946, and for cases on the subject, see 36 Digest (Repl) 423-447, 1-187.

For continuation of a partnership after expiry of a fixed term, see 28 Halsbury's Laws (3rd Edn) 502, 503, para 965, and for cases on the subject, see 36 Digest (Repl) 457, 272-280.

For the grounds on which the court may order the dissolution of a partnership, see 28 Halsbury's Laws (3rd Edn) 567-570, paras 1104-1112.

For the Partnership Act 1890, ss 1, 24, 27, see 24 Halsbury's Statutes (3rd Edn) 501, 513, 515.

---

a   Section 1 (1) is set out at p 470 b, post
b   Section 27 is set out at p 471 h, post

Cases referred to in judgment

Battley v Lewis (1840) 1 Man & G 155, 133 ER 286; sub nom *Battley v Bailey* 1 Scott NR 143, 4 Jur 537, 36 Digest (Repl) 484, *552*.

Burnell v Hunt (1841) 5 Jur 650, 36 Digest (Repl) 439, *114*.

Ellis v Joseph Ellis & Co [1905] 1 KB 324, 74 LJKB 229, 92 LT 718, CA, 36 Digest (Repl) 424, *13*.

Hill, Re, Claremont v Hill [1934] Ch 623, [1934] All ER Rep 617, 103 LJCh 289, 151 LT 416, CA, 43 Digest (Repl) 129, *1181*.

Marsh v Stacey (1963) 107 Sol Jo 512, [1963] Bar Library transcript 169, CA.

Price v Groom (1848) 2 Exch 542, 17 LJ Ex 346, 154 ER 606, 36 Digest (Repl) 424, *14*.

Syers v Syers (1876) 1 App Cas 174, 35 LT 101, HL, 36 Digest (Repl) 428, *46*.

Walker v Hirsch (1884) 27 Ch D 460, 54 LJCh 315, 51 LT 481, CA, 36 Digest (Repl) 433, *80*.

Watson, Ex parte (1815) 19 Ves 459, 34 ER 587, 36 Digest (Repl) 446, *176*.

Young, Re, ex parte Jones [1896] 1 QB 484, 65 LJQB 681, 3 Mans 213; sub nom *Re Young, ex parte Jones v Berry* 75 LT 278, 36 Digest (Repl) 437, *104*.

Cases also cited

David and Matthews, Re [1899] 1 Ch 378, [1895-99] All ER Rep 817.

Jennings v Jennings [1898] 1 Ch 378.

Miles v Clarke [1953] 1 All ER 779, [1953] 1 WLR 537.

Trego v Hunt [1896] AC 7, [1895-99] All ER Rep 804, HL.

Action

By a writ issued on 14th September 1971 Ronald Stekel brought an action against Charles Ellice claiming (i) a declaration that a partnership at will between the plaintiff and the defendant formerly carried on under the name of Stanley Kennard & Co had been dissolved in August 1970; (ii) an order that the affairs of the partnership be wound up; (iii) for those purposes all necessary accounts and enquiries to be taken and made. The facts are set out in the judgment.

Martin Buckley for the plaintiff.
Dennis G Rice for the defendant.

MEGARRY J. This is an unusual dispute between two chartered accountants which raises questions on the nature of what are usually called 'salaried partnerships', a subject on which there is little direct authority. The plaintiff qualified in 1964 and the defendant in 1929. They first met in September 1967. The defendant had been in partnership with a Mr Jennison under an oral partnership for life. They practised under the style of Stanley Kennard & Co, the name of the firm which the defendant had joined soon after the end of the War. Mr Jennison unfortunately fell ill, and in the summer of 1967, when he was about to return to work, he suddenly died. One result of his illness and death, and the departure of some members of the small staff, was that the work of the firm had fallen sadly in arrear, not least in the costing and billing of the work done, and the defendant by himself could not keep abreast of the work or make up the arrears. He accordingly answered an advertisement which the plaintiff had inserted in 'The Accountant'.

The plaintiff was at that time employed by a well-known firm of accountants, but was anxious to cease being a mere employee. The advertisement simply stated that a chartered accountant about to set up in practice wanted to contact others either to establish a joint practice or to 'affect economies of scale'. As a result of the defendant's reply to that advertisement, the plaintiff and the defendant met on 14th September 1967, and the defendant explained his position to the plaintiff. The plaintiff had with him his father, an experienced businessman from whom the plaintiff sought advice from time to time. At this meeting it was agreed that the defendant

would employ the plaintiff for a probationary period of some three months or so at a
salary of £2,000 a year; this represented an increase of about one-third over the salary
that the plaintiff was then receiving. This employment was to be with a view to
a partnership; and late in October 1967 the plaintiff began to work for the defendant
under this arrangement.

In about January 1968 there was a discussion between the plaintiff and the defendant. The plaintiff was understandably anxious to progress to the contemplated
partnership with the defendant. Things had gone well between the two, and the
younger man was making inroads on the arrears of work. The difficulty, or a
difficulty, that the defendant felt was in relation to the money that was due to
Mr Jennison's executors. The amount due to them ultimately came to be quantified
at a little less than £5,500; but until the books of the partnership had been written
up, this sum could not be ascertained. The defendant suggested that the question
of the partnership should be left over for another six months or so, by which time the
position as regards the executors ought to be clear and the partnership agreement
could be made on the footing of an ascertained state of affairs. According to the
evidence of the defendant, which I accept, he had told the plaintiff of the position as
to the executors at their initial discussion, and had also told him that he would expect
him to put capital of some £1,500 to £2,000 into the business when he became a
partner.

In July or August 1968, the plaintiff raised the matter of his partnership again. He
had potential clients for the firm, but they wanted him as a partner and not as a
mere employee, he said. However, the figures for the executors had still not been
finally agreed, and in the end there was a meeting at an hotel on 10th September,
with the plaintiff's father present. After some discussion he suggested a salaried
parnership for the plaintiff as a modus vivendi, and this suggestion was accepted,
with 5th April 1969 being ultimately agreed as the date when it was to come to an
end. Some while later a document was drafted by the defendant's solicitors, and
revised by the plaintiff's solicitors; and the plaintiff and the defendant both signed
this. It is dated 1st October 1968 and bears the title 'Heads of Terms': I shall call it
'the 1968 agreement'. It refers to the parties by their initials, 'R.S.' being the
plaintiff, and 'C.E.' the defendant. I shall have to discuss this agreement in greater
detail later, but for the present I need only say that it has some 3½ pages of foolscap
typescript in double spacing, with 23 clauses (some amended in manuscript) which
in their drafting vary between full conveyancing language and the abbreviated
phraseology of heads of agreement. Clause 2 reads as follows: 'Duration to 5th
April 1969. The Partners will enter into a deed or agreement on or before the
expiration whereby R.S. becomes a full Partner'. Clause 7 runs: 'R.S. shall be a
salaried partner at £2,000·00 p.a. payable monthly in arrear on the last day of each
month.'

After the 1968 agreement had been signed, the parties continued as before, save that
the plaintiff was being held out as being a partner, as was shown, for instance, by his
name appearing on the firm's notepaper as a partner. He also acted as a partner
within the firm. Further, when the first subsequent monthly payment of salary to
the plaintiff became due, he asked the defendant to make the payment without
deduction of tax, instead of deducting tax as had been done in the past; and the
defendant agreed. 5th April 1969 came and went without any deed or agreement for
a full partnership being entered into, and no such deed or agreement ever came
into being. The defendant was contemplating that in due course he would retire
from practice and that the plaintiff would carry on the business, and so when early
in 1969 attempts were made to find some other firm to amalgamate with, or make
some working arrangement with, the defendant left the initial stages of the negotiations to the plaintiff. In the end, an arrangement was made with a firm of accountants called Arthur Bass & Co, and under an office-sharing agreement with that firm
the plaintiff and defendant and their staff moved into the premises of that firm in

a April 1969. That arrangement did not work very well, and after some while Arthur Bass & Co gave notice to quit to Stanley Kennard & Co for the end of June 1970.

By this time relations between the plaintiff and defendant were breaking down. According to the plaintiff, the defendant asked him to pay off the amount due to the executors, nearly £5,500, for which the executors were by then pressing strongly; the plaintiff was amazed, and said that it was entirely contrary to their agreement.

b According to the defendant, he did no more than seek to get the plaintiff to put some capital into the partnership to match his own £1,500 or £2,000. He wanted this to help pay off the executors, though in evidence before me he seemed thoroughly confused as to how a contribution to the partnership capital by the plaintiff would help him, the defendant, to discharge his debt to the executors. At all events, there were then discussions about selling or valuing the practice, and a visit was made

c to a firm of agents who specialised in such sales: and it was suggested that the practice would fetch something like one and a half times the gross annual recurring fees. There was a further meeting at an hotel on 14th August 1970 with the plaintiff's father in order to try and reach some sort of agreement, and in a letter to the defendant dated 17th August 1970 the plaintiff's father set out the terms that he thought had been agreed at the meeting. Under these terms, the partnership was to cease

d at the end of August 1970, the plaintiff was to take a holiday forthwith and not return to Stanley Kennard & Co, and he was to take with him all the clients that he had introduced. The defendant was to pay the plaintiff £2,000, but if the valuation of Stanley Kennard & Co was less than £10,000, the £2,000 was to be reduced pro rata. This in effect was a provision for dividing the value of the practice into four-fifths for the defendant and one-fifth for the plaintiff, though with a ceiling of £2,000 for the plaintiff.

e The defendant replied to this letter, agreeing its terms in all save three points. One of these, in the last paragraph of the letter, was that the salaried partnership should be deemed to have ceased on 5th April 1969 and that thereafter the plaintiff should have one-fifth of the profits and bear one-fifth of the losses. In evidence, the defendant said that what he thought had been agreed was that the plaintiff should

f repay the salary he had received after 5th April 1969, and instead receive one-fifth of the profits. The last paragraph of his letter, he said, referred to this repayment of the salary, though he agreed it was not at all clear. On this basis, the result would apparently have been the plaintiff would have to pay the defendant something, and not vice versa, and not until the defendant had come away from the meeting did he realise how well he had done on this footing. At all events, no agreement was reached, but the plaintiff left and took his clients with him. The defendant's letter

g was never answered, and after correspondence between solicitors the plaintiff issued his writ on 14th September 1971.

By his statement of claim, served on 20th October 1971, the plaintiff alleges a partnership at will between himself and the defendant, and claims:

h '1. A declaration that the said partnership at will was dissolved at or about the end of August, 1970. 2. An Order that the affairs of the said partnership be wound up. 3. For the purposes aforesaid all necessary accounts and enquiries to be taken and made',

and further or other relief and costs are claimed. The claim is based on a partnership at will having been constituted on or about 6th April 1969. The defence, put broadly,

j is that there never was any full partnership between the parties, and that if there was, it incorporated the provisions of the 1968 agreement, so that the plaintiff had no interest in the property of the business apart from his salary of £2,000. The defendant further pleaded that if, which was denied, the plaintiff was entitled to any interest in the goodwill of the business, his claim was satisfied by the arrangement whereby the plaintiff had taken his own clients with him.

Counsel for the plaintiff contended that as from 5th April 1969 there was a true
partnership at will between the parties. In the end, he quite rightly accepted that he
must abandon any contention that at the meeting on 10th September 1968 there was
an agreement for a full partnership which would automatically begin to run from
5th April 1969. Clause 2 of the 1968 agreement expressly provided for the creation of
a full partnership by means of the parties entering into a deed or agreement, and
neither the state of the evidence nor the law provided any encouragement for a
contention based on an oral agreement inconsistent with the written contract.
However, counsel for the plaintiff stressed the definition of a partnership in the
Partnership Act 1890, s 1 (1), which runs as follows: 'Partnership is the relation which
subsists between persons carrying on a business in common with a view of profit.'
Here, from 5th April 1969 the parties were carrying on an accountancy business in
common with a view to profit, and from this de facto state of affairs there arose, he
said, a partnership. As no terms of this partnership were agreed, the terms were
those set out in s 24 of the Act, terms which included an equal share in the capital
and profits of the business.

Counsel for the defendant contended, first, that the plaintiff had failed to establish
that, apart from the 1968 agreement, any partnership had ever come into being
between the parties, either by agreement or by conduct. Second, if he was wrong in
that, the 1968 agreement, taken in conjunction with s 27 of the Act, continued in
being, so that the plaintiff continued a mere salaried partner. Counsel for the defendant advanced certain further contentions. One of those was that even if the plaintiff
had become a full partner, this gave him no right to any share in the goodwill, apart
from the right to take away his own clients, as in fact he had done. He further contended that if that was wrong and the plaintiff had any rights in the goodwill, the
goodwill had no real value. With a little difficulty I succeeded in discouraging
counsel for the defendant from pursuing this latter contention as far as he would
have wished; for this seemed to me to be a matter for the accounts and enquiries
which the plaintiff sought if he succeeded on the matters that are now before me,
namely, that there was a partnership that had been dissolved, and that the affairs of
the partnership should be wound up. Perhaps I should say that although the defendant was obviously muddled as to the means of paying off the executors, I accept him
as a witness of truth, and on the whole, to the limited extent to which their testimony
diverged, I preferred his evidence to that of the plaintiff. I do not think that the
plaintiff was doing anything but his best to relate what had happened; but he is
persuasive and voluble, with a fluency of speech which at times defeated both the
judicial pen and the shorthand writer, and in some respects I think he may have
unconsciously persuaded himself as to his recollections.

I turn, then, to the question whether, apart from the relationship established by
the 1968 agreement, the plaintiff has succeeded in showing that there ever was any
partnership between him and the defendant. As the evidence stands, I cannot see
that the plaintiff has shown that there ever was any agreement for such a partnership, apart from the terms of the 1968 agreement. He can point to nothing which can
be said to have amounted to such an agreement. In any case, in the circumstances of
the case the probabilities are heavily against the defendant having knowingly created
a partnership at will in place of the partnership for life that he had had with Mr
Jennison, particularly a partnership at will under which the plaintiff could at any
time dissolve the partnership and claim a partner's share of the partnership property.

Is there, then, a partnership established by conduct, especially after 5th April 1969?
I cannot see that there is. There is nothing of any significance in the evidence to show
that at or after that date there was any change in the conduct of affairs or in the
relationship between the parties as compared with the previous state of affairs.
If, for instance, the plaintiff's salary had been paid subject to deduction of tax before
5th April 1969 and without deduction of tax thereafter, that might well have been at
least a straw pointing to the establishment of a full partnership; but in fact this

^a change in the mode of payment had already been effected when the first payment of
the plaintiff's salary was made after 1st October 1968. If what happened after 5th
April 1969 is the same as what happened before, at a time when there plainly was a
salaried partnership, then there are manifest difficulties in saying that what happened
after that date shows that a new and different relationship had been entered into.
Quite apart from statute, a continuance of a state of affairs or relationship after the
^b date fixed for its expiration points more towards a tacit continuance of the same
state of affairs or relationship than towards the establishment of a new and significantly different state of affairs or relationship.

I return to cl 2 of the 1968 agreement. After stating 'Duration to 5th April 1969',
the clause continues with the words: 'The Partners will enter into a deed or agreement on or before the expiration whereby R.S. becomes a full Partner.' As a matter
^c of construction, this provision plainly provides for the parties to enter into some new
transaction, and for that to be a transaction 'whereby' the plaintiff becomes something different from what the 1968 agreement made him; instead of being a salaried
partner, he is to become a full partner. The process whereby the new replaces the
old is to be by the deed or agreement that the parties are to enter into; and there is
nothing to say what those terms are to be. As I have mentioned, counsel for the
^d plaintiff contended that as no terms were agreed, the terms would be those as set out
in the Partnership Act 1890, and especially s 24; and he relied on *Battley v Lewis*[1] and
Syers v Syers[2] and especially a passage in the speech of Lord Cairns LC[3]. As a result,
he said that there was a partnership at will between the parties.

I accept, of course, that an agreement to enter into a partnership on certain terms,
or on terms left to be found in the Partnership Act 1890, may constitute a partner-
^e ship forthwith or from any agreed date, even though the agreement contemplates
or provides for some formal agreement which is never in fact executed. However,
that proposition does not seem to me to be decisive in the present case. Here, on 5th
April 1969, there was some pre-existing relationship between the parties under the
1968 agreement; it is not a case of parties who were then linked by no agreement
other than an agreement for a partnership to commence on that date. Accordingly,
^f when 5th April came, and no agreement for a full partnership had been entered
into, it was equally open to the parties to agree either for the continuance of the
existing relationship (that is, that the plaintiff should continue a salaried partner) or
for the plaintiff to become a 'full partner' despite the failure of the parties to enter
into the 'deed or agreement' by that date in accordance with the 1968 agreement.
The very thing that they had agreed to do had not been done; they had not entered
^g into the contemplated deed or agreement. The question was what they did in place
of what they had agreed to do; and the answer seems to me to be that they
continued just as before.

With that in mind, I turn to s 27 of the 1890 Act. This reads as follows:

^h '(1) Where a partnership entered into for a fixed term is continued after the
term has expired, and without any express new agreement, the rights and duties
of the partners remain the same as they were at the expiration of the term, so
far as is consistent with the incidents of a partnership at will.

'(2) A continuance of the business by the partners or such of them as
habitually acted therein during the term, without any settlement or liquidation
of the partnership affairs, is presumed to be a continuance of the partnership.'

^j One question that arose during the argument was whether this section had any
application to the present case. Did the 1968 agreement for a salaried partnership
bring into being 'a partnership' for the purposes of s 27 (1)? Counsel for the plaintiff's

---

1   (1840) 1 Man & G 155
2   (1876) 1 App Cas 174
3   (1876) 1 App Cas at 182

answer was No, and counsel for the defendant's answer was Yes; and inevitably that led to a consideration of what is the nature of a salaried partnership? On this, I am especially indebted to counsel for the plaintiff for his researches, inconclusive though they turned out to be.

Certain aspects of a salaried partnership were not disputed. The term 'salaried partner' is not a term of art, and to some extent it may be said to be a contradiction in terms. However, it is a convenient expression which is widely used to denote a person who is held out to the world as being a partner, with his name appearing as partner on the notepaper of the firm, and so on. At the same time, he receives a salary as remuneration, rather than a share of the profits, though he may, in addition to his salary, receive some bonus or other sum of money dependent on the profits. Quoad the outside world it often will matter little whether a man is a full partner or a salaried partner; for a salaried partner is held out as being a partner, and the partners will be liable for his acts accordingly. But within the partnership it may be important to know whether a salaried partner is truly to be classified as a mere employee or as a partner.

On this, there is little clear guidance to be obtained from the books. I was referred to various passages in Lindley[1] and in Pollock[2]. I was also referred to *Ex parte Watson*[3], *Walker v Hirsch*[4] and *Re Hill, Claremont v Hill*[5]. Counsel for the plaintiff also mentioned in short form the three other cases cited in Lindley[6], namely, *Burnell v Hunt*[7], *Price v Groom*[8] and *Re Young, ex parte Jones*[9]. In Lindley[10] there is a somewhat inconclusive discussion as to whether a sharing in the profits is essential to the concept of partnership. The text seems to lean towards saying that a salaried partner is not a true partner, for although the division of profits is not a concept written into the statutory definition of partnership, the provisions of s 39 of the 1890 Act relating to dissolution import by implication some requirement of this sort. On the other hand, in a passage added by the editor of the 15th edition, Pollock[11] says this:

'. . . it is thought that a salaried partner is a true partner notwithstanding that he is paid a fixed salary irrespective of profits and that as between himself and his co-partner he is not liable for the partnership debts. The question will rarely be of importance, since he is clearly held out as a partner and will be liable accordingly (*infra*, s. 14), but unless a true partner he would not be liable to a creditor who was aware of his position when the debt was contracted, so that the question is not purely academic.'

The first sentence of that statement is vouched by a reference to the first three authorities I have just cited. This passage, I may say, seems to assume that the only questions of importance in this field are those between the partnership and the outside world, whereas, as this case shows, there may be internal questions of importance between the partners.

I have looked at certain other authorities, including *Marsh v Stacey*[12] and *Ellis v Joseph Ellis & Co*[13]. In the former case, A, by agreement with his sole co-partner B,

1   The Law of Partnership (13th Edn, 1971), pp 13, 14, 18, 26, 79
2   The Law of Partnership (15th Edn, 1952), pp 9-11
3   (1815) 19 Ves 459
4   (1884) 27 Ch D 460
5   [1934] Ch 623, [1934] All ER Rep 617
6   13th Edn (1971), pp 17, 18
7   (1841) 5 Jur 650
8   (1848) 2 Exch 542
9   [1896] 1 QB 484
10 13th Edn (1971), pp 13, 14
11 15th Edn (1952), p 11
12 (1963) 107 Sol Jo 512, [1963] Bar Library transcript 169
13 [1905] 1 KB 324

a   reduced his activities and instead of taking a fraction of the profits agreed to accept 'a fixed salary of £1,200 per annum as a first charge on the profits'[1]. The profits in one year fell far short of £1,200, and the Court of Appeal, in affirming Pennycuick J, held that the words 'as a first charge on the profits' meant that A was not entitled to sue B for £1,200 for that year; a first charge on the profits for £1,200 was one thing, a firm agreement to pay him £1,200 another. In the course of his judgment (with which Ormerod and Davies LJJ simply agreed), Upjohn LJ said[2] that A 'really

b   became a salaried partner, that is to say, an employee of the partnership'. Yet the order made by Pennycuick J included an order to wind up the partnership and directed the usual accounts and enquiries, which points to a true partnership rather than a mere relationship of master and servant: and perhaps 'salaried partner' is not really an apt term for someone who is entitled not to a fixed salary but to the profits (if any) up to a fixed limit. In *Re Hill*[3], I may say, the position

c   seems to have been similar despite the reference by Maugham LJ[4] to 'a salary of 600l. a year'. The *Ellis* case[5] merely holds that a true partner who in addition is paid a fixed wage for doing specific work does not thereby become a workman for the purposes of the Workmen's Compensation Act 1897, for he could not for that purpose be both master and servant.

   I have found it impossible to deduce any real rule from the authorities before me,

d   and I think that, while paying due regard to those authorities, I must look at the matter on principle. It seems to me impossible to say that as a matter of law a salaried partner is or is not necessarily a partner in the true sense. He may or may not be a partner, depending on the facts. What must be done, I think, is to look at the substance of the relationship between the parties; and there is ample authority for saying that the question whether or not there is a partnership depends on what the true

e   relationship is and not on any mere label attached to that relationship. A relationship that is plainly not a partnership is no more made into a partnership by calling it one than a relationship which is plainly a partnership is prevented from being one by a clause negativing partnership: see, for example, Lindley[6].

   If, then, there is a plain contract of master and servant, and the only qualification

f   of that relationship is that the servant is being held out as being a partner, the name 'salaried partner' seems perfectly apt for him; and yet he will be no partner in relation to the members of the firm. At the other extreme, there may be a full partnership deed under which all the partners save one take a share of the profits, with that one being paid a fixed salary not dependent on profits. Again, 'salaried partner' seems to me an apt description of that one: yet I do not see why he should not be a true partner, at all events if he is entitled to share in the profits on a winding-up, thereby

g   satisfying the point made by Lindley[7] on s 39. However, I do not think it could be said it would be impossible to exclude or vary s 39 by the terms of the partnership agreement, or even by subsequent variation (see s 19), and so I think that there could well be cases in which a salaried partner will be a true partner even though he would not benefit from s 39. It may be that most salaried partners are persons

h   whose only title to partnership is that they are held out as being partners; but even if 'salaried partners' who are true partners, though at a salary, are in a minority, that does not mean that they are non-existent.

   If I am right in this, then it seems to me that one must in every case look at the terms of the relationship to ascertain whether or not it creates a true partnership.

j   1   [1963] Bar Library transcript 169 at p 4
     2   [1963] Bar Library transcript 169 at p 7
     3   [1934] Ch at 624, 628, 630
     4   [1934] Ch at 632, [1934] All ER Rep at 622
     5   [1905] 1 KB 324
     6   13th Edn (1971), p 66
     7   13th Edn (1971), pp 13, 14

In this case, I have so far not said much about the terms of the 1968 agreement. It contains a number of features that strongly point to a partnership. Clause 6 recites that: 'C.E. and R.S. have agreed to enter into partnership upon the terms herein set out.' Clause 7 I have already mentioned. Clause 8 provides: 'The capital of the partnership shall be provided and shall solely belong to C.E.', with a somewhat trivial exception as to the plaintiff's furniture. There are further provisions for bringing all directors' fees into the partnership accounts, that all profits are to belong to the defendant, and that he, and not the plaintiff, is to bear all losses. Then there are provisions as to keeping up the books of account, full-time services, diligent attendance and so on, and restraining either partner without the consent of the other from being engaged in any other business, taking apprentices or hiring or dismissing any agent or servant of the firm, lending the firm's money, giving securities on account of the firm, endangering the partnership property, or drawing, accepting or endorsing bills of exchange or promissory notes on account of the firm. By cl 18 there is provision for either to give notice to the other of dissolution of the partnership for breach of certain terms of the agreement, committing a crime or acts of bankruptcy, and so on. By cl 19, on the expiration of the partnership or on the determination of the partnership under cl 18, the defendant is to be entitled to all the capital (save for the plaintiff's furniture) and to all the clients save those introduced by the plaintiff; but if either dies while the partnership continues, the other is to be entitled, without payment, to all the clients of the deceased. If the defendant dies, the practice is to belong to the plaintiff, and he is to pay the defendant's personal representative the amount of capital that the defendant has in the firm, and apportioned sums for the profits and work in progress, by payments of £250 every three months. There is then a remarkable clause, the best part of a page in length, providing for doubts and questions to be decided by an expert to be nominated (in default of agreement) by the President of the Institute of Chartered Accountants, with an extensive power to give directions, including directions dissolving the partnership.

Is this an agreement for employment or an agreement for partnership? If it is merely a contract for employment, then it is one of the most remarkable contracts for employment that I have seen. As I read it, it is very much more an agreement for a partnership than it is an agreement for employment. True, the provisions for a salary and for the ownership of capital are not the usual provisions to be found in a partnership agreement; but I do not think that they or anything else denature the agreement. Certainly the relationship between the parties under the agreement seems to me to satisfy the statutory definition in s 1 (1) of the 1890 Act as being 'the relation which subsists between persons carrying on a business in common with a view of profit.' True again, the plaintiff had no 'share of the profits' within s 2 (3), and so there is no prima facie evidence that he is a partner in the business under the head; but the absence of one possible head of prima facie evidence does not negative the other evidence of partnership. Furthermore, on the evidence before me, the actual conduct of the parties after 1st October 1968 fully accorded with the concept of partnership as recorded in the 1968 agreement. That being so, I think that there is a 'partnership entered into for a fixed term' for the purposes of s 27, and that this was continued without any express new agreement. That partnership was determined by mutual agreement in August 1970 when, with the defendant's consent, the plaintiff departed with all the papers relating to his clients. This accorded with cl 19 of the 1968 agreement. All the capital and all the clients of the defendant remain his.

Paragraphs 1 and 2 of the statement of claim allege as follows:

'1. On or about the 6th April 1969 the Plaintiff and the Defendant started to carry on in partnership at 35, Eagle Street, London, W.C.1. the business of Chartered Accountants which had previously been carried on by the Defendant alone, and of which the Plaintiff had previously been an employee.

'2. The said business had been and continued to be carried on under the name of Stanley Kennard & Co. No fixed term was agreed upon for the duration of the partnership, and accordingly the partnership was a partnership at will. No terms relating to the interests or duties of the partners were agreed, and accordingly the provisions of Section 24 of the Partnership Act, 1890, applied to the partnership.'

These allegations seem to me to be in a substantial degree contrary to what I have held. The relationship between the plaintiff and the defendant was in substance the same after 6th April 1969 as it was before. The plaintiff had no interest in the capital of the firm or in the clients, save those whom he took with him. He has, indeed, not done badly. The work that he did for the clients that he introduced was done prior to August 1970, in time for which he was receiving £2,000 a year from the defendant. The remuneration for that work, as work in progress (apart from any subsequent work), will be retained entirely by him. To that extent he will be being paid twice over for the same work; and I observe that the accounts for the firm for the years ended 30th June 1969 and 30th June 1970 each show a loss for the year after paying the plaintiff his £2,000. Nevertheless, the plaintiff is now seeking to have the partnership wound up, and is claiming an interest in the capital. Neither the plaintiff nor the defendant asserts that there is any continuing partnership between them, and both say that, whatever the relationship was, it came to an end in August 1970. With that state of affairs, I cannot see any real point in merely making a declaration that the partnership was dissolved on or about the end of August 1970. A plaintiff who claims a declaration that a relationship which the defendant says has never existed is at an end is claiming something which, per se, will usually have little or no value. However, it may be that counsel will consider such a declaration to be desirable, and I will hear them on the form of order.

I turn to the claim for an order for winding up, and for the accounts and enquiries. If there never was a partnership, then there is nothing to wind up; but if there was a partnership, there may be. However, nothing has been put before me to suggest that, on the facts as they appear to me, there would be any real practical utility in making such an order, though again if counsel wish to make any further submissions on the point I will readily hear them. The case was one which developed considerably during the course of argument and there was no exploration of the question whether a partnership arising merely from constituting one of the two persons concerned a salaried partner is one which is subject to winding up in the usual way. It seems to me, however, that even though there was no express mention of goodwill as such, the intention of the 1968 agreement was to exclude the plaintiff from any proprietary interest in the partnership, and I do not think that to hold that a relationship is a partnership for the purposes of s 27 can necessarily mean that the court is obliged to make an order to wind up at the suit of the partner who lacks any such interest. Indeed, it would not surprise me if the majority of salaried partners had no real claims to an order for the winding-up of a partnership. I do not want to involve the parties in any avoidable costs, and I do not propose to make an order which, so far as I can see, would serve no useful purpose. There are, indeed, a number of loose ends and puzzling discrepancies in the case which I have not attempted to explore in this judgment, but on the whole it seems to me that the plaintiff's claim has failed, and that subject to any further submissions that counsel may wish to make, the right course would be to dismiss the action.

Action dismissed.

Solicitors: *A Kramer & Co* (for the plaintiff); *Bircham & Co* (for the defendant).

Susan Corbett Barrister.

R v Croydon Juvenile Court Justices, ex parte Croydon London Borough Council

QUEEN'S BENCH DIVISION
LORD WIDGERY CJ, WILLIS AND TALBOT JJ
4th DECEMBER 1972

Children and young persons – Fine – Imposition – Court's power to order parent or guardian to pay fine instead of child or young person – Child placed in care of local authority pursuant to care order – Child then committing several offences – Child living in local authority home at time – Justices imposing fines for offences and ordering local authority to pay them as child's guardian – Whether local authority his 'guardian' – Children and Young Persons Act 1933, ss 55 (1), 107 (1).

X, a boy under the age of 14, was placed under the care of a local authority pursuant to a care order made under s 1 (3) (c) of the Children and Young Persons Act 1969. The local authority put X in a children's home which it owned and ran. Whilst there X committed several offences. He was charged and brought before a juvenile court. The justices decided that the case would be best met by the imposition of fines and, in the purported exercise of their power under s 55 (1)[a] of the Children and Young Persons Act 1933, ordered the local authority to pay the fines in respect of the offences committed by X. The local authority applied for an order of certiorari to quash the order of the justices on the ground that the justices had no jurisdiction to order it to pay the fines, as it was not the 'guardian' of X within the meaning of s 55.

Held – The application for an order of certiorari would be refused; the justices were entitled to make the order. In the context of s 55 the word 'guardian' was used in the way in which it was defined in s 107 (1)[b] of the 1933 Act, namely, as the person who had 'for the time being the charge of or control over the child'; the local authority came within the definition because (i) by virtue of the care order, it had been charged with the care and control of X and (ii) X was actually living in one of its homes at the time (see p 478 j to p 479 a and p 480 a e and g, post).

Notes
For the court's power to order a parent or guardian to pay a fine instead of a child or young person, see 10 Halsbury's Laws (3rd Edn) 516, para 940.

For the Children and Young Persons Act 1933, ss 55, 107, see 17 Halsbury's Statutes (3rd Edn) 473, 515.

For the Children and Young Persons Act 1969, s 1, see 40 Halsbury's Statutes (3rd Edn) 849.

Motion for certiorari
This was an application by way of motion by Croydon London Borough Council for an order of certiorari to bring up and quash an order made by the Croydon Juvenile Court justices on 28th September 1972 whereby they ordered the applicants

---

a Section 55 (1) is set out at p 478 d and e, post
b Section 107 (1), so far as material, is set out at p 478 h, post

a   to pay the fines incurred by a child in their care on the finding of guilt being recorded against that child pursuant to s 55 of the Children and Young Persons Act 1933. The grounds for the application were: (1) that the justices purported to order the fines to be paid pursuant to s 55 of the 1933 Act on the grounds that the applicants were the guardians of the child within the meaning of s 55; (2) that the words 'parent or guardian' in s 55 of the 1933 Act did not include a body corporate or local authority;

b   (3) that the context of s 55 of the 1933 Act did not permit the justices to hold the opinion that a body corporate or local authority had for the time being the charge or control over a child or young person having regard to the terms of s 107 of the 1933 Act; (4) that the motion and concept of care orders made under the Children and Young Persons Acts 1933 to 1969 did not permit of the construction being given to s 55 of the 1933 Act whereby the local authorities in whose care a child had been placed could be ordered to pay the fines of the child in the event of such child being

c   convicted of any offence; and (5) the justices had no jurisdiction to order the applicants to pay the fines. The matter first came ex parte before the court (Lawton LJ, Chapman and Wien JJ) on 20th October 1972 when leave to move for certiorari was granted. The facts are set out in the judgment of Lord Widgery CJ.

d   *D H Farquharson QC* and *Ian McCulloch* for the applicants.
    Gordon Slynn as amicus curiae.

e   **LORD WIDGERY CJ.** In these proceedings counsel moves on behalf of the applicants, Croydon London Borough Council, for an order of certiorari to bring up and quash a decision of the Croydon Juvenile Court made on 28th September 1972 whereby the applicants were ordered to pay fines incurred by a child in their care, pursuant to an order made under s 55 of the Children and Young Persons Act 1933 in respect of offences committed by the child. This is evidently a somewhat

f   novel and interesting point of principle beyond the confines of the borough of Croydon. It concerns a boy who was born on 4th June 1959 and who is now about 13, and being still under 14 is for the purposes of terminology a 'child' as opposed to a 'young person'. He was before the juvenile court in Croydon in July 1971 in respect of offences of wilful damage, and a supervision order was made in respect of him under the Children and Young Persons Act 1969. This however was not wholly

g   successful because in May 1972 he was back before the court and on that occasion there was made what is called a care order in respect of him under s 1 of the 1969 Act.

    Section 1 of the 1969 Act gives a wide discretion to justices and juvenile courts in regard to what are now generally called care proceedings, and one of the steps that can be taken is the making of a care order under s 1 (3) (c) of that Act. The local authority,

h   indeed the present applicants, as a consequence of that care order became responsible for the care and control of this boy. Initially they put him in a children's home in Croydon which was owned and run by them. Whilst he was in that home he continued to misbehave. On 24th May he played truant, took and drove away two motor cars and was charged in respect of those offences and also in regard to driving whilst under age and without insurance. On 8th June at the home where

j   he was living, he stole £7 from the housemother and on 21st June he played truant again and indulged in one offence of burglary and one of wilful damage to a telephone box. Faced with that course of conduct over a few weeks the local authority took him away from the children's home and sent him to a remand home and later to school at Redhill, the purpose of which transfer as I understand it was so that he might be classified with a view to his going to an approved school. He was in trouble again before the Oxted justices in August when a conditional discharge was made, and finally on 21st September 1972 he was before the Croydon Juvenile Court in respect of the six motoring offences to which I have already referred, and also in respect of his offences on 21st June when he committed burglary and damaged the telephone box.

The juvenile court, having to deal with him in respect of those charges on 21st September, was referred to s 55 of the Children and Young Persons Act 1933, to which I must return in a moment, and considered imposing fines and making an order that those fines should be paid by the local authority in whose care and control it was said that he had been at the material time. To give the applicants a fair opportunity of answering this claim, the matter was put over until 28th September, but then in purported exercise of their powers under s 55 of the Children and Young Persons Act 1933, the court imposed fines and ordered that they be paid by the applicants, hence the present application in which it is said that was an order made without jurisdiction, and consequently it should be quashed.

There is a great deal of statute law in regard to children and young persons. Counsel for the applicants has faced up to a difficult and unappetising task in taking us through a great deal of it. One must begin with the section under which the justices purported to act. Section 55 (1) of the Children and Young Persons Act 1933 provides:

'Where a child or young person is charged with any offence for the commission of which a fine, damages, or costs may be imposed, if the court is of opinion that the case would be best met by the imposition of a fine, damages, or costs. whether with or without any other punishment, the court may in any case, and shall if the offender is a child, order that the fine, damages, or costs awarded be paid by the parent or guardian of the child or young person instead of by the child or young person, unless the court is satisfied that the parent or guardian cannot be found or that he has not conduced to the commission of the offence by neglecting to exercise due care of the child or young person.'

The purpose of the legislation is clear enough in my judgment. It is to make provision whereby parents who have not exercised due care over the conduct of their children may be made to pay fines which would otherwise be imposed on the children. Several things are to be observed on reading this subsection. First of all it does not apply unless the court is of the opinion that the case would best be met by the imposition of a fine. Only then does the question arise at all. Secondly it is to be observed that the obligation is on the parent or guardian of the child, and thirdly that the parent or guardian has the opportunity if he can of showing that he has not conduced to the commission of the offence by neglecting the child.

In the light of those three points, one turns to s 107 (1) of the 1933 Act to see what 'guardian' means. It is defined in these words:

' "Guardian", in relation to a child or young person, includes any person who, in the opinion of the court having cognisance of any case in relation to the child or young person or in which the child or young person is concerned, has for the time being the charge of or control over the child or young person'.

That is an extremely wide definition; it extends to anybody who in the opinion of the court has for the time being the charge of or control over the child. It is perfectly clear that it is not intended to be restricted to what one might call legal guardians, because legal guardians recognised by the law are defined separately in the same section, so it must be intended to give the phrase 'parent or guardian' in s 55 a very wide meaning. For my part, when one looks at the language and gives the words their natural meaning, it seems to me clear that the local authority charged with the care and control of the child by virtue of the care order is the person for the time being in charge of or with control over the child if, as in the present case, the child is

a   physically in the home managed and run by that local authority. What the position
    may be where the child is in another situation under a care order, I leave for con-
    sideration on another day, but here we are concerned with a child who at the relevant
    time was in a home actually owned and organised by the local authority itself, and
    looking at the words which I have read and giving them their natural meaning, it
    seems to me that a strong case is made out for the proposition that in these circums-
b   tances the child was in the charge or control of the local authority, and the local
    authority is the guardian.

    That being a matter of first impression, one tends to ask oneself why it should not
    be so, as counsel for the applicants has so strenuously argued.   Apparently this
    power, although it has existed since 1933, has been sparingly used, but I do not get
    much assistance from that. Then it is said it will hamper the discretion of the local
c   authority in its decision in regard to the child if it is liable to find itself paying fines
    of this character; but I am not impressed by that argument because as I have said
    more than once, the local authority, like any other guardian, can be excused responsi-
    bility if it has exercised due care, and I would not have thought that in the rare cases
    where it fails to exercise due care the resultant fines would be likely to be so burden-
    some on the ratepayers as to be really a matter which Parliament cannot be assumed
d   to have intended. All the consequences of looking at the language and trying to
    apply common sense seem to me to point to the conclusion that the justices were
    entitled to do what they did. Whether they were wise in the individual case or not
    is not a matter for us.

    However, counsel for the applicants has shown us a number of other provisions
    designed to show that the local authority is in a special position in this kind of litiga-
e   tion, if only because it is driven into it willy nilly whether it likes it or not. He refers
    us to s 2 (3) of the Children and Young Persons Act 1969, which makes it perfectly
    clear that once care proceedings are being taken, the local authority has to come
    into those proceedings compulsorily. I accept that. Then he goes on to indicate a
    number of provisions in the legislation which show that the natural parent does not
    wholly lose his status, and authority, as a result of a care order. He showed us s 21 (2)
f   of the 1969 Act, which linked with s 70 (2) is a good illustration of that. Section 21 (2)
    provides:

> 'If it appears to a juvenile court, on the application of a local authority to
> whose care a person is committed by a care order or on the application of that
> person, that it is appropriate to discharge the order, the court may discharge
> it and on discharging it may, unless it was an interim order and unless the person
g   > to whom the discharged order related has attained the age of eighteen, make a
> supervision order in respect of him.'

    It does, however, as counsel for the applicants contends, illustrate that the natural
    parent continues to have some status. But I find a good deal of encouragement for my
h   own provisional view of this matter in s 24, which is concerned with the duty of the
    local authority under orders such as this. Section 24 (1) provides:

> 'It shall be the duty of a local authority to whose care a person is committed
> by a care order or by a warrant under subsection (1) of the preceding section to
> receive him into their care and, notwithstanding any claim by his parent or
j   > guardian, to keep him in their care while the order or warrant is in force.'

    It is evident there that the child has been taken out of the care of the parent or
    guardian and into the care of the authority. Section 24 (2) provides:

> 'A local authority shall, subject to the following provisions of this section, have
> the same powers and duties with respect to a person in their care by virtue of a

care order or such a warrant as his parent or guardian would have apart from
the order . . .'

Again one finds the local authority acting under the care order being equated in
its powers and duties to the natural parent.

If further reinforcement of what I have described as my own provisional view were
required I find it in s 49 of the 1969 Act, a section which introduces amendments to
s 13 of the Children Act 1948, and the relevant passage is in the new s 13 (2) of that
Act which provides:

'Without prejudice to the generality of subsection (1) of this section, a local
authority may allow a child in their care, either for a fixed period or until the
local authority otherwise determine, to be under the charge and control of a
parent, guardian, relative or friend.'

It seems to me to be absolutely conclusive that for the purposes of the Children
Act 1948 a local authority acting under a care order can properly be described as
having the child in its charge or control. True it is a different Act, but these Acts are
all related, and I get, as I say, reinforcement of my provisional view from reading
that section of the 1948 Act. I hope I shall not be thought disrespectful to counsel
for the applicants' argument if I do not go through his references in greater detail;
it suffices to say that in the circumstances of this case, which I stress was one in which
a child was actually living in the local authority home at the time, the child was within
the charge or control of the local authority sufficient to justify the justices in what they
did when they imposed the fines and ordered that the local authority should pay
them.

I would add in parenthesis, as it were, that I cannot believe that this is a practice
which is likely to be widely used in the country as a whole. If good sense prevented
the necessity for imposing fines on a local authority in the 36 years between the passing
of the two Acts, it is unlikely that a great outburst of such activity will now follow.
In any event, local authorities should not be unduly concerned, in my judgment,
because they have, as I have pointed out, a complete answer to this kind of imposition
if they have not been guilty of neglect in the care and control of the child. I would
therefore refuse the application for certiorari.

WILLIS J. I agree.

TALBOT J. I agree.

Application dismissed.

Solicitors: *Sharpe, Pritchard & Co,* agents for *Alan Blakemore,* Croydon (for the
applicants); *Treasury Solicitor.*

N P Metcalfe Esq Barrister.

Duke and others v Robson and others

CHANCERY DIVISION
PLOWMAN J
4th DECEMBER 1972

COURT OF APPEAL, CIVIL DIVISION
RUSSELL, STAMP AND ROSKILL LJJ
11th DECEMBER 1972

Mortgage – Sale – Exercise of power of sale by mortgagee – Sale overreaching prior dealing by mortgagor – Mortgagor contracting to sell mortgaged property to plaintiffs – Registration of contract by plaintiffs as land charge – Subsequent contract entered into by mortgagee in exercise of power of sale and with notice of the previous contract – Whether mortgagee can be restrained from exercising power of sale.

The mortgagors were the owners of a freehold house. The house was subject to a charge by way of legal mortgage to the mortgagees. There was due under that mortgage some £19,000; two subsequent incumbrances brought the total charge on the property to a figure approaching £27,000. In March 1972 the mortgagors contracted to sell the house to the plaintiffs for £25,000. On 28th September the mortgagees took possession of the property. On 9th October the plaintiffs registered their contract to purchase the house as a class C (iv)[a] land charge. A day or so later the plaintiffs, through their solicitors, offered to put into the joint names of their own solicitors and the mortgagees' solicitors the total amount owing to all three incumbrancers but with a top limit of £26,000. Subsequently the plaintiffs issued a writ against the mortgagors for specific performance. On 7th November the mortgagees, pursuant to their power of sale, contracted to sell the house to the fourth defendant for £45,000. The plaintiffs applied for an interlocutory injunction restraining the mortgagees and the fourth defendant from carrying out that contract.

Held – The application would be dismissed for the following reasons—
(i) the information given by the plaintiffs that they were prepared to put (up to a ceiling of £26,000) the total due to the incumbrancers into the joint names of solicitors was not equivalent to a tender or payment of what was due under the incumbrances sufficient to deprive the mortgagees of the power of sale (see p 487 g and j and p 489 e and g, post); *Lord Waring v London and Manchester Assurance Co Ltd* [1934] All ER Rep 642 applied;
(ii) a contract for sale by a mortgagor of the equity of redemption could have no possible effect on the rights and powers of a mortgagee, in particular the right of the mortgagee to exercise his power of sale, any more than could a conveyance by a mortgagor, unless in the course of completion the mortgage was redeemed (see p 488 g and p 489 e and g, post).

Notes
For the paramount effect of power of sale, see 27 Halsbury's Laws (3rd Edn) 294, para 551, and for cases on the subject, see 35 Digest (Repl) 587, 2596-2598.
For the circumstances in which a mortgagee may be restrained from exercising his power of sale, see 27 Halsbury's Laws (3rd Edn) 301, 302, para 566.
For the Land Charges Act 1925, s 10, see 27 Halsbury's Statutes (3rd Edn) 696.
Section 10 of the 1925 Act has been replaced by s 2 of the Land Charges Act 1972 as from 29th January 1973.

---

a   Under s 10 (1) of the Land Charges Act 1925

Cases referred to in judgments

Cuckmere Brick Co Ltd v Mutual Finance Ltd, Mutual Finance Ltd v Cuckmere Brick Co Ltd   a
   [1971] 2 All ER 633, [1971] Ch 949, [1971] 2 WLR 1207, CA.
Property and Bloodstock Ltd v Emerton, Bush v Property and Bloodstock Ltd [1967] 3 All ER
   321, [1968] Ch 94, [1967] 3 WLR 973, CA, Digest (Cont Vol C) 718, 2598a.
Waring (Lord) v London and Manchester Assurance Co Ltd [1935] Ch 310, [1934] All
   ER Rep 642, 104 LJCh 201, 152 LT 390, 35 Digest (Repl) 587, 2598.   b

Authority also cited

Megarry and Wade, The Law of Real Property (3rd Edn, 1966), p 582.

Motion

By a writ issued on 14th November 1972 the plaintiffs, (1) Anthony Duke, (2) Godfrey
Kenneth Sidney Paddick, (3) Renee Paddick, and (4) Andrew James Ramage-Gibson,   c
claimed against the defendants, (1) Jean Robson, (2) Paul John Robson, (3) Windsor Life
Assurance Co Ltd ('the mortgagees'), and (4) D Collins, inter alia, (1) specific performance of an agreement between the plaintiffs and the first defendant dated 17th March
1972 for the sale of certain freehold property at Burnham, Buckinghamshire, known
as the Abbey House, (2) further or alternatively damages for breach of contract,
and (3) an injunction restraining the mortgagees from completing the contract for   d
the sale of the Abbey House which they had entered into under purported exercise
of their power of sale after notice of the contract dated 17th March 1972 and restraining
the mortgagees from entering into any other contract for the sale thereof.   By
notice of motion dated 14th November 1972 the plaintiffs sought an interlocutory
injunction in the same terms as that claimed in the writ.   The facts are set out in   e
the judgment of Plowman J.

J R Macdonald for the plaintiffs.
T A C Coningsby for the first defendant.
Susan Burridge for the second defendant.
T R F Jennings for the mortgagees.
The fourth defendant did not appear and was not represented.   f

PLOWMAN J.   A sale by mortgagees under their power of sale is due to be completed tomorrow.   The question which I have to decide is whether the purchasers
under a contract for sale with the mortgagors are entitled to stop the sale by the
mortgagees by reason of the fact that the purchasers from the mortgagors had   g
registered their contract as a class C (iv) land charge before the mortgagees entered
into their contract with their purchaser.   The plaintiffs in this action are the purchasers from the mortgagors.   The first and second defendants, Mr and Mrs Robson,
are the mortgagors.   The third defendants, Windsor Life Assurance Co Ltd, are
the mortgagees, and the fourth defendant, Mr Collins, who has not appeared on this
motion, is the purchaser from the mortgagees.   The property in dispute in this case   h
is a property at Burnham called the Abbey House.   Mr and Mrs Robson, the first
two defendants, are the legal owners of that property.

   On 13th March 1968 they mortgaged it by a legal charge to the mortgagees to secure
the sum of £15,000 and interest.   Mr and Mrs Robson also executed a second
mortgage in favour of Lloyds Bank and a third mortgage in favour of Barclays Bank,
and the total amount currently owing on those three mortgages is said to be   j
something in the neighbourhood of £30,000.

   On 16th March 1972 Mr Robson contracted to sell his interest in the Abbey House
to his wife for the sum of £25,000.   On the following day she entered into a contract
to sell it to the plaintiffs at the same price, £25,000.   That was a contract for sale
with vacant possession and without reference to any of the mortgages affecting the

a property. On 9th October 1972 that contract was registered as a class C (iv) land
charge against Mrs Robson. On 7th November the mortgagees in exercising their
power of sale contracted to sell the property to the fourth defendant for £45,000
and, as I have already said, the date fixed for the completion of that contract is tomorrow. By the notice of motion which is before me the plaintiffs are seeking
to stop that completion taking place.

b I must go back a little way in time. In September 1971, when Mr and Mrs Robson
were in default, the mortgagees obtained an order against them in the Slough County
Court for possession. That order was not enforced for some time. On 7th April
1972 the solicitors for the mortgagees were informed by the solicitors who were then
acting for both Mr and Mrs Robson that the latter had entered into a contract for
sale of the house. By letter of that date Messrs Tyrrell Lewis & Co wrote to Messrs
c Metson, Cross & Co stating: 'Contracts have been exchanged for the sale of our
clients' house and it is hoped to complete the sale on the 11th April.' Various redemption statements were sent to the mortgagors on behalf of the mortgagees but
nothing happened, and on 19th September the mortgagees applied to the county
court for a warrant to enforce their order for possession. That warrant was in fact
enforced and possession given to the mortgagees on 28th September.

d Meanwhile on 22nd September Messrs Tyrrell Lewis & Co, who at that time
were acting solely on behalf of Mr Robson, wrote a letter to Messrs Metson, Cross &
Co, on behalf of the mortgagees, which I had better read because it is relied on by
the plaintiffs on this application. Among other things they said in that letter:

'Contracts have since been exchanged for the sale of the property to our
Client's wife who has herself entered into a Contract for the sub sale of the
e property at the same price to a property company.'

The property company in fact are the plaintiffs. The letter continued:

'Contracts were exchanged as long ago as 16th March 1972. Since that date
the principal owing under the first mortgage to your Clients the second mortgage
f to Lloyds Bank Limited, Maidenhead and the third mortgage to Barclays Bank,
Slough together with the interest which has accumulated and which is accruing
from day to day more than exceeds the £25,000. mentioned above. It is in
the respective interest of both our Client and his wife that your Clients should
enforce the Order for Possession which they have obtained from the Court and
then as mortgagees in possession sell the property to Mr C. Llewelyn of 2 The
g Limes, Mill Lane Windsor who has agreed to purchase the same for the sum
of £33,000. subject to contract. We would mention that our Clients have
also received another offer for the purchase of the property for the sum of £31,000
subject to contract showing that the present value of the property is well above
the price shown in the Contract for the sale of the property to Mrs. Robson.
Our respective Clients appreciate that in the event of your Clients enforcing the
h Order for Possession and selling the property to the person mentioned above it
would annul the contract for the sale of the property to Mrs. Robson and her
contract for the sub sale of the property to the consortium. This would fit
in with our Clients requirements and we should be obliged if you would obtain
your Clients instructions on the matter and confirm that they would be prepared
to proceed with the sale of the property to Mr. C. Llewelyn at the price of £33,000
j subject to contract.'

It was early in October 1972 that the plaintiffs learned that the mortgagees were
themselves proposing to dispose of the property, and on 10th or 11th October
the plaintiffs' solicitors informed the solicitors for the mortgagees that they were
issuing a writ for specific performance. On behalf of the plaintiffs—not the bor-
rowers but on behalf of the plaintiffs—they offered to place the amount due on

deposit in the joint names of solicitors. Then, as I have stated, on 7th November the mortgagees entered into a contract to sell the property to the fourth defendant for the sum of £45,000.

Counsel for the plaintiffs puts forward two reasons why an injunction should be granted. The first is on the ground of lack of good faith, bad faith, on the part of the mortgagees. Counsel referred me to a decision of Crossman J in *Lord Waring v London and Manchester Assurance Co Ltd*[1]. Crossman J said:

'The contract is an absolute contract, not conditional in any way, and the sale is expressed to be made by the company as mortgagee. If, before the date of the contract, the plaintiff had tendered the principal with interest and costs, or had paid it into Court in proceedings, then, if the company had continued to take steps to enter into a contract for sale, or had purported to do so, the plaintiff would, in my opinion, have been entitled to an injunction restraining it from doing so.'

I pause there to say that the offer to which I have referred to place the mortgage money on deposit in the joint names of solicitors is in my view a very different thing from either a tender of the mortgage money or the payment of the mortgage money into court. Crossman J continued[1]:

'After a contract has been entered into, however, it is, in my judgment perfectly clear (subject to what has been said to me to-day) that the mortgagee (in the present case, the company) can be restrained from completing only on the ground that he has not acted in good faith and that the sale is therefore liable to be set aside.'

That decision of Crossman J was expressly approved by the Court of Appeal in *Property and Bloodstock Ltd v Emerton*[2]. The improper motive or the lack of good faith which counsel for the plaintiffs seeks to attribute to the mortgagees arises principally, I think, out of that letter of 22nd September 1972, which I have read, in which Mr Robson was saying that it would be in the best interests of himself and Mrs Robson if the mortgagees sold as mortgagees, the point of course being that they could sell at a price considerably in excess of the sum of £25,000 for which the property had earlier been contracted to be sold, and therefore, of course, there would be more to go into the pockets of the owners of the equity of redemption. Counsel for the plaintiffs stressed the words in the paragraph that I read:

'Our respective Clients appreciate that in the event of your Clients enforcing the Order for Possession and selling the property to the person mentioned above it would annul the contract for the sale of the property to Mrs. Robson and her contract for the sub sale of the property to the consortium. This would fit in with our Clients requirements and we should be obliged if you would obtain your Clients instructions [and so on].'

Whatever the motives of Mr and Mrs Robson may have been—and whether those motives were proper or improper motives—that letter does not seem to me to be any evidence of improper motive on the part of the mortgagees. I see no evidence in this case which is sufficient to lead me to even a provisional conclusion that the mortgagees ought to be restrained from completing their sale on the ground of bad faith.

The other point which counsel for the plaintiffs relied on was this. He pointed out that the plaintiffs' contract had been registered as an estate contract before the mortgagees entered into any contract for the sale of the property to the fourth

1 [1935] Ch 310 at 317, [1934] All ER Rep 642 at 644
2 [1967] 3 All ER 321, [1968] Ch 94

a   defendant. He submitted that under the relevant provisions of the Land Charges Act 1925 the fourth defendant was therefore affected with and bound by notice of the plaintiffs' contract. But the answer to that, in my judgment, is this, that the plaintiffs' contract with Mr and Mrs Robson affected only their equity of redemption. That was all they had to sell, an equity of redemption. That equity of redemption, together with the plaintiffs' interest in it under their contract with the

b   mortgagors, is in my judgment overridden under the overriding powers of a mortgagee contained in the Law of Property Act 1925. I should refer to certain sections in that Act. First of all, s 2 (1) provides:

> 'A conveyance to a purchaser of a legal estate in land shall overreach any equitable interest or power affecting that estate, whether or not he has notice thereof...'

c   Then in para (iii) of that subsection it is stated that one of the cases to which that applies is—

> '[if] the conveyance is made by a mortgagee or personal representative in the exercise of his paramount powers, and the equitable interest or power is

d   capable of being overreached by such conveyance, and any capital money arising from the transaction is paid to the mortgagee or personal representative'.

Section 88 (1) provides:

> 'Where an estate in fee simple has been mortgaged by the creation of a term of years absolute limited thereout or by a charge by way of legal mortgage and the mortgagee sells under his statutory or express power of sale—(a) the con-

e   veyance by him shall operate to vest in the purchaser the fee simple in the land conveyed subject to any legal mortgage having priority to the mortgage in right of which the sale is made and to any money thereby secured, and thereupon; (b) the mortgage term or the charge by way of legal mortgage and any subsequent mortgage term or charges shall merge or be extinguished as respects the

f   land conveyed; and such conveyance may, as respects the fee simple, be made in the name of the estate owner in whom it is vested.'

Section 101 (1) provides:

> 'A mortgagee, where the mortgage is made by deed, shall, by virtue of this Act, have the following powers, to the like extent as if they had been in terms conferred by the mortgage deed, but not further (namely):—(i) A power, when the mortgage money has become due, to sell, or to concur with any other person in selling, the mortgaged property, or any part thereof, either subject to prior charges or not, and either together or in lots, by public auction or by private contract, subject to such conditions respecting title, or evidence of title, or other matter, as the mortgagee thinks fit, with power to vary any contract for sale, and to buy in at an auction, or to rescind any contract for sale, and to re-sell, without being answerable for any loss occasioned thereby...'

Finally, s 104 (1) provides:

> 'A mortgagee exercising the power of sale conferred by this Act shall have power, by deed, to convey the property sold, for such estate and interest therein as he is by this Act authorised to sell or convey or may be the subject of the mortgage, freed from all estates, interest, and rights to which the mortgage has priority, but subject to all estates, interests, and rights which have priority to the mortgage.'

The effect of those provisions, as I have indicated in my judgment, is that a sale by

a   a mortgagee under a charge by way of legal mortgage overreaches the equity of redemption and all rights subsisting in that equity, including the right of a purchaser from the mortgagor, and notwithstanding that he may have registered an estate contract in respect of his contract for sale.

In those circumstances I dismiss this motion.

Motion dismissed.

Solicitors: *Sharpe, Pritchard & Co*, agents for *W Norris, Bazzard & Co*, Amersham (for the plaintiffs); *C R Thomas & Son*, Maidenhead (for the first defendant); *Tyrrell Lewis & Co* (for the second defendant); *Metson, Cross & Co* (for the mortgagees).

Jacqueline Metcalfe   Barrister.

Interlocutory appeal

The plaintiffs appealed against the decision of Plowman J and, by notice of motion dated 5th December 1972, applied to the Court of Appeal for an order restraining the mortgagees until the hearing of the appeal from completing the contract for the sale of the Abbey House. With the consent of the parties the Court of Appeal agreed to treat the application as the hearing of the appeal. The grounds of appeal were as follows: (1) The plaintiffs as bona fide purchasers of the freehold property known as the Abbey House under a specifically performable contract dated 16th March 1972 made between the first defendant of the one part and the plaintiffs of the other part which was registered as a class C (iv) land charge in the land charges register on 9th October 1972 had a proprietary interest in the Abbey House which was enforceable against third parties. The judge was wrong in holding that the plaintiffs' interest was overreached by the contract for the sale of the property dated 7th November 1972 by the mortgagees purporting to act under their statutory power of sale to the fourth defendant. (2) The judge was wrong in holding on the authority of *Lord Waring v London and Manchester Assurance Co Ltd*[1] that the courts would only restrain a mortgagee from completing a contract for sale of the mortgaged property which the mortgagee had entered into on the ground that the mortgagee had not acted in good faith. The judge should have held that the court would restrain a mortgagee from completing a contract for the sale of the mortgaged property when the mortgagee had sold with the knowledge of a prior sale by the mortgagor to a bona fide purchaser because the equity vested in the bona fide purchaser prevailed over the subsequent equity of the purchaser from the mortgagee. (3) If, contrary to the contention of the plaintiffs, *Lord Waring v London and Manchester Assurance Co Ltd*[1] was authority for the judge holding that the courts would only restrain a mortgagee from completing a contract for the sale of the mortgaged property on the ground that the mortgagee had not acted in good faith, then *Lord Waring v London and Manchester Assurance Co Ltd*[1] was wrongly decided and should be reconsidered by the Court of Appeal in the light of the Court of Appeal's decision in *Cuckmere Brick Co Ltd v Mutual Finance Ltd*[2], which established that a mortgagee's duty in exercising his power of sale was not confined to acting in good faith. (4) A mortgagee in exercising his power of sale owed a duty of care to an existing bona fide purchaser from the mortgagor; the Court of Appeal should restrain the mortgagees from completing the sale to the fourth defendant in breach of the duty which they owed the plaintiffs.

J R Macdonald for the plaintiffs.
The first and second defendants did not appear and were not represented.
Gerald Godfrey QC and *T R F Jennings* for the mortgagees and fourth defendant.

---

1   [1935] Ch 310, [1934] All ER Rep 642
2   [1971] 2 All ER 633, [1971] Ch 949

RUSSELL LJ. This appeal from Plowman J raises a short point and the facts are in a limited field. The matter came before the learned judge on a motion by the plaintiffs to restrain the mortgagees from carrying out a contract of sale to the fourth defendant, Mr Collins, which is now due for completion, of a house, a freehold property, for the sum of £45,000. Plowman J refused the motion. The present application initially came before this court for an injunction to restrain the completion of that contract pending the hearing of the appeal. The parties have, however, agreed that we should treat the appeal, which has been set down as an interlocutory appeal, as being before us and to deal with the matter now.

The relevant facts are, as I have said, in a limited compass. The freehold house to which I have referred was owned by the first and second defendants, Mr and Mrs Robson, and it had been subject to a charge by way of legal mortgage to the mortgagees, the third defendants, since March 1968. There was due under that mortgage some £19,000 odd, and there were two subsequent incumbrances, bringing the total charge on the property to something approaching £27,000. On 17th March 1972 the mortgagors contracted to sell the property for £25,000 to the plaintiffs. In saying that the mortgagors so contracted I have short-circuited events, because on 16th March Mr Robson contracted to sell his beneficial interest in the house to Mrs Robson for £25,000; and on 17th March she contracted to sell the freehold to the plaintiffs. This sale, of course, would be a sale of the equity of redemption, albeit it was a contract for sale which no doubt as beneficial owner would impose on Mrs Robson the obligation to clear the incumbrances off the property.

On 28th September 1972 the mortgagees took possession of the property. On 9th October 1972 the plaintiffs registered their contract to purchase the house as a class C (iv) land charge. On 10th or 11th October 1972 the plaintiffs, through their solicitors, offered to put into the joint names of their solicitors and the solicitors for the mortgagees a total of what was owing to all the three incumbrancers, but in fact with a top limit of £26,000, which I apprehend was not enough. On 12th October the plaintiffs issued a writ against Mrs Robson for specific preformance of the contract to sell to them. On 7th November 1972 the mortgagees, pursuant to their power to sell under the mortgage, contracted to sell the property, as I have indicated, to the fourth defendant, for a sum of £45,000. Under that last contract completion was in fact due on 5th December, and, as I have said, Plowman J refused an injunction against completion of the contract.

It is perfectly plain that the information given on 10th or 11th October 1972 to the mortgagees' solicitors that the plaintiffs were prepared to put (up to a ceiling of £26,000) the total due to the three incumbrancers into the joint names of solicitors could not be described as equivalent to a tender or payment of what was due under the incumbrances, which would be necessary if someone was to say on that ground that the mortgagees no longer had their power to sell available to them. Crossman J in *Lord Waring v London and Manchester Assurance Co Ltd*[1] indicated that that was what was required if an injunction was to be obtained against a mortgagee purporting to exercise his power to sell by proposing to enter into a contract for sale thereunder. The reason for that, of course, is that tender or payment into court would be the equivalent of redemption, and if there was redemption no longer would the power to sell be exercisable at all.

It was sought to be argued before us that the fact that they had made this suggestion to the mortgagee about payments in joint names was the equivalent of a tender, combined with the fact that information had been given that there had been a contract for sale by the mortgagor to a bona fide purchaser at the market value. It appears to me that that is a total misconception of the possible effect of such a contract or such an offer. It cannot be described as the equivalent of tender, or payment into court, or redemption.

---

1   [1935] Ch 310, [1934] All ER Rep 642

It was further sought to be argued (although the facts here are not in accordance with it) that if such information as to a contract is given before the mortgagee purports to exercise his power to sell, and in particular when the proposed purchaser from the mortgagee has notice (owing to the registration of the land charge), then neither that purchaser nor the mortgagee is in a position to complain if the contract provided for enough purchase price to satisfy all the incumbrances. I should not be prepared to accept that proposition even if it fitted the facts of this case (which it does not), because it cannot possibly be said that a mortgagee is deprived of his power to sell by the fact that there is a contract which may be specifically enforceable, may be for enough to pay off all the incumbrances, but which is still in the field of contract and may not come to the stage of completion. I see no ground in principle or equity for saying that this would deprive a mortgagee of the right to exercise a power to sell; and so a fortiori if the only contract of which the mortgagee is given information is one which does not on the face of it provide a sufficient purchase price for the payment off of the incumbrances.

An argument was put before us which I must say I find extremely difficult to follow. It was said that the decision of Crossman J in the *Waring* case[1] (that after a mortgagee has contracted to sell the court will only restrain the sale on the ground that the mortgagee has not acted in good faith) was wrong, because the later case in this court of *Cuckmere Brick Co Ltd v Mutual Finance Ltd*[2] says that the mortgagee's duty is wider. What the *Cuckmere* case[2] says is that the mortgagee's duty is wider in this respect; that he has a duty not only to act bona fide, but to take reasonable care to obtain the true market value. That extension of the *Waring* case[1] cannot be of any relevance in the present case when the mortgagees are seeking to realise on their sale the sum of £45,000 and the plaintiffs are seeking to enforce a contract of sale at £25,000.

It does not seem to me that it is possible to say that the mortgagees, in respect of the exercise of their power to sell, can be in any worse position vis-à-vis the plaintiffs because the plaintiffs have a registered contract for the sale of the equity of redemption than they would be (without such a contract) vis-à-vis the mortgagors themselves —that is to say, Mr and Mrs Robson. Further, it seems to me that the mortgagees in this respect cannot be in a worse position than if the plaintiffs had actually got a conveyance, as distinct from their rights resting only in contract, the conveyance itself being subject to incumbrances. That would not affect at all the power to sell vested in the mortgagees by virtue of the still existing mortgage—and I stress 'still existing' if only to recall what I have said; that there cannot be in this case anything that can be described as redemption of the mortgage before the contract for sale in November 1972.

In short, it seems to me that a contract for sale by a mortgagor of the equity of redemption has no possible effect on the rights and powers of a mortgagee, and in particular the rights and powers of a mortgagee to exercise his power to sell, any more than can an actual conveyance by a mortgagor, unless of course the mortgage is in the course of completion redeemed, in which case no question of a subsequent exercise of power to sell by contract by the mortgagee will arise.

I am afraid that I have dealt rather briefly with the arguments that have been placed before us, but, with all respect to those arguments, I cannot see that there is any validity in them. One has only, as a test, to ask oneself the question: what has happened in this case in any way to cut down the rights and powers of sale of the mortgagees? In my opinion, nothing has happened. All that has happened is that the mortgagor has contracted with somebody else to sell the equity of redemption; and I do not see any ground in principle, equity or otherwise for saying that

1   [1935] Ch 310, [1934] All ER Rep 642
2   [1971] 2 All ER 633, [1971] Ch 949

somehow that puts the person to whom the mortgagor has contracted to sell the equity of redemption in a better position vis-à-vis the mortgagees and their power of sale than, say, the mortgagor himself or herself. In my view, the learned judge was quite right to refuse the injunction asked for, and I would entirely support his decision.

I say nothing as to what the situation may or may not be hereafter between the plaintiffs and the defendant mortgagor, Mrs Robson, because in due course, the mortgagees having obtained on completion the sum of £45,000 for the sale in the exercise of their power to sell, will have in their hands after paying off fully themselves and subsequent incumbrances a substantial sum. Prima facie they will become payable to the mortgagor. But it may be (I say nothing by way of decision, because the mortgagors are not before us) that the plaintiffs will be able to complain that they agreed to sell the property without any incumbrances for £25,000, and it may be that they will have a substantial claim for damages against the selling mortgagors. Further, it may be that they will be able to lay their hands in some way or other on the balance in the hands of the mortgagees after the payment off of all incumbrances. I do not know, and I do not propose to decide that. I only mention it because it may well be that they, the plaintiffs, are disappointed, because I understand that they have the possibility of a sale to another person for £60,000, and they may be able to formulate some claim in damages based on the mortgagor's inability to convey the property free from incumbrances for £25,000.

Accordingly, I would dismiss the appeal.

STAMP LJ. I agree. This seems to me a very simple case. The plaintiffs who purchased the equity of redemption can be in no better position to restrain a sale by the mortgagee than their vendor mortgagor. There has been neither a tender nor payment into court of the money to redeem the mortgage. The charge that the mortgagees are acting in bad faith is not pursued in this court. I can see no ground on which the mortgagees can be restrained from exercising the power to sell. I, too, would dismiss the appeal.

ROSKILL LJ. I agree with both judgments that have been delivered. It seems to me that Plowman J was abundantly right in refusing to grant the plaintiffs the injunction they sought to restrain the mortgagees from completing the sale to the fourth defendant, Mr Collins. In truth, the issue here is short and simple, namely, whether the plaintiffs are able to show that there is something which restricts or in some way cuts down the power to sell which the mortgagees would otherwise have as first mortgagees of the property in question. Like Stamp LJ, I am unable to find any ground on which the mortgagees can be restrained from exercising their power to sell. It seems to me that they have no claim for relief, and for the reasons given by Russell and Stamp LJJ I agree that the appeal should be dismissed.

Appeal dismissed.

Solicitors: *Sharpe, Pritchard & Co*, agents for *W Norris, Bazzard & Co*, Amersham (for the plaintiffs); *Metson, Cross & Co* (for the mortgagees and fourth defendant).

Mary Rose Plummer Barrister.

Byrne v E H Smith (Roofing) Ltd

COURT OF APPEAL, CIVIL DIVISION
BUCKLEY AND STEPHENSON LJJ
21st, 22nd, 23rd, 24th, 27th NOVEMBER, 20th DECEMBER 1972

Building – Construction regulations – Safe means of access – Roof – Weather conditions – Relevance – Heavy rainfall rendering means of access unsafe – Foreseeability of weather conditions – Relevance of fact that access route could be negotiated with safety – Construction (General Provisions) Regulations 1961 (SI 1961 No 1580), reg 7 (1).

Building – Building regulations – Roof – Roof work – Fragile materials covering roof – Work being done 'near' roof covered with fragile materials – Workmen having to 'pass over' fragile materials – Meaning of 'near' – Meaning of 'pass over' – Building (Safety, Health and Welfare) Regulations 1948 (SI 1948 No 1145), reg 31 (3).

The plaintiff was employed by the defendants as a roof sheeter's mate. He was working as the mate of a chargehand, B, cleaning out the gutters on the roof of a factory. The roof line of the main building of the factory consisted of three identical gables from the apices of which ridges ran back along the length of the building; the gutters in question ran along the valleys between those ridges. Abutting on to the face of the main building below the level of the gables was a loading bay of comparatively light construction, the roof of which was constructed of fragile asbestos sheeting bolted to purlins. At the point where the loading bay abutted on to the main building its roof was at approximately the same level as the bottoms of the valleys on the main roof. A lead lined gutter ran along the face of the main building at that level to take the water off the loading bay roof which rose away from the main building at an angle of 25 degrees. The base of the gutter was nine to ten inches wide. The lip of the asbestos roof overhung the gutter so that the open passage at the top of the gutter was not more than seven inches wide. The asbestos roofing was bolted to purlins running parallel to the loading bay gutter, the lower one being about eight inches up the roof from the lip overhanging the gutter; its presence was indicated on the roof by a line of bolts. B and the plaintiff reached the main building gutters by a route over the roof of the main building which was safe to walk on. They had almost completed their work of cleaning the main building gutters when there was a heavy storm of rain which made it unsafe for them to return to the ground by the route they had come. They therefore climbed into the loading bay gutter and proceeded along it to a platform surrounding a water tank at the end of the loading bay from which they descended to the ground by an access ladder permanently fixed to the platform. It was then midday. After lunch B decided to return to the roof to see if it would be possible to resume work and to check that the main building gutters were functioning satisfactorily. He returned by the route along the loading bay gutter. Unknown to B, the plaintiff followed him. Whilst B was inspecting the gutters he turned and saw the plaintiff standing either in the loading bay gutter or on the line of the lower purlin supporting the loading bay roof. He told the plaintiff to watch his step as the asbestos sheets were greasy. B then turned again to look at the main building gutters; he heard a crash and turning again saw that the plaintiff had fallen through the loading bay roof 17 feet to the floor of the loading bay and injured himself. The plaintiff brought an action against the defendants for, inter alia, breach of statutory duty under reg 7ᵃ of the Construction (General Provisions) Regulations 1961 on the ground that they had failed to

---

a Regulation 7 (1), so far as material, is set out at p 497 h, post

a provide a safe means of access and egress to and from his place of work. It was accepted by witnesses for the defendants that in consequence of the rain the asbestos roofing and the loading bay gutter were slippery.

Held – The plaintiffs were liable for breach of duty under reg 7 (1) of the 1961 regulations for the following reasons—

(i) the route along the loading bay gutter was a 'means of access' to the plaintiff's
b place of work within reg 7 (1) (see p 497 g and p 501 d and f, post);

(ii) even if it were the case that the route along the loading bay gutter was safe to walk along with one foot in the gutter and the other on the eight inch strip of asbestos below the lower line of bolts, it did not follow that it was a safe means of access; the fact that it would have been safely negotiated by a careful and experienced sheeter's mate did not mean that the defendants had discharged their duty under
c reg 7 (1); the weather conditions prevailing at the time of the accident were reasonably foreseeable by the defendants and no means of access which was safe in those conditions had been provided; accordingly the defendants were in breach of their duty under reg 7 (1) (see p 497 j to p 498 c and p 501 g and j to p 502 b, post).

Per Stephenson LJ (Buckley LJ dissenting). The defendants were also in breach of reg 31 (3)[b] of the Building (Safety, Health and Welfare) Regulations 1948 because
d (i) the use of the loading bay gutter as a means of access involved 'passing over' fragile materials covering the loading bay roof, and (ii) the asbestos sheet over which the plaintiff had to pass and through which he fell was 'near' the part of the main building gutter where the work was being done (see p 499 c and g to j and p 502 c e and g post).

e **Notes**

For safe means of access in work places, see 17 Halsbury's Laws (3rd Edn) 85-87, para 143, and for cases on the subject, see 24 Digest (Repl) 1075-1081, *324-364*.

For special regulations relating to building, see 17 Halsbury's Laws (3rd Edn) 125-128, para 206.

The Building (Safety, Health and Welfare) Regulations 1948, reg 31, and the Con-
f struction (General Provisions) Regulations 1961, reg 7, were revoked as from 1st August 1966 by the Construction (Working Places) Regulations 1966 (SI 1966 No 94), reg 1, and replaced respectively by regs 36 and 6 of the 1966 regulations.

Cases referred to in judgments

Palmer v Sheetcraft & Ovens Ltd (7th June 1961) unreported, [1961] Bar Library transcript 204A, CA.
g *Trott v W E Smith (Erectors) Ltd* [1957] 3 All ER 500, [1957] 1 WLR 1154, 56 LGR 20, CA, Digest (Cont Vol A) 597, *332a*.

Appeal

This was an appeal by the plaintiff, James Noel Byrne, against the judgment of Thesiger J given at the trial of the action on 9th December 1971 whereby he dismissed
h the plaintiff's claim for damages for personal injuries against the defendants, E H Smith (Roofing) Ltd. The facts are set out in the judgment of Buckley LJ.

C Fawcett QC and *G M Hamilton* for the plaintiff.
R G Rougier QC and *R A G Inglis* for the defendants.

Cur adv vult

j 20th December. The following judgments were read.

BUCKLEY LJ. This is an appeal from a judgment of Thesiger J given on 9th December 1971 whereby he dismissed the plaintiff's action for damages for personal injuries occasioned by an accident which occurred on 5th July 1966 when he fell

---

b Regulation 31 (3), so far as material, is set out at p 498 d, post

through an asbestos roof at a factory at Perivale where he was working in the employment of the defendants. The plaintiff was then 24 years of age. He had had about 2½ years' experience as a steel erector, and about one year's experience as a roof sheeter's mate, performing the function which is apparently described in the trade as that of a 'holder-upper'. He had been in the employment of the defendants for about eight weeks when the accident occurred, working as mate of a chargehand named Burrell. The day when the accident occurred was the plaintiff's first day on the job at Perivale. The site of this job was a factory belonging to a company named General and Industrial Paints Ltd. The operation on which Mr Burrell and the plaintiff were then engaged was the cleaning out of the gutters on the main roof of the factory in preparation for painting.

In order that the position may be understood it is necessary to describe the relevant parts of the factory. Facing the end with which we are concerned of the main building of the factory one would see that the roof line comprises three identical gables. Starting at the right hand end the roof line rises at an angle of 28 degrees to the horizontal to an apex from which it drops at a corresponding angle to the level from which it originally rose. From this point a second gable rises at a similar angle to a similar height as the first and drops to a similar level, from which point the third gable rises also at a similar angle to a similar height and drops to the same level. At the left-hand end of the third gable the main building abuts on an office block the wall of which rises vertically above the level of the third gable. This face of the main building consequently presents to the eye two broad valleys between the first and second gables and the second and third gables respectively and a narrow valley between the third gable and the vertical wall of the office block. From the apices of the three gables roof ridges run back from this face of the main building at right angles to it. The flank wall of the office block also runs back at right angles to this face of the main building parallel with the ridges just referred to. In the bottom of each of the two broad valleys is a dwarf wall running along the bottom of the valley, dividing the pitched roof on the one side from the pitched roof on the other side. On each side of each dwarf wall is a gutter running along beside it. In the narrow valley adjoining the office block there is a single gutter running along the line of division between the roof of the main building and the office block. To distinguish these five gutters from another gutter which I shall presently have to mention I will call them 'main building gutters'. It was these main building gutters which Mr Burrell and the plaintiff were engaged in cleaning. Mr Burrell, without the assistance of the plaintiff, had cleaned out the single gutter in the narrow valley and the two gutters in the more left-hand of the two broad valleys on the day preceding that of the accident. On the day of the accident Mr Burrell and the plaintiff were engaged in cleaning out the two gutters in the wide valley between the first and second gables.

Abutting on this face of the main building and below the level of the gables was a roofed loading bay of comparatively light construction extending along all, or nearly all, of the distance covered by the three gables. The roof of this loading bay was constructed of fragile asbestos sheeting bolted to purlins with glass lights inserted in it. Where the loading bay abutted on the face of the main building, the level of its roof was approximately the same as the level of the bottoms of the valleys in the main roof, that is, of the main building gutters. A lead-lined gutter ran along the face of the main building at this level to take the water off the loading bay roof, which rose away from the main building at an angle of 25 degrees to the horizontal. At the side of this gutter nearest to the main building along the whole length of the loading bay there was a lead flashing projecting some 6½ inches from the face of the main building and then falling vertically about six inches to the base of the gutter. Spanning the V-shaped spaces between the gables at their lower extremities in each of the wide valleys (and I think in the narrow valley also) were low walls about three feet high. These low walls projected about four inches from the face of the gables, and consequently, where there was such a wall, the lead flashing projected only very a slightly from the base of such wall in the horizontal plane before falling to the base of the gutter. This gutter, which I will call 'the loading bay gutter', was about 12 inches wide at its top, but the side of it further from the main building was at an angle from the perpendicular so that the level base of the gutter was about nine inches to ten inches wide. The lip of the asbestos roof of the loading bay overhung this gutter to the extent of about four inches to five inches. The open passage at the

b top of the gutter was accordingly not more than about seven inches wide.
    Glass roof lights were set all along this pitch of the roof of the loading bay. The distance between the lower edge of these lights and the lip of the asbestos roof over the loading bay gutter was three feet. This three foot wide strip of asbestos roofing was bolted to two purlins running parallel to the loading bay gutter. These purlins were two feet apart. That one of them which was nearer to the loading bay gutter

c was about eight inches up the asbestos roofing from the lip of the roof. The upper purlin was about four inches down the slope of the roof from the lower edge of the glass lights. The plaintiff fell through this roof between these two purlins.
    On the morning of the day when the accident occurred Mr Burrell and the plaintiff reached the main roof gutters on which they were to work by a route which did not involve going on to the roof of the loading bay or along the loading bay gutter. This

d route involved scaling a ridge of the roof of the main building. The roof of the main building was also of corrugated asbestos but was of a stouter construction than the roof of the loading bay and it was apparently safe to walk on it without using boards in good weather conditions. Mr Burrell and the plaintiff began to clean the gutters on which they were to work at the end of them furthest from the loading bay. They had cleaned all but about the last ten feet when there was a heavy storm of rain.

e This made it unsafe to return to the ground by the route by which they had come in the morning, for the rain made the roof of the main building too slippery. They therefore climbed over the three foot wall at the loading bay end of the valley in which they were working into the loading bay gutter, along which they proceeded in a direction leading away from the office block to a platform surrounding a water tank adjoining the end of the loading bay. This platform was at about the level of

f the end of the loading bay gutter. They climbed on to this platform and descended to the ground by an access ladder permanently affixed to the platform in question.
    It was then the middle of the day and they had some dinner. After about an hour and a half the rain stopped. Mr Burrell asked the plaintiff to go and find a broom which was needed to complete part of the work on the roof. There was a conflict of evidence about what happened with regard to this broom, but on the view

g which I take of the case it is not really important. Mr Burrell said that the plaintiff came back to him saying that he could not find a broom, whereupon he, Mr Burrell, went and found a broom which he took with him up to the roof. The plaintiff, on the other hand, said that he went to look for a broom, and when he returned Mr Burrell had already gone up on to the roof again, and that he, the plaintiff, followed Mr Burrell to report that he was unable to find a broom. The learned judge pre-

h ferred Mr Burrell's evidence in this respect. It is common ground that Mr Burrell told the plaintiff that he, Mr Burrell, was going up on to the roof to see if conditions were suitable for them to continue their work, and that he did not tell the plaintiff that he was not to follow him. The evidence, accepted by the learned judge, was that Mr Burrell, having found the broom, came back with it and passed close to the plaintiff, who was talking to another man. Mr Burrell, carrying the broom, ascended

j the ladder to the platform by the water tank from where he was able to see that conditions were not suitable for the work to be continued on account of the wet state of the roofs. He wanted, however, to take advantage of this state of affairs to check that the gutters were functioning satisfactorily, and so he proceeded along the loading bay gutter to the low wall spanning the mouth of the wide valley between the first and second gables over which he looked to see how the gutters were functioning. The plaintiff, unknown to Mr Burrell, followed Mr Burrell up to the platform and on to the loading bay gutter or the roof of the loading bay. Mr Burrell was unaware of the plaintiff's presence until the plaintiff spoke to him, when he turned and was surprised to find him standing either in the gutter or on the line of the lower purlin supporting the loading bay roof. He told the plaintiff to watch his step as the sheets were greasy, and said: 'The conditions are bad. We'll get back down.' Mr Burrell then turned again to look at the main building gutters in the valley; he heard a crash, and turning round again he found that the plaintiff had fallen through the roof of the loading bay at a point just short of the low wall spanning the first wide valley of the main roof. The plaintiff fell 17 feet to the floor of the loading bay and injured himself.

Mr Burrell in due course reported the accident to his superiors and two documents were prepared based on information received from him, on which considerable reliance has been placed. The first of these is a foreman's report which contains the following account of the accident:

'While following Burrell to working area, [the plaintiff] stepped on an asbestos sheet which disintegrated resulting in him falling 17-ft on to concrete floor. In actual fact this was not the roof they were working on and previously they gained access to their work by walking across the roof they were working on. The route taken at the time of the accident was only used twice and was not the usual means of access.'

In answer to a requirement that the report should specify exactly what the injured person was doing at the time of the accident, the report states: 'Making his way to roof gutter where working.' In answer to the question: 'Was employee obeying instructions?' the report says 'Yes'. The second document is a return made to the Ministry of Pensions and National Insurance signed by the secretary to the defendant company and relating to the plaintiff's claim to industrial injuries benefit. The return contains the following four questions and answers:

'4. Was the claimant authorised to be in that place at that time for the purpose of his work? Yes. 5. What was the claimant doing at the time of the accident? Returning to working area. 6. Was this something authorised or permitted to be done for the purpose of his work? Yes. 7. What was the accident and how did it happen? Accidentally stepped on asbestos sheet & fell 17 ft to concrete floor.'

The plaintiff's case was presented at the trial under three heads: first, breach by the defendants of a statutory duty under the Construction (General Provisions) Regulations 1961[1], reg 7; secondly, breach by the defendants of a statutory duty under the Building (Safety, Health and Welfare) Regulations 1948[2], reg 31 (3); and thirdly, common law negligence. The learned judge disposed of the last mentioned claim on the basis that the place where the plaintiff had his accident was not unsafe. The learned judge's actual words were:

'I do not consider in those circumstances that it would be right to hold that the defendants failed in their common law duty to take reasonable care for the plaintiff's safety. He was accustomed to steel erection work. I feel that one would have expected him to go quite safely along that gutter, by that asbestos roof, and not to fall between the purlins.'

This should be considered in conjunction with two other findings of the learned judge: first he said:

'On the way down from the roof the plaintiff and the chargehand, Burrell, successfully came along the gutter. I cannot myself see any danger in putting

1 SI 1961 No 1580
2 SI 1948 No 1145

a   one foot on the bottom end of the asbestos sheet between the bottom lip of the sheet overhanging the gutter and the line of bolts a few inches up the slope which are over the purlin.   One would keep one's weight on the left as one came down, in other words as one walked towards the water tank and the platform. It is not really like a girder, such as a steel erector walks along.   It seems to me a much simpler and safer operation,'

b   and, secondly:

'It also seems to me that a steel erector like the plaintiff could have come along that gutter with that flashing on one side, and then the lower end of the gable and the dwarf wall on the same side, without any difficulty, especially when one remembers that one could have rested one's foot on the bottom end
c   of the asbestos sheet below the lower line of bolts which were on a purlin.'

Although he does not expressly say so, the learned judge seems to have regarded the route by way of the loading bay gutter to the valley of the main roof where the men were working as a means of access to that area of the main roof. In the passage from the judgment which I have read the learned judge finds that for a
d   man with the plaintiff's experience of steel erection work this was a safe means of access. If this is right the plaintiff could not succeed either at common law or under reg 7 of the 1961 regulations. In this respect I am prepared to accept counsel for the plaintiff's formulation of the test, which was: 'Is the place of access a reasonably foreseeable cause of injury to a man of the type in question acting in a way in which such a man may reasonably be expected to act in circumstances which may reasonably be expected to occur'?
e   It seems to me with due deference to the learned judge, that the view which he formed pays insufficient attention to the physical conditions existing when the accident occurred. The plaintiff in his evidence in chief described the state of the gutter when he and Mr Burrell came down from the roof after the rain had come on, as 'gruesome', saying that there was a slimy stuff in it, leaves and such like.   In cross-
f   examination this state of affairs was put to him in this way:

'Q And what happened was what I might describe as a sharp and heavy shower around about the midday break?   A Yes.
'Q And of course this had the effect of making the sloping roofs wet and slippery did it not?   A Yes, sir.
'Q And it was for that reason, was it not, that when abandoning the job for
g   the moment because of the rain, rather than walk on the pitch of the roofs, which were wet and sloping, Mr Burrell and yourself hopped over the dwarf wall at the end and made your way along the gutter?   A Yes.

I omit three questions.

'Q Very well.   But as you told my Lord, it was a gutter which had not been
h   cleaned for some time?   A Yes, sir.
'Q And as one would expect there was a good deal of muck, if I may put it that way, at the bottom?   A Yes, sir.
'Q You walked along, but you had to take pretty good care how you stepped, didn't you?   A Yes, sir.'

j   The evidence-in-chief of Mr Wood, the plaintiff's expert witness, was as follows:

'Q The plaintiff told my Lord the gutter had not been cleaned out for a long time.   What would be the situation of that gutter if it had not been cleaned out and there was water in it?   A Well, I don't know, I wasn't there, but I should think it was certainly wet.   Whether there was any water lying about there I couldn't say.

'*Q* But assume it was there, would that in any way affect the foothold in the *a* gutter itself? *A* Oh, I'm sure it would, yes.

'*Q* In what way? *A* I think it would make it even more precarious.

'*Q* By reason of what risk? *A* By being far more slippery. Because in gutters of course one often gets slime which when it becomes wet becomes very slippery.'

He was not cross-examined on this aspect of the matter, but volunteered one relevant *b* answer as follows:

'*Q* Walking along that gutter is certainly no harder than walking on open steelwork of a comparable width, is it? *A* I think it may be in certain circumstances. I do not know what that gutter was like at the time. As I said previously, one very often gets slime in the bottom of a gutter and it is extremely *c* slippery when it becomes wet.'

Mr Burrell was called to give evidence for the defendants. The judge regarded him as an extremely fair witness. In cross-examination his evidence was:

'*Q* And you knew if you were going to walk on that bit of roof as shown in these photographs you ought to have had boards to walk on, did you not? *A* If *d* we were working there, sir, yes. But this was an emergency, pouring rain, sir.

'*Q* You say that in an emergency you came down that way? *A* Yes.

'*Q* Because it was an emergency. But if you were going to go up there again, or use that as a means of access to get to the place where you were going to work, did you know that you ought to have boards on it? *A* Yes, sir, I would *e* have had boards on it.

'*Q* You said to my Lord [referring to the witness's evidence-in-chief], "I would not have gone that way unless it had been sheeted out", is that right? *A* Yes, it wouldn't have worked that way.

'*Q* "I wouldn't have worked that way unless it had been sheeted out"? *A* Yes.

'*Q* And you said that because you knew perfectly well it is dangerous to walk *f* on that type of asbestos, is it not? *A* Yes.

'*Q* Because if your foot slips off the purlin line, it only requires a little slip and your leg is through and you are down, that is right, is it not? *A* Very good, sir.'

Mr Hunt, the defendants' expert witness, when asked in chief whether he considered *g* that there was unreasonable danger in walking along with one foot in the gutter and one either on the line of the bolts or a bit below it, said:

'I don't think it unreasonable when a person is merely passing along there as opposed to working there. The danger is not of going through where the feet are—the danger comes from slipping and falling over and coming down on an unsupported part of the sheeting.' *h*

In cross-examination he gave the following evidence:

'*Q* And if there is material in the gutter which is slippery, that is an additional hazard to his balance and stability? *A* Yes, certainly.

'*Q* And if the roof sheet is wet—it becomes very slippery in wet weather, does it not? *A* If it has some deposit on it, yes.

'*Q* Well, most old asbestos roofs have got some deposits on them? *A* Yes, certainly.'

Later:

'*Q* Let me put it to you this way—it is reasonably foreseeable that if a man a walks along that gutter in close proximity to the wall, with one foot in the gutter and one foot on the asbestos sheeting and there is wet stuff in the gutter and on the sheeting, he may well slip, is that not right? *A* Yes, I think that is right.

'*Q* And if he slips, is it not easily foreseeable that he may overbalance? *A* Yes, I think that is right.

b '*Q* And if he overbalances, is it not easily foreseeable that he may well fall on to the asbestos sheeting? *A* Yes, obviously this could occur.

'*Q* It could occur, and it is easily foreseeable that it may well occur? *A* Well, in my experience, it does not.'

Unless this last answer is to be so interpreted, no witness said that in the conditions existing at the time of the accident the loading bay gutter and the roof of the loading c bay afforded a safe means of access to the main roof, nor, in my opinion, was there any evidence from which this could be properly inferred On the contrary, to my mind, Mr Hunt's answers in cross-examination clearly indicate the contrary. In these circumstances I find myself unable to agree with the learned judge's findings. They were, in my judgment, unsupported by the evidence, and indeed against the weight of the evidence. Moreover, the evidence to which I have referred takes no d account of the additional hazard, recognised by both Mr Wood and Mr Hunt, that if anyone were to stand on the overhanging lip of the asbestos roof the chances would be that it would break. This would, I think, clearly involve a risk that the person would in those circumstances lose his balance.

In this court the defendants have contended that the loading bay gutter and roof ought not to be regarded as a means of access for the purposes of reg 7 because, as e they say, the plaintiff's presence there at the time of the accident was not to be expected or foreseen. I feel unable to accept this contention. Not only is it contrary to what is to be found in the documents to which I have referred, but also Mr Burrell in cross-examination agreed that for the plaintiff to come on to the roof of the loading bay was in the circumstances the very kind of thing one might have anticipated. The plaintiff had not been forbidden to follow Mr Burrell up on to the roof, and in f the absence of contrary instructions it was, in my opinion, clearly foreseeable that he might do so.

When Mr Burrell and the plaintiff came off the roof before their dinner break, they used the route along the loading bay gutter as a means of egress, and indeed on the evidence it appears that it was in the conditions that then existed the safest means of egress available. When Mr Burrell returned after the break to inspect the g gutters he used the same route in reverse as a means of access. The plaintiff followed him using the same route as a means of access to the place where, had conditions permitted, the work would have been continued. I feel no doubt that this route should be treated as a means of access within the meaning of reg 7.

I agree with the learned judge that this case does not fall within the proviso to reg 3 of the 1961 regulations and that reg 7 of whose regulations is accordingly h applicable. Regulation 7 (1) provides:

'Sufficient safe means of access and egress shall so far as is reasonably practicable be provided and maintained to and from every place at which any person has at any time to work ...'

j The learned judge held that a sufficient safe means of access was, so far as reasonably practicable, provided. As I understand his judgment this was because he considered that a man could safely walk along the loading bay gutter with one foot in the gutter and one on the asbestos roof below the line of the bolts holding the lower purlin. The learned judge had found as a fact that, Mr Burrell turned and saw the plaintiff on the loading bay roof he did not have one foot in the gutter but had both feet on the asbestos. To this finding I shall return when considering contributory negligence.

Since, on the view which I take of the evidence, the process of walking along the loading bay gutter with one foot in it and one on the asbestos was not safe in the weather conditions existing at the time of the accident, it is irrelevant for the purposes of reg 7 whether the plaintiff was proceeding in that way or with both feet on the asbestos. In my judgment, no means of access which was safe in the prevailing conditions was provided along the loading bay gutter, although it was, in the prevailing conditions and in the absence of any boards, the safest means of access available. A heavy rainstorm was clearly a foreseeable contingency, and the consequences of such a storm to the safety of the route across the ridge of the roof of the main building and of the route by way of the loading bay gutter should, in my opinion, have been apparent to the defendants. Either route could have been rendered safe by the simple expedient of laying boards over the asbestos roofs. In my judgment, the plaintiff succeeds in establishing a breach by the defendants of reg 7.

This really makes it unnecessary to determine whether there was also a breach of reg 31 (3) of the 1948 regulations, but as the point has been argued I should perhaps state my view on it. Regulation 31 (3), so far as relevant, is in these terms:

> 'Where work is being done on or near roofs or ceilings covered with fragile materials through which a person is liable to fall a distance of more than 10 feet —(a) where workmen have to pass over or work above such fragile materials, suitable and sufficient ladders, duck ladders or crawling boards, which shall be securely supported, shall be provided and used . . .'

The learned judge reached the conclusion that on the facts of this case the plaintiff did not have to 'pass over' a fragile roof. A decision of this court in *Palmer v Sheetcraft & Ovens Ltd*[1], which was brought to our attention but not to that of the learned judge, makes it impossible, I think, to sustain the learned judge's conclusion. In that case the plaintiff Palmer was one of a gang employed in installing ventilating ducts in the roof of a factory. The work consisted of inserting what were described as chimney stacks composed of very light sections of ducting into holes already made in the roof. The plan of the factory consisted of a number of bays at right angles to and on each side of a passageway running between them, which had a flat roof. That roof was 13 feet wide and to the extent of a little over 11 feet of its width was composed of fragile material, supported by four purlins. At one side of this roof was a gutter, which was not fragile, the opening of which was about nine inches wide. The men were carrying sections of ducting for a distance of about 100 feet along this gutter to a point opposite the place in the roof of one of the bays where the next ventilating duct was to be installed. Mr Palmer, having reached that point, fell through the roof of the passage in circumstances which nobody saw. Donovan J said that, since the gutter was not fragile, nor was that part of the roof which rested on the purlin nearest to the gutter, he doubted whether at that juncture the regulation applied. Of this Davies LJ, giving the leading judgment on appeal, said[2]:

> 'With the greatest respect to the learned judge, I am quite unable to agree that there was no breach of the regulations. When the plaintiff was ordered to go some 100 feet along this fragile roof he was undoubtedly, in my opinion, "passing over fragile materials", within the meaning of the regulation, for the whole length of his journey. The fact that the journey could be accomplished safely by an experienced man exercising great care by walking on the gutter and the purlin does not in any way detract from the mandatory effect of the regulation. It is this sort of risky journey, inter alia, that the regulation is designated to prevent. In my opinion, the regulation enjoined that boards should have been in position all the way along the route which the plaintiff was ordered to take'.

1   (7th June 1961) unreported
2   [1961] Bar Library transcript 204A at p 10

a The other two members of the court agreed. Upjohn LJ said[1]:

'The plaintiff was ordered to pass over a roof covered with fragile material. He could only do so with any degree of safety by carefully placing his feet in position at each step; his left foot had to travel along the gutter adjoining the roof, and his right foot had carefully to follow the line of studs which indicated the position of the purlin underneath. Essentially, however, he was passing

b over a roof covered with fragile material and a slip or fall, or a misplaced step, might be disastrous. Regulation 31 (3) was designed to cover that danger and to protect the workman from it.'

The physical features of *Palmer's* case[2] clearly bear a strong resemblance to those in the present case and, in my judgment, make it impossible to hold in this case that the

c use of the loading bay gutter as a means of access to the roof of the main building did not involve passing over fragile materials.

There seems in *Palmer's* case[2] to have been no discussion about whether the work was there being done 'near' the fragile roof of the passage. Donovan J is recorded by Davies LJ to have said 'This work was certainly being done on or near a fragile roof'. This suggests to me that the parties may have treated the work as comprising

d not merely the installation of the ventilating ducts but also the carriage to the place of installation of the parts to be installed, so that work was being done within the meaning of the regulation on the passage roof. This may well have been right. The point does not seem to have been raised in the Court of Appeal. In the present case, on the other hand, it is common ground that no work was being done on the loading bay gutter or roof. Regulation 31 (3) can only apply if work was being done

e 'near' to the loading bay roof. The plaintiff concedes that in a case in which there was a long means of access, if workmen had to pass over fragile materials at a point on the route which was remote from the place where the work was to be done, the regulation would not apply; but, he says, in the present case the valley on the main roof, where the work was to be done, was only just on the other side of the three foot wall across the mouth of the valley from the fragile roof of the loading bay;

f they were near to one another. The defendants, on the other hand, stress that the words 'such fragile materials' in reg 31 (3) must relate back to fragile materials covering a roof 'near' which 'work is being done'. They submit that the fragile materials must be near enough to constitute a hazard while work is being done. Clearly some principle must be discovered underlying the regulation which will make it possible to discover what degree or kind of propinquity will satisfy the word

g 'near'. The test submitted by the defendants appeals to me as eminently sensible. In the present case the workmen, that is Mr Burrell and the plaintiff, did not have to pass over or work above the loading bay roof when they were engaged on their work, that is, cleaning the main building gutters. The presence of the three foot wall closing the end of the valley excluded any risk of this occurring. When using the loading bay gutter as a means of access they did have to pass over the loading bay roof

h according to *Palmer's* case[2] but I can see no reason for supposing that the regulation was intended to apply to one area of a mere means of access (where the men could not be while at work) but not to another area of the same means of access because the former is only a short distance from the place of work and the latter a greater distance. If the present case turned on the application of reg 31 (3) I would accept this submission and hold the regulation not to be applicable.

j In my judgment, however, for reasons given earlier, the defendants are liable under reg 7, and also, I think, on the ground of common law negligence.

There remains the question of contributory negligence. This involves consideration of how and why the plaintiff fell. The learned judge found that when Mr Burrell saw the plaintiff on the loading bay roof the plaintiff had both feet on the asbestos

1 [1961] Bar Library transcript 204A at p 14
2 (7th June 1961) unreported

and none in the gutter. If that had been his position, I cannot believe that he would *a*
not have turned in a clockwise direction, that is, towards the main building. His
evidence was that he turned counter-clockwise and I see no reason to reject this.
His evidence was to the effect that he walked along the gutter one foot in front of
the other, as he said he had done on the reverse journey earlier in the day. The
space under the overhang of the asbestos above the gutter would give some room
to swivel a foot, standing in the gutter and pointing away from the water tank in a *b*
counter-clockwise direction, but the overhang would make a clockwise swivel impracticable. On the other hand, if the plaintiff had been minded to turn clockwise
he might have been able to make use of the lead flashing, but his evidence was that
when he turned he was beside the low wall at the end of the valley, at which point
the lead flashing would not have afforded a toe-hold. In view of the facts that the
only evidence supporting the judge's finding that the plaintiff had both feet on the *c*
asbestos was that of Mr Burrell, from whom the defendants must have elicited his
version of the occurrence before their pleading was settled or at the latest during
the preparations for trial, and that the defence, which sets out particulars of the
plaintiff's contributory negligence, contains no hint of this important allegation, which
moreover was never put to the plaintiff in cross-examination, I do not think, with
all due respect to the learned judge, that this finding can be regarded as satisfactory. *d*
    In this court the defendants relied on three grounds of contributory negligence:
first, having both feet on the asbestos roof, secondly, turning counter-clockwise
instead of clockwise, and thirdly, turning in such a way that he overbalanced and
fell. The first of these grounds has not been established as a fact to my satisfaction.
As to the second, if the plaintiff in doing so had made use of the lead flashing, turning
clockwise might have been marginally safer; but I do not think that turning counter- *e*
clockwise should in itself be regarded as an act of negligence. I think, however, that
the plaintiff, who had just been warned of the slippery state of the roof, must have
been guilty of some degree of carelessness in making his turn which I would assess
as making him 20 per cent responsible for the accident.
    The parties have agreed damages on a basis of full liability at £7,500. I would
therefore allow this appeal and award damages to the plaintiff in a sum of £6,000 *f*
with interest.

STEPHENSON LJ. I agree on every point but one.
    I find it extremely difficult to decide on the evidence how the plaintiff fell through
this roof. Where he fell was, on the contrary, clearly proved, namely, through the
asbestos sheet which looks dark in the photograph no 2, below the broken glass *g*
rooflight and between the two lines of bolts. I see no reason to reject his own evidence
that he was turning counter-clockwise to his left when he fell, and I conclude that he
must have been within reach of the dwarf wall at the end of the first main building
gutter on his right when he fell, having walked there from the access ladder past the
water tank without falling.
    I feel less certain where his feet were when he walked along the loading bay gutter *h*
and when he turned and fell. I think it unlikely that he walked along the gutter by
placing one foot directly in front of the other in the gutter itself, as he swore, or that
he walked along the lower line of bolts by placing one foot directly in front of the
other on the asbestos sheets immediately above the bolts, and I think it more likely
that he walked as the judge first suggested and finally found was safe, and as the
defendant's chargehand Mr Burrell swore that he himself had walked, with one foot *j*
in the gutter and the other on the asbestos sheets on his left below the lower line of
bolts, or, as Mr Burrell said was the way roofing people walked and as the plaintiff
Palmer in the unreported case[1] to which Buckley LJ has referred walked, with one
foot in the gutter and the other on the asbestos sheets immediately above the lower

---

1   I e *Palmer v Sheetcraft & Ovens Ltd* (7th June 1961) unreported

a line of bolts. I find it hard to accept the evidence of Mr Burrell that when he turned and saw the plaintiff, the plaintiff had both feet on the asbestos, for it was never pleaded or suggested until Mr Burrell gave evidence for the defendants, because, as Mr Burrell admitted, he had never told anyone this important 'fact' before. Further, as Buckley LJ has pointed out, it makes a counter-clockwise turn by the plaintiff incredible.

b I do not, however, think that it matters except in answering the question of the plaintiff's own negligence, which I shall consider last. For I doubt if the plaintiff could have turned to his left when he did without putting one foot on the asbestos, and wherever on the asbestos he put it he was bound to risk his foot slipping on the asbestos, as it was wet, and going through it, as it was fragile, and, if that happened, to risk also overbalancing and falling through the asbestos at a point where it had neither purlin nor gutter underneath it. I think it unlikely that he would have put

c both feet on asbestos at the same time, but probable that he would have had to rest his whole weight on the foot which was on the asbestos, and that would have been enough to cause his fall.

I agree that this gutter was a means of access and egress to and from the place at which the plaintiff had to work on 5th July 1966, and if (as counsel for the defendants submitted but contrary to Buckley LJ's opinion) it is implicit in the judge's judgment

d that it was not, I respectfully think that he was wrong. It had been used earlier that day as a means of egress from the first main building gutter where both he and his chargehand Mr Burrell had worked; it was used as a means of access to the same place of work by Mr Burrell when he returned just before the plaintiff, and it was so used by the plaintiff following him up. Whether or not Mr Burrell was surprised at his following him up or the plaintiff misunderstood his duties or instructions, and

e whatever the truth about the search for a broom, the plaintiff was not trespassing when he followed Mr Burrell up at a time when it was not decided that work for the day in the first main building gutter was at an end. I prefer Mr Burrell's own view embodied in the 14th answer given in the foreman's report (which Buckley LJ has read), that 'The route taken at the time of the accident was only used twice and was not the usual means of access'; an unusual means of access and one it may be which

f was used only once before in the emergency created by the rainstorm, but just as much a means of access on the return journey for the plaintiff as it was for Mr Burrell.

I must also respectfully differ fron the learned judge's view that it was safe. He may be right in holding that it was safe to walk along this route with one foot in this slimy gutter and one foot on the eight inch strip of asbestos below the lower line of bolts; but that does not, in my judgment, conclude the question whether

g this was a safe means of access so far as was reasonably practicable. The fact (if it be the fact) that it could have been safely negotiated and used in one particular way by a careful and experienced sheeter's mate does not mean that the defendants had discharged their duty under reg 7 (1) of the Construction (General Provisions) Regulations 1961, although it would go a long way to show that they had discharged their duty at common law to take reasonable care of the plaintiff. To permit even an

h experienced and careful roof worker to walk along a route which consisted of a slimy gutter of these dimensions overhung by slippery asbestos on one side, even with a flashing which might give foothold on the other, and to go back, which involved turning round either to his left by placing one foot on the slippery asbestos or to his right where he might risk overbalancing on to the asbestos seems to me to be failing to provide him with safe means of access and (more doubtfully) to be exposing

j him to unnecessary risk of injury through slipping, overbalancing and falling.

As it is beyond dispute that it was reasonably practicable to make the route safe by providing a double line of boards above the lower line of bolts, and that the judge was right in holding that the plaintiff's presence at the place where he fell was impliedly permitted by the defendants and that the proviso to reg 3 (1) (*a*) of the 1961 regulations did not apply, the defendants were in breach of reg 7 (1) and were negligent at common law. I agree with Buckley LJ that the judge did not pay suffi- *a* cient attention to the physical conditions when the accident occurred and I derive support for my conclusion that the defendants were guilty of breach of this statutory duty from the admissions made by the defendants' chargehand Mr Burrell and by the defendants' expert Mr Hunt in the passages from their evidence which Buckley LJ has read, and from *Trott v W E Smith (Erectors) Ltd*[1], and from *Palmer v Sheetcraft & Ovens Ltd*[2], both decisions on other regulations, but indicating, in my judgment, that *b* this means of access was unsafe for the plaintiff and might have been so even in more favourable weather.

On the next question, whether the defendants were also in breach of reg 31 (3) of the Building (Safety, Health and Welfare) Regulations 1948, I have the misfortune to differ from the learned judge on his construction of the words 'pass over' for the reason Buckley LJ has given, but also from Buckley LJ on his construction of the word *c* 'near'. This accident happened less than two months before the Construction (Working Places) Regulations 1966[3] revoked this regulation and gave persons passing across or near or working on or near fragile materials differently and perhaps more clearly and comprehensively worded protection: see regs 1 (2) (*a*) and 36. I am conscious that if any claims arising out of falls through fragile materials before 1st August 1966 are still undecided, this difference of opinion, ineffective in this case, may introduce *d* uncertainty into those others. But as counsel's argument for the plaintiff has convinced me, I feel bound to say so. I entirely agree with counsel for the defendants that the words 'such fragile materials' in reg 31 (3) (*a*) must relate back to 'fragile materials' covering roofs or ceilings where or 'near' which 'work is being done'. But I should have thought that the asbestos sheet over which the plaintiff had to pass and through which he fell was 'near' the part of the main building gutter where work was being *e* done. Indeed the end of the valley over the dwarf wall was nearer to the asbestos sheet through which the plaintiff fell than the place where work was being done was to the roof through which the plaintiff Palmer fell, as I understand the facts of that case[4]. There is, it is true, no discussion in the judgments of the meaning of the word 'near', or of the limits of the work being done. But there the work of installing ducts seems to have been done at the place or places where they were being installed, *f* and if it included carrying them to the place of installation along 100 feet of gutter, as Palmer was doing, the work of cleaning out the first main building gutter might include carrying a broom to that gutter or even reporting to the chargehand for duty at that gutter, as the plaintiff in effect was doing. And as I read the judgments in *Palmer's* case[2], the courts must not put so narrow a construction on the regulation as to exclude a journey of the kind which the plaintiff was making, at least where it would naturally be described as bringing him near the place where the work was *g* being done. This prevents me from adding the sensible gloss on the word 'near' which appeals to Buckley LJ, and fortifies me in giving the word its ordinary meaning and applying it to the facts of this case. Propinquity is, in my judgment, a matter of degree, but I find nothing in the regulation, or in the judgments in *Palmer's* case[2], to justify the selection of one kind of propinquity for the regulation to cover. *h*

I therefore hold the defendants liable to pay damages to the plaintiff.

The last question which remains I have found the most difficult to answer: was the plaintiff guilty of contributory negligence? The difficulty is increased by uncertainty as to the way in which the plaintiff used this means of access both in walking and in turning. Of the three matters relied on in this court by counsel for the defendants as contributory negligence—walking wholly on the asbestos roof, turning left *j* instead of right, and turning so that he overbalanced and fell—only the last was pleaded in the defence.

1 [1957] 3 All ER 500, [1957] 1 WLR 1154
2 (7th June 1961) unreported
3 SI 1966 No 94
4 I e *Palmer v Sheetcraft & Ovens Ltd* (7th June 1961) unreported

a On the whole I have come to the conclusion that although it might have been safer to turn clockwise, the plaintiff was not negligent in turning to his left instead of to his right, but was negligent in the way in which he executed this difficult manoeuvre. If I was satisfied on the balance of probabilities that he had put both feet on the asbestos in turning, I should find him guilty of contributory negligence to a high degree. But I am not so satisfied. As I have already indicated, I think it
b much more probable that he put one foot on it which caused him to overbalance and fall through it, and I agree that he was negligent in doing that to an extent which makes him 20 per cent responsible for his accident.

For these reasons I agree that this appeal succeeds and the plaintiff is entitled to judgment for four-fifths of the agreed sum with appropriate interest.

Appeal allowed. Judgment entered for the plaintiff for £6,000 damages plus £1,669·76
c *interest.*

Solicitors: *Clifford & Co* (for the plaintiff); *Rowleys & Blewitts* (for the defendants).

L J Kovats Esq Barrister.

d McGreevy v Director of Public Prosecutions

HOUSE OF LORDS
LORD REID, LORD MORRIS OF BORTH-Y-GEST, LORD HODSON, LORD SIMON OF GLAISDALE AND LORD CROSS OF CHELSEA
30th NOVEMBER, 1st, 4th, 6th, 7th DECEMBER 1972, 1st FEBRUARY 1973

e *Jury – Direction to jury – Burden of proof – Criminal proceedings – Prosecution case based on circumstantial evidence – Proof beyond reasonable doubt – Whether judge required to give further direction that facts proved must be inconsistent with any reasonable conclusion other than guilt of accused.*

f In a criminal trial it is the duty of the judge to make clear to the jury in terms which are adequate to cover the particular features of the case that they must not convict unless they are satisfied beyond reasonable doubt of the guilt of the accused. There is no rule that, where the prosecution case is based on circumstantial evidence, the judge must, as a matter of law, give a further direction that the jury must not convict unless they are satisfied that the facts proved are not only consistent with the guilt of the accused, but also such as to be inconsistent with any other reasonable
g conclusion (see p 504 c, p 508 c to e, p 509 h to p 510 a and j to p 511 a c and f to j post).
Dictum of Alderson B in *R v Hodge* (1838) 2 Lew CC at 228 explained.

Notes
For proof by circumstantial evidence, see 10 Halsbury's Laws (3rd Edn) 438-441, paras 813-815, and for cases on the subject, see 14 Digest (Repl) 497-499, 4792-4818.

h **Cases referred to in opinions**
Commonwealth v Webster (1850) 5 Cushing (59 Massachusetts Reports) 295.
Martin v Osborne (1936) 55 CLR 367.
Peacock v The King (1911) 13 CLR 619.
Plomp v The Queen (1963) 110 CLR 234.
j *R v Ducsharm* [1955] OR 824, (1955) OWN 817, 1 DLR (2d) 732, 22 CR 129, 113 Can Crim Cas 1, Digest (Cont Vol A) 358, *1933a.*
R v Hodge (1838) 2 Lew CC 227, 68 ER 1136, 14 Digest (Repl) 402, *3935.*
R v Onufrejczyk [1955] 1 All ER 247, [1955] 1 QB 388, 39 Cr App Rep 1, CCA, 14 Digest (Repl) 497, 4800.
Teper v R [1952] 2 All ER 447, 116 JP 502; sub nom *Lejzor Teper v R* [1952] AC 480, PC, 14 Digest (Repl) 451, 4377.

Appeal

a

William McGreevy appealed against an order of the Court of Criminal Appeal in Northern Ireland (Lowry LCJ, Curran and Gibson JJ) dated 3rd May 1972 dismissing his appeal against his conviction for murder at the County Down Autumn Assizes on 12th November 1971 before Jones J and a jury. The facts are set out in the opinion of Lord Morris of Borth-y-Gest.

R Appleton QC and *H P Kennedy* (both of the Northern Ireland Bar) for the appellant.   *b*
B Kelly QC, J M A Nicholson QC and *R Ferguson* (all of the Northern Ireland Bar) for the Crown.

Their Lordships took time for consideration.

1st February. The following opinions were delivered.

c

LORD REID. My Lords, for the reasons given by my noble and learned friend, Lord Morris of Borth-y-Gest, I would dismiss this appeal.

LORD MORRIS OF BORTH-Y-GEST. My Lords, the appellant was charged with murdering Margaret Magee in her house in High Street, Portaferry, on 17th *d* November 1970. When he was tried at the Spring Assizes in County Down in 1971, the jury failed to reach a verdict. He was thereafter tried at the Autumn Assizes before Jones J and a jury. The trial took place on 8th, 9th, 10th, 11th and 12th November 1971. The jury found the appellant guilty and he was sentenced to life imprisonment. He appealed to the Court of Criminal Appeal. The appeal was based on various grounds. It was contended that the learned judge had in many respects *e* misdirected the jury: particular prominence was given to a contention that the learned judge had failed to direct the jury or to give them guidance 'as to how they should view and approach circumstantial evidence'. It was further contended that in all the circumstances of the case the verdict of the jury was unsafe and unsatisfactory. The appeal was fully heard by the Court of Criminal Appeal on 25th, 26th, 27th and 28th April 1972. By their judgment delivered by Lowry LCJ on 3rd May *f* 1972, the court dismissed the appeal. The court dealt with the contentions as to misdirection and in particular with the argument relating to circumstantial evidence. The court rejected the submission that the verdict was unsafe and unsatisfactory. The court held that there was evidence on which the jury properly directed were fully justified in finding the appellant guilty. The charge of the learned judge earned the commendation of the court as having been 'full, accurate, careful and *g* conspicuously fair'.

The trial involved a consideration by the jury of the evidence of over 30 witnesses. There was no doubt that the deceased woman had been murdered by someone. The case for the Crown was that the appellant had gone into the deceased's shop with the intention of stealing money from the till and in the hope that he would not be heard by the deceased from her room at the back: that the deceased had come *h* into the shop and that thereupon the appellant had bolted the shop door, had pushed the deceased to the back room, and, in order to silence her, had struck her over the head with a bottle of lemonade and, after she had fallen, kicked or stamped her to death. All that was firmly denied by the appellant. The appellant had undoubtedly been in the vicinity of the shop and there was much detailed evidence relating to his movements during the time before he joined his fiancée: she had driven to *j* Portaferry to meet him and had then taken him to her house which was a few miles away. No occasion now arises to summarise the mass of the evidence. It suffices to say that there was much evidence relating to the issue whether the appellant had had the opportunity to do what the Crown suggested. He himself gave an account of his movements. There were witnesses who had seen him and spoken to him and been with him. He had paid one perfectly lawful visit to the deceased's

a shop. He made a purchase there. He accounted for a period of about ten minutes which, on the Crown case, was the most relevant time by saying that he had left the vicinity of High Street and had returned to his house. There was evidence dealing with the discovery of the body of the deceased and the time of such discovery. There was evidence as to the probable time of the death and evidence as to the state of the room where the deceased was found. There was evidence as to the route taken
b by the assailant when he left the rear of the premises. There was evidence that some blood stains were found on certain clothing and attire of the deceased and evidence as to the blood grouping of the stains. There was evidence as to what clothing was worn or was not worn by the appellant on the night in question and evidence as to how and when on a later day he visited the police and subsequently produced clothing for their inspection. The appellant gave explanations as to how blood stains came
c to be on the clothing. There was evidence that footprints were found in what was spilled on to the floor of the deceased's room and evidence on the question whether they were or were not of a size and nature that showed that they were made or could have been made by the appellant.

From this brief indication of the range of the evidence it is apparent that there were many matters which demanded the attention of the jury and further that it
d was open to them to draw conclusions from the evidence which would warrant them in deciding that the guilt of the appellant had been established.

On appeal to the Court of Criminal Appeal, some of the grounds of appeal were of misdirection in specific respects including (a) misdirection as to what was the Crown case in regard to the footprints; (b) misdirection as to what Dr Grant (an expert witness) had said in regard to the footprints; (c) misdirection by failing to direct the jury that there was no evidence that certain blue trousers (on which there were
e blood stains) had been worn by the appellant on the evening of 17th November 1970, and (d) misdirection as to a test relating to the blood on the appellant's car coat.

Counsel for the appellant renewed in this House certain of the specific submissions as to alleged misdirection which he had advanced in the Court of Criminal Appeal, but more especially he related them to the contention which, as I have stated above, formed so prominent a part of the case which he argued in the Court of Criminal
f Appeal and which became the basis of an appeal to this House. After the Court of Criminal Appeal had given judgment on 3rd May 1972, application was made, pursuant to the provisions of s 36 (2) of the Criminal Appeal (Northern Ireland) Act 1968, and the court certified that a point of law of general public importance was involved and the court granted leave to appeal to this House. The point of law so certified was as follows:
g

'Whether at a criminal trial with a jury, in which the case against the accused depends wholly or substantially on circumstantial evidence, it is the duty of the trial judge not only to tell the jury generally that they must be satisfied of the guilt of the accused beyond reasonable doubt, but also to give them a special
h direction by telling them in express terms that before they can find the accused guilty they must be satisfied not only that the circumstances are consistent with his having committed the crime but also that the facts proved are such as to be inconsistent with any other reasonable conclusion.'

In presenting his most careful and lucid argument counsel formulated his proposition of law in somewhat varied terms as follows: that in a criminal trial in which
j the prosecution case, or any essential ingredient thereof, depends, as to the commission of the act, entirely on circumstantial evidence, it is the duty of the trial judge, in addition to giving the usual direction that the prosecution must prove the case beyond reasonable doubt, to explain to the jury in terms appropriate to the case being tried that this direction means that they must not convict on circumstantial evidence unless they are satisfied that the facts proved are (a) consistent with the

guilt of the accused and (b) exclude every reasonable explanation other than the guilt of the accused.

I think that it is apparent that if the proposition were accepted there would hereafter be a rule of law which it would be obligatory on the judges to follow. As I will indicate it would, in my view, be a new rule. It would be a rule applicable in criminal cases where (as to the commission of the act) the prosecution case (or an essential ingredient of it) depended entirely on circumstantial evidence. It is not contended that the rule would apply if the case depended partly on direct and partly on circumstantial evidence. The application of the rule would therefore depend on defining and identifying what evidence is direct and what is circumstantial and deciding which label was applicable. If the rule existed then despite the qualification that the explanation need only be in 'terms appropriate to the case' it might well become a virtual necessity for a judge to employ the language of the concluding words of the proposition.

It has first to be considered whether the proposition would involve the formulation of a new rule binding on judges. If it would then the question arises whether such a new rule would be desirable.

Before examining these questions it will be convenient to refer to certain criticisms of the summing-up which were made by learned counsel: many of these were made by way of illustration of the need for a direction in the form propounded. It was further submitted that there were omissions in the summing-up in that although the evidence was referred to, there was lacking a critical analysis of it and an omission to make the jury understand that they were dealing with a different kind of evidence from direct evidence and that there was a failure to demonstrate or to discuss ways in which evidence which was consistent with the Crown case was also consistent with the innocence of the appellant. Thus, to give an example, evidence was given by a Mr McManus who said that at 9.20 to 9.25 he had left his home and had then walked to the shop of the deceased and had found the shop door shut at the top although there was a light in the shop. He thought that the deceased was probably having some tea and he had not wished to disturb her. Complaint was made that the learned judge did not discuss with the jury the possibility that the deceased was in fact having tea which would mean that the murder had not then already been committed and so must have been committed by someone else at a later time when admittedly the appellant was (in company with others) at a place some miles away. It was submitted that the summing-up was defective if the learned judge did not in connection with the various parts of the evidence (a) point to any explanations that were consistent with innocence on the part of the appellant and (b) refer to the possibilities of someone else being the killer and (c) warn the jury in terms that they must not convict unless they could exclude every reasonable explanation of the facts proved other than the guilt of the appellant. A further matter of complaint was that the learned judge did not adequately direct the jury on the issue whether the appellant was or was not wearing the blue trousers and did not discuss the inferences that they should draw if they decided that he was not. A further matter of complaint was that the learned judge treated lightly and inadequately the evidence of a Mr Dorrian whose evidence to the effect that at a certain time and place no one had passed was relied on as negativing the guilt of the appellant. Complaint was also made of the way in which the learned judge had dealt with the evidence of Dr Grant whose testimony, it was contended, if accepted, was such as to negative the guilt of the appellant. Unless these or other matters can be used to demonstrate the need for a specific direction in the form contended for I do not consider that it is shown that the summing-up was inadequate or unsatisfactory. The evidence was all before the jury and the Court of Criminal Appeal after its full examination of the case came to the conclusion that there was 'no circumstance which was inconsistent with guilt in the logical sense that the circumstance and the guilt of the [appellant] could not co-exist'. There were the court held 'few circumstances which could be

said to point towards innocence; the most favourable way from the point of view
of the [appellant] was to regard them as neutral.' Lowry LCJ indicated the general
style and pattern of the summing-up in the two following passages of his judgment:

(a) 'So far from failing to put the defence case, the judge put it twice, by giving
the main instances of where issue was joined in cross-examination of the Crown
witnesses and then giving a plain account of what the defence witnesses said
in their turn, and in this respect he dealt with the Crown case and the defence
case in the same way. It is not essential that the trial judge should make every
point that can be made for the defence. If he were to do so and were also to
follow each such point with the Crown's rebutting argument, he would run
the risk of breaking up the defence case in such a way as to destroy its effect.
There is no set formula for doing justice to the defence in the course of the
charge: the fundamental requirements are correct directions in point of law,
an accurate review of the main facts and alleged facts, and a general impression
of fairness. This was in fact an outstandingly fair charge, devoid of insinuation
and in its general approach helpful to the appellant. By concentrating on a
relation of facts to the virtual exclusion of argument the learned trial judge was
again being helpful to the appellant'.

And:

(b) 'It would have been open, and properly open, to the learned trial judge to
comment favourably on the circumstances which might seem helpful to the
[appellant] and to balance that comment with observations on the circumstances,
(which were more cogent as well as more numerous), pointing towards guilt.
Such a course would have been unexceptionable but would have told more
heavily against the [appellant] than the factual and uncoloured approach which
the judge actually adopted.'

The particular form and style of a summing-up, provided it contains what must
on any view be certain essential elements, must depend not only on the particular
features of a particular case but also on the view formed by a judge as to the form
and style that will be fair and reasonable and helpful. The solemn function of those
concerned in a criminal trial is to clear the innocent and to convict the guilty. It is,
however, not for the judge but for the jury to decide what evidence is to be accepted
and what conclusion should be drawn from it. It is not to be assumed that members
of a jury will abandon their reasoning powers and, having decided that they accept
as true some particular piece of evidence, will not proceed further to consider whether
the effect of that piece of evidence is to point to guilt or is neutral or is to point to
innocence. Nor is it to be assumed that in the process of weighing up a great many
separate pieces of evidence they will forget the fundamental direction, if carefully
given to them, that they must not convict unless they are satisfied that guilt has been
proved and has been proved beyond all reasonable doubt. The argument on behalf
of the appellant in the terms of the proposition of law which I have set out seems to
me inevitably to involve the suggestion that in the absence of a direction in the
terms propounded a jury would not be likely to consider evidence critically so as
to decide what it proves.

I must turn, therefore, to consider the two questions to which I have adverted:
(a) does the proposition formulated on behalf of the appellant state the existing
law and (b) if not—should there be a new rule which will be binding on judges?
Reliance was placed on the report of *R v Hodge*[1]. The accused in that case was charged
with murder and the trial in 1838 took place at the Assizes in Liverpool. The short
report of the case records what Alderson B[2] said in summing-up to the jury. He

---

1   (1838) 2 Lew CC 227
2   (1838) 2 Lew CC at 228

told them that the case was 'made up of circumstances entirely' and that before   *a*
they could find the prisoner guilty they must be satisfied—

> 'not only that those circumstances were consistent with his having committed
> the act, but they must also be satisfied that the facts were such as to be in-
> consistent with any other rational conclusion than that the prisoner was the
> guilty person.'

He also pointed out to the jury, to quote from the report, the proneness of the human   *b*
mind to look for (and often slightly to distort) the facts in order to establish a proposition while forgetting that a single circumstance which is inconsistent with such
a conclusion is of more importance than all the rest inasmuch as it destroyed the
hypothesis of guilt. In the report of the case it was said that the evidence was all
circumstantial and contained no one fact which taken alone would lead to a presumption of guilt. No one could doubt that the wise words used by the learned judge   *c*
were helpful and admirable and as such were worthy of being recorded. But there
is no indication that the learned judge was newly laying down a requirement for a
summing-up in cases where the evidence is circumstantial nor that he was himself
employing words so as to comply with an already existing legal requirement.

The painstaking research of counsel for the appellant showed that in some
countries in the Commonwealth both learned judges and also legal writers have   *d*
made reference to the 'rule' in *Hodge's* case[1]. I do not propose to refer to all the citations which counsel made. The singular fact remains that here in the home of the
common law *Hodge's* case[1] has not been given very special prominence: references
to it are scant and do not suggest that it enshrines guidance of such compulsive power
as to amount to a rule of law which if not faithfully followed will stamp a summing-
up as defective. I think that this is consistent with the view that *Hodge's* case[1] was   *e*
reported not because it laid down a new rule of law but because it was thought to
furnish a helpful example of one way in which a jury could be directed in a case where
the evidence was circumstantial.

In Kenny's Outlines of Criminal Law[2] it is said:

> 'No distrust of circumstantial evidence has been shewn by English law. It
> does not even require that direct evidence shall receive any preference over   *f*
> circumstantial.'

Memorable instances are cited of important capital convictions, whose correctness
is unquestioned, that were based solely on indirect evidence. There is a quotation[3] of
some words used by Shaw CJ in the American case of the trial of Professor Webster[4]
for murder in 1850 in reference to the reasonable doubt of a jury, viz: *g*

> 'It is the condition of mind which exists when the jurors cannot say that they
> feel an abiding conviction, a moral certainty, of the truth of the charge. For it is
> not sufficient for the prosecutor to establish a probability, even though a strong
> one according to the doctrine of chances: he must establish the fact to a moral
> certainty—a certainty that convinces the understanding, satisfies the reason, and
> directs the judgment. But were the law to go further than this, and require   *h*
> absolute certainty, it would exclude circumstantial evidence altogether.'

The conclusion is expressed in Kenny[4] that what is called the abstract, and therefore necessarily vague, direction that a jury must be satisfied beyond reasonable
doubt is the only restriction which in ordinary cases English criminal law imposes
on the discretion of juries in pronouncing on the sufficiency of evidence.

It would appear that in Canada it has been the practice to follow the wording   *j*
of Alderson B and to adopt what is regarded as the 'rule' in *Hodge's* case[1]: it appears

---

1   (1838) 2 Lew CC 227
2   15th Edn (1936), p397
3   Ibid at p 455
4   *Commonwealth v Webster* (1850) 5 Cushing 295 at 320
5   Op cit p 456

a to have become a settled rule that such a special direction as to the way in which circumstantial evidence is to be viewed should be given. Indeed, in *R v Ducsharm*[1] it was said that the rule regarding circumstantial evidence was quite distinct from the rule as to reasonable doubt and that a judge should separate his direction as to the one from his direction as to the other. It would appear that in Australia it is certainly customary where circumstantial evidence is relied on to prove guilt to

b give a direction[2]—

'that to enable a jury to bring in a verdict of guilty it is necessary not only that it should be a rational inference but the only rational inference that the circumstances would enable them to draw'.

In *Plomp v The Queen*[3], Dixon CJ referred to—

c 'the rule that you cannot be satisfied beyond reasonable doubt on circumstantial evidence unless no other explanation than guilt is reasonably compatible with the circumstances.'

He cited the following words[4]:

d 'In the inculpation of an accused person the evidentiary circumstances must bear no other reasonable explanation. This means that, according to the common course of human affairs, the degree of probability that the occurrence of the facts proved would be accompanied by the occurrence of the fact to be proved is so high that the contrary cannot reasonably be supposed.'

e In his judgment in the same case Menzies J[5] said that the customary direction was not something separate and distinct from the direction that the prosecution must prove its case beyond reasonable doubt. He considered that the giving of the particular direction stemmed from the more general requirement that proof must be established beyond reasonable doubt. In the earlier case of *Peacock v The King*[6] it was said that it was the practice of judges, whether they were bound to give such a direction or not, to tell the jury that, if there is any reasonable hypothesis consistent with the innocence of the prisoner, it is their duty to acquit.

f In Taylor on Evidence[7], in reference to circumstantial evidence, it is said that after the facts sworn to are proved a further and a highly difficult duty remains for the jury to perform:

'They must decide, not whether these facts are consistent with the prisoner's guilt, but whether they are inconsistent with any other rational conclusion; for

g it is only on this last hypothesis that they can safely convict the accused. The circumstances must be such as to produce moral certainty, to the exclusion of every reasonable doubt. Moral certainty and the absence of reasonable doubt are in truth one and the same thing.'

I see no advantage in using the phrase 'moral certainty' but I agree with the view

h expressed by Menzies J[5] and with the view expressed in Taylor[7] that the form of any particular direction stems from the general requirement that proof must be established beyond reasonable doubt. I consider that the form in which this general requirement is emphasised to a jury is best left to the discretion of a judge without his being tied down by some new rule which would be likely to have the effect that

---

j 1 [1955] OR 824
2 See *Plomp v The Queen* (1963) 110 CLR 234 at 252, per Menzies J
3 (1963) 110 CLR 234 at 243
4 From *Martin v Osborne* (1936) 55 CLR 367 at 375, per Dixon J
5 (1963) 110 CLR at 252
6 (1911) 13 CLR 619 at 630
7 11th Edn (1920) vol 1, p 74

a stereotyped form of words would be deemed necessary. In a case in which inferences may have to be drawn by a jury such facts as are found by them a judge will wish to give the jury guidance as to their approach and in giving that guidance he will certainly be assisted by having in mind what was said by Alderson B[1] and by Dixon CJ[2] and by others who have given expression to the same line of thought. To the same effect were the words used by Lord Normand in *Teper v R*[3] when he said:

> 'Circumstantial evidence may sometimes be conclusive, but it must always be narrowly examined, if only because evidence of this kind may be fabricated to cast suspicion on another. Joseph commanded the steward of his house, "put my cup, the silver cup, in the sack's mouth of the youngest," and when the cup was found there Benjamin's brethren too hastily assumed that he must have stolen it. It is also necessary before drawing the inference of the accused's guilt from circumstantial evidence to be sure that there are no other co-existing circumstances which would weaken or destroy the inference.'

So also were the words used by Lord Goddard CJ in *R v Onufrejczyk*[4] (in dealing with the situation where in a murder case no corpse had been found) when he said:

> 'Now it is perfectly clear that there is apparently no reported case in English law where a man has been convicted of murder when there has been no trace of the body at all. But it is equally clear that the fact of death, like any other fact, can be proved by circumstantial evidence, that is to say, evidence of facts which lead to one conclusion, provided that the jury are satisfied and are warned that it must lead to one conclusion only.

It is of interest to note that neither in *Teper v R*[5] nor in *R v Onufrejczyk*[6] does *Hodge's* case[7] appear to have been mentioned.

If, having regard to the facts and circumstances of a particular case, a summing-up is held to have been inadequate and to have failed to set the jury on their proper line of approach or to give them proper guidance a conviction might be held to be unsafe and unsatisfactory. But I am averse from laying down more rules binding on judges than are shown to be necessary.

In my view, the basic necessity before guilt of a criminal charge can be pronounced is that the jury are satisfied of guilt beyond all reasonable doubt. This is a conception that a jury can readily understand and by clear exposition can readily be made to understand. So also can a jury readily understand that from one piece of evidence which they accept various inferences might be drawn. It requires no more than ordinary common sense for a jury to understand that if one suggested inference from an accepted piece of evidence leads to a conclusion of guilt and another suggested inference to a conclusion of innocence a jury could not on that piece of evidence alone be satisfied of guilt beyond all reasonable doubt unless they wholly rejected and excluded the latter suggestion. Furthermore a jury can fully understand that if the facts which they accept are consistent with guilt but also consistent with innocence they could not say that they were satisfied of guilt beyond all reasonable doubt. Equally a jury can fully understand that if a fact which they accept is inconsistent with guilt or may be so they could not say that they were satisfied of guilt beyond all reasonable doubt.

In my view, it would be undesirable to lay it down as a rule which would bind judges that a direction to a jury in cases where circumstantial evidence is the basis

---

1 (1838) 2 Lew CC at 228
2 (1963) 110 CLR at 243
3 [1952] AC 480 at 489
4 [1955] 1 QB 388 at 394, cf [1955] 1 All ER 247 at 248
5 [1952] 2 All ER 447, [1952] AC 480
6 [1955] 1 All ER 247, [1955] 1 QB 388
7 (1838) 2 Lew CC 227

of the prosecution case must be given in some special form provided always that in suitable terms it is made plain to a jury that they must not convict unless they are satisfied of guilt beyond all reasonable doubt. In the present case there were only two possible verdicts: one was a verdict of not guilty and the other a verdict of guilty. In the judgment of Lowry LCJ it is noted that during the course of a long summing-up the learned judge had on at least ten occasions warned the jury of the need to be satisfied beyond reasonable doubt. The issue before the jury was whether it was the appellant or whether it was someone else who killed the deceased. If the jury were satisfied beyond reasonable doubt that it was the appellant they must have been satisfied beyond reasonable doubt that it was no one else. They could only have been satisfied beyond reasonable doubt of the appellant's guilt if the evidence which they accepted led them irresistibly to that conclusion.

To introduce a rule as suggested by learned counsel for the appellant would, in my view, not only be unnecessary but would be undesirable. In very many criminal cases it becomes necessary to draw conclusions from some accepted evidence. The mental element in a crime can rarely be proved by direct evidence. I see no advantage in seeking for the purposes of a summing-up to classify evidence into direct or circumstantial with the result that if the case for the prosecution depends (as to the commission of the act) entirely on circumstantial evidence (a term which would need to be defined) the judge becomes under obligation to comply when summing-up with a special requirement. The suggested rule is only to apply if the case depends 'entirely' on such evidence. If the rule is desirable why should it be so limited? And how is the judge to know what evidence the jury accept? Without knowing this how can he decide whether a case depends entirely on circumstantial evidence? If it were to apply not only when the prosecution case depends entirely on circumstantial evidence but also if 'any essential ingredient' of the case so depends there would be a risk of legalistic complications in a sphere where simplicity and clarity are of prime importance.

In agreement with the Court of Criminal Appeal I would reject the contention that there is a special obligation on a judge in the terms of the proposition of law that I have set out. There should be no set formulae which must be used by a learned judge. In certain types of cases there are rules of law and practice which require a judge to give certain warnings although not in any compulsory wording to a jury. But in the generality of cases I see no necessity to lay down a rule which would confine or define or supplement the duty of a judge to make clear to a jury in terms which are adequate to cover the particular features of the particular case that they must not convict unless they are satisfied beyond reasonable doubt.

I would dismiss the appeal.

LORD HODSON. My Lords, I have read the speech of my noble and learned friend, Lord Morris of Borth-y-Gest. I agree with it and that this appeal should be dismissed.

LORD SIMON OF GLAISDALE. My Lords, I have had the advantage of reading in draft the speech prepared by my noble and learned friend, Lord Morris of Borth-y-Gest. I agree with it; and would therefore dismiss the appeal.

LORD CROSS OF CHELSEA. My Lords, for the reasons given by my noble and learned friend, Lord Morris of Borth-y-Gest, in his speech which I have had an opportunity to read I would dismiss this appeal.

Appeal dismissed.

Solicitors: *Prothero & Prothero*, agents for *Alex Stewart & Son*, Newtownards, Co Down (for the appellant); *Director of Public Prosecutions*.

S A Hatteea Esq Barrister.

Charter and others v Race Relations Board

HOUSE OF LORDS
LORD REID, LORD MORRIS OF BORTH-Y-GEST, LORD HODSON, LORD SIMON OF GLAISDALE
AND LORD CROSS OF CHELSEA
20th, 21st, 22nd, 23rd, 27th, 28th NOVEMBER 1972, 1st FEBRUARY 1973

Race relations – Discrimination – Unlawful discrimination – Provision of goods, facilities and services – Discrimination by person concerned with provision of goods etc to a section of the public – Section of the public – Club – Members' club – Club providing facilities and services to members – Club rejecting application for membership on ground of applicant's colour – Conservative club – Adult male Conservatives eligible for membership – Club's rules providing for selection of members by process of nomination and election – Eligible applicants for membership always admitted in practice – No evidence that election process a facade – Whether members of club a 'section of the public' – Whether club providing facilities and services to a section of the public – Race Relations Act 1968, s 2 (1).

The East Ham South Conservative Club was a social members' club with premises in which members met for social intercourse and to enjoy the various services and facilities there provided. All male Conservatives of 18 years or over were eligible for membership, but members were mainly drawn from members of the East Ham Conservative Association. Under the club's rules an applicant for membership had to find a proposer and seconder among the members 'able to vouch for his respectability and fitness to become a member'. The completed nomination forms had then to be posted on the club notice board for at least seven days before the applicant was considered for membership. Thereafter the application was considered by the club's committee who decided whether to accept or reject the application. S, who was an Indian, and an adult male Conservative, applied for membership of the club. When the application came before the committee it was rejected by the casting vote of the chairman who, it was alleged, said that he was opposed to the application on the ground of S's colour. S complained to the Race Relations Board who brought proceedings against the club under the Race Relations Act 1968. The following preliminary issue was ordered to be tried: whether a refusal by the committee to elect a person to membership of the club on the ground of colour, race or ethnic or national origins where that person was eligible for membership would be unlawful under s 2 (1)[a] of the 1968 Act. For the purposes of the hearing of the preliminary issue it was admitted that 'any member of the [East Ham] Conservative Association who applied for membership of the Club and was otherwise eligible under the club's rules was admitted to membership of the Club', but there was no evidence that the process of election under the club's rules was a mere facade or that election to the club followed automatically from an application. It was common ground that the club was, within s 2 (1) of the 1968 Act, a person concerned with the provision of facilities and services to members of the club, the point at issue being whether the members constituted 'a section of the public' within s 2 (1).

Held (Lord Morris of Borth-y-Gest dissenting) – (i) The words 'section of the public' were words of limitation restricting the circumstances in which it would be unlawful under s 2 (1) for persons concerned with the provision of goods, facilities or services to discriminate on the grounds of colour etc. The word 'public' was used in contrast to 'private'; accordingly s 2 (1) did not apply to situations of a purely private character (see p 515 d, p 516 d and e, p 524 g to j, p 527 f, p 529 b and p 531 j to p 532 a, post).

(ii) It followed that a club, being essentially a private association of individuals, fell outside the scope of s 2 (1) provided that the club's rules concerning the election

---

a Section 2 (1) is set out at p 514 j, post

a of members made provision for a genuine process of selection and those rules were in practice complied with. In such a situation the club, in providing facilities or services to members, was not providing them to a 'section of the public' within s 2 (1) (see p 516 f to h, p 525 a to f, p 529 d f and h and p 534 a to h, post).

(iii) It could not be inferred from the admitted facts that there was no genuine selection of members of the East Ham South Conservative Club. Accordingly the facts did not disclose a situation to which s 2 (1) applied, with the consequence that a refusal by the club to elect a person to membership on the ground of colour would not be unlawful (see p 517 h and j, p 526 b and c, p 530 a, p 534 d and p 536 g and h, post).

Decision of the Court of Appeal sub nom *Race Relations Board v Charter* [1972] 1 All ER 556 reversed.

Notes

For discrimination on racial grounds in the provision of goods, facilities and services, see Supplement to 7 Halsbury's Laws (3rd Edn) para 1280, 2.

For the Race Relations Act 1968, s 2, see 40 Halsbury's Statutes (3rd Edn) 105.

Cases referred to in opinions

Compton, Re, Powell v Compton [1945] 1 All ER 198, [1945] Ch 123, 114 LJCh 99, 172 LT 158, CA, 8 Digest (Repl) 330, *123*.

Dingle v Turner [1972] 1 All ER 878, [1972] AC 601, [1972] 2 WLR 523, HL.

Hobourn Aero Components Ltd's Air Raid Distress Fund, Re, Ryan v Forrest [1946] 1 All ER 501, [1946] Ch 194, 115 LJCh 158, 174 LT 428, CA, 8 Digest (Repl) 321, *56*.

Jennings v Stephens [1936] 1 All ER 409, [1936] Ch 469, 105 LJCh 353, 154 LT 479, CA, 13 Digest (Repl) 119, *596*.

London Borough of Ealing v Race Relations Board [1972] 1 All ER 105, [1972] AC 342, [1972] 2 WLR 71, HL.

McMillan v Crouch [1972] 3 All ER 61, [1972] 1 WLR 1102, [1972] 2 Lloyd's Rep 325, HL.

Moose Lodge No 107 v K Leroy Irvis (1972) US 32 L Ed 2d 627, 92 Supreme Court.

Panama (Piccadilly) Ltd v Newberry [1962] 1 All ER 769, [1962] 1 WLR 610, 126 JP 140, 60 LGR 503, DC, Digest (Cont Vol A) 424, *8744a*.

Race Relations Board v Bradmore Working Men's Social Club and Institute (9th April 1970) unreported, Birmingham County Court.

Young's Will Trusts, Re, Westminster Bank Ltd v Sterling [1955] 3 All ER 689, [1955] 1 WLR 1269, Digest (Cont Vol A) 89, *31a*.

Appeal

Edward Reginald Marden Charter, Horace A Parker and William Albert English (sued on their own behalf and on behalf of all other members of the East Ham South Conservative Club between 27th April 1969 and 5th November 1969) appealed against an order of the Court of Appeal (Lord Denning MR, Megaw and Stephenson LJJ) dated 14th December 1971 and reported at [1972] 1 All ER 556, allowing the appeal of the respondents, the Race Relations Board ('the board'), against the judgment of his Honour Judge Herbert QC on 6th April 1971 in the Westminster County Court in favour of the appellants on two preliminary issues directed by consent to be tried before hearing of the action by the board against the appellants. The facts and the preliminary issues are set out in the opinion of Lord Reid.

David Hirst QC, Andrew Leggatt QC and *J F A Archer* for the appellants.
J P Comyn QC and *Anthony Lester* for the board.

Their Lordships took time for consideration.

1st February. The following opinions were delivered.

LORD REID. My Lords, the respondents, the Race Relations Board (whom I shall refer to as 'the board') sued the appellants on their own behalf and on behalf of all other members of the East Ham South Conservative Club in the Westminster County Court for damages and for a declaration that certain acts were unlawful by virtue of the provisions of s 2 of the Race Relations Act 1968. It is not disputed that the club is an ordinary social members' club with premises in which members meet for social intercourse and to enjoy the various services and facilities there provided. All male adult Conservatives are eligible for membership but members were mainly drawn from members of the East Ham Conservative Association.

In 1969 Mr Shah who was born in India and is a postal and telegraph officer applied for membership. When the application came before the club committee it was rejected by the casting vote of the chairman who it is alleged said that he was opposed to the application on the grounds of Mr Shah's colour. On complaint being made to the board they formed the opinion that the club had done an act which was unlawful. Failing to secure a settlement under s 15 of the 1968 Act they brought this action. Of consent the county court judge made the following order:

'By consent

'It is ordered that upon the [appellants] admitting the Rules of the East Ham South Conservative Club and admitting for the purposes only of the hearing of the preliminary issues hereinafter referred to the facts and matters alleged by paragraphs 1, 4 and 5 of the Particulars of Claim herein (subject to the qualification that (a) the admission to membership referred to by the said paragraph 4 was by means of the election procedure prescribed by the said Rules and (b) that the [appellants] do not admit that consideration of an application for admission to membership of the said Club or election to such membership are facilities or services within the meaning of Section 2 of the Race Relations Act, 1968) that the following preliminary issues, be set down to be tried by this Court namely (i) the issue whether consideration by the Committee of the said Club under the Rules of the said Club of an application for election to membership of the said Club is a "situation" to which Section 2, 3, 4 or 5 of the said Act applies, and (ii) the issue whether a refusal on the ground of colour race or ethnic or national origins by the said Committee to elect to membership of the said Club an applicant eligible under Rule 4 of the said Rules would be unlawful by virtue of Section 2 of the said Act.'

Paragraph 4 of the statement of claim stated:

'At all material times the members of the Club consisted wholly or mainly of members of the East Ham Conservative Association and any member of the said Conservative Association who applied for membership of the Club and was otherwise eligible under the club's rules was admitted to membership of the Club.'

The learned county court judge decided the preliminary issues in favour of the appellants and gave judgment in their favour. On appeal the Court of Appeal[1] set aside his decision and decided the preliminary issues in favour of the board. The case turns on the proper interpretation of s 2 (1) of the 1968 Act which is in the following terms:

'It shall be unlawful for any person concerned with the provision to the public or a section of the public (whether on payment or otherwise) of any goods, facilities or services to discriminate against any person seeking to obtain or use those goods, facilities or services by refusing or deliberately omitting to provide him with any of them or to provide him with goods, services or facilities of the like quality, in the like manner and on the like terms in and on which the former normally makes them available to other members of the public.'

1 [1972] 1 All ER 556, [1972] 1 QB 545

It is agreed that within the meaning of this subsection the club is a person, that it is concerned with the provision of facilities and services, that Mr Shah sought to obtain these facilities and services and that the club refused to provide him with them. The question at issue is whether the club provided these facilities and services to 'the public or a section of the public'. It provided them to its members and their guests, but are the members 'a section of the public'?

Read literally the words denote any two or more persons associated together in any way—perhaps any one person could be a section of the public but I shall assume not. But that cannot be the meaning of those words in this context. The head of a household provides facilities for all members of his household. Suppose he has in his household three servants one of whom is coloured, and although asked to do so, he refuses to the coloured servant facilities which he provides for the others and says that he does so on the ground of colour. The board admit that that is not within the scope of the Act. Plainly there is discrimination within the meaning of s 1 and the only possible ground for excluding such a case from the operation of the Act is that the household is not a section of the public. Various sections of the Act make it clear that it is not intended to interfere with people's domestic lives and counsel for the board both made it clear that they did not contend otherwise.

So the words 'a section of the public' are words of limitation. If they were not there would have been no point in inserting in the section the words 'the public or a section of the public'. The section would read perfectly well without them, but then the case which I have supposed of discrimination within a household would have been within the scope of the Act. The question then is how far does the exception in limitation extend. Counsel for the board contended that it only extends to the purely domestic sphere. For the appellants it was contended that the natural antithesis to public is private.

Before coming to the facts of the case I think it well to consider a few quite possible cases. Suppose that in the absence of a nursery school a woman with some knowledge of children lets it be known among her neighbours that she is willing (whether with or without payment) to take a few children into her house for some hours each day either just to look after them or to conduct some kind of kindergarten or its modern equivalent and she refuses to take the child of a coloured neighbour. Or suppose a small bridge club which meets in the houses of its members and which rejects an application for membership by a coloured person. Or suppose a man let it be known among his friends that he would like to take a congenial party abroad: a coloured friend of his seeks to be included in the party but he says some of the other members of his party would object and therefore he is sorry he cannot include his coloured friend. Counsel for the board argued that all these cases are within the Act so that the discrimination in all these cases would be actionable. Junior counsel, however, informed us that the board do not want to have to deal with such cases.

Now let me come to clubs. I leave out of account various societies or associations which call themselves clubs but have no premises where members meet for social intercourse. No doubt social clubs vary in character. Some are small, some large. Some are very exclusive, some less so. It is suggested in the judgment of the Court of Appeal[1] that a distinction can be drawn between those which restrict membership to persons who have certain qualifications and those which do not. This is linked to a distinction between personal and impersonal qualities which I must confess I do not understand. If the truth is that there is a careful selection of candidates for membership so that only those who are thought to be acceptable to other members are admitted, then I do not see how it can matter that candidates for membership of certain clubs must be Conservatives or members of particular universities or travellers or reformers whereas other similar clubs make no such restriction. Members are not admitted because they have these qualifications, but because on personal grounds they are thought to be acceptable. No doubt Conservatives or graduates of a particular university are a section of the public but it does not at all follow that a number of Conservatives or graduates selected for personal reasons must also be a section of the public. I would regard with the greatest suspicion any interpretation of the Act which required us to hold that of two apparently similar clubs one is within the Act because it restricts membership in this way but the other is not because it does not. The result would be absurd.

In determining the precise scope of s 2 we must read the Act as a whole in the light of any general policy which its terms disclose. Let me say at once that I get no help from either charity or copyright cases. Public policy has had much to do with developing the law as to charity, and there are obvious reasons for reading the words 'in public' in such a way as to give all reasonable protection to an author's rights. Where a word is capable of having several meanings or shades of meaning, it can seldom be profitable to consider the meaning which has been given to it in a different chapter of the law.

The 1968 Act was preceded by the Race Relations Act 1965 which forbade discrimination in relation to various places of public resort. The scope of the 1968 Act is obviously much wider but it still appears to me to be confined to situations in which there can be said to be some public element. I have already said that the words 'the public or a section of the public' in s 2 must have been intended to have some limiting effect. And the provisions in the Act which limit its scope in various particular contexts appear to me to flow from this general conception. I would infer from the Act as a whole that the legislature thought all discrimination on racial grounds to be deplorable but thought it unwise or impracticable to attempt to apply legal sanctions in situations of a purely private character.

Some clubs have a very domestic appearance and atmosphere, others less so. Suppose a club begins by meeting in members' houses and then acquires small premises of its own but preserves its former character. The mere move to its own premises does not seem to me to introduce any public element. I cannot see any reasonable or workable dividing line so long as there is operated a genuine system of personal selection of members. There is no public element where a personally selected group of people meet in private premises and the club which they constitute does not provide facilities or services to the public or any section of the public. So s 2 does not apply.

But a clear dividing line does emerge if entry to a club is no more than a formality. This may be because the club rules do not provide for any true selection or because in practice the rules are disregarded. There are, or at least have been, clubs which are in fact no more difficult to enter than a restaurant. There may be some delay, and there may be entry money and a subscription but that makes no difference. In fact the club services and facilities are provided to any one of the public who wishes to come in, provided that he does not have such obvious disqualification as might cause the manager of say a good restaurant to exclude him. And it would make no difference if entry were confined to a particular section of the public—Conservatives or graduates or any other.

The board say that this club falls within the latter class. So we must go to the admission set out in the order for the trial of the preliminary issues. The board found in the admission that at all material times any member of the East Ham Conservative Association who applied and was eligible under the club rules was admitted to membership. But that is qualified by the admission that such admission was by means of the election procedure prescribed by the rules: that must mean that the rules were not disregarded. So we must go to the rules. The most important are:

'6. An applicant for membership must be proposed and seconded by two members able to vouch for his respectability and fitness to become a member. The proposer, seconder and the candidate must sign the A.C.C. nomination form and the candidate by doing so shall undertake to support the Conservative Party and to abide by the rules and by-laws of the Club. Only those who have been members for at least six months immediately prior to the nomination shall be entitled to propose or second a candidate. In cases where an applicant for membership is not personally known to members as required by the foregoing conditions the Committee shall have powers to recommend the nomination of an applicant after such examination of the circumstances as may be necessary to satisfy them of his suitability and to depute two members of the Committee to act formally as proposer and seconder. All other procedure shall be as required for other candidates.

'7. All completed nomination forms shall be posted on the club notice board for at least seven days prior to the candidate being considered for election and any objection communicated to the Secretary, in writing and without prejudice, within that period.

'8. The Committee shall have the right to request the candidate and/or his proposer and seconder to appear before them and to answer any questions relevant to the application for membership. Failure to comply with this request or to provide a satisfactory excuse within four weeks shall render the nomination void.

'9. An elected candidate shall not be deemed a member until his first subscription has been paid.

'10. No rejected candidate shall again be proposed as a member until the expiration of twelve months from the date of such rejection. He shall not, during that period be admitted to the Club as a visitor except with the special consent of the Committee. No person who has been expelled from the Club shall again be proposed for membership or make use of the Club premises as a visitor or otherwise except with the special consent of the Committee. A person who has previously been a member of the Club shall not be eligible for re-election until a period of twelve months from the cessation of his membership has elapsed unless he shall have paid all subscriptions which would have been due had he remained a member over the period from the date of his last subscription to the date of his application for re-election.'

So the rules provide for three stages. First and perhaps most important, the applicant must find a proposer and a seconder who will vouch for his respectability and fitness to become a member. There is nothing to suggest that this is a formality or that members asked to propose or second an applicant do not take their responsibilities seriously. Then the nomination form must be posted on the club notice board. And thirdly the committee must consider each application. There is nothing to suggest that this has been a mere formality.

No doubt every applicant who has been vouched for by a proposer and seconder during the material time has been elected. But that by itself is quite inconclusive. Unsuitable aspirants to membership may have taken no steps because they knew they would not succeed, or they may have failed to find proposers and seconders. The most we could infer is that this club is not very exclusive. It cannot be inferred from the facts at which we are entitled to look at this stage that there is no genuine selection of members of this club.

So if the case has to be finally decided on the admissions I would hold on the first preliminary issue that they do not disclose a situation to which s 2 applies and that therefore on the second issue a refusal to elect to membership on the ground of colour would not be unlawful. But I understood counsel for the board to ask for an opportunity to consider whether to seek an amendment of their statement of claim.

I would therefore allow this appeal with costs here and below, and remit the case to the county court to proceed in accordance with the decision of this House.

LORD MORRIS OF BORTH-Y-GEST. My Lords, by enacting the Race Relations Acts 1965 and 1968 Parliament introduced into the law of England a new guiding
principle of fundamental and far-reaching importance. It is one that affects and must
influence action and behaviour in this country within a wide-ranging sweep of human
activities and personal relationships. In the terms decreed by Parliament, but subject
to the exceptions permitted by Parliament, discrimination against a person on the
ground of colour, race or ethnic or national origins has become unlawful by the law
of England. In one sense there results for some people a limitation on what could be
called their freedom: they may no longer treat certain people, because of their colour
race or ethnic or national origins, less favourably than they would treat others. But
in the interests of the same cause of freedom, although differently viewed, Parliament
has, in statutory terms now calling for consideration, proscribed discrimination (on
the stated grounds) as being unlawful.

The issue in the present case is whether, on the basis of certain stated facts, the
provisions of s 2 of the 1968 Act were applicable or not. A certain Mr Shah (who was
born in India) applied for membership of the East Ham South Conservative Club.
By the rules of the club only male Conservatives not being under the age of 18 years
are eligible for membership. There is no law which affects the legality of those limitations. Mr Shah was a Conservative and he was over 18. He was an applicant for
membership within the terms of a rule of the club. The election of members is vested
in the committee of the club. At a meeting of the committee which was considering
Mr Shah's application for membership, the chairman, in reply to a question from a
member of the committee, indicated that he regarded Mr Shah's colour as relevant to
the consideration of his application for membership of the club. Shortly stated the
issue in this appeal is whether that answer flouted the law of England if the answer
meant, as presumably it did, that an adverse vote could be solely based on the ground
of Mr Shah's colour.

The machinery which was adopted in order to ascertain the legal principle which is
applicable in the case was that of having a trial of two preliminary issues. The substance of the first is as follows: (1) Is the consideration by the committee of the club
(under its rules) of an application for election to membership a 'situation' to which
ss 2, 3, 4 or 5 of the Act applies? The question has reference to the words 'in any situation to which ss 2, 3, 4 or 5 applies' which are found in s 1 (1) of the 1968 Act. Effectively
the question became one whether the situation was one to which s 2 applies. Section
2 (1) begins with the words:

> 'It shall be unlawful for any person concerned with the provision to the public
> or a section of the public (whether on payment or otherwise) of any goods,
> facilities or services to discriminate against any person seeking to obtain or use
> those goods, facilities or services . . .'

For the purpose of the hearing of the preliminary issues it was expressly admitted
that at all material times the club provided and provides facilities and services (including facilities for entertainment recreation or refreshment) to members and visitors
at the club's premises which are at 187 High Street, South, East Ham. No question
now arises as to which persons could or would in law be liable if it is held that there
was a situation to which s 2 applied and that a refusal to elect on the ground of colour
would be unlawful and if at a later time it is proved that there was in fact a refusal on
such ground. As it is admitted that the club provided facilities for entertainment
recreation or refreshment to its members it follows that the decision whether the
club is within s 2 depends on the question whether the admitted provision is provision
'to the public or a section of the public'.

The other preliminary issue was framed as follows: (2) Whether a refusal on the
ground of colour race or ethnic or national origins by the committee to elect to
membership of the club an applicant eligible under r 4 of the rules would be unlawful

by virtue of s 2 of the 1968 Act. In regard to this issue as so stated I think that it must be clear that such a refusal would undoubtedly be unlawful if the club is within s 2 or, to be more precise, if a consideration by the committee of an application for membership is a 'situation' to which s 2 of the Act applies.

It seems to be beyond doubt therefore that it is on the answer to the first preliminary issue that decision rests. The contention of the appellants is that the 1968 Act does not have any application to the East Ham South Conservative Club or to any comparable clubs. But on the admissions made for the purposes of the preliminary issue the Act undoubtedly applies to the club if its provision to members and their visitors of facilities for entertainment recreation or refreshment is provision 'to the public or a section of the public'. The Court of Appeal[1] held, and in my view rightly held, that there was no such provision to 'the public'. They held that there was such provision to a section of the public. It is this finding that the appellants seek to challenge. They say that the 400 or more members of the East Ham South Conservative Club are not a section of the public. The whole issue depends on a consideration of the meaning of those words in their context in s 2.

I approach the case on the footing that the club is a genuine club having the attributes of a members' club and with a procedure for the election of new members which has no spurious element. The board desired to keep open for later consideration the question whether admission to the club was no more than a formality. For the purposes of the hearing of the preliminary issues there was an admission, but subject to a qualification, of the following paragraph in the particulars of claim:

'At all material times the members of the Club consisted wholly or mainly of members of the East Ham Conservative Association and any member of the said Conservative Association who applied for membership of the Club and was otherwise eligible under the club's rules was admitted to membership of the Club.'

The qualification was that the admission to membership was by means of election procedure prescribed by the rules. Naturally I cannot express any opinion in regard to any matter which may depend on an elucidation of facts. In some circumstances there could be 'election' to a club which was so speedy, and which was virtually so automatic on application, that the reality would be that the services or facilities provided by the club would be available for any member of the public who presented himself. In such circumstances it could be said that there was provision to the public. I express my opinion in the present case on the assumption that the process of becoming a member of the East Ham South Conservative Club was neither an immediate nor an automatic one.

Section 2 (1) refers to goods, facilities or services. Subsection (2) of the section gives examples of facilities or services. In connection with the provision either to the public or to a section of the public, of any goods or of any facilities or of any services it is 'unlawful' to discriminate (in the sense defined by [s 1) against anyone seeking to obtain or to use any such goods or facilities or services either (a) by refusing or deliberately omitting to provide such person with any of them or (b) by refusing or deliberately omitting to provide such person with goods, services or facilities of the like quality, in the like manner and on the like terms in and on which they are normally made available to other members of the public. If the members of the East Ham South Conservative Club are not a section of the public it follows that if the club did elect Mr Shah as a member they would therefore be free, subject only to their rules, to 'discriminate' against him within the club premises.

A study of the 'examples' of facilities and services covered by s 2 (1) (as set out in sub-s (2)) shows their very comprehensive nature. Section 2 (2) is in the following terms:

---

1   [1972] 1 All ER 556, [1972] 1 QB 545

'The following are examples of the facilities and services mentioned in sub-section (1) above, that is to say—

(a) 'access to and use of any place which members of the public are permitted to enter;

(b) 'accommodation in a hotel, boarding house or other similar establishment;

(c) 'facilities by way of banking or insurance or for grants, loans, credit or finance;

(d) 'facilities for education, instruction or training;

(e) 'facilities for entertainment, recreation or refreshment;

(f) 'facilities for transport or travel;

(g) 'the services of any business, profession or trade or local or other public authority.'

It will be seen that as regards services there are embraced the services of any business, of any profession, of any trade or the services of any local or other public authority. As regards facilities there are included, inter alia, those for education, instruction or training and those for entertainment, recreation or refreshment. Entertainment (to take one example) may be provided for the public or for a section of the public. There must be no 'discrimination' in the terms defined by the Act against any member of the public seeking to go to a theatre or to a cinema or to a restaurant. Equally once people are within a theatre or cinema or restaurant there must be no 'discrimination'. Those who have bought their tickets and taken their seats in a theatre or cinema will, in my view, constitute a section of the public. In similar fashion there must be no 'discrimination' against anyone seeking to obtain the facility of education. Section 2 must be read as a whole and it clearly covers both those facilities and services which a member of the public can use and also those which a member of the public can seek to obtain. A public park may be open for anyone to enter. A public reading room may be open for anyone to enter. In the case of an educational establishment or an institution for instruction or training it will ordinarily be necessary for a person to make application to join or to be admitted. If some educational standard or attainment is made a condition for acceptance or admission, that will not constitute 'discrimination' within the meaning of s 1. But there must be no 'discrimination' as defined by the Act on a consideration of an application to join or to be admitted. Nor within the establishment or institution must there be any discrimination. Those who have been admitted to a school or to a college or to an Inn of Court or to some comparable institution will surely constitute a section of the public for whom there is provided the facility of education, instruction or training. Similarly I see no reason why those who are members of a club are not properly described as being a section of the public. If they are not—it may be asked what they are. It is suggested that they might be described as a private group. But this is only to introduce another phrase, which is not found in the Act, and which requires definition. A private group may also be a section of the public and where Parliament has not provided that clubs are to be exempted from the Act no such exemption ought to be implied unless the implication is clearly necessary.

Not only are there reasons why there should not be any such implication; there is positive indication that the members of an association do constitute a section of the public. By s 6 (1) of the 1965 Act (which forms a part of what is cited as the Race Relations Acts 1965 and 1968) it is provided as follows:

'A person shall be guilty of an offence under this section if, with intent to stir up hatred against any section of the public in Great Britain distinguished by colour, race, or ethnic or national origins—(a) he publishes or distributes written matter which is threatening, abusive or insulting; or (b) he uses in any public place or at any public meeting words which are threatening, abusive or insulting, being matter or words likely to stir up hatred against that section on grounds of colour, race, or ethnic or national origins.'

By s 6 (2) it is provided that 'publish' and 'distribute' mean—

'publish or distribute to the public at large or to any section of the public not consisting exclusively of members of an association of which the person publishing or distributing is a member'.

The words 'public at large' and 'section of the public' are to be noted. Three things clearly appear from this section: (a) any group consisting of those of the same colour or of the same race or the same ethnic or national origins will be a 'section of the public'; (b) the members of any particular association are a 'section of the public'; (c) in the words 'the public at large or to any section of the public' the words 'section of the public' are used as a complement to the words 'the public at large'.

It is to be observed that ss 2, 3, 4, 5 and 6 of the Act all begin with the words 'It shall be unlawful'. There follows a group of sections which provide for certain exceptions and prescribe that certain Acts are 'not unlawful'. There are certain exceptions in the case of residential accommodation. There are certain exceptions in the case of employment. Other exceptions are contained in ss 9, 10 and 11. I can find no words in the Act which include clubs among the exceptions.

It is suggested that the Act should not be regarded as curtailing private freedom of action. But to a considerable extent the Act undoubtedly does do so. Someone who in his own business is concerned with the employment of others might wish to 'discriminate'. A perusal of s 3 of the Act shows that, save to the extent of the exceptions provided for by s 8, such a person must not discriminate. A special exception (see s 8 (6)) was enacted in regard to the employment of a person for the purposes of a 'private household'. Within his own home someone may have only such employees or such guests as he chooses. But if he decides to open his home or his garden to the public (whether on payment or otherwise) he must not discriminate against any visitor on the ground of colour, race or ethnic or national origins.

The sweeping contention of the appellants that 'the Act of 1968 was not intended to have nor does it have any application to clubs' cannot be correct. A club and those concerned on its behalf with the employment of servants must surely be bound by the provisions of s 3 which make discrimination unlawful.

The wording of s 2 of the Act makes it plain that the provision (to the public or a section of the public) which is referred to is a provision (of goods, facilities or services) which anyone may seek to obtain or use. The provision within the circle of a family of the facility of refreshment is clearly not a provision which anyone outside the family may seek to obtain or use. If a host has a dinner party to which he invites some of his friends there is clearly no provision of a facility which anyone may seek to obtain or use. If someone invites some personal friends to join him on a holiday or on an expedition there is clearly no provision of a facility for travel which anyone may seek to obtain or use. It is quite otherwise if a club has a rule (as by r 6 has the East Ham South Conservative Club) which shows that there may be applicants for membership. A person may then seek to obtain those facilities which the club provides for its members. A club which permits or even encourages applications for membership (as opposed to a club which only recruits new members by special personal invitations) may lay down qualifications for membership but these qualifications must not be framed so as to provide that on the ground of colour, race or ethnic or national origins one applicant for membership will be treated less favourably than any other.

It was suggested that the antithesis of 'public' is 'private' and on this basis it was contended that any group which could be described as a 'private' group was excepted from the operation of the Act. In support of this contention it was argued that the presence in s 2 of the words 'provision to the public or a section of the public' could only be justified on the basis that private groups were excepted. But the words 'provision to the public or a section of the public' so far from being words which warrant any exception or exclusion are words which are particularly all-embracing. They are not words of limitation but rather of further description. It would be a strange and roundabout procedure to extract an exception from the words which are employed in describing what is unlawful when no mention of the exception is to be found in the group of sections which specially provide for exceptions and which lay down what is not unlawful. Furthermore, the contention is, in my view, based on a misunderstanding of the phrase 'provision to the public or a section of the public'. The phrase was used because of the range and variety of the 'goods facilities or services' which are the subject of the section. No occasion arises for seeking to find the opposite of or the antithesis of 'public'. The section deals both with circumstances where there is a 'provision' to any member of the public and where there is provision to some only of the public. Any member of the public may enter a shop for the purpose of making a purchase. Any member of the public may enter licensed premises for the purpose of purchasing a drink during permitted hours. Any member of the public may visit a public museum or art gallery. But some facilities are not provided for any and every member of the public but only for a section of the public. An educational establishment may have its full complement. A member of the public cannot walk in and demand to be taught or demand to purchase refreshment. The provision of such facilities is only for those who compose the full complement; it is not provision to the public but to a section of the public. If any antithesis is to be sought it is between the situation where any and every member of the public may claim goods (whether on payment or otherwise) or may claim some facility or some service and the situation where the provision of the goods, facilities or services is only to a group or section of the public.

I have for my part not been assisted by considering cases in which for the purposes of the law of charities there has been discussion as to what constitutes benefit of the public or a section of the public. Special considerations are there applicable. Nor do I find need to decide whether there are personal or impersonal links between those who comprise a section of the public. The link between them may be temporary or more lasting: it may be designed or fortuitous.

I would consider that members of the Conservative party constitute a section of the public. Similarly that all male Conservatives over 18 years of age in East Ham constitute a section of the public. Similarly, I consider that the Conservatives in East Ham who have become members of the East Ham South Conservative Club are a section of the public. All in a theatre watching a play must surely be a section of the public. So too—all who are travelling on a particular train or a particular boat or a particular bus. So too—all who are at a particular school or college; or all who are members of a particular church.

But apart from all these considerations it seems to me that the whole policy of the Acts gives guidance as to the meaning of the phrase 'the public or a section of the public'. On the one hand, there is the public at 'large': and every ordinary member of the public is included. On the other hand, there are groups of the public which may or may not have been formed by some process of selection or election or elimination but which are groups which members of the public may seek to join. What Parliament has as a matter of policy provided is that, subject to certain defined exceptions, that type of discrimination which is made unlawful is just as unlawful where groups of the public are concerned as it is where members of the public at large are concerned.

It is I think to be remembered throughout that the Acts only make discrimination unlawful if it is on racial grounds. I suppose that practically every organisation or institution or club makes a practice of it, or is under a necessity of, discriminating. Any selective process inevitably involves making a distinction between one person and another. That is what discrimination is. But the Acts only forbid one variety *a* of selection or discrimination. A school or a college or a university may have a rule that only someone who has passed some particular examination will be admitted. There will be a differentation between the intelligent and the dullard. The Acts do not condemn such selection or differentiation. An organisation may be confined to those who carry on some particular trade or business or profession or occupation. The Acts do not condemn such differentiation or discrimination. A club may say *b* that only those skilled in a particular sport may join; or only those who owe allegiance to a particular political party; or only those who share the same religious faith; or only those who are under or over a certain age; or only those who will pay a certain amount of money. Discrimination on any of those or similar lines is not made unlawful. A club may say that out of those who apply to join only those will be selected who are considered by the committee to have qualities of personal acceptability. The Acts do not make such discrimination unlawful. What the Acts do *c* say is that other things being equal a man is not to be ruled out only because of the colour of his skin. As between one person and others a person is not to be treated less favourably than the others on the ground of his colour or of his race or his ethnic or national origins. There should be no exceptions from the new guiding principle unless Parliament has decreed them.

d In agreement with Lord Denning MR, Megaw and Stephenson LJJ[1], I can see no logical reason why the members of a club for whom there is the provision of facilities are not a section of the public. Where there is private hospitality there is not a situation where a member of the public can 'seek to obtain or use' the facilities provided by the host. There may, as Stephenson LJ pointed out, be some clubs which are so constituted that admission is by invitation only. A member of the public would not be entitled to seek to obtain the facilities of such a club. It is *e* otherwise in the present case. There will be male Conservatives in East Ham who will be applicants for membership of the East Ham South Conservative Club and who as such will be fully entitled to 'seek to obtain' the facilities which are provided. As between such applicants there must not be discrimination on the grounds of colour, race or ethnic or national origins although there may be selection or election or *f* discrimination in many other ways.

In my view, the Court of Appeal[1] reached the correct conclusion and I would dismiss the appeal.

LORD HODSON. My Lords, the question raised by the appeal is whether the *g* race relations legislation applies to clubs, that is to say, to associations of persons meeting periodically for social intercourse etc. A subsidiary question is whether if the first question is answered in the negative yet on the facts of the instant case the legislation is applicable because a particular association is not recognisable as a club.

The short facts are these. On 27th April 1969 Amarjit Singh Shah, who was born in India, applied for membership of the East Ham South Conservative Club *h* (represented in the action by the appellants). Mr Shah had been an active member of the Conservative Association for several years and was eligible for membership of the club in accordance with its rules. Finally, at a meeting held on 5th November 1969, the committee of the club considered Mr Shah's application. One of the members asked the chairman (the first appellant) 'Is colour relevant?' The chairman replied 'I regard it as relevant'. The application was put to the vote and on the casting *j* vote of the chairman was rejected. Mr Shah complained to the Race Relations Board who brought an action in the Westminster County Court claiming damages for lost opportunity and a declaration that the rejection of Mr Shah was unlawful. On 1st March 1971 an order was made for the trial of a preliminary issue. The principal question was—

1 [1972] 1 All ER 556, [1972] 1 QB 545

'whether a refusal on the basis of colour, race or ethnic or national origin by the said Committee to elect to membership ... would be unlawful by virtue of Section 2 of the said Act.'

This Act is the Race Relations Act 1968, and s 2 reads as follows:

'(1) It shall be unlawful for any person concerned with the provision to the public or a section of the public (whether on payment or otherwise) of any goods, facilities or services to discriminate against any person seeking to obtain or use those goods, facilities or services by refusing or deliberately omitting to provide him with any of them or to provide him with goods, services or facilities of the like quality, in the like manner and on the like terms in and on which the former normally makes them available to other members of the public ...'

Section 1 of the Act provides:

'(1) For the purposes of this Act a person discriminates against another if on the ground of colour, race or ethnic or national origins he treats the other, in any situation to which section 2 ... applies, less favourably than he treats or would treat other persons ...'

The first question to be decided is whether such a situation had arisen. The judge sat with two assessors and answered both questions in favour of the appellants. On appeal[1] this judgment was reversed and it was declared (1) an application for membership of the club is a situation to which s 2 of the Act applies; (2) a refusal to elect on the ground of colour, race or ethnic or national origins would be unlawful by virtue of s 2 of the Act.

I need not set out in detail the constitution of the club which is a members' club limited to persons holding specific qualifications who have been proposed and seconded and approved by the committee after their names have been presented to the club as candidates for election in case of any objection. The judge held that no doubt as a matter of practice an eligible candidate is elected but he may not be. He held the club to be a members' club not relevantly distinguishable from other members' clubs such as the Garrick or the Athenaeum.

The main question at issue depends on the construction of s 2 of the Act and, in particular, on the meaning of the words 'the public or a section of the public' in s 2. Taken in isolation it is plain that the public consists of individuals and that it cannot be denied that a single individual, certainly a few individuals, are a section of the public.

It is, however, also plain and not in dispute between the contesting parties that the words 'a section of the public' are not surplusage and must have a meaning which contrasts with the meaning to be found in the word 'public', that is to say, the public as a whole. If the words are, as they must be in some sense, words of limitation what are the boundaries of the limit? The antithesis of 'public' is 'private' and the enquiry there is as to who is fitted by the cap 'private'.

The main argument for the Race Relations Board is that s 2 seeks to contrast not public and private but public and domestic so that the family in the narrow sense is admittedly without the scope of the Act but private associations of individuals not connected by family ties or perhaps household ties are within the ambit. I find this limitation unacceptable and so far as authority is to be found relating to kindred topics unsupported. I may say that such support as can be found in charity and copyright cases, where the decisions are themselves unassailable, do not assist as they are concerned with different situations and different branches of the law where the relationship between the individuals concerned is manifestly different.

---

1 [1972] 1 All ER 556, [1972] 1 QB 545

It is plain to me, as I think it was to Megaw LJ in the Court of Appeal[1], that in this context one cannot differentiate between one club and another provided each is genuine in the sense that there is a process of selection or election carried out in accordance with the rules.

I do not understand the difference between personal and impersonal relied on by Lord Denning MR[2] as a foundation for the proposition that, if one club is easier to get into than another, in such a case the successful applicant is to be taken to be automatically or virtually automatically elected so that he is a member of the public or a section of the public, whereas if a member of a club to which election is based on personal qualifications he retains his privacy. This, with all respect to Lord Denning MR, appears to be an impossibility but, of course, not decisive of this case. One still has to construe the words 'section of the public' in the context of the Act, and I find the language not only of s 2 but of the whole Act consistent with the conclusion I have reached, namely, that 'private' is to be treated as the appropriate contrast to 'public' and that an association of individuals outside the domestic sphere can be properly, within the meaning and intent of the Act as gathered from its language, be described as private.

True it is that in the case of these associations which are commonly called clubs there may be cases where there is no election and no proper selection regulated by rules or at all. In such a case the Act cannot be evaded by calling a club something which is not qualified to receive that appellation and is in reality nothing more, so far as its so called members are concerned, than a section of the public. Such a case is illustrated by *Panama (Piccadilly) Ltd v Newberry*[3] which was concerned with a bogus club where any person was admitted as a so-called member by filling in a form and paying 25s.

I can find nothing in the Act which leads to the supposition that Parliament was concerned with the inclusion of private clubs in their activities as between some member and another. The activities of such clubs are not normally concerned with the provision to the general public of goods, facilities or services.

If one looks at the examples given of facilities and services mentioned in s 2 (2) one finds no indication that the legislature was aiming at private institutions more commonly called clubs. The board relies on the unrepealed section of the 1965 Act (s 6) which shows that members of an association 'may be' a section of the public, and would include some clubs. True enough, but this does not mean that members of every association must be regarded as a relevant section of the public by reason of their association with one another.

Your Lordships were referred to a decision of the Supreme Court of the United States in *Moose Lodge No 107 v K Leroy Irvis*[4]. This decision related to a private club and is not directly relevant to the problem here being considered but is interesting as showing that the nine judges were unanimous in regarding clubs as private institutions. The issue arose from the 14th Amendment to the Constitution which forbids a state to enforce a discriminatory rule because of the public element involved. The language is 'No State shall make or support any law nor deny to any person in its jurisdiction the equal protection of the law'.

There remains a further point taken by counsel for the board which is relevant to this case since whatever may be said about private clubs in general this particular club (it is said) composed of persons who are a section of the public. Membership is open to male Conservatives over 18 years of age. Associate membership is open to female Conservatives over 21 years of age. Junior associate members may be any male of 16 or 17 years of age willing to support Conservative principles. Honorary membership is open to any distinguished member of the Conservative party and temporary honorary membership is open to members of affiliated clubs.

---

1   [1972] 1 All ER 556 at 560, [1972] 1 QB 545 at 558
2   [1972] 1 All ER at 560, [1972] 1 QB at 556
3   [1962] 1 All ER 769, [1962] 1 WLR 610
4   (1972) US 32 L Ed 2d 627, 92 Supreme Court

It is not suggested that the political purpose of the club is relevant but it has been contended that since, as the judge said 'No doubt as a matter of practice, an eligible candidate is elected but he need not be' therefore there is, as it were, an impersonal element which makes the election no more than a facade which follows automatically or, as Lord Denning MR[1] puts it, virtually automatically from the applications for membership. It is agreed that the admission to membership was by means of the election procedure prescribed by the rules. No doubt the number of persons eligible for election is large but there is nothing impersonal about members and nothing to indicate that this club is to be differentiated from other clubs mentioned from time to time in the course of the argument. There is nothing to indicate that this particular club is bogus, as was the club in *Panama (Piccadilly) Ltd v Newberry*[2] and it has not been suggested that there is any suspicion of this. In these circumstances I am reluctant myself to pursue an enquiry into what may well be a task of difficulty in order to ascertain the history of election processes in particular cases but, in light of the views expressed by the majority of your Lordships, I do not dissent from the order proposed by my noble and learned friend, Lord Reid.

LORD SIMON OF GLAISDALE. My Lords, this appeal involves a short point of construction—the meaning of the words 'to the public or a section of the public' in s 2 (1) of the Race Relations Act 1968, involving whether the Act applies to members' clubs in general and to the East Ham South Conservative Club in particular. But, although the issues can be thus so shortly stated, they seemed to keep exploding in all directions; and, before we knew where we were, we were exploring the meaning of 'section of the public' in charity law, of 'in public' in relation to performing rights, the status of clubs in civil rights legislation in the United States, the Inns of Court, the Royal Automobile Club, the Caledonian Club, the London Welsh Rugby Football Club, the London Scottish Regiment, and hypothetical clubs formed by immigrant groups. This was inevitable; since the Act gives no explicit guidance on whether, and if so to what extent, it applies to clubs; so that it was necessary to investigate the repercussions of the rival interpretations, in order to adjudge the probable attitude of Parliament to such situations. In order to limit the necessity for such exploration counsel for the appellants argued that if Parliament had intended that the Act should apply to clubs, it could and would have said so expressly; while counsel for the board riposted that if Parliament had intended to exempt clubs from the provisions of the Act, it could and would have done so expressly. Neither contention seems to me more nor less valid than the other. But there was cited to your Lordships a judgment of his Honour Judge Nicklin in the Birmingham County Court in 1970 (*Race Relations Board v Bradmore Working Men's Social Club and Institute*[3]) from which it appears that the rules of many working men's clubs expressly operate a colour bar, and it is well known that the membership of many famous and reputable London clubs depends on national origin. In these circumstances I find it difficult to believe that during the passage of this Act through Parliament no member raised the question whether the Act would apply to members' clubs, or received no answer to such a question. In *London Borough of Ealing v Race Relations Board*[4] my noble and learned friend, Lord Kilbrandon, said:

> 'That one should be left groping for, or even speculating about, the meaning of a key phrase used in a recent Act of Parliament designed to remedy social grievances by assuring large groups of citizens of the protection of the law . . . is an unhappy feature of our present rules for the interpretation of statutes.'

1 [1972] 1 All ER at 561, [1972] 1 QB at 557
2 [1962] 1 All ER 769, [1962] 1 WLR 610
3 (9th April 1970) unreported
4 [1972] 1 All ER 105 at 119, [1972] AC 342 at 367

a   If I am right in my surmise that the very issue with which your Lordships are concerned may well have been the subject-matter of Ministerial assurance one way or
the other, Lord Kilbrandon's observations are even more in point.   I hope that I
may without seeming egotistical draw attention to my suggestion in *McMillan v
Crouch*[1], that Parliamentary proceedings or other preparatory material might be
made available to aid judicial interpretation of statutes in the really clinching case
at least, with the sanction of costs against misuse. But, in the meantime, it is necessary
b   to rely on traditional methods of interpretation.

   Since I agree with the speech prepared by my noble and learned friend on the
Woolsack, which I have had the advantage of reading in draft, I content myself with
reference only to certain aspects of the matter under your Lordships' consideration.
For the final impression which the Act makes on me I gratefully adopt the language
used by my noble and learned friend[2]:
c

> 'I would infer from the Act as a whole that the legislature thought all dis-
> crimination on racial grounds to be deplorable but thought it unwise or
> impracticable to attempt to apply legal sanctions in situations of a purely private
> character.'

d   The hesitations about carrying the general provisions into private, domestic and
intimate situations appear from ss 7 and 8.   I would only add that it seems also to
have been within Parliamentary contemplation that the law might perform in this
field one of its traditional functions—an educative one—namely, to raise moral
standards by stigmatising as henceforward socially unacceptable certain hitherto generally condoned conduct.   I refer particularly to transitional provisions such as s 8 (1),
e   whereby certain exemptions from the Act are gradually phased out.   These transitional provisions further emphasise the way in which Parliament hesitated to make
racial discrimination unlawful in every field of human intercourse.

   This is sufficient to dispose of the first argument of leading counsel for the board.
'The public or a section of the public' are, he said, words of description, not of limitation.   Everyone is a member of the public, so that any two or more persons gathered
f   together constitute 'a section of the public'.   Not only does such an interpretation
run counter to the general balance of the Parliamentary approach, but linguistic
examination, too, shows it to be unsupportable.   On such a reading, the words 'to
the public or a section of the public' would be quite superfluous: s 2 (1) could have
run, 'It shall be unlawful for any person concerned with the provision of any goods,
facilities or services to discriminate [etc]'.   It must be presumed that the words
g   'to the public or a section of the public' were inserted for some purpose.   To what
was the draftsman referring?

   We all have, we hope, a spark of unique personality.   But every one of us plays a
number of roles in life.   We are children, husbands or wives, mothers or fathers,
members of some association, passengers in a bus, cinema-goers, workers with
varying status in industry or commerce or profession, adherents of a religious de-
h   nomination, Parliamentary or local government electors, nationals of a state, together
with countless other personae in the course of a lifetime—many in the course of a
day—some, indeed, simultaneously.   Certain of these roles lie in the public domain;
others in the private or domestic.   When the draftsman used the words 'provision
to the public or a section of the public' he was contemplating, I think, provision to
persons aggregated in one or other of their public roles.   The words would thus
j   have some meaning, which would coincide with the general impression that the Act
makes on me and with the specific impression given by the exemptions from the
situations of unlawful discrimination.

---

1   [1972] 3 All ER 61 at 76, [1972] 1 WLR 1102 at 1119
2   See p 516 d, ante

Leading counsel for the board in the end accepted that the words 'to the public or a section of the public' must be given some force. He suggested, however, that they stood in contradistinction, not to 'private', but to 'domestic'. He relied on *Jennings v Stephens*[1]. This was a decision of the Court of Appeal concerned with the meaning of the words 'in public' in connection with performance of copyright material. A decision on even the same phraseology in a different branch of the law can be of value in only two ways. It is of direct significance if it seems likely that the draftsman of the provision under instant interpretation had in mind the other phrase and its judicial interpretations and intended the court to invoke them. That seems to me to be purely fanciful as regards this instance. But interpretation of a similar phrase in a different statute or from a different branch of the law may be indirectly of value by showing how a legal phrase has struck different judicial minds: the value, though, will vary directly with the closeness of the context. Here the contexts are so different as to make anything said in *Jennings v Stephens*[1] virtually irrelevant to your Lordships' instant task of interpretation. But if anything the authority is against the board's contention. In that case 'public' was in some passages contrasted with 'domestic' or 'quasi-domestic' (although in others with 'private'). The word 'quasi' is apt to confuse rather than clarify; although it may legitimately be used to denote a twilight area and to signify to which of the neighbouring areas the situation in question is more akin. Thus, domestic shades off into public life; and 'quasi-domestic' may properly be used to denote that part of the intermediate area which lies nearer the domestic. If this is a legitimate approach, I think that a members' club might properly be said to be 'quasi-domestic' rather than 'public' or 'quasi-public'—a home from home, so to speak.

Before I leave this part of the case I must notice the main ground of decision in the Court of Appeal[2], although it was barely supported before your Lordships. This proceeded on analogy from the use of the phrase 'section of the public' in the law of charity. Although s 9 of the Race Relations Act 1968 refers to charities, exempting them and acts done for charitable purposes from the provisions of the Act, it seems extravagant to suppose that the draftsman was intending thereby to signal to the courts that they should construe the phrase 'a section of the public' in s 2 (1) by reference to the law of charity. And, again here, the contexts are so widely different as otherwise to make anything said about the word 'public' in the one branch of the law of little value for the other. I share the difficulty expressed by my noble and learned friend on the Woolsack and to be expressed by my noble and learned friend, Lord Cross of Chelsea, about the concepts of personal and impersonal qualities in the judgment of Lord Denning MR[2]; although it is right to point out that the decision of the Court of Appeal was given before the decision of your Lordships' House in *Dingle v Turner*[3] discountenanced the personal or impersonal character of a relationship as a determinant of what is 'a section of the public' for the purpose of the law of charity. But again here, any such analogy as may be invoked is in reality against the board's contention. In *Re Young's Will Trusts, Westminster Bank Ltd v Sterling*[4] there was a trust for the relief of indigent members of the Savage Club. Danckwerts J held that it was a valid charitable trust for the relief of poverty (relief of poverty virtually importing a public element automatically); but it is apparent that were it not for the fact that the trust was for the relief of poverty he would not have held it to be charitable. In other words, he did not regard members of such a members' club as themselves constituting a section of the public.

But although analogies from other branches of the law tend to favour the appellants, I do not think the draftsman intended them to be invoked, and the contexts are so different that no judicial pronouncement about the meaning of words in such

1   [1936] 1 All ER 409, [1936] Ch 469
2   [1972] 1 All ER 556, [1972] 1 QB 545
3   [1972] 1 All ER 878, [1972] AC 601
4   [1955] 3 All ER 689, [1955] 1 WLR 1269

other context can provide any close guidance in the decision facing your Lordships. So I am left to interpret the phrase 'a section of the public' only with such assistance as I can get from the statutory context and how I think Parliament would be likely to have regarded the implications of the one interpretation or the other. Notwithstanding the paramount objective of discouragement of racial discrimination, I find it impossible to believe that Parliament would willingly have countenanced the implications involved in the wider contentions made on behalf of the board. I think 'a section of the public' in s 2 (1) was used to denote a group of persons in their public capacities or roles, in contrast to a group of persons in their private capacities or roles. If this is right it is conclusive against the wide argument addressed to your Lordships by the board's leading counsel. The East Ham South Conservative Club is admittedly a bona fide members' club. The nature of such an institution is thus stated in Halsbury's Laws of England[1]:

> 'A club may be defined as a society of persons associated together for social intercourse, for the promotion of politics, sport, art, science, or literature, or for any purpose except the acquisition of gain. *The association must be private and have some element of permanence.*' (My italics.)

A bona fide members' club is, in other words, in its juristic essence a private association and not a section of the public. This accords, too, with popular conception.

Junior counsel for the board put his case, alternatively to that of his learned leader, more narrowly and, in my view, more acceptably. He conceded, for the purpose of this argument, that 'to the public or a section of the public' in s 2 (1) must be given some force: that this involved some limitation of the word 'provision'; that the natural antonym of 'public' is 'private' (provision to persons associated in a private capacity being thus excluded); that the usual members' club is an association of persons in their private capacities; and that the traditional members' club would thus be outside the ambit of the Act. But he argued that these concessions do not preclude certain members' clubs from being sections of the public; and that the East Ham South Conservative Club, in particular, is an association which, on careful scrutiny, can be shown to be no more than a section of the public.

On this part of the case, too, I agree with the speech of my noble and learned friend on the Woolsack. I think that it is open to show that some so-called clubs —even some which purport to be private members' clubs—do in reality constitute merely a section of the public. The dividing line, in my view, lies in the personal selection of members with a view to their common acceptability. No doubt a club may be less or more selective according to whether its membership is under strength, on the one hand, or it has a long waiting list, on the other. No doubt some clubs will provide for election by all members, so many blackballs perhaps excluding; while others may vest election in a committee. Most will require a candidate in any event to be sponsored by one or more existing members; and no doubt the status, personality or popularity of the sponsor will be influential in forwarding the interest of his candidate. The essential feature is that there should be a genuine screening at some stage as a pledge of general acceptability to fellow members. It is this screening that determines that membership is a private role. Without it the association remains a section of the public (see *Panama (Piccadilly) Ltd v Newberry*[2]). The rules will determine prima facie whether the association is in this way a private club or a section of the public; omnia praesumuntur rite esse acta. But this is a rebuttable presumption; so it will always be open to any interested person (including the board) to show that the rules are a sham, that anyone who applies can join, that the mode of entry is, in other words, a mere formality. Equally it must be open to the club to show that the rules give an inadequate picture of the true degree of selectivity.

---

1 3rd Edn, vol 5, p 252, para 586
2 [1962] 1 All ER 769, [1962] 1 WLR 610

For the reasons given by my noble and learned friend on the Woolsack, as the issues were framed on the basis of the pleadings as they stand at the moment, I do not think that it is open to the board to say that entry to this club was a mere formality. Insufficient has been pleaded and agreed to displace the presumption in favour of the club constituted by the rules. But the terms of the issue indicate that there may have been some misunderstandings about what facts were really being agreed. I therefore concur with the order proposed by my noble and learned friend on the Woolsack.

LORD CROSS OF CHELSEA. My Lords, the question for decision in this case is whether the members of the East Ham South Conservative Club are concerned with the provision of facilities for recreation and refreshment to a section of the public within the meaning of s 2 of the Race Relations Act 1968. Whether the race relations legislation applies to clubs is a very important question and one would have expected to find the Act stating in clear terms either that all clubs or no clubs should be affected by it or what kind of club should or should not be affected by it. In fact, however, the Act contains no reference to clubs and it has been left to the courts to infer from the vague language of s 2 what the intentions of Parliament in this regard may be supposed to have been. In these circumstances it is not surprising that different judges should reach different conclusions on the point.

I will begin by setting out the parts of the Act which appear to be directly relevant to or possibly to shed some indirect light on the problem. Sections 1 and 2 are in the following terms:

'1.—(1) For the purposes of this Act a person discriminates against another if on the ground of colour, race or ethnic or national origins he treats that other, in any situation to which section 2, 3, 4 or 5 below applies, less favourably than he treats or would treat other persons, and in this Act references to discrimination are references to discrimination on any of those grounds.

'(2) It is hereby declared that for those purposes segregating a person from other persons on any of those grounds is treating him less favourably than they are treated.

'2.—(1) It shall be unlawful for any person concerned with the provision to the public or a section of the public (whether on payment or otherwise) of any goods, facilities or services to discriminate against any person seeking to obtain or use those goods, facilities or services by refusing or deliberately omitting to provide him with any of them or to provide him with goods, services or facilities of the like quality, in the like manner and on the like terms in and on which the former normally makes them available to other members of the public.

'(2) The following are examples of the facilities and services mentioned in subsection (1) above, that is to say—access to and use of any place which members of the public are permitted to enter; accommodation in a hotel, boarding house or other similar establishment; facilities by way of banking or insurance or for grants, loans, credit or finance; facilities for education, instruction or training; facilities for entertainment, recreation or refreshment; facilities for transport or travel; the services of any business, profession or trade or local or other public authority.'

Section 3 forbids discrimination in the sphere of employment subject to various exceptions which are set out in sub-s (2) and s 8. In the course of argument reference was made by both sides to s 8 (6) and (10). The former subsection provides that neither s 2 nor s 3 shall apply to the employment of any person for the purposes of a private household. The latter runs as follows:

'It shall not be unlawful by virtue of section 2 or 3 above to discriminate against any person in respect of employment on a ship, if compliance with either of a those sections in that respect would result in persons of different colour, race or ethnic or national origins being compelled to share sleeping rooms, mess rooms or sanitary accommodation.'

Section 4 is directed to trade unions and employers and trade organisations and makes it unlawful for such bodies, inter alia, to 'discriminate' against anyone who is not a member by refusing to admit him to membership. Section 5 forbids discrimination b in the disposal of housing accommodation or business premises but this is subject to the exception set out in s 7. Subsections (1) to (5) of s 7—speaking generally—except from the provisions of ss 2 and 5 what may be called small boarding houses or lodging houses where the proprietor or landlord lives on the premises and shares some of the accommodation with his boarders or lodgers. Subsections (6) and (7) provide as follows:

c
'(6) It shall not be unlawful by virtue of section 2 above to discriminate against any person in respect of the provision of sleeping cabins for passengers on a ship if compliance with that section in that respect would result in persons of different colour, race or ethnic or national origins being compelled to share any such cabin.

d '(7) It shall not be unlawful by virtue of section 5 above for any person to discriminate against another with respect to the disposal by the former of his interest in any premises owned and wholly occupied by him unless he uses the services of an estate agent for the purposes of the disposal, or publishes or displays or causes the publication or display, of an advertisement or notice in connection with the disposal.'

e   The only other part of the legislation to which reference need be made is part of s 6 (2) of the Race Relations Act 1965 (which has to be read together with the 1968 Act) which runs as follows:

'In this section the following expressions have the meanings hereby assigned to them, that is to say— . . . "publish" and "distribute" mean publish and distri-
f bute to the public at large or to any section of the public not consisting exclusively of members of an association of which the person publishing or distributing is a member . . .'

The starting point of the enquiry must be to ask oneself what Parliament meant by inserting in s 2 (1) the words 'to the public or a section of the public' and the later reference to 'other members of the public'. Every individual is a member of the g public and if not every individual, then at least any two or more individuals form a part of the public and may be said to be, in a sense, a 'section' of it. But if Parliament meant the section to apply to any provision of services to others it would surely have said simply that. The words in question would seem, prima facie, to have been used in order to make it clear that only what could be called the 'public' provision of facilities was within this section. I am confirmed in this view by the consideration
h that if this were not so, s 2 would render unlawful acts which Parliament cannot have intended to make unlawful. Take, for example, the case of a mother and daughter who share a small flat or even a single room. The daughter is often away from home and it is well known in the neighbourhood that when the mother is alone she is generally willing, in return for a small payment, to allow another woman to sleep in her daughter's bed and have breakfast with her. Having regard to the
j provisions of ss 7 (6) and 8 (6) it is clear that Parliament would have wished the mother, in the case supposed, to have complete freedom to accept or refuse any applicant for any reason including those specified in s 1; but the case would not fall under the exception in s 7 since s 7 (1) (c) would not be satisfied and if it is excluded from the Act it must be because the wording of s 2 (1) was intended to limit the provision contemplated to 'public' as opposed to 'private' provision. Leading

counsel for the board was indeed disposed to agree that the words were used in a
limiting sense, although he preferred to speak of provision of facilities in the 'domestic'
rather than in the 'private' sphere as being outside the section; but the natural
antithesis to 'public' is 'private'.

Next comes the question how and where to draw the line between the 'public' and
the 'private' provision of facilities. Social clubs are a form of 'association' and s 6 (4)
of the 1965 Act shows that the members of some associations at least are 'sections of
the public' for the purpose of the Acts. But 'associations' are of many different
kinds—different in the objects for which they are formed, different in the size of
their membership and different in the modes by which and the ease or difficulty
with which one can become a member and I do not myself derive any help in the
solution of the present problem from speculating as to the impact of the Act on
associations of a totally different character from social clubs such as the Automobile
Association or an Inn of Court. Again I derive no help in the task of deciding on
which side of the line between the 'public' and the 'private' provision of facilities
social clubs fall from the other sections of the Act. The appellants relied on the
express reference to refusal to admit to membership of an organisation in s 4 as an
indication that in general a refusal to admit to membership of an association was
not unlawful. But trade unions had been accorded special treatment by Parliament
in other fields and one cannot, I think, deduce from the fact that it was expressly
provided that they could not 'discriminate' by refusing to admit to membership
the consequence that any organisation not covered by s 4 can 'discriminate' in this way.

I turn now to the judgments in the Court of Appeal[1]. All three members of the
court said that some clubs were within and others outside the Act but they differed
as to the place where the line should be drawn. Lord Denning MR, with whose
judgment Megaw LJ agreed, said[2] that the members of a club to which a member is
elected on his personal qualifications—his personal acceptability to other members
(which I will hereafter refer to as a 'selective' club)—did not form a section of the
public for the purposes of s 2. That is a view with which, as will later appear, I
agree; but Lord Denning MR added the rider that if the club in question did not
select its members from a wide class such as adult males or adult females—but from
a narrower class distinguished by what he called an 'impersonal quality' such as
'Conservatives' or 'Roman Catholics' the members would constitute a section of the
public. That is a distinction which I cannot follow at all and counsel for the board
were themselves not enamoured of it. I do not in fact find the division of the qualities
which distinguish one individual from another into 'personal' and 'impersonal' at
all easy to grasp but if one must adopt it I would have thought that the quality of
being an adult male as it depends on nature not choice was 'impersonal' and that
such qualities as being a 'Conservative' or a 'Roman Catholic' which depend on choice
were personal. But be that as it may, the fact that a club selects its members from
a limited class does not prevent it from selecting them on personal qualifications.
The distinction drawn by Lord Denning MR would lead to the very odd conclusion
that some 'selective' clubs in St James's would be outside the Act while other equally
'selective' neighbours—such, for instance, as the Carlton—would be within it. Lord
Denning MR relied in support of his views on the 'charity' cases; but with all respect
to him, those cases, if and so far as any analogy can properly be drawn from them,
tell in favour of the appellants. In the course of the last 100 years or so Chancery
judges have been frequently called on to decide whether the class of beneficiaries
named in some trust was such a class that the trust could rank as a charitable—i e a
public—trust. In the field of trusts for the relief of poverty the courts have taken a
very benevolent attitude to this question and have admitted as 'charities' trusts in
which the class of beneficiaries was what in common parlance would be called a

---

1   [1972] 1 All ER 556, [1972] 1 QB 545
2   [1972] 1 All ER at 561, 562, [1972] 1 QB at 557

a 'private class'. But in all other fields they have insisted that a trust to be charitable must be for the benefit of the public or of a 'section of the public'. In *Re Compton, Powell v Compton*[1] and in *Re Hobourn Aero Components Ltd's Air Raid Distress Fund, Ryan v Forrest*[2], Lord Greene MR, while disclaiming any intention of defining the expression, suggested that no group united by a tie of personal relationship such as descent from a common ancestor or of employment by a common employer or of

b common membership of an association could be a section of the public for the purpose of the law of charity. In the recent case of *Dingle v Turner*[3] I ventured to suggest that the *Compton*[1] test was not very satisfactory when applied to large classes, such as the employees of big companies, which the ordinary man might be inclined to describe as sections of the public and that the refusal of charitable status to trusts for the benefit of such a class could be justified more satisfactorily on other grounds. But however

c that may be, there is no doubt whatever that the members of a social club are not 'a section of the public' for charity purposes. The argument in *Re Young's Will Trusts*[4] case—which was a 'poverty' case—proceeded and rightly proceeded, on that assumption. But the fact that the members of the East Ham South Conservative Club are not a section of the public for the purposes of the law of charity may not help the appellants very much. In the first place I doubt whether it is safe to draw from

d s 9 of the 1968 Act, which deals with charitable dispositions, the conclusion suggested by Stephenson LJ that Parliament in speaking of 'a section of the public' in s 2 had the charity cases in mind. But, secondly, even if the members of a social club are not themselves 'a section of the public' for the purpose of s 2, it can still be argued in the case of any given club—that s 2 applies to it because any member of the public or of some section of the public who wishes to become a member can become one at any

e time subject only to compliance with some formality and that accordingly the members of the club are concerned with the provision of facilities not only for themselves but also for such members of the public or a section of the public as choose to apply for membership. Stephenson LJ—to turn now to his judgment—thought, as I read his judgment, that while clubs which 'co-opt' their new members are outside s 2, all clubs to which a would-be member can apply to become a member—even though

f he has to be proposed and seconded—are within the section. I agree that a club of which you can only become a member by invitation must be outside the section but to draw a distinction between such a club and a 'selective' club to which you can apply for membership if you can find a proposer and seconder is to my mind somewhat unreal. Sometimes, no doubt, a man who wishes to join a particular club will start himself to look among the existing members for a proposer and seconder. On

g the other hand, there are certainly other clubs where, although new members are recruited by application supported by a proposer and seconder, many people would hesitate to search for a proposer but would rather wait until some friend said to him: 'We want some new members at the X club, and it occurred to me that you might like to join. I would be glad to propose you and Y to second you.' I find it hard to distinguish such a club from a club which co-opts its new members. That is one

h reason why, while rejecting his 'rider', I prefer to draw the line where Lord Denning MR drew it—rather than where Stephenson LJ drew it. A further reason is that like Megaw LJ and indeed Stephenson LJ himself, I am troubled at the extraordinary consequences which acceptance of the board's arguments would entail with regard to clubs the membership of which is confined to racial groups. There must, I imagine, be many such clubs—Scottish, Welsh, Irish and, I daresay, West

j Indian or Pakistani—formed to promote social intercourse or sporting or cultural activities among such members of the racial group in question as are considered suitable for membership by the committee or the other members. I cannot believe

1 [1945] 1 All ER 198, [1945] Ch 123
2 [1946] 1 All ER 501, [1946] Ch 194
3 [1972] 1 All ER 878 at 889, [1972] AC 601 at 623, 624
    [1955] 3 All ER 689, [1955] 1 WLR 1269

that Parliament intended to make it unlawful for such clubs to operate the membership provisions in their rules and to make it a statutory offence under s 7 for the club
to publish them.   In the result then the conclusion which I reach on the general
question of principle is that a club which is a 'selective' club (i e a club to which apart
from any question of racial discrimination entry is regulated by the personal acceptability of the applicant to the existing members) can practise 'discrimination' in
admitting to membership but that a club to which, apart from considerations of
colour, race or ethnic or national origins, any member of the public or of a section of
the public can become a member subject only to complying with certain formalities,
is no more entitled to 'discriminate' on those grounds than is a hotel or a restaurant.

The question on which side of the line any given club falls is, no doubt, a question of
fact to be decided by the judge on the evidence adduced by each side in the particular
case.   It is, however, as I see it, necessary to say something as to the proper approach
to the problem—if only because we have to decide what order to make in the light of
the facts assumed in the 'issue' submitted to the court.   First, of course, one must
consider the rules.   If they do not justify refusal of membership on grounds of personal
acceptability, then obviously it is not a 'selective' club.   But the rules of the club—
and probably the rules of most clubs—plainly justify refusal of membership on such
grounds.   Rule 4 provides that to be eligible for membership one must be a male
Conservative over 18 years of age.   Rule 6 provides that in general no one can apply
for membership unless two members of the club who know him personally, vouch
for his respectability and fitness to become a member—although if an applicant is not
known to any members, the committee can, if it thinks fit, enquire into his suitability
themselves and, if satisfied of it, depute two of their members to act as his proposer
and seconder.   Rule 7 requires the nomination forms to be posted on the club notice
board seven days before the candidate is considered for election in order to give
members an opportunity to lodge objections in writing with the secretary.   Finally,
r 3 provides that election of members is vested in the committee and that if a ballot is
called for, two or more adverse votes shall exclude.   But it is one thing for a club to
have rules and another for the rules to be complied with.   It is common knowledge
that many clubs—such as the club the subject of the decision in *Panama (Piccadilly)
Ltd v Newberry*[1]—are in truth open to the public since the election machinery laid
down in the rules is either neglected entirely or treated as a pure formality.   So, if it
could be shown that in a case such as this, applicants were admitted to membership
without proposers and seconders or with proposers and seconders to whom they were
not personally known or that the nominations were not screened or that the committee did not consider each application on its merits so far as known to those present,
but simply acted as a 'rubber stamp' then the club would, I think, be within s 2.
Furthermore one must bear in mind that even establishments which are open to the
public may practice 'selectivity' of a sort.   The proprietor of a restaurant, for example,
may well refuse to serve someone who, in point of cleanliness or sobriety, falls
markedly below the level maintained by the general run of his patrons.   If therefore
the board could prove in the case of any given club that although the rules as to
admission were fully observed yet—discrimination on racial grounds apart—no greater
degree of 'selectivity' in admitting members was exercised by any of those concerned
than would be exercised by the proprietor of a restaurant catering for a class of the
public broadly similar in habits to the membership of the club, then I think that it
might well be held that the club was within s 2.   In practice, however, it would be
very difficult for the board to prove this in any given case for the mere fact that
there were no recorded instances of the refusal of an application for membership
would not itself establish anything.   In the most 'selective' clubs it may be rare for
any applicant to be rejected since what maintains its 'selectiveness' is the fact that no
one will readily propose or second an applicant who is likely to be unacceptable to
any appreciable number of his fellow members.   From the size of the membership

---

1   [1962] 1 All ER 769, [1962] 1 WLR 610

a and the number of affiliated members with automatic rights of entry, it might, perhaps, be suggested that the court should draw the inference that proposers and seconders never look beyond such manifest signs of unsuitability as I have referred to, but to draw such an inference might be hazardous—especially since the standards applied by any given club may vary from time to time as the composition of the committee changes or the need of the club for new members increases or decreases.

b Finally, I turn to the facts—or, rather, the 'assumed' facts—in the present case. Paragraphs 1 to 5 of the particulars of claim ran as follows:

'1. At all material times the first named [appellant] was the Chairman, the second-named [appellant] was the Honorary Secretary, and the third-named [appellant] was the Honorary Treasurer of a members' club known as the East Ham South Conservative Club whose offices are at No. 1, Vicarage Lane, East

c Ham, E.6., in the London Borough of New Ham (hereinafter called "the Club").

'2. By rule 1 of the Club's rules the objects of the Club are to maintain and advance Conservative principles and the club is affiliated to and inter-affiliated with the Association of Conservative Clubs and in those respects is subject to the rules and regulations of the said Association. The [board] will refer at the trial to the Club's rules and to the rules and regulations of the said Association for their

d full terms and true effect.

'3. At all material times the following classes of persons were and are eligible for admission to membership of the Club in accordance with the Club's rules (hereinafter called "Members").

'(a) *Membership*: any male Conservative not being under the age of 18 years;

'(b) *Associate Membership*: any female Conservative not being under the age

e of 21 years;

'(c) *Junior Associate Membership*: any male person of 16 and 17 years of age who is willing to support Conservative principles;

'(d) *Honorary Membership*: any distinguished member of the Conservative Party;

'(e) *Temporary Honorary Membership*: any member of any other club affiliated

f to the said Association and holding an Inter-affiliated ticket of the said Association.

'4. At all material times the members of the Club consisted wholly or mainly of members of the East Ham Conservative Association and any member of the said Conservative Association who applied for membership of the Club and was otherwise eligible under the club's rules was admitted to membership of the

g Club.

'5. At all material times the Club provided and provides facilities and services (including facilities for entertainment, recreation or refreshment) to members and visitors at the Club's premises at 187, High Street, South, East Ham, E.6. aforesaid.'

Paragraphs 1 to 4 of the defence were as follows:

h '1. Paragraphs 1 and 2 of the Pacticulars of Claim are admitted. No admission is made as to the representative capacity in which purportedly the [appellants] are sued. The Club at all material times has been a private unincorporated members' club.

'2. Subject to reference for their terms and effect to the Club's Rules which are neither fully nor accurately pleaded by paragraph 3 of the Particulars of Claim

j that paragraph is admitted. By rule 3 of the Club's Rules the election of members shall be vested in the Committee; by rule 6 an applicant for membership shall be proposed and seconded by two members; and by necessary implication from the Rules (and in particular rule 10) a candidate for membership may be rejected.

'3. Save that at all material times the members of the Club consisted mainly of persons who were also members of the East Ham Conservative Association paragraph 4 of the Particulars of Claim is denied.

'4. Save that the Club's premises at all material times have been and are at 1 Vicarage Lane paragraph 5 of the Particulars of Claim is admitted.'

On 24th March 1971 the parties agreed to an order submitting two preliminary issues to the court, which ran as follows:

'IT IS ORDERED that upon the [appellants] admitting the Rules of the East Ham South Conservative Club and admitting for the purposes only of the hearing of the preliminary issues hereinafter referred to the facts and matters alleged by paragraphs 1, 4 and 5 of the Particulars of Claim herein (subject to the qualification that (a) the admission to membership referred to by the said paragraph 4 was by means of the election procedure prescribed by the said Rules and (b) that the [appellants] do not admit that consideration of an application for admission to membership of the said Club or election to such membership are facilities or services within the meaning of section 2 of the Race Relations Act, 1968) that the following preliminary issues, be set down to be tried by this Court namely (i) the issue whether consideration by the Committee of the said Club under the Rules of the said Club of an application for election to membership of the said Club is a "situation" to which Section 2, 3, 4 or 5 of the Act applies, and (ii) the issue whether a refusal on the ground of colour race or ethnic or national origins by the said Committee to elect to membership of the said Club an applicant eligible under Rule 4 of the said Rules would be unlawful by virtue of Section 2 of the said Act.'

On 6th April 1971 Judge Herbert answered both questions in the negative but on 14th December 1971 the Court of Appeal[1] reversed his judgment and answered both questions in the affirmative. I do not find it easy to state precisely the grounds on which the Court of Appeal reversed the decision of the judge. It was largely no doubt because Lord Denning MR and Megaw LJ thought that a club membership of which was confined to a class such as 'Conservatives' must be within s 2 and because Stephenson LJ thought that any club admission to which was by election following application as opposed to by invitation was within the section. As I have said, I cannot agree with either of those grounds. But the judgments of Lord Denning MR and Stephenson LJ appear also to proceed to some extent on the view that the admitted facts showed that any member of the East Ham Conservative Association who wished to become a member of the club was admitted to membership more or less automatically[2]. I cannot agree that the facts agreed for the purpose of the issues lead to that conclusion. All that is admitted is that any member of the association who applied for membership was admitted to membership; but that is not at all the same thing as saying that any member of the association who wanted to become a member could become one. The appellants, on the other hand, submitted that if the true view was—as in my judgment it is—that any 'selective' club is outside the Act then the admission for the purposes of the issues that admission to membership was by means of the election procedure prescribed by the rules concluded the case in their favour since it must be assumed that the election procedure was properly complied with. But as I have tried to point out it does not, to my mind, necessarily follow that compliance with the rules shows that a club is outside s 2—however difficult it may be in such a case for the board to prove that it is within it. In truth the pleadings and the issues framed do not raise the proper issues. Accordingly, I would be in favour of allowing the appeal and remitting the case to the county court where either side would be at liberty to amend its pleadings.

Appeal allowed. Case remitted to the county court to proceed in accordance with the opinions expressed by the majority.

Solicitors: *Vizards* (for the appellants); *Lawford & Co* (for the board).

S A Hatteea Esq   Barrister.

---

1   [1972] 1 All ER 556, [1972] 1 QB 545
2   See [1972] 1 All ER at 561, 565, [1972] 1 QB at 557, 561

Barry v Hughes (Inspector of Taxes)

CHANCERY DIVISION
PENNYCUICK V-C
1st DECEMBER 1972

Income tax – Relief – Children – Child over the age of 16 receiving full-time instruction – Instruction at any university, college, school or other educational establishment – Other educational establishment – Meaning of education – Training of mind in contradistinction to training in manual skills – Taxpayer's son attending a training unit for the mentally subnormal – Training predominantly in factory work – Academic training every day or every alternate day – Whether unit educational establishment – Income and Corporation Taxes Act 1970, s 10 (2).

The taxpayer claimed child relief in respect of his son who was over the age of 16 at the commencement of the year of assessment. The son was attending on a full-time basis at an intensive training unit ('the unit') for the mentally subnormal between the ages of 15 to 30. The unit, which formed part of a hospital management group, provided training mainly in factory work. Apart from an hour's teaching in history, geography and mathematics, daily or on alternate days, the unit provided no other academic training. On the evidence the commissioners came to the conclusion that the unit was not an educational establishment within the meaning of s 10 (2)[a] of the Income and Corporation Taxes Act 1970 and disallowed the taxpayer's claim. On appeal by the taxpayer,

Held – The question the court had to decide was whether the unit was some kind of educational establishment other than a university, college or school. An educational establishment was one whose primary function was that of education, which, in the context of s 10 (2) of the 1970 Act, denoted training of the mind in contradistinction to training in manual skills. As by far the greater part of the activities of the unit was devoted to training in manual skills and only a very small proportion of the time was addressed to the training of the mind in a direct sense, it was reasonable for the commissioners to conclude that the unit was not an educational establishment. Accordingly the taxpayer's appeal would be dismissed (see p 543 f h and j and p 544 b and c, post).

Notes

For relief in respect of children over the age of 16 receiving full-time education, see 20 Halsbury's Laws (3rd Edn) 441, 442, para 824, and for a case on the subject, see 28 (1) Digest (Reissue) 448, 1602.

For the Income and Corporation Taxes Act 1970, s 10, see 33 Halsbury's Statutes (3rd Edn) 43.

Case referred to in judgment

Heaslip v Hasemer (1927) 13 Tax Cas 212, 138 LT 207, 28 (1) Digest (Reissue) 448, *1602.*

Case stated

At a meeting of the Commissioners for the General Purposes of Income Tax for the Division of West Brixton held on 10th December 1970, Leonard Thomas Barry ('the taxpayer') claimed that he was entitled to child relief in respect of his son,

---

a   Section 10 (2), so far as material, is set out at p 538 g, post

Michael, who was over the age of 16 at the commencement of the year of assessment   a
1969-70. At the relevant time the son attended as a day patient at the Sherwood
Intensive Training Unit run by the Manor Hospital Management Committee. The
commissioners dismissed the claim on the ground that the unit was not a recognised
educational establishment, college, university or school and that the education was
not full-time. Following a formal declaration of dissatisfaction by the taxpayer,
they stated a case. On 2nd December 1971 the appeal on that case stated came before   b
Megarry J who remitted the case to the General Commissioners. The commissioners
reheard the appeal and again dismissed the taxpayer's claim on the ground that the
intensive training unit was not a 'university, college, school or other educational
establishment'. The taxpayer declared his dissatisfaction with that decision and
required them to state a supplemental case. The original and the supplemental
cases are set out in the judgment.   c

The taxpayer appeared in person.
Patrick Medd for the Crown.

PENNYCUICK V-C. I have before me an appeal by Mr Leonard Thomas Barry   d
('the taxpayer') against a decision of the General Commissioners of Income Tax for
the Division of West Brixton. The appeal relates to a claim for child relief made
by the taxpayer in respect of his son Michael for the year ended 5th April 1970.
Very summarily, Michael was rather educationally backward, and after attaining
the age of 15 he spent two years as a day boy at the Sherwood Intensive Training
Unit, which is a training unit run by the Manor Hospital Management Committee.   e
The question before me today is whether that unit represents a 'school or other
educational establishment' for the purpose of s 10 of the Income and Corporation
Taxes Act 1970. Before proceeding further, I will read the relevant provisions of
that section:

> '(1) If the claimant proves—(a) that there is living at any time within the year   f
> of assessment a child of his with respect to whom one of the conditions in sub-
> section (2) below is fulfilled ... he shall, subject to the provisions of this section
> and section 11 below, be entitled in respect of each such child to a deduction
> from the amount of income tax with which he is chargeable equal to income tax
> at the standard rate on the appropriate amount for the child ...
> '(2) The conditions referred to in subsection (1) above are ... (b) that the child
> is over the age of sixteen years at the commencement of that year of assessment,   g
> but is receiving full-time instruction at any university, college, school or other
> educational establishment.'

Subsection (3) sets out the appropriate amount.

> '(4) The reference in subsection (2) (b) above to a child receiving full-time   h
> instruction at an educational establishment shall include a reference to a child
> undergoing training by any person (hereinafter referred to as "the employer")
> for any trade, profession or vocation in such circumstances that the child is
> required to devote the whole of his time to the training for a period of not less
> than two years ...
> '(6) If any question arises as to whether any person is entitled to relief under   j
> this section in respect of a child who is over the age of sixteen years, as being a
> child who is receiving full-time instruction at an educational establishment, the
> Board may consult the Secretary of State for Education and Science ...'

The case has had rather a lengthy course. The taxpayer's appeal first came before
the General Commissioners in December 1970, and they stated a case. Then, the

taxpayer's appeal on that case stated came before Megarry J on 2nd December 1971, and Megarry J, for reasons which will become apparent, remitted the case to the General Commissioners. The same General Commissioners then reheard the appeal, and they stated a supplemental case as a result of that rehearing. The taxpayer's appeal is now once again before the court on that supplemental case stated.

I shall first read the original case stated. Paragraph 1 states the hearing of the appeal. Paragraphs 2-7:

'2. The question for our decision was whether the child [that is Michael] was receiving full time instruction at any University, College, School or other educational establishment within Section 10 (2) (b) Income and Corporation Taxes Act 1970.'

'3. Oral evidence was given before us by the [taxpayer] and by the Respondent Inspector of Taxes. Also a letter from Mr. A. R. Worters M.B., D.P.M., Physician Superintendent of The Manor Hospital, Epsom, Surrey, dated 8th September 1970 with an accompanying timetable as from 5th February 1970 was produced. [I shall refer to that in a moment.] . . .

'4. The following facts were admitted or proved before us:—(a) The [taxpayer] received Dependent Relative Relief of £75 in respect of the Child in the year of Assessment 1969/1970. (b) Following Medical examination it had been determined that the Child was educationally sub-normal. (c) The Child attended Sherwood Intensive Training Unit (hereinafter called "Sherwood") a training unit run by The Manor Hospital Management Committee as a day patient. (d) "Sherwood" functioned as a mixed residential intensive training unit for adolescent, and young adult, relatively high grade sub-normal patients. (e) Although it was situated apart from the main hospital, it constituted part of The Manor Hospital Group and was, therefore, a National Health Service Establishment. (f) "Sherwood" was not recognised as an educational establishment. (g) "Sherwood" held no examinations and there was no academic training. [I interpose that that last finding requires qualification, in that it is now accepted that there was academic training in history, geography and arithmetic for one hour every day or every other day.] (h) At Sherwood the emphasis was on factory work at which the child earned about £1 per week. (i) The Child was born on the 28th January 1952, and was therefore over 16 years of age at the commencement of the year assessment.

'5. The [taxpayer] contended:—(a) The instruction given was full time education at Sherwood Intensive Training Unit at the Manor Hospital, Epsom, Surrey. (b) "The Child" attended as a daytime pupil as he had failed his 11 plus. (c) "The Child" was not resident at "Sherwood". (d) "The Child" earned £1 weekly pocket money from the special centre. (e) That he was entitled to the Child Allowance for his Son under Section 10 (2) [of the 1970 Act.]

'6. The Respondent Inspector of Taxes contended:—(a) That the Child was not receiving full time education at a University, College, School or other educational establishment. (b) "Sherwood" School at the Manor Hospital was not a recognised educational establishment. (c) "Sherwood" was a part of a therapeutic centre for the treatment of mentally handicapped or sub-normal young people and was not ejusdem generis with a University, college, school or other educational establishment. (d) "Sherwood" was a vocational centre. The object of the training was to try to remedy the mental deficiencies of the person concerned. (e) Such "education" as there was, was remedial and in no sense full time. (f) Under the terms of Section 10 (2) [of the 1970 Act] "the Child" failed to qualify for Child Relief.

'7. We, the Commissioners who heard the Claim having considered all the arguments, gave the following decision:—Under Section 10 [of the 1970 Act] The Claim for Child Allowance fails because (a) The education was not full time.

(b) Sherwood is not a recognised educational establishment, College, University   *a*
or School.'

And there was a formal declaration of dissatisfaction.

I should refer next to the letter from Mr Worters, which is referred to in that case. It is dated 8th September 1970 and runs as follows:

'Thank you for your enquiry of the 27th August. "Sherwood" functions as a   *b* mixed, residential, intensive Training Unit for adolescent/young adult, relatively high-grade subnormal and, in the minority of instances, psychopathic patients. Although it is situated apart from our main hospital, it does constitute part of The Manor Hospital group; therefore it is a National Health Service Establishment. So far as training is concerned, the emphasis during the working week is on factory work—being machine production of chain-link fencing and brushes,   *c* printing, and the assembly of electronic components on a sub-contract basis, the patients' ages ranging between 15 and 30. We attempt to develop all aspects of our patients' personalities, concentrating on facets which are known to be relevant in a particular patient's social incompetence. Thus, in addition to the factory training already mentioned, those patients in need receive daily remedial tuition on a one-teacher-to-one-patient basis—say, for 30-40 minute sessions and,   *d* as you will see from the provisional time-table enclosed, all patients also receive tuition in basic cookery and pottery. There is no fixed criteria so far as the maximum age to which patients may continue to receive remedial tuition and the additional subjects shown. It is widely known that the subnormal can continue to make excellent progress educationally well after the age when most children have left school. We therefore tend to ignore a patient's age, and plan   *e* his or her training programme almost entirely on his existing level, and inherent ability to profit from further tuition. It may well be observed that the "education" we give is in no sense full-time. However, our patients are often so disturbed during the early part of their stay with us that they are only able to benefit from tuition given on the basis described. In fact, many of the patients concerned have previously attended a Special School for the educationally subnormal, and   *f* have made relatively little academic progress when taught within a full-time class setting.'

Then, the time-table shows the daily routine at Sherwood. It starts with the hour at which patients living at Sherwood are called, and so forth. Michael's routine begins with 'Clock on—8.30'. I will not go through the time-table in detail, but basically the items in it are 'Factory Training Unit' repeatedly; 'P.E.', which I take it means physical   *g* exercises, on every day; 'Cookery' on certain days; and on every day but one a period of 'Remedial Tuition'.

When the case came before Megarry J he very properly took the point that the two grounds for the decision given by the commissioners contained two plain errors; first, the question posed by the statute is not one of 'full-time education' but one of 'full-time instruction'; and, secondly, the statute refers to 'any university, college,   *h* school or other educational establishment', and the word 'recognised', which appears in the commissioners' decision, is no part of the statutory language. He accordingly remitted the case to the commissioners for further hearing.

Before the further hearing, the commissioners, as they were entitled to do under s 10 (6) of the 1970 Act, consulted the Permanent Secretary of the Department of Education and Science. I shall not read the letter written on behalf of the commis-   *j* sioners, but perhaps I should point out that it omits to mention the one hour's teaching, daily or on alternate days, of history, geography and arithmetic. The answer, which is dated 23rd February 1972, is as follows:

'In reply to Mr Robertson's letter of February 10, I am directed by the Secretary of State to say that she has given careful consideration to all the information about the Sherwood Intensive Training Unit contained in the letter and in the provisional timetable for the Unit which was enclosed. She does not regard the training provided in this institution as constituting education in the sense with which she is concerned in the exercise of her functions as the Minister responsible for the promotion of education in England and Wales. The provisions of the Education (Handicapped Children) Act 1970 for the transfer of staff and property were ancillary to provisions relating to the education and training of children of compulsory school age. The Order made under the Act (The Education of Handicapped Children (Transfer of Staff and Property) Order 1971[1]) applied only in relation to institutions for training children classified under section 57 of the Education Act 1944 as unsuitable for education at school, that is to say, children not over the upper limit of compulsory school age. Neither the Act nor the Order had any application to this institution and it has not been recognised by the Secretary of State as a special school within the meaning of section 9 (5) of the Education Act 1944. It is understood that the Unit is provided by the South West Metropolitan Regional Hospital Board.'

I must pay due attention to that letter as representing a statement by the Minister of the place of Sherwood in the educational scene of things, but, it is not in dispute that the conclusion whether the condition referred to in s 10 (2) (b) is or is not fulfilled rests with the court.

After their second hearing, the General Commissioners stated a supplemental case as follows.

'2. The [taxpayer] gave evidence which we accepted that:—(a) Up to the age of 11 years, his Son Michael (hereinafter called "the Child") the subject of the Claim for child allowance, had attended an ordinary primary school but was found to be unsuitable to take the "11-plus" examination. (b) The Child was subsequently sent to the lowest stream in a secondary modern school where he became bewildered, confused and reluctant to attend. (c) As a result, the [taxpayer] succeeded in getting the Child to a remedial school, Chartfield. It was not so rough there but the Child still did not learn much and there was pressure from that School to get the Child to leave when he reached the age of 16 years. (d) The [taxpayer] came to the conclusion that the Child was not then capable of earning his own living and with the assistance of a doctor and a psychiatrist he succeeded in getting the Child into "Sherwood" which the Child attended daily from April 1969 to April 1971. (e) "Sherwood" was a new venture set up originally to provide some occupation for children roaming the wards at the Manor Hospital proper, but "Sherwood" did accept a few others who attended daily among whom were the Child. (f) "Sherwood" stood on its own a short way from the main hospital but probably in the hospital grounds. The "Sherwood" residents lived above the main workshop and diningroom and together with those who attended daily never came into contact with the hospital patients. There were about 30-40 patients in the workshop. (g) The Child left home at 7.30. a.m. and returned home at 5.30. p.m. on a five day week throughout his 2 year stay at Sherwood. The [taxpayer] could have taken the Child away at any time but it was arranged that he would stay at "Sherwood" until he was fit to work. It was originally thought that this would take longer than two years. (h) There was at "Sherwood" one qualified teacher paid on the Burnham scale. The Child was taught history, geography and arithmetic for an hour a day, or an hour every other day. The rest of the time was spent on "factory" work. The Child was engaged successively on the printing machine, for which he made up print; on the chain link fence machine; in operating the fly press producing

---

chassis for electronic components and soldering fitting and wiring up electronic
components to specification. The Child was, to-day engaged in similar work
that is the assembly of electronic components. Instruction in the "factory
work" was carried out by two full-time male instructors in the workshop.
(i) The Child was paid "pocket money" of £1. per week, as were the Sherwood
residents but only so as to make no distinction between the Child and residents.
The hospital received payment for the items produced in the workshop. (j) The
Child never received any medical treatment at "Sherwood".

  '3. Mr. M. A. Walker, Assistant Secretary of the Department of Education
and Science gave evidence, which we accepted pursuant to Section 10 (6) [of the
1970 Act.] Mr. Walker produced a copy of a letter dated 10th February 1972
. . . and his reply [I have already referred to those.] Mr. Walker then expanded the opinion contained in his letter as follows:—Education was not
defined by the statutes but was considered to be wider than purely academic subjects. He said that a helpful definition of training (as contrasted with education)
produced in the Department was "the systematic development of the attitude/
knowledge/skill pattern required by an individual in order to perform adequately a given task or job". Further education was a mixture of education and
training and in order to decide whether a particular course was "education" or
"training", the particular course had to be analysed. He illustrated this by
reference to a secretarial course which in addition to instruction in typing, gave
lessons in spelling and use of English—this would be regarded as educational,
whereas courses consisting of typing practice alone would be regarded as training. In the Department's "Special schools", education was very broad—such as
would help develop powers and capabilities beyond intellectual ability to enable
the subject to take a place in society. Often this might mean no more than
nursery education. However this did not include training in a repetitive process.
The factory training at "Sherwood" would not be included in the Department's
"Special schools". He thought there was not a lot of tuition at "Sherwood". The
emphasis was on training rather than education. He did not consider that
"Sherwood" was an educational establishment although some people got more
tuition than others. There was some training at technical colleges but it was the
overall character of the college syllabus which decided whether it was an educational establishment or not. In a technical college education would predominate
although some individual students might only be engaged in training. He did
not consider that the instruction in electronics which took place at Sherwood was
educational. So far as he was concerned some of it could be regarded as training
within Section 10 (4) [of the 1970 Act].

  '4. The [taxpayer] contended that there was full-time instruction. While he
agreed that "Sherwood" was not a university or college he contended that it
was a school or of the same nature as a school; that it came within the term
"other educational establishment". He maintained that there could be no denying that "Sherwood" was an "Establishment" and one had to look at the purpose
of that Establishment and the sole purpose of the establishment at "Sherwood"
was to educate. The [taxpayer] maintained that Michael had learned more in 2
years at "Sherwood" than he did in the previous schools. Education meant
developing and drawing out such mental capabilities and skills as the student
might have. He, Michael, had been educated to a point where he could now work
for his living. He had been educated and trained at "Sherwood" for 2 years—on a
full time basis.

  '5. For the Respondent, H. M. Inspector of Taxes it was contended that: (i) there
were three questions involved in the construction of Section 10 (2) (b) [of the
1970 Act], namely:—(a) Was there instruction? (b) Was the instruction full time?
(c) Was the instruction received at a University, College, School or other educational establishment? (ii) for the purpose of the present case it was not proposed

to make any distinction between "instruction" in respect of the "remedial tuition" and any "instruction" in the "factory work". (iii) As a result of the [taxpayer's] evidence, it was accepted that there was "instruction" and that this instruction was "full time". (iv) On the third point as to whether "Sherwood" was within the term "university college school or other educational establishment" (a) Sherwood was not a "university college or school". (b) The words "other educational establishment" had to be construed ejusdem generis with "university college or school" and "Sherwood" was not an "other educational establishment" on this basis. (c) A "university college school or other educational establishment" meant an establishment set up to provide education in the sense that the Department of Education and Science understood it.

'6. The Case of *Heaslip v. Hasemer*[1] was cited to us.

'7. We the Commissioners who heard the Claim originally as well as the supplementary evidence and having considered all the arguments, gave the following decision. On remission we find that, notwithstanding that Michael was receiving full time instruction, the claim under Section 10 (2) (b) [of the 1970 Act] the Child allowance must fail as "Sherwood" was not a University, College, School or other educational establishment within that Section.'

It will be observed that before the commissioners the Crown abandoned the claim based on 'instruction' or 'full-time instruction' and confined its case to the contention that Sherwood was not within the term 'university, college, school or other educational establishment'.

On the present appeal the taxpayer again appeared in person and, if I may say so, conducted his appeal admirably. The Crown was represented by Mr Medd. I will get one or two points out of the way before reaching what I think is the decisive point. In the first place, I think it is clear that the facts as put in evidence show that it was not a school in any ordinary use of that term. The question is: was Sherwood an 'other educational establishment'? I do not think that the argument based on ejusdem generis takes one very far. That would be an extremely important argument if the expression were 'university, college, school or other establishment'. With the word 'educational' in, all one has to do, so far as I can see, is to determine whether or not Sherwood is some kind of educational establishment other than a university, college or school. I should also mention at this stage, as I think is common ground, that the only case[2] cited does not advance the present question. What had to be considered by the commissioners and what I now have to consider bearing in mind their decision is whether Sherwood is properly to be described as an educational establishment. I do not think there was any argument on whether it is an establishment or not—I have no doubt it can properly be so described—but is it an educational establishment?

Looking at the matter apart from any finding on the facts of this particular case, an educational establishment must, I think, be an establishment whose primary function is that of education. In this context, and especially against the background of the legislation which has now culminated in s 10 of the 1970 Act, I think it is clear that 'education' denotes training of the mind, in contradistinction to training in manual skills. In the present case, by far the greater part of the activities carried on at Sherwood was addressed to manual skills, and a very small proportion of the time was addressed to training of the mind in a direct sense; that is to say, the hour every day or every other day during which history, geography and arithmetic were taught. On those facts, which are not in dispute, prima facie it seems to me that Sherwood could not properly be described as an educational establishment. The only escape

---

1 (1927) 13 Tax Cas 212
2 *Heaslip v Hasemer* (1927) 13 Tax Cas 212

from this conclusion, and perhaps a possible one, would be to say that the training in manual skills at Sherwood represented a therapeutic training of the mind; that is, that the mind was being trained therapeutically through exercises in manual skills. I say that is a possible conclusion on the facts, but I do not think I would put it any higher.

The commissioners, after hearing the Assistant Secretary of the Department of Education and Science and after taking into account the full particulars of what was done at Sherwood, came to the conclusion that Sherwood was not an educational establishment. It seems to me, to put it at its very lowest, that that was a conclusion to which reasonable commissioners, acting judicially and properly instructed, might have come, and I do not think it is a conclusion which I am entitled to disturb, even if I would myself have come to a different conclusion. I am very far from saying that I would have come to a different conclusion. To avoid misunderstanding I stress that, while the commissioners were entitled to have regard to what was said by Mr Walker, I am certainly not saying, as was apparently argued on behalf of the Crown, that the expression 'university, college, school or other educational establishment' means an establishment set up to provide education in the sense that the Department of Education and Science understands it. I think it means an establishment set up to provide education in the sense in which a judicial tribunal, first the commissioners and then the court, understands it after receiving such guidance as the Department of Education and Science has been able to afford it. I must accordingly dismiss this appeal.

Appeal dismissed.

Solicitor: *Solicitor of Inland Revenue.*

Rengan Krishnan Esq Barrister.

Halfdan Grieg & Co A/S v Sterling Coal & Navigation Corporation and another

QUEEN'S BENCH DIVISION

KERR J

10th, 29th NOVEMBER 1972

Arbitration – Special case – Direction by court – Direction to arbitrator to state question of law or award in form of a special case – Discretion of court – Exercise of discretion – Issue involving question of law – Discretion of court to refuse to direct statement of special case – Factors governing exercise of discretion – Arbitration Act 1950, s 21 (1), (2).

On 21st January 1964 the owners chartered their vessel to the charterers for 24 months from 29th March 1964. By an agreement dated 4th November 1964 the parties agreed to treat the vessel as redelivered on 30th October 1964. The agreement further provided for the terms on which the vessel could be operated by the owners and for compensation by the charterers to the owners for any loss sustained by them as a result of the premature termination of the charterparty. Until July 1965 the vessel was employed on voyage charters; thereafter she was fixed on a time charter differing in certain respects from the original charter. A dispute arose as to the true construction and effect of the agreement concerning the basis on which the vessel's earnings under the subsequent time charter were to be measured and the ultimate adjustment made. On the extreme contentions of the parties the amount at stake was some £57,000. In 1966 the matter was referred to arbitration. The arbitration hearing did not take place until 1972, a delay of nearly three years between 1969 and 1972 being due to inaction on the part of the owners. The parties were represented by solicitors and counsel and the tribunal consisted of two arbitrators and an umpire who were very experienced. At the end of the hearing, the owners asked the tribunal to state their award as a special case. The charterers opposed that request although both parties ultimately agreed a question of law on a 'without prejudice' basis. The arbitrators declined to state a special case and gave their reasons in a letter to both parties in which they stated, inter alia, that the dispute was 'more suitable for decision by a commercial arbitration tribunal than by the Courts since its interpretation is so closely allied to commercial practice and the interpretation that commercial men would give it'. They felt that as no principle of law was involved it was unnecessary from the point of view of both time and expense to trouble the court further. They delayed their award, however, so that the parties could apply to the court. The owners thereupon applied for an order directing the arbitrators, under s 21 (1)[a] of the Arbitration Act 1950, to state a special case for the opinion of the court in the terms of the agreed question of law. It was contended by the owners that, once it had been shown to the satisfaction of the court that the question of law was clear-cut, seriously arguable, raised bona fide, and substantial in the sense of being important to the determination of the dispute and to the parties, then a party was in effect entitled as of right to an appeal to the courts by the machinery of the special case under s 21 (1) of the 1950 Act.

---

a Section 21, so far as material, provides:
    '(1) An arbitrator or umpire may, and shall if so directed by the High Court, state—
    (a) any question of law arising in the course of the reference; or (b) any award or any part
    of an award, in the form of a special case for the decision of the High Court.
    '(2) A special case with respect to an interim award or with respect to a question of law
    arising in the course of a reference may be stated, or may be directed by the High Court to
    be stated, notwithstanding that proceedings under the reference are still pending . . .'

Held – (i) Even when a dispute submitted to arbitration involved one or more substantial questions of law which a party bona fide desired to raise by way of a special
case, the court retained a residual discretion whether or not in all the circumstances
to direct the tribunal to state a special case (see p 551 a and b and p 554 a, post); dicta
of Collins LJ in *Re Nuttall and Lynton and Barnstaple Railway Co* (1899) 82 LT at 19, 20
and of Megaw J in *Orion Compagnia Espanola de Seguros v Belfort Maatschappij voor
Algemene Verzekgringeen* [1962] 2 Lloyd's Rep at 266 applied.

(ii) Although the issue between the parties raised a question of law, it related solely
to the proper comparison of the earnings of a vessel under two time charters and was
well within the experience and capacity of the tribunal; the amount at issue was
large but by no means unusually high; the issue of law involved no consideration of
legal authorities and no identifiable question of principle; and the proceedings had
already taken six years, due in part to the inaction of the owners, and the request
for a special case would delay still further the resolution of the dispute. Accordingly
the application would be dismissed (see p 544 c to f, post).

Per Kerr J. (i) The fact that arbitrators who are untrained in law have allowed
persons trained in law to address them on legal points is not a factor that should influence the court to exercise its discretion in favour of directing the arbitrators to
state their award in the form of a special case (see p 552 e and g, post); dictum of
Scrutton LJ in *Czarnikow v Roth, Schmidt & Co* [1922] All ER Rep at 50 disapproved.

(ii) The true construction of a document is a question of law and the ultimate
arbiters on questions of law are the courts. The methods of construction adopted
by arbitration tribunals should not, therefore, differ from those applicable in the
courts nor can there be any tribunals better qualified to decide those issues than
the courts (see p 553 b c and g, post); *Woodhouse AC Israel Cocoa Ltd SA v Nigerian
Produce Marketing Co Ltd* [9721] 2 All ER 271 applied.

Observations on the factors which are relevant to the exercise of the court's
discretion under s 21 of the 1950 Act (see p 551 f to j and p 552 a, post).

Notes

For applications to compare the statement of a special case, see 2 Halsbury's Laws
(3rd Edn) 40, 41, para 91, and for cases on the subject, see 2 Digest (Repl) 580-582,
1122-1134.

For the Arbitration Act 1950, s 21, see 2 Halsbury's Statutes (3rd Edn) 450.

Cases referred to in judgment

Compagnie d'Armement Maritime SA v Compagnie Tunisienne de Navigation SA [1970]
3 All ER 71, [1971] AC 572, [1970] 3 WLR 389, HL; rvsg sub nom *Compagnie
Tunisienne de Navigation SA v Compagnie d'Armement Maritime SA* [1969] 3 All ER
589, [1969] 1 WLR 1338, [1969] 2 Lloyd's Rep 71, CA, Digest (Cont Vol C) 140, 721b.

Czarnikow v Roth, Schmidt & Co [1922] 2 KB 478, [1922] All ER Rep 45, 92 LJKB 81,
127 LT 824, 28 Com Cas 29, CA, 2 Digest (Repl) 580, 1117.

Nuttall and Lynton and Barnstaple Railway Co, Re (1989) 82 LT 17, CA 2 Digest (Repl)
581, 1130.

*Orion Compagnia Espanola de Seguros v Belfort Maatschappij voor Algemene Ver-
zekgringeen* [1962] 2 Lloyd's Rep 257, Digest (Cont Vol B) 28, 1499a.

Union-Castle Mail Steamship Co Ltd v Houston Line (London) Ltd (1936) 55 Lloyd LR
136 CA.

Woodhouse AC Israel Cocoa Ltd SA v Nigerian Produce Marketing Co Ltd [1972] 2 All
ER 271, [1972] AC 741, [1972] 2 WLR 1090, 13 KIR 45, [1972] 1 Lloyd's Rep 439, HL.

Summons

By an originating summons dated 17th October 1972, the owners, Halfdan Grieg &
Co A/S, the respondents in an arbitration reference in which the charterers, Sterling
Coal & Navigation Corporation and A C Neleman's Handel-en Transportonder-
neming, were claimants, sought an order pursuant to s 21 of the Arbitration Act 1950
that the arbitrators, Commander R L Sumpton and J Chesterman Esq, be directed

a   to state a question of law arising out of the arbitration reference in the form of a special case for the decision of the court. The hearing was in chambers but at the request of counsel judgment was delivered in open court. The facts are set out in the judgment.

Basil Eckersley for the owners.
C S Staughton QC and *P N Legh-Jones* for the charterers.

b

Cur adv vult

29th November. **KERR J** read the following judgment. The parties to this summons have asked for judgment in open court because they consider that it raises a question of principle on which differing opinions are held and on which there is no clear rule of practice. This question, briefly, is as to the nature and scope of the discre-
c   tion which the courts exercise under s 21 of the Arbitration Act 1950 in directing arbitration tribunals to state an award in the form of a special case for the opinion of the court on a question of law when the arbitration tribunal declines to do so.

The matter arises out of a dispute between the plaintiffs as owners and both defendants as charterers of the vessel 'Lysland'. The charterparty was concluded on
d   21st January 1964, for a basic period of 24 months, and the vessel was delivered on 29th March 1964. The charter would therefore normally have terminated at about the end of March 1966. However, by an agreement dated 4th November 1964, the parties agreed to treat the vessel as redelivered at the end of her then current voyage, which terminated on 30th October 1964. This agreement provided for the terms on which the vessel could thereafter be operated by the owners and for compensation
e   by the charterers to the owners for any loss which the owners might ultimately be found to have sustained as the result of the premature termination of the charter-party. The charterers were to pay a certain deposit to the owners by way of security for any such loss, and there was then to be an adjustment of the amount due after the expiry of the period of the original charter. There were provisions about adjust-ment of the deposit according to the vessel's earnings (as referred to in the agreement)
f   during the balance of the charter period, but it is unnecessary to set these out here.

The dispute was as to the true construction and effect of the agreement concerning the basis on which the vessel's earnings during this period were to be measured and the ultimate adjustment made. The relevant points were of course not argued before me, and no views of mine about them should be inferred from any language used in this judgment in describing the issue, but it is necessary shortly to set out
g   the main provisions of the agreement on which the issue turns and to state the respective contentions of the parties. Clause 1 provided that from the date when the vessel was to be treated as redelivered under the charter—

> 'the Owners to operate the vessel at their discretion and Owners are entirely free to fix the ship at their discretion including fixing her on timecharter for any period also in excess of the expiry of the timecharter period under [charterparty]
h   > dated 21st January 1964 and at a rate lower than dollars 3.00.'

Clause 5 provided that the deposit was to be returned to the charterers—

> 'if, for the balance of the timecharter period as per Charterparty of the 21st January 1964, the Owners are able to earn an amount equivalent to or exceeding dollars 3.00 less 2½% address commission on T/C [i e 'time charter'] basis. If
j   > the Owners earn less, the difference to be deducted from the amount deposited and the balance of the deposit, if any, to be returned to Timecharterers.'

The nature of the issue was shortly as follows: the owners contended that for the purpose of the adjustment one is only concerned to see how much was in fact received by them from the employment of the vessel during the balance of the charter period and to compare this with what they would have received under the original

charter. The charterers contended that the substitute sums actually received must
be adjusted to take account of differences between the value to the owners of the
original charter and of the vessel's substitute employment.

What had happened on the facts was that from the vessel's agreed premature re-
delivery on 30th October 1964 until 29th July 1965 she had been on tramping employment under voyage charters, and the parties were able to agree how this period was
to be dealt with for the purpose of the computation under cl 5. But thereafter the
vessel was fixed on a time charter which considerably exceeded the remaining
period of the original charter and which also differed from it in certain other respects
which the charterers contended to be material. A dispute accordingly arose about
the construction and effect of the agreement in relation to this latter charter and
about the relevance and effect, if any, of its differing features. I was informed that,
on the extreme contentions of the parties, the amount at stake is about £57,000.

This dispute was referred to arbitration. The owners (the plaintiffs on the present
summons) appointed Mr John Chesterman as their arbitrator, and the charterers
(defendants) appointed Commander R L Sumpton. The two arbitrators appointed
Mr Cedric Barclay as umpire. There was a hearing at which the parties were represented by solicitors and counsel. As is often done, the umpire was present at
the hearing, to avoid the necessity of a further hearing before him if the arbitrators
should disagree, but there has been no disagreement. At the hearing both parties
argued their respective submissions on the question of construction, and there was
also a good deal of evidence about the financial consequences which the charterers
contended to be material in comparing the original time charter with the substitute
time charter. The fact that most of the hearing was taken up by evidence and argument on the latter issues is one of the matters relied on before me as a ground for
not ordering a special case. But in my view this is of little weight since it was no doubt
convenient to deal with this evidence de bene esse without prejudice to the question
whether, on the true construction of the agreement, the evidence was material. I
have no doubt that the tribunal fully appreciated this, and would not thereby have
been led to overlook that the primary issue was one of construction. More relevant
to the present application is that neither side cited any authority to the tribunal,
although this was of course to be expected in relation to an issue which, on any
view, is a relatively short issue of construction.

The hearing took two days. At the end of the first day counsel for the owners
indicated that his clients would be asking for a special case, and counsel for the
charterers said that this would be resisted. At the end of the hearing this request
on behalf of the owners was made formally. There was then some discussion as to
what would be the question of law, and counsel ultimately agreed a question of law
on a 'without prejudice' basis. This is the question which appears in the summons
before me in the following terms, and which I am asked to direct the arbitrators to
state in the form of a special case:

> 'Whether, upon the facts found and upon a true construction of the agreement
> dated 4th November 1964 the amount that the vessel was able to earn in respect
> of the period between the 29th July 1965 and the 31st March 1966 falls, for the
> purposes of clause 5 of the said Agreement, to be assessed as:—(a) The sums
> actually received by Owners during that period under the time-charter dated
> the 9th June 1965, or (b) the above sums adjusted to take account of the differences
> between timecharters dated the 21st January 1964 and the 9th June 1965 in
> respect of (i) expiry date, and/or (ii) redelivery range, and/or (iii) commissions
> payable, and/or (iv) quality of fuel to be used.'

The two arbitrators then considered the matter and wrote a joint letter to the
parties' solicitors which I should set out in full. They say this:

> 'With reference to the [owners'] request that we should state our award
> in the form of a special case we have to advise you that we have decided not to do

so, for the following reasons:

'We did not feel that this was a proper case to be so stated. Whilst it may well be that there is a question of law, it is our feeling that whilst we do not presume to usurp the functions of the Court, it is more suitable for decision by a commercial arbitration tribunal than by the Courts since its interpretation is so closely allied to commercial practice and the interpretation that commercial men would give it.

'Counsel agreed that the Court's decision would add nothing to the wealth of law which is already available to us, and as there is no further principle of law involved, we feel it unnecessary, from the point of view of both time and expense, to trouble their Lordships further. We have also decided to delay the issue of our award for fourteen days so that the parties may, if they wish, apply to the Court.'

On receipt of this letter the owners issued the present summons, which asks for an order directing the arbitrators to state a special case for the opinion of the court in the terms of the agreed question of law.

Before dealing with the arbitrators' letter insofar as it is relevant, I must make it clear that both parties emphasised before me their full confidence in the experience, ability and of course the complete impartiality of the members of the tribunal. Indeed, it was pointed out that two of its three members were described as 'very experienced arbitrators' by Lord Wilberforce in *Compagnie d'Armement Maritime SA v Compagnie Tunisienne de Navigation SA*[1]. But, quite apart from this, the Commercial Court would of course take judicial notice of the fact that arbitrations such as the present before tribunals of the London Maritime Arbitrators Association or of other well known trade associations are composed of persons who have great experience and expertise in acting as arbitrators. They perform an important function and play a vital part in the determination of commercial disputes in this country. Most of such disputes have an international character, and the services rendered by such tribunals have for many years greatly contributed to making this country, and in particular the City of London, the most important centre for the resolution of international commercial disputes. On the other hand, for over 80 years it has also been a fundamental feature of our jurisprudence that arbitrators are subject to the law, and in a number of respects to the control of the courts. Perhaps the most important of these is the machinery provided by s 21, whereby arbitral tribunals may state a special case for the opinion of the court on any question of law arising in in the course of the reference, and are required to do so if the court so directs.

On the present summons the charterers conceded that a material and substantial question of construction involving a large sum of money arose in this arbitration, that this was a question of law and that it could be clearly defined, as it was by agreement on a 'without prejudice' basis. The charterers also in effect conceded, or at least did not challenge, that the owners were acting bona fide in requesting an order for a special case, and were not doing so merely for the purpose of further delay. Counsel's submission on behalf of the owners was, in effect, that this was sufficient to entitle the owners to the order asked for. He conceded that when a question of law arises in an arbitration, the court has some residual discretion whether or not to order a special case. Indeed, this is obvious from the use of the words 'may' in sub-ss (1) and (2) of s 21, which in themselves only become relevant in the event of 'a question of law arising in the course of the reference'. But he submitted that once it was shown to the satisfaction of the court that the question of law was clear-cut, seriously arguable, raised bona fide, and substantial in the sense of being important to the determination of the dispute and to the parties, then a party was in effect entitled as of right to an appeal to the courts on such question of law by the machinery of the special case.

Counsel for the charterers on the other hand contended that the discretion

1 [1970] 3 All ER 71 at 83, [1971] AC 572 at 594

whether or not to order a special case is much wider even if these requirements are satisfied in a particular case, and that it depended in each case on all the circumstances whether the discretion to direct the statement of a special case should be exercised or not. In this connection he mentioned a number of factors, to which I shall have to return, which would in his submission be relevant to the exercise of the discretion. Both counsel said that the present practice of the courts was unclear as to which was the correct test.

It is convenient first to deal with the authorities. Counsel for the owners cited a number of cases. Most of these arose out of arbitrations in which one party had asked for a special case but the arbitrators, unlike in the present case, had then proceeded to make an award without giving opportunity for an application to the court to direct the statement of a special case. This was repeatedly held to constitute misconduct on the part of the arbitrators, with the result that such awards were set aside unless the court considered that there was in any event no basis for a special case.

Counsel for the owners drew attention in these and other (for present purposes) similar cases to the words used in some of the judgments in describing the question of law, such as 'real and substantial', 'bona fide', etc. I do not find expressions such as these helpful for present purposes, since the courts were there simply describing the particular question of law raised before them, without seeking to lay down any general principle or to circumscribe the limits of the court's discretion.

There are only two authorities which are in my view of any real assistance, and both counsel relied on both of them. The first was *Re Nuttall and Lynton and Barnstaple Railway Co*[1] where Collins LJ, having dealt with the arbitrators having jurisdiction to state a special case[2], said:

'Indeed it is not contended that the court had no jurisdiction in this case. I think that no case has gone so far as to say that, upon a party showing that there is a point of law, the court would *ex debito justitiæ* order the arbitrator to state a special case. Therefore the line must be drawn somewhere between those two points. It seems to me that the dominant factors are, what is the nature of the point of law and what are the qualifications of the arbitrator for deciding the point in question? I think that the decisions have gone to this length, that if the court is satisfied that there is a real point of law, and that the arbitrator is not specially qualified to decide that point, the court will order the arbitrator to state a special case under sect. 19 of the Act.'

That was the precursor of the present s 21.

Secondly, in *Orion Compagnia Espanola de Seguros v Belfort Maatschappij voor Algemene Verzekgringeen*[3], Megaw J was dealing with disputes relating to quota share and re-insurance agreements, in which one of the issues was whether an arbitration tribunal should be ordered to state a special case on either or both of two alleged issues of law which they declined to do. The learned judge was not satisfied that there were any sufficiently clearly defined questions of law as distinct from issues of fact, and considered that insofar as questions of construction arose, those turned mainly on the meaning of technical terms in this field of insurance. But on the assumption that there were questions of law which could be defined sufficiently clearly, he went on to say, in relation to those alleged questions of law[4]:

'... looking at them even now, it seems to me that such questions of law as there were were questions which the Court would more likely than not, if the whole matter had been expounded to them at the time of an application for an order to state a case, have said: "No; these are questions on which, in our

1 (1899) 82 LT 17
2 (1899) 82 LT at 19, 20
3 [1962] 2 Lloyd's Rep 257
4 [1962] 2 Lloyd's Rep at 266

discretion, even if technically questions of law, we would not require these arbitrators or this umpire to state a case." '

In my view, both these passages point to the conclusion that even when a dispute submitted to arbitration involves one or more substantial questions of law which a party bona fide desires to raise by way of special case, there remains in the court a residual discretion whether or not in all the circumstances to direct the tribunal to state their award in the form of a special case. This has also always been my understanding of the legal position. The general principle is fairly stated in Halsbury's Laws of England[1], and it would in my view be undesirable to define to any greater extent than there indicated the circumstances in which a court will exercise its discretion in favour of requiring a case to be stated. It is there put as follows:

'The Court will not direct the arbitrator or umpire to state a special case unless (1) the applicant has in the first instance requested him to state a case and the request has been refused, and (2) the question of law on which the opinion of the Court is desired is material to the issues between the parties, and, having regard to all the circumstances of the case, is such as should be determined by the Court.'

I should add that the cases cited for this proposition do not in fact contain any such statement of general principle, but they are consistent with it.

Without in any way derogating from the generality of the court's discretion in the particular circumstances of each case, I think that it may be helpful, as submitted by counsel for the charterers, to mention by way of illustration some of the more important factors which are likely to be relevant in deciding whether or not to exercise the discretion. Many of these may not apply in particular cases and the list is of course not intended to be exhaustive, nor are the factors mentioned intended to be listed in any particular order. I should add that, although Collins LJ referred to two such factors as 'the dominant factors' in the *Nuttall* case[2], I do not think that he was intending to lay down any general principle where the line should be drawn in individual cases, nor even as to what should be 'the dominant factors' in all cases: see also per Greer LJ in *Union-Castle Mail Steamship Co Ltd v Houston Line (London) Ltd*[3].

I think that the following factors would be relevant in considering how the exercise of the discretion should be approached insofar as they may be applicable in any particular case, but without any single one being by itself likely to be decisive: (a) the qualifications and experience, insofar as known to the court, of the arbitral tribunal, both in general and in relation to the particular dispute; (b) where the question is one of construction, whether the construction involves consideration of any technical terms or against the background of any particular industry, trade or market of which the tribunal has some specialised knowledge; (c) in general, and also where the question of law is one of construction, whether the answer requires or would be assisted by recourse to statutes, decided cases or textbooks; (d) whether an authoritative answer to the question of law by the court is likely to be of assistance in resolving future disputes or in introducing a measure of uniformity; for instance the construction of provisions in standard forms of contracts or the decision of issues on which the court is informed that different arbitrators have taken different views; (e) the amount involved in the dispute or the importance of the decision to the parties for any other reason; (f) the consequences of the delay likely to result from the special case procedure with its possibilities of further appeals, together with the question whether there has already been undue delay, in particular by the party seeking the statement of a special case; (g) whether the court forms the impression on any material before it that the arbitration tribunal is likely to reach a conclusion which is wrong in law or that it has shown any tendency in some way to behave unjudicially. This could arise in a variety of ways. There might, for instance, be

1 3rd Edn, vol 2, p 40, para 91
2 (1899) 82 LT at 19
3 (1936) 55 Lloyd LR 136 at 137

material indicating that the tribunal did not appreciate that any question of law was involved, or that it had refused a request for a special case out of hand without being willing to listen to the grounds on which it was requested; similarly, if the tribunal had in some way indicated that it was accepting a submission or proceeding on a basis which the court could see was likely to be erroneous in law.

There is one other general matter which I should mention. Counsel for the owners strongly relied on the well-known decision of the Court of Appeal in *Czarnikow v Roth, Schmidt & Co*[1]. This contains the classic passages in the judgments of Bankes, Scrutton and Atkin LJJ on the importance of maintaining the special case machinery as part of our legal system. It is unnecessary to set them out here; they were set out in the judgment in the *Orion* case[2]. But there is one passage in the judgment of Scrutton LJ which counsel for the charterers submits should not be put in the balance when considering whether or not to direct a special case. Speaking about lay arbitrators, Scrutton LJ said[3]:

> 'When they are persons untrained in law, [and then I italicise] *and especially when as in this case they allow persons trained in law to address them on legal points*, there is every probability of their going wrong, and for that reason Parliament has provided in the Arbitration Act [1889] that, not only may they ask the Courts for guidance and the solution of their legal problems in special cases stated at their own instance, but that the courts may require them, even if unwilling, to state cases for the opinion of the Court on the application of a party to the arbitration if the Courts think it proper.'

I have italicised the words which counsel for the charterers submits should not nowadays carry any weight. I agree with this submission. Times have changed since this judgment was delivered 50 years ago; so have the prevalence of arbitrations and the experience of persons who frequently or regularly act as arbitrators in specialist disputes. I think that arbitrators are nowadays probably much more used to being addressed by lawyers than in the past. There is now a close relationship and co-operation between specialist arbitration tribunals and the courts, in particular the commercial court. This is also shown by the fact that probably more than half of the work of the commercial court arises out of references to arbitration and that the new machinery set up by s 4 of the Administration of Justice Act 1970 is beginning to be used whereby judges nominated to be commercial judges can accept appointment as sole arbitrators or umpires subject to obtaining the permission of the Lord Chief Justice. I have no doubt that arbitration tribunals are now much more in touch with legal developments in their specialist fields than in the past. In these circumstances I cannot think that it would nowadays be right to suggest that they are more likely to go wrong in law as the result of having been addressed by counsel or solicitors. On the contrary, in cases of doubt this factor should in my view be placed in the other scale, although by itself it is in any event unlikely to play any major part in any individual case.

Finally, I would add two further points. First, it seems to me that all the foregoing remarks apply equally to the initial discretion exercised by an arbitration tribunal whether or not to accede to a request for a special case as they do to the controlling discretion exercised by the courts. Secondly, I think that borderline cases should be decided in favour of stating or directing special cases, because in cases of doubt parties should not be shut out from arguing a question of law in the courts.

Having dealt with the general principle, I now turn to consider how the discretion should be exercised in the present case. The first matter is the arbitrators' letter giving their reasons for declining to state a special case. This has been criticised by counsel for the owners. I agree that the middle paragraph is open to comment, if

1   [1922] 2 KB 478, [1922] All ER Rep 45
2   [1962] 2 Lloyd's Rep at 263, 264
3   [1922] 2 KB at 488, [1922] All ER Rep at 50

not criticism. It can be read to imply that this agreement should be interpreted in some special way, so as to give it a meaning other than that which would be given to it in the courts, because it is 'so closely allied to commercial practice and the interpretation that commercial men would give it'. Lay arbitrators are bound to hold views about the interpretation which commercial men would put on an agreement in their specialist field and about particular factors which would be regarded as relevant to its construction. But this is no ground whatever for declining to state a special case, since such material, if thought to be relevant, can thereby be placed before the court as part of the reasoning underlying the primary award. The important point about this passage in the arbitrators' letter is that there is always danger in any suggestion or tendency on the part of arbitration tribunals to employ methods of construction which differ from those applicable in the courts and which form part of the law of the land. The true construction of a document is a question of law, and the ultimate arbiters on questions of law are the courts. This elementary but fundamental principle was recently re-stated by the House of Lords in *Woodhouse AC Israel Cocoa Ltd SA v Nigerian Produce Marketing Co Ltd*[1]. That case also provides a clear illustration of the dangers inherent in any doctrine that the true legal meaning of documents may differ according to whether they are construed by commercial men or by the courts. The trade umpire in that case, in which very large sums of money were involved, held that one party had by certain letters made statements which the other party 'reasonably regarded' as representing that certain contractual terms had been varied. Counsel seeking to uphold the resulting special case did not even seek to argue that the correspondence on its true construction could constitute such a variation, and this court, the Court of Appeal and the House of Lords were unanimously of the same view. One of the main points in the case was accordingly whether the umpire's conclusions relating to the correspondence could amount to findings of fact which bound the courts. This was negatived because the meaning and effect of documents is a question of law for the courts and not one which could be concluded by any finding of fact in a special case, however expressed. It follows that if the award in that case had not been made in the form of a special case for the opinion of the court, then an issue of great importance to the parties, albeit only an issue of construction, would have been decided between them finally and without appeal and contrary to law.

The other point on which comment can in my view justifiably be made about the arbitrators' choice of language in the letter before me is that it suggests in the same passage that a commercial arbitration tribunal would be 'more suitable' than the courts to decide the question of construction which arises in the present case. I think that the arbitrators might have contented themselves with echoing the language of Smith LJ in the *Nuttall* case[2] referred to above, where he said: 'Some points of law can be as easily decided by the arbitrator as by the Court', although it is also to be noted that he added 'some points of law cannot'. Since issues concerning the true interpretation of documents are issues of law (apart from the ascertainment of the meaning of techical terms or of words having a particular meaning in a special context) it follows that there cannot by our legal system be any tribunals which are better qualified to decide these issues than the courts. Counsel for the charterers submitted that a passage in the judgment of the *Orion* case[3] suggests the contrary; but in my view this is not so. It will be seen that the learned judge there qualified his remarks by the express assumption that the arbitrators 'had directed themselves correctly in law'. Further, all that he was there saying was that, on this assumption, the views of an arbitration tribunal specialised in insurance business might be preferable to those of the court on the question whether certain alleged misrepresentations

---

1   [1972] 2 All ER 271, [1972] AC 741
2   (1899) 82 LT at 19
3   [1962] 2 Lloyd's Rep at 266

and non-disclosures would be material in influencing the judgment of a prudent insurer. As the learned judge pointed out, assuming that the tribunal had correctly directed itself on the law, such matters would then primarily be questions of fact. The governing passage of the judgment[1] for present purposes, which I have already set out and respectfully follow, is to the effect that even if a reference to arbitration involves the decision of questions of law, the court retains a discretion not to require the statement of a special case.

I have spent some time commenting on the language used by the arbitrators in their letter because it is important that this should not be allowed to give rise to any misunderstanding and because it is open to some criticism. But I do not regard the arbitrators' language as any indication that they are liable to misconstrue the agreement, so as to lead me to the conclusion that they should on this ground be directed to state a special case. I think that they merely mean that because this agreement lies in their specialist field, they are quite capable of interpreting it correctly. With this I agree. I have come to the conclusion that in all the circumstances of this case the proper exercise of the discretion is that I should not direct the statement of a special case. The sole issue is the proper comparison of the earnings of a vessel under two time charters. The problem of construction is simply whether under the agreement of 4th November 1964 these earnings are to be compared solely on a cash basis, or whether certain adjustments require to be made to achieve the comparison which the parties intended. Although this issue undoubtedly raises a question of law, I think that it is one which is well within the experience and capacity of this tribunal, which has great experience of legal disputes relating to shipping matters, including of course many questions of construction of agreements in this field. The amount involved is admittedly considerable, but by no means unusually high by present-day standards. The issue of law involves no consideration of legal authorities and no identifiable question of principle. I also attach importance to the fact that the dispute arises out of an agreement made eight years ago and that this arbitration was instituted as long ago as 1966. On the evidence before me, a delay of nearly three years between 1969 and 1972 appears to have been due to inaction on the side of the owners, who have been in possession of a substantial deposit for more than seven years since this was claimed back by the charterers. The owners' request for a special case at this stage would therefore inevitably still further delay the resolution of this long-standing dispute.

It is however necessary to emphasise that my decision not to direct the statement of a special case on this application should not be taken as any indication, any more than happened as the result of the decision in the *Orion* case[2] ten years ago, that special cases should be stated less frequently in future than in the past. If one takes the criteria put forward by counsel for the owners, that is to say, a clear-cut question of law which is seriously arguable, substantial in the sense of being important for the resolution of the dispute and to the parties, and which is raised bona fide and not merely for the purpose of delay, then I would expect that in the great majority of cases in which these criteria are satisfied, special cases will in future, as in the past, be stated on request or, if necessary, directed by the courts. All that I am deciding in this case is that: (a) even where these criteria are satisfied, there is no entitlement as of right to a special case but a residual discretion in the arbitrators and a controlling discretion in the courts; and (b) although these criteria are admittedly satisfied here, I consider that in the particular circumstances of this case the court's discretion should not be exercised.

Summons dismissed. Leave to appeal granted.

Solicitors: *Sinclair, Roche & Temperley* (for the owners); *Thomas Cooper & Stibbard* for the charterers).

Janet Harding   Barrister.

---

1   [1962] 2 Lloyd's Rep at 266
2   [1962] 2 Lloyd's Rep 257

Mavani v Ralli Brothers Ltd

QUEEN'S BENCH DIVISION
KERR J
27th OCTOBER, 6th NOVEMBER 1972

Arbitration – Costs – Security for costs – Claimant ordinarily resident out of the jurisdiction – Residence – Deemed residence under contract for purposes of arbitration – Claimant resident in Pakistan – Contract subject to trade association rules – Contract providing that party resident outside United Kingdom to be considered as resident in London – Whether court's jurisdiction to order security for costs may be ousted by agreement – Arbitration Act 1950, s 12 (6) (a) – RSC Ord 23, r 1.

Arbitration – Costs – Security for costs – Claimant ordinarily resident out of the jurisdiction – Just in all the circumstances to order security – Arbitration proceeding on basis of written documents – General practice not to order security unless oral hearing – Circumstances in which security should be ordered – Arbitration Act 1950, s 12 (6) (a) – RSC Ord 23, r 1.

By a contract incorporating the rules and regulations of the Refined Sugar Association ('the association') the sellers agreed to sell and the buyer to buy a quantity of sugar cif Karachi. The buyer ordinarily resided and carried on business in Karachi. The association's rules provided for the reference to arbitration of disputes. Such disputes were to be settled according to English law. Rule 6 (a) provided: 'Any party to a contract residing or carrying on business outside the United Kingdom shall, for the purposes of proceedings at law or in arbitration, be considered as ordinarily resident or carrying on business at the Consulate (or equivalent official residence) in London of the country of his residence or place of business'. The council of the association was empowered by the rules to decide a case on the written documents submitted to it without an oral hearing. A dispute arose out of the contract between the parties and the buyer gave notice of arbitration under the association's rules. The arbitration thereafter proceeded on written contentions with annexed supporting documents which had reached the stage of rejoinder. The issues raised by the dispute were complex and at the stage of reply the written contentions and annexed documents amounted to some 50 pages. The sellers applied under s 12 (6) (a)ᵃ of the Arbitration Act 1950 for an order for security for costs under RSC Ord 23, r 1ᵇ, on the ground that the buyer was ordinarily resident out of the jurisdiction. The buyer contended, inter alia, that the court had no jurisdiction to make the order, since, by virtue of r 6 (a) of the association's rules, he was to be considered as resident and carrying on business in England.

Held – (i) The jurisdiction of the court to order security for costs could not be ousted by agreement between the parties. Accordingly r 6 (a) of the association's rules did not preclude the court from proceeding on the basis of the undisputed fact that the buyer was ordinarily resident in Karachi. It followed that the court had jurisdiction to order security for costs against the buyer (see p 559 j and p 560 a d f and j, post).

(ii) The provisions of r 6 (a) were not such as to render an order for security for costs unjust. Although it would be unjust for the court to order security where the agreement provided that, in the event of arbitration proceedings, neither party would apply for such an order, no such agreement could be implied from the terms of r 6 (a). Furthermore r 6 (a) had nothing to do with the merits of the grounds of the application; the fact that the buyer was to be considered as resident in London did not secure the sellers' position on costs in any way (see p 560 f g and j to p 561 a d and e, post).

ᵃ Section 12 (6), so far as material, is set out at p 557 c, post
ᵇ Rule 1 (1) (a), so far as material, is set out at p 557 e, post

(iii) In the circumstances of the case it was just that an order for security for costs should be made. Although in general the courts would not order security more or less automatically in an arbitration proceeding on documents merely because one of the parties was resident outside the jurisdiction, in the instant case the circumstances were exceptional. Not only would an order for costs be difficult to enforce in Pakistan against the buyer, but the issues raised by the buyer on the written contentions were complex and, in consequence, the sellers had already reasonably incurred substantial costs in solicitors' and counsel's fees (see p 562 b to d and f to h, post).

Notes

For the power to order security for costs in arbitration proceedings, see 2 Halsbury's Laws (3rd Edn) 36-38, paras 82, 86.

For the circumstances in which security for costs may be ordered in the High Court, see 30 Halsbury's Laws (3rd Edn) 378-380, para 706, and for cases on security for costs when plaintiff resident abroad, see 51 Digest (Repl) 973-976, 5092-5074.

For the Arbitration Act 1950, s 12, see 2 Halsbury's Statutes (3rd Edn) 444.

Cases referred to in judgment

Aeronave SPA v Westland Charters Ltd [1971] 3 All ER 531, [1971] 1 WLR 1445, CA.
Becker, Shillan & Co and Barry Brothers, Re [1921] 1 KB 391 [1920] All ER Rep 644, 90 LJKB 316, 124 LT 604, DC, 2 Digest (Repl) 695, 2096.
British Controlled Oilfields Ltd v Stagg (1921) 127 LT 209, 11 Digest (Repl) 377, 412.
Hudson Strumpffabrik GmbH v Bentley Engineering Co Ltd [1962] 3 All ER 460, [1962] 2 QB 587, [1962] 3 WLR 758, [1962] 2 Lloyd's Rep 90, Digest (Cont Vol A) 45, 2423a.
Scott v Avery (1856) 5 HL Cas 811, [1843-60] All ER Rep 1, 25 LJEx 308, 28 LTOS 207, 2 Jur NS 815, 10 ER 1121, HL, 2 Digest (Repl) 465, 290.

Summons

By a summons dated 31st July 1972 the sellers, Ralli Brothers Ltd, the respondents to an arbitration reference by the buyer, Badrudin H Mavani, applied for an order that the buyer give security for the sellers' costs in the arbitration proceedings on the grounds that he was ordinarily resident out of the jurisdiction and that in the meantime all further proceedings in the arbitration be stayed. The summons was heard in chambers but at the request of both parties judgment was delivered in open court. The facts are set out in the judgment.

Stewart Boyd for the sellers.
M Dean for the buyer.

Cur adv vult

6th November. **KERR J** read the following judgment. I adjourned this summons into open court because it raises a question of some general importance in connection with applications for security for costs in arbitrations under the rules of certain trade associations. In this case the point arises under the 'Rules Relating to Arbitration' of the Refined Sugar Association. Under a contract made on 21st October 1965 the claimant in the arbitration was the buyer and the respondents the sellers of a quantity of Czechoslovakian sugar sold cif Karachi subject to the rules and regulations of the Refined Sugar Association. It is not disputed that the buyer ordinarily resides and carries on business in Karachi. A dispute arose under the contract in that the buyer contends that the documents tendered by the sellers against the letter of credit were tendered late or did not correspond with the contract and that the buyer suffered loss in consequence for which he is claiming damages. On 4th November 1971, about six years after the contract, the buyer gave notice of arbitration under the rules of the association. The arbitration is at present proceeding on written contentions with annexed supporting documents. I understand that these have reached the stage of rejoinder and that a surrejoinder is contemplated. I have seen a the contentions and annexed documents up to and including the stage of reply and they already amount to about 50 pages.

For convenience I will refer to the applicants and the respondent to this summons as the sellers and buyer to avoid confusion with the inverse positions as respondent and claimant which they occupy in the arbitration. On this summons the sellers apply for an order that the buyer should give security to cover the costs of the present b stage of the arbitration, that is to say up to the stage of the oral hearing if there is to be one, on the ground that the buyer is ordinarily resident out of the jurisdiction. The buyer resists this application, the main ground of objection being that under the rules relating to arbitration he is for the purpose of proceedings at law and by arbitration to be considered as resident here.

The application is made under s 12 (6) (a) of the Arbitration Act 1950. Section 12 (6) c provides:

'The High Court shall have, for the purpose of and in relation to a reference, the same power of making orders in respect of—(a) security for costs . . . as it has for the purpose of and in relation to an action or matter in the High Court: Provided that nothing in this subsection shall be taken to prejudice any power which may be vested in an arbitrator or umpire of making orders with respect d to any of the matters aforesaid.'

The court's powers in connection with the ordering of security for costs are now governed by RSC Ord 23, of which r 1 (1) (a) is the material provision for present purposes. Rule 1 (1) provides:

e 'Where, on the application of a defendant to an action or other proceeding in the High Court, it appears to the Court—(a) that the plaintiff is ordinarily resident out of the jurisdiction . . . then if, having regard to all the circumstances of the case, the Court thinks it just to do so, it may order the plaintiff to give such security for the defendant's costs of the action or other proceeding as it thinks just.'

f It is common ground between the parties that the provisions of this rule apply equally when the application for security is made in an arbitration as in an action. The authorities on this point were reviewed by Mocatta J in relation to the predecessor of the present rule in *Hudson Strumpffabrik GmbH v Bentley Engineering Co Ltd*[1]. This case was followed by the Court of Appeal and applied in relation to the present rule in *Aeronave SPA v Westland Charters Ltd*[2]. The later case also shows that the question g for the court under the present rule is simply to decide in each case which falls within its terms whether or not it is just in all the circumstances to order a plaintiff (or as here a claimant in an arbitration) to give security. Apart from the consideration that at present this is an arbitration proceeding purely on written submissions and may never come to an oral hearing, the claimant would no doubt normally be ordered to give security. But apart from the general question of discretion, the buyer relies h on the 'Rules Relating to Arbitration' of the association and submits that they are part of the contract between the parties (with which I agree) and that the sellers' application for security is inconsistent with them. The latter is the main point on this summons. I must read some of these rules. Rule 2 provides:

'A party to a contract which is subject to the Association Rules Relating to Arbitration who wishes to refer a dispute to arbitration shall, after giving to j the other party seven clear days' notice by registered mail . . . refer in writing the matter in dispute to the Council for arbitration. The Council shall thereupon have power to determine as hereinafter provided any such matter in dispute . . .'

---

1 [1962] 3 All ER 460, [1962] 2 QB 587
2 [1971] 3 All ER 531, [1971] 1 WLR 1445

Rule 4 provides:

> 'For determination of a dispute the Council shall appoint not less than five persons from the Panel of Arbitrators to act on its behalf . . .'

I must read rr 5, 6 and 7 in full.

> '5. For the purpose of all proceedings in arbitration, the contract shall be deemed to have been made in England, any correspondence in reference to the offer, the acceptance, the place of payment or otherwise notwithstanding, and England shall be regarded as the place of performance. Disputes shall be settled according to the law of England wherever the domicile, residence or place of business of the parties to the contract may be or become.
>
> '6. (a) Any party to a contract residing or carrying on business outside the United Kingdom shall, for the purposes of any proceedings at law or in arbitration, be considered as ordinarily resident or carrying on business at the Consulate (or equivalent official residence) in London of the country of his residence or place of business. (b) Any party to a contract residing or carrying on business either in Scotland or Northern Ireland shall, for the purpose of any proceedings at law or in arbitration, be considered as ordinarily resident or carrying on business at the offices of the Association, and he shall be held to have submitted to the jurisdiction of the English Courts.
>
> '7. The service of any proceedings, upon a party residing or carrying on business outside the United Kingdom by delivering the same at the appropriate Consulate (or equivalent official residence) and upon a party residing or carrying on business either in Scotland or Northern Ireland by delivering the same at the office of the Association together with the posting of a copy of such proceedings to the address abroad, or in Scotland or Northern Ireland, of such party, shall be deemed good service, any rule of law or equity to the contrary notwithstanding.'

Then r 8 contains a *Scott v Avery*[1] clause making arbitration a condition precedent to action and I need not read it. Rule 10 is a long rule which provides for the submission of disputes to the association by the delivery by the claimant of a statement of case, by the respondent of a defence, in each case with any supporting documents on which they wish to rely. It then gives each party a further period of 21 days or such extended time as the council may permit within which to submit further written comments and/or documents in reply to the other party's last submission (and then I quote) 'until the Council shall in its absolute discretion decide to proceed to make its award'. Rule 10 then goes on as follows, and I must read this:

> 'The Council may in its discretion decide the case on the written statements and documents submitted to it without a *viva voce* hearing. The Council may however, call the parties before it, and request the attendance of witnesses, or the provision of further documents, or information in written form, and may also consult the legal advisers of the Association. In the event of a hearing, with or without witnesses, each party shall appear either personally or by any agent engaged in the trade and duly appointed in writing, but shall not be represented or appear at the hearing by counsel or solicitor unless special leave shall have previously been obtained in writing from the Council, which leave the Council may grant or refuse in their absolute discretion and without assigning any reason. One party shall not, however, make any oral statement in the absence of the other, excepting in the case of his opponent's representative failing to appear after notice has been given him by the Secretary . . .'

Then I can pass to rules 11 and 12 which I must read in full:

---

1   (1856) 5 HL Cas 811, [1843-60] All ER Rep 1

a
'11. A non-returnable registration fee of £25 shall be paid to the Secretary upon any reference to arbitration. The Council may if it thinks fit at any time require either party to the arbitration to deposit with the Secretary such sum as the Council may think fit on account of the fees, costs and expenses in connection with or arising out of the arbitration.'

Rule 12 falls into three paragraphs. The first is as follows:

b
'The arbitration fees shall be in the discretion of the Council in every case, provided always that the amount of the fees payable in respect of any one arbitration shall not be less than £60 and shall be paid by whom the Council shall determine.'

Then:

c
'Any costs incurred by the Association or by the Council, including the expenses incurred in obtaining legal assistance, copies of the documents or evidence, short-hand notes, etc., may be added to such fees.'

And finally:

d
'In the event of either or both parties having been granted permission by the Council to be legally represented at the hearing, the Council may take into consideration any legal costs which have been incurred.'

The issues in the present summons turn mainly on rr 6 (a) and 12. On 23rd March 1972 the solicitors acting for the sellers applied to the association for security for costs under r 11 in the provisional sum of £300. On the following day the secretary of
e
the association replied that in the view of the legal adviser of the association r 11 dealt only with the costs of the association. It gave no power to order security for the costs incurred by the parties. He added that this was, and always has been, also the view of the association. It is settled law that unless a submission to arbitration expressly empowers an arbitral tribunal to order security for costs the tribunal has no such power. This is no doubt why the court was given this power under what
f
is now s 12 of the Arbitration Act 1950. Whether or not the construction placed on r 11 by the association and their legal adviser is correct is not an issue directly before me. But I can appreciate the reasons underlying this view, particularly in the context of r 12 to which I will come later.

In opposition to the present application two main points were taken by counsel for the buyer. First, he submitted that the application was inconsistent with r 6 (a),
g
so that the exercise of the general discretion under RSC Ord 23, r 1, could not arise and the application must fail in limine. He put his contention both on the agreement and on estoppel. He said that, the parties having agreed that the buyer was for the purpose of any proceedings at law or in arbitration to be considered as resident at the office of the High Commission of Pakistan in this country, the sellers could not now apply for security on the basis that the buyer was in fact ordinarily resident in
h
Karachi. Secondly and alternatively he said that by reason of r 12 no question of costs might in any event arise unless there was an oral hearing with legal representation, which there might never be. He therefore submitted that it was inconsistent with the association's rules to apply for security for costs to cover the present stage, which might be the final stage and not merely the interlocutory stage.

Counsel for the sellers submitted, first, that irrespective of the effect of the rules
j
relating to arbitration the power of the court under s 12 (6) (a) of the Arbitration Act 1950 could not be ousted by agreement between the parties. His submission was mainly founded on the fact that this provision does not contain words such as 'unless a contrary intention is expressed in the arbitration agreement' which one finds in many other provisions of the Act, in particular in s 12 (1), (2) and (3). He therefore submitted that no question of jurisdiction could arise in relation to the court's power

under s 12. Counsel for the buyer did not directly challenge this submission and in
my view it is right. Section 12 deals with much which Parliament may well have
regarded as fundamental for the proper administration of justice in arbitrations and
outside any agreement between the parties. It refers, for instance, in s 12 (4), (5) and
part of (6) to the right of the parties to summon witnesses to give evidence or to produce documents and to the powers of the court to order evidence to be given by
affidavit or to have witnesses examined otherwise than before the arbitrator. But
this is only the starting point. One then comes to RSC Ord 23 under which the court
exercises the discretion whether or not to order security which is conferred on it by
s 12 of the Arbitration Act 1950. As to this, counsel for the sellers submitted that the
jurisdiction underlying the exercise of the discretion vested in the court depends on
what appear to the court to be the true facts and not on any agreement between the
parties whereby fictitious facts are deemed to exist. He drew attention to the words
'if it appears to the court'. He cited as an illustration of a somewhat similar position a
dictum of Sargant J in *British Controlled Oilfields Ltd v Stagg*[1]. Sargant J there said
obiter that the court had no jurisdiction to give leave to issue a writ for service out of
the jurisdiction on the ground that a contract had been made in England when
the contract had in fact been made in New York but provided that it should be considered and held to have been made in England. Counsel therefore submitted that
r 6 (a) of the association's rules could not preclude the court from approaching the
sellers' application for security on the basis of the true facts and to decide on the basis
of the true facts whether or not it was just to order security. Counsel for the buyer
challenged this entirely. His argument in relation to RSC Ord 23 was in effect that at
this point the jurisdiction of the court either stopped or that in view of r 6 (a) the
court was bound to decline to make the order without being able to go into the
merits of whether or not it would be just to do so. He said that by agreement or
estoppel or both the sellers were in effect precluded from applying for security on
the ground that the buyer was resident outside the jurisdiction.

Having considered the matter I cannot accept counsel for the buyer's argument.
In my view the jurisdiction of the court under RSC Ord 23 is not ousted by a provision
such as r 6 (a). This is not to say that the parties cannot incorporate into their agreement or submission to arbitration provisions which would make it obviously unjust
in all the circumstances to order security. If for instance a contract provides that in the
event of proceedings neither party will apply for security, then although the court
would still technically have jurisdiction to exercise its discretion under RSC Ord 23,
it would obviously decline to make the order because in the face of the agreement
of the parties it would be unjust to do so. The question whether or not there should
be security for costs is one which only affects the parties inter se, not the administration of justice in general. The court would therefore in my view give effect to any
clear agreement between the parties which regulates this question. But does the
present case fall within this principle? The position can be tested as follows. Suppose
that it were clear that in all the circumstances security should be ordered in a certain
case and that the only factor militating against this conclusion is r 6 (a) itself. Would
r 6 (a) then be a ground for refusing security? In my view the answer is No. For
the reasons already stated r 6 (a) cannot touch the court's jurisdiction under RSC
Ord 23. In the present case it not only appears to the court that the buyer is
ordinarily resident in Karachi; the fact that he is so resident and carrying on business
there and not here is undisputed. There is therefore in my view no doubt about jurisdiction. Would it then be unjust to order security in all the circumstances? If the only
circumstance which could be placed in the scales against such an order is r 6 (a),
then the answer is in my view again No for two reasons. First, r 6 (a) has nothing
to do with the merits of the grounds of the application at all. If in all the circumstances
an order for security would be just and a refusal unjust, then r 6 (a) does not alter

---

1   (1921) 127 LT 209 at 210

the merits of the position in any way. The fact that the buyer is to be considered
a as resident at the office of the High Commission of Pakistan does not secure the sellers'
position on costs in any way. Secondly, I cannot extract from r 6 (a) any implication
to the effect that the parties have agreed that neither of them would apply for
security for costs, so as to render an order for security unjust. If that had been the
intention it would have been easy to say so, and I would have given effect to the
parties' agreement. I think that r 6, together with rr 5 and 7, forms part of a complex
b of provisions designed to remove all possible difficulty about the proper law of the
contract and about service of process under RSC Ord 11. The latter type of agreement
is now permitted to a limited extent by RSC Ord 10, r 3. I appreciate that r 7 can be
said, as counsel for the buyer submits, to deal with service of process independently
from r 6. But this is merely an argument based on the superfluity of certain provisions in these somewhat old-fashioned rules which is not strong. It can, for instance,
c equally be applied to the first sentence of r 5. It also seems to me, although I have
not considered this in detail since it was not mentioned by counsel, that the argument
addressed to me by counsel for the buyer on the basis of r 6 (a) cannot be applied to
r 6 (b) because residence in Scotland or Northern Ireland would not found an
application for security. It cannot therefore be contended that the whole of r 6 was
intended to oust any application for security for costs. For these reasons I cannot
d regard r 6 as an agreement, or in any event as a sufficiently clear agreement, that
neither party will apply for security for costs so as to have the effect of rendering an
order for security unjust if in all the circumstances apart from r 6 such an order
would be just.

I therefore reject the buyer's contentions that r 6 (a) in effect bars this application
or predestines the court's exercise of its discretion against such an application.
e Counsel for the buyer's second argument was that no order should be made because
the question of costs might never arise at all. He relied on the third paragraph of
r 12 and sought to infer from this and from that part of r 10 which I have read that
unless the arbitration went to an oral hearing, which it might not, no order for costs
would or could in any event be made. In my view this submission is untenable. An
arbitration on documents and written submissions is still an arbitration. Any award
f in such an arbitration, as in any other arbitration, is incomplete and will be remitted
to the arbitral tribunal if it does not deal with costs: see *Re Becker Shillen & Co and
Barry Brothers*[1] for the general principle. Further, to construe the rules in the way
submitted by counsel for the buyer would lead to the construction that if an arbitration ensues and is limited to written submissions and documents without an oral
hearing, then each party will in any event pay its own costs. But if this were the
g right construction of r 10 read with the third paragraph of r 12, then this result
would be void under s 18 (3) of the Arbitration Act 1950. This provides:

'Any provision in an arbitration agreement to the effect that the parties or
any party thereto shall in any event pay their or his own costs of the reference
or award or any part thereof shall be void, and this Part of this Act shall, in the
h case of an arbitration agreement containing any such provision, have effect as
if that provision were not contained therein: Provided that nothing in this subsection shall invalidate such a provision when it is part of an agreement to submit
to arbitration a dispute which has arisen before the making of that agreement.'

I therefore consider that the third paragraph of r 12 is not to be construed in the way
for which counsel for the buyer contends. As in the second paragraph of that rule,
j and in my view also in r 11, the reference to 'costs' is best regarded as a reference to
the costs of the association. The third paragraph of r 12 is not very clear, but I think
that it was probably intended to mean that if there is a hearing with legal representation, which is therefore likely to render the arbitration more complex and longer,

---

1   [1921] 1 KB 391, [1920] All ER Rep 644

then the additional costs thereby incurred can also be taken into consideration by the
association when fixing the level of its fees. I say this because it seems to me that the
whole of r 12 is concerned with the fees payable to the association. But whether
the arbitration goes to an oral hearing or not, and whether with or without legal
representation, it will be the duty of the association in its award to deal with costs
in the proper and usual manner, and I have no doubt that the association is fully
conscious of this.

There then remains the final question which is one of pure discretion. Is it just in
all the circumstances of this case to make an order for security as asked? Apart from
the fact that at the present stage this is still only an arbitration on written submissions
and documents, I have no doubt that the answer should be Yes. The buyer is ordinarily resident and carrying on business in Pakistan. There is no suggestion that he
has any assets within the jurisdiction. I unhesitatingly accept the evidence that an
order for costs would be difficult to enforce against him in Pakistan and that there
would be considerable difficulty in securing the remission of the proceeds of such
enforcement. But the point on which my mind has wavered is the factor that at
present this is only a contest on documents. Generally speaking I do not think
that the courts should order security for costs more or less automatically in an
arbitration proceeding purely on documents on the ground that one of the parties is
resident outside the jurisdiction, as it generally does in an action. I also do not believe
that this is the practice of the courts. Each year countless international arbitrations
are decided on the Baltic Exchange and before other trade associations on documents
alone between parties of whom one, and very often both, carry on business abroad
and not in this country. It may then be a matter of chance which party initiates the
proceedings as claimant. The purpose and value of such arbitrations is that they
should be conducted and decided with the minimum of complexity, delay and
expense. This purpose would be substantially weakened if the practice in such
arbitrations were to order the claimant more or less automatically to give security
for costs solely because he is not ordinarily resident within the jurisdiction, as is
the general practice in relation to actions in the courts. In an ordinary arbitration
which proceeds simply on documents and written submissions I would therefore
generally exercise my discretion against such an order. But this is not an ordinary
case. The written contentions have already reached the stage of rejoinder and are
likely to go at least as far as a surrejoinder. The issues raised by the buyer are complex.
I say nothing about their merits. The pleadings up to and including reply already
cover about 50 pages together with the annexed documents. The sellers have already
incurred substantial costs in solicitors' and counsel's fees, and in my view the employment of solicitors and counsel was perfectly reasonable in the light of the issues
raised by the buyer. I therefore consider that in these circumstances it would be just
to order security for costs and that it would be unjust to refuse such an order. I
will therefore hear counsel on the question of quantum, as to which there is some
conflicting evidence on the affidavits before me.

Order that the buyer give security for the sellers' costs.

Solicitors: *Clifford-Turner & Co* (for the sellers); *Stocken & Co* (for the buyer).

Janet Harding   Barrister.

a   # The Trustees Executors and Agency Co Ltd and others v Inland Revenue Commissioners

CHANCERY DIVISION
PENNYCUICK V-C

b   20th, 21st, 24th NOVEMBER 1972

Estate duty – Exemption – Property situate out of Great Britain – Ship – Ship situate within jurisdiction but registered abroad – Testator dying domiciled in Australia – Testator owner of yacht – Yacht berthed in England – Yacht registered in Jersey – Executors required to obtain probate and registration in Jersey in order to perfect title to yacht – Whether yacht to be
c   *treated as 'situate out of Great Britain' for estate duty purposes – Finance Act 1949, s 28 (2).*

The testator, a British subject, was the owner of a yacht registered in Jersey. He died domiciled in the State of Victoria in Australia. The yacht was normally berthed at Southampton and was there at the date of his death. The executors sold the
d   yacht but, in order to perfect their title under the Merchant Shipping Act 1894, they were obliged to obtain registration in Jersey. For that purpose they had to produce a Jersey probate to the registrar of ships in Jersey. The executors claimed that the yacht was exempt from estate duty since it was to be treated as being, at the date of the testator's death, 'situate out of Great Britain' within s 28 (2)[a] of the Finance Act 1949. They contended (i) that, prior to 1894, since title could only have been perfected by probate and registration in Jersey, a vessel registered in Jersey would
e   not have required probate in England and consequently probate duty would not have been payable in respect of her under the Stamp Act 1815; and (ii) that since 1894 estate duty covered the same field as probate duty, with the consequence that the exemption from estate duty in respect of property situate out of Great Britain was applicable to a ship registered in Jersey.

f   **Held** – The yacht was not 'property . . . situate out of Great Britain', within s 28 (2), and accordingly was not exempt from estate duty. Before 1894 a vessel registered in Jersey but situate in England would have been an item of personal estate within the jurisdiction of the English courts. As such, a grant of probate by the English court would have been required under the 1815 Act before a personal representative could have dealt with the vessel. That requirement would not have been displaced
g   by the need for probate in Jersey also. In consequence, probate duty would have been payable in respect of the vessel. Although in general there might be grounds for attributing to a vessel on the high seas an artificial situs at her port of registry, when she was within territorial or national waters the artificial situs was displaced by the actual situs (see p 565 d, p 566 d to g and p 568 g and h, post).

h   **Notes**
For exemption from estate duty in respect of property situate out of Great Britain, see 15 Halsbury's Laws (3rd Edn) 56-59, paras 111-116, for cases on foreign property where deceased domiciled abroad, see 21 Digest (Repl) 39, 147-149, and for cases on domicil and situs for the purpose of probate duty, see ibid 181-183, 1070-1088.
j   For the Finance Act 1949, s 28, see 12 Halsbury's Statutes (3rd Edn) 645.

Cases referred to in judgment
Attorney-General v Bouwens (1838) 4 M & W 171, 1 Horn & H 319, 7 LJEx 297, 150 ER 1390, 21 Digest (Repl) 181, 1072.

---

a   Section 28 (2), so far as material, is set out at p 564 j to p 565 b, post

Attorney-General v Dimond (1831) 1 Cr & J 356, 1 Tyr 243, 9 LJOSEx 90, 148 ER 1458,   *a*
   21 Digest (Repl) 181, *1070*.
Attorney-General v Hope (1834) 8 Bli NS 44, 2 Cl & Fin 84, 1 Cr M & R 530, 4 Tyr 878,
   5 ER 863, HL, 21 Digest (Repl) 181, *1071*.
Compania Naviera Vascongado v Steamship Cristina [1938] 1 All ER 719, [1938] AC 485,
   107 LJP 1, 159 LT 394, 19 Asp MLC 159, HL, 1 Digest (Repl) 129, *154*.
Stapleton v Haymen (1864) 2 H & C 918, 3 New Rep 481, 33 LJEx 170, 9 LT 655, 10   *b*
   Jur NS 497, 159 ER 380, 42 Digest (Repl) 638, *3916*.
Winans v Attorney-General [1910] AC 27, 79 LJKB 156, 101 LT 754, HL, 21 Digest (Repl)
   5, *1*.

Originating summons

The plaintiffs, The Trustees Executors and Agency Co Ltd, Sir George Whitecross   *c*
Paton, Sir Charles Gullan McGrath, Hugh Dean Thomas Williamson and John
Samuel Gale, surviving executors of the will dated 9th August 1960, and two codicils
thereto, of William Lionel Buckland, deceased, took out an originating summons,
asking the court to determine whether the motor yacht 'Natalie', which formed
part of the free estate of the deceased and whose port of registry was in the island
of Jersey, was property situate out of Great Britain within the meaning of s 28 (2) of   *d*
the Finance Act 1949 at the date of the death of the deceased and thereby exempt
from estate duty on his death.   The facts are set out in the judgment.

Martin Nourse QC and *J Maurice Price* for the executors.
N C H Browne-Wilkinson QC and *P L Gibson* for the Crown.

Cur adv vult   *e*

24th November.   **PENNYCUICK V-C** read the following judgment.   On this
summons the plaintiffs are the personal representatives of one William Lionel
Buckland (to whom I shall refer as 'the testator') and the defendants are the Commissioners of Inland Revenue.   The summons raises a single question as to the liability
for estate duty of a yacht called 'Natalie', whose port of registry was in Jersey but   *f*
which was ordinarily kept in a yard in Southampton and was there at the date of the
testator's death.
   The facts are not in dispute.   The testator died in the State of Victoria, Australia,
on 22nd November 1964.   It is accepted by the Crown that he died domiciled in
Victoria, and that the proper law regulating the disposition of his personalty was
that of Victoria.   In April 1959 the testator purchased the yacht from a Lady Crane,   *g*
who lived in Jersey.   The yacht was registered in Jersey, and remained so registered
at the death of the testator.   Jersey is one of the countries in which a register book
of British ships is kept pursuant to the Merchant Shipping Act.
   The testator made cruises of about two months average duration in the yacht from
1959 to 1963 inclusive, but during the remainder of the time the yacht was normally
berthed in the yard of Camper and Nicholsons Ltd at Southampton, where it was at   *h*
his death.   Particulars of the yacht's movements are in evidence.   In 1965 the testator's executors sold the yacht for £40,000.   In order to perfect their title under the
Merchant Shipping Act, they were obliged to obtain registration in Jersey, and for
this purpose they had to obtain a probate in Jersey and produce it to the registrar of
ships there.   There was unchallenged evidence as to Jersey law on this matter.
   The relevant fiscal provisions in force at the date of the testator's death are the   *j*
general charging provision in s 1 of the Finance Act 1894, which I need not read, and
the exempting provision now contained in s 28 (2) of the Finance Act 1949, which reads
as follows:

   'As respects property passing on the death of a person dying after the commencement of this Part of this Act, subsection (2) of section two of the Finance

a Act, 1894 (which exempts from estate duty property situate abroad and not chargeable with legacy duty or succession duty), and section twenty-four of the Finance Act, 1936 (which restricts the exemption conferred by the said sub-section (2)), shall not have effect; but that property shall be deemed for the purposes of estate duty not to include any property passing on the death which is situate out of Great Britain if it is shown that the proper law regulating the devolution of the property so situate, or the disposition under or by reason of *b* which it passes, is the law neither of England nor of Scotland and that one at least of the following conditions is satisfied, namely,—(*a*) that the deceased did not die domiciled in any part of Great Britain . . .'

I need not read any further. The sole question is whether the yacht should be treated as having been situate out of Great Britain at the date of death. As I have indicated, *c* the remaining conditions of exemption are admittedly satisfied.

There is no doubt that the yacht was physically situate in Great Britain at the death of the testator. Equally, in case that should be relevant, there is no doubt that it was not there for some merely temporary purpose. I should mention at the outset that admittedly a ship does not, for the general purposes of the law, possess an artificial local situation, e g a situation dependent on its port of registry. *d* For the purposes of the general law, a ship situate locally in England is treated as indeed possessing that local situation. Contrast the position of choses in action, such as shares in a company, which have no actual local situation and to which, accordingly, an artificial local situation has to be attributed.

Counsel for the plaintiff executors based his case on the law prevailing before 1894 in relation to probate duty. His arguments may, I think, be fairly summarised in *e* this way. Probate duty would not have been payable in respect of a ship registered in Jersey; and estate duty covers the same field as probate duty. Therefore, one must construe the exemption from estate duty in respect of property situate out of Great Britain as applicable to a ship registered in Jersey.

Probate duty was an ad valorem stamp duty reimposed by the Stamp Act 1815: see ss 2, 37 et seq and Part 3 of the Schedule to that Act. Before the passing of the *f* Probate Act 1857 probate was granted by the ecclesiastical court. Broadly, the subject matter of probate was personal estate and effects within the jurisdiction of the ecclesiastical court. Section 37 of the 1815 Act prohibits any person from taking possession of any part of the personal estate and effects of any person who is deceased without obtaining probate. Section 38 provides that no ecclesiastical court shall grant probate without receiving from the applicant an affidavit that the estate and effects of the *g* deceased for or in respect of which probate is to be granted are under the value of the sum which is therein specified. Part 3 of the Schedule sets out the rates.

On the face of these provisions, it appears perfectly clear that probate duty was chargeable in respect of the entire personal estate and effects of the deceased person situate at his death within the jurisdiction of the relevant ecclesiastical court, i e in effect, the United Kingdom. On the other hand, it was early established that probate *h* duty was not chargeable in respect of assets situate at the death outside the United Kingdom, since these were not assets in respect of which probate fell to be granted: see *Attorney-General v Dimond*[1] and in particular per Lord Lyndhurst CB[2]:

'But probate is not granted in respect of the assets generally, but in respect of such part of them as are at the testator's death within the jurisdiction of the spiritual judge by whom it is granted';

j and, again[3]:

'It could not be granted for or in respect of it, because the property was, at

---

1 (1831) 1 Cr & J 356
2 (1831) 1 Cr & J at 370
3 (1831) 1 Cr & J at 371

the death of the testator, in a foreign country, and consequently out of the
jurisdiction of the spiritual judge.'

And contrast *Attorney-General v Bouwens*[1] and in particular per Lord Abinger CB[2]:

'By [the 1815 Act] a certain duty is granted on probates, "in proportion to the
value of the estate and effects for and in respect of which such probate shall be
granted;" and the law has been settled by the two cases of *The Attorney-General
v. Dimond*[3] and *Attorney-General v. Hope*[4] that the duty is to be regulated, not by
the value of all the assets which an executor or administrator may ultimately
administer by virtue of the will or letters of administration, but by the value of
such part as are at the death of the deceased within the jurisdiction of the spiritual
judge by whom the probate or letters of administration are granted. The question is, therefore, whether these securities are to be considered as assets locally
situate within the province of Canterbury at the time of the testatrix's death.'

The securities were bonds of a foreign government, and it was held that they were
situate in this country.

Counsel for the executors contended that inasmuch as title to a ship registered in
Jersey could be perfected only by registration in Jersey on production of a Jersey
probate, such a ship would not have been an asset in respect of which probate had to
be granted in England and accordingly probate duty would not have been payable in
respect of it. It is difficult to be over-positive as to the ambit of a long since obsolete
statute; but it seems to me that the requirement of probate and registration in Jersey
could in no way displace the requirement of probate in England under the 1815
Act. The ship would have been an item of personal estate within the jurisdiction
of the relevant ecclesiastical court in this country, and as such would have required
a grant of probate by the ecclesiastical court before a personal representative could
deal with it in this country. That appears to be the clear effect of the provisions of
the 1815 Act. I do not see why this requirement should be displaced by the need for
probate elsewhere. There is, of course, nothing unusual in a grant of probate being
required in more than one country. That is the ordinary position where a foreigner
leaves personal property in this country. What is unusual is the need for a further
grant of probate in the country of registration. Once it is accepted that the ship
would fall within the requirement of probate by the ecclesiastical court, it must
unequivocally fall within the charge of probate duty.

I should mention two statutory provisions enacted between 1815 and 1894, in which
latter year estate duty supplanted probate duty. The Revenue (No 2) Act 1864,
s 4, provides:

'... Be it enacted, that the said stamp duties [that includes probate duty] shall be
charged and paid in respect of the value of any ship or any share of a ship belonging to any deceased person which shall be registered at any port in the United
Kingdom, notwithstanding such ship at the time of the death of the testator or
intestate may have been at sea or elsewhere out of the United Kingdom; and
for the purpose of charging the said duties such ship shall be deemed to have
been at the time aforesaid in the port at which she may be registered.'

That section imposes a notional local situation on ships registered at any port in
the United Kingdom. One might perhaps have expected a corresponding provision
with regard to ships registered at a foreign port, but such a provision is conspicuously
absent and it seems to me impossible to imply such a provision.

1 (1838) 4 M & W 171
2 (1838) 4 M & W at 190, 191
3 (1831) 1 Cr & J 356
4 (1834) 8 Bli NS 44

a

Then, the Revenue Act 1884, s 11, provides:

> 'Notwithstanding any provision to the contrary contained in any local or private Act of Parliament, the production of a grant of representation from a court in the United Kingdom by probate or letters of administration or confirmation shall be necessary to establish the right to recover or receive any part of the personal estate and effects of any deceased person situated in the United
b   Kingdom . . .'

That section imposes in express terms an obligation to produce a probate in order to establish the right to receive any part of the personal estate and effects of any deceased person situated in the United Kingdom. It is not clear precisely why it was thought necessary to enact that express provision over and above the provisions contained in the 1815 Act. The section is significant in that it contains, so far as
c   counsel have been able to ascertain, the first use of the expression 'situated in the United Kingdom' in connection with duty. Counsel for the executors contends that probate duty would not have been payable on a ship registered in Jersey, and that accordingly such a ship cannot be regarded as situated in the United Kingdom within the meaning of those words in that section. Section 11 is not a new charging
d   section, but its wording rather underlines the difficulty in the way of counsel's previous contention.

Although the view which I have taken as to the scope of probate duty concludes the matter against counsel's contentions, I should mention the final step in those contentions. Section 2 (2) of the Finance Act 1894, now superseded by s 28 (2) of the Finance Act 1949, ran as follows:

e

> 'Property passing on the death of the deceased when situate out of the United Kingdom shall be included only, if, under the law in force before the passing of this Act, legacy or succession duty is payable in respect thereof, or would be so payable but for the relationship of the person to whom it passes.'

Counsel for the executors pointed out, truly, that estate duty has taken the place of
f   probate duty and relied on *Winans v Attorney-General*[1] where the members of the House of Lords made a full analysis of the relationship between probate duty and estate duty: see, for example, per Lord Loreburn LC[2]:

> 'The Act of 1894 is in that respect analogous not to the Legacy and Succession Duty Acts, but to the old Probate Duty Acts, which it supersedes in so far as they cover common ground. No doubt the estate duty covers more than did the
g   probate duty.'

The other learned Lords made statements to a similar effect, although one at least is perhaps slightly more favourable to counsel's view. I refer to the speech of Lord Atkinson[3].

h   Counsel for the executors then contended that, since a ship registered in Jersey would not have been within the charge of probate duty, it should likewise be treated as property situate outside the United Kingdon for the purposes of estate duty. For the reasons given, I do not think the premise of this argument is well founded. If the premise were correct, the conclusion would not on the face of it follow from the premise. But at this stage s 11 of the Revenue Act 1884 might have a considerable impact. If indeed a ship registered in Jersey was not to be treated as 'situated in the
j   United Kingdom' within the meaning of s 11, that would be a weighty argument for putting a corresponding limitation on the scope of the words 'situate out of the

---

1   [1910] AC 27
2   [1910] AC at 30
3   [1910] AC at 35

United Kingdom' in s 2 of the 1894 Act; and likewise, of course, the words 'situate out of Great Britain' in s 28 of the 1949 Act. It would not be useful to pursue this hypothetical question further.

On the facts of the present case, it is immaterial whether an asset brought to the United Kingdom for a purely temporary purpose, and coincidentally in the United Kingdom when its owner dies, should be regarded as situate in Great Britain for the purpose of duty. I deliberately abstain from expressing any view on that question.

I have in this judgment referred simply to the Merchant Shipping Act. The Act now in force is that of 1894: but the 1894 Act is a consolidating Act, and the merchant shipping legislation goes back far before that date, and accordingly into the period when probate duty was in force. I was taken in some detail through certain provisions of the 1894 Act, but I think it is only useful to refer specifically, without reading them, to ss 27 and 28, which deal with transmission. Nothing in those sections could affect the liability of personal representatives to probate duty.

I was referred to authority which established that the purchaser of a ship acquires ownership irrespective of registration although under the Merchant Shipping Act his title requires to be perfected by registration: see *Stapleton v Haymen*[1]. The significance of these cases seems to me to be only marginal here, and I do not intend to quote from them.

It is common ground that the point raised by the summons is not covered by judicial authority. Perhaps I may conclude with two textbook citations. Dymond on Death Duties[2], in a chapter headed 'Locality of Assets' and a paragraph headed 'Ships and Aircraft' states:

'Ships and shares of ships, registered at a British port, were for Probate Duty purposes deemed to be situate there under s.4 of the Revenue (No. 2) Act, 1864, but it is doubtful whether s. 4 was incorporated for Estate Duty purposes by the Finance Act, 1894 . . .'

Dicey and Morris on The Conflict of Laws[3] contains this paragraph:

'*Exception* 1.—A merchant ship may at some times be deemed to be situate at her port of registry. Comment: "A ship is not like an ordinary personal chattel", and although the question has never fallen for decision in England there are dicta indicating that a ship is situate in law at her port of registry and not where she is physically situate from time to time. This rule has been adopted for a limited purpose by the legislature [and it then refers to s 4 of the 1864 Act] and would seem to be both convenient and sound in principle when the vessel is upon the high seas. Where, however, a vessel is within territorial or national waters the reasons for ascribing her a *situs* at her port of registry are less compelling, and it would seem that the artificial *situs* is displaced by the actual *situs*. Thus the English courts will not recognise the validity of a foreign government's interference with vessels wearing its flag present within English waters.'

For the reasons which I have given, I agree with the statement in the penultimate sentence of that comment, i e so far as a ship registered abroad and locally situate here is concerned, the artificial situs is displaced by the actual situs.

In view of its high authority, I should quote a sentence from Lord Wright's dictum in *Compania Naviera Vascongado v Steamship Cristina*[4] which is among the dicta referred to by Dicey. What Lord Wright said was this[5]:

---

1 (1864) 2 H & C 918
2 14th Edn (1965), p 1055
3 8th Edn (1967), pp 516, 517
4 [1938] 1 All ER 719, [1938] AC 485
5 [1938] 1 All ER at 733, [1938] AC at 509

a 'It must also be noted in the present case that the Cristina, even when in Cardiff docks, may have, as being a foreign merchant ship, a status different from that of an ordinary chattel on land.'

That statement does not go very far.

I propose to make a declaration on the present summons that the motor yacht known by the name of 'Natalie' (following the wording of the summons) was property
b not situate out of Great Britain within the meaning of s 28 (2) of the Finance Act 1949, and was accordingly liable for estate duty on the death of the testator.

Declaration accordingly.

Solicitors: *Radcliffes & Co* (for the executors); *Solicitor of Inland Revenue.*

c   Rengan Krishnan Esq Barrister.

Tak Ming Co Ltd v Yee Sang Metal Supplies Co

PRIVY COUNCIL
d LORD WILBERFORCE, VISCOUNT DILHORNE AND LORD PEARSON
25th OCTOBER, 11th DECEMBER 1972

Judgment – Order – Correction – Accidental slip or omission – Res judicata – Claim by plaintiffs for damages and interest – Judgment awarding damages only – Accidental omission of award of interest – Application by summons inter partes for award of interest – Summons
e *dismissed for want of jurisdiction – Subsequent application under slip rule for amendment of judgment by inclusion of award of interest – Whether court precluded from amending judgment by reason of dismissal of earlier summons.*

The respondents brought an action against the appellants in the Supreme Court of Hong Kong. By their statement of claim the respondents claimed the balance of a sum of money owing to them and interest thereon. Pickering J gave judgment
f in favour of the respondents on the issue of liability, the amount owing to be assessed, but omitted to make an award of interest. The judgment was not read but handed down in open court and the omission was not noticed by counsel before leaving court. Subsequently the balance owing was assessed and a few days later the respondents applied by a summons inter partes for an order that interest should be paid by the appellants on that sum. The summons was heard by Briggs J in chambers
g and dismissed on the ground that he had no jurisdiction to make an award of interest after delivery of judgment. Subsequently the respondents applied by notice of motion for an order that Pickering J's judgment be amended under the slip rule by the inclusion of an award of interest. The application was heard by Pickering J and he decided that the correction should be made. His decision was affirmed by the Full Court. On appeal the appellants contended that Pickering J was
h precluded from correcting his judgment by the subsequent judgment of Briggs J.

Held – The order correcting his judgment had been properly made by Pickering J. The matter was not res judicata since the claim for interest had not been adjudicated on by Briggs J, there being only a denial of jurisdiction (see p 574 c and f and p 575 a, post).

j   *Pinnock Brothers v Lewis & Peat Ltd* [1923] 1 KB 690 applied.
      Reichel v Magrath (1889) 14 App Cas 665, *Ayscough v Sheed Thomson & Co* (1923) 92 LJKB 878, and dictum of Lush J in *Ord v Ord* [1923] All ER Rep at 212 distinguished.

Notes
For correction of clerical and accidental mistakes, see 22 Halsbury's Laws (3rd Edn) 786-788, para 1666, and for cases on the subject, see 50 Digest (Repl) 530-535, 1970-2022.

Cases referred to in opinion

Ayscough v Sheed Thomson & Co (1923) 92 LJKB 878, 129 LT 429, 39 TLR 206, CA;
    affd (1924) 93 LJKB 924, 131 LT 610, 30 Com Cas 23, HL, 2 Digest (Repl) 450, *183*.

Hatton v Harris [1892] AC 547, 62 LJPC 24, 67 LT 722, HL, 50 Digest (Repl) 531, *1977*.

Inchcape, Re, Craigmyle v Inchcape [1942] 2 All ER 157, [1942] Ch 394, 111 LJCh 273,
    167 LT 333, 50 Digest (Repl) 533, *1998*.

Moore v Buchanan, Buchanan v Moore-Pataleewa [1967] 3 All ER 273, [1967] 1 WLR 1341,
    CA, Digest (Cont Vol C) 1091, *2013a*.

Ord v Ord [1923] 2 KB 432, [1923] All ER Rep 206, 92 LJKB 859, 129 LT 605, DC, 21
    Digest (Repl) 198, *1*.

Pinnock Brothers v Lewis & Peat Ltd [1923] 1 KB 690, 92 LJKB 695, 129 LT 320, 28 Com
    Cas 210, 2 Digest (Repl) 450, *187*.

Reichel v Magrath (1889) 14 App Cas 665, 59 LJQB 159, 54 JP 196, HL, 50 Digest (Repl)
    85, *698*.

Appeal

Tak Ming Co Ltd appealed against an order of the Supreme Court of Hong Kong
in its appellate jurisdiction (Blair-Kerr, Mills-Owens and McMullin JJ) dated 1st
December 1970 dismissing an appeal against the decision of Pickering J dated 7th
July 1970 whereby it was ordered that the judgment of Pickering J dated 3rd January
1969 against the appellants, who were the second defendants in an action brought
by the respondents, Yee Sang Metal Supplies Co, as plaintiffs, be corrected by the
inclusion of an order that the appellants pay interest to the respondents on the
judgment debt of $332,635·17 at the rate of 8 per cent per annum from the date of
commencement of the action to the date of payment. The facts are set out in the
opinion of the board.

R A R Stroyan QC for the appellants.
M L M Chavasse QC and D G Valentine for the respondents.

LORD PEARSON. On 7th July 1970 in the Supreme Court of Hong Kong
Pickering J made an order under the 'slip rule' correcting his own earlier judgment
in favour of the present respondents (plaintiffs in the action) against the present
appellants (second defendants in the action) by including in it an award of interest
on the sum found to be due. His order was affirmed (except as to costs) by the Full
Court. In the present appeal the questions raised are (1) whether Pickering J was
precluded from making the order by a decision of another judge on a previous
application relating to such interest; (2) whether Pickering J's discretion was wrongly
exercised when he decided to make the order, having regard to the relevant events
and circumstances including the respondents' delay in applying for the order. It
will be convenient first to trace the sequence of events, then to refer to the relevant
procedural provisions and then to consider the two questions raised in this appeal.
In October 1964 Defag Construction Co contracted with the appellants to erect for
them a 16 storey building, and Defag Construction Co engaged the respondents as
sub-contractors to carry out steel work. For the work which they did the respondents
received payments on account amounting to $884,000, but there was still a large
balance due to them. On 16th November 1966 they brought an action against Defag
Construction Co as first defendants and the appellants as second defendants claiming
$367,654·75 as the balance due. The respondents recovered judgment against Defag
Construction Co but the judgment was not satisfied. The respondents proceeded
with their action against the appellants, claiming that the appellants had by an undertaking given in correspondence assumed liability to the respondents. In their statement of claim against the appellants dated 13th March 1967 the respondents claimed
the balance of $367,645·75 and interest thereon at the rate of 8 per cent per annum

a from the commencement of the action to payment under Ord 15, r 7 of the Code of Civil Procedure. The appellants denied liability.

The action was tried by Pickering J in the Supreme Court of Hong Kong. At the request of both parties he agreed to determine the issue of liability before evidence was adduced on the issue of quantum. On 3rd January 1969 he gave a judgment, dealing at length with the issue of liability and deciding it in favour of the respondents.

b He held that the appellants were liable to the respondents for the balance, if any, of the price of work done on the site by the respondents in excess of the sum of $884,000 already received by the respondents. He said:

'The amount of any such balance is a matter for future determination and, at counsel's request, there will be liberty to either side to apply for directions regarding the manner of such determination.'

c
He awarded costs to the respondents. The learned judge did not in this judgment award interest and he was not then asked to do so. The judgment was not read but was handed down in open court.

On 8th February 1969 the learned judge in response to an application by the parties appointed an expert to determine the amount of the balance owing. At the

d hearing of this application counsel for the respondents asked for it to be put on record that he was intending to make an application for interest at the appropriate time.

The appellants had appealed against the judgment on the issue of liability but their appeal was dismissed by the Full Court of the Supreme Court of Hong Kong on 2nd June 1969. On 20th June 1969 the Full Court granted leave for the appellants to appeal to Her Majesty in Council.

e On 30th July 1969 the expert assessed the balance owing to the respondents at $332,635·17. On 6th August 1969 the respondents applied by a summons inter partes for an order that interest should be paid by the appellants to the respondents on the sum of $332,635·17 at the rate of 8 per cent per annum from the commencement of the action on 16th November 1966 until payment of the judgment debt. The summons was supported by an affirmation of the respondents' solicitor. On 16th

f August 1969 it was heard by Briggs J in chambers and was dismissed with costs. On 23rd August 1969 final judgment was entered for the amount assessed.

Then about nine months later, on 26th May 1970, the respondents applied by notice of motion for an order that Pickering J's judgment of 3rd January 1969 should be corrected by the inclusion of an award of interest pursuant to the claim in the statement of claim, the ground of the application being that owing to an accidental omis-

g sion the judgment did not provide for this part of the plaintiffs' (the respondents') claim. At the time when this application was made the appeal to Her Majesty in Council on the issue of liability was still pending; it was ultimately dismissed by Order in Council dated 27th October 1971. The application for correction of Pickering J's judgment of 3rd January 1969 was heard by him on 7th July 1970 and he decided that the correction should be made. On appeal his decision was affirmed,

h except as to costs, by the Full Court on 1st December 1970. The present appeal is from that decision of the Full Court.

As to costs, Pickering J had directed on 7th July 1970 that each party should pay their own costs of the application to him for correction of the judgment, but the Full Court substituted a direction that the respondents should pay the appellants' costs of that application and also directed that one-third of the appellants' costs of the

j appeal to the Full Court should be borne by the respondents and that two-thirds of the respondents' costs of that appeal should be borne by the appellants. Now it is necessary to refer to certain procedural provisions. The claim for interest in the statement of claim dated 13th March 1967 was made under Ord 15, r 7, of the Code of Civil Procedure, which was then in force and provided:

'When the action is for a sum of money due to the plaintiff the court may in

the judgment order interest at such rate as the court may think proper to be
paid on the principal sum adjudged from the commencement of the action to
the date of the judgment, in addition to any interest adjudged on such principal
sum for any period prior to the commencement of the action; and further
interest, at such rate as may for the time being be fixed by the court, shall be
recoverable on the aggregate sum so adjudged, from the date of the judgment
to the date of payment.'

The Code of Civil Procedure was repealed and replaced by the Rules of the Supreme
Court 1967 coming into force on 1st September 1967. By an amendment coming into
force on 1st May 1968 those rules included Ord 6, r 2A, and this was identical with the
former Ord 15, r 7, which has been set out above. Consequently, when Briggs J gave
his decision in August 1969, the relevant provision was that '. . . the court may in the
judgment award interest . . .' There was then no power to make an award of interest
separate from the judgment.

New provisions were introduced in January 1970. RSC Ord 6, r 2A was repealed
on 6th January 1970, and on 9th January 1970 the Supreme Court Ordinance (Cap 4
of the Laws of Hong Kong) was amended by the addition of ss 30A and 30B. Sections
30A and 30B included the following provisions:

> '30A.—(1) Subject to subsection (2), the Court may, in any proceedings brought
> in the Court for the recovery of any debt or damage, order that there shall be
> included in the sum for which judgment is given interest at such rate as it thinks
> fit on the whole or any part of the debt or damage for the whole or any part of
> the period between the date when the cause of action arose and the date of the
> judgment . . .
> '(3) The powers conferred by subsection (1) may be exercised:—(a) whether or
> not interest is expressly claimed; (b) at any time after judgment is entered in any
> case in which it appears that the failure to apply for or to award interest was
> through inadvertence . . .
> '30B.—(1) A judgment debt shall carry interest at the rate of eight per cent
> per annum, or at such other rate as may be prescribed by rules of Court, on the
> aggregate amount thereof, or on such part thereof as for the time being remains
> unsatisfied, from the date of the judgment until satisfaction . . .'

There was thus in 1970 the possibility of making an application under s 30A (3).
But the respondents, presumably for tactical reasons—seeking to avoid a plea of
res judicata—did not adopt this course and preferred to apply under the 'slip rule' for
correction of Pickering J's judgment of 3rd January 1969. The 'slip rule', in Hong Kong
as in England, was at all material times contained in Ord 20, r 11 and worded as
follows:

> 'Clerical mistakes in judgments or orders or errors arising therein from any
> accidental slip or omission, may at any time be corrected by the Court on motion
> or Summons without an appeal.'

The requirements for acting under the slip rule were satisfied. Pickering J said:

> 'A most important matter for me to consider is what I would have done at the
> time I gave judgment had this matter of interest been in my mind. After a
> lengthy trial, in the course of which both sides asked me to confine my decision
> to the issue of liability, and having written a long judgment which occasioned to
> me no small difficulty, my mind was on the issue of liability rather than upon
> any figures. But had I thought the matter through further, as I should have done,
> I am in no doubt whatever, having a very clear recollection of the case and
> the evasiveness of Mr. Cheng, witness for the [appellants], that I would have
> made an award of interest. Unfortunately for the [respondents], I did not read

the lengthy judgment in court but handed it down so that the omission was not obvious to counsel for the [respondents] before I had left the court.'

On the basis of that explanation it can be said both that there was an accidental omission by the judge to order interest in his judgment of 3rd January 1969 and that there was an accidental omission by counsel to ask for it. Under the slip rule an accidental omission by counsel can suffice to bring the rule into operation: *Re Inchcape, Craigmyle v Inchcape*[1] per Morton J.

The first question raised in this appeal is whether Pickering J was precluded from making the order of 7th July 1970, correcting his judgment of 3rd January 1969, by the decision of Briggs J on 16th August 1969. The answer must depend very largely on what Briggs J decided. This was considered both by Pickering J and by the Full Court. According to the judge's notes of the arguments the respondents' counsel said he was instructed that Briggs J's reason for dismissing the application was that he had no jurisdiction—that an order for interest must be made in the judgment and it was too late for interest to be awarded after delivery of the judgment—and appellants' counsel said 'Briggs J refused as having no jurisdiction'. Pickering J said in his judgment:

'... my brother Briggs refused the application being, I am informed by counsel, of the view that he had no jurisdiction to make the order sought and that a successful plaintiff could either obtain an order for interest at the time of his judgment or not at all.'

Counsel who appeared on the appeal to the Full Court had not appeared on the application before Briggs J but one of them had been informed by counsel who did appear on that application that the entire proceedings took only three minutes. There was produced to the Full Court the endorsement on counsel's brief, reading as follows:

'Briggs J. in Chambers 16/8/69 at 10 o'clock. Application refused with costs. Certificate for counsel. Court said it had no power to grant interest at this stage of proceeding and it should have been done at time of Judgment.'

The Full Court consulted Briggs J, but he, understandably, owing to the lapse of time, was not able to say what arguments were presented to him on the application. The Full Court's conclusion was:

'From the brief note of the proceedings set out above the preferable view would seem to be that the learned judge came swiftly to the conclusion that he had simply no jurisdiction to deal with the matter at all.'

On the materials available that was a reasonable conclusion. In effect there is a finding of fact by both courts below that Briggs J's reason for rejecting the application was that he had no jurisdiction to entertain it. He did not decide whether on some different application—e g an application for correction of the judgment—he would have had jurisdiction to decide whether interest should be awarded. There was no adjudication on the merits of the claim for interest. In principle this case resembles *Pinnock Brothers v Lewis & Peat Ltd*[2], where the arbitrator held that he had no jurisdiction to entertain the claim, and differs from *Ayscough v Sheed Thomson & Co*[3], where the arbitrator considered and dismissed the claim. The distinction on the facts between these two cases may seem tenuous, but the principle is quite clear. In *Pinnock Brothers v Lewis & Peat Ltd*[4] Roche J said, referring to *Ayscough's* case[3]:

---

1   [1942] 2 All ER 157 at 160, [1942] Ch 394 at 399
2   [1923] 1 KB 690
3   (1923) 92 LJKB 878; *affd* HL (1924) 93 LJKB 924
4   [1923] 1 KB at 695, 696

'In that case the arbitrator decided—whether rightly or wrongly is immaterial
for the present purpose—that by reason of a clause as to time contained in the
contract, the plaintiffs had no claim, and therefore he dismissed it. In the present
case the arbitrator merely decided that he had no jurisdiction, and that being so
the award does not and cannot determine the substance of the plaintiff's claim . . .
The mere presence of an arbitration clause is no defence to an action on the
contract. An award following on the arbitration clause may be an answer to the
claim, and it will be an answer where it deals with the claim. *Ayscough's Case*[1]
is an authority for that. But where, as in this case, the award does not deal with the
claim but merely with the jurisdiction of the arbitrator, it is no answer.'

In the present case there was no res judicata. The claim for interest had not been
adjudicated by Briggs J.

There is, however, also a wider principle to be considered. In *Ord v Ord*[2] Lush J
said:

'It remains for me to deal with the other, the wider principle to which I have
referred and which is often treated as falling within the plea of res judicata.
The maxim "nemo debet bis vexari" prevents a litigant who has had an opportunity of proving a fact in support of his claim or defence and chosen not to rely
on it from afterwards putting it before another tribunal. To do that would be
unduly to harass his opponent, and if he endeavoured to do so he would be met
by the objection that the judgment in the former action precluded him from raising that contention. It is not that it has been already decided, or that the record
deals with it. The new fact has not been decided; it has never been in fact submitted to the tribunal and it is not really dealt with by the record. But it is,
by reason of the principle I have stated, treated as if it had been.'

That wider principle is not properly applicable in the present case. It would have
applied if Briggs J had adjudicated on the claim for interest and respondents' counsel,
having omitted to rely in the proceedings before Briggs J on some fact or argument,
had afterwards sought in other proceedings to rely on that fact or argument. In the
present case there was simply a refusal to adjudicate on the ground of lack of
jurisdiction.

The appellants have placed some reliance on *Reichel v Magrath*[3]. In that case Mr
Reichel had, in an action against the bishop and the patrons of a benefice from which
he had resigned, failed to prove that he was still the vicar of the benefice, and he
afterwards refused to give up possession of the parsonage house and glebe lands, and
in defence to an action by his successor he sought to raise the same case as he had unsuccessfully put forward in his own action against the bishop and the patrons. An order
that the defence be struck out was affirmed by the Court of Appeal and the House of
Lords. Lord Halsbury LC said[4]:

'I think it would be a scandal to the administration of justice if, the same question having been disposed of by one case, the litigant were to be permitted by
changing the form of the proceedings to set up the same case again. It cannot be
denied that the only ground upon which Mr. Reichel can resist the claim by Mr.
Magrath to occupy the vicarage is that he (Mr. Reichel) is still vicar of Sparsholt.
If by the hypothesis he is not vicar of Sparsholt and his appeal absolutely fails,
it surely must be in the jurisdiction of the Court of Justice to prevent the defeated
litigant raising the very same question which the Court has decided in a separate

1   (1923) 92 LJKB 878; *affd* HL (1924) 93 LJKB 924
2   [1923] 2 KB 432 at 443, [1923] All ER Rep 206 at 212
3   (1889) 14 App Cas 665
4   (1889) 14 App Cas at 668

action. I believe there must be an inherent jurisdiction in every Court of Justice to prevent such an abuse of its procedure and I therefore think that this appeal must likewise be dismissed.'

The principle in that case does not apply here, because the claim for interest was not considered and decided and disposed of in the earlier proceedings, there being only a denial of jurisdiction.

Finally there is the question of discretion. Even though the requirements of the slip rule are satisfied, and the court is not precluded from making an order under it by any res judicata in the narrow or the extended sense, there is nevertheless a discretion in the court to refuse an order under the slip rule if something has intervened which would render it inexpedient or inequitable to do so: *Moore v Buchanan*[1] following Lord Watson in *Hatton v Harris*[2].

In this case there was considerable delay by the respondents before they made their application under the slip rule. It does not appear, however, that the delay caused the appellants to take any step which they would otherwise have refrained from taking or to omit any step which they would otherwise have taken. The liability for interest was of course dependent on the liability for the principal sum, the balance due to the respondents, and there was no final decision as to the appellants' liability for the principal sum until the appeal to Her Majesty in Council was dismissed by Order in Council on 27th October 1971. There were also factors in favour of making the order under the slip rule. The respondents had been kept out of their money— the balance due to them, for which the appellants have been held responsible—for several years, and it is just that they should have interest on it. Also they had asked for interest in their statement of claim, and had indicated when directions were given on 8th February 1969 that they intended to apply for interest 'at the appropriate time', and they had made the application for interest on 6th August 1969, which was rejected by Briggs J for want of jurisdiction on 16th August 1969, and they made their application under the slip rule on 26th May 1970. Thus they had taken several steps with a view to recovering interest. This question of discretion was carefully considered by both courts below, and no sufficient ground has been shown to their Lordships for interfering with the exercise of the discretion which was made by Pickering J and affirmed by the Full Court.

Their Lordships will humbly advise Her Majesty that the appeal should be dismissed. The appellants must pay the respondents' costs of the present appeal. The special orders made by the Full Court with regard to the costs of the application and the costs of the appeal to the Full Court remain unaltered.

Appeal dismissed.

Solicitors: *Nabarro, Nathanson & Co* (for the appellants); *Sharpe, Pritchard & Co* (for the respondents).

S A Hatteea Esq   Barrister.

---

1   [1967] 3 All ER 273, [1967] 1 WLR 1341
2   [1892] AC 547 at 560

Commissioner of Stamp Duties v Atwill and others

PRIVY COUNCIL

LORD REID, LORD MORRIS OF BORTH-Y-GEST, VISCOUNT DILHORNE, LORD SIMON OF GLAISDALE AND SIR RICHARD WILD

10th, 11th, 12th JULY, 7th NOVEMBER 1972

Privy Council – Australia – New South Wales – Death duty – Dutiable estate – Classes of property – Property disposed of by deceased by a settlement – Settlement containing trust to take effect after deceased's death – Property deemed to be included in estate being property subject to trust at time of death – Whether limited to actual property disposed of by deceased remaining subject to trust at time of death – Stamp Duties Act 1920-1964 (New South Wales), s 102 (2) (a).

Statute – Construction – Proviso – Function of proviso to limit or qualify substantive provision – Circumstances in which proviso may be construed as adding to and not merely qualifying what goes before – Stamp Duties Act 1920-1964 (New South Wales), s 102 (2) (a).

In November 1953 the deceased created a trust fund for the benefit of his wife and family. The trust fund consisted of £200 provided by the deceased. That sum was invested by the trustees in the purchase of 20 shares in a company and those shares continued to be held by the trust at the time of the deceased's death in November 1965. Their value then was $276,458. The deceased had at all material times been domiciled and resident in the State of New South Wales. Since the trust was to take effect after the deceased's death it was common ground that it was caught by s 102 (2) (a)[a] of the Stamp Duties Act 1920-1964 of New South Wales. The executors of the deceased's estate, however, claimed that, since the proviso to s 102 (2) (a) only had the effect of limiting the substantive part of s 102 (2) (a) and thus operating only on so much of the property disposed of by the deceased as remained subject to the trust, the consequence was that s 102 (2) (a) only operated to bring into account as part of the dutiable estate so much of the actual property made subject to the trust as was in existence and subject to the trust at the date of death; and that accordingly only £200 could have been included in the dutiable estate and as that sum was not at the date of death subject to the trust nothing should be included.

Held – On the true construction of s 102 (2) (a) the 20 shares were to be included in the deceased's dutiable estate. Although it was often the function of a proviso merely to limit or qualify rather than to add to the substantive provision, a proviso did not necessarily have that restricted effect. The words of the proviso to s 102 (2) (a) were clear and unambiguous and were to be construed with the preceding words. To come within s 102 (2) (a) there must have been property disposed of by a will or settlement containing a trust in respect of that property to take effect after death; if that were so then the property which at the time of death was subject to the trust was to be deemed to be included in the deceased's estate. The scope of that description of property was not in any way restricted by the fact that it was contained in a proviso and there was no valid ground for implying that it should be read as 'property which at the time of his death is subject to such trust and which was disposed of by the deceased' (see p 579 j and p 580 f and h to p 581 a and f to h, post).

Dicta of Lord Loreburn LC in *Rhondda UDC v Taff Vale Railway Co* [1909] AC at 258 and of Viscount Maugham and Lord Wright in *Jennings v Kelly* [1939] 4 All ER at 470, 477 applied.

---

a   Section 102 (2) (a) is set out at p 579 c, post

Notes

For interests ceasing on death under the estate duty legislation in England and Scotland, see 15 Halsbury's Laws (3rd Edn) 13, 14, para 22.

For the effect of provisos in statutes, see 36 ibid 399-401, para 604, and for cases on the subject, see 44 Digest (Repl) 246-248, 696-722.

Cases referred to in opinion

Comr of Stamp Duties (NSW) v Perpetual Trustee Co Ltd (Watt's Case) (1926) 38 CLR 12, *rvsg* (1925) 25 SRNSW 467.

Falkiner v Comr of Stamp Duties p 598, post.

Jennings v Kelly [1939] 4 All ER 464, [1940] AC 206, 109 LJPC 38, 162 LT 1, HL, 44 Digest (Repl) 247, 714.

Rhondda UDC v Taff Vale Railway Co [1909] AC 253, 78 LJKB 647, 100 LT 713, 73 JP 257, 7 LGR 616, HL, 38 Digest (Repl) 312, 141.

West Derby Union v Metropolitan Life Assurance Society [1897] AC 647, 66 LJCh 726, 77 LT 284, 61 JP 820, HL, 44 Digest (Repl) 247, 704.

Appeal

On 3rd April 1970 the Commissioner of Stamp Duties of the State of New South Wales ('the commissioner') stated the following case for the opinion of the Court of Appeal of the Supreme Court of New South Wales.

1. Milton Spencer Atwill ('the deceased') died on 24th November 1965.

2. At the time of his death and at all material times theretofore the deceased was domiciled and resident in the State of New South Wales.

3. Probate of the last will of the deceased was on 2nd March 1966 granted by the Supreme Court of New South Wales in its Probate Jurisdiction to Alan Cavaye Atwill, Milton John Napier Atwill and David Nairn Reid, the executors therein named ('the executors').

4. On 27th November 1953 the deceased paid to himself, Alan Cavaye Atwill and Milton John Napier Atwill ('the trustees') the sum of £200 contemporaneously with the execution by the deceased and by the trustees of a deed dated 27th November 1953 and made between the deceased of the one part and the trustees of the other part whereby, inter alia, the deceased directed and declared that the trustees and their successors in office should stand possessed of that sum of £200 on the trusts (which should be irrevocable) and with and subject to the discretions powers and provisions therein contained. The terms of the deed[1] were set forth in the schedule to the case.

5. The trustees, in exercise of the powers conferred on them by the deed, invested the sum of £200 in the acquisition by application and allotment of 20 shares in the capital of Langton Pty Ltd, a company incorporated in the State of New South Wales, and thereafter continued to hold those shares as the trust funds referred to in the deed until, and so held them at, the time of the death of the deceased.

6. The value of the shares at the time of the death of the deceased was $276,458.

7. At the time of the death of the deceased and at all material times 17 of the 20 shares were registered on the New South Wales register of Langton Pty Ltd and three of the shares were registered on the Australian Capital Territory register of Langton Pty Ltd.

8. The deceased was survived by his widow, Isabella Caroline Atwill, his sons, Alan Cavaye Atwill and Milton John Napier Atwill, and five grandchildren and no more. The grandchildren of the deceased were all children either of Alan Cavaye Atwill or Milton John Napier Atwill and were all under the age of 21 years at the time of the death of the deceased. No grandchildren of the deceased predeceased him.

---

1 The terms of the deed are not material for the purposes of this report and are not reproduced here

9. The commissioner in assessing the death duty payable in respect of the estate of the deceased claimed that by virtue of ss 102 (2) (a) and 102 (2A) of the Stamp Duties Act 1920-1964, the 20 shares in Langton Pty Ltd were included in the dutiable estate of the deceased, and the commissioner accordingly assessed the death duty payable in respect of the estate at the sum of $124,938·06.

10. The executors claimed that the 20 shares in Langton Pty Ltd should not be included in the dutiable estate of the deceased.

11. The executors being dissatisfied with the assessment of death duty in respect of the estate of the deceased, pursuant to s 124 of the 1920-1964 Act and within the time therein limited delivered to the commissioner a notice in writing requiring him to state a case for the opinion of the Court of Appeal.

12. If the 20 shares in Langton Pty Ltd were not to be included in the dutiable estate of the deceased, the death duty payable would be reduced by the sum of $77,926·04, to the sum $47,012·02.

13. The questions for the decision of the court were: (1) whether the 20 shares in Langton Pty Ltd should be included in the dutiable estate of the deceased for the purposes of the assessment and payment of death duty; (2) whether the amount of death duty which should properly be assessed in respect of the estate of the deceased was (a) $124,938·06, or (b) $47,012·02, or (c) some other, and if so what, amount?; (3) how the costs of the case were to be borne and paid.

On 27th November 1970 the Court of Appeal (Asprey, Mason and Moffitt JJA) unanimously answered the questions raised by the case as follows: (1) yes; (2) $124,938·06; (3) by the executors. The executors appealed to the High Court of Australia and on 3rd December the court (Barwick CJ, Windeyer and Owen JJ; Menzies and Walsh JJ dissenting) allowed the appeal and answered the questions in the case stated as follows: (1) no; (2) (a) no; (b) yes; (c) unnecessary to answer; (3) by the commissioner. By special leave of Her Majesty in Council the commissioner appealed against that decision.

F J D Officer QC and M H McLelland (both of the New South Wales Bar) for the commissioner.

A B Kerrigan QC, T R Morling QC and W E Reddy (all of the New South Wales Bar) for the executors.

VISCOUNT DILHORNE. Milton Spencer Atwill ('the deceased') who died on 24th November 1965, on 27th November 1953 created a trust fund for the benefit of his wife and family. After the death of the survivor of himself, his wife and his sons the trust fund was to be divided. It is not disputed that the trust deed contained a trust to take effect after his death and so was caught by s 102 (2) (a) of the Stamp Duties Act 1920-1964 of New South Wales.

The trust fund in 1953 consisted of £200 provided by the deceased. That sum was invested by the trustees in the purchase of 20 shares in Langton Pty Ltd, a company incorporated in New South Wales, and those shares continued to be held by the trust and were held by the trust at the deceased's death. Their value then was $276,458.

The Commissioner of Stamp Duties in assessing the death duty payable in respect of the deceased's estate claimed that the 20 shares were to be included in his dutiable estate and on that basis assessed the duty payable at $124,938·06. If the shares are not to be so included that sum will be reduced by $77,926·04 so that the duty will be $47,012·02. The executors required the commissioner to state a case and on 27th November 1970 the Court of Appeal of the Supreme Court of New South Wales (Asprey, Mason and Moffitt JJA) dismissed their appeal holding that the duty payable was $124,938·06. The executors then appealed to the High Court of Australia and by a majority their appeal was allowed (Barwick CJ, Windeyer and Owen JJ; Menzies and Walsh JJ dissenting).

The commissioner now appeals with special leave. At the time leave was granted *a* an appeal from the Court of Appeal of the Supreme Court of New South Wales was pending which raised precisely the same question. Counsel for the appellants in that case (*Falkiner v Comr of Stamp Duties*[1]) was heard in the course of the argument in this case.

The question to be determined is the proper interpretation to be placed on the relevant parts of s 102 of the Stamp Duties Act of New South Wales. They read as *b* follows:

'For the purposes of the assessment and payment of death duty but subject as hereinafter provided, the estate of a deceased person shall be deemed to include and consist of the following classes of property:— ...

'(2) (*a*) All property which the deceased has disposed of ... by a settlement containing any trust in respect of that property to take effect after his death: *c* ... Provided that the property deemed to be included in the estate of the deceased shall be the property which at the time of his death is subject to such trust ...'

The executors in this case and the appellants in the *Falkiner* case[1] contend that s 102 (2) (*a*) only operates to bring into account as part of the dutiable estate so much of the actual property made subject to a settlement containing a trust to take effect *d* after the settlor's death as was in existence and subject to the settlement at the date of the death. The executors therefore say that at most only £200 could have been included, and that as that sum was not at the date of death subject to the trust, nothing should be included. The commissioner on the other hand contends that the value of the 20 shares at the date of death must be included in the dutiable estate.

e Barwick CJ said that he agreed with the conclusions of Owen J and with his reasons. He held that it was an inadmissible method of construction of the statute to read the words of the proviso as if they were a substantive provision; that the proviso ought not to be read and construed apart from the terms of the section; that the governing words of the whole provision were the opening words of s 102 (2) (*a*) 'All property which the deceased has disposed of ... by a settlement ...' and that the reference to property in the proviso was to that property. In his opinion the proviso *f* ensured that only the property made subject to the settlement which is at the date of the death still subject to the settlement is brought into the valuation.

Owen J said that it appeared to him odd that what on its face appears in the form of a proviso should be regarded as adding to and not merely qualifying what went before. 'If it is itself a substantive enactment then the legislature has, in the form of a proviso, added to s 102 (2) a new category of "notional estate" consisting of pro- *g* perty over which the deceased never had any power of disposition.' He thought the second part of s 102 (2) (*a*) was a true proviso limiting the operation of the first part and operating only on so much of the property disposed of by the deceased as remains subject to the trusts of the settlement.

Windeyer J agreed with the judgment of Barwick CJ and Owen J. In his view the shares not being property the deceased disposed of were not by virtue of s 102 (2) (*a*) *h* to be included in his dutiable estate. In his view the property subjected to duty was the property that the deceased had disposed of by the settlement, or so much of it as was still subject to the trust when he died.

The decision of the majority of the High Court was thus based on the view that the proviso was a true proviso limiting or qualifying what preceded it.

Their Lordships are not able to agree with this conclusion. While in many cases *i* that is the function of a proviso, it is the substance and content of the enactment, not its form, which has to be considered, and that which is expressed to be a proviso may itself add to and not merely limit or qualify that which precedes it. In *Jennings v Kelly*[2] Viscount Maugham said:

1 Page 598, post
2 [1939] 4 All ER 464 at 470, [1940] AC 206 at 217

'In coming to his conclusion, ANDREWS, L.C.J., was influenced by his view that   *a*
the first part of the section was the operative portion of it, and that the proviso
could not properly be used to explain the words as to increase of population
in the operative part. He therefore relied on the principle of construction to be
found in the case of *West Derby Union* v. *Metropolitan Life Assurance Society*[1].
The principle is thus stated by Lord Watson[2]: "... I am perfectly clear that if the
language of the enacting part of the statute does not contain the provisions   *b*
which are said to occur in it, you cannot derive these provisions by implication
from a proviso." I am sure that none of your Lordships would desire to depart
from this principle where it is applicable—namely, where the enacting part of
the section is unambiguous and complete and is followed by a true proviso (that
is, a qualification or an exception out of it). In my view that is not the case here,
and, as LORD HERSCHELL pointed out in the *West Derby Union* case[3]: "Of course a   *c*
proviso may be used to guide you in the selection of one or other of two possible
constructions of the words to be found in the enactments, and show when there
is doubt about its scope, when it may reasonably admit of doubt as to its having
this scope or that, which is the proper view to take of it . . ." My Lords, that is
precisely the method of construction which, in my view, is applicable in the
present case. I will add that the words beginning "Provided that" are, in my   *d*
opinion, additional and explanatory words, necessary for the purpose of giving
a more definite meaning to the preceding words—namely, for the purpose
of removing doubt as to its scope—and they might easily have been incorporated
in the earlier part of the section, at the risk of making it rather more cumbrous
than it is. We are not dealing here with a true proviso, or, at any rate, not with
such a proviso as this House was considering in the *West Derby Union* case[1]. It   *e*
cannot, I think, be disputed that in construing a section of an Act of Parliament,
it is constantly necessary to explain the meaning of the words by an examination of
the purport and effect of other sections in the same Act . . . . This principle is
equally applicable in the case of different parts of a single section, and none the
less so because the latter part is introduced by the words "provided that," or
like words. There can, I think, be no doubt that the view expressed in KENT'S   *f*
COMMENTARIES ON AMERICAN LAW[4] (cited with approval in MAXWELL ON THE
INTERPRETATION OF STATUTES[5]), is correct: "The true principle undoubtedly is,
that the sound interpretation and meaning of the statute, on a view of the enacting clause, saving clause, and proviso, taken and construed together, is to
prevail".'

In the same case Lord Wright said[6]:   *g*

'It is said that, where there is a proviso, the former part, which is described
as the enacting part, must be construed without reference to the proviso. No
doubt there may be cases in which the first part is so clear and unambiguous
as not to admit in regard to the matters which are there clear any reference
to any other part of the section. The proviso may simply be an exception out of   *h*
what is clearly defined in the first part, or it may be some qualification not
inconsistent with what is expressed in the first part. In the present case, however,
not only is the first part of the section deficient in express definition, but the
second part is complementary and necessary in order to ascertain the full intention of the legislature. The proper course is to apply the broad general rule of
construction, which is that a section or enactment must be construed as a whole,   *j*

1   [1897] AC 647
2   [1897] AC at 652
3   [1897] AC at 655
4   (12th Edn) vol 1, p 463n
5   (8th Edn, 1937), p 140
6   [1939] 4 All ER at 477, [1940] AC at 229

each portion throwing light, if need be, on the rest. I do not think that there is any other rule, even in the case of a proviso in the strictest or narrowest sense, and still less where, as here, the introduction of the second part by the word "provided" is, in a strict sense, inapt.'

In a strict sense the use of the words 'Provided that' in s 102 (2) (*a*) may also be disregarded as inapt. The meaning of that provision and the proviso would be the same if instead of the words 'Provided that' there had appeared the word 'and' or the words 'in which case' and to ascertain the true effect of the provision the second part, that is to say, the proviso, is complementary and necessary in order to ascertain the full intention of the legislature. In *Rhondda Urban District Council v Taff Vale Railway Co*[1] the House of Lords had to consider the effect of a section which was framed as a proviso on preceding sections. In that case Lord Loreburn LC said[2]:

'But it is also true that the latter half of it, though in form a proviso, is in substance a fresh enactment, adding to and not merely qualifying that which goes before.'

Other examples of such provisos are to be found in the Stamp Act itself in the first proviso to s 102 (2) (*ba*) where the commissioner is given power to reduce the value of any property in certain circumstances; in the first proviso to s 102 (2) (*l*) and to s 102 (2B) where the commissioner is given a similar power. In each of these instances the proviso contained what is called a substantive enactment (see also the Wheat Marketing Act 1920, s 11 (1), and the Workmen's Compensation (Amendment) Act 1920 of New South Wales, s 4).

Examples of such a use of a proviso can also be found in conveyancing precedents (see Hallett's Conveyancing Precedents[3] and the Encyclopaedia of Forms and Precedents[4]). The words of the proviso to s 102 (2) (*a*) are in their Lordships' opinion clear and unambiguous. They must be construed with the words which precede them and their effect would not be different if instead of the words 'Provided that', the section, as has been said, had read 'and' or 'in which case'. To come within s 102 (2) (*a*) there must have been property disposed of by the deceased by a will or settlement containing a trust in respect of that property to take effect after death. If that is so, then the property which at the time of the death is subject to such trust is to be deemed to be included in the deceased's estate.

The word 'property' is used four times in s 102 (2) (*a*). In each case the subsection makes clear beyond doubt what is the property referred to. On the first two occasions on which it is used it is property which the deceased had disposed of. On the third occasion it is property 'deemed to be included in the estate' and on the fourth 'property which at the time of his death is subject to such trust'.

The scope of that description of property is not in their Lordships' view in any way restricted by the fact that it is contained in a proviso and there is no valid ground for implying that it should be read as 'property which at the time of his death is subject to such trust and which was disposed of by the deceased'.

In *Watt's Case*[5] Ferguson J expressed the opinion that the intention of the legislature was that if there was existing some property which the deceased had disposed of but which at his death was still subject to a trust to take effect after a death the effect of the proviso was to secure that that was treated as part of his dutiable estate. On appeal Higgins J[6] agreed with this. That was a case where a trust to take effect on

---

1 [1909] AC 253
2 [1909] AC at 258
3 (1965), p 846, 3 (b)
4 20 Ency Forms & Precedents (4th Edn) 617, Form I:H:24; ibid 627, Form I:H:41; ibid 640, Form I:L:6
5 (1925) 25 SRNSW 467
6 (1926) 38 CLR 12 at 36

death was extinguished and the commissioner's contention was that once property had been disposed of by a will or settlement on a trust to take effect after death that property was stamped irrevocably with liability to death duty. That contention was rejected. The court in that case did not have to consider the problem raised in this case and while what Ferguson J said was clearly right, their Lordships do not consider that the effect of the proviso is limited to such a case.

If in this case the decision of the High Court is right, then it means that a very large gate is open for the avoidance of duty. Directly the disposition of property is made by a settlement on a trust to take effect on the settlor's death the trustees of the settlement, by changing the form of the property held, e g by selling the shares transferred by the settlor and buying further shares with the money realised, can free the trust fund from all liability to estate duty. It cannot have been the intention of the legislature so to provide.

In the Stamp Duties Act 1898, s 58, it was provided that within six months of the death of any person who had executed a settlement containing a trust to take effect after his death, notice of the settlement had to be lodged 'together with a declaration specifying the property thereby settled and the value thereof' and duty was payable on that value. Section 58 (2) gave the Supreme Court power to order a sufficient part of 'the property included in such settlement' to be sold to pay the duty.

When the Stamp Act 1920, an Act to amend and to consolidate, was prepared, it may have been appreciated that the language of s 58 which was replaced by s 102 (2) (a) left it open to argument whether the property thereby settled was to be interpreted as the property disposed of and whether duty was or was not payable on the value of the property included in the settlement at the time of death. It may well have been in order to clarify the position that the proviso to s 102 (2) (a) was inserted.

For the reasons stated their Lordships are of the opinion that the views expressed by Menzies and Walsh JJ were correct and they will humbly advise Her Majesty that this appeal should be allowed, the order of the High Court set aside and the order of the Court of Appeal restored. The executors must pay the costs of the appeal to the High Court and of this appeal.

Appeal allowed.

Solicitors: *Light & Fulton* (for the commissioner); *Coward, Chance & Co* (for the executors).

Rengan Krishnan Esq Barrister.

a

O'Brien and another v Robinson

HOUSE OF LORDS

LORD REID, LORD MORRIS OF BORTH-Y-GEST, LORD DIPLOCK, LORD SIMON OF GLAISDALE
AND LORD CROSS OF CHELSEA

b 11th, 12th, 13th DECEMBER 1972, 19th FEBRUARY 1973

*Landlord and tenant – Repair – Implied covenant – Short lease of dwelling-house – Defect
requiring repair – Knowledge of defect – Relevance – Latent defect in ceiling – Ceiling falling
in and injuring tenant – Tenant having no knowledge of defect before fall – Tenant not in
a position to inform landlord of defect – Landlord having no knowledge of defect – Whether
landlord liable for breach of implied covenant to keep structure of dwelling-house in repair –*
c *Housing Act 1961, s 32 (1).*

The first plaintiff was the lessee of a dwelling-house consisting of the basement and
ground floor of a house which belonged to the defendant. The lease was one to
which s 32 of the Housing Act 1961 applied and in consequence, under s 32 (1)*[a]*, there
was implied in the lease a covenant that the defendant, as lessor, would keep the
d structure of the dwelling-house in repair. The first plaintiff and his wife, the second
plaintiff, were in bed one night when the ceiling of their bedroom fell in causing them
injuries. The fall was caused by a latent defect in the ceiling of which neither the
plaintiffs nor the defendant were aware until the fall took place. The plaintiffs,
contending that the defendant was in breach of his implied covenant to keep the
structure of their dwelling-house in repair, brought an action against him in respect
e of the injuries and damage which they had suffered.

Held – Under the covenant implied by s 32 of the 1961 Act a lessor's obligation to
start carrying out any work of repair to premises occupied by his lessee did not arise
until he had information about the existence of a defect in the premises such as would
put a reasonable man on enquiry whether works of repair were needed. That was
f the case even where, because the defect was latent, the lessee was not in a position to
bring it to the attention of the lessor. Accordingly, since the defendant had no
knowledge of the defect in the ceiling he could not be held liable for the damage which
the plaintiffs had sustained (see p 584 g, p 588 h, p 589 e and f, p 592 b c and h, p 593 e
to g and p 594 b and c, post).

    McCarrick v Liverpool Corpn [1946] 2 All ER 646 applied.
g   *Morgan v Liverpool Corpn* [1926] All ER Rep 25 approved.

    Quaere. Whether, if the lessor has previous information from a source other
than the lessee about the existence of a defect, his obligation to start carrying out
works arises before he is given notice of the defect by the lessee (see p 589 f to h and
p 592 d, post).

h **Notes**

For covenants to repair by landlords generally, see 23 Halsbury's Laws (3rd Edn)
586, 587, paras 1268, 1269.

    For the condition implied by statute that a house is reasonably fit for habitation,
see ibid 575-578, paras 1251-1253, and for cases on the subject, see 31 Digest (Repl)
198, 199, 3303-3310.

j   For the covenant to repair implied in short leases of dwelling-houses, see
Supplement to 23 Halsbury's Laws (3rd Edn) para 1253A.

    For the Housing Act 1961, s 32, see 16 Halsbury's Statutes (3rd Edn) 351.

---

a   Section 32 (1), so far as material, provides: 'In any lease of a dwelling-house, being a lease
    to which this section applies, there shall be implied a covenant by the lessor—(a) to keep
    in repair the structure . . . of the dwelling-house . . .'

Cases referred to in opinions

Fisher v Walters [1926] 2 KB 315, 95 LJKB 846, 135 LT 411, 90 JP 195, 24 LGR 327, DC, 31 Digest (Repl) 198, 3306.

Griffin v Pillet [1926] 1 KB 17, 95 LJKB 67, 134 LT 58, 31 Digest (Repl) 383, 5106.

McCarrick v Liverpool Corpn [1946] 2 All ER 646, [1947] AC 219, [1947] LJR 56, 176 LT 11, 111 JP 6, 45 LGR 49, HL, 31 Digest (Repl) 199, 3308.

Makin v Watkinson (1870) LR 6 Exch 25, [1861-73] All ER Rep 281, 40 LJEx 33, 23 LT 592, 31 Digest (Repl) 346, 4768.

Morgan v Liverpool Corpn [1927] 2 KB 131, [1926] All ER Rep 25, 96 LJKB 234, 136 LT 622, 91 JP 26, 25 LGR 79, CA, 31 Digest (Repl) 198, 3307.

Summers v Salford Corpn [1943] 1 All ER 68, [1943] AC 283, 112 LJKB 65, 168 LT 97, 107 JP 35, 41 LGR 1, HL, 31 Digest (Repl) 198, 3305.

Appeal

The appellants, Lawrence Joseph O'Brien and Doris Muriel O'Brien, claimed damages against the respondent, Martin C Robinson, for personal injuries sustained by them when the bedroom ceiling of the premises in which they were residing collapsed and fell on them. They claimed that the collapse was due to the breach by the respondent, as landlord of the premises, of the repairing covenant implied by virtue of s 32 (1) (*a*) of the Housing Act 1961. On 6th March 1972 Bristow J dismissed the appellants' claim but certified, pursuant to s 12 of the Administration of Justice Act 1969, that the decision involved a point of law of general public importance in respect of which he was bound by a decision of the House of Lords in previous proceedings in which the point had been fully considered, and granted the appellants' application for a certificate for leave to appeal to the House of Lords. On 26th April 1972 the appeal committee granted leave to appeal. The facts are set out in the opinion of Lord Morris of Borth-y-Gest.

David Turner-Samuels QC and *Barbara Calvert* for the appellants.
Michael Turner for the respondent.

Their Lordships took time for consideration.

19th February.   The following opinions were delivered.

LORD REID.   My Lords, for the reasons given by my noble and learned friend, Lord Diplock, I would dismiss this appeal.

LORD MORRIS OF BORTH-Y-GEST.   My Lords, this appeal raises issues of no little importance. The appellants were injured when the ceiling of their bedroom fell on them. In no way were they to blame. They were occupying premises belonging to the respondent. Payment was being made to him for the use of them by the appellants. Is he responsible for injuries, loss and damage which they sustained?

The first appellant was the tenant of a dwelling-house (being the basement and ground floor of a house in East Croydon) to which s 32 of the Housing Act 1961 applied. In his tenancy there was, by virtue of the implication resulting from that section, a covenant by the respondent which required him, inter alia, to keep in repair the structure and exterior of the dwelling-house. The question arises as to what is the meaning of the obligation of a landlord to his tenant 'to keep in repair' the structure of demised premises. In the present case the ceiling which fell on 26th November 1968 must have been out of repair at the time immediately before it fell. If the obligation of the respondent was an absolute one in the sense that ignorance of any condition of disrepair was immaterial, then there would clearly be liability in him. But the meaning of an obligation on the part of a landlord 'to keep in repair' or of comparable obligations has been the subject of much judicial consideration.

There is a statutory restriction on contracting out of the statutorily implied covenant. By s 33 (7) of the 1961 Act any covenant or agreement is void so far as it purports to exclude or to limit the obligations of a lessor under s 32. There is, however, power in the county court, if the parties consent, to authorise provisions excluding or modifying in relation to the lease the provisions of s 32 with respect to the repairing obligations if the court, in the terms of s 33 (6), considers it reasonable to do so. In the present case no such authorisation was sought and there was no purported exclusion of the respondent's obligations as lessor. So the question remains as to what is the meaning of a covenant to keep in repair.

The restriction on contracting out which is contained in s 33 (7) of the 1961 Act is in line with a provision contained in the previous Housing Act. By s 6 (2) of the Housing Act 1957, the covenant there provided for is to be implied 'notwithstanding any stipulation to the contrary'. There was a comparable provision in s 2 of the Housing Act 1936; so also in s 1 of the Housing Act 1925.

The obligation on a lessor under s 32 (1) of the 1961 Act to 'keep in repair' may be compared with the obligations on a lessor under earlier Acts. Thus, under the 1957 Act (see s 6) the implications include a condition that the house is, at the commencement of the tenancy, and an undertaking that the house will be kept by the landlord during the tenancy, fit for human habitation. Under the 1936 Act there was a comparable provision (see s 2) as there was in the Housing Act 1925 (see s 1). See also s 15 of the Housing, Town Planning, etc, Act 1909. In the 1936 Act the implied condition was that at the commencement of the tenancy the house was, and the implied undertaking that during the tenancy it would be kept, in all respects reasonably fit for human habitation.

So under all these Acts since 1909 the obligation of a lessor where it has by statute been implied has been to keep the premises in a certain condition and for the purpose of considering the issue now arising it is immaterial whether the obligation imposed is to keep in repair or to keep premises in all respects reasonably fit for human habitation. Questions as to the nature of a lessor's obligations and liabilities have of course arisen where apart from any statute there has been a covenant by a lessor to keep in repair: see e g *Makin v Watkinson*[1].

On a consideration of the meaning of a lessor's obligation to keep premises in repair there has been scope for much reasonable competitive argument. The various authorities (which I do not propose fully to cite) show that every point of view has been explored. The following are some of the contentions that have been pressed. On the one hand, it has been said that it would be wholly unreasonable to make a lessor liable for failing to remedy a defect of which he was unaware. So the liability to repair is one that arises only on notice that there is a need to repair. Where by contract between lessor and lessee there has been a covenant to keep in repair the parties must have intended that the obligation of the lessor would only arise if the lessor had notice of want of repair and a condition or stipulation to that effect should be imported into the contract. The lessee in occupation would be in the best position to know of any state of disrepair. On the other hand, it has been said that if a lessor chooses or is required to covenant to keep premises in repair then there is an absolute obligation on him. Alternatively, even if ordinarily there is no obligation on the part of a lessor until he is told by his lessee of a need for repair a lessee can only give notice of any condition of which he is aware and accordingly cannot give notice of some unknown or unseen condition or latent defect: if, in these circumstances, the lessee suffers injury by reason of the premises not being in repair liability should rest on the lessor.

At times an argument was pressed to the effect that a lessor ought not to be held liable on a covenant because he would have no right of entry to inspect the condition of the premises and so would be dependent on being told if something needed to

---

1   (1870) LR 6 Exch 25, [1861-73] All ER Rep 281

be done. But by the Housing, Town Planning, etc, Act 1909 (see s 15 (2)) a right on notice was given in cases to which the Act applied to enter for the purpose of viewing the state and condition of the premises. Similar powers were given in later Acts and by s 32 (4) of the 1961 Act a right of entry (in the terms provided) is given in the case of any lease in which the lessor's repairing covenant is implied. But even if there is a right of entry for the purpose of viewing the condition of the premises it has been argued that frequent visits by a lessor would not be expected or desired and in order to acquire knowledge of any want of repair a lessor would in fact be dependent largely on receiving information from his lessee.

It may here be stated that in the present case the learned judge held that the second appellant was not a tenant. As a consequence of this any liability of the respondent to her would have to be established in reliance on the provisions of s 4 of the Occupiers' Liability Act 1957.

In *Morgan v Liverpool Corpn*[1] one basis of claim was that there had been a failure to perform the statutory undertaking that the house would be 'kept in all respects reasonably fit for human habitation'. As I have shown, there was at that date a statutory right in a landlord to enter for the purposes of inspection. The accident which gave rise to the claim was that when the upper portion of a window was being opened one of the cords of the window sash broke with the result that the top part of the window slipped down and caught and injured the plaintiff's hand. In the argument on behalf of the plaintiff in the Court of Appeal it was admitted that the defect was a latent one (of which the plaintiff did not know and about which accordingly he could not give any notice) but it was contended that there was a statutory obligation on the landlord which was different from that contained in an ordinary covenant and that in the Act (Housing Act 1925) there were no words requiring that any notice should be given to the landlord. Furthermore reliance was placed on the statutory right of the landlord to enter and inspect. Apart from any such statutory right the facts of the case showed that there was a notice posted up in the house containing certain conditions which included a reservation by the landlord of the right of entering the house at any time without previous notice in order to view the state of repair. The Court of Appeal held that the landlord was not liable and that any liability was conditional on his having been given notice of any defects even though they were latent ones and that this result was not affected by the fact that the landlord had a right to enter in order to inspect. There were divisions of opinion on certain points which arose: in particular on the point whether by reason of the breaking of the sash cord the particular dwelling (which was most limited in size) was rendered unfit for human habitation. But all three Lords Justices were of the opinion that the claim failed because the landlord did not have notice and because in such a case as that under consideration notice was required before the liability of the landlord to repair existed. Lord Hanworth MR said[2] that it had long been established that where there is a covenant on the part of a landlord to keep premises in repair the tenant must give notice to the landlord of what is out of repair. He held that notice was required whether or not the landlord had means of access; he said that the fact that the origin of a covenant was statutory did not give the covenant any higher authority than one inserted in a contract by the parties. Atkin LJ said that in ordinary circumstances the obligation of a landlord to do repairs does not come into existence until he has had notice of the defect which his contract to repair requires him to make good. He said[3]:

'I think the power of access that is given, extensive though it may be, does not take the case away from the principle from which the Courts have inferred the condition that the liability is not to arise except on notice. The position is quite

---

1 [1927] 2 KB 131, [1926] All ER Rep 25
2 [1927] 2 KB at 141, [1926] All ER Rep at 29
3 [1927] 2 KB at 151, [1926] All ER Rep at 34

a satisfactory one, because as soon as the tenant is aware of the defect he must then give notice, and if the landlord does not repair it, the landlord will be liable. If in fact the tenant is not able to ascertain the defect, there seems to be no reason why the landlord should be exposed to what remains still the same injustice of being required to repair a defect of which he does not know, which seems to me to be the real reason for the rule. This was a case in which notice was not given to the landlord. As I have said, it appears to me that, as soon as the defect became so known by the fall of the sash, the tenant was able to give notice to the landlord and did give notice. In my view the landlord then became under a liability to repair in the circumstances of this case, because if he did not, the house would be in a state not in all respects fit for human habitation; but as no notice was given, I think the landlord was not liable.'

Lawrence LJ said[1]:

'On the question of notice I am in complete agreement with the judgments delivered by the Master of the Rolls and Atkin L.J. and have very little to add. In my opinion the established rule is that the obligation of the landlord to keep the premises in repair is not broken unless notice has been given to him of the want of repair, and that mere knowledge is not sufficient to saddle the landlord with liability. The foundation of such rule is that the tenant in occupation is generally in a far better position to know of any want of repair. I am further of opinion that for the reasons stated by Atkin L.J. the rule applies to latent as well as to patent defects, and certainly applies to the defect which existed in the present case.'

The decision in *Fisher v Walters*[2] (a case where the defects in the ceiling were latent), which counsel for the landlord had submitted had gone too far, was not expressly mentioned in the judgments.

If the decision in *Morgan's* case[3] is correct it would, I think, govern the present case. Although all three Lords Justices agreed as to the necessity for notice it did not become necessary for the court to decide whether such notice had to be given by the tenant or whether knowledge in the landlord of a necessity to do repairs or notice from some other source to him of such necessity would also suffice to create a liability in the landlord to do repairs. There was in that case neither notice to the landlord of the existence of the defective or broken sash-cord nor was there knowledge in the landlord of the state of affairs.

In *Summers v Salford Corpn*[4] a case came to this House in which the tenant did give notice to the landlord's agent that one sash-cord in the only window of a bedroom had broken. No repair was effected and about two months later the second sash-cord broke in circumstances causing injury to the tenant. The issue that arose was whether there was a breach by the landlord of the implied undertaking (see s 2 (1) of the Housing Act 1936) that the house would be kept by the landlord during the tenancy in all respects fit for human habitation. In his speech Lord Atkin said[5]:

'In the present case the point upon which the Court of Appeal in *Morgan's* case[3] decided for the defendant does not arise, viz., that notice of the lack of repair complained of must be given to the landlord before his statutory obligation arises. I can see that different considerations may arise in the case of an obligation to repair imposed in the public interest; and I think that this question must be left open, and I reserve to myself the right to reconsider my former decision if the necessity arises.'

---

1 [1927] 2 KB at 153, [1926] All ER Rep at 35
2 [1926] 2 KB 315
3 [1927] 2 KB 131, [1926] All ER Rep 25
4 [1943] 1 All ER 68, [1943] AC 283
5 [1943] 1 All ER at 71, [1943] AC at 290

Lord Thankerton also expressly kept the same question open. So did Lord Russell of Killowen. So did Lord Wright. So did Lord Romer.

Then in *McCarrick v Liverpool Corpn*[1] the question whether *Morgan's* case[2] was correctly decided was presented for consideration in this House. The tenant's wife had fallen by reason of the defective condition of two stone steps leading from the kitchen to the back kitchen. The provisions of the Housing Act 1936 were applicable. It was held that the house was not kept in the state required by s 2 of that Act. No notice of want of repair was given to the landlords. They had the statutory right of entry to view the state of the premises. The defects would appear to have been patent. The tenant could therefore be aware of them; so also could the landlords have been had they exercised their right of entry. It was argued that *Morgan's* case[2] was wrongly decided, that the Housing Act 1936 contained no provision requiring notice, that the duty imposed on a landlord by the Act (particularly as he was given a right of entry to inspect) was absolute and was analogous to that imposed on a factory occupier by the Factories Acts, and that the effect of the legislation should not be minimised or neutralised by introducing notions inspired by the old law.

Very important questions of principle were therefore raised. The significant previous authorities were considered. It was held that the decision in *Morgan's* case[2] was correct. Lord Thankerton said that the effect of s 2 (1) of the 1936 Act was to incorporate the prescribed condition in the contract so that it became an integral part of it and the statutory origin of the condition did not differentiate it, in any question of construction, from any of the conventional stipulations in the contract: it followed, therefore, that a condition as to notice of the material defect (established by a long line of authority) fell to be implied. Lord Porter said that whatever view might have been taken of the section if no previous history lay behind it it had to be remembered that similar provisions in earlier Acts had been interpreted as only requiring the landlord to repair after notice: he considered that it was too late to reinterpret its meaning. That was in 1946. Since then there have been the Housing Act 1957, and the Act now being considered. Lord Simonds's speech was concurred in by Lord Thankerton and by Lord Macmillan; after reviewing the authorities he clearly held that the provision which the 1936 Act imported into the contract of tenancy fell to be construed in the same way as any other term would be construed and that the correct construction of the provision was that no obligation was imposed on the landlord unless and until he had notice of a particular defect. Lord Uthwatt said that it was an implied term (resulting from the comprehensiveness of the statutory term and the circumstances necessarily involved in the tenancy) that in a case where the tenant knows the defect and the landlord does not, the obligation to do a specific act directed to repairing the defect does not arise until at least the landlord becomes aware of the need for it.

The decision in *McCarrick's* case[1] must have guided landlords and tenants in their business transactions in the years since 1946. Later legislation has followed. In my view, it would not be within the intendment of the power reserved in 1966[3] now to disturb a decision which as Lord Porter indicated was given in 1946 'finally to determine' the point first decided in *Morgan's* case[2] in 1927 and then left open in *Summers's* case[4] in 1943. The question does, however, arise whether the decision of this House in *McCarrick's* case[1] governs the present appeal which concerns a latent defect.

In *McCarrick's* case[1] the defects were there to be seen by the tenant. In the present case no defect was visible and so there was no visible defect to which the landlord's attention could be called. In *McCarrick's* case[1] Lord Simonds said that the decision

---

1 [1946] 2 All ER 646, [1947] AC 219
2 [1927] 2 KB 131, [1926] All ER Rep 25
3 See *Note* [1966] 3 All ER 77, [1966] 1 WLR 1234
4 [1943] 1 All ER 68, [1943] AC 283

in *Fisher v Walters*[1] could not stand and his speech was concurred in by Lord Thankerton and by Lord Macmillan. Lord Porter said that no question of the latency of
the defect came in issue as it did in *Fisher v Walters*[1] and that if it did the decision in
that case would require to be 'carefully scrutinized'. Lord Uthwatt remarked that
latent defects were not in question and he expressed no opinion as to their position.

Although there were these reservations, *Morgan's* case[2] was approved and *Morgan's*
case[2] must, I think, be regarded as a case in which the defect was latent, even though
some defects in a window sash-cord might be visible. I have cited above a passage
from the judgment of Atkin LJ[3]. He also said[4]:

> 'Here is a case of something which arose quite suddenly. It is possible that a
> very careful inspection of the window cords might have revealed the state in
> which they were, but there are many other defects which arise quite suddenly,
> leaks quite suddenly spring up in joints of water pipes and gas pipes, and so on,
> and to say that the landlord is responsible for the consequences of those not being
> in repair in circumstances in which no time could have elapsed between the time
> when the defect first arose and the time when the injury from it occurred, would
> certainly be to impose a very harsh obligation upon a landlord which the Courts
> do not impose except subject to a condition that he must receive notice of the
> defect. To my mind in those circumstances it is clear that, if the landlord gives
> the exclusive occupation to the tenant, the landlord does not in fact know, and in
> this case could not know of the defect.'

In my view, these and other parts of the judgment of Atkin LJ were based on the
reasoning that it is only when defects (although previously latent or invisible) become
patent and are made known to the landlord that his liability to repair arises. Furthermore, it seems to me that both the words of Lord Simonds and his reasoning in
McCarrick's case[5] show that a landlord's obligation to take action only arises when
he has notice of a defect. He will not have notice if no one knows that there is a
defect.

The question does not now arise for express decision whether a landlord's obligation
to repair will arise not only when he receives notice from his tenant of a defect but
also if he receives such notice aliunde or if he has knowledge of it: but I observe that
in *Griffin v Pillet*[6] where a lessee gave notice that steps to a dwelling-house needed
attention but where the lessee did not know that the steps were in fact actually
dangerous, Wright J held that a liability rested on the lessor when subsequently
he, although not his lessee, did acquire knowledge that the steps were actually
dangerous. The purpose of a notice is to impart knowledge that the moment for
action under a covenant to repair has or may have arisen. If a lessor who is under
an obligation to keep premises in repair acquires knowledge that there is a state of
disrepair which may be dangerous then even if such knowledge is not shared by the
lessee I would consider that there arises an obligation on the part of the lessor to
take appropriate action.

I pass, then, to consider whether the respondent had either knowledge or notice
that the ceiling of the bedroom was defective. It is impossible to consider the facts
of the case without entertaining great sympathy with the appellants. Those who as
tenants of the respondent in the early part of 1965 were in occupation of the rooms
above the rooms of the appellants undoubtedly caused disturbance and annoyance
for the appellants. There were frequent parties with music and dancing and there

1   [1926] 2 KB 315
2   [1927] 2 KB 131, [1926] All ER Rep 25
3   [1927] 2 KB at 151, [1926] All ER Rep at 34
4   [1927] 2 KB at 150, [1926] All ER Rep at 33, 34
5   [1946] 2 All ER 646, [1947] AC 219
6   [1926] 1 KB 17

was noise and banging on the floors; even the windows were caused to rattle and
the lights to swing. The appellants complained both to the upstairs tenants and to
the respondent. In his evidence the first appellant said:

> 'I told him that I could not get any sleep at night through banging and jumping
> upstairs and if there was not something done, that the ceiling would eventually
> fall down.'

Further complaint followed:

> 'I told him if something was not done about the all-night parties that my
> wife would be in bad health and so would I and also that probably the ceiling
> would fall down.'

Matters were sufficiently serious as to involve the bringing of proceedings, relating to
the nuisance of noise, in the Croydon County Court. On the giving of specific undertakings to the court the action was, in July 1965, withdrawn. Shortly afterwards
those who had been responsible for the nuisance moved away. That was in 1965.
No defects in the ceiling were or became visible. Three years passed. Then on
26th November 1968 the ceiling fell. The learned judge considered that it was
probable, although perhaps difficult to prove conclusively, that it was the behaviour
of the young people in 1965 rather than old age alone which brought the ceiling down
in 1968. But once the nuisance and the annoyance of the noise had ceased in 1965
there is nothing to suggest that either lessor or lessee thought that there was need to
take any action in regard to the ceiling. There is no evidence that there was any
apprehension or any nervousness concerning its condition. The question naturally
arises whether by reason of the events to which I have referred the respondent had
such measure of knowledge or notice as would require that he should take some
action. But it does not appear that anyone thought that the ceiling had in fact been
weakened: the fear had been expressed that it might or would become affected if the
nuisance continued. The nuisance was then abated. Much as I regret that recovery
of damages by the appellants is not possible I am unable to say that the decision of the
learned judge was in any way erroneous.

I would dismiss the appeal.

LORD DIPLOCK. My Lords, when Parliament first decided by s 12 of the Housing
of the Working Classes Act 1885 to impose on landlords of dwelling-houses for the
working classes obligations as to the physical state of the demised premises, the
method chosen was to provide by statute that a term should be implied in every
contract for letting for habitation a house or part of a house to which the Act applied.
The term originally implied related only to the physical condition of the house at
the commencement of the letting, viz, that it was at that time in all respects reasonably fit for human habitation. It did not impose on the landlord any duty to do any
work on the premises to make them reasonably fit for human habitation after the
commencement of the letting nor did it give him any right to do so, unless a right of
entry for this purpose was reserved to him by the contract of letting. Any breach
of this implied contractual term occurred once and for all at the commencement of
the letting and any right to damages accrued then.

By the Housing, Town Planning, etc, Act 1909, s 15, the landlord's obligations were
extended to the physical state of the premises during the continuance of the letting.
Again the method chosen was to provide by statute for a further term to be implied
in the contract for letting, viz, 'an undertaking that the house shall, during the holding,
be kept by the landlord in all respects fit for human habitation'.

This implied term did impose on the landlord an obligation owed to the tenant to
carry out such work on the premises during the continuance of the tenancy as might
from time to time be needed to keep them reasonably fit for human habitation.

a   But although created by statute the legal nature of this obligation was contractual. Its characteristics were the same as those of an obligation created by a repairing covenant in a lease. What the statute was providing was that any contract for the letting of premises to which it applied should be read and given effect to as if it contained an express covenant by the landlord to keep the premises in such a state of repair as would make them reasonably fit for human habitation. The landlord's

b   obligation lies in the field of contract not of tort. His duty is not one of reasonable care to avoid injury to the tenant. It is a duty to perform his contract.

Provisions in substantially the same form were re-enacted in the Housing Acts of 1925 and 1936. Their legal effect was the subject of consideration by the Divisional Court in *Fisher v Walters*[1], by the Court of Appeal in *Morgan v Liverpool Corpn*[2] and finally by this House in *McCarrick v Liverpool Corpn*[3] where the decision in *Morgan's*

c   case[2], and in particular the reasoning of Atkin LJ in that case, were approved. I shall be returning to these cases later. At this stage it is sufficient to say that as I read *Morgan's* case[2] and *McCarrick's* case[3] their ratio decidendi was based on (a) the contractual nature of the landlord's obligation resulting from the statutory requirement that it should be implied as a term in the contract of letting and (b) the legal characteristics of a repairing covenant by a landlord in a lease or tenancy agreement.

d   My Lords, s 32 (1) of the Housing Act 1961, which your Lordships have now to construe, is not in the same terms as the earlier legislation. But it has the same essential characteristics: (a) that the landlord's obligation results from a statutory requirement that it should be implied as a term in the contract of letting and (b) that the term to be implied has the legal characteristic of a repairing covenant by a landlord in a lease. I can see nothing in s 32 or s 33 of the Housing Act 1961 which alters either of these essential characteristics of the obligation imposed on the landlord by

e   s 32 (1). Reliance has been placed by the appellants on s 33 (7) which avoids any covenant or agreement 'so far as it purports to exclude or limit the obligations of the lessor' under s 32 (1). But this merely refers one back to s 32 (1) to see what are the obligations of the lessor thereunder.

At the root of any analysis of the landlord's obligations under a repairing covenant lies the initial question whether it is an undertaking by the landlord to prevent the

f   premises ever getting out of repair during the continuance of the tenancy or whether it is an undertaking to do work of repair on the premises from time to time as and when they have become out of repair. If it is the former the breach occurs as soon as the premises are in fact out of repair and continues until he has put them back into repair. If it is the latter, there is involved the subsidiary question as to the time at which the landlord's obligation to do the necessary work of repair first arises. Until

g   that time arrives there can be no breach of the obligation; nor can there be any breach thereafter if the landlord then carries out the necessary work of repair with reasonable expedition.

In all the cases on this subject decided before *Fisher v Walters*[1] to which attention has been directed in the argument, starting with *Makin v Watkinson*[4] and ending

h   with *Griffin v Pillet*[5], it has been assumed, even though not expressly stated, that a landlord's repairing covenant is of the latter kind, viz, an undertaking to do work of repair on the premises from time to time if and when they have become out of repair. This appears most clearly in a passage in the judgment of Wright J in *Griffin v Pillet*[6] where he says:

'. . . the lessor in my judgment was not liable for breach of covenant until

j   ——————————————————————————————————————

1   [1926] 2 KB 315
2   [1927] 2 KB 131, [1926] All ER Rep 25
3   [1946] 2 All ER 646, [1947] AC 219
4   (1870) LR 6 Exch 25, [1861-73] All ER Rep 281
5   [1926] 1 KB 17
6   [1926] 1 KB at 22

he had been able to ascertain the nature of the repairs required. This he knew
by April 8, and I think he acted at his peril if he did not at once remedy the non-   *a*
repair, either by temporary measures, if the permanent repairs could not be
immediately effected, or by doing the permanent repairs, if this was practicable.
If he did not do this he committed a breach of covenant.'

The cases to which I have referred were concerned with the time at which the
obligation of the landlord to start works of repair arose. I do not propose to deal   *b*
with them individually. They do not show a continuing logical development in the law
nor any great consistency in reasoning. But by 1926 the result of half a century of judicial
decision was that it was well established that, at any rate where the state of disrepair
was known to the tenant, the landlord's obligation to start carrying out any works
of repair did not arise until he had information about the existence of a defect in the
premises such as would put a reasonable man on enquiry whether works of repair   *c*
were needed.

Although this at least was well-established by 1926, two matters remained open to
doubt. The first is whether, notwithstanding that the landlord has previous information from some other source about the existence of a defect, his obligation to start
carrying out works of repair arises until he has been given notice of the defect by the
tenant. It is unnecessary to decide this in the instant appeal, because the only infor-   *d*
mation relied on is that which was given to the landlord by the tenant. But the
second is a much broader question. It is whether the rule that the landlord must
have information of the existence of a defect in the premises before any obligation
on his part to start carrying out works of repair arises, applies at all when the defect
is latent, i e is of such a nature that the tenant did not know and could not have discovered by reasonable examination that the premises were out of repair. In such a   *e*
case is the landlord under an obligation to start carrying out works of repair as soon
as the premises are in fact out of repair even though he has no such information as
would put a reasonable man on enquiry whether works of repair are needed?

This question arose in the Divisional Court in *Fisher v Walters*[1]. It was a case of
latent defect—a falling ceiling, as in the instant appeal. The tenant relied on the
undertaking of the landlord implied under s 15 of the Housing, Town Planning, etc,   *f*
Act 1909, that the house should be kept by the landlord in all respects fit for human
habitation. Finlay J decided it in favour of the tenant on the broad ground that
irrespective of whether the defect were patent or latent the common law rule that
the landlord must have information about the existence of the defect did not apply
to the covenant implied by statute. Mackinnon J held that the common law rule
did not apply to latent defects, but left it open whether it would apply to patent   *g*
defects.

In the same year a similar question came before the Court of Appeal in *Morgan v
Liverpool Corpn*[2]. It was a case of a broken window cord which was held by the
trial judge to be a latent defect. All three members of the Court of Appeal held
that the implied covenant under the Housing Act 1925 was to be treated as creating
a contractual obligation on the landlord to keep the premises in repair and that the   *h*
landlord's obligation to start to carry out works of repair did not arise until he had
notice of the defect. While Lord Hanworth MR expressed doubt whether the defect
was truly latent, Atkin and Lawrence LJJ decided the case on the basis that the defect
was latent and held expressly that the common law rule applied to all defects,
latent as well as patent.

Finally, there is the decision of your Lordships' house in *McCarrick v Liverpool*   *j*
Corpn[3]. Although the defect in that case was patent the appeal was brought to

---

1   [1926] 2 KB 315
2   [1927] 2 KB 131, [1926] All ER Rep 25
3   [1946] 2 All ER 646, [1947] AC 219

a   this House, as Lord Simonds said[1], to test the correctness of the decision of the Court of Appeal in *Morgan's* case[2]. Lord Simonds's speech was concurred in by Lords Thankerton and Macmillan. He approved expressly the decision in *Morgan's* case[2] and in particular the judgment of Atkin LJ. He drew no distinction between latent and patent defects and said that the decision in *Fisher v Walters*[3] was inconsistent with higher authority and could not stand. He summarised the law as follows[4]:

b

'I conclude, then, that the provision imported by statute into the contractual tenancy must be construed in the same way as any other term of the tenancy and, so construed, does not impose any obligation on the landlord unless and until he has notice of the defect which renders the dwelling not "reasonably fit for human habitation". That is the only question which your Lordships have to decide and I do not think it desirable or necessary to consider what may constitute such notice.'

c

Lord Porter and Lord Uthwatt delivered separate speeches. Although Lord Porter contented himself with expressing the view that *Fisher v Walters*[3] would have required to be carefully scrutinised if the latency of the defect had been in issue in *d*   *McCarrick's* case[5] he concluded by expressing his agreement with the reasoning and decision of Atkin LJ in *Morgan's* case[2] which was on the basis that the defect there was latent. Lord Uthwatt simply said that he expressed no opinion as to latent defects.

My Lords, unless your Lordships are prepared to overrule *Morgan v Liverpool Corpn*[2] despite its express approval by this House in *McCarrick v Liverpool Corpn*[5], and to hold that Lord Simonds's statement of the law that I have cited was wrong, I *e*   think you are compelled to hold that this appeal must fail unless the tenant can show that before the ceiling fell the landlord had information about the existence of a defect in the ceiling such as would put him on enquiry whether works of repair to it were needed.

While it would be open to your Lordships to do so, this is not I think a suitable *f*   case in which to exercise the recently asserted power[6] of this House to refuse to follow one of its own previous decisions[6]. An examination of the reasoning in the judgments in the cases of this subject during the last 100 years suggests that the law might easily have developed on different lines from those which it in fact followed. But, for my part, I am not persuaded that this development was clearly wrong or leads to results which are clearly unjust. *McCarrick's* case[5] has stood for 25 years; *Morgan's* case[2] for 45 years. Landlords and tenants and their insurers have entered *g*   into leases and contracts and Parliament has passed statutes on the basis that the law is as stated in those judgments. This House would not be justified in altering it now.

The only remaining question in this appeal is whether what the tenant said to the landlord in 1965 at a time when the tenants of the flat above were still holding parties *h*   which involved stamping on the ceiling, $3\frac{1}{2}$ years before the ceiling fell, would have put a reasonable landlord on enquiry whether works of repair were needed at that time. Bristow J who heard the evidence of the plaintiffs, found that the complaints which the tenant then made were not to the effect that the structure of the ceiling might already be defective, but that if the stamping continued it would one day

j

1   [1946] 2 All ER at 649, [1947] AC at 227
2   [1927] 2 KB 131, [1926] All ER Rep 25
3   [1926] 2 KB 315
4   [1946] 2 All ER at 650, 651, [1947] AC at 229, 230
5   [1946] 2 All ER 646, [1947] AC 219
6   See *Note* [1966] 3 All ER 77, [1966] 1 WLR 1234

bring down the ceiling while it was going on. This finding was amply supported by   *a*
the evidence and was, I think, clearly right.

My Lords, I would dismiss this appeal and in doing so express my entire concurrence
with the judgment of Bristow J.

LORD SIMON OF GLAISDALE. My Lords, I have had the advantage of
reading in advance the speech prepared by my noble and learned friend, Lord Dip-   *b*
lock. I agree with it; and I would therefore dismiss the appeal.

LORD CROSS OF CHELSEA. My Lords, for the reasons given by my noble
and learned friends, Lord Morris of Borth-y-Gest and Lord Diplock in their speeches
which I have had the opportunity of reading I would dismiss this appeal.
                                                                                   c

Appeal dismissed.

Solicitors: *B M Birnberg & Co* (for the appellants); *Herbert Smith & Co* (for the
respondent).

                                                        S A Hatteea Esq Barrister.   *d*

R v Chief Immigration Officer of Manchester airport, ex parte Insah Begum
                                                                                   e

COURT OF APPEAL, CIVIL DIVISION
LORD DENNING MR, MEGAW LJ AND SIR GORDON WILLMER
3rd NOVEMBER 1972

Commonwealth immigrant – Admission – Refusal of admission – Notice of refusal – Delivery   *f*
of notice to immigrant – Notice delivered by immigration officer to immigrant's legal adviser at
airport – Immigrant illiterate and having no knowledge of English – Whether necessary that
notice should be delivered by hand to immigrant personally – Commonwealth Immigrants Act
1962, Sch 1, para 2 (1).

Commonwealth immigrant – Admission – Refusal of admission – Notice of refusal – Time within   *g*
which notice to be given – Notice to be given not later than 12 hours after conclusion of immi-
grant's examination – Examination not concluded until all information to hand – Common-
wealth Immigrants Act 1962, Sch 1, para 2 (3).

The applicant, a woman, who was illiterate and had no knowledge of English, arrived   *h*
from Pakistan at Manchester airport at 2.00 p m on 14th September 1971, seeking admission into the United Kingdom. She produced a passport and entry certificate and
said that she was the wife of a Commonwealth citizen resident in the United Kingdom.
The immigration officer having examined the entry certificate thought that it was a
forgery. He made enquiries; he interviewed the man said to be the applicant's husband, and a friend, and had a telex sent to Lahore about the entry certificate. At 9.00
p m on 14th September the immigration officer told the applicant, through an inter-   *i*
preter, that he thought the entry certificate was a forgery, he said that he was expecting a reply to the telex he had sent to Lahore, and that no decision would be taken to
admit or refuse to admit the applicant until a reply to the telex had been received.
Later that day the applicant got in touch with a solicitor. On the next day, 15th
September, the solicitor's managing clerk went with the applicant to see the

a immigration officer at the airport. Whilst they were interviewing the officer he received a telex message from Lahore confirming his suspicion that the entry certificate was a forgery. The message was received at 1.30 pm on 15th September. Thereupon the officer told his assistant to make out a notice of refusal of admission into the United Kingdom and the notice was immediately given to the managing clerk who had lent across the table saying, 'I will take this: I am [the applicant's] legal repre-
b sentative'. The applicant applied for an order of certiorari to quash the decision of the immigration officer refusing to admit her to the United Kingdom contending (i) that the immigration officer had not complied with the procedure laid down by para 2 (1)*a* of Sch 1 to the Commonwealth Immigrants Act 1962, in that the notice refusing admission should have been given to the applicant herself and not to the managing clerk, and (ii) that under para 2 (3)*b* of Sch 1 to the 1962 Act the notice refus-
c ing admission was invalid because it was not given until more than 12 hours after the conclusion of the applicant's examination, it being contended that the examination was concluded at 9.00 p m on 14th September.

Held – The applicant was not entitled to the order sought because—
(i) para 2 (1) of Sch 1 to the 1962 Act did not require personal service on the person concerned of a notice refusing his admission to the United Kingdom; the giving of a
d notice complied with the Act if it was served on the person's legal adviser in circumstances from which it could be presumed that he had authority to accept it; since the applicant could not speak English, it was good service of the notice to give it to the managing clerk who was acting for the applicant and was present with her (see p 596 h and p 597 b f g and h, post); dictum of Lord Campbell CJ in *R v Deputies of the Freemen of Leicester* (1850) 15 QB at 675, and *Burt v Kirkcaldy* [1965] 1 All ER 741 applied;
e (ii) service of the notice was not out of time under para 2 (3) of Sch 1; examination of a person pursuant to para 1 of Sch 1 was not concluded until all information was to hand; accordingly the applicant's examination had not been concluded at 9.00 pm on 14th September but had merely been adjourned pending receipt of the telex from Lahore; it was concluded on receipt of the telex when the notice refusing admission was immediately given (see p 597 d e and h, post).
f Decision of the Divisional Court [1972] 1 All ER 6 affirmed.

Notes
For examination of Commonwealth immigrants, see Supplement to 5 Halsbury's Laws (3rd Edn) para 1514.
For the Commonwealth Immigrants Act 1962, Sch 1, para 2, see 4 Halsbury's
g Statutes (3rd Edn) 48.

Cases referred to in judgment
Burt v Kirkcaldy [1965] 1 All ER 741, [1965] 1 WLR 474, 129 JP 190, DC, Digest (Cont Vol B) 677, 376a.
R v Deputies of the Freemen of Leicester (1850) 15 QB 671, 117 ER 613; sub nom *R v*
h *Goodrich* 19 LJQB 413, 15 LTOS 248, 14 JP 415, 33 Digest (Repl) 333, 1584.

Appeal
This was an appeal on behalf of the applicant, Insah Begum, against the judgment of the Divisional Court (Lord Widgery CJ, Bridge and Shaw JJ) given on 8th October 1971 and reported at [1972] 1 All ER 6, dismissing a motion on behalf of the applicant (i) for an order of certiorari to quash a decision made by the respondent, Her Majesty's
j immigration officer at Manchester airport, refusing the applicant admission into the United Kingdom and (ii) for an order of mandamus directed to the immigration officer requiring him to hear and determine fully, according to law and natural

---

a Paragraph 2 (1), so far as material, is set out at p 596 g, post
b Paragraph 2 (3), so far as material, is set out at p 597 c, post

justice, the facts relevant to the applicant's admission into the United Kingdom and requiring him to admit the applicant into the United Kingdom. The facts are set out in the judgment of Lord Denning MR

Martin Collins QC and *G S Khan* for the applicant.
Gordon Slynn for the respondent.

LORD DENNING MR. Insah Begum, a woman, came from Pakistan to England. On 14th September 1971 about 2.00 pm she arrived at the airport at Manchester. She could not speak English at all. She produced a passport and an entry certificate. (The Commomwealth Immigrants Act 1962, s 2 (2), entitles a woman, a Commonwealth citizen, to enter this country if she holds an entry certificate and is the wife of a Commonwealth citizen who is resident here at the time.) This woman said her husband was a Mr Hussain, who was here, and she produced an entry certificate. The immigration officer, Mr Fuller, examined the entry certificate and thought that it was a forgery. It appeared to him that some one had manufactured a rubber stamp purporting to be an entry certificate issued by the British High Commission. This one was different from the genuine stamp. The lines were uneven and there was a difference in shape. The immigration officer made enquires. He interviewed a man who was said to be her husband and a friend. He also had further interviews. He had a telex sent to Lahore about the entry certificate. At about 9.00 p m he told the woman and her friends, through an interpreter, that he thought that the entry certificate was a forgery and that he was expecting a reply to the telex. He said that no decision would be taken to admit or to refuse her until this had been received.

Later that day the woman got in touch with a solicitor. He got in touch with counsel. On the next day, 15th September, the solicitor's managing clerk, with the woman, went along to see the immigration officer at Manchester airport. Whilst they were interviewing the immigration officers there, a telex message was received from Lahore. It confirmed the suspicions about the entry certificate. It was a forgery. The authorities there had previously refused to issue her with a certificate. So she had got a forged one. Thereupon the immigration officer told his assistant to make out a notice of refusal saying she could not be admitted. When the assistant produced it, the solicitors' managing clerk lent across the table and took it from him, saying: 'I will take this: I am [the applicant's] legal representative.' It was then 1.30 p m on 15th September.

On that procedure two points are taken before us. The first point was that the officers had not complied with the procedure laid down by para 2 (1) of Sch 1 to the Commonwealth Immigrants Act 1962, which says:

> 'The power of an immigration officer . . . to refuse admission into the United Kingdom . . . shall be exercised by notice in writing; and . . . any such notice shall be given by being delivered by the immigration officer to the person to whom it relates.'

The argument was based on the words 'to the person to whom it relates'. It is said that the notice ought to have been given to the woman herself and not to the solicitor's clerk. I do not agree. I think the notice is sufficient to comply with the statute if it is given to the person herself or to her agent, in this sense, that is he authorised to receive it on her behalf or may from his position be presumed to have such authority. Thus, when husband and wife are living together, the wife may be presumed to have authority to receive service of a document for her husband. It was so held in *R v Deputies of the Freemen of Leicester*[1]. Lord Campbell CJ said[2]:

> 'In general, when personal service is required by an Act, it is so said in express

[1] (1850) 15 QB 671
[2] (1850) 15 QB at 675

a   words; but here the words used are "give or deliver notice in writing unto such deputy," which have no such force.'

Similarly in *Burt v Kirkcaldy*[1] a police constable served a notice of intended prosecution on a husband by leaving it with the wife or at the house. It was held to be sufficient. Likewise I think a notice is sufficiently served if it is served on a person's solicitor or on his solicitor's clerk in such circumstances that he may be presumed to have

b   authority to accept it. In this case, when you remember that the women could not speak English, it was perfectly good service—indeed the best service—to deliver it to the solicitors who was acting for her and present with her.

The second point is this: para 2 (3) of Sch 1 says that a notice—

c   'under this paragraph shall not be given to any person unless he has been examined . . . and shall not be given to any person later than twelve hours after the conclusion of his examination (including any futher examination) . . .'

It was said that the examination of Insah Begum was concluded at 9.00 p m on 14th September, and that the notice was not given until 1.30 p m on the next day, 15th September; and that it was therefore more than 12 hours, and was invalid. The answer is however that the examination was not 'concluded' at 9.00 p m on the 14th. It was

d   then adjourned pending the telex communication from Lahore. Very often an examination may have to be adjourned pending further enquiries, and then resumed after the replies are received. It is not 'concluded' until all information is to hand. In this case it was not concluded until the telex reply was received at 1.30 p m on the 15th. It was there and then said: 'Here and now the examination is concluded and this notice is given refusing entry.' It was well in time.

e   I do not think that either of these points is good. I think the decision of the Divisional Court[2] was right and I would dismiss this appeal.

MEGAW LJ. I agree. As to the first point, I agree with the proposition put forward by counsel for the respondent, that it is not a case in which service is required to be

f   personal service on the particular individual concerned. Of course, it must be shown that if it is service on someone else, that other person is an authorised agent for that purpose. I agree entirely with the view which Lord Denning MR has expressed that nobody could be more properly regarded as the authorised agent for that purpose than the solicitor's managing clerk who was dealing with the matter in this case and to whom the notice was given.

g   With regard to the second point, as to the period of time which had elapsed after the conclusion of this examination, I regard the view expressed by Lord Widgery CJ in the Divisional Court[3] as being, if I may say so with respect, completely apposite. The irresistible conclusion is that the examination had not been concluded on the previous evening—that is 14th September. Accordingly I agree that both points fail and that the appeal should be dismissed.

h

SIR GORDON WILLMER. I agree with both the judgments that have been delivered. I have nothing further of my own to add.

Appeal dismissed.

j   Solicitors: *Amelan & Roth*, Manchester (for the applicant); *Treasury Solicitor*.

Wendy Shockett Barrister.

---

1   [1965] 1 All ER 741, [1965] 1 WLR 474
2   [1972] 1 All ER 6
3   [1972] 1 All ER at 9

Falkiner and another v Commissioner of Stamp Duties

PRIVY COUNCIL

LORD REID, LORD MORRIS OF BORTH-Y-GEST, VISCOUNT DILHORNE, LORD SIMON OF GLAISDALE
AND SIR RICHARD WILD

10th, 11th, 12th, 13th JULY, 7th NOVEMBER 1972

*Privy Council – Australia – New South Wales – Death Duty – Dutiable estate – Classes of
property – Property disposed of by deceased by a settlement – Settlement containing trust to
take effect after deceased's death – Settlement containing trust to take effect on failure of
preceding trusts – Trust for next-of-kin of settlor – 'Next-of-kin' meaning next-of-kin at
time of settlor's death – Trust to take effect after deceased's death – Stamp Duties Act 1920-
1959 (New South Wales), s 102 (2) (a).*

On 4th October 1961 the settlor executed a settlement of a sum of $100,000 which
he paid to the trustees of the settlement. By cl 3 (b)[a] the trustees were to hold the
fund on trust for the settlor's son, contingent on his attaining the age of 22 years,
or if he should die before that age, on trust for such of his children as should attain
21 years or marry under that age. On the failure of the preceding trusts, the fund
was, by cl 3 (b) (iv), to be held on trust for children of the settlor, or the children
or remoter issue of any deceased child; cl 3 (b) continued: '. . . and should the Trust
Fund not vest as aforesaid then (v) UPON TRUST for the next of kin of the Settlor as
determined by the provisions now in force of the Wills Probate and Administration
Act 1898-1954 of the State of New South Wales.' The settlor died on 15th October
1961 domiciled and resident in the State of New South Wales. The Commissioner
of Stamp Duties of New South Wales claimed that the property subject to the settlement formed part of the dutiable estate of the settlor in that the settlement was
one which contained a trust (i e the trust in cl 3 (b) (v)) 'to take effect after [the
settlor's] death' within s 102 (2) (a)[b] of the Stamp Duties Act 1920-1959.

Held – The prima facie rule of construction was that the words 'next-of-kin' referred
to the persons who were the next-of-kin at the date of the death of the person whose
next-of-kin they were. The construction of those words in cl 3 (b) (v) in that sense
was reinforced by the reference to the relevant statute of distribution. There was
nothing in the terms of cl 3 (b) to rebut the prima facie meaning; the word 'then'
at the conclusion of cl 3 (b) (iv) was to be construed as referring to an event and not
as an adverb of time, and the fact that there might be a hiatus between the contingent
failure of the preceding trusts and the ascertainment of the next-of-kin was not
sufficient to demonstrate that by 'next of kin' the settlor meant the next-of-kin to be
ascertained as at the contingent failure of the trust and not at the time of his death. It
followed that the trust in cl 3 (b) (v) had to await the settlor's death before it could
take effect and, accordingly the property which was subject to the settlement was
to be included in the deceased's dutiable estate (see p 604 c and f, p 606 b c f and g,
p 607 j and p 608 b c e and g, post).

Gundry v Pinniger [1843-60] All ER Rep 403, *Bullock v Downes* [1843-60] All ER Rep
706, *Re Winn, Brook v Whitton* [1908-10] All ER Rep 593, *Hutchinson v National Refuges
for Homeless and Destitute Children* [1920] All ER Rep 701, and dicta of Sir Raymond
Evershed MR and of Jenkins LJ in *Re Gansloser's Will Trusts* [1951] All ER at 940,
945, applied.

---

a Clause 3 (*b*) is set out at p 601 c to g, post

b Section 102 (2) (*a*) is set out at p 602 c and d, post

Notes

a For interests ceasing on death under the estate duty legislation in England and Scotland, see 15 Halsbury's Laws (3rd Edn) 13, 14, para 22.

For gifts to next-of-kin in wills, see 39 Halsbury's Laws (3rd Edn) 1042, 1043, para 1564, and for cases on the subject, see 49 Digest (Repl) 794-796, 7467-7484.

Cases referred to in opinion

b Bullock v Downes (1860) 9 HL Cas 1, [1843-60] All ER Rep 706, 3 LT 194, 11 ER 627, HL, 49 Digest (Repl) 790, 7429.

Comr of Stamp Duties v Atwill p 576, ante; rvsg (1971) 45 ALJR 703; rvsg (1970) 92 NSWWN 869.

Deane v Lombe (1925) 25 SRNSW 502, 42 NSWWN 119, 49 Digest (Repl) 666, *2130.

Gansloser's Will Trusts, Re, Chartered Bank of India, Australia and China v Chillingworth *c* [1951] 2 All ER 936, [1952] Ch 30, CA, 49 Digest (Repl) 797, 7492.

Gundry v Pinniger (1852) 1 De GM & G 502, [1843-60] All ER Rep 403, 21 LJCh 405, 18 LTOS 325, 16 Jur 488, 42 ER 647; affg (1851) 14 Beav 94, 51 ER 222, 49 Digest (Repl) 794, 7467.

Hooper, Re, Hooper v Carpenter [1936] 1 All ER 277, [1936] Ch 442, 105 LJCh 298, 154 LT 677, CA, 49 Digest (Repl) 775, 7267.

d Hutchinson v National Refuges for Homeless and Destitute Children [1920] AC 795, [1920] All ER Rep 701, 89 LJCh 469, 123 LT 439, HL, 49 Digest (Repl) 796, 7489.

Keighley v Comr of Stamp Duties (NSW) (1971) 45 ALJR 620; rvsg [1971] NSWLR 229.

Kent v Comr of Stamp Duties (NSW) (1961) 106 CLR 366.

Nicholas (decd), In the estate of [1955] VLR 291.

Ranking's Settlement Trusts, Re (1868) LR 6 Eq 601, 40 Digest (Repl) 635, 1282.

e Rosenthal v Rosenthal (1910) 11 CLR 87, 21 Digest (Repl) 179, *509.

Toldervy v Colt (1836) 1 M & W 250, 1 Y & C Ex 621, Tyr & Gr 324, 5 LJExEq 25, 150 ER 427, 49 Digest (Repl) 1120, 10390.

Warburton v Loveland d Ivie (1828) 1 Hud & B 623; affd (1832) 6 Bli NS 1, [1824-34] All ER Rep 589, 2 Dow & Cl 480, 5 ER 499, HL, 17 Digest (Repl) 277, *371.

Wharton v Barker (1858) 4 K & J 483, 4 Jur NS 553, 70 ER 202, 49 Digest (Repl) 798, *f* 7501.

Winn, Re, Brook v Whitton [1910] 1 Ch 278, [1908-10] All ER Rep 593, 79 LJCh 165, 101 LT 737, 49 Digest (Repl) 795, 7483.

Appeal

On 12th November 1970 the Commissioner of Stamp Duties of the State of New South Wales ('the commissioner') stated the following case for the opinion of the *g* Court of Appeal of the Supreme Court of New South Wales.

1. George Brereton Sadleir Falkiner ('the settlor') died on 15th October 1961 leaving him surviving three children and no more, namely, George Brereton Sadleir Falkiner, Frances Dorothy Falkiner and Suzanne Enid Falkiner, each of whom was then under 21 years of age and unmarried.

2. At the time of his death and at all material times theretofore the settlor was *h* domiciled and resident in the State of New South Wales.

3. Probate of the last will of the settlor was on 14th February 1962 granted by the Supreme Court of New South Wales in its probate jurisdiction to Pauline Arnold Falkiner, Perpetual Trustee Co Ltd ('the appellants') and to Alexander Burnett Ramsay, who died on 25th September 1965.

4. Canberra Estates Property Ltd ('the trustee') was and at all material times had *j* been a company incorporated in the Australian Capital Territory.

5. On 4th October 1961 and within the Australian Capital Territory: (a) the settlor paid to the trustee ten separate sums of $100,000 each, and (b) the settlor and the trustee executed ten separate deeds[1], each dated 4th October 1961 and made between the settlor of the one part and the trustee of the other part.

---

1 The terms of the deeds, so far as material, are set out at p 601, post

6. Thereafter, also on 4th October 1961 and within the Australian Capital Territory, the trustee, in exercise of the powers conferred on it by the respective deeds, applied each of the ten separate sums of $100,000 in the acquisition by application and allotment of 10,000 fully paid ordinary shares of $2 each in Booka Pty Ltd (a company which was incorporated in the Australian Capital Territory) at par and 32,000 fully paid ordinary shares of $2 each in Senior Park Pty Ltd (a company which was incorporated in the Australian Capital Territory) at a premium of 50 cents per share. Thereafter the trustee continued to hold each of the ten parcels of 10,000 shares in Booka Pty Ltd, and 32,000 shares in Senior Park Pty Ltd as the trust fund referred to in the respective deeds until, and so held them at, the time of the death of the settlor.

7. At the time of the death of the settlor, the value of each of the ten parcels of shares was $100,000 and the total value of all of the shares was $1,000 000.

8. From the time of allotment until the death of the settlor and at all other material times all of the shares acquired and held by the trustee were registered in the share registers of the respective companies maintained in the Australian Capital Territory.

9. The commissioner, in assessing the death duty payable in respect of the estate of the settlor, claimed that, by virtue of ss 102 (2) (a) and 102 (2A) of the Stamp Duties Act 1920-1959, each of the ten parcels of shares (a total of 100,000 shares in Booka Pty Ltd and 320,000 shares in Senior Park Pty Ltd) was included in the dutiable estate of the settlor, and the commissioner accordingly assessed the death duty payable in respect of the estate at the sum of $735,899 (subject to an allowance or refund $4,390·23 pursuant to the provisions of s 103A of the 1920-1959 Act).

10. The appellants claimed that none of the shares should be included in the dutiable estate of the settlor.

11. The appellants, being dissatisfied with the assessment of death duty in respect of the estate of the settlor, pursuant to s 124 of the 1920-1959 Act and within the time therein limited, delivered to the commissioner a notice in writing requiring him to state a case for the opinion of the Court of Appeal.

12. If none of the shares were to be included in the dutiable estate of the settlor the death duty payable in respect of the estate would be reduced by the sum of $270,000 to $465,899·26 (subject to an allowance or refund of $4,390·23 pursuant to s 103A of the 1920-1959 Act).

13. The questions for the decision of the Court of Appeal were: (1) whether the whole of the 100,000 shares in Booka Pty Ltd and 320,000 shares in Senior Park Pty Ltd should be included in the dutiable estate of the settlor for the purpose of the assessment and payment of death duty; (2) if the answer to question (1) was in the negative, whether any, and if so which, of those shares should be included in the dutiable estate of the settlor for the purpose of the assessment and payment of death duty; (3) whether the amount of death duty which should properly be assessed in respect of the estate of the settlor (subject to any allowance or refund pursuant to s 103A of the 1920-1959 Act) was (a) $735,899·26 or (b) $465,899·26 or (c) some other, and if so what, amount; (4) how the costs of the case were to be borne and paid.

On 20th May 1971 the Court of Appeal (Asprey, Mason and Taylor JJ) held that in view of the provisions of para (v) of cl 3 (b) of each of the trust deeds the settlor had disposed of property by settlements each of which contained a trust to take effect after his death, within s 102 (2) (a) of the 1920-1959 Act, and accordingly ordered that the questions asked in the case stated be answered as follows: (1) yes; (2) does not arise; (3) (a) yes; (4) by the appellants. By leave of the Court of Appeal the appellants appealed against that decision.

P J Kenny QC and *C V Cullinan* (both of the New South Wales Bar) for the appellants.
F J D Officer QC and *M H McLelland* (both of the New South Wales Bar) for the commissioner.

LORD SIMON OF GLAISDALE. On 4th October 1961 the deceased settlor, George Brereton Sadleir Falkiner, executed ten settlements in relation respectively a   to ten separate sums of $100,000 which he paid that day to Canberra Estates Property Ltd (a company incorporated in the Australian Capital Territory), named as the trustee of the settlements. Clause 3 of the first settlement reads as follows:

'3. The Trustees shall hold all moneys from time to time forming part of the Trust Fund UPON TRUST to invest the same in any one or more of the modes of investment hereinafter authorised and subject thereto shall hold the Trust
b   Fund and the income thereof upon the trusts hereinafter expressed concerning the same that is to say: (a) During the minority of any person or persons who under the trusts hereinafter declared would for the time being if of full age be entitled to receive the income of the Trust Fund the Trustees shall invest the rents profits and income of and from the Trust Fund in or upon investments in or upon which the Trustees are by this Deed authorised to invest money and may
c   from time to time vary such investments and (subject as hereinafter provided) shall accumulate the yearly produce of the said investments in the way of compound interest by from time to time similarly investing the same and the yearly produce of the investments thereby from time to time acquired. (b) Subject as hereinafter provided the Trustees shall stand possessed of the Trust Fund and all accumulations of income derived from such rents profits and income as
d   aforesaid and the investments representing the same: (i) UPON TRUST subject to and contingent upon GEORGE BRERETON SADLEIR FALKINER the son of the Settlor (hereinafter called "the Contingent Beneficiary") attaining the age of twenty-one (21) years thereafter TO PAY the income arising therefrom to the Contingent Beneficiary until he shall attain the age of twenty-two (22) years or die under such age. (ii) UPON TRUST subject to and contingent upon the Contingent Beneficiary
e   attaining the age of twenty-two (22) years as to the corpus of the said Trust Fund and all accumulations thereof for the Contingent Beneficiary absolutely, (iii) UPON TRUST should the Contingent Beneficiary die before attaining the age of twenty-two (22) years leaving children him surviving for such of his children as shall attain the age of twenty-one years or marry under that age in equal shares or should no such child attain that age or marry under that age or should
f   the Contingent Beneficiary die before attaining twenty-one years of age leaving no children him surviving then (iv) UPON TRUST for such of the children of the Settlor as shall be living at the date of the death of the survivor of the persons in this Clause previously mentioned and the children or remoter issue then living of any then deceased child of the Settlor in equal shares per stirpes and should the Trust Fund not vest as aforesaid then (v) UPON TRUST for the next of kin of
g   the Settlor as determined by the provisions now in force of the Wills Probate and Administration Act 1898-1954 of the State of New South Wales.'

The other nine settlements were similar, except that in place of the age of 22 years specified in cl 3 (b) (i), (ii) and (iii) the ages specified ran respectively from 23 to 31 years. Thereafter, also on 4th October 1961, the trustee of the settlements applied
h   the whole of the settled sums in the purchase of shares in companies incorporated in the Australian Capital Territory.

The settlor died on 15th October 1961, domiciled and resident in the State of New South Wales. He left surviving him three children, namely George Brereton Sadlier Falkiner (the person called 'the Contingent Beneficiary' in the settlements), Frances Dorothy Falkiner and Suzanne Enid Falkiner; all were under the age of 21 years
j   and were unmarried. The record is silent as to other kindred. Probate of the last will of the settlor was on 14th February 1962 granted to the two appellants and to one other joint executor since deceased.

The commissioner in assessing the death duty payable in respect of the estate of the settlor, claimed that by virtue of ss 102 (2) (a) and 102 (2A) of the Stamp Duties Act 1920-1959, the shares the subject-matter of the ten settlements of 4th October 1961 were to be included in the dutiable estate of the settlor, and the commissioner

assessed the death duty payable in respect of the estate accordingly. The appellants,
being dissatisfied with the assessment and claiming that the shares should not be
included in the dutiable estate of the settlor, required the commissioner to state a
case for the judgment of the Court of Appeal of New South Wales. On this being
done, the Court of Appeal unanimously upheld the assessment of the commissioner.
By their leave the appellants have appealed to Her Majesty in Council. Section 102
(2) (a) is in the following terms:

> 'For the purposes of the assessment and payment of death duty but subject
> as hereinafter provided, the estate of a deceased person shall be deemed to
> include and consist of the following classes of property:—
> '(1) ...
> '(2) (a) All property which the deceased has disposed of, whether before or
> after the passing of this Act, by will or by a settlement containing any trust in
> respect of that property to take effect after his death, including a will or settle-
> ment made in the exercise of any general power of appointment, whether exer-
> cisable by the deceased alone or jointly with another person: Provided that the
> property deemed to be included in the estate of the deceased shall be the property
> which at the time of his death is subject to such trust.'

(It is unnecessary to set out s 102 (2A); it is common ground that its effect is to make
the shares part of the dutiable estate of the settlor notwithstanding that they are
in companies, and held by a trustee, incorporated outside New South Wales, if they
would have been part of it had the trustee been resident in, and the shares been in
companies incorporated within, New South Wales.)

Before the Court of Appeal the appellants took three points: (1) the effect of the
proviso to s 102 (2) (a) is that there is brought into the dutiable estate by the main
provision of the paragraph only so much of the actual property 'disposed of' by way
of settlement as was, at the time of the death of the settlor, still subject to the
trusts of the settlement; and that, the property in the instant case which was so
disposed of being cash which was converted into shares (so that no cash remained at
the time of death subject to the trusts of the settlement), none of the property disposed of by way of settlement on 4th October 1961 was part of the dutiable estate of
the settlor; (2) for s 102 (2) (a) to take effect, the relevant trust must be expressly
conditioned to take effect after the death of the settlor—in other words, the condition
precedent of the settlor's death must be expressed in the settlement in literal terms;
(3) on their proper construction the settlements did not contain any trust, either
expressly or impliedly, to take effect after the death of the settlor—in particular, the
trust in cl 3 (b) (v) in each of the settlements for next-of-kin did not give rise to any
trust to take effect after the death of the settlor within the meaning of s 102 (2) (a).

On the first point—namely, the relevant construction of the proviso to s 102 (2) (a)—
the Court of Appeal followed their previous decision in *Comr of Stamp Duties v Atwill*[1]
holding that the effect of the proviso on its proper construction was not to exempt,
the shares from duty under the paragraph merely because they were the proceeds
of the property originally settled, and not that property itself. Subsequent to the
decision of the Court of Appeal in the instant case their decision in *Atwill's* case[1] was
reversed by a majority of the High Court of Australia[2]. The commissioner appealed
to Her Majesty in Council from the judgment of the High Court in *Atwill's* case[2];
and the appeal of the instant appellants on this point was argued before the Board
in conjunction with the appeal in *Atwill's* case[3]. The point is covered in the reasons
which their Lordships have given for the advice which they have humbly tendered
to Her Majesty in *Atwill's* case[3].

1   (1970) 92 NSWWN 869
2   (1971) 45 ALJR 703
3   See p 576, ante

On the second point the Court of Appeal also followed a previous decision of their
court (*Keighley v Comr of Stamp Duties (NSW)*[1]), which itself purported to follow earlier
decisions such as *Rosenthal v Rosenthal*[2] and *Kent v Comr of Stamp Duties (NSW)*[3]; they
held that, for a trust to be caught by s 102 (2) (*a*), the death of the settlor need not be
an express condition precedent to its operation—it is enough that the settlement
contains any trust the provisions of which make it impossible to operate on the trust
property before the settlor's death.   The decision of the Court of Appeal in New
South Wales in *Keighley's* case[1] was also reversed by the High Court of Australia[4],
but on the ground that, on the proper construction of the relevant trust of the settlement in that case, its taking effect was neither expressly nor impliedly conditional on
the settlor's death.   Menzies J[5] (Windeyer J agreeing) cited with approval Herring
CJ in *In the estate of Nicholas (decd)*[6]: 'Settlements were . . . caught . . . if any trust contained therein had to await the death of the settlor before it could take effect . . .'
Gibbs J[7] (McTiernan, Windeyer and Owen JJ agreeing) cited with approval from *Kent v
Comr of Stamp Duties (NSW)*[8]: '. . . the expression "containing any trust to take effect
after his death" postulates a trust which at the death is still capable of taking effect.'
Before their Lordships these were accepted on behalf of the appellants as correct
statements of the law; so that, where any will or settlement contains a trust which
either expressly or impliedly depends on the settlor's death as a condition precedent
to the vesting in possession or enjoyment of the trust property and interest therein
in a beneficiary, the provisions of s 101 (2) (*a*) are satisfied.

The point argued independently in the instant appeal was therefore whether the
settlements on their proper construction contained any trust which was still capable
of taking effect at the death of the settlor, and which had to await the death of the
settlor before it could take effect—specifically, whether the trust for next-of-kin
contained in cl 3 (*b*) (v) had such effect.

Certain words have been legally construed as having a prima facie meaning (not,
generally, differing from their most ordinary meaning) when contained in documents
intended to have legal effect—particularly, wills and settlements.   In the absence of
a contrary intention appearing, the court will assume that it is this prima facie meaning which was intended.   Such a rule has manifest advantages.   In the first place,
the existence of the rule will enable legal advisers to predict how a court will construe
the words in various circumstances within the contemplation of client and advisers;
and, if the prima facie legal meaning does not represent the client's intention, to make
that intention plain.   Secondly, the rule leads to economy; the meaning need not
be spelled out at length, but words can rather be used in the knowledge that they
will prima facie carry the meaning put on them by the law.   Thirdly, if, as often
happens, the actual forensic situation was probably not foreseen by settlor or testator,
the court is relieved from a purely impressionistic interpretation, which might well
vary from judge to judge; and the unsuccessful litigant will at least have the con-
solation of knowing that his case has been adjudged by an objective standard, which
has been applied in the past to others in a similar situation to his, and which will be
so applicable to others in future.   (In this connection, their Lordships bear in mind
that there is no evidence of the present ages or status of the settlor's children; and
that cl 3 (*b*) (v) of the settlements, or some of them, might still be invoked to
determine private interests of parties not now before the court.)

Such reasons as these are still potent to recommend the prima facie rules of construction to which their Lordships have referred, even if those rules were not, as
their Lordships think, so firmly established in law as to compel adherence.   But they
are, of course, only prima facie rules; and it is always open to a settlor or testator to

---

1 [1971] NSWLR 229   5 (1971) 45 ALJR at 621
2 (1910) 11 CLR 87   6 [1955] VLR 291 at 294
3 (1961) 106 CLR 366   7 (1971) 45 ALJR at 623
4 (1971) 45 ALJR 620   8 (1961) 106 CLR at 374

demonstrate that he intends his words to bear a meaning other than the prima facie
one which the law ascribes to them.

So far as the expression 'next-of-kin' is concerned, there are numerous statements
of the rule; the earlier cases were extensively reviewed by Page Wood V-C in *Wharton
v Barker*[1] and by Viscount Finlay in *Hutchinson v National Refuges for Homeless and
Destitute Children*[2]. It is unnecessary to refer to other than some of the more illuminating and authoritative decisions and pronouncements. *Gundry v Pinniger*[3] was
decided at first instance by Sir John Romilly MR. There was a bequest to AB for
life and afterwards to her children; but, in default of children, to CD if living, but
if dead, then to his next-of-kin in legal course of distribution, ex parte materna.
Sir John Romilly MR said[4]:

> 'The rule has very properly been admitted to be, that in ordinary cases of a
> gift to the next of kin of a person, such a class is to be ascertained at the death
> of the person himself, unless there be some special words to shew that such a
> construction cannot properly apply. I never accurately understood how the
> "next of kin" of a person could properly be ascertained at any other period than
> at the death of such person himself. The words "next of kin" have a distinct
> legal meaning. They naturally point to persons to be ascertained at a fixed
> period—viz., at the death of the person whose next of kin they are, and not
> to different persons, existing at different periods. When, therefore, you speak
> of the next of kin of a person, meaning that they should be ascertained at a
> period when he did not die, you really are giving no sensible meaning to the
> expression, unless you designate the class as the persons, who *would have been*
> the next of kin of a person, if he had died at a period other than when he did
> actually die.'

(The case is also of importance for another part of the instant appeal, since the word
'then' was construed as pointing to the event and not to the time.) The decision was
affirmed on appeal[5], Lord Cranworth LJ saying[6]:

> 'My conclusion (founded on the rule of Mr. Justice Burton [in *Warburton v
> Loveland d Ivie*[7] cited by Parke B in *Toldervy v Colt*[8]]) is, that the meaning of the
> "next of kin" is next of kin at the death of the person whose next of kin is spoken
> of.'

In *Bullock v Downes*[9] the testator left the residue of his property on various trusts,
on failure of which—

> 'then to stand possessed of the same, in trust for such person or persons of
> the blood of me, as would by virtue of the Statutes of Distributions of Intestates'
> Effects have become, and been *then* entitled thereto, in case I had died intestate.'

It was held that the word 'then' (i e the second 'then': the first was accepted as referring to the event and not the time), even if treated as an adverb of time, referred only
to the time when the persons entitled would come into possession of what had been
bequeathed to them, but that the persons entitled were to be ascertained at the death
of the testator. Lord Campbell LC said[10]:

---

1   (1858) 4 K & J 483
2   [1920] AC 795, [1920] All ER Rep 701
3   (1851) 14 Beav 94
4   (1851) 14 Beav at 98, 99
5   (1852) 1 De GM & G 502, [1843-60] All ER Rep 403
6   (1852) 1 De GM & G at 506, [1843-60] All ER Rep at 405
7   (1828) 1 Hud & B 623 at 648
8   (1836) 1 M & W 250 at 264
9   (1860) 9 HL Cas 1, [1843-60] All ER Rep 706
10   (1860) 9 HL Cas at 12, [1843-60] All ER Rep at 709

'Generally speaking, where there is a bequest to one for life, and after his decease to the testator's next of kin, the next of kin who are to take are the persons who answer the description at the death of the testator, and not those who answer that description at the death of the first taker.'

Lord Cranworth said[1]:

'Where a testator, having by his will, made contingent dispositions of his estate or of any part of it to take effect after the termination of particular interests for life, has proceeded to direct that if the contingencies do not arise, on which those dispositions are to take effect, then the property shall go to his next of kin according to the statute, the courts have in modern times held that *prima facie* his language is to be taken to refer to those who are his next of kin at his death, not to those who may happen to answer that description at the determination of the preceding particular interests.'

Lord Kingsdown said[2]:

'There is no expression of the interest which any of the persons who may answer the description are to take, except by reference to their title under the statute. They are to take according to their title under the statute. The words seem to me, according to their natural import, to mean this: "My trustees shall transfer the funds according to the title created by the statute amongst my next of kin", and I think that this is the construction settled by the decided cases.'

In *Re Winn, Brook v Whitton*[3] Parker J said:

'... in every case of a gift "to my next of kin," or "my nearest relations," or any gift of that kind, prima facie the rule is, and I think it is not only a rule of construction, but the natural meaning of the words, that the class is to be ascertained at the death of the testator.'

Those words were quoted by Greene LJ in *Re Hooper, Hooper v Carpenter*[4]—although his was a dissenting judgment applying the general rule, whilst the majority of the court felt that there was sufficient manifestation of an intention to exclude the general rule (in that case relating to the meaning of the word 'heir' which similarly prima facie means the person who would have been the heir at the date of the death of the propositus). In *Hutchinson v National Refuges for Homeless and Destitute Children*[5] Viscount Finlay said:

'It is for those who assert that the class is to be ascertained at a date other than that of the death of the testator to show that this is the fair result of the language of the will.'

Re Gansloser's Will Trusts[6] was a case where the general rule that the class (there 'relations') was to be ascertained as at the death of the propositus was excluded by indications that another date was intended. But Sir Raymond Evershed MR said[7]:

'I agree ... that in an ordinary case, and apart from something in the context which would lead to a different result, if a fund is given to "A's relations," by which, by the operation of the rule, is meant those relations who would be comprehended in an application of the Statutes of Distribution, then, *prima facie*, one would find who constituted the class at A's death, since it is only on that event that the Statutes of Distribution properly provide an answer to the question

1 (1860) 9 HL Cas at 18, [1843-60] All ER Rep at 711
2 (1860) 9 HL Cas at 28, [1843-60] All ER Rep at 715
3 [1910] 1 Ch 278 at 286, [1908-10] All ER Rep 593 at 596
4 [1936] 1 All ER 277 at 281, [1936] Ch 442 at 449
5 [1920] AC at 802, [1920] All ER Rep at 704
6 [1951] 2 All ER 936, [1952] Ch 30
7 [1951] 2 All ER at 940, [1952] Ch at 37

notionally put. But it must be clear, I think, that the testator who uses this loose *a*
phrase may well, by the context in which the phrase is used, produce the result
that the class is to be ascertained albeit by reference to the Statutes of Distribution,
yet at some date other than that at which in ordinary circumstances the Statutes
of Distribution would come into operation . . .'

('Next-of-kin' is a less loose, more legalistic, phrase than 'relations'.) Jenkins LJ
said[1]:   *b*

'. . . the rule in *Gundry* v. *Pinniger*[2]. . . comes to this, that, inasmuch as the
proper time for the operation of the Statutes of Distribution in relation to the
estate of any person is the death of that person, therefore, *prima facie*, the reference
to next of kin according to the statutes involves by implication the ascertainment of those persons at the proper time, namely, the death of the person whose
next of kin according to the statutes are referred to.'   *c*

Morris LJ expressed himself in full agreement with the judgments of Sir Raymond
Evershed MR and Jenkins LJ.

The prima facie rule of construction of the expression 'next-of-kin' applies as much
to settlements as to wills—indeed, in that settlements are more universally drawn
formally than wills, the rule might be thought to be even more relevant. In *Re*   *d*
Ranking's Settlement Trusts[3] Giffard V-C followed *Bullock v Downes*[4], saying:

'. . . where, either in a will or a settlement, there is a reference to the statute,
the statute regulates the nature of the interest as well as the persons who are
to take under it.'

This in turn was followed in New South Wales in another settlement case, *Deane v*
Lombe[5]. Norton on Deeds[6] states: *e*

'The "next-of-kin" or "next-of-kin or persons entitled according to the Statute",
are to be ascertained at the death of the propositus.'

Certainly in the present case the rule of legal presumption accords with the ordinary
sense of the language of cl 3 (*b*) (v) of the settlements. The trusts are 'for the next of
kin of the Settlor as determined by the provisions now in force of the Wills Probate *f*
and Administration Act 1898-1954 of the State of New South Wales'. Section 63 of
that Act refers to grants of administration to the husband or wife of the deceased
or one or more of his next-of-kin. This refers back to s 61A (2), which substituted
a new s 49 (1) in 1954 for the original provisions in the 1898 Act. The relevant part
reads as follows:

'49 (1) . . . the real and personal estate, . . . as to which any person (in this *g*
section referred to as "the intestate") dies intestate shall—(*a*) be held by the
administrator on intestacy, or in the case of partial intestacy by the executor or
administrator with the will annexed, as the case may be—(i) as to the real and
personal estate—(*a*) where the intestate leaves issue, in statutory trust for the
issue of the intestate; (*b*) where the intestate leaves no issue but both parents,
in trust for the father and the mother in equal shares; (*c*) where the intestate *h*
leaves no issue but one parent, in trust for the surviving father or mother; (*d*)
where the intestate leaves no issue or parent, in trust for the following persons
living at the death of the intestate, and in the following order and manner,
namely:—First in statutory trust for the brothers and sisters of the whole blood
of the intestate; but if there is no member of this class; then Secondly, in statutory *j*

1   [1951] 2 All ER at 945, [1952] Ch at 44
2   (1852) 1 De GM & G 502, [1843-60] All ER Rep 403; *affg* (1851) 14 Beav 94
3   (1868) LR 6 Eq 601 at 604
4   (1860) 9 HL Cas 1, [1843-60] All ER Rep 706
5   (1925) 25 SRNSW 502
6   2nd Edn (1928), p 446

trust for the brothers and sisters of the half blood of the intestate; but if there is no member of this class; then Thirdly, for the grandparents of the intestate and, if more than one survive the intestate, in equal shares; but if there is no member of this class; then Fourthly, for the uncles and aunts of the intestate (being brothers or sisters of the whole blood of a parent of the intestate) and, if more than one survive the intestate, in equal shares; but if there is no member of this class; then Fifthly, for the uncles and aunts of the intestate (being brothers or sisters of the half blood of a parent of the intestate) and, if more than one survive the intestate, in equal shares; but if there is no member of this class; then Sixthly, for the surviving husband or wife of the intestate; . . .

'(2) (a) Where under this section real and personal estate of an intestate or any part thereof is directed to be held in statutory trust for the issue of the intestate, the same shall be held upon the following trusts, namely:—(i) In trust, in equal shares, if more than one, for all or any the children or child of the intestate, living at the death of the intestate, and for all or any of the issue living at the death of the intestate of any child of the intestate who predeceases the intestate, such issue to take through all degrees, according to their stocks, in equal shares if more than one, the share which their parent would have taken if living at the death of the intestate, and so that no issue shall take whose parent is living at the death of the intestate and so capable of taking . . . (b) Where under this section real and personal estate of an intestate or any part thereof is directed to be held in statutory trust for any class of relatives of the intestate, other than issue of the intestate, the same shall be held in trust corresponding to the statutory trust for the issue of the intestate (other than the provision for bringing any money or property into account) as if such trust (other than as aforesaid) were repeated with the substitution of references to the members or member of that class for references to the children or child of the intestate . . .'

The statute refers to the intestate *leaving* issue and parents; while the remaining classes of next-of-kin under s 49 (1) (a) (i) (d) are specifically *persons living at the death of the intestate*. The same expression is used in relation to the description of the statutory trusts in sub-s (2).

The appellants have not sought to argue that the time of distribution could be any earlier than the time for ascertainment of the next-of-kin entitled under cl 3 (b) (v). But they rely on three matters which, they claim, suffice to rebut the presumption that, when the settlor referred to his next-of-kin in cl 3 (b) (v), he was referring to his statutory next-of-kin (i e living at his death), and demonstrate that he was referring to those who would have been his next-of-kin if he had died at the time of failure of the preceding trusts: (1) the word 'now' in the phrase 'determined by the provisions *now* in force of the Wills Probate and Administration Act'; (2) the word 'then' at the end of cl 3 (b) (iv), which they would read as an adverb of time to denote that the trust in cl 3 (b) (v) ensued immediately on a failure of the preceding trust, so that next-of-kin must be ascertained as at that time; (3) since the settlor might still be living on the failure of the trust under cl 3 (b) (iv), he cannot have intended a hiatus until his death before the next beneficiaries under (v) are ascertained; there is a presumption in favour of early vesting.

With regard to the use of the word 'now' in cl 3 (b) (v), their Lordships agree with the Court of Appeal that it does not in any way indicate that the settlor, in specifying his next-of-kin as beneficiaries, meant anything other than those who would be his next-of-kin at the date of his death; but that it is merely identifying to which statutory provision he wished reference to be made for the purpose of ascertaining who were his next-of-kin, and guarding against a possible change in the law subsequent to the execution of the settlement. As such it is against, rather than for, the contention of the appellants; since the particular statutory provision to which he wished reference to be made specifies 'persons living at the death of the intestate'.

As for the argument based on the use of the word 'then' at the end of cl 3 (b) (iv), *a*
Norton on Deeds[1] states:

'Where the interest of the next-of-kin does not take effect in possession at the
death of the propositus the word "then" is not alone sufficient to prevent the
rule [that they are to be ascertained at the death of the propositus] applying,
and to cause the next-of-kin to be ascertained at the time they take in possession.'
b

Moreover, this argument for the appellants was that rejected in *Gundry v Pinniger*[2]:
see also *Bullock v Downes*[3]. The present case is stronger than those. The statute
to which reference is to be made itself uses 'then' in the sense of 'in that event', not in
the sense of 'at that time'. Their Lordships agree with the Court of Appeal that
the word 'then' at the end of cl 3 (b) (iv) means 'in that event' and not 'at that time',
and are of opinion that neither in itself nor in conjunction with any other matter is *c*
the use of this word there any contra-indication to the application of the presumption
that the settlor intended his next-of-kin entitled under the trust to be ascertained as
at his death.

The third argument for the appellants on this part of the case was that unless
'the next of kin of the Settlor' meant those who would have been his next-of-kin if
he had died on the happening of the last event causing the failure of the preceding *d*
trusts there would, if the settlor had survived such event, be a hiatus between the
failure of the preceding trusts and the ascertainment of the beneficiaries under the
trust contained in cl 3 (b) (v). Their Lordships accept that the law leans in favour
of early vesting. But none of the discussions of these matters to which their Lordships' attention has been drawn suggests that the fact that there might be a hiatus
between the contingent failure of preceding trusts and the ascertainment of who are *e*
next-of-kin (heir, relations, etc) of the propositus is sufficient to demonstrate that the
settlor meant the next-of-kin (etc) to be ascertained as at the contingent failure of
trust and not at the time of the death of the propositus.

Their Lordships do not consider that, because the settlor in the instant appeal might
have survived the happening of the events which caused the failure of the trusts
preceding that for the next-of-kin, that phrase should be read as meaning 'those who *f*
would have been the next-of-kin of the settlor if he had died at the time of the failure
of the preceding trusts', rather than in the ordinary sense of the words actually used
which is also the presumptive sense—namely, his next-of-kin living at the date of
his death.

It follows that their Lordships agree with the Court of Appeal that the settlement
contained a 'trust in respect of . . . property to take effect after [the settlor's] death'. *g*
The trust in cl 2 (b) (v) had to await the death of the settlor before it could take effect.
The settlement postulated a trust which at the settlor's death was still capable of
taking effect.

For the foregoing reasons, as well as the reasons which their Lordships have given
for humbly advising Her Majesty in *Atwill's* case[4], their Lordships will humbly
advise Her Majesty that the instant appeal should be dismissed with costs. *h*

Appeal dismissed.

Solicitors: *Allen & Overy* (for the appellants); *Light & Fulton* (for the commissioner).

Rengan Krishnan Esq Barrister. *j*

1 2nd Edn (1928), p 448
2 (1852) 1 De GM & G 502, [1843-60] All ER Rep 403; *affg* (1851) 14 Beav 94
3 (1860) 9 HL Cas 1, [1843-60] All ER Rep 706
4 See p 576, ante

Eckman and others v Midland Bank Ltd and another

NATIONAL INDUSTRIAL RELATIONS COURT
SIR JOHN DONALDSON P, MR R DAVIES AND MR H ROBERTS
28th NOVEMBER, 7th DECEMBER 1972

Contempt of court – Sequestration – Position of third parties in relation to writ of sequestration – Third party holding contemnor's assets – Duty to pay over contemnor's assets on demand by sequestrators – Circumstances in which specific order of court required – Trade union fined for contempt of court – Writs of sequestration issued – Demand by sequestrators to union's bankers for payment of fine and costs – Banks declining to pay without first receiving specific order from court to comply with sequestrators' demands – Whether banks under duty to pay fine and costs without specific order from court.

A trade union was fined £5,000 for contempt of an order of the National Industrial Relations Court. The fine remained unpaid and writs of sequestration were issued addressed to four sequestrators requiring them to recover the amount of the fine and costs against the assets of the union. The sequestrators wrote to the union's bankers requiring them to pay forthwith the sum of £5,000 together with that of £275 in respect of the sequestrators' fees and expenses. The banks, having taken legal advice, replied stating that they felt they should take no action to comply with the sequestrators' demands pending an order of the court that the writ of sequestration be enforced against such of the union's assets as were held by the banks. The sequestrators then applied on motion to the National Industrial Relations Court for orders that the banks should (a) make disclosure of the union's assets and (b) pay the sum of £5,000 together with a sum covering the sequestrators' fees and expenses. The banks did not resist the making of orders against them but contended that they should not be required to pay the sequestrators' costs of the motion on the grounds that they had acted reasonably in making the sequestrators apply for a specific order of the court since they had to have regard to their duty to the union not to breach the confidence inherent in a bank-customer relationship and to act in accordance with their customers' instructions unless compelled to do so and a writ only entitled and did not oblige a third party to transfer possession of the contemnor's property.

Held – Although a writ of sequestration did not of itself bind a third party, a third party was nonetheless under a duty to refrain from knowingly assisting in the breach of any order of the court. Thus the banks were subject to a duty not knowingly to take any action which would obstruct compliance by the sequestrators with the terms of the writ of sequestration which required them to take possession of the union's assets. It followed that the banks should have made full disclosure to the sequestrators and paid over to them the sums originally demanded without a specific order to that effect (see p 615 f to g and p 616 e and g, post). However, the attitude of the banks was not unreasonable in view of the state of the law and of the advice received by them and no order would be made in respect of the costs of the motion (see p 617 a and b, post).

Re Pollard, Pollard v Pollard (1902) 87 LT 61 considered.

Seaward v Paterson [1895-99] All ER Rep 1127 applied.

Per Curiam. A requirement by sequestrators to transfer possession of a contemnor's property need not be complied with by a third party if (a) someone other than the contemnor has, or may have, an interest in the property, or (b) there is doubt whether the property is liable to sequestration. In those exceptional cases the third party must explain to the sequestrators the reason for his failure to comply with their demand in order that they may decide whether or not to seek a specific order from the court (see p 616 e to g, post).

Notes

For the form and effect of a writ of sequestration, and for the enforcement of the writ, see 16 Halsbury's Laws (3rd Edn) 70, 75, paras 107, 113.

Cases referred to in judgment

Bucknell v Bucknell [1969] 2 All ER 998, [1969] 1 WLR 1204, Digest (Cont Vol C) 717, 2560a.

Goad v Amalgamated Union of Engineering Workers (Engineering Section) (No 2) [1973] ICR 42, NIRC.

Pollard, Re, ex parte Pollard [1903] 2 KB 41, 72 LJKB 509, 10 Mans 152; sub nom *Re Pollard, ex parte Trustee* 88 LT 652, CA, 21 Digest (Repl) 687, 1816.

Seaward v Paterson [1897] 1 Ch 545, [1895-99] All ER Rep 1127, 66 LJCh 267, 76 LT 215, CA, 28 (2) Digest (Reissue) 1127, 1266.

Tournier v National Provincial and Union Bank of England [1924] 1 KB 461, 93 LJKB 449, 130 LT 682, CA, 3 Digest (Repl) 343, 1108.

Ward v Booth (1872) LR 14 Eq 195, 41 LJCh 729, 27 LT 364, 21 Digest (Repl) 699, 2001.

Motion

On 3rd October 1972, having heard a complaint of unfair industrial practice made under s 101 (1) of the Industrial Relations Act 1971 by James Henry Goad against the Amalgamated Union of Engineering Workers ('the union'), the National Industrial Relations Court made an order against the union that Mr Goad, so long as he remained a member of the union, should not by way of arbitrary or unreasonable discrimination be excluded from attending and taking part in meetings of any branch or section of the union in breach of his rights as a member. On 8th November 1972 the Industrial Court fined the union the sum of £5,000 for wilfully disobeying the order of 3rd October and issued writs of sequestration to Maurice Isidor Eckman, Martin Richard Harris, Alfred Henry Chapman and George Anthony Cherry ('the sequestrators') to keep the union's property and assets under sequestration until the union had cleared its contempt. The sequestrators applied to the court on motion for orders (i) that the union's bankers, Midland Bank Ltd and Hill Samuel & Co Ltd ('the banks') verify by affidavit the balances on the union's accounts with them and all deeds, documents of title, stock and share certificates and other securities held by them on behalf of the union and (ii) that the banks or either of them pay to the sequestrators or any two or three of them the sum of £5,000 together with a sum sufficient to cover the sequestrators' reasonable or proper fees and expenses (including the sequestrators' costs of the motion on a solicitor and client basis). The facts are set out in the judgment of the court.

Richard Southwell for the sequestrators.
Thomas Bingham QC and *Timothy Walker* for the banks.
Peter Perrins for Mr Goad.

Cur adv vult

7th December. **SIR JOHN DONALDSON P** read the following judgment of the court. On 8th November 1972, in *Goad v Amalgamated Union of Engineering Workers (Engineering Section) (No 2)*[1], the union was ordered to pay a fine of £5,000 for failing to comply with an order of this court. The fine was payable on or before 21st November 1972 and, in accordance with s 47 of the Criminal Justice Act 1967 as

---

1   [1973] ICR 42

a   applied by para 28 (1) of Sch 3 to the Industrial Relations Act 1971, Bow Street Magistrates' Court was specified as the place of payment.   The order further provided that, should the fine not be paid within this period, writs of sequestration would issue to enforce both the payment of the fine and of the fees and expenses of the commissioners acting under the writs.

     The fine was not paid and writs of sequestration were issued addressed to the four applicants.   The writs were in classic form and, in the operative part, authorised *b*   and commanded the applicants as the commissioners, or any two or three of them:

> *c*   '. . . to enter upon and take possession of all the real and personal estate of [the union] and to collect, receive and get into your hands the rents and profits of their real estate and all their goods, chattels and personal estate and keep the same under sequestration in your hands until [the union] shall clear their contempt and [the court] make other order to the contrary.'

     The wide powers and duties of the commissioners under these writs were, however, limited by the order of the court dated 8th November 1972, which provided that the writs should be executed 'only to the extent and for the purposes herein or as hereinafter ordered by this Court'. The effect of this limitation was that at all material *d*   times the writs were only to be executed to the extent necessary to recover the amount of the fine and the costs of execution.

     The writs of sequestration are sued out by the person complaining of the breach of the court's order and are served by him on the commissioners named in the writs. Thereafter the commissioners (to whom we will refer as 'the sequestrators') act as officers of the court.   Historically the involvement of the complainant may stem *e*   from the fact that he or she usually has an interest in the execution of the writs. This is the case, for example, when such writs are issued at the suit of a wife to enforce a maintenance order against her husband.   Where, however, the writs are issued to enforce payment of a fine the complainant has no such interest.   In the present case the writs were issued to the sequestrators' solicitors who, for this purpose only, acted as London agents for Mr Goad's solicitors.   Thus the formalities were observed, *f*   but the reality is that it is the court as representing the law and the public, and not Mr Goad, which is interested in enforcing the payment of fines which it has imposed. This aspect should be borne in mind if and when revision of the law relating to sequestration or of the Industrial Relations Act 1971 is under consideration.   Mr Goad and his solicitors had to sue out the writs of sequestration in the present case whether he wanted to or not, because the court had ordered him to do so.

g   On 22nd November 1972, Clifford-Turner & Co, solicitors for the sequestrators, wrote to the Midland Bank and Hill Samuel & Co as follows:

> 'Dear Sirs,
>
>   *Goad—v—Amalgamated Union of Engineering Workers—(Engineering Section)*
>   'We act for the [sequestrators] named in the Writs of Sequestration issued out of the National Industrial Relations Court on 8th November 1972. We *h*   enclose a copy of the Writ and the Order of the Court, also dated 8th November 1972, together with a copy of a letter received from the Secretary of the Court addressed to Messrs. Marshall and Sutton of to-day's date.
>   'As you will see the fine referred to in paragraph 1 of the Order was not paid on or before 21st November 1972, and it is therefore necessary in execution of the Writ of Sequestration, and under the Order, that the Commissioners do take *j*   possession of so much of the real and personal estate of the Union as is necessary to meet the said fine.   It is understood that you are one of the Union's bankers, and we hereby require you to pay forthwith to the [sequestrators] the sum of £5,000 and also the sum of £275 to cover the reasonable and proper fees and expenses of the [sequestrators] as provided by paragraph 6 of the Order.
>   'You will probably wish to seek legal advice as to your position. However,

we think it right to warn you that should you allow the Union's balances to be _a_
diminished or securities to be withdrawn so as to make it impossible for the full
amount of the fine to be paid, and the reasonable and proper fees and expenses
of the [sequestrators] also to be paid, you might have interfered with
the [sequestrators] in the performance of their duties, and have put yourself in
danger of being held in contempt of Court.

Yours faithfully . . .'   _b_

Next day, Coward, Chance & Co replied on behalf of the Midland Bank in these
terms:

'Dear Sirs,
    Goad v Amalgamated Union of Engineering Workers—(Engineering Section)
    'We write with reference to your letter of 22nd November, 1972 to our clients   _c_
Midland Bank Limited enclosing a copy of a Writ of Sequestration issued out
of the National Industrial Relations Court on 8th November, 1972.
    'Having considered its position in all the circumstances, and having taken advice,
the Bank feels that it should take no action pending an order of the Court and
that the Writ be enforced against such assets (if any) held by it.
    'Should application be made to the Court, the Bank will attend and make such   _d_
representations as may seem appropriate.

Yours faithfully . . .'

A similar reply was sent by Hill Samuel & Co who were also advised by Coward,
Chance & Co.
    On receipt of these replies the sequestrators applied to the court on motion for   _e_
orders:

    '1.   That Midland Bank Limited and Hill, Samuel & Co. Limited do verify
by affidavit of the balances of the [union's] accounts with them and all deeds
documents of title stock and share certificates and other securities held by
them on behalf of the [union],   _f_
    '2.   That Midland Bank Limited and Hill, Samuel & Co. Limited or either of
them do pay to the [sequestrators] or any two or three of them the sum of
£5,000 and a sum sufficient to cover the reasonable or proper fees and expenses
of the [sequestrators] (including the [sequestrators'] costs of this motion on a
solicitor and client basis).'

                                                                                 _g_
    On the hearing of the motion, counsel who appeared for both banks did not resist
the making of orders requiring them to verify by affidavit the balances of the union's
accounts and the deeds, documents of title, stock and share certificates and other
securities held by them on behalf of the union. He also expressed the banks' willingness to pay or transfer any moneys or other property held by them on behalf of the
union in accordance with the orders of the court.   _h_
    The affidavits filed in response to the court's order disclosed that the union had
accounts with a number of branches of the Midland Bank and that overall the union
was overdrawn. Midland Bank also held securities belonging to the union. Part
of these securities were held by the bank for safe custody and part as security for the
general balance of the union's indebtedness to the bank. The affidavits also disclosed that the union had two deposit accounts with Hill Samuel & Co Ltd. The   _j_
first, described as being part of the union's 'General Fund (Unprotected)' was held to
the order of the Midland Bank as additional security for the union's indebtedness.
The second was described as the union's 'Political Fund (Protected)'. The references
to 'Protected' and 'Unprotected' are, we assume, references to 'protection' under
ss 153 and 154 of the Industrial Relations Act 1971. Section 153 applies to registered
and s 154 to unregistered trade unions. Both provide that if, under the rules of the

a union, property comprised in any fund cannot be used for financing strikes or other industrial action that property is not available to satisfy 'an award of compensation or damages, or for the payment of any costs or expenses'. These sections have no application to sequestration, to the payment of fines imposed for contempt of court or, in our judgment, to the payment of costs or expenses ordered to be paid in connection with contempt proceedings. For such purposes resort may be had to any and every part of the union's property.

b The value of the securities held by the Midland Bank and the precise amounts of the balances on the current and deposit accounts are not material to the present proceedings. In the circumstances, we did not think that we should require the affidavits to be read in open court and will only say that the balances on each of the two deposit accounts with Hill Samuel & Co were sufficient to meet the sequestrators' demands. This being the case, we ordered Hill Samuel & Co to pay into

c court the sum of £5,000 for payment out in satisfaction of the fine and to pay the further sum of £1,000 to the sequestrators to cover the costs and expenses of the execution of the writs. This latter sum the sequestrators were ordered to pay into court pending a determination of what was due to them. A more usual order would have required the £5,000 to be paid to the sequestrators and have been coupled

d with an order requiring the sequestrators to pay that sum into court, but in the circumstances of the present case such a procedure seemed an unnecessary complication. Hill Samuel & Co asked us to specify which of the union's accounts should be debited with these payments, but this we refused to do as this was not the concern of the court.

This left only the issue of whether the two banks should be ordered to pay the sequestrators' costs of the motion. Counsel for the banks submitted that when the

e banks received the letters from the sequestrators and saw copies of the writs they were placed in a dilemma. In their view—and counsel for the banks told the court that he had so advised them—the writs of sequestration entitled the banks to give the sequestrators the information for which they had asked, but probably did not oblige them to do so. Similarly, the writs entitled the banks to make payments to the sequestrators out of any balances standing to the credit of the union, but again

f probably did not oblige them to do so. Faced with a choice whether or not to comply with the sequestrators' requirements, the banks had to have regard to their duty to the union not to breach the confidence which is inherent in the banker-customer relationship and to act in accordance with their customers' instructions. In counsel's submission, the banks had acted reasonably and should not be required to pay the sequestrators' costs, although he did not go so far as to ask for an order for

g costs against the sequestrators.

It is quite clear that the duty of a banker to maintain secrecy concerning his customers' affairs is not absolute but is subject to qualification. This qualification was summarised by Bankes LJ in *Tournier v National Provincial and Union Bank of England*[1] under four heads, namely:

h '(a) Where disclosure is under compulsion by law; (b) where there is a duty to the public to disclose; (c) where the interests of the bank require disclosure; (d) where the disclosure is made by the express or implied consent of the customer.'

The latter two heads are not material, for the banks' interests were not involved in the present case and both banks knew that any disclosure would be contrary to the

j wishes of the union. In relation to payment out of funds or the transfer of securities held by a banker for his customer, the banker's primary duty is to act in accordance with his mandate. That duty again is not absolute but is at least subject to the banker's duty to act otherwise under compulsion by law or where there is a duty to the public so to act. It is therefore necessary to consider the effect of receipt by

1 [1924] 1 KB 461 at 473

a banker of notice of writs of sequestration affecting property, including bank balances, held on behalf of his customer.

A somewhat similar problem confronted Brandon J in *Bucknell v Bucknell*[1]. There the bank had refused, in the absence of a specific order, to pay over to the sequestrators a sum which stood to the credit of their customer's account. However, when the matter came to be argued the bank conceded that it could safely have paid the sum concerned, since notice of the writs of sequestration would have provided it with a complete defence to any complaint by their customer. A specific order was in fact made against the bank and the argument, as in the present case, was concerned with whether the conduct of the bank in forcing the sequestrators to apply to the court was so unreasonable as to merit an award of costs against them. In the course of a reserved judgment, Brandon J reviewed the authorities and pointed out[2]:

> 'If they [the sequestrators] had been obliged in every case to obtain a specific court order against the third party concerned, with the costs of both sides coming out of the sequestrated assets, much time and effort would have been wasted, and the moneys ultimately available to be paid to the wife would have been materially reduced.'

He continued:

> 'I should be reluctant to accept that the law requires such a pointless and wasteful procedure to be followed in a straightforward case where there is no doubt or dispute about the liability of the chose in action to sequestration or about the contemnor's title to it.'

The learned judge concluded that there was no such requirement in law, although the bank did not act unreasonably in thinking that there might be and accordingly requiring the sequestrators to obtain a specific order. In these circumstances no order for costs was made, but it was made quite clear that a repetition of such conduct would probably be considered unreasonable.

The banks were no doubt aware of this decision when they required the sequestrators to come to this court. Their justification for adopting this course is that they wished to advance an argument which was not put forward before Brandon J and which, indeed, appears to be completely novel. They accept, as Brandon J held, that in law they were entitled to act without any specific order of the court and that, had they done so, the union would have had no complaint of which any court would have taken cognisance. Nevertheless, they say that the relationship between banker and customer is not one which consists wholly of legal rights and duties. It is much more than that. By commercial custom and practice, whether or not amounting to a legal duty, a banker should not take any action of which his customer would disapprove, unless compelled to do so. Unless and until a specific order was made, they were not compelled to do anything and commercial custom and practice prevented their doing so.

It is certainly a fact that bankers, underwriters, merchants and other members of the commercial community recognise and act on the basis of extra-legal obligations where there is no conflict with their legal obligations. Indeed, strict compliance with obligations which bind in honour only is one of the hallmarks of the most respected members of that community. The banks' argument is therefore attractive. But is it really sound?

No problem arises in cases in which there is doubt whether the property concerned is liable to sequestration or as to the contemnor's title. The third party is not a

---

1   [1969] 2 All ER 998, [1969] 1 WLR 1204
2   [1969] 2 All ER at 1006, [1969] 1 WLR at 1212, 1213

a party to the proceedings in which the writ of sequestration is issued and in such cases he is entitled to await a specific order of the court made in proceedings to which he is a party. The problem only arises when, as the banks admit in the present case, the contemnor's title is clear and the property is without doubt liable to sequestration. The authorities seem to establish the following propositions: (1) A writ of sequestration does not create a charge on the contemnor's property (Re Pollard, ex parte

b Pollard[1]). (2) The collusive creation of a mortgage with a view to preventing the enforcement of a sequestration is ineffective (Ward v Booth[2]). (3) A writ of sequestration affects possession not title. Accordingly, money paid into court for the credit of a sequestration account under authority of the writ is available to the contemnor's creditors, but it is otherwise if pursuant to a specific order of the court the money is paid out or paid into court for the general credit of an action (Re Pollard[1]). (4) If a third

c party pays or transfers money or property to sequestrators on their demand, he is protected from claims by the contemnor. (5) No court has ever declared that a third party should pay money or transfer property to the sequestrators without also making a specific order to that effect. (6) In one case (Re Pollard, Pollard v Pollard[3]) Joyce J took the view that he had no power on motion to order the payment of a sum equal to the money which had been paid to the contemnor by the third party after notice

d of the writ of sequestration and in breach of an undertaking given to the sequestrators, but it seems from a report of subsequent proceedings[1] that his order to pay over the money remaining in the hands of the third party was without prejudice to the sequestrators' rights to take further proceedings against the third party.

The banks seek to rationalise these propositions by their contention that a writ of sequestration entitles, but does not oblige, the third party to transfer possession of the contemnor's property. Bearing in mind that the writ of sequestration not

e only authorises, but requires, the sequestrator to take possession of the property, this is a strange situation. It is not made any the less strange by the fact that the only beneficiaries seem to be the lawyers who will be employed to seek specific orders from the court, although the making of the orders cannot be resisted and give the third party no added protection. Nevertheless, if this is the only basis on which

f the authorities can be reconciled, the banks' argument must be accepted.

However, in our judgment there is a fallacy in the banks' argument. The writ of sequestration itself does not bind the third party, since he is not privy to the action in which it is issued and it is not addressed to him. If it is to bind him, he must be brought before the court and a specific order made against him. But this does not explain why it protects the third party from claims by the contemnor if he parts with property to the sequestrators. The answer is to be found in the indirect effect

g of court orders. For example, if A obtains an order against B requiring B to refrain from committing certain acts, only B is bound by the order itself. However, if C knows of the order, he will assist B to commit the prohibited acts at his peril. This is not because C is bound by the order, for he is not. It is because C, and every other member of the public, is under a duty to refrain from knowingly assisting B to

h break an order of the court. If he does so he will be called to account, not for a breach of the order, but for contempt of court, the court having an inherent jurisdiction to take action to prevent its process being set at naught and treated with contempt (see Seaward v Paterson[4]).

In our judgment, the position of a third party in relation to a writ of sequestration is analogous to that of a third party in relation to an injunction, namely that he is

j subject to a duty not knowingly to take any action which will obstruct compliance by the sequestrators with the terms of the writ of sequestration which require them to take possession of the assets. It is the existence of this duty which provides the

1 [1903] 2 KB 41 at 43
2 [1872] LR 14 Eq 195
3 (1902) 87 LT 61
4 [1897] 1 Ch 545 at 555, 556, [1895-99] All ER Rep 1127 at 1131, per Lindley LJ

third party with a complete defence to any complaint by the contemnor when he
parts with the possession of property to the sequestrators. That no action has ever
been taken by sequestrators against a third party on this basis is explained by the fact
that it is easier and more profitable to obtain a specific order against the third party
than to proceed against him for contempt of court. If and insofar as the decision of
Joyce J in Re Pollard[1] is inconsistent with this view, we think that it must be regarded
as turning on its special facts or the procedure invoked.

Counsel for the banks has asked that we define the duty of banks and other third
parties in relation to their dealings with a contemnor's property following the issue
of writs of sequestration. We do not think that we can do this exhaustively, but in
our judgment it at least extends to the following: (1) The third party is completely
unaffected unless and until he knows of the issue of the writ of sequestration. (2) The
only duty which arises out of mere knowledge that a writ of sequestration has been
issued is a duty to refuse to take any action the object of which is known by the third
party to be the frustration of the object of the writ. Thus, in the absence of express
instructions from the sequestrators banks can continue to honour cheques and
stockbrokers can sell securities on the authority of the contemnor, unless they
know that the transactions are exceptional and designed to obstruct or prevent the
sequestration. If they have any doubts they can protect themselves by reporting
the facts to the sequestrators. (3) A demand by sequestrators for disclosure of
property held for account of the contemnor not only may but must be answered
promptly, fully and accurately. The duty of disclosure extends to revealing, on
request, that no such property is held, or, if it has been but is no longer held, when,
in what manner and to whom it was disposed of. If there is doubt as to the contemnor's title or the property is or may be subject to a charge, the full facts must be given
to the sequestrators, who are as much entitled to the information as is the contemnor.
(4) If sequestrators require the transfer of possession of property which is or may be
held for account of the contemnor or (which is the same) that the property be held
to their order, the requirement must be strictly complied with unless (a) someone
other than the contemnor has or may have an interest in the property, e g the bank
itself has a charge on securities possession of which is demanded by the sequestrators
or money is held on the joint account of the contemnor and others or there is notice
of a trust in favour of others; or (b) there is doubt whether the property is liable to
sequestration; in these exceptional cases it is the duty of the third party to explain
the reasons for its failure to comply with the sequestrators' demand in order that the
sequestrators may decide whether or not to seek a specific order from the court.

In the present case, both banks should have made full disclosure to the sequestrators and Hill Samuel & Co should have paid over the sums originally demanded
without a specific order. The position of the Midland Bank in relation to payment
may have been different in that the union was overdrawn. The right to the overdrawn balance is that of the bank and not of the contemnor. If, however, a bank has
contracted with the contemnor in terms which entitle him to draw on the bank up
to a limit and that limit has not been reached, this facility is part of the property of
the contemnor which the sequestrators are entitled to have transferred to them and
which they can operate by authority of the writ of sequestration. Clearly, securities
held to secure an overdraft are part of the property of the contemnor. In this case
neither bank was required to transfer possession of securities, but a bank could, consistently with its duty, refuse to transfer possession of the securities unless and until the
overdraft was paid off or the court made a specific order which would, of course,
ensure that the bank's position was not prejudiced.

Although the point was not raised in the present case, we wish to emphasise that
third parties are not concerned with any limitations which may have been placed
by the court on the execution of the writs of sequestration. Any excess of execution

---

1   (1902) 87 LT 61

a is a matter for the sequestrators, the contemnor and the court.   So far as third parties are concerned, the writ takes effect according to its terms.

The present proceedings became necessary solely because of the attitude adopted by the banks.   However, in the light of the advice which they had received and the state of the law, we do not think that they acted unreasonably on this occasion. Should such a situation arise again, their position will be quite different.   We there-
b fore thought it right to make no order in respect of the costs of the motion, leaving the sequestrators to recover their costs from the sequestrated funds, that is to say from the union.

Order accordingly.

Solicitors: *Clifford-Turner & Co* (for the applicants); *Coward, Chance & Co* (for the
c banks); *Marshall & Sutton*, Colchester (for Mr Goad).

Gordon H Scott Esq Barrister.

Pritam Kaur (administratrix of Bikar Singh
d (deceased)) v S Russell & Sons Ltd

COURT OF APPEAL, CIVIL DIVISION
LORD DENNING MR, KARMINSKI LJ AND MEGARRY J
4th, 14th DECEMBER 1972

e *Limitation of action – When time begins to run – Actions of tort – Computation of three year limitation period – Whether day of event causing injuries excluded – Limitation Act 1939, s 2 (1), as amended by the Law Reform (Limitation of Actions, etc) Act 1954, s 2 (1).*

Writ – Issue – Time – Limitation period prescribed by statute – Period expiring on day court offices closed – Writ issued on first day thereafter that court offices open – Effect – Fatal
f *Accidents Act 1846, s 3, as amended by the Law Reform (Limitation of Actions, etc) Act 1954, s 3 – Limitation Act 1939, s 2 (1), as amended by the Law Reform (Limitation of Actions, etc) Act 1954, s 2 (1).*

The plaintiff's husband was killed at work on 5th September 1967.   On 7th September 1970, the plaintiff issued a writ against her husband's employers claiming damages for negligence and breach of statutory duty under the Fatal Accidents Acts 1846
g to 1959 and the Law Reform (Miscellaneous Provisions) Act 1934.   It was impossible for the plaintiff to issue her writ on 5th or 6th September 1970 for, being a Saturday and Sunday, the court offices were closed on those days.   The defendants contended that the plaintiff's action was barred by s 3[a] of the Fatal Accidents Act 1846, as amended, and s 2 (1)[b] of the Limitation Act 1939, as amended, on the grounds
h (i) that the date on which the accident occurred was to be included in the three year limitation period, which therefore expired on Friday, 4th September 1970; and (ii) that in any event the three year period expired on 5th September 1970, and therefore the writ was issued out of time.

a Section 3, as amended and so far as material, provides: '... every ... action shall be commenced within three years after the death of [the] deceased person.'
j b Section 2 (1), as amended and so far as material, provides: 'The following actions shall not be brought after the expiration of six years from the date on which the cause of action accrued, that is to say:—(a) actions founded on simple contract or on tort ... Provided that, in the case of actions for damages for negligence ... or breach of duty ... where the damages claimed by the plaintiff for the negligence ... or breach of duty consist of or include damages in respect of personal injuries to any person, this subsection shall have effect as if for the reference to six years there were substituted a reference to three years.'

Held – (i) In computing the period of three years within which the action had to
be brought the date on which the accident occurred was to be excluded. Accordingly   *a*
the last day of the three year period was 5th September 1970 (see p 619 e, p 620 g and
p 621 e and f, post); *Marren v Dawson Bentley & Co Ltd* [1961] 2 All ER 270 applied.

  (ii) Where a statute prescribed a period within which an act was to be done and
the act was one which could only be done on a day on which the court offices were
open, the period would be extended, if the court office was closed for the whole of   *b*
the last day of the prescribed period, until the next day on which the court offices
were open. It followed that the plaintiff had until 7th September 1970 in which to
issue her writ, and she was therefore in time (see p 620 d f and g and p 626 f and g,
post); *Hughes v Griffiths* (1862) 13 CBNS 324 applied; *Hodgson v Armstrong* [1967]
1 All ER 307 considered; *Morris v Richards* (1881) 45 LT 210 and *Gelmini v Moriggia*
[1911-13] All ER Rep 1115 not followed.   *c*

Decision of Willis J [1972] 3 All ER 305 reversed.

Notes

For the time when a period of limitation begins to run, see 24 Halsbury's Laws
(3rd Edn) 193-196, paras 347, 348, and for cases on the subject, see 32 Digest (Repl)
385-410, 147-338.

For the effect where periods of time expire on days when court offices are closed,   *d*
see 37 Halsbury's Laws (3rd Edn) 97-99, paras 172, 173, and for cases on the subject,
see 45 Digest (Repl) 268, 269, 349-359.

For the Fatal Accidents Act 1846, s 3, see 23 Halsbury's Statutes (3rd Edn) 784.

For the Limitation Act 1939, s 2, see 19 Halsbury's Statutes (3rd Edn) 61.

Cases referred to in judgments   *e*

Clarke v Bradlaugh (1881) 8 QBD 63, [1881-85] All ER Rep 1002, 51 LJQB 1, 46 LT 49,
  46 JP 278, CA, 45 Digest (Repl) 272, 411.
Dechène v Montreal (City) [1894] AC 640, 64 LJPC 14, 71 LT 354, PC, 45 Digest (Repl)
  258, *219.
Gelmini v Moriggia [1913] 2 KB 549, [1911-13] All ER Rep 1115, 82 LJKB 949, 109 LT   *f*
  77, 32 Digest (Repl) 389, 179.
Henderson v Henderson (1888) 16 R 5.
Hodgson v Armstrong [1967] 1 All ER 307, [1967] 2 QB 299, [1967] 2 WLR 311, CA,
  Digest (Cont Vol C) 955, 358a.
Hughes v Griffiths (1862) 13 CBNS 324, 32 LJCP 47, 143 ER 129, 45 Digest (Repl) 268,
  349.
Hutton v Garland (1883) 10 R (J) 60.   *g*
M'Niven v Glasgow Corpn 1920 SC 584, 38 Digest (Repl) 138, *541.
M'Vean v Jameson (1896) 23 R (J) 25.
Marren v Dawson Bentley & Co Ltd [1961] 2 All ER 270, [1961] 2 QB 135, [1961] 2 WLR
  679, 32 Digest (Repl) 403, 277.
Morris v Richards (1881) 45 LT 210, 46 JP 37, 32 Digest (Repl) 389, 178.
Mumford v Hitchcocks (1863) 14 CBNS 361, 2 New Rep 122, 32 LJC P168, 8 LT 282,   *h*
  9 Jur NS 1200, 143 ER 485, 45 Digest (Repl) 268, 358.
Prideaux v Webber (1661) 1 Lev 31, 1 Keb 204, 83 ER 282, 32 Digest (Repl) 410, 340.

Appeal

This was an appeal by the plaintiff, Pritam Kaur, the widow and administratrix of   *i*
Bikar Singh, against the judgment of Willis J given at the trial of a preliminary
point of law on 2nd June 1972 and reported at [1972] 3 All ER 305 whereby it was
adjudged that the plaintiff's causes of action against the defendants, S Russell & Sons
Ltd, under the Fatal Accidents Acts 1846 to 1959 and the Law Reform (Miscellaneous
Provisions) Act 1934 for negligence and/or breach of statutory duty in respect of the
deceased's death did not accrue within three years before the commencement of the

proceedings and were barred by s 2 of the Limitation Act 1939, as amended, and s 3 of the Fatal Accidents Act 1846, as amended. The facts are set out in the judgment of Lord Denning MR.

Patrick Bennett QC and *A T Smith* for the plaintiff.
H Tudor Evans QC and *W C Woodward* for the defendants.

Cur adv vult

14th December. The following judgments were read.

LORD DENNING MR. On 5th September 1967 Mr Bikar Singh was working in a pit in a foundry. A skip suddenly fell on him and killed him then and there. On 7th September 1970 his widow issued a writ against his employers claiming damages for breach of statutory duty and for negligence. Her claim was under the Fatal Accidents Acts 1846 to 1959 and the Law Reform (Miscellaneous Provisions) Act 1934.

We are asked to decide this preliminary point of law. Was the action commenced within the period of three years allowed by the statute of limitations? or is it statute-barred? The Limitation Act 1939, s 2 (1), as amended by the Law Reform (Limitation of Actions, etc) Act 1954, says that the action *'shall not be brought after* the expiration of three years from the date on which the cause of action accrued'. The Fatal Accidents Act 1846, s 3, as amended by the 1954 Act, says that it 'shall be *commenced within* three years after the death'. Nothing turns on the difference in wording. The period is the same in either case. The first thing to notice is that, in computing the three years, you do not count the first day, 5th September 1967, on which the accident occurred. It was so held by Havers J in *Marren v Dawson Bentley & Co Ltd*[1]. The defendants here, by their cross-notice, challenged that decision; but I think it was plainly right.

If you count three years from 5th September 1967, you get the last day as 5th September 1970. The writ here was issued on 7th September 1970. If you looked at the dates, therefore, and nothing else, the action would appear to be two days out of time. But, when you look at the days of the week, you see that 5th September 1970 was a Saturday, and 6th September 1970 was a Sunday. On both those days the offices of the court were closed. As soon as they re-opened on Monday, 7th September 1970, the plaintiff issued the writ. That is to say, her solicitors took the writ to the offices of the district registry at Leicester. A clerk in the registry stamped it with the official stamp in the proper place (*locus sigillare*). It was then duly issued. But, was it in time?

At the outset I would emphasise that the period of limitation (three years) is prescribed by the statutes. It is not prescribed by the rules of court. If it had been prescribed by rules of court, there is a rule in the High Court (RSC Ord 3, r 4) and in the county court (CCR Ord 48, r 10 (3)), which says that, if the court offices are closed, the time is extended until the next day. But neither of those rules, as I read them, applies to cases when the time is prescribed by statute. I am aware that the county court rule only uses the words 'time prescribed', but I think that it implies 'time prescribed by these rules'. I am afraid that I do not agree with the contrary view expressed by Davies LJ in *Hodgson v Armstrong*[2].

The arguments on each side are evenly balanced. The defendants can say: 'The plaintiff has three years in which to bring his action. If the last day is a Saturday or Sunday, or other *dies non*, he ought not to leave it until the last day. He ought to make sure and issue it the day before when the offices are open.' The defendants can rely

---

1   [1961] 2 All ER 270, [1961] 2 QB 135
2   [1967] 1 All ER 307 at 316, [1967] 2 QB 299 at 317

for this view on the reasoning of Russell LJ in *Hodgson v Armstrong*[1] and the cases
to which he refers. The plaintiff can say: 'The statute gives me three years in which I
can bring my action. If I go in to the offices on the last day, and find them closed, I
ought not to be defeated on that account. I should be allowed to go next day when
the offices are open. Otherwise, I should be deprived of the three years which the
statute allows me.' The plaintiff can rely for their view on the reasoning of Sellers LJ
in *Hodgson v Armstrong*[2], and the cases to which he refers.

Those arguments are so evenly balanced that we can come down either way.
The important thing is to lay down a rule for the future so that people can know
how they stand. In laying down a rule, we can look to parallel fields of law to see the
rule there. The nearest parallel is the case where a time is prescribed by the rules
of court for doing any act. The rule prescribed both in the county court and the
High Court is this: if the time expires on a Sunday or any other day on which the
court office is closed, the act is done in time if it is done on the next day on which the
court office is open. I think we should apply a similar rule when the time is prescribed
by statute. By so doing, we make the law consistent in itself; and we avoid confusion
to practitioners. So I am prepared to hold that, when a time is prescribed by statute
for doing any act, and that act can only be done if the court office is open on the day
when the time expires, then, if it turns out in any particular case that the day is a
Sunday or other dies non, the time is extended until the next day on which the
court office is open.

In support of this conclusion, I would refer to *Hughes v Griffiths*[3]. It was on a
different statute, but the principle was enunciated by Erle CJ[4]:

'Where the act is to be done by the court, and the court refuses to act on that
day, the intendment of the law is that the party shall have until the earliest day
on which the court will act.'

Insofar as *Morris v Richards*[5] and *Gelmini v Moriggia*[6], proceed on the footing that the
time was not extended, they are no longer to be followed.

In my opinion, therefore, the plaintiff here had until 7th September 1970 in which
to issue her writ. She issued it on that day. She is, therefore, in time. I would allow
the appeal accordingly.

KARMINSKI LJ. I have read the judgment of Lord Denning MR, and agree
entirely with it.   In *Hughes v Griffiths*[3] Byles J, dealing with a different statute which
gave a creditor seven days to set the court in motion, said this[7]:

'Consequently, the seventh day must be one upon which the court can be set
in motion; otherwise, the party would not have that which the legislature
contemplated that he should have.'

Applying these words to the present case, the legislature here gives the widow three
years to bring her action from the date of the death of the deceased husband. Through
the last two days of the three years happening on days when the court offices were
closed, the writ could not be issued. It was in fact issued on the next day when the
court offices were opened.

I do not know why it was left to the very last day of the three years to issue the
writ, and I want to say nothing to encourage parties or their solicitors to leave the

---

1   [1967] 1 All ER at 320, [1967] 2 QB at 323, 324
2   [1967] 1 All ER at 311, 312, [1967] 2 QB at 309, 310
3   (1862) 13 CBNS 324
4   (1862) 13 CBNS at 333
5   (1881) 45 LT 210
6   [1913] 2 KB 549, [1911-13] All ER Rep 1115
7   (1862) 13 CBNS at 337

a issue of the writ to the very last day. In the result I agree that the writ was issued in time, and that this appeal should be allowed.

MEGARRY J. As a bird of passage in this court I feel a proper diffidence in expressing my views at any length when Lord Denning MR and Karminski LJ have been able to dispose of the appeal with brevity. I have the excuse that we are differ-
b ing from Willis J[1]; but in truth what I have succumbed to is the temptation of an interesting and not unimportant point of law, together with the support to be found in some further authorities.

The case arises on two similar statutory provisions. There is a claim under the Fatal Accident Acts 1846 to 1959; and by s 3 of the 1846 Act, as amended by the Law Reform (Limitation of Actions, etc) Act 1954, s 3, 'every such action shall be com-
c menced within three years after the death of such deceased person'. There is also a claim in tort for negligence and breach of statutory duty which falls within the Limitation Act 1939, s 2 (1), as amended by the 1954 Act, s 2 (1); and this provides that the action 'shall not be brought after the expiration of three years from the date on which the cause of action accrued'. No point, I may say, has been taken in argument on the difference in wording between 'within three years after the death' and
d 'after the expiration of three years from the date'. At one time there was some argument on whether or not the period was to be reckoned by excluding the date on which the accident occurred, but in the end the point was not pressed. The decision of Havers J in *Marren v Dawson Bentley & Co Ltd*[2], based on the Limitation Act 1939, s 2 (1), was that the day of the accident was to be excluded in the computation of the time; and in the present case the judge applied that decision. The language of s 2 (1),
e with the phrase 'after the expiration of three years from the date', plainly supports that view. If the wording of the Fatal Accidents Acts, with the phrase 'within three years after the death', is less apt, it would nevertheless be regrettable to introduce any fine distinctions, especially as the period of three years was inserted into each statute by the same Act, that of 1954. I would therefore agree with the judge in excluding the day of the accident from the computation under both heads.

f The accident occurred on Tuesday, 5th September 1967. The writ was not issued until Monday, 7th September 1970. Excluding the day of the accident, the statutory three years thus expired at the end of 5th September 1970: and that was a Saturday. Both on that day and on the next day the offices of the Supreme Court and the district registry were closed, by virtue of RSC Ord 64, rr 7, 8. The writ was thus too late, and the action must fail, unless there is some general principle that will in effect
g extend the time until Monday, 7th September 1970, or there is some other ground for doing so. The point was taken as a preliminary issue, and in a careful reserved judgment Willis J held that there was nothing to extend the time, and the claim of the plaintiff, the administratrix of the deceased, was thus out of time. In so deciding he welcomed the prospect of the point being taken to appeal. At the centre of the argument was a decision of this court, *Hodgson v Armstrong*[3]; and both before the
h judge and in this court much of the attention of counsel for the plaintiff and counsel for the defendants was rightly directed to that case.

Hodgson v Armstrong[3] was concerned not with any of the Acts in point in this case, but with the different language of a special procedure laid down by a special Act, the Landlord and Tenant Act 1954, Part II, relating to business tenancies. Section 24 (1) authorises a tenant of business premises to apply to the court for a new tenancy,
j and s 29 (3) provides that:

'No application under subsection (1) of section twenty-four of this Act shall be entertained unless it is made not less than two nor more than four months

---

1   [1972] 3 All ER 305, [1972] 3 WLR 663
2   [1961] 2 All ER 270, [1961] 2 QB 135
3   [1967] 1 All ER 307, [1967] 2 QB 299

after the giving of the landlord's notice under section twenty-five of this
Act . . .'   *a*

The landlords served their notice on the tenant on 19th December 1964, and on
Thursday, 15th April 1965, the tenant's solicitors attempted to deliver to the county
court an originating application seeking a new tenancy under CCR Ord 48, r 8 (1),
but found the offices shut. Not until the court offices opened again after the Easter
weekend, on Thursday, 20th April 1965, was the originating application received   *b*
by the county court. The county court judge held that he had no jurisdiction, but
this court, by a majority, reversed that decision. Russell LJ, dissenting, would have
dismissed the appeal. Davies LJ held that the matter was governed by CCR Ord 48,
r 10. This has three sub-rules. Sub-rule (1) provides that where 'anything is required
by these Rules to be done' within a specified period, or after a particular event has
happened, the day of the event is normally to be excluded from the computation of   *c*
the period. Sub-rule (2) provides for the exclusion of days when the court offices are
closed where anything 'is required by these Rules to be done' within a period not
exceeding three days, or after the elapse of such a period. Sub-rule (3) provides
that 'Where the time prescribed for doing any act expires' on a day on which the
court office is closed, the act is to be in time if done on the next day on which
the office is open. Davies LJ[1] pointed to the contrast in wording between these   *d*
sub-rules, whereby the first two are restricted to the requirements of the rules, and
the third is free from any such limiting words. Sub-rule (3) was thus in his view
capable of applying to a time laid down by statute, and so applied to the originating
application in question.

In the leading judgment, Sellers LJ[2] took a different view, but said that if he was
wrong in that, he would take substantially the same view on the effect of CCR Ord 48,   *e*
r 10 (3). His primary view, however, was that although the court cannot enlarge a
period of time laid down by statute, the court can and should define the period. If
the period expires on a day when the offices of the court are closed, the plaintiff
will not have the full period intended by Parliament, but a shorter period, unless
he is able to commence the proceedings on the next day that the offices are open.
Despite a number of authorities which allowed no extension of time, there were   *f*
other authorities, concerned with short periods, in which extensions had been allowed.
To the most important of these, *Hughes v Griffiths*[3], Lord Denning MR and Karminski
LJ have already referred. The conclusion of Sellers LJ was that the period extended
so as to include the next day on which the offices were open.

A somewhat odd procedural point emerged during the hearing of this appeal.
The present Rule of the Supreme Court on the expiry of time, RSC Ord 3, r 4,   *g*
provides that 'Where the time prescribed by these rules, or by any judgment, order
or direction' for doing any act at an office of the Supreme Court expires on a day on
which the office is closed, the act is to be in time if done on the next day on which
the office is open. That provision is plainly confined to times prescribed by the
rules, and so on, and cannot be read as applying to times laid down by statute. The
rule in this form was introduced by the Rules of the Supreme Court (Revision)   *h*
1962[4]. Before that, the rule had been RSC Ord 64, r 3, and it began, 'Where the time
for doing any act or taking any proceeding' expires on a day on which the offices
are closed, and so on. This former wording closely corresponds with the county
court rule that was construed in *Hodgson v Armstrong*[5], so that on the footing that
that rule was decisive in that case, the result of other cases might well, by the change
in the wording of the Rules of the Supreme Court, be made to depend on whether the   *f*

1   [1967] 1 All ER at 316, [1967] 2 QB at 317
2   [1967] 1 All ER at 311, [1967] 2 QB at 309
3   (1862) 13 CBNS 324
4   SI 1962 No 2145
5   [1967] 1 All ER 307, [1967] 2 QB 299

a case falls within the county court or High Court jurisdiction; if the former, time would in effect be extended under the rules; if the latter, not. Such a distinction would hardly be creditable to the law.

    With great respect, I find much difficulty in following the view that CCR Ord 48, r 10 (3) applies to periods fixed by Act of Parliament. The corresponding provisions in the old Rules of the Supreme Court had long been construed as being confined to b periods prescribed by the rules: see, e g, *Morris v Richards*[1], and *Gelmini v Moriggia*[2], a case which was cited to this effect in the old White Books (see, for example, The Annual Practice 1963[3]). Davies LJ cited these cases, I may say, but said that he would not follow them. The verbal contrast in the County Court Rules is, of course, obvious: yet if the Rules Committee had any real intention to make so significant a distinction in the operation of the rules, it may be doubted whether they would have entrusted it to so frail and inferential a carrier. Furthermore, it is inconceivable c that the County Court Rule should be taken in its full and literal width: for, read literally, the time would be extended for all purposes, whether or not the case in question was being brought in the county court. The rule must at least be limited to county court cases; and once one begins to read implied limitations into the rules, a limitation to periods prescribed by the rules seems probable and perhaps inevitable. d In any case, it may well be questioned whether the Rules Committee has any power to make a rule which in effect extends a time limit laid down by Parliament. The power to make rules is given by the County Courts Act 1959, s 102, and this, unlike the Supreme Court of Judicature (Consolidation) Act 1925 for the Supreme Court (see s 99 (1) (g)), includes no express power to repeal enactments. On this part of the case I would express my respectful agreement with the dissenting judgment of e Russell LJ in *Hodgson v Armstrong*[4]. The change in the wording of the Rules of the Supreme Court did no more, I think, than give effect to the case law which had stood for some 80 years, and the County Court Rules, expressed in similar terms, seem to me to have the same effect.

    All these difficulties are avoided if there is a general principle such as has been suggested. Whether the statute is imperative in form ('shall be commenced within . . .') f or negative ('shall not be brought after . . .'), what Parliament must be contemplating is that the plaintiff shall not be shut out until the statutory period has run. Parliament must also be taken to contemplate that there will be days and short periods during which it will not be possible to issue a writ because under the rules of court the offices of the court will be closed. If, then, the period expires when the offices are closed, is the period in effect to be curtailed by the days of closing, or is it to be extended? The operation of the Statutes of Limitation has sometimes been called an g act of peace, in that the statutes prevent long dormant claims being stirred up. An arbitrary period has to be fixed in order to make the Act certain and workable; but in applying that period to cases where the courts are shut on the last day, the policy of the statute seems better effectuated by allowing an extra day or two than by subtracting a day or two. The difference between three years and three years h and a day cannot normally make much difference to a defendant; it may be disastrous to a plaintiff. It is true, as Russell LJ pointed out in *Hodgson v Armstrong*[5], that as the offices of the court close each afternoon, a litigant does not get his full period, and may fail to issue his writ in time if he arrives an hour or two after the offices have closed on what for him is the last day; but I think that the legislature may be safely assumed to have contemplated that the offices will not remain open until j midnight each day, and that a litigant will get the full period intended if the offices are open during the prescribed hours on his last day.

1 (1881) 45 LT 210
2 [1913] 2 KB 549, [1911-13] All ER Rep 1115
3 Vol 1, p 1812
4 [1967] 1 All ER at 319, [1967] 2 QB at 322
5 [1967] 1 All ER at 320, [1967] 2 QB at 323

There are indeed authorities which support the view that no extension of time is possible.   These include *Morris v Richards*[1] and *Gelmini v Moriggia*[2], which I have already mentioned; and in these the point was disposed of somewhat shortly.   There is the Judicial Committee case of *Dechène v City of Montreal*[3], which turned on the construction of the Quebec legislation there in point.   There is also *M'Niven v Glasgow Corpn*[4], of which I shall say something later in relation to other Scottish cases.

On the other hand, there is some authority for holding that the period may in effect be extended.   Lord Denning MR and Karminski LJ have already referred to *Hughes v Griffiths*[5], with its distinction between acts to be done by a party and acts to be done by the court.   I entirely agree with what they say about that case, and I need only add that I think that counsel for the plaintiff was putting it too high in opening when he said that issuing a writ of summons was an act not of the litigant but of the court.   This proposition is at least difficult to reconcile with *Clarke v Bradlaugh*[6] and in any case it suffices counsel to say that although the issue of a writ is the act of the litigant, it requires some action by the court for its validity, in the affixing of the seal of the court, and so on.   It is thus not, in the phrase of Erle CJ in *Hughes v Griffiths*[7] 'a mere act of the party'.

Hughes v Griffiths[5] is not an authority that stands in isolation.   A similar view was taken in *Mumford v Hitchcocks*[8], where the eight days for appearing to a specially indorsed writ under the Common Law Procedure Act 1852 expired on a Good Friday.   It was held that the defendant could validly enter an appearance when the offices of the court first reopened, which was on the following Wednesday.   Erle CJ[9] said that the appearance to the writ of summons 'is the combined act of the court and of the party; it cannot be done by the party unless the office is open and the officer ready to receive it'; and he equated the days of the holiday to Sundays, on which no juridical act can be done.

A similar view has also been taken in Scotland.   The cases establish that although a Sunday or other dies non occurring during the period is not to be disregarded in computing the period (*Hutton v Garland*[10]), there are circumstances in which the period will be extended if the last day of the period is dies non.   These circumstances correspond to those envisaged in *Hughes v Griffiths*[5], namely, where some activity of the court is requisite for the doing of the necessary act.   In *Henderson v Henderson*[11], Lord President Inglis referred to the exercise of the right under the Personal Diligence Act 1838, s 20, to lodge a reclaiming note within ten days of a judgment in a case in which the ten days expired on a Saturday when the offices of the court were closed, as they had been the day before as well.   He said[12]:

'It seems to me that when a limited time is allowed by the Legislature for the exercise of a privilege of this kind, that must always be subject to the implied condition that it is possible to perform the act in question within the specified time. Here that was impossible. If we were to hold that in consequence of the impossibility of implementing the statutory obligation to lodge the reclaiming note within the specified period there was an obligation to lodge it within a

---

1   (1881) 45 LT 210
2   [1913] 2 KB 549, [1911-13] All ER Rep 1115
3   [1894] AC 640
4   1920 SC 584
5   (1862) 13 CBNS 324
6   (1881) 8 QBD 63, [1881-85] All ER Rep 1002
7   (1862) 13 CBNS at 333
8   (1863) 14 CBNS 361
9   (1863) 14 CBNS at 368
10 (1883) 10 R (J) 60
11 (1888) 16 R 5
12 (1888) 16 R at 6

a   shorter time, we should be construing the statute in a manner quite unprecedented.   In this case it would limit the reclaiming days to eight instead of to ten, which are given by the statute.'

The next day on which the office was open was thus in time; and with this view the other members of the First Division concurred.

M'Vean v Jameson[1] was similarly concerned with a time limit fixed by statute,
b   namely, for the giving of notice of appeal; and the court made the same sort of distinction as appeared in Hughes v Griffiths[2]. Lord M'Laren said[3]:

'When some step of judicial procedure has to be performed by the litigant within a definite number of days fixed by statute, and the last day is a Sunday, our decisions have sanctioned the completion of the step on the Monday, where
c   the step is one which requires the co-operation of the Clerk of Court or other official, as the giving in of a report or document of any kind ... But where the act is something which the litigant can do at his own hand—where he has it in his power to complete the act so far as his own share in it is concerned without the co-operation of a second party, as in the case of the notice required—I see no reason why Sunday should be discounted.'

d   I should perhaps say that these Scottish cases were not cited in argument, although they were mentioned in the next case, which was duly cited; but as they merely reinforce the view that could be formed without their aid, I think I may properly refer to them.

This line of cases was distinguished in M'Niven v Glasgow Corpn[4] on the ground that the rule established for periods expressed in days did not apply to periods
e   expressed in months, unless, indeed, the courts were shut for the entire last month, as was theoretically possible. The statutory period of six months in that case was thus not extended even though it ended on a Sunday. The extension, it was said, must be founded on the construction of the statute, or it must fail. A difficulty in that sort of approach is that if 'days' is to be construed as 'days upon which the offices of the court are open', that would mean that Sundays during the period would be excluded
f   in computing the period; yet that is what is not done. However, if instead of looking at the units of which the period is composed, whether days, months or years, the period is regarded as a whole, and attention is directed to ascertaining the point of time at which the period expires, the difficulty disappears; and that is the approach that I would favour.

It is true that most of the cases have been concerned with short periods, and that
g   in the present case even three years minus a day or two is an ample period in which to issue a writ: no question of impossibility arises. But distinctions between long periods and short are difficult to make and justify, and although they may be made by statute, they are obviously unsatisfactory for establishing by case law. It is also true that there has long been a rule, dating from Prideaux v Webber[5], that once time begins to run, it runs continuously, even when the courts are not open. That, however,
h   does not trench upon the question of when the period expires. What matters most is the last day; days during the period when the plaintiff cannot issue his writ are of little importance if some time still remains, as, indeed, must have been obvious to Parliament. The last day is another matter, and without affecting the rule that time runs continuously, it seems to me to be open to the courts to determine upon what day any period expires, and how that day is to be ascertained.

j

1   (1896) 23 R (J) 25
2   (1862) 13 CBNS 324
3   (1896) 23 R (J) at 27
4   1920 SC 584
5   (1661) 1 Lev 31

I do not think that I need refer to the other cases cited in *Hodgson v Armstrong*[1]. As Willis J in effect pointed out in the court below[2], that case was decided upon a statute which imposed upon the court a prohibition against entertaining an application unless it complied with the time limit. No doubt this form of wording was adopted because, unlike the ordinary cases of limitation, the prohibition is against making an application not merely too late but also too early ('not less than two nor more than four months...'). Be that as it may, the language differs significantly from language which provides that an action shall not be brought after a stated time, or shall be commenced within a stated time. It may be, too, that statutory prohibitions against the court doing certain acts are more closely linked to the rules of court than statutory provisions relating to the commencement of an action. In any case, I would prefer the rule which Sellers LJ put in the forefront of his judgment, based on *Hughes v Griffiths*[3], and I would not treat *Hodgson v Armstrong*[1] as laying down for cases other than those under the Landlord and Tenant Act 1954 a binding rule based on the dominance of the County Court Rules, especially as Sellers LJ concurred with this view only as a dernier ressort. I appreciate that the existence of a general principle to this effect may make unnecessary express statutory provisions to the like effect, such as the Bankruptcy Act 1914, s 145, discussed in *Hodgson v Armstrong*[1]; but like Sellers LJ[4] I do not think that the enactment of such provisions, which at least remove any possible doubt within their sphere, can really be said to demonstrate that in other cases no such principle could exist.

Accordingly, in my judgment the result is as follows. There are a number of cases which support the general rule that a statutory period of time, whether general or special, will, in the absence of any contrary provision, normally be construed as ending at the expiration of the last day of the period. That rule remains; but there is a limited but important exception or qualification to it, which may be derived from a line of authorities which include *Hughes v Griffiths*[3], *Mumford v Hitchcocks*[5], the judgment of Sellers LJ in *Hodgson v Armstrong*[1] and the Scottish cases. If the act to be done by the person concerned is one for which some action by the court is requisite, such as issuing a writ, and it is impossible to do that act on the last day of the period because the offices of the court are closed for the whole of that day, the period will prima facie be construed as ending not on that day but at the expiration of the next day upon which the offices of the court are open and it becomes possible to do the act. In this appeal, there is nothing in the facts of the case which ousts the prima facie application of this exception, which accordingly applies. I therefore concur in allowing the appeal.

Appeal allowed with costs in the Court of Appeal and below. Leave to appeal on condition that the defendants do not attempt to disturb the order for costs in the Court of Appeal and in the court below and pay all the costs in the House of Lords.

Solicitors: *Rowe & Maw*, agents for *Salusbury & Co*, Leicester (for the plaintiff); *Ironsides*, Leicester (for the defendants).

L J Kovats Esq Barrister.

1   [1967] 1 All ER 307, [1967] 2 QB 299
2   [1972] 3 All ER 305, [1972] 3 WLR 663
3   (1862) 13 CBNS 324
4   [1967] 1 All ER at 314, [1967] 2 QB at 313, 314
5   (1863) 14 CBNS 361

R v Patents Appeal Tribunal, ex parte Beecham Group Ltd

COURT OF APPEAL, CIVIL DIVISION
LORD DENNING MR, EDMUND DAVIES AND STEPHENSON LJJ
18th, 19th, 20th OCTOBER, 30th NOVEMBER 1972

Patent – Grant – Opposition – Prior use – Invention used in United Kingdom before priority date of claim – Used – Use without appreciating qualities of product or principles on which based – Product blended with other substances to make it commercially saleable – Identity of product lost in blended article – Manufacture and sale of blended product in commercial quantities – Ampicillin trihydrate – Ampicillin trihydrate blended with other substances to make it commercially saleable in form of capsules – Special qualities of ampicillin trihydrate unknown to manufacturers – Whether manufacturers 'used' ampicillin trihydrate – Patents Act 1949, s 14 (1) (d).

Patent – Grant – Opposition – Prior use – Secret use – No account to be taken of any secret use – Secret – Secrecy connoting conscious or intentional concealment of use – Product blended with other substances to make it commercially saleable – Identity of product lost in blended article – No intention to conceal use of product – Patents Act 1949, s 14 (3).

In 1962 Beechams discovered ampicillin, an improved form of penicillin. During 1962 they produced ampicillin mixed with water in various forms, e g mixed with one, two or three parts of water, but at that time they were not concerned with the amount of water mixed with the ampicillin (which made no difference to the sufferer taking the drug), being then more concerned with the curative properties of ampicillin. Records kept by Beechams showed that in 1962 they produced a considerable quantity of ampicillin mixed with three parts of water (ampicillin trihydrate) although at the time they did not recognise it as such or appreciate its advantages. Four batches of ampicillin trihydrate amounting to one hundredweight, enough for 10,000 doses, were manufactured at their Worthing factory in the course of regular commercial manufacture, and more batches may have been manufactured of which there were no records. The four batches of ampicillin trihydrate were transmitted to another Beechams' factory where they were blended with other substances to make the ampicillin trihydrate commercially saleable in the form of capsules. The capsules were put on the market and sold in commercial quantities. After the blending process the identity of the ampicillin trihydrate was lost; analysis of the capsules would not disclose that they had been made with ampicillin trihydrate rather than with any other form of ampicillin. It was conceded by Beechams that the effect of the blending was to extinguish the purchaser's means of knowledge of the constituents of ampicillin trihydrate. Late in 1963 Beechams discovered that ampicillin trihydrate had special advantages over the other forms of ampicillin; it retained its efficacy longer and thus had a longer 'shelf life'. Beechams thereafter switched their production entirely to ampicillin trihydrate. On 21st March 1963 their American rivals, Bristol-Myers Co, who had been working on ampicillin trihydrate, applied for a patent for that product, one of the claims of the specification being a claim to the product, ampicillin trihydrate, itself. Beechams lodged an opposition to the grant of the patent under s 14 (1)[a]

of the Patents Act 1949, inter alia, on the ground in para (*d*) of s 14 (1), that the invention (ampicillin trihydrate) had been 'used' in the United Kingdom before 21st
March 1963, the priority date of Bristol-Myers' claim; for that purpose Beechams
relied on the production of ampicillin trihydrate on a commercial scale by themselves
before the priority date. Bristol-Myers contended that even if Beechams had 'used'
the product, that use was a 'secret use', and so, by virtue of s 14 (3)[b] of the 1949 Act,
was to be disregarded in opposition proceedings.

Held – Beechams' opposition to the grant of the patent should be upheld for the
following reasons—
  (i) Beechams had 'used' ampicillin trihydrate, within s 14 (1) (*d*) of the 1949 Act,
before the priority date of the claim. In order to establish prior use it had to be shown
that the use had been substantial rather than minimal, and intentional rather than
merely accidental. It was immaterial that the user had used the product without
recognising it or knowing or appreciating its qualities or the principles on which it was
based; further, it was unnecessary to show that the prior use had been such as to give
the means of knowledge of the constituents of the product to the public; (per Lord
Denning MR) the test was, if the patent were granted, would it stop the prior user
from doing what he had been doing before. The evidence established that, before the
priority date, Beechams had made and used ampicillin trihydrate in commercial
quantities and accordingly had 'used' the product within s 14 (1) (*d*) even though
they did not then recognise the ampicillin trihydrate as such and the product had been
blended with other substances before it was sold to the public with the result that it
could not be discovered by analysis (see p 632 b and j to p 633 b d and f, p 636 f to
p 637 b and p 638 g, post); *Harwood v Great Northern Railway Co* (1864) 11 HL Cas 654
applied; *Boyce v Morris Motors Ltd* (1926) 44 RPC 105 distinguished.
  (ii) The prior use by Beechams was not a 'secret use' within s 14 (3) of the 1949
Act. The word 'secret' connoted conscious or intentional concealment of the use of the
product, and thus was a matter to be judged subjectively. There was no evidence of
conscious concealment by Beechams; the blending was done for commercial
convenience and not to keep the product secret (see p 633 g to j and p 637 j to p 638
b h and j, post).

Notes
For prior use, see 29 Halsbury's Laws (3rd Edn) 29-39, paras 62-88; for prior secret
use, see ibid 39-41, paras 89-91, and for cases on prior use, see 36 Digest (Repl) 710-721,
544-659.
  For the Patents Act 1949, s 14, see 24 Halsbury's Statutes (3rd Edn) 565.

Cases referred to in judgments
Boyce v Morris Motors Ltd (1927) 44 RPC 105, CA, 36 Digest (Repl) 697, 451.
Carpenter v Smith (1841) 1 Web Pat Cas 530; *subsequent proceedings* (1842) 9 M & W
  300, 36 Digest (Repl) 719, 647.
Crane v Price (1842) 4 Man & G 580, 5 Scott NR 338, 12 LJCP 81, 1 Web Pat Cas 393,
  134 ER 239, 36 Digest (Repl) 684, 351.
Fomento Industrial SA, Biro Swan Ltd v Mentmore Manufacturing Co Ltd [1956] RPC 87,
  CA, Digest (Cont Vol A) 1237, 603a.
Gill v Coutts and Sons and Cutler (1895) 13 RPC 125, 23 R 371, 33 Sc LR 218, 3 SLT 205,
  36 Digest (Repl) 1038, *609.
Harwood v Great Northern Railway Co (1864) 11 HL Cas 654, 35 LJQB 27, 12 LT 771,
  11 ER 1488, HL; *affg* (1862) 2 B & S 222, 31 LJQB 198, 121 ER 1056; *rvsg* (1860)
  2 B & S 194, 29 LJQB 193, 121 ER 1044, 36 Digest (Repl) 691, 399.

---

b Section 14 (3), so far as material, provides: '. . . for the purposes of paragraph (*d*) . . . of . . .
  subsection (1) no account shall be taken of any secret use.'

Heath v Smith (1854) 3 E & B 256, 2 Web Pat Cas 268, 2 CLR 1584, 23 LJQB 166, 22 LTOS 257, 18 Jur 601, 118 ER 1136, 36 Digest (Repl) 716, 607.

International Nickel Co Inc v Ford Motor Co (1958) 119 USPQ 72.

Monsanto Co (Brignac's) Application [1971] RPC 153.

Plimpton v Malcolmson (1876) 3 Ch D 531, 45 LJCh 505, 34 LT 340; *previous proceedings sub nom Plympton v Malcolmson* (1875) LR 20 Eq 37, 36 Digest (Repl) 653, 78.

Stahlwerk Becker Aktiengesellschaft's Patent, Re (1918) 36 RPC 13, HL, 36 Digest (Repl) 720, 658.

Tilghman v Proctor (1880) 102 US 707.

Cases and authority also cited

Miller's Patent, Re (1898) 15 RPC 205, CA.

Reymes-Cole v Elite Hosiery Co Ltd [1965] RPC 102, CA.

Terrell on the Law of Patents (12th Edn, 1971), pp 110, 113, paras 274, 283.

Appeal

The applicants, Beecham Group Ltd ('Beechams'), appealed against the order of the Divisional Court (Lord Widgery CJ, Bridge and Shaw JJ) dated 13th October 1971, dismissing their motion for an order of certiorari to remove into the High Court for the purpose of there being rescinded and quashed (1) the decision of the Patents Appeal Tribunal (Whitford J) dated 30th November 1970, given in proceedings concerning an application by the respondents, Bristol-Myers Co ('Bristol-Myers'), for a patent for ampicillin trihydrate (letters patent 1,100,843) and the opposition thereto of Beechams; and (2) the decision of the hearing officer acting on behalf of the Comptroller General of Patents, dated 24th March 1970. The Comptroller General and the Patents Appeal Tribunal severally but on different grounds had rejected Beechams' opposition to the grant to Bristol-Myers of the patent for ampicillin trihydrate. Beechams' grounds of appeal were that the Divisional Court was wrong in law (i) in holding that commercial sales to diverse persons, without any bond of secrecy by Beechams, of a quantity of ampicillin trihydrate exceeding one hundredweight, constituted a secret user of the invention within the meaning of s 14 (3) of the Patents Act 1949; and (ii) in refusing to quash the decisions appealed against, allowing the grant of the letters patent for ampicillin trihydrate, when if the patent was granted it would have the effect, contrary to s 6 of the Statute of Monopolies 1623[1], of granting a patent monopoly in the manufacture, use and sale of a substance, ampicillin trihydrate, which others at and prior to the date of the application for the patent monopoly were in fact making, using and selling on a substantial commercial scale. Bristol-Myers gave notice that on the hearing of the appeal they would contend that the Divisional Court's judgment should be affirmed on grounds additional or alternative to those relied on by that court, namely, on the grounds (1) on which the Patents Appeal Tribunal and/or the superintending examiner acting for the Comptroller General of Patents found for Bristol-Myers on the issue of prior user; (2) that the sale of ampicillin trihydrate material blended and mixed beyond recognition with other substances could not be held to be prior user for any purposes of the Patents Act 1949; (3) that the sale of ampicillin trihydrate material blended and mixed beyond recognition could not and did not give anybody the means of knowledge required to constitute prior user; (4) that Beechams' own prior manufacture of ampicillin trihydrate was accidental, fortuitous, unintended and unappreciated so that in fact they did not discover it at all but passed it by and blended the material beyond recognition with other material; (5) that the decision in *Boyce v Morris Motors Ltd*[2] and in *Re Stahlwerk Becker Akt's Patent*[3] were decisive against Beechams; and (6) that the appeal related to s 14 and not s 32 of the Patents Act 1949 and the decisions in *Dollond's Case*[4]

1 21 Jac 1 c 3
2 (1927) 44 RPC 105
3 (1918) 36 RPC 13
4 (1766) unreported; cited in Terrell on the Law of Patents (12th Edn, 1971), p 111, para 274

and *Carpenter v Smith*[1] were properly to be regarded as referable to s 32 and validity, not to s 14 and opposition to grant. The facts are set out in the judgment of Lord Denning MR.

S Gratwick QC, R A Lunzer and *B C Reid* for Beechams.
J P Comyn QC and *A E Turner* for Bristol-Myers.

Cur adv vult

30th November. The following judgments were read.

LORD DENNING MR. The great discovery of penicillin by Fleming has been followed by many developments. In 1962 Beechams discovered an improved form of penicillin known as ampicillin. They patented it under specification 902,703. They produced it in a form mixed with water, but Beechams did not at that time worry about the amount of water mixed with it. They were more concerned with the curative properties of ampicillin itself, the correct dosage, and so forth. The ampicillin which they produced might have no water with it (anhydrous) or one part of water (monohydrate); or two parts (dihydrate); or three parts (trihydrate), or so forth. But this made no difference to the sufferer who took the drug. All that mattered to him was the ampicillin itself. When he took the capsules, the water disappeared, leaving the ampicillin to do its work.

In 1962 Beechams were producing ampicillin in the form of ampicillin monohydrate; but they were also producing a considerable quantity of ampicillin trihydrate. They did not recognise it as ampicillin trihydrate at the time, but they kept records which show that it must have been. It was in the form of fine colourless needles which had an infra-red spectrum now known to be ampicillin trihydrate. Beechams manufactured several batches of it at their Worthing factory and transmitted it to their Brentford factory. Each batch was there blended with another batch or with ingredients conventionally used by pharmaceutical manufacturers. By this blending the ampicillin trihydrate was made into saleable form as capsules. It was then put on to the market. It was sold in commercial quantities. We do not know the exact amount. The reason is because records were not taken of all batches but only of some of them for another purpose altogether.

But we do know that four batches made at Worthing amounted to 37 kilograms (about one hundredweight)—enough for 10,000 doses—and were ampicillin trihydrate. There may have been more. But at least those four batches were ampicillin trihydrate.

Nevertheless, after the blending at Brentford, the identity of the ampicillin trihydrate was lost. The capsules, when blended, were of course, ampicillin capsules, but no analysis would disclose that they had been made with ampicillin trihydrate. They might have been made with ampicillin monohydrate or ampicillin in any other form. The superintending examiner said that '. . . the evidence establishes that substantial quantities of ampicillin trihydrate were sold commercially during 1962.'

Late in 1963 Beechams discovered that ampicillin trihydrate had special advantages over the other forms of ampicillin. It had a 'longer shelf-life'. It retained its efficacy longer than the other forms. So they decided to switch their production to ampicillin trihydrate entirely. Since 1963 they have done so. So have all other manufacturers of ampicillin. The trihydrate has not only a longer shelf-life. It is also the form most likely to appear in manufacture.

I must now return to 1962 and early 1963. At that time Beechams were busy producing ampicillin in any form. But their American rivals, Bristol-Myers Co, were concentrating on ampicillin trihydrate. On 21st March 1963 Bristol-Myers applied for a patent for ampicillin trihydrate. It is specification 1,011,843. Claims 1 to 11 were all claims to various processes for making ampicillin trihydrate. Claim 12 was a claim

---

1 (1841) 1 Web Pat Cas 530

a to the product ampicillin trihydrate itself. If it is good, it means that the American corporation will have the exclusive right to make, vend or use this compound ampicillin trihydrate; and Beechams will have to stop making or selling it, although they have done so for the last nine years; or else Beechams will have to seek a compulsory licence.

b Beechams naturally object to the granting of this application. They have now their own process for producing ampicillin trihydrate. So they do not challenge the processes in claims 1 to 11 in the Bristol-Myers' specification. But they do challenge the product claim, no 12. They lodged an opposition to it under s 14 (1) of the Patents Act 1949. They opposed it on the ground that it was published in the United Kingdom before the priority date, 21st March 1963. They relied for this purpose on their own prior specification 902,703. They also opposed it on the ground that it was used in the c United Kingdom before the priority date. They relied for this purpose on the ground that they had themselves produced ampicillin trihydrate on a commercial scale before the priority date. To this, however, Bristol-Myers replied that it was a secret use and therefore no account had to be taken of it in opposition proceedings under s 14; although it might be in revocation proceedings under s 32.

d The superintending examiner upheld the opposition of Beechams on the ground that there was prior publication. The Patents Appeal Tribunal rejected Beechams' opposition on the ground that there was no prior publication and no prior use. The Divisional Court rejected Beechams' opposition on the ground that there was a secret use. No question arises before us on prior publication. The only questions are: (1) prior use; (2) secret use.

e **1 Prior use**

Section 14 (1) (d) of the 1949 Act says that any person interested may oppose the grant of a patent on the ground that the invention, so far as claimed in any claim of the complete specification, *was used* in the United Kingdom before the priority date of that claim. The statute does not define what is meant by 'used'. But one thing is quite clear. The statute does not say 'publicly used', nor 'used in a public manner', f nor does it say 'knowingly used' or 'intentionally used'. I see no reason whatever for introducing any of those glosses into the statute. Whenever the statute wished to specify a particular kind of use, it did so: as, for example, 'secret use' or 'use for reasonable trial or experiment'.

To determine the meaning of 'use', I look to the Statute of Monopolies 1623[1], which is the foundation of our patent law today. It authorises the grant of letters g patent and grants of privilege—

'of the sole working or making of any manner of new manufactures within this realm, to the true and first inventor and inventors of such manufactures, which others at the time of making such letters patents and grants shall not use . . .'

h Those words 'shall not use' mean in modern parlance 'do not use' or 'have not used'. They are expressly inserted so as to give protection to a person who is already manufacturing the thing, or has previously manufactured it, and has put it into use. He is not to be stopped from doing what he has done before. So letters patent are not to be issued to an inventor if the result would be to stop a prior user from continuing his use. It may be that the prior user (who has manufactured the thing previously) j did so in complete ignorance of the scientific phenomenon involved. He may not have had the least idea of the chemical properties of the ingredients. He may have manufactured the thing simply by chance, and then found out that it had particular advantages, or was useful for particular purposes. Later on some other person may quite independently invent a process for manufacturing the very same thing. He may find

1 21 Jac 1 c 3

that it has other special advantages, or can be put to other extra purposes. Yet that   *a*
discovery does not entitle him to stop the prior user from continuing to manufacture
it. He cannot get a patent for the product; so as to stop the prior user from doing
what he did before.

I take the test to be: if this patent were granted, would it stop the prior user from
doing what he was doing before? That is shown, I think, by *Harwood v Great
Northern Railway Co*[1]. The prior use had there been of channelled iron which had   *b*
been in use for a considerable period anterior to the patent, but for a different
purpose (for joining timbers on a bridge) instead of the new purpose (for joining railway lines together). Hill J said[2] that he was prepared to apply the test—

'whether, if this patent were upheld, it would interfere with or prevent the
parties, who are alleged to have used the subject-matter of the invention before,
from continuing to enjoy that which they say was a prior use of it . . .'   *c*

That test was accepted by Lord Westbury LC, when that case reached the House of
Lords. He said[3]:

'. . . the true mode of trying the question of course would be to reverse the
order of time of the two productions, and to inquire whether if any one had now   *d*
introduced the channelled iron it would or would not have been an infringement
of the Plaintiff's patent.'

Apply that test here. Suppose that Bristol-Myers had obtained a patent in 1961
for the product ampicillin trihydrate, and then in 1962 Beechams had made and used
ampicillin trihydrate, as they in fact did, that is to say, they made it and used it in
commercial quantities, but did not recognise that it was ampicillin trihydrate, nor   *e*
appreciate all of its advantages. Would that be an infringement? Clearly it would.
The fact that Beechams made and used it, by accident as it were, or fortuitously,
would be no defence in an action for infringement. I know that in *Harwood's case*[4]
Blackburn J in the Court of Queen's Bench said:

'A man cannot be said to "use" a manufacture . . . when accidentally, and with-   *f*
out any knowledge or intention, he produces that which, if it were knowingly
and intentionally done, and for the purpose of trade, would be a manufacture.'

But his views were not endorsed in the Exchequer Chamber or in the House of Lords.
Quite the contrary. In the Exchequer Chamber[5] Willes J, giving the judgment of
the whole court, said that prior use of an invention might well avail a prior user even   *g*
though 'the principle upon which it acts was either unknown or misapprehended'.

Boyce v Morris Motors Ltd[6] is no authority to the contrary. Rolls-Royce (the alleged
prior user) had never 'used' the thermometer with its bulb out of the water. They
put it there by way of trial or experience. They thought that the splashing of the
water would have the same effect as if it had been put into the water. Whereas
here Beechams had deliberately 'used' the ampicillin trihydrate, even though they   *h*
did not know or appreciate its qualities.

I am prepared to hold, therefore, that, if there has been a prior use of the product,
it is a bar to a subsequent inventor of it, even though the prior user has used it without
knowing or appreciating its qualities or the principles on which it was based. The
prior user must have been substantial and not minimal; and it must have been an

j

---

1 (1864) 11 HL Cas 654
2 (1860) 2 B & S 194 at 212
3 (1864) 11 HL Cas at 681
4 (1860) 2 B & S at 215
5 (1862) 2 B & S 222 at 231
6 (1927) 44 RPC 105

a   intentional use of the same product intending to put it to use—and not a chance encounter. The reason being that it is the policy of the law that a prior user should not be prevented from continuing to use it as he did before.

It seems to have been thought at one time that the prior user, to be of any avail, must have been made known to some one or other of the public, so that, if he wished, he could, by examination or analysis, get to know how to make it himself. In short, b   the prior user should be such as to give the means of knowledge. That was supposed to follow from *Carpenter v Smith*[1]; and *Re Stahlwerk Becker Akt's Patent*[2]. But I do not think that is right. I agree with the observations of Whitford J on this point in *Monsanto Co (Brignac's) Application*[3]. A man may make a product in his own factory and sell it on a commercial scale—but it may be so compounded that it defies analysis by others. No one who buys it may be able to discover how it is made or what the ingredients are. Then some newcomer stumbles on a method of making c   it himself, and seeks a patent for it. But it is then too late. He cannot get a patent. He cannot stop the prior user from going on with his manufacture as he has always done. The prior user is a bar to the patent sought.

Likewise here. The prior sales of ampicillin trihydrate were in a blended form. It was blended with other substances—so that the ampicillin trihydrate could not be d   discovered by analysis. But that does not alter the fact that the ampicillin trihydrate was 'used'—and used on a commercial scale—to make the blended article. It is just like the blending of various teas. Each tea is 'used', even though it is afterwards mingled inextricably with the others.

I must mention, however, a point made by counsel for Bristol-Myers. He put this test. Suppose that Beechams in December 1963 applied for a patent for ampicillin trihydrate. Would they have been defeated by their own prior use in 1962? e   The answer is Yes, they would. It is just the same question. There might have been a practical difficulty in any third person proving this prior use. But it does not affect the principle. I would hold, therefore, that in this case, on the facts found by the superintending examiner, there was a prior use of ampicillin trihydrate by Beechams before the priority date.

f   2   *Secret use*

There remains the question of 'secret use'. The Divisional Court held that the use by Beechams was 'secret' for this reason: the ampicillin trihydrate was blended with other substances before it was sold to the public; and in the blended form it could not be detected by analysis. This blending made the use of it 'secret', even though it was not intentionally kept secret. The Divisional Court said that 'secret' was a g   matter to be judged objectively, and not subjectively.

I am afraid that I cannot agree with the Divisional Court on this point. The statute does not contain any definition of the word 'secret'. But I must say that it connotes to my mind the conscious concealment of the use of the thing. It is, in that sense, a matter to be judged subjectively. The Shorter Oxford English Dictionary gives as its meaning, in regard to actions 'Done with the intention of being concealed'. The h   test is: did the prior user *keep* the use of it 'secret'? If he expressly imposed on his servants an obligation of confidence that they should not disclose the use of it to others—then it would be a secret use. But, if he manufactured it by his workmen, without any obligation of confidence on them, I do not see that it could be regarded as secret. There is no evidence of any conscious concealment by Beechams in this case. They certainly did not do the 'blending' so as to keep it secret. They did j   'blending' only for commercial convenience, so as to make it into capsules ready for sale.

I would hold, therefore, that there was prior use by Beechams—which was not secret—and that the opposition should be upheld.

---

1   (1842) 9 M & W 300   2   (1918) 36 RPC 13   3   [1971] RPC 153

EDMUND DAVIES LJ. In this appeal two questions arise for determination from the facts already related by Lord Denning MR: (1) was ampicillin trihydrate 'used in the United Kingdom' by Beechams before 21st March 1963, the priority date of Bristol-Myers' claim (Patents Act 1949, s 14 (1) (d))? (2) If so, has it nevertheless to be disregarded as being a 'secret use' (s 14 (3))?

Before dealing with these questions, it may be helpful to consider in some detail how the relevant facts have been regarded during the earlier stages of this litigation. The superintending examiner, who upheld on the ground of 'prior publication' the opposition of Beechams, rejected their claim to prior user on the ground that they—

> 'did not dispute that the blending ... would prevent any identification by analysis of any ampicillin trihydrate which may have been present in the finished product, so that no question would arise of the public being given the means of knowledge.'

But, while also rejecting Beechams' opposition, the Patents Appeal Tribunal declined to adopt this approach, which was founded on the decision of the House of Lords in *Re Stahlwerk Becker Akt's Patent*[1] where Lord Finlay LC said[2]:

> 'The law as to prior user seems to be this, that, if the article has been manu-factured and sold, that gives the means of knowledge to the purchaser, and that that is enough to establish prior user.'

It being conceded by Beechams that the effect of blending their ampicillin with other materials extinguished 'the means of knowledge of the purchaser', could there nevertheless be said to be any prior user? Whitford J answered that question in the affirmative, saying:

> 'I do not for my own part think that the decision in the House of Lords can be taken as establishing that no case of prior use can possibly be made out unless it is shown that means of knowledge of the invention is given to the public.'

In *Monsanto Co (Brignac's) Application*[3] he added:

> 'I do not think *Stahlwerk Becker*[1] decides anything more than this if a prior use gives means of knowledge it will invalidate a subsequent patent by publica-tion. Their lordships in that case were *not* considering the question of the effect of prior use alone.'

It may here be usefully noted that such question *was* considered in *Gill v Coutts and Sons and Cutler*[4], Lord Trayner saying:

> '... I think the Sheriff Substitute has fallen into error by misapprehending the statement often made that there must be disclosure as well as use. But that disclosure does not mean that the public shall know as much about the article used as the maker of it knows. It means that the thing must be disclosed to the public and not kept by the maker to himself. It is the use of the thing in public as distinguished from the use in private by the inventor. Public user involves disclosure ... It is quite true ... that in order to obtain Letters Patent, the inventor must disclose his secret to the public in return for the monopoly conferred upon him. But such a disclosure as that is not necessary to the prior use which will anticipate and so void a patent.'

Whitford J concurred with the examiner in rejecting Beechams' opposition, but he did so on the quite different ground that:

1   (1918) 36 RPC 13
2   (1918) 36 RPC at 19
3   [1971] RPC 153 at 163
4   (1895) 13 RPC 125 at 136, 137

a   'I fail to find any evidence at all which to my mind satisfactorily establishes any intention by the opponents prior to the relevant date to manufacture the trihydrate form in their commercial premises . . . assuming for present purposes the opponents are right when they say that prior user can be tested on a wider basis . . . if it is established that there is an intention to use which may not have given means of knowledge to the public but nonetheless was an intention relating to commercial use . . . then they have not really got over the hurdle which

b   they must surmount because they have failed to establish the requisite intention . . . . the whole conception of the grant of monopoly is contrary to the idea that by such grant somebody else could be stopped from carrying on a pre-existing intention to manufacture because such production of the trihydrate as did occur, which was a very minor proportion of the total production was not . . . the result of any deliberate intention, it was purely fortuitous . . .'

c   While the Divisional Court likewise rejected Beechams' opposition, Lord Widgery CJ and Shaw J declined to follow this reasoning of Whitford J. After reviewing the authorities, and in particular *Boyce v Morris Motors Ltd*[1], Lord Widgery CJ said:

d   '. . . I do not think one can deduce from an authority of that kind . . . a general proposition that if you do not intend to produce the inventive result, that of necessity prevents your user from being user within the section. Indeed, as we are considering a relatively new Act of Parliament, I would myself try to construe it in accordance with the broadest basic principles of patent law.'

Bridge J did not deal with this matter of user and restricted himself to giving his reasons for holding that, in any event, any prior user that might be regarded as

e   having occurred was 'secret' and therefore had to be disregarded, a view shared by all three members of the court.

Counsel for Bristol-Myers has sought to uphold before us both conclusions of Whitford J, i e (1) that there can be 'prior use' even though the product does not of itself provide a means of knowledge as to its constituents; but (2) that in the present case the lack of knowledge and *intention* on the part of Beechams led to the conclusion

f   that there was no user by them before the priority date. In relation to the findings of the Divisional Court, he submits (a) that their finding of 'prior user' was erroneous but (b) they were right in holding that any user which had taken place was 'secret'. Counsel for Beechams, on the other hand, seeks to uphold the Divisional Court's favourable finding as to 'prior user', but submits that they fell into error in holding that it was 'secret'.

g   After this somewhat lengthy introduction, I turn to consider the two questions raised, pausing only to point out that, if Beechams are to succeed in their opposition, the burden rests on them of establishing that, in the circumstances of this case, the first question demands an affirmative answer and the second a negative one.

(1) *Was there a 'prior user' by Beechams?*

h   Ampicillin trihydrate was sold by Beechams, and the superintending examiner made an unchallenged finding to that effect. But, because of their ignorance at the relevant time of its superiority in one respect, they paid no attention to the water content of the ampicillin molecules they blended and sold, and it may be that their records are not as ample as they would have been had they been knowledgeable about the matter. Nevertheless, they did make four batches of ampicillin trihy-

j   drate, weighing a hundredweight and being sufficient to constitute 10,000 doses. This is surely a substantial quantity; it seems to me irrelevant that it was small in comparison with their total output of ampicillin, and it was produced in the course of regular commercial manufacture; so that no question of mere experiment and trial arises.

---

1   (1927) 44 RPC 105

It is true that, in the words of Lord Widgery CJ:

a

'... the trihydrate was not sold in its virgin state, it was sold mixed with the other unidentified substances in such a way as in my judgment to destroy its identity altogether ... What they sold was a compound obscured in which was some ampicillin trihydrate. It did not survive in recognisable form ...'

But, as already noted, counsel for Bristol-Myers concedes (and rightly, in my judgment) that this fact would not, of itself, eliminate the possibility of prior user. Purporting to base himself on the judgment of Whitford J, he invokes s 6 of the Statute of Monopolies 1623, with its reference to 'the true and first inventor' of new manufactures. He submits that anyone who accidentally and unknowingly makes ampicillin trihydrate is not its 'true inventor', and that, Beechams lacking all knowledge of the superiority of ampicillin trihydrate until some six months after the priority date and until then not even realising that they had been manufacturing and selling it, they cannot be regarded as its 'true inventor'. He understandably relies on *Harwood v Great Northern Railway Co*[1] where Blackburn J said:

b

c

'I cannot think that a man can use a manufacture ... because accidentally and, without in the least degree intending it, he does that thing which, if it were habitually done on purpose, and for the purpose of trade, would be a manufacture. I cannot think there is a use, either public or private ... unless there be some knowledge and some intention.'

d

But the reference to the Statute of Monopolies in this context is with respect, misleading. I may stumble on a splendid invention, and it is nihil ad rem that I wholly lacked prior art or even simple industry, the way in which it was arrived at being of no importance: see, for example, *Crane v Price*[2]. Even so, I cannot patent it unless I have, through native intelligence or by the advice of another, come to realise what it is that I have discovered and have acquired sufficient knowledge of what has happened to be able to furnish the particulars required in a specification. Granted this, I can then claim to be the 'true and first inventor'. But even less is required of me in order that I may properly be described as a 'prior user'. For this purpose, I may be completely unaware of the novelty or special qualities of that which I am using in a public manner. For example, I may be the importer to this country of goods manufactured abroad and I may lack all but the broadest knowledge of what I am selling. Even so, I am entitled to oppose the grant of a patent in respect of that which I have been selling before the priority date. Indeed, in some circumstances, I may even claim that I was myself a first and true inventor within the 1623 Statute (*Plimpton v Malcomson*[3], per Sir George Jessel MR).

e

f

g

As to the observations of Blackburn J in *Harwood v Great Northern Railway Co*[4] in reversing the judgment of the Queen's Bench Court, Willes J said in the Exchequer Chamber[5] '... we by no means say that prior use of an invention is to be of no avail because the principle upon which it acts was either unknown or misapprehended'. It will not do if the user is merely accidental, as in *Boyce v Morris Motors Ltd*[6], but the user may be intentional even without knowledge of that which is being used, and that, as I see it, is the position here. Insofar as the American case of *International Nickel Co Inc v Ford Motor Co*[7] is authority to the contrary, I must respectfully decline to follow it. In my judgment prior use of ampicillin trihydrate by Beechams before the

h

j

---

1 (1860) 29 LJQB 193 at 202; cf (1860) 2 B & S 194 at 215
2 (1842) 1 Web Pat Cas 393 at 411
3 (1876) 3 Ch D 531 at 555
4 (1860) 29 LJQB at 202; cf (1860) 2 B & S at 215
5 (1862) 2 B & S 222 at 230, 231
6 (1927) 44 RPC 105
7 (1958) 119 USPQ 72

a   priority date was established, and I think that counsel for Beechams was accordingly right in conceding that, had they applied for a patent in December 1963, when they discovered its special properties, they would have been defeated by their own prior user even though they alone had put it on the market, just as the first and true inventor was defeated in *Fomento Industrial SA, Biro Swan Ltd v Mentmore Manufacturing Co Ltd*[1].

b   (2) *Was the prior user 'secret'?*

Counsel for Bristol-Myers was right in submitting that it was for Beechams to establish that their prior user was non-secret. The Divisional Court held that he was also right in submitting that they had failed to do this. Indeed, that court went further, holding that such user as had occurred was clearly 'secret' within the meaning of s 14 (3). Lord Widgery CJ said:

c

'It seems to me ... that in construing 'secret use' in the context of s 14, one ought to bear in mind that what Parliament was almost certainly trying to do was to bring in, in perhaps more modern and simple language, the ... concept that a use which has not in any sense made the secret available to the public is a non-open use, a secret use if you like, which ought not to qualify as a ground for
d   objection ... I am prepared to accept that ... the mere fact that the qualities of the trihydrate would not reveal themselves on an analysis of the substance sold is not by itself enough to cause the user to be secret. But even that is not far enough in my judgment for the objectors to go, because here the trihydrate was not sold in its virgin state, it was sold mixed with the other unidentified substances in such a way as in my judgment to destroy its identity altogether ...
e   this really cannot be treated as a case in which the objectors sold ampicillin trihydrate at all for the present purpose. What they sold was a compound obscured in which was some ampicillin trihydrate. It did not survive in recognisable form, and I think it is taking the matter too far to say that a manufacture and sale of that kind is not a secret manufacture under the section. I regard "secret" as being a matter to be judged objectively and not subjectively. I would
f   have thought this was clearly a secret use for present purposes.'

Bridge J said in concurring:

'In the end, I ask myself the question: in any sense in which the word "secret" can reasonably be used in the English language, what more could [Beechams]
g   have done if they had appreciated the existence of the trihydrate and wanted to use it as an ingredient in a product they were going to sell without the public knowing about it—what more could they have done to keep the existence of the trihydrate secret? It seems to me the answer is: nothing.'

Supporting this finding, counsel for Bristol-Myers submitted that whether or not user is secret is independent of knowledge, for one can unconsciously and unwit-
h   tingly make 'secret use', so that, as the Divisional Court held, the test is simply an objective one. Putting the matter with his customary clarity, counsel for Bristol-Myers submitted that no user could be more secret than that of which even the user himself is unaware. I have to say that I do not accept this. The phrase 'secret use' appears, of course, not only in s 14 (3) but also in s 32 (2) and it must surely be interpreted in the same way in both cases. Section 32 (1) (*l*) provides for the revocation
j   of a patent if it 'was *secretly* used in the United Kingdom, otherwise than as mentioned in subsection (2) of this section, before the priority date of that claim'.

It appears to me that the adverb brings out possibly more clearly than the adjective the necessity for there to be both knowledge and deliberate concealment before

---

1 [1956] RPC 87

a person can be said to be secretly using. And if he is not secretly using he is not making a secret use. For my part, at one stage I had some difficulty in accepting *a* that there was 'prior use' in this case because of the absence of knowledge in Beechams of what they were manufacturing and selling. The Divisional Court appear not to have had the same difficulty. I have to say in my turn that, this being so, I cannot follow them when they say that, however unwittingly Beechams concealed the qualities of ampicillin trihydrate by their blending process, they were thereafter *b* making secret use of it. I hold, as Lord Denning MR has done, that there was not only a prior use but that the very facts which counsel for Bristol-Myers relied on in challenging that conclusion serve to satisfy me that the user was non-secret.

For these reasons, I concur in upholding the opposition of Beechams and in allowing their appeal.

c

STEPHENSON LJ. This appeal turns on the meaning of two words found together in s 14 of the Patents Act 1949, 'secret' and 'use'. On the very special facts of this case, was ampicillin trihydrate 'used' by Beechams in the United Kingdom before 21st March 1963? If it was, was its use by them a 'secret use'?

In the ordinary understanding of words he who uses a thing made up of different ingredients uses them all, whether he knows what each is and even if he intends to *d* use the thing but not a particular ingredient in its composition because he does not know of its existence. I see no good reason for understanding the word 'used' differently when the thing is an invention and that invention is a product: see what Lord Trayner said about the opposite view by the Sheriff Substitute in *Gill v Coutts*[1].

Processes and products may be used in such a way that some features or ingredients of them cannot be said to be used by A before being invented by B. Such a case was *e* *Boyce v Morris Motors Ltd*[2], which I respectfully agree with Lord Widgery CJ was decided rightly, but is clearly distinguishable from this. The American case of *International Nickel Co Inc v Ford Motor Co*[3], which was not cited to the Divisional Court, is nearer this case and supports the decision of the Patents Appeal Tribunal on this point. There the district court of New York, following a decision of the Supreme Court in *Tilghman v Proctor*[4], held that the production of magnesium induced nodular *f* iron by A by chance, unrecognised and unappreciated, did not anticipate its discovery by B or prevent him from patenting it. However, if that decision, or the language of the judgment in that case or of the judgment of Blackburn J in *Harwood's* case[5], covers this, I prefer to follow the view of the Divisional Court that Beechams' use of ampicillin trihydrate, although fortuitous, unrecognised and unappreciated, was nevertheless a prior use. *g*

Was then that prior use a secret use? On this second question I also agree with Lord Denning MR. The very special circumstance that ampicillin trihydrate had been blended out of recognisable existence when Beechams used it does not, in my opinion, make their use of it secret. It was hidden, and in a sense it was hidden by them because they mixed it beyond recognition in the present state of scientific knowledge. But they hid it by accident in ignorance of what it was and not by *h* design with the intention of concealing it, and it is intentional concealment which the words naturally connote and which the Act means when it speaks in s 14 (3) and again in s 32 (2) of 'secret use', and in s 32 (1) (*l*) of 'secretly used'.

This means that ignorance may be irrelevant to use but relevant to secret use and the test for use essentially objective, for secret use subjective. We are, however, in a field where the secrecy of inventions is protected (see the sidenote to s 18 of the *j*

1 (1895) 13 RPC 125 at 137
2 (1926) 44 RPC 105
3 (1958) 119 USPQ 72
4 (1880) 102 US 707
5 (1860) 2 B & S 194 at 215, 29 LJQB 193 at 202

a Act); and where a line of cases has distinguished public use or use in public, which anticipates a subsequent patent, from use kept private and secret, which does not. In 1841 Lord Abinger CB directed the jury in *Carpenter v Smith*[1] to find for the defendant if 'he makes no secret' of the lock he used, but 'the exercise of the invention was public, and not kept secret, so that the public might have no benefit from it'. Fourteen years later the question whether prior use, even if secret, invalidated a subsequent

b patent was argued in the Court of Queen's Bench in *Heath v Smith*[2]. The court found that if the user had to be public it was public because some of those who applied carburet of manganese to steel 'made no attempt at concealment' (per Lord Campbell CJ[3]). 'As to secrecy', said Erle J[4]—

> 'three of the firms practised no concealment whatever. That of itself is ground enough for discharging the rule. I should, however, be disposed to go
c further. If one party only had used the process, and had brought out the article for profit, and kept the method entirely secret, I am not prepared to say that then the patent would have been valid. But for the purpose of the present case it is enough to say, that here was an user without any concealment.'

And the same sort of language was used by Lord Trayner in holding a patent invalid
d by anticipation in his judgment in *Gill v Coutts*[5], to which I have already referred. Considering that the prior use had to be in public, he said that—

> 'the thing must be disclosed to the public and not kept by the maker of it to himself. It is the use of the thing in public as distinguished from the use in private by the inventor.'

e It is, of course, true that those judges, like Whitford J in the recent case of *Monsanto*[6] to which Lord Denning MR has referred, had not to consider the kind of use with which we are concerned. But when the legislature declared that any secret use was to be disregarded, it would be likely to have in mind the kind of secret use which had been considered to be outside the Statute of Monopolies. If nevertheless it had used words which would naturally or necessarily cover use of a different kind, such as the
f use of a component unknowingly or unwittingly, undiscovered and undiscoverable, we should have to give effect to the words. But I respectfully differ from the opinion of the Divisional Court that the legislature has done so. Section 32 read as a whole confirms my view that it has not.

I therefore concur in allowing this appeal on this point.

g **Appeal allowed; order of Patents Appeal Tribunal (Whitford J) quashed; matter remitted to tribunal. Leave to appeal to the House of Lords.**

Solicitors: *Simmons & Simmons* (for Beechams); *Herbert Smith & Co* (for Bristol-Myers).

Wendy Shockett Barrister.

h 1 (1841) 1 Web Pat Cas 530 at 540
2 (1854) 3 E & B 256
3 (1854) 3 E & B at 270
4 (1854) 3 E & B at 273
5 (1895) 13 RPC at 136
6 [1971] RPC 153

Redspring Ltd v Francis

COURT OF APPEAL, CIVIL DIVISION
SACHS, BUCKLEY AND ORR LJJ
9th, 10th NOVEMBER 1972

Rent restriction – Alternative accommodation – Suitable alternative accommodation – Suitable to needs of tenant having regard to character – Environmental matters – Relevance – Noise and smell – Tenant of small flat in quiet residential street – Claim for possession by landlords – Tenant offered more spacious flat by landlords – New flat in busy traffic thoroughfare subject to noise from traffic and other sources and to smell from nearby fish and chip shop – Whether noise and smell relevant matters in considering suitability of new flat to needs of tenant – Rent Act 1968, s 10 (1), Sch 3, Part IV, para 3 (1).

The tenant had lived for 30 years in a small flat in a converted house, sharing a bathroom with another tenant in the same house; she was permitted to enjoy the use of the back garden although without any legal right to do so. The house was in a quiet residential road. The landlords gave her notice to quit. They offered her alternative accommodation consisting of a top floor flat, also in a converted house, with somewhat larger rooms and exclusive possession of a bathroom, but no garden. However the new flat was in a busy traffic thoroughfare with people coming and going at all hours, there was a fried fish shop next door, a hospital in the neighbourhood, a cinema and a public house close by, and at the back a yard or open space, previously occupied by a tram shed, but which the local authority were proposing to use as a transport depot. The landlords brought proceedings in the county court for possession of the tenant's existing flat on the ground that they had made available to her 'suitable alternative accommodation' within the Rent Act 1968, s 10 (1)[a] and Sch 3, paras 2[b] and 3 (1)[c]. The judge made a possession order and in his judgment stated that, in considering whether the alternative accommodation was such as to reasonably satisfy the tenant's needs, within Sch 3, para 3 (1), he had to exclude consideration of any environmental matters such as the smell from the fish and chip shop, noise from the public house and from traffic, and matters of that kind. The tenant appealed.

Held – The appeal would be allowed for the following reasons—

(i) in determining whether alternative accommodation offered to a tenant was suitable for the purposes of s 10 of the 1968 Act, the court could properly take into account not only the physical character of that accommodation but also environmental matters, either as a consideration affecting its suitability to the needs of the tenant as regards its character, under Sch 3, para 3 (1), or as being a matter which affected the question whether it would be proper for the court to regard it as reasonable to make a possession order under s 10 (see p 643 c to f and p 644 g, post);

(ii) the flat offered to the tenant was not reasonably suitable to her needs as regards character, in view of the fact that, whereas her existing flat was in a quiet residential road, the new flat was in a situation where it was subject to offensive smell and noise (see p 644 b and f to g and p 645 c and d, post).

Notes
As to alternative accommodation on recovery of possession of a dwelling-house

---

a   Section 10 (1), so far as material, is set out at p 641 j to p 642 a, post
b   Paragraph 2 is set out at p 642 b and c, post
c   Paragraph 3 (1), so far as material, is set out at p 642 d, post

subject to a statutory tenancy, see 23 Halsbury's Laws (3rd Edn) 815-818, para 1594, and for cases on the subject, see 31 Digest (Repl) 714-719, *7995-8033*.

For the Rent Act 1968, s 10 and Sch 3, Part IV, see 18 Halsbury's Statutes (3rd Edn) 798, 911.

Appeal

The tenant, Mrs M Francis, appealed against an order of his Honour Judge Curtis-Raleigh made in Bloomsbury and Marylebone County Court on 29th February 1972, adjudging that the landlords, Redspring Ltd, should recover possession of the tenant's top floor rooms at 47 Lisburne Road, London NW3, on 29th May 1972. The facts are set out in the judgment of Buckley LJ.

F Reynold for the tenant.
R A Payne for the landlords.

BUCKLEY LJ delivered the first judgment at the invitation of Sachs LJ. This is an appeal against a decision of his Honour Judge Curtis-Raleigh on 29th February 1972 under s 10 of the Rent Act 1968 by which he ordered the tenant of certain property to give up possession within three months from the date of the order, i e by 29th May 1972. The tenant, Mrs Francis, who is the appellant in this court, had lived for, I think, some 30 years in premises at 47 Lisburne Road, London NW3, which was a small flat in a converted house, in connection with which she had a share only of a bathroom with another tenant who had accommodation in the same house, and while she enjoyed the use of the garden she had no legal right in that respect.

The landlord company, Redspring Ltd, served a notice to quit and offered as alternative accommodation premises in Fleet Road, London NW3, which is a busy traffic thoroughfare not far distant from Lisburne Road. The accommodation offered was again a flat in a converted house, rooms on the top floor, somewhat larger in size than the rooms which the tenant had occupied, and still occupies, in Lisburne Road, which included a bathroom of which she would have had exclusive possession. But the house had no garden. Not only is Fleet Road a busy traffic thoroughfare, but immediately next door to no 108, in which the accommodation was offered to the tenant, there is a fried fish shop; there is a hospital in the neighbourhood, a cinema and a public house close by, and it is an area where at all hours of the day and night there are people coming and going and where there is a lot of traffic. The fried fish shop emits smells of a kind which one would expect to be emitted from an establishment of that sort. Lisburne Road, on the other hand, is a quiet residential road, as I gather, and at the back of the house there is the garden which the tenant is permitted to use. At the back of 108 Fleet Road there is a yard or open space, previously occupied by a tram shed, but which the local authority are proposing to use as a transport depot, where presumably there would be large motor vehicles coming and going from time to time. It is conceded on the part of the tenant that the physical accommodation afforded at 108 Fleet Road is more spacious and better in respect of the bathroom than the accommodation enjoyed by the tenant in Lisburne Road. But it is said that because of the environment in which it stands it does not satisfy the tenant's needs.

The statutory provisions which have to be considered in connection with a case of this kind are to be found in s 10 of, and Sch 3 to, the Rent Act 1968. Section 10 (1) is in the following terms:

'Subject to the following provisions of this Part of this Act, a court shall not make an order for possession of a dwelling-house which is for the time being let on a protected tenancy or subject to a statutory tenancy unless the court considers it reasonable to make such an order and either—(a) the court is satisfied that suitable alternative accommodation is available for the tenant or will be available for him when the order in question takes effect, or [and I need not read para (b)]'.

One then turns to Sch 3, Part IV. Paragraph 1 deals with the issue of a certificate by a housing authority certifying that the authority will provide suitable alternative accommodation. Then para 2 provides:

'Where no such certificate as is mentioned in paragraph 1 above is produced to the court, accommodation shall be deemed to be suitable for the purposes of section 10 (1) (a) of this Act if it consists of either—(a) premises which are to be let as a separate dwelling such that they will then be let on a protected tenancy, or (b) premises to be let as a separate dwelling on terms which will, in the opinion of the court, afford to the tenant security of tenure reasonably equivalent to the security afforded by Part II of this Act in the case of a protected tenancy, and, in the opinion of the court, the accommodation fulfils the relevant conditions as defined in paragraph 3 below.'

Then one goes to para 3, which is the relevant paragraph for the purposes of this case, and sub-para (1) provides:

'For the purposes of paragraph 2 above, the relevant conditions are that the accommodation is reasonably suitable to the needs of the tenant and his family as regards proximity to place of work, and either [and I need not trouble to read sub-para (a)]; or (b) reasonably suitable to the means of the tenant and to the needs of the tenant and his family as regards extent and character.'

So we have to consider whether in the present case the accommodation offered at 108 Fleet Road is reasonably suitable to the needs of the tenant as regards extent and character. No point arises in this case in relation to proximity to the place of work or the means of the tenant. We are concerned only with the question whether the accommodation is reasonably suitable to her needs as regards extent and character. Extent, as I have already stated, is conceded. So the question is whether the accommodation is reasonably suited to her needs in respect of its character.

The learned county court judge in referring to those statutory provisions said this in the penultimate paragraph of the note of his judgment:

'The "needs" contemplated by the Act Para 3 (1) (b) of Part IV [of Sch 3 to] the 1968 Rent Act, cited in argument, are not the same as tastes and inclinations: they are needs of an urgent, compelling nature—space, transport, a bathroom etc. Peripheral amenities are of a different category; by this I am not saying that [the tenant's] objections are fanciful, but I find that her needs are met, apart from the environmental aspect. One must look at the whole of the picture, and I have not forgotten the hospital, the fish and chip shop and the public house and the cinema.'

Having reached that conclusion that the tenant's needs were satisfied by the accommodation that was offered, the learned county court judge made the order for possession.

Before I comment on those observations by the learned county court judge I should perhaps complete the statement of facts of the case, because certain things have occurred since the matter was heard in the court below. It appears that in about May 1972, which was after the date of the hearing, the local authority put out a circular to all local residents indicating that the area at the back of 108 Fleet Road was going to be used as a transport depot. It also has transpired since the hearing that in September 1972 the landlords sold their interest in 108 Fleet Road, having at the date of the sale carried out none of the repairs which the learned county court judge held in his judgment to be necessary to put the accommodation which was offered to the tenant into a proper state of repair so as to render it suitable alternative accommodation. So the position has changed in those two respects since the learned county court judge gave his decision.

The contention of the tenant has been that in considering the character of alternative accommodation not only the physical characteristics of the premises containing the accommodation fall to be considered, but also such matters as neighbourhood, noise, smell and other considerations of a kind which one can perhaps best describe as environmental considerations; and we have been referred to certain authorities bearing on that aspect of the matter, with none of which do I think it necessary to deal in any detail in this judgment because it is conceded on the part of the landlords that environmental questions are matters relevant to the character of the proposed alternative accommodation. That concession was, in my judgment, properly made. For if a tenant who occupies accommodation in a residential area is offered other accommodation which may be physically as good as or better than the accommodation which he is required to vacate, but is situated in an area which is offensive as the result of some industrial activity in the neighbourhood, which perhaps creates offensive smells or noises, or which is extremely noisy as a result of a great deal of traffic passing by, or in some other respect is clearly much less well endowed with amenities than the accommodation which the tenant is required to vacate, then it seems to me that it would be most unreal to say that the alternative accommodation is such as to satisfy the needs of the tenant with regard to its character. What he needs is somewhere where he can live in reasonably comfortable conditions suitable to the style of life which he leads, and environmental matters must inevitably affect the suitability of offered accommodation to provide him with the sort of conditions in which it is reasonable that he should live.

Under the section it is possible that this sort of consideration might be regarded as coming into consideration under one of two heads: either as a consideration which affects the suitability of the accommodation as regards its character, or as being a matter which affects the question of whether it is proper for the court to regard it as reasonable to make a possession order under s 10. For my part, I do not think it very much matters under which head one regards it as coming. I am, for myself, satisfied that such environmental questions are proper matters to be taken into consideration in deciding whether or not a possession order should be made.

The landlords in the present case have contended that in fact the learned county court judge did take the environmental aspects of this case into consideration in arriving at his conclusion. Counsel points with some force to the last sentence that I read from the judgment: 'One must look at the whole of the picture, and I have not forgotten the hospital, the fish and chip shop and the public house and the cinema.' It is clear that the learned judge had not forgotten those features. But when one comes to look at the way in which he treats the question he has to answer, it seems to me to be clear from the note of his judgment that he regarded those environmental matters as not matters to be taken into consideration, certainly in relation to the character of the alternative accommodation, and to whether that accommodation was of a character reasonably to satisfy the needs of the tenant: for after saying that 'needs' are 'needs of an urgent, compelling nature', he says in terms that 'peripheral amenities'—and here he is clearly referring to the environmental matter—'are of a different category'. That, as I understand it, means that the learned judge is saying that he does not think they are matters to be taken into consideration as forming part of the matters relevant to the needs of the tenant. Then he goes on to say that he finds that the tenant's 'needs are met, apart from the environmental aspect'. He is there saying, as I understand it: 'I consider her needs apart from environmental matters, and I find that this accommodation satisfies her needs.' I cannot read this passage in the learned judge's judgment without coming to the conclusion that he was directing himself that, in considering whether the alternative accommodation was such as to reasonably satisfy the tenant's needs, he was to shut out from his mind environmental matters such as the smell from the fish and chip shop, the noise from the public house, noise perhaps from vehicles going to and from the hospital and matters of that kind. In so doing, with respect to the learned judge, I think he misdirected himself. Those, I think, are all matters properly to be taken into consideration in connection with the making of such an order as was sought in this case.

Having regard to the evidence which was given at the hearing, the finding of the learned judge with regard to the fish and chip shop, which he said produced the smells that one would expect, and his finding that Fleet Road was a busy street and people were around day and night, in my view, the conclusion at which the learned judge should have arrived on the facts of the case was that the accommodation at 108 Fleet Road was not such as reasonably to satisfy the tenant's needs, from which it would follow that the order should not have been made.

It has been contended that, in the light of the subsequent events, and in particular the sale of the property without the repairs ever having been done, the order for possession was one which could never have been enforced by the landlords and that the tenant should not have prosecuted this appeal but should have either allowed the matter to rest where it was or perhaps have gone back to the county court under s 11 of the Act and asked for an indefinite stay of the order. But, if I am right in the views which I have expressed on the legal aspect of the case, the order which the learned judge made was one which should not have been made and therefore was clearly an appealable order. Had he made the order which he should have made—i e an order dismissing the application for an order for possession—no doubt he would have ordered the landlords to pay the tenant's costs. In fact, he made no order for costs, the tenant being legally aided. But in this state of affairs it seems to me that the tenant was perfectly reasonable in pursuing her appeal, the notice of which had in fact been served before either the local authority's circular with regard to the transport depot had been circulated or the sale of 108 Fleet Road had taken effect. Having launched her appeal, in my judgment, the tenant was not under any obligation to refrain from prosecuting it merely because of those changes in the situation.

For those reasons, in my judgment, this appeal should be allowed, the order of the learned county court judge should be discharged, and there should be substituted for it an order dismissing the landlords' proceedings, with costs here and below.

ORR LJ. I agree.

SACHS LJ. I too agree that this appeal should be allowed, with the consequences as to costs which Buckley LJ has proposed. As we are differing from an experienced county court judge, and in none of the series of recognised law reports is there any satisfactory reported authorities on the effect of the words, 'needs of the tenant and his family as regards . . . character', in para 3 (1) (b) of Part IV of Sch 3 to the Rent Act 1968 it is appropriate to add some observations. It is clear that, perhaps to some extent because even such authorities as do exist were not cited to him, the learned county court judge when deciding whether the accommodation offered was suitable quite deliberately excluded from consideration what has been termed the environmental aspect of that accommodation. He plainly considered that aspect as something which in law could not be regarded as relevant to the needs of the tenant in relation to the character of the premises offered to her.

Counsel for the landlords started by somewhat gallantly attempting to persuade us that the learned county court judge did regard that environmental aspect as relevant and had merely found as a fact that in this particular instance there was nothing in that aspect which rendered the accommodation unsuitable. Persuasive though his efforts were, counsel wholly failed to convince us on that point. Thereafter he felt himself unable—having heard the full argument put before us and the citation of all available authorities—to contend that the relevant words in para 3 (1)

(b) did not include environmental considerations in relation to character. That concession on counsel's part was in essence inevitable, remembering, however, that the difference in character must of course normally relate to a difference in kind rather than a difference of lesser degree. In each case it is a question of fact having regard to the needs of the tenant in the circumstances as a whole.

The view which I have just expressed coincides with the tenor of those sparsely reported decisions of the court (e g in the Estates Gazette) to which reference has already been made. Any other view of the meaning of the relevant words would, indeed, produce astonishing results, some of which were canvassed in the course of argument. It would result in accommodation on the third floor of premises facing on to Edgware Road being necessarily held to be equivalent in character to a quiet third floor flat in nearby Montagu Square. Another example was put of a cottage in a quiet country lane which has one character and that of a cottage of identical construction which found itself implanted in or entangled with a new M-road.

In this particular case the difference is in my judgment one of kind and not merely one of some modest degree. Even if that were not so, it would, as Buckley LJ has pointed out, in the circumstances of this case, be unreasonable to make an order against this particular tenant that she should occupy premises which, having regard to her way of life, she not unnaturally spoke of as being 'horrible'.

In those circumstances it is that, agreeing with everything that Buckley LJ has said, and adding only some observations on the question of law that has been discussed, this appeal should also in my judgment be allowed.

Appeal allowed. Order dismissing landlord's proceedings substituted for order in court below.

Solicitors: *Edward Moeran & Partners* (for the tenant); *Bailey & Peltz* (for the landlords).

F A Amies Esq Barrister.

Middlegate Properties Ltd v Messimeris

COURT OF APPEAL, CIVIL DIVISION
LORD DENNING MR, MEGAW LJ AND SIR GORDON WILLMER
6th, 7th NOVEMBER 1972

Landlord and tenant – Lease – Forfeiture – Repairing covenant – Notice – Statement of lessee's right to serve counter-notice – Statement in characters not less conspicuous than those used in any other part of notice – Statement to specify manner in which counter-notice may be served – Name and address for service of lessor to be specified – Notice served on tenant – Standard form used – Blank spaces for insertion of details – Details filled in in bigger blacker type – Statement of tenant's rights in ordinary type – Statement only specifying some of the ways in which counter-notice could be served – Statement only giving name and address for service of landlords' solicitor – Whether statutory requirements complied with – Law of Property Act 1925, s 146 – Leasehold Property (Repairs) Act 1938, s 1 (4).

A house was let to the tenant on a 28 year lease. The lease contained the usual repairing covenants and a proviso for re-entry. When it still had more than three years to run, the landlords' solicitors served on the tenant a notice under s 146 of the Law of Property Act 1925 informing him, in para 1, that there had been breaches of the covenants in the lease and, in para 5, stating, as required by s 1 (4)[a] of the Leasehold Property (Repairs) Act 1938, that he was entitled, under that Act, to serve on the landlords a counter-notice claiming the benefit of the Act, and, inter alia, that

---

a Section 1 (4), so far as material, is set out at p 647 a and b, post

such notice should be addressed to the landlords' solicitors and might be 'left at or sent by registered post' to the solicitors at their registered office, the address of which was set out. The solicitors used for the notice a stock form containing certain blank spaces which required filling in in each case to give the details of the premises, the name of the lessor and the particulars of the lease, etc. Those details were inserted in the notice in bigger, blacker type than the printed type in the rest of the notice. The tenant claimed that the notice was invalid on the grounds that the statement in para 5 did not comply with s 1 (4) of the 1938 Act in that (i) it was in less conspicuous characters than those used in the rest of the notice; (ii) it did not specify (a) in full the 'manner' in which the counter-notice might be served or (b) the lessors' name and address.

Held – (i) The statement in para 5 was not in 'less conspicuous' characters than those used in any other part of the notice; the words 'not less conspicuous' in s 1 (4) meant 'equally readable' or 'equally sufficient' to tell the tenant of his right to a counter-notice and so construed para 5 passed the test; further (per Megaw LJ) the words typed into the form did not themselves constitute a 'part of the notice' within s 1 (4) (see p 648 a to c and f h j and p 649 a and b, post).

(ii) The statement (a) was not required to specify all manner of service; it was sufficient if it specified one good manner (see p 648 d and p 649 b, post); and (b) was sufficient if it specified an appropriate name and address for service, such as that of the lessor's solicitor (see p 648 e and p 649 b, post).

(iii) It followed that the landlords' notice was valid.

Notes

For requirements of notice by landlord before action and the effect of counter-notice by the tenant, see 23 Halsbury's Laws (3rd Edn) 588, 589, paras 1271, 1272, and 675, 676, para 1401, and for cases on the subject, see 31 Digest (Repl) 538-541, 6620-6638.

For the Law of Property Act 1925, s 146, see 27 Halsbury's Statutes (3rd Edn) 563.

For the Leasehold Property (Repairs) Act 1938, s 1, see 18 Halsbury's Statutes (3rd Edn) 473.

Appeal

Spyridon Messimeris, the defendant tenant in an action by the plaintiff landlords, Middlegate Properties Ltd, for possession of premises at 96 Hereford Road, London W2, appealed against the judgment of his Honour Judge Edgar Fay QC, sitting as Official Referee, given on the hearing of a preliminary issue in the action on 26th June 1971 whereby it was adjudged that the notice, under s 146 of the Law of Property Act 1925, dated 28th January 1971 and served by the plaintiffs on the defendant was a sufficient and valid notice. The facts are set out in the judgment of Lord Denning MR.

J R *Peppitt* for the defendant.
P R *Oliver* QC and *Lindsay Megarry* for the plaintiffs.

LORD DENNING MR. In the 1930s there were some ruthless landlords who used to buy the leaseholds of small houses, serve oppressive schedules of dilapidations on the tenants, forfeit the leases and claim damages. To remedy this mischief Parliament passed the Leasehold Property (Repairs) Act 1938, now amended by the Landlord and Tenant Act 1954. It provided that, where more than three years were left to run in a lease—if the landlord served a notice under s 146 of the Law of Property Act 1925—then the tenant could serve a counter-notice. If a counter-notice was served, the landlord could not go ahead for forfeiture or damages unless he got the leave of the court. That provision would have been useless unless the tenant knew *a* of his right to give a counter-notice.   So Parliament imposed a duty on the landlord to tell the tenant about it.   Section 1 (4) of the 1938 Act says:

b 'A notice served under subsection (1) of section one hundred and forty-six of the Law of Property Act, 1925, ... shall not be valid unless it contains a statement, in characters not less conspicuous than those used in any other part of the notice, to the effect that the lessee is entitled under this Act to serve on the lessor a counter-notice claiming the benefit of this Act, and a statement in the like characters specifying the time within which, and the manner in which, under this Act a counter-notice may be served and specifying the name and address for service of the lessor.'

c The question in this case is whether a notice served by the landlords satisfied those requisites.   The facts are these.   In 1953 the Church Commissioners let 96 Hereford Road, W2, to the defendant for 28 years from 25th December 1950 at a rent of £126 a year.   The lease contained the usual repairing covenants and a proviso for re-entry. A few years ago the Church Commissioners sold their interest to Middlegate Properties Ltd.   On 28th January 1971 the solicitors for Middlegate Properties served a notice under s 146 on the defendant.   The lease had then some nine years to run.

d So the notice had to comply with s 1 (4) of the 1938 Act.   The solicitors used a stock form of notice, duplicated in quantities, but with blanks.   They filled in the blanks for each particular case.   I will set it out, italicising the fillings in:

'STATUTORY NOTICE OF BREACH OF COVENANT TO REPAIR

Relating to premises known as:	*96 Hereford Road, London W.2.*
This Notice is served on behalf of:	*Middlegate Properties Limited.*
(hereinafter called "the Company")	
the registered office of which is at:	*25 Harley Street, London, W.1.*
Particulars of the lease under which	
the said premises are held	

e

f *A lease made the 28th December 1953 between the Church Commissioners for England of the one part and SPYRIDON MESSIMERIS of the other part whereby the said premises were demised for a term of 14 years from 25th December 1950 and extended to 28 years by a Deed dated 29th December 1953.*

g 'WE LIEBERMAN LEIGH & CO of 8 Museum House, Museum Street London W.C.1 Solicitors for the Company, HEREBY GIVE YOU NOTICE as follows:

'1.   There have been breaches of the covenants contained in the Lease ...

'5.   By virtue of the Leasehold Property (Repairs) Act 1938 you are entitled if you so desire to serve upon us a Counter-Notice in writing claiming the benefit of that Act.   Such Notice must be served upon us within 28 days of the service

h hereof and be to the effect that you claim the benefit of that Act.   The Notice should be addressed to us Lieberman Leigh & Co ... and may be left at or sent by registered post to our office at 8 Museum House, Museum Street, London, W.C.1.

'Dated this 28th day of *January 1971*.

'To: *Spyridon Messimeris, Esq.,*   Lieberman Leigh & Co.

j   8 Museum House,
                                 Museum Street, London W.C.1., Solicitors
                                 for the Company.'

The parts I have italicised were in bigger, blacker type than the rest of the notice.

The defendant says that the notice did not comply with s 1 (4).   In the first place he says that the statement in para 5 ought to have been in characters not less conspicuous

than those used in any other part of the notice; and he says that it was not, because
it was a smaller lighter type than the big black type which I have italicised.

If the Act is to be read with literal strictness, I suppose that the characters of para 5
were a little less conspicuous than the blacker type; but they were perfectly legible
and easy to read. No one could possibly overlook para 5 or be misled in any way. It
told the defendant plainly all that the Act required. The Act was aimed at a different
mischief altogether—the mischief of putting clauses in small print or on the back—
which no ordinary person would read. Seeing that this case is not within the mischief,
I do not think we should construe the Act so as to invalidate the notice. We should
construe 'not less conspicuous' so as to mean 'equally readable' or 'equally sufficient'
to tell the defendant of his right to give a counter-notice. So construed, this para 5
passes the test. Were it otherwise, we should fall into the danger spoken of by
Harman LJ—we should catch the virtuous in the net which is laid for the sinner.

The second point is this. Section 1 (4) says that the notice must contain a statement
'in the like characters specifying the time within which, *and the manner* in which . . . a
counter-notice may be served and specifying the *name and address for service of the
lessor'*. The tenant says that para 5 was bad because it only specified registered post
and not also recorded delivery service. He points out that under the Recorded
Delivery Service Act 1962 recorded delivery is equal to registered post. I think this
point is bad also. The statement is sufficient if it specifies one good manner of
service. It need not specify all.

The third point is this. The defendant says that the statement is to specify the 'name
and address for service of the lessor'; and here it did not do so. It only specified
the name and address of the solicitor. I think this point is equally bad. The statement is sufficient if it specifies an appropriate name and address for service; and none
could be more appropriate than the address of the lessor's solicitor.

We have been referred to some of the precedent books. Some give forms with
more detail than others. All I would say is that these notices should be construed
reasonably. If they tell the tenant with sufficient clearness what the statute requires,
they are good.

I agree with the Official Referee and would dismiss the appeal.

MEGAW LJ. I agree. The first point relates to the requirement of s 1 (4) of the
Leasehold Property (Repairs) Act 1938. In the notice given by the landlord under
s 146 of the Law of Property Act 1925 the tenant must be told that he is entitled under
the Act to serve on the lessor, the landlord, a counter-notice. He must be so told
'in characters not less conspicuous than those used in any other part of the notice'.
It is clear to my mind that the comparison there to be made cannot fairly or legitimately be done by taking, say, one word or two words out of some other part of the
notice and saying that those words are more conspicuous than individual words in
the part of the notice which is telling the lessee of his rights. The reference in the
subsection to 'any other part of the notice' must be construed so as to give a sensible
meaning to 'any part'. Now if one looks at the notice with which we are concerned
in the present case, the first words which are typed in in the larger typescript and
the darker colour are the words '96 Hereford Road, London W.2'. That in my view
is not in itself 'a part' of the form within the meaning of those words. To make it
a part of the form you have to read it with the context; and the context includes the
words on the left hand side of the form 'Relating to premises known as', and then
'96 Hereford Road, London W.2'. The minimum that can be described as a 'part
of the notice' for the purposes of this subsection is the totality of those words. I
should be disposed to say that even that may be less than the minimum. To make it
a 'part of the notice', one should go on to include also the following words: 'This
Notice is served on behalf of'. That is typed in what I will call normal type. And
then in the larger type, 'Middlegate Properties Limited.' Then, after further words

in the normal type, one gets in the larger and blacker type, '25 Harley Street' and so on. When one takes the totality of those words as constituting a 'part of the notice', I do not think that they can be described as being in any substantial degree in characters more conspicuous than those in para 5 of the notice.

With regard to the second point taken as to the invalidity of the notice, I have nothing to add to the reasons given by Lord Denning MR with which on both points I entirely agree.

SIR GORDON WILLMER. I agree and have nothing further to add.

Appeal dismissed.

Solicitors: *Alexanders* (for the defendant); *Lieberman Leigh & Co* (for the plaintiffs).

L J Kovats Esq Barrister.

R v Osborne   R v Virtue

COURT OF APPEAL, CRIMINAL DIVISION
LAWTON LJ, MELFORD STEVENSON AND BRABIN JJ
7th, 8th DECEMBER 1972

Criminal law – Evidence – Admissibility – Judges' Rules – Interrogation – Caution – Police officer having evidence affording reasonable grounds for suspicion – Evidence – Police officer having reasonable grounds for suspecting accused – Officer not having evidence which could be put before court – Whether officer required to administer caution – Judges' Rules (1964), r 2.

Criminal law – Evidence – Identity – Identification parade – Witness picking out accused at identification parade – Witness denying at trial that she had picked out accused – Evidence of police officer in charge of identification parade – Evidence that witness had picked out accused – Whether evidence of police officer admissible.

Police officers investigating a robbery arrested the appellants, O and V, and took them to a police station where they were interrogated by a chief inspector. The interrogation took place without any caution being administered to the appellants. At the time of the arrest the chief inspector had reasonable grounds for suspecting that the two appellants had been members of the gang responsible for the robbery, but he had no evidence to justify that suspicion. After the interrogation both the appellants were put up for an identification parade, which was carried out strictly in accordance with police regulations. Both appellants were identified by two female witnesses who had been present when the robbery took place. The appellants were then duly cautioned and charged. Their trial did not take place until some 7½ months later. The two witnesses who had identified the appellants gave evidence; one said that she did not remember picking out any one, and the other, who was in a highly nervous and emotional condition, proved in consequence to be a very unsatisfactory witness, first stating that she had picked out the appellant V and then denying that fact. The appellants' defence at the trial was an alibi and a great deal of the evidence against them was provided by what they had said to the chief inspector at their interrogation. The appellants submitted that that evidence was inadmissible since they had not been cautioned in accordance with r 2[a] of the Judges' Rules (1964)[b].

---

a Rule 2, so far as material, provides: 'As soon as a police officer has evidence which would afford reasonable grounds for suspecting that a person has committed an offence, he shall caution that person or cause him to be cautioned before putting to him any questions, or further questions, relating to that offence ...'

b See *Practice Note* [1964] 1 All ER 237

The recorder overruled that submission, stating that if there had been a breach of the Judges' Rules he would have exercised his discretion to exclude the evidence. The trial proceeded and the officer who had conducted the identification parade was asked who it was that the two female witnesses had picked out at the parade. Counsel for the appellant O objected to that question on the ground that the officer's evidence would contradict that of the two witnesses concerned. The recorder rejected the objection and admitted the officer's evidence. The appellants were convicted and appealed.

Held – (i) Rule 2 of the Judges' Rules did not require a police officer to administer a caution to a suspected person whom he was questioning until he had got some information which could be put before the court as the beginnings of a case. Since at the time when he started to question the appellants the chief inspector had no information which would have enabled him to put evidence against them before the court, the evidence of the interrogation had been rightly put before the jury (see p 655 e to h and p 656 d, post).

(ii) The evidence of the officer conducting the identification parade had been properly admitted. Evidence of identification other than identification in the witness box was admissible. The officer's evidence did not contradict the evidence of the two witnesses who attended the identification parade. There was no objection to a witness with a better memory testifying that another witness had identified an accused at an identification parade some months previously even though that witness could not himself remember doing so (see p 656 h and p 657 a b d and e, post); *R v Christie* [1914-15] All ER Rep 63 applied.

(iii) It followed that the appeals should be dismissed and the convictions affirmed.

Note

For the Judges' Rules, see 10 Halsbury's Laws (3rd Edn) 470-473, para 865.

Cases referred to in judgment

R v Christie [1914] AC 545; sub nom *Public Prosecutions Director v Christie* [1914-15] All ER Rep 63, 83 LJKB 1097, 111 LT 220, 78 JP 321, 24 Cox CC 249, 10 Cr App Rep 141, HL, 14 Digest (Repl) 405, 3962.

R v Richardson [1971] 2 All ER 773, [1971] 2 QB 484, [1971] 2 WLR 889, 135 JP 371, 55 Cr App Rep 244, CA.

Cases also cited

R v Prager [1972] 1 All ER 1114, [1972] 1 WLR 260, CA.
R v White [1964] Crim LR 720, CCA.
Sumner and Leivesley v John Brown & Co (1909) 25 TLR 745.

Appeals

Colin Osborne and John Graham Virtue appealed against their convictions on 9th July 1971 at the Central Criminal Court before the Recorder of London (Sir Carl Aarvold) and a jury. The facts are set out in the judgment of the court.

H J Leonard QC and *M Sherborne* for the appellant Osborne.
J B R Hazan QC and *I J Lawrence* for the appellant Virtue.
Brian Watling for the Crown.

LAWTON LJ delivered the following judgment of the court. On 9th July 1971 at the Central Criminal Court, after a trial before the Recorder of London and a jury which lasted a month, the appellants were convicted of taking a conveyance without authority (count 1), robbery (count 2), having a firearm with intent (count 3), wounding with intent (count 4), and assault occasioning actual bodily harm (count 5). In addition, the appellant Osborne pleaded guilty to handling stolen goods *a* (count 11), and the appellant Virtue was convicted of having an offensive weapon, namely, a flick knife (count 8). There were two other counts in the indictment against the appellant Osborne, but they were not proceeded with. The appellant Osborne was sentenced to seven years' imprisonment on counts 2, 3 and 4, to 12 months' imprisonment on counts 1 and 5 and six months' imprisonment on count 11. All the sentences were ordered to run concurrently. The appellant Virtue was sentenced

b to seven years' imprisonment on counts 2, 3 and 4, 12 months' imprisonment on counts 1 and 5, and six months' imprisonment on count 8, and again all the sentences were ordered to run concurrently. The appellants had been indicted with two other men. One was named Lloyd and the other Baldessare. These two men were acquitted on all the counts against them and discharged. These two appellants by leave of the full court now appeal against conviction. They do not appeal against

c sentence.

The events out of which the appellants' convictions arise can be stated shortly because the points which arise in the appeal are only on the fringes of the main facts of the case. On Monday, 16th November 1970, at about 9.30 a m a gang of at least four men (I say 'at least' because there may have been a fifth) entered the South Suburban Co-operative Society's shop in Penge High Street in South London. Some

d of these men wore masks; others wore hats. One of them is said by witnesses to have worn a bowler hat.

They went into the general office and one or more of the gang told the staff to lie on the floor. When that had been done, they went through the counter drawers and took a total of £858 in cash. Having got this money, the gang then ran from the office and some of the staff courageously tried to intercept them. One of them was

e a Mr Reader, who was struck with some object and knocked to the ground with a cut over his right eye. The manager, a Mr Aikman, hit one of the men with a mirror with sufficient force to break it over the man. Thereupon one of the gang shouted out 'Shoot him'. A gun was produced and at fairly close range Mr Aikman was shot. Fortunately for him, and perhaps fortunately for the two appellants, the shots went into Mr Aikman's leg and did not do him serious damage. Mr Aikman having

f been shot down, the men ran out into the road and got into a Triumph motor car which had been stolen on 14th November from the Hyde Park underground car park.

It is relevant at this stage to say that one of the employees in that store, a Mrs Head, was standing close to Mr Aikman when he was shot. That must have been a terrifying experience for her, and it seems, as I shall be recounting later in this

g judgment, to have affected her emotionally to a considerable extent.

As so frequently happens in this kind of gang robbery, the robbers got away from the scene of the crime. Fortunately for justice the police had some reason to think that they knew who at least four of the robbers were and they got to know by the early hours of Friday, 20th November. What information they had which led them to think that they knew who the robbers were was not put in evidence at the trial.

h It may have been information from an informer. It may have been nothing more than a hunch.

When the police are dealing with suspected gunmen they must act quickly and they must act with resolution; and on this occasion the police did act quickly and they did act with resolution. They took the very wise tactical step of trying to arrest the suspects all at the same time. At 6.30 a m on 20th November 1970 two police

j officers went to the house where the appellant Osborne was living with a woman. They found him in bed. They asked him questions and ultimately took him into custody. The questions which they asked him at the place of arrest play an important part in this case and it is convenient, therefore, that I should here and now deal shortly with them. The details of the questioning are set out in the learned recorder's summing-up from which I shall quote, and no criticism was made before this court that the recorder had in any way in this passage in the summing-up or in other passages

to which I shall be referring made any material omission. The interview with the
appellant Osborne started in this way. One of the officers said:

'I told him who we were ... showed him a search warrant to search the
premises for stolen money and [the appellant Osborne] said "Well, you've
come early enough. I can't stop you. What's it all about?".'

One of the officers said to him: 'Get up. We want to talk to you.' Thereupon the
appellant Osborne got out of bed and dressed. They went into the front room and
they looked round and found a watch which was later identified as stolen property.
That was the watch mentioned in count 11 of the indictment, a count to which the
appellant Osborne pleaded guilty.

Shortly after they found the watch the appellant Osborne said to the police officers:
'All right, you've got yourself a capture. I'll get my coat and off we go.' That comment could be related to the finding by the police officers of a watch subsequently
proved to have been stolen to the knowledge of the appellant Osborne and could
have been intended to get the officers out of the house before they found anything else.

The appellant Osborne not unnaturally wanted more information as to why
they were there and he was told: 'Well, as you have seen on the warrant, we are
looking for stolen cash which in fact I can tell you was from a robbery.' The appellant
Osborne's reply to that was: 'I've got no cash here. I'm skint. Which blagging are
you interested in? There's been so many lately.' The police officer replied: 'The
one we believe you are involved in was last Monday at the Co-op. in Penge High
Street.' The appellant Osborne said: 'I haven't heard about that one. Where's
Penge?'

After that the police officers started searching for money and in the end they found
£265 in £10 and £5 notes. When that money was found one of the police officers
said to the appellant Osborne: 'I thought you said you didn't have any money here.
What about this lot? Where does it come from?' to which the appellant Osborne
replied words to the effect that 'I had a nice few quid. That's what's left.'

The senior officer present said: 'Well, who was holding it for you?' to which the
appellant Osborne replied: 'It wasn't the bloody bank manager, I can tell you. You
are wasting your time.' The officer then said: 'Have you been working lately?',
to which the appellant Osborne said: 'You mean "legit"-like? No, not since the
beginning of the year. I've done a bit of gambling to keep going.'

That answer is of some importance in this case because the police knew that the
appellant Osborne for some months had been trying to earn his living as a professional
gambler and they appreciated that he might have acquired a substantial sum of
money by gambling and that even if he had not, that negative would be impossible
to prove.

The search went on and in the course of it one of the officers found a black homburg
hat in a cupboard. When it was shown to the appellant Osborne he came out with
an expletive and said: 'I can see you mean business.' The sergeant said: 'Is it yours?'
and the appellant Osborne made an answer which amounted to an admission that
it was.

What does all that come to in terms of material on which to base a prosecution?
The most that can be said about it is this, that the appellant Osborne had told lies
to the police when they told him that they were going to search his premises for
money which they believed to have been stolen in the course of a robbery at Penge.
When he had been told where it was believed the money had come from, he said
he knew nothing about any such robbery at all. Again when the money was found, he
put up an explanation which could have been true. Beyond that the police got nothing
out of that interview. So much for the arrest of the appellant Osborne.

The appellant Virtue was arrested in the following circumstances. The police
knew that he was serving a sentence at Pentonville Prison and that he was to be
released at 7.00 a m or thereabouts on 20th November. They were waiting for him

a and arrested him at the prison gates. To most members of the public the reaction would be 'Well, he could not have taken part, could he, in the robbery because he was in prison on 16th November?' but that is not modern life. This man, for some six months or so before 16th November, had been on a release scheme from the prison and, therefore, he would have been able to carry out this armed robbery on 16th November if he had had the inclination. When he was searched on arrest he was found to be in possession only of a very small sum of money to which no significance

b can be attached.

These two men were then taken off to a police station in South London. There the officer in charge of the case, Chief Inspector Gittus, started to interrogate them and one of the points in the case which is common to both appellants is this. During that interrogation the chief inspector did not caution them. It has been submitted to the court that his failure to do so was a breach of the Judges' Rules (1964)[1] and

c that all the evidence relating to these interrogations should have been ruled inadmissible, and if that had been done, it was submitted, there would have been little satisfactory evidence left. So the first point which has to be dealt with in this appeal is whether the chief inspector should have cautioned the two appellants before he started to ask them questions.

d At the trial this matter was gone into with care by the recorder. The chief inspector and his colleague who assisted him in the interrogation both admitted when they were asked by defending counsel that they had reasonable grounds for suspecting that the two appellants had been members of the gang, but what the chief inspector denied was that he had any evidence to justify his reasonable suspicion.

Two points arise: first of all what is meant by the word 'evidence' in the context of r 2 of the Judges' Rules; and, secondly, on the facts of this case was there any

e evidence within such meaning as could properly be put to the word 'evidence'? A further point was made that even if there was not any evidence at the beginning of the interrogation of the appellant Virtue, some evidence became available before the end of it and, therefore, during the course of the interrogation a caution should have been given.

After the interrogation the two appellants were put up for identification on an

f identification parade. It is necessary to say something about what happened at that parade. The two appellants had a solicitor's representative present at the parade. The parade, it would appear, was carried out strictly in accordance with the regulations relating to identity parades. No criticism of any kind has been made about the way in which the parade was conducted.

Members of the staff at the South Suburban Co-operative Store attended the

g identification parade. A number, indeed I think the majority, failed to pick out anybody, which was not surprising, as some of the gunmen were wearing masks. Others picked out the wrong person. That again in the experience of this court in this class of case is not unusual. A few, including Mrs Brookes and Mrs Head, picked out one or more. So far as Mrs Head was concerned, the evidence at the trial clearly established that when she attended the identity parade she was in a very upset and dis-

h tressed condition, which was not to be wondered at as she had been standing near her manager when he was gunned down. At one stage of the parade she nearly fainted. Unfortunately the trial did not take place for 7½ months after the identity parade so there was a long interval of time before the two ladies whom I have mentioned went into the witness box and were called on once again to identify the men

j whom they had seen only for moments when they were escaping from the Co-operative store. But to return to the sequence of events immediately after the identity parade. No doubt because of the identifications made at it (which included identifications by Mrs Brookes and Mrs Head) the appellants were duly cautioned and then charged. No further point arises with regard to the procedure carried out by the police.

---

1 See *Practice Note* [1964] 1 All ER 237, [1964] 1 WLR 152

At the trial, and it is necessary to refer to the events at the trial, Mrs Brookes gave
evidence on the first day, and she was asked in the witness box, as all identifying   *a*
witnesses are always asked, whether she could pick out the man in the dock whom
she had identified at the identity parade 7½ months before. According to the
summing-up, she gave this answer. She said that she did not remember that she
had picked out anyone on the last parade, which may have been a somewhat
surprising answer in all the circumstances, but that was what she said.

When Mrs Head was in the witness box, according both to the summing-up and   *b*
a note taken by one of the prosecuting counsel, which has been accepted in this
court as an accurate note, she was very nervous, her hands were shaking and at
one stage she got emotional. According to the note which counsel made in his notebook, her voice shook when she gave some important answers. I think it right that
I should read some extracts from counsel's note. She said she had picked out the
appellant Virtue, but a few moments later she corrected that and said, 'I didn't   *c*
pick the fair man out'. That was the appellant Virtue. 'I recognised him but didn't
point the finger. On another parade I spoke to the officer. I pointed to a man.'
She said she had spoken to the police inspector in charge of the parade and pointed
to someone. Then she went on to say, 'I don't think the man I picked out is here
today'. A moment or two later in her evidence she said again, 'The man I picked
out, I don't think he is in the dock today'. She also said in cross-examination 'I do   *d*
not see anybody else here whom I recognise'. She was a very unsatisfactory witness,
not because she wanted to prevaricate or be difficult, but because she was in an
emotional state.

When the recorder came to sum up the case to the jury he reminded them in
the clearest possible terms of the weaknesses in her evidence and left them in no
doubt at all that virtually no weight of any kind should be attached to what she   *e*
said insofar as she purported to identify any of the men then in the dock. That
being so, on any view of this case, if the issue before this court had been whether the
verdict was unsafe or unsatisfactory, it could not have been adjudged that, because
of Mrs Head's evidence, it was. But that does not reflect the point which has been made
by the appellant Osborne.

That point arises in this way. After Mrs Brookes and Mrs Head had given evidence   *f*
—as has been common for many years—the officer in charge of the parade, Chief
Inspector Stevenson, was called to give evidence and he was asked by prosecuting
counsel whom Mrs Brookes and Mrs Head had pointed out. Thereupon counsel defending the appellant Osborne objected, and the basis of his objection was that the
evidence of the chief inspector would contradict the evidence which had been given
by the two ladies. The recorder rejected that objection and admitted the evidence.   *g*
The objection has been repeated in this court.

So far as the case itself was concerned, all I need say about it is this that a great
deal of the case against both appellants was provided by what they had said to the
inspector when they were being interrogated at the police station because the chief
inspector very sensibly asked both of them where they had been at the time when   *h*
the robbery had taken place, and they both gave accounts of their movements.
When they came to trial they both sought to set up alibis which conflicted with
what they were alleged to have said to the chief inspector in the police station before
they had any time to arrange alibis as the Crown alleged. So the main issue at the
trial was this: were the police officers accurate and reliable in their recollections
as to what had been said at the interrogations? Or did a real doubt arise because of   *j*
the alibi evidence? No criticism of any kind has been made about the summing-up
on that very important issue. But that being the issue, it is understandable why
such strenuous efforts have been made both before the recorder and before this
court to get the evidence of the chief inspector as to the interrogation about their
movements rejected.

Now I turn to the basis of the submission with regard to the rejection of the evidence *a* of the interrogation. It is said on behalf of both appellants that by the time the chief inspector came to carry out the interrogation he had evidence which would have afforded reasonable grounds for his suspecting that they had committed an offence. The first problem which arises in this case is what is meant by evidence in this context?

It is important for the court to remind itself that the Judges' Rules are intended for the guidance of police officers. They have to comply with the rules. If a police *b* officer looks at the rules and asks himself the question 'What do they mean?' he would answer in the light of his own police experience. In police experience evidence means information which can be put before a court; and it means that not only to police officers but to the general public, as is shown clearly by one of the meanings given to the word 'evidence' in the Shorter Oxford English Dictionary, which under the sub-heading 'Law' defines 'evidence' in these terms: 'Information that is given *c* in a legal investigation, to establish the fact or point in question.' If the police officer, who was trying to understand what the word 'evidence' meant in the Judges' Rules, felt that he ought to turn to a standard legal textbook in case the Oxford Dictionary definition was too wide, and he turned to Phipson on Evidence[1], he would have found 'evidence' defined as follows:

d 'Evidence, as used in judicial proceedings, has several meanings. The two main senses of the word are: first, the means, apart from argument and inference, whereby the court is informed as to the issues of fact as ascertained by the pleadings; secondly, the subject-matter of such means.'

In the judgment of this court, that is how a police officer would understand these rules. There are other indications in the rules that that is the right way for them to be construed. The rules contemplate three stages in the investigations leading *e* up to somebody being brought before a court for a criminal offence. The first is the gathering of information, and that can be gathered from anybody, including persons in custody provided they have not been charged. At the gathering of information stage no caution of any kind need be administered. The final stage, the one contemplated by r 3 of the Judges' Rules[2], is when the police officer has got enough (and I stress the word 'enough') evidence to prefer a charge. That is clear from the *f* introduction to the Judges' Rules which sets out the principle. But a police officer when carrying out an investigation meets a stage in between the mere gathering of information and the getting of enough evidence to prefer the charge. He reaches a stage where he has got the beginnings of evidence. It is at that stage that he must caution. In the judgment of this court, he is not bound to caution until he has got some information which he can put before the court as the beginnings of a case.

g On that view of the Judges' Rules the next question is: what information had the chief inspector when he started his interrogation which would have enabled him to put evidence before the court? The answer is in both these cases none. The inspector, in the judgment of this court, was right when he told the recorder that he had no evidence. That can be demonstrated in both cases.

So far as the appellant Osborne was concerned, the statement to the effect that the *h* police had got themselves 'a good capture' was entirely equivocal. It could have referred, and probably did refer, to the fact that they had found him in possession of a stolen watch. I have dealt already with the matter of the lie about the money. That was equivocal. The fact that he had been found in possession of a black homburg when witnesses said that one of the gang was wearing a bowler hat could not be the beginnings of a case. In the case of the appellant Virtue there does not begin *j* to be even enough to justify reasonable suspicion. The court has reminded itself that it is not concerned with whether there was enough to justify arrest; that is a different problem altogether. All the police had in the case of the appellant Virtue was the fact that he answered the description of one of the men wanted.

---

1   11th Edn (1970), p 2, para 3
2   See [1964] 1 All ER at 238, [1964] 1 WLR at 154

The court has not seen all the descriptions given by the witnesses who were taken to the identity parade, but it has seen a few, and it is clear that no police officer would be justified in bringing a man before a court because he answered a vague description of the type which the court has knowledge of from the transcripts in this case.

It follows so far as the appellant Virtue was concerned that the interrogation could properly start without any caution. It was said that during the interrogation the appellant Virtue behaved in such a way and made statements which should have led the officer to stop the interrogation and administer a caution. It was said that he began to tremble and went very white. That was nothing in itself. When the officer was asking questions as to where the appellant Virtue had been on the Saturday afternoon he said: 'Can you tell me or not because the car was stolen that day?', thereupon the appellant Virtue interposed to say 'I did not take the car if that is what you mean', and the officer said 'I never said anything about your taking the car'. It is impossible to think that that could be regarded by any responsible police officer as evidence of any real value. There was another passage to which I should also refer. He said something like, 'Well, I will tell you about it later'. That again is not evidence which could be the foundation of a case.

So in all the circumstances, in the judgment of this court, the recorder was right in the approach which he made to this problem and right in his conclusion that there was no evidence in the possession of the chief inspector which called for a caution. It follows that the evidence of interrogation was rightly put before the jury and, because the jury accepted that evidence and rejected the evidence in support of the alibis, it follows that there is nothing wrong with the conviction arising from the omission to caution.

Now I turn to the point which was taken on behalf of the appellant Osborne about the admissibility of Chief Inspector Stevenson's evidence. It is right that I should stress that the point was that such evidence was inadmissible. Its weight was another matter altogether and, as I have pointed out already, the recorder advised the jury to attach little, if any, weight to Mrs Head's evidence of identification. He reminded the jury of Mrs Brookes's lapse of memory. It was strenuously argued before the recorder and equally strenuously argued before us that such evidence was not admissible at all and that its wrongful admission made the conviction unsafe. An analogy was drawn between the situation which arose in this case with these two ladies and the situation which can arise in the witness box when a witness for the prosecution gives evidence which the Crown does not like. Our attention was drawn to the Criminal Procedure Act 1865. The situation envisaged by s 3 of that Act did not arise in this case at all because nobody suggested that these two ladies were acting in the way envisaged by that Act, namely, adversely, or, to use the modern term, hostilely, but it was said that the judge allowed the Crown to call evidence to contradict them, which is not admissible.

We do not agree that Chief Inspector Stevenson's evidence contradicted their evidence. All that Mrs Brookes had said was that she did not remember, and, as I have already indicated, that is very understandable after a delay of $7\frac{1}{2}$ months. She had, however, done something. Within four days of the robbery she had attended an identification parade. She had been told in the presence and hearing of the appellant Osborne, as is the usual practice, what she was to do, namely, point out anybody whom she had seen at the time of the raid. She did point somebody out and it was the appellant Osborne. One asks oneself as a matter of common sense why, when a witness has forgotten what she did, evidence should not be given by another witness with a better memory to establish what, in fact, she did when the events were fresh in her mind. Much the same situation arises with regard to Mrs Head. She said in the witness box that she had picked somebody out. She did not think the man she had picked out was in court, but that again is understandable because appearances can change after $7\frac{1}{2}$ months, and, if the experience of this court is anything to go by, accused persons often look much smarter in the dock than they do when they are first arrested. This court can see no reason at all in principle why evidence of that kind should not be admitted.

It was submitted that the admission of that evidence was contrary to a decision of the House of Lords in *R v Christie*[1]. This case has long been regarded as a difficult one to understand because the speeches of their Lordships were not directed to the same points; but this can be got from the speeches—evidence of identification other than identification in the witness box is admissible.

All that the Crown were seeking to do was to establish the fact of identification at the identity parade held on 20th November. This court can see no reason why that evidence should not have been admitted. The court is fortified in that view by a passage in the judgment of Sachs LJ which appears in *R v Richardson*[2]. The case was a very different case from this one, but the principle enunciated by Sachs LJ is applicable. He said[3]:

'The courts, however, must take care not to deprive themselves by new, artificial rules of practice of the best chances of learning the truth. The courts are under no compulsion unnecessarily to follow on a matter of practice the lure of the rules of logic in order to produce unreasonable results which would hinder the course of justice.'

It is pertinent to point out that in 1914 when the House of Lords came to consider *R v Christie*[1] the modern practice of identity parades did not exist. The whole object of identity parades is for the protection of the suspect, and what happens at those parades is highly relevant to the establishment of the truth. It would be wrong, in the judgment of this court, to set up artificial rules of evidence, which hinder the administration of justice.

The evidence was admissible. Accordingly there is no substance in the point which was taken on behalf of the appellant Osborne. In these circumstances the court dismisses the appeals.

Appeals dismissed. Leave to appeal to the House of Lords refused.

Solicitors: *Sampson & Co* (for the appellants); *Solicitor, Metropolitan Police.*

N P Metcalfe Esq   Barrister.

---

1 [1914] AC 545, [1914-15] All ER Rep 63
2 [1971] 2 All ER 773, [1971] 2 QB 484
3 [1971] 2 All ER at 777, [1971] 2 QB at 490

Potters (a firm) v Loppert

CHANCERY DIVISION
PENNYCUICK V-C
30th, 31st OCTOBER, 8th NOVEMBER 1972

Estate agent – Deposit – Interest – Liability to account – Contract for sale of land – Deposit prior to contract – Deposit paid by prospective purchaser of property pending negotiation of contract – Deposit held by estate agents as stakeholders – Agents paying deposit into deposit account with bank – Prospective purchaser deciding not to proceed with purchase – Estate agents returning deposit to prospective purchaser – Interest earned on deposit while held by agents – Whether agents liable to account for interest.

Estate agents, on behalf of clients, placed a freehold property on the market. In March 1971 a prospective purchaser informed the agents that she would be willing to buy the property, subject to contract and survey, for £32,500. The agents wrote to her stating that their clients had instructed them to accept the offer. The letter concluded: 'We should be glad to receive the usual 10% deposit of £3,250 which we will hold as stakeholders.' On 19th March the prospective purchaser sent them a cheque for that amount. On 2nd April the agents paid the cheque into a deposit account with their bank and sent a receipt for £3,250 'in part payment of the purchase price . . . To be held by us as Stakeholders'. On 9th August the prospective purchaser informed the agents that she had decided not to purchase the property and requested the return of the deposit. On the following day the agents sent her a cheque for £3,250 drawn on their current account and gave the bank seven days' notice to transfer £3,250 from their deposit account to their current account. The interest earned on the deposit account in respect of the £3,250 between 2nd April to 10th August amounted to some £45. The prospective purchaser claimed that the agents were liable to account to her for that sum.

Held – The agents were not liable to account to the prospective purchaser for interest on the deposit. The only basis on which a stakeholder could be held liable to account for interest was that he held the deposit as a trustee or in some other fiduciary capacity. The capacity in which an estate agent held a deposit in the pre-contract as well as the post-contract period was contractual or quasi-contractual. His only obligation was to pay over, on demand, a fixed sum equal to the amount of the deposit. In the absence of an express agreement to the contrary, he was under no obligation to account for any profit derived from the deposit while held by him (see p 662 a, p 665 b, p 667 g, p 668 d h and j and p 669 a to e and g, post).

Harington v Hoggart [1824-34] All ER Rep 471, *Burt v Claude Cousins & Co Ltd* [1971] 2 All ER 611 and *Barrington v Lee* [1971] 3 All ER 1231 applied.

Brown v Inland Revenue Comrs [1964] 3 All ER 119 distinguished.

Dictum of Cross J in *Skinner v Trustee of Property of Reed* [1967] 2 All ER at 1289 explained.

Dicta of Diplock J in *Royal Norwegian Government v Constant & Constant and Calcutta Marine Engineering Co Ltd* [1960] 2 Lloyd's Rep at 443 and of Sachs LJ in *Burt v Claude Cousins & Co Ltd* [1971] 2 All ER at 622 disapproved.

Notes

For the liability of auctioneers to pay interest on deposits held by them as stakeholders, see 2 Halsbury's Laws (3rd Edn) 75, para 152, and for cases on the subject, see 3 Digest (Repl) 26, 27, 193-199.

For the terms on which deposits are received in contracts for the sale of land, see 34 Halsbury's Laws (3rd Edn) 234, 235, 322, 323, paras 393, 394 and 545.

Cases referred to in judgment

Barrington v Lee [1971] 3 All ER 1231, [1972] 1 QB 326, [1971] 3 WLR 962, CA.

Brown v Inland Revenue Comrs [1964] 3 All ER 119, [1965] AC 244, [1964] 3 WLR 511, 42 Tax Cas 42, [1964] TR 269, 43 ATC 224, [1964] SLT 302, [1964] SC (HL) 180, HL, Digest (Cont Vol B) 420, *1320a*.

Browne v Southouse (1790) 3 Bro CC 107, 29 ER 437, 1 Digest (Repl) 519, *1530*.

Burt v Claude Cousins & Co Ltd [1971] 2 All ER 611, [1971] 2 QB 426, [1971] 2 WLR 930, CA.

Chedworth (Lord) v Edwards (1802) 8 Ves 46, 32 ER 268, 1 Digest (Repl) 497, *1349*.

Farquhar v Farley (1817) 7 Taunt 592, 1 Moore CP 322, 129 ER 236, 3 Digest (Repl) 26, *194*.

Goding v Frazer [1966] 3 All ER 234, [1967] 1 WLR 286, Digest (Cont Vol B) 640, *2074a*.

Harington v Hoggart (1830) 1 B & Ad 577, [1824-34] All ER Rep 471, 9 LJOSKB 14, 109 ER 902, 1 Digest (Repl) 520, *1536*.

Lonsdale (Earl) v Church (1790) 3 Bro CC 41, 29 ER 396, 7 Digest (Repl) 219, *566*.

Maloney v Hardy and Moorshead (1970) 216 Estates Gazette 1582, CA; noted at [1971] 2 All ER 630, [1971] 1 QB 442, [1971] 2 WLR 942.

Quistclose Investments Ltd v Rolls Razor Ltd [1968] 1 All ER 613, [1968] Ch 540, [1968] 2 WLR 478, CA; *affd sub nom Barclays Bank Ltd v Quistclose Investments Ltd* [1968] 3 All ER 651, [1970] AC 567, [1968] 3 WLR 1097, HL, Digest (Cont Vol C) 35, *401a*.

Rogers v Boehm (1798) 2 Esp 702, 170 ER 502, 1 Digest (Repl) 519, *1531*.

Royal Norwegian Government v Constant & Constant and Calcutta Marine Engineering Co Ltd [1960] 2 Lloyd's Rep 431.

Salisbury (Lord) v Wilkinson (undated) cited 8 Ves 48, 32 ER 268, 1 Digest (Repl) 521, *1544*.

Skinner v Trustee of Property of Reed [1967] 2 All ER 1286, [1967] Ch 1194, [1967] 3 WLR 871, Digest (Cont Vol C) 30, *213a*.

Smith v Hamilton [1950] 2 All ER 928, [1951] Ch 174, 66 (pt 2) TLR 937, Digest (Cont Vol A) 287, *2666a*.

Cases also cited

Ellis v Goulton [1893] 1 QB 350.

Gray v Gutteridge (1828) 3 C & P 40, 172 ER 313.

Hardwicke (Earl) v Vernon (1808) 14 Ves 504, 33 ER 614.

Page v Newman (1829) 9 B & C 378, 109 ER 140.

Rayner v Paskell and Cann (1948) 152 Estates Gazette 270; noted at [1971] 2 All ER 628, [1971] 2 QB 439.

Originating summons

By a summons dated 25th May 1972, as amended, the plaintiffs, Potters (a firm), sought, inter alia, the determination of the following questions: whether in the events which had happened Potters were (a) chargeable by the defendant, Susan Loppert, with any and if so what interest on the sum of £3,250 which had been paid by Miss Loppert by a cheque received by Potters on 22nd March 1971 and presented by them for payment on 2nd April 1971 and which sum was returned by Potters to Miss Loppert on 10th August 1971, (b) accountable to Miss Loppert for the sum of £48·82 (being the amount of interest earned by the sum of £3,250 placed by Potters on deposit account with the Hampstead branch of Lloyds Bank Ltd from 2nd April to 17th August 1971 inclusive), (c) under any duty to Miss Loppert in respect of the sum of £3,250 other than to repay that sum to her on demand. The facts are set out in the judgment.

Jeremiah Harman QC and *Oliver Lodge* for Potters.
N C H Browne-Wilkinson QC and *Richard Scott* for Miss Loppert.

Cur adv vult

8th November. **PENNYCUICK V-C.** On this summons the plaintiffs are Potters,   *a*
a firm of estate agents, and the defendant is Miss Susan Loppert. The summons
raises a question of some general importance concerning the liability of an estate agent
to account for interest on a pre-contract deposit paid to him expressly as stakeholder
by the prospective purchaser, where no contract is made and the deposit is returned
to the prospective purchaser.

The facts are not in dispute and may be stated as follows. In January 1971 Potters,   *b*
on behalf of a client, placed on the market a property known as 104 Heath Street,
Hampstead. On or about 15th March 1971 Miss Loppert informed Potters on the
telephone that, subject to contract and survey, she was willing to purchase at the
price of £32,500. By a letter dated 17th March 1971, Potters, on the instructions of
their clients, wrote in the following terms:

'With further reference to your recent telephone conversation we write to   *c*
inform you that our client has instructed us to accept your offer of £32,500 for
the freehold interest in this property subject to Contract and survey. [They
concluded:] We should be glad to receive the usual 10% deposit of £3,250
which we will hold as stakeholders.'

On 19th March Miss Loppert replied, enclosing her cheque for £3,250 expressed   *d*
to be 'as a deposit of 10%'. On 2nd April Miss Loppert orally informed Potters that
her offer was no longer subject to survey and on the same day Potters paid her cheque
into the firm's deposit account with the Hampstead branch of Lloyds Bank. On the
same day Potters sent Miss Loppert a receipt in the following terms:

'Received from Miss Susan Loppert...cheque value £3,250...being on
account of the 10% deposit and in part payment of the purchase price of £32,500   *e*
...agreed to be paid for the above-mentioned freehold property subject to
contract. To be held by us as Stakeholders.'

On 9th August the solicitors acting for Miss Loppert informed Potters that she had
decided not to proceed with the purchase of the property and requested the return of
her deposit. On 10th August Potters sent Miss Loppert a cheque on the firm's current   *f*
account for £3,250. On the same date Potters gave seven days' notice to the bank to
transfer £3,250 from the firm's deposit account to its current account, and this
transfer was effected on 17th August. Mr Field, the partner in Potters who swore an
affidavit in support of the summons, states:

'Between 17th March 1971 and 10th August 1971 my firm made no attempt
to find any other purchaser for the Property, it being contrary to the practice   *g*
of my firm to do so while a property is under offer to an intending purchaser.'

Subsequently Miss Loppert's solicitors demanded interest on the sum of £3,250
for the period during which it was held by Potters. The interest on the deposit
account from 2nd April to 17th August amounted to £48·82, but one week's interest
is attributable to the period after Potters repaid Miss Loppert £3,250, and it is   *h*
accepted, on her behalf, that that week's interest must be deducted, reducing
the interest to approximately £45.

Potters contend that they are not accountable for interest, and they issued the
present summons on 25th May 1972. The questions sought to be determined (as
amended at the hearing in order to correct an obvious slip) are, inter alia, as follows:

'1. Whether in the events which have happened [Potters] are:—(a) Chargeable   *j*
by [Miss Loppert] with any and if so what interest upon the sum of £3,250...
(b) Accountable to [Miss Loppert] for the sum of £48·82 (being the amount of
interest earned by the said sum of £3,250)...'

During the hearing counsel for Miss Loppert abandoned the first claim for interest
as such and concentrated exclusively on the second claim, that is, accountability for

interest actually earned on the deposit account between 2nd April and 10th August.

One further affidavit was sworn on behalf of Potters by Mr Wilcox, who is the Departmental Secretary of the Practice and Conduct Department of the Royal Institution of Chartered Surveyors. Mr Wilcox exhibited an announcement[1] made by his institution to its members in the present connection which should be looked at, but I will not take up time reading it. Mr Wilcox also explained that his institution and the Incorporated Society of Valuers and Auctioneers are paying Miss Loppert's costs in any event in this cause.

Summarily, counsel for Potters contended that on the proper view of the mutual obligations between a purchaser and a stakeholder, as laid down by judicial decision, Potters were liable to Miss Loppert in contract or quasi-contract for the amount of the deposit and were not accountable to her for any profit, including income profit, derived from the deposit while held by them. Counsel for Miss Loppert contended that Potters received the deposit in a fiduciary capacity and that on general principles they were so accountable.

It is necessary for the understanding of this matter to recognise at the outset the difference between a pre-contract deposit and a deposit paid on or after the conclusion of a contract. I refer to the latter as a contract deposit. The practice of requiring a purchaser to pay a deposit on the conclusion of a contract is of long standing. Such a deposit serves the dual purpose of an earnest to bind the bargain and as part-payment of the purchase price. The deposit is frequently paid to some person, usually the estate agent or a solicitor employed by the vendor, as a stakeholder. Broadly, it is the duty of the stakeholder to deal with the deposit according to the event. In comparatively recent times—put as approximately the last 40 years—a practice has arisen of requiring the prospective purchaser to pay a deposit in advance of the conclusion of a contract. Unless and until the contract is concluded, the prospective purchaser is entitled to require the return of his deposit at any time. On conclusion of a contract, the deposit stands in the same position as a contract deposit. Such a deposit is frequently paid to some person—again, usually the estate agent or solicitor employed by the vendor—expressed to be a 'stakeholder', although doubt has been cast on the accuracy of that expression in relation to a pre-contract deposit. It is the duty of the stakeholder to deal with the deposit according to the event, that is, to return the deposit to the prospective purchaser on request before the conclusion of a contract and thereafter, on conclusion of the contract, to deal with it according to how the contract works out.

I propose in the first place to consider the law in relation to contract deposits. Looking at the position apart from authority, one might perhaps at first sight rather expect that where any property is placed in medio in the hands of a third party to await an event as between two other parties the third party receives that property as trustee and that the property and the investments for the time being representing it represent his trust estate. Where the property is something other than money—for example, an investment—that must in the nature of things almost certainly be the position. But where the property is money—that is, cash or a cheque resulting in a bank credit—this is by no means necessarily so. Certainly the money may be paid to the third party as trustee, but equally it may be paid to him as principal on a contractual or quasi-contractual obligation to pay the like sum to one or other of the parties according to the event. It must depend on the intention of the parties, to be derived from all the circumstances, including any written documents, in which capacity the third party receives the money. It should be observed that, apart from some express or implied agreement between the parties, on the one hand, a trustee is accountable for profit derived from the trust property, including income profit from its investment; on the other hand, a party liable for money had and received is not accountable for profit derived from that money, nor is he liable for interest on it.

---

1 See the Chartered Surveyor (January 1968), p 340

Turning now to authority, it is to my mind conclusive that, apart from agreement
to the contrary, a contract deposit paid to a stakeholder is not paid to him as trustee,   *a*
but on a contractual or quasi-contractual liability with the consequence that the
stakeholder is not accountable for profit on it. The decisive case on this point is
Harington v Hoggart[1], heard by a full King's Bench Court in 1830. The headnote
reads[2]:

> 'An auctioneer who is employed to sell an estate, and who receives a deposit   *b*
> from the purchaser, is a mere stake-holder, liable to be called upon to pay the
> money at any time; and, therefore, although he place the money in the funds
> and make interest of it, he is not liable to pay such interest to the vendor when
> the purchase is completed; though the vendor (without the concurrence of the
> vendee) gave him notice to invest the money in Government securities.'

The plea against the estate auctioneer was in assumpsit for the amount of the deposit   *c*
with interest. The deposit was paid into court and the only question outstanding
for decision was whether the auctioneer was liable for interest. I should refer to one
statement in counsel's argument for the auctioneer[3], because it contains a quotation
from something said by Lord Eldon LC in a connected suit which was proceeding
in the Court of Chancery: *d*

> 'When the present case was before Lord Chancellor Eldon in the suit men-
> tioned in the special case, he said, "Adverting with deference to the dictum of
> Sir V. Gibbs [CJ in *Farquhar v Farley*[4]], I must say I cannot readily give in to that
> doctrine. The strong inclination of my own opinion is, that it makes no difference
> whether interest were made or not."'

Lord Tenterden CJ said[5]:   *e*

> 'I am of opinion that the plaintiff, in this case, is not entitled to recover. There
> is an essential distinction between the character of an agent and that of a stake-
> holder. The case of *Rogers v. Boehm*[6] was the case of an agent, and what Lord
> Kenyon there said must be understood to apply to a person filling that character.   *f*
> If an agent receive money for his principal, the very instant he receives it, it
> becomes the money of his principal. If, instead of paying it over to his principal,
> he thinks fit to retain it, and makes a profit of it, he may, under such
> circumstances, as occurred in that case, be liable to account for the profit. Here
> the defendant is not a mere agent, but a stakeholder. A stakeholder does not
> receive the money for either party, he receives it for both; and until the event is   *g*
> known, it is his duty to keep it in his own hands. If he think fit to employ it
> and make interest of it, by laying it out in the funds or otherwise, and any loss
> accrue, he must be answerable for that loss; and if he is to answer for the loss, it
> seems to me he has a right to any intermediate advantage which may arise.
> The defendant here has not laid out or made a profit of the plaintiff's money,
> for at the time he laid it out it was not the plaintiff's, and it was doubtful whether   *h*
> it would ever become so or not.'

Then Lord Tenterden CJ said[7]:

> 'As to the cases that have been cited upon this subject, there certainly is none
> in which interest has been recovered from an auctioneer. The strong inclination

1 (1830) 1 B & Ad 577, [1824-34] All ER Rep 471
2 (1830) 1 B & Ad at 577
3 (1830) 1 B & Ad at 585
4 (1817) 7 Taunt 592
5 (1830) 1 B & Ad at 586, 587, [1824-34] All ER Rep at 472
6 (1798) 2 Esp 702
7 (1830) 1 B & Ad at 587, 588, [1824-34] All ER Rep at 472, 473

of Lord Eldon's opinion was, that it could not be recovered in this particular case, even although it should appear that a profit had been made, and all who know that noble and learned Lord, know that he was exceedingly cautious in delivering a positive opinion upon any point, and that he forbore to do so until it became absolutely necessary for the decision of the cause. By deciding now that the defendant is not liable, we certainly do not vary from any principle which has been laid down by a Judge in equity, or make the law in this Court different from the rule in equity. I have observed, that there is no case in which interest has been recovered against an auctioneer.'

Parke J said[1]:

'The simple question for the consideration of the Court is, whether the defendant, as an auctioneer, and in that character having received a deposit of 2000*l*. for the estate sold by the plaintiff to Mr. Secretan, is liable, under the circumstances stated in this case, to pay interest to the vendor of the estate for any part of the time during which the money was in his hands before the purchase was completed. He has paid into Court interest for the subsequent period. It appears to me that the situation of an auctioneer is this: he receives a sum of money which is to be paid in one event to the vendor, that is, provided the purchase is completed; and in the other, if it is not completed, to the vendee: he holds the money, in the mean time, as stakeholder; and he is bound to keep it, and pay it over, upon either of those events, immediately. He is clearly not responsible for interest upon that money, if he makes it, (as he is supposed to have done in this case,) and the principle upon which he is exempt from responsibility was settled in a case of *Lord Salisbury* v. *Wilkinson*[2], cited and recognized by Lord Eldon in *Lord Chedworth* v. *Edwards*[3], and by Lord Alvanley in *The Earl of Lonsdale* v. *Church*[4]. These cases, and that of *Browne* v. *Southouse*[5], which is to the same effect, establish that a man who holds money as an agent or banker, bound to produce it at a moment's notice to the person who deposits the money in his hands, is not liable to pay interest if he makes it. Here the auctioneer was liable to produce the money deposited with him at a moment's notice, when the event took place on which he was to pay it to one party or the other; he would be responsible in case the fund was lost during any part of the time he ought to keep it in his possession; and if he was responsible for loss, he had a right to the interest accruing if he employed the fund. That appears to me to have been the original situation of the defendant as auctioneer.'

Then[6]:

'There is no case in which it has been decided that interest is recoverable under such circumstances. Certainly it cannot be recovered here upon the ground of the money having been the plaintiff's; because, at the time it was laid out, it was not his money, and he had no title to it till the purchase was completed.'

Taunton J said[7]:

'Then, with respect to this being money had and received to the plaintiff's use, it is perfectly clear that, when the defendant laid the money out, he did so at his peril. If he laid the money out in the funds, and received the intermediate

1 (1830) 1 B & Ad at 588, 589, [1824-34] All ER Rep at 473
2 (Undated) cited 8 Ves 48
3 (1802) 8 Ves 46
4 (1790) 3 Bro CC 41
5 (1790) 3 Bro CC 107
6 (1830) 1 B & Ad at 590, [1824-34] All ER Rep at 473, 474
7 (1830) 1 B & Ad at 591, 592, [1824-34] All ER Rep at 474

dividends, he must have borne the loss, if between the investment and the *a*
completion of the contract the funds had fallen. Then, if the money was laid
out at the risk and peril of the defendant, it appears to me that, in conscience
and equity, he is entitled to any profit which he may have derived from running
that risk. Under these circumstances, I am of opinion the plaintiff is not entitled
to recover the sum claimed, either as interest, or as money had and received to
his use.'   *b*

Finally, Patteson J said[1]:

'The defendant, being a stakeholder, was bound to pay to the party ultimately
entitled the sum deposited with him, without any deduction, as soon as it was
determined which of the parties was entitled to it. It seems to me wholly
inconsistent with such a liability that he should be bound to pay interest, for if   *c*
he were bound to pay interest, and to make interest, by laying out the principal,
the principal should be laid out at the risk of the party entitled to it.'

The claim for principal and interest was based on assumpsit for money had and
received. No doubt the common law court in 1830 could not have entertained a
claim based on trust. But, most significantly, Lord Eldon LC is quoted as having
reached the same conclusion as to interest. Lord Tenterden CJ in terms said[2]:   *d*

'. . . we certainly do not vary from any principle which has been laid down by a
Judge in equity, or make the law in this Court different from the rule in equity.'

No doubt seems to have been cast on that decision, apart from an obiter dictum
by Sachs LJ in the recent case of *Burt v Claude Cousins & Co Ltd*[3]. That was a case
of pre-contract deposit, to which I will refer in a few moments.   *e*
In *Williams on The Contract of Sale of Land*[4]—a textbook of high authority—
the following passage occurs. Dealing with the position of a stakeholder, it says:

'Where a deposit is paid to any person as stakeholder, he shall hold it to abide
the event of the contract, and shall be bound to pay the amount thereof to the
vendor upon (but not before) the completion of the sale or the forfeiture of the
deposit, or to the purchaser if and when the purchaser shall acquire the right to   *f*
the return of the deposit; but until the event of the contract shall be decided
the stakeholder shall not pay over the deposit to either party without the other
party's consent. The stakeholder shall be accountable to the parties accordingly;
but he shall not be chargeable with any interest for any time during which he
shall rightfully retain the deposit, or accountable for any profit which he may
make, in the way of interest or otherwise, by the use of the deposit money during   *g*
that time.'

In *Smith v Hamilton*[5], Harman J said[6]:

'The stake-holder is not bound to pay interest: he retains the benefit of it:
that is his reward for holding the stake. The position seems to me an odd one,
but I do not see why I should not order the vendor to pay interest on the money   *h*
in the meantime.'

Before coming to *Burt v Claude Cousins & Co Ltd*[7], I should refer to something
that was said in two other recent cases. In *Royal Norwegian Government v Constant &
Constant and Calcutta Marine Engineering Co Ltd*[8] Diplock J said:

1 (1830) 1 B & Ad at 592, [1824-34] All ER Rep at 474
2 (1830) 1 B & Ad at 587, 588, [1824-34] All ER Rep at 473
3 [1971] 2 All ER 611 at 621, 622, [1971] 2 QB 426 at 449, 450
4 (1930), p 104
5 [1950] 2 All ER 928, [1951] Ch 174
6 [1951] Ch at 184; cf [1950] 2 All ER at 935
7 [1971] 2 All ER 611, [1971] 2 QB 426
8 [1960] 2 Lloyd's Rep 431 at 443

a 'Mr. Eckersley seems to get nervous at the idea of such a Chancery notion as a trust being mentioned in the Commercial Court, but, whenever money is paid to a stakeholder, where the legal ownership is in the stakeholder and the beneficial ownership in someone else, the stakeholder holds the money as trustee...'

b *Harington v Hoggart*[1] was not cited to the learned judge, nor were any other authorities directly in point cited to him. With respect to him, the statement which I have quoted, if intended to be of universal application, is too wide. It is certainly possible for money to be paid to a stakeholder without his becoming a trustee. In relation to the accountability for income profit, which would follow from the capacity of a trustee, the statement in relation to a contract deposit is irreconcilable with the decision in *Harington v Hoggart*[1].

c In *Skinner v Trustee of Property of Reed*[2] Cross J reviewed the position of a contract stakeholder in these terms:

'The purchaser pays his deposit both as an earnest to bind the bargain and in part payment of the purchase price and, if the deposit is paid to a stakeholder, then subject to any express term in the contract, the stakeholder holds the *d* deposit on trust to deal with it in different ways in different contingencies.'

He then goes on to state the duty of the stakeholder in various contingencies. In the next paragraph he refers to the trust on which the stakeholder in the event holds the deposit. So in that otherwise unexceptional statement about a stakeholder the learned judge twice refers to trust. But, here again, *Harington v Hoggart*[1] was not *e* cited to him, and I do not think he can be treated as having addressed his mind to the capacity—that is, whether in trust or in contract—in which the stakeholder receives a deposit.

I come now to *Burt v Claude Cousins & Co Ltd*[3]. In that case a pre-contract deposit had been paid to an estate agent, not expressly as stakeholder, who subsequently became insolvent. No contract was concluded as between the intending purchaser *f* and intending vendor. The case gave rise to a difference of opinion between the members of the Court of Appeal, all of whom reviewed to some extent the relation of purchaser or intending purchaser, vendor or intending vendor, and stakeholder generally, and not only in relation to pre-contract deposits. In the course of his dissenting judgment, Lord Denning MR said[4]:

'If an estate agent or solicitor, being duly authorised in that behalf, receives a *g* deposit "as stakeholder", he is under a duty to hold it in medio pending the outcome of a future event. He does not hold it as agent for the vendor, nor as agent for the purchaser. He holds it as trustee for both to await the event: see *Skinner v Trustee of Property of Reed*[2], per Cross J. Until the event is known, it is his duty to keep it in his own hands; or to put it on deposit at the bank; in which case he is entitled to keep for himself any interest that accrues to it: see *h* *Harington v Hoggart*[1].'

I find the collocation in that passage of the statement that the stakeholder is a trustee and is not liable for interest arising from the deposit rather perplexing; but I need not dwell on that, because in the subsequent case of *Barrington v Lee*[5], to which I will refer later, Lord Denning MR comes down squarely on liability in contract or quasi-*j* contract.

---

1   (1830) 1 B & Ad 577, [1824-34] All ER Rep 471
2   [1967] 2 All ER 1286 at 1289, [1967] Ch 1194 at 1200
3   [1971] 2 All ER 611, [1971] 2 QB 426
4   [1971] 2 All ER at 615, [1971] 2 QB at 435, 436
5   [1971] 3 All ER 1231, [1972] 1 QB 326

It is Sachs LJ who alone expresses doubts on the decision in *Harington v Hoggart*[1]. He says[2]:

'For the purpose of coming to a conclusion on the status or capacity in which the deposit is received, it has not seemed to me necessary on this occasion to consider the precise nature of the claim the purchaser has against that estate agent if he demands his deposit back in the pre-contract period though I am still disposed to the views expressed in *Goding v Frazer*[3]. It matters not whether that claim sounds in the old common count for money had and received (and is so whether in contract or quasi contract), or whether it lies against the estate agent in some other form in which there would be pleaded a contract or a trust. A claim manifestly does lie against the estate agent whatever the answer to the question as to status or capacity. It is apt to note that in Bullen and Leake[4], in reference to money had and received, the following passage is to be found: "This is the most comprehensive of all the common counts. It is applicable wherever the defendant has received money which in justice and equity belongs to the plaintiff, under circumstances which render the receipt of it a receipt by the defendant to the use of the plaintiff." Suffice it accordingly to say that whatever the status or capacity, in my judgment a claim would correctly lie for money had and received. That conclusion does not militate against the co-existence of an equitable remedy (cf *Quistclose Investments Ltd v Rolls Razor Ltd*[5]) if, as may well be the case, the deposit money is impressed with a trust. Nor, likewise, did it seem necessary for the purpose of determining the relevant status to decide who is entitled to any interest earned or benefit gained by the use of the deposit money in the pre-contract period. Such views as I expressed on this point in *Goding's* case[6] stemmed from the reasoning in *Brown v Inland Revenue Comrs*[7] (which concerned solicitors). They naturally require reconsideration insofar as they were based on a wrong premise as regards the terms on which estate agents receive deposits. In the circumstances I prefer to say no more on this point which was not argued before us (though it may have been mentioned) save that I still very much doubt whether an estate agent is entitled to retain interest he receives by putting deposit money on deposit. The old leading Court of Queen's Bench case of *Harington v Hoggart*[1] as to interest on auctioneers' deposits may need review in the light of the principles on which *Brown's* case[7] was based (as illustrated by the speech of Lord Upjohn[8]) at any rate if the deposit money is impressed with a trust.'

In *Barrington v Lee*[9] the Court of Appeal had once again to consider the position of pre-contract deposits, this time paid to two estate agents expressly as stakeholders, one of whom became insolvent. Here again, no contract was concluded, and the issue lay between the intending purchaser and the intending vendor. In this case Lord Denning MR reaffirmed his minority view in *Burt v Claude Cousins & Co Ltd*[10], and Edmund Davies and Stephenson LJJ, with obvious reluctance, reaffirmed the majority view in that case, but distinguished it on its facts. The judgments are important in the present connection for their insistence that the liability of a

---

1   (1830) 1 B & Ad 577, [1824-34] All ER Rep 471
2   [1971] 2 All ER at 621, 622, [1971] 2 QB at 449, 450
3   [1966] 3 All ER 234, [1967] 1 WLR 286
4   Precedents of Pleading (3rd Edn, 1868), p 44
5   [1968] 1 All ER 613 at 620, 629,630, [1968] Ch 540 at 554, 568, 569
6   [1966] 3 All ER at 238, [1967] 1 WLR at 292
7   [1964] 3 All ER 119, [1965] AC 244
8   [1964] 3 All ER at 127, [1965] AC at 265
9   [1971] 3 All ER 1231, [1972] 1 QB 326
10 [1971] 2 All ER 611, [1971] 2 QB 426

a   stakeholder receiving a pre-contract deposit lies in contract or quasi-contract.   Lord Denning MR said[1]:

> 'To my mind, the claim to the return of the deposit lies in contract and nothing else.   When the purchaser pays a deposit to an estate agent, in the course of negotiations before any contract is concluded, there is clearly an implied promise *by someone* to repay it if the negotiations break down.   But who is that someone?
b   Who makes the promise to repay it?   The estate agent or the vendor?   If the estate agent receives the deposit "as stakeholder", then it is the estate agent who makes the promise to repay, and he alone can be sued for it.'

Edmund Davies LJ said[2]:

> "In such cases as the present, the basis of liability of either estate agent or
c   prospective vendor to return a deposit paid can, as I see it, only be on the basis of money had and received to the use of the depositor.'

Stephenson LJ said[3]:

> 'This may be thought a surprising sort of agency; surprising not because it renders both agent and principal liable, for that is not unique, as Megaw LJ pointed out in *Burt's* case[4] but because the principal is apparently liable to
d   repay money had and received by his agent to the plaintiff's use which he has not only never himself had or received, but of which he may know nothing and had he known of it could not have received it from his agent without the consent of the plaintiff.'

Later he said[5]:

e
> 'However it seems reasonably certain that the plaintiff's cause of action against Elliotts [the defendant's agents] would have been for money had and received for Mr Bohener's use, as the judge assumed, and that is the cause of action on which she bases her claim against the defendant, although not expressed in those actual words.'

f   Their Lordships in that case were of course concerned with a pre-contract deposit but, so far as their observations relate to the nature of a stakeholder's liability lying in contract, they appear equally applicable to the case of any contract deposit.

I conclude that so far from casting any doubt on the decision in *Harington v Hoggart*[6] the two recent decisions on pre-contract deposits, when read together, tend to affirm the correctness of that decision; that is, by their insistence on the contrac-
g   tual nature of a stakeholder's liability.   I must also conclude that the doubt expressed by Sachs LJ[7] on that decision is not well founded.

Counsel for Miss Loppert advanced an argument based on the Supreme Court of Judicature Act 1873, s 25 (11).   He contended that before 1873 there existed a rule in equity, which he formulated as follows: when moneys are received by a stakeholder,
h   he receives them in circumstances in which he becomes either the trustee or agents for both parties.   Then he contended that, by virtue of s 25 (11), this rule must now prevail over the rule of the common law as applied in *Harington v Hoggart*[6].   He was however unable to point to any case in which the rule which he formulated had been applied in equity before 1873.   It seems to me that, in view of the comments made by Lord Eldon LC, as quoted in *Harington v Hoggart*[6], it is impossible to suppose

j   1   [1971] 3 All ER at 1237, 1238, [1972] 1 QB at 337
   2   [1971] 3 All ER at 1242, [1972] 1 QB at 343
   3   [1971] 3 All ER at 1243, [1972] 1 QB at 344
   4   [1971] 2 All ER at 627, [1971] 2 QB at 455
   5   [1971] 3 All ER at 1247, [1972] 1 QB at 347, 348
   6   (1830) 1 B & Ad 577, [1824-34] All ER Rep 471
   7   [1971] 2 All ER at 622, [1971] 2 QB at 449, 450

that any such rule existed.   Of course, it has always been a rule of equity that a trustee
is accountable for profit derived from his trust estate; but an attempt to apply this   *a*
rule to a stakeholder begs the question of the capacity of the stakeholder.

Counsel for Miss Loppert placed reliance on *Brown v Inland Revenue Comrs*[1].   That
was a case relating to interest on money in the hands of a solicitor.   In particular he
relied on the statement by Lord Upjohn in these terms[2]:

'One of the most settled principles of the law of Scotland, as of the law of   *b*
England, is that a person who is in a fiduciary relationship to another may not
make a profit out of his trust, and the contrary was not argued.   A professional
adviser, whether he be solicitor, factor, stockbroker or surveyor is of course
in a fiduciary relationship to his client, and if and when he is entrusted with his
client's money he can make no profit out of it.'

No one would dispute the validity of that statement, but, again, its application to a   *c*
stakeholder begs the question of the capacity of a stakeholder, and it does not seem
to me that that statement advances the present question.

I turn now to the law in relation to pre-contract deposits.   When such a deposit
is paid to someone, expressed to be a stakeholder, the duties of the latter are as I have
already stated.   Unless and until a contract is concluded, the prospective purchaser   *d*
can require the return of the deposit at any time, and on conclusion of the contract
the deposit assumes the position of an ordinary contract deposit.

In *Maloney v Hardy and Moorshead*[3] Russell LJ criticised the use of the term 'stakeholder' in relation to a pre-contract deposit.   That criticism was echoed by Megaw
LJ in *Burt's* case[4].   I appreciate the force of that criticism, but the term is that used
by estate agents themselves and, so long as one appreciates the distinction between   *e*
the duties of a depositee in relation to a pre-contract deposit and those in relation to a
contract deposit, I think that the term may be used as a convenient label.   It is
difficult to think of a better one.

Counsel for Miss Loppert's first contention was that, irrespective of the capacity
of a stakeholder in regard to a contract deposit, the stakeholder receives a pre-contract
deposit as bare trustee for the prospective purchaser and holds the deposit in that   *f*
capacity unless and until a contract is concluded.   Counsel for Miss Loppert formulated that contention in these terms: the pre-contract deposit is a mere show of
means by the purchaser and remains his money throughout; the depositee holds as
bare trustee for the depositor.   Quite apart from the question whether the obligation of the stakeholder lies in trust or in contract, I doubt whether that is a correct
analysis of the position.   It is true that the stakeholder is bound to return the deposit   *g*
to the prospective purchaser on request; but immediately and automatically on
conclusion of a contract his obligation is altered, not by reason of any new instructions
given to him by the prospective purchaser, but by virtue of the terms impliedly
imposed on him on receipt of the deposit.   It seems to me that, from the moment
of receipt, the stakeholder must be treated as subject to the entirety of obligations
imposed on him by the receipt.   However one analyses the obligations of the stake-   *h*
holder, it seems to me that the stakeholder's capacity must remain constant throughout.   I find it impossible to suppose that, pending the conclusion of a contract, the
stakeholder holds the deposit as a trust estate and then, on conclusion of the contract,
the deposit loses that character and the obligation of the stakeholder is transmuted
into a contractual obligation to pay a sum of money.   This contention also seems to
me to be irreconcilable with the statements of the law in *Barrington v Lee*[5].   *j*

1   [1964] 3 All ER 119, [1965] AC 244
2   [1964] 3 All ER at 127, [1965] AC at 265
3   (1970) 216 Estates Gazette 1582, noted at [1971] 2 All ER 630, [1971] 2 QB 442
4   [1971] 2 All ER at 627, [1971] 2 QB at 455
5   [1971] 3 All ER 1231, [1972] 1 QB 326

Counsel for Miss Loppert's next contention was that throughout—that is, before and after the conclusion of a contract—the capacity of the stakeholder is in its nature that of a trustee. He formulated the proposition that if a deposit is paid to a stakeholder, that involves the concept that the depositee holds the stake in medio pending the outcome of an event, and the stakeholder holds on behalf of one or other of the vendor and purchaser and, as such, is an agent or a trustee. For the reasons which I have already given in relation to a contract deposit, it seems to me that authority is conclusive against this contention, and it would not be useful to go over the ground again in relation to pre-contract deposits.

I must refer to one other contention made by counsel for Miss Loppert, namely, that a remedy in contract is not inconsistent with the existence of other equitable rights. That contention echoes what was said by Sachs LJ in the passage I quoted from *Burt v Claude Cousins & Co Ltd*[1]. Obviously a legal right may co-exist with an equitable remedy; but I find great difficulty in seeing how the receipt of a deposit by a stakeholder could impose on the latter simultaneously an obligation to hold the specific deposit and its investment as trust property, and a liability to repay a fixed sum equal to the amount of the deposit. At any rate, I see no ground, apart from the dictum of Sachs LJ, for saying that that is the legal position in regard to a deposit. Unless a stakeholder occupies the capacity of a trustee during whatever is the relevant period, there can be no ground on which he could be made accountable for profit, including income profit, derived from the deposit and its investment. I think the contrary is not contended, and counsel for Miss Loppert abandoned any claim to interest as such.

The question raised by the summons is one of law, but one would be reluctant to reach a conclusion at variance with what is fair and reasonable between the parties. How can one justify the retention by a stakeholder of interest on what is in substance someone else's money? I have already quoted the explanation given by the King's Bench judges in *Harington v Hoggart*[2]. The ground on which they say that a stakeholder is not liable for interest is neatly summarised by Patteson J[3]. Harman J puts it rather differently in the passage I have cited from *Smith v Hamilton*[4]. I venture to think that that statement might be rather elaborated on the evidence in this case, namely, that the interest represents not merely a reward for the agents' trouble, but also a recompense for the sterilisation of the property vis-à-vis the estate agent during the period between the payment of the deposit and the conclusion of a contract or its breakdown, with the consequences that the agent has no prospect of earning a commission on its sale to any other party so long as the property remains sterilised.

It is not for me to say more about the ethics of the situation. For the reasons which I have given, I propose to answer the three questions (a), (b) and (c) in the summons in the negative.

Declaration accordingly.

Solicitors: *Beale & Co* (for Potters); *Birkbeck, Montagu's & Co* (for Miss Loppert).

Susan Corbett Barrister.

---

1 [1971] 2 All ER at 621, 622, [1971] 2 QB at 449, 450
2 (1830) 1 B & Ad 577, [1824-34] All ER Rep 471
3 (1830) 1 B & Ad at 592, [1824-34] All ER Rep at 474
4 [1951] Ch at 184; cf [1950] 2 All ER at 935

Fakes v Taylor Woodrow Construction Ltd

COURT OF APPEAL, CIVIL DIVISION
LORD DENNING MR, MEGAW LJ AND SIR GORDON WILLMER
2nd, 3rd NOVEMBER 1972

Arbitration – Stay of court proceedings – Refusal of stay – Grounds for refusal – Insolvency of plaintiff – Availability of legal aid in court proceedings – Insolvency alleged to have been caused by defendant's breach of contract – Plaintiff unable to afford arbitration proceedings by reason of insolvency – Reasonable grounds for believing that insolvency caused by defendant's breach – Effect of granting stay a denial of justice to plaintiff.

Arbitration – Stay of court proceedings – Legal aid – Relevance – Legal aid not available in arbitration proceedings – Rights of person receiving legal aid not to affect rights or liabilities of other parties or principles on which court's discretion normally exercised – Plaintiff insolvent – Plaintiff granted legal aid for court proceedings – Application by defendant for stay – Defendant having no right to stay – No principles on which court's discretion exercised – Court not precluded from refusing stay on ground plaintiff having legal aid for court proceedings but unable to afford arbitration proceedings – Legal Aid and Advice Act 1949, s 1 (7) (b).

The plaintiff carried on business as a plumbing contractor. He was engaged by the defendants under sub-contracts made in 1967 and 1969 to carry out plumbing work on building sites where the defendants were the main contractors. The sub-contracts contained an arbitration clause which provided that any dispute, question or difference arising between the contractor and the sub-contractor in connection with the sub-contract 'shall be referred to arbitration'. The plaintiff carried out a great deal of work under the sub-contracts. He alleged, however, that because of breaches of contract by the defendants in delaying his work and in failing to pay him sums due at the times when payment should have been made, he was made insolvent and his business was ruined. It appeared that in 1970 the plaintiff was sued to judgment by various creditors and that he was in consequence without means. In May 1971 the plaintiff obtained a full certificate for legal aid to bring an action against the defendants. A writ was issued in February 1972 and a statement of claim was delivered in March 1972 alleging breaches of contract and claiming over £80,000 from the defendants for moneys due under the sub-contracts and as damages for the delay in paying the sums due. The defendants denied breach of contract. They took out a summons to stay the action on the ground of the arbitration clause in the sub-contracts; they wished to take the dispute to arbitration. The plaintiff resisted the summons on the ground that legal aid was not available for an arbitration and because of his insolvency he had not got the means to go to arbitration; he alleged that if he was forced to go to arbitration it was tantamount to losing the claim. The judge in chambers ordered the action to be stayed. The plaintiff appealed against the stay. There was before the court an affidavit sworn by the defendants and an affidavit in reply sworn by the plaintiff. The defendants admitted they had sought a stay because, believing the claim to be ill-founded and that the plaintiff could not afford to take the case to arbitration, it was the quickest way to stop the claim.

Held (Megaw LJ dissenting) – The appeal would be allowed for the following reasons—

(i) although in general the poverty or insolvency of a plaintiff would not per se justify the court in refusing a stay, that rule was not applicable in circumstances where the plaintiff showed that there were grounds sufficient to raise a triable issue that his insolvency had been caused by the defendant's breach of contract; the plaintiff was not required to establish a prima facie case that the insolvency had been caused by the

a breach; on the material before the court there were reasonable grounds for believing
the plaintiff's allegation regarding the cause of his insolvency or that there was at least
a triable issue about it; accordingly, if the action were stayed there would be a denial
of justice (see p 674 a b and p 678 d g and h, post); *Smith v Pearl Assurance Co Ltd* [1939]
1 All ER 95 distinguished;

(ii) the provision of s 1 (7) (b)ᵃ of the Legal Aid and Advice Act 1949 that the rights
conferred on a person receiving legal aid were not to 'affect the rights . . . of other
b parties to the proceedings or the principles on which the discretion of any court . . .
is normally exercised', had no application; the defendants had no 'rights' by which
they could demand a stay, and there were no principles on which the discretion to
refuse a stay was 'normally exercised'; it was for the court to exercise its discretion
in the way which justice required in the circumstances of each case; accordingly
there was nothing in s 1 (7) (b) to prevent the court from exercising its discretion, as
c justice required to refuse the stay (see p 674 d and p 678 j to p 679 a, post).

Notes

For refusal of an application to stay proceedings where there is an arbitration agreement, see 2 Halsbury's Laws (3rd Edn) 26-28, para 61, and for cases on the subject,
see 2 Digest (Repl) 486-495, 396-443.
d For the effect of legal aid on the rights of other parties and on the exercise of a
court's discretion, see 30 Halsbury's Laws (3rd Edn) 484, 485, para 904.

For the Legal Aid and Advice Act 1949, s 1, see 25 Halsbury's Statutes (3rd Edn) 757.

Cases referred to in judgment

Cook v S [1967] 1 All ER 299; sub nom *Cook v Swinfen* [1967] 1 WLR 457, CA, Digest
e (Cont Vol C) 1088, 1779a.
Farrer v Lacy, Hartland & Co (1885) 28 Ch D 482, 54 LJCh 808, 52 LT 38, CA, 51 Digest
(Repl) 846, 3999.
Ford v Clarksons Holidays Ltd [1971] 3 All ER 454, [1971] 1 WLR 1412, CA.
Law v Garrett (1878) 8 Ch D 26, 38 LT 3, CA, 2 Digest (Repl) 479, 360.
Saxton, Re, Johnson v Saxton [1962] 2 All ER 618, [1962] 1 WLR 859; rvsd [1962] 3
f All ER 92, [1962] 1 WLR 968, CA, 51 Digest (Repl) 609, 2291.
Smith v Pearl Assurance Co Ltd [1939] 1 All ER 95, 55 TLR 335, 83 Sol Jo 113, CA, 2
Digest (Repl) 485, 394.
Willesford v Watson (1873) 8 Ch App 473, 42 LJCh 447, 28 LT 428, 37 JP 548, 2 Digest
(Repl) 482, 378.

g **Interlocutory appeal**

This was an appeal by the plaintiff, John Malcolm Fakes, trading as John M Fakes &
Co, against the order of Griffiths J made in chambers on 28th June 1972, affirming
the order made by Master Bickford Smith on 30th May 1972, that all further proceedings in the plaintiff's action against the defendants, Taylor Woodrow Construction Ltd, be stayed pursuant to s 4 of the Arbitration Act 1950. The facts are set out
h in the judgment of Lord Denning MR.

D G *Wright* for the plaintiff.
H J *Lloyd* for the defendants.

LORD DENNING MR. Mr John M Fakes is a plumber. He did a lot of work for
Taylor Woodrow Construction Ltd and now seeks to be paid. His claim comes to over
j £80,000. He has brought an action for it. Taylor Woodrow dispute the claim and wish
it to be referred to arbitration.

The claim arises out of several buildings for which Taylor Woodrow were the main
contractors. They employed Mr Fakes as a sub-contractor for the plumbing work.

---

a Section 1 (7) (b) is set out at p 674 c, post

The sub-contracts were on Taylor Woodrow's usual forms of sub-contract. One of these buildings was a college of architecture called Mexborough House. In May 1967 Taylor Woodrow employed Mr Fakes to do the plumbing and drainage work for £37,353. Another building was for the Commercial Union in Leadenhall Street. In March 1969 Taylor Woodrow employed Mr Fakes to provide and fit flashings for £653. Another building was an extension for Fords at Dagenham. In April 1969 Taylor Woodrow employed Mr Fakes to do work for £365.

The sub-contract with which we are most concerned is the work at the college of architecture. It contained stipulations as to the plumbing programme. By an order dated 25th January 1967 (which formed part of the contract) Taylor Woodrow set out a plumbing programme by which Mr Fakes was to commence work on 13th February 1967 and complete it by June 1969. Unfortunately the building itself was much delayed. So much so that Taylor Woodrow could not give Mr Fakes access to it so as to do his plumbing work. He says that his men were only engaged in dribs and drabs—a few at a time and at intervals—which made the work much more expensive for him. Furthermore he says that Taylor Woodrow did not pay him the moneys for the work as and when he did it. He points to cl 17 (b), in the sub-contract which says that—

'the Contractor shall pay to the Sub-Contractor the total value of work executed by him in respect of which payment has been made to the Contractor on the certificate of the Engineer/Architect and such payments to the Sub-Contractor shall be made within 4 days of the receipt of any such payment by the Contractor.'

Mr Fakes also says that it was agreed in a letter of 1st February 1967 (which formed part of the contract) that the retention would only be 5 per cent (instead of the usual 10 per cent) and the remaining 5 per cent to be retained for six months only—and applied to each section as it was completed. Mr Fakes says that the sections were not completed in time through no fault of his; and so he was kept out of his money in that way.

I need not, however, go into the details. The long and short of it is that Mr Fakes says that Taylor Woodrow did not pay him the sums which they should have done, at the times when they should have done, and that on this account he was unable to pay his men or keep them going on the work. For instance, he says that at the end of 1969 there was some £7,000 which he ought to have been paid, but he had not been. He was put into such grave difficulty that by April 1970 he had, in effect, to cease work. He said it was all Taylor Woodrow's fault. He alleges that by reason of Taylor Woodrow's fault he himself was made insolvent and his business was ruined. It does appear that later on in 1970 he was sued to judgment by various creditors, and that he is without means.

In that plight, Mr Fakes in August 1970 sought legal aid. He was given it—in the first instance—to get counsel's opinion. That opinion was so strong in his favour that in May 1971 Mr Fakes was given a full certificate to bring an action against Taylor Woodrow. The lawyers did a great deal of work on his case. In February 1972 a writ was issued on his behalf against Taylor Woodrow. On 3rd March 1972 there was a statement of claim running into 18 pages, with schedules of 23 pages. It set out his claim coming to over £80,000. Some of it was for money actually due to him. Other of it was for damages for the delay and for the damage to his business.

Faced with this formidable statement of claim, Taylor Woodrow took out a summons to stay the proceedings on the ground that there was an arbitration clause in their form of sub-contract. It says: 'If any dispute question or difference arises between the Contractor and Sub-Contractor in connection with this Sub-Contract, it shall . . . be referred' to arbitration.

So Taylor Woodrow wish to go to arbitration. Mr Fakes resists it. He says that if he is forced to go to arbitration, it will be tantamount to losing his claim altogether. He gets legal aid for this action in the courts: but he cannot get it for an arbitration. Legal aid is not available in arbitration. He is advised that it would cost him some

a £4,000 to go to arbitration, which he has not got. Even then he could not take up any
award; because he would have to pay the arbitrator's fees of about £1,200, which he
has not got. Even if he had the money, his other creditors would take it rather than
let him spend it on an arbitration. Both the master and the judge ordered the action
to be stayed. The judge said:

b   'I, like Master Bickford Smith, have great sympathy with the plaintiff. But I
      take the view, as did the master, that I am clearly bound by the decisions of the
      Court of Appeal.'

So I turn to the previous decisions. The first is *Smith v Pearl Assurance Co Ltd*[1]. It
was long before legal aid. It was under the Poor Persons Rules. A poor man issued
a writ against an insurance company under the Third Parties (Rights against Insurers)
c Act 1930. The insurance company disputed liability and demanded that the matter
should go to arbitration. This court held that the action must be stayed. It said in
effect: 'We are sorry, but your poverty is a personal disability of yours. We cannot
do anything to help a poor man. You must go to arbitration.' The next case is *Ford v
Clarksons Holidays Ltd*[2]. The plaintiff brought an action in the county court. It was
only for £200 damages. He said that it would cost less in the county court than in an
d arbitration. The county court judge refused a stay because of the extra expense.
Stephenson LJ said[3] that reason 'might have been cogent but for the decision of this
court in *Smith v Pearl Assurance Co Ltd*[4]'.

I must confess that I am not at all content with the reasoning in *Smith v Pearl Assurance Co Ltd*[4]. In any case I am not prepared to extend it to cases where a man is legally
aided. One of the objects of legal aid is to remove the reproach that 'there is one law
e for the rich and another for the poor'. It is bad enough for a poor man to be faced with
an arbitration clause, usually in a printed form which he has never read. It is much
worse if the courts then insist that he is to go off to arbitration where there is no legal
aid. That would mean that he is denied a remedy simply because he cannot afford it.
The rich man, who can afford arbitration, has his remedy there. The poor man, who
cannot afford arbitration, has no remedy. That will not do. If the poor man cannot
f afford arbitration, he should not be compelled to go there. He should be allowed to
continue his action in the courts which is the only place where he can obtain justice,
situated as he is.

Apart from this, however, this case is quite distinguishable from *Smith v Pearl
Assurance Co Ltd*[4]. Mr Fakes says that his misfortune and in particular, his insolvency,
has been brought about by Taylor Woodrow's breaches of contract, in that they did
g not give him the work as and when they should: so they did not pay him as and when
they should. It would be indeed 'the most unkindest cut of all' if they in the first
place break their contract and by doing so make him insolvent, and then in the
second place say to him, 'owing to your insolvency, which we have brought about, we
are going to make you go to arbitration, which you cannot afford'. A parallel can be
found in the cases in which this court orders security for costs. In *Farrer v Lacy,
h Hartland & Co*[5], Bowen LJ said:

      'Suppose the plaintiff in that case had been right on the point of law, his in-
      solvency would have arisen from the wrongful act complained of in the action.
      To have required security for costs on the ground of an insolvency which (if the
      plaintiff was right) the defendant had wrongly caused, might have been a denial
j   of justice.'

---

1 [1939] 1 All ER 95
2 [1971] 3 All ER 454, [1971] 1 WLR 1412
3 [1971] 3 All ER at 459, [1971] 1 WLR at 1418
4 [1939] 1 All ER 95
5 (1885) 28 Ch D 482 at 485

So here also, if Mr Fakes's insolvency arose by reason of Taylor Woodrow's breach, it would be a denial of justice to require him now to go to arbitration—which he cannot afford—instead of proceeding in the courts—where he can get legal aid.

Counsel for Taylor Woodrow was inclined to accept this proposition, but he said there must be a strong prima facie case that the insolvency was caused by the breach. I think it is sufficient if there are reasonable grounds for believing that Mr Fakes's assertions may be correct or there is a triable issue about it. On the materials before us, I think there are reasonable grounds. At any rate there is an issue fit to be tried. It can only be tried if he is allowed to continue this action. I would therefore hold that the action should not be stayed.

All this is subject to a point raised by counsel for Taylor Woodrow on the Legal Aid and Advice Act 1949. Section 1 (7) provides:

'Save as expressly provided by this Part of this Act or by regulations made thereunder . . . (b) the rights conferred by this Part of this Act on a person receiving legal aid shall not affect the rights or liabilities of other parties to the proceedings or the principles on which the discretion of any court or tribunal is normally exercised.'

We had to consider that subsection in Re Saxton, Johnson v Saxton[1], and we had it in mind in Cook v S[2]. I do not think the subsection applies to this case. Taylor Woodrow have no 'rights' conferred on them by which they can demand a stay. And, there are no principles on which the discretion 'is normally exercised'. It all depends on the circumstances of each case. It is open to the court to exercise its discretion in the way which justice requires. In this case justice requires that this action should not be stayed.

I asked counsel for Taylor Woodrow why they were so keen to insist on the case going to arbitration. I pointed out to him that the matter in dispute would be just as well tried by an official referee. Counsel for Taylor Woodrow very frankly admitted that the reason was because they thought the claim was ill-founded and that the quickest way to stop it was to stay the action—believing that Mr Fakes had no money to take it to arbitration. That would make Taylor Woodrow judges in their own cause. By staying his action at law, they would get rid of his claim. This attitude makes me very unwilling to stay the action—especially as the legal aid authorities consider that he has a case fit to be tried. I think this is a case where, if the action were stayed, justice would be denied.

I would therefore allow the appeal. The action should continue. It should not be stayed.

MEGAW LJ. It is with very real regret and diffidence that I find myself unable to agree with the conclusion which Lord Denning MR has just expressed. If the matter were to arise afresh without the hampering effect of a past decision of this court and without the effect of legislation passed by Parliament, there would indeed in my view be much to be said in favour of allowing this plaintiff to pursue his claim by litigation in the courts and not requiring him to carry out the agreement in the clause of the contract whereby it was provided that such disputes should be referred to arbitration. But there is the decision of this court to which Lord Denning MR has referred, Smith v Pearl Assurance Co Ltd[3], which is binding on this court. The principle is I think clearly set out in the judgment of Clauson LJ. The learned Lord Justice, having clearly indicated that the only reason put forward for not enforcing the agreement as to reference to arbitration was the financial position of the plaintiff, went on to say this[4]:

'In my judgment, it can only be in some very exceptional case indeed that the court would be justified in holding that one party's mere personal disability

1 [1962] 3 All ER 92, [1962] 1 WLR 968
2 [1967] 1 All ER 299, [1967] 1 WLR 457
3 [1939] 1 All ER 95
4 [1939] 1 All ER at 98

a   of this character would be sufficient reason for the court to exercise the power, given by the Arbitration Act, 1889, s. 4, of overriding the contractual right of arbitration.'

I do not find it necessary because of the view that I take of the effect of the statute, to express a final view whether or not the exception to the principle which Lord Denning MR has suggested is one which ought to be treated as being an exception:

b   that is to say, that the potential plaintiff may be able to show that his poverty has been caused by the wrongful act of the potential defendant.

Assuming that that be a permissible exception, in my view counsel for the defendants is right in saying that that exception could only properly be brought into operation if in the particular case the plaintiff showed a prima facie case that his poverty was brought about by the wrongful act of the defendant on which he seeks to litigate against the defendant. We have in the present case an affidavit sworn on behalf of the

c   defendants. We have an affidavit in reply sworn on behalf of the plaintiff. Without going into detail, in my view the plaintiff falls short of showing a prima facie case that his lack of means was caused by some fault in law on the part of the defendants. It may or may not ultimately turn out to be so, but all we can deal with at the moment is the evidence as it stands before the court as it appears in those two affidavits and the

d   exhibits thereto, including such of the correspondence as has been brought to our notice.

In passing, I would say that in my judgment it would be wrong to take into account, in deciding whether or not there is such a prima facie case, the question whether or not the plaintiff has been granted legal aid. Just as it would be wrong, in general, to make an assumption against a party in any matter because he had been refused a

e   legal aid certificate, so the opposite must apply. It would be wrong to make an assumption in a party's favour as to the merits because he has been granted such a certificate.

Apart, however, from any question arising out of the decision in *Smith v Pearl Assurance Co Ltd*[1], there is the legislative provision of s 1 (7) of the Legal Aid and Advice Act 1949. That subsection, so far as is relevant, reads in these terms:

f   'Save as expressly provided by this Part of this Act or by regulations made thereunder [Then I omit para (*a*) as irrelevant:] (*b*) the rights conferred by this part of this Act on a person receiving legal aid shall not affect the rights or liabilities of other parties to the proceedings or the principles on which the discretion of any court or tribunal is normally exercised.'

g   That provision fell to be considered by this court in *Re Saxton, Johnson v Saxton*[2]. In that case Wilberforce J in the court below in an order for directions had given a direction that the defendants should make available a document to the plaintiffs in order that that document might be examined by a handwriting expert on behalf of the plaintiffs. The plaintiffs were legally aided. The defendants were not. The learned judge, in making that order, had imposed a condition that the report of the

h   handwriting expert when it was received should be shown to the other party. The learned judge in giving his decision to that effect had said[3]:

        'I should not lose sight of the fact that the plaintiffs are legally aided, so that costs incurred by the defendants in relation to this matter are likely to rest on them whatever the result of the action is.'

j   This court varied that order by removing the condition that the report of the expert should be made available to the other party. In dealing with that matter, Lord Denning MR said this[4]:

---

1   [1939] 1 All ER 95
2   [1962] 3 All ER 92, [1962] 1 WLR 968
3   [1962] 2 All ER 618 at 620, [1962] 1 WLR 859 at 862
4   [1962] 3 All ER at 94, [1962] 1 WLR at 971

'The judge seems to have been influenced by the fact that the plaintiffs were
legally aided; and I must say that I sympathise with his point of view. It seems
very hard on the defendants that the plaintiffs should be able to conduct their
case at the expense of the state, including the cost of employing a handwriting
expert to make highly skilled scientific tests and yet not disclose the result to the
defendants. For it means that the defendants, in order to meet the case, will
have to employ a handwriting expert of their own, who will also have to make
scientific tests, all at great expense, which they will have little or no chance of
recovering from their legally aided opponents. Yet the legislature has said that
this aspect of the case must be ignored. The courts must disregard the fact that
the plaintiffs are legally aided and must exercise their discretion in the way in
which it would be exercised if they were not legally aided. This is made clear by
s. 1 (7) (b) of the Legal Aid and Advice Act, 1949, which says that the rights conferred on a person receiving legal aid "shall not affect the rights or liabilities of
other parties to the proceedings or the principles on which the discretion of any
court or tribunal is normally exercised".'

Now, that provision of s 1 (7) of the Legal Aid and Advice Act 1949 normally falls
to be considered in this aspect—that a party to legal proceedings must not be at a
disadvantage by reason of the fact that he is legally aided or by reason of the fact that
while he is legally aided his opponent is not. But the provision which Parliament has
made is not confined to preventing that discrimination against a party who is legally
aided; it applies equally to prevent discrimination against a party who is not legally
aided by reason of the fact that the other party is legally aided. In the present case,
therefore, as I see it, that statutory provision involves that in dealing with the question
of discretion whether or not proceedings in the courts should be stayed and the
disputes referred to arbitration because of an agreement as to arbitration in a contract
between the parties, we have to disregard the fact that one party is legally aided, or,
if proceedings are allowed to proceed in the court, may be legally aided. We have to
decide the matter, because Parliament has said so, on the principles on which the
discretion of the court is normally exercised. That involves disregarding for this
purpose any consideration of the right conferred by this Part of this Act on a person
receiving legal aid.

Now, what is the principle on which the courts normally act? It is set out in a
passage from the speech of Lord Selborne LC in *Willesford v Watson*[1], as follows:

'If parties choose to determine for themselves that they will have a domestic
forum instead of resorting to the ordinary Courts, then since that Act of Parliament [the Common Law Procedure Act 1854] was passed a *prima facie* duty
is cast upon the Courts to act upon such an agreement.'

As it is put in Russell on the Law of Arbitration[2]:

'Once the party moving for a stay has shown that the dispute is within a valid
and subsisting arbitration clause, the burden of showing cause why effect should
not be given to the agreement to submit is upon the party opposing the application to stay.'

Lord Selborne LC's statement of the law was approved by this court in *Law v
Garrett*[3]. It has been cited recently by Davies LJ in *Ford v Clarksons Holidays Ltd*[4]. In
that same case Edmund Davies LJ stated[5] what I conceive to be the same principle
in different words:

1 (1873) 8 Ch App 473 at 480
2 18th Edn (1970), p 153
3 (1878) 8 Ch D 26 at 37
4 [1971] 3 All ER 454 at 457, [1971] 1 WLR 1412 at 1416
5 [1971] 3 All ER 459, [1971] 1 WLR at 1418

a   '. . . but I would certainly direct my mind in the way in which the court has done in a number of the reported cases, namely, that, once the party moving for a stay has shown that the dispute is within a valid and subsisting arbitration clause, the burden of showing cause why effect should not be given to the agreement to submit is on the party opposing the application to stay.'

b   Is it permissible in this case to take into account, not merely the plaintiff's poverty, but also the fact that if he is allowed to proceed by litigation he will have the advantage of legal aid, whereas if he has to go by arbitration, he will not have that advantage? Unless it is permissible to take that factor into account, then there is nothing put forward in this case which enables the court, in my view, to depart from the general principle to which I have referred. Poverty in itself clearly would not be such a matter:
c   the proof of poverty by a party who is seeking arbitration or is opposing arbitration would be totally irrelevant in itself to the question whether arbitration or litigation is the proper course for the court to order where there is a discretion. It is equally irrelevant whether or not the poverty was caused by the default of the opposite party. That factor taken by itself, and omitting the consequence in respect of legal aid, is totally irrelevant to the question whether arbitration or litigation is the proper course for the
d   court to order. Accordingly, as I see it, if we were to give effect here to the only point put forward in favour of litigation rather than arbitration, we should be doing the very thing which, as I interpret it, Parliament has said that we may not do by what it has said in s 1 (7) (b) of the Legal Aid and Advice Act 1949. We should be departing from the principles which the court normally applies; and we should be doing so because of, and by reference to, the rights conferred on a person receiving legal aid.
e   Accordingly, as I say, with regret and diffidence, I would dismiss this appeal.

SIR GORDON WILLMER. The judgments which Lord Denning MR and Megaw LJ have delivered put me in the embarrassing position of having to cast the decisive vote on what I too regard as a very difficult question. Like my Lords, I think we must start from the principles laid down by this court in *Smith v Pearl Assurance Co Ltd*[1].
f   I take that decision to be a decision of principle as to what may and what may not properly be taken into consideration by a court exercising its discretion whether or not to stay proceedings where there is an arbitration clause. It was held in that case that the mere fact of the plaintiff's poverty, which would have rendered it financially impossible for him to go to arbitration, was not per se a sufficient ground on which the court could refuse to order a stay. In the present case the position is perhaps even
g   stronger against the plaintiff than it was in *Smith's* case[1]. For there the plaintiff was suing under the Third Parties (Rights against Insurers) Act 1930 which gave him, as a passenger in a motor car, a right to sue the owner-driver's insurers for the damages which he had sustained. There was an arbitration clause in the contract between the owner-driver and the insurers. The plaintiff was, of course, a stranger to that contract, but he was nonetheless held to be bound by its terms. In the present case, however,
h   the plaintiff is in no way a stranger to the arbitration clause, because it forms part of the contract into which he himself entered. He says that he signed the contract without reading it and without noticing that it did in fact contain an arbitration clause. But on well-established principle that statement will not avail him.
    That was the position in 1939, at a time when there was no legal aid scheme in force. The particular plaintiff in *Smith's* case[1] was taking advantage of the Poor Persons Rules.
j   But, as I see it, the principle decided in that case remained unaltered with the advent of the legal aid scheme. We are therefore in this position, that the mere fact of the plaintiff's poverty or insolvency is not per se a sufficient ground on which this court, or the court below, could exercise its discretion by refusing a stay.

1 [1939] 1 All ER 95

On the hearing before us, however, a new point has been raised which was not before
the learned master or the learned judge below. It arises from the plaintiff's allegation
that his poverty and indeed insolvency were directly induced by the very breaches of
contract on the part of the defendants of which he complains. No such point as that
was before the court in *Smith v Pearl Assurance Co Ltd*[1]; but I do note that in the passage which has already been cited by Megaw LJ, Clauson LJ[2] did express the view
that there might be very exceptional cases in which the rule he was applying should
not be applied. The question arises, therefore, whether the plaintiff's allegation as to
the way in which his poverty was induced does make this case an exceptional case so
as to take it out of the ordinary rule exemplified in *Smith v Pearl Assurance Co Ltd*[1].
It has to be recognised that the plaintiff's allegations of breach of contract on the part
of the defendants are denied. It also has to be recognised that that conflict between
the two parties cannot be finally resolved in these present interlocutory proceedings
before us. It has been urged by counsel for the defendants that at least the plaintiff
ought to be able to show a strong prima facie case before such an allegation can be
relied on to prevent the application of the ordinary rule. For my part, I think that is
putting it rather too high. Clearly the court must examine the charges of breach of
contract which are made, and clearly, if the court can readily see that they are manifestly trumped-up charges, it would have to disregard them. But it seems to me that
if the court, after examining the charges, comes to the conclusion that there is some
reasonable probability that the charges, or some of them, may be well founded, that
is sufficient at the present stage of this litigation. This is not altogether an unusual task
for the court to have to undertake at the interlocutory stage. I am reminded of the
days when I sat in the matrimonial court and had occasion from time to time to consider applications brought before the court on originating summons for leave to
institute divorce proceedings within three years of the date of the marriage. The Act
then in force provided that such leave could be obtained in cases of exceptional
hardship or exceptional depravity. The application would be supported by an affidavit
in which allegations would be made, whether going to depravity or hardship; but
it was clearly impossible at that stage to reach any final conclusion whether the allegations which were made were well founded or not. But the approach of the court in
such cases was that which I have just suggested, namely, looking at the whole background of the case, to ask whether there is some reasonable probability that the
charges may be true. In the present case I think it is right to approach the question
now raised at the interlocutory stage in the same way. I confess that I have had some
difficulty in making up my mind whether there is in the present case a sufficient
probability that the plaintiff's charges of breach of contract may be true. But, on the
whole, I have come to the conclusion, for the reasons stated by Lord Denning MR,
that there is sufficient material here to justify us in saying that there is a reasonable
probability that the defendants' breaches of contract did induce the plaintiff's present
poverty and insolvency. If that is right, then it seems to me that it would be a positive
denial of justice if in these exceptional circumstances we were to apply the strict rule
as laid down in *Smith v Pearl Assurance Co Ltd*[1]. The circumstances which I have
mentioned are, as I see them, sufficient to make this an exceptional case, such as was
envisaged by Clauson LJ in *Smith's* case[2] in the passage to which Megaw LJ has already
referred.

That, however, does not quite end all the difficulties of this case, because my Lords
in their judgments have disagreed as to the effect of s 1 (7) (*b*) of the Legal Aid and
Advice Act 1949. I do not want to repeat in detail the arguments put forward in
relation to that. I think it will be sufficient if I say that, after much hesitation, I have
come to the conclusion that the view expressed by Lord Denning MR is the right
view, and that in the circumstances of this case there is nothing in s 1 (7) (*b*) of the

1   [1939] 1 All ER 95
2   [1939] 1 All ER at 98

a Legal Aid and Advice Act 1949 to prevent us from giving effect to the very exceptional circumstances of the case to which I have already referred. In those circumstances, not without hesitation and diffidence, I have come to the conclusion, in agreement with Lord Denning MR, that this appeal ought to be allowed.

Appeal allowed; stay removed; action allowed to proceed. Leave to appeal to the House of
b *Lords refused.*

Solicitors: *Denton, Hall & Burgin* (for the plaintiff); *McKenna & Co* (for the defendants).

Wendy Shockett   Barrister.

c

Chesterfield Football Club Ltd v Secretary of State for Social Services

d QUEEN'S BENCH DIVISION
BEAN J
16th NOVEMBER, 1st DECEMBER 1972

National insurance – Contributions – Employer's contributions – Liability to pay – No services rendered by employee in contribution week – Employee incapable of work and would but for
e *that incapacity have been working – Incapable of work – Employer a football club – Employee a professional footballer – Employee incapable of playing football in consequence of injury – Employee capable of doing other work – Whether employer liable to pay contributions where employee incapable of following his regular occupation – National Insurance Act 1965, s 8 (5) – National Insurance (Industrial Injuries) Act 1965, s 3 (2) (b).*

f S was employed by a football club as a professional footballer. He played for the club from 1952 until 1968. In October 1968 a medical examination of S revealed that, in consequence of injuries that he had received, he was incapable of work as a footballer but capable of other work. It was subsequently agreed that S should give up football and leave the club. He left in May 1969. During the period 21st October 1968 to 9th May 1969 S was paid wages by the club and did not work for anyone else. During that period S continued to be included in the class of employed persons for
g the purposes of the National Insurance Act 1965 and the club remained liable to pay insurance contributions in respect of S unless, during the relevant period he was, within s 8 (5) (b) (i)ᵃ of the 1965 Act, 'incapable of work and would but for the incapacity have been working'. The Secretary of State held that the club was not exempt from liability since S, although incapable of playing football, was capable of other work. The club appealed.
h

Held – The appeal would be allowed. Since the 1965 Act imposed a pecuniary burden on the club it was to be construed strictly. During the relevant period S was 'incapable of work' within s 8 (5) (b) (i) since he was incapable of following his regular occupation as a professional footballer (see p 684 f and g, post).

j a Section 8 (5), so far as material, provides: 'Where, as respects any employed contributor's employment—(a) no services are rendered by an employed person in any contribution week; and (b) no remuneration is paid wholly or partly in respect of any day in that week other than a day on which he either—(i) is incapable of work and would but for the incapacity have been working; (ii) or does not work in a normal week, then that employment shall, in relation to that week be disregarded for the purposes of subsections (3) and (4) of this section . . .'

Notes

For national insurance contributions by insured persons and employers, see 27
Halsbury's Laws (3rd Edn) 690, 691, para 1249.

For the National Insurance Act 1965, s 8, see 23 Halsbury's Statutes (3rd Edn) 262.

Cases referred to in judgment

Cape Brandy Syndicate v Inland Revenue Comrs [1921] 1 KB 64, 90 LJKB 113, 125 LT 108,
    12 Tax Cas 358; *affd* [1921] 2 KB 403, 90 LJKB 461, CA, 44 Digest (Repl) 255, 798.

Padgett v Minister of Pensions and National Insurance (22nd July 1960) unreported.

Appeal

On 29th August 1969 Arthur Gordon Sutherland, secretary/manager of the Chesterfield Football Club Ltd of the Recreation Ground, Chesterfield, Derbyshire ('the
club') applied for the decision of the Secretary of State for Social Services under s 64 (1)
of the National Insurance Act 1965 and s 35 (1) of the National Insurance (Industrial
Injuries) Act 1965 of the question whether the club was liable as employer to pay
contributions under s 3 of the National Insurance Act 1965 and s 2 (1) (a) of the
National Insurance (Industrial Injuries) Act 1965 in respect of Gerald Sears for the
period from 21st October 1968 to 9th May 1969. On 28th January 1970 the
Secretary of State appointed Mr P E Abbott, barrister and member of the Solicitor's
Office of the Department of Health and Social Security, to hold an inquiry into
questions arising on the application and to report thereon. Mr Abbott held an
inquiry at Chesterfield on 3rd March 1970.

On consideration of the evidence given at the inquiry the Secretary of State found
the following facts: (1) The club was incorporated on 20th August 1919. (2) Mr Sears
was 35 years of age. He joined the club as a professional footballer at the age of 17
in 1952 and continued to play football for the club until 1968. (3) Successive written
agreements were in force between Mr Sears and the club, the last being dated 14th
August 1967. In May 1968 the club exercised its option in writing under the agreement whereby the agreement was continued to 30th June 1969. (4) On commencement of the agreement Mr Sears attended the club for all forms of physical and other
training. He played for the club at home and away matches. He received orders
from the club's team manager and trainers. (5) A club doctor was available to attend
to players as necessary, and to supervise medical treatment. (6) On 23rd December
1967 Mr Sears sustained an injury to his back during a game of football. He was
treated by the club's doctor. He continued to train and play for the club. (7) In
February 1968, following consultation with the club's doctor, he entered hospital
for 2½ weeks. (8) On discharge from hospital he was unable to play football. He was
under the care of an orthopaedic specialist as an out-patient. He attended at the
club on almost every weekday for physiotherapy under the supervision of the club's
doctor. He attended matches for his own amusement. He was not required to, nor
did he do anything for the club, other than attend for physiotherapy. (9) In June
1968 Mr Sears re-entered hospital for an operation on his ankle. On discharge he
continued to attend the club for physiotherapy and to attend matches, as described
in (8) above. His attendance for physiotherapy was on the instructions of the club's
doctor. (10) On 12th September 1968 Mr Sears was examined by a medical officer
of the Ministry of Health, who said that in his opinion Mr Sears was unfit for work as
a professional footballer, but was fit for other work within certain limits. (11) On
14th October 1968 Mr Sears was examined by a different medical officer of the
Ministry of Health, who said that in his opinion Mr Sears was incapable of work as a
professional footballer, but was capable of other work. (12) On 10th December 1968
the Chesterfield Local Tribunal dismissed the appeal of Mr Sears against a decision of
the insurance officer that sickness benefit was not payable from 22nd October 1968
to 23rd October 1968 on the grounds that Mr Sears had not proved incapacity for
work owing to some specific disease or bodily or mental disablement. (13) On 3rd

a   February 1969 the Football League orthopaedic specialist reported that Mr Sears was unlikely to recover enough to return to first class football. Accordingly, it was agreed between Mr Sears and the club that it would be in his interests to give up professional football. (14) Until the receipt of the report both Mr Sears and the club had hoped that he would eventually be able to resume playing for the club. (15) About the end of February 1969 compensation in the sum of £750 was paid to

b   Mr Sears under an insurance scheme operated by the Football League. The club received £1,000 under the same scheme for the loss of Mr Sears's services. Mr Sears continued to attend the club for physiotherapy. He remained under the supervision of the club's doctor. (16) In May 1969 Mr Sears completed negotiations for a window cleaning business which he wished to buy. Accordingly, Mr Sears and the club agreed orally that his contract should be terminated. (17) Throughout the period 21st October

c   1968 to 9th May 1969 Mr Sears was paid by the club in accordance with the agreement. On leaving the club he received a gratuity in view of his past services. (18) Throughout the period following his discharge from hospital in February 1968 until the termination of his contract, Mr Sears was unfit to play professional football by reason of his injury. During that period he did not work for anyone else.

    It was not disputed by the club or by Mr Sears that the contract of employment between Mr Sears and the club continued in operation throughout the period from

d   21st October 1968 to 9th May 1969, that that contract was a contract of service and that Mr Sears continued to be paid remuneration in respect of each day in that period. It was accordingly accepted that Mr Sears continued to be included in the class of employed persons for the purposes of the National Insurance Act 1965 and to be employed in insurable employment within the meaning of the National Insurance (Industrial Injuries) Act 1965 and that the club remained liable as employer to pay

e   contributions for Mr Sears under those Acts unless Mr Sears's employment by the club fell, in relation to any contribution week in the period, to be disregarded by reason of s 8 (5) of the National Insurance Act 1965 or unless no contribution was payable for any week in the period by reason of s 3 (2) (b) of the National Insurance (Industrial Injuries) Act 1965.

f   It was contended on behalf of the club that Mr Sears was incapable throughout the period in question of following his regular occupation as a professional footballer and, having regard to the fact that he had been a professional footballer (a special and technical occupation) from the age of 17 and that it was therefore unreasonable to require him to seek other employment outside football, he should be treated as incapable of work for the purposes of s 8 (5) of the National Insurance Act 1965 and s 3 (2) (b) of the National Insurance (Industrial Injuries) Act 1965. In effect the club

g   contended that the words 'incapable of work' in those sections should be interpreted as meaning 'incapable of following his regular occupation'. On consideration of the above facts and the contentions of the club the Secretary of State concluded that during the period from 21st October 1968 to 9th May 1969: (1) Mr Sears was employed by the club under a contract of service and was gainfully employed in employment thereunder in Great Britain; (2) by virtue of s 1 (2) (a) of the National Insurance

h   Act 1965 Mr Sears was included in the class of employed persons for the purposes of that Act; (3) by virtue of s 1 of, and para 1 of Part I of Sch 1 to, the National Insurance (Industrial Injuries) Act 1965 Mr Sears was employed in insurable employment within the meaning of that Act; (4) by virtue of ss 3 and 11 (1) of the National Insurance Act 1965 ss 2 and 3 (1) of the National Insurance (Industrial Injuries) Act 1965 the club was liable as employer to pay contributions for Mr Sears under those

j   Acts unless Mr Sears's employment by the club fell, in relation to any contribution week in that period, to be disregarded by reason of s 8 (5) of the National Insurance Act 1965 or unless no contribution was payable for any week in that period by reason of s 3 (2) (b) of the National Insurance (Industrial Injuries) Act 1965; (5) Mr Sears was not incapable of work for any day in the period and accordingly Mr Sears's employment, in relation to any contribution week in the period, did not fall to be

disregarded by reason of the provisions of s 8 (5) of the National Insurance Act 1965
and s 3 (2) (b) of the National Insurance (Industrial Injuries) Act 1965. Accordingly *a*
the Secretary of State decided that the club was liable as employer to pay contributions in respect of Mr Sears under s 3 of the National Insurance Act 1965 and under
s 2 (1) (a) of the National Insurance (Industrial Injuries) Act 1965 for the period from
21st October 1968 to 9th May 1969.

By letter dated 22nd July 1970 the club required the Secretary of State to state a
case under s 65 (3) of the National Insurance Act 1965 and s 35 (3) of the National *b*
Insurance (Industrial Injuries) Act 1965 and in accordance with RSC Ord 111. By
notice of motion dated 15th May 1972, the club applied for an order reversing
the decision of the Secretary of State as set forth in the case stated by the Secretary
of State dated 26th April 1972.

M J Mustill QC and *D R Harter* for the club.   *c*
R A Gatehouse QC and *Gordon Slynn* for the Secretary of State.

Cur adv vult

1st December.   **BEAN J** read the following judgment. This is a motion by *d*
Chesterfield Football Club Ltd (who I will refer to as 'the club') for an order to
reverse the decision of the Secretary of State for Social Services dated 22nd April
1970, as set out in the case stated by the Secretary of State dated 26th April 1972,
that the club was liable as employer to pay contributions in respect of Gerald Sears,
under s 3 (b) of the National Insurance Act 1965 and under s 2 (1) (a) of the National
Insurance (Industrial Injuries) Act 1965, for the period from 21st October 1968 to 9th
May 1969.   *e*

The relevant facts taken from the case stated are these: (1) Gerald Sears joined
the club as a professional footballer in 1952, when he was 17, and played for the club
until 1968. (2) Successive written agreements were in force between Mr Sears and
the club. (3) On 23rd December 1967 Mr Sears sustained an injury to his back during
a game of football, but he continued to train and play for the club. (4) In February *f*
1968, following consultation with the club's doctor, Mr Sears entered hospital for
2½ weeks and then became an out-patient under the care of an orthopaedic specialist.
He also attended at the club regularly for physiotherapy under the supervision of the
club doctor. (5) In June 1968 Mr Sears entered hospital for an operation on his ankle.
On discharge he continued to attend the club for physiotherapy. (6) On 12th September 1968 and 14th October 1968 Mr Sears was examined by medical officers of
the Ministry of Health who found him to be incapable of work as a professional *g*
footballer, but capable of other work. (7) Mr Sears was held not entitled to sickness
benefit from 22nd to 23rd October 1968 on the ground that he had not proved
incapacity for work owing to some specific disease or bodily or mental disablement.
(8) On 3rd February 1969 the Football League orthopaedic specialist reported that
Mr Sears was unlikely to recover enough to return to first class football and it was
agreed between him and the club that it would be in his interest to give up professional *h*
football. He received £750 compensation and the club received £1,000 under an
insurance scheme operated by the Football League. (9) In May 1969, Mr Sears having
completed negotiations for the purchase of a business, he and the club agreed orally
that his contract should be terminated. (10) Throughout the period 21st October
1968 to 9th May 1969 Mr Sears was paid wages by the club and did not work for
anyone else. *j*

It is accepted that during this period (21st October 1968 to 9th May 1969) Mr Sears
continued to be included in the class of employed persons for the purpose of the
National Insurance Act 1965 and to be employed in insurable employment within
the meaning of the National Insurance (Industrial Injuries) Act 1965 and that the
club remained liable as employer to pay contributions in respect of Mr Sears under

those Acts unless his employment by the club fell, in relation to any contribution week in that period, to be disregarded by reason of s 8 (5) of the National Insurance Act 1965 or unless no contribution was payable for any week in the period by reason of s 3 (2) (b) of the National Insurance (Industrial Injuries) Act 1965. Put in simple language, the club was liable to pay contributions for Mr Sears during the relevant period unless he was, in the words of s 8 (5) (b) (i) of the National Insurance Act 1965, 'incapable of work and would but for the incapacity have been working'.

At the inquiry held by direction of the Secretary of State, the club contended that the words 'incapable of work' should be interpreted as meaning 'incapable of following his regular occupation' (i e as a professional footballer). The Secretary of State decided that Mr Sears was not incapable of work for any day in the period and accordingly the club was not exempted from liability to pay contributions and had to pay them under s 3 of the National Insurance Act 1965 and under s 2 (1) (a) of the National Insurance (Industrial Injuries) Act 1965 for the period from 21st October 1968 to 9th May 1969. The club now appeals to the High Court.

The narrow point in issue between the parties is surprisingly devoid of direct authority. The interpretation section, s 114 of the National Insurance Act 1965, defines 'incapable of work' as meaning 'incapable of work by reason of some specific disease or bodily or mental disablement or deemed, in accordance with regulations, to be so incapable'. That definition scarcely helps in this case because the club argues that Mr Sears was indeed incapable of work as a professional footballer, whilst the Secretary of State replies that Mr Sears was nonetheless not incapable of any work. He could, for example, have done clerical work in the relevant period.

I was referred to an unreported case, *Padgett v Minister of Pensions and National Insurance*[1], heard by Salmon J. That was an appeal by Mr Padgett, a former tax inspector, who in 1945 had been compulsorily retired from the Board of Inland Revenue on the ground of ill-health, he being a chronic sufferer from writer's cramp and prone to attacks of asthma. Mr Padgett took the view that if the board were correct in compulsorily retiring him, it followed that he was medically incapable of any kind of work and should accordingly be credited with national insurance contributions as a person incapable of work. The Minister thought otherwise and was upheld by Salmon J. In the course of his judgment, the learned judge said:

'I think it ought to be fairly obvious to any reasonable person that it is quite possible that anyone could have the misfortune to be in such a state of health as not to be incapable of carrying out the duties, for example, as a tax inspector, whereas he might well be physically or mentally fit enough to be employed in a vast variety of other occupations.'

Whilst I respectfully agree with that observation by the learned trial judge, it does not provide an answer to my problem.

Counsel for the club argued that the sensible reading of s 8 (5) (b) (i) of the National Insurance Act 1965 would be:

'Where as respects any employed contributor's employment [here, professional footballing] (a) no services are rendered by an employed person in any contribution week; and (b) no remuneration is paid wholly or partly in respect of any day in that week other than the day on which he either—(i) is incapable of work [as a footballer] and would but for the incapacity have been working [at his normal job] then that employment shall . . . be disregarded . . .'

Thus, the argument goes, if the club continued to pay Mr Sears's wages during a period in which he could not play football, no contribution is payable for that period by the club.

---

1   22nd July 1960

Counsel for the Secretary of State says that it is necessary to look at the benefits *a* section of the Insurance Acts for a key to the problem. It will be seen that the phrases 'incapable of work' and 'incapacity for work' are used interchangeably. If an insured person is not capable of work then no payment is made by him on his insurance card. He is credited with his contribution and becomes entitled to sickness benefit under s 19 (1) (*b*) of the National Insurance Act 1965 or to industrial injury benefit under s 5 (1) (*a*) of the National Insurance (Industrial Injuries) Act 1965. But, argued counsel, *b* as from 21st October 1968 Mr Sears was no longer entitled to sickness benefit because he was no longer incapable of work (even though he was incapable of playing football). Thus it will be seen that the arguments are nicely balanced.

It seems to me that the wording of the Acts is quite ambiguous on the narrow point I have to decide. Both the interpretations put before me are equally attractive depending whether they are seen through the eyes of the employer or through the *c* eyes of the insurance authority, and the Insurance Acts being statutes, parts of which impose pecuniary burdens, those parts have to be construed strictly. I cannot do better than quote a short passage from Maxwell on the Interpretation of Statutes[1]:

'It is a well-settled rule of law that all charges upon the subject must be imposed by clear and unambiguous language, because in some degree they operate as penalties: the subject is not to be taxed unless the language of the *d* statute clearly imposes the obligation, and language must not be strained in order to tax a transaction which, had the legislature thought of it, would have been covered by appropriate words. "In a taxing Act," said Rowlatt J.[2], "one has to look merely at what is clearly said. There is no room for any intendment. There is no equity about a tax. There is no presumption as to a tax. Nothing is to be read in, nothing is to be implied. One can only look fairly at the language *e* used".'

The matter does not quite end there. The good sense of the situation favours the club who were being good employers by continuing to pay the wages of an employee injured in the course of his employment as a footballer and unable for a period to play football. If, for part of that period, the club is to be made liable to *f* pay insurance contributions because the footballer might have done some other and different work (for example, as a clerk or a watchman) then I think that requires the clearest possible wording in the appropriate statute, so that the employers know exactly where they stand.

For these reasons, I make an order quashing the decision of the Secretary of State dated 22nd April 1970.

g

Appeal allowed. Decision of the Secretary of State quashed.

Solicitors: *Herbert Smith & Co* (for the club); *Solicitor, Department of Health and Social Security.*

h

E H Hunter Esq   Barrister.

1   12th Edn (1969), p 256
2   In *Cape Brandy Syndicate v Inland Revenue Comrs* [1921] 1 KB 64 at 71

a

Ubsdell v Paterson

NATIONAL INDUSTRIAL RELATIONS COURT

SIR SAMUEL COOKE, MR F J FIELDING AND MR W C McDOWALL

7th, 14th DECEMBER 1972

b

Employment – Redundancy – Dismissal by reason of redundancy – Change of ownership of business – Re-engagement – Sale of business by former employer – Condition that purchasers of business make written offer of re-engagement to all employees in business on same terms as in existing contracts – No written offer made – Employee working for purchasers for two weeks for same wages paid by former employer – Employee's wages then changed by purchasers – Employee subsequently dismissed by purchasers – Whether conduct of purchasers

c

and employee amounting to offer and acceptance of re-engagement on terms not differing from previous contract – Whether employee entitled to redundancy payment from former employer – Redundancy Payments Act 1965, ss 3 (2) (a), 13 (2).

From 1960 to the end of 1971 the employee worked for his employer as the head waiter in an hotel. His remuneration was £10 per week plus a share of the 'tronc'. On 3rd January 1972 the employer sold the hotel business to M P Ltd. The contract for the

d

sale of the business provided that M P Ltd should, before the completion date, make to each employee in the business an offer in writing to re-engage him on terms which did not differ from those of his existing contract of employment. M P Ltd made no such written offer of re-engagement to the employee. For two weeks following 3rd January the employee worked for M P Ltd and received wages from them calculated on the same basis as that on which he had been paid by his former employer. He was

e

then told that his terms of employment would be changed so that his remuneration would be £20 a week and no more. He agreed to the change. On 18th February M P Ltd dismissed the employee who then claimed a redundancy payment from his former employer. It was contended by the former employer that by virtue of ss 3 (2)*ᵃ*

and 13 (2)*ᵇ* of the Redundancy Payments Act 1965 the employee was not entitled to a redundancy payment because his contract of employment had been renewed by M P

f

Ltd on the same terms and conditions as those in his contract with the former employer.

Held – (i) The mere fact that the employee had for a short period worked for M P Ltd and accepted wages from them on the same basis as under his former contract of employment was not necessarily conclusive evidence that there had been an offer

g

by conduct by M P Ltd to re-engage the employee on all the terms and conditions of his previous contract, or that the employee had accepted such an offer. The requirements of s 3 (2) (a) of the 1965 Act were not satisfied unless the new employer had offered, by words or conduct, to re-engage the employee on terms which did not differ from those of the previous contract and the employee had, by words or conduct,

h

accepted that offer; if a previous employer wished to rely on s 3 (2) (a), the burden rested on him to show that there had been such offer and acceptance (see p 687 g to j, post).

(ii) On the evidence the former employer had not discharged the burden of proving that the requirements of s 3 (2) (a) had been satisfied. Accordingly the employee was entitled to a redundancy payment (see p 688 d, post).

j **Notes**

For redundancy payments after a change in the ownership of a business, see Supplement to 38 Halsbury's Laws (3rd Edn) para 808c, 3.

---

a   Section 3 (2) is set out at p 687 c to e, post

b   Section 13 (2) is set out at p 686 j to p 687 a, post

For the Redundancy Payments Act 1965, ss 3, 13, see 12 Halsbury's Statutes (3rd *a* Edn) 240, 249.

Case cited
Havenhand v Thomas Black Ltd [1968] 2 All ER 1037, [1968] 1 WLR 1241, DC.

Appeal   *b*
This was an appeal by Ronald Edward Ubsdell against the decision of an industrial tribunal (chairman K R Eldin Taylor Esq) sitting at Southampton, dated 24th August 1972, that the appellant was not entitled to a redundancy payment from the respondent, Nora Irene Paterson. The facts are set out in the judgment of the court.

R N Titheridge for the appellant.
Christopher Whybrow for the respondent.   *c*

Cur adv vult

14th December.   **SIR SAMUEL COOKE** read the following judgment of the court. This is an appeal from a decision of an industrial tribunal, sitting at Southampton, whereby they dismissed an application by the appellant claiming that he was entitled *d* to a redundancy payment under the Redundancy Payments Act 1965.

The appellant had been employed at the Redroof Hotel since 1945. In about 1960, the respondent, Mrs Paterson, became the owner of the hotel, and she remained the owner of it until the end of 1971. On 20th December 1971 she entered into a contract to sell the hotel and the business to a company called Micro Properties Ltd and that company took control on or about the completion date specified in the contract, which *e* was 3rd January 1972. Immediately before the completion of the purchase the appellant held the position of head waiter at the hotel. Indeed, he had probably held that position for many years. His remuneration consisted of £10 a week plus a share of the 'tronc'—a fund into which all the tips received at the hotel were paid.

Now the respondent did her best to safeguard the position of her employees, and there was included in the contract for the sale of the hotel a clause, cl 14, which *f* provided that the purchasers should, before completion, make to each employee at the hotel an offer in writing to re-engage him on terms which did not differ from those of his existing contract of employment, or on certain other terms which may be ignored for the purposes of this case. It seems likely that the appellant knew of that clause, for his evidence was that he understood that he was to be retained after the sale. However, the purchasers did not comply with cl 14, and they made no written *g* offer of employment to the appellant. What happened was that after completion the appellant continued to work for the purchasers and for a short time there was no express contract between them. For two weeks he received wages calculated on the same basis as that on which he had been paid under the respondent. Then, according to the chairman's notes of the evidence, he was told that his terms of employment would be changed so that his remuneration would consist of £20 a week certain, no *h* more and no less. The appellant agreed to the change, which does not appear to have made a significant financial difference. On 18th February 1972 the purchasers dismissed him. There is no suggestion that he was dismissed on any ground of complaint. The respondent was represented at the hearing, but no oral evidence was adduced on her behalf.

It is clear that in this case there was a change in the ownership of a business taking *j* place in such circumstances that the provisions of s 13 of the Redundancy Payments Act 1965 apply. Section 13 (2) provides as follows:

'If, by agreement with the employee, the person who immediately after the change occurs is the owner of the business or of the part of the business in question, as the case may be (in this section referred to as "the new owner") renews the employee's contract of employment (with the substitution of the new owner for the previous owner) or re-engages him under a new contract of employment, section 3 (2) of this Act shall have effect as if the renewal or re-engagement had been a renewal or re-engagement by the previous owner (without any substitution of the new owner for the previous owner).'

Counsel for the appellant has argued that the words 'by agreement with the employee' in s 13 (2) must be construed as meaning 'by express agreement'. He then says that since there was no express agreement in this case s 13 (2) does not apply. We reject that argument. We think that the word 'agreement' in the subsection must be construed in its ordinary meaning, which includes an agreement to be implied from conduct. It follows that s 3 (2) of the 1965 Act must be applied to this case as if the renewal or re-engagement had been by the previous owner. Section 3 (2) provides as follows:

'An employee shall not be taken for the purposes of this Part of this Act to be dismissed by his employer if his contract of employment is renewed, or he is re-engaged by the same employer under a new contract of employment, and— (a) in a case where the provisions of the contract as renewed, or of the new contract, as the case may be, as to the capacity and place in which he is employed, and as to the other terms and conditions of his employment, do not differ from the corresponding provisions of the previous contract, the renewal or re-engagement takes effect immediately on the ending of his employment under the previous contract, or (b) in any other case, the renewal or re-engagement is in pursuance of an offer in writing made by his employer before the ending of his employment under the previous contract, and takes effect either immediately on the ending of that employment or after an interval of not more than four weeks thereafter.'

The tribunal appear to have considered this case on the footing that the applicable provisions of the 1965 Act were not those of s 3 (2), but those of s 2 (3). That is, we think, an error. The tribunal held that the purchasers of the business had renewed the appellant's contract of employment, albeit for a very brief period, on the same terms and conditions as those which had previously prevailed. If that is right, then the applicable provisions would be those of s 3 (2) (a) of the 1965 Act and the appellant would not be entitled to a redundancy payment. The tribunal describe the result as unfortunate and express their sympathy with the appellant.

We approach the matter by considering whether the tribunal were right in their decision that the purchasers had renewed the appellant's contract of employment on the same terms and conditions as those on which he was employed by the respondent. In our view the mere fact that an employee for a short period accepts wages calculated on the same basis as his wages under his contract with the previous employer is by no means necessarily conclusive evidence that there has been an offer by conduct by the new employer to re-engage the employee on all the terms and conditions of the previous contract, or that the employee has accepted such an offer. The new employer's conduct may mean no more than this: 'If you will work for me for the time being I will pay you reasonable remuneration.' That is a perfectly possible interpretation, especially in these days when it is known that the transfer of a business is frequently followed by staff reorganisations carried out in the interests of economy. It may be necessary to look at the new employer's conduct over a number of weeks following the transfer to determine what is the correct inference to be drawn from that conduct. The requirements of s 3 (2) (a) of the 1965 Act are not satisfied unless the new employer has offered, by words or conduct, to re-engage the employee on terms which do not differ from those of the previous contract and the employee has, by words or conduct, accepted that offer. If the previous employer wishes to rely on s 3 (2) (a) of the 1965 Act, the burden rests on him to show that there has been such an offer and such acceptance.

a

In this case, there are factors to be weighed against the fact that the employee, for a short period, accepted wages calculated on the same basis as before. One such factor is that the new employer did not comply with cl 14 of his contract with the respondent. If he intended to employ the old staff on the same terms and conditions as before, why did he not make a written offer to that effect in compliance with cl 14? Another such factor is that the new employer appears to have assumed that he was entitled to change the basis of the appellant's remuneration without notice. If the terms and conditions of the appellant's employment did not differ from those previously applicable, how can he have been entitled to do that? It is true that the appellant accepted the changed basis when it was put to him, but he may have felt that he had no alternative.

b

The question whether there has been an offer and acceptance of the terms of employment which were previously applicable is in all cases a question of fact. We have therefore considered whether the proper course is to remit the case to the tribunal for reconsideration of that question in the light of the matters to which we have drawn attention. But we think that on the application of proper principles to the evidence available to them (which, as we have said, included no oral evidence adduced on behalf of the respondent) the tribunal must inevitably have come to the conclusion that the respondent had not discharged the burden of proving that the requirements of s 3 (2) (*a*) of the 1965 Act were satisfied.

c

d

We therefore propose to allow the appeal and uphold the appellant's claim to a redundancy payment. If the amount of it cannot be agreed, the matter must be remitted to the tribunal in order that they may assess it.

Appeal allowed.

e

Solicitors: *Ward, Bowie & Co*, agents for *Woodford & Ackroyd*, Southampton (for the appellant); *Preston & Redman*, Bournemouth (for the respondent).

Gordon H Scott Esq Barrister.

Attorney-General (on the relation of McWhirter) v Independent Broadcasting Authority

COURT OF APPEAL, CIVIL DIVISION
LORD DENNING MR, CAIRNS AND LAWTON LJJ
16th, 19th, 25th, 26th, 29th JANUARY, 5th FEBRUARY 1973

Attorney-General – Relator action – Dispensing with relator procedure – Circumstances in which procedure may be dispensed with – Claim for injunction or declaration – Claim against statutory corporation – Claim that corporation in breach of statutory duty – Claim by member of public – Sufficiency of interest – Injunction to restrain breach of statutory duty – Unreasonable refusal by Attorney-General to give consent to relator proceedings – Insufficient time for procedural steps necessary for relator action – Aggrieved member of public entitled to bring action in own name as a last resort.

Broadcasting – Authority – Statutory duty – Content of programmes – Independent Broadcasting Authority – Duty of authority to satisfy themselves so far as possible that programmes include nothing offending good taste or decency or offensive to public feeling – Authority not required to see every filmed programme before broadcast – Decision of authority that programme suitable for broadcasting in general conclusive – Circumstances in which authority themselves should see programme before making decision – Circumstances in which decision of authority may be questioned in courts – Authority's decision unreasonable or based on a misdirection as to statutory requirements – Television Act 1964, s 3 (1) (a).

The plaintiff was a member of the public who owned a television set in respect of which he had paid a licence fee. The Independent Broadcasting Authority ('the authority') was a statutory body constituted under the Television Act 1964. The authority proposed to broadcast on Tuesday, 16th January 1973, at 10.30 pm, a television film about the American artist and film-maker, Andy Warhol. The plaintiff had not seen the film but he had evidence in the shape of newspaper reports which indicated that the film (which had been shown to the press) contained matter offending against good taste and decency and likely to be offensive to public feeling. On 15th January 1973 the plaintiff placed that evidence before the Attorney-General, claiming that the authority were in breach of the duty imposed on them by s 3 (1) (a)[a] of the 1964 Act to satisfy themselves so far as possible that such matter was not included in television programmes. The Attorney-General, however, declined to take action against the authority ex officio. Thereupon the plaintiff, in view of the urgency of the matter, did not seek to obtain the Attorney-General's leave to institute relator proceedings, but on the following day issued a writ against the authority claiming an injunction to restrain them from broadcasting the film on 16th January on the ground that they had failed to comply with s 3 (1) (a) of the 1964 Act. On 16th January the judge in chambers refused to grant the plaintiff an interim injunction to restrain the broadcast on the ground that the plaintiff had no locus standi. On the same day the plaintiff appealed to the Court of Appeal, claiming that he had a sufficient interest to apply for an injunction. The court heard argument for the authority; there was evidence that the authority had accepted the recommendation of their staff that the film was suitable for transmission on television without themselves seeing the film, despite the press criticisms and the announcement by one of the programme companies that they would not show the film as it was likely to offend public feeling. On the evidence before it the court, by a majority, held that it had jurisdiction at the

---

a Section 3 (1), so far as material, is set out at p 693 c, post

plaintiff's suit to grant an interim injunction restraining the broadcast and would
grant an injunction as an urgent and temporary measure since there was a prima facie
case that the authority had not fulfilled their statutory duty and that many people
might be caused offence, and damage would be done, if the film were broadcast.
On 19th January, before the interim injunction had been perfected, the court agreed
to restore the plaintiff's appeal to the list for further hearing, and the appeal came on
again on 25th January. At the further hearing it became clear there there had in fact
been time on 15th and 16th January for the plaintiff to have complied with the
procedural requirements necessary for obtaining the Attorney-General's consent to
bring relator proceedings and to have sought his consent to bring such proceedings
but that the plaintiff had chosen not to take that course. Consent to bring relator
proceedings had subsequently been given by the Attorney-General prior to the hearing on 25th January. There was evidence that before the further hearing the authority
had seen the film themselves and had unanimously affirmed their previous decision
that it was suitable for transmission on television and complied with s 3 (1) (a) of the
1964 Act. There was also evidence that the authority's general advisory council had
also seen the film, and by a majority of 17 to one had decided that it was suitable to
be shown on television. The advisory council represented a broad cross-section of the
public and was a responsible body. The court itself saw the film at the further hearing.
It purported to show what kind of artistic and film work Andy Warhol did. The film
lasted 45 minutes; there were five incidents in it, each lasting about 45 to 60 seconds,
which could be regarded as indecent and as likely to be offensive to many people.

Held – (i) (Cairns LJ dissenting) Although the relator procedure should be taken in
every case where it was reasonably available to a member of the public aggrieved
by non-observance of the law, in the last resort, if the Attorney-General refused improperly or unreasonably to exercise his powers to initiate proceedings, or if there was
not sufficient time, an aggrieved member of the public who had a sufficient interest,
could himself come to the courts and seek a declaration and, in a proper case, an
injunction, joining the Attorney-General, if need be, as defendant; (per Lord Denning
MR) the circumstances in which a person might be held to have a sufficient interest
should not be restricted. Accordingly on 16th January, when the case presented to
the court was of an exceptional character in that there was evidence from which it
could be inferred that the authority were in breach of their statutory duty, that the
Attorney-General had refused to take action himself ex officio and that there was no
time for the procedural steps necessary for a relator action, the court was entitled to
hear the plaintiff, for it appeared at that date that no other remedy was reasonably
available to him (see p 698 b d and g, p 699 c and d, p 704 h and j and p 705 f and g,
post); *Dyson v Attorney-General* [1911] 1 KB 410 considered.

(ii) Since the evidence at the further hearing showed, however, that the plaintiff had
had time on 15th and 16th January to obtain the Attorney-General's consent to relator
proceedings, he had no locus standi to apply for the injunction himself (see p 699 g
and h, and p 705 b, post).

(iii) On the basis that the proceedings had been properly constituted, the court was
justified in granting an interim injunction on 16th January for, on the evidence then
before the court, there appeared to be a prima facie case that the authority were in
breach of the duty imposed on them by s 3 (1) (a) of the 1964 Act; having regard to
the press reports, the authority ought to have seen the film for themselves and in
failing to do so they had not done what was reasonably sufficient to satisfy themselves,
so far as possible, that there was nothing indecent or offensive in the film (see p 700 j,
p 703 g and h and p 706 a and c, post).

(iv) On the evidence before the court at the further hearing the authority had
fulfilled their statutory duty under s 3 (1) (a), and unless their decision could be
impugned on the ground that it was unreasonable, or that they had misdirected
themselves in reaching it, it was decisive and the court had no right to interfere.

a Having regard to the film itself, and to the standing of the authority and their advisory council, it could not be said that the authority had come to a decision to which they could not reasonably have come nor (per Lawton LJ) could it be said that their decision was perverse. Furthermore it was not possible to infer that in coming to their decision the authority had only had regard to the film as a whole and had overlooked their duty to ensure that nothing indecent was included in the film. It followed that an

b injunction restraining the authority from broadcasting the film should not be granted, and the injunction granted on 16th January would be discharged (see p 700 a, p 701 d and h, p 706 a and e and p 707 d, post).

Notes

For the relator procedure, see 30 Halsbury's Laws (3rd Edn) 310-312, para 570, and for
c cases on the subject, see 16 Digest (Repl) 537, 538, 3770-3785.
For the grant of interlocutory injunctions, see 21 Halsbury's Laws (3rd Edn) 364-368, paras 763-772, for injunctions against corporations and associations, see ibid, 371-372, paras 777-782, and for cases on interlocutory injunctions, see 28 (2) Digest (Reissue) 966-980, 60-161.
For the duties of the Independent Broadcasting Authority with regard to
d programmes, see 36 Halsbury's Laws (3rd Edn) 651, para 1036.
For the Television Act 1964, s 3, see 35 Halsbury's Statutes (3rd Edn) 123.

Cases referred to in judgments

Attorney-General v Great Eastern Railway Co (1879) 11 Ch D 449, 48 LJCh 428, 40 LT 265, CA; *affd* (1880) 5 App Cas 473, 49 LJCh 545, 42 LT 810, HL, 38 Digest (Repl) 384, 519.
e *Attorney-General v Pontypridd Waterworks Co* [1908] 1 Ch 388, 77 LJCh 237, 98 LT 275, 72 JP 48, 6 LGR 39, 16 Digest (Repl) 545, 3862.
Attorney-General v Westminster City Council [1924] 2 Ch 416, [1924] All ER Rep 162, 93 LJCh 573, 131 LT 802, 88 JP 145, 22 LGR 506, CA, 16 Digest (Repl) 537, 3776.
Boyce v Paddington Borough Council [1903] 1 Ch 109, 72 LJCh 28, 87 LT 564, 67 JP 23,
f 1 LGR 98; *subsequent proceedings* [1903] 2 Ch 556, 72 LJCh 695, 89 LT 383, CA; *sub nom Paddington Corpn v Attorney-General* [1906] AC 1, [1904-7] All ER Rep 362, 75 LJCh 4, 93 LT 673, HL, 16 Digest (Repl) 543, 3842.
Caldwell v Pagham Harbour Reclamation Co (1876) 2 Ch D 221, 3 Char Pr Cas 119, 45 LJCh 796, 50 Digest (Repl) 116, 972.
Deare v Attorney-General (1835) 1 Y & C Ex 197, 160 ER 80, Ex Ch, 11 Digest (Repl) 592, 311.
g *Dyson v Attorney-General* [1911] 1 KB 410, 81 LJKB 217, 105 LT 753, CA; *subsequent proceedings* [1912] 1 Ch 158, CA, 11 Digest (Repl) 593, 314.
Lewisham Metropolitan Borough and Town Clerk v Roberts [1949] 1 All ER 815, [1949] 2 KB 608, 113 JP 260, 47 LGR 479; *sub nom Roberts v Lewisham Borough Council* [1949] LJR 1318, CA, 17 Digest (Repl) 443, 124.
h *Liversidge v Anderson* [1941] 3 All ER 338, [1942] AC 206, 110 LJKB 724, 116 LT 1, HL, 17 Digest (Repl) 422, 27.
London County Council v Attorney-General [1902] AC 165, 71 LJCh 268, 86 LT 161, 66 JP 340, HL, 16 Digest (Repl) 537, 3775.
Prescott v Birmingham Corpn [1954] 3 All ER 698, [1955] Ch 210, 119 JP 48, 53 LGR 68, CA, 33 Digest (Repl) 100, 623.
j *R v Metropolitan Police Comr, ex parte Blackburn* [1968] 1 All ER 763, [1968] 2 QB 118, [1968] 2 WLR 893, CA, Digest (Cont Vol C) 279, 1113a.
Secretary of State for Employment v Associated Society of Locomotive Engineers and Firemen (No 2) [1972] 2 All ER 949, [1972] 2 QB 455, [1972] 2 WLR 1370, 13 KIR 1, NIRC and CA.
Thorne v British Broadcasting Corpn [1967] 2 All ER 1225, [1967] 1 WLR 1104, CA, Digest (Cont Vol C) 243, 7272c.

Cases also cited   *a*
Attorney-General (on the relation of Hornchurch Urban District Council) v Bastow [1957]
　1 All ER 497, [1957] 1 QB 514.
N (Infants), Re [1967] 1 All ER 161, [1967] Ch 512.
R v Comrs of Customs and Excise, ex parte Cooke and Stevenson [1970] 1 All ER 1068,
　[1970] 1 WLR 450, DC.
                                                                                          b

Interlocutory appeal
On 16th January 1973 Alan Ross McWhirter, a member of the public, issued a writ
claiming an injunction against the Independent Broadcasting Authority ('the
authority'), to restrain them, their servants, agents or programming companies under
their control, from broadcasting on television, on 16th January 1973 at 10.30 p m, a
programme about the American film-maker and artist Andy Warhol, on the ground   *c*
that transmission of the programme was a breach of the Television Act 1964. On 16th
January Forbes J refused an ex parte application by Mr McWhirter for an interim
injunction to restrain the authority from broadcasting the programme on the ground
that Mr McWhirter did not have any locus standi to bring the proceedings. Later on
the same day Mr McWhirter appealed against that decision. The facts are set out
in the judgment of Lord Denning MR.   *d*

Mr McWhirter appeared in person.
David Kemp for the authority.

LORD DENNING MR. This is an urgent case which we have heard at short notice   *e*
at this late hour. There is advertised to be shown on several independent television
channels this evening at 10.30 a programme entitled 'Warhol: Artist and Film-
maker.' Mr McWhirter, a member of the public, has issued a writ today in which he
seeks an injunction against the Independent Broadcasting Authority to restrain them
from broadcasting this programme. We are grateful to the authority for instructing   *f*
Mr Kemp on their behalf, and to Mr Kemp for attending to assist us.
　Towards the end of last week a film of this programme was shown privately to a
number of journalists. I expect that there was an embargo forbidding comment until
Sunday. In the Sunday newspapers the journalists made very severe criticisms of the
proposed programme. On the front page of the News of the World it was said:

> 'This TV shocker is the worst ever. A Programme which goes further than   *g*
> anything I have ever seen on TV is to be screened on Tuesday night. Millions
> of viewers will find its frankness offensive.'

In the Sunday Mirror it was said:

> 'Andy Warhol film shocker for ITV. Television viewers are about to see what   *h*
> many will consider to be the most permissive shocker to be shown on British
> screens . . . I have been shown a preview of this remarkable documentary. It
> includes: A FAT GIRL stripping to the waist, daubing her breasts with paint and
> then painting a canvas with them. She also throws paint down a lavatory pan to
> form weird patterns. This one she calls Flush Art.'

And then another paragraph almost equally indecent. It goes on: 'A DISCUSSION   *j*
between a young girl and a man dressed as a Hell's Angel on how they can have sex.
She says she will only do it at 60 m.p.h. on his motor cycle.' A little later on: 'Conversations are laced with four-letter words . . . It's there all right. Especially trans-
vestites, lesbianism and the whole freaky scene which surrounds Warhol.' In the Daily
Express on Monday it was said: 'Shocking world of TV by James Thomas.' It finishes:

a 'The public still has to see the Andy Warhol programme. It may then turn itself into an indignant jury. Or viewers may merely find these infant antics funny. Is it art for Andy's sake—or for the sake of the I.B.A.'s ratings? We shall judge tomorrow. It could be that ITV, by throwing slush at the public, has made its biggest mistake in a decade.'

b Mr McWhirter says that those comments are typical and that there are others to the same effect. He has not himself seen the programme. He asked to see it but he was not allowed to do so. So he relies on those comments in the press as the best evidence he can obtain about the contents of the programme. On the basis of them, he says that the Independent Broadcasting Authority are about to break the duty laid on them by statute. Section 3 (1) of the Television Act 1964 provides:

c 'It shall be the duty of the Authority to satisfy themselves that, so far as possible, the programmes broadcast by the Authority comply with the following requirements, that is to say—(a) that nothing is included in the programmes which offends against good taste or decency or is likely to encourage or incite to crime or to lead to disorder or to be offensive to public feeling . . .'

d Mr McWhirter says that there is evidence here from these newspaper reporters that this programme contains matter which offends against good taste and decency and is likely to be offensive to public feeling. He stresses the word 'likely'. I must say that the evidence of those who have seen the film, that is, the evidence of the newspaper reporters, does warrant the inference—it leads almost inevitably to the inference—that this programme includes some matter which will offend against good taste and decency and is likely to be offensive to the public feeling: whereas the Act

e requires the authority to satisfy themselves that *nothing* in it should do so.
In answer counsel for the authority says: the authority are the supreme arbiters on this matter. He relies on the words 'It shall be the duty of the Authority to satisfy themselves . . . so far as possible . . .' He says that it is for the authority and not for the courts to sit in judgment over the programmes. To this I would answer that if the authority do not carry out their duty, the courts can enquire into it. The Act does not

f provide any specific way for enforcing the duty. It defines no offence. It provides no punishment. It gives no remedy for a breach. When a statutory duty is imposed, but no means of enforcing it, the courts are the one body which can see that the duty is fulfilled: and when called on, they must do so. Counsel for the authority referred to the wide powers of the Postmaster General, now the Minister of Posts and Telecommunications, under s 18 (3) of the Act. But that does not seem to me to meet the

g present problem. That section enables him to give general directions, but it does not enable him to intervene at short notice in a matter of this kind. It is, in my judgment, the province of the courts to see that the duties laid down by Parliament are obeyed.
The next point is, who can bring the matter to the notice of the court? Can it be done by an ordinary member of the public such as Mr McWhirter? This is the most difficult part of the case. It is said in our law books[1]:

h 'An injunction will only be granted at the suit of a party having sufficient interest in the relief sought. If the injury complained of affects the public interest the Attorney-General must be joined . . .'

So it is said that Mr McWhirter cannot come here on his own. In answer Mr McWhirter

j says that he has been to the Attorney-General's office, and, although he has not been given leave to bring a relator action—that is, an action on the relation of the Attorney-General—nevertheless it is not out of the question that he might obtain leave. But the machinery of obtaining leave takes some little time to get to work. If he waited until he obtained leave, it would be too late for the court to take action; because by that

---

1 See 21 Halsbury's Laws (3rd Edn), 407, 408, para 855

time the film would have been shown and the damage would have been done. I
think there is sufficient in his answer for us to anticipate that he may get leave and
to act in advance of it. The obtaining of leave is just a matter of procedure. In these
days we have to mould procedural requirements so as to see that the duty which the
statute ordains is fulfilled. At any rate, for the time being, even at the suit of Mr
McWhirter, we have jurisdiction to grant an injunction if such be the only way of
seeing that the statutory duty is fulfilled.

In this particular case it seems to me that we can and should grant an injunction
to stop the performance of this film this evening. I would emphasise in particular
that the statutory requirement is that it is the duty of the authority to satisfy *themselves*. I should have thought that on Sunday or Monday—when there had been all
these Press criticisms saying that it would be offensive to great numbers of the public—
the authority themselves should have considered whether there was anything in it
which was likely to be offensive to public feeling. I should have thought that the
authority themselves—the members of that authority—would have intervened and
said: 'We must see this: we must see this for ourselves before it goes out—we must
see whether it is as offensive as the newspaper reports say.' But we are told they did
not do so. They considered the matter, but they did not see the film.

We are told that the authority had before them a report from the staff. It said that
the programme was prefaced with a statement that 'some people may find Warhol's
views unusual and possibly offensive'; and that in the light of the modifications that
had been made, the staff felt able to recommend that the programme be transmitted.
On the faith of that report the authority seems to have authorised the transmission.
But that report was made before the newspaper reporters saw the film. After the
newspaper reporters saw the film and made these very severe criticisms of it, a new
situation arose. At that stage it seems to me that the authority, in order to do their
duty properly as the statute requires, should have seen it and satisfied themselves
personally that *nothing* in it was likely to be offensive to public feeling. They may, of
course, delegate many things to the staff, but occasions may arise—and this may be
one—when no delegation will suffice. They must satisfy themselves personally.

I realise that it is an important case; but as a temporary measure, I think an injunction should be granted. We are told—and it is really not contradicted—that on the
television channels there are standby programmes ready to be inserted. We are also
told that one channel, Anglia Television, has already decided not to show this programme but to put something else in. It seems to me that the others should follow
suit.

Although it is a difficult case, it seems to me that, on the evidence of the newspaper
reports, there are some things included in this programme which are likely to be
offensive to public feeling. There is evidence from which it can be inferred that the
authority have mistaken the extent of their duties in the matter, and therefore the
court should intervene by granting an injunction for a week or a fortnight. It need
only be be adjourned for that short time. Meanwhile the matter can be further
considered. If need be, the Attorney-General can be brought in by relator proceedings,
if he agrees. Then the matter can be fully debated on the various issues that arise.
I would be glad for that to be done. But, to keep the matter open for the time being,
I would grant the injunction as asked.

CAIRNS LJ. I should be very glad if I could agree that an injunction should be
granted in this case, because I think it is very much against the public interest that this
programme should be broadcast. I am, however, of opinion that it is still the law
that where the injury complained of affects only the public interest, the Attorney-
General must be joined. In my view the fact that it has not been possible in the time
available to persuade the Attorney-General to take action is no sufficient ground for
saying that the private individual is to be allowed to enforce the matter of public
interest. For that reason only I must dissent from Lord Denning MR's judgment.

a **LAWTON LJ.** I agree with Lord Denning MR that an injunction should be granted in this case, and I agree with the reasons which he has given. It seems to me that the point which is troubling Cairns LJ is one in which, under the changing conditions of the modern world, in which there are powerful statutory bodies like the Independent Broadcasting Authority, whose activities affect the public generally, the time has come to look at the procedural rules of law which hitherto seem to have restricted the right **b** of the ordinary citizen to complain about their activities; in other words, there is a case worthy of consideration; and this is not one where there is a mere shadowy claim to an injunction. In my judgment the evidence is clear that the authority have not applied the right test. It has long been accepted by the courts that where a statutory body has the duty of satisfying itself, that body must act in a reasonable manner. There is evidence—and I stress that I am going no further than saying that there is evidence— that the statutory body has not applied reasonable standards in saying that it has **c** satisfied itself. One illustration will show that. According to the Sunday Mirror— and it is uncontradicted on behalf of the authority—this film has in it the incident relating to the fat girl which Lord Denning MR read out; there is no need for me to read it out. The authority have taken the view that that incident is not likely to be offensive to the public. One has only got to ask oneself what would have happened if **d** that incident had taken place in a shop window or in any other part of a shop; and the answer is that the shopkeeper who organised such an exhibition would almost certainly have found himself charged with and convicted of wilfully exposing an indecent exhibition, contrary to s 4 of the Vagrancy Act 1824; and, as I pointed out in the course of the argument, if a television retailer had in his shop window a set with this particular programme coming through on it, he too might find himself charged with the same offence. In those circumstances it seems unlikely that the authority **e** can have applied their minds in a proper way to this programme.

Interim injunction granted.   Undertaking by Mr McWhirter as to damages.

Motion

By notice of motion dated 19th January 1973 the authority applied for an order **f** that Mr McWhirter's appeal against the order of Forbes J refusing him an interim injunction be restored to the Court of Appeal's list for further hearing and that no order be perfected until after that hearing. Before the hearing of the motion Mr McWhirter took steps to obtain the leave of the Attorney-General to institute relator proceedings and counsel gave his certificate that it was a proper case for leave. The Attorney-General was present at the hearing as amicus curiae and intimated to the court that he would give his consent to relator proceedings. **g** Leave was given to amend Mr McWhirter's writ by joining the Attorney-General as plaintiff. The proceedings then being properly constituted and under the sole control of Mr McWhirter, the Attorney-General withdrew and the hearing of the appeal proceeded on the substantive issue.

J G Le Quesne QC and *Stuart McKinnon* for Mr McWhirter.
h *R J Parker QC* and *David Kemp* for the authority.
The Attorney-General (Sir Peter Rawlinson QC), Gordon Slynn with him, as amicus curiae.

Cur adv vult

5th February. The following judgments were read.

j **LORD DENNING MR.** When Mr McWhirter came on Tuesday, 16th January 1973, he represented to us that it was a matter of great urgency. The Independent Broadcasting Authority were proposing, he said, that very evening, to broadcast a television film which did not comply with the statutory requirements laid down by Parliament. He produced evidence, in the shape of newspaper reports, which showed that it contained matter which offended against decency and was likely to be offensive to public feeling. He said that he had put that evidence before the Attorney-General's

office, but the Attorney-General had declined to take action ex officio. So he had himself come to the courts to seek an injunction. He claimed that he had a sufficient
interest. He was himself the owner of a television set; he had paid his licence fee.
When he switched it on, he was entitled to expect that the programme would comply
with the statutory requirements. There were thousands like him sitting at home
watching. All were entitled to have their privacy respected.

On that occasion this court, acting by a majority, granted the injunction. It was
essentially a 'holding operation' so as to enable the important issues to be discussed
when there was more time to do it. By granting an injunction—for a very short time—
no irreparable damage would be done. The television companies are able to change
programmes at short notice. They have substitute films standing by ready for use.
We thought that if it was found, after enquiry, that the programme did comply with
the statutory requirements, it could be shown a little later. But if it was broadcast at
once, without complying with the statutory requirements, much damage might be
done, much offence might be caused to many. So, on balance, as an urgent and
temporary measure, we granted the injunction. I do not suppose that this has done
the programme any disservice. On the contrary, it has given it publicity, so that if it
is shown many more will watch it than would have done so previously. Moreover, it
has enabled us to debate two points of much importance. The first is whether Mr
McWhirter had any locus standi to come to the court at all. The second is whether the
injunction should be continued.

Locus standi

This is a point of constitutional significance. We live in an age when Parliament
has placed statutory duties on government departments and public authorities—for
the benefit of the public—but has provided no remedy for the breach of them. If a
government department or a public authority transgresses the law laid down by
Parliament, or threatens to transgress it, can a member of the public come to the court
and draw the matter to its attention? He may himself be injuriously affected by the
breach. So may thousands of others like him. Is each and every one of them debarred
from access to the courts? The law is clear that no one of them can bring an action for
damages, unless he has suffered special damage over and above everyone else. That
was settled in 1535 in a case in the Year Books[1]. That rule was laid down in order to
avoid multiplicity of actions. The argument was put in this way: 'If one of those
injured were allowed to sue, a thousand might do so': and that was considered
intolerable. Sir William Blackstone in his Commentaries[2] said:

'... it would be unreasonable to multiply suits, by giving every man a separate
right of action, for what damnifies him in common only with the rest of his
fellow-subjects.'

But does this rule—which prevents anyone suing for damages—also prevent any
member of the public from seeking a declaration or an injunction? There are discretionary remedies, to which no one has a right, but which the court can grant if it
thinks fit. The usual course, no doubt, is for the member of the public who is aggrieved
to go to the Attorney-General and ask him to intervene—either ex officio or by granting leave to use his name in a relator action. In all proper cases the Attorney-General
will, no doubt, give his leave. But it is a matter for his discretion. Suppose that, in a
very rare case, he exercises his discretion wrongly and declines to intervene for no
good reason or on entirely wrong grounds; or suppose he is away and cannot be
reached in time, or suppose that the machinery works too slowly. I do not suggest
that it was so in this case. I only put the point so as to test the position. But before
doing so, it is necessary to consider the role of the Attorney-General in these matters.

1 *Anon* (1535) YB Mich 27 Hen 8, f 27, pl 10; see Fifoot, History and Sources of the Common
Law, Tort and Contract (1949), p 98
2 4th Edn (1770), bk IV, p 167

The role of the Attorney-General

It is settled in our constitutional law that in matters which concern the public at large the Attorney-General is the guardian of the public interest. Although he is a member of the government of the day, it is his duty to represent the public interest with complete objectivity and detachment. He must act independently of any external pressure from whatever quarter it may come. As the guardian of the public interest, the Attorney-General has a special duty in regard to the enforcement of the law.

His duty has been thus stated by members of this court who, each in his turn, had held the office of Attorney-General. In 1879 in *Attorney-General v Great Eastern Railway Co*[1] Baggallay LJ said:

'It is the interest of the public that the law should in all respects be respected and observed, and if the law is transgressed or threatened to be transgressed ... it is the duty of the Attorney-General to take the necessary steps to enforce it, nor does it make any difference whether he sues *ex officio*, or at the instance of relators.'

In 1924 Sir Ernest Pollock MR repeated those very words with approval: see *Attorney-General v Westminster City Council*[2]. To these I would add the words of Lord Abinger CB who had himself been Attorney-General in *Deare v Attorney-General*[3]:

'... it has been the practice, which I hope never will be discontinued, for the officers of the Crown to throw no difficulty in the way of any proceeding for the purpose of bringing matters before a Court of justice, where any real point of difficulty that requires judicial decision has occurred.'

Before the Attorney-General gives leave, however, there are certain regulations which any private individual is required to observe. These regulations go back a long time and are set out in Robertson's Civil Proceedings By and Against the Crown[4] and repeated in the White Book[5]. The member of the public must instruct solicitor and counsel. He must get them to prepare a writ and statement of claim. The counsel must certify that 'this writ and statement of claim are proper for the allowance of Her Majesty's Attorney-General'. The solicitor must certify that the relator is a proper person to be relator, and that he is competent to answer the costs of the proposed action. It sounds to me that that would all take some time, as well as money, but the Attorney-General assured us that it could be, and had been, carried through, sometimes within minutes, and certainly within hours.

At any rate, when all that is done and the Attorney-General gives his consent, he virtually drops out of the proceedings. As Sir Jocelyn Simon, when he was a law officer[6], told the House of Commons: '.... the Attorney-General is the nominal plaintiff in the action, but, in reality, the action is brought by the complainant.' Once the consent of the Attorney-General is obtained, the actual conduct of the proceedings is entirely in the hands of the relator who is responsible for the costs of the action.

In all this, however, one thing is clear. In exercising his functions, the Attorney-General is not subject to the control of the courts. It was so laid down by the Earl of Halsbury LC, in *London County Council v Attorney-General*[7], when he said:

'... but the initiation of the litigation, and the determination of the question whether it is a proper case for the Attorney-General to proceed in, is a matter

---

1 (1879) 11 Ch D 449 at 500
2 [1924] 2 Ch 416 at 420, [1924] All ER Rep 162 at 165
3 (1835) 1 Y & C Ex 197 at 208
4 (1908), p 835
5 The Supreme Court Practice 1973, p 196, notes to RSC Ord 15, r 11
6 Solicitor-General; see Hansard, Parliamentary Debates, HC, vol 631, col 691 (1st December 1960)
7 [1902] AC 165 at 169

entirely beyond the jurisdiction of this or any other Court. It is a question which   *a*
the law of this country has made to reside exclusively in the Attorney-General.'

The role of the private individual

Such is the relator procedure by which any member of the public can, in a proper
case, take steps to secure that the law is observed. It is a procedure which should be
taken in every case where it is reasonably available. But the question that arises for
consideration here is, suppose a case should arise in which the relator procedure is not   *b*
reasonably available; suppose the machinery works too slowly. In the present case
Mr McWhirter told us that the Attorney-General refused to take action ex officio,
and that he, Mr McWhirter, considered the matter was so urgent that he came direct
to this court. Was he entitled to come here? Test it by an extreme case. Suppose the
Attorney-General refuses to give leave for no good reason or on entirely wrong
grounds, mistaking, maybe, the interpretation of a statute. Would a private individual   *c*
be entitled to come to the court? Such a situation was not in Lord Halsbury LC's
mind in 1902. But it happened in 1910. There was a great case[1] then in which
this court, to quote a learned author[2], 'struck a blow which is still reverberating fifty
years later'.

In such a situation I am of opinion—and I state it as a matter of principle—that the
citizen who is aggrieved has a locus standi to come to the courts. He can at least   *d*
seek a declaration. That is the view expressed in a resourceful book to which the
Attorney-General himself referred us, Zamir on The Declaratory Judgment[3].
It is based on the celebrated case of *Dyson v Attorney-General*[4] to which I have just
referred. In 1910 the Commissioners of Inland Revenue sent out a questionnaire which
they required eight million people to answer. It was illegal. It was contrary to an
Act of Parliament. A private individual, Mr Dyson, objected to it. He came to the   *e*
courts and sought a declaration. At that time he could not sue the Commissioners of
Inland Revenue themselves. So he sued the Attorney-General as representing them.
The Attorney-General regarded his action as frivolous and vexatious. He sought to
strike it out. It is plain that he would never have given leave to Mr Dyson to bring the
action. This court refused to strike the action out. It declared that the questionnaire
was illegal and that Mr Dyson was under no obligation to comply with it.   *f*

Since that case there have been many others, such as *Prescott v Birmingham Corpn*[5],
when a private individual has successfully sought a declaration against a public
authority, and there is a valuable discussion of the whole question by Professor de
Smith in his book[6].

In the light of all this I am of opinion that, in the last resort, if the Attorney-General
refuses leave in a proper case, or improperly or unreasonably delays in giving leave,   *g*
or his machinery works too slowly, then a member of the public, who has a sufficient
interest, can himself apply to the court itself. He can apply for a declaration and, in a
proper case, for an injunction, joining the Attorney-General if need be, as defendant.
In these days when government departments and public authorities have such great
powers and influence, this is a most important safeguard for the ordinary citizens of
this country; so that they can see that those great powers and influence are exercised   *h*
in accordance with law. I would not restrict the circumstances in which an individual
may be held to have a sufficient interest. Take the recent cases[7] when Mr Raymond
Blackburn applied to the court on the ground that the commissioner of police was not

---

1 *Dyson v Attorney-General* [1911] 1 KB 410, [1912] 1 Ch 158
2 See Edwards, The Law Officers of the Crown (1964), p 295
3 (1962), p 275
4 [1911] 1 KB 410, [1912] 1 Ch 158
5 [1954] 3 All ER 698, [1955] Ch 210
6 Judicial Review of Administrative Action (2nd Edn, 1968), pp 464-479
7 I e R v *Metropolitan Police Comr, ex parte Blackburn* [1968] 1 All ER 763, [1968] 2 QB 118;
   R v *Metropolitan Police Comr, ex parte Blackburn (No 3)* p 324, ante, [1973] 2 WLR 43

a
doing his duty in regard to gaming or pornography. Mr Blackburn had a sufficient interest, even though it was shared with thousands of others. I doubt whether the Attorney-General would have given him leave to use his name: see *R v Metropolitan Police Comr, ex parte Blackburn*[1]. But we heard Mr Blackburn in his own name. His intervention was both timely and useful.

b
It was suggested that if Mr McWhirter could come to the court complaining of indecent films, so could others come objecting to boxing films or anyone else who had his own particular dislikes. But none of those could get past the sieve afforded by the Attorney-General's office. None of those would be able to produce the slightest evidence that the Independent Broadcasting Authority had not fulfilled their statutory duty. But, as Mr McWhirter's case was presented to us, it was of a highly exceptional character. There was evidence from which it could be inferred that the Independent Broadcasting Authority had not done their duty; that the Attorney-General had

c
refused to take action himself ex officio; and that there was no time to do all the things necessary for a relator action. It was a case of the last resort; and I hold that we were entitled to hear him as we did. I have said so much because I regard it as a matter of high constitutional principle that if there is good ground for supposing that a government department or a public authority is transgressing the law, or is about to transgress it, in a way which offends or injures thousands of Her Majesty's subjects, then in

d
the last resort any one of those offended or injured can draw it to the attention of the courts of law and seek to have the law enforced. But this, I would emphasise, is only in the last resort when there is no other remedy reasonably available to secure that the law is obeyed.

e
It was suggested that the person aggrieved should approach the Minister so that he should give a notice under s 18 (3) of the Television Act 1964, or should approach his member of Parliament so that he could ask a question in the House. But those do not seem to me to be remedies that are reasonably available. They are not so accessible. They are not so speedy or effective. They are not so independent as the courts of law.

This present case

f
On the case, as it appeared to us on Tuesday, 16th January 1973, Mr McWhirter had no other remedy reasonably available to him. But the Attorney-General has thrown more light on the circumstances. It appears that at about 2.00 p m on the Monday Mr McWhirter was told that the Attorney-General would not take action ex officio, but that this was without prejudice to any application that Mr McWhirter might wish to make for the Attorney-General's consent to relator proceedings. There was time then for Mr McWhirter to get the procedure moving. During the rest of that day and

g
the next morning, he could have instructed solicitors and counsel, and sought leave; and if it was a proper case he would have got leave. But Mr McWhirter deliberately decided not to take that course. He came straight to this court. That was a mistake. There was another remedy reasonably available to him, and he did not take it.

So he was in the wrong. But it has all been cured now. He took steps to get the leave of the Attorney-General, as we intimated he should do. Counsel gave his certificate

h
that it was a proper case for leave. The Attorney-General has told us that he would give leave. The necessary amendment can be made at any time, and will date back retrospectively to the issue of the writ: see *Caldwell v Pagham Harbour Reclamation Co*[2]. So all is now in order from the beginning. I turn, therefore, to the substantive question, should the injunction be continued?

j
In s 3 of the Television Act 1964 Parliament specified several requirements with which programmes should comply. The first (s 3 (1) (a)) is this: '. . . that nothing is included in the programmes which offends against good taste or decency or is likely . . . to be offensive to public feeling'. I would stress the words 'nothing is included'.

1   [1968] 1 All ER at 770, 771, [1968] 2 QB at 137, 139
2   (1876) 2 Ch D 221

Those words show that the programme is to be judged, not as a whole, but in its several parts, piece by piece. If a documentary dealt with life in the underworld on a restrained level, but then included by way of illustration 30 seconds of pornographic photographs, it would be a breach of the statutory requirements. It would not be cured by words being said at the beginning that 'some parts of this programme may be offensive to some people'. Viewers may switch on in the middle of the programme, and, in any case, the statute does not permit of a warning being an excuse for non-compliance.

Such being the statutory requirements, Parliament puts a duty on the Independent Broadcasting Authority to 'satisfy themselves' that they are complied with 'so far as possible'. This does not mean, of course, that the members of the authority are themselves to see every programme or go through it. They can and must leave a great deal to the staff. They are entitled in the ordinary way to accept the advice of their staff on the programmes in general, and on any programme in particular: see *Lewisham Metropolitan Borough and Town Clerk v Roberts*[1]. It is only in a most exceptional case that they may be expected to see a programme for themselves in order to be 'satisfied'. But there are such exceptional cases, just as there are exceptional cases when a Minister must satisfy himself personally. It depends how serious is the case: see *Liversidge v Anderson*[2].

Was this film a programme which they ought to have seen for themselves? Let me state the circumstances. (i) The programme was prepared by one of the programme companies called ATV Network Ltd. In its original form, the staff of the Independent Broadcasting Authority were so unhappy about it that they thought that the programme should be seen by the authority itself. (ii) ATV Network Ltd thereupon deleted some of the material and introduced the film with a warning that 'some people may find Warhol's views unusual and possibly offensive'. (iii) In the light of those modifications, the Director-General and staff of the Independent Broadcasting Authority felt able to recommend that the programme be transmitted as the usual network documentary on Tuesday, 16th January 1973, at 10.30 p m. They made an intervention report to that effect. The Independent Broadcasting Authority accepted that recommendation but did not see the film themselves. (iv) On 12th or 13th January journalists were invited to a preview of the film. (v) On Sunday, 14th January, and Monday, 15th January, some of the journalists in their papers made severe criticisms of the film. If their accounts were correct, it included incidents which were indecent and likely to be offensive to public feeling. The News of the World, in particular, said that 'Millions of viewers will find its frankness offensive'. (vi) On reading those newspaper reports, the chairman and directors of one of the channels, Anglia Television, determined to have the film screened privately for them to see. They came to the unanimous conclusion that the programme, if broadcast, was likely to be offensive to public feeling. They announced that they were not going to supply it for broadcasting. (vii) The Independent Broadcasting Authority, however, did not see it. Some of them had an informal discussion with the senior staff, and, on their assurances, were prepared to let it be broadcast.

The question is: did the Independent Broadcasting Authority do what was sufficient, or ought they not to have seen the film for themselves, as the chairman of Anglia Television did and their directors? When the matter was brought before this court on Tuesday, 16th January, it appeared that there was a prima facie case for saying that they had not done what was reasonably sufficient to satisfy themselves that 'so far as possible' there was nothing indecent or offensive in the programme. It was better to postpone its showing for a little while, using a substitute film, rather than let it go out that evening. Meanwhile, the matter could be properly considered in all its

---

1   [1949] 1 All ER 815 at 824, 828, 829, [1949] 2 KB 608 at 621, 629
2   [1941] 3 All ER 338 at 348, [1942] AC 206 at 223, 224

a aspects, both as to the locus standi of Mr McWhirter and as to the fulfilment of the statutory requirements.

In the circumstances I think that the Independent Broadcasting Authority ought to have seen the film for themselves on the Monday or Tuesday before passing it. Since that time they have done so. So have the General Advisory Council. The members of the General Council are drawn from a broad cross-section of the people,

b and are as representative and responsible a body as you could find anywhere. The General Council, by a majority of 17 to one, passed this resolution: 'The Council felt that the staff were right to advise the Authority that the film which they had seen was suitable to be shown at the suggested time'. The members of the Independent Broadcasting Authority are likewise most representative and responsible. Ten out of the eleven saw the film and unanimously reaffirmed the decision—

c
'that the programme is suitable for transmission in the 10.30 p.m. documentary slot, and that it is satisfied that the programme complies with the requirements of Section 3 (1) (a) of the Television Act 1964.'

d If those decisions are to be accepted as valid, they are decisive. The Independent Broadcasting Authority are the people who matter. They are the censors. The courts have no right whatever—and I may add no desire whatever—to interfere with their decisions so long as they reach them in accordance with law: see *Secretary of State for Employment v Associated Society of Locomotive Engineers and Firemen (No 2)*[1]. Counsel for Mr McWhirter submitted, however, that the Independent Broadcasting Authority had misdirected themselves. He said that they had regarded the film as a whole, and

e not piece by piece as the statute required. Alternatively, he said that their decision was one to which they could not reasonably have come.

To test these submissions we ourselves saw the film. I hesitate to express my own views on it, but it is part of the evidence before us and I feel I should do so. I can understand that some people would think it entertaining, but I must speak as I find. Viewing it as a whole, the film struck me as dreary and dull. It shows the sort of

f people— the perverts and homosexuals—who surround Mr Warhol and whom he portrays in his work. But, taken as a whole, it is not offensive. Viewing it piece by piece, there are some incidents which seemed to me to be inserted in an attempt to liven up the dullness—an attempt which did not succeed, at least so far as I was concerned. These are the incidents which struck the newspaper reporters and were described by them, and which, no doubt, struck the chairman of Anglia Television and his col-

g leagues. They only form about one-tenth of the whole. Speaking for myself, I would take the same view as the newspaper reporters and the chairman and directors of Anglia Television. I should have thought that those individual incidents could be regarded as indecent and likely to be offensive to many. But my views do not matter, unless they go to show that the Independent Broadcasting Authority misdirected themselves or came to a conclusion to which they could not reasonably come. I am

h certainly not prepared to say that. Quite the contrary. On seeing the film, they came to a decision to which they might reasonably come, and this court has no right whatever to interfere with it.

I would therefore lift the injunction. The programme can be shown as soon as can be arranged. No doubt many will wish to see it to form their own view. Some will write to the Independent Broadcasting Authority and tell them. It should give the

j Independent Broadcasting Authority a good guide to public feeling, and so help them in the difficult decisions which they have to make in the future. But they should always remember that there is a silent majority of good people who say little but view a

---

1 [1972] 2 All ER 949 at 967, 968, [1972] 2 QB 455 at 493

lot. Their feelings are to be respected as well as those of the vociferous minority who, *a* in the name of freedom, shout for ugliness in all its forms.

So let the programme be shown. We will not stop it.

CAIRNS LJ. When Mr McWhirter appeared before this court on 16th January to appeal against the refusal by Forbes J to grant him an interlocutory injunction, *b* I was of the opinion that he was not entitled to the relief he sought because his action was an action aimed at enforcing the public duty of the authority and not at protecting any private right of the plaintiff. That being so, the proper plaintiff would be the Attorney-General suing on behalf of the public as a whole and not Mr McWhirter or any other private individual.

I remain of opinion that that is the law. The cases that have been cited, *Boyce v* *c* *Paddington Borough Council*[1], *Attorney-General v Pontypridd Waterworks Co*[2] and *Thorne v British Broadcasting Corpn*[3], all support it. There is no single authority, and no sentence in any judgment, that points the other way.

What the majority of the court held on 16th January was that when the matter was one of urgency, when it appeared to the court that there had been no reasonable opportunity of obtaining the fiat of the Attorney-General for a relator action, an *d* injunction to cover a short period could be granted on the application of the individual plaintiff. It did not seem to me then and does not seem to me now that this is a sustainable proposition. As is shown by *Thorne*'s case[3], the plaintiff has no cause of action; the defendants could have moved to have the writ set aside on that ground. There would then have been no proceedings in being within which interlocutory relief could have been sought. It cannot be supposed that an action which the plaintiff *e* has no right to bring can enable him to get an injunction merely because the defendants have not had an opportunity of getting it struck out. Counsel for Mr McWhirter suggested that there was an analogy with RSC Ord 29, r 1 (3), under which an injunction can be obtained before action brought by a person who undertakes to issue a writ. That rule is clearly not directly applicable here because a writ had in fact been issued, and if it had not it would be quite improper for the court to accept an undertaking by *f* a person to issue a writ, naming himself as plaintiff, claiming relief to which he was not entitled. The suggestion made by counsel was rather that the undertaking should be an undertaking to apply for relator proceedings. This, however, affords no parallel to RSC Ord 29, r 1 (3), or to the common law rule to the same effect which existed before the Supreme Court of Judicature Act 1873. The issue of a writ by a plaintiff for relief which he is entitled to claim is a purely ministerial act; whether he *g* applies to the judge for an injunction before or after he has gone to the central office to issue his writ is a difference of form and not of substance. It is very different with the application to the Attorney-General for relator proceedings. There is no right to obtain his fiat. It is a matter for his absolute discretion whether he gives it or not, and in this function he is controllable only by Parliament and not by the courts (*London County Council v Attorney-General*[4], per Lord Halsbury LC[5] and per Lord *h* MacNaghten[6]).

In adhering to the view that the Attorney-General must be a party to the action, and in holding that no application for an injunction can be made before he is joined (or at least before he has given his fiat, which then creates a situation akin to that dealt with in RSC Ord 29, r 1 (3)), I do not consider that I am upholding a mere archaic

j

---

1   [1903] 1 Ch 109
2   [1908] 1 Ch 388
3   [1967] 2 All ER 1225, [1967] 1 WLR 1104
4   [1902] AC 165
5   [1902] AC at 168, 169
6   [1902] AC at 170

a   piece of red tape. Everybody, and every statutory or other authority, is liable to be sued by any person who claims that his individual interests have been interfered with. It does not follow that a person or authority should be liable to action at the suit of any person (and it might be a multitude of different people bringing separate actions) to enforce a public duty. If there is a difference of opinion between an individual and an authority as to what the authority ought to do or refrain from doing, there may well *b*   be a difference of opinion between members of the public about it. The requirement for the consent of the Attorney-General is a useful safeguard against merely cranky proceedings and against a multiplicity of proceedings. While there may be cases in which a person seeks to restrain some action of an authority and has no time or money or opportunity to take the steps necessary to obtain the Attorney-General's consent, I think this will be rare, and on the whole the risk of damage to the public interest by *c*   allowing a right to apply for relief to such a person without such consent is greater than the risk of damage to the public interest (which is all we are concerned with) in withholding it. Take this case. If Mr McWhirter's contention were right, he might have obtained his injunction from a judge in chambers on an ex parte application at a moment leaving no time for an appeal. The application might have been based on apparently convincing but in fact misleading newspaper reports. The programme *d*   might really be an innocent one, and the cost of cancelling it far more than Mr McWhirter could afford to pay. And millions of viewers might be deprived of pleasure and instruction against their will.

The weapon of the interlocutory injunction is at all times a powerful one, the use of which involves risks. It is a valuable weapon for the protection of private rights and protecting the welfare of children. While it is a weapon that may well have *e*   its uses in relation to the protection of the public interest, I think it is right that it should not be immediately available for that purpose to any member of the public. However that may be, I am quite satisfied that the present law does not allow such an application, and if a change of the law is desirable it is for Parliament to say so.

If ever a case arose in which it appeared that the Attorney-General had failed to give proper consideration to an application for his fiat, or had refused it on wholly improper *f*   grounds, then consideration would have to be given to the question of whether any remedy is available other than control by Parliament as envisaged by Lord Halsbury LC. No such problem arises in the present case.

Since I consider that Mr McWhirter's action and his application for an injunction and his appeal to this court were all misconceived, I should be inclined to refuse to answer the hypothetical question of whether in other circumstances the evidence before the court on 16th January was such as to justify the grant of an injunction. But *g*   the matter has been fully argued and the parties are anxious to have an answer. I will simply say that as the description in the newspaper cuttings was in my view sufficient evidence, at any rate on an urgent interlocutory application, that indecent material was to be broadcast, and as there was evidence that the Independent Broadcasting Authority had not seen the film before giving their consent to its being shown, *h*   I consider that we were then entitled to take the view that the authority had not complied with their duty under s 3 (1) (*a*) of the 1964 Act.

It is, however, necessary to consider whether an injunction should be granted in a relator action on the evidence now before this court. This includes the two affidavits of Lord Aylestone and the view which the members of the court have had of the film.

j   I adhere to the opinion which I formed on the basis of the newspaper descriptions and which I found amply confirmed by seeing the film, that in my opinion it contains a substantial amount of indecent material. It is a matter of surprise to me that 11 members of the authority were unanimously of the opinion that it does not offend against good taste or decency; and a matter of greater surprise that 17 out of 18 members of the advisory council took the same view of it. But they did.

The position here is not comparable to that which exists when a court holds that the

verdict of a jury is perverse; because the court there knows nothing of the character *a*
or background of individual members of the jury and 11 rather weak jurymen may
have been persuaded by one prejudiced strong-minded man. Here we know that
the people who formed this opinion are intelligent, cultured people with a wide range
of types of background. To say that they must all but one have applied some wrong
test or that they must themselves be lacking in good taste and decent feeling would
be a bold statement. The authority are the censors, I am not. The advisory council *b*
has the duty of advising them, I have not.

The strongest part of counsel for Mr McWhirter's argument was, I thought, the
contention based on certain passages in Lord Aylestone's first affidavit and on some
of the documents produced that the authority, their staff and advisers, had directed
their minds only to the programme as a whole, coupled with the warning broadcast
at the beginning of it, and may have overlooked their duty to ensure as far as possible *c*
that nothing indecent is *included* in a programme. I do not, however, in the end
think that that would be a proper inference. I observe in particular that in a letter
written by Lord Aylestone in March 1972, he drew the attention of programme
companies to an increase in the introduction of bad language into programmes,
and I also bear in mind that when the staff of the Independent Broadcasting Authority
considered the first version of the Andy Warhol programme they recommended *d*
the deletion of parts that appeared to them objectionable. It seems to me clear
that neither the authority nor their staff limited their consideration to the general
effect of the programme as distinct from examining its various parts. I would therefore not grant an injunction in relator proceedings.

LAWTON LJ. When at about 3.00 p m on 16th January 1973 Mr McWhirter applied *e*
to this court for an interim injunction against the Independent Broadcasting Authority
to restrain them from broadcasting at 10.30 p m the same evening a programme
about a man named Andy Warhol, it seemed to me on the evidence and information
then available that the court might have to solve the grave and important constitutional problem, if it could, of how a powerful statutory body like the authority
could be made to obey the law if the Attorney-General was not willing to act ex *f*
officio, as the court was told correctly he was not, and the shortness of time made
what I then believed to be the complicated and cumbersome procedure of a relator
action unavailable. Mr McWhirter put before the court three newspaper reports
which gave factual details about the contents of the programme. These reports
were not the best evidence of what was in the programme but under the rules of
court they were admissible in support of an interlocutory application; and when
at the court's invitation the authority appeared at 5.00 p m represented by counsel, *g*
it was not suggested on their behalf that these factual details were untrue or
inaccurate.

Counsel then submitted that Mr McWhirter, as a private citizen, had no right in
law to apply to the court to stop the authority from breaking the law (if they were
going to do so, which they denied) by broadcasting a programme which did not
comply with s 3 of the Television Act 1964. As in my judgment Mr McWhirter's *h*
evidence established a prima facie case that the authority were about to break the
law, and as no irreparable damage would be done to them if they were ordered not
to broadcast the programme that evening, I agreed with Lord Denning MR that an
interlocutory injunction should be granted pending a full examination of the legal
position, which it was impossible to make there and then.

At a hearing starting on 25th January 1973, the court had the help of counsel for *i*
both Mr McWhirter and the authority and of the Attorney-General himself. In
the course of this hearing the Attorney-General gave the court information about
the attitude which he and his predecessors in modern times have taken towards
relator actions, and the speed with which he can and will act in such actions if he
is satisfied that the relator has a case which is worthy of consideration by a court.

a   Much of this information is not available as far as I know in any of the practitioners' textbooks. In the present case Mr McWhirter was told about midday on 15th January that the Attorney-General would not act ex officio but that his refusal was without prejudice to Mr McWhirter's right to ask for his co-operation in a relator action. Mr McWhirter elected not to make any request for relator proceedings. The next day he issued his writ in his own name and came before this court as a

b   private citizen. Had he asked the Attorney-General for leave to start a relator action forthwith, and had the Attorney-General been satisfied both as to the urgency of the matter and the prima facie merits of his case, he could have appeared before the court without there being any challenge to his standing. He decided to proceed on his own. There has been a challenge, and in my judgment the challenge must be held to have been established.

c   The leading authorities on the right of a private citizen to apply to the court to ensure that the law is obeyed have been reviewed by Lord Denning MR. I have only this to add. The problem of what to do about powerful persons or bodies who seem to be above the law is not new. So far the flexibility of our constitution has been such that the weapons used for cutting down the over mighty to size have varied from age to age. The early Tudors used their executive powers through the pre-

d   rogative courts to curb the feudal barons. In the last two centuries Parliament has used its legislative powers to restrain the misuse of economic strength, and in the last 50 years the courts by means of the so-called prerogative orders of certiorari, man-damus and prohibition and by the granting of injunctions have succeeded in keeping statutory bodies within the limits of the law and of making them perform their duties according to the law. The courts, however, cannot initiate action: they have to be moved to action, and they can only be moved by private citizens or corporations

e   who have suffered some harm or damage over and above that suffered by the public at large. This might be a serious flaw in our constitution were it not for the office of the Attorney-General who by constitutional convention puts himself above politics in his appearances before the courts and in his administration of the law. As long as he is prepared to act ex officio whenever he himself considers that a statutory

f   body or even a Minister has been flouting the law or to give consent to the starting of a relator action on the application of a private citizen if he is satisfied that there is a case worthy of consideration, members of the public are reasonably well protected against abuses and misuses of power. Further, there is an advantage in having him as a sieve for complaints; statutory bodies such as the Independent Broadcasting Authority can get on with the job Parliament has given them to do without having to occupy themselves with fighting off interfering busybodies. I agree with Lord

g   Denning MR that if at any time in the future (and in my judgment it is not the fore-seeable future) there was reason to think that an Attorney-General was refusing improperly to exercise his powers, the courts might have to intervene to ensure that the law was obeyed.

I turn now to the main issue, it having been agreed by the Attorney-General that if the court decided against Mr McWhirter on status he would give his consent to

h   relator proceedings. In order to avoid an adjournment so that Mr McWhirter could get his action in proper form, counsel for the authority argued their case on the basis that relator proceedings had been started.

In my judgment it is important to underline the differences between the authority, the British Broadcasting Corporation, the theatre and the cinema as

j   sources of entertainment. The duties of the authority are set out in a statute; the duties of the other institutions are not. If the latter broadcast, perform or show anything to which objection is made, they must be judged by the law which applies generally; but if objection is made to what the authority does, the courts have to construe and apply the Television Act 1964.

It has not been suggested by counsel for the authority at any stage of these pro-ceedings that the courts have no jurisdiction to restrain the authority from breaches

of that Act. Their submissions have been directed to establishing the limits of the **a**
court's jurisdiction to interfere and that this case does not come within those limits.
Lord Denning MR and Cairns LJ have dealt with the principles of law applicable.
I have nothing to add on the law. On the application of the law to the facts of this
case I would like to make a few observations.

I accept counsel for the authority's submission that the authority when satisfying
themselves that programmes comply with s 3 (1) of the Television Act 1964 are **b**
entitled to rely on evidence and that there is no statutory obligation on them to look
at every programme. The evidence which they can rely on includes the reports of
members of their staff, and in most cases such evidence would be the best and only
evidence before them. They should, however, remember that such reports are
only evidence. If at any time credible evidence to the contrary effect to a staff
report becomes available, then they should look at the programme themselves and **c**
make up their own minds. In my judgment this is what they should have done,
and did not do, on 15th January 1973, when the press reports came to their notice.
They are not bound to pay overmuch attention to adjectives used in newspapers to
attract the attention of readers; but when newspaper reports contain factual details,
as the ones relied on by Mr McWhirter did, the position is different. After the interlocutory injunction had been granted, both the authority and their General Advisory **d**
Council each looked at the programme separately, and with one dissentient on the
advisory council they all agreed that it complied with what they understood to be
the requirements of the Act. Counsel for Mr McWhirter submitted that there was
evidence that they had misdirected themselves as to the construction of the Act. I
am not satisfied that they did. It follows that there remains only one question to
be answered. Was their decision to broadcast the programme, if the court dis- **e**
charged the interlocutory injunction, one which no reasonable authority could have
made? In simpler terms, did they make a perverse decision?

Before this court could adjudge that the authority had made a perverse decision
there would have to be very strong evidence indeed. The only evidence we have
had, besides the newspaper reports, has been a showing of the programme itself;
and now that it has been put in evidence it has become the best evidence, and the **f**
newspaper reports can be put aside.

In fairness to the authority, it is right to point out that there is some basis for their
chairman's complaint made in an affidavit sworn on 24th January 1973, that by
stressing certain incidents an entirely false impression of the programme had been
given. It lasts about 45 minutes; the incidents, five in number, to which reference
was made in the newspaper reports, occupy between 10 and 12 per cent of the running **g**
time. Three lasted about 45 to 60 seconds each; one which showed a woman trying
to apply paint to a piece of paper with one of her breasts lasted between one to two
minutes; and the remaining incident, which was concerned with a conversation
having homosexual implications between two men, one naked, sharing a bed, lasted
about 2½ minutes. In my judgment these incidents provided strong evidence that the
authority intended to broadcast matter which, in the words of the statute, offended **h**
'against good taste or decency'; but I have reminded myself that my judicial task is
to adjudge whether my assessment of the evidence is the only reasonable one, if it
be a reasonable one at all. For this purpose it is necessary to consider the programme
as a whole.

It purports to show what kind of artistic and film work Andy Warhol does and the
kind of people he mixes with. Insofar as it shows his artistic work there can be no **i**
doubt that many would find it attractive. His film work was illustrated by extracts
from films he had made; three of the incidents complained of came from these
extracts. Finally there were shots showing his friends and associates. Most of these
people, who included the woman using one of her breasts to apply paint to paper,
seemed very weird indeed. A possible appreciation of the programme could be that
it was an attempt to give the television viewing public an opportunity of seeing

something of, and understanding, what, in modern idiom, has come to be called a 'sick society'. If this was the intention the distasteful and indecent incidents become relevant. It would be no answer to a charge of disregarding the Television Act 1964 for the authority to say that their motives in broadcasting indecent matter were worthy; but whether an incident is indecent must depend on all the circumstances, including the context in which the alleged indecent matter occurs. Save for the incident involving the woman, which had aspects of both bathos and pathos, all the others were concerned with indecency in words, not in acts, and show how depraved some people can become. I am far from being satisfied that the major part of the British public is willing to have broadcast to their homes the kinds of conversations which occur in this programme; the authority seem to think they are. They may be right. In the realm of good taste and decency, whose frontiers are ill-defined, I find it impossible to say that the authority have crossed from the permissible into the unlawful. They have got perilously near to doing so, and in a society with constantly changing standards of outlook and behaviour they would be unwise to assume that the frontiers will always be pushed nearer licentiousness, as the history of morals in this country shows. The ribaldry and bawdiness which was enjoyed at Drury Lane Theatre up to the end of the reign of Queen Anne had gone by David Garrick's time some 50 years later; his public liked plays with a marked moral flavour.

As I can envisage, albeit with difficulty, a reasonable authority thinking that this programme complied with s 3 (1) of the Television Act 1964, I cannot say that their decision to broadcast it was perverse. I would discharge the injunction.

Appeal restored to list for further hearing. Leave given to amend writ. Appeal dismissed; injunction discharged; damages under the undertaking given by Mr McWhirter remitted to be assessed by a master.

Solicitors: *Trower, Still & Keeling* (for Mr McWhirter); *Allen & Overy* (for the authority); *Treasury Solicitor*.

Wendy Shockett Barrister.

John Bishop (Caterers) Ltd and another v National Union Bank Ltd and others

CHANCERY DIVISION

PLOWMAN J

1st, 2nd NOVEMBER 1972

Costs – Security for costs – Company – Limited company as plaintiff – Company likely to be unable to pay costs of defendant if successful in his defence – Co-plaintiff with company – Plaintiff company in liquidation and alleged to be hopelessly insolvent – Second plaintiff a secured creditor of plaintiff company – Overlap of plaintiffs' claims comparatively small – Whether presence of second plaintiff justifying refusal of order for security for costs – Companies Act 1948, s 447.

The plaintiff company and the second plaintiff brought an action against the defendants. The second plaintiff was a secured creditor of the plaintiff company. There were large areas of the claim raised by the plaintiff company in which the second plaintiff appeared to have no interest. The plaintiff company was in liquidation and was alleged to be hopelessly insolvent. The defendants applied for an order for security for costs against the plaintiff company under s 447[a] of the Companies Act

─────────────

a Section 447 is set out at p 709 b, post

1948. The plaintiff company conceded that the court had jurisdiction to make an
order but contended that no order should be made because of the presence of the *a*
second plaintiff.

Held – The plaintiff company should give security for costs. Since the overlap
between the claim of the plaintiff company and that of the second plaintiff appeared
to be comparatively small, it was possible that, if the action went to trial and the
plaintiff company lost, the second plaintiff would not necessarily be ordered to pay *b*
the defendants all the costs which they had incurred against the plaintiff company
(see p 710 h j and p 711 b, post).

   M'Connell and Varlett v Johnston (1801) 1 East 431, *Sykes v Sykes* (1869) LR 4 CP 645
and *D'Hormusgee & Co and Isaacs & Co v Grey* (1882) 10 QBD 13 distinguished.

c

Notes
For security for costs by a company, see 6 Halsbury's Laws (3rd Edn) 451-453, para
875, and for cases on the subject, see 9 Digest (Repl) 731, 732, 4853-4864.
   For the Companies Act 1948, s 447, see 5 Halsbury's Statutes (3rd Edn) 425.

Cases referred to in judgment
D'Hormusgee & Co and Isaacs & Co v Grey (1882) 10 QBD 13, 52 LJQB 192, 51 Digest *d*
(Repl) 976, 5125.
M'Connell and Varlett v Johnston (1801) 1 East 431, 102 ER 167, 51 Digest (Repl) 976,
5121.
Sykes v Sykes (1869) LR 4 CP 645, 38 LJCP 281, 20 LT 663, 51 Digest (Repl) 973, 5085.
Winthorp v Royal Exchange Assurance Co (1755) 1 Dick 282, 21 ER 277, 51 Digest (Repl)
976, 5120. *e*

Cases also cited
Bilcon Ltd v Fegmay Investments Ltd [1966] 2 All ER 513, [1966] 2 QB 221.
Diamond Fuel Co, Re (1879) 13 Ch D 400.
Green v Rozen [1955] 2 All ER 797, [1955] 1 WLR 741.
Jones & Saldanha v Gurney [1913] WN 72. *f*
Photographic Artists' Co-operative Supply Association, Re (1883) 23 Ch D 370, CA.
Pure Spirit Co v Fowler (1890) 25 QBD 235, DC.
Selangor United Rubber Estates Ltd v Cradock [1967] 2 All ER 1255, [1967] 1 WLR 1168.

Procedure summonses
These were applications under s 447 of the Companies Act 1948, the first by *g*
a summons dated 25th February 1972, by National Union Bank Ltd, and the second
by a summons dated 23rd February 1972, by Bernard Phillips, for orders for security
for costs against the plaintiff company, John Bishop (Caterers) Ltd. The applicants
were, respectively, the first and second defendants in an action brought against them
and the third defendant, Lonetree Properties Ltd, by the plaintiff company and
William Cleland Sneddon, a secured creditor of the plaintiff company, seeking *h*
various declarations and enquiries. A third and similar summons by the third
defendant was dismissed in default of prosecution.

W A Macpherson QC and *Frank J White* for the plaintiffs.
J L Knox for the first defendant.
Jack Hames QC for the second defendant. *j*

PLOWMAN J. There are two summonses before me, one by the first defendant,
National Union Bank Ltd, asking for an order for security for costs against the plaintiff
company, John Bishop (Caterers) Ltd, and another by the second defendant, Mr
Bernard Phillips, asking for a similar order. There was a third and similar summons

a in my list, issued at the instance of the third defendant, Lonetree Properties Ltd, again asking for a similar order, but they have not appeared to support their summons and I have, in the course of these proceedings, dismissed it.

The basis of the application in each of the two cases with which I am concerned is that the plaintiff company is in compulsory liquidation and hopelessly insolvent. The applications are made under s 447 of the Companies Act 1948 which provides

b as follows:

'Where a limited company is plaintiff or pursuer in any action or other legal proceeding, any judge having jurisdiction in the matter may, if it appears by credible testimony that there is reason to believe that the company will be unable to pay the costs of the defendant if successful in his defence, require sufficient security to be given for those costs, and may stay all proceedings until

c the security is given.'

The summons are opposed on the ground that there is a second plaintiff, namely William Cleland Sneddon. It is not, I think, seriously disputed that if the plaintiff company were the only plaintiff an order for security for costs would follow almost as a matter of course. Also, it is conceded—and, in my view, rightly conceded—

d that notwithstanding the presence of a second plaintiff I have a discretion whether or not to make orders for security. But what is said is that in the present case, owing to the presence of Mr Sneddon as plaintiff, I ought to exercise my discretion by declining to make any order for security for costs, and in this connection I was referred, amongst others, to three cases, which I will mention briefly.

The first was *M'Connell and Varlett v Johnston*[1] decided in 1801 and very briefly

e reported. The headnote states:

'If one of the plaintiffs reside within reach of the process of the Court, security will not be required for the costs, though the other plaintiff be a foreigner residing abroad: and though the first-mentioned plaintiff be a bankrupt in execution for debt.'

f The report is simply this[2]:

'Lambe moved for a rule to stay proceedings in an action of assumpsit, till security was given by the plaintiffs for the costs; one of them (Varlett) being a foreigner residing abroad, and the other a bankrupt in custody in execution for a debt. But the Court denied the motion in the first instance, one of the plaintiffs being within the jurisdiction of the Court, and within reach of its process, and

g not coming under any of the rules requiring security to be given for the costs.'

That is the whole of the report. It is not very informative and does not say what the facts were; it does not disclose whether the plaintiffs were suing in respect of the same cause of action or not, but I suspect, having regard to the rules as to joinder of parties which were current at that time, that the action was a joint action of

h assumpsit.

The second case to which I was referred was *Sykes v Sykes*[3]. The headnote says this:

In an action by two executors, one of whom is out of the jurisdiction and the other insolvent, the defendant is not entitled to a stay of proceedings until they

j give security for costs.'

And the facts, very briefly, are stated in the first paragraph of the report:

---

1   (1801) 1 East 431
2   (1801) 1 East at 431, 432
3   (1869) LR 4 CP 645

'Action by the plaintiffs, as executors and executrix of Ellen Sykes, against the *a*
sheriff of Yorkshire and one Love for seizing and selling goods belonging to the
testatrix under an execution at the suit of Love upon a judgment recovered by
him against W. H. Shaw, the husband of the executrix.'

It is clear from that that in that case there was a complete identity of interests between
the two plaintiffs; they were suing in respect of one and the same cause of action.
    The other case was in 1882 called *D'Hormusgee & Co and Isaacs & Co v Grey*[1]. I *b*
will read the headnote:

'An action was brought against the defendant as a common carrier by two
plaintiffs, one residing abroad. The statement of claim alleged a contract by
the defendant with the plaintiffs jointly, and in the alternative with each of the
plaintiffs separately:—*Held*, that the plaintiff residing abroad could not be *c*
ordered to give security for costs.'

The relative facts were these[2]:

'It appeared that the first paragraph of the statement of claim alleged that the
plaintiffs, D'Hormusgee & Co., were merchants at Bombay, and the plaintiffs,
Isaacs & Co., merchants in London, and the defendant a lighterman in London, *d*
and the second and third paragraphs that the plaintiffs delivered to the defendant
as a common carrier 246 bales of cotton, which the defendant undertook to
convey safely and securely to St. Katherine Dock, and that in breach of his
undertaking he allowed them to become damaged by water. Fourth paragraph.
"In the alternative the plaintiffs repeat the second and third paragraphs of the
statement of claim, substituting for the word 'plaintiffs' the words 'the said *e*
Messrs. D'Hormusgee & Co.', and in the further alternative again repeat them,
substituting for the word 'plaintiffs' the words 'the said Messrs. Isaacs & Co.'".'

So that that was the claim by the plaintiffs, either jointly or by each of them severally,
in respect of the same subject-matter and there was a complete overlap in that case.
    Counsel for the second defendant invited me to say that that decision, which was a *f*
decision of the Divisional Court, was wrong. But it is one which has stood now for
90 years and is still cited as an authority, for example, in the White Book which
states[3]:

'No order will be made [for security of costs] if there are co-plaintiffs resident
in England (*Winthorp* v. *Royal Exchange Assurance Co*[4]; *D'Hormusgee* v. *Grey*[1]);
but they must be genuine co-plaintiffs and not merely the English attorney *g*
joined to avoid giving security . . .'

I am not prepared to express the view that *D'Hormusgee & Co v Grey*[1] was wrongly
decided, but there are, I think, two observations to be made about those cases. In
the first place, they were quite different on the facts from the present case. There, as I
have indicated when going through them, there was a complete identity or overlap *h*
of claim. In the present case—and I say this without attempting to analyse the long
and complicated statement of claim which has been served—it seems to me that there
are very large areas of claim raised by the plaintiff company, in which Mr Sneddon,
whose interest is that of a secured creditor, appears to have no locus standi. In other
words, unlike the cases to which I have referred, in the present case the overlap seems
to me to be comparatively small. And if that is so and this action goes to trial and *j*
the plaintiff company loses, I am not satisfied that Mr Sneddon will necessarily be
ordered to pay to the defendants all the costs which they incurred vis-à-vis the plaintiff

1   (1882) 10 QBD 13
2   (1882) 10 QBD at 13
3   The Supreme Court Practice 1973, vol I, p 378
4   (1755) 1 Dick 282

a company. The second observation to be made about the cases which I quoted is that none of them is a case under the Companies Acts. In fact, I am told that the researches of counsel on both sides have failed to disclose any case of an application under s 447 or its predecessors where there were two plaintiffs. And it does not necessarily follow that the cases which were cited to me are applicable to an application under s 447, an application which the legislature has singled out for special treatment.
b But, in a sense, the question whether those cases are applicable to an application under s 447 or not is academic because once it is conceded that I have a discretion, it is implicit that it is open to me to decide either way.

All I propose to say about the matter is this, that, taking into account all the circumstances here, I propose to exercise my discretion by ordering security on both summonses.

c *Order accordingly.*

Solicitors: *J Hird Williams* (for the plaintiffs); *A Kramer & Co* (for the first defendant); *Charles Mazillius & Co* (for the second defendant).

d Jacqueline Metcalfe Barrister.

R v Swabey (No 2)

e COURTS-MARTIAL APPEAL COURT
LORD WIDGERY CJ, ASHWORTH AND WILLIS JJ
11th DECEMBER 1972

Court-martial – Appeal – Reference of cases by authorities – Costs – Costs of defence –
f *Expenses properly incurred by defendant for the purposes of his appearance before Appeal Court – Costs restricted to costs incurred in his appearing physically before the court – Courts-Martial (Appeals) Act 1968, s 35 (1).*

The applicant, an officer in the Royal Navy, was convicted in 1956 on two charges and dismissed the service. In 1972, on a reference by the Home Secretary under s 34[a]
g of the Courts-Martial (Appeals) Act 1968, the first of the two convictions was quashed by the Courts-Martial Appeal Court[b] and a sentence of severe reprimand was substituted. No order for costs was made or asked for, however, it being assumed on behalf of the applicant that such an order would be automatic by virtue of the terms of s 35 (1)[c] of the 1968 Act which required the court to order the Secretary of State to pay 'such sums as appear to them reasonably sufficient to compensate [the applicant]
h for any expenses properly incurred by him for the purposes of his appearance'. A dispute arose as to the true construction of s 35 (1) and the matter was referred to the court for decision. The applicant also sought the adjudication of the court on the question whether the effect of the quashing of his conviction was to restore his status from the date of the original court-martial in 1956.

j **Held** – (i) The expenses referred to in s 35 (1) were merely the expenses involved in the applicant making his way to court and subsisting during the hearing of the reference, i e the costs incurred in his appearing physically before the court; they did not refer

---

a   Section 34, so far as material, is set out at p 712 *j* to p 713 *a*, post
b   See *R v Swabey* [1972] 2 All ER 1094
c   Section 35 (1) is set out at p 712 *g*, post

to the costs incurred by being represented by counsel and solicitor. Accordingly, the
applicant was only entitled to such expenses and not to costs generally (see p 715 c,
post).

(ii) The court had no jurisdiction to entertain an application to restore the applicant's status to what it had been at the date of his court-martial (see p 715 g, post).

Notes
For special references to the Courts-Martial Appeal Court, see 33 Halsbury's Laws
(3rd Edn) 1113, 1114, para 1849, and for costs generally on courts-martial appeals,
see ibid, 1125, 1126, para 1866.

For the Courts-Martial (Appeals) Act 1968, ss 34, 35, see 29 Halsbury's Statutes
(3rd Edn) 894, 895.

Case referred to in judgment
R v Swabey [1972] 2 All ER 1094, [1972] 1 WLR 925, C-MAC.

Application
This was an application on behalf of Christopher Carlisle Swabey for an order for
costs in his favour arising out of a reference by the Secretary of State to the Courts-
Martial Appeal Court under s 34 of the Courts-Martial (Appeals) Act 1968 to consider
the findings of guilty against the applicant at a court-martial on 17th April 1956.
On 3rd May 1972 the court quashed a finding of guilty of indecent assault but upheld
a finding of guilty of conduct to the prejudice of naval discipline, and substituted
for the sentence of dismissal from the service (passed in accordance with service law
on the charge sheet as a whole) a sentence of severe reprimand.   At the conclusion
of the hearing of the reference counsel for the applicant did not ask for costs and no
order was made.   The matter was referred to the court for decision whether there
was power under s 35 of the 1968 Act to award the applicant the costs incurred by
him on the reference.   The facts are set out in the judgment of the court.

J N Hutchinson QC and Colin Nicholls for the applicant.
J P Comyn QC and Felix Waley for the Crown.

LORD WIDGERY CJ delivered the judgment of the court.   Section 35 (1) of the
Courts-Martial (Appeals) Act 1968 reads as follows:

'Where on a reference under section 34 of this Act the person who was tried
by court-martial appears before the Appeal Court, the Court shall direct the
payment by the Secretary of State of such sums as appear to them reasonably
sufficient to compensate that person for any expenses properly incurred by him
for the purposes of his appearance.'

It is unnecessary to go in any kind of detail into the long and extremely complex
history of this case. It suffices to say that in 1956 the applicant, Lieutenant-Commander
Swabey, was convicted by court-martial of two charges and sentenced to be
dismissed the service.   After a lapse of some 16 years, namely on 3rd May 1972, the
matter came before this court[1], not for the first time, but in this instance on a reference
by the Secretary of State under s 34 of the Act to which I have just referred.   That
section provides, omitting irrelevant words:

'(1) If, in the case of the conviction of a person by court-martial ... (b) it appears
to the Secretary of State, upon consideration of matters appearing to him not to
have been brought to the notice of the court-martial at the trial, to be expedient
that the finding of the court-martial should be considered or reconsidered by the
Appeal Court ... the Secretary of State ... may refer the finding to the Court.

1   See R v Swabey [1972] 2 All ER 1094, [1972] 1 WLR 925

a '(2) A reference to the Appeal Court under this section shall, for all purposes other than those of sections 31 and 32 of this Act, be treated as an appeal by the person convicted against his conviction . . .'

Following the hearing of the appeal, as it is properly described, in this court, on 3rd May 1972, counsel for the applicant, although successful in securing the quashing of the first of two convictions, did not make any application for costs. His failure to
b do so is, if I may say so, fully understandable because he took the view that an order for costs would be automatic by virtue of the terms of s 35 (1). It now appears that this view is not universally held and an issue has arisen between the applicant and the Ministry, as one may properly now describe them, as to the true effect of s 35 (1).

It is contended on behalf of the applicant through counsel that it really is a provision which entitles him to his costs in the ordinary legal sense of that word, in other
c words counsel urges on us a construction of s 35 (1) whereby the court would be bound to make an order that the applicant receive his costs of the proceedings, including of course the expenses incurred by him in instructing counsel and solicitor in the matter.

On the other side it is argued by counsel on behalf of the Ministry that the operation of s 35 (1) is very much more limited and that the only expenses properly incurred in
d respect of which an order can be made under that subsection are the expenses incurred in the applicant's physically travelling to this court and being physically present in the court in the course of his three day hearing. In terms of cash, of course, the different effect of the two constructions would no doubt be very wide. First of all, since this is a Courts-Martial Appeal Court jurisdiction, one must look at the structure of the Courts-Martial (Appeals) Act 1968 in regard to costs. It is to be observed that
e there is a provision in s 31 for dealing with the costs of a successful appeal. Section 31 (1) provides:

'Where the Appeal Court allow an appeal they may if they think fit, direct the payment by the Secretary of State of costs to the appellant.'

The nature of the costs which may so be ordered are further defined in sub-s (2)
f which refers to them as—

'The costs which may under this section be directed to be paid are such sums as appear to the Appeal Court reasonably sufficient to compensate the appellant for any expenses properly incurred by him in the case . . .'

There is no argument at all but that what is contemplated by that section is an
g order for costs in the ordinary sense in which lawyers understand that phrase.

Section 32 makes provision for costs against the appellant in an ordinary appeal under the Act, and it provides that:

'(1) Where the Appeal Court dismiss an appeal or an application for leave to appeal they may, if they think fit, order the appellant or applicant (as the case may be) to pay to the Secretary of State the whole or any part of the costs of
h the appeal . . .'

So one gets again a common form discretionary power to the court in the event of the appeal proving unsuccessful, to order the costs of the respondent to be paid by the appellant. It is to be noted at once, as is clear from my reading of s 34 (2), that both ss 31 and 32 are excluded from the present proceedings, which are proceedings on a
j reference. Parliament has quite deliberately decided that those discretionary powers, one might think commonly to be expected in proceedings of this kind, are not to apply. There can be no doubt about that. It is equally clear that Parliament has substituted for the discretionary powers in ss 31 and 32 a mandatory obligation on the court to make an order in favour of, in this case, the applicant in respect of the expenses properly incurred by him for the purposes of his appearance. We should have much more confidence in deciding this case if the court, or counsel, were able

to provide a clear and really cogent explanation of why that alteration is made, and
what purpose it is sought to achieve.   The court finds it difficult to determine precisely what was the purpose in the draftsman's mind, and counsel have not been
able to assist us either.   But that there is a wholly different approach to costs on a
reference is clear enough.   Exactly why the difference is made, and exactly why there
is this single mandatory provision in respect of references, whatever the merits
which are reposed in them, and whatever the outcome of them, is something which
we do do not find easy to determine.

One must look around in the legislation to see whether assistance is to be obtained
from any other place.   We have been referred, amongst other provisions of the
Act, to s 47, which deals with costs on an appeal from this court to the House of Lords
following a conviction by court-martial.   There are in s 47 what one might call the
normal discretionary powers for awarding costs, and there is no doubt here that the
award is for costs in the conventional sense, because the amount which is to be paid
is that which is reasonably sufficient to compensate the accused for any expenses
properly incurred by him in resisting the application, not just appearing in their
Lordships' House but in resisting the application.   One finds again if one goes back
to s 35 (2), a somewhat similar provision, because in sub-s (2) it is said that:

'In any such case [which means of course the disposal of a reference] the Appeal
Court may, if they think fit, also direct the payment by the Secretary of State of
such sums as appear to them reasonably sufficient to compensate the person
who was tried by court-martial for any expenses properly incurred by him in
carrying on his defence before the court-martial . . .'

That again can only mean, we think, an award of costs, and one at once asks oneself
why, if in s 35 (1) Parliament was seeking again to refer to costs in the ordinary conventional sense, a phrase such as that appearing in s 47 or in s 35 (2) or in s 31 should
not have been used.   It seems to us to be a clear and deliberate choice exercised by
the draftsman not to use any one of the three or four conventional phrases about
which no dispute would arise at all.

In a further effort to achieve the correct construction of this provision we have
looked at the earlier legislation contained in the Criminal Appeal Act 1907 and later
contemporaneously in the Criminal Appeal Act 1968.   It is not without interest to
observe that in s 13 (1) of the Criminal Appeal Act 1907 there was a single peremptory
provision that in proceedings under that Act no costs should be allowed to either
side.   The whole conventional use of costs and an order for costs is excluded.   But
in s 13 (2) of the 1907 Act we get something not altogether different from the provisions of s 35 (1) of the current Courts-Martial (Appeals) Act 1968, because s 13 (2)
provides:

'The expenses of any solicitor or counsel assigned to an appellant under this
Act, and the expenses of any witnesses attending on the order of the court or
examined in any proceedings incidental to the appeal, and of the appearance
of an appellant on the hearing of his appeal or on any proceedings preliminary
or incidental to the appeal, and all expenses of and incidental to any examination
of witnesses conducted by any person appointed by the court for the purpose, or
any reference of a question to a special commissioner appointed by the court,
or of any person appointed as assessor to the court, shall be defrayed, up to an
amount allowed by the court, but subject to any regulations as to rates and
scales of payment made by the Secretary of State . . .'

So again one finds in the 1907 Act a clear distinction between costs and expenses, because they are dealt with by different provisions with wholly different consequences.

Finally, our attention has been drawn to the fact that in the Criminal Appeal
Act 1968, which contains conventional discretionary powers in the court both for
ordinary appeals and for references, there is a special provision in s 27 dealing with the
expenses of an appellant's appearance.   Section 27 provides:

a
'Where an appellant who is not in custody appears before the Court of Appeal, either on the hearing of his appeal or in any proceedings preliminary or incidental thereto, the Court may direct that there be paid to him out of local funds the expenses of his appearance.'

Counsel for the applicant has urged, and we have considerable sympathy with his argument, that in this case, and perhaps in many like it, it really is quite an extra-

b ordinary thing that the court shall not only be deprived of any discretionary power to compensate the applicant for his costs in the conventional sense, but should rather be required to make an order in respect of the expenses of his appearance. But nevertheless we find the language of these provisions too strong to reach a different conclusion and in our judgment, if the matter is to be altered, it must be altered by Parliament.

c
Our determination on the application before us is that the expenses referred to in s 35 (1) are merely the expenses involved in the applicant making his way to this court and subsisting during the period of the hearing; in other words the costs incurred in his appearing physically in this building and not the other costs incurred in being represented by counsel and solicitor. The court hopes that that decision in principle having been given, the form of the consequential order may perhaps be a matter of

d agreement between the parties. The court will make an order for payment to the applicant of whatever the correct sum is.

[There followed argument on sentence under s 13 of the 1968 Act.]

LORD WIDGERY CJ. The outcome of the hearing in this court on 3rd May 1972 was, as I have already indicated, that the court quashed the applicant's conviction on

e the first of the two counts which were then before it, and confirmed his conviction on the second count. It thereupon varied the sentence which had been a combined or composite sentence on both counts, to one of a severe reprimand in lieu of the previous sentence of dismissal from the service.

The court's authority for quashing the conviction is to be found in s 12 of the Courts-Martial (Appeals) Act 1968 which provides in terms in sub-s (2): 'If the Appeal Court

f allow an appeal against conviction, they shall quash the conviction.' This is a statutory tribunal; it has no powers except those conferred on it by statute, and it has done in this case in terms what the Act said it was to do.

Counsel for the applicant has asked us to adjudicate on what is no doubt an extremely important consequential issue, namely whether the effect of the quashing of the conviction restores the applicant's status as it were from the original court-martial

g date or only restored it from the date of the hearing in this court or from some other date. Whilst we have some sympathy with the desire of the parties to obtain a ruling on that issue, the plain fact is that this court has no jurisdiction in our view to entertain such an application. There are other procedures proper to be used, but in this court, whether we wish to do it or not, we do not enjoy the power and authority to do it.

h
Before leaving the matter, I would like to observe that no challenge has been made to the power of this court to substitute a sentence of severe reprimand for one of dismissal from the service under s 13 of the Act. There being no challenge to that determination, and more important, no question of an appeal from it, then it stands for the purposes of this case, but we would wish it known to those who come to this matter in other cases that our decision on the facts of this case that we had jurisdiction

j to vary the sentence is one which was reached without argument and should be viewed with appropriate caution in the event of reference being made to it hereafter.

Order accordingly.

Solicitors: *Thomas Eggar & Son*, Chichester (for the applicant); *Treasury Solicitor*.

N P Metcalfe Esq Barrister.

R v Lymm Justices, ex parte Brown

QUEEN'S BENCH DIVISION

LORD WIDGERY CJ, MELFORD STEVENSON AND BRABIN JJ

6th NOVEMBER 1972

Crown Court – Committal of offender to Crown Court for sentence – Jurisdiction – Summary trial for indictable offence – Accused charged with offences of theft – Accused of previous good character – Justices having no other information about accused's antecedents and character – Justices agreeing to summary trial – Accused pleading guilty – Justices subsequently discovering accused police officer – Offences committed whilst accused on duty – Justices committing accused for sentence – Power of justices to commit for sentence – Magistrates' Courts Act 1952, ss 19, 29.

The applicant was charged with (i) stealing a lady's twin set and (ii) on divers dates committing a number of offences of theft, and brought before the justices. The prosecution intimated that the case could be dealt with summarily. At that stage of the proceedings the only knowledge that the justices had about the applicant was that he had been charged with the offences alleged in the informations and that he was of previous good character. Accordingly they agreed to a summary trial under s 19[a] of the Magistrates' Courts Act 1952. The applicant did not object and pleaded guilty to both counts. The prosecution then outlined the details of the case, whereupon the justices learned that the applicant was a police officer, that the offences had been committed by him whilst on duty, and that over a period of time he had stolen property from persons whom he had been employed to protect. In view of those disclosures the justices decided, in the purported exercise of their power under s 29[b] of the 1952 Act, to commit the applicant to quarter sessions for sentence. The applicant moved, inter alia, for an order of certiorari to quash the committal order on the ground that the justices had in the circumstances no jurisdiction to make it.

Held – Before exercising their power under s 19 (2) to proceed with a case summarily, justices were under a duty to make a proper enquiry into the circumstances of the case. Facts which became known to the justices as a result of that enquiry, and before the decision had been made to proceed summarily, could not thereafter be taken into consideration when the justices came to decide whether to commit for sentence under s 29. Where, however, justices had failed to make a proper enquiry before deciding to proceed summarily under s 19, they could have regard to facts relating to the character and antecedents of the accused which had emerged subsequently when deciding whether to commit for sentence under s 29. In the applicant's case the justices were entitled to take into account the additional facts relating to his character and antecedents which they had learned after he had pleaded guilty; accordingly the committal order had been properly made (see p 719 e to j, p 720 g and p 721 d and f, post).

R v King's Lynn Justices, ex parte Carter [1968] 3 All ER 858 applied.

R v Tower Bridge Magistrate, ex parte Osman [1971] 2 All ER 1018 explained.

Notes

For committal to quarter sessions for sentence for indictable offences triable summarily, see 25 Halsbury's Laws (3rd Edn) 226, 227, para 421, and for cases on the subject, see 33 Digest (Repl) 187, 188, 356-364.

For the Magistrates' Courts Act 1952, ss 19, 29, see 21 Halsbury's Statutes (3rd Edn) 203, 215.

---

a   Section 19, so far as material, is set out at p 718 d, post

b   Section 29, so far as material, is set out at p 718 g, post

Cases referred to in judgments

a R v King's Lynn Justices, ex parte Carter [1968] 3 All ER 858, [1969] 1 QB 488, [1968] 3 WLR 1210, 133 JP 83, 53 Cr App Rep 42, DC, Digest (Cont Vol C) 650, 361e.

R v Tower Bridge Magistrate, ex parte Osman [1971] 2 All ER 1018, [1971] 1 WLR 1109, 135 JP 427, 55 Cr App Rep 436, DC.

Cases and authority also cited

b R v Thompson [1914] 2 KB 99, CCA.

R v Vallett [1951] 1 All ER 231, CCA.

Archbold's Criminal Pleading, Evidence and Practice (37th Edn, 1969), pp 45, 46, para 122.

Motion for certiorari

c This was an application on behalf of Donald William Brown for an order of certiorari (i) to bring up and quash an order made by the justices sitting at Lymm Magistrates' Court under s 29 of the Magistrates' Courts Act 1952 on 30th June 1971 whereby the justices committed the applicant on bail to the Knutsford Quarter Sessions for sentence; and (ii) to bring up and quash the conviction on the second charge recorded by the justices. The grounds on which the relief was sought were as follows: (1) that *d* the justices on summary trial had no power to commit the applicant to the Knutsford Quarter Sessions for sentence because that power was dependent on their having regard, on conviction, to the applicant's character and antecedents which, being excellent, mitigated rather than aggravated the two offences to which he pleaded guilty and the one offence which he asked the court to take into consideration; (2) that the justices, having accepted that their powers of punishment for the offences *e* charged were adequate pursuant to s 19 (2) of the Magistrates' Courts Act 1952 were not entitled to include the facts of the offences charged in their considerations when determining that the applicant be committed for sentence to Knutsford Quarter Sessions; (3) that the one other offence the applicant requested to be taken into consideration did not materially add to the gravity of the offences charged such as to entitle the justices to commit the applicant for sentence; (4) that if, which was *f* denied, the justices did have a discretion to commit the applicant pursuant to s 29, they did not appear to exercise that discretion judicially; (5) that no information as to the applicant's character and antecedents was adduced before the court, or existed such as to enable the justices to commit him for sentence to the Knutsford Quarter Sessions, and (6) that on the record of conviction an error of law was disclosed, namely, that the second charge was bad in law for duplicity, and should *g* have been quashed notwithstanding the applicant's plea of guilty to it.

R J S Fairley for the applicant.
Gordon Slynn as amicus curiae.
The respondent justices did not appear and were not represented.

h **LORD WIDGERY CJ.** In these proceedings counsel for the applicant moves for an order of certiorari to remove into this court with a view to its being quashed an order made by justices sitting at Lymm Magistrates' Court on 30th June 1971 whereby, purporting to act under s 29 of the Magistrates' Courts Act 1952, they committed the applicant on bail to the Knutsford Quarter Sessions for sentence on two offences. Also he asks for an order of certiorari to bring up and quash the conviction on the second of those two offences.

j On 29th June 1971 the applicant was arrested, one gathers almost caught in the act, when opening a showcase at Manchester airport and stealing certain articles therein. That by itself, perhaps, would not be unduly serious, until one knows that the applicant was at the time a police officer employed at Manchester airport, that he picked the lock in order to steal, and that he had committed a very large number of similar offences in the preceding four or five months. The arrest having

taken place on 29th June, the applicant was before the justices the following day, *a*
30th June, and the prosecution intimated that this was a proper case for summary
trial.

In the absence of those who made that decision, one would not wish unfairly to
criticise them when they have not had an opportunity of being heard, but I must
say, speaking for myself, that this looks very much like the type of case, all too
common in practice, in which the prosecution are far too ready to accept that a case *b*
is suitable for summary trial and sometimes exercise a greater influence than they
ought on the justices in that decision. For my part, if anyone had known at the
beginning the brief details of these cases to which I have already referred, no possible
conclusion that this case was fit for summary trial could have been reached, and
the whole thing seems to have been carried through with indecent haste, the trial,
such as it was, taking place on the very day after the arrest.   *c*

However, the matter has got to be dealt with under the appropriate statutory
provisions, and I remind myself of what they are. Section 19 (2) of the Magistrates'
Courts Act 1952 provides:

> 'If at any time during the inquiry into the offence it appears to the court, having
> regard to any representations made in the presence of the accused by the pro-
> secutor or made by the accused, and to the nature of the case, that the punish- *d*
> ment that the court has power to inflict under this section would be adequate
> and that the circumstances do not make the offence one of serious character and
> do not for other reasons require trial on indictment, the court may proceed
> with a view to summary trial.'

That subsection enables the justices, as is well known, to try summarily an offence *e*
which is of its nature an indictable offence, and no doubt the section contemplates
that the justices will do their best before reaching their decision to discover whether
the case is truly suitable for summary trial having regard to the considerations
mentioned in s 19 (2). As a safeguard against the justices mistakenly exercising
this power, that is to say exercising this power in a case in which in the event it is
clear that they should have treated the case as an indictable one, s 29 of the same *f*
Act, as amended, provides:

> 'Where on the summary trial under subsection (3) of section eighteen or
> section nineteen of this Act of an indictable offence . . . a person who is not less
> than seventeen years old is convicted of the offence, then, if on obtaining informa-
> tion about his character and antecedents the court is of opinion that they are *g*
> such that greater punishment should be inflicted for the offence than the court
> has power to inflict, the court may, in accordance with section 56 of the Criminal
> Justice Act 1967, commit him in custody or on bail to quarter sessions for sentence
> in accordance with the provisions of section twenty-nine of the Criminal Justice
> Act, 1948.'

h

What happened in this case was that, when the justices sat, the individual responsible for the prosecution intimated that this was a case which could be dealt with
summarily. The justices had before them the information, and whilst they knew
that in the first information it was alleged against the applicant that he had on 29th
June 1971 stolen one lady's twin set, and that in the second information he was
charged that on divers dates he had committed a large number of offences of theft, per- *j*
haps 20 or some such number as that, at any rate a large number, they did not know
that he was a police officer, they did not know that these offences were alleged to
have been committed by him whilst on duty; but they did know that he was a
person of previous good character, and in the face of the prosecution's suggestion
that this was a proper case for summary trial and knowing nothing of the matter
save that he was of previous good character, they made at that time what was not

a   a wholly unreasonable decision that this was a case for summary trial under s 19; so they began. The applicant pleaded guilty to both counts and then details were provided for the justices prior to their passing sentence. As the justices' affidavit discloses, they then discovered for the first time that this man was a policeman employed by the Manchester Ringway Airport Authority, and he had over a period of time stolen property from the persons whose property he had been employed to protect. It is quite clear that the justices—one does not want to use too strong a word—were shocked to discover this and they decided this was a proper case for the employment of s 29 and they made the committal order accordingly. It is said that they erred in law in committing this case, and the substance of the argument is that on the facts of this case they were virtually in possession of all the relevant information before they decided to try the case summarily, and it is said, and rightly said, that if justices having been informed of the full facts before they decided to try the case summarily, they cannot use those same facts, as it were, as a justification for committal under s 29. The whole question for us is whether on the facts disclosed, this is a case in which, subsequent to conviction, the justices receive additional information as to the character and antecedents of the accused, thus justifying their proceeding under s 29.

b

c

d   For my part I think one can restrict the reference to authority to two of the more recent cases. The first to which I refer is *R v King's Lynn Justices, ex parte Carter*[1]. This again was a case where justices had allowed the summary trial of a person charged with theft, and after conviction, and when they were hearing evidence of antecedents, it became apparent that the case was much more serious than it had at first appeared and where the justices considered themselves entitled to act under s 29. Lord Parker CJ expressed the rule in my judgment not only accurately but compactly in these words. He said[2]:

e

> 'Of course, in the ordinary way where justices do their duty under s. 19 (2) of the Act of 1952, the circumstances of the offence which reflect on character and antecedents will already have emerged, and if, notwithstanding that, the justices decide to deal with the case summarily, they cannot take those matters into consideration again when they are considering committal under s. 29; there must be something more than has been revealed at the stage when they decided to deal with the case summarily. On the other hand, where, as in the present case, they have either been persuaded to deal with the case summarily, or have embarked on the summary trial without making any proper inquiry, or without conducting their inquiry as examining magistrates far enough to understand the nature of the case, then, as it seems to me, they are fully entitled to take into consideration those matters relating to the offence which had been revealed at the trial and which do reflect on the character and antecedents.'

f

g

Lord Parker CJ was saying in the clearest terms that although it is right and desirable for justices to make as full an enquiry as possible before committing themselves to a decision to try the case summarily, yet if they do not do that, either because they have been over-persuaded by the prosecution, or for any other reason, they can have regard to facts subsequently emerging in deciding whether or not to apply s 29, and that in my judgment is exactly what the justices did in this case. They discovered after they had agreed to try the case summarily and after the conviction that the applicant was a policeman and had committed these offences when on duty. Those were matters of antecedents for the purpose of s 29, as is not disputed, and in my judgment they were perfectly within the direction given by Lord Parker CJ in deciding to commit under s 29.

h

j

Some confusion may have arisen by reason of a later decision, *R v Tower Bridge*

---

1   [1968] 3 All ER 858, [1969] 1 QB 488
2   [1968] 3 All ER at 862, [1969] 1 QB at 498

Magistrate, ex parte Osman[1]. I find it unnecessary to deal with the particular cir- **a**
cumstances of that case save to say that in the end the court was of the opinion that
the magistrate had been seised of all the relevant information before he decided
to try the case summarily. Accordingly the committal order was quashed. But
it is said that perhaps some difference is to be discovered in the principle laid down
by this court in the *Tower Bridge* case[1] when compared with the *King's Lynn* case[2].
I for my part see no difference. Lord Parker CJ in *R v Tower Bridge Magistrate, ex parte* **b**
Osman[3] explains his anxiety lest justices be tempted to try summarily cases which
ought to be tried on indictment, relying on their power to commit under s 29 if
the events prove that this is desirable. He points out, and this I am sure is right,
that justices should not take an easy view of their duty under these sections and
consent to summary trial in the belief that s 29 will get them out of all their difficulties. They ought to try first of all to decide whether the case is a case for summary **c**
trial or not. But beyond that warning, I see nothing in Lord Parker CJ's judgment
to produce any principle different from that which he had enunciated in the *King's
Lynn* case[2]. I was a party to the later case and simply agreed with Lord Parker CJ.
Bridge J, who was the third member of the court in *R v Tower Bridge Magistrate,
ex parte Osman*[4], said this:

> 'Before they [that is the justices] assume jurisdiction to try an indictable **d**
> offence summarily, whatever the plea is to be, magistrates have a plain duty
> under section 19 to make sufficient inquiry into the facts of the case to satisfy
> themselves that, so far as those facts are concerned, their powers of punishment
> are adequate. The decision of this court in *Reg* v. *King's Lynn Justices, Ex parte
> Carter*[2], should not be read as derogating from that duty. A conscientious decision
> under section 19, as to whether a case is appropriate for summary trial, will **e**
> automatically avoid any difficulty, of the kind exemplified in the present
> application, arising on committal for sentence under section 29.'

What Bridge J is saying there in my judgment is this, first that the justices should
make an enquiry—I agree with that and I do not think anyone would doubt it.
Secondly, that *R v King's Lynn Justices, ex parte Carter*[2] should not be regarded as **f**
derogating from the justices' duty to make a proper enquiry—I agree with that
too. Thirdly he says that if they make a proper enquiry, then this kind of difficulty
will probably be avoided, and I agree with that as well. But I can find nothing in any
of the judgments in *R v Tower Bridge Magistrate, ex parte Osman*[1] to suggest that if
the failure to disclose the fact at an earlier stage is due to the justices' failure to make
a proper enquiry, this in any way inhibits their power to use s 29. I would reiterate **g**
the correctness of Lord Parker CJ's dictum in *R v King's Lynn Justices, ex parte
Carter*[2], and applying it to the present case, it seems clear to me that the
committal order was made with jurisdiction and in accordance with s 29.

That does not conclude the application because, as I have already indicated, there
is a further claim that the conviction on the second charge was bad in any event, and
that the conviction on this count should be set aside. The basis of the argument is **h**
that the information offended against r 12 (1) of the Magistrates' Courts Rules 1968[5],
which provides:

> 'Subject to any Act passed after 2nd October 1848, a magistrates' court
> shall not proceed to the trial of an information that charges more than one
> offence.'   **j**

---

1 [1971] 2 All ER 1018, [1971] 1 WLR 1109
2 [1968] 3 All ER 858, [1969] 1 QB 488
3 [1971] 2 All ER at 1020, [1971] 1 WLR at 1111
4 [1971] 1 WLR at 1112, cf [1971] 2 All ER at 1020, 1021
5 SI 1968 No 1920

a   In this case the second information did charge more than one offence, and it did so because it alleged that on divers dates over a period of months the applicant had stolen this great list of articles. That that was including more than one offence in a single information is clearly right, but the facts of this matter cannot be overlooked; all the information on which these charges were based came from the applicant himself, and when they were put wrongly in a single information, he was clearly not prejudiced thereby and he pleaded guilty without objection.

b   In view of those circumstances, I turn back to s 100 (1) of the Magistrates' Courts Act 1952, which provides: 'No objection shall be allowed to any information or complaint, or to any summons or warrant to procure the presence of the defendant, for any defect in it in substance or in form . . .' Subject to amendment and with the giving of particulars, that is a principle which could be applied here as in any other case. It seems to me therefore that in this case the conviction is not a bad convic-

c   tion and, having regard to s 100, it is certainly too late to take advantage of the breach of r 12, and accordingly since the conviction on that footing is a valid conviction, I would say that the order of certiorari prayed in respect of that conviction should also be refused.

d   **MELFORD STEVENSON J.** I wholly agree. I would only add this by way of emphasis, and perhaps at the risk of repetition. The application to this case of the language of Lord Parker CJ which Lord Widgery CJ has read from the report of *R v King's Lynn Justices, ex parte Carter*[1] is vividly demonstrated when one looks at the first sentence of para 4 of the affidavit of the chairman of the justices. I will read the one sentence:

e   'The Justices were told nothing, and from enquiries I have made of the two Justices who sat under me I am satisfied that we knew nothing of the Applicant's character and antecedents before he consented to summary trial and pleaded guilty to the offence with which he was charged.'

     That fact is in my view conclusive of the matter and plainly enables one to apply
f   the language of Lord Parker CJ in the *King's Lynn* case[1].

     BRABIN J. I agree.

     Certiorari refused.   Leave to appeal to the House of Lords refused.

g   Solicitors: *Alsop, Stevens, Batesons & Co*, agents for *W Stuart Hague & Co*, Knutsford (for the applicant); *Treasury Solicitor.*

                                                                'N P Metcalfe Esq Barrister.

---

1   [1968] 3 All ER 858, [1969] 1 QB 488

F v S (adoption: ward)   *a*

COURT OF APPEAL, CIVIL DIVISION
DAVIES, MEGAW AND ORR LJJ
7th, 8th DECEMBER 1972

b

Adoption – Consent – Ward of court – Leave to institute adoption proceedings – Leave of court required – Question to be determined by court on application for leave – Whether application for adoption having reasonable likelihood of success.

In September 1969 the mother of a child, a girl born in 1964, left the father with whom she had been living taking the child with her and leaving no message as to where *c*
she had gone. After unsuccessful attempts to trace them the father in January 1970 issued a wardship summons to which the mother eventually entered an appearance in November 1970. At the hearing of the summons in January 1971 the judge made an order that the wardship should continue, that the mother should have the care of the child and that the father should have access to the child once a month at the home of friends of both parties. Three months later the mother married and went to *d*
live with her husband. The mother applied for leave to commence adoption pro-ceedings with a view to adoption of the child by herself and her husband; the father made a cross-application for increased access. The judge found that the mother would have liked the father not to see the child any more (which would have been the result of adoption). The judge considered that it would be a grave responsibility to set some kind of seal of approval on adoption proceedings which might end the *e*
child's visits to her father, which she enjoyed, and that he ought not to make the order unless satisfied that it was in the child's interests for him to make it. Since he was not so satisfied he refused leave to commence the proceedings. The mother appealed.

Held – The appeal would be allowed and leave given to commence proceedings *f*
for the following reasons—
   (i) since the Family Division were in loco parentis to a ward of court, an applica-tion to the court for leave was a necessary preliminary to the commencement of adoption proceedings; where such an application was made, however, the proper function of the judge was limited to considering whether an application for adoption was one which might reasonably succeed; it was not his function to decide the ultimate question whether it was in the child's interests to be adopted, for that *g*
question fell to be decided by the court hearing the adoption proceedings (see p 724 j to p 725 a d and e and p 726 b, post);
   (ii) the mother's application for adoption was one which might reasonably succeed, for adoption in circumstances such as those before the court offered advantages to the child, against which would fall to be weighed any corresponding disadvantages *h*
through being deprived of association with her natural father; although the judge had found that one of the mother's motives in seeking adoption was to put an end to the natural father's rights of access, the evidence did not show that she entertained that motive out of ill will or spite towards the father rather than on a consideration of what was in the best interests of the child, or that it was her only motive; even if it were her only motive, there was no ground for saying that adoption would *j*
offer no advantage for the child (see p 725 f to j and p 726 b, post).

Notes

For the persons whose consent is necessary to adoption proceedings, see 21 Halsbury's Laws (3rd Edn) 231-233, para 506, and for cases on the subject, see 28 (2) Digest (Reissue) 826, 827, 1366, 1367.

a **Cases referred to in judgment**

E (P) (an infant), Re [1969] 1 All ER 323, [1968] 1 WLR 1913, 133 JP 137, 67 LGR 73, CA, 28 (2) Digest (Reissue) 824, 1359.

M (an infant), Re [1955] 2 All ER 911, [1955] 2 QB 479, [1955] 3 WLR 320, 119 JP 535, 53 LGR 497, CA, 28 (2) Digest (Reissue) 832, 1390.

b **Appeal**

The mother appealed against an order of Stirling J made on 18th May 1972, refusing her leave to commence adoption proceedings for the adoption by herself and her husband of her child of whom the respondent was the father. The facts are set out in the judgment.

c A B Hollis QC and I L R Romer for the mother.
Gerald Godfrey QC and Anita Ryan for the father.

ORR LJ delivered the first judgment at the request of Davies LJ. This is an appeal by the mother of a ward of court now aged eight, an illegitimate child, of d whom the respondent is the father, against an order of Stirling J made on 18th May 1972, by which he refused an application by the mother for leave to commence adoption proceedings with a view to the adoption of the child by herself and her husband whom she married on 16th October 1971, many years after the child's birth. On the same date and in the same hearing the judge also made an order granting to the father increased access to the child, but against that part of the order the e mother does not seek to appeal.

The facts of the case are briefly these. In November 1963 the mother, then 21 years of age, whose parents had separated when she was 16 and who had already given birth to two illegitimate children who were given in adoption, one born in 1960 and the other in 1962, met the father, who was a man of 31, unmarried, who had come to England from Singapore some years before. Very shortly after that f they began to live together as man and wife, the mother assuming the father's surname. The child was born on 20th September 1964, and it is not in dispute that the respondent was the father. It is also not in dispute that on 15th September 1969 the mother left the address where they were then living, taking the child with her but leaving no message as to where she had gone. She claimed in the wardship proceedings, which were heard by Stirling J on 15th July 1971, that she had been g driven to leave by violence on the part of the father, and she made other complaints against him, as to the poor standard of the accommodation in which they lived and as to his gambling and drinking; but all those allegations were denied by him. She also claimed that the reason why she left no message for him as to where she was going was that she was afraid that he would take the child away with him to Singapore.

h After she and the child had left, the father made numerous attempts to trace them, but without success, and eventually, on 8th January 1970 issued a wardship summons, to which the mother eventually entered an appearance on 9th November 1970. That summons came before Stirling J, as I have said, in July 1971 when he heard oral evidence of the two parties and also had before him sworn statements by supporting witnesses for the mother, on whose evidence I need not pause for the present pur- j poses. The learned judge at that hearing made an order that the wardship should continue, that the mother should have the care of the child, and that the father should have access to the child once a month at the home of friends of both of them, a Mr and Mrs W.

Some three months after that hearing, in October 1971, the mother married her husband who is in good employment and they have their home in a three-bedroomed house, which they rent furnished and which was described by the welfare officer as being an attractive home. The father is living with another woman in accommodation comprising a bed-sitting room with a partitioned kitchenette and a bathroom.

On the hearing of the mother's application for leave to take adoption proceedings and of the father's cross-application for increased access, there were before the judge a welfare report and two sworn statements, one by the father, which dealt solely with the question of increased access, and the other by the mother and her husband; and no oral evidence was given at that hearing. The welfare report describes the child as an attractive, bright-eyed girl with an easy, happy disposition, and showing at school both a readiness to integrate and bright intelligence. It goes on to say:

> '[She] seems at this stage refreshingly unaware of the conflicting feelings between her parents. She sees her natural father happily on access days and enjoys these occasions unquestioningly. She commented in "the same breath' that she enjoyed playing with Mrs [W's] two youngest daughters on these occasions as well.'

That information was no doubt obtained by the welfare officer from Mr and Mrs W at whose house the access took place. As to the access, it is clear on the report that it was proving successful and that the child enjoyed it.

As to the adoption proceedings, the welfare officer records the mother as feeling that the child's best interests would lie in her being acknowledged as a secure member of a united family and that to have an extra father figure from earlier years reintroduced would be confusing to the child and reminiscent of previous conflicts. In their joint sworn statement the mother and her husband say with regard to the adoption that spite did not in any way enter into their desire to adopt the child, but that they both very strongly felt that it was in her best interests that they should adopt her, so that she could be brought up as their own daughter and enjoy a happier and more peaceful childhood than would be the case if she were to remain a ward of court divided between two households.

On the material which I have summarised, the learned judge, in a brief but careful judgment, recorded that at the earlier hearing he had been satisfied that what the mother would have liked best was really that the father should not see the child any more; and he recognised, what was not in dispute, that if the adoption ultimately went through its effect would be to terminate the father's rights to see his child; and bearing in mind that she appeared to enjoy the visits to her father he thought that it would be a grave responsibility to make an order which by setting what he called some kind of seal of approval on adoption proceedings might lead to a situation in which the child would not see her father again. He considered that he ought not to make such an order unless he was satisfied that it was in the child's interests that he should make it, and the conclusion he reached was that he was left unconvinced that it would be in the child's interests to give leave for adoption proceedings to be commenced.

In the mother's notice of appeal a number of grounds are set out but in argument before this court only one has been relied on, namely, that the judge, in holding that it was not in the child's interests to allow adoption proceedings to be commenced, was deciding the very point which would fall to be determined in those proceedings if leave were granted; that in doing that he went beyond his function in deciding whether leave should be granted; and that the question which he ought to have asked himself was not, is it in the child's interests? but, might it reasonably be held on a subsequent hearing in adoption proceedings that it would be in her interests to be adopted? and that it was only if he answered that question in the negative that he would be justified in refusing leave.

There is no authority as to which of these questions falls to be asked on an application for leave to commence adoption proceedings, nor indeed on the question whether an application for such leave is necessary. But Atkin's Encyclopaedia of Court Forms[1],

---

1   3rd Edn (1955), vol 21, p 202

a   under the heading 'Who may be adopted', states that leave is required; and a similar passage appeared in a footnote in the 1963 White Book[1]. As a matter of common sense I think that this is right, since the Family Division are, as the Chancery Division formerly were, in loco parentis to a ward.

As to the status in adoption proceedings of the father of an illegitimate child, he is by definition in the Adoption Act 1958 included in the terms 'father' and 'relative'
b   as used in that Act, and therefore entitled, under s 2 to apply for an adoption order; but he is not a person whose consent to adoption is required, since the term 'parent' as used in the 1958 Act is nowhere defined; and it was held in *Re M (an infant)*[2], a decision of this court under the comparable Adoption Act 1950, that that term did not include the father of an illegitimate child. It is however clear that the Official Solicitor, as guardian ad litem of the ward, would be under a duty by the Adoption
c   Rules to get in touch with the father, whose views and wishes would therefore be canvassed and brought to the notice of the court.

As to the function of a judge dealing with an application for leave to bring adoption proceedings, we have, as I have said, to arrive at a conclusion in the absence of any direct authority. The argument for the mother has been that the proper function of the judge is not to decide the ultimate question which, if he gave leave, would
d   fall to be decided by the court hearing the adoption proceedings, but only to consider whether the application is one which reasonably might succeed. The argument advanced by counsel for the father was that it is the duty of the court on such an application to come to a conclusion as to what is in the best interests of the ward, and that by refusing or failing to come to such a conclusion the judge would be abdicating his functions.

e   As between these two arguments I have no hesitation in preferring, with great respect to the argument of counsel for the father, the submission of counsel for the mother that the function of the judge on this application was not to decide the very point which would later fall to be decided on adoption proceedings if they were taken; and, in my judgment, in the circumstances of this case it was wrong to refuse leave for the proceedings to be brought.

f   Clearly, as held by this court in *Re E (P) (an infant)*[3], adoption, in circumstances such as those with which we are here concerned, offers advantages to the child, and those advantages would fall, on the hearing of adoption proceedings, to be weighed against any corresponding disadvantage which would be caused to the child by being deprived of association with her natural father.

The judge in the present case plainly came to the conclusion, as I think that he
g   was entitled to do on the evidence, that it was one of the mother's motives in seeking adoption that the making of an adoption order would put an end to the natural father's rights of access. This was also a matter which would fall to be weighed in the balance with everything else on the hearing of adoption proceedings; but in my judgment it could not be said on the evidence that this was the mother's sole motive or that in entertaining that motive she did so out of ill will or spite to the
h   father rather than on a consideration of what she thought was in the best interests of the child. Nor, even if it was her sole motive, was there any ground for saying that the adoption would offer no advantage for the child.

In these circumstances, while I can understand the reasons which the learned judge had in mind in refusing leave, I do not think he was right to conclude that this application was one in which leave should be refused. I for my part would
j   therefore allow this appeal and substitute an order granting leave, but in coming to that conclusion I do not indicate any view of mine as to what the result of the adoption proceedings ought to be. In argument before this court junior counsel for the mother

---

1   The Annual Practice 1963, vol 2, p 3509
2   [1955] 2 All ER 911, [1955] 2 QB 479
3   [1969] 1 All ER 323, [1968] 1 WLR 1913

suggested that it would be open to a judge dealing with an application for leave to   *a*
grant leave on terms that the mother should issue a summons in wardship proceedings to come on for hearing with the adoption application and that by that means
the father would have a right of representation or of making representations himself
to the court. If in this case the father wishes to take out such a summons, I think
that it should come on and be heard together with the adoption application.

b

DAVIES LJ. I entirely agree.

MEGAW LJ. I also agree.

*Appeal allowed. Leave granted for the mother and her husband to apply in the High Court for
an adoption order.*   *c*

Solicitors: *Dale & Newbery*, Feltham (for the mother); *Cecil Altman & Co* (for the
father).

F A Amies Esq   Barrister.

d

English Exporters (London) Ltd v Eldonwall Ltd

CHANCERY DIVISION
MEGARRY J   *e*
8th, 9th, 10th, 13th NOVEMBER 1972

*Landlord and tenant – Business premises – Rent – Interim rent – Continuation of tenancy
following application for new tenancy – Determination of interim rent – Application by landlord – Discretion of court – Rent which it would be reasonable for tenant to pay – Market
rent of hypothetical yearly tenancy – Regard to be had to rent payable under terms of existing   f
tenancy – Landlord and Tenant Act 1954, ss 24A (added by the Law of Property Act 1969,
ss 3 (1)), 34.*

*Valuer – Evidence – Expert evidence – Hearsay – Admissibility – Evidence of comparables –
Expression of opinion on values – Opinion formed in part by matters of which valuer having
no first-hand knowledge – Evidence of transactions of which valuer having no first-hand   g
knowledge – Extent to which evidence admissible.*

The landlords held a lease dated 19th April 1962 from superior landlords of certain
premises at a rent of £15,100 per annum. That lease was due to expire on 29th
September 1981 but it contained a break clause whereby the superior landlords could   *h*
determine it on 29th September 1974, by giving six months' notice in writing. By an
underlease dated 30th December 1966 the landlords granted a tenancy of part of those
premises to the tenants at a rent of £7,655 per annum for a seven year term due to
expire 1st March 1972. The tenants occupied the premises for the purposes of their
business. On 19th August 1971 the tenants served on the landlords a request under
s 26 of the Landlord and Tenant Act 1954 for a new tenancy commencing on 1st March   *j*
1972 at a rent of £10,206·66 per annum but otherwise on the terms of the existing
lease. The landlords served no counter-notice and on 14th December 1971 the tenants
issued an originating summons specifying 29th September 1981 as the date for termination with provision for termination on 29th September 1974 should the superior
landlords exercise their right of determination under the break clause. By a summons issued on 29th December 1971 the landlords asked for an interim rent to be

a   determined under s 24A*ᵃ* of the 1954 Act. The parties concurred in taking 1st April 1973 as the probable date for the commencement of the new tenancy. The issues to be decided were: (i) the rent to be reserved under the new tenancy, and (ii) whether an interim rent should be fixed and, if so, how much it should be. At the trial expert evidence was given by chartered surveyors on behalf of both parties and a number of comparables was adduced on behalf of the landlords.

b   **Held** – (i) On the evidence the rent at which, having regard to the terms of the tenancy, the holding might reasonably be expected to be let on the open market by a willing lessor was £16,000 per annum; in accordance with s 34 (1)*ᵇ* of the 1954 Act, the rent of the new tenancy would, therefore, be determined at that figure (see p 735 g, post).

(ii) The power of the court under s 24A (1) of the 1954 Act to determine an interim rent while the existing tenancy continued was discretionary and accordingly the court *c*   was not bound to determine an interim rent in every case where the landlord applied to it to do so. However, in most normal cases the court's discretion ought to be exercised, in that to do so would usually promote justice (see p 736 d and h and p 742 j, post).

(iii) In determining what would be a reasonable interim rent for the tenant to pay while the existing tenancy continued, in accordance with s 24A (1), the court was *d*   enjoined by s 24A (3) to determine the market rent, in accordance with s 34, on the assumption that the court was determining the rent of a hypothetical new yearly tenancy on the same terms as those of the existing tenancy, so far as compatible with a yearly tenancy; for that purpose the court was precluded by s 34 (1) from having regard to the rent of the hypothetical new tenancy, but there was nothing to exclude the rent of the existing tenancy if it was of assistance for valuation purposes. Having *e*   determined the 'market rent' in accordance with that formula the court was then further required by s 24A (3) to 'have regard' to the rent payable under the existing tenancy; the effect of that provision was to enable the court to determine an interim rent which was less than the full 'market rent' calculated in accordance with the s 34 formula, if, having regard to the existing rent, the court felt it reasonable to do so *f*   (see p 739 h to p 740 e, p 741 d and j to p 742 b and p 743 g, post); *Regis Property Co Ltd v Lewis & Peat Ltd* [1970] 3 All ER 227 not followed.

(iv) Having regard to the rent of £16,000 determined for the new tenancy the market rent for a hypothetical yearly tenancy would be £15,000. On the facts there was not much of a case for tempering the market rent by reference to the existing rent of £7,655 per annum by any very substantial amount; the appropriate figure was £14,000 per annum (see p 743 a h and j, post).

g   Per Megarry J. (i) In determining the interim rent in accordance with s 24A (3) of the 1954 Act the values to be applied should be those existing when the interim period begins to run (see p 741 f, post).

(ii) Apart from anything made admissible under the Civil Evidence Act 1968 or in consequence of questions asked in cross-examination, a valuer giving expert evidence in chief or in re-examination (a) may express the opinions that he has

h   ————————————————————

a   Section 24A, so far as material, provides:
'(1) The landlord of a tenancy to which this Part of this Act applies may, ... (b) if the tenant has made a request for a new tenancy in accordance with section 26 of this Act; apply to the court to determine a rent which it would be reasonable for the tenant to pay while the tenancy continues by virtue of section 24 of this Act, and the court may *j*   determine a rent accordingly ...
'(3) In determining a rent under this section the court shall have regard to the rent payable under the terms of the tenancy, but otherwise subsections (1) and (2) of section 34 of this Act shall apply to the determination as they would apply to the determination of a rent under that section if a new tenancy from year to year of the whole of the property comprised in the tenancy were granted to the tenant by order of the court.'
b   Section 34 (1), so far as material, is set out at p 730 b, post

formed as to values even though substantial contributions to the formation of those *a*
opinions have been made by matters of which he has no first-hand knowledge;
(b) may give evidence as to the details of any transactions within his personal knowledge, in order to establish them as matters of fact; and (c) may express his opinion
as to the significance of any transactions which are or will be proved by admissible
evidence (whether or not given by him) in relation to the valuation with which he is
concerned; but (d) may not give hearsay evidence stating the details of any transac- *b*
tions not within his personal knowledge in order to establish them as matters of fact
(see p 732 b to e and p 733 b to e, post); *Wright v Sidney Municipal Council* (1916) 16
SRNSW 348 approved.

Notes
For the rent payable under a new tenancy of business premises, see 23 Halsbury's *c*
Laws (3rd Edn) 898, 899, para 1725, and for a case on the subject, see Digest (Cont
Vol A) 1063, 7417ya.
   For applications to determine an interim rent, see Supplement to 23 Halsbury's
Laws (3rd Edn) para 1714A.
   For the Landlord and Tenant Act 1954, ss 24A, 26, 34, see 18 Halsbury's Statutes
(3rd Edn) 559, 561, 573. *d*

Cases referred to in judgment
Julius v Bishop of Oxford (1880) 5 App Cas 214, [1874-80] All ER Rep 43, 49 LJQB 577,
   42 LT 546, HL; *affg* sub nom *R v Oxford (Bp)* (1879) 4 QBD 525, CA, 44 Digest (Repl)
   310, 1415.
Koscot Interplanetary (UK) Ltd, Re, Re Koscot AG [1972] 3 All ER 829.
Regis Property Co Ltd v Lewis & Peat Ltd [1970] 3 All ER 227, [1970] Ch 695, [1970] *e*
   3 WLR 361, 21 P & CR 761, [1970] RVR 805, Digest (Cont Vol C) 614, 7417yab.
Sheen v Bumpstead (1862) 1 H & C 358, 158 ER 924; *affd* (1863) 2 H & C 193, 2 New Rep
   370, 32 LJEx 271, 8 LT 832, 10 Jur NS 242, 159 ER 80, Ex Ch, 35 Digest (Repl) 39, 326.
Wright v Sydney Municipal Council (1916) 16 SRNSW 348.

Summonses *f*
By an originating summons dated 14th December 1971, the tenants, English Exporters
(London)Ltd, sought against the landlords, Eldonwall Ltd, the grant of a new tenancy,
pursuant to Part II of the Landlord and Tenant Act 1954, of the premises known as
rooms on the first floor and part of the second floor at 66-70 Baker Street, London
W1, for a specified period and on specified terms. By a summons dated 29th December 1971, the landlords sought an order that the tenants pay such rent as to the court *g*
seemed meet whilst the tenancy of the premises continued, as provided by s 24A of
the 1954 Act. The facts are set out in the judgment.

Gavin Lightman for the tenants.
Stanley Ibbotson for the landlords.

h

MEGARRY J. This is a case under the Landlord and Tenant Act 1954, Part II,
as amended. The holding consists of the first floor and most of the second floor of
66-70 Baker Street, London W1. The plaintiffs are English Exporters (London) Ltd,
the tenants; and I shall refer to them as 'the tenants'. The defendants are Eldonwall
Ltd, the landlords, to whom I shall refer as 'the landlords'. On 19th August 1971 the *j*
tenants served on the landlords a request under the 1954 Act for a new tenancy
commencing on 1st March 1972 at a rent of £10,206·66 per annum, but otherwise
on the terms of the existing lease. The landlords served no counter-notice, and on
14th December 1971 the tenants issued their originating summons under the Act,
specifying 29th September 1981 as the date of termination of the proposed tenancy,
and including an additional clause to be inserted in the lease relating to the

a contractual right of termination: to this I shall return shortly. The rent under the existing tenancy was stated to be £7,650 per annum, though this seems to be £5 too little. The only issues before me are, first, as to the rent to be reserved under the new tenancy, and, second, under a summons issued by the landlords on 29th December 1971, whether an interim rent should be fixed under s 24A of the Act, and, if so, at how much. In the course of the argument, however, points of law of some impor-
b tance have arisen as to valuation evidence and as to the process of fixing interim rents.

There is a hierarchy of leases concerning these premises. No doubt there is a free-holder somewhere, but the highest interest before me is that of the Liverpool Victoria Friendly Society, which I understand holds a head lease. That society granted an underlease of the first, second, third and fourth floors at a rent of £9,750 per annum, and at present that lease is vested in Gonville and Caius College, Cambridge.
c Out of that under-leasehold interest there was granted an underlease dated 19th April 1962 of the same premises at a rent of £15,100 a year, and this is now vested in the landlords. By an underlease dated 30th December 1966 the landlords granted the underlease with which I am concerned, whereby part of the premises vested in the landlords was demised to the tenants; the part consists of the holding, which appears to have rather less than half the total floor area comprised in the landlords'
d underlease. The rent reserved is £7,655 per annum, and the term was seven years from 1st March 1965, so that apart from the Act the term expired on 1st March 1972. The tenants occupy the whole of the holding for their business of importers and exporters.

The leasehold interest immediately superior to the lease which is vested in the landlords, namely, that now vested in Gonville and Caius College, is for a term of 21 years from 29th September 1960, and this, subject to the Act, will expire on 29th
e September 1981. However, it contains a break clause whereby either the reversioners or the leaseholders may determine the lease at the expiration of the 14th year of the term (namely, on 29th September 1974) by giving six months' prior notice in writing. This provision is in substance repeated in the lease under which the landlords now hold, their term being ten days shorter than the term vested in Gonville and Caius College. In consequence, the tenants, in their originating summons, ask for the
f inclusion of a provision in the new lease which they seek that if the landlords' imme-diate landlords duly exercise the right of determination on or before 29th September 1974, then the new tenancy claimed by the tenants is to determine on 29th September 1974. In short, the tenants seek a new tenancy which, apart from the Act, will deter-mine either on 29th September 1974 or on 29th September 1981, depending on whether or not the landlords' own leasehold interest is determined on or before
g 29th September 1974 under the break clause. Having regard to the provisions of s 64 of the 1954 Act relating to the interim continuation of tenancies, the parties have very sensibly concurred in taking 1st April 1973 as the probable date of commence-ment for the new tenancy which the tenants claim under the Act. I am thus concerned with a tenancy commencing on that date for a term of about either one and a half years or eight and a half years. I may say that although the tenants occupy
h the holding for their business, and so their tenancy is one to which the Act applies, the landlords occupy none of the premises comprised in the lease to them, and so their tenancy is not within the Act. The small part of the second floor not comprised in the holding is, I understand, vacant, and the third and fourth floors are each of them let, one to one tenant and the other to another.

I will deal first with the rent under the proposed new tenancy, leaving the interim
j rent until later. As I have mentioned, the rent for the holding proposed by the tenants in their request for a new tenancy and their originating summons is £10,206·66 per annum. The landlords, on the other hand, seek a rent of £16,600 per annum. The holding has an agreed area of 3,274 square feet, and at the landlords' figure this comes out at £5·07 per square foot. I need not trouble with the conversion of the tenants' figure, as they have not sought to establish it before me. The Master

made an order for one expert witness on each side, and counsel for the tenants called
Mr Martin French, a Fellow of the Royal Institution of Chartered Surveyors, while
counsel for the landlords called Mr Laurie, also a Fellow of the Royal Institution of
Chartered Surveyors. There was a considerable measure of agreement between
their views, although, of course, there was also much on which they did not agree.
One of the problems that each witness had to face was that of making a valuation
today for a tenancy beginning on 1st March 1973 which might last for a mere one and
a half years or might endure for eight and a half years. The standard applicable is,
of course, that laid down by s 34 (1) of the 1954 Act, namely, such rent as may be
determined by the court to be 'that at which, having regard to the terms of the
tenancy (other than those relating to rent), the holding might reasonably be expected
to be let in the open market by a willing lessor', subject to disregarding a number of
factors about which I need say nothing, as there has been no argument about them
before me.

As is usual in these cases, a number of comparables was adduced. Eight were put
forward by the landlords: the tenants put in none of their own. As is also far from
unknown, some of the comparables were less comparable than others, and some
turned out to be supported only by hearsay evidence, or by evidence that was in
other respects less than cogent. There was no formal process of a ruling being made to
exclude those comparables which were supported only by hearsay evidence; but
I was discouraging, and in the event counsel for the landlords, though rueful, did not
seriously argue the point, or press it. I nevertheless think that I ought to make more
explicit the reasons for my having been discouraging, for in my experience the status
of hearsay evidence of comparables in valuation cases is a matter that is often misunderstood, and not only by valuers. For all I know, that misunderstanding may in
recent years have been fostered by a passage in Woodfall's Law of Landlord and
Tenant[1], to which counsel for the tenants very properly referred me. There, the
editors take the view that when a valuer is giving his opinion on rental value under
the Act of 1954—

> 'he should state his reasons for holding that opinion even if this involves
> reference to comparisons of which he only knows at second-hand, that surely
> going to weight rather than admissibility.'

There are further passages amplifying that view, but I think that this is a sufficient
indication of the general import of a paragraph which seems to contend that valuers
are entitled to give hearsay evidence of comparables.

Let me put on one side the cases in which exceptions to the rule excluding hearsay
evidence have grown up, whether by case law or by statute (and sometimes almost
by a side-wind; see, for example, Re Koscot Interplanetary (UK) Ltd[2]); and in particular
I exclude cases in which, subject to observing the statutory safeguards, hearsay
evidence has been made admissible under the Civil Evidence Act 1968. Let me
further ignore cases in which questions in cross-examination may have let in evidence
that otherwise would be inadmissible, and confine myself to the admissibility of
hearsay in chief and in re-examination in these valuation cases. In such circumstances,
two of the heads under which the valuer's evidence may be ranged are opinion
evidence and factual evidence. As an expert witness, the valuer is entitled to express
his opinion about matters within his field of competence. In building up his opinions
about values, he will no doubt have learned much from transactions in which he has
himself been engaged, and of which he could give first-hand evidence. But he will
also have learned much from many other sources, including much of which he could
give no first-hand evidence. Textbooks, journals, reports of auctions and other
dealings, and information obtained from his professional brethren and others, some

---

1 27th Edn (1968), vol 2, p 1350, para 2495
2 [1972] 3 All ER 829

related to particular transactions and some more general and indefinite, will all have contributed their share. Doubtless much, or most, of this will be accurate, though some will not; and even what is accurate so far as it goes may be incomplete, in that nothing may have been said of some special element which affects values. Nevertheless, the opinion that the expert expresses is none the worse because it is in part derived from the matters of which he could give no direct evidence. Even if some of the extraneous information which he acquires in this way is inaccurate or incomplete, the errors and omissions will often tend to cancel each other out; and the valuer, after all, is an expert in this field, so that the less reliable the knowledge that he has about the details of some reported transaction, the more his experience will tell him that he should be ready to make some discount from the weight that he gives it in contributing to his overall sense of values. Some aberrant transactions may stand so far out of line that he will give them little or no weight. No question of giving hearsay evidence arises in such cases; the witness states his opinion from his general experience.

On the other hand, quite apart from merely expressing his opinion, the expert often is able to give factual evidence as well. If he has first-hand knowledge of a transaction, he can speak of that. He may himself have measured the premises and conducted the negotiations which led to a letting of them at £x, which comes to £y per square foot; and he himself may have read the lease and seen that it contains no provisions, other than some particular clause, which would have any material effect on the valuation; and then he may express his opinion on the value. So far as the expert gives factual evidence, he is doing what any other witness of fact may do, namely, speaking of that which he has perceived for himself. No doubt in many valuation cases the requirement of first-hand evidence is not pressed to an extreme: if the witness has not himself measured the premises, but it has been done by his assistant under his supervision, the expert's figures are often accepted without requiring the assistant to be called to give evidence. Again, it may be that it would be possible for a valuer to fill a gap in his first-hand knowledge of a transaction by some method such as stating in his evidence that he has made diligent enquiries of some person who took part in the transaction in question, but despite receiving full answers to his enquiries, he discovered nothing which suggested to him that the transaction had any unusual features which would affect the value as a comparable. But basically, the expert's factual evidence on matters of fact is in the same position as the factual evidence of any other witness. Further, factual evidence that he cannot give himself is sometimes adduced in some other way, as by the testimony of some other witness who was himself concerned in the transaction in question, or by proving some document which carried the transaction through, or recorded it; and to the transaction thus established, like the transactions which the expert himself has proved, the expert may apply his experience and opinions, as tending to support or qualify his views.

That being so, it seems to me quite another matter when it is asserted that a valuer may give factual evidence of transactions of which he has no direct knowledge, whether per se or whether in the guise of giving reasons for his opinion as to value. It is one thing to say 'From my general experience of recent transactions comparable with this one, I think the proper rent should be £x': it is another thing to say 'Because I have been told by someone else that the premises next door have an area of x square feet and were recently let on such and such terms for £y a year, I say the rent of these premises should be £z a year'. What he has been told about the premises next door may be inaccurate or misleading as to the area, the rent, the terms and much else besides. It makes it no better when the witness expresses his confidence in the reliability of his source of information: a transparently honest and careful witness cannot make information reliable if, instead of speaking of what he has seen and heard for himself, he is merely retailing what others have told him. The other party to the litigation is entitled to have a witness whom he can cross-examine on oath as to the reliability

of the facts deposed to, and not merely as to the witness's opinion as to the reliability
of information which was given to him not on oath, and possibly in circumstances
tending to inaccuracies and slips. Further, it is often difficult enough for the courts
to ascertain the true facts from witnesses giving direct evidence, without the added
complication of attempts to evaluate a witness's opinion of the reliability, care and
thoroughness of some informant who has supplied the witness with the facts that he
is seeking to recount.

It therefore seems to me that details of comparable transactions upon which a valuer
intends to rely in his evidence must, if they are to be put before the court, be confined
to those details which have been, or will be, proved by admissible evidence, given
either by the valuer himself or in some other way. I know of no special rule giving
expert valuation witnesses the right to give hearsay evidence of facts: and notwithstanding many pleasant days spent in the Lands Tribunal while I was at the Bar,
I can see no compelling reasons of policy why they should be able to do this. Of
course, the long-established technique in adducing expert evidence of asking hypothetical questions may also be employed for valuers. It would, I think, be perfectly
proper to ask a valuer 'If in May 1972 no 3, with an area of 2,000 square feet, was let for
£10,000 a year for seven years on a full repairing lease with no unusual terms, what
rent would be appropriate for the premises in dispute?' But I cannot see that it
would do much good unless the facts of the hypothesis are established by admissible
evidence; and the valuer's statement that someone reputable had told him these
facts, or that he had seen them in a reputable periodical, would not in my judgment
constitute admissible evidence.

On principle, therefore, I would not accept the proposition in Woodfall[1]; and in
this I do not think I would be alone. To the end of the passage in question, Woodfall[1] very properly appends a footnote which reads: 'See, however, *Wright* v. *Sydney
Municipal Council*[2]'. The case cited seems to me to provide much support for the
views that I have expressed; and Woodfall[1] does not attempt to discuss or refute
the decision. In that case, *Wright v Sydney Municipal Council*[2], much the same sort of
point came before Sly, Gordon and Ferguson JJ. The case concerned a sale and not a
tenancy but that seems immaterial. It was contended[3] that an expert valuer 'was
entitled to state what sales he had knowledge of, even from hearsay, and to give the
details of such sales, including price, etc., in evidence'; but this contention was
rejected. Sly J said that the expert could, in addition to giving direct evidence of
sales of other comparable land, provided there was legal evidence of these, testify
that (inter alia) he had kept in touch with sales not made by himself in the district,
to show that he was competent to give evidence of values in the particular case.
The learned judge added[3]:

> 'But he has no privilege beyond any other witness to speak in detail of the
> prices realised for other lands unless he can give legal evidence of such sales, or
> that evidence has already been given by the witnesses. It would be a most
> dangerous thing to allow an expert to speak of the details of sales of which he
> really knows nothing, and see the difficulty the plaintiff in a case like this would
> be in if he had to answer such evidence not knowing whether the sales were
> really existent or not. I think the same principle applies whether the evidence
> is given in chief or in reply.'

Gordon J[4] took a similar view, and Ferguson J[5] rejected the contention that the witness
could 'give hearsay evidence of the particulars of the transactions in question'. See

1   Woodfall's Law of Landlord and Tenant (27th Edn, 1968), vol 2, p 1350, para 2495
2   (1916) 16 SRNSW 348
3   (1916) 16 SRNSW at 359
4   (1916) 16 SRNSW at 365
5   (1916) 16 SRNSW at 366

also Phipson on Evidence[1]. Bramwell B, I may say, apparently would have put
a matters on an even narrower basis, saying that a valuer may state his opinion of the
value of land, but that he must not in chief add that he says this because some other
land sold for such-and-such a price, although he may say this in cross-examination;
see *Sheen v Bumpstead*[2]. However, this, I think, was an obiter remark in a dissenting
judgment (although Phipson[3] does not reveal this), and for many years now such
evidence has not been rejected in chief when the witness has been speaking from his
b first-hand knowledge.

Putting matters shortly, and leaving on one side the matters that I have mentioned,
such as the Civil Evidence Act 1968 and anything made admissible by questions in
cross-examination, in my judgment a valuer giving expert evidence in chief (or in
re-examination)—

c (a) may express the opinions that he has formed as to values even though
substantial contributions to the formation of those opinions have been made by
matters of which he has no first-hand knowledge;

(b) may give evidence as to the details of any transactions within his personal
knowledge, in order to establish them as matters of fact; and

(c) may express his opinion as to the significance of any transactions which are
d or will be proved by admissible evidence (whether or not given by him) in relation to the valuation with which he is concerned; but

(d) may not give hearsay evidence stating the details of any transactions not
within his personal knowledge in order to establish them as matters of fact.

To those propositions I would add that for counsel to put in a list of comparables
ought to amount to a warranty by him of his intention to tender admissible evidence
e of all that is shown on the list.

I have spent some little time on dealing with this matter of evidence as it appears
to be the subject of no direct modern authority, and experience suggests that it is a
matter upon which there is considerable misunderstanding. When a list of comparables is being prepared for the trial, as is usual and convenient, it is all too common
to include in the list transactions upon which there will be no admissible evidence
f but only hearsay of a greater or lesser degree of reliability. If the parties exchange
lists of comparables at an early date, often much time and money can be saved by
the experts on each side agreeing such of the transactions in each list as, after any
necessary enquiry, they feel they can accept as being reliably summarised; and in
this way the additional expense of proving a favourable comparable not within an
expert's own knowledge can be avoided. But if the other side will not accept the
g facts, then either the transaction must be proved by admissible evidence or it must
be omitted as a comparable.

In the present case, Mr Laurie's evidence as to the eight comparables that he put
forward was in some cases unsatisfactory. He admitted that he had failed to read
with any degree of care the leases under which some of the comparable properties
were held; and of other comparables he had little or no knowledge save hearsay.
h However little effect this had upon his general knowledge and opinions of value, it
seriously weakened what otherwise would have been an impressive list of comparables. In his evidence Mr French also pointed to a number of respects in which
the comparables were not truly comparable. Apart from the comparables, however,
I found Mr Laurie a convincing witness. I have re-read my notes of the evidence, and
I do not propose to discuss it in any detail; but after allowing for all the frailties in
j the expert evidence that was tendered on each side, it seemed to me that, in broad

---

1 11th Edn (1970), p 518, para 1297
2 (1862) 1 H & C 358 at 365
3 11th Edn (1970), p 519, para 1299

terms, Mr Laurie's evidence was the more cogent.   In saying this, I do not forget
that Mr Laurie has some personal interest in the prosperity of the landlords, by means
of an interest in a holding company, so that, unlike Mr French, he cannot come
forward as a wholly disinterested expert.

I have already mentioned that the landlords are seeking a rent of £16,600 per
annum, which devalues at £5·07 per square foot; and it was this figure to which
Mr Laurie resolutely adhered in his evidence.   Mr French's evidence was different.
By the time his cross-examination had concluded, he had put forward a range of
figures which depended upon the circumstances.   His basic figure was £4·40 per
square foot, which produced a rent of just over £14,400 per annum.   This was on
the footing of a tenancy expiring under the break clause on 29th September 1974.
In answer to questions, he then put forward other figures for other circumstances.
At times during his evidence there was some degree of confusion, and I am not at all
sure that the answers given always matched the questions asked.   What it came
down to, I think, was this.   The rate of £4·40 per square foot was for a rent assessed
now, on s 34 terms, for a term to begin on 1st April 1973 and end on 29th September
1974.   If the assessment was to be made not now, but as at 1st April 1973, the rate
would be £4·60; and the rate for a term of comparable length, assessed at 29th
September 1974, would be somewhere about £5·00. If instead of this short term there
were to be a lease expiring in September 1981 with no break, the £4·40 would become
£4·75, the £4·60 would become £5·00, and the £5·00 would become £5·50; and
at any rate initially Mr French said that the same increased figures would apply if
instead of the certainty of a term enduring until 29th September 1981 there was a
term which might be broken, with the tenant able to seek a new tenancy under the
Act, though without the certainty of success. Mr French converted some of these values
per square foot into rent for the holding by hurried calculations in the witness box,
but later worked them out more accurately: and I take these more accurate figures
in the place of the initial calculations, which in at least one case proved markedly too
low.   £5·00 per square foot comes out in the revised version to £16,370, whereas
originally it had been put at a rounded-off figure of £15,000.   I should at once add,
however, that at least part of the explanation is that Mr French's original figures
were calculated on a floor area which was a little less than that which came to be
agreed between the parties and was used in the revised calculations.   The relevant
figures, rounded off, are as follows: for £4·40, £14,400; for £4·60, £15,060; for £4·75,
£15,550; for £5·00, £16,370; and for £5·50, £18,000.

There was no direct evidence as to whether the break clause in the superior lease
is likely to be operated.   On the facts before me, however, it seems highly probable
that it will.   Gonville and Caius College is at present paying £9,750 a year for the
four floors in its lease, and is receiving £15,100 a year for them.   If the college exercises its power to break the lease and the landlords do not occupy the premises for
their business, the landlords will not be protected by the Act, and the college will
then become the direct landlord of the occupying tenants.   The present rent of
the third and fourth floors alone comes to £19,100, and even on the lowest of Mr
French's figures, the rent of the holding (and ignoring the unlet part of the second
floor) would be £14,400.   If, then, a landlord at present receiving a rent of £15,100
can, by operating a break clause, become entitled to rents totalling at least £33,500,
is the landlord likely to exercise the power to break the lease? Of course, money is
not everything: but in the absence of evidence of any other consideration of any
cogency, I can see only one answer to that question.

What, then, I have to consider is the rent at which the holding might reasonably be
expected to be let in the open market by a willing lessor for a term commencing on
1st April 1973 and running until 29th September 1981 (that is, a term of eight and a
half years), but subject to determination on 29th September 1974 if (which is highly
probable) the superior landlord exercises its power to break the superior lease on
that date.   If this happens, then of course the tenants can exercise their rights under

the Act if they satisfy the necessary conditions, and obtain new tenancies at new
rents unless their landlord has any valid ground for opposing the grant of the new
tenancies.

Mr French was pressed as to his distinction between a rate of £4·40 for a
lease granted now to commence on 1st April 1973, and a rate of £4·60 for a lease
granted on 1st April 1973 to commence forthwith, and correspondingly for his
equivalent of those rates for other conditions; and in the end he abandoned the distinction, accepting that the rate must be £4·60. He then had second thoughts
about this and decided in the end to split the difference, putting forward a rate of
£4·50 for a rent assessed now, to begin on 1st April 1973; and despite questions in re-
examination which went to the full length of the permissible, he stuck to his guns,
both on this and on the increased rates for a term which was not merely a bare one
and a half years but was for eight and a half years, determinable at one and a half
years, yet with the prospect of obtaining a new tenancy under the Act. In the end,
though Mr French made no admission to this effect, I think he had no very substantial
reasons for disagreeing violently with Mr Laurie's £16,600 per annum. The most
that could be said was put by counsel for the tenants in his reply. He urged that the
fourth floor of the same building provided the only safe comparable, and that there
were four elements which called for a reduction of the rent of the holding by comparison. The rent of the fourth floor is the equivalent of £5·02 per square foot
under a lease which has just been granted for a term of nine years determinable in
September 1974. A rate of £5·02, when applied to the holding, comes out at less than
£200 below Mr Laurie's £16,600. The four elements which appeared in the evidence
of Mr French and were stressed by counsel for the tenants were that the lease of the
fourth floor was some four and a half months longer than the tenancy would be in the
present case; that the natural lighting and prospect of the fourth floor were better
than that of the holding, which was on the first and second floors; that the fourth
floor was a single unit, and did not consist of one floor and part of another; and
that the fourth floor had been let to a somewhat special tenant, in that the tenant
also occupied nearby premises. Counsel for the tenants contended that those
comparisons brought the rate for the holding down from £5·02 per square foot to
£4·60 per square foot, and thus to a rent of just over £15,000; but I think that this
is much too heavy a discount. Even if the fourth floor is the best comparable, it is
not the only comparable supported by admissible evidence, and the others, even
when suitably discounted, provide some support for a higher rent. On the evidence
as a whole, I think a rate of a little under £5·00 is appropriate; a rate of exactly £5·00
would yield £16,370, and rounding that down I come to £16,000. I accordingly
determine the rent at £16,000 per annum.

That brings me to the second important point, that of the interim rent. This is a
convenient term to apply to the rent during the period 'while the tenancy continues
by virtue of section 24 of this Act': see s 24A (1) of the 1954 Act, inserted by the Law
of Property Act 1969, s 3 (1). The date specified in the tenants' request for a new
tenancy for the beginning of the new tenancy is 1st March 1972 and so, under s 26 (5),
that is the date immediately before which the existing tenancy ended, subject to
s 64. Under s 64, the continuation of the tenancy under s 24 of the 1954 Act is until
the expiration of three months after the application is finally disposed of: and on
the footing of this case being decided today, the period under s 64 is three months
after the expiration of the six weeks allowed for appealing. As I have mentioned,
the parties have agreed that for practical purposes the date to be taken is 1st April
1973. On this footing, the interim rent will run from 1st March 1972 until 1st April
1973, a period of one year and one month.

With that I come to two interesting points taken by counsel for the tenants, one of
them far from simple. The first contention was that whereas the court is bound to
fix the rent under the new tenancy, the fixing of an interim rent under s 24A is not
obligatory but discretionary. The second point was that if an interim rent is to be

fixed, the method laid down by Stamp J in *Regis Property Co Ltd v Lewis & Peat Ltd*[1]
is wrong.

On the issue of discretion, counsel for the tenants pointed to the provisions relating
to what I may call the permanent rent. Under s 29 (1), subject to the provisions of
the Act, on an application under s 24 (1) for a new tenancy—

> 'the court shall make an order for the grant of a tenancy comprising such
> property, at such rent and on such other terms, as are hereinafter provided:'

the lame punctuation is that of the statute book. Section 34 (1) provides for the
ascertainment of the rent at such a rent as may be agreed between the landlord
and the tenant, 'or as, in default of such agreement, may be determined by the court'.
Plainly, said counsel for the tenants, this is the language of obligation. The court
'shall' make the order; the 'may' goes only to quantum. This is to be contrasted
with s 24A (1), under which the landlord in the cases cited—

> 'may . . . apply to the court to determine a rent which it would be reasonable
> for the tenant to pay while the tenancy continues by virtue of section 24 of this
> Act, and the court may determine a rent accordingly.'

Clearly the landlord is under no obligation to apply to the court, and his 'may' must
be merely permissive. The court's 'may' seems equally permissive: it relates not
merely to quantum but to whether or not a determination is to be made at all. Thus
ran the argument.

In my judgment this argument, in its essentials, is sound. In saying this, I do not
forget the long line of cases (in which *Julius v Bishop of Oxford*[2] is prominent) which
show that language which grammatically is merely permissive, such as 'may', 'if
they think fit', or 'shall have power', may nevertheless be coupled with a duty to
exercise the power or discretion, so that the apparently permissive becomes obligatory. In this case, however, I do not think that the material exists which would
bring these authorities into play. Section 24A was introduced in order to meet the
mischief of tenants seeking to drag out proceedings under the 1954 Act because it
continued their existing tenancies at their existing rents until three months after the
application was finally disposed of: and under market conditions in recent years the
rents under the existing tenancies were in many cases far below the current level of
rents. The court's power to fix interim rents meets the justifiable complaint of
landlords under this head. Nevertheless, there may be many cases in which proceedings for the fixing of an interim rent might be unreasonable or even oppressive.
Thus the gap between the rent being paid and the rent sought by the landlords may
be small: or the proceedings may have marched on apace, so that the period for
which any interim rent could operate would be trivial. Furthermore, once the court
has ordered a new tenancy to be granted and has fixed its terms, under s 36 (2) the
tenant can within 14 days require the court to revoke the order, as, for instance, he
may well wish to do if the rent has been fixed at a level far above what he can afford
to pay; yet in the case of an interim rent the 1954 Act provides the tenant with no
such means of escape. Nor is it always the tenant who delays proceedings under the
Act. Considerations such as these seem to me to support the view, based on the
language of the statute, that the jurisdiction is merely discretionary. I may say that
counsel for the landlords did not contest that this was the case.

I have considered this first point at length as it links up with the second. Before
I turn to the *Regis* case[3], I must refer to s 24A. I have already set out the relevant
part of s 24A (1), whereby the landlord may apply to the court 'to determine a rent
which it would be reasonable for the tenant to pay' for the interim period, 'and the

---

1   [1970] 3 All ER 227, [1970] Ch 695
2   (1880) 5 App Cas 214, [1874–80] All ER Rep 43
3   [1970] 3 All ER 227, [1970] Ch 695

a   court may determine a rent accordingly'. Section 24A (2) deals with the period for which the interim rent is payable. It is to begin with the later of two dates, the date on which the proceedings for the determination of the interim rent were commenced (here, 29th December 1971), and the date specified in the tenant's request: here, that date is 1st March 1972, so that this, being the later, is the relevant date. There is then s 24A (3); and this is important. It runs as follows:

b   'In determining a rent under this section the court shall have regard to the rent payable under the terms of the tenancy, but otherwise subsections (1) and (2) of section 34 of this Act shall apply to the determination as they would apply to the determination of a rent under that section if a new tenancy from year to year of the whole of the property comprised in the tenancy were granted to the tenant by order of the court.'

c   I pause at that point to comment. Under s 24A (1), what has to be determined is what the landlord has applied for, namely, 'a rent which it would be reasonable for the tenant to pay' during the interim period. The word 'accordingly' makes that clear. However, s 24A (3) lays down what has to be done in determining a rent under that section; and two different tenancies have to be kept in mind. First, there is the existing tenancy for which the interim rent under the section is to be

d   determined, and second, there is the hypothetical tenancy under the concluding words of the subsection, the 'new tenancy from year to year'. In determining the interim rent for the existing tenancy, the court must 'have regard' to the existing rent payable under the terms of that tenancy, but otherwise sub-ss (1) and (2) of s 34 are to apply in determining the interim rent under the existing tenancy in the same way as they would apply if, instead of fixing an interim rent under the existing

e   tenancy, the court were fixing the rent under a new tenancy from year to year.
        With that, I turn to the *Regis* case[1]. Let me say at the outset that I share to the full the sentiments expressed by Stamp J as to the difficulties of construing s 24A (3). Indeed, I would add my own comment that the term 'have regard' is almost of necessity bound to create difficulties. How much regard is to be had, and what

f   weight is to be attached to the regard when it has been had? Put shortly, the contentions before the learned judge in the *Regis* case[1] were on one side that the emphasis should be on the word 'reasonable' in s 24A (1), thereby giving the court power to provide a 'cushion' for the tenant against the full impact of s 24A (3); and on the other side there was the argument that s 24A (3) predominated and made s 34, with its formula based on the open market rent, apply to the determination, without any cushion from s 24A (1) or the opening words of s 24A (3). The learned judge

g   rejected the cushion argument. He said[2]:

          'If there is a construction of sub-s (3) which leads to a more satisfactory result I must, I think, adopt it; for otherwise, notwithstanding the formula prescribed by the second limb of sub-s (3), the rent will in the end be fixed by the length of the judge's foot. I cannot infer, unless compelled to do so, that the legislature,

h   having laid down the formula at the end of sub-s(3), intended to enable the court to depart from it to an unspecified and arbitrary extent.'

        I think I ought to read most of the remainder of the learned judge's closely reasoned judgment. It continues as follows[3]:

          'I have come to the conclusion, not without hesitation, that sub-s (3) does
i   not contemplate a reconciliation of two elements or an adjustment of the rent ascertained by the formula at the end of the subsection by reference to

---

1   [1970] 3 All ER 227, [1970] Ch 695
2   [1970] 3 All ER at 228, [1970] Ch at 698
3   [1970] 3 All ER at 228, 229, [1970] Ch at 698, 699

the existing rent mentioned at the beginning of the subsection. The process
contemplated by the subsection is, in my judgment, a single process to be carried
out by applying s 34 (1) and (2), but by applying those subsections with a modification of their language. The clue is, in my judgment, to be found in the
wording of s 34 (1). Under that subsection, the court, in determining what I
might call the permanent rent, is to determine the rent—"... at which, *having
regard to the terms of the [new] tenancy* (other than those relating to rent), the holding might be expected to be let in the open market ..." In relation to the determination of a rent under a new tenancy the phrase "having regard to the terms of
the [new] tenancy" would be nonsensical if there were not excluded from it the
terms relating to rent. The words which are in parenthesis ("other than those
relating to rent") are there inserted to make it sensible. Section 24A, however,
is not concerned with the rent under a new tenancy but with a rent to be paid
under an existing tenancy; and although often the rent under the existing
tenancy will like other terms of the tenancy be no guide and will be irrelevant
in determining at what rent the holding might reasonably be expected to be let
on a tenancy from year to year, it may sometimes be a relevant consideration
for that purpose.'

I pause at that point to stress the phrase 'not concerned with the rent under a new
tenancy', to which I must return. The judgment continues[1]:

'It would, for example, be relevant if the property had been let on a tenancy
from year to year at a rent of £x and there was evidence that, since the creation
of the tenancy, there had been a rise of 20 per cent in rents of comparable
properties. The existing rent would be relevant if the holding and another
comparable holding had been let on the same day at the same rent and the
comparable holding had lately been let on a tenancy from year to year. If
s 34 (1) had been applicable without modification to the determination of the
interim rent, the court would, in relation to both examples, have been precluded
from looking at a rent which would in those cases be a fact leading to the elucidation of the problem. The introductory words of s 24A (3) are, in my judgment,
designed to introduce that modification. The process of determination is to be
a single process under which s 34 (1) is to be applied, but just as the court is
enjoined under that subsection to have regard to the terms of the new tenancy,
under s 24A (3) it is likewise to have regard to those terms of the existing tenancy,
but in the latter case including and not excluding the term as to rent. So construed, sub-s (3) becomes sensible and the court is not to be precluded, in determining the rent at which the holding might reasonably be expected to be let on
a tenancy from year to year, from such assistance as it may derive from the fact that
at such and such a time the rent was agreed at £x. If, as I think, the introductory
words of sub-s (3) do no more than, in effect, strike out the words in parenthesis
in s 34 (1) and substitute for those words the words "including those relating to
rent"[and again I pause to emphasise those words], then it follows that, if the
existing terms as to rent throw no light on the rent at which the holding might
reasonably be expected to be let under a tenancy from year to year, one is no
more bound to take the actual rent into account as a relevant element in determining the rent than one would an irrelevant covenant such as a covenant
in a lease of office tenancies against assignment without the consent of the landlord. On finding that some of the terms of the existing tenancy and the existing
rent do not on the facts of a particular case assist one in determining what the
interim rent ought to be, one ignores them. I am assisted to my conclusion as
to the true construction of sub-s (3) by the words "but otherwise", which suggest
to me that s 34 (1) and (2) is to apply with the modification that the rent payable

---

1 [1970] 3 All ER at 229, [1970] Ch at 699, 700

a is not to be disregarded for they are words which, in my judgment, would be quite inappropriate if two processes were contemplated. I am also assisted by the consideration that, unless the introductory words of sub-s (3) operate in the way that I think they do, one is faced with a contradiction; for under the introductory words one is to have regard to the existing rent, whereas in applying s 34 (1) one is precluded from doing so.'

b This reasoning is, if I may say so, both persuasive and powerful, making sense out of an obscure subsection. The force of that reasoning is strengthened by the judgment being a reserved judgment. There is, however, one aspect in particular that I have difficulty in following. The statement that s 24A 'is not concerned with the rent under a new tenancy but with a rent to be paid under an existing tenancy' seems to me to give scant weight to the concluding words of s 24A (3), as well as to *c* other parts of the section. True, it is the rent to be paid under the existing tenancy that is to be determined; but, quite apart from the opening requirement to 'have regard' to the existing rent, that determination is to be made not by applying s 34 simpliciter to the existing tenancy but by applying it to that tenancy in the same way as it would apply to the determination of the rent of a new (and hypothetical) tenancy from year to year. (I may say that in relation to s 24A (3) I shall for brevity use *d* 's 34' as meaning s 34 (1) and (2).) Not until the mode of application of s 34 to the hypothetical yearly tenancy has been determined can it be said how s 34 is to apply to the existing tenancy.

The start, then, must be to apply s 34 to that notional yearly tenancy. In doing this, s 34 requires the court to determine the rent to be that at which, having regard to the terms of that hypothetical tenancy (other than those relating to rent), the holding *e* might reasonably be expected to be let in the open market. The parenthetical words are needed here as they are needed in the ordinary case under s 34, in order to prevent the formula from being 'nonsensical', to use the language of Stamp J. The words in the early part of s 24A (3) which require the court to 'have regard to the rent payable under the terms of the tenancy' plainly refer to the existing tenancy that is continuing, and not to the hypothetical yearly tenancy conjured up by the *f* latter part of s 24A (3). A requirement to have regard to the existing rent under an existing tenancy does not seem to me to 'do no more than, in effect, strike out the words in parenthesis' in s 34 (1), namely, the words which, in their application to s 24A, speak not of the terms relating to the existing rent of the existing tenancy, but the terms relating to the nonexistent rent of the hypothetical yearly tenancy. In short, it may be said that the judgment in the *Regis* case[1] does not give effect to *g* the fact that the two provisions are speaking of different tenancies. One can without difficulty obey the direction to ignore terms as to rent in the new hypothetical tenancy and at the same time obey the direction to have regard to the rent payable under the existing tenancy.

The statutory concept is undeniably complex, and at the risk of inaccuracy I think I ought to attempt to state in general terms the manner in which it seems to me *h* that s 24A works:

(1) What has to be determined is 'a rent which it would be reasonable for the tenant to pay while the tenancy continues by virtue of section 24'. Section 24A (3) gives directions as to the mode of determination, but it is the words just quoted that constitute the basic requirement.

(2) In making the determination, s 24A (3) lays down two separate requirements: *j* (a) the court must 'have regard' to the existing rent under the existing tenancy; and (b) in other respects the court must apply s 34 in a specified manner.

(3) That specified manner is first to determine how s 34 would apply to a hypothetical new yearly tenancy granted by the court. In doing that, the court must have regard to the terms of that hypothetical tenancy (other than those relating to rent);

---

1   [1970] 3 All ER 227, [1970] Ch 695

but at this stage there is nothing to exclude the terms of the existing tenancy as to *a*
rent, though these may or may not provide any valuation assistance. (Presumably
the other terms of the hypothetical tenancy which are to be assumed should be those
of the existing tenancy so far as they are compatible with a yearly tenancy.)

(4) The specified manner of applying s 34 then requires that the section shall be
applied to the existing tenancy in the same way as it applied to the hypothetical
tenancy; and as that meant an application excluding terms relating to the rent under *b*
the hypothetical tenancy but not terms relating to rent under the existing tenancy,
those latter terms, for what they are worth, are still not excluded, even at this stage.

(5) Having thus applied s 34 in the specified manner required by the concluding
words of s 24A (3), the opening words of that subsection come into play and impose
a positive requirement to 'have regard' to the rent payable under the existing tenancy.

(6) That positive requirement forms no part of the process of ascertaining the
market rent in the specified manner; it is a separate and independent requirement, *c*
emphasised by the words 'but otherwise' in s 24A (3). It is therefore to be applied
in all cases, and not merely in those envisaged in the *Regis* case[1], namely, those in
which the rent under the existing tenancy throws some light on the market rent.

(7) This accords with the basic requirement to determine the rent that it would be
'reasonable' for the tenant to pay during the interim period; in determining what *d*
rent is reasonable for the tenant to pay, the determination must be made in accordance with the requirements of s 24A (3). The court is not given a roving commission
to consider every fact that might bear on reasonableness, but must determine what
rent it would be reasonable for the tenant to pay according to the market value
formula of s 34 (as modified by s 24A (3)), but 'having regard' to the rent payable
under the existing tenancy.

To these propositions I would append five comments. First, a major difficulty *e*
in the *Regis* case[2] is that it appears to give inadequate weight to two phrases in s 24A,
namely, 'a rent which it would be reasonable for the tenant to pay' under s 24A (1),
and 'the court shall have regard to the rent payable under the terms of the tenancy'
under s 24A (3). The *Regis*[2] construction virtually reduces the elaborate formula
of s 24A to a simple application of the open market formula of s 34. The words
'reasonable for the tenant to pay' in s 24A (1) do nothing either to reconcile two *f*
elements or to adjust the rent ascertained under s 24A (3) according to s 34. The
requirement to 'have regard' to the existing rent does nothing, for if that rent threw
any light on the open market rent it would be admissible quite apart from the
'have regard' phrase. When s 34 applies in determining a permanent rent, the parenthetic words in s 34 (1) plainly do not prevent the court from looking at the terms of
the existing tenancy; they speak only of the new tenancy that is to be granted. *g*
Similarly, in determining the rent for the hypothetical yearly tenancy under s 24A (3),
the parenthetic words, so as to avoid nonsense, exclude the rent under that hypothetical new tenancy, but not under the existing tenancy. Having determined how
s 34 applies to the hypothetical new tenancy, the provisions of that section must be
applied in the same way ('shall apply . . . as they would apply') to the determination
of the interim rent; and for this the rent under the existing tenancy could, when *h*
relevant, be taken into account quite apart from the direction in s 24A (3) to 'have
regard' to it. The direction to have regard to the existing rent is thus not needed
to prevent the court from being 'precluded . . . from such assistance as it may derive
from the fact that at such and such a time the rent was agreed at £x' (see the *Regis*
case[1]), for there is nothing which precludes the court from doing this. I would only *j*
add that the process of applying s 34 to a hypothetical yearly tenancy is one that, at
least under present conditions, may often have an air of unreality about it that would
puzzle the most expert of valuers.

Second, if all that s 24A achieves is to provide for an interim rent to be fixed on the
basis of market value, it is difficult to see why Parliament adopted the complex

---

1   [1970] 3 All ER at 229, [1970] Ch at 699   2   [1970] 3 All ER 227, [1970] Ch 695

formula of s 24A. All that was needed was a provision allowing the permanent rent
to be back-dated, or, if the interim rent is being fixed before the final hearing, a
provision for fixing the interim rent on the s 34 basis, on the footing of a tenancy
from year to year in each case. Instead of that, there is the requirement of a rent
that it would be 'reasonable' for the tenant to pay, to be fixed by a formula which
qualifies the market rent basis of s 34 by the direction to 'have regard' to the existing
rent. I find it hard to believe that in trying to ascertain the meaning of Parliament,
as expressed in the language it has used, this elaboration is to go for nothing.

Third, I cannot attach any great weight to the 'length of the judge's foot' mentioned
in the *Regis* case[1] as a ground for rejecting the statutory provision for determining
the rent 'which it would be reasonable for the tenant to pay'. For one thing, Parliament has not infrequently consigned matters to the decision of the courts with little
more than the word 'reasonable' or its equivalent to guide them. One has only to
look at the decisions under the Inheritance (Family Provision) Act 1938 to see a trail
of reasonableness which has been trodden by the feet of many judges. For another
thing, s 24A seems to me to lay down a far more restricted formula than would be
indicated by the phrase 'which it would be reasonable for the tenant to pay' simpliciter.
As I have mentioned, the section gives the court no roving commission, but provides
(I put it shortly) for the rent that it would be reasonable for the tenant to pay to be
worked out in a particular way, namely, by taking the market rent and then having
regard to the existing rent; and that is all. Reasonableness thus operates within a
narrowly defined field, though I do not know that this necessarily makes the problem
much easier.

Fourth, there is a question of time. A determination under s 34 alone is necessarily
prospective, fixing a new rent as from the future commencement of the new tenancy,
whereas a determination under s 24A will usually, if not always, be in some degree
retrospective, applying in part to a period that has already run. In a market of changing values, as at what date should the determination of the rent under s 24A to be
made? Counsel for the landlords submitted that the values existing at the date of
determination ought to be applied; but I do not think that the accident of when that
date occurs ought to affect the result, with a higher interim rent being fixed if the
market is rising and the determination is late rather than early. The facts that s 34 is
prospective, and that under s 24A (3) there is a hypothetical yearly tenancy, seem
to me to provide sufficient grounds for holding that the values to be applied should
be those existing when the interim period begins to run.

Fifth, I should emphasise that, in differing from Stamp J, I do so with great hesitation. I have attempted to avoid obscurity and prolixity by refraining from tentative
language and from prefacing every reference to his views with the words 'with the
greatest of respect', 'with much hesitation' and the like; but the thought is there in
full measure. The section is indeed difficult and puzzling; but having groped my way
to a conclusion, I think I ought to give effect to it. When no statute is concerned, a
judge owes the duty of comity, if no more, to the decisions of his brethren; but if
the question is one of the construction of a statute, the judge owes a duty of obedience
to Parliament as well. He must always go back to the words of the statute, and not
merely stop at what the courts have said those words mean, unless subject to binding
authority to do so. Furthermore, I have had certain advantages which Stamp J lacked.
His was the first reported decision on this difficult section, so that he lacked the assistance of having before him the firmness and clarity of outline that a reported judgment
gives to the problem and to its possible solutions. There is a proclaimed doctrine to
support and attack, and not merely a cloud of indefinite ideas. He also, so far as is
disclosed by the report of the argument[2], lacked the advantage of having before him
any argument on the jurisdiction under s 24A being discretionary: and if, as I have
held, the jurisdiction is indeed discretionary, this is all of a piece with the section
not merely providing for a rigid valuation according to market values, but including

1 [1970] 3 All ER at 228, [1970] Ch at 698   2 [1970] Ch at 696, 697

within it some provision for tempering market values by reference to the existing rent. If this were not so, the discretion would have to be exercised on a footing that the court must either refuse to fix an interim rent at all, and so leave the existing rent to continue, or else fix an interim rent at the full market value, with no intermediate rent possible. To me, s 24A does not read as if it were intended in this way to provide for all or nothing. The wording seems to me to indicate the intention of Parliament to make it possible to provide the 'cushion' for the tenant that was discussed in argument in the *Regis* case[1]. In view of the ambit of the 1954 Act, applying alike to great and small, I do not find this surprising.

With those considerations in mind, I return to the facts of this case. First, is this a case in which any interim rent ought to be determined? If yes, then, second, what ought that rent to be? On the first point, the period with which I am concerned is no trivial period; it is at least a year and a month. The disparity between the existing rent of £7,655 and the rent that will be payable under the new tenancy that is to be granted is again no small matter, for the new rent is £16,000 and so is more than double the existing rent. On the other hand, there has been no suggestion that the tenants have been delaying the proceedings in any attempt to prolong the advantage of the present rent. However, counsel for the tenants contended that the 1954 Act in its original form gave the tenant a vested right to continue during the interim period at the existing rent, and that, in the absence of any delay or other misconduct on his part, the amendment introduced by the Law of Property Act 1969 ought not to be used to alter his vested rights.

I do not think that this contention can be right. At common law, the tenancy would have expired on 1st March 1972. The 1954 Act in its original form gave the tenant the right to remain during the interim period at the existing rent, and while that Act remained unamended it may have been possible to regard a tenant as having a vested right to this effect. However, after the Law of Property Act 1969 had inserted s 24A, the 1954 Act became an Act which gave no unqualified right to the tenant to remain at his existing rent, but instead gave him a right qualified by s 24A. As soon as the Act spoke in its amended form, I cannot see how it could be said that any tenant then had a vested right to remain at his existing rent during the interim period: his common law liability to be evicted at the end of his contractual term had been modified by a statute which, giving him the right to remain, gave him only a qualified right to continue at his existing rent. The most that could be said is that where, as here, the tenancy began before the 1969 Act was passed, the tenant initially had a reasonable expectation of being able to remain for some indefinite period at the end of the term at the existing rent if he wanted to, an expectation dependent upon whether or not the statute was amended, and also, of course, dependent for its benefit on whether rents continued to rise.

In those circumstances, it seems to me that the court ought in this case to determine an interim rent. The choice lies between leaving the tenants to pay their existing rent, which is admittedly far below the value of what they are getting, and requiring them to pay a rent which, by statutory definition, is the rent 'which it would be reasonable' for the tenants to pay. In the absence of considerations pointing to any different conclusion, why should the court prefer the inadequate to the reasonable? Without laying down any formal rule that the onus lies on the tenant to show why the discretion should not be exercised, I would say that in most normal cases the court's discretion under s 24A ought to be exercised, in that to do so will usually promote justice.

That brings me to the second question, that of quantum. The matters of law that I have been discussing had not been fully deployed when the evidence was being given, but I think that the figure on which in the end the experts were not far from agreeing was that of a pure valuation figure based on s 34 as applied by s 24A, without (I think rightly) giving effect, or attempting to attribute proper weight, to the words in s 24A

---

1   [1970] Ch 695 at 697

a (3) which require the court to 'have regard to the rent payable under the terms of the tenancy'. Mr Laurie's figure was £15,500, and Mr French accepted that this was right if Mr Laurie's figure of £16,600 for the new tenancy was right; and having regard to the rent that I have determined for the new tenancy, I think I can take £15,000 as the starting point for determining the interim rent. With that point of departure, then, the question for the court is, with whatever aid it can obtain from the evidence and having regard to the existing rent of £7,655, what rent it would be reasonable for b the tenants to pay during the interim period in accordance with the statutory formula. It will be observed that the statute is expressed, not in terms of what rent 'would be a reasonable rent'. Such language would require a consideration of the interests of both landlord and tenant. Instead, the wording looks to the tenant who pays the rent; the rent is to be the 'rent which it would be reasonable for the tenant to pay'. The rent will be a rent under an existing tenancy which binds the tenant; he must pay the c rent, and he has no escape from it such as he has under s 36 (2) in the case of a new tenancy. In such circumstances, what interim rent ought to be determined in the present case? What is the effect on £15,000 of having regard to the existing rent of £7,655?

Counsel for the tenants' contention was that a rent half way between the two figures would be appropriate; and he stressed that an interim tenancy was not a d marketable commodity. Yet the tenants are enjoying something which on the valuation evidence is worth £15,000 per annum; and it may indeed be asked why it would be reasonable for the tenants to pay some £11,300 per annum for what is worth some £3,700 per annum more. A possible reply lies in the reasonable expectation which the tenants had when their lease was granted in 1966, well before the 1969 Act was passed, namely, that the rent agreed would probably continue to apply for e some while after the contractual end of their term; I have already mentioned this in relation to the court's discretion. If a tenant enters into a lease with such an expectation and subsequently statute confers on the court a discretionary power to order the tenant to pay what in the event is a higher rent, but expresses that power in terms of 'a rent which it would be reasonable for the tenant to pay', and in working this out requires the court to 'have regard' to his existing rent, may it not be said that f there are grounds on which the court may hold it reasonable for the tenant to pay less than the full market rent? Yet if so, how much less? It is here that I feel most acutely the pinch of Stamp J's comments[1] on the judge's foot.

I doubt if the two elements of market rent and existing rent are intended to be given equal weight. Section 24A (3) provides that s 34 'shall apply' to the determination in the manner stated and merely requires the court to 'have regard' to the existing rent. g I think the process envisaged is not that of striking a balance between two factors of equal weight, but of applying one factor, that of the market rent, and, where appropriate, suitably tempering it by reference to the existing rent. On the facts before me, I do not think that much of a case for tempering the market rent by any very substantial amount has been made out; there is some case, but not much. What, then, is the right figure, closer to the interim market rent of £15,000 than to the existing h rent of £7,655, that will duly reflect the intention of s 24A in relation to the facts of this case? Doing the best I can in this very difficult jurisdiction, I can only say that, for reasons which defy any detailed analysis, I would, on the facts of this case, fix the interim rent at £14,000 a year; and I therefore determine the rent under s 24A at this figure. I would only add that, obvious though my reasons for regretting the length of this judgment must be, part of the responsibility may not unfairly be laid at the j door of Parliament.

Judgment accordingly.

Solicitors: *Fallons* (for the tenants); *Berwin Leighton* (for the landlords).

Susan Corbett   Barrister.

1   [1970] 3 All ER at 228, [1970] Ch at 698

R v Lovett

COURT OF APPEAL, CRIMINAL DIVISION

EDMUND DAVIES LJ, CANTLEY AND BRISTOW JJ

30th NOVEMBER, 20th DECEMBER 1972

Criminal law – Evidence – Character of accused – Character of witness for prosecution – Defendant conducting defence so as to involve imputation on character of prosecution witness – Defendant also giving evidence against co-accused – Co-accused charged with different offence – Co-accused cross-examining defendant about his criminal record without first seeking leave to do so – Whether in circumstances co-accused entitled to cross-examine defendant without leave – Criminal Evidence Act 1898, s 1 (f), provisos (ii), (iii).

The appellant and G were jointly indicted. The appellant was charged with entering a house as a trespasser and stealing therein a television set (count 1), and G with dishonestly assisting in the disposal of the set knowing or believing it to be stolen (count 2). At their trial (i) the appellant in the course of his examination-in-chief gave evidence against his co-accused, G, and (ii) his counsel in cross-examining a Crown witness made imputations on the character of that witness within the terms of proviso (ii) to s 1 (f)[a] of the Criminal Evidence Act 1898. Without intimating to the trial judge that he intended to do so, G's counsel cross-examined the appellant about his criminal record. G was acquitted on count 2 and the appellant was convicted on count 1. He appealed on the grounds (i) that G's counsel could not cross-examine him under proviso (iii) of s 1 (f) as the two co-accused were not charged with the same offence and the facts were not such that the two offences could in law amount to the same offence, and (ii) no ruling in law had been asked for or given on the question whether the appellant and G were charged with the same offence before the appellant was cross-examined about his previous convictions. Counsel for the Crown informed the court that he would have sought the trial judge's permission to cross-examine the appellant on his criminal record, if he had not been forestalled by G's counsel.

Held – (i) G's counsel had acted irregularly in cross-examining the appellant without first seeking and obtaining the court's leave to do so; he could not rely on proviso (iii) to s 1 (f) as the offence charged against the appellant and the offence charged against G could not in law amount to the same offence within the meaning of that proviso, and he was not entitled as of right to cross-examine the appellant under proviso (ii) on the ground that the character of a Crown witness had been impugned (see p 747 a to c, p 750 b and p 751 e, post).

(ii) The case was however a proper one for applying the proviso to s 2 (1)[b] of the Criminal Appeal Act 1968 and the appeal would accordingly be dismissed because (a) on the evidence the imputation on the character of the Crown witness was of

---

a   Section 1 (f), so far as material, provides: 'A person charged and called as a witness in pursuance of this Act shall not be asked, and if asked shall not be required to answer, any question tending to show that he has committed or been convicted of or been charged with any offence other than that wherewith he is then charged, or is of bad character, unless . . . (ii) . . . the nature or conduct of the defence is such as to involve imputations on the character of the prosecutor or the witnesses for the prosecution; or (iii) he has given evidence against any other person charged with the same offence'.

b   Section 2 (1), so far as material, provides: '. . . the Court may, notwithstanding that they are of opinion that the point raised in the appeal might be decided in favour of the appellant, dismiss the appeal if they consider that no miscarriage of justice has actually occurred.'

a such gravity that had counsel for the Crown applied under proviso (ii) to cross-examine the appellant the application would undoubtedly have been granted, with the result that the appellant's record would in any event have been revealed to the jury and (b) in the circumstances no miscarriage of justice had resulted from the irregularity of the course adopted by G's counsel (see p 751 f and g, post).

Per Curiam. Where evidence has been given by one co-accused against another
b co-accused in circumstances which do not come within proviso (iii), it may be that the court of trial can in the exercise of its discretion grant the co-accused who has been attacked leave to cross-examine the other co-accused pursuant to proviso (ii) on the ground that the latter has made imputations against a Crown witness (see p 750 b and c, post).

   R v Cook [1959] 2 All ER 97 applied.
   Murdoch v Taylor [1965] 1 All ER 406 considered.
c

Notes

For cross-examination of defendant as to character, see 10 Halsbury's Laws (3rd Edn) 449-451, para 828, and for cases on the subject, see 14 Digest (Repl) 511-513, 4942-4968, 515-518, 4987-5016.
d   For the Criminal Evidence Act 1898, s 1, see 12 Halsbury's Statutes (3rd Edn) 865.
   For the Criminal Appeal Act 1968, s 2, see 8 Halsbury's Statutes (3rd Edn) 690.

Cases referred to in judgment

Murdoch v Taylor [1965] 1 All ER 406, [1965] AC 574, [1965] 2 WLR 425, 129 JP 208, 49 Cr App Rep 119, HL, Digest (Cont Vol B) 175, 4957b.
e *R v Cook* [1959] 2 All ER 97, [1959] 2 QB 340, [1959] 2 WLR 616, 123 JP 271, 43 Cr App Rep 138, CCA, Digest (Cont Vol A) 374, 4942a.
R v Francis, R v Murphy (1959) 43 Cr App Rep 174, CCA, Digest (Cont Vol A) 368, 4448a.
R v Hadwen [1902] 1 KB 882, 71 LJKB 581, 86 LT 601, 66 JP 456, 20 Cox CC 206, CCR, 14 Digest (Repl) 519, 5018.
f *R v Jenkins* (1945) 114 LJKB 425, 173 LT 311, 110 JP 86, 44 LGR 42, 31 Cr App Rep 1, CCA, 14 Digest (Repl) 512, 4950.
R v Meek (1966) 110 Sol Jo 867, CA, Digest (Cont Vol B) 177, 5019a.
R v Roberts [1936] 1 All ER 23, 154 LT 276, 100 JP 117, 25 Cr App Rep 158, 34 LGR 147, CCA, 14 Digest (Repl) 519, 5019.
R v Russell [1970] 3 All ER 924, [1971] 1 QB 151, [1970] 3 WLR 977, 135 JP 78, CA, Digest (Cont Vol C) 218, 5019b.
g *R v Sargvon* (1967) 51 Cr App Rep 394, CA, Digest (Cont Vol C) 217, 5016c.
R v Seigley (1911) 6 Cr App Rep 106, CCA, 14 Digest (Repl) 512, 4953.
Selvey v Director of Public Prosecutions [1968] 2 All ER 497, [1970] AC 304, [1968] 2 WLR 1494, 132 JP 430, 52 Cr App Rep 443, HL, Digest (Cont Vol C) 217, 5016b.

h **Appeal**

On 3rd May 1972 at Nottingham Crown Court before the recorder (D G A Lowe Esq QC) and a jury the appellant, Barry Lovett, was convicted of burglary (count 1) and theft (count 5) and sentenced to 12 months' imprisonment consecutive on each count, a suspended sentence of six months' imprisonment imposed on 14th July 1970 for theft was ordered to be activated and to run consecutively with the other sentences making 2½ years' imprisonment in all. He appealed against his conviction
j with leave of the single judge. His grounds, inter alia, were as follows: (i) that he was cross-examined by counsel for his co-accused, Arthur Gregory, about his previous convictions, after he, the appellant, gave evidence against Gregory within the meaning of the proviso to s 1 (f) (iii) of the Criminal Evidence Act 1898; the appellant had been charged with burglary and Gregory with handling and therefore they were not charged with the same offence within the meaning of s 1 of the 1898 Act, nor

were the facts such that the two offences could in law amount to the same offence;
and (ii) no ruling in law was asked for or given on the question whether the appellant   a
had given evidence against his co-accused and was charged with the same offence
before the appellant was cross-examined about his previous convictions. He also
applied, after refusal by the single judge, for extension of time to appeal against
sentence on the ground of disparity with the sentence imposed on Gregory of 12
months' imprisonment in all. The facts are set out in the judgment of the court.   b

J R Hopkin for the appellant.
R A D Payne for the Crown.

Cur adv vult

20th December. **EDMUND DAVIES LJ** read the following judgment of the   c
court. Barry Lovett appeals by leave of the single judge from his conviction at Nottingham Crown Court in May 1972 for burglary and theft of a television set (count 1), for
which he was sentenced to 12 months' imprisonment. He also appeals against his
conviction on another charge of theft (count 5), relating to a vacuum cleaner, for which
he received a 12 months consecutive sentence. He further applies for leave to appeal
against his sentences which (together with a six months suspended sentence put   d
into operation) total 30 months' imprisonment.

The appellant was jointly indicted and tried with Arthur Gregory. Count 1 of
the indictment charged the appellant with burglary, contrary to s 9 of the Theft
Act 1968, the particulars being that 'on the 13th of June, 1971, in the City of Nottingham, having entered a dwellinghouse as a trespasser [he] stole therein a Sobell
television set'. Count 2 charged Gregory with handling, contrary to s 22, the   e
particulars being that—

'on a day unknown between the 1st and 30th June, 1971 ... [he] dishonestly
assisted in the disposal of stolen goods, namely a Sobell television set, by or for
the benefit of [the appellant], knowing or believing the same to have been
stolen.'   f

The appellant was convicted, Gregory acquitted.

The case for the prosecution was that on 13th June 1971, the appellant telephoned
a Mrs Griffiths and in the course of the conversation she said she would be away
from home that evening. Her little daughter testified that, during her mother's
absence, the appellant and another man came to the house and took away the television set. Another prosecution witness said that the appellant and Gregory brought   g
him the set in July and he paid them £90 for it. In August the appellant admitted
to the police that he had stolen the set, saying that Gregory had put him up to it,
and that they had both taken the set from the house of Mrs Griffiths and later sold
it. But at the trial he testified that Gregory, who said he had formerly been associating with Mrs Griffiths, had claimed the set as his property and wanted it back.
Believing Gregory, he and Gregory's brother had collected the set and he was paid   h
£25 for his trouble. Gregory, on the other hand, testified that he had nothing to do
with the matter at all and, as we have already said, the jury acquitted him on count 2.

The trial of this commonplace type of case developed on lines which are
fortunately far from common. The appellant having in the course of his examination-
in-chief clearly given evidence against his co-accused, counsel for Gregory (whom we
have not heard) seemingly took the view that this entitled him as of right to cross-   j
examine the appellant on his bad criminal record. And, without giving any intimation to the learned recorder of his intention, that is what he in fact did. We have
to say that this was quite contrary to the established proper practice, which is for
counsel to tell the presiding judge (in the absence of the jury) that he proposes to
cross-examine the accused as to his previous convictions unless the court rules that he

a may not do so: see the observations of Lord Morris of Borth-y-Gest in *Murdoch v Taylor*[1]. This enables the court to consider the position that has arisen and rule whether, having regard to the proviso to s 1 (*f*) of the Criminal Evidence Act 1898, the proposed cross-examination should be permitted. Had this been done in the present case and had Gregory's counsel relied on proviso (iii), the proper ruling would clearly have been that it had no application and could not be invoked. Proviso (iii)

b applies when the co-accused sought to be cross-examined has given evidence against another co-accused 'charged with the same offence'. This matter was considered in *R v Roberts*[2] and *R v Russell*[3] but no authority is necessary to establish that in the present case the offences of theft and handling charged against the appellant and Gregory respectively were not the 'same offence', even though the same Sobell television set was the subject-matter of both charges. Indeed, s 22 (1) of the Theft Act 1968 puts the matter beyond all doubt by defining handling as being 'otherwise

c than in the course of stealing'.

The first ground of appeal raises this very point, and it follows that it is well-founded. It has been suggested (and not without good reason) that the law on this matter is unsatisfactory, and that the mischief aimed at in proviso (iii) would be more satisfactorily dealt with if it applied whenever two accused are jointly tried, even though they are not charged with the same offence (Cross on Evidence[4]). But we

d have to deal with the law as it is, and if the proceedings before this court had stopped with the foregoing submission of counsel for the appellant, this would have been a straightforward appeal which must clearly have been allowed. But a complication arose when counsel for the Crown was called on. He drew our attention to the fact that Det Con Everitt, a witness for the prosecution, was cross-examined by counsel for the appellant to the effect that, during the appellant's interrogation at the police

e station, the detective had threatened him with physical violence unless he gave a statement, an allegation which the officer denied. Counsel submitted that this cross-examination clearly involved imputations on the character of a prosecution witness within the terms of proviso (ii), and before us counsel for the appellant immediately conceded that this was so. That having occurred, counsel for the Crown informed this court that, when his turn to cross-examine the appellant came, he

f was proposing to cross-examine the appellant on his criminal record. Instead, counsel for Gregory forestalled him by doing that very thing. But he submitted that, since the appellant's record would thus in any event have been brought out, the ultimate result must have been the same and that this appeal should accordingly be dismissed.

To this, counsel for the appellant retorted that whether or not the Crown would

g have been permitted to cross-examine him under proviso (ii) depended on the recorder's discretion (*R v Jenkins*[5], *R v Cook*[6]); that it was not permissible for this court to guess what he would have done regarding a discretion he was never asked to exercise; and that, for all we know, the recorder might have disallowed the proposed cross-examination of the appellant.

The final stage was reached with the submission of counsel for the Crown that it

h is open to a co-accused, just as much as the Crown, to invoke proviso (ii) if the other co-accused makes imputations against a prosecution witness; that even though in the present case counsel for Gregory wrongly had proviso (iii) in mind when cross-examining the appellant as he did, he would nevertheless have been entitled to rely on proviso (ii) in justification; furthermore, that although the recorder could have

j

---

1   [1965] 1 All ER 406 at 410, [1965] AC 574 at 585
2   [1936] 1 All ER 23, 25 Cr App Rep 158
3   [1970] 3 All ER 924, [1971] 1 QB 151
4   3rd Edn (1967), p 356
5   (1945) 114 LJKB 425
6   [1959] 2 All ER 97, [1959] 2 QB 340

prevented the Crown from cross-examining as to the appellant's record, he had no
more power to stop Gregory's counsel from cross-examining the appellant as he
did than the recorder would have had under proviso (iii) if the two men had in fact
been 'charged with the same offence'; and that, in the result, counsel for Gregory
had done no more than that which he was entitled as of right to do. For these
reasons, the Crown submitted that the conviction of the appellant for theft should
stand.

These conflicting submissions present this court with a problem which apparently
has hitherto been unsolved. There have been many statements in judgments to the
effect that it is in the public interest that, where there is a conflict of interest between
the prosecution and the defence and the latter makes imputations against witnesses
called for the Crown, the court should know what kind of a person the accused
is in order to enable the court to judge whom to believe. This point was stressed
in *R v Sargvon*[1] and *Selvey v Director of Public Prosecutions*[2]. But where there is the
additional complication of a contest between co-accused, the course of justice is not
so clear. For guidance, we naturally turn to *Murdoch v Taylor*[3] which finally
established that in cases coming within proviso (iii) the attacked co-accused is entitled as of right to cross-examine his co-accused as to his past criminal record once
he has given evidence against his co-accused. Lord Donovan said[4]:

'Proviso (*f*) (iii) ... in terms confers no ... discretion and, in my opinion,
none can be implied. It is true that in relation to proviso (*f*) (ii) such a discretion does exist; that is to say, in the cases where the accused has attempted
to establish his own good character or where the nature and conduct of the
defence is such as to involve imputations on the character of the prosecutor or
of a witness for the prosecution. In these cases it will normally, if not invariably,
however, be the prosecution who will want to bring out the accused's bad
character—not some co-accused; and in such cases it seems to me quite proper
that the court should retain some control of the matter. For its duty is to secure
a fair trial and the prejudicial value of evidence establishing the accused's bad
character may at times wholly outweigh the value of such evidence as tending
to show that he was guilty of the crime alleged. These considerations lead me
to the view that if, in any given case (which I think would be rare), the prosecution sought to avail itself of the provisions of proviso (*f*) (iii) then here, again,
the court should keep control of the matter in the like way ... but when it is
the co-accused who seeks to exercise the right conferred by proviso (*f*) (iii)
different considerations come into play. He seeks to defend himself; to say
... that the man who is giving evidence against him is unworthy of belief;
and to support that assertion by proof of bad character. The right to do this
cannot, in my opinion, be fettered in any way.'

Commenting on this passage, Widgery LJ said in *R v Russell*[5]:

'[Lord Donovan] clearly contemplated the possibility that a co-accused
might take advantage of proviso (ii) and also that the prosecution might take
advantage of proviso (iii). But the case is not authority on any of these points ...'

In *R v Russell*[6] one co-accused had not only given evidence against another co-
accused charged, as the court held, with the same (albeit not joint) offence, but he
had also made imputations against a witness for the prosecution, and counsel for
the attacked co-accused had at the trial unsuccessfully sought to cross-examine his

---

1   (1967) 51 Cr App Rep 394
2   [1968] 2 All ER 497, [1970] AC 304
3   [1965] 1 All ER 406, [1965] AC 574
4   [1965] 1 All ER at 416, [1965] AC at 592, 593
5   [1970] 3 All ER at 926, [1971] 1 QB at 154
6   [1970] 3 All ER 924, [1971] 1 QB 151

a attacker as to his past record under both (ii) and (iii) of proviso (f). But, holding that the latter clearly applied, the court found it unnecessary to decide whether the former could also have been invoked.

We know of only one reported case where it appears that the prosecution was permitted to cross-examine one of the two co-accused under proviso (iii). This is
b *R v Seigley*[1]. The case is in some ways an odd one, but Hamilton J[2] said that the course adopted was 'clearly permissible under the third sub-section of s. 1 (f) of the Criminal Evidence Act, 1898'. On the other hand, we have no knowledge of any case where a co-accused who has not been attacked in circumstances coming within proviso (iii) has proceeded to cross-examine his co-accused pursuant to proviso (ii) on the ground that the latter has made imputations against a Crown witness.

In principle, ought he to be allowed to do so? We think that under the existing
c law circumstances could well arise when he should, and those of the present case afford one example. Gregory could not legitimately cross-examine the appellant on his previous record, despite his extremely damaging evidence, solely because they were not, as we have held, 'charged with the same offence'. But the resulting prejudice against Gregory was nonetheless real on that account.

In *R v Roberts*[3] Talbot J, giving the judgment of the Court of Criminal Appeal,
d said:

> 'One can easily conceive an argument for ... allowing a further exception to the exemption of prisoners from this particular line of cross-examination, but one must interpret the Act as it is.'

And a 'liberal' interpretation could lead to injustice. For example, A and B are jointly charged with the same offence; A (who has a criminal record) gives no
e evidence against B, but he does make imputations against a Crown witness. On the other hand, B (with a clean record) has it in mind to throw all the blame on A and, for this purpose, it would obviously be helpful to him if he could discredit A by cross-examining him on his bad record. In such circumstances, the Crown themselves may or may not have it in mind to cross-examine A on these lines, but in either case they unquestionably must first seek and obtain the court's permission. Then ought
f B, against whom A has alleged nothing, to be in a position to cross-examine A *as of right* on these matters? We think that justice demands a negative answer to that question.

In *R v Meek*[4] Winn LJ said in relation to proviso (iii):

> '... the whole purpose of the provision is to assist one of two co-accused who
g is in peril of being convicted upon the same charge upon which a co-accused has been charged, by evidence given against him by that co-accused without being able to demonstrate to the jury that that co-accused is unworthy of credibility.'

Mr I G Carvell has pointed out[5] that the same reason was given as early as 1902 in *R v Hadwen*[6]. But in the hypothetical case we have given, A did nothing to pre-
h judice B's defence. In the instant case, on the other hand, the appellant placed Gregory in peril, and the two cases are in that respect dissimilar. But since neither comes within proviso (iii), to allow cross-examination of the appellant by Gregory as of right would mean that B also should be accorded that same right. This would involve that the sheer fortuity that A has made an imputation against a Crown witness would always mean that B could cross-examine him as of right, whereas the

j

1   (1911) 6 Cr App Rep 106
2   (1911) 6 Cr App Rep at 107, 108
3   (1936) 25 Cr App Rep at 161, cf [1936] 1 All ER at 25
4   (1966) 110 Sol Jo 867
5   See 'The Criminal Evidence Act 1898, s 1 (f) (iii)' [1965] Crim LR 419 at 420
6   [1902] 1 KB 882

Crown could be prevented by the court from following that course if it felt that injustice to A might result. We regard such a state of affairs as contrary to the whole tenor of proviso (*f*) and consider that it must be condemned.

Having reflected on the matter, the conclusion we have accordingly come to in relation to the present case is this: Although a final decision on the point is not now called for, we incline to the view that the circumstances were such as to empower the court to rule that cross-examination of the appellant on his past history by Gregory was permissible under proviso (ii). But we are firmly of the view that Gregory was not entitled as of right to do this, and that all would depend on whether the court in the exercise of its discretion granted him leave to follow that course. The court of trial not having been called on to rule on the matter and its discretion accordingly never having been exercised, the question that arises is what course this court should now take.

In *R v Francis, R v Murphy*[1], the Court of Criminal Appeal quashed a conviction when the recorder had failed to rule on the admissibility of alleged confessions, but we are here concerned not with admissibility but with discretion to exclude evidence despite its strict admissibility. The latter point was involved in *R v Cook*[2], where imputations had been made by the defence on the character of a police officer within the meaning of proviso (ii). The following passages from the judgment of the five judge court delivered by Devlin J are relevant to the present case:

(a)[3]'[The court] ... has laid it down that in cases which fall within the words [of s 1 (*f*)] the trial judge must not allow as a matter of course questions designed to show bad character; he must weigh the prejudicial effect of such questions against the damage done by the attack on the prosecution's witnesses and must generally exercise his discretion so as to secure a trial that is fair both to the prosecution and to the defence.'

(b)[4] '"... in the ordinary and normal case, he may feel that if the credit of the prosecutor or his witnesses has been attacked it is only fair that the jury should have before them material on which they can form their judgment as to whether the accused is any more worthy to be believed than those he has attacked ... The essential thing is a fair trial, and that the legislature sought to ensure by s. 1 (*f*)"'.

(The foregoing passage, thus cited with approval, is from the judgment of Singleton J in *R v Jenkins*[5].)

(c)[6] 'The issue, therefore, becomes one of discretion. It is well settled that this court will not interfere with the exercise of a discretion by the judge below unless he has erred in principle or there is no material on which he could properly have arrived at his decision; but in this case we are not satisfied that the learned judge really exercised his discretion at all. He allowed the questions to be put because he thought that counsel was strictly entitled to do so, although he, the learned chairman, queried whether it was necessary. *Accordingly, it falls to us to exercise our own discretion in the matter.*' [The emphasis is ours.]

(d)[7] 'In cases of this sort, where there is no hard and fast rule, some warning to the defence that it is going too far is of great importance; and it has always been the practice for prosecuting counsel to indicate in advance that he is going to claim his rights under s. 1, proviso (*f*) (ii), or for the judge to give the

---

1 (1959) 43 Cr App Rep 174
2 [1959] 2 All ER 97, [1959] 2 QB 340
3 [1959] 2 All ER at 99, [1959] 2 QB at 345
4 [1959] 2 All ER at 100, [1959] 2 QB at 347
5 (1945) 114 LJKB at 431
6 [1959] 2 All ER at 101, [1959] 2 QB at 348
7 [1959] 2 All ER at 101, 102, [1959] 2 QB at 349

a defence a caution . . . We have come to the conclusion that the questions ought not to have been put.'

The court nevertheless applied the proviso to s 4 (1) of the Criminal Appeal Act 1907 and dismissed the appeal, Devlin J saying[1]:

b '. . . we are satisfied that the only reasonable and proper verdict on the facts was one of guilty and that there has been no miscarriage of justice.'

In the present case, assuming the correctness of our tentative view that it was open to Gregory to invoke proviso (ii), it does not follow that the court would deal in the same way with applications made on his behalf and by the Crown to cross-examine the appellant as to character in reliance on that proviso. It might, for example, have taken the view that the appellant's imputations against Det Con c Everitt did Gregory no harm and that it would not be fair to allow him to cross-examine the appellant as, through his counsel, he did. But the imputation against the detective was as grave as it was direct and we regard it as highly unlikely that the court would have refused the Crown leave to cross-examine the appellant. It is true that the trial took so unusual a turn that counsel for the prosecution never had an opportunity to seek leave, but it is not disputed that he proposed to do so at d the proper time, nor has it been submitted that there would have been any likelihood of the recorder's refusing such an application. In these circumstances we propose to follow the course adopted in R v Cook[2] by exercising our own discretion for that which the learned recorder was never called on to exercise.

Adopting that approach, in our judgment the sensible outcome of this appeal may be thus stated: (1) counsel for Gregory acted irregularly in cross-examining the e appellant as he did without first seeking and obtaining the court's leave to do so; (2) the conduct of the appellant's defence admittedly involving an imputation on an important Crown witness, it was clearly open to prosecuting counsel to apply under proviso (ii) to cross-examine the appellant on his criminal record; (3) the gravity of the imputation was such that we entertain no doubt that the application would have been granted; (4) the appellant's record thus becoming revealed to the f jury, counsel for the appellant has made no submission that on the totality of the evidence they were not entitled to convict him, as they in fact did; (5) in the result, while there was an irregularity in the trial, no miscarriage of justice resulted there-from; (6) it is accordingly a proper case to apply the proviso to s 2 (1) of the Criminal Appeal Act 1968; (7) applying it, we dismiss the appeal against conviction.

As to the application for leave to appeal against sentence, what is said is that, while g the recorder committed no error in principle, there was such a disparity between the sentences totalling 30 months' imprisonment passed on the appellant and the concurrent sentences of 12 months' imprisonment passed on Gregory in respect of the theft of two other television sets charged in the same indictment that this court should now interfere. Gregory had, indeed, a bad criminal record and was sentenced to 14 years' imprisonment in 1960 for robbery with violence, and it may be that the h recorder treated him with excessive leniency. However that may be, we do not in all the circumstances consider that interference is called for, and the appellant's application is therefore dismissed.

Appeal against conviction dismissed. Application for leave to appeal against sentence refused.

j Solicitors: *Registrar of Criminal Appeals* (for the appellant); *D W Ritchie*, Nottingham (for the Crown).

N P Metcalfe Esq Barrister.

---

1   [1959] 2 All ER at 102, [1959] 2 QB at 349
2   [1959] 2 All ER 97, [1959] 2 QB 340

Barclays Bank Ltd v Taylor and another   *a*

COURT OF APPEAL, CIVIL DIVISION
RUSSELL, CAIRNS AND STAMP LJJ
24th, 27th, 28th, 29th, 30th NOVEMBER 1972, 24th JANUARY 1973

b

Land registration – Priority – Entries protecting dealings off the register – Deposit of land certificate with bank by registered proprietors to secure debt – Notice of deposit registered – Agreement by registered proprietors to execute legal mortgage in favour of bank on demand – Subsequent execution of mortgage under seal – Registered proprietors thereafter contracting to sell land – Purchasers entering caution against dealings on register in their favour – Subsequent application by bank to register mortgage as a charge – Whether bank entitled to rely   *c*
on notice of deposit to protect mortgage – Whether mortgage subject to purchasers' interest under contract – Land Registration Act 1925, s 106.

In 1961 the registered proprietors of certain land being indebted to their bank deposited the land certificate with the bank as security for their liabilities to the bank and undertook to execute a legal mortgage in favour of the bank whenever called on to   *d*
do so. In June 1961 the bank gave notice of the deposit of the land certificate by way of security to the Land Registry and on 19th June that was entered on the charges register. On 29th August 1962 the registered proprietors executed a legal mortgage in favour of the bank. No step was taken by the bank to register that mortgage but they still held the land certificate and its deposit with them remained on the charges register. On 29th February 1968 the registered proprietors contracted to sell the   *e*
property to the defendants who paid them the full purchase price without obtaining a transfer of the land. As a result of steps taken by the bank in the exercise of its power of sale under the 1962 mortgage, the defendants, on 19th August 1968, registered a caution against dealing in the proprietorship register until notice had been served on them. On 10th October the bank applied to register the 1962 mortgage as a charge. The defendants were duly notified and objected contending that the   *f*
registration should be made subject to their contract of purchase of 29th February 1968. Goulding J[a] held that the bank's mortgage was to be treated as having been made under s 106[b] of the Land Registration Act 1925 and, since it could therefore only be protected by a mortgage caution, it could not be registered as a prior charge since no mortgage caution had been lodged. On appeal,

g

Held – Although, under s 106 of the 1925 Act, until the mortgage was protected on the register under that section, it was capable of taking effect only in equity and of being overridden as a minor interest, the defendants' estate contract was itself only a similar minor interest and the caution lodged on behalf of the defendants had no effect whatever by itself on priorities. It followed that the failure by the bank to

h

---

a   [1972] 2 All ER 752
b   Section 106, so far as material, provides:
    '(1) The proprietor of any registered land may, subject to any entry to the contrary on the register, mortgage, by deed or otherwise, the land or any part thereof in any manner which would have been permissible if the land had not been registered and with the like effect ...   *j*
    '(2) A mortgage made under this section may, if by deed, be protected by a caution in a specially prescribed form and in no other way, and if not by deed, by a caution.
    '(3) The entry of a caution in a specially prescribed form under this section shall be deemed a dealing capable of being restrained by caution.
    '(4) Until the mortgage is protected on the register under this section, it shall be capable of taking effect only in equity and of being overridden as a minor interest ...'

lodge a caution was irrelevant and the ordinary rules of priority between persons
a equitably interested in land applied, there being nothing in the conduct of the bank
to justify postponement of its equity. The bank was therefore entitled to be registered in respect of the mortgage without being subject to the defendants' contract
and the appeal would be allowed (see p 757 c d g and h, post).

   Decision of Goulding J [1972] 2 All ER 752 reversed.

b **Notes**

For the protection of mortgages on registered land, see 23 Halsbury's Laws (3rd Edn)
293-296, paras 694-704, and for the creation of a lien by deposit of the land charge
certificate, see ibid 327, 328, paras 801-808.

   For the Land Registration Act 1925, s 106, see 27 Halsbury's Statutes (3rd Edn)
c 876.

Cases cited

Gallie v Lee [1969] 1 All ER 1062, [1969] 2 Ch 17, CA; *on appeal sub nom Saunders*
   (Executrix of Estate of Gallie) v Anglia Building Society (formerly Northampton Town and
   County Building Society) [1970] 3 All ER 961, [1971] AC 1004, HL.
James v Rice (1854) 5 De G M & G 461, 43 ER 949.
d *Kensington, Ex parte* (1813) 2 Ves & B 79, [1803-13] All ER Rep 398, 35 ER 249, LC.
Molton Finance Ltd, Re [1967] 3 All ER 843, [1968] Ch 325, CA.
Morelle Ltd v Wakeling [1955] 1 All ER 708, [1955] 2 QB 379, CA.
Parkash v Irani Finance Ltd [1969] 1 All ER 930, [1970] Ch 101.
White Rose Cottage, Re [1964] 1 All ER 169, [1964] Ch 483; *affd in part, rvsd in part* [1965]
   1 All ER 11, [1965] Ch 940, CA.
e *Young v Bristol Aeroplane Co Ltd* [1944] 2 All ER 293, [1944] KB 718, CA; *affd* [1946]
   1 All ER 98, [1946] AC 163, HL.

Appeal

On 7th January 1957 John Frank Duxbury and Hazel Dawn Duxbury, his wife, were
f registered as proprietors of the property known as 32 Westdown Drive, Thurmaston,
Leicestershire, title no P 186571, which they had purchased with the assistance of a
mortgage from the Leicester Permanent Building Society. In 1961 Mr Duxbury
was carrying on business as a builder and contractor under the name of 'John Duxbury' and had an account with Martins Bank Ltd in connection with his trading and
also a small private account. On 15th March 1961 the bank at the request of Mr and
Mrs Duxbury paid off the balance due to the building society of some £1,604 and that
g sum was debited to a new joint account in the names of Mr and Mrs Duxbury. The
land certificate was handed to the bank as security for the overdraft, and also to
secure the overdraft on the trading account in the name of 'John Duxbury'. In
June 1961 the bank gave notice of the deposit with them of the land certificate to
the land registry under s 66 of the Land Registration Act 1925, and on 19th June
notice of deposit of the land certificate with the bank was entered in the charges
h register. On 13th September Mr and Mrs Duxbury signed a memorandum of
deposit addressed to Martins Bank Ltd acknowledging that the land certificate was
in the possession of the bank as security for the liabilities to the bank on their joint
account and on the account under the name of 'John Duxbury'. They also undertook
to execute a legal mortgage in favour of the bank whenever called on to do so. In
December 1961 Mr Duxbury formed a company to take over his business, John Dux-
j bury Ltd, and in August 1962 the bank agreed to open an account in the name of
the company and allow it overdraft facilities up to £3,000 on the personal guarantee
of its directors who were Mr and Mrs Duxbury, supported by a mortgage on the
house. On 29th August 1962 Mr and Mrs Duxbury executed a mortgage on the house
by way of legal charge to secure all moneys owing to the bank on any account whether
as principals or sureties. On the same day they signed a guarantee to the bank for

the company's liabilities to the bank up to £3,000.   At that date Mr and Mrs Duxbury's trading account with the bank was overdrawn by £1,043 14s and the joint   *a*
account by £1,488 18s 10d.   On 4th September 1962 a company account was opened
by the transfer of £1,000 from Mr Duxbury's personal business account to the company account and on 5th September Mr Duxbury's trading account was closed.
Final payment out was made on that date.

   The bank, in accordance with its normal banking practice, did not register the   *b*
mortgage of 29th August 1962 under s 26 of the Land Registration Act 1925 as they
were entitled to.   In May 1965 the bank agreed to increase the overlimit on the
company's account to £7,500 and on 26th May 1965 Mr and Mrs Duxbury signed a
further guarantee to cover the increase.   On 29th February 1968 Mr and Mrs Duxbury entered into a contract for the sale of their house to the defendants, Clarence
Kitchener Taylor and his wife Marjorie Taylor ('the Taylors'), for £3,500, Mrs Taylor
being the sister of Mrs Duxbury.   In March 1968 the bank made a formal demand to   *c*
the company and on the Duxburys' joint account for payment of the overdrafts and
also for payment by Mr and Mrs Duxbury on the guarantees.   On 18th April 1968
the overdraft on the joint account was paid off and the account closed.   The only
outstanding liability to the bank was therefore under the guarantees on the company's account.   In December 1968 the company went into compulsory liquidation.
In August 1968 the bank with a view to exercising its power of sale of the property   *d*
instructed estate agents to find a purchaser for the property.   On 19th August 1968
the Taylors registered a caution against dealing in the property in the proprietorship
register pursuant to s 54 of the Land Registration Act 1925 and r 215 of the Land
Registration Rules 1925[1].   On 25th September their solicitors wrote to the bank
stating that the Taylors had paid the full purchase price for the property.   On 10th
October 1968 the bank's solicitors lodged for registration the charge dated 29th August   *e*
1962.   The Land Registry gave notice of that application to the Taylors, who objected
to the registration in priority to their rights under the contract of 29th February 1968.
The matter was referred to the Chancery Division by an order of the Chief Land
Registrar dated 22nd January 1969 made under the provisions of r 220 (4) of the Land
Registration Rules 1925.   On 18th February 1969 an originating summons was
issued pursuant to that order seeking the determination of the court on the following   *f*
matters: (i) whether the charge dated 29th August 1962 and made between Mr
Duxbury and Mrs Duxbury (the registered proprietors of the property) and Martins
Bank Ltd should be registered;   (ii) if so, whether the registration should be subject
to the contract expressed to be protected by the caution registered by the Taylors.
By virtue of the Barclays Bank Act 1969 the plaintiffs, Barclays Bank Ltd ('the bank'),
had become the universal successors of Martins Bank Ltd for all purposes relevant to   *g*
the proceedings.   On 23rd February 1972 Goulding J, reported at [1972] 2 All ER 752,
answered both questions in the summons in the affirmative.   The bank appealed.

H E Francis QC and *John Monckton* for the bank.
P M H Mottershead and *T J Craven* for the Taylors.

                                                              Cur adv vult *h*

24th January.   **RUSSELL LJ** read the following judgment of the court.   This
appeal is from a decision of Goulding J[2] determining a question referred to the court
by the Chief Land Registrar by his order dated 22nd January 1969 under r 220 (4) of
the Land Registration Rules 1925.
                                                                                    j
   A couple called Duxbury were registered in 1957 as proprietors with absolute
title of a freehold property, 32 Westdown Drive, Thurmaston, having acquired the
property with the assistance of a building society mortgage, which itself was registered

---

1   SR & O 1925 No 1093
2   [1972] 2 All ER 752, [1972] 2 WLR 1038

in the charges register.   In June 1961 the bank (which was Martins Bank Ltd and is
now the appellant Barclays Bank Ltd), at the request of the Duxburys, paid off the
building society by a sum of £1,604, which was debited to a Duxbury joint account.
In order to secure moneys due on the overdrawn joint account and on Mr Duxbury's
separate trading account, the land certificate was deposited with the bank.   Not
long afterwards (in September 1961) the Duxburys signed a memorandum of deposit
acknowledging that the land certificate was in the possession of the bank as security
for the liabilities to the bank on the Duxbury joint account and on the account of
Mr Duxbury trading as 'John Duxbury', and by the memorandum the Duxburys
undertook on demand to execute a legal mortgage in favour of the bank whenever
called on to do so.   It is to be observed that this document is the only reliable evidence
of the extent of the security created by the earlier deposit of the land certificate; that
it is in terms limited to moneys due to the bank on two accounts; and that the undertaking to execute a legal mortgage would not in a contractual sense oblige the Duxburys to execute a legal mortgage wider in the extent of the moneys to be secured.
On the other hand, if the bank called for a legal mortgage wider in extent, the
Duxburys would no doubt as a practical matter find it difficult to resist.

The ability so to charge the land by deposit of the certificate is conferred on the
registered proprietors by s 66 of the Land Registration Act 1925.   This provides
that the proprietor of the land may, subject to any estates, interests, charges or
rights registered or protected before the date of the deposit, create a lien on the land
by deposit of the land certificate, such lien being equivalent to that created in the case
of unregistered land by deposit of the title deeds.

Notice of the deposit of the land certificate by way of security was given to the
Land Registry on behalf of the bank in June 1961, and this was entered in the charges
register.   This was pursuant to r 239, which provides that the notice shall operate as
a caution under s 54 of the Act.   This rule is made under s 144 (1) (xi) of the Act.
There is no requirement that the notice of deposit, given or entered in the charges
register, shall indicate the extent of the security.   The operation of the notice of a
caution under s 54 is that it indicates that no dealing with the land is to be registered
until notice has been served on the person giving notice of the deposit of the land
certificate: see also s 55.

Apart from the value of notice of deposit registered in the charges register as
operating as a caution, possession of the land certificate by way of security effectively
prevents any entry on the register for which production of the land certificate is
required.

In December 1961 Mr Duxbury formed a private limited company to take over his
business.   On 29th August 1962 the situation as between the Duxburys and the bank
was as follows: Mr Duxbury's trading account was overdrawn by £1,043 and the
Duxbury joint account by £1,488.   On 29th August 1962 (i) the bank agreed to open
an account in the name of the Duxbury company with overdraft facilities; (ii) the
Duxburys signed, in consideration of the bank giving credit facilities to the Duxbury
company, a joint and several guarantee of that company's liabilities to the bank up
to £3,000; and (ii) the Duxburys executed a charge by way of legal mortgage in
favour of the bank.   Clause 6 of the guarantee document provided that the bank—

'shall be entitled to a lien for all moneys payable under this guarantee on all
securities belonging to us . . . now or hereafter held by you (otherwise than for
safe custody only) . . .'

The charge by way of legal mortgage was in the bank's common form.   The Duxburys covenanted jointly and severally on demand to pay to the bank any balance
due on any account of them or either of them and to pay and discharge all other
liabilities to the bank of them or either of them for the time being, whether as principal
or surety, and charged the scheduled property with their covenanted obligations.

The schedule referred to 32 Westdown Drive 'and all other if any the freehold . . .
hereditaments described in . . . the following . . . documents . . .' and then, under   *a*
the heading 'Particulars of Documents', is written 'Land Certificate Title No.
P. 186571'. Clause 7 is in the following terms:

> 'Nothing herein contained shall operate so as to merge or otherwise prejudice
> or affect any lien charge or other security . . . which the Bank now or at any time
> hereafter may have or would apart from this security have for any money   *b*
> intended to be hereby secured or any right or remedy of the bank thereunder.'

On 4th September 1962 the Duxbury company's account was debited with substantially the balance due on Mr Duxbury's trading account, which was then closed. In
May 1965 the bank agreed to increase the overdraft facilities on the Duxbury company's account to £7,500 and the Duxburys signed a guarantee in similar form for   *c*
an additional £4,500.

In February 1968 the Duxburys contracted to sell the property to the Taylors
for £3,500 plus £1,500 for fixtures and fittings, which apparently was paid without
attempting to get a transfer or inspecting any entry in the Land Registry. Mrs
Duxbury and Mrs Taylor are sisters. No step in connection with the Land Registry
had been taken by the bank in relation to the legal charge, although of course the   *d*
bank still held the land certificate, and the notice of its deposit with the bank remained on the charges register. In March 1968 the bank called in the bank overdrafts
(on the Duxbury company's account and on the Duxburys' joint account) and called
for payment by the Duxburys under their guarantees. On 18th April 1968 the amount
owing on that joint account was paid off and the account closed. Thus, neither of
the two accounts mentioned in the 1961 memorandum of deposit remained in   *e*
existence, but the bank still held the land certificate and the legal charge extended
to the guarantees of the Duxbury company's indebtedness.

As a result of steps taken by the bank with a view to exercising its power of sale
of the property, where, we understood, the Taylors were living, the Taylors took the
step in August 1968 of registering a caution against dealings, by applying that no dealings
with the land should be registered until notice had been served on them: the requisite   *f*
statutory declaration by their solicitor stated that they were interested in the land as
contracting purchasers under the contract between the Duxburys and the Taylors.
On 19th August 1968 this caution was entered in the proprietorship register. This
was pursuant to s 54 of the Act.

The bank then applied to register the legal mortgage. Section 25 of the Act enables
a registered proprietor of land by deed to charge the land; and s 26 provides that such   *g*
a charge shall be completed by registration of the chargee as proprietor of the charge
together with particulars thereof. The cautioning Taylors were given notice and
the dispute brought to a head. The question ordered to be referred to the court for
determination was—

> 'whether the said charge dated the 29th August 1962 . . . shall be registered   *h*
> and, if so, whether such registration shall be subject to the contract expressed
> to be protected by the caution registered on the 19th August 1968 in favour of
> [the Taylors].'

These questions were in due course formulated in the form of an originating
summons. The order made by Goulding J[1] declared (a) that the charge dated 29th
August 1962 should be registered, and (b) that such registration should be subject   *j*
to the Taylors' contract.

We must confess that the outcome of such an order is obscure to us. Have the
Taylors any right to require the bank to hand over the land certificate if they obtain

---

1   [1972] 2 All ER 752, [1972] 2 WLR 1038

a   a transfer executed by the Duxburys? Is the registration of the legal charge an
empty formality, the Taylors having paid the contract price to the Duxburys? Is
there deadlock as to the ability to deal with the legal estate in the land?

Now, quite apart from the question of deposit of the land certificate, and on the
footing that the mortgage of 29th August 1962, until registration, cannot take effect
save in equity, we ask ourselves what provision is there in the Act which reverses the
b   ordinary rule that as between equities—for the Taylors have only an interest in equity
under their contract of purchase—priority is governed by the time sequence?

The learned judge based his decision on the language of s 106 relating to a mortgage
made by deed which is not registered, which provides that it may be protected by a
caution in specially prescribed form 'and in no other way'.   The section also provides
that until the mortgage is protected on the register under that section it shall
c   be capable of taking effect only in equity and of being overridden as a minor interest.
The judge, simply on the ground that this mortgage was 'made under' s 106 (which
we will assume without deciding) and had not been made the subject of a caution in
special form, held that it must be postponed to the estate contract presumably
because it was not 'protected' against it.   But the estate contract was itself only a
similar minor interest: see s 101. The caution lodged on behalf of the Taylors had
d   no effect whatever by itself on priorities: it simply conferred on the Taylors the
right to be given notice of any dealing proposed to be registered (see ss 54 and 55)
so that they might have the opportunity of contending that it would be a dealing
which would infringe their rights and to which the applicants for the registration
were not as against them entitled.   The limited function of such a caution is stressed
by s 56 (2), which enacts that a caution lodged in pursuance of this Act shall not
prejudice the claim or title of any person and shall have no effect whatever except as
e   in this Act mentioned.   See also s 102 (2), which provides that save in a limited field
of minor interests 'priorities as between persons interested in minor interests shall
not be affected by the lodgment of cautions'.

In truth the bank in respect of its mortgage, albeit taking effect as a minor interest
only in equity, did not need any protection against the subsequent equitable interest
f   of the Taylors: it only needed protection against a registration of the Taylors as
proprietors (and, for this, possession of the land certificate was at least de facto protection), or against a subsequent mortgagee whose charge was registered or perhaps
who lodged a caution in special form (although again here there would, we apprehend
be the same de facto protection).

Consequently, in our view, and quite apart from the fact that the land certificate
was in the possession of the bank, (a) failure by the bank to lodge a caution in special
g   form is irrelevant, (b) the Taylors' caution did not and could not confer on their
equitable entitlement or interest any priority over the bank's equitable charge,
(c) the ordinary rules of priority between persons equitably interested in the land
must apply, there being nothing in the conduct of the bank (which was sitting on
the land certificate, notice of deposit of which remained on the register) to justify
h   postponement of its equity, and (d) consequently the bank is entitled to be registered
in respect of the mortgage without being subject to the contract to the Taylors.   We
should add that counsel for the Taylors was quite unable to point to any provision
in the statute which stated that their caution as such gave them priority in respect of
their equitable interest over the earlier equitable interest of the bank under its
mortgage. If such had been the intention of the legislature, it would not have been
j   difficult for the statute to have so provided: see the express provision in s 29 on
priorities between registered charges; and in s 106 (2) already mentioned.

Consequently, in our judgment, the appeal must be allowed. That part of the
order below which declared that the registration of the bank's mortgage dated
29th August 1962 should be subject to the Taylors' contract will be set aside, and in
lieu it will be declared that the registration of the mortgage will not be subject to
the Taylors' contract.

We have not dealt with the situation arising in law from the notice of deposit of the land certificate and the subsequent events that we have recited, including arguments founded on cl 6 of the guarantees and cl 7 of the mortgage. It is not necessary that we should do so. On our view of the case, the question does not arise, and in those circumstances it is all too easy to state propositions which overlook points that would not be overlooked when the matter is necessary to the actual decision of the case. We therefore refrain.

Appeal allowed; declaration set aside, substituting therefor a declaration that the registration of the mortgage will not be subject to the Taylors' contract. Leave to appeal to the House of Lords refused.

Solicitors: *Durrant Cooper & Hambling* (for the bank); *Adam Burn & Metson*, agents for *Rich & Carr*, Leicester (for the Taylors).

Mary Rose Plummer Barrister.

R v Newton

COURT OF APPEAL, CRIMINAL DIVISION
MEGAW LJ, O'CONNOR AND PHILLIPS JJ
12th, 15th JANUARY 1973

Criminal law – Sentence – Extended term of imprisonment – Conditions to be satisfied – Previous convictions – Qualifying sentences – Sentence of imprisonment for a term of three years or more – Two sentences of imprisonment each for a term of two years or more – Sentence of imprisonment – Whether including a sentence of corrective training – Criminal Justice Act 1967, s 37 (2), (4) (c) (ii).

In 1960 the appellant was sentenced to three years' corrective training for storebreaking and larceny, in 1968 to 15 months' imprisonment for burglary with intent and in 1970 to 12 months' imprisonment for burglary and theft. In 1972 the appellant was again convicted of theft and the court imposed on him an extended term of imprisonment for three years under s 37 (2)^a of the Criminal Justice Act 1967. On appeal against sentence,

---

a Section 37, so far as material, provides:
'. . . (2) Where an offender is convicted on indictment of an offence punishable with imprisonment for a term of two years or more and the conditions specified in subsection (4) of this section are satisfied, then, if the court is satisfied, by reason of his previous conduct and of the likelihood of his committing further offences, that it is expedient to protect the public from him for a substantial time, the court may impose an extended term of imprisonment under this section . . .
    '(4) The conditions referred to in subsection (2) of this section are:—(a) the offence was committed before the expiration of three years from a previous conviction of an offence punishable on indictment with imprisonment for a term of two years or more or from his final release from prison after serving a sentence of imprisonment, corrective training or preventive detention passed on such a conviction; and (b) the offender has been convicted on indictment on at least three previous occasions since he attained the age of twenty-one of offences punishable on indictment with imprisonment for a term of two years or more; and (c) the total length of the sentences of imprisonment, corrective training or preventive detention to which he was sentenced on those occasions was not less than five years and—(i) on at least one of those occasions a sentence of preventive detention was passed on him; or (ii) on at least two of those occasions a sentence of imprisonment (other than a suspended sentence which has not taken effect) or of corrective training was so passed and of those sentences one was a sentence of imprisonment for a term of three years or more in respect of one offence or two were sentences of imprisonment each for a term of two years or more in respect of one offence . . .'

Held – The appeal would be allowed and a sentence of three years' imprisonment, not extended, substituted for the extended term. The words ɛntence of imprisonment' where they occurred in s 37 (4) (*c*) (ii) of the 1967 Act did not include a sentence of corrective training. Accordingly the appellant did not qualify for the imposition of an extended sentence under s 37 (4) (*c*) (ii) since his previous sentences did not include either (1) 'a sentence of imprisonment for a term of three years or more', or (2) 'two ... sentences of imprisonment each for a term of two years or more' (see p 760 h to p 761 c and f, post).

Notes

For extended sentences, see Supplement to 10 Halsbury's Laws (3rd Edn) para 932A. For the Criminal Justice Act 1967, s 37, see 8 Halsbury's Statutes (3rd Edn) 600.

Cases referred to in judgment

R v Grant [1951] 1 All ER 28, [1951] 1 KB 500, 115 JP 36, 34 Cr App Rep 230, 49 LGR 146, CCA, 14 Digest (Repl) 585, *5822*.

R v McCarthy [1955] 2 All ER 927, [1955] 1 WLR 856, 119 JP 504, 39 Cr App Rep 118, CCA, 14 Digest (Repl) 592, *5896*.

Appeal

On 20th April 1972 at Nottingham Crown Court before Judge Irvine and a jury the appellant, Barry John Newton, was convicted of theft and sentenced to three years' imprisonment. The court issued a certificate under s 37 (5) of the Criminal Justice Act 1967 certifying that the sentence had been imposed as an extended term of imprisonment under s 37 (2). The appellant applied for leave to appeal against both conviction and sentence. On 28th November 1972 the court (Orr LJ, Milmo and Phillips JJ) refused him leave to appeal against conviction, but granted him leave to appeal against sentence. The facts are set out in the judgment of the court.

M A O'Connell for the appellant.
J R Hopkin for the Crown.

MEGAW LJ delivered the judgment of the court. This is yet another case of difficulty arising under s 37 of the Criminal Justice Act 1967 relating to extended terms of imprisonment.

The appellant, Barry John Newton, was convicted of theft at Nottingham Crown Court on 20th April 1972. He was sentenced to three years' imprisonment certified to be an extended term of imprisonment. It was ordered that the sentence should be concurrent with a sentence already being served by the appellant. He applied for leave to appeal against conviction and sentence. After refusal by the single judge, he renewed the applications. The full court on 28th November 1972 refused the application as regards conviction, but gave leave to appeal against sentence. Although the point had not been raised in the grounds of appeal, the court itself raised the question. It was of opinion that a question arose as to the legality of the extended sentence, depending on the construction of words in s 37 (4) of the Criminal Justice Act 1967.

It is not necessary to go into the facts of the offence. It is sufficient to say that a sentence of three years' imprisonment was fully justified. No attempt has been made before us to argue otherwise. The only question is whether, on the true construction of the Act, an extended sentence could lawfully be imposed on the basis of the appellant's relevant past convictions and sentences. On that question we have had the benefit of submissions by counsel for the appellant and the Crown. At the end of the argument we allowed the appeal and substituted a sentence of three years' imprisonment, not extended, for the extended term imposed by the judge. The sentence will, as before, be concurrent with the sentence already being served. We now give the reasons for our decision.

The point of construction which arises is in connection with cases where one of the previous sentences of the accused person, considered for the purpose of an extended sentence, had been corrective training. That type of custodial sentence, introduced by s 21 (1) of the Criminal Justice Act 1948, was abolished by s 37 (1) of the Criminal Justice Act 1967 with effect from 1st October 1967. But sentences of that type passed during the period when corrective training was a statutorily authorised type of custodial sentence may still be relevant because the conditions laid down for the imposition of extended terms of imprisonment involve the accused person's past record of convictions and sentences which may go back for many years.

Section 37 (4) of the 1967 Act sets out the conditions which have to be fulfilled before an extended sentence may be imposed. We do not propose to analyse, to a greater degree than is strictly necessary for the decision of this appeal, the complexities of that subsection with its numerous specified conditions, some of which are cumulative and others of which are alternative to one another, or indeed in one instance involve an alternative within an alternative.

One of the conditions is that on at least two occasions 'a sentence of imprisonment . . . or of corrective training' (those are the words used in sub-para (ii) of s 37 (4) (c)) should have been passed. The sub-paragraph continues:

'. . . and of those sentences one was a sentence of imprisonment for a term of three years or more in respect of one offence or two were sentences of imprisonment each for a term of two years or more in respect of one offence.'

In the present case the appellant's past offences and sentences on the basis of which the extended sentence was passed were these: 6th January 1960, storebreaking and larceny, etc, three years' corrective training; 6th August 1968, burglary with intent, 15 months' imprisonment; 26th February 1970, burglary and theft, 12 months' imprisonment.

We turn again to the words of s 37 (4) (c) (ii). Unless in the words 'of those sentences one was a sentence of imprisonment for a term of three years or more' the phrase 'a sentence of imprisonment' can be construed as including a sentence of corrective training, the relevant second condition laid down in s 37 (4) (c) (ii) has not been fulfilled in respect of the appellant. So the sentence of an extended term could not lawfully be imposed. Nor was the alternative condition of the latter part of the sub-paragraph fulfilled, for there were not two sentences of imprisonment of two years or more, even if it were permissible (which is the very issue in this appeal) to treat 'a sentence of imprisonment' as including 'sentence of corrective training'.

For the Crown it is contended that the phrase 'a sentence of imprisonment', where that phrase appears for the second time in s 37 (4) (c) (ii), ought to be construed as including a sentence of corrective training. Reliance was placed by counsel for the Crown on R v McCarthy[1]. We do not think that that authority assists us in the present question. There are other contexts, no doubt, in which it would be right to construe 'sentence of imprisonment' as including a sentence of corrective training. But not in this context, for in this context such a construction would, in our judgment, involve a departure from the plain and ordinary meaning of the words.

The reason for that conclusion is quite simple. It can be expressed in two sentences. In s 37 (4) (a), and again in the opening words of s 37 (4) (c), and yet again in the earlier part of the very sentence in s 37 (4) (c) (ii) which we are now construing, the phrase 'corrective training' has been used in collocation with the phrase 'sentence of imprisonment' in such a way as to show that for the purpose of those provisions 'corrective training' is different from, and is not included in, 'sentence of imprisonment'. It is impossible to suppose that, where the legislature uses the same phrase 'sentence of imprisonment' in the latter part of s 37 (4) (c) (ii), it intended that

---

1   [1955] 2 All ER 927, [1955] 1 WLR 856

a the phrase should be given a different and wider meaning as compared with the meaning which the phrase clearly bears elsewhere in the same subsection, and, in particular, in the earlier part of the self-same sentence. There are no other provisions in the 1967 Act or in any other legislation to which we were referred which in any way support a different view.

b The necessary result of this interpretation is that, when a sentence of an extended term of imprisonment is being considered, a past sentence of corrective training, whatever its length between the statutory limits for such a sentence of two to four years[1], may be relevant if, but only if, there has also been a past sentence of three years' imprisonment. In no other case can a past sentence of corrective training properly be taken into account for the purpose of an extended sentence.

c Even if there were no rational explanation for this differentiation which, on our interpretation of the words in s 37 (4) (c) (ii), has been made by the legislature between the effect, for this purpose, of the two types of custodial sentence, we should not think it right for that reason to depart from the natural and ordinary meaning of the words in their context. This is a penal provision. In those circumstances it is not necessary to examine laboriously the question of a possible explanation for this discrimination against sentences of corrective training in respect of their availability as qualifying sentences for extended terms of imprisonment under the 1967 Act. It occurs to us,

d however, that a partial explanation may be found in some decisions of the Court of Criminal Appeal relating to the appropriate length of a sentence of corrective training. Between *R v Grant*[2] and the *Practice Direction*[3] of the Court of Criminal Appeal of 20th February 1961, a sentence of corrective training might have been imposed for a longer term than the appropriate sentence of imprisonment, had imprisonment been awarded, for the same offence.

e However that may be, and whether or not good reason could be found for this additional complexity in a sphere where simplicity is desirable, we have no doubt that the true interpretation of the provision is as we have stated; and that a sentence of three years' corrective training is not 'a sentence of imprisonment for a term of three years or more' for the purposes of s 37 (4) (c) (ii) of the Criminal Justice Act

f 1967.

Appeal allowed. Sentence varied.

Solicitors: *Registrar of Criminal Appeals* (for the appellant); *D W Ritchie*, Nottingham (for the Crown).

N P Metcalfe Esq Barrister.

g

---

1 See s 21 (1) of the Criminal Justice Act 1948
2 [1951] 1 All ER 28, [1951] 1 KB 500
3 [1961] 1 All ER 619, [1961] 1 WLR 463

MFI Warehouses Ltd v Nattrass

QUEEN'S BENCH DIVISION

LORD WIDGERY CJ, ASHWORTH AND WILLIS JJ

11th, 21st DECEMBER 1972

Trade description – False or misleading statement – Provision of services etc – Statement made recklessly – Recklessly – Meaning – Statement made regardless of whether it is true or false – Statement in trade advertisement – Advertiser failing to appreciate that advertisement reasonably capable of being understood in sense different to that intended – Whether statement made regardless of truth or falsity – Trade Descriptions Act 1968, s 14 (1), (2).

The appellants, a mail order firm, had for some time been selling a wooden door described as a 'louvre' door. Subsequently they began to market a set of sliding door gear designed to be used with the louvre doors. They issued an advertisement offering louvre doors on 14 days' free approval on the terms that, if retained thereafter, the price stated in the advertisement would become payable together with the carriage charge stated. The advertisement also offered on 14 days' free approval 'Folding Door Gear (Carriage Free)'. It was the appellants' intention that when the door gear was sold with the louvre doors no extra carriage charge should be made and that the same period of approval should be available for the door gear as for the doors. Before publication the advertisement was considered by the appellants' chairman for some five or ten minutes before he approved it but he did not think through its implications sufficiently to appreciate that the advertisement could reasonably be understood as offering the door gear as an item which could be purchased separately on the stated terms; it had not been the appellants' intention to offer the door gear separately on those terms. On the strength of the advertisement a purchaser ordered the door gear on its own but was required by the appellants to pay the purchase price and carriage charge before despatch. The appellants were charged with recklessly making a statement which was false as to the provision in the course of their trade of a facility, contrary to s 14 (1)*a* of the Trade Descriptions Act 1968. They were convicted by the justices and appealed contending that the statement in the advertisement had not been made 'recklessly', within s 14 (1), (2), of the 1968 Act in that recklessness implied a lack of care whether the statement was true or false.

Held – The statement in the advertisement had been made 'recklessly' within s 14 (1) since the appellants had not had regard to the falsity or otherwise of the statement; s 14 (2) placed on an advertiser a positive obligation to have regard to whether his advertisement was true or false. It was immaterial that the appellants' chairman had not deliberately closed his eyes to the truth or had any kind of dishonest mind. Accordingly the justices were entitled to convict and the appeal would be dismissed (see p 768 c to f, post).

Dictum of Lord Parker CJ in *Sunair Holidays Ltd v Dodd* [1970] 2 All ER at 411 disapproved.

Notes

For false or misleading statements as to services, see Supplement to 10 Halsbury's Laws (3rd Edn) para 1314c, 3.

For the Trade Desctripions Act 1968, s 14, see 37 Halsbury's Statutes (3rd Edn) 959.

---

a Section 14, so far as material, is set out at p 766 g and h, post

Cases referred to in judgment

Derry v Peek (1889) 14 App Cas 337, [1886-90] All ER Rep 1, 58 LJCh 864, 61 LT 265, 54 JP 148, 1 Meg 292, HL, 9 Digest (Repl) 127, 685.

R v Bates [1952] 2 All ER 842, 36 Cr App Rep 175, *on appeal* sub nom *R v Russell* [1953] 1 WLR 77, CCA, 44 Digest (Repl) 444, 480.

R v Clarksons Holidays Ltd [1972] Crim LR 653, CA.

R v Mackinnon [1958] 3 All ER 657, [1959] 1 QB 150, [1958] 3 WLR 688, 123 JP 43, 43 Cr App Rep 1, 44 Digest (Repl) 444, 482.

Sunair Holidays Ltd v Dodd [1970] 2 All ER 410, [1970] 1 WLR 1037, 134 JP 507, DC, Digest (Cont Vol C) 1023, 1100b.

Case stated

This was an appeal by way of case stated by justices for the county of Chester acting in and for the petty sessional division of Chester Castle and Ellesmere Port in respect of their adjudication as a magistrates' court sitting at Chester on 27th March 1972.

1. On 10th December 1971 informations were preferred by the respondent, William Kenneth Nattrass, against the appellants, MFI Warehouses Ltd, as follows: (a) that the appellants in the course of a trade, namely that of selling goods by mail order, did recklessly make a statement which was false as to the provision in the course of that trade of a facility by means of an advertisement on p 99 of the August 1971 edition of Practical Householder containing the words 'Folding Door Gear (Carriage Free)' whereas a carriage charge of 25p per set was made in respect of four sets of folding door gear supplied to Ian William Luxton in fulfilling an order given by him on 24th August 1971, contrary to s 14 (1) of the Trade Descriptions Act 1968; (b) that the appellants in the course of a trade, namely that of selling goods by mail order, did recklessly make a statement which was false as to the provision in the course of that trade of a facility by means of an advertisement on p 99 of the August 1971 edition of Practical Householder which offered folding door gear sets on 14 days' free approval whereas payment before despatch was required in fulfilling an order for four sets of folding door gear by Ian William Luxton on 24th August 1971, contrary to s 14 (1) of the Trade Descriptions Act 1968.

2. The justices found the following facts: (a) that the advertisement referred to in the informations offered louvre doors on 14 days' free approval on the terms that, if retained thereafter, the price stated in the advertisement would become payable together with the carriage charge there stated; (b) that the advertisement further offered folding door gear at the prices therein stated on the terms that the carriage thereof would be free and that the same could be had on 14 days' free approval; (c) that there was no statement or indication in the advertisement that the door gear could not be separately purchased and that accordingly a reasonable person would interpret the advertisement as offering, inter alia, the folding door gear as a separate item for 14 days' free approval carriage free; (d) that the wording of the advertisements had been drafted by a director of the appellant company and approved by the appellants' chairman; (e) that the appellants had for many years sold louvre doors on the terms stated in (a) above but had not sold folding door gear therefor or at all; (f) that recently as appeared from the advertisement, the appellants began to offer for sale louvre doors and folding door gear; (g) that the appellants intended the folding door gear to be an ancillary to their main product, namely the louvre doors, and to be capable of being purchased only as such and not as a separate item; (h) that the appellants did not expect that any person would wish to buy the folding door gear as a separate item even though many of the appellants' customers were 'do-it-yourself' enthusiasts who would be likely to make their own doors and would only require to buy from the appellants folding door gear; (i) that the folding door gear was in fact capable of being used on doors other than the louvre doors; (j) that the appellants by their chairman studied the advertisement for five or ten minutes or thereabouts prior to approving it but did not think

through sufficiently the implications thereof and did not appreciate that it in fact offered the folding door gear as an item which could be separately purchased on the terms stated in (b) above; (k) that the appellants' invariable practice was to impose a carriage charge on goods which they sold and in accordance therewith would have imposed a carriage charge on the folding door gear if they had realised that it was being offered for sale as a separate item; (l) that by reason of the foregoing the advertisement did contain statements made by the appellants which were false as to the provision of facilities in the course of the trade of selling goods by mail order in that the advertisement purported to offer the folding door gear on the terms stated in (b) above, whereas they were not intended by the appellants to be on offer as a separate item on those or any terms despite the terms of the advertisement; (m) that a carriage charge of 25p per set was made by the appellants in respect of four sets of the folding door gear supplied to Ian William Luxton in fulfilling an order given by him on 24th August 1971 and that payment therefor before despatch was required by the appellants in fulfilling the order; (n) that in fulfilling a similar order for four sets of the folding door gear without doors by Kenneth J Davison of Irby, Wirral, Cheshire, placed on 9th August 1971 the appellants had also imposed a carriage charge of 25p per set and required payment before despatch; (o) that the order of Mr Luxton was dealt with in that way because the clerk who processed it did not seek the assistance of his superiors in dealing therewith or inform them of a letter from Mr Davison dated 16th August 1971 complaining of the imposition of the carriage charge and the requirement of payment in advance, but assumed (i) that the carriage charge on the louvre doors applied to the folding door gear ordered separately; and (ii) that the offer of 14 days' free approval which applied to the louvre doors did not apply to the folding door gear ordered as a separate item; (p) that if the clerk had referred the order of Mr Luxton or Mr Davison to the appellants' chairman he would then have appreciated that the advertisement offered, inter alia, the folding door gear as a separate item for 14 days' free approval carriage free and would have instructed the clerk to honour the terms of the advertisement; (q) that the appellants' current advertisement relating to folding door gear made it clear that such gear would only be sold together with doors.

3. It was admitted by the appellants that the advertisement did contain the false statements specified in para 2 (l) above and that they had been negligent in that they had failed to appreciate that the advertisement in fact offered the folding door gear as an item which could be separately purchased on the terms stated in para 2 (b). It was contended by the appellants that they had thereby negligently made the false statements specified in the informations but that they had not thereby made them 'recklessly' within the meaning of that expression in s 14 of the 1968 Act. The offence of recklessly making a false statement under s 14 of the 1968 Act required the statement to have been made not caring whether it was true or false; that is, a dishonest or fraudulent statement as distinct from one which was made with an honest belief in its truth. The evidence showed that the appellants had been at worst negligent in failing to appreciate that a reasonable person would interpret the advertisement as offering, inter alia, the folding door gear as a separate item for 14 days' free approval carriage free. It had not been, and could not have been, suggested by the respondent that the appellants had been dishonest or fraudulent in regard to the advertisement (cf *R v Mackinnon*[1]). Moreover, the Divisional Court in *Sunair Holidays Ltd v Dodd*[2] had decided in connection with an alleged offence under s 14 that the mere fact that a customer did not subsequently get what had been originally offered to him did not constitute an offence.

4. It was contended by the respondent that the facts specified in para 2 above showed that the appellants had committed the two offences charged. The appellants

---

1   [1958] 3 All ER 657, [1959] 1 QB 150
2   [1970] 2 All ER 410, [1970] 1 WLR 1037

had admitted that the statements were false and in failing to appreciate that a reason-
a able person would interpret the advertisement as offering folding door gear as a
separate item on 14 days' free approval carriage free the appellants had made the
statements regardless of whether they were true or false. The appellants could easily
have qualified the wording of the advertisement to make it clear that the relevant
statements did not apply to door gear bought separately. The fact that that was
their current practice indicated that the appellants had not previously had regard
b to the truth or falsity of the statements. Their main concern had been simply to
induce the public to do business with them. *R v Mackinnon*[1] had been decided in
the context of the language of the Prevention of Fraud (Investments) Act 1939. The
offences under s 12 of that Act had the common characteristic of dishonesty and it
was for that reason that the court had decided that for the purposes of s 12 'reckless' necessarily involved dishonesty. Section 14 of the Trade Descriptions Act 1968,
c however, specifically defined 'recklessly' with no reference to dishonesty and it
would be wrong to impute the element of dishonesty into that word. *Sunair Holidays
Ltd v Dodd*[2] was also inapplicable to the present issues for there the statement in
question was true when first made whereas the statements by the appellants about
which complaint was made had never been true.

[Paragraph 5 listed the cases to which the justices were referred.]
d 6. The justices were of the opinion that the contentions of the respondent were
to be preferred to the contentions of the appellants in that the appellants had made
the two statements regardless of whether they were true or false and accordingly
found the appellants guilty on both informations; imposed a fine of £50 in respect
of each thereof; and ordered the appellants to pay £10 costs.
7. The question for the opinion of the High Court was whether on the facts found
e the appellants made the statements 'recklessly' within the meaning of that expression
in s 14 of the 1968 Act.

Alexander Irvine for the appellants.
N W Lyell for the respondent.

f
                                                                    Cur adv vult

21st December. **LORD WIDGERY CJ** read the following judgment. This is an
appeal by case stated by justices for the county of Chester acting in and for the petty
sessional division of Chester Castle and Ellesmere Port, in respect of their adjudication
g as a magistrates' court sitting at Chester on 27th March 1972. On that date the justices
convicted the appellants of two offences contrary to s 14 (1) of the Trade Descriptions
Act 1968. The offences were as follows: first, that in the course of a trade, namely
that of selling goods by mail order, the appellants did recklessly make a statement
which was false as to the provision in the course of that trade of a facility by means
of an advertisement on p 99 of the August 1971 edition of 'Practical Householder'
h containing the words 'Folding Door Gear (Carriage Free)' whereas a carriage charge
of 25p per set was made in respect of four sets of folding door gear supplied to Ian
William Luxton in fulfilling an order given by him on 24th August 1971; second,
that in the course of a trade, namely that of selling goods by mail order, the appellants did recklessly make a statement which was false as to the provision in the
course of that trade of a facility by means of an advertisement on p 99 of the August
j 1971 edition of 'Practical Householder' which offered folding door gear sets on 14
days' free approval whereas payment before despatch was required in fulfilling an
order for four sets of folding door gear by Ian William Luxton on 24th August 1971.

---

1   [1958] 3 All ER 657, [1959] 1 QB 150
2   [1970] 2 All ER 410, [1970] 1 WLR 1037

The circumstances of the case were these. For some time the appellants had
been selling by mail order a wooden door which is described as a louvre door because
it had slats in it through which air could pass for purposes of ventilation. The terms
on which these doors were advertised and sold was that they could be had on 14
days' approval without pre-payment and that 25p carriage should be charged on each
door. After a while the appellants marketed a set of sliding door gear designed to
be used with the louvre doors, the purpose of which was to enable these doors to be
assembled in such a way as to make a sliding partition. The intention of the appellants
was that these sliding door sets should be sold only with a set of louvre doors and not
separately. Their intention when the door gear was sold with the doors was that no
extra carriage charge should be made in respect of the inclusion of the sliding door
gear, and that the same period of approval should be available for the door gear as
was for the doors. The advertisement complained of referred to the doors as being
'carriage free' which was intended by the appellants to indicate that no additional carriage charge would result if the door gear was ordered with the doors.
Furthermore, the advertisement in referring to 14 days' free approval did not distinguish between an order for doors and door gear respectively, it not having been
in the minds of the appellants that the gear should be sold separately in any instance.

The purchaser referred to in this case read the advertisement as meaning that
the sliding door gear could be bought separately. One may say at once that he
was not to be blamed for reaching that conclusion because it was one which might
well have been reached by an intelligent reader of the advertisement itself. Accordingly he placed an order for door gear and was surprised to find that he was expected
to pay carriage on the door gear notwithstanding the reference to 'carriage free' in
the advertisement, whereas in the other case the purchaser was surprised to find
that he could not obtain the door gear on 14 days' free approval but was required
to make payment before despatch.

The explanation of this is that the clerk who dealt with the order treated it as one
which did not entitle the buyer to the facilities of free approval or free carriage
because it was an order for the gear in isolation and not coupled with an order for
doors. The justices found that if the clerk in question had referred the matter to
the appellants' chairman the latter would then have appreciated that the advertisement was ambiguous and would have instructed the clerk to honour the terms of
the advertisement. In fact the matter was not referred to the appellants' chairman
and the purchaser raised complaint, which resulted in the bringing of these charges.

Section 14 of the Trade Descriptions Act 1968, so far as relevant, reads as follows:

> '(1) It shall be an offence for any person in the course of any trade or business
> ... (b) recklessly to make a statement which is false; as to any of the following
> matters, that is to say,—(i) the provision in the course of any trade or business of
> any services, accommodation or facilities ...
>
> '(2) For the purposes of this section ... (b) a statement made regardless of
> whether it is true or false shall be deemed to be made recklessly, whether or
> not the person making it had reasons for believing that it might be false ...'

The justices found that the advertisement constituted a false statement made by
the appellants in the course of their trade or business in regard to the provision
of facilities within the meaning of s 14 (1). The only remaining question, therefore,
was whether that statement had been made 'recklessly' within the meaning of the
section. The only further finding which goes to the thought given by the appellants
to the correctness or otherwise of their advertisement is to be found in para 2 (j)
of the stated case which states:

> 'that the [appellants] by their Chairman studied the said advertisement for 5 or
> 10 minutes or thereabouts prior to approving it but did not think through
> sufficiently the implications thereof and did not appreciate that it in fact offered

a   the said folding door gear as an item which could be separately purchased on the terms stated.'

Argument in the court below, as in this court, centred on the meaning of the word 'reckless'. For the appellants it was argued that 'reckless' here had its familiar common law meaning derived from *Derry v Peek*[1], that is to say, that 'recklessness' implies a total irresponsibility and a total lack of consideration whether the state-
b   ment was false or true. It was argued that on this construction a statement could not be made recklessly unless the conduct of the maker was on the threshold of fraud or he had shown himself ready to run a risk with the truth. Such conduct, it was said, could not be found against the appellants on the facts which the justices had accepted and, in particular, having regard to the consideration given to the advertisement by the appellants' chairman.

c   For the respondent it was contended that the word 'reckless' in the present con-text had a wider meaning than that in *Derry v Peek*[1]. It was contended that if the draftsman had intended the word 'reckless' to have its normal common law meaning, he would not have thought it necessary to include a specific definition clause in the section. Furthermore, when the definition clause was examined again it was to be observed that it referred to a statement made 'regardless of whether it is true or
d   false'. It was contended that the normal meaning of 'regardless' is 'without having regard to'. It was accordingly contended that this Act placed on sellers a duty to give active consideration to whether their advertisements were true or false, and that unless the advertisement had been examined with this end in view it was open to the prosecution to contend that the advertisement was issued without regard to whether it was true or false. Attention was also directed to the final phrase in
e   s 14 (2) (*b*) namely, 'whether or not the person making it had reasons for believ-ing that it might be false'. It is argued that this phrase shows the intention of the legislature to require sellers to examine their advertisements for falsity even though it is not shown that they had any independent reason for suspecting that the advertisement was false.

The only reference to this question in authority on this particular section is to be
f   found in Lord Parker CJ's judgment in *Sunair Holidays Ltd v Dodd*[2]. There, after reading the section, Lord Parker CJ observed[2]:

'In other words this by statute is importing the common law definition of "recklessly" as laid down in *Derry v Peek*[1] and adopted ever since.'

g   It does not appear that this dictum was essential to the decision in the case with which Lord Parker CJ was concerned and there is no reason to suppose that there had been argument on it. For these reasons I would be disinclined to accept Lord Parker CJ's word as being the final pronouncement on this question, and think that it behoves this court to look into the matter again. I am supported in this view by a comment made by Roskill LJ in giving the judgment of the court in *R v Clarksons Holidays*
h   *Ltd*[3]; it was not necessary for him to express any final view on the point but he indicated his impression that Lord Parker CJ's observation[2] would not be accepted if the matter were fully argued. That the word 'reckless' may have more than one meaning in law is apparent from a consideration of the judgment of Salmon J in *R v Mackinnon*[4], and the judgment of Donovan J in *R v Bates*[5]. I am inclined to think that it was the fact that the word 'reckless' has more than one meaning which

j

---

1   (1889) 14 App Cas 337, [1886-90] All ER Rep 1
2   [1970] 2 All ER 410 at 411, [1970] 1 WLR 1037 at 1040
3   [1972] Crim LR 653
4   [1958] 3 All ER 657 at 658, [1959] 1 QB 150 at 152
5   [1952] 2 All ER 842

prompted the draftsman to give a special definition of that word in the Act with which we are presently concerned, and I think, therefore, that we should approach the problem of construction by having regard to that definition rather than to preconceived notions of what the word 'reckless' should mean. I have much sympathy with the view of Salmon J[1] that where a criminal offence is being created and an element of the offence is 'recklessness', one should hesitate before accepting the view that anything less than '*Derry v Peek*[2] recklessness' will do. On the other hand, it is quite clear that this Act is designed for the protection of customers and it does not seem to me to be unreasonable to suppose that in creating such additional protection for customers Parliament was minded to place on the advertiser a positive obligation to have regard to whether his advertisement was true or false.

I have accordingly come to the conclusion that 'recklessly' in the context of the 1968 Act does not involve dishonesty. Accordingly it is not necessary to prove that the statement was made with that degree of irresponsibility which is implied in the phrase 'careless whether it be true or false'. I think it suffices for present purposes if the prosecution can show that the advertiser did not have regard to the truth or falsity of his advertisement even though it cannot be shown that he was deliberately closing his eyes to the truth, or that he had any kind of dishonest mind. If I had taken the contrary view I would have held that the facts found in this case would not support the conviction. On the opinion which I have just expressed, however, I think that the justices were entitled to convict in this case, and that the explanation of their decision is that they considered that the appellants' chairman did not have regard to the falsity or otherwise of what was written on his behalf. Accordingly, I would dismiss the appeal.

ASHWORTH J. I agree.

WILLIS J. I agree.

Appeal dismissed.

Solicitors: *D J Freeman & Co* (for the appellants); *Sharpe, Pritchard & Co*, agents for *J K Boynton*, Clerk to Cheshire County Council (for the respondent).

N P Metcalfe Esq Barrister.

---

1 [1958] 3 All ER at 658, [1959] 1 QB at 152
2 (1889) 14 App Cas 337, [1886-90] All ER Rep 1

The Brimnes
Tenax Steamship Co Ltd v The Brimnes (Owners)

QUEEN'S BENCH DIVISION (ADMIRALTY COURT)

BRANDON J

20th, 21st, 22nd, 23rd, 26th, 27th, 28th, 29th, 30th JUNE, 3rd, 4th, 5th, 7th, 10th, 28th JULY 1972

Shipping – Charterparty – Time charter – Withdrawal – Waiver – Default in payment of hire – Right to withdraw ship arising on default – Hire payable in advance – Late payment – Acceptance by shipowner's bank – Hire relating in part to period after right of withdrawal has arisen – Shipowner's knowledge at time payment accepted that right of withdrawal has arisen – Shipowner's bank bound to accept payments tendered by charterers – Whether acceptance of hire accrued due before right of withdrawal arising constituting waiver – Whether acceptance by bank amounting to waiver.

Shipping – Charterparty – Time charter – Withdrawal – Default in payment of hire – Right to withdraw ship 'failing punctual payment' – Late payment made before right of withdrawal exercised – Whether shipowners entitled to withdraw in any event once payment overdue.

Bank – Payment – Time of payment – Transfer order – Payer and payee both having accounts with bank – Payer sending order to transfer money from his account to payee's account – Whether time of payment moment when transfer order received by bank or moment when decision to credit and debit accounts made by bank.

The charterers chartered a vessel from the shipowners for a period of 24-26 months from 18th December 1968 under a time charterparty, cl 5 of which provided (i) that hire was to be paid in advance on the first day of each month; (ii) that payment was to be made to the shipowners' bank ('the bank') in New York; and (iii) that 'otherwise failing the punctual and regular payment of the hire' the shipowners were to be at liberty to withdraw the vessel from the charterers' service. The charterers were late almost every month in paying the hire when it fell due, usually by no more than a few days. One of the methods of payment was for the charterers' agents, who also had an account with the bank, to instruct the bank to transfer the amount of the hire from their own to the shipowners' account. Following the receipt of the usual application form on the morning of 2nd April 1970, the charterers' agents sent an order by telex at 10.53 BST to the bank instructing it to transfer the amount of hire due for April 1970. Because of the difference in time in New York and because of the internal procedures that had to be carried out in the bank, the transfer was not effected until 18.07 BST on 2nd April. Meanwhile at 17.45 BST on the same day, the shipowners sent a telex message to the charterers withdrawing the vessel from their service. Although the message had been sent, and received instantaneously on the charterers' telex machine, during normal business hours, no member of the charterers' staff saw the telex message until the start of business on the following day, 3rd April. The amount of the April hire was retained by the bank in the shipowners' account and on 6th April the shipowners wrote to the charterers informing them that it was being retained by the shipowners as security for cross-claims for damages arising out of the charterparty. The charterers claimed damages from the shipowners on the ground that they had wrongfully withdrawn the vessel, contending (a) that payment of the hire due for April had been made when the bank received the instructions from the agents to transfer the money from one account to another, i e before the withdrawal of the vessel; (b) that the shipowners' right to withdraw the vessel under cl 5 subsisted only so long as default in payment continued, and by the time they withdrew the vessel they no longer had the right to do so; (c) that the obligation to pay hire punctually was not an essential term of the contract so that breach of it did not entitle the shipowners to treat the contract as at an end; (d) that the charterers' conduct in relation to late payment of hire did not amount to a repudiation of the contract entitling the shipowners to regard it as terminated; (e) that the acceptance by the bank of the late payment of the hire due on 1st April, assuming that it had taken place before notice of withdrawal had been given, amounted to waiver by the shipowners of their right to withdraw the vessel; and (f) that the retention of the hire by the shipowners after withdrawal was evidence of a new contract between the parties.

Held – The charterers' conduct in relation to late payment did not clearly evince an intention not to be bound by the contract and did not, therefore, amount to a repudiation of the contract (see p 791 e, post). Nevertheless the shipowners were entitled to withdraw the vessel for the following reasons—

(i) payment was made when the bank decided to debit the agents' account and credit the shipowners' account, i e at 18.07 BST on 2nd April, and not when the order to transfer was received, for the receipt of the transfer order by the bank was not analogous to the receipt of a cheque, which would constitute conditional payment; nor was there any evidence that the parties had accepted that the time of receipt of the transfer order should be treated as the time of payment (see p 784 e to h and p 788 a, post); *Zim Israel Navigation Co Ltd v Effy Shipping Corpn, The Effy* [1972] 1 Lloyd's Rep 18 applied; since the telex message was sent during business hours, it was to be considered as having arrived when it was received by the charterers' telex machine, i e at 17.45 BST on 2nd April, even though it was not seen by the charterers until the following day (see p 786 h j and p 787 e and j, post); *Entores Ltd v Miles Far East Corpn* [1955] 2 All ER 493 applied; consequently the withdrawal had taken place before payment (see p 787 j, post); *Empresa Cubana de Fletes v Lagonisi Shipping Co Ltd, The Georgios C* [1971] 1 All ER 193 applied;

(ii) the bank, as the shipowners' banker, was bound to receive any payment tendered to it by the charterers for the credit of the shipowners' account and, therefore, the bank's act in retaining the hire did not amount to a waiver of the shipowners' right of withdrawal (see p 795 b and f, post);

(iii) no common intention of the parties to enter into a fresh agreement on the same terms as the old could be inferred from the retention of the hire by the shipowners, since it was clear from the shipowners' letter that it was being retained as security for cross-claims under the charterparty (see p 796 b, post); *Wulfsberg & Co v Weardale (Owners)* (1916) 85 LJKB 1717 applied.

Per Brandon J. (i) There was nothing in cl 5 which showed clearly that the parties intended the obligation to pay hire punctually to be an essential term of the contract as distinct from being a term for breach of which an express right to withdraw was given but the words 'failing punctual payment', on their ordinary and natural meaning, meant 'when there has been a failure to pay punctually' and the right to withdraw subsisted, subject to waiver, despite any late tender or payment of hire made after the due date but before withdrawal (see p 789 h to p 790 a and h j, post); *Empresa Cubana de Fletes v Lagonisi Shipping Co Ltd, The Georgios C* [1971] 1 All ER 193 distinguished.

(ii) Acceptance by a shipowner of hire payable in whole or in part in respect of a period after a right to withdraw has to his knowledge arisen would constitute a waiver of that right even though, because the hire is payable in advance, it has accrued due before the date on which the right of withdrawal arose (see p 793 h to p 794 a and c f, post); *Langfond (Owners) v Canadian Forwarding and Export Co* (1907) 96 LT 559 applied.

Notes

For stipulations as to hire in time charters, see 35 Halsbury's Laws (3rd Edn) 281-284, para 423, and for cases on the subject, see 41 Digest (Repl) 220-229, 472-539.

Cases referred to in judgment

Central Estates (Belgravia) Ltd v Woolgar (No 2) [1972] 3 All ER 610, [1972] 1 WLR 1048, CA.

Clarke v Grant [1949] 1 All ER 768, [1950] 1 KB 104, [1949] LJR 1450, CA, 31 Digest (Repl) 507, 6322.

Dies v British and International Mining and Finance Corpn Ltd [1939] 1 KB 724, 108 LJKB 398, 160 LT 563, 39 Digest (Repl) 826, 2881.

Doe d Nash v Birch (1836) 1 M & W 402, 2 Gale 26, Tyr & Gr 769, 5 LJEx 185, 150 ER 490, 31 Digest (Repl) 561, 6819.

Ellis v Rowbotham [1900] 1 QB 740, [1900-3] All ER Rep 299, 69 LJQB 379, 82 LT 191, CA, 31 Digest (Repl) 286, 4208.

Empresa Cubana de Fletes v Lagonisi Shipping Co Ltd, The Georgios C [1971] 1 All ER 193, [1971] 1 QB 488, [1971] 2 WLR 221, [1971] 1 Lloyd's Rep 7, CA.

Entores Ltd v Miles Far East Corpn [1955] 2 All ER 493, [1955] 2 QB 327, [1955] 3 WLR 48, [1955] 1 Lloyd's Rep 511, CA, 50 Digest (Repl) 341, 688.

Green's Case (1582) Cro Eliz 3, 78 ER 269, 31 Digest (Repl) 555, 6741.

Italian State Railways v Mavrogordatos [1919] 2 KB 305, 88 LJKB 1099, 121 LT 183, 14 Asp MLC 504, CA, 41 Digest (Repl) 215, 436.

Langfond (Owners) v Canadian Forwarding and Export Co (1907) 96 LT 559, 10 Asp MLC 414, PC, 41 Digest (Repl) 229, 539.

McDonald v Dennys Lascelles Ltd (1933) 48 CLR 457.

Maclaine v Gatty [1921] 1 AC 376, [1920] All ER Rep 70, 90 LJPC 73, 124 LT 385, HL, 21 Digest (Repl) 472, 1663.

Matthews v Smallwood [1910] 1 Ch 777, [1908-10] All ER Rep 536, 79 LJCh 322, 102 LT 228, 31 Digest (Repl) 419, 5483.

Mayson v Clouet [1924] AC 980, 93 LJPC 237, 131 LT 645, PC, 40 Digest (Repl) 261, 2201.

Pennant's Case (1596) 3 Co Rep 64a, [1558-1774] All ER Rep 634, 76 ER 775; sub nom *Harvey v Oswald*, Moore KB 456, Cro Eliz 553, 572, 72 ER 692, 31 Digest (Repl) 282, 4167.

Tankexpress A/S v Compagnie Financière Belge des Petroles SA, The Petrofina [1948] 2 All ER 939, [1949] AC 76, [1949] LJR 170, HL, 41 Digest (Repl) 221, 482.

Tonnelier v Smith (1897) 77 LT 277, 8 Asp MLC 327, 2 Com Cas 258, CA, 41 Digest (Repl) 222, 483.

Ward v Day (1863) 4 B & S 337, 2 New Rep 444, 33 LJQB 3, 28 JP 197, 122 ER 486; affd Exch Ch (1864) 5 B & S 359, 4 New Rep 177, 33 LJQB 254, 10 LT 578, 122 ER 865, 31 Digest (Repl) 556, 6753.

Wehner v Dene Steam Shipping Co [1905] 2 KB 92, 74 LJKB 550, 10 Com Cas 139, 41 Digest (Repl) 277, 948.

Wulfsberg & Co v Weardale (Owners) (1916) 85 LJKB 1717, 115 LT 146, 13 Asp MLC 416, CA, 41 Digest (Repl) 229, 538.

Zim Israel Navigation Co Ltd v Effy Shipping Corpn, The Effy [1972] 1 Lloyd's Rep 18.

Cases also cited

Anon (1586) Godb 47, 78 ER 29.

Blumberg v Life Interests & Reversionary Securities Corpn [1897] 1 Ch 171.

British and Benningtons Ltd v North Western Cachar Tea Co Ltd [1923] AC 48, [1922] All ER Rep 224, HL.

Car and Universal Finance Co Ltd v Caldwell [1964] 1 All ER 290, [1965] 1 QB 525, CA.

Creery v Summersell and Flowerdew & Co Ltd [1949] Ch 751.

Elson (Inspector of Taxes) v Prices Tailors Ltd [1963] 1 All ER 231, [1963] 1 WLR 287.

Financings Ltd v Baldock [1963] 1 All ER 443, [1963] 2 QB 104, CA.

Foster (E) & Co v J P Best & Co (1921) 8 Lloyd LR 502.

Hadley (Felix) & Co Ltd v Hadley [1898] 2 Ch 680.

Heisler v Anglo-Dal Ltd [1954] 2 All ER 770, [1954] 1 WLR 1273, CA.

Henderson v Arthur [1907] 1 KB 10.

Hone (a bankrupt), Re, ex parte The Trustee v Kensington Borough Council [1950] 2 All ER *a*
716, [1951] Ch 85.
Keith, Prowse & Co v National Telephone Co [1894] 2 Ch 147.
Leslie Shipping Co v Welstead, The Raithwaite [1921] 3 KB 420.
Maredelanto Compania Naviera SA v Bergbau-Handel GmbH, The Mihalis Angelos [1970]
3 All ER 125, [1971] 1 QB 164, CA.
Spargo's Case, Re Harmony and Montague Tin & Copper Mining Co Ltd (1873) 8 Ch App *b*
407, [1861-73] All ER Rep 261, CA.
Stewart (C A) & Co v Phs Van Ommeren (London) Ltd [1918] 2 KB 560, CA.
Stockloser v Johnson [1954] 1 All ER 630, [1954] 1 QB 476, CA.
Suisse Atlantique Société d'Armement Maritime SA v N V Rotterdamsche Kolen Centrale
[1966] 2 All ER 61, [1967] 1 AC 361, HL.

c
Action

This was an action by the plaintiffs, Tenax Steamship Co Ltd of London, who had
chartered the motor vessel Brimnes from the defendant shipowners, Reinante Transoceanica Navegacion SA of Panama, under a time charterparty, claiming damages for
the wrongful withdrawal of the vessel from the charterers' service on the ground that
the hire had not been paid by the due date. The facts are set out in the judgment.   *d*

R L A Goff QC and *Basil Eckersley* for the charterers.
A H M Evans QC and *M O Saville* for the shipowners.

Cur adv vult

e
28th July.   **BRANDON J** read the following judgment.   The court has before it
claims and counterclaims arising out of a time charterparty relating to the motor
vessel Brimnes made between the plaintiffs as charterers and the defendants as shipowners.   The main question is whether the defendants were entitled to withdraw
the ship from the plaintiffs' service on the ground of the plaintiffs' admitted failure
to pay hire punctually.   On the footing that the defendants were not so entitled, *f*
the plaintiffs have a claim for damages the amount of which is in dispute.   On the
footing that the defendants were so entitled, the defendants have a counterclaim for
moneys due on a quantum meruit or otherwise the amount of which is also in dispute.
Other claims and counterclaims are raised on the pleadings but the parties have
reached agreement as to how these should be disposed of and the court does not
therefore have to adjudicate on them.   It has further been agreed that, in relation *g*
to the claim and counterclaim arising out of the withdrawal of the ship, the question
of liability shall be decided first, and the question of the amount of the claim or
counterclaim, as the case may be, decided later.

The Brimnes is a Liberian motor vessel belonging to the port of Monrovia of
15,756 tons deadweight capacity.   I shall refer to her as 'the ship'.   The plaintiffs
are Tenax Steamship Co Ltd, an English company carrying on business at 85 London *h*
Wall, London EC2.   I shall refer to them as the charterers.   The defendants are
Reinante Transoceanica Navegacion SA, a Panamanian company carrying on business
in Greece and dealing in relation to the charterparty through agents in London.   I
shall refer to them as the shipowners.

The history of the matter, as I find it, is as follows.   The ship was originally owned
by the charterers.   In or about November 1968 the charterers agreed to sell the ship
to the shipowners on the basis that she would be immediately time chartered back *j*
to the charterers.   The purchase of the ship by the shipowners was financed by a
loan from their bankers, Morgan Guaranty Trust Co of New York, whom I shall
call 'MGT'.   Repayment of the loan and payment of interest on it were secured,
first, by a mortgage of the ship and, second, by an assignment of the charter hire by
the shipowners to MGT.

The charterparty which came into being pursuant to these arrangements was made in London on 22nd November 1968. Its main terms were: (1) that the charter period should be 24-26 months; (2) that hire should be at the rate of US $3.80 per deadweight ton per calendar month and should be paid monthly in advance in cash to MGT, New York, for the credit of the shipowners' Brimnes account; and (3) that, failing punctual payment of hire, the shipowners should have the right to withdraw the ship.

The ship was delivered to the charterers under the charterparty on 18th December 1968. The shipowners' agents were at that time and until the end of November 1969, SG Embiricos Ltd, of Dunster House, 17-18 Mark Lane, London EC2. They were changed, as from 1st December 1969 to Embiricos Shipping Agency Ltd, of Boston House, 132 Cheapside, London EC2.

Although the ship was delivered on 18th December 1968 the first monthly period of hire was treated as being from 16th December 1968 to 16th January 1969. The next two monthly periods of hire were treated as being from 16th January to 16th February 1969, and from 16th February to 16th March 1969. In March 1969, however, payment was made and accepted for the period from 16th March to 30th April 1969, and after that the monthly hire period was treated as being the period beginning on the first day and ending on the last day of each calendar month. It follows that, as from 1st May 1969, the charterers were under an obligation to pay hire monthly in advance by the first day of each month.

The charterers' bankers were Hambros Bank Ltd, of 41 Bishopsgate, London EC2, whom I shall call 'Hambros'. The method of paying hire used by the charterers was to instruct Hambros to transfer the amount due to MGT, New York, for the credit of the shipowners' Brimnes account. These instructions would be given in writing on a printed form issued by Hambros and headed 'Application for mail transfer'. The form would be completed by the charterers' accountant, Mr Sanders, by filling in the name and address of the beneficiary's bankers, the name of the beneficiary and the amount in US dollars to be transferred. The form by its printed terms provided only for transfer by mail or air mail, but Mr Sanders would cross out the printed words and substitute a request for transfer by cable. After completing the form in this way he would obtain the signatures of two directors of the charterers to it and send it to Hambros, who would then take steps to effect the transfer requested.

For this purpose Hambros used at different times two methods, which I shall call the direct transfer method and the indirect transfer method. The procedure when they used the direct transfer method was this. Hambros would send by telex an order to MGT, New York, with whom they had an account, to pay the amount concerned to the shipowners' Brimnes account by order of the charterers. This order to pay would include a statement of the value date, meaning the date for the delivery of the US dollars under the exchange sale involved. Having done this, Hambros would send to the charterers an exchange sale advice, confirming in effect that they had complied with the charterers' application for transfer. This would show the value date in relation to the exchange sale, and confirm that Hambros had instructed their correspondents, MGT, New York, to pay the amount of US dollars concerned to the shipowners' Brimnes account. It would also show the sterling amount debited to the charterers' account in respect of the transfer, including a charge for cabling the instructions to New York.

Hambros' order to pay would be received on a telex machine at MGT, New York. Following such receipt various processes would be gone through in MGT, the end product of which would be that Hambros' account with MGT would be debited, and the shipowners' Brimnes account credited, with the amount in US dollars concerned. Debit and credit advices showing this would come into being, and would be sent by MGT to Hambros and the shipowners' London agents respectively. The credit advice note, when received by the shipowners' agents, would show the date of crediting

and the source of payment, namely cable instructions from Hambros by order of the   *a*
charterers bearing a certain date.

This direct transfer method of payment was used by Hambros on 13 out of 16
occasions of payment of hire, including the last eight such occasions from August 1969
to April 1970. On one of these 13 occasions, however, in June 1969, Hambros' order
to MGT, New York, to pay was sent by letter instead of telex, with consequent
delay.   *b*

The indirect transfer method, which was used on the three remaining occasions
of payment of hire, in February, March and August 1969, was similar in general to the
direct transfer method. It differed, however, in this respect, that Hambros' order
to pay the amount concerned to the shipowners' Brimnes account at MGT, New
York, was sent not to MGT, New York, itself, but to another New York bank acting
as correspondents for Hambros. That other bank would, in response to such order,   *c*
send a bankers' cheque to MGT, New York, for the credit of the shipowners' Brimnes
account, and, on receipt of such cheque, MGT would credit that account accordingly.
The fact that the transfer had been effected indirectly through another New York
bank would be apparent from the wording, first, of the exchange sale advice sent
by Hambros to the charterers, and, secondly, of the credit advice sent by MGT to
the shipowners' London agents.   *d*

It was the practice of Mr Sanders, when dealing with the payment of hire each
month, and at or about the time of the application to Hambros for transfer, to send
a letter to the shipowners' London agents, setting out his calculation of the amount
of hire due, and stating that such amount had been paid or transferred.

The contentions put forward on either side in this case make it necessary, for reasons
which will become apparent later, to decide if possible the precise time at which,   *e*
under the methods of payment used, the payment of hire was effected. Where
the indirect transfer method was used it is, I think, reasonably clear that payment
was effected when the bankers' cheque issued by the other New York bank was
received by MGT. It was so contended by counsel for the shipowners, and I did not
understand counsel for the charterers to submit otherwise. When the direct transfer
method was used, the question of the precise time of payment is more difficult and   *f*
the parties are in disagreement about it.

For the charterers it was contended that, where the date of receipt by MGT of
Hambros' order to pay was no earlier than the value date specified in it, the time of
payment was the time of arrival of such order on MGT's telex machine (or, at the
latest, the time when MGT first opened for business thereafter); and that, where
the date of such receipt was earlier than the value date, the time of payment was
the start of the value date (or, at the latest, the time when MGT first opened for   *g*
business on that date). For the shipowners, on the other hand, it was contended
that the time of payment was the time when MGT, in the course of processing
Hambros' order to pay, took the decision to debit Hambros' account and credit the
shipowners' Brimnes account. It will be necessary later to resolve the conflict between
these two views, but for the time being it is sufficient merely to indicate its existence   *h*
and nature.

On either view of the precise time of payment it is clear that the charterers' payments of hire under the charterparty were almost invariably late. Even assuming,
in charterers' favour, that the time of payment was as they contend, the payments
were late by the following number of days:

1968	December	11
1969	January	nil
	February	1
	March	4
	May	1
	June	9

a

1969	July	70
	August	10
	September	4
	October	5
	November	5
	December	2
1970	January	5
	February	3
	March	1
	April	1

It is right to observe, however, that the lateness of the payment for June 1969 was due, mostly, although not wholly, to the fact that Hambros' order to pay was sent by
c letter instead of telex; and that the delay of over two months in making the July payment was due to a dispute whether, having regard to off-hire periods, any hire was payable at all.

The shipowners' London agents appear to have tolerated the late payments of hire made in this way without complaint until January 1970. On 2nd January Mr Patsalides, who was the secretary and also a director of Embiricos Shipping Agency
d Ltd, and dealt with the charterparty accounts for them, spoke to Mr Sanders on the telephone and made two complaints. The first complaint was about deductions being made from the hire for disbursements not previously submitted to the shipowners' agents for their agreement. The second complaint was about hire being paid late.

On 3rd February 1970 Mr E G E Embiricos, the managing director of Embiricos
e Shipping Agency Ltd, wrote a letter to the charterers making a further and more formal complaint about the matter. That letter read:

> 'In reviewing accounts for this vessel, we notice that you have repeatedly effected payments of monthly hire several days late. Hire was due on the 1st. instant, but to the time of writing this letter we have no advice either from our Bankers
> *f* or from your goodselves that payment of the monthly hire has been effected. We have your letter of the 2nd. instant together with enclosures which are receiving our attention, but even in that letter, you do not say that payment of hire has already been effected. Will you please ensure that all future payments of hire are effected on the 1st of the month.'

No answer to that letter was sent by the charterers.
g The next payment of hire due after that letter was the fifteenth under the charterparty, payable by 1st March 1970. This was a Sunday and the shipowners' agents took the view that they would in these circumstances be content if payment was made by Monday, 2nd March. They had instructions, however, from the shipowners that, if payment was not effected by the latter date, they were to withdraw
h the ship from the service of the charterers.

In order to be able to act promptly on these instructions Mr Embiricos spoke on the telephone to Mr Valli, an assistant treasurer of MGT, New York, and enquired when was the earliest time MGT could be sure whether payment had been made on a particular day or not. He was told that there was a delay between a payment being made and the account being credited, and that a definite answer could not be given before 11.00 New York time on the day following the day in question. This was the
i equivalent of 17.00 BST.

Following this conversation Mr Embiricos made two requests to MGT to inform Embiricos Shipping Agency Ltd as soon as possible whether hire had been paid by 2nd March 1970. The first request was made in a letter to the London office of MGT dated 26th February 1970, after a meeting between Mr Embiricos and Mr Noble, an assistant vice-president of MGT in charge at that office. The second request was

made by telex to MGT, New York, dated 2nd March 1970.   The substance of the   *a*
request was the same in either case and it will therefore be sufficient to refer only
to the telex of 2nd March.   It reads:

> 'Owners motor vessel "Brimnes" have instructed us withdraw subject vessel
> from time charter dated 22nd November, 1968, as per their rights pursuant to
> Clause (5) of subject time charter, if hire for month March 1970 not paid by close
> business, New York on Monday, 2nd March, 1970, said hire being due on 1st   *b*
> March.   Therefore essential you telex advise us soonest after close business
> New York today, 2nd March, and in any case before 5 p.m. London time 3rd
> March, whether hire "Brimnes" paid by [the charterers] to [the shipowners]
> before close business New York on Monday 2nd March.   We must emphasise
> that what you must advise us is whether you have received the funds and not
> whether the funds have been credited to vessel's account, since payment of funds   *c*
> to you constitutes payment.   In view of gravity of this matter imperative that
> greatest care be exercised on your part to avoid any mistake. Please confirm that
> above well received and understood and that you will act accordingly.'

In response to these requests MGT, New York, on 2nd March, sent the following
telegram to the shipowners' agents: *d*

> 'Re Embiricos Shipping Agency and Reinante and Brimnes dollars 58,027·57
> received A.M. of March 2nd from Hambros London order of [the charterers].'

In view of this information the shipowners' agents regarded the hire for March as
having been paid punctually and took no action to withdraw the ship.   They prepared themselves, however, to do so a month later if the April payment should be   *e*
late.   To this end they once again requested MGT to inform them as soon as possible
whether payment had been made by 1st April 1970.   This was not a Sunday and no
question therefore arose of allowing an extra day for payment as on the previous
occasion.   Again two requests in similar terms were made, one by letter to MGT,
London, and the other by telex to MGT, New York.   The telex was dated 31st March
1970 and read: *f*

> 'Kindly telex advise us soonest after close business New York 1st April and in
> any case before 5 p.m. London time 2nd April, whether hire Brimnes paid by
> [the charterers] to [the shipowners] before close business New York on Wednes-
> day 1st April.   We must emphasise that what you must advise us is whether you
> have received the funds and not whether the funds have been credited to
> vessel's account since payment of funds to you constitutes payment. In view of   *g*
> gravity of this matter, imperative that greatest care be exercised.   Kindly
> acknowledge that message well received.'

Meanwhile Mr Sanders was taking steps on behalf of the charterers to pay the
April hire by the same method as before.   On 31st March 1970 he completed
Hambros' form of application requesting them to transfer by cable to MGT, New   *h*
York, for the benefit of the shipowners' Brimnes account US $51,210·95. He was not,
however, able to obtain both the directors' signatures to the form which were necessary until the morning of the next day, 1st April, and because of this the form did not
reach Hambros until later that morning.

Following receipt of the transfer application form Hambros sent an order to pay
by telex to MGT.   This was sent at 10.53 BST or 04.53 New York time on 2nd April.   *i*
It read:

> 'Value 2/4. Pay [the shipowners] account m.v. "Brimnes" order [the
> charterers] U.S. $51,210·95.'

Since the order to pay was not received until 2nd April, it is clear that, even on the *a*   charterers' contention as to time of payment under the direct transfer method, the payment of the April hire, which should have been made by 1st April, was late.

At 14.06 BST on 2nd April the shipowners' agents sent a telex reminder to MGT, New York, reading:

> 'M.V. Brimnes. Kindly do not fail to advise us by telex before 5 p.m. London time today whether charter hire of m.v. Brimnes received before close of business yesterday, in New York.'

b

The reason for the emphasis in this and earlier requests on 17.00 as the latest time for giving the answer sought was the information given earlier to Mr Embiricos by Mr Valli that a definite answer could not be given until that hour. Despite the request for an answer by 17.00, no message from MGT was received by the shipowners' *c* agents by that hour. In these circumstances at some time after 17.00 Mr Embiricos spoke on the telephone to Mr Noble at MGT's London office and asked for news. Mr Noble rang off in order to telephone direct to New York, and spoke to someone there who informed him that no payment of hire had been made by 1st April. He then telephoned back to Mr Embiricos and passed that information on to him. Mr Embiricos, although empowered to act without further instructions from the *d* shipowners, decided to report the situation first to one of the shipowners' directors who happened to be in London at the time. He did so and had his instructions to withdraw the ship confirmed. He thereupon dictated a notice of withdrawal to his secretary, Miss Rangecroft, for despatch by telex to the charterers at their London office. He used for this purpose, with necessary alterations, a draft notice prepared for him by the shipowners' solicitors in late February when withdrawal on the ground *e* of late payment of the March hire had been in contemplation. Miss Rangecroft took down the notice as dictated and then typed it on a telex tape and sent it off to the charterers.

The time when this telex notice of withdrawal was sent is seriously in dispute. The evidence for the shipowners was that it was shortly before 17.30, when the charterers' office was, or might be expected to have been open. The evidence for the charterers *f* was that the time was after 18.30, when their office was, and might be expected to be, closed.

Whatever may have been the precise time of the telex notice of withdrawal—and it will be necessary to make a finding about it if possible later—at 18.00 that evening the shipowners' agents received further information from MGT, New York, about the payment of the April hire. This came in the form of a telephone message from *g* S G Embiricos Ltd, passsing on a telex message sent by Mr Valli to the shipowners' agents at about 11.30 New York time, or 17.30 BST. This telex message had been addressed to Embiricos Shipping Agency Ltd, but sent in error to S G Embiricos Ltd, who telephoned its contents through to the former at about 18.00. The telex read:

> 'Most urgent. Re M.V. Brimnes dollars 51,210·95 received by MGT this *h* morning April 2nd, 1970. Regards Filippo Valli Assistant Treasurer.'

In addition to sending the telex notice of withdrawal, the shipowners' agents also sent a confirmatory letter to the charterers quoting the contents of the telex. This letter was typed by Miss Rangecroft the same evening and posted by her by registered post on her way home from the office. On the morning of 3rd April 1970 the telex *j* and letter giving notice of withdrawal were brought to the attention of Mr Sanders in the charterers' office by the secretary, Mrs Sayce.

On the same day Mr Valli sent a further telex to the shipowners' agents reading:

> 'Payment for M.V. Brimnes from [the charterers] received after 10 a.m. April 2 1970 from Hambros Bank London and was processed soon thereafter. For your information we do not time every step of payment orders received through

the flow of work but you may rest assured that orders are processed with
maximum possible dispatch.'

In the evening the charterers replied by telex to the shipowners' agents as follows:

'Shocked to learn contents of your telex in which you advise that you intend
to exploit the fact that the hire was only transferred to your account on the 2nd
April instead of on the first.   As you know we have always paid the hire in this
way as in the present case viz. by asking our bank to transfer the hire to your
bank, but the transfer has apparently been delayed somewhat.   As you will
appreciate we remit hire telegraphically from our London bank to your bank
each month.   View you have accepted such method of payment and in view
of you having previously accepted minor delays we certainly protest strongly
against your unwarranted action and trust you will reconsider same.   March
hire paid exactly same time and manner as April.   We therefore advise that it
is clear in law that your withdrawal unjustified.'

On 6th April 1970 the shipowners' agents wrote to the charterers as follows:

'We acknowledge your Telex, received in the evening of the 3rd. instant·
As you admit in subject Telex, you have repeatedly in the past paid the hire of
the M/V "Brimnes" late.   This is totally unacceptable to Owners and we therefore advised you by our letter of the 3rd. February, 1970 that you must ensure
that all future payments of hire were effected on the first of the month, i.e. on
the due date in accordance with the Time Charter.   Following our above-
mentioned letter, the March hire was paid promptly on the first business day on
March, i.e. March 2nd., March 1st. being a Sunday and Owners' New York Bankers
being of course closed on Sundays.   Now, however, you have begun repeating
your past practice of paying the hire late and in spite of our letter to you of the
3rd. February, the April hire was not paid on the due date.   Owners therefore
have decided to withdraw vessel from Charterers' service in exercise of their
rights under the Time Charter and this withdrawal is confirmed.   Owners
advise that the sum paid by you to their account with Morgan Guaranty Trust
Company of New York on April 2nd. 1970, will be provisionally held by Owners
as a payment on account of Owners' claim for damages against Charterers for
Charterers' breach of contract.'

On the same day the shipowners' agents received a letter from Mr Sanders dated
2nd April, informing them that hire amounting to US $51,210.95 had been transferred
to the shipowners' account with MGT on 1st April 1970.   The dispute was then
referred to solicitors on either side and letters were exchanged between them to
which I shall refer later.

It was contended for the charterers: (1) that the shipowners did not withdraw the
ship until after the charterers had made their admittedly late payment of hire on
2nd April 1970; (2) that the shipowners' right to withdraw the ship under cl 5 of the
charterparty only subsisted so long as default in payment of hire continued; accordingly, by the time the shipowners withdrew the ship, they no longer had the right to
do so; (3) that the obligation to pay hire punctually was not an essential term of the
contract, so that breach of it did not entitle the shipowners to treat the contract as
at an end; (4) that the charterers' conduct in relation to late payment of hire during
the charterparty did not amount to repudiation of the contract, so as to entitle the
shipowners to treat it as at an end; (5) that, if the charterers were wrong about (2),
(3) or (4) above, the acceptance by MGT of the late payment of hire before the ship
was withdrawn amounted to a waiver by the shipowners of any or all rights of withdrawal which they would otherwise have had; (6) that, if the charterers were wrong
about (1) above and the ship was withdrawn before the late payment of hire was

a made, then the acceptance and retention of the hire by the shipowners after withdrawal of the ship was evidence of a new contract between the parties on the same terms as the old.

It was contended for the shipowners: (1) that they withdrew the ship before the charterers made their late payment of hire on 2nd April 1970; (2) that they had a right to withdraw the ship under the express power given to them by cl 5 of the charterparty because of the charterers' admitted failure to pay hire punctually by

b 1st April; (3) that, apart from their right under cl 5, they had a right to withdraw the ship on two other grounds: (a) because the obligation to pay hire punctually was an essential term of the contract, on breach of which the shipowners were entitled to treat the contract as at an end; (b) because the charterers' conduct in relation to late payment of hire, taken as a whole, amounted to a repudiation of the contract, which the shipowners were entitled to accept by treating the contract as at an end;

c (4) that even if, contrary to (1) above, the late payment of hire was made before the withdrawal: (a) the making of such payment did not deprive the shipowners of their right to withdraw under cl 5; (b) the acceptance of the payment by MGT did not constitute a waiver by the shipowners of their right to withdraw under cl 5 or otherwise; (5) that, on the footing that the ship was withdrawn before the late payment of hire was made, the acceptance and retention of such payment by the shipowners

d did not evidence the making of a new contract on the same terms as the old.

I shall consider first the question whether the withdrawal of the ship took place before or after the late payment of hire on 2nd April. This involves establishing, if possible, the precise times of both events, which might seem a simple task but is in fact a distinctly difficult one. I take first, the time of payment. I indicated earlier the cases put forward on either side with regard to this. The charterers' case, in

e relation to the payment on 2nd April was, that it was made when Hambros' telex order to pay arrived on the telex machine at MGT, New York, which was 04.53 New York time or 10.53 BST; alternatively, that it was made when MGT next opened for business which was 09.00 New York time or 15.00 BST. The shipowners' case was that payment was made when, in the course of the processing by MGT of Hambros' order to pay, the decision was taken to debit Hambros' account and credit the

f shipowners' account. For reasons which I shall now explain, the precise time of this decision cannot be fixed with certainty but its probable time can be established within certain limits.

The court had evidence from Mr Felton, a vice-president of MGT, about the practice of his bank in relation to a telex transfer order of the kind sent by Hambros. That practice is as follows. (1) On receipt of the telex if it is received during business hours,

g or as soon as possible after 09.00 if it is received earlier, the order is sent to the test section of the telegraph and cable department for verification of the test key. (2) After verification the telex is given to a control clerk in the money transfer department to be logged in and assigned a control number. (3) A multiple form known as a fan-fold is then typed containing the relative account numbers, debit and credit advices, and internal control documents. (4) After a sufficient number of transfer

h orders have been prepared in this way (usually between ten and 20 depending on the volume of such business), they are taken to the bookkeeping department for a determination whether sufficient funds are available in the remitting account to effect payment. If everything is found to be in order, funds are held against the account and the multiple forms are returned to the money transfer department.

j (5) On such return, which is normally two to three hours after the telex was sent to the test section of the telegraph and cable department, the final decision is made to credit the amount of the beneficiary. (6) During the remainder of the business day the multiple form is broken up, debit and credit balances are mailed and internal advices are posted in a journal. This journal is then taken to the data processing department where, between 18.00 and 21.00, punch cards are made out for each transaction and the information is transferred to a magnetic tape. (7) Computer records are then up-dated by a night-work force between 24.00 and 05.00 on the next day and a print-out listing all transactions and final balances for the previous day is available between 04.00 and 08.00. The average number of transfer orders processed by MGT in this way in one day is about 6,000.

Mr Felton said that MGT believed themselves to be the agents of the payer until the decision to debit his account was taken. At that point of time the position changed and MGT acted as agents for the payee. Accordingly, if MGT were to receive instructions from the payer revoking the transfer order while there was still time to act on them, MGT would regard themselves as bound to obey such instructions. As regards the ability of the beneficiary to draw on the funds being transferred, Mr Felton said that MGT would, if specially asked, allow him to do so from the time when the decision to credit his account had been taken but not earlier. Any permission to draw earlier would involve, in effect, the extension of credit by MGT to the beneficiary, for which special authority would be required.

In the present case the telex transfer order of 2nd April was clocked in by the telegraph and cable department at 09.37 New York time and by the money transfer department at 10.10 New York time. It follows that, if the time taken in processing was normal, the decision to debit Hambros' account and credit the shipowners' account was made at some time between 11.37 and 12.37 New York time, or between 17.37 and 18.37 BST. Both sides sought to derive some indication of the actual time of the decision from Mr Valli's telex message relating to the receipt of the money sent to the shipowners' agents through S G Embiricos Ltd at about 11.30 New York time or 17.30 BST. With regard to this Mr Valli said that, when he sent the message, he did not know how far the process had got; he knew only that the telex transfer order had been received by the money transfer department. He had only asked to be informed as soon as the bank knew that the money in some form was there, not whether the shipowners' account had been credited. All his message meant was that they knew that 'the money was in'. In view of this evidence I do not consider that I should be justified in inferring that, by the time of the message, the process had already reached the stage when the decision to debit Hambros' account and credit the shipowners' account had been taken. It is to my mind more likely that the information that the money was in some form there was given to Mr Valli by the money transfer department at a somewhat earlier stage, but how much earlier it is impossible to say. For these reasons I do not consider that this message assists in fixing the time when the decision to debit and credit was taken, and one is left in the position that the time is likely to have been somewhere between the normal limits of 11.37 and 12.37 New York time.

In considering at what time payment was in principle made under the direct transfer method, regard must be had to the hire payment clause in the charterparty and to the accepted method, if any, of the parties of operating it. Clause 5 provided:

'Payment of said hire to be made in New York in cash in United States Currency to Morgan Guaranty Trust Co. of New York, 23 Wall Street, New York, for the credit of the account for [the shipowners] of Panama re m.s. "Brimnes" monthly in advance . . .'

Until a late stage in the hearing before me the case was argued on either side on the footing that what was involved was a payment of hire by the charterers to the shipowners. At a late stage, however, after a reamendment of the statement of claim which I thought it right to allow despite opposition, counsel for the charterers contended that, by reason of the assignment of charter hire by the shipowners to MGT by way of security to which I referred earlier, what was involved was not a payment by the charterers to the shipowners but a payment by the charterers to MGT. He further contended that, even if, in relation to a payment by the charterers to the shipowners, the time of payment was the time of MGT's decision to debit and credit

a (which he strongly disputed), in relation to a payment by the charterers to MGT different considerations, leading to the conclusion that the time of payment was the time of receipt of the transfer order, applied.

The assignment of charter hire was made by a written assignment dated 16th December 1968. It is by its terms an absolute assignment governed by English law. Written notice of it was given by the shipowners to the charterers on the day it was made. The

b effect of the assignment and notice, under s 136 of the Law of Property Act 1925, was to transfer from the shipowners to MGT the right to be paid the hire by the charterers. In practice, however, the three parties concerned behaved in all respects as if the assignment had not been made. The reason for this was that MGT regarded the assignment as being no more than a security for the performance by the shipowners of their obligations under the loan agreement between MGT and them, and had no intention, so long as the shipowners were not in default, of enforcing their rights under it.

c For the charterers it was argued that the court should give effect to the true position in law, and treat the payment of hire as being a payment by the charterers to MGT pursuant to the assignment. For the shipowners it was argued that the court should regard the situation in the same way as the three parties concerned regarded it, and treat the payment of hire as being a payment by the charterers to the shipowners, notwithstanding the legal effect of the assignment. In my view the argument for the

d shipowners on this point should prevail. Parties to a transaction may always, by mutual arrangement, waive temporarily the strict legal rights arising under it and, if they do so, they are thereafter estopped, until appropriate notice has been given, from insisting on such rights. I think that that is what happened in this case. All three parties, the charterers, shipowners and MGT, were content to behave as if the assignment was in suspense, and I do not think that any of them could, except by giving

e appropriate notice, have terminated this arrangement and insisted on the assignment being acted on. In these circumstances I am of opinon that the payments of hire under the charterparty should be treated by the court in the same way as they were treated by the parties, namely as payments by the charterers to the shipowners through MGT, and not as payments by them to MGT direct. In further considering the question of

f time of payment, I proceed on that basis.

In support of the shipowners' contention that, under the direct transfer method, the time of payment was the time of MGT's decision to debit Hambros' account and credit the shipowners' account, counsel argued as follows: (1) the words 'payment ... to be made ... in cash' in cl 5 of the charterparty did not mean that payment had to be made in dollar bills. The expression 'payment in cash', as used in a modern charterparty, included any commercially recognised method of transferring funds,

g the result of which was to give the transferee an unconditional right to the immediate use of such funds. Both the direct and indirect methods of transfer used by the charterers at different times in this case constituted payments in cash within the meaning of cl 5. (2) Since the methods of transferring funds used were within cl 5, as properly construed, there was no need to infer, nor any room for inferring, an

h accepted method of payment not covered by the charterparty of the kind found by the arbitrator in *Tankexpress A/S v Compagnie Financière Belge des Petroles SA*[1]. (3) While the expression 'payment in cash' covered the methods of transferring funds used in this case, a payment by such methods could not be regarded as having been made until the payee had an unconditional right to the immediate use of the funds transferred. (4) Under the direct transfer method the shipowners did not have an

j unconditional right to the immediate use of the funds transferred until MGT's decision to debit the one account and credit the other was taken.

In support of (3) above, reliance was placed on *Zim Israel Navigation Co Ltd v Effy Shipping Corpn, The Effy*[2]. The facts in that case differed materially from those in the

---

1 [1948] 2 All ER 939, [1949] AC 76
2 [1972] 1 Lloyd's Rep 18

present case, but the decision of Mocatta J appears to be an authority for the proposition that, where a charterparty requires payment in cash, and the method of payment used is a transfer of funds between banks A and B ending in the crediting of the payee's account with bank B, payment is not effected until the payee is in a position to draw on that account for the amount of the funds transferred. Counsel for the shipowners argued that the situation was the same when the transfer of funds took place entirely within a single bank, with which both the payor's agents and the payee himself had accounts.

In support of the charterers' contentions with regard to the time of payment, counsel argued as follows: (1) The words 'payment . . . to be made . . . in cash' in cl 5 of the charterparty meant what they said, namely that payment should be made in US dollar bills or other legal tender. They did not have the wider meaning contended for by the shipowners. (2) In the present case, however, there was an accepted method of payment of the kind found by the arbitrator in the *Tankexpress* case[1]. This was the direct transfer method operated by Hambros as agents for the charterers. (3) Under this method the receipt by MGT of the transfer order was for all practical purposes equivalant to payment, except where the value date was later than the date of receipt, in which case the payment became effective at the start of the value date. Accordingly the time of receipt in the one case, or the start of the value date in the other case, was, or should be treated as being, the time of payment. (4) Payment by transfer order was analogous to payment by cheque. Thus, where payment was made by cheque it was a conditional payment which, provided the cheque was met, was effective from the time of receipt of the cheque. Similarly, where payment was made by transfer order, it was a conditional payment, which, provided there was sufficient funds in the transferor's account to meet the transfer, was effective from the time of receipt of the transfer order. (5) It was clear from the documents that both the shipowners' agents and MGT regarded payment as having been made when the transfer order was received. This showed that the parties accepted this time as the time of payment. (6) Alternatively, where the transfer order was received before MGT opened for business, the time of payment was the time when MGT next opened for business thereafter.

I consider first the meaning of payment in cash in cl 5 of the charterparty. In my view these words must be interpreted against the background of modern commercial practice. So interpreted it seems to me that they cannot mean only payment in dollar bills or other legal tender of the USA. They must, as the shipowners contend, have a wider meaning, comprehending any commercially recognised method of transferring funds, the result of which is to give the transferee the unconditional right to the immediate use of the funds transferred. This would include both the direct and the indirect transfer methods used by Hambros as agents for the charterers in this case.

If my view on that point is wrong, it would, I think, follow that the alternative view put forward by the charterers, that the direct and indirect transfer methods of payment, while not strictly speaking contractual methods, were accepted methods between the parties, would be the right one. As I see it, however, this would not produce any different legal result from the other view, unless it could be shown that acceptance of the direct transfer method as a method of payment was accompanied by acceptance of a particular stage in the carrying out of such method as the time of payment.

Insofar as the charterers' case is based on treating the receipt of a transfer order as analogous to the receipt of a cheque, I see two main objections to it. First, when it is said that receipt of a cheque is conditional payment, the receipt meant is receipt by the payee. In this case the receipt of the transfer order was not receipt by the payee but receipt by MGT as Hambros' correspondents, i e as sub-agents of the agents of

---

1   [1948] 2 All ER 939, [1949] AC 76

the charterers.   That this was so is, I think, apparent, from the form of the exchange
sale advices sent by Hambros to the charterers, in which it was stated that Hambros
had instructed their correspondents MGT to pay the amount concerned to the shipowners' account. In this connection comparison can usefully be made with the position when the indirect transfer method was used, under which the instructions were
given to another New York bank as correspondents; it could hardly be suggested, in
that case, that the receipt of the instructions by the other bank was a receipt by the
payee.   The inference to be drawn in this respect from the exchange sale advices is
supported by Mr Felton's evidence as to MGT's belief that, when first dealing with
the transfer order, they acted as agents for Hambros.

Secondly, it seems to me that a cheque, being a negotiable instrument on which
a payee who receives it can sue, is something quite different from an order to transfer,
which does not have these attributes.   While it is therefore appropriate to treat
receipt of a cheque as conditional payment, it would not be appropriate to treat receipt
of a transfer order in the same way.

For both these reasons I do not consider that the analogy which counsel for the
charterers sought to draw between payment by cheque and payment by transfer
order under the direct transfer method is a valid one.

Insofar as the charterers' case is based on the assertion that the time of the receipt of
the transfer order by MGT was accepted between the parties as the time of payment,
I have difficulty in seeing what is the evidence of such acceptance. Mr Sanders, in his
letters relating to hire sent each month to the shipowners' agents, used language
which suggested that he regarded payment as having been made when the charterers'
application for transfer of funds was sent to Hambros, a time which often preceded
by several days the date of the transfer order or the value date specified in it. Mr
Embiricos said in evidence that these letters were treated by the shipowners' agents
as something of a joke, and as signifying no more than that the machinery for transferring the funds had been set in motion.   It might, I suppose, have been argued for
the charterers that the shipowners' agents, by failing to take exception to the language of Mr Sanders's letters in this respect, were accepting his approach. That point,
however, was neither pleaded nor argued by the charterers and is not therefore open
to them.   In any case, I do not think that a finding that the shipowners accepted a
notional time of payment of that kind could justly be based on the mere fact that
their agents took no exception to the terms of Mr Sanders's letters.

Reliance was, however, placed by counsel for the charterers on the terms of the
letters and telexes exchanged between the shipowners' agents and MGT with regard
to the shipowners' agents being informed by MGT at the earliest opportunity whether
hire from March and April had been paid punctually or not. I referred to these
in the account of the facts which I gave earlier and set out the terms of some of the
relevant messages. There is no doubt that in these exchanges both Mr Embiricos and
Mr Valli drew a distinction between a later time when the shipowners' account was
credited, and an earlier time when payment was made to, or received by, MGT, and
that Mr Embiricos was content, for the purpose of the enquiries which he was making,
to treat the earlier of these two times as the time of payment.

In drawing inferences, however, from these exchanges about the state of mind of
Mr Embiricos, it is important to have regard to two matters.   The first matter is
that Mr Embiricos was not concerned in the enquiries which he was making with
the time of payment as such. By that I mean that he was not trying to find out at what
time, if any, on 2nd March or 1st April the hire was paid. He was only trying to find
out whether it had been paid at any time on those two days at all. In these circumstances he was not, by what he said, treating the time of receipt of the funds by MGT as
the time of payment to the shipowners; he was only treating the day of such receipt
as the day of payment, in preference to the day following when, the shipowners'
account would be credited.   The second matter is that Mr Embiricos was not, at the
time of those exchanges, fully aware of the precise method of transferring funds used

by the charterers, or of the detail of the processes employed by MGT in imple- a
menting such method of tranfer. The inference which I draw from this is that, when
Mr Embiricos referred in his letters and telexes to receipt of funds by MGT, and treated
such receipt as equivalant to payment to the shipowners, he was referring to
receipt of the funds by MGT in their capacity as bankers for the shipowners. He was
not referring, and, because, he did not know enough about the method and processes
of transfer involved, could not have been referring, to receipt of Hambros' transfer b
order by MGT in their capacity as bankers for Hambros.

Having regard to these two matters, I think that it would be wrong to regard the
letters and telexes relied on by counsel for the charterers as showing that Mr Embiricos,
as agent for the shipowners, accepted, even in his own mind, that receipt by MGT of
Hambros' transfer order constituted payment to the shipowners. Apart from this,
however, what the charterers have to show in order to make good their case on this c
point is not an acceptance by Mr Embiricos in his own mind, but an acceptance between the parties. The documents here concerned are not documents between
the parties, but documents between the shipowners' agents and their New York
bankers. I can find no documents passing between the parties which evidence, or
could even be suggested to evidence, such an acceptance.

For the various reasons which I have given, I consider that the charterers' case, that d
it was accepted between them and the shipowners that the time of receipt of Hambros' transfer order was, or should be treated as being, the time of payment, has not
been made out.

On the footing that receipt of the transfer was not analogous to receipt of a cheque,
and that no special or notional time of payment was accepted between the parties,
I can see no answer to the shipowners' contention that the time of payment was the
time of MGT's decision to debit Hambros' account and credit the shipowners' account. e
Apart from authority it seems to me that, when payment of a debit is effected by a
transfer of funds within a bank from the account of customer A to that of customer B
pursuant to an order given to the bank by customer A, the time of the payment
must, in principle, be the time when the order to transfer it is executed and not the
time when it is given or received. According to the evidence of MGT's practice given f
before me, the effective time of execution of the order, from the point of view of availability of the funds to customer B, is the time of the decision to debit the one account
and credit the other. That is, accordingly, in my view, the time of transfer or payment.
That view, which I should hold apart from authority, is, in my opinion, supported by
the judgment of Mocatta J in *The Effy*[1] the effect of which, so far as this point is concerned, I set out earlier. I therefore find that the late payment of hire on 2nd April
1970 was made between 11.37 and 12.37 New York time, or 17.37 and 18.37 BST. I g
further find that there is no evidence, or at least no satisfactory evidence, to show at
what precise time between those limits it took place. I shall consider later how the
court, faced with this lack of evidence, should deal with the matter.

I turn, second, to the time of withdrawal. Counsel for the shipowners, while
reserving the point for argument in the House of Lords if necessary, conceded that I
was bound by authority in the Court of Appeal to hold first, that, in order to exercise a h
right to withdraw a ship under a time charter like the one here concerned, the shipowners must give notice to the charterers, and, secondly, that the withdrawal only
operates from the time when such notice is received by the charterers. The relevant
decision is *Empresa Cubana de Fletes v Lagonisi Shipping Co Ltd, The Georgios C*[2], to which
I shall have to refer later on other points. It follows that the question here is at what
time was the telex notice of withdrawal, which was sent by the shipowners' agents j
on the late afternoon or evening of 2nd April 1970, received by the charterers.

The nearest approach to contemporaneous evidence on this question is to be found

1 [1972] 1 Lloyd's Rep 18
2 [1971] 1 All ER 193, [1971] 1 QB 488

a in certain letters written soon after the withdrawal. On 10th April 1970 the
   charterers' solicitors sent to the shipowners' agents a letter protesting about the withdrawal. In the second paragraph of that letter they said:

   'Investigations made by us disclose that the hire was in fact paid into the Owner's
   bank account in New York not less than two hours before you sent the telex in
   question, which incidentally was not received on our clients' machine until after
b their office had closed.'

   Mr Embiricos received the letter on the same day as it was written and passed it to
   the shipowners' solicitors under cover of an explanatory letter of his own. In the
   second paragraph of his letter he wrote:

   '... Owners' bankers advised us shortly after 11 p.m. New York time on the 2nd
c April, that is shortly after 5 p.m. London time on the 2nd April that the April
   hire of the m.v. "Brimnes" was not received by them by close of business in New
   York on the 1st April, 1970. After communicating with Owners we sent a telex to
   [the charterers] at Owners' instructions advising the [charterers] of the withdrawal of the m.v. "Brimnes" from time charter pursuant to Owners' rights
   under the said time charter, some time between 5.30 p.m. and 6 p.m. on the 2nd
d April. Due to circumstances explained above it was, of course, not possible for us
   to advise [the charterers] of the withdrawal of the m.v. "Brimnes" before such
   a time.'

   This information was passed on by the shipowners' solicitors to the charterers' solicitors in a letter of 13th April, but in a somewhat modified form, for they stated
e that the notice of withdrawal was sent 'sometime before 6 p.m. London time'. The
   charterers' solicitors replied to this on 14th April, and stated in the third paragraph
   of their letter:

   'So far as concerns the timing of the withdrawal notice, a secretary in our clients'
   office was sitting a short distance from their telex machine until 6.30 p.m. on 2nd
f April, and her evidence is that the notice had not been received up to that time.'

   Direct oral evidence on the question was given for the charterers by two witnesses
   from their office, the secretary, Mrs Sayce, and the crewing superintendent, Mr Buck;
   and for the shipowners by three witnesses from their agents' office, Miss Rangecroft,
   Mr Embiricos and Mr Patsalides, to all of whom I have already referred. The charterers also put in a written statement from Mr Sanders. Indirect evidence bearing on the
g matter was given by two other witnesses. These were Mr Van der Hoven, a postal
   and telegraph officer, who was called by the charterers to establish the time when Miss
   Rangecroft posted the registered letter confirming the notice of withdrawal on her
   way home from the office, and Mr Noble, of MGT's London office, who was called
   by the shipowners to deal with the telephone conversations which he had with Mr
   Embiricos soon after 17.00.
h I have already set out, in my earlier statement of the facts, the sequence of events
   in the shipowners' agents' office from 17.00 onwards. The question is at what time
   in this sequence did the sending of the telex notice come. As to this, Miss Rangecroft
   put the time at about 17.20, Mr Embiricos at shortly before 17.30 and Mr Patsalides
   at about 17.20 to 17.25. It was clear that each of these three witnesses was making an
   estimate of time based on a reconstruction of events from 17.00 onwards, rather
j than on a recollection of an observation made at the time.
   The evidence of Mrs Sayce and Mr Buck was very different. Mrs Sayce said that she
   did not leave the charterers' office until after 18.30, perhaps as late as 18.45 or 18.50; that
   she looked for any message on the telex machine before leaving; and that the notice
   of withdrawal had not yet arrived on it. She returned to the office at 08.55 the following day, 3rd April, and then saw the notice on the machine for the first time. She

   HH

took it off the machine, read it and then took it to Mr Sanders. Shortly afterwards she opened the letter confirming the telex notice and took this also to Mr Sanders. She said that the machine was always left switched on by day and night, and that there would usually be someone in the office to receive messages on it until 18.30 or 19.00.

Mr Buck said that he first saw the telex notice and the confirmatory letter at between 10.00 and 11.00 on 3rd April when Mr Sanders showed them to him. He could not remember when he left the office on the evening of 2nd April, but his ordinary practice was to leave about 18.15 to 18.30 and to look on the machine for any message before doing so.

I have given careful consideration to the whole of the evidence on this matter and have reached the conclusion that I prefer, in general, the evidence for the shipowners. There are two main reasons for this. The first reason is that it seems to me that the witnesses who were in the shipowners' agents' office had more reason to remember what happened on 2nd April than did the witnesses who were in the charterers' office. This is because it was the first time that any of those in the agents' office had been concerned in withdrawing a ship, which was a serious and important step to take, and they were all to some extent keyed up about it. By contrast 2nd April was an uneventful day in the charterers' office. The second reason is that I thought that the evidence of the shipowners' witnesses, taken as a whole, was better and more convincing than that of the charterers' witnesses. In particular I thought that Mr Buck was not at all an impressive witness.

Preferring as I do, in general, the evidence of the shipowners' witnesses, I reject the evidence of the charterers' witnesses that the notice of withdrawal did not arrive on the charterers' telex machine until after 18.30. I am satisfied that it arrived not only before 18.30 but before 18.00 as well. I am not satisfied, however, that it was as early as 17.20 or 17.25 or 17.30. As stated earlier, Mr Embiricos, in his letter to the shipowners' solicitors written eight days after the event, gave the time as 17.30 to 18.00. I think that his estimate made then is likely to be more accurate than estimates made by him and others who were with him later. It is impossible to be sure of the precise time, but I must do the best I can, and, approaching the matter in that way, I think a reasonable estimate, on the whole of the evidence, is that the notice was sent and arrived at about 17.45, and I so find.

The further question remains whether arrival of the notice on the charterers' telex machine constituted reception of the notice by the charterers. It was conceded by counsel for the charterers that, if Mrs Sayce, Mr Buck or Mr Sanders had been aware of the arrival of the notice on the machine before they left the office, the notice would have been received by the charterers at the time when they became so aware. But, he argued that, if the notice arrived as late as after 17.30, and none of those in the charterers' office were, for whatever reason, aware of its arrival, then there was no reception of the notice by the charterers that evening, but only the following morning at about 08.55 when the message was first seen by Mrs Sayce. In this connection counsel for the charterers said that the shipowners' agents could easily have obtained an acknowledgment of the telex if they had wished to do so, and, having chosen not to do so, could not claim that the message was received when in fact it was not.

Counsel for the shipowners on the other hand argued that the charterers, by leaving their telex machine on and able to receive, represented to all those who could normally be expected to communicate with them by telex, including the shipowners' agents, that messages sent in that way would be received; that the shipowners' agents, relying on that representation, had sent the notice by telex and made no attempt to effect early communication by other means; and that, in these circumstances, the charterers were estopped from saying that the notice, although it arrived, was not received. Counsel for the shipowners said that this would be so even if the message had been sent outside business hours; but, in any case, it was so when, as here, the message was sent during business hours.

a   In support of his submissions on this point counsel for the shipowners relied on
    Entores Ltd v Miles Far East Corpn[1]. In that case a contractual offer had been accepted
    by a telex message sent from Amsterdam to London, and the question arose whether
    the contract so formed had been made in Amsterdam or London. The Court of
    Appeal held that it had been made in London, on the ground that, where an accept-
    ance is communicated by instantaneous means of communication such as telex, the
b   contract is only complete when the message of acceptance is received. Denning LJ
    discussed the situation which might arise if the sender of a message thought that it
    had been received but in fact it had not. He said[2]:

        'In all the instances I have taken so far, the man who sends the message of
    acceptance knows that it has not been received or he has reason to know it. So
    he must repeat it. But suppose that he does not know that his message did not
c   get home. He thinks it has. This may happen if the listener on the telephone
    does not catch the words of acceptance, but nevertheless does not trouble to ask
    for them to be repeated: or if the ink on the teleprinter fails at the receiving end,
    but the clerk does not ask for the message to be repeated: so that the man who
    sends an acceptance reasonably believes that his message has been received. The
    offeror in such circumstances is clearly bound, because he will be estopped from
d   saying that he did not receive the message of acceptance. It is his own fault that
    he did not get it. But if there should be a case where the offeror without any fault
    on his part does not receive the message of acceptance—yet the sender of it
    reasonably believes it has got home when it has not—then I think there is no
    contract.'

    In my view, counsel for the shipowners' argument, so far as it relates to a telex
e   message sent during business hours, is correct. Whether it is also correct in relation
    to a message sent outside business hours is more doubtful, but, for the reasons which
    I am about to give, I do not think that it is necessary to decide that point in this case.
    The evidence was that the charterers' office was regularly open for business until
    18.00 or later, and there was some evidence that other shipping offices were also
    normally open until that hour. I therefore find that, so far as the charterers were
f   concerned, the message containing the notice of withdrawal was sent during what
    were, and could reasonably be supposed by the shipowners' agents to be, ordinary
    business hours.

    I am not sure that the observations of Denning LJ in the *Entores* case[2], with regard
    to fault on the part of those at the receiving end, are relevant to a case like the
    present one. He was dealing with the possibility of a mechanical breakdown, such as
g   lack of ink, on the receiving machine, which prevented the message from arriving at
    all. He was not dealing with failure to notice or read a message which had arrived.
    If it be necessary, however, for the principle of estoppel to operate, that there should
    have been some fault of those in the charterers' office, I should be prepared to find
    that their failure to notice the arrival of the message amounted to such fault. In this
    connection, if one accepts the evidence of Mrs Sayce and Mr Buck that they were not
h   aware of the arrival of the message before they left the office that evening, which I am
    inclined to do, one is driven to one or other of two conclusions: either that, contrary
    to their recollection, they left the office early that night, well before the end of
    ordinary business hours; or that, if they stayed until 18.00 or later, they were busy
    with other matters and neglected to pay attention to the telex machine in the way
    that they claimed it was their ordinary practice to do.

j   For the reasons which I have given, I hold that the notice of withdrawal was
    received by the charterers at about 17.45 on 2nd April, when the telex message con-
    taining it arrived on the machine in their office. It follows, on the authority of *The
    Georgios C* case[3], that the withdrawal was effected at that time.

1   [1955] 2 All ER 493, [1955] 2 QB 327
2   [1955] 2 All ER at 495, [1955] 2 QB at 333
3   [1971] 1 All ER 193, [1971] 1 QB 488

It remains to consider whether that withdrawal at 17.45 was before or after the late a
payment of hire. I found earlier that the latter was made between 17.37 and 18.37,
and that there was no evidence to show precisely when, between those limits, it took
place. In these circumstances I think that the court can only do its best by taking a
mean time of about 18.07, and on that basis I find that the payment was after the
withdrawal. If that is wrong, the court could, I think, say that, with the time of
withdrawal established as being about 17.45, and the time of payment as being b
between seven minutes earlier and 53 minutes later than that, it is more likely that
the time of payment was after the time of withdrawal than before it. I arrive at the
same finding, if necessary, on this alternative basis. Finally, if neither of these two
approaches is justified, the position is that, whichever side needs, for the purpose of
its case, to establish affirmatively that one of the two events preceded the other, has
failed to discharge the burden of proof resting on it. c
    In dealing with the rights of the parties, I shall proceed primarily on the basis
that the withdrawal was before the payment. I shall, however, consider also what
those rights would be if I am wrong about that, and either the payment was before
the withdrawal, or the evidence leaves in doubt which of the two events preceded
the other.
    I turn now to the construction of cl 5 of the charterparty. I have already set out d
the earlier part of it, in which the obligation to pay hire is stated. After further words
relating to payment of hire during the last month of the charterparty period, the
clause continues:

> '. . . otherwise failing the punctual and regular payment of the hire . . . or
> any breach of this Charterparty, the Owners shall be at liberty to withdraw the
> vessel from the service of the Charterers, without prejudice to any claim they e
> (the Owners) may otherwise have on the Charterers . . .'

    As appears from the rival contentions of the parties which I set out earlier, two
points of construction arise on this clause. The first point is whether the obligation
to pay hire punctually was an essential term of the contract, so that breach of it
entitled the shipowners to treat the contract as at an end. Counsel for the ship- f
owners argued that it was, and counsel for the charterers that it was not. The second
point is whether the right to withdraw was conditional not only on there being a
failure to pay hire by the due date, but also on there being no subsequent tender or
payment of hire after the due date but before withdrawal. Counsel for the charterers
argued that both conditions had to be fulfilled; counsel for the shipowners that
fulfilment of the first condition alone was sufficient. g
    The answer to both points depends on whether the present case is governed by,
or should be distinguished from, *The Georgios C*[1] to which I referred earlier. In this
connection also counsel for the shipowners, while reserving his right to contend in the
House of Lords that that case was wrongly decided, accepted that I was bound by it.
In *The Georgios C*[1] the charterparty by cl 6 provided:
h

> '. . . Payment of hire to be made in Pounds Sterling to National Westminster
> Bank Ltd. 27 St. Mary Axe, London, EC3, for account [the shipowners] without
> discount half-monthly in advance . . . In default of payment the [shipowners]
> to have the right of withdrawing the Vessel from the services of the Charterers
> . . . without prejudice to any claim the [shipowners] may otherwise have on the
> Charterers under the Charter . . .' j

Hire for a certain period was not paid by the due date, but payment was tendered two
days after the due date and before the ship was withdrawn. The shipowners thereafter
withdrew the ship and the question was whether they had the right to do so. It was

---

1 [1971] 1 All ER 193, [1971] 1 QB 488

a   held by Donaldson J[1] that they did not have such right, and his decision was affirmed by the Court of Appeal[2].

Both courts held, on the authority of the *Tankexpress* case[3], that, where a charter-party required payment by a certain date, the obligation was not performed by payment made one day, or even one hour, after that date. They went on to hold, however, first, that the obligation to pay hire by the due date was not an essential

b   term of the contract and, second, that, if hire was tendered late but nevertheless before withdrawal, the shipowners' right to withdraw under cl 6 no longer subsisted. With regard to the first point Donaldson J said[4]:

c   'It is important to remember that in relation to the payment of hire under a time charterparty, time is of the essence of the contract only in the sense that there is a breach of contract if payment is a moment late. It is not of the essence of the contract in the sense that late payment goes to the root of the contract and is a repudiating breach giving rise to a common law right in the owners to treat the contract as at an end. The right to withdraw the vessel and thus bring the charterparty to an end is contractual and the situations in which this right is exercisable depend upon the true construction of the contract.'

d   In the Court of Appeal Lord Denning MR said[5]:

'The effect of a stipulation as to time always depends on the true construction of the contract. A default in payment does not automatically give the other a right to determine it. Usually it does not do so. It only does so if there is an express provision giving the right to determine, or if the non-payment is such as to amount to a repudiation of the contract.'

e   It was argued by counsel for the shipowners that there were two features of cl 5 of the charterparty in this case, not present in cl 6 of *The Georgios C*[2] charterparty, which showed that the parties intended the obligation to pay hire by a certain date to be of the essence of the contract. These were, first, the use in relation to the word 'payment' of the epithets 'punctual' and 'regular', and, second the presence of the

f   words 'or any breach of the charterparty'. As regards the epithets 'punctual' and 'regular' he said that these emphasised the importance of the obligation, and he relied, in support of this proposition, on *Maclaine v Gatty*[6] and particularly on the observations of Viscount Finlay[7]. As regards the words 'or any breach of the charter-party' he said that it was necessary to imply the words 'in the event of' between the words 'or' and 'any', and that what was then meant was that, in the event of a breach

g   of any essential term of the charterparty other than failure to pay hire punctually, the shipowners should have the right to withdraw the ship. It followed that failure to pay hire punctually was being treated as being in the same category as breach of any other essential term. Against that counsel for the charterers argued that the use of the epithets 'punctual' and 'regular' added nothing or little to the word 'payment' standing alone; and that reservation of an express right of withdrawal for failure to

h   pay hire tended to show that the obligation was not otherwise of such a character as to be an essential term.

I have considered these arguments carefully and I have reached the conclusion that there is nothing in cl 5 which shows clearly that the parties intended the obligation to pay hire punctually to be an essential term of the contract, as distinct from being a

j   1 [1971] 1 QB at 490–493
2 [1971] 1 All ER 193, [1971] 1 QB 488
3 [1948] 2 All ER 939, [1949] AC 76
4 [1971] 1 QB at 494
5 [1971] 1 All ER at 197, [1971] 1 QB at 504
6 [1921] 1 AC 376, [1920] All ER Rep 70
7 [1921] 1 AC at 389, [1920] All ER Rep at 76, 77

term for breach of which an express right to withdraw was given. It follows that I   *a*
decide the first point of construction in favour of the charterers.

Turning to the second point on cl 5, it appears to me that the basis of the decision
in *The Georgios C*[1] was that the words 'in default of payment' meant, on their true
construction, 'whilst there is default in payment' (per Donaldson J[2]), or 'in default
of payment and so long as default continues' (per Lord Denning MR[3]). It seems that
Donaldson J thought that, if the words had been 'in default of punctual payment',   *b*
they would not have meant 'whilst there is default in payment' but 'when there has
been default in punctual payment' (see his observations[2]). The judges of the Court
of Appeal, however, did not refer to this possible distinction. The words in the
present case are 'failing the punctual and regular payment', and the question is
whether they mean 'failing punctual or any payment' or 'failing punctual payment'
simpliciter.   *c*

Counsel for the charterers, contending for the first meaning, argued as follows.
An obligation to pay by a certain day had the same meaning as an obligation to pay
punctually by a certain day: see the *Tankexpress* case[4]. It followed that a default in
payment, or a failure to pay, meant the same as a default in punctual payment or a
failure to pay punctually. The Court of Appeal in *The Georgios C*[1] had held that
'in default of payment' meant, in effect, 'in default of punctual or any payment'. It   *d*
followed that 'failing punctual payment, meant 'failing punctual or any payment'.
This view, counsel said, was supported by the consideration that the Court of Appeal
in *The Georgios C*[1] appeared to see no distinction, for this purpose, between the words
'in default of payment' in the charterparty in that case, and the words 'in default of
such payment' in the charterparty in the *Tankexpress* case[4]. Finally counsel for the
charterers urged on me the undesirability, especially in the commercial field, of   *e*
drawing fine distinctions, on the basis of minor verbal differences, between clauses the
general purpose of which was the same.

Counsel for the shipowners, contending for the second meaning, relied on the
dictum of Donaldson J[2] to which I have referred. He further argued that the
words of the present charterparty differed materially from the words in the charterparty in *The Georgios C*[1] and that they could not, on their ordinary and natural   *f*
meaning, have the same effect as the latter.

I have found this point a difficult one. I accept fully that I am bound by the decision
of the Court of Appeal in *The Georgios C*[1], so far as it is applicable. I agree that fine
distinctions, based on minor verbal differences, are, in principle, undesirable. On
the other hand it seems to me that I must try to construe the words used in the
present charterparty, and not to allow myself to be over-influenced by the construction put by the Court of Appeal on different words in a different charterparty.   *g*
I can, if I may most respectfully say so, readily understand the Court of Appeal in
The Georgios C[1] giving the words 'in default of payment' the less drastic of the two
possible meanings canvassed before it. I find it difficult to see, however, how the
words 'failing punctual payment' can be fairly said to be capable of the same two
meanings. Rather do I think that they can, on the ordinary and natural interpretation   *h*
of the words used, have only one meaning, namely 'when there has been a failure to
pay punctually'.

For these reasons I hold that, as regards the second point of construction on cl 5,
the present case is distinguishable from *The Georgios C*[1], and the shipowners' right
to withdraw under cl 5 subsisted (subject to waiver) despite any late tender or
payment of hire made after the due date but before withdrawal.

If my finding that the time of the belated payment of hire on 2nd April was later   *j*
than the time of withdrawal is correct, the second point of construction on which

1   [1971] 1 All ER 193, [1971] 1 QB 488
2   [1971] 1 QB at 494
3   [1971] 1 All ER at 197, [1971] 1 QB at 504
4   [1948] 2 All ER 939, [1949] AC 76

a I have just expressed my opinion does not arise. If that finding is wrong, however, and the correct view is that the time of payment was before the time of withdrawal, or that the shipowners, having the burden of proving otherwise, have not discharged such burden, then the result of my opinion on the second point of construction is that it makes no difference.   In either case, there having been a failure by the charterers to pay the hire punctually by 1st April, the shipowners were (subject to the question of waiver which I shall discuss later) entitled under cl 5 to withdraw the

b ship when they did.

My decision on the first point of construction means that the shipowners were not also entitled to withdraw the ship on the ground that the charterers' failure to pay hire by 1st April was a breach of an essential term of the contract, which gave them the right to treat the contract as at an end.   It is necessary to consider, however, the shipowners' alternative contention that the charterers' conduct in relation to late

c payment of hire, taken as a whole, amounted to a repudiation of the contract, which they were entitled to accept by withdrawing the ship.

The question whether the charterers' conduct in this respect was repudiatory or not is a question of fact and of degree. I set out earlier all the relevant primary facts concerning late payment. In assessing their weight I think that the following matters are relevant. Of the first 14 payments, 13 were late by a varying number of days.

d No complaint on this score was made at all until after the 13th payment, and no written complaint until after a further late payment. The next payment (for March 1970) was technically a day late, but, for what I accept were sensible commercial reasons, it was treated by the shipowners' agents as being in time. The April payment was only one day late. In order to justify a decision that the charterers' conduct was repudiatory it would be necessary to find that they evinced clearly by it an intention

e not to be bound by the terms of the contract. I am not satisfied that, on an objective view, their conduct in relation to late payment, although persisted in over a long time, went so far as this. For this reason I am not prepared to hold that the charterers repudiated the contract, so as to entitle the shipowners to treat it as at an end.

I come now to the question of waiver. In order to make good their case on waiver, the charterers must establish that their late payment of hire was made before the

f withdrawal. On my findings they have not done so, and their case on waiver must therefore fail on that ground alone. That is so, moreover, whether the evidence justifies, as I think it does, an affirmative finding that the withdrawal was before the payment, or leaves the matter in doubt, so that the charterers, on whom the burden of proof for this purpose lies, have failed to discharge such burden.

g Since I may be wrong about the relative times, however, and the correct conclusion on the evidence may be that the payment was made before the withdrawal, it is desirable, I think, that I should examine the question of waiver on that alternative hypothesis. In doing so I shall be considering primarily whether, assuming that the late payment was made before the withdrawal, there was a waiver by the shipowners of the express right of withdrawal given to them by cl 5 of the charterparty.

h I shall, however, consider at the same time whether, if the shipowners (contrary to the views which I have expressed earlier) had rights to withdraw the ship on other grounds (namely breach of an essential term or repudiation), there was a waiver of those rights also.

The argument for the charterers on waiver was as follows: (1) The hire payable by 1st April 1970 was hire in advance payable in respect of the use of the ship's services during the period of 30 days from 1st to 30th of that month. (2) In the event of

j the ship being withdrawn by the shipowners at some time during 2nd April, then (a) if the hire had not by then been paid, only so much as was payable in respect of 1st and part of 2nd April up to the time of withdrawal would have been due, and the remainder would not have been due; (b) if the hire had by then been paid, only so much as was payable in respect of 1st and part of 2nd April up to the time of withdrawal would have been retainable as hire by the shipowners, and the remainder would have been immediately repayable. (3) This would be the position, as a matter of law, whether the withdrawal was effected under the express power given by cl 5, or on the ground of breach of an essential term or of repudiation. (4) By accepting, through the agency of MGT, the whole month's hire on 2nd April, the shipowners did an unequivocal act inconsistent with the subsequent exercise by them of any right to withdraw the ship under cl 5 or otherwise. It was inconsistent because, on the footing that they were going to exercise such right, they would not be entitled to be paid, or, if they had been paid, would not be entitled to retain but would be obliged immediately to repay by far the larger part of the whole month's hire. (5) That unequivocal act, done by the shipowners with knowledge of the facts giving them the right to withdraw, constituted, as a matter of law, a waiver by them of such right, just as the acceptance of rent by a landlord with knowledge of a breach of covenant giving rise to a right of forfeiture constituted a waiver by him of the right to forfeit.

In support of propositions (2) and (3) above, counsel for the charterers relied on a number of authorities. In relation to withdrawal under the express power, he relied on *Wehner v Dene Steam Shipping Co*[1] and *Italian State Railways v Mavrogordatos*[2]. In relation to withdrawal on the ground of breach of an essential term or of repudiation, he relied on *Mayson v Clouet*[3], *McDonald v Dennys Lascelles Ltd*[4], and *Dies v British and International Mining and Finance Corpn*[5].

In support of propositions (4) and (5), counsel for the charterers relied, in relation to acceptance of hire under a time charterparty, on *Langfond (Owners) v Canadian Forwarding and Export Co*[6]; and, so far as the analogy of landlord and tenant cases is concerned, on *Matthews v Smallwood*[7] and the recent decision of the Court of Appeal in *Central Estates (Belgravia) Ltd v Woolgar (No 2)*[8].

Counsel for the shipowners strongly disputed that there was any waiver by the shipowners. In doing so, he argued two main points: (1) that acceptance of hire which had already accrued due before any right to withdraw had arisen was not inconsistent with a subsequent exercise of such right and did not therefore amount to waiver; and (2) that, in any case, the receipt of the hire by MGT was a ministerial act and did not constitute an acceptance of the hire as hire by the shipowners themselves.

As regards point (1), counsel for the shipowners said that the shipowners were entitled to be paid by 1st April a full month's hire in advance and that this was so even though it could be foreseen that the charterparty would come to an end before the full month had run, and that, as a result of its doing so, part of the amount paid would be repayable: *Tonnelier v Smith*[9]. In these circumstances there was nothing inconsistent between accepting the full amount due, and later, having done so, withdrawing the ship. The only result was that the shipowners could not thereafter retain, as hire, so much of the amount paid as was payable in respect of the period after withdrawal, but would have to account for it to the charterers. In fact the shipowners had never claimed to retain this element in the payment as hire, but only to set it off against their cross-claim for carrying the charterers' cargo to destination after the ship had been withdrawn. As regards point (2), counsel for the shipowners said that MGT's authority from the shipowners was limited to that arising from the ordinary relationship of banker and customer. Accordingly, while MGT had authority to credit to the shipowners' Brimnes account any funds paid or transferred to them

1   [1905] 2 KB 92
2   [1919] 2 KB 305
3   [1924] AC 980
4   (1933) 48 CLR 457
5   [1939] 1 KB 724
6   (1907) 96 LT 559
7   [1910] 1 Ch 777, [1908-10] All ER Rep 536
8   [1972] 3 All ER 610, [1972] 1 WLR 1048
9   (1897) 77 LT 277

a by the charterers for the benefit of that account, they had no authority to accept hire either as hire or otherwise than as hire, or, by accepting it as hire, to waive any of the shipowners' rights under the charterparty. In this connection counsel relied on *Doe d Nash v Birch*[1], where it was held that a son who demanded rent when his father was too ill to attend to business did not have authority to waive a right of forfeiture which had arisen. There is, I think, a close analogy between the situation where

b a landlord, by accepting rent, waives a right of forfeiture under a lease, and that where shipowners, by accepting hire, waive a right of withdrawal under a time charterparty. It is, however, necessary to bear in mind that there are essential differences between a lease of land and a contract for the use of a ship's services, and that authorities on waiver in the landlord and tenant field may not therefore necessarily be applicable in the shipowner and time charterer field.

c In the landlord and tenant field a clear distinction has been drawn between acceptance of rent which has accrued due after, and acceptance of rent which had accrued due before, the cause of forfeiture arose. Where a landlord, with knowledge of a cause of forfeiture, accepts rent which has accrued due after the cause of forfeiture, he waives the forfeiture: *Matthews v Smallwood*[2]. But where a landlord, with the same knowledge, accepts rent which had accrued due before the cause of forfeiture,

d he does not waive the forfeiture. This is so, moreover, where the rent which he accepts is the very rent for non-payment of which he has the right to forfeit: *Ward v Day*[3], *Green's Case*[4] and *Pennant's Case*[5].

The cases on the second of these two situations appear to be cases where the rent which had accrued due was not only rent payable before the time when the cause of forfeiture arose, but also, being rent in arrears, rent payable in respect of a period antecedent to that time. Counsel were unable to refer me to a landlord and tenant

e case in which it had been considered whether, where a landlord, with knowledge of a cause of forfeiture, accepts rent which has accrued due before the time when the cause of forfeiture arose, but, being rent in advance, was payable (in whole or in part) in respect of a period subsequent to that time, he thereby waives the forfeiture. The answer to that question may, however, depend on whether so much of the rent

f as is payable in respect of a period subsequent to the time when the cause of forfeiture arose ceases to be payable (if unpaid) or becomes repayable (if paid) on the right of forfeiture being exercised. It seems that, under a lease, rent payable in advance which has accrued due before the time when a cause of forfeiture arose, but is referable in part to a period subsequent to that time, is not, when paid, repayable on forfeiture: *Ellis v Rowbotham*[6]. The position therefore differs in this respect from that which arises with regard to hire payable in advance under a time charter when

g withdrawal occurs: *Wehner v Dene Steam Shipping Co*[7].

Counsel for the shipowners suggested that, while there appeared to be no landlord and tenant case on the point, it was covered, so far as withdrawal under time charterparties was concerned, by *Wulfsberg & Co v Weardale (Owners)*[8]. It seems to me, however, that, since in that case the act relied on as waiver, namely the issue of a

h writ claiming a full month's hire, was done after withdrawal, the decision is no authority on the effect of a comparable act done before withdrawal.

Looking at the matter as one of principle, apart from authority, I am of opinion that there is an inconsistency between shipowners accepting hire payable in whole or part in respect of a period after a right to withdraw has to their knowledge arisen

1   (1836) 1 M & W 402
j 2   [1910] 1 Ch 777, [1908-10] All ER Rep 536
3   (1863) 4 B & S 337
4   (1582) 1 Cro Eliz 3
5   (1596) 3 Co Rep 64a, [1558-1774] All ER Rep 634
6   [1900] 1 QB 740, [1900-3] All ER Rep 299
7   [1905] 2 KB 92
8   (1916) 85 LJKB 1717

(even though, because such hire is payable in advance, it has already accrued due), and then later, after such acceptance, exercising such right. The reality of the matter becomes apparent, I think, if one visualises, by reference to the facts of this case, a meeting on 2nd April between Mr Sanders for the charterers and Mr Embiricos for the shipowners, and assumes, for the purpose of argument, that payment by sterling cheque was a contractual or accepted method of payment. Let it be supposed that, at such meeting, Mr Sanders tenders to Mr Embiricos, by way of late payment of the hire due by 1st April, a sterling cheque for the full amount. Mr Embiricos accepts the cheque without comment or reservation. Immediately afterwards he hands to Mr Sanders a notice of withdrawal taking effect from the moment when it is received by the latter. These two pieces of conduct by Mr Embiricos are, I should have thought, plainly inconsistent with each other. First, he accepts hire for the whole period of 30 days from 1st to 30th April. Then he says that he is withdrawing the ship from the charterers' service as from 2nd April. I think that the common sense view of the matter is that the acceptance of the advance payment for the whole month is an unequivocal act inconsistent with withdrawing the ship during that month for cause already known. If that is correct, it follows that such acceptance is, as a matter of law, a waiver of the right to withdraw for such cause. This view, which I have formed independently of authority, seems to me to be supported by the decision of the Privy Council in *Langfond (Owners) v Canadian Forwarding and Export Co.*[1] There was some discussion before me whether that case was decided on the basis of waiver, or on the basis of a construction of the withdrawal clause similar to that adopted in *The Georgios C*[2]. While Donaldson J and Phillimore LJ appear to have regarded the case as having been decided on the latter basis, it has, I think been generally regarded in the past as having been decided on the former basis: see, for example, Scrutton on Charterparties[3] and Carver's Carriage by Sea[4]. The true view, however, may be that the decision can be justified on either ground.

The view which I have just expressed, if correct, disposes of counsel for the shipowners' first main point on waiver, that acceptance by the shipowners of advance hire already accrued due, would not, as a matter of law, amount to waiver of their right of withdrawal for failure to pay such hire punctually. It remains to consider his second main point, that receipt of the hire by MGT did not constitute acceptance of hire as hire by the shipowners.

In relation to that point, there are, I think, two ways in which the charterers' case can be put. First, it can be said that, since MGT were the agents of the shipowners to receive hire when tendered, receipt by them had the same effect in law as receipt by the shipowners themselves would have done. Secondly, it can be said that the shipowners, insofar as they did not instruct MGT not to receive hire tendered late, thereby themselves accepted late payment, or caused or permitted it to be accepted.

As regards the first way of putting the case, I am impressed with counsel for the shipowners' argument that MGT was acting in a purely ministerial capacity and had no authority, actual or ostensible, to waive the shipowners' rights under the charterparty. Against that argument it was said for the charterers that, where waiver by acceptance of rent under a lease is concerned, the intention of the landlord in accepting the rent is irrelevant. The acceptance operates, as a matter of law, as waiver. So here, the absence of any intention on the part of MGT to waive the shipowners' rights, or of any authority from the shipowners to do so, was immaterial. The act of the agent was the act of the principal and amounted in law to waiver.

I do not think that it is entirely correct to say that, where waiver by acceptance of rent under a lease is concerned, the intention of the landlord is irrelevant. I think

---

1   (1907) 96 LT 559
2   [1971] 1 All ER 193, [1971] 1 QB 488
3   17th Edn (1964), p 354
4   12th Edn (1971), vol 1, para 391 (2 British Shipping Laws p 337)

a it is more accurate to say that intention is an essential element in waiver, but that, in such a case, the landlord's intention to waive is conclusively presumed against him. It does not follow that, because a particular act by a landlord results in a certain intention being conclusively presumed against him, the same act done for him by an agent with limited authority, has the same effect. MGT were bound, as the shipowners' bankers, to receive any payments tendered to them by the charterers

b for the credit of the shipowners' account, whether they were in respect of hire or anything else. They had no authority to refuse or make reservations on such receipt. In these circumstances, I do not see why, as a matter of principle, MGT's act in receiving the hire when paid late on 2nd April should of itself lead to a conclusive presumption against the shipowners that they intended to waive their right of withdrawal.

c As regards the second way of putting the charterers' case, it would, no doubt have been possible for the shipowners, if so minded, to have instructed MGT on or before 1st April not to accept any late payment of hire tendered after that date. This would, however, have involved the shipowners in making an election between withdrawing and not withdrawing before any right to withdraw had arisen. I do not think it can be the law that shipowners, in order to avoid being held to have

d waived such a right, must, in effect, elect to exercise it in advance. Assuming that to be right, the question remains whether it would have been possible for the shipowners, after learning that hire had not been paid by 1st April, to instruct MGT, in sufficient time for the instruction to have been acted on, not to accept any hire tendered late. For this purpose it is necessary to assume, contrary to my findings, that the late payment of hire was made before 17.45 on 2nd April, possibly a few hours before. On such a timetable I do not see how the shipowners, who only knew

e for certain that hire had not been paid by 1st April soon after 17.00 on 2nd April, could possibly have given MGT effective instructions not to accept the late payment.

Little authority appears to be available on these matters, but I agree with counsel for the shipowners that *Doe d Nash v Birch*[1], so far as it goes, tends to support this argument. The facts, however, were very different, and the judgments deal only

f shortly with the question.

While the matter is not easy, I have come to the conclusion that counsel for the shipowners' argument on this second point is right, and that MGT's receipt of the hire, assuming it to have occurred before withdrawal, was not an acceptance of the hire as hire by the shipowners so as to amount to a waiver by them of their right to withdraw the ship.

g There is one further question to consider, which is whether there should be inferred from the shipowners' acceptance or retention of the hire after withdrawal a fresh agreement between the parties on the same terms as the old. For the charterers it was contended that such an agreement should be inferred, for the shipowners that it should not.

Here again there is an analogy with landlord and tenant cases. In this field it has

h been held that acceptance of rent after forfeiture, or after expiry of notice to quit, may be evidence of the creation of a new tenancy. In such a case, however, there is no presumption of law that the landlord, by accepting rent, intends to create a new tenancy; the intention of the parties is a question of fact to be determined, like any other question of fact, on the evidence: *Clarke v Grant*[2] and *Central Estates (Belgravia) Ltd v Woolgar (No 2)*[3]. The same principle, in my view, applies to a case where ship-owners, who have withdrawn a ship from a time charter, accept or retain hire after

j such withdrawal.

---

1 (1836) 1 M & W 402
2 [1949] 1 All ER 768, [1950] 1 KB 104
3 [1972] 3 All ER 610, [1972] 1 WLR 1048

In the present case the basis on which the shipowners retained the hire received
by MGT on their behalf appears from the letter from the shipowners' agents to the
charterers dated 6th April 1970, and the letter from the shipowner's solicitors to
the charterers' solicitors dated 13th April 1970. It is clear from these letters that the
hire was not being retained as hire, but as security for cross-claims under the charterparty. In these circumstances I do not consider that the court would be justified in
inferring, from the retention of the hire, any common intention of the parties to
enter into a fresh agreement on the same terms as the old, or to treat the withdrawal
as if it had not been made. This conclusion, which I should reach apart from authority,
is supported by *Wulfsberg & Co v Weardale (Owners)*[1]. I decide this point also,
therefore, against the charterers.

I shall now summarise my decisions on the various questions raised before me. I
decide: (1) that the shipowners became entitled, under cl 5 of the charterparty, to
withdraw the ship on the ground of the charterers' failure to pay the April hire punctually by 1st April 1970; (2) that the shipowners were not also entitled to withdraw
the ship on the ground of breach of an essential term or of repudiation; (3) that the
shipowners withdrew the ship before the charterers made their belated payment
of hire on 2nd April 1970; (4) that, even if the belated payment of hire was made
before the withdrawal, the shipowners' right of withdrawal under cl 5 remained,
and was not waived as a result of MGT's receipt of such payment; (5) that no fresh
contract on the same terms as the old is to be inferred from the shipowners' retention,
after withdrawal, of the hire paid.

The result of these decisions is that the shipowners were entitled to withdraw the
ship when they did, and there must be judgment for them on the issue of liability
accordingly.

Judgment for the shipowners.

Solicitors: *Sinclair, Roche & Temperley* (for the charterers); *Constant & Constant* (for
the shipowners).

N P Metcalfe Esq Barrister.

Practice Direction

CHANCERY DIVISION

*Landlord and tenant – Business premises – Agreement for lease – Contracting out – Court's
power to authorise contracting out of statutory provisions where tenancy for term of years
certain – Joint applications for authorisation – Appointments for hearing – Urgent cases –
Landlord and Tenant Act 1954, s 38 (4) (added by the Law of Property Act 1969, s 5).*

The Chancery masters have arranged to give priority of hearing to joint applications
for authorisation of agreements excluding ss 24 to 28 of the Landlord and Tenant Act
1954, made pursuant to s 38 (4) of that Act, in cases of urgency. Appointments for
hearing will be given at two or three days' notice, if necessary outside the normal
hearing hours, unless the applicants indicate that there is no urgency or the master
concerned is quite unable to give an early date.

R E Ball
Chief Master
19th February 1973

---

1   (1916) 85 LJKB 1717

a Re a debtor, ex parte the debtor v Hungerford Rural District Council

CHANCERY DIVISION

UNGOED-THOMAS AND GOULDING JJ

b 30th OCTOBER, 27th NOVEMBER 1972

County court – Judgment or order – Satisfaction – Payment into court – Bankruptcy notice – County court exercising bankruptcy jurisdiction – Notice specifying agent to receive payment on behalf of creditor – Validity – Whether payment required to be made into court – Bankruptcy Act 1914, s 2 – County Courts Act 1959, s 99 (3).

c

Section 99 (3)*ᵃ* of the County Courts Act 1959, which requires all moneys payable under a judgment or order of a county court to be paid into court, has no application to a county court exercising its bankruptcy jurisdiction. Accordingly a bankruptcy notice on a judgment or order of a county court may, in accordance with the Bankruptcy Act 1914, s 2, proviso (i)*ᵇ*, specify an agent of the creditor, e g his solicitor, to *d* whom payment of the amount due on the judgment or order is to be made (see p 799 h to p 800 a and d f g, post).

Notes

For form of bankruptcy notice, see 2 Halsbury's Laws (3rd Edn) 279-281, para 522.

For payment into court of moneys due under a county court judgment, see 9 *e* Halsbury's Laws (3rd Edn) 260, para 607.

For the Bankruptcy Act 1914, s 2, see 3 Halsbury's Statutes (3rd Edn) 42.

For the County Courts Act 1959, s 99, see 7 Halsbury's Statutes (3rd Edn) 363.

Case cited

Debtor (No 16 of 1922), Re, ex parte the debtor (1922) 92 LJCh 410, DC.

f

Appeal

This was an appeal by a judgment debtor against the order of the Newbury County Court dated 14th August 1972 dismissing his application to set aside a bankruptcy notice dated 15th June 1972. The respondents were Hungerford Rural District Council. The facts are set out in the judgment of Ungoed-Thomas J.

g

Geoffrey Jaques for the appellant.

Anthony King for the respondents.

UNGOED-THOMAS J. This is an appeal by a judgment debtor from the order *h* of the Newbury County Court, which has bankruptcy jurisdiction, dismissing an application to set aside a bankruptcy notice. The bankruptcy notice was founded on an order of the Newbury County Court exercising its bankruptcy jurisdiction. That order provided for the payment by the appellant of costs of an appeal which he had made in respect of an earlier bankruptcy notice. The order was made on 22nd May 1972, and the costs were taxed on 6th June at £70·25. On 14th August *j* the appellant's application to set aside the bankrupcty notice was dismissed by the Newbury County Court exercising its bankruptcy jurisdiction. Appeal was then made to this court.

---

a Section 99 (3), so far as material, is set out at p 798 f, post
b Section 2, so far as material, is set out at p 800 b and e, post

There have been three grounds of appeal canvassed before us, two of them mentioned in the notice of appeal, and the third raised subsequently. The first ground of appeal was that there was evidence before the Newbury County Court showing that less than £50 was due to the respondents at the time of the issue of the bankruptcy notice. That ground of appeal was abandoned. It was, however, maintained that the statement was inaccurate and the appellant relied on that inaccuracy. But s 2, proviso (ii), of the Bankruptcy Act 1914 provides:

'A bankruptcy notice ... shall not be invalidated by reason only that the sum specified in the notice as the amount due exceeds the amount actually due, unless the debtor within the time allowed for payment gives notice to the creditor that he disputes the validity of the notice on the ground of such misstatement ...'

There is no evidence that the appellant within the time allowed gave notice to the respondents that he disputed the validity of the notice on the ground on which he now relies. The result, therefore, is that this ground of appeal fails. The second ground was that there was no final judgment or order, but that ground was abandoned.

The substantial dispute in this case arises on the third ground that was subsequently raised, namely, that the bankruptcy notice provides for payment to the respondents' solicitors instead of, as it is claimed it should have been, for payment into court. The order dated 22nd May 1972 is an order headed 'IN THE NEWBURY COUNTY COURT IN BANKRUPTCY. Re [the appellant] Ex parte [the respondents]'. It reads:

'Upon hearing the [appellant] in person and counsel for the respondents it is ordered that the application to set aside the bankruptcy notice be dismissed and that the costs be taxed and paid by the [appellant]';

and it is signed by the registrar.

Section 99 (3) of the County Courts Act 1959 provides:

'All moneys payable under a judgment or order shall be paid into court: Provided that ... the money shall, if the court so directs, be paid by one party to the other party or his solicitor ...'

It is claimed for the appellant that in view of that section the effect of the order which I have just read, of 22nd May, provides for the payment in this case into court, and it is quite clear and is not disputed that where no direction is made as to payment then payment under a county court order within s 99 does require payment into court.

Subsequently on 6th June the registrar—incidentally the same registrar—taxed the costs and issued a form called a 'Notification as to amount of taxed costs'. It is headed 'In the Newbury County Court' and underneath are the words 'In Bankruptcy —BETWEEN Hungerford Rural District Council, Creditor and [the appellant]'. It provides: 'Pursuant to an Order ... dated the 22nd day of May 1972 the costs of this application [the printed word "Action" being crossed out, and the written word "application" being substituted for it] have this day been taxed and allowed at the sum of £70·25 which amount is payable [and then in the form appear the words "into Court" which are crossed out and above are written the words "to the creditors"] (within 3 days of the date of this notification)'. Again it is addressed to the 'applicant' inserted in writing instead of the printed words 'defendant' or 'plaintiff' which are crossed out. It is dated and signed by the registrar.

In view of the substitutions which I have mentioned, and the addition of the words 'In Bankruptcy' under the words 'In the Newbury County Court', this document is an adaptation of an ordinary county court form to make it applicable to the taxation of costs in bankruptcy jurisdiction.

a Assuming s 99 applies to the order made on 22nd May, yet this notification is not converted into an order merely by reason of its being signed by the same registrar as signed the order. It is here merely notifying the taxation of costs which has taken place within the ambit of the order of 22nd May, which is the only order which exists for the payment of costs. The taxation becomes effective by virtue of the order, but it is not itself the order. Therefore, in my view the reference to the 'amount is payable to the Creditors' (instead of 'into Court') would, if s 99 applies, be nugatory.

b The question, however, arises whether s 99 does apply to the bankruptcy jurisdiction of the county court. Section 99 appears in Part III of the County Courts Act 1959, which commences at s 78, and is headed 'Procedure'. It follows on Part II of the Act, which commences at s 39, and which is headed 'Jurisdiction and Transfer of Proceedings'. It is recognised that there is no reference in Part II to bankruptcy at all.

c Section 96 (1) of the Bankruptcy Act 1914 provides: 'The courts having jurisdiction in bankruptcy shall be the High Court and the county courts.' Then s 96 (2) provides that the Lord Chancellor may specify which county courts are to have bankruptcy jurisdiction. Under the statutory instrument[1] made under that section it is well known that not all county courts have bankruptcy jurisdiction and that some are given jurisdiction which extends over more than one county court district. The *d* source of the bankruptcy jurisdiction for the county court is thus clearly to be found not in the County Courts Act 1959, but in the Bankruptcy Act 1914. By s 103 of the 1914 Act it is provided:

'A county court shall, for the purposes of its bankruptcy jurisdiction, in addition to the ordinary powers of the court, have all the powers and jurisdiction of the *e* High Court, and the orders of the court may be enforced accordingly in manner prescribed.'

(Section 105 (1) does in fact produce a small limitation on the bankruptcy jurisdiction which the county court may exercise, but the limitation is immaterial for present purposes.) We therefore have in s 103 the county courts and the High Court being *f* given identical jurisdiction (subject only in the case of the county courts to that small limitation, to which I have referred).

Rule 390 of the Bankruptcy Rules 1952[2] provides: 'Save as provided by these Rules, the Rules of the Supreme Court shall not apply to any proceedings in bankruptcy.' So the High Court and the county court, if selected by the Lord Chancellor, namely, selected county courts, both have bankruptcy jurisdiction. They both have identical *g* jurisdiction, subject to the modification I have indicated, and in the case of the High Court it has been made clear that the Rules of the Supreme Court shall not apply. Section 103 of the County Courts Act 1959 provides: 'In any case not expressly provided for by or in pursuance of this Act, the general principles of practice in the High Court may be adopted and applied to proceedings in a county court', and the County Court Rules can be made in respect of those matters for which the Rules of the *h* Supreme Court can be made in the case of the High Court. The result is, in my view, that just as the Rules of the Supreme Court do not apply to the High Court's bankruptcy jurisdiction, so similarly the County Court Rules do not apply to bankruptcy jurisdiction. The result of that is that the provision in s 99 of the County Courts Act 1959 requiring all moneys payable under a judgment or order to be paid into court, does not apply to the county court when exercising its bankruptcy jurisdiction. *j* The result is that the order of 22nd May does not have the effect of requiring payment

---

1 The County Courts (Bankruptcy and Companies Winding-up Jurisdiction) Order 1971, SI 1971 No 656
2 SI 1952 No 2113

into the county court, which is what is relied on for defeating the bankruptcy *a*
rules.

Thus the provision of s 2 of the Bankruptcy Act 1914 comes into operation without
it in any way being thwarted by the judgment of 22nd May requiring under the 1959
Act payment into the county court. Section 2 provides: 'A bankruptcy notice under
this Act shall be in the prescribed form . . .' Pausing there, 'the prescribed form'
which is referred to is form 7 which provides for—and I quote from the heading of *b*
the form—'Bankruptcy Notice on Judgment or Order of a County Court'. It
provides:

> 'Take Notice, that within Seven days after Service of this Notice on you, ex-
> cluding the day of such Service, you must pay to the Registrar of the . . . County
> Court at . . . the sum of £ . . . claimed [and so forth].'
c

That form follows, of course, the requirements of s 99 of the 1959 Act, and that section
and the form are limited to a judgment or order of a county court exercising its
ordinary county court jurisdiction. It is not a form which is directed to an order for
payment made by a county court exercising its bankruptcy jurisdiction. So that the
reference to the prescribed form at the beginning of s 2 does not, in my view, in any
way limit or affect the operation of s 2. Section 2 then goes on to provide as follows: *d*

> '. . . and shall require the debtor to pay the judgment debt or sum ordered
> to be paid in accordance with the terms of the judgment or order, or to secure
> or compound for it to the satisfaction of the creditor or the court, and shall state
> the consequences of non-compliance with the notice, and shall be served in the
> prescribed manner: Provided that a bankruptcy notice—(i) may specify an agent
> to act on behalf of the creditor in respect of any payment or other thing required *e*
> by the notice to be made to, or done to the satisfaction of, the creditor . . .'

In this case the bankruptcy notice specified payment to the respondents' solicitors who
were 'agents' within proviso (i) of s 2.

In my view the notice complied with all the statutory and procedural requirements
and was a good bankruptcy notice. The submissions on behalf of the appellant *f*
fail.

GOULDING J.   I agree with Ungoed-Thomas J's judgment and with the reasons
which he has given. For myself, I would add only this. I have felt considerable
doubt whether we ought to have exercised our discretion to allow a point of such
mere technicality to be raised at the hearing when notice of it was not given in proper *g*
time by the notice of appeal. I say that only because I am anxious that the course
we have adopted in the present case should not be regarded as a precedent to the
effect that the court's discretion ought generally to be exercised in favour of such a
late argument on technical grounds.

Appeal dismissed.   *h*

Solicitors: *Haywards* (for the appellant); *Charles Lucas & Marshall*, Newbury (for
the respondents).

Jacqueline Metcalfe Barrister.

H v H (child in care: court's jurisdiction)

FAMILY DIVISION
WRANGHAM J
13th OCTOBER 1972

Divorce – Custody – Jurisdiction of court – Child in care of local authority – Child committed to care of local authority under a fit person order – Father and mother subsequently divorced – Application to court by mother for direction that child should continue to live with foster parents found by her – Court's jurisdiction to intervene on matters within the discretion of local authority – Children and Young Persons Act 1933, ss 62 (1) (b), 76 (1) – Matrimonial Proceedings and Property Act 1970, s 18 (1).

The parties were divorced in 1969. Three years prior to the divorce a juvenile court, acting under ss 62 (1) (b) and 76 (1) of the Children and Young Persons Act 1933, committed the infant son of the parties to the care of a local authority. The local authority looked after the boy in various ways until July 1971 when the mother, with whom he had been staying with the permission of the authority, kept him. Subsequently she took out a summons asking for the court's direction that the boy should continue to live with the foster parents whom she had found for him until further order, contending that the direction asked for was within the jurisdiction of the court by virtue of s 18 (1) of the Matrimonial Proceedings and Property Act 1970.

Held – The court would not exercise its own jurisdiction in respect of matters already confided to the discretion of a local authority, even though that jurisdiction was conferred on it by statute. Accordingly the mother would not be granted the direction asked for in her summons, since it was in respect of a matter which was well within the discretion of the local authority by virtue of the order made under ss 62 and 76 of the 1933 Act (see p 804 b and c, post).

Re T (A J J) (an infant) [1970] 2 All ER 865, and *Re M (an infant)* [1961] 1 All ER 788 considered.

Notes

For the custody of and access to children in divorce proceedings, see 12 Halsbury's Laws (3rd Edn) 392-397, paras 868-880, and for cases on the subject, see 27 (2) Digest (Reissue) 738-742, 5780-5826.

For fit person orders, see 21 Halsbury's Laws (3rd Edn) 258, 259, para 558, and for reception of children into care by local authorities, see ibid, 275, 276, para 590.

For the Children and Young Persons Act 1933, ss 62, 76, see 17 Halsbury's Statutes (3rd Edn) 477, 486, and for the Matrimonial Proceedings and Property Act 1970, s 18 (1), see 40 ibid, 821.

Cases referred to in judgment

Hall v Hall [1963] 2 All ER 140, [1963] P 378, [1963] 2 WLR 1054, CA, Digest (Cont Vol A) 765, 4437b.

M (an infant), Re [1961] 1 All ER 788, [1961] Ch 328, [1961] 2 WLR 350, 125 JP 278, 59 LGR 146, CA, 28 (2) Digest (Reissue) 940, 2433.

T (A J J) (an infant), Re [1970] 2 All ER 865, [1970] Ch 688, [1970] 3 WLR 315, 134 JP 611, CA, 28 (2) Digest (Reissue) 913, 2239.

Summons

This was a summons taken out by the mother which, as amended, asked the court to *a*
direct that her infant son, who was in the care of the East Sussex County Council by
virtue of an order made by a juvenile court under ss 62 and 76 of the Children and
Young Persons Act 1933, should continue until further order to live with the foster
parents whom she had arranged to look after him, without the consent of the council.
The facts are set out in the judgment.   *b*

F P Shier for the mother.
Gilbert Rodway for the father.
T Ian Payne for the council.

c

WRANGHAM J. This case concerns the future of a little boy of 11, the son
of a former wife and husband, whose marriage was terminated by divorce in
1969. Before that, of course, the marriage had broken down; indeed, the parties
had separated, I think, as long ago as 1962. In that year the child was taken into care
by the East Sussex County Council under s 1 of the Children Act 1948. That order
was discharged in 1963. But on 10th June 1966 this child again came into the care of *d*
the East Sussex County Council, this time under an order of the magistrates' court
made under s 62 of the Children and Young Persons Act 1933, the East Sussex County
Council being nominated as a fit person under s 76 of that Act. The effect of ss 62
and 76 was to provide that the child was committed to the care of the council, and
the council was required by statute to undertake care of him as having been so
committed. The child has been looked after by the council in various ways since that *e*
time, until July 1971, when the mother of the child, with whom the child had been
staying under the direction, or with the permission, of the council, kept the child.
On 11th July his Honour Judge Beresford made an order, ex parte, that the child
should continued to live, or should go to live with the parents of the mother. That
has ultimately proved impracticable, and the child has for not very long been living
with foster parents found for him by his mother; in effect, foster parents on behalf *f*
of the mother.

The mother has in her summons applied for custody of the child. On that application there have appeared in opposition counsel on behalf of the father and counsel on
behalf of the council. On my suggestion, the summons of the mother has been
amended, because her summons for custody would appear by itself not adequately
to describe what it was she really wanted. Indeed, she still has, in common with *g*
the father, the custody of this child. They were by nature joint custodians of this
child and nobody has yet made any order depriving either of them of the custody
of the child, although, of course, the effect of the order under s 62 of the 1933 Act
was to suspend the right of either of them to care and control of the child. Accordingly, it seemed right that the mother should specify in her summons that which
she really wanted the court to order, and the summons was accordingly amended *h*
to ask for a direction that the child should live until further order at the home of
the foster parents who are at the moment caring for him.

Before the merits of this application could be considered at all, it seemed to me to
be necessary to investigate the position at law, because as the order under s 62 had
never been discharged or varied, the position was that the council were still under a
duty, a duty under s 76 of that Act, to undertake his care. Now, in *Re M (an infant)*[1] the *j*
Court of Appeal had to consider what the position was when a child whom the local
authority had taken into their care under s 1 of the Children Act 1948 was made a
ward of court. In that case it was argued that the jurisdiction of the court to deal

---

1 [1961] 1 All ER 788, [1961] Ch 328

a with children as wards, an inherent jurisdiction which is derived from the prerogative right of the Queen as parens patriae, was ousted or abrogated by reason of the duties imposed and the rights conferred on the local authority by s 2 of the Children Act 1948. Under s 2 of that Act the rights and liabilities of the parents are, of course, transferred to the local authority. The decision of the Court of Appeal was that the jurisdiction of the Chancery Court over a child as a ward was not ousted or abrogated *b* for all purposes by the existence of the jurisdiction conferred on the local authority by s 2 of the Children Act 1948. But, although the jurisdiction was not ousted, it was held that the judge exercising that jurisdiction ought not to exercise control over any duty or discretion which was vested clearly by statute in the local authority. In other words, although jurisdiction still existed, to a large extent it could only be exercised properly one way. There was, indeed, a limitation on that, namely, that if it *c* could be said that the local authority had not exercised a discretion at all, or refused to exercise a discretion, then the Chancery Court exercising the wardship jurisdiction would, no doubt, step in; but that was limited to cases in which the local authority had been shown to be acting in some way in breach or in disregard of its statutory duties. That limitation, it is conceded, does not apply in this case, because it cannot be said, and is not said, that this local authority, the East Sussex County Council, has *d* at any point acted in breach or in disregard of its statutory duties, although it would no doubt be sought to be contended on the merits of the matter that that discretion might rather more sensibly have been exercised in a different way.

The principles laid down in *Re M*[1] were applied to a case arising out of s 62 of the Children and Young Persons Act 1933, *Re T (A J J) (an infant)*[2]. It was there held in terms that the legislature had confided to the discretion of the administrative *e* body (that is the local authority) all decisions as to the custody, care and control of the child, and the Chancery Court would not, save in exceptional circumstances (that I understand to be a case where a local authority had disregarded its obligations in some way) intervene in the exercise of that discretion. In these respects, there was no difference between the case of a child committed to the care of a local authority under s 62, and that of a child in respect of whom a resolution had been passed by *f* the local authority under s 2 of the Children Act 1948. And the principles laid down in *Re M*[1] were duly applied. In those circumstances, it would appear that if I were being asked to exercise a wardship jurisdiction, there could be no question that this application would have failed on the ground that the matters to which it is directed are matters confided to the discretion of the local authority which can only properly be determined by them. And indeed, counsel for the mother candidly admitted *g* that at the very outset of his argument. But, he contended, the position is different where the judge is exercising not the inherent jurisdiction of wardship, but the statutory jurisdiction conferred on this court by the Matrimonial Proceedings and Property Act 1970, s 18 (1). He said: 'A statutory jurisdiction prevails over an inherent jurisdiction where the two are in any sense in conflict.' Now, had it been held in *Re M*[1] that the inherent jurisdiction ceased to exist at all in cases under s 2 *h* of the Children Act 1948 or had it been consequentially held in *Re T*[2] that the inherent jurisdiction ceased to exist at all in cases arising under s 62 of the 1933 Act, there would, I think, have been some plausibility in the argument of counsel for the mother, because it might be said that that which is enough to destroy altogether an inherent jurisdiction is not enough to destroy a jurisdiction founded on statute, and founded indeed on recent statute. But I think the fallacy of his argument is that there is no *j* conflict between the jurisdiction conferred on this court by the statute, namely, s 18 of the 1970 Act, and the discretion conferred on the local authority by s 62 of the

---

1 [1961] 1 All ER 788, [1961] Ch 328
2 [1970] 2 All ER 865, [1970] Ch 688

1933 Act. In referring to that section, I should in passing say that it has to some extent no doubt been replaced or affected by s 1 of the Children and Young Persons Act 1969, superseded perhaps by that, and affected in its previous operation by para 8 of Sch 4 to, and s 20 of, that Act. But whatever the result is of para 8 of Sch 4 to, and s 20 of, that Act, it is common ground that that does not affect the questions arising in this case.

The real position no doubt is that the statutory jurisdiction of this court continues, just as the inherent jurisdiction of the Chancery Court continued, in cases arising under s 62. But that jurisdiction, whether it be inherent or statutory, must be exercised so as not to be in conflict with the discretion expressly conferred on the local authority. That means, of course, that in any case covered by the discretion conferred on the local authority, this court will not exercise its own discretion, but will leave the matter to be decided by the local authority. It is plain that the direction for which the mother by her learned counsel now asks is a matter well within the discretion conferred on the local authority by ss 62 and 76 of the 1933 Act. It follows that it is a matter on which this court will not exercise an independent discretion at all, but will leave the matter to be determined by the local authority.

Counsel for the council, to whom as to counsel for the mother I am much indebted for their arguments, pointed out that in *Hall v Hall*[1] the existence of a concurrent jurisdiction over similar matters in the Chancery Division dealing with wardships, and what was then the Probate, Divorce and Admiralty Division dealing with matrimonial affairs, was recognised, and it was in effect left to the judges exercising the jurisdiction in each of those Divisions to exercise their discretion in cases which came before them, so as not to conflict with any orders made by the judges in the other Divisions. Secondly, it appeared from that case that there was no real distinction to be drawn between an inherent jurisdiction on the one side and the statutory jurisdiction on the other. In those circumstances it seems to me plain that it would be quite wrong for me to make the order for which the mother asks. That is a matter on which she should apply to the council, or make such application to put an end to the operation of the order under s 62, as she may be advised to do. The procedure for that has not been investigated here. But such procedure no doubt exists. For these reasons, I think it right, without investigating the merits of this case at all, to dismiss this application.

Application dismissed.

Solicitors: *Sampson & Co* (for the mother); *Wilkins, Rohan & Co* (for the father); *Sharpe, Pritchard & Co* (for the council).

Rengan Krishnan Esq   Barrister.

1   [1963] 2 All ER 140, [1963] P 378

R v Lowe

COURT OF APPEAL, CRIMINAL DIVISION
PHILLIMORE LJ, CUSACK AND MARS-JONES JJ
11th, 12th, 23rd JANUARY 1973

Criminal law – Manslaughter – Wilful neglect of child – Neglect causing death of child – Accused having failed to foresee consequences of neglect – Neglect deliberate in sense of not being inadvertent – Whether death of child automatically giving rise to charge of manslaughter.

Criminal law – Wilful neglect of child – Wilful – Neglect causing unnecessary suffering and injury to health of child – Accused failing to realise possible consequences of neglect – Neglect deliberate in sense of not being inadvertent – Whether neglect wilful – Children and Young Persons Act 1933, s 1 (1).

The appellant, a man of low intelligence, was alleged to have neglected his daughter, a baby of nine weeks old, by failing to call a doctor when she became ill. The child died some ten days later of dehydration and gross emaciation. The woman with whom the appellant had been living had four other children and was of subnormal intelligence. The appellant stated that he had told her to take the child to the doctor, but she had not done so because she was afraid that the child would be taken into care by the local authority. The appellant was charged with manslaughter (count 1) and cruelty by wilfully neglecting the child so as to cause her unnecessary suffering or injury to health, contrary to s 1 (1)[a] of the Children and Young Persons Act 1933 (count 2). The judge directed the jury that in order to constitute the offence charged on count 2 it was not necessary that the appellant should have foreseen the probable or possible result of his failure to call a doctor. He further directed them that, if they found the appellant guilty on count 2 and death had resulted from the neglect, they were bound, as a matter of law, to find him guilty of manslaughter on count 1 and it was not necessary to prove that the appellant had been reckless. The appellant was convicted on both counts and appealed.

Held – (i) The conviction for wilful neglect would be affirmed. It did not matter what the accused ought to have realised as the possible consequences of his failure to call a doctor; the sole question was whether his failure to do so was (a) deliberate and (b) the cause of the child's unnecessary suffering or injury to health (see p 807 j, post).

(ii) The conviction for manslaughter would be quashed. A clear distinction was to be drawn in relation to an act of commission and an act of omission; mere neglect, even though deliberate, which caused injury to a child's health and resulted in its death, did not necessarily constitute manslaughter where the accused had failed to foresee the consequences of his neglect (see p 809 c and d, post); dictum of Lord Atkin in *Andrews v Director of Public Prosecutions* [1937] 2 All ER at 555, 556 applied; *R v Senior* [1895-99] All ER Rep 511 not followed.

Notes

For neglect of children, see 10 Halsbury's Laws (3rd Edn) 760-762, paras 1470, 1471, for manslaughter of a child by neglect, see ibid 718-720, paras 1376, 1377, and for cases on the subject, see 15 Digest (Repl) 957-958, 9250-9279.

---

a Section 1 (1), so far as material, provides: 'If any person who has attained the age of sixteen years and has the custody, charge, or care of any child . . . under that age, wilfully . . . neglects . . . him, or causes . . . him to be . . . neglected . . . in a manner likely to cause him unnecessary suffering or injury to health . . . that person shall be guilty of [an offence] and shall be liable—(a) on conviction or indictment, to . . . imprisonment for any term not exceeding two years . . .'

For the Children and Young Persons Act 1933, s 1, see 17 Halsbury's Statutes (3rd   *a*
Edn) 438.

Cases referred to in judgment

Andrews v Director of Public Prosecutions [1937] 2 All ER 552, [1937] AC 576, 106 LJKB
 370, 101 JP 386, 26 Cr App Rep 34, sub nom *R v Andrews* 156 LT 464, 30 Cox CC
 576, HL, 45 Digest (Repl) 85, *281*.
R v Bateman (1925) 94 LJKB 791, [1925] All ER Rep 45, 133 LT 730, 89 JP 162, 28 Cox CC   *b*
 33, 19 Cr App Rep 8, CCA, 15 Digest (Repl) 966, *9369*.
R v Senior [1899] 1 QB 283, [1895-99] All ER Rep 511, 68 LJQB 175, 79 LT 562, 63 JP 8,
 19 Cox CC 219, CCR, 14 Digest (Repl) 55, *198*.

Cases and authority also cited

Buck v Buck [1965] 1 All ER 882, [1965] Ch 745, CA.   *c*
Director of Public Prosecutions v Smith [1960] 3 All ER 161, [1961] AC 290, HL.
Phillips v R [1969] 2 AC 130, [1969] 2 WLR 581.
R v Cascoe [1970] 2 All ER 833, CA.
R v Church [1965] 2 All ER 72, [1966] 1 QB 59, CCA.
R v Large [1939] 1 All ER 753, CCA.
R v Larkin [1943] 1 All ER 217, [1943] 1 KB 174, CCA.   *d*
R v Wallett [1968] 2 All ER 296, [1968] 2 QB 367, CA.
R v Watson [1962] Crim LR 783, CCA.
Archbold's Criminal Pleading, Evidence and Practice (37th Edn, 1969), pp 782, 783,
 868, paras 2498, 2739.

Appeal
On 25th July 1972 in the Crown Court at Nottingham before May J and a jury the   *e*
appellant, Robert Lowe, was convicted of manslaughter (count 1) and wilful neglect
of a child, contrary to s 1 (1) of the Children and Young Persons Act 1933 (count 2).
He was sentenced to five years' imprisonment on count 1, and to two years' imprisonment (the maximum) on count 2, the sentences to run concurrently. He appealed
against the convictions and sentences with leave of Browne J. His grounds of appeal   *f*
were as follows: on count 1 that the trial judge was wrong in law in directing the jury
that if they convicted the appellant of wilful neglect as charged in count 2 of the
indictment, they must also convict him of manslaughter on count 1 provided that
they, the jury, found that the death of the child had resulted from or was accelerated
by the wilful neglect; on count 2 that the trial judge had misdirected the jury on
the question what at law constituted 'wilful neglect'. The facts are set out in the
judgment of the court.   *g*

Ronald M Bell QC and *S E Herman* for the appellant.
R G Rougier QC and *T T Dineen* for the Crown.

                                                                          Cur adv vult

23rd January. **PHILLIMORE LJ** read the following judgment of the court.   *h*
Robert Lowe appeals against his convictions at Nottingham Crown Court on 25th
July 1972. He also appeals against the sentences imposed on him. He obtained leave
to appeal from the single judge both against convictions and sentences. As to the
convictions, he was convicted on count 2 of the indictment of cruelty to a child by
wilfully neglecting it so as to cause unnecessary suffering or injury to health contrary
to the provisions of s 1 (1) of the Children and Young Persons Act 1933. He was also   *j*
convicted on count 1 of manslaughter of the child on the grounds that his cruelty
alleged under count 2 caused its death. He was sentenced to two years' imprisonment
on count 2 and to five years' imprisonment on count 1.

   Two points have been argued in regard to the convictions, namely: (1) As to count 2
charging cruelty, do the words 'wilful neglect' in s 1 (1) of the Children and Young
Persons Act 1933 involve proof that the accused intended the consequences of his acts

or do they merely mean that the neglect must be deliberate as opposed to inadvertent? (2) Assuming a conviction on count 2 charging wilful neglect—if death results, is the person guilty of that neglect necessarily liable in manslaughter?

In regard to sentence it is argued that the sentence of two years on count 2, being the maximum sentence for that offence, was not warranted on the facts and that since the jury negatived reckless behaviour by the appellant as being the cause of death and made it clear that the conviction of manslaughter was solely due to the direction by the judge that if guilty on count 2 and death resulted a finding of manslaughter was an inevitable concomitant, five years was excessive for the same conduct that only carried a maximum of two years under the 1933 Act. It is convenient to take first the point under s 1 (1) of the Children and Young Persons Act 1933 on which count 2 was founded.

Counsel for the appellant, in a conspicuously able argument, submitted that in the light of s 8 of the Criminal Justice Act 1967 the test of wilful neglect by omission to call a doctor must be a subjective test, as indeed the judge accepted and that the question for the jury must involve the question of whether the appellant foresaw the probable or possible results of a failure to call a doctor. Did he foresee the likelihood of unnecessary suffering or injury to health? He submitted that there was no evidence to suggest that he foresaw the results of his omission. He complained that passages in the summing-up suggesting that the appellant ought to have foreseen such a result were in conflict with the words of s 8 which involve a subjective test. He emphasised the facts, namely that the appellant and Miss Marshall had been living together for several years and had had four previous children, only one of whom had been taken into care. This particular child was born on 28th August 1971 and was not apparently ill until about ten days before its death, which occurred early on the morning of Thursday, 4th November 1971.

The child was last seen by a social worker on 5th October, when it was observed that she was vomiting up her milk. According to the appellant he was not troubled about the state of the child until Saturday, 30th October, when he suggested that Miss Marshall should take it to the doctor—later that day she said she had done so, that the doctor had been out when she went to his surgery but that she had got some medicine. On the Monday he said that he had again urged her to take the child to the doctor and again later in the day she said that she had done so. After the child had been found dead from dehydration and gross emaciation on the Thursday morning Miss Marshall had said words indicating that she had been unwilling to risk disclosing its state of health lest it should be removed from her and taken into care as had happened with one of her previous children. Her intelligence was subnormal and the appellant's low average. Counsel for the appellant contended that the woman had done her best to deceive the appellant as to the state of health of the child.

Counsel for the Crown, in answer to this argument, contended that the section merely involved neglect which was deliberate as opposed to accidental or inadvertent. Any direction to the effect that the appellant must foresee the consequences of his neglect was unduly benevolent to him. It was only necessary to show that his failure had been intentional but not inadvertent. Section 8 only applied where a specific intent was in question. He also argued that there was ample material on which the jury could find that the neglect of the appellant, who was unemployed and living at home on social benefits, was deliberate as opposed to inadvertent.

We think that counsel for the Crown is right to the extent that the complaints of the summing-up and the references to what the appellant ought to have realised, were unduly benevolent to the appellant on count 2. It did not matter what he ought to have realised as the possible consequences of his failure to call a doctor—the sole question was whether his failure to do so was deliberate and thereby occasioned the results referred to in the section. We are quite satisfied that the conviction on count 2 was justified both on the law and the facts.

The trial judge, in a summing-up which was not conspicuous for its clarity, proceeded

to deal with the count of manslaughter. He left it to the jury to say whether they   *a*
thought that the appellant's conduct towards the child had been reckless and whether
its death had been caused thereby. Quite separately, however, he directed the jury
that if they found the appellant guilty of the second count they must, as a matter
of law, find him guilty of the first, namely of manslaughter. Having found him
guilty of the second count they also found him guilty of the first and made it clear
that they did so solely as a result of the direction by the trial judge; in other words,   *b*
they did *not* find the appellant guilty of reckless conduct resulting in the child's death.

Counsel for the Crown defends the direction given by the trial judge, namely that
if they found the appellant guilty on the second count the jury must as a matter of law
convict him of manslaughter on count 1, even though they acquitted him of conduct
which was reckless. He based his argument on the decision in *R v Senior*[1], a case where
a child had died following the failure of the father to call in a doctor in circumstances   *c*
where it was contrary to his religious beliefs so to do. In that case the court held that
there was evidence that the prisoner had wilfully neglected the child in a manner likely
to cause injury to its health and having thereby caused or accelerated its death he
was rightly convicted of manslaughter. It is to be observed that in a passage in his
judgment in *R v Senior*[2] Lord Russell of Killowen CJ interpreted the words 'wilful
neglect' in the manner contended for by counsel for the Crown in his argument on   *d*
count 2 and indeed in the manner which this court accepts.

Counsel for the appellant's answer is that the decision in *R v Senior*[1] cannot be regarded as good law in the light of the unanimous decision of the House of Lords in
Andrews v Director of Public Prosecutions[3]. True, that case involved motor manslaughter
as a result of neglect, but the speech of Lord Atkin is in the widest terms and is clearly
intended to apply to every case of manslaughter by neglect. In the course of citing   *e*
R v Bateman[4], Lord Atkin said[5], quoting Lord Hewart CJ[6]:

'In explaining to juries the test which they should apply to determine whether
the negligence, in the particular case, amounted or did not amount to a crime,
judges have used many epithets, such as "culpable," "criminal," "gross,"
"wicked," "clear," "complete." But, whatever epithet be used and whether an
epithet be used or not, in order to establish criminal liability the facts must be   *f*
such that, in the opinion of the jury, the negligence of the accused went beyond a
mere matter of compensation between subjects and showed such disregard for
the life and safety of others, as to amount to a crime against the State and conduct
deserving punishment.'

Lord Atkin then went on to say[7]:   *g*

'Here, again, I think, with respect, that the expressions used are not, indeed
they probably were not intended to be, a precise definition of the crime. I do
not myself find the connotations of *mens rea* helpful in distinguishing between
degrees of negligence, nor do the ideas of crime and punishment in themselves
carry a jury much further in deciding whether, in a particular case, the degree of
negligence shown is a crime, and deserves punishment. But the substance of   *h*
the judgment is most valuable, and, in my opinion, is correct. In practice, it has
generally been adopted by judges in charging juries in all cases of manslaughter
by negligence, whether in driving vehicles or otherwise. The principle to be
observed is that cases of manslaughter in driving motor cars are but instances of a

---

1 [1899] 1 QB 283, [1895-99] All ER Rep 511   *j*
2 [1899] 1 QB at 290, [1895-99] All ER Rep at 514
3 [1937] 2 All ER 552, [1937] AC 576
4 (1925) 94 LJKB 791, [1925] All ER Rep 45
5 [1937] 2 All ER at 555, 556, [1937] AC at 582, 583
6 In *R v Bateman* (1925) 94 LJKB at 793, 794, [1925] All ER Rep at 48
7 [1937] 2 All ER at 556, [1937] AC at 583

general rule applicable to all charges of homicide by negligence. Simple lack of care such as will constitute civil liability is not enough. For purposes of the criminal law there are degrees of negligence, and a very high degree of negligence is required to be proved before the felony is established. Probably of all the epithets that can be applied "reckless" most nearly covers the case.'

Now in the present case the jury negatived recklessness. How then can mere neglect albeit wilful amount to manslaughter?

This court feels that there is something inherently unattractive in a theory of constructive manslaughter. It seems strange that an omission which is wilful solely in the sense that it is not inadvertent, the consequences of which are not in fact foreseen by the person who is neglectful should, if death results, automatically give rise to an indeterminate sentence instead of the maximum of two years which would otherwise be the limit imposed.

We think there is a clear distinction between an act of omission and an act of commission likely to cause harm. Whatever may be the position in regard to the latter it does not follow that the same is true of the former. In other words if I strike a child in a manner likely to cause harm it is right that if the child dies I may be charged with manslaughter. If, however, I omit to do something with the result that it suffers injury to health which results in its death, we think that a charge of manslaughter should not be an inevitable consequence, even if the omission is deliberate.

In regard to sentence we have been troubled by the contrast in the sentences passed on the man and the woman. She was put on probation whereas he was sentenced to five years' and two years' imprisonment, yet she had set out deliberately to deceive him.

No doubt he was gravely to blame, but in all the circumstances we think that a sentence of 12 months should be substituted for the sentence of two years. We would, of course, quash the sentence of five years for manslaughter, the conviction on which we also quash.

Appeal allowed in part. Conviction on count 1 quashed. Conviction on count 2 to stand. Sentence varied. The court certified under s 33 (1) of the Criminal Appeal Act 1968 that a point of law of general public importance was involved, namely, whether the conviction of a person of wilfully neglecting a child, contrary to s 1 (1) of the Children and Young Persons Act 1933, necessarily involved a conviction of manslaughter if the child died as a result of that neglect, irrespective of negligence or the degree thereof, and granted the Crown leave to appeal to the House of Lords obtaining an assurance from counsel for the Crown that, whatever the decision of the House of Lords, he would not seek any increase in the sentence of one year's imprisonment.

Solicitors: *Berryman & Co*, Nottingham (for the appellant); *Director of Public Prosecutions.*

N P Metcalfe Esq   Barrister.

Chelmsford Auctions Ltd v Poole

COURT OF APPEAL, CIVIL DIVISION
LORD DENNING MR, KARMINSKI AND BUCKLEY LJJ
18th, 19th DECEMBER 1972

Auctioneer – Rights against purchaser – Action for price – Right to sue in own name – Purchaser having paid deposit – Deposit sufficient to cover auctioneer's commission – Auctioneer having paid balance of deposit and sum representing balance of purchase price to vendor – Whether auctioneer entitled to sue purchaser in own name for balance of purchase price.

The plaintiffs were motor car auctioneers. At an auction held at their premises in accordance with their printed conditions of sale, the defendant made a bid for a car; it was 'knocked down' to him at £57. The defendant paid £7 deposit on the car; the plaintiffs retained £3·50 of it for their commission and they paid the vendor the other £3·50 and the balance of the purchase price of the car out of their own money. When the defendant came to collect the car from the plaintiffs' premises five days later, he refused to accept it on the ground that it was not in a roadworthy condition. He never got the car. The plaintiffs brought an action against him for the balance of the purchase price. At the hearing the judge dismissed the action on a preliminary issue without hearing the merits, holding that, once the plaintiffs had received enough from the defendant by way of deposit to satisfy their own charges, their lien on the proceeds of sale had gone and they were not entitled to sue in their own name for the balance of the purchase price. On appeal,

Held – At common law a contract was implied between an auctioneer and a purchaser whereby the purchaser agreed to pay the price into the hands of the auctioneer. The auctioneer had a lien on the goods for the whole price until it had been paid. Accordingly, in the event of the purchaser's default, he was entitled to sue for the price in his own name even though he had received a deposit which covered his commission. Since the plaintiffs' conditions of sale proceeded on the basis of the common law, they were entitled to sue in their own name and the appeal would be allowed (see p 812 j to p 813 c and e and p 814 c to h, post).

Williams v Millington [1775-1802] All ER Rep 124, *Robinson v Rutter* (1855) 4 E & B 954 and dictum of Salter J in *Benton v Campbell, Parker & Co* [1925] All ER Rep at 189 applied.

Notes

For the auctioneer's right to maintain an action in his own name for price of goods sold, see 2 Halsbury's Laws (3rd Edn) 88, para 181, and for cases on the subject, see 3 Digest (Repl) 41-44, *293-314*.

Cases referred to in judgment

Benton v Campbell, Parker & Co [1925] 2 KB 410, [1925] All ER Rep 187, 94 LJKB 881, 134 LT 60, 89 JP 187, DC, 3 Digest (Repl) 48, *339*.
Coppin v Walker (1816) 7 Taunt 237, 2 Marsh 497, 129 ER 95, 3 Digest (Repl) 42, *304*.
Grice v Kenrick (1870) LR 5 QB 340, 39 LJQB 175, 22 LT 743, 3 Digest (Repl) 42, *306*.
Holmes v Tutton (1855) 5 E & B 65, 24 LJQB 346, 25 LTOS 177, 1 Jur NS 975, 3 CLR 1343, 119 ER 405, 3 Digest (Repl) 43, *312*.
Robinson v Rutter (1855) 4 E & B 954, 24 LJQB 250, 25 LTOS 127, 1 Jur NS 823, 3 CLR 1195, 119 ER 355, 3 Digest (Repl) 42, *305*.
Williams v Millington (1788) 1 Hy Bl 81, [1775-1802] All ER Rep 124, 126 ER 49, 3 Digest (Repl) 41, *293*.

Cases also cited

Freeman v Farrow (1886) 2 TLR 547.
Lupton v Potts [1969] 3 All ER 1083, [1969] 1 WLR 1749.
Manley & Sons Ltd v Berkett [1912] 2 KB 329.
Webb v Smith (1885) 30 Ch D 192, CA.
Wilson & Sons v Pike [1948] 2 All ER 267, [1949] 1 KB 176, CA.
Woolfe v Horne (1877) 2 QBD 355.

Interlocutory appeal

The plaintiffs, Chelmsford Auctions Ltd, brought an action in the Chelmsford County Court against the defendant, F Poole, claiming the value of goods bargained and sold. By their particulars of claim the plaintiffs alleged that at their vehicle auction held in the New Livestock Market, Chelmsford, on 15th September 1971, lot 280 was a Fiat car, registration no 281 ELE; that the defendant made a bid for the lot and it was 'knocked down' to him at £57; that the defendant signed the bid sheet and paid a deposit of £7 but failed to settle the bid; that the vehicle, being sold for less than £100, was 'sold as seen' under the plaintiffs' conditions of sale; that the plaintiffs had sent the vehicle log book to the defendant in error and the defendant had refused to return it to them; and the plaintiffs claimed £51 being the balance of the purchase price plus an indemnity fee of £1 less the deposit paid. By his defence the defendant claimed, inter alia, that the plaintiffs had no cause of action against him in that they were not the vendors but were acting on behalf of a disclosed principal and the loss, if any, had not been suffered by the plaintiffs.

At the trial of the action on 27th March 1972, his Honour Judge Corley raised a preliminary issue of his own motion and dismissed the plaintiffs' claim without hearing the merits, holding that, as the defendant had paid enough by way of deposit to cover the plaintiffs' commission of £3·50, he was entitled to assume that the £3·50 had been retained by the plaintiffs in satisfaction of their charges; that the plaintiffs' right to sue had gone if their lien on the proceeds of sale had gone; that the lien had gone because the plaintiffs' charges had been satisfied, and that the plaintiffs were not, therefore, entitled to sue for the price of the vehicle in their own name.

The plaintiffs appealed against that decision on the following grounds: (i) that the judge had misdirected himself in law in holding that an auctioneer's right to sue a purchaser in his own name determined as soon as the auctioneer had received payment from the purchaser of a sum sufficient to satisfy his commission; (ii) that the judge had misdirected himself in law in holding that the plaintiffs had a lien on the proceeds of sale and that such lien had been discharged when a sum sufficient to discharge their commission had been paid by the defendant but ought to have held that the lien of the plaintiffs attached to the property sold and had not been discharged at any material time; (iii) that the judge had misdirected himself in law in holding that the sum paid by the defendant to the plaintiffs amounted to a discharge of the plaintiffs' commission and therefore determined their right to sue in their own name for the price of the goods, but ought to have held that such sum was a part payment of the purchase price and an earnest by the defendant that he would pay the balance of the purchase price; (iv) that the judge had misdirected himself in law in holding that the plaintiffs had no right to sue the defendant in their own name and ought to have held that it was an express term of the contract between the plaintiffs and the defendant that the purchase price would be paid by the defendant direct to the plaintiffs and that the plaintiffs therefore had the right to sue the defendant in their own name.

J E A Samuels for the plaintiffs.
M D Beckman for the defendant.

LORD DENNING MR. On 15th September 1971 auctioneers called Chelmsford Auctions Ltd held an auction at Chelmsford for the sale of cars. They put up for sale a Fiat motor car. It was knocked down by the hammer to the highest bidder, Mr Poole. The price of the car was £57. There was an extra £1 as an idemnity fee. The total was £58. Mr Poole paid a deposit of £7 on the vehicle. The auctioneers retained £3·50 of it for their commission. They paid the vendor the other £3·50 and also £51 of their own money, thus making the £58 for the car. Mr Poole did not take delivery of the car or pay the balance of £51 which was owing. On 20th September 1971 he saw the car on the auctioneers' premises. He thought that it was not in a roadworthy condition. So he refused to accept it. He never got the vehicle or the log book or the keys. The auctioneers retained them.

On 2nd October 1971 the auctioneers sued Mr Poole in the Chelmsford County Court for the price of the car. The case was heard on 27th March 1972. A preliminary issue arose. It was suggested that the auctioneers were unable to sue in their own name because they had taken a deposit which covered their own commission; and that the only person who could sue was the true owner of the goods. This point was raised in para 8 of the defence, which said:

'. . . the Plaintiffs [that is the auctioneers] were not the Vendor but expressly acting on behalf of a disclosed principal, and the loss (if any) was not suffered by the Plaintiffs. In the premises the Defendant denies that the Plaintiffs have a cause of action against him.'

The case was heard at short notice. The lawyers at Chelmsford had not an opportunity to look up the books. The judge held that the auctioneers had no right to sue. He said:

'The plaintiffs' right to sue has gone if the auctioneers' lien on the proceeds of sale has gone. I hold that the auctioneers' lien on the proceeds of sale has gone because they [that is the charges] have been satisfied.'

The auctioneers appeal to this court.

It seems to me that the case depends largely on the conditions of sale which were exhibited on the premises, and which it was conceded, govern the transaction. But in order to understand those conditions, it is useful to set out the common law apart from conditions. On a sale by auction, there are three contracts. The first is the contract between the owner of the goods (the vendor) and the highest bidder to whom the goods are knocked down (the purchaser). That is a simple contract of sale to which the auctioneer is no party. That was made clear by Salter J in *Benton v Campbell, Parker & Co*[1]: 'To that contract [of sale] the auctioneer who sells a specific chattel as an agent, is in my opinion, no party.' The second is the contract between the owner of the goods (the vendor) and the auctioneer. The vendor entrusts the auctioneer with the possession of the goods for sale by auction. The understanding is that the auctioneer should not part with the possession of them to the purchaser except against payment of the price; or, if the auctioneer should part with them without receiving payment, he is responsible to the vendor for the price. As Lord Loughborough CJ said in *Williams v Millington*[2]:

'In the common course of auctions, there is no delivery without actual payment, if it is otherwise, the auctioneer gives credit to the vendee, entirely at his own risk.'

The auctioneer is given as against the vendor, a lien on the proceeds for his commission and charges. The third is the contract between the auctioneer and the highest bidder (the purchaser). The auctioneer has possession of the goods and he has a lien on them for the whole price. He is not bound to deliver the goods to the purchaser except on receiving the price in cash; or, if he is willing to accept a cheque, on receiving a

---

1   [1925] 2 KB 410 at 416, [1925] All ER Rep 187 at 189
2   (1788) 1 Hy Bl 81 at 85, [1775-1802] All ER Rep 124 at 125

a cheque payable to himself, the auctioneer, for the price.   If he does allow the purchaser to take delivery without paying the price—or if the purchaser gets delivery clandestinely or by a trick—the auctioneer can sue in his own name for the full price. That was established in 1788 in *Williams v Millington*[1].

If the purchaser, who has bid the highest, afterwards changes his mind and refuses to take delivery, the auctioneer can sue him for the whole price.   The reason is because:

b

'The auctioneer sues for the price by virtue of his special property and his lien, and also, in most cases, by virtue of his contract with the buyer, that the price shall be paid into his hands . . . '

(see *Benton v Campbell, Parker & Co*[2]).

c Under this third contract, the purchaser cannot avoid his liability to the auctioneer by paying the vendor direct without telling the auctioneer.   If he does so, the auctioneer can make the purchaser pay him the full price again, even though it means that the purchaser pays twice over: see *Robinson v Rutter*[3].   The only cases where the purchaser can avoid paying the auctioneer are those where he can pray in aid some equity against the auctioneer.   That happened in two cases where the auctioneer d had already received his commission, and the purchaser had a set-off against the vendor: see *Holmes v Tutton*[4], *Grice v Kenrick*[5], and in another case where the auctioneer has deceived the purchaser as to the ownership of the goods: see *Coppin v Walker*[6].

Turning now to the conditions of sale in this case, they seem to proceed on the basis of the common law that the auctioneer can sue in his own name for the price.   Take condition 5.   It can be divided into two parts.   The opening sentences deal with the e contract between the vendor and purchaser:

'A Contract of Sale shall be deemed to have been completed on the fall of the hammer between the person or persons signing the entry form in respect of the Vehicle concerned [that is the vendor] and the Purchaser thereof.   The Auctioneers shall not be a party to or liable in any way whatsoever on such f Contract.   The Vendor and the Purchaser shall have no legal rights of action except against each other in respect of any matter arising out of the sale or the legal ownership of the vehicle.   The name and address given by the Vendors will be furnished by the Auctioneers to the Purchasers on request and the Auctioneers shall be regarded as agents for a disclosed principal.'

g The later sentences of condition 5 cover all three of the common law contracts:

'Any person who makes a bid for any lot which is accepted by the Auctioneers agrees in consideration of the Auctioneers accepting his bid that the conditions contained herein shall govern his rights against and his liabilities to the Auctioneers and to the Vendor.   These conditions also govern the rights and liabilities of the Vendors to the Purchaser and the Auctioneers.   The Auctioneers h and their servants and agents shall not be liable for injury loss or damage however caused and whether caused by negligence or otherwise.'

The third of the common law contracts, that between the auctioneers and the purchasers, is elaborated in the opening words of condition 6:

'All Lots purchased shall be paid for in cash by the Purchaser to the Auctioneers j as Stakeholders on the day of sale before 5.30 p.m. and no Lot shall be removed

1   (1788) 1 Hy Bl 81, [1775-1802] All ER Rep 124
2   [1925] 2 KB at 416, [1925] All ER Rep at 189
3   (1855) 4 E & B 954
4   (1855) 5 E & B 65 at 82
5   (1870) LR 5 QB 340
6   (1816) 7 Taunt 237

until the total price is so paid. [I think the words "as Stakeholders" are inappropriate and should be rejected.] If the purchase price be not so paid, the Auctioneers may without notice to the Purchaser rescind the Contract of Sale on behalf
of the Vendor . . . The Auctioneers may at their discretion re-auction . . . and in
such case any deficiency . . . shall represent the damages attributable to the
Purchaser's breach of contract and *be forthwith recoverable by the Auctioneers
by action.*'

Then condition 6 goes on to deal with payment by cheque.   It says that if the cheque
is dishonoured—

'the Purchaser shall be deemed to have waived until the cheque is paid any
claim whatsoever against the Auctioneers or the Vendor without prejudice to
the *right of the Auctioneers* or the Vendor against the Purchaser or other party
to the cheque and *the rights of the Auctioneers* or the Vendor to *recover the* purchase
price.'

That condition clearly contemplates that the auctioneers can recover the purchase
price.

I need only mention condition 7, which provides for the purchaser to pay premium
for insurance in respect of title: 'The premium for this Insurance shall be paid *to the
Auctioneers* before the lot is removed . . .'

Those conditions fit in well with the common law. The auctioneer has a lien
on the goods for the whole price until the whole price is paid. If it is not paid, he
himself can sue in his own name for that price. He may have received a deposit
which covers his commission, but that does not debar him from suing for the balance
of the price in his own name.

The reason is because there is a contract implied by law, between the auctioneer
and the purchaser, whereby the purchaser has agreed to pay the price into the hands
of the auctioneers and he must honour that promise. I realise that condition 6 in
these conditions does say it is to be paid to the auctioneers 'as Stakeholders'. But I
do not think that is an accurate description. The auctioneers hold the money to
apply it in payment to the vendor, after satisfying their commission. The words
'as Stakeholder' are a *falsa demonstratio*. The fact remains that the purchaser has
agreed to pay the price to the auctioneers. If he does not pay, the auctioneers can
sue him for it. So I think the preliminary point taken by the defendant was not
right. I think the auctioneers are entitled to sue in their own names for the balance
of the price, and I would hold accordingly.

KARMINSKI LJ. I agree and have nothing to add.

BUCKLEY LJ. I also agree.

*Appeal allowed. Order of the county court judge set aside. Action remitted to the county
court for hearing on the merits.*

Solicitors: *Redmayne, Wyatt & Kershaw*, Chelmsford (for the plaintiffs); *G D Bishop
& Co*, Westcliff-on-Sea (for the defendant).

L J Kovats Esq Barrister.

a Attorney-General v Times Newspapers Ltd

COURT OF APPEAL, CIVIL DIVISION
LORD DENNING MR, PHILLIMORE AND SCARMAN LJJ
30th, 31st JANUARY, 1st, 2nd, 16th FEBRUARY 1973

b

Contempt of court – Publications concerning legal proceedings – Pending proceedings – Litigation actively in suit before the court – Public interest in fair comment on issues raised by litigation – Issues raised by litigation of national concern – Writs issued but proceedings dormant for several years – No evidence that parties intending to bring proceedings to trial – Children injured by drug – Claims against drug manufacturer – Newspaper wishing to publish article concerning drug manufacturer – Article critical of delay in settling claims and accusing drug manufacturer of not facing up to responsibilities.

Contempt of court – Publications concerning legal proceedings – Pending proceedings – Discussion in Parliament – Practice of Parliament in relation to proceedings sub judice – Rules applied by court in contempt proceedings – Desirable that rules should correspond to practice of Parliament.

In 1958 Distillers, a drug company, started to manufacture and market a drug known as thalidomide which was intended as a sedative for pregnant mothers. By 1961, when the drug was taken off the market, over 451 babies had been born with gross deformities in consequence of their mothers taking the drug. Parents of 62 of those babies brought actions against Distillers within the three year limitation period. In February 1968 those actions were settled. Meanwhile parents of a further 266 got leave to issue writs out of time; a further 123 did not issue writs at all. At the time of the 1968 settlement Distillers recognised that they had a moral responsibility to the remaining 389 children and announced that they would provide a substantial sum. Distillers, however, made it a condition that all the parents should accept it. A minority refused to do so. Thereafter negotiations continued but no agreement was reached. No steps were taken however to bring any of the actions against Distillers to trial. By 1972 the editor of the Sunday Times had become increasingly concerned about the long delay in providing compensation for the children, who were by then ten or more years old. He had investigations made and launched a campaign against Distillers. On 24th September 1972 the paper published an article headed 'Our Thalidomide Children: A Cause for National Shame'. Distillers complained to the Attorney-General suggesting that the article was in contempt of court. The Attorney-General asked the Sunday Times for their observations. The editor replied justifying the publication and in addition sent the Attorney-General a draft of a further article which he proposed to publish. It contained a detailed analysis of the evidence against Distillers, suggesting that they had not measured up to their responsibilities; it also summarised the arguments that could be made for Distillers. A copy of the article was also sent to Distillers. On 12th October the Attorney-General issued a writ claiming an injunction restraining the defendants, the proprietors of the Sunday Times, from publishing the article on the ground that it constituted contempt of court. On 17th November the Divisional Court[a] granted an injunction and the defendants appealed. On 29th November a debate took place in the House of Commons on the plight of the thalidomide children, in which speeches were made alleging that Distillers were gravely at fault and had not faced up to their moral responsibilities. Those speeches were widely reported in the newspapers. The debate was followed by much comment, some very critical of Distillers. The hearing of the appeal against the order of the Divisional Court

---

a [1972] 3 All ER 1136

began in January 1973. Distillers instructed counsel, with a watching brief, who
was allowed to address the court. He alleged that there were serious errors in the   *a*
article but did not provide any further information on the state of the litigation or of
the negotiations for a settlement.

Held – The appeal would be allowed and the injunction removed for the following
reasons—

(i) When litigation was pending and actively in suit before the court, it would   *b*
constitute contempt of court for anyone to comment on it in such a way that there
was a real and substantial danger of prejudice to the trial of the action, or to the settlement of it, e g by influencing the judge, the jurors or the witnesses, or by prejudicing
mankind in general against a party to the cause. The interests of the parties were,
however, to be weighed against the public interest; where the issues raised by the
litigation were of national concern, public comment on those issues was permissible   *c*
provided that it was fair and based on an accurate statement of the facts. Such comment would not amount to contempt unless there was real and substantial prejudice
to pending litigation which was actively in suit before the court (see p 821 f, p 822 a b
and d to f, p 825 e and p 827 a f and g, post); *Re Truth and Sportsman Ltd, ex parte Bread
Manufacturers* (1937) 37 SRNSW 242 and *Ex parte Dawson, Re Australian Consolidated
Press Ltd* [1961] SRNSW 573 applied.   *d*

(ii) The publication of the article by the Sunday Times would not amount to contempt; the case was so unique that public interest in discussion of the matters which
it raised outweighed the prejudice which might thereby be occasioned to Distillers.
The article contained comments which the Sunday Times honestly believed to be
true, and it did not prejudice pending litigation because the litigation between the
parents and Distillers had been dormant for several years and there was no evidence   *e*
that either party wished or intended to bring it before the court. Insofar as the
article sought to bring pressure to bear on Distillers to settle for more than they
would otherwise have paid, that pressure was, in the light of all that had happened,
legitimate (see p 822 j, p 823 j to p 824 a, p 825 e and j and p 827 a and g, post).

(iii) Furthermore it was desirable that the rules applied by the courts in relation to
proceedings for contempt should correspond to the practice adopted by Parliament   *f*
in relation to the discussion of matters sub judice, since matters discussed in Parliament could be reported at large in the newspapers. In view of the debate which had
taken place in the House of Commons it was evident that the Commons accepted
that the sub judice rule did not apply in relation to the actions against Distillers, so
as to forbid discussion. In the light of the newspaper comment which had followed
the debate it would be unfair discrimination to prohibit the defendants by injunction   *g*
from publishing their article (see p 823 b to d and f to h, p 826 b c and j and p 828 d
and e, post).

Per Lord Denning MR and Phillimore LJ. In a civil action the Attorney-General
should not bring proceedings for contempt except in a quite unusual situation when
he thinks he should do so in the public interest. Normally the complainant should
be left to take proceedings himself at his own expense and risk as to costs (see p 820 e   *h*
and h to p 821 a and p 824 g, post); dictum of Lord Goddard CJ in *R v Hargreaves,
ex parte Dill* (1953) The Times, 4th November, explained.

Decision of the Divisional Court of the Queen's Bench Division [1972] 3 All ER
1136 reversed.

Notes

For contempt of court in relation to pending proceedings, see 8 Halsbury's Laws   *j*
(3rd Edn) 7-10, paras 11, 12, and for cases on the subject, see 16 Digest (Repl) 6, 7, *1-9,*
25-28, 180-336.

Cases referred to in judgments

Bradlaugh v Gossett (1884) 12 QBD 271, 53 LJQB 209, 50 LT 620, 36 Digest (Repl) 394,
415.

a   *Dawson, Ex parte, Re Australian Consolidated Press Ltd* [1961] SRNSW 573.

Dingle v Associated Newspapers Ltd [1960] 1 All ER 294, [1960] 2 QB 405, [1960] 2 WLR 430; on appeal [1961] 1 All ER 897, [1961] 2 QB 162, [1961] 2 WLR 523, CA; *affd* sub nom *Associated Newspapers Ltd v Dingle* [1962] 2 All ER 737, [1964] AC 371, [1962] 3 WLR 229, HL, Digest (Cont Vol A) 1223, *415a*.

O'Shea v O'Shea and Parnell (1890) 15 PD 59, 59 LJP 47, 62 LT 713, 17 Cox CC 107, CA,

b   16 Digest (Repl) 8, *11*.

R v Hargreaves, ex parte Dill [1954] Crim LR 54, (1953) The Times, 4th November, DC.

St James's Evening Post Case, The, Roach v Garvan (or Hall) (1742) 2 Atk 469, 26 ER 683, Dick 794, 16 Digest (Repl) 6, *1*.

Skipworth's Case (1873) LR 9 QB 230, 28 LT 227; sub nom *R v Skipworth, R v De Castro* 12 Cox CC 371, DC, 16 Digest (Repl) 23, *171*.

c   *Taylor's Application, Re* [1972] 2 All ER 873, [1972] 2 QB 369, [1972] 2 WLR 1337, CA.

Tichborne v Mostyn, Tichborne v Tichborne (1867) LR 7 Eq 55, 17 LT 5, 16 Digest (Repl) 32, *268*.

Tichborne v Tichborne (1870) 39 LJCh 398, 22 LT 55, 16 Digest (Repl) 29, *216*.

Truth and Sportsman Ltd, Re, ex parte Bread Manufacturers (1937) 37 SRNSW 242, 54

d   NSWNN 98, 9 Digest (Repl) 75, **98*.

Vine Products Ltd v Mackenzie & Co Ltd (or Green or Daily Telegraph) [1965] 3 All ER 58, [1966] 1 Ch 484, [1965] 3 WLR 791, Digest (Cont Vol B) 206, *275a*.

William Thomas Shipping Co Ltd, Re, H W Dillon & Sons Ltd v The Company, Re Sir Robert Thomas [1930] 2 Ch 368, 99 LJCh 560, 144 LT 104, 16 Digest (Repl) 31, *251*.

e   **Cases also cited**

Alliance Perpetual Building Society v Belrum Investments Ltd [1957] 1 All ER 635, [1957] 1 WLR 720.

Attorney-General v London Weekend Television Ltd [1972] 3 All ER 1146, [1973] 1 WLR 202, DC.

Cheltenham & Swansea Railway Carriage & Wagon Co, Re (1869) LR 8 Eq 580.

f   *Church of Scientology of California v Burrell* (30th July 1970) unreported.

Coats (J & P) v Chadwick [1894] 1 Ch 347.

Crown Bank, Re, Re O'Malley (1890) 44 Ch D 649.

Daw v Eley (1868) LR 7 Eq 49.

Hubbard v Vosper [1972] 1 All ER 1023, [1972] 2 QB 84, CA.

Hunt v Clarke (1889) 58 LJQB 490, CA.

g   *Ilkley Local Board v Lister* (1895) 11 TLR 176.

Kitcat v Sharp (1882) 52 LJCh 134.

S v Distillers Co (Biochemicals) Ltd, J v Distillers Co (Biochemicals) Ltd [1969] 3 All ER 1412, [1970] 1 WLR 114.

South Shields (Thames Street) Clearance Order 1931, Re (1932) 173 LT Jo 76, DC.

h   *Thomson v Times Newspapers Ltd* [1969] 3 All ER 648, [1969] 1 WLR 1236, CA.

Webster v Bakewell Rural District Council [1916] 1 Ch 300.

Wood v Georgia (1962) 370 US 375.

Appeal

j   On 12th October 1972 the Attorney-General as plaintiff issued a writ against the defendants, Times Newspapers Ltd, the publishers of the Sunday Times newspaper, claiming an injunction to restrain the defendants by themselves, their servants or agents or otherwise from publishing or causing or authorising to be published or printed an article dealing, inter alia, with the development, distribution and use of the drug thalidomide, a copy of which article had been supplied to the Attorney-General by the defendants. The action was brought by the Attorney-General following a

complaint by Distillers Co (Biochemicals) Ltd ('Distillers'), the distributors of thalidomide. By a summons also dated 12th October 1972 the Attorney-General applied to   *a*
the judge in chambers for an interim injunction restraining the defendants from
publishing or causing or authorising the publication or printing of the article until
the trial of the action or further order. By consent of the parties on 20th October
1972 the matter was ordered to be transferred to the Divisional Court of the Queen's
Bench Division. By consent the hearing of the application was treated as the trial   *b*
of the action. By its judgment dated 17th November 1972 and reported at [1972]
3 All ER 1136, the Divisional Court granted an injunction in the terms claimed until
further order. The defendants appealed.

Brian Neill QC and *Edward Adeane* for the defendants.
The Attorney-General (Sir Peter Rawlinson QC), Gordon Slynn and *N D Bratza* for the   *c*
  plaintiff.
John Wilmers QC, D D H Sullivan and *Marcus Edwards* held watching briefs on behalf
  of Distillers.

Cur adv vult

16th February. The following judgments were read.   *d*

LORD DENNING MR.

Introduction

Nearly 12 years ago an overwhelming tragedy befell hundreds of families in this
country. Mothers when pregnant had taken thalidomide as a sedative to help   *e*
them rest. All believed it was safe. The manufacturers had proclaimed it to be
so. The doctors had accepted their assurances. But, unknown to anyone, if a
pregnant woman took it between the fourth and twelfth weeks it would affect the
limbs of the foetus in the womb. In consequence some 451 babies were born
deformed. Some without arms or legs. Others with gross distortions.
Some of the parents were advised to bring actions for damages against Distillers   *f*
(Biochemicals) Ltd who marketed the drug. They had three years allowed by the
Statute of Limitations in which to bring their actions. Only 62 of them did. In
February 1968 a settlement was reached under which £1 million was paid to those 62.
Distillers, no doubt, thought that was the end of their legal liabilities; because, after
the expiry of three years, the claims of the remaining 389 would normally be statute-
barred. Distillers must have realised, however, that they were not altogether clear   *g*
of liability. A few parents, after the expiry of the three years, had got leave to bring
actions out of time. These were still pending in February 1968 when the 62 actions
were settled. And more perhaps might follow. Eventually 266 got leave to issue
writs out of time; but another 123 did not issue writs at all. That makes a total of
389 not provided for by the settlement. At any rate, Distillers, at the time of the
settlement, recognised that they had a moral responsibility to those remaining 389   *h*
children who did not benefit from the settlement. So in February 1968 they
announced that they would provide a substantial sum for the benefit of the other
children. To honour that pledge they later proposed to form a charitable trust
and to pay to trustees a sum of £3,250,000 for the benefit of all the malformed
children.
But this proposal failed to win acceptance, because Distillers insisted that all parents   *j*
must agree to it. The great majority of the parents did agree to it. Many were
hesitant, but agreed because they thought it was the best they could get. But five
did not agree. They stood out. The majority tried to get the five to agree, but
they would not. Much pressure was brought to bear on them. One of the majority
actually brought proceedings to get the parents of the five removed as next friends,

a and to be replaced by the Official Solicitor, knowing that he would agree to the
settlement. The court refused to remove the parents of the five. We gave our
decision on 12th April 1972. It is reported as *Re Taylor's Application*[1]. It was the
turning point in the whole matter.

The editor of the Sunday Times tells us that the report of that case caused him
great anxiety. Over ten years had passed since the children were born with these
b deformities, and still no compensation had been paid by Distillers. He determined
to investigate the matter in depth and to do all he could, through his newspaper,
to persuade Distillers to take a fresh look at their moral responsibilities to all the
thalidomide children, both those where writs had been issued and those where they
had not. He had investigations made and launched a campaign against Distillers.

On 24th September 1972 the Sunday Times published an article headed 'OUR
THALIDOMIDE CHILDREN: A CAUSE FOR NATIONAL SHAME'. It drew attention to the
c long drawn-out legal proceedings, and said:

> 'It seeems clear that in the new term lawyers acting for Distillers Biochemicals,
> who made thalidomide, will appear with lawyers acting for the children, to seek
> court approval for a settlement which has been worked out in private over the
> past few months. Unhappily, the settlement is one which is grotesquely out of
d > proportion to the appalling injuries the thalidomide children suffered. Essenti-
> ally, the offer is that Distillers set up a trust for the children and their families,
> worth some £3·25 million. This is not a large sum in the context of Distillers'
> commercial operations (a little less than 10 per cent. of last year's after-tax
> profits, a little more than 1 per cent. of the money made in the ten years since
> thalidomide).'

e As soon as that article was published, Distillers made a formal complaint to the
Attorney-General suggesting that it was a contempt of court. On 27th September
1972 the Attorney-General asked the Sunday Times for their observations. On
28th September 1972 the editor replied justifying the publication of the article. In
addition he sent to the Attorney-General the draft of another article which he pro-
f posed to publish. It is the very one which is in question in these proceedings. It has
not yet been published. But we have seen it. It contains a detailed analysis of the
evidence against Distillers. It marshals forcibly the arguments for saying that
Distillers did not measure up to their responsibility. Although, to be fair, it does
summarise the arguments which could be made for Distillers. The editor realised
that this article—with its detailed analysis—was in a different category from the
g article of 24th September 1972. So he wrote this letter to the Attorney-General:

> 'I should be very grateful for any observations you may have upon it. You
> may take it that we are entirely satisfied with its factual accuracy in every respect
> but it is our intention to give the representatives of the parties the opportunity
> of commenting thereon before making a decision as to whether to publish it.'

h On 10th October the Sunday Times delivered a copy of the draft article to Distillers;
and invited their comments or objections. Distillers replied that the matter was
receiving consideration, but they did no more. On 12th October the Attorney-
General issued a writ against the Sunday Times claiming an injunction to restrain
them from publishing the draft article. This step was welcomed by the Sunday
Times as being 'both sensible and constructive'. So it seemed at the time, because
j it would enable the Sunday Times to see where they stood. But, as things have
turned out, I think it was a pity.

The motion of the Attorney-General

The application is made by the Attorney-General, and not by Distillers. I should
have thought myself that it should have been made by Distillers. After all, it is

---

1 [1972] 2 All ER 873, [1972] 2 QB 369

that company which will be prejudiced by the publication of the proposed article. *a*
It is their litigation which may be affected by it. Yet we have no affidavit from
Distillers telling us of the prejudice to them or of the pressures on them by reason
of the article. We have little knowledge of the state of the litigation or of the negotiations for a settlement. Before us Distillers instructed leading counsel with a watching
brief. We allowed him to address us. He pointed out the serious errors which, he
said, were contained in the proposed article. But he did not add to our knowledge *b*
of the state of the litigation or of the negotiations for a settlement.

The Attorney-General explained why he had himself made the application. It
was because of *R v Hargreaves, ex parte Dill*[1]. A man was charged with conspiracy.
A magazine contained an article about it. The man moved for a writ of attachment
against the editor. Lord Goddard CJ said:

'I have said on more than one occasion that it would be a good thing if such *c*
motions were made on the application of the Attorney-General . . . Such motions
should only be made by the law officers . . .'

Those remarks were made in regard to criminal cases. But they were interpreted
as extending to civil cases in the Queen's Bench Division. In 1959 a committee
presided over by Lord Shawcross recommended that no proceedings for such con- *d*
tempt 'should be instituted except by or with the consent of the Attorney-General':
see the Report by Justice on Contempt of Court[2]. Accordingly, since that time it
has become the practice for the Attorney-General himself to institute proceedings.
That is the reason, no doubt, why he did it in the present case.

I must say that I think the time has come to revert to the previous practice in regard
to civil proceedings. In the civil courts the practice for well over two centuries was *e*
for the party to the action himself to make the application. He moved the court
to commit the newspaper for contempt. That was done in every case that I can
discover. The notice of motion was entitled in the cause in regard to which the
contempt had arisen, and it was made to the court in which the cause was proceeding
That is to say, to the Chancery Division, the Queen's Bench or the Divorce Court, as
the case might be. Thus in the divorce suit to which Mr Parnell was a party, the *f*
application was made by the petitioner Captain O'Shea against the newspaper and
was entitled in the suit of *O'Shea v O'Shea and Parnell*[3], and in the civil proceedings
brought by the claimant in the *Tichborne* suit the application was made by the
claimant himself against the newspapers and was entitled in the cause: see *Tichborne
v Mostyn*[4] and *Tichborne v Tichborne*[5]. But when words were spoken to the prejudice
of the proceedings in the criminal proceedings, the application was made by the *g*
prosecution: see *Skipworth's Case*[6].

This is as it should be. When a man is on trial in a criminal court, the Crown
itself is a party. It is concerned itself to ensure the fairness of the trial. It is only
right and proper that the Attorney-General should take the responsibility of proceeding for contempt of court. But a civil action is different. The Attorney-General
will, as a rule, have no knowledge of the course of a civil action—or of any interference *h*
with it—unless it is brought to his knowledge by one of the parties to it. If the
Attorney-General then himself takes proceedings for contempt, it means that he is
putting the authority of the Crown behind the complaint. No doubt he can do so
if he thinks it proper to do so. But I venture to suggest that he should not do so

j

1 (1953) The Times, 4th November, [1954] Crim LR 54
2 (1959) p 34
3 (1890) 15 PD 59
4 (1867) LR 7 Eq 55
5 (1870) 39 LJCh 398
6 (1873) LR 9 QB 230

a except in a plain case. When the case is open to controversy or to argument, it would be better to follow the previous practice. The complainant should be left to take proceedings himself at his own expense and risk as to costs.

The pending actions

b What do we know about the pending actions? We are told that since the 62 actions were settled in February 1968, 266 writs have been issued against Distillers. The parents must have got leave ex parte from a judge to bring these actions. I expect that they made affidavits saying that they did not know they had a worthwhile cause of action until February 1968. They had to issue their writs within 12 months of getting to know. So I expect these 266 writs were issued in 1968. But we have been told very little of what has happened to those 266 actions. In one case there was a statement of claim and a defence was delivered in March 1969; but nothing more has happened. In many of the cases, by agreement, pleadings have not been served. All that has happened is that the writs have been issued and served; appearances have been entered, but nothing more done in the actions. So far as the courts are concerned, these 266 actions have gone soundly to sleep and have been asleep for these last three or four years. No one has awakened them. I think I can see why. Both *d* sides have been hoping for a settlement. We do not know the dates on which the writs were issued, nor when they were served. The plaintiffs have not pressed forward in the courts because of the difficulties in surmounting the Statute of Limitations, and the enormous expense involved in a contest. Distillers have not applied to strike out the actions because they, too, are anxious for a settlement and shudder at the prospect of a fight. So the litigation remained dormant. So far as *e* appears, it was still dormant in April 1972 when we heard *Re Taylor's Application*[1]. So far as we know, it was still dormant when the Sunday Times started in September 1972 publishing its articles on the thalidomide children. It is still dormant today.

The law

f It is undoubted law that, when litigation is pending and actively in suit before the court, no one shall comment on it in such a way that there is a real and substantial danger of prejudice to the trial of the action, as for instance by influencing the judge, the jurors, or the witnesses, or even by prejudicing mankind in general against a party to the cause. That appears from the case before Lord Hardwicke in 1742, *The St James's Evening Post Case*[2], and by many other cases to which the Attorney-General drew our attention. Even if the person making the comment honestly believes it to *g* be true, still it is a contempt of court if he prejudges the truth before it is ascertained in the proceedings: see *Skipworth's Case*[3] per Blackburn J. To that rule about a fair trial, there is this further rule about bringing pressure to bear on a party, none shall, by misrepresentation or otherwise, bring unfair pressure to bear on one of the parties to a cause so as to force him to drop his complaint, or to give up his defence, or to come to a settlement on terms which he would not otherwise have been pre-*h* pared to entertain. That appears from *Re William Thomas Shipping Co Ltd*[4] and *Vine Products Ltd v Mackenzie & Co Ltd*[5], to which I would add an article by Professor Goodhart[6].

I regard it as of the first importance that the law which I have just stated should be maintained in its full integrity. We must not allow 'trial by newspaper' or 'trial by

j
1 [1972] 2 All ER 873, [1972] 2 QB 369
2 (1742) 2 Atk 469
3 (1873) LR 9 QB at 234
4 [1930] 2 Ch 368
5 [1965] 3 All ER 58, [1966] 1 Ch 484
6 (1935) 48 Harvard Law Review 895, 896

television' or trial by any medium other than the courts of law. But, in so stating the
law, I would emphasise that it applies only 'when litigation is pending and is actively
in suit before the court'. To which I would add that there must appear to be 'a real
and substantial danger of prejudice' to the trial of the case or to the settlement of it.
And when considering the question, it must always be remembered that, besides the
interest of the parties in a fair trial or a fair settlement of the case, there is another
important interest to be considered. It is the interest of the public in matters of
national concern, and the freedom of the Press to make fair comment on such matters.
The one interest must be balanced against the other. There may be cases where the
subject-matter is such that the public interest counter-balances the private interest
of the parties. In such cases the public interest prevails. Fair comment is to be allowed.
It has been so stated in Australia in regard to the courts of law: see *Re Truth and Sportsman Ltd, ex parte Bread Manufacturers*[1] and *Ex parte Dawson, Re Australian Consolidated
Press Ltd*[2]. It was so recommended by a committee presided over by Lord Salmon
in regard to tribunals of inquiry[3]. Take this present case. Here we have a matter
of the greatest public interest. The thalidomide children are the living reminders of
a national tragedy. There has been no public enquiry how it came about. Such
enquiry as there has been, has been done in confidence in the course of private litigation between the parties. The compensation offered is believed by many to be too
small. Nearly 12 years have passed and still no settlement has been reached. On such
a matter the law can and does authorise the newspapers to make fair comment.
So long as they get their facts right, and keep their comments fair, they are without
reproach. They do not offend against the law as to contempt of court unless there is
real and substantial prejudice to pending litigation which is actively in suit before the
court. Our law of contempt does not prevent comment before the litigation is started,
nor after it has ended. Nor does it prevent it when the litigation is dormant and is
not being actively pursued. If the pending action is one which, as a matter of public
interest, ought to have been brought to trial long ago, or ought to have been settled
long ago, the newspapers can fairly comment on the failure to bring it to trial or to
reach a settlement. No person can stop comment by serving a writ and letting it lie
idle; nor can he stop it by entering an appearance and doing nothing more. It is
active litigation which is protected by the law of contempt, not the absence of it.

Apply these considerations to the present case. Take the first 62 actions which were
settled in February 1968. The newspapers can fairly comment on those settlements,
saying that in making them Distillers did not measure up to their moral responsibilities. Take the last 123 children in regard to whom writs have never been issued.
The newspapers can fairly press for compensation on the ground that Distillers were
morally responsible. That leaves only the 266 actions in which writs were issued four
years ago but have never been brought to trial. Does the existence of those writs
prevent the newspapers from drawing attention to the moral responsibilities of
Distillers? If they can comment on the first 62 or the last 123, I do not see why they
cannot comment on these intervening 266. There is no way of distinguishing between
them. The draft article comments on all the thalidomide children together. It is
clearly lawful in respect of the first 62 and the last 123. So also it should be in respect
of the middle 266.

I have said enough to show that this case is unique. So much so that in my opinion
the public interest in having it discussed outweighs the prejudice which might thereby
be occasioned to a party to the dispute. At any rate, the High Court of Parliament has
allowed it to be discussed. So why should not we in these courts also permit it?
There is no possible reason why Parliament should permit it and we refuse it.

1 (1937) 37 SRNSW 242
2 [1961] SRNSW 573
3 Report of the Interdepartmental Committee on the Law of Contempt as it Affects
   Tribunals of Inquiry (1969), Cmnd 4078, para 26

The proceedings in the House of Commons

a   On 29th November 1972 there was a debate in the House of Commons on the thalidomide children. As the Attorney-General reminded us, we must be careful in speaking of it. The Bill of Rights says: ' . . . the freedom of speech and debates or proceedings in Parliament ought not to be impeached or questioned in any court or place out of Parliament.' It is plain that Parliament has the exclusive right to regulate its own proceedings. What is said or done within the walls of Parliament cannot be

b   enquired into in a court of law: see *Bradlaugh v Gossett*[1] and *Dingle v Associated Newspapers Ltd*[2].

Nevertheless, I hope I may say this without giving offence. It is desirable that the convention of Parliament as to matters sub judice should, so far as possible, be the same as the law administered in the courts. The object of each is the same—to prevent prejudice to pending litigation and the parties to it—and the rules for achieving it

c   should be the same, and for this very good reason: as soon as matters are discussed in Parliament, they can be, and are, reported at large in the newspapers. The publication in the newspapers is protected by the law. Whatever comments are made in Parliament, they can be repeated in the newspapers without any fear of an action for libel or proceedings for contempt of court. If it is no contempt for a newspaper to

d   publish the comments made in Parliament, it should be no contempt to publish the self-same comments made outside Parliament.

Take this very case. On 29th November 1972 speeches were made in Parliament and reported in the newspapers in which Distillers were said to be gravely at fault and had not faced up to their moral responsibility. If the reports of those speeches were not a contempt of court, nor should the self-same matter be a contempt when published in the form of an article.

e   In view of the debate which took place in Parliament, I feel sure that all present on that occasion must have accepted that the sub judice rule did not apply so as to forbid discussion. The reason was, no doubt, because none of these actions had been set down for trial or otherwise brought before the court. All that had happened was that writs had been issued in 266 out of 389 cases, and nothing more done. It did not appear that there was a real and substantial danger or prejudice to the trial of the

f   cases. So the discussion was allowed to take place.

If we in this court apply rules as to sub judice which are on the same lines as Parliament, we shall not go far wrong.

The subsequent events

After the debate in Parliament, there was a spate of comment of all kinds. Some for

g   Distillers. Others against them. In the Daily Mail of 8th December 1972 there was an article which was very critical of Distillers—on much the same lines as the article which the Sunday Times proposed to publish. No steps have been taken against the Daily Mail. Seeing that all those comments have been let through without any steps being taken by anyone to stop them, it is plain to my mind that this injunction against

h   the Sunday Times cannot stand. The proposed article is in the same category as all these others. It would be discrimination of the worst kind if the Sunday Times was the only paper to be stopped by injunction. But I would not rest my decision on this ground alone. I go back to last September, when the Sunday Times submitted the article to the Attorney-General. Even at that time I think its publication would not amount to a contempt of court. The reason is because it dealt with a matter of the greatest public interest and contained comments which the newspaper honestly

j   believed to be true. It drew attention to the moral responsibilities of Distillers for all the 451 children, and not merely the 266 who had issued writs. It did not prejudice pending litigation because that litigation was dormant—and had been dormant for

1   (1884) 12 QBD 271
2   [1960] 1 All ER 294, [1960] 2 QB 405

years. No doubt the article was intended to bring pressure to bear on Distillers to *a* increase their offer—but that pressure was legitimate in the light of all that had happened. It would be open to Distillers to reply to it. If they had submitted their reply to the Sunday Times, I should expect it to have received equal publicity. But, all in all, it was a matter which warranted debate, not only in Parliament, but also in the Press. I would not restrict it.

I would only add this. Fair comment is one thing. Unfair comment or unfair *b* pressure is another. However good the cause—and however much the sympathy for the children—no one should resort to unfair tactics to force a settlement when they do not know—and cannot know—the rights and wrongs of the dispute. But this article, as I see it, does not come into that category. It exerts pressure, but legitimate pressure. I would, therefore, allow the appeal and discharge the injunction.

c

PHILLIMORE LJ.   The Divisional Court[1] granted an injunction on the ground that if the article prepared by the Sunday Times was published there was a serious risk that unfair pressure would be put on Distillers to settle litigation or to settle on terms to which they would not otherwise have agreed. Questions such as whether pressure is unfair or whether there is a serious risk obviously involve important questions of fact. *d*

If only because questions of fact are involved, I am troubled by the procedure which has been followed. The motion for an injunction was moved by the Attorney-General, who cannot know much about the facts. Moreover, there is no affidavit by any member of Distillers dealing with the facts. In such circumstances ought the court to speculate on what the facts may be and in particular whether any pressure put on Distillers is unfair. *e*

In 1954 in *R v Hargreaves, ex parte Dill*[2] Lord Goddard CJ said in terms that if there was any question of moving for attachment the motion should be moved by the Attorney-General. Now, of course, in a criminal case, where the issue is between the Crown and a subject, there is obvious sense in an intervention by the Attorney-General, although I should have thought that if he refused to intervene, it should be open to the subject to move the court himself. In fact, the case in which Lord Goddard *f* CJ made that observation involved an article commenting on a criminal case, and was no authority for intervention by the Attorney-General in a civil case.

In a civil case, when the facts and issues are all important, why should the Attorney-General move? In the ordinary way it should be for the party who considers its interests affected to move the court. The Attorney-General should only move in some quite unusual situation when he thinks he should do so in the public interest. *g*

What do we know about the facts? We have been told that Distillers started to manufacture and market the drug in 1958. The results were soon apparent and by the winter of 1961, when the drug was withdrawn, over 400 thalidomide children had been born in this country. It is unnecessary to detail their deformities; counsel has said that this was a national tragedy. I do not think that that is any exaggeration.

Some 62 parents started actions against Distillers. After lengthy negotiations these *h* were settled in February 1968 on the basis that Distillers would pay 40 per cent of the full sum which each case would have attracted in damages if liability was established. These sums have been paid and anyone is now free to comment on those proceedings and their outcome.

We were told that since then something like 260 other actions have been started. It is not clear whether any of these have proceeded beyond the stage of a writ issued *j* pursuant to leave granted ex parte, save that it is said that in one case pleadings have been delivered. We do not know whether any of these actions, other than perhaps the one mentioned, is effective and can be brought to court.

1   [1972] 3 All ER 1136, [1972] 3 WLR 855
2   (1953) The Times, 4th November, [1954] Crim LR 54

a   We were told that there are something like 120 further claims which have been put forward in correspondence but no writs having been issued; they would appear to be hopelessly statute barred. Anyone is, of course, free to comment on these cases, since they are in no sense sub judice.

As I said during the argument, I have no doubt that all this so-called litigation is somewhat unreal. No parent dares to bring one of these cases to trial for fear of losing, whilst Distillers are most unwilling to fight one of these cases lest they lose, when,
b   quite apart from the moral obloquy, the damages might well be enormous. In a sense we are dealing with something akin to shadow boxing dressed up as litigation.

What then of the serious risk or the unfair pressure? I do not think that any party intends to bring any case into court—there is no evidence to the contrary—any more than there is any evidence as to what additional pressure this article would apply to Distillers if it were published.
c   Of course, the article—worded with skill—is in effect saying to Distillers: you may or may not have some technical defence in law, but for the following detailed reasons you cannot deny that you were negligent. Here are these children now getting to the ages of 10 and 11, and their claims—to which there is no moral answer—are still unsettled. Why—if this article exerts pressure—is it unfair? Here is a national tragedy which has lingered on for years. Whether Distillers were negligent or not (and they
d   have not sworn they were not) they sold this drug with these terrible results.

I do not question that if a party to a genuine lawsuit is subjected to unfair pressure to force him to settle or to settle on terms on which he would not otherwise agree, there would be a contempt of court. But this problem is unique—we are talking of claims many of which have never been the subject of proceedings—we are dealing with a matter of great public interest—a national tragedy. I am not satisfied on the
e   material before the court that there was any serious risk of this article compelling Distillers to settle or settle for more than they would otherwise have paid or that if any pressure would have been applied by it that that pressure was unfair. As I have said, they have not attempted to indicate in evidence what the effect of the article would have been.

Looking at the history of all this, a number of parents who must have been dis-
f   traught and overwhelmed with worry have had to bring their claims against this powerful corporation. Apart from concern for their child or children, they have had the worry of being unable to plan for the future. On the other hand, Distillers have been able to sit back and wait while pressure on the parents has mounted until it may force them to agree to the terms Distillers have offered. How is pressure on this corporation unfair? In my opinion these claims ought to have been settled years ago
g   and on generous terms.

I am, of course, very conscious of the mass of authority put before us by the Attorney-General showing that an attempt to stir up public feeling against a party is a serious contempt. In the ordinary case I would accept these authorities as binding, but, as I have said, this is no ordinary case. This litigation is dormant and has been now for several years. Both sides have displayed a masterly inactivity in its pursuit. Neither
h   wishes to bring one of these claims into court. Delay exerts pressure on the parents rather than on Distillers. The whole problem is inevitably of public interest and rightly so. Is no one ever to be free to comment on such matters as the delay, the size of Distillers' offer or the question of their legal and moral responsibility? If it is true that Distillers are putting pressure on the parents, is no one to be permitted to say so and to give reasons for suggesting that pressure should be put on Distillers?
i   If in any single case I was satisfied that there was a real intention to bring the matter to court, I would not for a moment countenance an article designed to prejudice the public against a party or to put pressure on that party so as to force a settlement. But this as I see it is not that sort of situation at all. In the absence of evidence that this is or that these are normal lawsuits and that the parties are prepared to bring ordered an injunction against the publication of this article.

However, since the judgment of the Divisional Court[1] on 17th November 1972, matters have not stood still. The House of Commons debated the whole subject on 29th November, and since then articles and comment have appeared in the newspapers, some in favour of Distillers and some against, including two articles in the Daily Mail which in effect reproduced the article prepared for the Sunday Times and banned by the order of the Divisional Court[1]. The Attorney-General has not moved the court in respect of any of these articles, and it is obviously quite unreal in this situation to continue the injunction. I would accordingly discharge it.

I desire to add a word or two in regard to the debate in the House of Commons since it was this debate that precipitated the flood of articles and has made the order of the Divisional Court[1] impossible to maintain. I am, of course, well aware that it is not for us to criticise in any way the conduct of a debate in the House of Commons. Article 9 of the Bill of Rights forbids me to do so; and in any event, for the reasons I have already given, I cannot see that these claims ought in all the circumstances to be regarded as sub judice, and accordingly I see no possible objection to the debate.

It seems to me, however, that it is important that the sub judice rules applied in the House of Parliament and in the courts should be broadly in line. In fact, the House of Commons sub judice rules would seem to have been more restrictive of comment than those applied by the courts. Thus the Select Committee appointed to consider and make recommendations on matters sub judice in its report dated 5th March 1963 recommended[2]:

'Matters awaiting or under adjudication in a civil court should not be referred to in any motion or debate on a motion or in any Parliamentary Question, including any supplementary question, from the time that the case has been set down for trial or otherwise brought before the court, as for example by notice of motion for an injunction: such matters may be referred to before such date unless it appears to the Chair that there is a real and substantial danger of prejudice to the trial of the case.'

The report continued[3]:

'In using the word "prejudice" your Committee intend the word to cover possible effect on the members of the Court, the jury, the witnesses and the parties to any action.'

Reading the evidence of the Speaker given to the committee, it is to be observed that he had in mind the possible effects of comment when one party had made a payment into court. The comment might destroy all hope of settlement.

These recommendations seem to me to be quite admirable. The limitation of all comment after a case has been set down for trial is eminently sensible. It goes beyond the rule of the courts which would apply the test of 'real and substantial degree of prejudice' to a comment made even after that stage—a stage when there is every indication that the parties intend to bring their dispute before the court, but this is right. Anything said in Parliament is liable to be widely reported and therefore it is all the more important to be careful as to what may be said.

In short, however, as it seems to me, no one could seriously suggest that the debate transgressed the recommendations of the Select Committee; and to attempt to maintain this injunction in the face of what has been said in Parliament would not merely be an idle exercise, but would mean that the courts were seeking to impose a standard at variance with that imposed by Parliament. I should regard such a situation as deplorable.

For these reasons I would allow this appeal and discharge the injunction ordered by the Divisional Court.

---

1 [1972] 3 All ER 1136, [1972] 3 WLR 855
2 See para 10 of the First Report from the Select Committee on Procedure: The Rule relating to reference in the House of Commons to matters considered as sub judice
3 See ibid, para 11

a **SCARMAN LJ.** In my opinion, this injunction should be discharged. I have had an opportunity of reading the judgment of Lord Denning MR. Since I agree with it, I propose to add only a very few comments of my own limited to the pending actions and to the relationship between the courts and Parliament.

The pending actions

b Distillers withdrew the thalidomide drug from the market in 1961, when evidence was coming forward of terrible deformities suffered by children whose mothers had taken the drug during pregnancy. Some 60 writs were issued on behalf of children who, it was claimed, had been born deformed because of the drug. By 1968 their cases were settled. But public apprehension continued to mount; in particular many thought the settlement was grossly inadequate.

c In the same year, encouraged no doubt by the public agitation, the parents of other grievously deformed children issued writs against Distillers. By the time the Attorney-General applied for this injunction, 266 writs had been issued and some 120 further claims notified. This court knows very little about the litigation thus begun, but two features are startlingly clear: each writ is out of time unless it can be brought within some exception allowed by the Limitation Acts; and each case, if fought, will have to meet formidable difficulties of proof. The reality of the situation, therefore, is that d no one expects a trial; the writs were issued as moves towards a settlement. And it is obvious from what we were told in the course of the appeal that an overall settlement is very likely in the reasonably near future.

If the writs had not been issued, nothing could have prevented publication of the proposed article. Speech is free subject to the safeguards of the law of libel and slan-e der; and, if an editor (as in this case) is prepared to justify, no injunction will issue to stop him publishing. The defamed person's remedy is only in damages after the event, if in fact the published matter turns out to be untrue.

Does the issue of these writs make such a difference? Does a writ put a stop to comment that could otherwise be made with freedom? It all depends. It is not the writ that matters but the situation that develops thereafter; and in any event the f issue of a writ cannot stifle all comment, but only some in certain circumstances.

Contempt is an interference with the course of justice. It is necessary, therefore, to prove that the course of justice is being actively pursued. A writ is the formal act which begins a civil action. But not every writ is followed by further legal proceedings; very often a writ is no more than a step in a tactical manoeuvre designed to help towards a settlement. Since there is in this case no evidence of any litigation g actively in suit, it is being unrealistic to treat this article as constituting a real or substantial danger of prejudice to the course of justice; which, as Lord Denning MR has shown, is, when considered in conjunction with the public interest in freedom of speech, the test for contempt. Further, these writs are only a minor feature in a situation which deeply disturbs the nation, and in which the public have a very great interest in freedom of discussion. I believe a valuable approach to the problem of h contempt of court when the issues raised are of great public moment is to be found in a passage from the judgment of Owen J in *Ex parte Dawson, Re Australian Consolidated Press Ltd*[1]; the learned judge said:

'. . . if in the course of the ventilation of a question of public concern matter is published which may prejudice a party in the conduct of a law suit, it does not follow that a contempt has been committed.'

j And then, a little later:

'The discussion of public affairs . . . cannot be required to be suspended merely because the discussion . . . may, as an incidental but not intended by-product,

---

1 [1961] SRNSW 573 at 575, quoting Jordan CJ in *Re Truth and Sportsman Ltd, ex parte Bread Manufacturers Ltd* (1937) 37 SRNSW 242 at 249

cause some likelihood of prejudice to a person who happens at the time to be a litigant.'

Parliament

'...the freedom of speech and debates or proceedings in Parliament ought not to be impeached or questioned in any court or place out of Parliament.'

So declares art 9 of the Bill of Rights. Parliament has an absolute right to forbid publication of its proceedings. But when, as at present, Parliament publishes its proceedings and puts an official report on sale to the public, it is the duty of the court in an appropriate case to inform itself of what goes on within Parliament. The present is an appropriate case. On 29th November, 12 days after the judgment of the Divisional Court[1], the House of Commons debated a motion drawing attention to the plight of the thalidomide children. It is clear that the House was not inhibited from discussing the sort of questions that the Sunday Times would raise in the article, if published. It is also clear that the Commons took the view that their debate did not transgress their own sub judice rule. The courts, subject only to the legislative power of Parliament, determine what constitutes contempt of court and have a discretion as to remedy and punishment. Nevertheless, a serious and, perhaps, dangerous situation could arise if the practice of the courts differed substantially from that of Parliament. On the view of the law taken by Lord Denning MR, which I share, such a situation is unlikely to arise. It is, I suggest, the duty of the courts, in an area which enjoys the attention of both Parliament and the courts, and where discretion is a major element in the process of decision, to note the practice of the two Houses of Parliament and to act in harmony with it, so far as the law allows. For myself, even if I had thought the Divisional Court to have come to a correct decision on 17th November, the state of public discussion following the Commons debate is such that I would have thought it right to discharge the injunction in the exercise of the court's discretion.

Appeal allowed: injunction removed. Leave to appeal to the House of Lords refused.

1st March 1973. The appeal committee of the House of Lords gave leave to appeal.

Solicitors: *J Evans* (for the defendants); *Treasury Solicitor; Wilkinson, Kimbers & Staddon* (for Distillers).

L J Kovats Esq   Barrister.

---

1   [1972] 3 All ER 1136, [1972] 3 WLR 855

Wachtel v Wachtel

COURT OF APPEAL, CIVIL DIVISION

LORD DENNING MR, PHILLIMORE AND ROSKILL LJJ

29th, 30th NOVEMBER, 1st DECEMBER 1972, 8th FEBRUARY 1973

Divorce – Financial provision – Matters to be considered by court when making order – Family assets – Assets comprising capital assets and parties' earning power – Reallocation of family assets so as to do broad justice between parties – Starting point of reallocation one-third of capital assets and one-third of earnings – Circumstances in which 'one-third rule' not applicable – Prospect of remarriage – Relevance – Matrimonial Proceedings and Property Act 1970, ss 2-5.

Divorce – Financial provision – Conduct of parties – Duty of court to have regard to conduct – Circumstances in which regard to be had to conduct – Conduct obvious and gross – Conduct only affecting award of financial provision where obvious and gross – Court not required to conduct a lengthy post mortem in order to establish respective guilt of parties – Matrimonial Proceedings and Property Act 1970, s 5 (1).

Divorce – Financial provision – Contributions by each of parties to welfare of family – Duty of court to have regard to contributions in making provision – Contribution by wife – Wife looking after home and family but not going out to work – Wife contributing to family assets – Wife entitled to share of assets on breakdown of marriage – Matrimonial Proceedings and Property Act 1970, s 5 (1) (f).

Divorce – Financial provision – Lump sum payment – Lump sum provision to be considered in every case – No order for lump sum where insufficient assets – Lump sum payment should be ordered where sufficient assets – Payment to be outright except where there are children and a settlement may be desirable – Transfer of matrimonial home – Effect on lump sum payment – Matrimonial Proceedings and Property Act 1970, s 5 (1) (c).

The following principles should be applied when granting ancillary relief pursuant to the powers conferred by ss 2-5 of the Matrimonial Proceedings and Property Act 1970:

(i) *Conduct of the parties.* Divorce on the ground of irretrievable breakdown of the marriage pursuant to the 1969 Act is a misfortune befalling both parties; no longer is one party to be regarded as guilty and the other party as innocent. Although s 5 (1)[a] of the 1970 Act requires the court to have regard to the conduct of the parties,

---

[a] Section 5 (1) provides: 'It shall be the duty of the court in deciding whether to exercise its powers under section 2 or 4 of this Act in relation to a party to the marriage and, if so, in what manner, to have regard to all the circumstances of the case including the following matters, that is to say—(a) the income, earning capacity, property and other financial resources which each of the parties to the marriage has or is likely to have in the foreseeable future; (b) the financial needs, obligations and responsibilities which each of the parties to the marriage has or is likely to have in the foreseeable future; (c) the standard of living enjoyed by the family before the breakdown of the marriage; (d) the age of each party to the marriage and the duration of the marriage; (e) any physical or mental disability of either of the parties to the marriage; (f) the contributions made by each of the parties to the welfare of the family, including any contribution made by looking after the home or caring for the family; (g) in the case of proceedings for divorce or nullity of marriage, the value to either of the parties to the marriage of any benefit (for example, a pension) which, by reason of the dissolution or annulment of the marriage, that party will lose the chance of acquiring; and so to exercise those powers as to place the parties, so far as it is practicable and, having regard to their conduct, just to do so, in the financial position in which they would have been if the marriage had not broken down and each had properly discharged his or her financial obligations and responsibilities towards the other.'

this does not mean that the judge in chambers must hold a lengthy post mortem into the marriage to find out what killed it; in most cases both parties have contri- *a* buted to the breakdown. Therefore, except in the residue of cases where the conduct of one party has been so obvious and gross that it is repugnant to justice to order the other party to give financial support, the court should not reduce its order for financial provision merely because of what was formerly regarded as guilt or blame (see p 835 e g and j to p 836 b, post).

   (ii) *Family assets.* The phrase 'family assets' refers to things acquired by one or *b* other or both parties with the intention that they should be continuing provision for them and their children during their joint lives and used for the benefit of the family as a whole. Family assets include (a) capital assets, such as the matrimonial home and the furniture in it, and (b) revenue-producing assets, such as the earning power of husband and wife. When the marriage ends the family assets have to be reallocated. Section 5 (1) (*f*) of the 1970 Act recognises that a wife who has looked after the *c* home and family for many years is entitled to a share in the matrimonial home if the court concludes that the home has been acquired and maintained by the joint efforts of both husband and wife. Accordingly the wife will usually be entitled to a share of the capital assets as well as a share of the earnings (by way of periodical pay- ments for herself and maintenance for the children). In calculating the share in the family assets to which the wife is entitled, the fairest way is to start with one-third of *d* the capital assets and one-third of the parties' joint earnings. That is only a starting point, however, and not a rule; it will serve in cases where the marriage has lasted for many years and the wife has been in the home bringing up the children; it may not be applicable where the marriage has lasted only a short time or where there are no children and the wife can go out to work (see p 836 c and d, p 838 j to p 839 a and p 840 b to d, post). *e*

   (iii) *Lump sum provision.* In every case the court should consider whether to order a lump sum to be paid by the husband to the wife under s 2 (1) (*c*)[b] of the 1970 Act, but no such order should be made unless the husband has capital assets out of which to pay a lump sum without crippling his earning power. When he has available assets sufficient for the purpose the court should not hesitate to order him to pay a lump sum; the payment should be outright and not subject to conditions except *f* where there are children, when it may be desirable to make it the subject of a settle- ment. Where the matrimonial home is the principal or only capital asset, and where the wife has left the home and the husband remains in it, the house should be vested in the husband absolutely, free of any share in the wife, the husband alone being responsible for the payment of mortgage instalments; the wife should be com- pensated for the loss of her share in the house by the award of a lump sum sufficient *g* to enable her to acquire her own home; that sum should be such as the husband can raise by a further mortgage on the matrimonial home. Conversely, if the husband leaves the matrimonial home and the wife remains, and is likely to be there indefinitely, the house should be vested in the wife absolutely free of any share in the husband; or if there are children it should be settled on the wife and children; provision should be made for the husband to pay or to guarantee the mortgage *h* instalments; if this is done, there may be no necessity for a lump sum payment as well, and the periodical payments will be less than they would otherwise be (see p 840 e and g to p 841 c, post).

   (iv) *Remarriage.* The prospect of the wife's remarriage should not reduce her share in the capital assets. Periodical payments should be assessed without regard to the prospects of remarriage but if the wife in fact remarries they will cease, and if *j*

---

b   Section 2 (1), so far as material, provides: 'On granting a decree of divorce . . . (whether . . . before or after the decree is made absolute), the court may . . . make . . . (*c*) an order that either party to the marriage shall pay to the other such lump sum or sums as may be [specified in the order].'

a she goes to live with another man without marrying him, they may be reviewed (see p 841 d and f, post).

The husband and wife were married in 1954. They had one son and one daughter. At first they lived in a flat, pooling their earnings to get the flat and furniture and to keep it going. In 1956 the matrimonial home was purchased in the husband's name. The purchase price was £5,000; it was paid by means of a 100 per cent mortgage, *b* the husband paying the mortgage instalments. The wife continued working until 1958 when the son was born. Thereafter she stayed at home looking after the children; she also helped the husband, who was a dentist, in his practice as a receptionist and with clerical work. The marriage broke down in March 1972. The wife left the matrimonial home, but the husband continued to live there. In July 1972 the marriage was dissolved, cross-decrees being granted to each party under s 2 (1) (*b*) *c* of the Divorce Reform Act 1969. The parties arranged that the son should stay with the husband; he was at boarding school at his grandfather's expense but the husband had to provide a home for him and to clothe and maintain him in the holidays; the daughter, who was aged 11 and attended a day-school, was to be with the wife. The current market value of the matrimonial home was £22,000 or more; the outstanding mortgage on it was £2,000. The husband's earning capacity was *d* not less than £6,000 per annum and the wife had a potential earning capacity as a dental nurse of £750 per annum. They were both aged 46; the wife's remarriage was thus a possibility although not an imminent probability. For 18 years she had contributed to the matrimonial home by looking after the home and the family and helping her husband, and had been an excellent mother. The wife applied under ss 2 and 3 of the Matrimonial Proceedings and Property Act 1970 for periodical pay- *e* ments for herself and the daughter, secured provision and a lump sum or sums, and, under s 4 of the 1970 Act for a settlement, transfer of property or variation of settlement order. The judge, having found that responsibility for the breakdown of the marriage rested equally on both parties, determined that the only capital asset, the matrimonial home, should be divided approximately equally between the parties and he ordered the husband to pay the wife a lump sum of £10,000 or half the net *f* value of the house, if sold, whichever was the less. He further ordered, on the basis that the husband's gross earning capacity was £4,000 to £5,000, that the husband should make periodical payments to the wife of £1,500 per annum less tax, and should pay a further £500 per annum less tax to the wife in respect of the daughter. The husband appealed.

g **Held** – The appeal would be allowed and the order varied. Looking at the situation broadly, the following provisions met the justice of the case: the order for periodical payments to the wife of £1,500 should stand on the basis that the husband's earning capacity was £6,000 per annum; one-third of the parties' joint earnings, i e £6,750, gave the figure of £2,250; from that figure the wife's earning capacity of £750 per annum should be deducted resulting in a figure of £1,500 per annum; on the basis *h* that the order for periodical payments of £1,500 per annum stood, the proper lump sum, taking everything into account that the 1970 Act required, was £6,000, i e nearly one-third of the value of the matrimonial home; the wife should have that sum free of any trust or other terms; £500 per annum was too high a figure for the daughter's maintenance and it would be reduced to £300 per annum. There was no reason for making any reduction in the wife's financial provision on the ground that *i* the wife had been equally responsible with the husband for the breakdown of their marriage (see p 841 j to p 842 a and f to p 843 a, post).

Per Curiam. For the purpose of interpreting statutory provisions regard may be had to reports of the Law Commission to show the mischief which Parliament intended to remedy (see p 838 h, post).

Decision of Ormrod J p 113, ante, varied.

Notes

For financial provision on granting a decree of divorce and the matters to be con-　*a*
sidered by the court in exercising its powers, see Supplement to 12 Halsbury's Laws
(3rd Edn) para 987A, 1-4.

　For the Matrimonial Proceedings and Property Act 1970, ss 2-5, see 40 Halsbury's
Statutes (3rd Edn) 800-804.

b

Cases referred to in judgment

Ackerman v Ackerman [1972] 2 All ER 420, [1972] Fam 225, [1972] 2 WLR 1253, CA;
　varying [1971] 3 All ER 721, [1972] Fam 1, [1971] 3 WLR 725.
Balfour v Balfour [1919] 2 KB 571, [1918-19] All ER Rep 800, 88 LJKB 1054, 121 LT 346,
　CA, 27 (1) Digest (Reissue) 237, *1738*.
Buckley v John Allen & Ford (Oxford) Ltd [1967] 1 All ER 539, [1967] 2 QB 637, [1967]　*c*
　2 WLR 759, Digest (Cont Vol C) 754, *1194h*.
Goodburn v Thomas Cotton Ltd [1968] 1 All ER 518, [1968] 1 QB 845, [1968] 2 WLR 229,
　CA, Digest (Cont Vol C) 754, *1194ca*.
Hazell v Hazell [1972] 1 All ER 923, [1972] 1 WLR 301, CA.
Kershaw v Kershaw [1964] 3 All ER 635, [1966] P 13, [1964] 3 WLR 1143, 128 JP 589, DC,
　27 (2) Digest (Reissue) 974, *7829*.　　　　　　　　　　　　　　　　　　　　　　*d*
Pettitt v Pettitt [1969] 2 All ER 385, [1970] AC 777, [1969] 2 WLR 966, 20 P & CR 991,
　HL, 27 (1) Digest (Reissue) 102, *707*.
Porter v Porter [1969] 3 All ER 640, [1969] 1 WLR 1155, CA, 27 (2) Digest (Reissue)
　823, *6594*.
Rogers' Question, Re [1948] 1 All ER 328, 205 LT Jo 118, CA, 27 (1) Digest (Reissue)
　308, *2294*.　　　　　　　　　　　　　　　　　　　　　　　　　　　　　　　　*e*

Cases also cited

Brett v Brett [1969] 1 All ER 1007, [1969] 1 WLR 487, CA.
Curtis v Curtis [1969] 2 All ER 207, [1969] 1 WLR 422, CA.
Davis v Davis [1967] 1 All ER 123, [1967] P 185, CA.
Dean v Dean [1923] P 172.　　　　　　　　　　　　　　　　　　　　　　　　　　　*f*
Duchesne v Duchesne [1950] 2 All ER 784, [1951] P 101.
Gilbey v Gilbey [1927] P 197, [1927] All ER Rep 662.
Hakluytt v Hakluytt [1968] 2 All ER 868, [1968] 1 WLR 1145, CA.
Iverson v Iverson [1966] 1 All ER 258, [1967] P 134.
Jones v Jones [1971] 3 All ER 1201, CA.
N v N [1928] All ER Rep 462, 44 TLR 324.　　　　　　　　　　　　　　　　　　　　*g*
Powys v Powys [1971] 3 All ER 116, [1971] P 340.
Roberts v Roberts [1968] 3 All ER 479, [1970] P 1, DC.
Schlesinger v Schlesinger [1960] 1 All ER 721, [1960] P 191.
Stibbe v Stibbe [1931] P 105, CA.
Trestain v Trestain [1950] 1 All ER 618, [1950] P 198, CA.
Von Mehren v Von Mehren [1970] 1 All ER 153, [1970] 1 WLR 56, CA.　　　　　　　　*h*
Wood v Wood [1891] P 272, [1891-94] All ER Rep 506, CA.

Appeal

By a petition dated 18th April 1972 the husband sought the dissolution of his marriage
and by her answer dated 9th May 1972 the wife cross-petitioned for a decree.　On　*j*
21st July 1972 Ormrod J granted each party a decree nisi. By an order dated 3rd
October 1972 and reported at p 113, ante, Ormrod J ordered the husband to
pay the wife (i) a lump sum of £10,000 or half the net value of the matrimonial
home, whichever was the less; (ii) periodical payments at the rate of £1,500 per
annum less tax, and (iii) a further £500 per annum less tax in respect of the daughter

a of the marriage. The husband appealed against that order and the wife cross-appealed contending that a lump sum payment of £10,000 or half the net value of the house, whichever was the greater, should have been ordered. The facts are set out in the judgment of the court.

A B Ewbank QC for the husband.

b *Roger Gray QC* and *E S Cazalet* for the wife.

Cur adv vult

8th February. **LORD DENNING MR** read the following judgment of the court. Mr and Mrs Wachtel were married on 9th January 1954. They were both then 28 years of age. They have two children, a son now aged 14 and a girl of 11.
c The husband is a dentist in good practice. On 31st March 1972 the wife left the home. On 21st July 1972 there was a divorce on the ground that the marriage had irretrievably broken down. In consequence many things have to be settled. The parties have made arrangements for the children. The son is with the father. He is a boarder at Epsom College, where his fees are paid by his grandfather. The daughter is with the mother. She goes to day-school. There remain the financial conse-
d quences. The parties have not agreed on them. So they have to be settled by the courts.

On 3rd October 1972 Ormrod J ordered the husband to pay to his wife (i) a lump sum of £10,000, or half the value of the former matrimonial home in Norwood, South London, whichever be the less; (ii) a periodical payment of £1,500 per annum, less tax; and (iii) a further payment of £500 per annum, less tax, in respect of the
e 11 year old daughter. The husband appeals to this court.

The appeal raises issues of wide importance. This court is asked to determine, for the first time, after full argument, the principles which should be applied in the Family Division when granting ancillary relief pursuant to the powers conferred by the Matrimonial Proceedings and Property Act 1970 (in this judgment called 'the 1970 Act') following dissolution of marriage pursuant to the Divorce Reform Act
f 1969 (in this judgment called 'the 1969 Act'). We were told by counsel both for the husband and for the wife that it was hoped that this court might feel able, to quote the phrase used in the argument, 'to lay down some guide lines' which would be of help in the future. There are divergences of view and of practice between judge and registrars. Furthermore, counsel and solicitors are unable to advise their clients with a reasonable degree of certainty as to the likely outcome of any contested pro-
g ceedings. It is very desirable to remove that uncertainty and to assist parties to come to agreement.

The parties separated on 31st March 1972. The husband's petition was filed on 18th April 1972, and alleged adultery by the wife with a doctor whose patient she was. By her answer dated 9th May 1972, the wife denied the adultery and cross-petitioned on the ground that her husband had behaved in such a way that she could not reason-
h ably be expected to continue to live with him. Her answer was amended later to add two charges of adultery against the husband. The husband denied all the allegations against him. The co-respondent doctor also filed an answer denying the alleged adultery. These contested proceedings were heard before Ormrod J on five days between 3rd and 7th July 1972. The learned judge reserved his judgment at the conclusion of the hearing. He delivered the judgment on 21st July. He had, it
j seems, previously indicated to the parties that he was not satisfied that any relevant charge of adultery had been proved on either side, but he had given the husband leave to amend his petition so as to rely in the alternative on s 2 (1) (b) of the 1969 Act.

The learned judge granted cross-decrees to both parties under s 2 (1) (b) of the 1969 Act. He then proceeded to deal with the ancillary matters. He again reserved

judgment, and delivered it after the Long Vacation, on 3rd October 1972[1]. It is
against that second reserved judgment that the present appeal is brought.

The crucial finding of fact is that the responsibility for the breakdown of the marriage rested equally on both parties. The learned judge, having made that finding,
determined that the only capital asset, namely the matrimonial home, should be
divided more or less equally between the parties. Since the evidence before the
judge showed that the equity of the house in Norwood (after discharging the outstanding mortgage amounting to some £2,000) was about £20,000, he ordered the
husband to pay to his wife a lump sum of £10,000 or half the net value of the house
if and when sold, whichever was the less. So far as the periodical payment of £1,500
per annum is concerned, the learned judge appears to have worked on an earning
capacity on the part of the husband of £4,000 to £5,000 gross taxable income. He
appears not to have allowed anything for the wife's earning capacity, at least in terms
of monetary value. On this basis the £1,500 represents about one-third of the learned
judge's assessment of the husband's earning capacity. But if one adds to that figure
of £1,500 the further sum of £500 gross which the judge ordered to be paid by the
husband to the wife in respect of the 11 year old daughter, the total is £2,000 gross,
considerably more than one-third of the figure which the judge took as the husband's
earning capacity.

The husband's appeal was founded on the ground that in effect he had been ordered
to pay his wife one-half of his capital, and about one-half of his income. Particular
criticism was levelled in this respect at an important passage in the learned judge's
judgment[2] stating that Parliament had intended in the 1970 Act to bring about a
shift of emphasis from the old concept of maintenance to one of redistribution of
assets and of purchasing power. Counsel for the husband contended that the judge
had but lightly concealed his view that the 1970 Act had brought about a new concept
of community of property so that it was just to give every wife—or at least almost
every wife—half the value of the matrimonial home on the break-up of the marriage,
and about half her husband's income. If that were right in the case of a wife held
equally to blame with her husband for the breakdown of the marriage, what, he
asked rhetorically, was the position of a wife who was wholly innocent of responsibility for such a breakdown. He further asked this: if, as in the past, one-third of
the combined available income of the parties had been regarded as proper maintenance for a blameless wife, with a reduction (we avoid the use of the word 'discount') in the case of a wife who was not free from blame, how could periodical
payments totalling nearly one-half of the husband's earning capacity be justified in
a case where the wife was found equally to blame with the husband for the breakdown?

Counsel for the husband also complained that the judge had really started from a
presumption that equal division was right and had worked back from the starting
point and, allowing nothing—or almost nothing—for 'conduct', had arrived at the
determination we have stated. He contested the judge's view that it was right to
disregard conduct where blame had been found to exist, especially as Parliament in
s 5 (1) of the 1970 Act had enjoined the courts to have regard to the conduct of the
parties. He also said that no, or no sufficient, account had been taken of the wife's
earning capacity and that the £500 ordered to be paid for the child was in any event
too high. He offered a lump sum of £4,000, together with a guarantee of any mortgage instalments which the wife might have to pay in connection with the acquisition
of a new home for herself and the child. He urged this court in any event to reduce
the £1,500 to £1,000; and the £500 to £300, or less.

Counsel for the wife supported the judgment on the broad ground that the long
line of cases decided over the last century and more, which dealt with the issue of
conduct, especially in relation to a guilty or blameworthy wife, were all decided

1   [1973] 1 All ER 113, [1973] 2 WLR 84
2   [1973] 1 All ER at 116, [1973] 2 WLR at 88

when the foundation of the right to relief in matrimonial causes was the concept of a matrimonial offence. Now that concept had been swept away by the 1969 Act, the whole question of conduct in relation to ancillary relief required to be reconsidered, even though s 5 (1) of the 1970 Act preserved the obligation on the courts to have regard to the 'conduct' in language not easily distinguishable from that of the earlier statutes from 1857 onwards. Although judges and former judges of the present Family Division of great experience have recently said that s 5 (1) was only 'codifying' the preceding law and practice, counsel for the wife contended that that was wrong and that the new provisions contained in s 5 (1) (f) showed it to be wrong. Any approach to questions arising out of the 1970 Act founded on decisions before that Act and the 1969 Act were passed was wrong, since the 1970 Act ought not to be considered apart from the fundamental change wrought by the 1969 Act. Counsel for the wife particularly criticised the continued application of the so-called 'one-third rule' under present day conditions, and drew attention to the fact (as is undoubtedly the case) that in *Ackerman v Ackerman*[1], where this court recently proceeded on the basis that that so-called rule was still applicable to cases arising under the 1970 Act, it had done so without the matters which have been argued on this appeal having been argued. We will deal with these issues in order.

The conduct of the parties

When Parliament in 1857 introduced divorce by the courts of law, it based it on the doctrine of the matrimonial offence. This affected all that followed. If a person was the guilty party in a divorce suit, it went hard with him or her. It affected so many things. The custody of the children depended on it. So did the award of maintenance. To say nothing of the standing in society. So serious were the consequences that divorce suits were contested at great length and at much cost.

All that is altered. Parliament has decreed: 'If the marriage has broken down irretrievably, let there be a divorce'. It carries no stigma, but only sympathy. It is a misfortune which befalls both. No longer is one guilty and the other innocent. No longer are there long contested divorce suits. Nearly every case goes uncontested. The parties come to an agreement, if they can, on the things that matter so much to them. They divide up the furniture. They arrange the custody of the children, the financial provision for the wife, and the future of the matrimonial home. If they cannot agree, the matters are referred to a judge in chambers.

When the judge comes to decide these questions, what place has conduct in it? Parliament still says that the court has to have 'regard to their conduct': see s 5 (1) of the 1970 Act. Does this mean that the judge in chambers is to hear their mutual recriminations and go into their petty squabbles for days on end, as he used to do in the old days? Does it mean that, after a marriage has been dissolved, there is to be a post mortem to find out what killed it? We do not think so. In most cases both parties are to blame—or, as we would prefer to say—both parties have contributed to the breakdown.

It has been suggested that there should be a 'discount' or 'reduction' in what the wife is to receive because of her supposed misconduct, guilt or blame (whatever word is used). We cannot accept this argument. In the vast majority of cases it is repugnant to the principles underlying the new legislation, and in particular the 1969 Act. There will be many cases in which a wife (although once considered guilty or blameworthy) will have cared for the home and looked after the family for very many years. Is she to be deprived of the benefit otherwise to be accorded to her by s 5 (1) (f) because she may share responsibility for the breakdown with her husband? There will no doubt be a residue of cases where the conduct of one of the parties is in the judge's words[2] 'both obvious and gross', so much so that to order one party to support another whose conduct falls into this category is repugnant to anyone's

---

1   [1972] 2 All ER 420, [1972] Fam 225
2   [1973] 1 All ER at 119, [1973] 2 WLR at 90

sense of justice. In such a case the court remains free to decline to afford financial *a*
support or to reduce the support which it would otherwise have ordered. But, short
of cases falling into this category, the court should not reduce its order for financial
provision merely because of what was formerly regarded as guilt or blame. To do
so would be to impose a fine for supposed misbehaviour in the course of an unhappy
married life. Counsel for the husband disputed this and claimed that it was but
justice that a wife should suffer for her supposed misbehaviour. We do not agree. *b*
Criminal justice often requires the imposition of financial and indeed custodial
penalties. But in the financial adjustments consequent on the dissolution of a
marriage which has irretrievably broken down, the imposition of financial penalties
ought seldom to find a place.

The family assets

The phrase 'family assets' is a convenient short way of expressing an important *c*
concept. It refers to those things which are acquired by one or other or both of the
parties, with the intention that they should be continuing provision for them and their
children during their joint lives, and used for the benefit of the family as a whole.
It is a phrase, for want of a better, used by the Law Commission, and is well understood. The family assets can be divided into two parts: (i) those which are of a capital *d*
nature, such as the matrimonial home and the furniture in it; (ii) those which are of
a revenue-producing nature, such as the earning power of husband and wife. When
the marriage comes to an end, the capital assets have to be divided: the earning power
of each has to be allocated.

Until recently the courts had limited powers in regard to the capital assets. They
could determine the property rights of the parties. They could vary any ante-
nuptial or post-nuptial settlements. But they could not order a transfer of property *e*
from one to the other. They could not even award a lump sum until 1963. The
way in which the courts made financial provision was by way of maintenance to the
wife. This they often did by way of the 'one-third' rule.

Now under the 1970 Act the court has power after a divorce to effect a transfer
of the assets of the one to the other. It set out in s 5 various criteria. It was suggested
that these were only codifying the existing law. Despite what has been said, we do *f*
not agree. The 1970 Act is not in any sense a codifying statute. It is a reforming
statute designed to facilitate the granting of ancillary relief in cases where marriages
have been dissolved under the 1969 Act, an even greater measure of reform. It is
true that in certain of the lettered sub-paras of s 5 (1) of the 1970 Act one can find
reflections of certain earlier well-known judicial decisions. But this was not to ensure
that earlier decisions on conduct should be slavishly followed against a different *g*
jurisdictional background. Rather it was to secure that the common sense principles
embodied in the lettered sub-paragraphs, which found their origin in long standing
judicial decisions, should continue to be applied where appropriate in the new situation. We regard the provisions of ss 2, 3, 4 and 5 of the 1970 Act as designed to accord
to the courts the widest possible powers in readjusting the financial position of the
parties and to afford the courts the necessary machinery to that end, as for example *h*
is provided in s 4. It must not be overlooked in this connection that certain of the
provisions of the 1970 Act are new. See for example s 7 (2). Further, so far as we are
aware, the principles clearly stated in s 5 (1) (*f*) have nowhere previously found comparable statutory enactment.

The matrimonial home

The matrimonial home is usually the most important capital asset. Often the only
one. This case is typical. When the parties married in 1954 they started in a flat. He
was a dentist. She a receptionist. They both went out to work. They pooled such
money as they had to get the flat and furniture and keep it going. Two years later, in
1956, they bought a house, 37 Pollards Hill North, Streatham, and moved in there.

a It has been their matrimonial home ever since. The purchase price in 1956 was £5,000. They did not put any money cash down, but bought it with a 100 per cent mortgage. It was taken in the husband's name. The husband paid the mortgage instalments. The mortgage over the years has been reduced from £5,000 to £2,000. The house has increased in value from £5,000 to £22,000, or more.

b After they moved into the house in 1956, the wife continued to go out to work until the son was born in 1958. She then stayed at home and looked after the children. But she helped her husband in various ways in his practice, such as by filling in the National Health forms, and helping as a receptionist from time to time. He put down a salary to her as part of his expenses against tax. This continued for all the years until 31st March 1972 when the wife left the house.

c During the divorce proceedings the wife took out a summons under s 17 of the Married Women's Property Act 1882 claiming that, by reason of her financial contributions, she was entitled to one-half of the equity in the house. Alternatively she claimed that, under s 4 of the 1970 Act, there should be a transfer to her of half the house or its value by way of a lump sum.

d Before the 1970 Act there might have been much debate whether the wife had made financial contributions of sufficient substance to entitle her to a share in the house. The judge said[1] that it 'might have been an important issue'. We agree. But he went on to say[1] that since the 1970 Act it was 'of little importance' because the powers of transfer under s 4 enabled the court to do what was just having regard to all the circumstances. We agree. We feel sure that registrars and judges have been acting on this view; because, whereas previously we had several cases in our list each term under s 17 of the 1882 Act: now we have hardly any.

e How is the court to exercise its discretion under the 1970 Act in regard to the matrimonial home. We will lead up to the answer by tracing the way in which the law has developed. Twenty-five years ago, if the matrimonial home stood in the husband's name, it was taken to belong to him entirely, both in law and in equity. The wife did not get a proprietary interest in it simply because she helped him buy it or to pay the mortgage instalments. Any money that she gave him for these purposes would be
f regarded as gifts, or, at any rate, not recoverable by her: see *Balfour v Balfour*[2]. But by a long line of cases, starting with *Re Rogers' Question*[3], and ending with *Hazell v Hazell*[4], it has been held by this court that, if a wife contributes directly or indirectly, in money or money's worth, to the initial deposit or to the mortgage instalments, she gets an interest proportionate to her contribution. In some cases it is a half-share. In others less.

g The court never succeeded, however, in getting a wife a share in the house by reason of her other contributions; other, that is, than her financial contributions. The injustice to her has often been pointed out. Seven members of the Royal Commission on Marriage and Divorce presided over by Lord Morton of Henryton[5] said:

h 'If, on marriage, she gives up her paid work in order to devote herself to caring for her husband and children, it is an unwarrantable hardship when in consequence she finds herself in the end with nothing she can call her own.'

In 1965 Sir Jocelyn Simon P[6] used a telling metaphor: 'The cock can feather the nest because he does not have to spend most of his time sitting on it.' He went on to give reasons in an address which he gave to the Law Society[7]:

j 1   [1973] 1 All ER at 119, [1973] 2 WLR at 91
2   [1919] 2 KB 571, [1918-19] All ER Rep 800
3   [1948] 1 All ER 328
4   [1972] 1 All ER 923, [1972] 1 WLR 301
5   (1956), Cmd 9678, para 652, at p 178
6   Cited by Lord Hodson in *Pettitt v Pettitt* [1969] 2 All ER 385 at 404, [1970] AC 777 at 811
7   The Seven Pillars of Divorce Reform (1965) 62 Law Society Gazette at p 345

'In the generality of marriages the wife bears and rears children and minds the *a*
home. She thereby frees her husband for his economic activities. Since it is her
performance of her function which enables the husband to perform his, she is in
justice entitled to share in its fruits.'

But the courts have never been able to do justice to her. In April 1969 in *Pettitt v
Pettitt*[1] Lord Hodson said: 'I do not myself see how one can correct the imbalance
which may be found to exist in property rights as between husband and wife without *b*
legislation.'

Section 5 (1) (f)
Now we have the legislation. In order to remedy the injustice Parliament has
intervened. The 1970 Act expressly says that, in considering whether to make a
transfer of property, the court is to have regard, among other things, to— *c*

'(f) the contributions made by each of the parties to the welfare of the family,
including any contribution made by looking after the home or caring for the
family'

Counsel for the husband suggested that there was nothing new in these criteria in *d*
s 5 (1)(f). He referred us to *Porter v Porter*[2], where Sachs LJ said: '... the court must
always take into account how long the marriage has lasted and to what extent the wife
has rendered her domestic services to the husband.' But in saying that, Sachs LJ
was only anticipating the report of the Law Commission which was printed in the very
week in which *Porter v Porter*[3] was reported. In their Report on Financial Provision in
Matrimonial Proceedings[4] the Law Commission emphasised the importance of s 5 *e*
(1) (f) and the change which it would make. They said:

'... we recommend that in the exercise of the court's armoury of powers to
order financial provision it should be directed to have regard to various criteria.
Among these there is one of outstanding importance in regard to the adjustment
of property rights as between the spouses. This is the extent to which each has
contributed to the welfare of the family, including not only contributions in *f*
money or money's worth (as in the determination of rights to particular items
of property) but also the contribution made (normally by the wife) in looking after
the home and family. This should meet the strongest complaint made by married
women, and recognised as legitimate by the Morton Commission in 1955, namely
that the contribution which wives make towards the acquisition of the family
assets by performing the domestic chores, thereby releasing their husbands for *g*
gainful employment, is at present wholly ignored in determining their rights.
Under our proposal this contribution would be a factor which the court would be
specifically directed to take into account.'

It has sometimes been suggested that we should not have regard to the reports of
the Law Commission which lead to legislation. But we think we should. They are *h*
most helpful in showing the mischief which Parliament intended to remedy.
In the light thus thrown on the reason for s 5 (1) (f), we may take it that Parliament
recognised that the wife who looks after the home and family contributes as much to
the family assets as the wife who goes out to work. The one contributes in kind. The
other in money or money's worth. If the court comes to the conclusion that the
home has been acquired and maintained by the joint efforts of both, then, when the *j*

---

1   [1969] 2 All ER at 404, [1970] AC at 811
2   [1969] 3 All ER 640 at 644, [1969] 1 WLR 1155 at 1160
3   [1969] 3 All ER 640, [1969] 1 WLR 1155
4   (1969) Law Com No 25, para 69

a   marriage breaks down, it should be regarded as the joint property of both of them, no matter in whose name it stands. Just as the wife who makes substantial money contributions usually gets a share, so should the wife who looks after the home and cares for the family for 20 years or more.

The one-third rule

b   In awarding maintenance the divorce courts followed the practice of the ecclesiastical courts. They awarded an innocent wife a sum equal to one-third of their joint incomes. Out of it she had to provide for her own accommodation, her food and clothes, and other expenses. If she had any rights in the matrimonial home, or was allowed to be in occupation of it, that went in reduction of maintenance.

     That one-third rule has been much criticised. In *Kershaw v Kershaw*[1] Sir Jocelyn
c   Simon P spoke of it as 'the discredited "one-third rule" '. But it has retained its attraction for a very simple reason: those who have to assess maintenance must have some starting point. They cannot operate in a void. No better starting point has yet been suggested that the one-third rule. In *Ackerman v Ackerman*[2] Phillimore LJ said: '. . . the proper course is to start again. I would begin with the "one-third rule"—bearing in mind that it is not a rule.'

d   There was, we think, much good sense in taking one-third as a starting point. When a marriage breaks up, there will thenceforward be two households instead of one. The husband will have to go out to work all day and must get some woman to look after the house—either a wife, if he remarries, or a housekeeper, if he does not. He will also have to provide maintenance for the children. The wife will not usually have so much expense. She may go out to work herself, but she will not usually employ
e   a housekeeper. She will do most of the housework herself, perhaps with some help. Or she may remarry, in which case her new husband will provide for her. In any case, when there are two households, the greater expense will, in most cases, fall on the husband than the wife. As a start has to be made somewhere, it seems to us that in the past it was quite fair to start with one-third. Counsel for the wife criticised the application of the so-called 'one-third rule' on the ground that it no longer is
f   applicable to present-day conditions, notwithstanding what was said in *Ackerman v Ackerman*[3]. But this so-called rule is not a rule and must never be so regarded. In any calculation the court has to have a starting point. If it is not to be one-third, should it be one-half? or one-quarter? A starting point at one-third of the combined resources of the parties is as good and rational a starting point as any other, remembering that the essence of the legislation is to secure flexibility to meet the justice of particular cases, and not rigidity, forcing particular cases to be fitted into some so-called
g   principle within which they do not easily lie. There may be cases where more than one-third is right. There are likely to be many others where less than one-third is the only practicable solution. But one third as a flexible starting point is in general more likely to lead to the correct final result than a starting point of equality, or a quarter.

h   There is this, however, to be noted. Under the old dispensation, the wife, out of her one-third, had to provide her own accommodation. If she was given the right to occupy the matrimonial home, that went to reduce the one-third. Under the new dispensation, she will get a share of the capital assets; and, with that share, she will be able to provide accommodation for herself, or, at any rate, the money to go some way towards it.

j   If we were only concerned with the capital assets of the family, and particularly with the matrimonial home, it would be tempting to divide them half and half, as the judge did. That would be fair enough if the wife afterwards went her own way, making no

---

1   [1964] 3 All ER 635 at 637, [1966] P 13 at 17
2   [1972] 2 All ER at 426, [1972] Fam at 234
3   [1972] 2 All ER 420, [1972] Fam 225

further demands on the husband. It would be simply a division of the assets of the *a*
partnership. That may come in the future. But at present few wives are content with
a share of the capital assets. Most wives want their former husband to make periodical
payments as well to support them; because, after the divorce, he will be earning far
more than she; and she can only keep up her standard of living with his help. He
also has to make payments for the children out of his earnings, even if they are with
her. In view of these calls on his future earnings, we do not think she can have both— *b*
half the capital assets, and half the earnings.

Under the new dispensation, she will usually get a share of each. In these days of
rising house prices, she should certainly have a share in the capital assets which she has
helped to create. The windfall should not all go to the husband. But we do not
think it should be as much as one-half, if she is also to get periodical payments for her
maintenance and support. Giving it the best consideration we can, we think that the *c*
fairest way is to start with one-third of each. If she has one-third of the family assets
as her own—and one-third of the joint earnings—her past contributions are adequately
recognised, and her future living standard assured so far as may be. She will certainly
in this way be as well off as if the capital assets were divided equally—which is all
that a partner is entitled to.

We would emphasise that this proposal is not a rule. It is only a starting point. It *d*
will serve in cases where the marriage has lasted for many years and the wife has been
in the home bringing up the children. It may not be applicable when the marriage
has lasted only a short time, or where there are no children and she can go out to
work.

The lump sum provision

In every case the court should consider whether to order a lump sum to be paid *e*
by her husband to her. Before 1963 a wife, on a divorce, could not get a lump sum paid
to her. All that she could get was weekly or monthly payments secured or unsecured.
By s 5 (1) of the Matrimonial Causes Act 1963 the court was empowered to make an
order for the payment of a lump sum. This is now contained in s 2 (1) (c) of
the 1970 Act. This court has decided many cases about lump sums. They will be found *f*
usefully set out in Mr Joseph Jackson's chapter on the subject in his book on Matrimonial Finance and Taxation[1]. The circumstances are so various that few general
principles can be stated. One thing is, however, obvious. No order should be made
for a lump sum unless the husband has capital assets out of which to pay it—without
crippling his earning power.

Another thing is this: when the husband has available capital assets sufficient for
the purpose, the court should not hesitate to order a lump sum. The wife will then *g*
be able to invest it and use the income to live on. This will reduce any periodical
payments, or make them unnecessary. It will also help to remove the bitterness which
is so often attendant on periodical payments. Once made, the parties can regard the
book as closed. The third thing is that, if a lump sum is awarded, it should be made
outright. It should not be made subject to conditions except when there are children. *h*
Then it may be desirable to let it be the subject of a settlement. In case she remarries,
the children will be assured of some part of the family assets which were built up for
them.

But the question of a lump sum needs special consideration in relation to the
matrimonial home. The house is in most cases the principal capital asset. Sometimes
the only asset. It will usually have increased greatly in value since it was acquired. *j*
It is to be regarded as belonging in equity to both of them jointly. What is to be done
with it? This is the most important question of all.

Take a case like the present when the wife leaves the home and the husband stays
in it. On the breakdown of the marriage arrangements should be made whereby it

1 (1972), pp 116-131

a is vested in him absolutely, free of any share in the wife, and he alone is liable for the mortgage instalments. But the wife should be compensated for the loss of her share by being awarded a lump sum. It should be a sum sufficient to enable her to get settled in a place of her own, such as by putting down a deposit on a flat or a house. It should not, however, be an excessive sum. It should be such as the husband can raise by a further mortgage on the house without crippling him.

b   Conversely, suppose the husband leaves the house and the wife stays in it. If she is likely to be there indefinitely, arrangements should be made whereby it is vested in her absolutely, free of any share in the husband; or, if there are children, settled on her and the children. This may mean that he will have to transfer the legal title to her. If there is a mortgage, some provision should be made for the mortgage instalments to be paid by the husband, or guaranteed by him. If this is done, there may be c no necessity for a lump sum as well. Furthermore, seeing that she has the house, the periodic payments will be much less than they otherwise would be.

Remarriage

     In making financial provision, ought the prospects of remarriage to be taken into account? The statute says in terms that periodical payments shall cease on remarriage: d see s 7 (1) (b). But it says nothing about the prospects of remarriage. The question then arises: ought the provision for the wife to be reduced if she is likely to remarry?

     So far as the capital assets are concerned, we see no reason for reducing her share. After all, she has earned it by her contribution in looking after the home and caring for the family. It should not be taken away from her by the prospect of remarriage. In *Buckley v John Allen & Ford (Oxford) Ltd*[1] Phillimore LJ showed that it was a guessing e game, which no judge was qualified to put his—or her—money on. His observations were disapproved by this court in *Goodburn v Thomas Cotton Ltd*[2]. But they have been vindicated by Parliament.

     So far as periodical payments are concerned, they are, of course, to be assessed without regard to the prospects of remarriage. If the wife does in fact remarry, they cease. If she goes to live with another man—without marrying him—they may be f reviewed.

The present case

     Coming now to the facts of the present case. The matrimonial home belongs in law to the husband. On the figures before the learned judge, its gross value was about £22,000; and, as already stated, the equity is worth about £20,000. Counsel for the g wife sought to reopen these figures. We saw no justification for allowing him to do so, since these figures could have been challenged before the learned judge had it then been desired to do so. But we allowed counsel for the wife to cross-appeal to argue that the judge, consistently with the principles which he sought to apply, should have ordered a lump sum payment of £10,000, or half the net value of the house, whichever was the greater, and not, as the learned judge in fact ordered, whichever was the less.

h   So far as the husband's earning capacity is concerned, we venture to think that the learned judge's findings are self-contradictory; for, if the husband was spending at the rate of £4,000 to £5,000 per annum without incurring debts and was, in fact, at the same time making savings, his gross taxable income must have been considerably more than the £4,000 to £5,000 found by the judge. We propose to proceed on the basis of the husband's earning capacity (i e his gross taxable income) being not less j than £6,000 per annum. This may well be too favourable to the husband who appears not to have disclosed part of his income as a dentist. We put the wife's potential earning capacity on part-time work as a dental nurse at £15 per week gross—say £750 per annum. The combined total earning capacity is thus £6,750 per annum gross, of

---

1   [1967] 1 All ER 539 at 542, [1967] 2 QB 637 at 645
2   [1968] 1 All ER 518, [1968] 1 QB 845

which one-third (if that be the right starting point) is £2,250. If one deducts the £750 a
from that latter figure of £2,250, the result is £1,500—the same figure as the learned
judge arrived at although he reached that figure by a different route.

The husband is presently living at the former matrimonial home. The son of the
marriage, aged 14, is now at a boarding school at the grandfather's expense. The boy
lives with his father in the holidays. The father has to clothe and maintain him in the
holidays. Clearly this requires the father to maintain a home for the son. Both parties
gave their ages as 46. Remarriage is thus a possibility, although not it seems an imminent b
probability. The wife undoubtedly contributed to the home for some 18 years and,
so far as the evidence goes, was in every respect an excellent mother. This is clearly a
case in which the wife has made a substantial contribution to the home, as of course
the husband has out of his earnings.

Any lump sum ordered to be paid will, we were told, be raised by the husband by
increasing the sum for which the house is mortgaged. To require him to pay a lump c
sum of £10,000 raised in this way might cost him around £900 per annum in interest;
and, of course, he will have to repay the principal as well. If £900 is added to the total
of £1,500, plus the £500 (i e £2,000), the result is the equivalent of an order for a
periodical payment of almost half of what we have taken to be the husband's gross
taxable income. We think an order for a periodical payment on this scale (omitting d
any consideration of a lump sum payment) would be too high, having regard to the
wife's needs and to the husband's needs. But, even if the matter be approached by a
different route, we still think the £10,000 figure is too high. The wife should be able
to make a substantial deposit in order to purchase suitable accommodation (assuming
she wishes to buy, and not to rent) with the aid of a considerably smaller sum; and,
if the order for £1,500 as a periodical payment is upheld, there seems to us to be a e
margin within that figure beyond the requirements of ordinary living expenses out of
which repayments of mortgage, principal and interest could be made. On the other
hand, we think the husband's offer of £4,000 is too low in a period of notoriously
inflationary house prices. The offer of a guarantee of the wife's mortgage repayments
does not improve the wife's day-to-day position, although it might make the obtaining
of mortgage facilities easier. f

On the basis that the order for a periodical payment of £1,500 per annum is left
untouched, we think the proper lump sum, taking everything into account that the
1970 Act requires, is £6,000, and we would vary the learned judge's order for £10,000
accordingly. We think the wife should have that sum, £6,000, free of any trust, or
other terms.

We, therefore, see no reason to interfere with the order for £1,500 in favour of the
wife on the basis of the figures we have just mentioned. But, with all respect to the g
learned judge, we think the figure of £500 for the child is considerably too high. We
would substitute a figure of £300 per annum, which we would express as £6 per week
so that the payment should be made gross of tax. We see no reason whatever on the
facts of this case, as found by the learned judge, for making any reduction of any
kind on the ground that the judge found the wife equally responsible with the husband
for the breakdown of their marriage. To do so would be quite inconsistent with the h
principles which we think should be adopted in future in relation to conduct.

Looking at it broadly

In all these cases it is necessary at the end to view the situation broadly and see if the j
proposals meet the justice of the case. On our proposals here the wife gets £6,000
(nearly one-third of the value of the matrimonial home). She gets it without any
conditions at all. This seems to represent a fair assessment of her past contributions,
when regard is had to the fact that she will get periodical payments as well. She also
gets £1,500 a year by way of periodical payments, which is about one-third of their
joint incomes. She will also have the management of £300 a year for the daughter

a who is at a good school, and aged 11. These provisions are as much as the husband can reasonably be expected to make. It will mean that each will have to cut down their standard of living: but it is as much as can be done in the circumstances.

The appeal should be allowed to the extent indicated. The wife's cross-appeal will be dismissed.

b *Appeal allowed; order below varied. Wife's cross-appeal dismissed. Leave to appeal to the House of Lords refused.*

Solicitors: *Malcolm Fraser & Co* (for the husband); *Cowles & Co* (for the wife).

Wendy Shockett   Barrister.

c

Re Endericks' Conveyance
Porter and another v Fletcher

d

CHANCERY DIVISION
GOULDING J
22nd NOVEMBER 1972

e *Restrictive covenant – Restrictive covenant affecting land – Construction – Covenant affecting freehold property – Covenant by purchaser not to use burdened property 'for any purpose other than that of a single private dwelling-house' – Dwelling-house already on property at date of purchase – Purchaser obtaining planning permission to erect a second dwelling-house on part of burdened property – Whether covenant preventing erection of second private dwelling-house on burdened land.*

f E agreed to sell to M certain freehold property comprising just under five acres and M agreed to sell to the defendant 1½ acres of that property. By one conveyance E conveyed to M the larger part ('the green land') of the five acres on which a house had been erected, and by a second conveyance made between E, M and the defendant, E, by the direction of M, conveyed to the defendant in fee simple, the other 1½ acres. By

g cl 4 of the second conveyance M covenanted with the defendant 'so as to bind so far as may be the [green land] into whosoever hands the same may come and so that this covenant shall be for the benefit and protection of the [1½ acres] . . . that he [M] and those deriving title under him will not at any time . . . (a) use the [green land] or any part thereof or any messuage or building now erected or hereafter to be erected thereon or on any part thereof for any purpose other than that of a single private dwelling-

h house . . .' M obtained outline planning permission for the erection of a dwelling-house on a half acre site on the green land. He conveyed that site to the plaintiff. The issue arose whether, on the true construction of cl 4 of the second conveyance, the restrictive covenant permitted the plaintiff to build a second house on the green land provided it was used only for the purposes of a single private dwelling-house.

j **Held** – Clause 4 prohibited the green land from being used for any purpose other than that of a single private dwelling-house; the addition of the references to 'any part' of the property, and to a 'messuage or building', present or future, were strictly unnecessary in that they merely added emphasis to the initial overriding prohibition and did not curtail it in any way; it followed that the plaintiff would be in breach of covenant if he erected a dwelling-house on his land as it would involve the green

land as a whole being used for the purpose of two single private dwelling-houses (see   *a*
p 846 g and h and p 848 d f and g, post).

Barton v Keeble [1928] All ER Rep 198, *Berton v Alliance Economic Investment Co* [1922]
1 KB 742, *Berton v London and Counties House Property Co* (17th November 1920)
unreported, and *Dobbs v Linford* [1952] 2 All ER 827 explained.

                                                       b

Notes
For the court's jurisdiction to declare what on the true construction of an instrument is
the nature and extent of a restrictive covenant, see 14 Halsbury's Laws (3rd Edn)
571, 572, para 1062 and for cases on the subject, see 40 Digest (Repl) 364-367, 2925-2936;
for cases on restriction as to number of dwelling-houses on a site, see ibid 348,
2808-2812.

                                                       c

Cases referred to in judgment
Barton v Keeble [1928] Ch 517, [1928] All ER Rep 198, 97 LJCh 215, 139 LT 136, 31 Digest
  (Repl) 168, 3027.
Berton v Alliance Economic Investment Co [1922] 1 KB 742, 91 LJKB 748, 127 LT 422, CA,
  31 Digest (Repl) 160, 2980.
Berton v London and Counties House Property Co (17th November 1920) unreported.   *d*
Dobbs v Linford [1952] 2 All ER 827, [1953] 1 QB 48, [1952] WN 485, CA, Digest (Cont
  Vol A) 1006, 3027a.
Kemp v Bird (1877) 5 Ch D 974, 46 LJCh 828, 37 LT 53, 42 JP 36, CA, 31 Digest (Repl)
  180, 3128.

                                                       e

Originating summons
By an originating summons taken out under s 84 of the Law of Property Act 1925,
the plaintiffs, William Gerald Porter and Christine Marina Porter, the successors in
title to Edmund James Mander to part of the land comprised in a conveyance dated
5th July 1967 and made between (1) Ivy Endericks, (2) Mr Mander, and (3) the defendant, Peter John Fletcher (who claimed to be entitled to the benefit of a restrictive   *f*
covenant contained in that conveyance), applied to the court for the determination of
the question whether on the true construction of the conveyance and in the events
that had happened a private dwelling-house might be erected on the land comprised
in a conveyance dated 27th July 1970 and made between (1) Mr Mander, (2) the
Lambeth Building Society, and (3) the first plaintiff. The facts are set out in the
judgment.

                                                       g

D M Burton for the plaintiffs.
John P Brookes for the defendant.

                                                       h

GOULDING J. This originating summons is taken out under s 84 of the Law of
Property Act 1925 and relates to a restrictive covenant affecting the use of freehold
property at Northam in Devonshire.

    The controversy between the parties lies in a very small compass. There is no
dispute that the land now owned by the plaintiffs is subject to the burden of the
covenant in question, and there is no dispute that the defendant is entitled to the bene-   *j*
fit of the covenant. The problem is one of interpretation of the words of the covenant.
The defendant has included in his evidence certain contentions relating to the discussions that preceded the execution of the deed containing the covenant and to
the intention of the parties at the time. However, the defendant does not claim
rectification of the instrument and I dismiss such evidence from my mind because I
think that on accepted principles it is not admissible on a question of interpretation.

a   Accordingly my task must be to construe the deed in the light of the principles stated nearly 100 years ago by James LJ in *Kemp v Bird*[1]. The learned Lord Justice said[2]:

'Persons ought to look after their own interests in framing their own contracts and their own covenants. Persons who are men of business, as they were here, are able to get protection and advice, and they must make their covenants express, so as to state what they really mean, and they cannot get a Court of Law or of
b   Equity to supply something which they have not stipulated for in order to get a benefit which is supposed to have been intended.'

So I have to look at the language of the deed in question and see what the parties mean according to that language.

c   The covenant is contained in a conveyance dated 5th July 1967 made between Ivy Endericks therein called the vendor, of the first part, Edmund James Mander therein called the purchaser, of the second part, and Peter John Fletcher, therein called the sub-purchaser, who is the defendant, of the third part. The conveyance recites that the vendor lately agreed with the purchaser for the sale of certain property at Northam comprising in all a little less than five acres, and that the purchaser had agreed with the sub-purchaser for the sale to the sub-purchaser of a part of that property. The
d   part so sub-sold contains about 1½ acres. The larger part of the five acres was conveyed to the purchaser, that is Mr Mander, by another conveyance also dated 5th July 1967. Then, after the recitals, whose effect I have stated, the conveyance to the defendant showed that the vendor, by the direction of the purchaser, conveyed to the sub-purchaser in fee simple the part that had been bought by him, that is to say 1½ acres. Clauses 4 and 5 of the conveyance that I am reciting contain mutual restrictive coven-
e   ants between the purchaser and the sub-purchaser. Clause 4 is that which is now in question. It reads as follows:

'The Purchaser hereby covenants with the Sub-Purchaser so as to bind so far as may be the said property edged green on the said plan Numbered 1 annexed hereto into whosoever hands the same may come and so that this covenant shall be for the benefit and protection of the said property hereby conveyed or any
f   part or parts thereof but so that the Purchaser and those deriving title under him shall not be personally liable for a breach of this covenant occurring on or in respect of the said property edged green on the said plan Numbered 1 annexed hereto [that is the property being retained by the purchaser] or any part or parts thereof after he or they shall have parted with all interest therein that he the Purchaser and those deriving title under him will not at any time after the date
g   hereof (a) use the said property edged green on the said plan Numbered 1 annexed hereto or any part thereof or any messuage or building now erected or hereafter to be erected thereon or on any part thereof for any purpose other than that of a single private dwelling-house or as the professional residence of a medical practitioner dentist solicitor or architect and (b) carry on or permit or suffer to be carried on any business trade school or club upon the said land edged green on
h   the said plan Numbered 1 annexed hereto or any part or parts thereof.'

Clause 5 contains a parallel covenant by the sub-purchaser burdening the land conveyed to him and benefiting the land retained by the purchaser expressed in almost identical terms, but omitting the words (after the word 'building') 'now erected or'. The reason for that omission was evidently that whereas the land retained by the pur-
j   chaser included a dwelling-house already erected and known as 'Old Pastures', the parcel conveyed to the sub-purchaser was at the time merely a building site. The purchaser, Mr Mander, towards the end of the year 1968 obtained outline planning permission for the erection of a dwelling-house on a part of the property

1   (1877) 5 Ch D 974
2   (1877) 5 Ch D at 976

burdened by his covenant. That site, in respect of which planning permission was *a*
obtained, comprises a little over half an acre and at present contains a disused tennis
court. Having obtained that planning permission, Mr Mander on 27th July 1970
conveyed the site having the benefit of the planning permission to the first-named
plaintiff Mr William Gerald Porter. At a later date in 1970 Mr Porter conveyed the
site to himself and his wife, the second-named plaintiff, as joint tenants legally and
beneficially.   *b*

The defendant claims that the restrictive covenant entered into by the plaintiffs'
predecessor in title, Mr Mander, prevents building of a second dwelling-house on the
land burdened by the covenant. The defendant says that the true meaning of the
covenant is that the whole of the 3½ acres or so retained by Mr Mander can be used
only for the purposes of one dwelling-house and no more. The plaintiffs say that any
number of dwelling-houses can be erected on the burdened land without breach of *c*
covenant so long as each building when erected is used only as a single private
dwelling-house. That is the dispute which I now have to resolve.

Counsel for the plaintiffs says emphatically that the covenant is in terms restrictive
only of user. In sub-para (a) of the covenant, the operative word which covers all
that follows is 'use'. He says that the covenant does not purport to limit or regulate
future building operations or the quantitative aspects of development. All that is hit *d*
at by sub-para (a) is the quality of use to which the existing or future buildings may be
put. Further, counsel for the plaintiffs says the language of sub-para (a) in terms contemplates further building. It refers to 'any messuage or building now erected or
hereafter to be erected'. The other sub-paragraph, sub-para (b), is likewise directed
solely to the quality of use of the premises, prohibiting any business, trade, school or
club. Both counsel, I think, generally agreed that whichever is the correct construc- *e*
tion of sub-para (a), sub-para (b) can add very little to it from a practical point of
view.

Counsel for the plaintiffs says that the defendant's argument renders a good deal
of the language entirely otiose. It would have been enough to say, if the defendant is
right, that the purchaser should not use the property edged green on the plan for any
purpose other than that of a single private dwelling-house. There is no need on the *f*
defendant's construction, says counsel for the plaintiffs, for referring to any part of the
property edged green 'or any messuage or building now erected or hereafter to be
erected thereon or on any part thereof'. Counsel for the plaintiffs emphasises that a
strict and literal construction of such restrictive covenants is of great importance since
they are intended to, and in the present case do, affect third parties who were not
contracting parties under the original agreement itself.   *g*

Counsel for the defendant says that on a true and literal reading of the covenant, it
prohibits any divided occupation of the burdened land taken as a unit. The important
part of the covenant in his submission is that the property edged green on the plan
shall not be used for any purpose other than that of a single private dwelling-house.
References to any part of the property, to a messuage or building, present or future,
and to any part of a messuage or building are intended to fortify and add emphasis *h*
to the initial and general overriding prohibition and do not cut it down in any way.
Counsel for the defendant founded himself on a case decided in the Court of Appeal,
Berton v London and Counties House Property Co[1]. That case is referred to in a later
case in the Court of Appeal, *Berton v Alliance Economic Investment Co*[2]. Both those
actions related to leases on the Dulwich College Estate and such leases contained a
covenant by the lessee that the lessee would[3]—   *j*

'not without the lessors' previous licence in writing use the premises or any part
thereof or permit the same to be used for any purpose whatsoever other than for

1 (17th November 1920) unreported
2 [1922] 1 KB 742
3 [1922] 1 KB at 743

a   the purpose of a private dwelling house wherein no business of any kind is carried on.'

Atkin LJ in the reported *Berton* case[1] referred to its predecessor with evident approval in these terms[2]:

b   'In *Berton v. London and Counties House Property Co.*[3] this Court held that to let in separate tenements a precisely similar house in the same neighbourhood was a breach of a covenant to use the house only as a private dwelling house.'

That decision was followed by Eve J in *Barton v Keeble*[4] which was likewise the case of a lease on the Dulwich College Estate with a covenant in identical terms. There are others in the same series of authorities. I was referred to *Dobbs v Linford*[5], a decision of the Court of Appeal on an appeal from Chichester County Court, where the

c   covenant in a tenancy agreement was in these terms[6]:

'. . . not to use the said premises for any purpose other than as a private dwelling-house and not to sub-let or part with the possession of the premises (except as a furnished house) without the consent of the landlord such consent not to be unreasonably withheld . . .'

d   Romer LJ, with whom the other members of the Court of Appeal agreed, said this[7]:

'The covenant was to use the premises for no other purpose than that of "a private dwelling-house." It was not disputed that the premises had been used partly as a dwelling-house by the tenant and partly as a dwelling-house by the sub-tenant. That was a plain breach of that covenant. There was the authority

e   of Eve J. in *Barton v. Keeble*[8], that a covenant in this form did not authorize the subletting of part of the premises.'

Counsel for the defendant, on those authorities, submits that in each case the covenant was held to prohibit sub-division of the demised building in relation to which the restriction was imposed. He says that, by parity of reasoning, the covenant in the

f   present case must be construed as prohibiting sub-division of the property as a whole and, on its language, does indeed justify that interpretation. The reference to buildings, in counsel's reading of the deed, allows demolition of the existing dwelling-house and its replacement by a new one. It may also allow the erection of additional buildings for purposes merely ancillary to the occupation of the main house. The reference to buildings does not however detract from the force of the covenant as prohibiting sub-division.

g   I do not think I can regard the authorities which counsel for the defendant has cited as concluding the matter in his favour. There are many differences of circumstance or of language. For one thing, the authorities related to leases or tenancy agreements. The present case is one of a conveyance in fee simple. Again, the leasehold property in the Dulwich College cases was in each instance a house in an area developed by the

h   lessors and there can be little doubt to my mind that the leases prohibited structural alterations or building without the lessors' licence. In the present case the party burdened is a freeholder and the words of the covenant expressly contemplate the erection of additional buildings. Accordingly I cannot regard the interpretation of the

---

j   1   [1922] 1 KB 742
2   [1922] 1 KB at 758
3   (17th November 1920) unreported
4   [1928] Ch 517, [1928] All ER Rep 198
5   [1952] 2 All ER 827, [1953] 1 QB 48
6   [1952] 2 All ER at 827, [1953] 1 QB at 48
7   [1952] WN at 485; cf [1952] 2 All ER at 830, [1953] 1 QB at 52, 53
8   [1928] Ch at 523, [1928] All ER Rep at 200

particular deed before me as decided by something the Court of Appeal has said about
quite different properties in a different relationship between the covenanting parties. *a*

Nonetheless counsel for the defendant can get this out of the Dulwich College
cases: that a covenant not to use a house or any part thereof for any purpose other than
for the purpose of a private dwelling-house is, on a proper reading of the language,
apt to forbid sub-division. It is unfortunate that there is no report of the leading case
which decided that. It seems to me however that there is no violence to grammar
in the view taken by the Court of Appeal. The court must, I think, have read the obli- *b*
gation not to use the premises or any part thereof for prohibited purposes as consisting
of two limbs: not to use the premises for a prohibited purpose, and not to use any
part of the premises for a prohibited purpose; so that, although sub-division into
separate tenements might not infringe the second limb, it would still infringe the first
alternative. It may be said indeed that the second limb was strictly unnecessary but
as in everyday speech so in the more careful language of conveyancers tautology *c*
serves the useful purpose of clarity.

Now, here, looking at the restriction quite literally and sub-dividing it, there are
several branches of the promise under sub-para (a). First that the purchaser and his
successors in title will not use the property edged green for any purpose other than
that of a single private dwelling-house. Secondly, that they will not use any part of the *d*
property edged green for any such other purpose. Thirdly, that they will not use any
existing or future messuage or building on the property for any such other purpose
and, fourthly, that they will not use any part of any such messuage or building for
any such other purpose.

Counsel for the defendant's interpretation, I think, makes all but the first of those
alternatives strictly unnecessary because if you use any part of the land or any building,
present or future, on the land otherwise than as a private dwelling-house, you neces- *e*
sarily use the land itself for other purposes. But on the other hand counsel for the
plaintiffs' interpretation does involve the rejection or in some way the rendering
ineffectual of the first branch of all, because his proposals, if carried into effect, will not
involve the use of any building for a purpose other than that of a single private
dwelling-house nor the use for such a purpose of any sub-divided curtilage of the land *f*
edged green, but they will involve a use of the land edged green for a purpose other
than that of a single private dwelling-house, since the land edged green as a whole
will be used for the purpose of two single private dwelling-houses.

Accordingly, although I have not found the problem at all an easy one, it seems to
me that in the end the argument of counsel for the defendant leads to a conclusion
more consonant with a strictly grammatical and literal reading of the covenant without the rejection of any words. It is clearly better, if one has a choice, to read some *g*
words as unnecessary rather than to reject some altogether. The result is that the
defendant succeeds and I must make a declaration on the originating summons that
on the true construction of the conveyance and in the events that have happened
a dwelling-house may not be erected on the site now owned by the plaintiffs.

Declaration accordingly. *h*

Solicitors: *Herbert Smith & Co* (for the plaintiffs); *Cripps, Harries, Willis & Carter*,
agents for *Dunn & Baker*, Exeter (for the defendant).

Susan Corbett   Barrister.

Re Wilson (I D) (a bankrupt), ex parte Bebbington Easton

CHANCERY DIVISION

GOULDING J

4th DECEMBER 1972

Vexatious proceedings – Institution – Restriction – Bankruptcy proceedings – Proof of debt in pending proceedings by non-petitioning creditor – Order in force requiring creditor to obtain leave of High Court before instituting legal proceedings – Whether creditor required to obtain leave before proving debt or appealing against rejection of proof – Supreme Court of Judicature (Consolidation) Act 1925, s 51 (1), as amended by the Supreme Court of Judicature (Amendment) Act 1959, s 1 (1).

A person who exercises his statutory right to prove a debt in bankruptcy proceedings instituted by a petitioning creditor other than himself is taking part in pending proceedings and not 'instituting' proceedings within s 51 (1)[a] of the Supreme Court of Judicature (Consolidation) Act 1925. Accordingly, where an order has been made under s 51 (1) prohibiting such a person from instituting legal proceedings without leave of the High Court or a judge thereof, that person does not require leave to prove a debt in bankruptcy proceedings, or to appeal against the rejection by the trustee in bankruptcy of his proof (see p 851 e to g, post).

Notes

For restriction on vexatious actions, see 1 Halsbury's Laws (3rd Edn) 19, 20, para 29, and for a case on the subject, see 44 Digest (Repl) 193, 57.

For the Supreme Court of Judicature (Consolidation) Act 1925, s 51, as amended by the Supreme Court of Judicature (Amendment) Act 1959, s 1, see 25 Halsbury's Statutes (3rd Edn) 723.

Case referred to in judgment

Boaler, Re [1915] 1 KB 21, [1914-15] All ER Rep 1022, 83 LJKB 1629, 111 LT 497, 24 Cox CC 335, 78 JP 280, CA, 44 Digest (Repl) 193, 57.

Application

On 31st January 1969 an order was made, under s 51 (1) of the Supreme Court of Judicature (Consolidation) Act 1925, by a Divisional Court of the Queen's Bench Division, prohibiting the applicant, Ann Marjorie Bebbington Easton, from initiating proceedings in any court without the leave of the High Court or a judge thereof. In bankruptcy proceedings in the Brighton County Court instituted by a petitioning creditor other than the applicant, Ian David Wilson was on 20th September 1971 adjudicated bankrupt; and the applicant submitted a proof of debt in Mr Wilson's bankruptcy. On 18th November 1971 the applicant's proof was rejected by the

---

a   Section 51 (1), as amended, provides: 'If, on an application made by the Attorney-General under this section, the High Court is satisfied that any person has habitually and persistently and without any reasonable ground instituted vexatious legal proceedings, whether in the High Court or in any inferior court, and whether against the same person or against different persons, the court may, after hearing that person or giving him an opportunity of being heard, order that no legal proceedings shall without the leave of the High Court or a judge thereof be instituted by him in any court and that any legal proceedings instituted by him in any court before the making of the order shall not be continued by him without such leave, and such leave shall not be given unless the court or judge is satisfied that the proceedings are not an abuse of the process of the court and that there is prima facie ground for the proceedings.'

trustee in bankruptcy. Her appeal against rejection was dismissed by his Honour Judge Wingate at the Brighton County Court on 22nd December 1971; the judge apparently dealt with the matter without reference to the Divisional Court order. On 26th June 1972 the applicant applied to the Brighton County Court for a rehearing of her appeal against rejection on the ground that since December 1971 fresh evidence had come to light, such a rehearing being within the court's discretion by virtue of the Bankruptcy Act 1914, s 108. On that occasion, regard was had to the Divisional Court order and consequently, on 12th July 1972, Mr Registrar Hankinson rejected the applicant's application. On 10th October 1972 the applicant made an ex parte application to the High Court in Bankruptcy for leave to appeal to the Brighton County Court against the rejection of her proof of debt by the trustee in bankruptcy, notwithstanding the order of the Divisional Court.

The applicant appeared in person.

GOULDING J. I am about to give judgment on an ex parte application made to me in chambers by a lady who is not professionally represented and whom I will call 'the applicant'. The application was made to me as the judge exercising, during the present sittings, the jurisdiction of the High Court in Bankruptcy. It arose in the following circumstances.

On 31st January 1969 a Divisional Court of the Queen's Bench Division on the motion of the Attorney-General made an order against the applicant in these terms:

'It is ORDERED that [the applicant] be and she is hereby prohibited from initiating proceedings in the High Court or in any other Court unless she obtains the leave of the High Court or a Judge thereof and satisfies the Court or a Judge that such legal proceedings are not an abuse of the process of the Court and that there is a prima facie ground for such proceedings AND IT IS ORDERED that any legal proceedings initiated by her in any Court before the making of this Order shall not be continued by her without such leave as aforesaid.'

That order was of course made under s 51 (1) of the Supreme Court of Judicature (Consolidation) Act 1925, as extended by the Supreme Court of Judicature (Amendment) Act 1959. In my view the words 'initiating proceedings' which occur in the order must be construed as equivalent to the words 'instituting proceedings'. 'Institute' is the verb used in the 1925 Act.

On 20th September 1971 one Ian David Wilson was adjudicated bankrupt in the Brighton County Court. The applicant submitted a proof of debt in Mr Wilson's bankruptcy. In due course, on 18th November 1971, her proof was rejected by the trustee in bankruptcy. The applicant appealed against such rejection to the court, i e the Brighton County Court, and her appeal was heard by his Honour Judge Wingate on 22nd December 1971. The learned judge appears to have dealt with the matter on the merits and without reference to the order of the Divisional Court in 1969. He dismissed the appeal with costs. On 26th June 1972 the applicant made a further application to the Brighton County Court. I understand that she sought thereby a rehearing of her appeal against the rejection of her proof in December 1971, on the ground that fresh evidence had come to light. Such a rehearing is within the discretion of the court under s 108 of the Bankruptcy Act 1914. On this second occasion, so far as I can ascertain, solicitors acting for the trustee in bankruptcy produced the 1969 order to the county court and submitted that the applicant was not at liberty to proceed with her application without leave of the High Court or a judge thereof, pursuant to that order. Consequently Mr Registrar Hankinson on 12th July 1972 dismissed, or in the terms of his order rejected, the applicant's second application with costs.

On 10th October 1972 the applicant made the present application to the High Court in Bankruptcy, for leave to appeal to the Brighton County Court against the rejection *a*   of her proof of debt by the trustee, notwithstanding the order of the Divisional Court in 1969.

If in law the applicant requires the leave she seeks then she has in my judgment come to the wrong court to obtain it. Under s 103 of the Bankruptcy Act 1914 a county court has, for the purpose of its bankruptcy jurisdiction, all the powers and jurisdiction of the High Court. If then the application for leave under the 1969 order is properly regarded in the circumstances as a step in bankruptcy proceedings,

b   it should in my view be disposed of by the county court judge in whose court such proceedings are pending. But if, as I think, it is altogether outside and preliminary to bankruptcy proceedings, then it is useless to apply to any bankruptcy court, whether the High Court or the county court. The proper forum on that assumption is the High Court in its general jurisdiction governed by the 1925 Act, and convenience

c   demands that the application be made in the Queen's Bench Division where the 1969 order was pronounced and where the applicant seems to have obtained leave to institute proceedings on at least one subsequent occasion.

In my opinion, however, the application is wholly misconceived, because the 1969 order does not prevent the applicant from appealing against the rejection of her proof by the trustee in bankruptcy. Wide though the language is of s 51 of the 1925 Act,

d   it imposes a serious restriction on civil rights and should not be construed more widely than its words clearly require: see *Re Boaler*[1]. In that case the Court of Appeal held, by a majority, that an order under the enactment now replaced by s 51 was no bar to the initiation of private criminal prosecutions by the person subject to the order. Similarly, although I know of no authority on the point, I doubt whether an order made under s 51 (1) will deprive the subject of his right to appeal without leave against an assessment to income tax.

e   Now, what is the applicant's position here? By appealing against the rejection of her proof of debt does she institute, or initiate, legal proceedings in a court? I think not. The relevant proceedings are those described as Bankruptcy no 63 of 1971 in the Brighton County Court. They were instituted by a petitioning creditor other than the applicant. In exercising her statutory right to prove her debt in the bank-

f   ruptcy and not to accept the trustee's decision as final, the applicant is taking part in pending proceedings in a court, not instituting fresh ones. Thus on a fair interpretation of the words of s 51 of the 1925 Act and of the order made thereunder, I am of opinion that no leave of the High Court is required to appeal against the rejection of a proof of debt. In the result, I must dismiss the applicant's application, but I have thought it right to state my reasons in open court in case she can make use of them elsewhere.

g   In conclusion, I should make these three observations. (1) I have no power to set aside Mr Registrar Hankinson's order of 12th July 1972. Any appeal from that order would lie to the Divisional Court in Bankruptcy under s 108 of the Bankruptcy Act 1914. (2) I express no opinion at all on the merits of the applicant's case for a re-hearing by the county court, which I have not investigated. (3) Since the application

h   has been, quite properly, made ex parte by the applicant in person, I have not had the benefit of argument by counsel. Accordingly I direct that my order dismissing the application shall not be drawn up until the registrar—and I mean the registrar here, not the county court registrar—has informed the Attorney-General of the matter and ascertained whether he wishes to be represented herein. If he does, then the application will be heard de novo[2]. Otherwise it will stand dismissed.

j   *Application dismissed.*

Susan Corbett Barrister.

---

1   [1915] 1 KB 21, [1914-15] All ER Rep 1022
2   It is understood that the Attorney-General did not wish to intervene

Re M (a minor) (adoption: removal from jurisdiction)

FAMILY DIVISION

BRANDON J

15th DECEMBER 1972, 12th JANUARY 1973

Adoption – Care and possession before adoption – Provisional adoption by person resident outside Great Britain – Restriction on removal of child outside British Islands – Prohibition on removal of child out of Great Britain with a view to adoption – Prospective adopters making child ward of court – Adopters domiciled and resident in Denmark – Adopters applying for leave to remove child to Denmark in order to establish requisite period of care and possession – Whether court having jurisdiction to give leave – Adoption Act 1958, ss 3 (1), 52 (1), 53 (5).

The husband and wife, who were of Danish nationality, domiciled and resident in Denmark, wished to adopt an illegitimate girl of two who was in the care of a local authority and was living with foster parents in England. The Danish couple made the child a ward of court and in the same proceedings sought an order for the removal of the child to Denmark so that they could have continuous care and control of her for six months, as required by ss 3 (1)*a* and 53 (5)*b* of the Adoption Act 1958, before applying to the court for a provisional adoption order. The question arose whether the court could give leave for the removal of the child to Denmark in view of the prohibition contained in s 52 (1)*c* of the 1958 Act on the removal of an infant who was a British subject 'to any place outside the British Islands with a view to the adoption of the infant'. The applicants contended that the removal would not be a removal 'with a view to the adoption' of the child but only a removal with a view to returning the child to England after six months and then applying for a provisional adoption order; they further contended that, the child being a ward of court, the court could make it a condition of granting leave that the applicants furnish guarantees and undertakings for her subsequent return to England.

Held – The application would be dismissed for the following reasons—

(i) s 52 (1) of the 1958 Act imposed an absolute prohibition against the removal of infants who were British subjects from the British Islands with a view to their adoption except under the authority of a provisional adoption order; the expression 'with a view to adoption' was a broad and comprehensive expression covering not only cases where the removal was for the immediate purpose of adoption but also cases where, although immediate adoption was not contemplated, the removal was one step in a larger process the ultimate purpose of which was adoption (see p 856 c and d, post);

(ii) it was irrelevant that, because the child was a ward of court, the court could make any permission for removal subject to an undertaking or guarantee; no distinction could be drawn between wards of court and children who were not wards in that respect (see p 856 e, post).

Notes

For the restrictions on the removal of infants out of the British Islands for the purpose of adoption, see 21 Halsbury's Laws (3rd Edn) 226, para 496.

For the Adoption Act 1958, ss 3, 52, 53, see 17 Halsbury's Statutes (3rd Edn) 639, 677.

---

a Section 3 (1), so far as material, is set out at p 854 h, post

b Section 53 (5) is set out at p 854 b, post

c Section 52 (1) is set out at p 855 g and h, post

Cases referred to in judgment

M (an infant), Re [1964] 2 All ER 1017, [1965] Ch 203, [1964] 3 WLR 609, 128 JP 522, 28 (2) Digest (Reissue) 836, 1404.

W (an infant), Re [1962] 2 All ER 875, [1962] Ch 918, [1962] 3 WLR 544, 126 JP 445, 61 LGR 113, 28 (2) Digest (Reissue) 825, 1365.

Preliminary issue

The plaintiffs, wishing to adopt a child aged two, issued an originating summons dated 1st July 1971 seeking, inter alia, an order that she be made a ward of court, and that care and control of her be committed to the plaintiffs. The defendants were the child's mother and Birmingham Social Services Department. The plaintiffs, a husband and wife, were resident and domiciled in Denmark. A preliminary issue arose whether the court had jurisdiction to give leave for the removal of the child to Denmark. The facts are set out in the judgment.

J A R Finlay for the plaintiffs.
D K Rattee for the Official Solicitor.
The defendants did not appear and were not represented.

Cur adv vult

12th January. **BRANDON J** read the following judgment. The court has before it a preliminary question of law in wardship proceedings. The ward concerned is a little girl of two, born to an unmarried mother in England in 1970. She is at present in the care of the city of Birmingham and living with foster parents there. The plaintiffs are a married couple of Danish nationality, domiciled and resident in Denmark. They wish to adopt the child in Denmark and for this purpose to obtain what is called a provisional adoption order under s 53 of the Adoption Act 1958 which I shall refer to as 'the Act'.

It is necessary for the plaintiffs, in order to satisfy one of the requirements of the Act for the grant of such an order, to have the care and possession of the child for six months before the date of the order. They desire to have such care and possession in Denmark and to remove the child from England for this purpose. In order to further their plan for adopting the child, the plaintiffs have made her a ward of court and seek an order from the court in the wardship proceedings permitting them to remove the child from England to Denmark so that they may have the care and possession of her for six months in that country, prior to bringing her back and applying for a provisional adoption order.

The question has, however, been raised whether, in view of certain provisions of the Act, the court can, whatever the merits of the proposal from the point of view of the child's welfare, lawfully give the plaintiffs the permission which they seek. In order to explain more fully how that question arises and to determine the answer to it, it is necessary to refer in some detail to a number of provisions of the Act which have a bearing on the matter. Section 53, which is in Part V of the Act, provides:

'(1) If the court is satisfied, upon an application being made by a person who is not domiciled in England or Scotland, that the applicant intends to adopt an infant under the law of or within the country in which he is domiciled, and for that purpose desires to remove the infant from Great Britain either immediately or after an interval, the court may, subject to the provisions of this section, make an order (in this section referred to as a provisional adoption order) authorising the applicant to remove the infant for the purpose aforesaid, and giving to the applicant the custody of the infant pending his adoption as aforesaid.

'(2) An application for a provisional adoption order may be made, in England to the High Court or the county court, and in Scotland to the Court of Session or the sheriff court.

'(3) A provisional adoption order may be made in any case where, apart from the domicile of the applicant, an adoption order could be made in respect of the infant under Part I of this Act, but shall not be made in any other case.

'(4) Subject to the provisions of this section, the provisions of this Act, other than this section and sections sixteen, seventeen and nineteen, shall apply in relation to a provisional adoption order as they apply in relation to an adoption order, and references in those provisions to adoption, to an adoption order, to an application or applicant for such an order and to an adopter or a person adopted or authorised to be adopted under such an order shall be construed accordingly.

'(5) In relation to a provisional adoption order section three of this Act shall have effect as if for the word "three", both where it occurs in subsection (1) and where it occurs in subsection (2), there were substituted the word "six".

'(6) . . .'

The reference in s 53 (3) to cases where, apart from the domicil of the applicant, an adoption order could be made in respect of the infant under Part I of the Act, is a reference to the making of adoption orders (a) under s 1 on the application of persons who are both domiciled and resident in England or Scotland, and (b) under s 12 on the application of persons who are domiciled in England or Scotland but are not ordinarily resident in Great Britain. The reference in s 53 (4) to other provisions of the Act applicable in relation to adoption orders, is a reference to a number of such provisions, including s 3, which deals with the care and possession of infants before adoption and notification of the local authority in the case of applicants both domiciled and resident in England or Scotland, and s 12 which deals with the modification of various earlier sections, including s 3, in the case of applicants domiciled in England or Scotland but not ordinarily resident in Great Britain. The effect of s 53 (5) is to make further modifications in the requirements of s 3 in the case of applicants for a provisional, as distinct from an ordinary, adoption order.

The nature of a provisional adoption order under s 53 was explained by Buckley J in *Re M (an infant)*[1] where he said:

'Such an order is not really an adoption order at all and does not create any relation between the applicants and the infant but merely empowers the applicants to remove the infant from this country to another jurisdiction for adoption outside England.'

While this important distinction between a true adoption order and a provisional adoption order exists, however, the same requirements of the Act with regard to, among other things, the care and possession of infants before the making of an order, and the notification of local authorities, apply, with some variations, to applications for both types of order.

Thus, in relation to an application for a provisional adoption order under s 53 by persons who are not domiciled in England or Scotland, s 3, as made applicable by s 53 (4) and modified by s 53 (5), must be read as providing:

'(1) [A provisional] adoption order shall not be made in respect of any infant unless he has been continuously in the care and possession of the applicant for at least [six] consecutive months immediately preceding the date of the order . . .

'(2) Except where the applicant or one of the applicants is a parent of the infant, [a provisional] adoption order shall not be made in respect of an infant who at the hearing of the application is below the upper limit of compulsory school age unless the applicant has, at least [six] months before the date of the order, given notice in writing to the local authority within whose area he was then resident of his intention to apply for [a provisional] adoption order in respect of the infant.'

---

1   [1964] 2 All ER 1017 at 1018, [1965] Ch 203 at 210

a   Further, in cases where the applicants for a provisional adoption order, besides not
being domiciled in England or Scotland, are also not ordinarily resident in Great
Britain, the provisions of s 3 set out above become further modified by s 12 (as also made
applicable by s 53 (4)). That section must, in such a case, be read as providing:

b   '(1) [A provisional] adoption order may, notwithstanding anything in this Act,
        be made on the application of a person who is not ordinarily resident in Great
        Britain; and in relation to such an application—(a) . . . (b) subsection (2) of section
        three of this Act applies with the substitution of the word "living" for the word
        "resident" . . .
        '(3) Where an application for [a provisional] adoption order is made jointly by
        spouses who are not, or one of whom is not, ordinarily resident in Great Britain,
        the notice required by subsection (2) of section 3 of this Act (as modified by
c   subsection (1) of this section) may be given by either of the applicants . . .'

The effect of these provisions is that the plaintiffs in the present case, in order to
qualify for the grant of a provisional adoption order in respect of the ward under s 53,
must first satisfy two requirements. First, they must have had the child continuously
in their care and possession for at least six consecutive months immediately preceding
d   the date of the order (s 3 (1) as modified by s 53 (5)). Secondly, one of them must, at
least six months before the date of the order, have given notice to the local authority
within whose area he or she was then living of their joint intention to apply for a
provisional order in respect of the child (s 3 (2) as modified by s 12 (1) and (3) and s 53
(5)).
No difficulty arises with regard to the plaintiffs fulfilling the second requirement.
e   One of them can come over to England and live there for a short period, and, while
doing so, give the necessary notice to the local authority within whose area he or she
will then be living. Difficulty does arise, however, with regard to the plaintiffs fulfilling the first requirement relating to six months' prior care and possession, if such care
and possession is to be had in Denmark as they desire.
The difficulty referred to does not arise because s 3 (1) requires care and possession
f   in such a case to be had in England rather than abroad, for it has been decided that
there should not be implied into that subsection any requirement to that effect: see
Re W (an infant)[1]. The difficulty arises rather out of s 52 of the Act, which imposes
restrictions on the removal of minors for adoption outside the British Islands (meaning
in this connection the United Kingdom, the Channel Islands and the Isle of Man).
Section 52 (1) provides:

g   'Except under the authority of an order under section fifty-three of this Act,
        it shall not be lawful for any person to take or send an infant who is a British
        subject out of Great Britain to any place outside the British Islands with a view to
        the adoption of the infant (whether in law or in fact) by any person not being a
        parent or guardian or relative of the infant; and any person who takes or sends
h   an infant out of Great Britain to any place in contravention of this subsection, or
        makes or takes part in any arrangements for transferring the care and possession
        of an infant to any person for that purpose, shall be liable on summary conviction
        to imprisonment for a term not exceeding six months or to a fine not exceeding
        one hundred pounds or to both.'

It has been argued on behalf of the Official Solicitor, who acts as guardian ad litem
j   of the child and considers it his duty to put the difficulty arising out of s 52 before the
court, that the effect of s 52 is to make it unlawful for the plaintiffs to remove the child
to Denmark in order to have the care and possession of her there as a preliminary to
a later application for a provisional adoption order under s 53, and that, in these

---

1   [1962] 2 All ER 875, [1962] Ch 918

circumstances, the court, in the exercise of its wardship jurisdiction, cannot properly *a* give the plaintiffs permission for such removal.

On the other side it has been argued for the plaintiffs that the proposed removal would not be a removal with a view to the adoption of the child within the meaning of s 52. It would, it is said, only be a removal with a view to returning the child to England after six months and then applying for a provisional adoption order under s 53. In this connection it is further said, that whatever might be the situation if the *b* child were not a ward of court, the circumstances that she is enables the court to make it a condition of any leave given for removal that the plaintiffs should furnish undertakings or guarantees satisfactory to the court for the subsequent return of the child to England and for the making of an application under s 53 before the taking of any steps to effect the adoption of the child in Denmark.

In my judgment the argument put forward on behalf of the Official Solicitor must *c* prevail. The purpose of s 52 is plain. It is to prohibit absolutely the removal of a child who is a British subject from the British Islands with a view to its adoption, except under the authority of a provisional adoption order under s 53. The expression 'with a view to adoption' is a very broad and comprehensive one. It covers, in my view not only cases where the removal is for the immediate purpose of adoption, but also cases where, although immediate adoption is not intended, the removal *d* constitutes one step in a larger process the ultimate purpose of which is adoption. I consider that the words should be interpreted as having this wider meaning despite the fact that the subsection concerned makes breach of the prohibition a criminal offence.

It is I think irrelevant that, because in the present case the child is a ward of court, the court can make any permission for removal subject to undertakings or guarantees. If the child were not a ward of court, so that undertakings or guarantees could not be *e* insisted on, the same question of construction would arise, and I do not see how it can be determined in one way in relation to a child who is not a ward and in another way in relation to a child who is a ward.

For the reasons which I have given I determine the preliminary question of law raised before me by holding that the court cannot properly, whatever the merits of the case from the point of view of the child's welfare, give the leave for removal which *f* is sought, because to do so in the present state of affairs would involve a breach of s 52 of the Act.

I use the expression 'in the present state of affairs' advisedly, for it appears to me that there could, in theory at least, be certain changes of circumstances in the future which would alter the position. One change of circumstances which would alter the position would be if the plaintiffs were to be appointed the guardians of the child, *g* because the prohibition against removal in s 52 does not apply to a guardian. Another change of circumstances would be if the Secretary of State gave his consent to the emigration of the child under s 17 of the Children Act 1948, for in that case, by virtue of s 55 of the Children and Young Persons Act 1963, s 52 would not apply.

While I do not desire to encourage the plaintiffs, and must not be taken as encouraging them, to follow any particular course, it may be that they and their legal advisers *h* would wish to consider at least the possibilities arising from the two matters to which I have referred.

Determination accordingly.

Solicitors: *Sharpe, Pritchard & Co*, agents for *Wragge & Co*, Birmingham (for the *j* plaintiffs); *Official Solicitor*.

R C T Habesch Esq   Barrister.

a

R v Andrews

COURT OF APPEAL, CRIMINAL DIVISION
LORD WIDGERY CJ, MEGAW LJ AND TALBOT J
30th NOVEMBER 1972

b

Criminal law – Obstructing course of justice – Incitement – Perversion of course of public justice – Accused offering to give false evidence on behalf of potential defendant in criminal proceedings in return for payment – Nexus between incitement and contemplated offence – Whether perversion of justice an offence.

c The appellant and R were involved in a motor accident in circumstances which were such as to render R liable to prosecution. Some days later the appellant visited R and intimated that R was in trouble with the police and would need a good witness. The appellant invited R to pay him money as a consideration for giving false evidence on behalf of R. The appellant was charged with soliciting and inciting R 'to pervert the course of justice by offering in consideration for a reward to make a false state-
d ment to the police relating to [the] accident . . . in which criminal proceedings were being instituted' against R. The appellant was convicted and appealed.

Held – The conviction would be affirmed for the following reasons—
    (i) to produce false evidence with a view to misleading the court and perverting the course of justice was a substantive offence at common law; an incitement so to act
e was also a charge known to the law and could properly be preferred in appropriate circumstances (see p 859 f, post); *R v Vreones* [1891] 1 QB 360 and *R v Grimes* [1968] 3 All ER 179 applied;
    (ii) there were no grounds for saying that the incitement by the appellant to R to pay money to obtain false evidence was so remote that it lacked a sufficient nexus with the contemplated perversion of justice to constitute the offence charged (see
f p 859 j to p 860 a, post).

Notes

For conspiracy to obstruct the course of justice, see 10 Halsbury's Laws (3rd Edn) 631, para 1198, and for cases on the subject, see 15 Digest (Repl) 843, 844, 8069-8090.
    For incitement to crime, see 10 Halsbury's Laws (3rd Edn) 309, 310, para 568, and
g for cases on the subject, see 14 Digest (Repl) 119, 822-831.

Cases referred to in judgment

R v Grimes [1968] 3 All ER 179, Digest (Cont Vol C) 247, 8066a.
R v Vreones [1891] 1 QB 360, 60 LJMC 62, 64 LT 389, 55 JP 536, 17 Cox CC 267, CCR, 15 Digest (Repl) 842, 8058.
h *Shaw v Director of Public Prosecutions* [1961] 2 All ER 446, [1962] AC 220, [1961] 2 WLR 897, 125 JP 437, 45 Cr App Rep 113, HL, Digest (Cont Vol A) 339, 919a.

Appeal

Edward John Andrews appealed against his conviction on 8th June 1972 in the Crown Court at Woodford before his Honour Judge Basil Hobson and a jury on a count
j charging him with incitement to pervert the course of public justice. He also appealed against the sentence of 18 months' imprisonment imposed on him. The facts are set out in the judgment of the court.

A W Lyon for the appellant.
Patricia Coles for the Crown.

LORD WIDGERY CJ delivered the following judgment of the court. At Woodford Crown Court in June 1972 the appellant was convicted on one count of incitement to pervert the course of public justice and he was sentenced to 18 months'
imprisonment. He appeals against conviction and sentence by leave of the single
judge, and in regard to his appeal against conviction the points raised are exclusively
points of law. They have to be decided against this factual background which at
this stage of the matter counsel for the appellant does not feel able to dispute. There
was a traffic accident on 6th September 1971; a Mr Watling was riding a moped in
Romford and as he approached a road junction two other cars were at or in the vicinity
of the junction. One car was driven by the appellant and the other car was driven by
a man called Reeves. The appellant's car seems to have been stationary at the
time, and no one suggested he was responsible for the collision which Mr Watling
suffered from, but Mr Reeves's car was in motion, and an immediate appreciation
of the situation after the accident was that the moped had been knocked over by
Mr Reeves's car and Mr Reeves was a potential defendant in proceedings in respect
of that accident. That being the case, according to Mr Reeves some seven days later
the appellant sought Mr Reeves out in the shop which Mr Reeves kept. He told Mr
Reeves that he had a directive from the police to call at the police station urgently,
and that Mr Reeves was in a lot of trouble and would need a good witness. Mr
Reeves, according to his evidence, said: 'What do you mean, what are you getting
at?' or words to that effect. The appellant said: Well, it is obvious, isn't it.' The
appellant then said: 'I'm in your hands' and made a reference to making an offer.
Mr Reeves said: 'Well £20'; that was not satisfactory to the appellant and no bargain
was struck. The next day two police officers were in the shop when the appellant
returned, and one must approach this case on the footing that there was no doubt
that the appellant was inviting Mr Reeves to make him, the appellant, a payment to
give evidence at the prospective prosecution which was contrary to the fact.

In the appeal against conviction two points of law are taken in regard to the conviction entered on those facts. Before I turn to the arguments, I should read the terms
of the count in the indictment on which the conviction was entered. It alleges that the
appellant was guilty of incitement to pervert the course of public justice, contrary
to common law. The particulars were that on or about 13th September 1971 in
the county of Essex he—

> 'solicited and incited Adrian Kenneth Cuthbert Reeves to pervert the course
> of public justice by offering in consideration for a reward to make a false state-
> ment to the police relating to an accident involving ... Reeves on the 6th Sep-
> tember, 1971, in which criminal proceedings were being instituted against the
> said ... Reeves.'

It is said first of all that that count assumes the existence of a substantive offence
of perverting the course of public justice, and we are invited to say in the present
day such an offence does not exist. There are two authorities, both I think relied
on below but both brought to our attention by counsel for the appellant in accordance
with his duty although neither is favourable to him. I refer first to *R v Grimes*[1]
which was decided in the Liverpool Crown Court by Judge Kilner Brown. This was
a case in which a charge had been preferred against an accused man of attempting
to defeat the due course of justice by inducing a named person falsely to report to
an officer of the Lancashire Constabulary that he had found in his house moneys
which he had previously reported to be unlawfully taken therefrom. In essence the
charge was an attempt to defeat the due course of justice by giving false evidence.
Judge Kilner Brown, having referred to the textbooks, said[2]:

> 'In my view useful assistance is to be gained from the arguments in the judg-
> ments on criminal law, as it then was, and the speeches of their lordships in the

1   [1968] 3 All ER 179
2   [1968] 3 All ER at 181

a   case of *Shaw* v. *Director of Public Prosecutions*[1]. Certain actions such as cheating
or behaving obscenely may not be offences in a private connotation, but once
the public is involved, either by agreement with one of its number or more
diversely, the law regards such conduct as criminal. Perversion of the course
of justice is per se an offence against the public weal. It is recognised as an
unlawful act for the purpose of framing a charge of conspiracy to pervert the

b   course of justice and I am of the opinion, whichever way one approaches it,
that common law does, and has for many years, recognised an act to pervert
the course of justice, or an attempt so to do, as an unlawful act in itself.'

Accordingly he refused to quash the count in that case.

In so doing he was in our opinion following authority in the form of *R v Vreones*[2].
In that case the allegation was that the accused had interfered with evidence before

c   arbitrators, and the count, very prolix as they often were in those days, set out in
great detail the interference which was alleged to have been committed by him and
then charged it as[3]:

> '. . . and thereby to injure and prejudice the said Sidman Thomas Stephens and
> others, and by the means aforesaid to pervert the due course of law and justice,
d   > against the peace of our Lady the Queen . . .'

So that the question arose whether it was possible to have an attempt to pervert the
course of justice. Lord Coleridge CJ said[4]:

> 'The first count of the indictment in substance charges the defendant with the
> misdemeanour of attempting, by the manufacture of false evidence, to mislead
e   > a judicial tribunal which might come into existence. If the act itself of the defen-
> dant was completed, I cannot doubt that to manufacture false evidence for the
> purpose of misleading a judicial tribunal is a misdemeanour . . . I think that an
> attempt to pervert the course of justice is in itself a punishable misdemeanour;
> and though I should myself have thought so on the grounds of sense and reason,
> there is also plenty of authority to shew that it is a misdemeanour in point of
f   > law.'

Accordingly, to produce false evidence with a view to misleading the court and perverting the course of justice is a substantive offence; an attempt so to act can be
charged as such, and in our judgment an incitement so to act is also a charge
known to the law and properly to be preferred in appropriate circumstances.

However, it is said, and this is the second submission against conviction, that the
g   charge here does not justify a conviction on the basis of the facts to which I have
referred. The argument is that the incitement which is to be assumed is an incitement to Mr Reeves to pay money in order to obtain false evidence from the appellant,
and it is argued that there is no sufficient nexus between that incitement and the
ultimate perversion of justice to make the particulars of this charge come within the
frontiers of the recognised offence to which I have already referred. We do not
h   accept that submission. It seems to us that if Mr Reeves had paid the money and as a
result the appellant had given false evidence there would there have been a perversion
of the course of justice or at least an attempt so to do, and one can regard the offering
of the reward by Mr Reeves and its acceptance by the appellant and his subsequent
conduct as contemplated by the bargain between them, as being all one matter.
j   Undoubtedly on the facts of this case the appellant incited Mr Reeves to enter into that
course of conduct, and we can see no reason to say that the incitement is so remote

---

1   [1961] 2 All ER 446, [1962] AC 220
2   [1891] 1 QB 360
3   [1891] 1 QB at 362
4   [1891] 1 QB at 366, 367

or lacks a sufficient nexus with the contemplated perversion of justice to say that this
count should not be allowed to stand. It follows therefore that the appeal against
conviction must be dismissed.

As to sentence, the appellant is a man of 49 years of age who had some criminal
record years ago in the 1940s, when he went to prison on four occasions, all for dishonesty except in one instance which was for malicious damage. Since 1948 he has
had no convictions; he has undoubtedly improved his position. In December 1971
he became general manager of an engineering company, and the court has been
supplied with testimonials by his employer and others to show that he has been an
honest and law abiding man now for a great number of years, and as the trial judge
said it is clearly a case in which one ought to approach him as being a man of
substantially good character for the purposes of sentence.

However, there are few more serious offences possible in the present day, if one
excludes violent offences, than those which tend to distort the course of public justice
and prevent the courts producing true and just results in the cases before them.
This sort of action is akin to perjury, which is always regarded as serious, and we do
not think even having regard to this man's good character that a sentence of 18
months' imprisonment is excessive. Accordingly the appeal against sentence is
also dismissed.

Appeals dismissed.

Solicitors: *Registrar of Criminal Appeals* (for the appellant); *Director of Public
Prosecutions.*

N P Metcalfe Esq Barrister.

Ray v Sempers

QUEEN'S BENCH DIVISION
LORD WIDGERY CJ, WILLIS AND TALBOT JJ
4th, 5th, 19th DECEMBER 1972

*Criminal law – Obtaining pecuniary advantage by deception – Deception – Representation
by words or conduct – Proof of an actual representation required – Accused ordering meal
in restaurant – Accused deciding during course of meal to leave without paying – Accused
remaining at table until waiter out of room before leaving restaurant – Whether
pecuniary advantage obtained by deception – Theft Act 1968, ss 15 (4), 16 (1).*

The accused went to a restaurant and ordered a meal. At the time of ordering he
intended to pay for the meal and had sufficient means to pay. During the course
of the meal he changed his mind and decided to leave without paying. Having
made that decision he remained at his table until the waiter had gone out of the
room, whereupon he left the restaurant. He was charged with obtaining a pecuniary
advantage by deception, contrary to s 16 (1)[a] of the Theft Act 1968. The Crown
contended that, by remaining at his table as an ordinary customer after he had
decided not to pay and failing to inform the waiter that he had changed his mind
about paying, the accused had made a false representation by conduct within s 15
(4)[b] of the 1968 Act and had therefore practised a deception within s 16 (1) whereby
he had obtained a pecuniary advantage, i e the evasion of his debt to the restaurant.

a Section 16 (1) is set out at p 862 j, post
b Section 15 (4) is set out at p 863 b, post

a **Held** – In order to prove a deception under s 16 it was necessary to show that the accused had actually made, by words or conduct, a false representation. The act of the accused in waiting until the waiter was out of the room in order to leave without paying did not amount to a representation; accordingly, although the accused had evaded his debt, he had not done so by deception (see p 865 g to p 866 a, post).

b **Notes**
For the offence of obtaining a pecuniary advantage by deception and the meaning of deception, see Supplement to 10 Halsbury's Laws (3rd Edn) para 1586A, 2, 3.
For the Theft Act 1968, ss 15, 16, see 8 Halsbury's Statutes (3rd Edn) 792, 793.

Cases referred to in judgment
c *R v Aston, R v Hadley* [1970] 3 All ER 1045, [1970] 1 WLR 1584, 135 JP 89, 55 Cr App Rep 18, CA, Digest (Cont Vol C) 262, 10,264a.
R v Collins [1972] 2 All ER 1105, [1972] 3 WLR 243, 56 Cr App Rep 554, CA.
R v Locker [1971] 2 All ER 875, [1971] 2 QB 321, [1971] 2 WLR 1302, 135 JP 437, 55 Cr App Rep 375, CA.
R v Page [1971] 2 All ER 870, [1971] 2 QB 330, [1971] 2 WLR 1308, 135 JP 376, 55 Cr
d App Rep 184, CA.
With v O'Flanagan [1936] 1 All ER 727, [1936] Ch 575, 105 LJCh 247, 154 LT 634, CA, 35 Digest (Repl) 32, *233.*

Case stated
This was an appeal by way of case stated by justices for the county of Lincoln, parts of Lindsey, acting in and for the petty sessional division of Gainsborough, in respect of
e their adjudication as a magistrates' court sitting at Gainsborough on 1st February 1972.
On 27th October 1971 the respondent, Arthur Sempers, a chief inspector of police, preferred an information against the appellant, Roger Anthony Ray, that he at Gainsborough on 30th September 1971, by a certain deception, namely by his conduct
f in ordering and being served with a meal in the Wing Wah restaurant and impliedly holding out at the time of ordering the meal an intention and an ability to pay on demand on receipt of the bill, dishonestly obtained for himself a pecuniary advantage, namely a meal consisting of prawn chop suey and fried rice, to the value of 47p and evaded the debt by running out of the restaurant without payment, contrary to s 16 (1) of the Theft Act 1968.
The following facts were found. (a) On the evening of 30th September 1971 the
g appellant (who was a university student) and four other young men entered the Wing Wah restaurant and four of them, including the appellant, ordered a meal. (b) At the time he entered the restaurant the appellant had only 10p on him, which was insufficient for a meal; one of the other men had agreed to lend him some money to pay. (c) The appellant was served with a meal, which he ate without
h making any complaint to the restaurant staff. A discussion took place between the other young men who had had a meal, which the appellant joined, and they decided not to pay for the meal and to run out of the restaurant. Some ten minutes later, and after being in the restaurant for nearly an hour and maintaining the demeanour of ordinary customers, the appellant and his four companions ran out of the restaurant whilst the waiter had gone to the kitchen. No payment was offered or made, and no money was left, for the meals served. Each of the four had consumed only
j a main course. After leaving the restaurant the appellant and the others ran away, and hid from sight of an approaching police vehicle.
It was contended by the appellant: (a) that there had been no deception since he had made arrangements for one of his companions to pay for the meal, and had no intention to evade payment at the time he entered the restaurant; (b) that a meal was not within the definition of a 'pecuniary advantage' contained in s 16 of

the Theft Act 1968; (c) that his running away from the restaurant was no evidence of a deception; (d) that in order to establish the appellant's guilt, the respondent had *a* to prove beyond reasonable doubt that the appellant intended his conduct to be a deception and that the deception was effective in obtaining a pecuniary advantage, namely the evasion of a debt.

It was contended by the respondent: (a) that as soon as the appellant had been served with a meal he incurred a debt which was a pecuniary advantage within the *b* statute; (b) that it was immaterial whether the deception occurred either when ordering the meal, eating the meal, or after the meal; (c) that as soon as the intent to evade payment was formed and the appellant still posed as an ordinary customer the deception had been made.

The justices were of the opinion: (a) that the appellant entered the restaurant intending that his meal should be paid for by one of his companions; (b) that he had *c* no complaint on the quality of the meal, and consumed it all; (c) that when his companions indicated a desire to evade payment, the appellant concurred in this and joined in the discussion of how that was to be done; (d) that having changed his mind as regards payment, by remaining in the restaurant for a further ten minutes as an ordinary customer who was likely to order a sweet or coffee, the appellant practised a deception, and (e) that the appellant had made himself liable for a debt *d* in respect of a meal, and by his deception dishonestly evaded payment. Accordingly the justices found the case proved, convicted the appellant, and ordered him to pay a fine of £1.

H A Skinner QC and *C C Colston* for the appellant.
Charles McCullough QC and *Igor Judge* for the respondent.

Cur adv vult *e*

19th December. **TALBOT J** read the first judgment at the request of Lord Widgery CJ. This is an appeal by way of case stated from the Gainsborough justices who on 1st February 1972 convicted the appellant on an information alleging that on 30th September 1971, by a dishonest deception, he obtained for himself a pecuniary advantage, namely a meal in the Wing Wah restaurant, and evaded the debt by *f* running out of the restaurant without payment, contrary to s 16 (1) of the Theft Act 1968. He was ordered to pay a fine of £1.

The facts which the justices found were as follows. On 30th September 1971 the appellant with four other young men went to the restaurant and the appellant and three of them ordered a meal. The appellant arranged to borrow sufficient money to pay for his meal from one of the other men. One course of the meal was served *g* and eaten whereupon a discussion took place between the appellant and the others about paying and it was decided that they would not pay and would run out of the restaurant without paying.

The justices accepted, therefore, that initially the appellant intended that his meal should be paid for and their finding was that he changed his mind. They also found that by remaining in the restaurant as an ordinary customer until the waiter *h* was out of the room he practised a deception and by his deception evaded payment. The justices seek the opinion of this court as to whether, on a true construction of s 16 of the Theft Act 1968, the appellant was rightly convicted.

Before proceeding to consider the case it is necessary that I should refer to the relevant parts of ss 15 and 16 (1), (2) (a) and (3). Section 16 provides:

'(1) A person who by any deception dishonestly obtains for himself or another *j* any pecuniary advantage shall on conviction on indictment be liable to imprisonment for a term not exceeding five years.

'(2) The cases in which a pecuniary advantage within the meaning of this section is to be regarded as obtained for a person are cases where—(a) any debt or charge for which he makes himself liable or is or may become liable (including *a* one not legally enforceable) is reduced or in whole or in part evaded or deferred ...

'(3) For purposes of this section "deception" has the same meaning as in section 15 of this Act.'

Section 15 (4) defines the nature of deception:

b 'For purposes of this section "deception" means any deception (whether deliberate or reckless) by words or conduct as to fact or as to law, including a deception as to the present intentions of the person using the deception or any other person.'

c Therefore what the respondent sought to prove was that the appellant by deception dishonestly obtained for himself a pecuniary advantage whereby the debt was evaded.
    Briefly the main contentions before us on behalf of the appellant were, first, that there was no deception, the appellant having entered the restaurant and ordered a meal with honest intentions; secondly, that no deception was proved by virtue of which the debt was evaded; and thirdly, that to evade a debt under the section meant
d to extinguish it and the respondent had failed to prove that the mind of the creditor, i e the waiter, had been moved to extinguish the debt. For the respondent it was argued that the appellant practised a deception by continuing to sit in the restaurant as a normal customer and by failing to correct the originally true representation that he was an honest customer. This deception, counsel for the respondent submitted, induced the waiter to grant the appellant credit to the extent of ten minutes more than he would otherwise have done had he been told that the appellant was not
e going to pay and the appellant therefore gained the opportunity to run out and evade the debt. I will return to these contentions a little later. In the course of the argument certain authorities were cited to the court. First in point of time was the decision of the Court of Appeal in *R v Aston, R v Hadley*[1]. That was the case where two men went to a betting shop and placed a bet on a greyhound race with no intention of paying. The deception alleged was that one of them so slowly counted
f out the money to be paid over that they were able to hear on the shop's broadcast relay that the dog named was not going to win, whereupon they left the shop without paying. The offence alleged was that contrary to s 16 (2) (*a*) they dishonestly obtained a pecuniary advantage, namely, the evasion of the debt for which one of them had made himself liable by false representations that he intended to pay the money immediately. The conviction was quashed on two grounds: first, that the
g slow counting of the money could not safely or satisfactorily be a deception involving a representation of an intention to make an immediate payment; secondly, that the jury could not properly be asked to find that it operated on the shop manager's mind in such a way as to bring about the evasion of the debt. Megaw LJ said[2]:

h 'Whatever representation the slow counting might be thought to involve, it could hardly be a representation of an intention to make an immediate payment. Moreover, to be relevant, the deception, for the purposes of s 16 (2) (*a*), must at least normally be a deception which operates on the mind of the person deceived so as to influence him to do or to refrain from doing something whereby the debt is deferred or evaded.'

j There followed *R v Page*[3]. That was a case where the appellant was convicted of obtaining a pecuniary advantage by deception in that he represented that certain cheques were good and valid orders for payment and thereby evaded a debt. The

1 [1970] 3 All ER 1045, [1970] 1 WLR 1584
2 [1970] 3 All ER at 1048, [1970] 1 WLR at 1588
3 [1971] 2 All ER 870, [1971] 2 QB 330

principal point taken on his behalf was that the debt was not evaded because it
remained, but the court decided that what was evaded was payment of the debt. *a*
That was the point of decision in that case together with a finding that if the cheques
were drawn recklessly and without regard to whether there was any chance of their
being met, they were drawn dishonestly and there was therefore a dishonest deception. No point was taken in that appeal on the question whether the deception
operated on the mind of the victim.

Finally there was the authority of *R v Locker*[1]. The charge in point there was *b*
obtaining a pecuniary advantage by deception whereby payment of a debt was deferred. The five-judge Court of Appeal quashed the conviction. It was a case where a
cheque had been given in payment of rent due when in fact the appellant had no
account at the bank. The ground on which the court quashed the conviction was
that there was no deferment of the debt by reason of the fact that the creditor's
remedy was suspended whilst the worthless cheque was in process of being presented. *c*
In the course of his judgment Widgery LJ dealt with the element of the offence
which is pertinent to this present appeal, namely, that the deception must operate
so as to bring about the deferment. He said[2]:

> 'In our judgment, dealing with antecedent debts (and I emphasise that we
> are dealing with debts antecedent to the alleged deception) we think that the *d*
> Crown has got to prove two essentials. In reaching this conclusion, we are in-
> fluenced by the fact that s 16 is concerned primarily with the advantage obtained
> by an accused and not with the detriment to the victim. The phraseology of
> the section makes that perfectly clear, and looking at the section as a whole
> and confining ourselves to antecedent debts, the two matters in our judgment
> which the Crown has to prove are these. First they must show that the accused *e*
> practised a deception with the intention of inducing the creditor to refrain from
> requiring payment on the due date. The whole basis of the offence is deception
> and dishonesty. There must therefore be a deception by the accused, and we
> think that it must be a deception which is intended to induce the creditor to
> refrain from enforcing the payment of the debt on its due date. Secondly, it
> must be shown that the deception was effective, in other words it must be shown *f*
> that the deception has caused the creditor to refrain from requiring payment
> on the date when the debt was originally due. If it can be shown that the neces-
> sary deception has been practised with the intent to which we have referred,
> and that in fact and as a matter of cause and effect the creditor has been induced
> to refrain from requiring payment on the due date, that in our judgment satis-
> fies the requirements of the section in regard to obtaining the deferment of an *g*
> antecedent debt by deception in the statutory terms.'

It should, I think, be pointed out that certainly when dealing with an allegation
of evasion of a debt one is dealing with what is potentially a unilateral act. The
authority of *R v Aston, R v Hadley*[3] and that of *R v Locker*[1] both show that what is
required is some deception by words or conduct in the terms of s 15 (4) which, as a *h*
matter of cause and effect, induces the victim either to do or refrain from doing
something whereby the accused is enabled to evade the debt. Returning to the
parties' contentions: the appellant accepts the proposition that a person who enters
a restaurant and orders a meal impliedly represents that he has the means and intention of paying for it. In the present case, however, this representation was not false
when made, because the justices accept that these young men intended to pay for *j*
their meal when they first ordered it. The appellant goes on to contend that there
was no subsequent deception because following the decision not to pay for the meal

1 [1971] 2 All ER 875, [1971] 2 QB 321
2 [1971] 2 All ER at 879, [1971] 2 QB at 328
3 [1970] 3 All ER 1045, [1970] 1 WLR 1584

a all that the appellant and his friends did was simply to walk out of the restaurant.
It is conceded that by walking out of the restaurant they evaded payment of the
debt which they had incurred, but the appellant's contention is that there was no
deception which led to this evasion.

The respondent seeks to support the conviction. He accepts that there was no
deception in the first instance because the young men intended to pay for their meal
b when they ordered it, but it is contended that a deception occurred when the decision
to leave without paying was taken and the diners decided to wait until the waiter was
out of the room and the coast was clear before they made their escape. The argument
that there was a deception at this point is based on such cases as *With v O'Flanagan*[1],
and on the principle that having made a true representation of intention to pay
there was a duty on the diners to inform the waiter of their changed intention as
soon as they made that change. Put another way, it is argued that having made a
c misrepresentation which was true at the time but which has been falsified by their
own change of mind, they then perpetrated a deception by not informing the waiter
of their change of mind, and by deliberately remaining in the restaurant with an
innocent appearance until the opportunity of leaving presented itself to them. If
this be true, the consequences would be somewhat surprising. Thus, if they had
changed their minds and decided to go out without paying at a moment when the
d waiter was not present, and had there and then left the premises, no offence would
have been committed. There being no opportunity to communicate their change
of mind to the waiter, they would not have been guilty of any deception. On the
other hand, if the change of mind occurs whilst the waiter is in the room, and they
fail to inform him, and wait with innocent appearance until the waiter has gone, a
deception has been practised and the offence has been committed. I do not think
e there is room for niceties of this kind in the application of the criminal law as contained in the Theft Act 1968, and I am reinforced in that view by the attitude of the
Court of Appeal in *R v Collins*[2]. That was a case in which a young man was charged
with burglary on the basis that he had entered premises as a trespasser with the
intention of committing rape. Much legal argument was addressed to this court on
the common law of trespass and such doctrines as that of a trespasser ab initio were
f invoked. This submission was summarily rejected, and in giving the judgment of
the court Edmund Davies LJ said[3]: 'Whatever be the position in the law of tort, to
regard such a proposition as acceptable in the criminal law would be unthinkable.'
I think that similar considerations apply to questions of deception under s 16 of the
Theft Act 1968. No doubt the law of tort remains as the background in cases of
deception, and as has been observed by one of the learned textbook writers it is not
g possible to understand the Theft Act 1968 without some basic knowledge of the
civil law. That does not mean, however, that all the intricacies and difficulties of
the civil law are to be imported into this relatively simple statute, and in my opinion
juries should be instructed not to find a deception under s 16 unless the accused has
actually made a representation by words or conduct which representation is found
to be false. The reality of the present case is that the appellant intended to evade
h his obligations by the simple expedient of walking out in the belief that he would
not be traced. To make this possible he waited until the waiter went out of the room.
His plan was totally lacking in the subtlety of deception and to argue that his remaining in the room until the coast was clear amounted to a representation to the
waiter is to introduce an artificiality which should have no place in the Act.

In these circumstances in my judgment the justices were wrong in convicting
j the appellant as the evidence did not support any finding that there had been a
deception whereby there was an evasion of the debt and the appeal should be allowed
and the conviction quashed.

1   [1936] 1 All ER 727, [1936] Ch 575
2   [1972] 2 All ER 1105, [1972] 3 WLR 243
3   [1972] 2 All ER at 1111, [1972] 3 WLR at 249

WILLIS J. I agree.

a

LORD WIDGERY CJ. I also agree. I have listened with sympathy to the suggestion of counsel that we might take the advantage of this judgment to clear up some other outstanding difficulties in s 16, and although I have thought about this, I have come to the conclusion that the time is not appropriate, and that we cannot perform the service requested.

b

Appeal allowed. Leave to appeal to the House of Lords refused, but the court certified under s 1 (2) of the Administration of Justice Act 1960 that a point of law of general public importance was involved, namely, whether a deception within s 15 (4) of the Theft Act 1968 is proved when a person, who initially obtains credit honestly by representing his willingness to pay, later dishonestly decides to evade payment but fails to correct the original representation.

c

Solicitors: *Sergeant & Collins*, Scunthorpe (for the appellant); *Burton & Dyson*, Gainsborough (for the respondent).

N P Metcalfe Esq   Barrister.

d

Argyle Motors (Birkenhead) Ltd v Birkenhead Corporation

COURT OF APPEAL, CIVIL DIVISION

RUSSELL, BUCKLEY AND ORR LJJ

9th, 10th, 11th OCTOBER, 15th DECEMBER 1972

e

Compensation – Injurious affection – Land – Land or interest therein injuriously affected by the execution of works – Scope of compensation – Business carried on on land – Damage to business – Loss of profits – Execution of works by local authority in exercise of statutory powers – Works carried out in street adjoining plaintiffs' business premises – Whether plaintiffs entitled to compensation for loss of profits of business in consequence of works – Lands Clauses Consolidation Act 1845, s 68, as amended by the Compulsory Purchase Act 1965, s 39 (4), Sch 8, Part III.

f

The plaintiffs were tenants of a building in Birkenhead where they carried on the business of dealing in new and secondhand motor cars. The building was bounded on one side by Conway Street. Under s 20 of the Birkenhead Corporation (Mersey Tunnel Approaches) Act 1965 the defendant corporation were authorised to carry out certain specified works and by s 22 they were authorised to carry out subsidiary and incidental works. Section 22 (3)[a] provided that the corporation were to 'make reasonable compensation for any damage caused by the exercise' of the powers conferred by s 22. The 1965 Act incorporated s 68[b] of the Lands Clauses Consolidation Act 1845. The corporation commenced certain works pursuant to the powers conferred on them by s 22 of the 1965 Act including the reconstruction of Conway Street in the area adjoining the plaintiffs' property. The plaintiffs claimed to be entitled to compensation for injurious affection to their premises in consequence of those works including compensation under s 22 (3) of the 1965 Act for loss of profits of their business.

g

h

j

---

a   Section 22 (3) is set out at p 869 d, post

b   Section 68, as amended, provides: 'If any party shall be entitled to any compensation in respect of any lands, or of any interest therein which shall have been taken for or injuriously affected by the execution of the works, and for which the promoters of the undertaking shall not have made satisfaction under the provisions of this or the special Act, or any Act incorporated therewith, such party may have the same settled.'

Held – (i) Loss of profits as such was not a head of damage of a kind which could
ground a claim to compensation under s 68 of the 1845 Act; compensation under
s 68 was confined to injury to land or an interest in land. The fact that a claimant
was entitled to compensation on the ground that his land had been injuriously
affected did not entitle him to include a claim for compensation for injury suffered
in respect of his business (see p 876 f and p 877 c and e, post).

b
(ii) On its true construction s 22 (3) of the 1965 Act gave no wider right to compensation than that contained in s 68 of the 1845 Act. Accordingly the plaintiffs were
not entitled to compensation for loss of profits of their business (see p 878 a b e and f,
post).

Dicta of Lord Chelmsford LC and Lord Cranworth in *Ricket v Directors, etc, of Metropolitan Railway Co* (1867) LR 2 HL at 187, 198, of Lord Chelmsford and Lord Penzance
in *Metropolitan Board of Works v McCarthy* (1874) LR 7 HL at 256, 262, of Lord Selborne
c
LC in *Caledonian Railway Co v Walker's Trustees* [1881-85] All ER Rep at 595, 598, 599,
and of Lord Esher MR and Cotton LJ in *Ford v Metropolitan and Metropolitan District
Railway Companies* (1886) 17 QBD at 19, 25, applied.

Per Curiam. If injury to a business can be shown to have occasioned a diminution
in the value of the land where the business is carried on, compensation may be
d
recoverable for that injurious affection of the land (see p 877 e, post).

Notes

For compensation for injurious affection when no land is taken from the claimant,
see 10 Halsbury's Laws (3rd Edn) 155-162, paras 270-280, and for cases on the subject,
see 11 Digest (Repl) 145-158, *239-338*.

For the Lands Clauses Consolidation Act 1845, s 68, see 6 Halsbury's Statutes (3rd
e
Edn) 27.

Cases referred to in judgments

Beckett v Midland Railway Co (1867) LR 3 CP 82, 37 LJCP 11, 17 LT 499, 11 Digest (Repl)
151, *287*.
Caledonian Railway Co v Ogilvy (1855) 2 Macq 229, 25 LTOS 106, HL, 11 Digest (Repl)
f
149, *276*.
Caledonian Railway Co v Walker's Trustees (1882) 7 App Cas 259, [1881-85] All ER Rep
592, 46 LT 826, 46 JP 676, HL, 11 Digest (Repl) 149, *274*.
Ford v Metropolitan and Metropolitan District Railway Companies (1886) 17 QBD 12,
55 LJQB 296, 54 LT 718, 50 JP 661, CA, 11 Digest (Repl) 153, *295*.
Hammersmith and City Railway Co v Brand (1869) LR 4 HL 171, [1861-73] All ER Rep 60,
38 LJQB 265, 21 LT 238, 34 JP 36, HL, 11 Digest (Repl) 106, *29*.
g
Lingké v Christchurch Corpn [1912] 3 KB 595, 82 LJKB 37, 107 LT 476, 76 JP 433, 10 LGR
773, CA, 11 Digest (Repl) 151, *285*.
Metropolitan Board of Works v McCarthy (1874) LR 7 HL 243, 43 LJCP 385, 31 LT 182,
38 JP 820, HL; *affg sub nom McCarthy v Metropolitan Board of Works* (1873) LR 8 CP
191, 28 LT 417, Ex Ch; *affg* (1872) LR 7 CP 508, 42 LJCP 81, 26 LT 772, 11 Digest
h
(Repl) 152, *289*.
Ricket v Directors, etc, of Metropolitan Railway Co (1867) LR 2 HL 175, 36 LJQB 205,
16 LT 542, 31 JP 484, HL, 11 Digest (Repl) 150, *281*.

Cases also cited

Blundy, Clark & Co Ltd v London and North Eastern Railway Co [1931] 2 KB 334, [1931]
All ER Rep 160, CA.
j
Colac (President etc) v Summerfield [1893] AC 187, PC.
Dudley Corpn, Re (1881) 8 QBD 86, [1881-85] All ER Rep 565, CA.
Fritz v Hobson (1880) 14 Ch D 542, [1874-80] All ER Rep 75.

Interlocutory appeal

The plaintiffs, Argyle Motors (Birkenhead) Ltd, brought an action against the defendants, Birkenhead Corporation ('the corporation'), claiming a declaration that they

were entitled to compensation under s 10 (1) of the Compulsory Purchase Act 1965
as applied by s 39 (3) of, and Sch 7 to, the Birkenhead Corporation (Mersey Tunnel
Approaches) Act 1965, for injurious affection to their premises situated at 12 Conway
Street, Birkenhead, by the execution of works authorised by the 1965 Act. They
also claimed to be entitled to compensation under s 22 (3) of the 1965 Act for damage
suffered by them in respect of the property and the business carried on by them on
the property, including loss of profits of the business, by the execution of works both
temporary and permanent. On 30th July 1971 the Liverpool District Registrar
directed that the claims under s 22 of the 1965 Act should be determined as preliminary issues and that pending such determination all further proceedings in the
action should be stayed. On 18th November 1971 Foster J, on the hearing of the
preliminary issues, held, inter alia, that the corporation were not liable to pay compensation to the plaintiffs in respect of loss of profits of their business. The plaintiffs
appealed.

Iain Glidewell QC and *E H Wells* for the plaintiffs.
Martin Nourse QC and *Joseph Turner* for the corporation.

Cur adv vult

15th December.   **BUCKLEY LJ** read the following judgment of the court at
the invitation of Russell LJ.   In this case the plaintiff company appeals from a judgment of Foster J on two preliminary questions which the district registrar at
Liverpool had ordered to be tried as preliminary issues.

The plaintiffs were at the relevant time, and we think still are, tenants from year
to year of a building in Conway Street, Birkenhead, where it carried on the business
of dealing in new and secondhand motor cars.   This building was bounded by
Conway Street on its southern side and on its eastern and western sides by William
Street and Henry Street respectively, which run northward from Conway Street
to another street called Hinson Street.   Conway Street is intersected at right angles
by Argyle Street at a point which is not very far distant from the plaintiff company's
building and to the west of it.   In about March 1967 Birkenhead Corporation ('the
corporation'), under certain powers conferred on them by a local Act, the Birkenhead
Corporation (Mersey Tunnel Approaches) Act 1965 (which in this judgment we will
call 'the local Act'), commenced certain works authorised by the local Act, including
the reconstruction of Conway Street in the area adjoining the plaintiffs' property
and the intersection of Conway Street and Argyle Street.

Section 20 of the local Act, so far as relevant to the works in question in this action,
is in the following terms:

'(1) Subject to the provisions of this Act, the Corportion may within the
borough make and maintain, in the lines or situations shown on the deposited
plans and according to the levels shown on the deposited sections, the works
hereinafter described with all necessary works and conveniences connected
therewith— . . . Work No. 16   A new street commencing in Argyle Street
near its northerly junction with Conway Street and terminating at the Haymarket
. . .'

Section 21 authorised the corporation in executing the works to deviate from the
deposited plans and sections within specified limits.   Section 22 has the marginal
note 'Power to make subsidiary works'.   The section, so far as it is necessary to read
it, is in the following terms:

'(1) Subject to the provisions of this Act and within the limits of deviation, the
Corporation in connection with the works may—(*a*) make and maintain all such
approaches, subways, roundabouts, flyovers, underpasses, overpasses, stairs,

a   ramps, passages, means of ingress or egress, shafts, stagings, buildings, apparatus, plant and machinery as may be necessary or convenient; (b) make junctions and communications (including the provision of steps or ramps for the use of persons on foot) with any existing or proposed streets which may be intersected or interfered with by or be contiguous with the works or any of them; (c) make diversions, widenings or alterations of lines or levels of any existing streets for

b   the purpose of connecting the same with the works or any of them or of crossing under or over the same or otherwise; (d) construct and provide carriageways, footways, reserved areas, vaults, cellars, arches, sewers, drains, subways, sunken or other ornamental gardens and all such bridges, piers, viaducts, embankments, aprons, tunnels, abutments, retaining walls, wing walls, culverts and other works as may be necessary or convenient for the works or for carrying the same over or under any railway, any stream or watercourse, any street or any land; (e) stop

c   up and appropriate the site and soil of so much of any streets as they may consider unnecessary to retain or necessary to throw into the works . . . together with all necessary or convenient subsidiary and incidental works . . .

'(3) In the exercise of the powers conferred by this section the Corporation shall cause as little detriment and inconvenience as circumstances admit to any person and shall make reasonable compensation for any damage caused by the exercise

d   of such powers . . .

'(5) Any question of disputed compensation payable under the foregoing provisions of this section shall be determined under and in accordance with the Land Compensation Act, 1961 . . .'

That Act relates to compensation for compulsory acquisition of land, not to injurious
e   affection. Section 22 (5) has not been relied on in this case.

Section 24, so far as material, provides:

'(1) The Corporation may stop up the whole or such portion or portions as they think fit of so much of the streets mentioned in Part I of the schedule to this Act as is shown on the deposited plans as intended to be stopped up and thereupon all rights of way over or along the same shall be extinguished and

f   the Corporation may appropriate and use the site thereof: Provided that the Corporation shall not under the powers of this section stop up any part of the said streets unless—(a) such part is bounded on both sides by lands belonging to the Corporation; or (b) the Corporation obtain the consent of the owners, lessees and occupiers of the houses and lands on both sides thereof . . .

'(3) Any person who suffers loss by—(a) the appropriation of any site of which
g   he is the owner; or (b) the extinguishment of any private right; under this section shall be entitled to be paid by the Corporation compensation to be determined in case of dispute under and in accordance with the Land Compensation Act, 1961 . . .'

Then s 26, so far as applicable, provides:

h   '(1) The Corporation during and for the purpose of the execution of the works may—(a) temporarily stop up and divert and interfere with any street; (b) execute and do all necessary works and things for or in connection with such stopping up or diversion and for keeping any such street open for traffic; and (c) for any reasonable time divert the traffic from any such street and prevent persons using the same . . .

j   '(3) Any question or dispute arising under this section shall be determined by the Minister . . .'

The works authorised by the local Act constituted an extensive scheme for the improvement of the approaches to the Mersey Tunnel. At the intersection of Argyle Street and Conway Street they include a flyover carrying traffic travelling east and west along Conway Street over Argyle Street. There also remains a roadway crossing

Argyle Street at ground level at this point. Work no 16 is shown on the deposited   *a*
plans as a new street starting from the east side of Argyle Street a short way north of
the previous intersection of Argyle Street and Conway Street, curving in a south-
easterly direction into the line of the previous Conway Street and then proceeding
in a straight line approximately in the same direction as the original Conway Street.
This new street, which is called in the statement of claim 'the new Conway Street',
is not shown on the deposited plans as passing immediately south of the plaintiffs'   *b*
building; nor in the form in which it was eventually constructed, which deviates
slightly from the lines indicated on the deposited plans, does it pass immediately
south of the plaintiffs' building. This new street is so sited that a sufficient space
is left between it and the southern entrance to Henry Street, the southern face of the
plaintiffs' building and the southern entrance to William Street, to permit the construction of a traffic road running from the southern end of Henry Street past the   *c*
plaintiffs' building and past the southern end of William Street and so on in an
easterly direction. Such a traffic road has been constructed as part of the works.
This is called in the statement of claim 'the old Conway Street'. Both the new Conway Street and the old Conway Street are at ground level, but they are separated by
a kerb and railing which makes it impossible for wheeled traffic to pass from one to
the other. Consequently, vehicular traffic which has come down Argyle Street and   *d*
turned left into the new Conway Street cannot get access to the plaintiffs' building.
It seems there are traffic regulations in force which require traffic coming eastward
along Conway Street to turn left up Argyle Street at the intersection of the two roads,
but that is, we think, irrelevant to the present proceedings. If traffic coming eastwards down Conway Street were free to proceed at ground level in an easterly
direction across Argyle Street (as the existing physical features would allow) it still   *e*
would be unable to reach the plaintiffs' building because of the kerb and fence to
which we have referred.

We have stated these details of the changes occasioned by the works in the neighbourhood of the plaintiffs' building because we think they make the position easier
to understand, but in fact the questions which we have to consider must be answered
in the light of the pleadings. Paragraph 1 of the statement of claim deals with the   *f*
geographical situation of the plaintiffs' building. Paragraphs 2, 3, 4, 5 and 6 deal
with sections of the local Act to which we have referred. Paragraph 7 is in the
following terms:

'In the course of the execution of the Works the [corporation] by their contractors obstructed access to the property by closing the Old Conway Street and
by excavations and other works at the junction of the Old Conway Street and   *g*
Henry Street thereby obstructing access to the property whereby the Plaintiff
suffered loss and damage in respect of the business carried on by it at the property.
Such damage included loss of profits of the said business and the Plaintiff will at
the trial of the action contend that by virtue of Section 22 of the [local] Act
the Plaintiff is entitled to compensation in respect of such damage.'

Paragraph 9 of the statement of claim is as follows: *h*

'The Works were completed in or about the month of July 1969. As appears
from the plan marked "B" annexed hereto the Works now prevent vehicular
access to the Plaintiff's premises from the New Conway Street whereby the
Plaintiff's premises have been injuriously affected and the Plaintiff has suffered
loss and damage in respect of the business carried on by it on the property such   *j*
damage consisting of loss of profits of the said business.'

The district registrar ordered that the following questions raised by the pleadings
should be tried as preliminary issues, namely (1) whether on the true construction
of s 22 of the local Act and on the facts pleaded in paras 1, 2, 3, 4, 5 and 7 of the statement of claim the corporation are liable to pay compensation to the plaintiffs in

a respect of loss of profits of the business carried on by the plaintiffs in the plaintiffs' building; and (2) whether on the true construction of the local Act and on the facts pleaded in paras 1, 2, 3, 4, 5 and 9 of the statement of claim the corporation are liable to pay compensation to the plaintiffs in respect of loss of profits of the business.

It is relevant to note that s 4 of the local Act provides that the Lands Clauses Acts, except certain irrelevant sections, were incorporated in the local Act. Section 68
b of the Lands Clauses Consolidation Act 1845 was not one of the excepted sections and, consequently, that section was incorporated in the local Act so far as it was applicable for the purposes of the local Act and not inconsistent with its provisions.

Foster J in his judgment dealt with each of these preliminary questions quite shortly. Of the temporary obstructions alleged in para 7 of the statement of claim he said:

c 'In my judgment, the temporary obstruction of and closing of Old Conway Street and other works could only have been done by the corporation under s 26 of the [local] Act, which provides for no compensation but only the right to refer to the Minister. I do not think that these works were carried out as subsidiary works under s 22 (3), which has no application to them. It is true that s 68 [of the Lands Clauses Consolidation Act 1845] can apply to temporary works (compare *Lingké v. Mayor &c. of Christchurch*[1]), and therefore the question which
d I discuss below remains, namely, whether damages for loss of profits as such come within the ambit of s 68.'

Of the permanent damage alleged in para 9 of the statement of claim the learned judge said this:

e 'In this case, too, I do not think that the plaintiffs can rely on s 22 (3) of the [local] Act. Their complaint, in my judgment, is in respect of the carrying out of Work no 16 in s 20. The prevention of vehicular access to the plaintiffs' property was the result of the carrying out of that work. It was not the result of any subsidiary works within the meaning of s 22. Even if I am wrong about that, I do not think that s 22 (3) gives the plaintiffs any wider remedy than that
f given to it by s 68 [of the 1845 Act].'

On the question whether damages for loss of profits of the business were within the ambit of s 68 the learned judge considered three decisions of the House of Lords: *Ricket v Directors, etc, of Metropolitan Railway Co*[2], *Metropolitan Board of Works v McCarthy*[3] and *Caledonian Railway Co v Walker's Trustees*[4]. On the authority of those decisions he held that the proper compensation in such a case as this was compensa-
g tion for the injurious affection of the plaintiffs' land and that the plaintiffs were not entitled to damages for loss of profits as such.

The learned judge's answers to both questions turned to some extent on the inter-pretation placed by him on s 22 of the local Act. His view was that neither the temporary obstructions referred to in para 7 of the statement of claim nor the permanent features referred to in para 9 of the statement of claim were works carried
h out under s 22. He considered that the temporary obstructions were authorised by s 20 of the local Act. Section 22, in his view, applied to none of them. In this court the plaintiffs have contended that s 22 extends to all operations necessary to imple-ment s 20. The corporation has contended that s 22 only relates to features of a permanent character which are ancillary to and not comprised in the works expressly authorised in s 20.

j Section 20 is the principal authorising section in the local Act. It authorises the corporation to make and maintain 17 distinct works which are individually shortly

1   [1912] 3 KB 595
2   (1867) LR 2 HL 175
3   (1874) LR 7 HL 243
4   (1882) 7 App Cas 259, [1881-85] All ER Rep 592

described. These works the corporation is authorised to make 'in the lines or situations shown on the deposited plans and according to the levels shown on the deposited sections', but neither s 20 nor the deposited plans and sections contain any detail whatsoever relating to the engineering methods or operations necessary for the construction of the works authorised by the section. The section must, however, by inference authorise these operations if they are not expressly authorised elsewhere. Moreover, the authority of the section is not restricted to the 17 numbered works: it extends to 'all necessary works and conveniences connected therewith'. Section 20, therefore, looked at alone, would seem to authorise the corporation to carry out all those operations which may be necessary to construct or effect the 17 numbered works and also all operations necessary to carry out any further incidental works which may be necessary or convenient for the scheme. It also authorises the corporation to maintain all those features which result from carrying out the operations referred to.

Turning now to s 22, this authorises the corporation to do certain things 'in connection with the works'. 'The works' means by definition the works authorised in Part III of the local Act, which consist of ss 20 to 35 inclusive. Consequently, unless the context otherwise requires (which does not seem to be the case), the works referred to in the opening words of s 22 include not only the 17 numbered works, but also all necessary works and conveniences connected therewith. The subject-matter of the various sub-paragraphs of s 22 (1) strongly suggests that the features there referred to are intended to form permanent features of the works to be carried out under the Act. Although it is perhaps possible that an underpass, for example, might be constructed as a temporary feature for use only during the period when the work was going on, we cannot think that s 22 is directed only to temporary operations. Indeed, sub-para (e) of s 22 (1) seems to us clearly to negative any such idea. In our judgment, s 22 is included in the Act for the purpose of authorising in terms those engineering operations which, as we have already remarked, would otherwise be inferentially authorised by s 20. The marginal note to the section is, in our opinion, misleading. 'Incidental' would, we think, have been a more appropriate word than 'subsidiary'; and we observe that the closing words of s 22 (1) are, 'all necessary or convenient subsidiary and incidental works'. Section 22, in our judgment, authorises the corporation to do all those things necessary to produce the results contemplated by s 20. Support for the view that the powers conferred by s 22 are linked with the works authorised by s 20 is, we think, to be found in the fact that the matters authorised by s 22 can only be pursued 'within the limits of deviation'. This relates back to s 21, which provides that 'In executing the works the Corporation may deviate' from the lines indicated on the deposited plans and sections within certain specified limits. This, in our opinion, indicates that the operations authorised by s 22 are to be operations carried out in executing 'the works'.

The closure of a street while operations under the local Act were going on might well not fall within the terms of s 22. It would not seem to be within the language of sub-para (e) of s 22 (1), which we think refers to a permanent stopping up and appropriation. It might also very well be thought not to fall within the expression 'all necessary or convenient subsidiary and incidental works', for excluding traffic from a street would not be aptly described as a 'work'. A separate power temporarily to stop up, divert and interfere with streets is accordingly found in s 26 (1). Paragraph 7 of the statement of claim alleges that in the course of the execution of the works access to the plaintiffs' property was obstructed by closing the old Conway Street and by excavations and other works at the junction of old Conway Street and Henry Street. If and so far as this obstruction was occasioned merely by closing the old Conway Street in the sense of excluding traffic from it, this was presumably done under the authority of s 26; but the excavations and other works referred to, which are alleged to have been made in the course of the execution of the works, must, in our opinion, fall within s 22 (1). So far as the matters complained of in

a
para 7 of the statement of claim fall within s 22 (1), s 22 (3) is applicable, but to the extent that they were done under the authority of s 26, s 22 (3) is not applicable.

Moving now to the permanent obstructions alleged in para 9 of the statement of claim, the physical features which prevent vehicular access to the plaintiffs' building from the new Conway Street consist of the kerb and railing referred to earlier. These are not shown on the deposited plans and they must, in our opinion, either con-

b
stitute 'necessary or convenient subsidiary and incidental works' within the terms of s 22 (1) of the local Act, in which case sub-s (3) of that section would be applicable, or they may be regarded as 'necessary works and conveniences connected therewith' within the terms of s 20 (1) of the local Act. In the latter alternative, we think that s 22 (3) is again applicable because, (a) for reasons which we have already given the operations of laying and erecting this kerb and railing, thereby bringing the alleged obstruction into existence, were operations authorised by s 22, and (b) to the extent

c
that the matters complained of constituted a permanent stopping up of the previous Conway Street, this was something expressly authorised by s 22 (1) (e). We should perhaps mention at this point that s 24 (1) of the local Act, which authorises the stopping up of various streets mentioned in Part I of the schedule to the local Act, including Conway Street, has no application in the present case because the case does not fall within the terms of the proviso to that subsection.

d
For these reasons, in our judgment, matters alleged in both paras 7 and 9 of the statement of claim attract compensation under s 22 (3) of the local Act.

The Lands Clauses Consolidation Act 1845, s 68, has been treated in the argument before us as a section which may confer a right to compensation, but it is not so in terms. It provides machinery for measuring the amount of compensation payable to someone who is entitled to compensation. Where s 68 is found operating in

e
conjunction with a section conferring a right to compensation in wide terms, such as s 16 of the Railways Clauses Consolidation Act 1845 or s 22 (3) of the local Act in the present case, the scope of s 68 may by contagion and as a matter of construction limit the kind of compensation recoverable under the entitling section.

Section 68 only applies in a case in which a claimant is entitled to compensation

f
'in respect of any lands, or of any interest therein which shall have been taken for or injuriously affected by the execution of the works'. The plaintiffs concede that they cannot successfully claim compensation within that section unless it is established that the plaintiffs' property has been injuriously affected by the works, but it is contended that once this has been established the compensation recoverable is not confined to compensation for injurious affection of the land, but can extend to com-

g
pensation for loss of profits of the plaintiffs' business. The plaintiffs draw attention to the difference between the language of s 68 of the 1845 Act and the language of s 22 (3) of the local Act which refers to 'reasonable compensation for any damage caused by the exercise of' the powers under the Act. It is submitted that this language is used in order to confer a right to compensation in respect of any and every kind of damage suffered which, but for the authority of the Act, would support a claim to

h
damages at common law. The defendant corporation, on the other hand, contend that s 22 (3) of the local Act confers no greater right to compensation than can be assessed under s 68 of the 1845 Act, and that neither section confers any right to compensation for loss of profits of a business, even if that business is carried on on land which is injuriously affected.

Before we turn to consideration of the authorities to which we have been referred,

j
it is perhaps desirable to emphasise that the question with which we are concerned in this case is whether in any circumstances the plaintiff company is entitled to compensation in respect of loss of profits of its business. We are not concerned with the question whether, if it can be shown that the plaintiffs' property has been injuriously affected, the plaintiffs are entitled to compensation in respect of that injurious affection of their land or their interest in the land.

In *Ricket v Directors, etc, of Metropolitan Railway Co*[1] Lord Chelmsford LC indicated

1   (1867) LR 2 HL at 187

that under the Railways Clauses Consolidation Act 1845, s 6, which for present pur- *a*
poses uses similar language to the Lands Clauses Consolidation Act 1845, s 68, no
compensation can be claimed unless the particular injury would have been actionable
but for the statutory powers under which the act complained of was done, but that it
does not follow that a party would have a right to compensation merely because,
but for the statutory powers, an action for damages would lie.

In *Caledonian Railway Co v Walker's Trustees*[1], which was a case arising under the *b*
Railways Clauses Consolidation (Scotland) Act 1845 in which similar language is
employed, Lord Selborne LC, after referring to *Caledonian Railway Co v Ogilvy*[2],
Ricket v Directors, etc, of Metropolitan Railway Co[3] and *Metropolitan Board of Works v
McCarthy*[4], said this[5]:

'With this preface, I think it right to say that all the three decisions of this
House, to which I have referred, appear to me to be capable of being explained *c*
and justified upon consistent principles; the propositions which I regard as
having been established by them, and by another judgment of your Lordships
in the case of *Hammersmith Railway Co. v. Brand*[6], being these:—1. When a right
of action, which would have existed if the work in respect of which compensation
is claimed had not been authorized by Parliament, would have been merely
personal, without reference to land or its incidents, compensation is not due *d*
under the Acts.   2. When damage arises, not out of the execution, but only out
of the subsequent use of the work, then also there is no case for compensation.
3. Loss of trade or custom, by reason of a work not otherwise directly affecting
the house or land in or upon which a trade has been carried on, or any right
properly incident thereto, is not by itself a proper subject for compensation.'

e

On behalf of the plaintiffs it is said that loss of profits was not canvassed in that case,
and this is correct; but the observations of Lord Selborne LC in the passage we have
cited obviously carry great weight, and the more so because he was there seeking to
reconcile three earlier decisions of the House of Lords. In the same case Lord
Blackburn said[7]:

'And it must, I think, also be now considered as settled that the construction of *f*
[the Lands and Railways Clauses Acts of 1845] is confined to giving compensation
for an injury to land or an interest in land; that it is not enough to shew that an
action would have lain for what was done if unauthorized, but it must also be
shewn that it would have lain in respect of an injury to the land or an interest
in land.'

g

In *Caledonian Railway Co v Ogilvy*[2], the earliest of the three cases referred to by
Lord Selborne LC, which was concerned with the interruption of access to a private
residence, no question of loss of profits was involved. But in *Ricket v Directors, etc, of
Metropolitan Railway Co*[3] a jury had found that, whereas no damage had been done
to the structure of the plaintiff's house, he had sustained damage in respect of the
interruption to his business in respect of which he was awarded a sum of £100 *h*
compensation. The case was later removed by certiorari into the Court of Queen's
Bench, where the question for the court was, 'whether the loss of customers by the
Plaintiff in his trade, under the above-mentioned circumstances, was such damage
as entitled him to recover from the company?'   When the case reached the House of

1   (1882) 7 App Cas 259, [1881-85] All ER Rep 592
2   (1855) 2 Macq 229
3   (1867) LR 2 HL 175
4   (1874) LR 7 HL 243
5   (1882) 7 App Cas at 275, 276, [1881-85] All ER Rep at 595
6   (1869) LR 4 HL 171, [1861-73] All ER Rep 60
7   (1882) 7 App Cas at 293, [1881-85] All ER Rep at 602

j

a   Lords, Lord Chelmsford LC decided it primarily on the ground that the damage which was the foundation of the claim to compensation made by the plaintiff, namely, the falling off in public attendance at his public house, allegedly due to certain obstructions of neighbouring highways, would have been too remote to be the subject of an action, but he went on to consider the meaning and effect of the Lands Clauses Consolidation Act 1845, s 68, and the Railways Clauses Consolidation Act 1845,

b   ss 6 and 16. He reached the conclusion that s 68 and s 6 were inapplicable to the case on the ground that the damage had arisen from temporary operations of the company and not from their permanent works. He held that no compensation was payable under s 16 on the ground that the damage was not of such a nature as to entitle the plaintiff to compensation, the interruption of persons who would have resorted to his house but for the obstruction of the highway being a consequential injury to the plaintiff too remote to be within the provisions of that section. Lord

c   Cranworth, who with Lord Chelmsford LC constituted the majority by whom the case was decided (Lord Westbury dissenting), held that no distinction was to be drawn between the kind of damage in respect of which compensation could be recovered under s 6 and the kind of damage in respect of which compensation could be recovered under s 16 of the Railways Clauses Consolidation Act 1845. He went

d   on[1]:

> 'Both principle and authority seem to me to shew that no case comes within the purview of the statute, unless where some damage has been occasioned to the land itself, in respect of which, but for the statute, the complaining party might have maintained an action.'

e   Of this decision Lord Selborne LC said in *Caledonian Railway Co v Walker's Trustees*[2]:

> 'But both these noble and learned Lords agreed that the damage by loss of custom, of which the plaintiff complained, was a consequence of the works of the railway company, too remote and indefinite to bring it within the scope of any of the compensation clauses of the Acts; and this I consider to have been the true ground of that decision . . .'

f   Later Lord Selborne LC said[3]:

> 'I may add that the same view of *Ricket's Case*[4] was afterwards taken by Willes and Byles, JJ., in the case of *Beckett*[5], where the former of those learned judges spoke of it as deciding that an injury for which compensation is due "must be in respect of the property itself, and not of any particular use to which it may

g   from time to time be put;" and the latter, as proceeding on the ground that the injury was not only temporary but "indirect, and to the trade only."'

In *Metropolitan Board of Works v McCarthy*[6], the third of the House of Lords' cases discussed by Lord Selborne LC in *Caledonian Railway Co v Walker's Trustees*[7], McCarthy was the occupier of a house in close proximity to a draw dock opening

h   into the River Thames, which he had no right to use except as one of the public, but his use of it for the purposes of a business which he carried on from his house was constant. This dock was destroyed in the course of the construction of the Thames Embankment. In proceedings under the Lands Clauses Consolidation Act 1845 damages were assessed in a sum of £1,900 in respect of diminution in the value of

---

j   1 (1867) LR 2 HL at 198
2 (1882) 7 App Cas at 283, 284, [1881-85] All ER Rep at 598
3 (1882) 7 App Cas at 284, [1881-85] All ER Rep at 598, 599
4 (1867) LR 2 HL 175
5 I e *Beckett v Midland Railway Co* (1867) LR 3 CP 82
6 (1874) LR 7 HL 243
7 (1882) 7 App Cas 259, [1881-85] All ER Rep 592

McCarthy's house resulting from the destruction of the dock. No mention is made
in the report of any claim to compensation in respect of loss of profits. The matter
had been dealt with in the Court of Common Pleas on a case stated containing a finding that by reason of the stopping up of the dock the plaintiff's premises became and
were as premises permanently damaged and diminished in value. McCarthy, as
plaintiff, succeeded in the Court of Common Pleas[1], whose decision was affirmed on
appeal by the Court of Exchequer Chamber[2]. On a further appeal to the House of
Lords[3] McCarthy was again successful. Lord Chelmsford said[4]:

> 'It may be taken to have been finally decided that in order to found a claim
> to compensation under the Acts there must be an injury and damage to the
> house or land itself in which the person claiming compensation has an interest.
> A mere personal obstruction or inconvenience, or a damage occasioned to a
> man's trade or the goodwill of his business, although of such a nature that but
> for the Act of Parliament it might have been the subject of an action for damages,
> will not entitle the injured party to compensation under it.'

Lord Penzance said[5]:

> 'There is another rule, which is, I conceive, well settled in these cases, namely,
> that the damage or injury, which is to be the subject of compensation, must not
> be of a personal character, but must be a damage or injury to the "land" of the
> claimant considered independently of any particular trade that the claimant
> may have carried on upon it.'

Notwithstanding that in *Ricket v Directors, etc, of Metropolitan Railway Co*[6] the circumstances were such that no action might have lain at common law but for the
statutory authority for the works, and that in neither *Metropolitan Board of Works v
McCarthy*[3] nor *Caledonian Railway Co v Walker's Trustees*[7] was any claim in respect
of loss of profits put forward, the citations which we have made from these cases,
in our opinion, clearly show that a number of learned Lords have taken the view that
loss of profits as such is not a head of damage of a kind which can ground a claim
to compensation within the Lands Clauses Consolidation Act 1845, s 68, or other
statutory provisions using similar language.

In *Ford v Metropolitan and Metropolitan District Railway Companies*[8] the point arose
more directly in this court. In that case the plaintiffs, whose access to their offices had
been interfered with by works carried out under statutory authority by the defendant
companies, claimed compensation under various heads, including interference with
their business. The arbitrator awarded a sum of £600 compensation, but did not
indicate in respect of which heads of claim the award was made. The defendants
claimed that the award was bad because to some extent the sum awarded related to
matters which were not proper heads of compensation. Lord Esher MR said[9]:

> 'Several points were urged as shewing that the claim was in certain particulars
> beyond the jurisdiction of the arbitrator. Some points with regard to these
> matters are quite clear: the mere personal inconvenience or injury, the mere
> injury to the business of the person claiming, must not be taken into account.'

---

1   (1872) LR 7 CP 508
2   (1873) LR 8 CP 191
3   (1874) LR 7 HL 243
4   (1874) LR 7 HL at 256
5   (1874) LR 7 HL at 262
6   (1867) LR 2 HL 175
7   (1882) 7 App Cas 259, [1881-85] All ER Rep 592
8   (1886) 17 QBD 12
9   (1886) 17 QBD at 19

a　He went on to hold that on the facts the inadmissible heads of claim had not affected the amount of the award. Cotton LJ said[1]:

> b　'But then I come to another point. It has been urged that evidence was given which referred to injuries sustained by the plaintiffs personally, injuries sustained by them in carrying on their business, and that that evidence would offend against the law laid down by Lord Cairns[2] in the passage which I read[3] (and it was repeated by other judges), that the inconvenience or injury which arises solely from the particular use to which the particular occupier puts the building, must not be regarded.'

He went on to hold, like Lord Esher MR, that such matters had not been shown to have affected the award. The award was accordingly held to have been valid.
c　Inferentially the court clearly considered that, if the award had contained any element of compensation for injury to the plaintiff's business, this would have vitiated it.

Although none of these authorities may technically bind us in the present case, we consider that we should follow the views expressed in them. It seems to us to be exceedingly improbable that Parliament should have intended to enact that, if a
d　claimant's land had been injuriously affected, he should be entitled to compensation not only for that injury but also for injury, if he could show any, which he had suffered in respect of his business, but that a claimant who had suffered no injury in respect of his land but had suffered injury in respect of his business could claim no compensation. Yet it is conceded that no claim could be brought within s 68 in the latter case. In our judgment, no claim to compensation can be brought within s 68 relating to
e　injury to a business. To avoid confusion, however, we add that this does not mean that, if injury to a business can be shown to have occasioned a diminution in the value of the land where the business is carried on, compensation cannot be recovered for that injurious affection of the land.

We now reach the question whether s 22 (3) of the local Act should be construed as conferring any wider right to compensation than such as falls within s 68. Section
f　68 having been incorporated by reference to the local Act, that section and s 22 (3) must be construed together as though s 68 were found in the local Act as one of its sections. On the construction of s 22 which we have adopted earlier in this judgment s 22 (3) has a wide application to acts done by the defendant corporation under the authority of the local Act: it extends to all acts done to produce the results indicated in the descriptions of the 17 numbered works referred to in s 20 or covered by the words 'all necessary works and conveniences connected therewith' appearing in that
g　section. It extends to all such acts down to the moment when those works are brought to final completion. It consequently extends to the establishment of the physical features so brought into existence. We are not concerned in this case with any injury to the plaintiff company arising after that stage had been reached in consequence of the way in which those physical features have been used.

h　We are consequently concerned with a statute which contains a provision in the terms of s 22 (3) of the local Act requiring the defendant corporation to make reasonable compensation for any damage caused by the exercise of its statutory powers, and contains a provision in the terms of s 68 of the 1845 Act which provides how any party entitled to compensation may have his compensation assessed. The latter provision is, for reasons already stated, to be treated as confined to compensation for injury to
j　land or an interest in land. If s 22 (3) should be construed as extending to compensation for some wider class of injuries, Parliament would have provided no machinery for assessing compensation in respect of any such injury falling outside the ambit of

---

1　(1886) 17 QBD at 25
2　See *Metropolitan Board of Works v McCarthy* (1874) LR 7 HL at 253
3　(1886) 17 QBD at 21

s 68. This would indeed be strange. In our judgment, however, s 22 (3) should not be so construed. We think the learned judge was right in holding that s 22 (3) does not *a* give any wider remedy than such as falls within s 68. The language of s 22 (3) differs in detail but not in substance from the language of the proviso to the Railways Clauses Consolidation Act 1845, s 16, which was considered in *Ricket v Directors, etc, of Metropolitan Railway Co*[1]. Of that proviso, comparing it with s 6 of the same Act, Lord Cranworth said[2]:

b

> 'The only material difference in the language by which relief is given in the one section and in the other is, that in the 6th section relief is in terms confined to the case of lands *injuriously affected*, whereas in the 16th relief is given to all parties interested for all *damage* by them sustained by reason of the exercise of the powers thereby authorized. I cannot, however, believe that the damage intended to be compensated in the latter case is a damage of a nature different *c* from that contemplated in the former case. I cannot believe that the Legislature could have intended to give relief in respect of acts done for a short and limited period while works are in progress, and to refuse it in respect of the same acts when they are to have effect permanently. The damage contemplated in sect. 6 must, I think, be *damnum cum injuriâ*. It must be damage occasioned by the land having been injuriously affected.' *d*

He therefore held that s 16 was similarly restricted. We have in the present case no section precisely corresponding with s 6 of the Railways Clauses Consolidation Act 1845, but in the same case Lord Chelmsford LC remarked[3] that (for the purposes there under consideration) there appeared to be no substantial difference between the language of the Lands Clauses Consolidation Act 1845, s 68, and the language of *e* s 6 of the Railways Clauses Consolidation Act 1845. In our judgment, in the present case the incorporation of s 68 in the local Act affords a context which indicates that Parliament intended by s 22 (3) of the local Act to require the corporation to make compensation under that subsection only in respect of injury coming within the terms of s 68, that is to say, injury affecting the claimant's land or his interest in some land.

For these reasons, we are of opinion that both the preliminary questions should be *f* answered in the negative. We reach the same conclusion as the learned judge, although for different reasons. The appeal will be dismissed.

Appeal dismissed. Leave to appeal to the House of Lords granted.

Solicitors: *Field, Fisher & Co*, agents for *Berkson & Berkson*, Birkenhead (for the plaintiffs); *Ian G Holt*, Town Clerk, Birkenhead (for the defendant corporation). *g*

Mary Rose Plummer   Barrister.

---

1   (1867) LR 2 HL 175
2   (1867) LR 2 HL at 198
3   (1867) LR 2 HL at 189

a

Franklin v Attorney-General

QUEEN'S BENCH DIVISION
LAWSON J
24th, 27th OCTOBER 1972

b *Petition of right – Colonial stock – Claim by stockholder for interest on stock – Remedy – Procedure – Plaintiff claiming to be interested in Government of Southern Rhodesia stock – Bank of England paying agents and registrars of stock – Government of Southern Rhodesia failing to provide bank with funds to pay interest – Whether plaintiff limited to civil proceedings against bank in respect of funds held by them as registrars – Whether plaintiff entitled to present petition of right – Form of petition – Colonial Stock Act 1877, s 20 – Crown Proceedings Act 1947, ss 39, 40, Sch 2 – Cyprus Act 1960, s 3, Sch, para 9.*

c

F was the holder of certain Government of Southern Rhodesia 6 per cent stock 1976-79, to which the Colonial Stock Act 1877 applied. He had not been paid any interest on that stock since 1965. Since then the Government of Southern Rhodesia had not put the Bank of England, their paying agents in London and the registrars of the *d* stock, in funds to pay the interest due on it. F sought a declaration that, as a person interested in the stock, he was entitled, under s 20*ᵃ* of the Colonial Stock Act 1877, to present a petition of right to HM the Queen for consideration by the Attorney-General whether to advise her to grant a fiat notwithstanding the provisions of s 3 (2)*ᵇ* of, and para 9 (2)*ᶜ* of the Schedule to, the Cyprus Act 1960 and s 39*ᵈ* of the Crown Proceedings Act 1947.

e **Held** – The declaration would be granted for the following reasons—
(i) the provisions of the 1947 Act (enabling a subject to bring legal proceedings against the Crown without obtaining the fiat of the Attorney-General) had no application as the alleged liability of the Crown arose 'otherwise than in respect of [Her] Majesty's Government in the United Kingdom' within the meaning of s 40 (2) (*b*)*ᵉ* (see p 882 d and h, post);
f (ii) on the true construction of s 3 of and para 9 of the Schedule to the 1960 Act, s 20 of the 1877 Act was amended only in relation to Cyprus; accordingly F could still proceed under s 20, as originally enacted (see p 887 e and f and p 888 c and d, post); dictum of Lord Simonds in *Smith v London Transport Executive* [1951] 1 All ER at 669 applied;
(iii) the petition of right would however have to be in the old form used prior to *g* the Petitions of Right Act 1860, as that Act had been repealed by s 39 of, and Sch 2 to, the Crown Proceedings Act 1947 (see p 882 h and p 888 g, post).

Notes
For colonial and other stocks, see 36 Halsbury's Laws (3rd Edn) 561, para 881.
For redress by way of petition of right, see 11 Halsbury's Laws (3rd Edn) 3, 5, *h* paras 1, 4.
For the Colonial Stock Act 1877, s 20, as originally enacted, see 6 Halsbury's Statutes (2nd Edn) 537.
For the Crown Proceedings Act 1947, s 40, see 8 Halsbury's Statutes (3rd Edn) 871, and for s 39 of, and Sch 2 to, that Act, see 6 Halsbury's Statutes (2nd Edn) 73, 76.
For the Cyprus Act 1960, s 3, see 4 Halsbury's Statutes (3rd Edn) 286, and for para 9 *j* of the Schedule to that Act, see 40 Halsbury's Statutes (2nd Edn) 253.

---

a   Section 20, so far as material, is set out at p 881 b to d, post
b   Section 3, so far as material, is set out at p 884 b, post
c   Paragraph 9 is set out at p 884 j to p 885 a, post
d   Section 39, so far as material, is set out at p 881 j, post
e   Section 40, so far as material, is set out at p 881 j to p 882 c, post

Case referred to in judgment

Smith v London Transport Executive [1951] 1 All ER 667, [1951] AC 555, 115 JP 213, 49 *a*
LGR 478, HL, 45 Digest (Repl) 3, 1.

Originating summons

By an originating summons dated 16th May 1972 the plaintiff, Henry Franklin,
applied to the court for the determination of the following question; whether on
the proper construction of s 20 of the Colonial Stock Act 1877 the plaintiff, being a *b*
person claiming to be interested in Government of Southern Rhodesia 6 per cent
stock 1976-79 and interest thereon, might present a petition of right in England
to HM the Queen notwithstanding the provisions of s 3 (2) of the Cyprus Act 1960,
para 9 (2) of the Schedule to that Act and the relevant sections of the Crown Proceedings Act 1947. The defendant was the Attorney-General. The facts are set out in the
judgment.   *c*

B H Anns for the plaintiff.
Gordon Slynn for the defendant.

Cur adv vult

27th October.   **LAWSON J** read the following judgment.   This is an originating
summons issued on 12th July 1972 in which the plaintiff is Henry Franklin and the *d*
defendant the Attorney-General.   The point of the summons is to determine a
question which arises out of the failure of the Government of Southern Rhodesia
since the year 1965 to put their paying agents in London, the Bank of England, in
funds to pay the interest due on the 1964 issue of Southern Rhodesian 6 per cent
stock redeemable 1976-79 of which the Bank of England are registrars.

In 1958 the plaintiff bought stock of the then Federation of Rhodesia and Nyasaland, *e*
and when that federation was dissolved and its component territories became the
states (as they were subsequently known) of Zambia, Malawi and Southern Rhodesia,
the earlier stock was replaced by issues of separate stock by each of the territorial
governments in proportions laid down under the provisions of an Order in Council
made in 1963.   Accordingly on 19th March 1964 the plaintiff had issued to him a
stock certificate for £521 4s of the 6 per cent Rhodesian stock which I mentioned. *f*
No interest having been paid since 1965 the question is what course, if any, is open
to the plaintiff and other stockholders in the same position, of whom there are many,
to recover what is due to them by proceedings in this country.

At first sight it seems anomalous that any such proceedings in this country should
lie, but that this is the fact immediately appears by reference to the Colonial Stock
Acts 1877 to 1948.   The first of those Acts, the Act of 1877, was passed to encourage *g*
English investors to invest in colonial stocks.   The scheme of the 1877 Act is broadly
this.   That a colonial government, pursuant to colonial legislation, can make a declaration that certain stock has been issued.   This declaration is left with the Commissioners of Inland Revenue and the commissioners, on payment of a fee, record the
same, and on the declaration being recorded the Colonial Stock Act 1877 applies to
the stock specified in the declaration. There are certain privileges given in respect *h*
of stamp duty on transfers and issue of stock: these are set out in s 2 of the Act.
Sections 4 to 18 of the Act make provision for a number of matters, including transfers
of stocks, dividends, issues of stocks, stock certificates, the entries in the registers of
stocks which have to be kept under the Act, and other matters.   Section 19 is an important section.   It provides that every prospectus and certificate relating to a colonial
stock registered under that Act has got to contain a declaration to the effect—   *j*

'that the revenues of the colony alone are liable in respect of the stock and
the dividends thereon, and that the Consolidated Fund of the United Kingdom
and the Treasury are not directly or indirectly liable or responsible for the
payment of the stock or of the dividends thereon, or for any matter relating
thereto . . .'

a   Section 20 is a section which as originally enacted contains two paragraphs. The first paragraph deals with the jurisdiction of the English courts to entertain legal proceedings in relation to the register of those colonial stocks to which the Act applies, or to entries in or omissions from the register, and to rights or titles or interests in such stocks and dividends thereon. It provides in effect that the jurisdiction of the English court cannot be objected to on the ground that the registrar of the stocks is

b   the agent of the colonial government. That paragraph still stands as originally enacted. The second paragraph of s 20 of the 1877 Act as enacted provides that 'Any person claiming to be interested in colonial stock to which this Act applies' or dividends on them 'may present a petition of right in England in relation to such stock or dividend', and proceed on the petition of right as proceedings would normally go on the petition of right under the then Petitions of Right Act 1860—

c
> 'subject to this qualification, that the certificate of the judgment decree rule or order of the court may be left with the registrar instead of with the Treasury, and such judgment decree rule or order shall be complied with by the registrar or other agent of the colonial government having possession in England of moneys of such government . . .'

d   The question that I have to determine on this summons depends on the second paragraph. It is this: whether the second paragraph of the 1877 Act as originally enacted is still extant, or whether that second paragraph has been repealed and replaced as a matter of general law by the provisions of the Cyprus Act 1960 to which I shall shortly come.

There are certain later Colonial Stock Acts, an Act of 1892; an Act of 1900; an Act
e   of 1934, which has since been repealed; and an Act of 1948. All of these are cited as the Colonial Stock Acts 1877 to 1948. In my judgment these later Acts have little importance in the present case except that they accomplish two results. First, they place, colonial stocks issued by what I will call the 'old dominions' in a more favourable position than colonial stocks issued by what I will call the 'old colonies'. And secondly, those later Acts had the effect of making registered colonial stock a 'trustee security'.

f   The next Act to which I have to turn is the Crown Proceedings Act 1947 which, as is well known, conferred the right on ordinary subjects to bring legal proceedings against the Crown in the normal form and without the fiat of the Attorney-General as had been necessary under the Petitions of Right Act 1860. This was mainly affected by s 1 of the Crown Proceedings Act 1947. There are also certain other provisions of that Act to which it is necessary to make reference, specifically s 23 (1):

g
> 'Subject to the provisions of this section, any reference in this Part of this Act to civil proceedings by the Crown shall be construed as a reference to [certain] proceedings only . . .'

and amongst them are those proceedings which prior to the passage of the 1947 Act had to be taken by way of one of the forms of remedy which are set out in Sch 1
h   to the 1947 Act—this included in effect petitions of right.

The other sections of the 1947 Act to which it is necessary to refer are ss 39 and 40. Section 39 is the repeal section. It provides:

> '(1) The enactments set out in the Second Schedule to this Act are hereby repealed to the extent specified in the third column of that Schedule.'

j   The repeal schedule includes the whole of the Petitions of Right Act 1860. It does not include or contain any reference to the Colonial Stock Act 1877 or to any of the other Colonial Stock Acts. Section 40 (1) provides:

> 'Nothing in this Act shall apply to proceedings by or against, or authorise proceedings in tort to be brought against, His Majesty in His private capacity.'

Section 40 (2), so far as is relevant, makes this provision:

'Except as therein otherwise expressly provided, nothing in this Act shall . . . (b) authorise proceedings to be taken against the Crown under or in accordance with this Act in respect of any alleged liability of the Crown arising otherwise than in respect of His Majesty's Government in the United Kingdom, or affect proceedings against the Crown in respect of any such alleged liability as aforesaid . . .'

Section 40 (2) concludes with the general words:

'. . . and, without prejudice to the general effect of the foregoing provisions, Part III of this Act shall not apply to the Crown except in right of His Majesty's Government in the United Kingdom.'

Part III of the Act is the part which in effect deals with judgments and execution of judgments against the Crown.

I should say this. It is, as I understand it, conceded that a failure to pay interest by the Government of Southern Rhodesia results in the liability of the Crown arising otherwise than in respect of Her Majesty's Government in the United Kingdom within the terms of s 40 (2) (b) of the 1947 Act which I have read. The conclusion from that is that nothing in the 1947 Act is applicable to proceedings in which a claim is made to enforce the liability which exists in this case.

At this point it is convenient to look historically at the position of colonial stock-holders' remedies for non-payment of interest or non-payment of capital. This can be done as follows. Until 1877 it seems pretty clear that a colonial stockholder of stock of the kind to which the 1877 Act was applicable would have had no remedy in this country by way of petition of right or otherwise in respect of non-payment of interest or non-repayment of capital. This proposition is supported by passages in Robertson's work, Civil Proceedings by and against the Crown[1], which were relied on by counsel for the defendant. I understand that counsel for the plaintiff accepts that that was the position. I am indebted to the Treasury Solicitor for lending me his copy of Robertson during the few days when I have been reading my notes and considering this matter. The second period historically is from 1877 to 1947. The remedy available to the stockholder was the remedy conferred by the second paragraph of s 20 of the 1877 Act as enacted, and that paragraph with its reference to petitions of right attracted the provisions of the Petitions of Right Act 1860. Thus the procedure for a petition of right during that period (1877 to 1947) was the procedure laid down in the 1860 Act; and that procedure would be followed with its deviation as to how the judgment was to be dealt with and from what funds it was to be paid, which is set out at the end of the second paragraph of that section. During the period 1947 to 1960 it seems to me that the remedy, because of s 40 (2) (b) of the Crown Proceedings Act 1947, was a petition of right, but a petition of right in the old pre-1860 Act form. This was not the only petition of right in the old form available after 1947 because by virtue of s 40 (1) of the 1947 Act it would seem that a claim against the Crown in its private capacity would be a claim which would have to be proceeded with by way of old petition of right, unless it could be argued—as in my judgment it cannot, but I will refer to this later—that for certain purposes, that is to say, for the purposes of those petitions of right which survive the 1947 Act, in some way or other the Act of 1860 was saved. The last period is the period 1960 to date, and it is in respect of this period that the question arises. This brings me at once to the Cyprus Act 1960. Of course it does strike one as very odd at first blush that the Cyprus Act 1960, the object of which as indicated by its s 1 was to establish the Republic of Cyprus as an independent sovereign state, should have anything at all to do with Southern Rhodesia or that it should have anything at all to do with other overseas territories,

1 (1908), pp 340, 341

a   formerly colonies and dominions of the Crown, and later as they became, most of them, Commonwealth countries. But of course that is by no means conclusive of the question—although it is in the forefront of counsel for the plaintiff's argument.

The sections of the 1960 Act to which it is necessary to refer are s 1, which I have already mentioned, and I think some emphasis is to be attached to the fact that it enacts there shall be established in the island on the appointed day—which is to be appointed by Order in Council—an independent sovereign republic. The appointed

b   day is defined in s 7 (2) of the Act as the day which is specified by the Order in Council under s 1 of the Act establishing the independence of Cyprus. Section 2 of the 1960 Act deals with the sovereign base areas, and nothing turns on that matter. The important sections are s 3, possibly s 6, and of course the Schedule. Section 3 (1) is designed to adapt existing laws to the changed situation brought about by an Order

c   in Council under s 1:

> 'On and after the appointed day any existing law which operates as a law of, or of any part of, the United Kingdom, being a law applying in relation to Cyprus or persons or things in any way belonging thereto or connected therewith, shall, save as provided after the passing of this Act by the authority having power to amend or repeal that law or by the following provisions of this Act, continue

d   > to apply in like manner in relation to the Republic of Cyprus or persons or things in any way belonging thereto or connected therewith . . .'

Any existing law is defined by sub-s (6) of s 3:

> ' "existing law" means any Act of Parliament (other than this Act) or other enactment or instrument whatsoever, and any rule of law, which is in force on the

e   > appointed day . . .'

So in order to find what an existing law is within s 3 (1), one has got to look at the relevant bundle of law and disregard the 1960 Act for the purpose of ascertaining what the existing law was.

Applying s 3 (1) to the Colonial Stock Acts therefore, one reaches the conclusion that

f   the Colonial Stock Acts 1877 to 1948, as they stood before the Cyprus Act 1960, were an existing law of the United Kingdom, which applied in relation to Cyprus or persons or things in any way belonging thereto or connected therewith; and that existing law continues to operate subject to two things, subject to any subsequent amendment by a body having the appropriate legislative authority—and we are not concerned in this case with any subsequent amendment to the Colonial Stock Acts; and 'subject to the

g   following provisions of this Act.' The following provisions of the Act, I agree with the submission of counsel for the defendant, include not only the provisions of the Act itself—that is those contained in its body, the seven sections—but also the provisions contained in the Schedule. The proviso to s 3 (1) is as follows:

> 'Provided that, save as aforesaid and subject to the provisions of the Schedule to

h   > this Act, any such law which contains different provision with respect to a Commonwealth country mentioned in subsection (3) of section one of the British Nationality Act, 1948, and with respect to parts of Her Majesty's dominions outside the United Kingdom not so mentioned, or expressly excludes any such Commonwealth country to any extent, shall apply in like manner and to the like extent (if any) with respect to the Republic of Cyprus as it applies with

j   > respect to the said Commonwealth country.'

The 'said Commonwealth country' means a Commonwealth country mentioned in s 1 (3) of the British Nationality Act 1948, which for present purposes one can broadly describe as being the 'old dominions'. The effect of that proviso to s 3 (1) on the Colonial Stock Acts 1877 to 1948 is in my judgment this: those Acts did contain provisions which were different in relation to the dominions and in relation to the

other overseas territories of the Crown. Therefore the effect of the proviso is that the   *a*
Colonial Stock Acts, as they applied to the dominions, and again subject to the provisions of the Schedule—which is what the proviso to the subsection says—would apply to Cyprus. In other words it would be treated as a dominion rather than as a colonial country. Section 3 (2) brings the Schedule into operation:

> 'As from the appointed day, the provisions of the Schedule to this Act shall
> have effect with respect to the enactments therein mentioned.'   *b*

I have already referred to s 3 (6). I think nothing more turns on the other provisions of that section. Section 4 is concerned with citizenship, and s 5 with the abolition of appeals to the Privy Council. Both of those matters have no bearing on the present question. Section 6 makes provision for the issue of Orders in Council to give effect to the change of status in Cyprus within the Commonwealth. Counsel for the plaintiff   *c*
has relied in support of his argument in this way: if s 6 is to be read as having general application, as the Attorney-General suggests that the Schedule should be read in its relevant parts, then Her Majesty by Order in Council would have jurisdiction under s 6 to make an Order in Council amending any law in any way. I do not accept that submission. I think with respect to counsel for the plaintiff you just cannot spell this out of s 6 of the Act, because the power to make Orders in Council under that section   *d*
is one to make Orders in Council which are related to the main Order in Council— or to include such provisions in the main Order in Council which is referred to in s 6 (1)—'as appear to Her Majesty in Council expedient for the purposes or in consequence of the Order' under s 6 (1). That is to say, there is a very clear limiting provision on the right of Her Majesty to make Orders in Council under the provisions of s 6 (2).

I have referred to the appointed day section and it is now necessary to look at the   *e*
Schedule. The relevant provisions of the Schedule are those which are contained in para 9 which has four sub-paragraphs. I am going to deal with those in a little more detail later.

It is, however, interesting to observe that in relation to all the other provisions of the Schedule all that they are doing is to include or exclude the Republic of Cyprus from various territorial lists which are incorporated or referred to in other statutes   *f*
of general application. This is a common form type of operation which has been conducted ever since 1947, when the old colonies and dominions started to come into independence. It is always necessary to make adaptations, to meet the new Commonwealth and international constitutional situation, to legislation which broadly speaking had Commonwealth operation, such as the British Nationality Acts, the Army Acts, the Visiting Forces Acts, Merchant Shipping Acts, Diplomatic Immunity Acts, and so   *g*
on; those are the type of Acts which figure in the paragraphs of the Schedule other than para 9. Paragraph 9 (1) provides:

> 'Subject to the provisions of this paragraph, the Colonial Stock Acts, 1877 to
> 1948, shall apply in relation to the Republic of Cyprus as they apply in relation
> to a Dominion within the meaning of the Colonial Stock Act, 1934.'   *h*

That is precisely what in my judgment is being said by s 3 (1) and its proviso in relation to the Colonial Stock Acts as they stood unamended by the Act of 1960. Paragraph 9 (2) provides:

> 'In section twenty of the Colonial Stock Act, 1877 (which relates to the jurisdiction of courts in the United Kingdom as to colonial stock) for the second paragraph   *j*
> there shall be substituted the following subsections, that is to say—
>   "(2) Any person claiming to be interested in colonial stock to which this Act
> applies, or in any dividend thereon, may institute civil proceedings in the United
> Kingdom against the registrar in relation to that stock or dividend.
>   (3) Notwithstanding anything in the foregoing provisions of this section
> [i e s 20], the registrar shall not by virtue of an order made by any court in the

a   United Kingdom in any such proceedings as are referred to in this section be liable to make any payment otherwise than out of moneys in his possession in the United Kingdom as registrar." '

Now, the important changes which are thus made in the old second paragraph of the 1877 Act are obviously these; first, that whereas under the second paragraph of s 20 as enacted the remedy was to be by way of petition of right against the Crown, *b* the remedy is henceforth by an action against the registrar. Secondly, that assuming relief were obtained in any such proceedings instead of *any moneys* of the colonial government in the hands or in the possession of the registrar or other agent in England being liable to be taken to satisfy an order, the only moneys under the new sub-s (3) which may be taken to satisfy such an order are moneys which are in the possession of the registrar in the United Kingdom *as registrar*. That is to say, funds remitted by the *c* colonial government in question to the registrar for the purpose of satisfying liabilities in respect of interest or capital repayment of the stocks of which the registrar is the registrar under the 1877 Act. As to sub-paras (3) and (4) of para 9: the first of them, sub-para (3), applies the Colonial Stock Act 1934 to Cyprus, in other words giving effect to the dominion status of Cyprus for the purpose of the Colonial Stock Acts. Sub-paragraph (4) deals with certain detailed provisions of the 1934 Act, but it seems *d* to me that nothing turns on this.

It has been a long approach but I felt it was better to deal with all these matters before I actually came to the question which is set out in the originating summons. The question itself is difficult to follow unless one has looked at the material which I have examined. The question is this:

e   'Whether upon the proper construction of Section 20 of the Colonial Stock Act 1877 the Plaintiff being a person claiming to be interested in Government of Southern Rhodesia 6% stock, 1976/1979 and interest thereon may present a Petition of Right in England to Her Majesty the Queen notwithstanding the provisions of Section 3 (2) of the Cyprus Act 1960, paragraph 9 (2) of the Schedule to the said Cyprus Act 1960 and the relevant sections of the Crown Proceedings *f*   Act 1947.'

The reason why this is important is that the effect of the new sub-s (3) in para 9 (2) of the Schedule to the Cyprus Act 1960 is to narrow down the funds against which any order obtained in proceedings by a stockholder who is entitled to the benefit of the 1877 Act from the general funds of the colonial government in question to those specific funds provided for the purpose of meeting the stockholders' claims. It is not *g* in dispute that under the new subsection the plaintiff would have a remedy in respect of his claim in this country. This would be, as the Attorney-General submits, that which is provided for in the new sub-s (2), the action or proceedings against the registrar in lieu of the old petition of right provided for by the second paragraph as enacted of the 1877 Act. I am also asked to decide an ancillary question should I find the answer to the question would be Yes, that is to say an answer favourable to *h* the plaintiff. This ancillary question is whether, assuming the plaintiff can present a petition of right to Her Majesty, this petition of right should be governed by the Petitions of Rights Act 1860 or whether it has to go back to the procedures and principles and rules which were available before the 1860 Act introduced the statutory procedure for the petition of right and which were specifically saved by that Act.

It is not without interest to observe that the learned editors of Halsbury's Statutes *j* on the one hand, and the learned editors of Halsbury's Laws on the other, have both considered this matter and have reached diametrically opposite conclusions. Taking Halsbury's Statutes first, because in point of time this seems to have been the first consideration, if one looks at volume 4 of Halsbury's Statutes[1], where the Colonial

---

1   3rd Edn (1968), p 491

Stock Act 1877 as allegedly amended is reproduced, one sees that the old s 20 has, so
far as its second paragraph is concerned, completely disappeared and the text is
replaced by sub-ss (2) and (3) set out in para 9 (2) of the Schedule to the 1960 Act.
And the note beneath it reads[1]:

'Sub-ss. (2) and (3) were substituted by the Cyprus Act 1960, s. 3 (2) and Schedule,
para. 9 (2), for the second paragraph of this section.'

Although sub-s (1) is reproduced exactly in the form in which it was enacted in 1877,
square brackets have been put around the (1)—the reason for that is of course that as
sub-ss (2) and (3) were specifically introduced by para 9 (2) of the Schedule to the 1960
Act it was necessary to insert the number (1) before the first subsection, as it became.
On the other hand according to the learned editors of Halsbury's Laws[2]:

'A further exception [that is an exception to the abolition of the petition of
right by the 1947 Act] exists in that a petition of right still lies under the Colonial
Stock Act 1877, s. 20 . . '

So one does not find this conflict really very helpful, but it is interesting to observe
that the point has been considered and different conclusions reached on it. This is
precisely the question I have to determine.

There is one other matter I should mention and that is that in the Ghana (Consequential Provision) (Colonial Stock Acts) Order in Council 1960[3], which is made
pursuant to the provisions of the Ghana (Consequential Provision) Act 1960, specific
provision is made for the modification of the Colonial Stock Acts 1877 to 1948—the
word 'modifications' is the word which is used in the Order in Council in the Ghana
case. Article 2 (1) reads:

'On and after the date on which Ghana becomes a Republic, the Colonial Stock
Acts, 1877 to 1948, shall apply in relation to Ghana subject to the modifications
set out in paragraphs (2), (3) and (4) of this Article.'

The relevant paragraph is paragraph 2 (4) of the Ghana Order in Council, which in
effect is in the same terms as para 9 (2) of the Schedule to the Cyprus Act. And again
one can also put the question in this way: did para 9 of the Schedule to the 1960 Act
change s 20 of the 1877 Act as a matter of general law, or did it only change it in relation to Cyprus? It is suggested that it would be very odd, particularly in view of comparison with the provision in the Ghana Order in Council, that you would have one
specific provision relating only to Ghana and Cyprus, whereas para 2 in its originally
enacted form would continue to apply to the rest of the overseas governments which
fall under the umbrella of the Colonial Stock Act 1877.

I approach the answer to the question by two stages. Stage one is this: is the meaning of the Cyprus Act in this respect clear and unambiguous, and if so, what does it
mean? At this stage I look at the words of the enactment as a whole, including the
Schedule, and I use no further aids, no further extrinsic aids in order to reach a conclusion as to the clear and unambiguous meaning of the words. At this stage, however,
I am entitled to take into consideration the general principles which apply when one
finds something which on the face of it might seem to be conflicting between the body
of the statute and provisions included in a schedule. Counsel for the defendant,
who as always has been most helpful, has referred me to passages in Craies on Statute
Law[4], which I have taken into account. If I find that the answer on the first stage in my
enquiry is the meaning of the Act in this respect is ambiguous, then I have to go on
to the second stage and consider two possible different meanings. That is to say
the meanings for which counsel for the plaintiff contends on the plaintiff's side and

1   3rd Edn (1968), vol 4, p 491
2   Supplement (1972) to 11 Halsbury's Laws (3rd Edn), para 2
3   SI 1960 No 969
4   7th Edn (1971), pp 224, 225, 376, 377

a for which counsel for the defendant contends for the Attorney-General. Now if I get to this second stage then, in my judgment, and then only, am I entitled to look at extrinsic aids, such as the long title, the heading, the side notes, other legislation; then only am I entitled to resort to maxims of construction, of which counsel for the plaintiff gave me a useful list. I have got to construe the words so that they have a reasonable effect. I have got to avoid absurdity or repugnance. I have got to avoid

b hardship and injustice. I have got to be sure that the meaning I select, if the meaning is ambiguous, is a meaning which does not unduly and unjustly interfere with subsisting rights. I can also, if I get to stage two, as I see the matter, consider what the consequences of a meaning selected between two would in practice be. But in my judgment I cannot use any of those extrinsic aids, and I cannot resort to those maxims, unless my answer on stage one is the meaning of these words is not clear and not unambiguous. So I concentrate now on stage one.

c I have already discussed s 3 (1) of the 1960 Act in some detail, and that subsection and its proviso mean in my judgment that the Colonial Stock Acts 1877 to 1948, as they were before the 1960 Act became effective, apply to Cyprus as they applied to the dominions, subject to the provisions of para 9. So far as s 3 (2) is concerned, the Schedule is effective from the appointed day and it is that Schedule which makes

d adaptations of the Colonial Stock Act 1877 as from that day. Section 6 as I have indicated really gives no help. Therefore, I must turn now to para 9 itself. It is interesting to observe that para 9 (1) commences with the words: 'Subject to the provisions of this paragraph . . .' Those words, as Lord Simonds said in a passage which again counsel for the defendant drew most helpfully to my attention, in his speech in *Smith v London Transport Executive*[1]: '[These] are . . . words that are apt to enact that the

e powers thereafter given are subject to restrictions or limitations . . .' In my judgment, it is important to observe that only para 9 (2) is introducing any restriction or limitation. Sub-paragraphs (3) and (4) are in fact extending, not limiting or restricting, the provisions of the Colonial Stock Acts in their application to Cyprus; and in my view, therefore, one is entitled to take the view—and this is the plaintiff's submission—that the Colonial Stock Acts are to be applied to Cyprus subject

f to the provisions of sub-para (2). And if they are to be applied to Cyprus, subject to the provisions of para 9 (2), it would follow that sub-para (2) has not general application but has application limited to Cyprus only.

The plaintiff has a further point, which in my judgment is not a sound one. He submits that there is no express repeal of s 20 of the 1877 Act contained in the Schedule, and that there is no repeal schedule in the normal form set out to the 1960 Act. I do not think that that is a valid point. The words which are used in para 9 (2) are the

g words 'shall be substituted the following subsections', and the use of that expression— I made a very quick random check on this—is a formula whereby subsections of sections can be changed as a matter of general law, or whereby words can be introduced into subsections with general effect which were not in there before. For this purpose I looked at two enactments in the 1960 volume of the statutes and I find, for example, in Sch 6 to the Charities Act 1960 entitled 'Consequential Amendments' the

h following: 'Enactment amended . . . The Places of Worship Registration Act, 1855— Section nine . . .'Amendment: For the words from "wholly freed" onwards there shall be *substituted* the words', and then it gives the substitution. And there are other examples in the same schedule. Another good example is the schedules to the Betting and Gaming Act 1960[2] where one finds the substitution of words dealt with in a large number of cases. For example, Sch 5 to the Betting and Gaming Act 1960, para 4:

j 'In each of the following enactments [and it specifies certain enactments], there shall be substituted the words "without his consent or connivance and that he exercised all due diligence to prevent it".' In other words, the formula of 'substitution' is a way of amending existing law by way of amendments of general application.

---

1 [1951] 1 All ER 667 at 669 [1951] AC 555 at 565
2 Halsbury's Statutes (2nd Edn, 1960) vol 40, pp 363-384

I now turn to the arguments of counsel for the defendant. He submits first of all that the words 'in relation to' are used in para 9 (1) and (3) of the Schedule to the Cyprus Act 1960 but are not used in para 9 (2). On my reading of para 9 (1) the way in which that applies because of my construction of the introductory phrase 'subject to the provisions of this paragraph', sub-para (2) being the only qualification or limitation in para 9, it would be quite unnecessary to put the words 'in relation to' Cyprus stock or 'in relation to Cyprus' in that subparagraph. Those words are unnecessary because of the meaning which I attach to para 9 (1) in the light of s 3 (1) of the 1960 Act.

Again counsel for the defendant makes the point, and it is a forcible point, that if you look at s 3 (2), which is the section which brings the Schedule into operation, you see that that is enacted in perfectly general terms. It does not for example say 'come into operation in relation to Cyprus'. It is a general enacting formula. Similarly he submits that one should have regard to the generality of para 9 (2) as opposed to what I am calling the specificity of the other paragraphs in the schedule. But again, on my reading of s 3 (1) its main paragraph and its proviso, the purpose of para 9 (2) of the Schedule is merely to effect a change in the Colonial Stock Acts as originally enacted in the specific case of Cyprus.

The answer therefore to the question which I have to determine on the originating summons is Yes, an answer which is in the plaintiff's favour. In that situation I have not reached, and I do not consider it is necessary for me to deal with, the stage two process. In my judgment the words are clear and unambiguous so that the answer to the question is Yes. But had I reached stage two I feel bound to say this: that I think that if the words had been susceptible on proper construction of the alternative meanings contended for, the arguments one way and the other would be very evenly and finely balanced and it by no means follows that the plaintiff would have been right on the stage two examination. But I am not going to decide that and I think it would be unnecessary for me to go beyond the conclusion I have reached on the main question.

As to the procedural form, counsel for the defendant has endeavoured to submit—and if he will forgive me for saying so—really half-heartedly because it really is not a submission which in my judgment can be supported, that in some way or other the Petitions of Right Act 1860 was saved for the purposes of petitions of right which remained available to the subject after the passing of the 1947 Act. I just cannot get that by any process of construction of the 1947 Act. It therefore follows that the plaintiff on this summons is thrown back to the position of a petitioner proceeding by way of petition of right before 1860. I conclude my judgment just by referring to another passage in Robertson[1] on this point. He is referring to the 1860 Act procedure:

'It is not even a substitute for the cumbrous old practice, but merely an alternative, since, by sect. 18, it is lawful for a suppliant to proceed as before the passing of the Act. It is so unlikely that anyone would wish to do so that it appears to be unnecessary to discuss the earlier practice. Those who are curious with regard to it will find specimens [in a number of authorities cited]. After perusing these precedents, probably no one would be desirous of adopting a similar procedure.'

So that is I think as far as I can take it and the quotation is somewhat ominous.

Question answered in the affirmative. Petition of right to be in pre-1860 form.

Solicitors: *Allan Jay & Co* (for the plaintiff); *Treasury Solicitor.*

E H Hunter Esq Barrister.

1 (1908), p 367

a

Re Cohen (deceased)
Cowan v Cohen and others

CHANCERY DIVISION

TEMPLEMAN J

b   9th, 10th, 23rd NOVEMBER 1972

Charity – Relief of poverty – Poor relations – Relatives 'in special need' – Direction in will – Trustees to pay and apply whole or any part or parts of residuary estate for or towards the maintenance and benefit of any relatives of testatrix whom the trustees 'shall consider to be in special need' – Residuary estate to be paid and applied 'in such manner and at such time
c   *or times as my Trustees shall in their absolute and uncontrolled discretion think fit' – Proviso that trustees under no legal obligation nor accountable in relation to carrying out of bequest – Whether charitable trust of final residue for relief of poverty among relations of testatrix – Whether special power of appointment exercisable in favour of relations of testatrix who were 'in special need'.*

d   The testatrix died in June 1966. By her will she gave her residuary estate to her trustees on the usual trusts for conversion, investment and payment of debts, funeral and testamentary expenses, and directed her trustees to hold the balance as to four-tenths for one of her sons, and as to three-tenths for another son. Clause 6 (b) (iii) provided: 'As to the remaining Three-tenths of my Residuary Estate (herein referred to as "the final residue") as to both capital and income thereof . . . (c) Upon Trust as to the
e   balance of the final residue to pay and apply the whole or any part or parts thereof in such manner and at such time or times as my Trustees shall in their absolute and uncontrolled discretion think fit for or towards the maintenance and benefit of any relatives of mine whom my Trustees shall consider to be in special need Provided that my Trustees shall be under no legal obligation whatsoever nor accountable to any other person or persons in relation to the carrying out of this bequest nor shall
f   any beneficiary under this my Will or any relative of mine or any of my next of kin be entitled to particulars from my Trustees as to the mode in which they have carried out this bequest.' The testatrix was survived by three sons, her next-of-kin, and about 50 relations, i e her grandchildren and remoter issue and her nephews and nieces and their issue, all of whom shared with her a common ancestor. Since her death the number of relations had increased to about 60. Her net estate, valued at about £1,500
g   at her death, had subsequently increased in value to between £10,000 and £15,000. The question arose whether the will created a charitable trust of the final residue for the relief of poverty among her relations, or a special power of appointment exercisable in favour of such of her relations as were 'in special need'.

Held – Paragraph (c) created a charitable trust for the relief of poverty among the
h   relations of the testatrix born before or after her death whom the trustees considered to be in special need, because—

(i) the instruction to the trustees to consider persons 'in special need' was to be construed as an instruction to satisfy the special needs of a selected beneficiary by alleviating poverty; accordingly para (c) was a gift for the relief of poverty among a special class (see p 895 f to h, post);

j   (ii) the trustees were under a duty to devote the final residue to the objects specified in that clause; the proviso was intended to smooth the path of the trustees in performing their duties and not to indicate that they were not subject to a trust or direction (see p 896 b to d, post);

(iii) there was nothing in the will to show that the term 'relative' was limited to persons living at the death of the testatrix (see p 896 e and f, post).

Re Scarisbrick, Cockshott v Public Trustee [1951] 1 All ER 822 applied.

Notes

For the relief of the poor being a charitable purpose, see 4 Halsbury's Laws (3rd Edn) 213-218, paras 492-495, and for cases on the subject, see 8 Digest (Repl) 316-319, 13-48.

Cases referred to in judgment

Compton, Re, Powell v Compton [1945] 1 All ER 198, [1945] Ch 123, 114 LJCh 99, 172 LT 158, CA, 8 Digest (Repl) 330, 123.

Dingle v Turner [1972] 1 All ER 878, [1972] AC 601, [1972] 2 WLR 523, HL.

Scarisbrick, Re, Cockshott v Public Trustee [1951] 1 All ER 822, [1951] Ch 622, CA; rvsg [1950] 1 All ER 143, [1950] Ch 226, 8 Digest (Repl) 316, 18.

Cases also cited

A-G v Duke of Northumberland (1877) 7 Ch D 745.

Baden's Deed Trusts (No 2), Re [1972] 2 All ER 1304, [1973] Ch 9, CA; affg [1971] 3 All ER 985, [1972] Ch 607.

Berkeley (deceased), Re [1968] 3 All ER 364, [1968] Ch 744, CA.

Blausten v Inland Revenue Comrs [1972] 1 All ER 41, [1972] Ch 256, CA.

Bridgen, Re, Chaytor v Edwin [1937] 4 All ER 342, [1938] Ch 205.

Coates, Re, Ramsden v Coates [1955] 1 All ER 26, [1955] Ch 495.

Cole v Wade (1807) 16 Ves 27, 33 ER 894.

Combe, Re, Combe v Combe [1925] Ch 210, [1925] All ER Rep 159.

Gibson v South American Stores (Gath & Chaves) Ltd [1949] 2 All ER 985, [1950] Ch 177, CA.

Goff v Webb (1602) Toth 30, 21 ER 114.

Grant v Lynam (1828) 4 Russ 292, 38 ER 815.

Green v Howard (1779) 1 Bro CC 31, 28 ER 967, LC.

Gulbenkian's Settlement Trusts, Re [1968] 3 All ER 785, [1970] AC 508, HL.

Hamley v Gilbert (1821) Jac 354.

Harding v Glyn (1739) 1 Atk 469, 26 ER 299.

Hughes, Re, Hughes v Footner [1921] 2 Ch 208, [1921] All ER Rep 310.

Isaac v Defriez (1754) Amb 595, [1803-13] All ER Rep 468n, 27 ER 387, LC.

Londonderry's Settlement, Re, Peat v Walsh [1964] 3 All ER 855, [1964] Ch 918, CA.

McPhail v Doulton [1970] 2 All ER 228, [1971] AC 424, HL; rvsg sub nom Re Baden's Deed Trusts [1969] 1 All ER 1016, [1969] 2 Ch 388, CA.

Oppenheim v Tobacco Securities Trust Co Ltd [1951] 1 All ER 31, [1951] AC 297, HL.

Perowne, Re, Perowne v Moss [1951] 2 All ER 201, [1951] Ch 785.

Pilkington v Inland Revenue Comrs [1962] 3 All ER 622, [1964] AC 612, HL.

Robinson, Re, Davis v Robinson [1950] 2 All ER 1148, [1951] Ch 198.

Sayer Trust, Re, MacGregor v Sayer [1956] 3 All ER 600, [1957] Ch 423.

Supple v Lowson (1773) Amb 729, 27 ER 471.

Tiffin v Longman (1852) 15 Beav 275, 51 ER 543.

Widmore v Woodroffe (1766) Amb 636, 27 ER 413.

Wilson v Duguid (1883) 24 Ch D 244.

Wootton's Will Trusts, Re [1968] 2 All ER 618, [1968] 1 WLR 681.

Adjourned summons

This was an application by originating summons dated 14th May 1969, as amended on 22nd February 1971, by the plaintiff, Maurice Cowan, an executor and trustee and one of the next-of-kin of Rachel Cohen, deceased ('the testatrix'), who died on 9th June 1966, seeking, inter alia, the determination of the following among other questions: (1) whether the words 'in special need' in the passage 'as my Trustees shall in their absolute and uncontrolled discretion think fit for or towards the maintenance and benefit of any relatives of mine whom my Trustees shall consider to be in special need' quoted from para (c) of cl 6 (b) (iii) of the will of the testatrix were (a) void for uncertainty, or (b) equivalent to the word 'poor'; (2) if the question in (1) above be *a* answered in the second alternative whether the trustees held the balance of the final residue (a) on trust for such of the statutory next-of-kin living at the date of the testatrix' death as were for the time being poor, or (b) subject to a bare power of appointment exercisable for 21 years in favour of the statutory next-of-kin of the testatrix living at her death who for the time being were poor and subject thereto in trust for the statutory next-of-kin of the testatrix living at the date of her death, or (c)

b subject to a bare power of appointment exercisable for 21 years in favour of the statutory next-of-kin and relations more remote of the testatrix living at the date of her death who for the time being were poor, and subject to and in default of the exercise of such power of appointment held the balance of the final residue in trust for the statutory next-of-kin of the testatrix living at the date of her death, or (d) subject to a bare power of appointment exercisable for 21 years in favour of the statutory

c next-of-kin and relations more remote of the testatrix for the time being in existence and subject to and in default of the exercise of such power of appointment held the balance of the final residue on trust for the statutory next-of-kin of the testatrix living at her death, or (e) created a valid charitable trust in favour of the persons who were related to the testatrix and were for the time being poor, or (f) in what manner the trustees held the balance of the final residue. The defendants were (1) Philip

d Solomon Cohen, a son of the testatrix, (2) John Cowan, a grandson of the testatrix born before her death, (3) Emanuel Cohen, a son of the testatrix and an executor and trustee, (4) Maurice Ellis, a nephew of the testatrix and an executor and trustee, (5) Richard Iain Cowan, an infant great grandson of the testatrix born after her death, and (6) the Attorney-General. The facts are set out in the judgment.

John Silberrad and *A E J Perrett* for the plaintiff.
e *Theodore Wallace* for the second defendant.
L L Ware for the third defendant.
Guy Seward for the fourth defendant.
Angus Nicol for the fifth defendant.
Andrew Morritt for the Attorney-General.
The first defendant did not appear and was not represented.

f

Cur adv vult

23rd November.   **TEMPLEMAN J** read the following judgment. The principal question raised by this originating summons is whether the will of the testatrix, Rachel Cohen, created a charitable trust of her final residue for the relief of poverty

g among her relations, or a special power of appointment exercisable in favour of her relations, who are 'in special need'.

By her will dated 11th February 1960 the testatrix appointed as her executors and trustees her nephew John and two of her sons, the third defendant, Emanuel Cohen, and the plaintiff, Maurice, who changed his name from Cohen to Cowan. The testatrix gave three small legacies totalling £60, which she described as charitable legacies.

h By cl 4 she authorised her trustees—but, as she said, without thereby imposing any trust or direction—to allow her son, Emanuel, to reside rent-free for a period of five years in a flat on property then owned by the testatrix. She gave her residuary estate to her trustees on the usual trusts for conversion, investment and payment of debts, funeral and testamentary expenses and to hold the balance as to four-tenths for Emanuel, as to three-tenths for Maurice, and in cl 6 (b) (iii), she continued:

j   'As to the remaining Three-tenths of my Residuary Estate (herein referred to as "the final residue") as to both capital and income thereof: (A) [£250 to be paid] to my grandchild Moira Cohen upon her marrying a person . . . of the Jewish Faith . . . (B) [£250 to be paid to Emanuel] being repayment to him of money borrowed from him on the occasion of the wedding of my grandchild Shirley Cohen. (c) Upon Trust as to the balance of the final residue to pay and

apply the whole or any part or parts thereof in such manner and at such time or   a
times as my Trustees shall in their absolute and uncontrolled discretion think fit
for or towards the maintenance and benefit of any relatives of mine whom my
Trustees shall consider to be in special need Provided that my Trustees shall be
under no legal obligation whatsoever nor accountable to any other person or
persons in relation to the carrying out of this bequest nor shall any beneficiary
under this my Will or any relative of mine or any of my next of kin be entitled   b
to particulars from my Trustees as to the mode in which they have carried out
this bequest.'

In cl 8 of her will, the testatrix declared—

'that in relation to the commission or omission of any act or otherwise howsoever in execution of the trusts of this my Will or of any Codicil hereto or in relation   c
to the exercise by my Trustees of any powers or discretion vested in them (whether
as Personal Representatives or Trustees) the opinion or decision of the majority
of such Trustees shall prevail notwithstanding that any one or more of such
Trustees may be personally interested or concerned.'

The testatrix made one codicil dated 30th August 1963 and thereby appointed an-   d
other nephew, the fourth defendant, Maurice Ellis, to be an executor and trustee in
the place of her nephew John, who had died.

The testatrix died on 9th June 1966, survived by three sons, Maurice, Emanuel
and the first defendant, Philip Solomon Cohen, who has not appeared to argue on this
summons. The three sons are the next-of-kin of the testatrix. The testatrix was also
survived by seven grandchildren and by great grandchildren, who have, since the   e
death of the testatrix, increased in number to 16. The second defendant, John Cowan,
is a grandson of the testatrix and was born before her death. The fifth defendant,
Richard Cowan, is an infant great grandson of the testatrix and was born after her
death. The testatrix was also survived by nephews and nieces and their issue, who
also have increased in number since the death of the testatrix. The relations of the
testatrix, that is to say, her children and remoter issue and her nephews and nieces   f
and their issue, all of whom share with the testatrix a common ancestor, now number
about 60 and must have numbered about 50 when the testatrix died.

The estate of the testatrix consisted almost entirely of two freehold properties, one
of which was heavily mortgaged, and her net estate at her death was only valued at
about £1,500. The value of the net estate, even after allowing for capital gains tax,
has since increased to between £10,000 and £15,000, partly because the lease of one of
the properties has been surrendered and partly because of the general rise in the value   g
of real property.

Counsel for the second defendant submitted that para (c) of cl 6 (b) (iii) of the will
created a special power of appointment exercisable in favour of relatives descended
from a common ancestor and living at the death of the testatrix and considered by the
trustees to be in special need.

Counsel for the third defendant submitted that the powers conferred on the   h
trustees were so wide that the trustees were absolutely entitled to the final residue.
Alternatively, he submitted that para (c) created a special power of appointment exercisable only in favour of next-of-kin. I cannot accept either of those submissions.
The trustees were plainly directed to hold on trust and not beneficially. In para (c)
the testatrix herself distinguished between relatives on the one hand and next-of-kin
on the other, and the authorities which construe relations as next-of-kin in order to   j
prevent a disposition being void for uncertainty are not applicable here. Counsel
also submitted, in the alternative, that the will created a special power of appointment in favour of relatives living at the death of the testatrix, and I will deal with that
submission later.

Counsel for the fourth defendant, on instructions, took no part in the argument.

Counsel for the fifth defendant submitted that para (c) created a charitable trust, or *a* alternatively a special power of appointment, in either case in favour of relations born before or after the death of the testatrix. By virtue of the Perpetuities and Accumulations Act 1964 any such special power of appointment is exercisable during the period of 21 years after the death of the testatrix.

Counsel for the sixth defendant, the Attorney-General, submitted that para (c) created a charitable trust for the relief of poverty among the relations of the testatrix.

b Finally, counsel who appeared for the plaintiff, but on this point was instructed to argue also for the interests of the absent first defendant, submitted that para (c) create a special power which was void for uncertainty and, in any event, did not created a charitable trust.

Some assistance on the distinction between, on the one hand, a charitable trust and, on the other, a special power of appointment, in the present context, is provided by the decision of the Court of Appeal in *Re Scarisbrick, Cockshott v Public Trustee*[1]. The *c* headnote reads[2]:

d 'A testatrix in disposing of her residuary estate, directed her trustees, after the death of her son and two daughters, to whom the income was to be paid during their lives in a specified way, to "hold the same upon trust for such relations of my said son and daughters as in the opinion of the survivor of my said son and daughters shall be in needy circumstances and for such charitable objects either in Germany or Great Britain . . . for such interest and in such proportions . . . as the survivor of my said son and daughters shall by deed or will appoint".'

Sir Raymond Evershed MR said[3]:

e '. . . what, on the true construction of the relevant part of [the will], was the intention of the testatrix? Did she, primarily, intend a benefit to such of a wide and otherwise unascertainable class of her children's "relations" as the survivor of her children should appoint subject only to the qualification that those selected should, in his or her opinion, be "in needy circumstances"—a qualification not by any means the same as that of the objective standard of poverty, and not having the effect of limiting the amount appointed to the relief of poverty?'

f He contrasted that with the other question[3]:

'Did the testatrix, on the other hand, intend primarily to relieve poverty, the persons to be relieved being chosen from the class of "relations" of the three children?'

g Sir Raymond Evershed MR therefore pointed a contrast between a charitable trust for the relief of poverty among relations and a special power of appointment exercisable in favour of relations who are poor.

In *Re Scarisbrick*[1] Sir Raymond Evershed MR came to the conclusion that there was a charitable trust largely because the direction to benefit relations in needy circumstances formed part of a disposition the other objects of which were expressly restricted *h* to charitable objects. His reasoning appears in the judgment[4] and, of course, the circumstance on which he relied is not present in the instant case. Jenkins LJ[5] gave a more general ground for distinguishing between, on the one hand, a charitable trust for the relief of poverty amongst a particular description of poor people, and, on the other hand, a gift to particular poor people, the relief of poverty being the motive of the gift. Jenkins LJ said this[5]:

j _____

1 [1951] 1 All ER 822, [1951] Ch 622
2 [1951] Ch at 622, 623
3 [1951] 1 All ER at 825, [1951] Ch at 630
4 [1951] Ch at 635, cf [1951] 1 All ER at 828
5 [1951] 1 All ER at 838, [1951] Ch at 650, 651

'It is, no doubt, true that a gift or trust is not necessarily charitable as being in
relief of poverty because the object or objects of it in order to take must be poor. *a*
Such a gift or trust may be no more than an ordinary gift to some particular
individual or individuals limited to the amount required to relieve his or their
necessities if in necessitous circumstances. One can conceive of a testator making a
limited provision of this character for a child or children whose conduct, in his
view, had reduced their claims on his bounty to a minimum. A disposition of *b*
that sort would obviously not be for the relief of poverty in the charitable sense.
The same must be said of gifts to named persons if in needy circumstances, or to a
narrow class of near relatives, as, for example, to such of a testator's statutory
next of kin as at his death shall be in needy circumstances. It is difficult to draw
any exact line, but I do not think the trust here in question can fairly be held disqualified as a trust for the relief of poverty in the charitable sense on grounds *c*
such as those illustrated above.'

Although in the instant case the class of relatives is narrower than the class of
relations in *Re Scarisbrick*[1], persons described in para (c) of the present will are not so
few in number or such a narrow class that a sensible distinction can be drawn between the present case and the reasoning of Jenkins LJ in *Re Scarisbrick*[1] on these
grounds. The decision in *Re Scarisbrick*[1] was approved in *Dingle v Turner*[2]. In *d*
that case there was a trust to apply income in paying pensions to poor employees
of a company. Megarry J held that the trust was a valid charitable trust; and the
House of Lords, in dismissing the appeal, held[3]—

'... that a trust for "poor employees" was capable of being a valid charitable
trust; that in the field of "poverty" trusts the distinction between a public or *e*
charitable trust and a private trust depended on whether as a matter of construction the gift was for the relief of poverty amongst a particular description
of poor people or was merely a gift to particular poor persons, the relief of
poverty among them being the motive of the gift; and that the trust in the
instant case was a valid charitable trust.'

Re Scarisbrick[1] was approved. Lord Cross of Chelsea referred to *Re Scarisbrick*[1] and *f*
said[4]:

'Most of the cases on the subject were decided in the 18th or early 19th centuries and are very inadequately reported but two things at least were clear.
First, that it never occurred to the judges who decided them that in the field of
"poverty" a trust could not be a charitable trust if the class of beneficiaries was *g*
defined by reference to descent from a common ancestor. Secondly, that the
courts did not treat a gift or trust as necessarily charitable because the objects
of it had to be poor in order to qualify, for in some of the cases the trust was
treated as a private trust and not a charity. The problem in *Re Scarisbrick*[1]
was to determine on what basis the distinction was drawn. Roxburgh J[5]...
had held that the distinction lay in whether the gift took the form of a trust *h*
under which capital was retained and the income only applied for the benefit
of the objects, in which case the gift was charitable, or whether the gift was one
under which the capital was immediately distributable among the objects, in
which case the gift was not a charity. The Court of Appeal[1] rejected this
ground of distinction. They held that in this field the distinction between a
public or charitable trust and a private trust depended on whether as a matter *j*

---

1 [1951] 1 All ER 822, [1951] Ch 622
2 [1972] 1 All ER 878, [1972] AC 601
3 See [1972] AC at 601
4 [1972] 1 All ER at 883, [1972] AC at 616, 617
5 [1950] 1 All ER 143, [1950] Ch 226

a of construction the gift was for the relief of poverty amongst a particular description of poor people or was merely a gift to particular poor persons, the relief of poverty among them being the motive of the gift. The fact that the gift took the form of a perpetual trust would no doubt indicate that the intention of the donor could not have been to confer private benefits on particular people whose possible necessities he had in mind; but the fact that the capital of the gift was

b to be distributed at once did not necessarily show that the gift was a private trust. The appellant in the instant case, while of course submitting that the judges who decided the old cases were wrong in not appreciating that no gift for the relief of poverty among persons tracing descent from a common ancestor could ever have a sufficiently "public" quality to constitute a charity, did not dispute the correctness of the analysis of those cases made by the Court of Appeal in *Re Scarisbrick*[1].'

c
And later Lord Cross of Chelsea said[2]:

'... wherever else it may hold sway the *Compton*[3] rule has no application in the field of trusts for the relief of poverty and ... there the dividing line between a charitable trust and a private trust lies where the Court of Appeal drew it in

d *Re Scarisbrick*[1].'

The other members of the House in *Dingle v Turner*[4] agreed with the conclusions and reasons of Lord Cross of Chelsea, with one reservation which is not here material. In drawing the dividing line the greatest help appears to be provided by the test laid down by Jenkins LJ[5].

Counsel for the second defendant, third defendant and the plaintiff sought to

e distinguish *Re Scarisbrick*[1] by arguing that while a person in needy circumstances is a person who is poor, a person who is in special need is not necessarily poor. Witness, they submit, the affluent parent who, debarred from state aid, is nevertheless in special need of money to send his son to university. And witness also, they submit, the testatrix who may or may not have been poor when, as appears from her will, she was on one occasion in special need of £250 which she borrowed from her son

f on the occasion of the marriage of a granddaughter.

In my judgment, where, in the context of a testamentary power of selection, trustees are instructed to consider persons in needy circumstances or persons in special need, no sensible or logical distinction can be drawn between the two expressions. Moreover, having regard to the size of the estate of the testatrix and what is revealed by her will, I do not consider that this testatrix envisaged the possibility that persons

g who were not poor could or would be selected by the trustees, nor do I consider that this testatrix envisaged that her final residue could or would be used otherwise than in an endeavour to satisfy the special needs of a selected beneficiary by alleviating poverty in some manner and in some measure. In my judgment, para (c) is a gift for the relief of poverty amongst a class and is indistinguishable from *Re Scarisbrick*[1], provided that on the true construction of para (c) the trustees are under a duty to

h devote the final residue to the objects specified in para (c). It is clear that the trustees are not bound to exhaust capital, because in relation to capital at any rate the trustees may devote the whole or any part of the final residue to the purposes indicated in the clause. This is not, however, fatal in a charitable trust provided it appears that the trustees were under a duty to consider the exercise of the power with regard to capital, and certainly to carry out the objects specified in para (c) with regard to income.

j
1 [1951] 1 All ER 822, [1951] Ch 622
2 [1972] 1 All ER at 888, [1972] AC at 623
3 In *Re Compton, Powell v Compton* [1945] 1 All ER 198, [1945] Ch 123
4 [1972] 1 All ER 878, [1972] AC 601
5 [1951] 1 All ER at 838, [1951] Ch at 650, 651

Paragraph (c) directs the final residue to be held 'Upon trust' as the trustees shall think fit for relations whom the trustees 'shall consider' to be in special need. The proviso to *a* para (c) protects the trustees in carrying out 'this bequest' and absolves them from giving particulars 'as to the mode in which they have carried out this bequest'. This is the language of a positive duty rather than the language of a power. Moreover, although it is common ground that the will was drafted by a professional draftsman and is guilty of some repetition and overlapping, there is no trust to take effect in default of appointment of the final residue, and I find it impossible to believe that *b* this could have been overlooked. In the same way that the testatrix intended that Emanuel and Maurice should take between them seven-tenths of her residuary estate, so she intended that the remaining three-tenths should be held on the trusts declared by para (c) and on no other trusts. This seems to me to impose on the trustees a duty to devote the three-tenths to the objects specified in para (c). The proviso in para (c) is intended to smooth the path of the trustees in performing *c* their duties and, unlike the plain indication in cl 4 of the will, the proviso in para (c), in my judgment, was not intended to indicate that the trustees are not subject to a trust or direction but can simply consider and then do as they please, and if they do not please, produce the bizarre results in the present instance of a partial intestacy.

Counsel for the plaintiff submitted that the testatrix only intended to make some discretionary provision for her third son, Philip, without disturbing his entitlement *d* to state assistance. There is certainly no evidence of this in the will, but, of course, there is nothing to prevent the trustees considering the special needs of Philip Solomon Cohen if he qualifies for consideration under para (c).

If, as I have indicated, in my judgment, para (c) creates a charitable trust for the relief of poverty among the relatives of the testatrix, there is nothing in the will to *e* show that the term 'relative' is limited to a person living at the death of the testatrix. There can be no logical distinction in the mind of the testatrix between a grandchild born immediately before her death and a grandchild born immediately after. Both will constitute relatives; both may be in special need at the date when the trustees from time to time consider relatives who are in special need.

It follows, in my judgment, that para (c) creates a charitable trust for the relief of poverty among the relatives of the testatrix born before or after her death whom the *f* trustees consider to be in special need.

Declaration accordingly.

Solicitors: *S R Freed & Co* (for the plaintiff and the second and fifth defendants); *Allan Jay & Co* (for the third defendant); *Edgley & Co* (for the fourth defendant); *Treasury* *g* *Solicitor.*

Jacqueline Metcalfe   Barrister.

Wroth and another v Tyler

CHANCERY DIVISION
MEGARRY J
16th, 17th, 20th, 22nd, 27th, 28th, 29th NOVEMBER, 20th DECEMBER 1972, 11th JANUARY
1973

*Specific performance – Sale of land – Sale with vacant possession – Duty of vendor to bring
proceedings to obtain possession – Matrimonial home – Vendor's spouse's right of occupation –
Right registered as a charge – Husband owner of home – Husband contracting to sell home –
Wife subsequently registering right of occupation as a charge – Husband and wife living together – Wife unwilling to leave home – Wife's right of occupation personal to herself – Husband
attempting without success to persuade wife short of litigation to remove notice of charge –
Purchasers having alternative remedy in damages – Whether husband should be compelled to
take proceedings to terminate wife's right of occupation – Whether purchasers entitled to
specific performance subject to wife's right of occupation – Matrimonial Homes Act 1967,
ss 1, 2.*

*Sale of land – Contract – Breach – Damages – Loss of bargain – Defect in vendor's title –
Vendor unable without any fault to show good title – Nominal damages for loss of bargain
– Defect in title – Wife's right to occupy matrimonial home – Wife entering in charges register
a notice of right of occupation after exchange of contracts – Vendor unable to persuade wife
to remove notice – Vendor withdrawing from contract – Whether purchaser limited to nominal
damages for loss of bargain.*

*Sale of land – Contract – Breach – Damages – Damages in substitution for specific performance
– Damages for loss of bargain – Date for assessment – Date of breach or date of hearing of action
for specific performance – Increase in value of property between date of breach and date of
hearing – Chancery Amendment Act 1858, s 2.*

*Contract – Breach – Damages – Measure – Foreseeability – Head or type of damage in con-
templation of parties at date of breach – Quantum of damage under that head not foreseeable –
Whether plaintiff entitled to damages in respect of whole of damage sustained under that
head.*

The defendant lived with his wife and grown-up daughter in a bungalow in Surrey.
His title to the bungalow was registered at the Land Registry as absolute; the bungalow
was mortgaged to a building society. In or about March 1971 the defendant decided
to sell the bungalow and to buy one in Norfolk. His wife and daughter were un-
enthusiastic about the proposed move. The bungalow was placed in the hands of
estate agents and the plaintiffs visited the premises with a view to purchase. On that
occasion the defendant's wife explained to the plaintiffs the working of the cooker,
gas drier, etc. The plaintiffs eventually agreed to buy the bungalow for £6,050, a
figure that included £50 for fittings, etc. They visited the bungalow on two or three
occasions subsequently. The defendant's wife may have been present on at least
one of those occasions. On 27th May 1971 contracts were exchanged for the sale of the
bungalow, the defendant as beneficial owner contracting to sell with vacant possession
at the agreed price, completion to take place on or before 31st October. On the same
day, the defendant entered into a contract for the purchase of the Norfolk bungalow.
On 28th May the defendant's wife, unknown to the defendant, entered in the charges
register against the defendant's title at the Land Registry a notice of her rights of
occupation under ss 1 and 2 of the Matrimonial Homes Act 1967. At no time had the
defendant's wife given any indication to the plaintiffs that she was unwilling to leave
the bungalow. Neither the defendant's wife nor the Land Registry disclosed the

registration of the notice directly to the defendant, but on 11th June the building
society to which the bungalow was mortgaged wrote to the defendant's solicitors
enclosing a notice of the wife's rights of occupation which had been received by them
from the Land Registry; and on 18th June the defendant learnt of the notice for the
first time when he received notification of the registration from his solicitors. There
followed an argument between the defendant and his wife over the notice. On the
following day the defendant instructed his solicitors to withdraw from his contract
with the plaintiffs and to cancel the purchase of the Norfolk bungalow. Subsequently
the defendant made various attempts to persuade his wife to withdraw her notice
but she was adamant. On 13th July the defendant's solicitors wrote to the plaintiffs'
solicitors confirming that the defendant would not complete the contract with the
plaintiffs. 31st October passed without completion taking place and in January 1972
the plaintiffs issued a writ claiming, inter alia, specific performance of the contract
and damages in lieu or in addition. It was common ground that at the date fixed for
completion of the contract the market value of the house was £7,500; at the date of
judgment in January 1973 it had risen to £11,500, i e £5,500 above the contract price.
Although at the date when the contract was made the parties had contemplated that
there would be a rise in house prices they had not contemplated that the market price
of the bungalow would almost have doubled during the following 18 months.

Held – (i) The plaintiffs were not entitled to an order for specific performance of the
contract with vacant possession. Although it was a vendor's duty to obtain necessary
consents to a sale and, where he had sold with vacant possession, to take proceedings to
obtain possession from any person in possession who had no right to be there, he would
not usually be required to embark on difficult or uncertain litigation in order to secure
any requisite consent or obtain vacant possession. An order in favour of the plaintiffs
for specific performance with vacant possession would require the defendant to apply
to the court, in accordance with s 1 (2) of the 1967 Act, for an order terminating his
wife's rights of occupation under the Act and the outcome of such an application would
depend on the exercise of the court's discretion. Furthermore it was undesirable to
require a husband to take legal proceedings against his wife, especially while they were
still living together. Since the defendant had sufficiently attempted to obtain the wife's
consent, short of litigation, it would, in the circumstances, be highly unreasonable to
make an order for specific performance if some other form of order could do justice
(see p 913 e to g and p 914 b to d, post); dictum of Lord Redesdale LC in *Costigan v
Hastler* [1803-13] All ER Rep at 558 applied.

(ii) The plaintiffs were not entitled to an order for specific performance of the
contract subject to the rights of occupation of the defendant's wife, with damages
or an abatement of the purchase price in respect thereof. There was at least a real
possibility that a decree of specific performance subject to the wife's right not to be
evicted or excluded would enable the plaintiffs, by taking suitable proceedings, to
evict the defendant, and perhaps the daughter, and thus split up the family. Those
circumstances made the case one in which the court would be slow to decree specific
performance if any reasonable alternative existed (see p 915 f and g, post).

(iii) The plaintiffs were not precluded from recovering damages for loss of bargain
by the rule that only nominal damages under that head were recoverable for a breach
of contract which had been occasioned by the defendant's inability, without his own
fault, to show a good title. The rule itself was anomalous and was not to be extended
to analogous cases. The instant case did not fall within the spirit or intendment of
the rule, for at the date of the contract the wife's charge was unregistered, and even
if an unregistered charge under the 1967 Act could be described as a 'defect in title',
it was a defect which could be removed merely by the defendant completing the
contract. The fact that, after the contract had been made, the wife had registered her
charge should not affect the damages to which the plaintiffs were entitled for breach
of the contract (see p 917 g to p 918 c and f g, post); dictum of Lord Lindley MR and

a   Rigby LJ in *Day v Singleton* [1899] 2 Ch at 329 applied; *Bain v Fothergill* [1874-80] All ER Rep 83 distinguished.

(iv) The damages for loss of bargain were to be computed as at the date of assessment, i e at £5,500, and not as at the date of breach of contract. Since the plaintiffs had a proper claim for specific performance, the case fell within the Chancery Amendment Act 1858, s 2*ᵃ*, under which the court had jurisdiction to award such damages

b   as would put the plaintiffs into as good a position as if the contract had been performed, even if to do so meant awarding damages assessed by reference to a period subsequent to the date of the breach (see p 919 c to g, p 920 f, p 921 d g and h and p 922 b, post); dicta of Fry J in *Fritz v Hobson* [1874-80] All ER Rep at 82 and of Fry LJ in *Dreyfus v Peruvian Guano Co* (1889) 43 Ch D at 342, and dicta of Viscount Finlay and Lord Dunedin in *Leeds Industrial Co-operative Society Ltd v Slack* [1924] All ER Rep at 263, 264, 266, applied.

c   (v) An award of £5,500 damages for loss of bargain was not precluded by reason of the fact that, although the parties had contemplated a rise in house prices, they had not foreseen a rise of an amount approaching that which had in fact taken place. It was in principle wrong to limit damages flowing from a contemplated state of affairs to the amount that the parties could be shown to have had in contemplation. In order

d   to establish a claim to damages for breach of contract it was only necessary to show a contemplation of circumstances which embraced the head or type of damage in question; there was no need to demonstrate a contemplation of the quantum of damages under that head or type (see p 922 f g and h and p 923 g, post); *Hadley v Baxendale* [1843-60] All ER Rep 461 and *Great Lakes Steamship Co v Maple Leaf Milling Co Ltd* (1924) 41 TLR 21 applied.

e   (vi) It followed therefore that the plaintiffs were entitled to damages of £5,500 in substitution for a decree of specific performance (see p 923 h, post).

Semble. If a protected spouse knowingly stands by and assists while the owning spouse contracts to sell the house with vacant possession, it may be that the protected spouse will thereafter be precluded from asserting his or her rights under the 1967 Act. In the case of registered land the court has power under s 139 (1)*ᵇ* of the Land

f   Registration Act 1925 to compel a protected spouse to appear in the action and show cause why the contract should not be specifically performed (see p 910 d to g, post).

Notes

For specific performance where performance by defendant impossible by reason of circumstances, see 36 Halsbury's Laws (3rd Edn) 313, 314, 318, 319, paras 449, 457, and for cases on the subject, see 44 Digest (Repl) 103-106, 828-839, 844-856.

g   For damages for loss of bargain on breach of contract for the sale of land, see 11 Halsbury's Laws (3rd Edn) 248, 249, para 420, and 34 ibid 336, 337, para 569, and for cases on the subject, see 40 Digest (Repl) 284-286, 2358-2377.

For the measure of damages in contract, see 11 Halsbury's Laws (3rd Edn) 241, 242, para 409, and for cases on the subject, see 17 Digest (Repl) 91-99, 99-154.

For the date by reference to which damages are measured, see 11 Halsbury's Laws

h   (3rd Edn) 237, 238, para 405.

For the Chancery Amendment Act 1858, s 2, see 25 Halsbury's Statutes (3rd Edn) 703.

For the Land Registration Act 1925, s 139, see 27 Halsbury's Statutes (3rd Edn) 902.

For the Matrimonial Homes Act 1967, ss 1, 2, see 17 Halsbury's Statutes (3rd Edn) 139, 141.

j

Cases referred to in judgment

Bain v Fothergill (1874) LR 7 HL 158, [1874-80] All ER Rep 83, 43 LJ Ex 243, 31 LT 387, 39 JP 228, HL; *affg* (1870) LR 6 Exch 59, Ex Ch, 17 Digest (Repl) 104, *188*.

---

a   Section 2 is set out at p 919 h, post

b   Section 139 (1) is set out at p 910 c, post

Braybrooks v Whaley [1919] 1 KB 435, 88 LJKB 577, 120 LT 281, 63 Sol Jo 373, DC, 40 Digest (Repl) 286, *2374*.

Capital and Counties Bank Ltd v Rhodes [1903] 1 Ch 631, 72 LJCh 336, 88 LT 255, CA, 20 Digest (Repl) 533, *2442*.

Chapman, Morsons & Co v Guardians of Auckland Union (1889) 23 QBD 294, 58 LJQB 504, 61 LT 446, 53 JP 820, CA, 28 (2) Digest (Reissue) 1015, *415*.

Compton, Re, Powell v Compton [1945] 1 All ER 198, [1945] Ch 123, 114 LJCh 99, 172 LT 158, CA, 8 Digest (Repl) 330, *123*.

Costigan v Hastler (1804) 2 Sch & Lef 160, [1803-13] All ER Rep 556, 44 Digest (Repl) 52, *175*.

Daniel, Re, Daniel v Vassall [1917] 2 Ch 405, [1916-17] All ER Rep 654, 87 LJCh 69, 117 LT 472, 40 Digest (Repl) 285, *2372*.

Day v Singleton [1899] 2 Ch 320, 68 LJCh 593, 81 LT 306, CA, 31 Digest (Repl) 429, *555b*.

Dreyfus v Peruvian Guano Co (1889) 43 Ch D 316, 62 LT 518, 6 Asp MLC 492, CA; *on appeal sub nom Peruvian Guano Co Ltd v Dreyfus Brothers & Co* [1892] AC 166, HL, 28 (2) Digest (Reissue) 1015, *421*.

Eastwood v Lever (1863) 4 De G J & Sm 114, 3 New Rep 232, 33 LJCh 355, 9 LT 615, 28 JP 212, 46 ER 859, 28 (2) Digest (Reissue) 1018, *447*.

Engell v Fitch (1869) LR 4 QB 659, 10 B & S 738, 38 LJQB 304, Ex Ch; *affg* (1867) LR 3 QB 314, 40 Digest (Repl) 285, *2369*.

Flureau v Thornhill (1776) 2 Wm Bl 1078, [1775-1802] All ER Rep 91, 96 ER 635, 40 Digest (Repl) 146, *1116*.

Fritz v Hobson (1880) 14 Ch D 542, [1874-80] All ER Rep 75, 49 LJCh 321, 42 LT 225, 17 Digest (Repl) 125, *353*.

Gainsford v Carroll (1824) 2 B & C 624, 4 Dow & Ry KB 161, 2 LJOSKB 112, 107 ER 516 39 Digest (Repl) 816, *2793*.

Glasbrook v Richardson (1874) 23 WR 51, 44 Digest (Repl) 111, *913*.

Graf v Hope Building Corporation (1930) 254 NY 1.

Great Lakes Steamship Co v Maple Leaf Milling Co Ltd (1924) 41 TLR 21, PC, 41 Digest (Repl) 425, *2097*.

Hadley v Baxendale (1854) 9 Exch 341, [1843-60] All ER Rep 461, 23 LJ Ex 179, 23 LTOS 69, 18 Jur 358, 2 CLR 517, 156 ER 145, 17 Digest (Repl) 91, *99*.

Howell v George (1815) 1 Madd 1, 56 ER 1, 44 Digest (Repl) 69, *542*.

Huxham v Llewellyn (1873) 21 WR 570, 28 LT 577, *subsequent proceedings* 21 WR 766, 44 Digest (Repl) 113, *930*.

J W Cafés Ltd v Brownlow Trust Ltd [1950] 1 All ER 894, 94 Sol Jo 304, 40 Digest (Repl) 257, *2156*.

Keeves v Dean, Nunn v Pellegrini [1924] 1 KB 685, [1923] All ER Rep 12, 93 LJKB 203, 130 LT 593, 22 LGR 127, CA, 31 Digest (Repl) 694, *7865*.

Leeds Industrial Co-operative Society Ltd v Slack [1924] AC 851, [1924] All ER Rep 259, 93 LJCh 436, 131 LT 710, HL; *rvsg sub nom Slack v Leeds Industrial Co-operative Society Ltd* [1923] 1 Ch 431, CA; *subsequent proceedings sub nom Slack v Leeds Industrial Co-operative Society Ltd* [1924] 2 Ch 475, CA, 28 (2) Digest (Reissue) 1012, *396*.

Lehmann v McArthur (1868) 3 Ch App 496, 37 LJ Ch 625, 32 JP 660; *sub nom Lechmann v McArthur* 18 LT 806, 44 Digest (Repl) 113, *933*.

Long v Bowring (1864) 33 Beav 585, 10 LT 683, 10 Jur NS 668, 55 ER 496, 44 Digest (Repl) 133, *1087*.

Miles v Bull [1968] 3 All ER 632, [1969] 1 QB 258, [1968] 3 WLR 1090, 20 P & CR 42, Digest (Cont Vol C) 426, *621 cc*.

Miles v Bull (No 2) [1969] 3 All ER 1585, 21 P & CR 23, Digest (Cont Vol C) 428, *621ggc*.

National Provincial Bank Ltd v Ainsworth [1965] 2 All ER 472, [1965] AC 1175, [1965] 3 WLR 1, HL; *rvsg sub nom National Provincial Bank Ltd v Hastings Car Mart Ltd* [1964] 1 All ER 688, [1964] 2 WLR 751, CA; *rvsg* [1964] 3 All ER 93, [1964] Ch 665, [1964] 3 WLR 463, CA, Digest (Cont Vol B) 343, *621e*.

a   *Robinson v Harman* (1848) 1 Exch 850, [1843-60] All ER Rep 383, 18 LJEx 202, 13 LTOS
     141, 154 ER 363, 17 Digest (Repl) 81, *33*.

     Thomas v Kensington [1942] 2 All ER 263, [1942] 2 KB 181, 111 LJKB 717, 167 LT 133,
     40 Digest (Repl) 285, *2373*.

     Vacwell Engineering Co Ltd v B D H Chemicals Ltd (formerly British Drug Houses Ltd)
     [1969] 3 All ER 1681, [1971] 1 QB 88, [1969] 3 WLR 927; *compromised* [1970] 3 All ER
b   553, [1971] 1 QB 112, [1970] 3 WLR 67, CA, Digest (Cont Vol C) 729, *109ba*.

     Watts v Waller [1972] 3 All ER 257, [1972] 3 WLR 365, CA.

     West Riding of Yorkshire Rivers Board v Linthwaite Urban Council (No 2) (1915) 84 LJKB
     1610, sub nom *West Riding of Yorkshire Rivers Board v Linthwaite Urban District Council
     (No 2)* 113 LT 547, 79 JP 433, 13 LGR 772, DC, 28 (2) Digest (Reissue) 1000, *303*.

     Williams v Glenton (1866) 1 Ch App 200, 44 Digest (Repl) 95, *778*.

c   **Cases also cited**

     Aronson v Mologa Holzindustrie A/G Leningrad (1927) 138 LT 470, CA.

     Atkin v Rose [1923] 1 Ch 522.

     Berton v Alliance Economic Investment Co Ltd [1922] 1 KB 742, CA.

     Celia (Steamship) v Volturno (Steamship) [1921] 2 AC 544, [1921] All ER Rep 110, HL.

     Diamond v Campbell-Jones [1960] 1 All ER 583, [1961] Ch 22.
d   *Doleman & Sons v Ossett Corpn* [1912] 3 KB 257, CA.

     Domsalla v Barr (trading as AB Construction) [1969] 3 All ER 487, [1969] 1 WLR 630, CA.

     Du Sautoy v Symes [1967] 1 All ER 25, [1967] Ch 1146.

     General and Finance Facilities Ltd v Cooks Cars (Romford) Ltd [1963] 2 All ER 314, [1963]
     1 WLR 644, CA.

     Heron II, The, Koufos v C Czarnikow Ltd [1967] 3 All ER 686, [1969] 1 AC 350, HL.
e   *Lehmann v McArthur* (1867) LR 3 Eq 746.

     Lipmans Wallpaper Ltd v Mason & Hodghton Ltd [1968] 1 All ER 1123, [1969] 1 Ch 20.

     McMurray v Spicer (1868) LR 5 Eq 527.

     Parkin v Thorold (1852) 16 Beav 59, 51 ER 698.

     Perestrello e Companhia Limitada v United Paint Co Ltd [1969] 3 All ER 479, [1969] 1 WLR
     570, CA.
f   *Philipps v Philipps* (1878) 4 QBD 127, CA.

     Philips v Ward [1956] 1 All ER 874, [1956] 1 WLR 471, CA.

     Pounsett v Fuller (1856) 17 CB 660, 139 ER 1235.

     Rock Portland Cement Co Ltd v Wilson (1882) 52 LJCh 214.

     Sachs v Miklos [1948] 1 All ER 67, [1948] 2 KB 23, CA.

     Startup v Cortazzi (1835) 2 Cr M & R 165, 150 ER 71.
g   *Victoria Laundry (Windsor) Ltd v Newman Industries Ltd* [1949] 1 All ER 997, [1949]
     2 KB 528, CA.

     Action

     By a writ issued on 25th January 1972 the plaintiffs, Colin Percy Wroth and Mary
     Rose Wroth, claimed, inter alia, (i) specific performance of an agreement in writing
h   dated 27th May 1971 and made between the defendant, Edmund Arthur Tyler, of
     the one part and the plaintiffs of the other part whereby it was agreed that the defen-
     dant should sell with vacant possession, and the plaintiffs should purchase, the defen-
     dant's bungalow in Ashford, Surrey, at the price of £6,050; (ii) damages in lieu of or
     in addition to specific performance. The facts are set out in the judgment.

j   *W A Blackburne* for the plaintiffs.
     M A F Lyndon-Stanford for the defendant.

                                                                    Cur adv vult

     20th December.   **MEGARRY J** read the following judgment.   The facts in this
     case are as simple as the law is complex. With one exception, the facts are common-
     place and do not differ from those in the great majority of sales of dwelling-houses;

yet the case has taken seven days to argue, and well over 50 authorities have been put
before me. It may be that the case will lead to changes in conveyancing practice
and amendments in the law; but I have to deal with it on the law and practice as they
stand. The case illustrates how modern statutory changes in the law, intended to
reform it, may, if imperfectly executed, create conditions of great hardship for
innocent people.

The plaintiffs, for whom Mr Blackburne appeared, are a young married couple
who, while still engaged, were seeking to buy a home. The defendant, for whom Mr
Lyndon-Stanford appeared, is a married man aged 62 who wished to retire from his
Civil Service employment. The plaintiffs and the defendant are all of modest means.
The premises concerned are a bungalow in Ashford, formerly in Middlesex but now
in Surrey; and the defendant lives there with his wife and grown-up daughter. His
title to the bungalow is registered as absolute at the Land Registry.

In or about March 1971 the defendant decided to sell the bungalow and purchase
a bungalow being built (or about to be built) in Norfolk. He had already disestablished
himself in the Civil Service, and had taken his gratuity; but although he is still
employed as a civil servant this is on an unestablished basis, and he can retire at any
time. The principal attraction of the move was that he could sell his Ashford bungalow
for over £2,000 more than he would have to pay for the Norfolk bungalow, and this
would suffice to discharge the amount due under the existing mortgage on the Ashford bungalow, some £1,250, and cover the moving and incidental expenses. He
would thus begin his retirement in a state of financial freedom.

The defendant put his bungalow in the hands of agents, and very soon the plaintiffs
came to see it. This was their first purchase of a house. Their initial visit was on 6th
March 1971, and the next day they returned. On this visit, among other things, the
defendant's wife explained to the plaintiffs the working of the cooker, gas drier,
extractor fan and other articles that would go with the bungalow. Two days later the
first plaintiff (the husband) visited the bungalow alone. The price asked by the
defendant was £6,050, a figure which included £50 for the various fittings and chattels
that would go with the bungalow. The first plaintiff saw the defendant, telling him
that they could not afford £6,050, and trying to persuade him to reduce the price by
£200. The plaintiffs were expecting to be able to raise £4,600 on mortgage, and they
had £950 of their own. The defendant would not reduce his price, and the first plaintiff went away. He then discussed matters with the second plaintiff, and they agreed
to pay the £6,050. The next day he informed the agents and put down a deposit of
£25.

Some weeks later the plaintiffs made two more visits to the bungalow; and
although the discussions were in the main with the defendant, the defendant's wife
may at least have been in the bungalow on one or more of these visits. Finally, after
the defendant had begun to press for a contract to be signed, contracts for the sale
of the bungalow by the defendant to the plaintiffs were exchanged on 27th May 1971,
in a form which incorporated the current edition of the National Conditions of Sale,
with modifications. Neither side, I may say, has relied on any provision in those
conditions. The sale was by the defendant as beneficial owner, and the property was
sold with vacant possession. Completion was to take place 'on or before' 31st October
1971, that being the date by which the defendant expected the Norfolk bungalow
to be ready for him. The price was £6,050, with a deposit of £605 which was duly
paid to the defendant's solicitors as stakeholders. The plaintiffs and the defendant
each had solicitors acting for them on the sale. On the same day, the defendant entered
into a contract for the purchase of the Norfolk bungalow. I have not seen this contract,
but on the defendant's evidence the price was about £3,800 and he paid a deposit of
£100.

Thus far, the transaction was wholly unremarkable, with nothing to distinguish it
from thousands of other transactions. However, the next day, on 28th May 1971,
the event occurred from which all the difficulty stems. The defendant's wife, no doubt

a acting through solicitors, caused the entry in the charges register against the defendant's title at the Land Registry of a notice of her rights of occupation under the Matrimonial Homes Act 1967. I have heard evidence from both the plaintiffs and the defendant, but not from the defendant's wife, so that what I say must be taken subject to that qualification. I should say at once that the evidence given by the plaintiffs and by the defendant was given frankly and openly, and I accept all three as witnesses of truth. There was, indeed, very little conflict of evidence.

b On the evidence before me, it is perfectly plain that the defendant's wife had never given any indication whatever to the plaintiffs that she was not willing to move out of the bungalow. Indeed, by explaining to them the working of the apparatus in the kitchen, she had given them the justifiable impression that she was concurring in the proposed move. Within the home, she had shown no enthusiasm for the move. The defendant said that his wife and daughter were very close to each other, and the

c attitude of both of them to the sale of the bungalow was 'very cool'. The defendant had discussed the sale of the bungalow and the move to Norfolk with them before he had put the bungalow into the hands of the agents, and they, though very cool about the move, had in some sort of way agreed to it. On this, the defendant had proceeded with his plan; and he had thought that they would have come with him when he moved.

d On the evidence as it stands, the picture is one of reluctance but not of any open opposition to the move. The defendant's wife and daughter had lived with him in the area since 1949, and in this particular bungalow since 1963; and they understandably did not want to be uprooted from their friends, and in the case of the daughter, from her employment. The wife, I may say, is 52 and the daughter 25.

The registration of the notice was not disclosed to the defendant. His wife said nothing about it to him; and for nearly three weeks she continued her life with the

e defendant without his having any knowledge or suspicion of what she had done. One can only speculate on the wife's thoughts as she lived her daily life with the defendant, with this unrevealed secret in her mind. During this time the solicitors were proceeding with the necessary conveyancing steps; the requisitions on title were duly delivered and answered, and the defendant's solicitors returned the draft transfer

f duly approved. Subject to the one question of the rights of the defendant's wife, counsel for the plaintiffs told me that the defendant's title to the bungalow was accepted. However, on 11th June 1971 the building society to which the bungalow was mortgaged wrote to the defendant's solicitors enclosing a notice of the wife's rights of occupation which had been received by the society from the Land Registry.

I pause there. In *Watts v Waller*[1] the Court of Appeal was critical of the absence of any provision requiring notification to the landowner if rights under the Matrimonial

g Homes Act 1967 are registered under the Land Charges Act 1925 or the Land Registration Act 1925. I do not know whether the attention of that court was drawn not merely to the absence of any statutory requirement of notification to the landowner, but also to the positive practice of the Land Registry to the contrary. In Ruoff and Roper on the Law and Practice of Registered Conveyancing[2], it is said: '. . . in no circumstances will a notice of a wife's application be served on the registered proprietor of the

h land.' A practice which warns a mortgagee of the registration of a charge over which his mortgage takes priority, but leaves unwarned the landowner, who may proceed to act to his detriment in ignorance of his wife's application, is a practice which seems to me (and I speak temperately) to deserve further consideration.

Having received the letter from the building society, the defendant's solicitors telephoned the plaintiffs' solicitors on 16th June 1971 to tell them of this letter; and

j on the same day the plaintiffs' solicitors by letter raised an additional requisition on the point. The defendant's solicitors replied the next day, saying that they would make arrangements for the removal of the notice in due course. The defendant had

1 [1972] 3 All ER 257, [1972] 3 WLR 365
2 3rd Edn (1972), p 784

gone to Norfolk that day to get the dimensions of the windows of the new bungalow
for curtaining, and so on. It is not without significance that his wife and daughter had
never been to see the district in Norfolk in which they were to live when they moved.
The defendant left home for work the next day, Friday, 18th June 1971, before the
arrival of a letter from his solicitors telling him of his wife's registration of the notice.
He found this letter on his return that evening. Its contents came as a complete
surprise to him.

That evening there was a row about the notice between the defendant and his wife,
after which he decided to withdraw from both transactions. The next day, Saturday,
19th June, he telephoned the Norfolk vendors to say that he would not be buying
the Norfolk property, and he wrote to his solicitors asking them to cancel the Norfolk
purchase and also the sale of his bungalow. That day he and his wife hardly spoke
to each other. The next day, Sunday, there was a worse row between the defendant
and his wife about the cost to the defendant of breaking his contracts. It ended with
the defendant slapping his wife, who thereupon sent for the police and called for a
doctor. In addition to these two rows, the defendant made some further attempts to
persuade his wife to withdraw her notice, though he could not recall the details
beyond saying that he did it when she seemed to be in an amiable mood; but she
was adamant.

As a result of the defendant's withdrawal, the plaintiffs were taken by an estate
agent to visit the defendant on the following Saturday, 26th June; and while they were
there the defendant's wife and daughter came in from shopping. The burden of the
discussion was whether the defendant and his wife would be willing to buy some other
property in the Ashford area and carry through the sale of the bungalow to the
plaintiffs. The defendant, his wife and daughter all agreed to look at other properties
in the district, and the agent offered his services in driving them to see suitable properties. The plaintiffs came away from the discussion with the impression that all would
be well after all.

The same day, and probably after that meeting, the defendant's wife wrote a letter
to the defendant's solicitors. It reads as follows:

'Dear Sir, I understand from my husband that we will probably have to pay
about £800 due to withdrawal of the sale of the above address. This is nonsense,
and as his solicitor it is up to you to see that he doesn't pay anything. Many of
my friends have withdrawn sale of their houses, and not had to pay any compensation. I know I started all this business, but will you please make sure that my
husband doesn't lose any money over it. I would also be grateful if you would
refrain from telling my husband that I have written to you.'

The defendant's wife was critical of the defendant's solicitors; but as the letter shows,
she expected them to achieve the impossible, and she must have had a complete lack
of understanding of the great difference between withdrawing from a transaction
before any contract is made, and withdrawing after contract.

As arranged with the plaintiffs and the agent, the defendant and his wife did inspect
some other houses in the district. The defendant thought that they were all more
expensive and in poorer condition than his own bungalow. With rising prices, he
found he would have to pay some £500 more to buy an equivalent, and with the
expense of repairs and redecorations, and the costs of purchase, he would have to pay
something like £1,000 more to obtain an equivalent. He saw nothing that he would
consider buying, and he preferred to pay damages for breach of his contract with the
plaintiffs. Accordingly, although on 2nd July 1971 the plaintiffs' solicitors had written
to the defendant's solicitors saying that they understood that the defendant had
decided, in view of the consequences of a breach of contract by him, that the sale of
the bungalow should proceed to completion, on 13th July the defendant's solicitors
wrote to say that the defendant would not complete after all.

a At this stage I can pass over the subsequent events quite quickly, although I shall have to return to some of them later. The plaintiffs' solicitors consulted counsel, and then applied for legal aid, although in the event their application was unsuccessful on financial grounds. In the meantime, on 18th September 1971 the plaintiffs intermarried. 31st October came and went without completion taking place. On 25th January 1972 the writ was issued, claiming specific performance and damages in lieu or in addition, together with other relief. The writ was served on 31st January, b and on 9th February the statement of claim was served. The defendant's solicitors then asked for time to take counsel's opinion before serving a defence; and the extension was agreed and later extended. Unsuccessful negotiations for a settlement then took place, and finally on 1st May 1972 the defence was served.

On 21st June 1972 the plaintiffs issued a summons for judgment on admissions in the defence, and for specific performance under RSC Ord 86. It can hardly be a matter c of surprise that when this summons came on before the Master on 7th July it did not prosper. Of the alternatives of adjourning the summons into court and setting the action down for trial, the plaintiffs elected for the latter. There was then a muddle about setting the case down for trial. The plaintiffs' solicitors had employed un-qualified legal agents, who informed the solicitors that the case could not be set down d for trial during the Long Vacation, and that even if it could, it would do no good. A note to RSC Ord 34, r 3, in the Supreme Court Practice 1970, which was then current (and to which one is led by a mere glance at the index), says in terms: 'Actions may be set down in vacation'. I hope that this verity may in future illuminate the plaintiffs' solicitors and their agents. On 4th October 1972 the action was set down for hearing, and after a successful application for expedition at the end of October, the hearing began on 16th November 1972.

e By his defence the defendant admits that at the date for completion and at the date of the defence he was unable to give vacant possession of the bungalow, and that he was thereby in breach of his agreement; and he states his willingness to submit to an enquiry as to damages for the breach. By an amendment made on 13th November, shortly before the hearing began, the defendant contends that if (which is denied) the plaintiffs are otherwise entitled to judgment for specific performance, they f have disentitled themselves to it by delay. The plaintiffs' primary claim is to specific performance, with damages as an alternative.

The issues before me may be summarised as follows. (1) Delay apart, are the plain-tiffs entitled to specific performance of the contract with vacant possession? If they are, a form of order is sought that will require the defendant to make an application to the court for an order against his wife terminating her rights of occupation under the g Matrimonial Homes Act 1967, in accordance with s 1 (2). (2) Delay apart, are the plain-tiffs, as an alternative, entitled to specific performance of the contract subject to the rights of occupation of the defendant's wife, with damages or an abatement of the purchase price in respect thereof? If they are, they will be able to make the application to the court under the 1967 Act, by virtue of ss 1 (2) and 2 (3). (3) If, apart from delay, the plaintiffs would be entitled to an order for specific performance under either of h these two heads, is their right to it barred by delay? (4) If the plaintiffs have no right to specific performance, then it is common ground that they are entitled to damages. There is, however, an acute conflict as to the measure of damages. The primary con-tention of the defendant is that the damages are limited by the rule in Bain v Fothergill[1], so that the defendant need only release the deposit to the plaintiffs and pay their costs of investigating title, and is not liable to them for more than nominal damages for j loss of their bargain. Is this contention sound? (5) If Bain v Fothergill[1] does not apply, then the defendant accepts that damages for loss of the bargain are payable; but there is a dispute as to the computation of those damages. The defendant says that the damages must be assessed as at the date of the breach, in accordance with the normal

___

1 (1874) LR 7 HL 158, [1874-80] All ER Rep 83

rule; the plaintiffs say that this is a case where damages must be assessed as at the date of assessment, that is, today, if I assess the damages. The valuers on each side have not given evidence, but very sensibly they have agreed a graph which shows the figures at successive dates, and counsel put this in as an agreed document. I can ignore £50 of the contract price, for that was for the various fittings and chattels; and on that footing the contract price was £6,000. It is agreed that at the date fixed for completion the bungalow was worth £7,500; and it is agreed that at the time of the hearing before me it was worth £11,500. Damages assessed as at the date of the breach would be £1,500, but as at the date of the hearing would be £5,500. At which figure should damages for the loss of the bargain be assessed? The defendant says that the former figure applies, in accordance with the general rule, but the plaintiffs say that the latter figure applies, for unless it does, they will be unable to acquire an equivalent house at today's prices.

Those are the main questions; there are others which I shall consider in their appropriate places, including an issue on the operation of the rule in *Hadley v Baxendale*[1] on which direct authority seems scanty. The third main issue, as to delay, stands in a separate category; but to a greater or lesser extent the other main issues all have this in common, that it is impossible to reach any conclusion on them without some understanding of the operation of the Matrimonial Homes Act 1967 and the nature of the interest under it that the defendant's wife has. Accordingly, I turn to that Act.

As is well known, the 1967 Act was passed after the House of Lords had held in *National Provincial Bank Ltd v Ainsworth*[2] that there was no such thing as the so-called deserted wife's equity. Over the previous ten or 15 years there had been much controversy about this alleged equity. The idea that a husband might desert his wife and then sell the former matrimonial home over her head, leaving her homeless, was obviously repugnant to the ideas of any civilised society, and plainly ought to be made impossible. One difficulty of the courts dealing with the matter was that any doctrine evolved by the courts was likely to take many years, and much litigation involving heavy costs, before a workable doctrine emerged in an established and fully-fledged form; and there was much uncertainty about many of the features of the equity. Did the equity arise only on desertion, or did it subsist throughout the marriage? Did it apply to constructive desertion, where the wife had been driven out by her husband? Was it dependent on desertion, or would it arise when there was some other matrimonial offence, such as adultery or cruelty? Was there a deserted husband's equity? Above all, how far were purchasers, mortgagees and others obliged to investigate the state of the marriage in order to be protected? It would have been intolerable if, when an overdraft was secured on the husband's house, the bank had to make enquiries as to the husband's matrimonial behaviour before honouring his cheques.

Statute could avoid all the difficulties, expenses and delays of a doctrine evolved by the courts by laying down a complete system uno ictu. In truth, the institution of what might amount to a new right of property, however badly needed, is a reform which the courts are ill-equipped to make. The 1967 Act could thus have brought certainty and clarity into what was a confused and contentious field. Whether in fact it has done so is another matter.

The 1967 Act is in far wider terms than the alleged equity ever was. It is in no way confined to desertion or any other matrimonial offence, but confers all the rights that it gives forthwith on marriage. It is not confined to wives, but applies to husbands as well; and it is not confined to one house, but applies to all dwelling-houses owned by either spouse, except 'a dwelling house which has at no time been

---

1   (1854) 9 Exch 341, [1843-60] All ER Rep 461
2   [1965] 2 All ER 472, [1965] AC 1175

a matrimonial home of the spouses in question': s 1 (8). The mainsprings of the
a Act for the purposes of this case are ss 1 (1) and 2 (1). Section 1 (1) provides as follows:

'Where one spouse is entitled to occupy a dwelling house by virtue of any
estate or interest or contract or by virtue of any enactment giving him or her
the right to remain in occupation, and the other spouse is not so entitled, then,
subject to the provisions of this Act, the spouse not so entitled shall have the
b following rights (in this Act referred to as "rights of occupation"):—(a) if in
occupation, a right not to be evicted or excluded from the dwelling house or
any part thereof by the other spouse except with the leave of the court given by
an order under this section; (b) if not in occupation, a right with the leave of the
court so given to enter into and occupy the dwelling house.'

c I pause there to say that in relation to the present case the right that the defendant's
wife has is 'a right not to be evicted or excluded' from the bungalow or any part of
it by the defendant. Despite the statutory phrase 'rights of occupation', an occupying
wife is given no positive right of occupation; the Act works by giving her a shield
against eviction or exclusion by her husband.
Section 2 (1) is as follows:

d 'Where, at any time during the subsistence of a marriage, one spouse is entitled
to occupy a dwelling house by virtue of an estate or interest, then the other
spouse's rights of occupation shall be a charge on that estate or interest, having
the like priority as if it were an equitable interest created at whichever is the
latest of the following dates, that is to say,—(a) the date when the spouse so
entitled acquires the estate or interest; (b) the date of the marriage; and (c) the
e commencement of this Act.'

In the present case, the concluding words of the subsection brought the wife's 'rights
of occupation' into being as a charge on 1st January 1968 when the Act came into
operation. It is on that date that she acquired 'a charge' on the defendant's fee
simple under his absolute title. That charge is not declared to be an equitable
f interest, but merely to have 'the like priority as if it were an equitable interest' created
(in this case) on 1st January 1968. The charge seems to be neither legal nor equitable,
but a pure creature of statute, with a priority (though not a nature) defined by
reference to equity.
The duration of the wife's rights of occupation are limited by s 2 (2), which brings
them to an automatic end, subject to any order of the court, on the termination of
g the marriage by death or otherwise. There is also provision by s 1 (2) for either
spouse to apply to the court for an order 'declaring, enforcing, restricting or terminating those rights', or regulating the exercise by either spouse of the right to
occupy the house. Section 1 (3) provides that on such an application—

'the court may make such order as it thinks just and reasonable having regard
to the conduct of the spouses in relation to each other and otherwise, to their
h respective needs and financial resources, to the needs of any children and to all
the circumstances of the case';

and some particular powers are then set out. In the High Court, all proceedings
under these provisions have, since 1st October 1971, been assigned to the Family
Division: Administration of Justice Act 1970, s 1 (2), Sch 1; and for the procedure,
j see RSC Ord 89, r 3. This Division accordingly cannot, at any rate normally, exercise
the jurisdiction under s 1 (2) and (3).
The status of the spouse's right as a charge is amplified by s 2 (3), which provides
for the effect of the charge as against successors in title. It runs as follows:

'Where a spouse's rights of occupation are a charge on the estate or interest
of the other spouse—(a) any order under section 1 above against the other spouse

shall, except in so far as the contrary intention appears, have the like effect
against persons deriving title under the other spouse and affected by the charge; *a*
and (*b*) subsections (2) to (5) of section 1 above shall apply in relation to any
person deriving title under the other spouse and affected by the charge as they
apply in relation to the other spouse.'

A successor in title to the defendant may thus make an application to the court
under s 1 (2) and (3) for the termination of the rights of occupation of the defendant's *b*
wife, and so on.   Section 2 (6) makes a charge under the Act registrable as a Class F
land charge.   Section 2 (7) provides for registered land; registration of a land charge
by virtue of this Act is to be effected by 'registering a notice or caution' under the
Land Registration Act 1925, and the spouse's rights of occupation are not to be an
overriding interest, even if the spouse is in actual occupation of the dwelling-house.
By s 2 (5), even if a charge under the Act on the estate or interest of a spouse is *c*
registered, it is to be void against the trustee in bankruptcy of that spouse.
    Finally, I should read s 3:

> 'Where one spouse is entitled by virtue of section 2 above to a charge on the
> estate or interest of the other spouse in each of two or more dwelling houses,
> only one of the charges to which that spouse is so entitled shall be registered *d*
> in accordance with subsection (6) or (7) of that section at any one time, and if
> any of those charges is registered in accordance with the said subsection (6) or (7),
> the Chief Land Registrar, on being satisfied that any other of them is so registered,
> shall cancel the registration of the charge first registered.'

Taken with ss 1 (1), (8) and 2 (1), this makes it plain that although rights of occupation
under the Act may attach to every house owned by either spouse which he or she is *e*
entitled to occupy, if at any time it has been a matrimonial home of theirs, no spouse
is entitled to have his or her statutory rights protected by registration for more than
one dwelling-house at a time.   I should also mention s 6 (1), which provides:

> 'A spouse entitled to rights of occupation may by a release in writing release
> those rights or release them as respects part only of the dwelling house affected *f*
> by them';

and by s 6 (3), a spouse entitled to a charge 'may agree in writing' that any other
charge or interest shall rank in priority to the spouse's charge.
    I can now say something about the nature of the charge and the mode of operation
of the 1967 Act.   First, for a spouse in occupation, the right seems to be a mere
statutory right for the spouse not to be evicted.   There appears to be nothing to *g*
stay the eviction of others.   For example, if a wife is living in her husband's house
with their children and her parents, her charge, even if registered, appears to give no
protection against eviction to the children or parents.   (I shall return to this point.)
Nor if the wife takes in lodgers does there seem to be anything to prevent the husband
from evicting them.   If, for example, the husband is himself living in the house, it
would be remarkable if the Act gives the wife the right to insist on having other *h*
occupants in the home against his will.   The statutory right appears in essence to be
a purely personal right for the wife not to be evicted; and it seems wholly inconsistent with the Act that this right should be assignable or otherwise disposable.   I
may add that there is nothing to require the wife to make any payment to the husband for her occupation, unless ordered by the court under s 1 (3), though if she is in
occupation against his will and by virtue of her statutory rights, it may be that she *j*
will be in rateable occupation.
    Second, although the right given to an occupying wife by s 1 (1) is merely a right
not to be evicted or excluded 'by the other spouse', and so at first sight does not
appear to be effective against anyone except that other spouse, s 2 (1) makes the right
'a charge' on the husband's estate or interest; and it is this and s 2 (3), rather than the

a   provisions for registration, which make the right binding on successors in title. The
operation of the provision for registration seems to be essentially negative; the right
is a charge which, if not duly protected by registration, will become void against
subsequent purchasers, or fail to bind them. In this, the right seems not to differ
from other registrable charges, such as general equitable charges or puisne mortgages. Yet there is this difference. For other charges, the expectation of the statute
b   is plainly that they will all be protected by registration, whereas under the 1967 Act
there does not seem to be the same expectation.

The case of multiple matrimonial homes illustrates this point. If a husband owns
three houses that either are or have been a matrimonial home for him and his wife,
under s 3 she can only have one of her charges protected by registration at any one
time. For the unregistered two, the Act plainly contemplates that although each is
subject to a charge under the Act in favour of the wife, if the husband sells them her
c   charges, for want of registration will not bind the purchaser. Furthermore, it may
well be doubted whether in the ordinary case of single matrimonial homes the Act
contemplated that there would be mass registrations in respect of all matrimonial
homes, however happy and stable the marriage. In such cases, it may well be that
the expectation was that there would be no registration, and so no need for any release
of the statutory rights or cancellation of the registration when the home was sold; for
d   although the wife held a charge on the husband's estate in the house, that charge
would be void against the purchaser. There is no evidence before me on what has
in fact happened, but it would not be surprising if in fact the Act in the main has
been operating on a basis of the mass invalidation of the statutory charges for want
of registration, with registration being effected only in cases of actual or impending
disputes.
e   Third, the Act has put into the hands of all spouses with statutory rights of occupation a weapon of great power and flexibility. Registration is a relatively simple,
speedy and secret process, as compared with the necessarily more complex, protracted and less private process of selling a house and carrying through the contract
to completion. As this case illustrates, Parliament has made it possible for the
f   protected spouse to go far towards having his or her way as to not moving from the
matrimonial home, at the expense of the other spouse and innocent purchasers.
No doubt, too, the protected spouse may, by registering the statutory charge, and
particularly by registering it at an inconvenient moment, require the owning spouse
to buy off the charge. In some cases this may be very proper; in others it may be
less so: but the power to do it is a unilateral power, free from any restraints. Of
course, the owning spouse always has the possibility of redress by means of an applica-
g   tion to the court under s 1 (2); but problems of time and costs will often make it
prudent to bow to even the more unreasonable demands. The Act thus offers a
financial temptation to the protected spouse which may impair marital relations.
In the case of multiple matrimonial homes, there are possibilities of the protected
spouse frustrating each attempted sale by a timely change of registration. Nor is it
easy to see why, for instance, if the husband leaves a friend in occupation of matri-
h   monial home A as licensee, moving with his wife's full assent to matrimonial home B,
it is reasonable for the protection of the wife that she should have a charge under the
Act on A which at any time she can protect by registration, thereby making it impossible for her husband to sell A without incurring expense and delay. But I forbear
from exploring in any detail questions on multiple homes that do not arise in this
case.
j   At this stage I may summarise my conclusions as to the essentials of the right given
by the Act to an occupying spouse as follows. The right is in essence a personal and
non-assignable statutory right not to be evicted from the matrimonial home in
question during marriage or until the court otherwise orders; and this right constitutes a charge on the estate or interest of the owning spouse which requires protection
against third parties by registration. For various reasons, the right may be said to

be one which readily fits into no category known to conveyancers before 1967; the phrase sui generis seems apt, but of little help.

With that in mind, I turn to the first question before me. Delay apart, are the plaintiffs entitled to specific performance of the contract with vacant possession? If they are, the form of order sought will require the defendant to make an application to the court under s 1 (2) to terminate his wife's rights of occupation which arose and became a charge on the defendant's estate on 1st January 1968, and were protected by registration on 28th May 1971. Under this head, there is a preliminary point that I should mention, namely, the Land Registration Act 1925, s 139 (1), replacing the Land Transfer Act 1875, s 93. The subsection reads as follows:

> 'Where an action is instituted for the specific performance of a contract relating to registered land, or a registered charge, the court having cognizance of the action may, by summons, or by such other mode as it deems expedient, cause all or any parties who have registered interests or rights in the registered land or charge, or have entered up notices, cautions, restrictions, or inhibitions against the same to appear in such action, and show cause why such contract should not be specifically performed, and the court may direct that any order made by the court in the action shall be binding on such parties or any of them.'

Although this provision has been on the statute book for nearly a century, there seems to be no authority on it. In *Capital and Counties Bank v Rhodes*[1] the section was mentioned, but no more. At one time counsel for the plaintiffs advanced quite a vigorous argument on the possibility of applying the section so as to bring in the defendant's wife to show cause why her notice should not be removed. There were obvious difficulties in this, and counsel for the defendant said that all the wife need do under the section was to say that she had her rights under the 1967 Act, and that then the Chancery Division could do no more, since the High Court's jurisdiction under the 1967 Act was assigned to the Family Division. In any case, this point had not been raised in the pleadings, and in the end counsel for the plaintiffs abandoned it.

I shall therefore do no more than make two comments on this point which may be of assistance in other cases. First, in a case under s 139 (1), as well as in other cases, it may be that the owning spouse may be able to make out a case of estoppel against the protected spouse. If the protected spouse knowingly stands by or assists while the owning spouse contracts to sell the house with vacant possession, it may be that the protected spouse will thereafter be precluded from asserting his or her rights of occupation under the 1967 Act. No case of estoppel, I may say, has been advanced before me, either between spouses or quoad the plaintiffs: the defendant's wife, of course, is not a party to these proceedings. Second, in the case of unregistered land, there appears to be no counterpart to s 139.

With that out of the way, I turn to the main question of specific performance. It seems to me that where a third party has some rights over the property to be sold, there are at least three categories of cases. First, there are those cases where the vendor is entitled as of right to put an end to the rights of the third party, or compel his concurrence or co-operation in the sale. Second, and at the other extreme, there are cases where the vendor has no right to put an end to the third party's rights, or compel his concurrence or co-operation in the sale, and can do no more than to try to persuade him to release his rights or to concur in the sale. An example of the first category would be the vendor's right, as mortgagor, to pay off a mortgage, or his right, as a mortgagee, to obtain possession from the mortgagor. An example of the second category would be when the third party is entitled to an easement over the land.

In between those two categories there is a third category, namely, where the vendor cannot as of right secure the requisite discharge or concurrence, but if it is refused

---

1 [1903] 1 Ch 631 at 657

a he can go to the court, which has power, on a proper case being shown, to secure the release or concurrence. Examples would be a restrictive covenant which may be modified or discharged under the Law of Property Act 1925, s 84 (as amended), or the requisite consent of a landlord to an assignment of a lease where there is a contractual or statutory requirement that the landlord's consent is not to be unreasonably withheld. The powers of the court under s 1 (2) of the 1967 Act seem to me to

b bring the present case within this third and intermediate category.

In the end, I do not think that there was much disagreement between counsel as to the first two categories; the real issue was whether the third category was to be aligned with the first or with the second. Counsel for the defendant did not contend that a decree of specific performance would be refused in every case in which the defendant was required to take proceedings to enforce some right; the burden of his contention was that only in clear cases would specific performance be decreed.

c Relying on the similarity between injunctions and specific performance, at one stage he cited *West Riding of Yorkshire Rivers Board v Linthwaite Urban Council (No 2)*[1] and Halsbury's Laws of England[2] for the proposition that the court would never grant a mandatory injunction (and so would never decree specific performance) if in effect the order would require the defendant to take legal proceedings against a third party.

d However, I do not think that the authorities carry so general a proposition, at any rate in relation to specific performance; and in the end I think counsel for the defendant accepted this, or at any rate did not violently dissent from it.

On the other hand, I do not think counsel for the plaintiffs contended that specific performance would be decreed if there were no means of compelling the concurrence of some requisite third party. It is true that there are some very old cases in which

e specific performance was decreed against a husband when his wife's consent was requisite, and if he failed to procure it he was committed to prison in order to induce her consent out of compassion for her husband. It does not appear what happened to the husband if his wife lacked compassion or, worse, was actuated by malevolence. However, for well over a century this approach has been abandoned: see, for example, *Howell v George*[3] and Fry's Specific Performance[4]. The modern doctrine seems to me

f to be stated in Fry[5]:

'As the consent of a third party is, or may be, a thing impossible to procure, a defendant who has entered into a contract to the performance of which such consent is necessary, will not, in case such consent cannot be procured, be decreed to obtain it, and thus perform an impossibility.'

g Nevertheless, as Plumer V-C said in *Howell v George*[6]:

'Those cases in which a husband was compelled to make his wife concur have been where he has agreed she should convey, and her consent might be supposed to have been previously obtained';

h and that is not wholly without relevance when, as here, a husband sells, believing his wife to have consented, albeit without enthusiasm.

Counsel for the defendant drew on various authorities, some of them concerned with the rule in *Bain v Fothergill*[7], for illustrations of the extent to which he accepted that specific performance could be decreed against a vendor in cases where he would

j 1 (1915) 84 LJKB 1610 at 1618
2 3rd Edn, vol 21, p 362, para 758
3 (1815) 1 Madd 1 at 6, 7
4 6th Edn (1921), pp 466, 467
5 At p 466
6 (1815) 1 Madd at 7
7 (1874) LR 7 HL 158, [1874-80] All ER Rep 83

be required to embark on litigation in order to fulfil his contract. In dealing with
Bain v Fothergill[1], Williams on Vendor and Purchaser[2] summarises the position
thus:

> '... although a vendor who has contracted to give vacant possession is bound
> at his peril to eject a tenant by sufferance, a tenant at will or a trespasser who
> refuses to give up possession, he is not obliged to engage in litigation with persons
> asserting in good faith and with apparent or reasonably possible right, claims
> adverse to his title.'

One of the principal authorities cited is *Williams v Glenton*[3], which was in fact a
vendor's action for specific performance. There Turner LJ said[4]:

> 'I am not aware of any case in which the Court has gone the length of saying
> that a vendor shall be compelled to enter into litigation with an adverse claimant
> in order to perfect his title, and so enable himself to complete a contract which he
> has entered into for sale of the property. The vendor, however, is bound to
> complete the contract, and if he does not take the steps which are necessary to
> enable him to do so, he is liable for damages upon the contract; and heavy
> damages would be given if, having the means of completing the sale, he should
> decline to take the proceedings necessary for that purpose.'

All that had to be decided in that case were questions of interest and costs, so that the
passage was obiter; but it has often been cited with approval: see, for example,
Day v Singleton[5]. *Engell v Fitch*[6] was a case in which mortgagees who sold a house
with vacant possession were held liable for full damages, not limited by the ancestor
of *Bain v Fothergill*[1] (namely, *Flureau v Thornhill*[7]), for failing to recover vacant possession from the mortgagor in order to complete the contract; and their ability to do so
was demonstrated by their recovery of possession from the mortgagor after writ issued.
No question of specific performance arose; but counsel for the defendant accepted
this as an instance of a case in which the vendor's duty to perform the contract by
delivering vacant possession might properly be enforced by a decree of specific
performance.

In *Bain v Fothergill*[8] itself, Lord Hatherley referred to *Engell v Fitch*[6], and, speaking
of the vendor, said that it was a case in which—

> 'if a bill had been filed in Equity, he would have been compelled by the Court
> to take proceedings in order to obtain the delivery up of possession according to
> his contract with his vendee...'

In *Day v Singleton*[9], another case on damages, the vendor of a leasehold interest
failed to obtain the consent of the lessors to the assignment which the unqualified
covenant against assignment made requisite. On one view, he had not really
tried to obtain it; on another, he had actually induced the lessors to withhold it. On
that footing, specific performance at the suit of the purchaser was impossible[10]. On
any view, the vendor's duty was to do his best to get the lessor's consent, and damages
were awarded on the footing that the vendor was in breach of his duty. To that case

---

1   (1874) LR 7 HL 158, [1874-80] All ER Rep 83
2   4th Edn (1936) Vol II, p 1020
3   (1866) 1 Ch App 200
4   (1866) 1 Ch App at 208, 209
5   [1899] 2 Ch 320 at 333
6   (1869) LR 4 QB 659; *affg* (1867) LR 3 QB 314
7   (1776) 2 Wm Bl 1078, [1775-1802] All ER Rep 91
8   (1874) LR 7 HL at 209, [1874-80] All ER Rep at 88
9   [1899] 2 Ch 320
10   See [1899] 2 Ch at 327

a   I shall have to return. One of the authorities cited in it was *Lehmann v McArthur*[1]. In that case, unlike *Day v Singleton*[2], the covenant against assignment was qualified by an obligation for the lessor not to withhold his consent unreasonably or vexatiously. The lessee sold the lease 'subject to the landlord's approval'; but the landlord refused it because he wanted to purchase the lease himself. The purchasers sued for specific performance, and the Court of Appeal in Chancery, reversing Stuart V-C,

b   held that the claim failed. In the leading judgment Page Wood LJ[3] said that the main question was the effect of the expression 'subject to the landlord's approval', and that it was the vendor's duty 'to do his best to obtain the landlord's consent'; and he said[4] that he—

> *c*   'was only bound to try to get the landlord's consent without going into the question whether the refusal was reasonable or unreasonable, and without taking the risk of legal proceedings to enforce his consent.'

The other member of the court, Selwyn LJ, took a similar view.

Although the point before me is not clearly governed by any of the authorities cited, I think that the cases provide some measure of support for counsel for the defendant's contentions. The matter is perhaps summed up as well as is possible by

d   Lord Redesdale LC in *Costigan v Hastler*[5]:

> 'When a person undertakes to do a thing which he can himself do, or has the means of making others do, the Court compels him to do it, or procure it to be done, unless the circumstances of the case make it highly unreasonable to do so.'

e   See also *Howell v George*[6], where Plumer V-C cited this passage with approval. A vendor must do his best to obtain any necessary consent to the sale; if he has sold with vacant possession he must, if necessary, take proceedings to obtain possession from any person in possession who has no right to be there or whose right is determinable by the vendor, at all events if the vendor's right to possession is reasonably

f   clear; but I do not think that the vendor will usually be required to embark on difficult or uncertain litigation in order to secure any requisite consent or obtain vacant possession. Where the outcome of any litigation depends on disputed facts, difficult questions of law or the exercise of a discretionary jurisdiction, then I think the court would be slow to make a decree of specific performance against the vendor which would require him to undertake such litigation. In such a case, the vendor cannot know where the litigation will end. If he succeeds at first instance, the defen-

g   dant may carry him to appeal; if he fails at first instance, the purchaser may say that there ought to be an appeal. No doubt the line between simple and difficult cases will sometimes be hard to draw; and it may be that specific performance will be readily decreed only where it is plain that the requisite consent is obtainable without difficulty. The form of decree appropriate to such cases might specifically require the defendant to undertake such litigation; the court moulds the decree

h   as need be. But it may be that the court will do no more than direct the defendant to procure the requisite consent: see *Long v Bowring*[7]; Seton's Forms of Judgments and Orders[8].

---

1   (1868) 3 Ch App 496
j   2   [1899] 2 Ch 320
3   (1868) 3 Ch App at 500
4   (1868) 3 Ch App at 501
5   (1804) 2 Sch & Lef 160 at 166, [1803-13] All ER Rep 556 at 558
6   (1815) 1 Madd at 11
7   (1864) 33 Beav 585
8   7th Edn (1912), vol 3, p 2204

In the present case the defendant has endeavoured to persuade his wife to concur *a* in the sale, but has failed. It is true that after the failure of his initial attempt on the Friday night he then instructed his solicitors to withdraw from both the sale and his Norfolk purchase; but he again tried to persuade his wife on the Sunday, and there is some evidence of later attempts. As the evidence stands, I think that the defendant has sufficiently attempted to obtain her consent, short of litigation. The mere fact that he sought to withdraw from the contract before he had made all his *b* attempts does not seem to me to make much difference; if a later attempt had succeeded, he could still have completed at the date fixed for completion.

Persuasion having failed, I think that the court should be slow to grant a decree of specific performance that would require an unwilling husband to make an application to the court under s 1 (2) of the 1967 Act, particularly as the decision of the court depends on the application of phrases such as 'just and reasonable' under s 1 (3). In *c* any case, the court would be reluctant to make an order which requires a husband to take legal proceedings against his wife, especially while they are still living together. Accordingly, although this is a contract of a type which the court is normally ready to enforce by a decree of specific performance, in my judgment it would, in Lord Redesdale LC's phrase, be 'highly unreasonable' to make such a decree if there is any other form of order that could do justice; and that I must consider in due course. *d* Let me add that I would certainly not regard proceedings under the Act by the defendant against his wife as being without prospects of success. As the evidence stands (and of course I have not heard the defendant's wife) there is at least a real prospect of success for the defendant. He does not in any way seek to deprive his wife of a home; the difference between them is a difference as to where the matrimonial home is to be. In that, the conduct of the wife towards the plaintiffs and the defendant must *e* play a substantial part.

I turn to the second main question, that of counsel for the plaintiffs' alternative claim to specific performance for which he contended if he failed in his main claim to specific performance, and if he also was limited either to *Bain v Fothergill*[1] damages, or else to damages assessed as at the date of the breach. This alternative claim was for specific performance of the contract, but with the plaintiffs taking subject to the *f* charge in favour of the defendant's wife, and receiving damages or an abatement of the purchase money. By virtue of s 2 (3) of the 1967 Act, s 1 (2) to (5) would apply to the plaintiffs as they apply to the defendant, in that the plaintiffs would be persons deriving title under the defendant, and affected by the charge. If the plaintiffs took subject to the charge in favour of the defendant's wife, the result would be remarkable, for reasons which I have already indicated. The defendant has no rights *g* of occupation under the 1967 Act, for his right of occupation stems from his estate in the land, and so s 1 (1) of the Act gives him no statutory rights of occupation. The defendant's daughter has no rights of occupation under the Act, for the Act does not purport to confer such rights on anyone except a spouse. The defendant's wife alone has statutory rights of occupation, and on the facts of this case, these are expressed as being no more than 'a right not to be evicted or excluded from the dwelling house *h* or any part thereof'. It has not been contended that this language is wide enough to empower the wife to authorise others to occupy the house with her, so that on that footing the plaintiffs, after completion, would be unable to evict the wife without an order of the court made under the Act, whereas the defendant and the daughter would have no defence to proceedings to evict them.

There seems to be considerable force in the contention that this would be the *i* result. Neither the defendant nor the daughter would have any rights of their own to remain in the house, and what the statute gives the wife is not a positive right of occupation, whether a licence or otherwise, but a mere negative right not to be evicted or excluded. A person who is given a positive right of occupation might be

---

1   (1874) LR 7 HL 158, [1874-80] All ER Rep 83

a envisaged as having been given the right to permit others to occupy with him or her; but a mere negative right not to be evicted or excluded cannot so readily be construed in this sense.

On the other hand, there are two other factors to be borne in mind. First, the negative right not to be evicted or excluded is given by s 1 (1) (a) where, as in the present case, the spouse is in occupation of the dwelling. If the spouse is not in b occupation, the right given by s 1 (1) (b) is a positive right of occupation, 'a right with the leave of the court so given to enter into and occupy the dwelling house'. This cuts both ways. It forms at least a contrast in language with s 1 (1) (a), and so emphasises the difference, yet on the other hand it would be remarkable if a spouse out of occupation were intended to have wider rights than a spouse in occupation. Second, on an application for an order under the Act, under s 1 (3), the court is to have regard (inter alia) 'to the needs of any children'; and this language seems to assume that c children may be in occupation. I do not know that this goes very far, for even if technically the children had no right of their own to be there, they might well in fact be there; and an owning husband or wife who is unable to evict his or her spouse may well see no point in trying to evict the children. In any case, a requirement to consider the needs of the children in any application under the Act does not impose any bar to proceedings to evict the children dehors the Act.

d If one leaves the position of the children on one side as being debatable, there remains the position of the defendant vis-à-vis the plaintiffs. Even if the wife not only is protected against eviction or exclusion, but also has the right to permit others to occupy the dwelling with her, the defendant has contracted to give vacant possession to the plaintiffs. Could he, then, in breach of his contract, remain in occupation under cover of his wife's statutory right not to be evicted or excluded? Would a e decree of specific performance of the contract subject only to his wife's statutory rights in effect be nugatory as to his contractual obligation not himself to remain in occupation but to give vacant possession? The Act seems to me to have created much doubt and uncertainty in this sphere, but there is at least a real possibility that a decree of specific performance subject to the wife's right not to be evicted or excluded would enable the plaintiffs, by taking suitable proceedings, to evict the defendant and f perhaps the daughter, and thus split up the family. These circumstances seem to me to make the case one in which the court should be slow to decree specific performance if any reasonable alternative exists. I shall accordingly turn in due course to the question of damages to see whether they would provide the plaintiffs with an adequate remedy.

g Before I consider damages, I must deal with the third main point, that of laches, which is a defence to specific performance, although not, of course, to damages. In the end, counsel for the defendant relied only on the delay between 17th August 1971 and the issue of the writ on 25th January 1972. On 17th August the plaintiffs' solicitors wrote to the defendant's solicitors saying that they were taking counsel's advice and would write further when they obtained it. Not until 30th November h 1971 did the plaintiffs' solicitors write to the defendant's solicitors to say that proceedings for specific performance or damages (or both) would be instituted shortly, and that the delay had been occasioned by the plaintiffs' unsuccessful application for legal aid. The period in question was thus some 3½ months or 5½ months, according to whether the terminus ad quem was the letter before action, or the writ. Counsel for the defendant's strongest cases were *Huxham v Llewellyn*[1] and *Glasbrook v Richardson*[2], where periods of unexplained delay for over five months and some j 3½ months respectively were held to be a bar to specific performance. However, as counsel for the plaintiffs pointed out, in this case the date fixed for completion was 31st October 1971, and it must, he said, at least be open to the plaintiffs to refrain

---

1 (1873) 21 WR 570
2 (1874) 23 WR 51

from suing for specific performance until the defendant had broken the contract. *a*
Time therefore ought to run not from 17th August but from 31st October, with a
consequent reduction of some 2½ months in each of the periods. In any case, the
authorities cited were cases of the sale of interests in a colliery, and so sales of highly
speculative interests, approaching a trade, to which special considerations applied.
It seems plain to me that there has been no unexplained delay of an order which, in
the circumstances of this case, would justify holding the remedy of specific *b*
performance barred by laches or acquiescence.

I turn to damages. The fourth main point is whether the damages are limited
to those recoverable under the rule in *Bain v Fothergill*[1]. The rule is conveniently
stated in Williams's Contract of Sale of Land[2]:

'Where the breach of contract is occasioned by the vendor's inability, without
his own fault, to show a good title, the purchaser is entitled to recover as damages *c*
his deposit, if any, with interest, and his expenses incurred in connection with
the agreement, but not more than nominal damages for the loss of his bargain.'

What is said by counsel for the defendant is, quite simply, that the statutory charge
in favour of the defendant's wife is a defect in title within the rule, just as much as
any other charge would be, whether legal or equitable, and so the rule applies. *d*

In *Bain v Fothergill*[1] itself, a distinction was drawn between matters of conveyancing
and matters of title. Lord Hatherley said[3]:

'Whenever it is a matter of conveyancing, and not a matter of title, it is the
duty of the vendor to do everything that he is enabled to do by force of his own
interest, and also by force of the interest of others whom he can compel to concur
in the conveyance.' *e*

This was said in relation to *Engell v Fitch*[4], where the principle of *Bain v Fothergill*[1],
as exemplified in its ancestor, *Flureau v Thornhill*[5], was held not to apply to mortgagees who sold with vacant possession but refused to evict the mortgagor who was
in possession. The right to vacant possession may be regarded as a matter of conveyancing rather than of title, in that vacant possession is required to be delivered only *f*
on completion, and a title may be in perfect order even though the vendor is out of
possession. By contrast, in *Bain v Fothergill*[1] the vendor had a mere equitable title
to the lease of the mining royalty that he had contracted to sell, and he unexpectedly
failed to obtain the lessor's consent to the assignment that would have enabled him
to convey what he had contracted to sell. That was plainly a matter of title, and the
rule applied. That in turn may be contrasted with *Day v Singleton*[6], where the *g*
lessors' consent was requisite for the assignment of the lease which had been sold,
and, as I have mentioned, the vendor either did not really try to obtain the consent,
or else had induced the lessors to withhold it. The Court of Appeal held
that damages for loss of the bargain were recoverable in that the vendor had failed
in his duty to obtain the lessors' consent. Lord Lindley MR and Rigby LJ said of
the rule in *Bain v Fothergill*[1] that it was[7]— *h*

'an anomalous rule based upon and justified by difficulties in shewing a good
title to real property in this country, but one which ought not to be extended
to cases in which the reasons on which it is based do not apply.'

1   (1874) LR 7 HL 158, [1874-80] All ER Rep 83   *j*
2   (1930) p 128
3   (1874) LR 7 HL at 209
4   (1869) LR 4 QB 659
5   (1776) 2 Wm Bl 1078, [1775-1802] All ER Rep 91
6   [1899] 2 Ch 320
7   [1899] 2 Ch at 329

a   Certainly the courts have proved ready to find grounds for holding that cases do not fall within the rule. In *Re Daniel, Daniel v Vassall*[1] a testator had, before his death, contracted to sell land which, with other property, was comprised in a mortgage. The mortgagees refused to release the land on payment of an appropriate fraction of what was due under the mortgage, and the testator's estate was insufficient to pay off the entire mortgage. Sargant J held that the rule in *Bain v Fothergill*[2] did

b   not apply, for the failure of the executors to perform the contract was due not to any defect in title, but to the insufficiency of the testator's estate, and he refused to extend the anomalous rule in *Bain v Fothergill*[2] (or *Flureau v Thornhill*[3]) to a case which was not within the spirit of the rule. In *Braybrooks v Whaley*[4] a mortgagee contracted to sell land, but without obtaining, either before or after the contract, the leave of the court made requisite by the Courts (Emergency Powers) Act 1914. Again the

c   rule was held not to apply. Horridge J said that the failure to seek leave of the court was not a matter of title within the rule, but a matter of completing the contract by conveyance, and Salter J held that the contention that the application, if made, would have failed had not been established. Counsel for the defendant submitted that this decision was wrong, at all events insofar as it proceeded on the footing that the vendor was under a duty to take proceedings to remove the obstacle

d   to completion, for he had no clear right to the grant of leave by the court but merely a hope or prospect that the discretionary powers of the court would be exercised in his favour.

     Various other cases were cited, including *Thomas v Kensington*[5] and *J W Cafés Ltd v Brownlow Trust Ltd*[6], but I do not think I need discuss them. None of the cases cited to me plainly covers the facts of the present case, or answers the question whether the wife's right is a defect in title within the principle of *Bain v Fothergill*[2].

e   At one stage counsel for the defendant observed that her right was a very strange right, but whatever it was, it was a defect in title within the rule; and counsel for the plaintiffs was constrained to accept that it constituted some sort of defect in title, though he said that it was not a defect of a type which brought *Bain v Fothergill*[2] into play, particularly as the rule was anomalous and ought not to be extended.

f   Let me consider the consequences of holding that the rule applies, in days when a new verb of doubtful etymology has been attracting considerable attention, namely, the verb 'to gazump'. The most helpful approach seems to me to take the matter by stages. First, if the mere existence of the wife's charge, before registration, creates a defect in title within the rule, then Parliament has at a blow imposed a defect in title on many millions of homes vested in one or other of the parties to a marriage. On 1st January 1968 millions of perfectly good titles became defective.

g   I should be slow indeed to impute to Parliament any intention to produce this result. This is all the more striking in the case of registered land, where the operation of the rule in *Bain v Fothergill*[2] might be expected to be minimal; for the main purpose of the Land Registration Acts is to simplify titles and conveyancing. Furthermore, if the mere existence of an unregistered charge under the 1967 Act constitutes a

h   defect in title, it is a singularly impotent defect, for on completion of a sale it will be void against the purchaser for want of registration. If instead the vendor refused to complete, plainly he would be refusing to take a step which would remove the defect from his title; and on the principle of *Day v Singleton*[7] he would appeal to *Bain v Fothergill*[2] in vain. As at the date of the contract in this case, I therefore cannot see

---

j 1 [1917] 2 Ch 405, [1916-17] All ER Rep 654
   2 (1874) LR 7 HL 158, [1874-80] All ER Rep 83
   3 (1776) 2 Wm Bl 1078, [1775-1802] All ER Rep 91
   4 [1919] 1 KB 435
   5 [1942] 2 All ER 263, [1942] 2 KB 181
   6 [1950] 1 All ER 894
   7 [1899] 2 Ch 320

how the rule in *Bain v Fothergill*[1] could have applied.   In other words, looking at   *a*
matters immediately after the contract had been made, the case could not, in my
judgment, be said to fall within either the spirit or the letter of the rule in *Bain v
Fothergill*[1].

When in this case the wife's rights were registered the day after the contract had
been made, a different situation arose; for then her rights could no longer be destroyed by completing the sale.   On the footing that the wife's rights thereupon   *b*
became capable of attracting the rule in *Bain v Fothergill*[1], does the rule apply to
cases where, at the date of the contract, the necessary conditions for the application
of the rule did not exist, but those conditions first came into being after the contract
had been made?   It has not been suggested that there is any authority bearing
directly on this point.   The action is an action for damages for breach of contract,
and I should be slow to hold that some supervening event could bring within the   *c*
rule a case initially outside it.   Furthermore, the basis of the rule is that of the contract having been made against a background of the uncertainty of titles to land in
England; see, for example, *Bain v Fothergill*[2], per Lord Hatherley.   In *Engell v
Fitch*[3] Kelly CB said that the rule was—

> 'founded entirely on the difficulty that a vendor often finds in making a title to
> real estate, not from any default on his part, but from his ignorance of the strict   *d*
> legal state of his title.'

As I have indicated, a rule laid down for defects in title which lay concealed in title
deeds which were often, in the phrase attributed to Lord Westbury, 'difficult to read,
disgusting to touch, and impossible to understand', seems singularly inapposite to
the effect of a modern statute on registered land, with its aseptic certainty and clarity   *e*
of title.

Furthermore, the rule is anomalous, and, as was shown by the Court of Appeal
in *Re Compton, Powell v Compton*[4] (in an entirely different field), where the court
encounters an anomalous rule, it is in general better to confine the anomaly within
its established sphere than to extend the anomaly to analogous cases.   Here, the
wife's rights are the creature of statute, imposed generally, and in no way dependent   *f*
on the vicissitudes of a particular title to property.   The charge itself is sui generis.
The wife has personal rights of occupation which she cannot deal with, thus differing
greatly from other charges, such as legal or equitable charges for money.   If her
rights are rights of property at all, they are at least highly idiosyncratic.   They do not
seem to me to fall within the spirit or intendment of the rule in *Bain v Fothergill*[1];
and so I hold.

That brings me to the fifth main point.   If *Bain v Fothergill*[1] does not apply, what   *g*
is the measure of damages?   It was common ground that the normal rule is that the
general damages to which a purchaser is entitled for breach of a contract for the sale
of land are basically measured by the difference between the contract price and the
market price of the land at the date of the breach, normally the date fixed for completion.   On the facts of this case, the damages under this rule would be of the order   *h*
of £1,500.   The real issue was whether that rule applies to this case, or whether some
other rule applies.

Now the principle that has long been accepted is that stated by Parke B in *Robinson
v Harman*[5], in which, incidentally, the rule in *Flureau v Thornhill*[6] was considered.
Parke B said[7]:

1   (1874) LR 7 HL 158, [1874-80] All ER Rep 83   *j*
2   (1874) LR 7 HL at 210, [1874-80] All ER Rep at 88
3   (1869) LR 4 QB at 666
4   [1945] 1 All ER 198 at 206, [1945] Ch 123 at 139, 140
5   (1848) 1 Exch 850, [1843-60] All ER Rep 383
6   (1776) 2 Wm Bl 1078, [1775-1802] All ER Rep 91
7   (1848) 1 Exch at 855, [1843-60] All ER Rep at 385

a   'The rule of the common law is, that where a party sustains a loss by reason of a breach of contract, he is, so far as money can do it, to be placed in the same situation, with respect to damages, as if the contract had been performed.'

In the present case, if the contract had been performed, the plaintiffs would at the date fixed for completion have had the house, then worth £7,500, in return for the contractual price of £6,000. If in lieu of the house they had been paid £1,500 damages *b* at that date, they could, with the addition of the £6,000 that they commanded, have forthwith bought an equivalent house. I am satisfied on the evidence that the plaintiffs had no financial resources of any substance beyond the £6,000 that they could have put together for the purchase of the defendant's bungalow, and that the defendant knew this when the contract was made. The plaintiffs were therefore, to the defendant's knowledge, unable at the time of the breach to raise a further *c* £1,500 in order to purchase an equivalent house forthwith, and so, as events have turned out, mitigate their loss. Today, to purchase an equivalent house they need £5,500 in addition to their £6,000. How, then, it may be asked, would the award today of £1,500 damages place them in the same situation as if the contract had been performed? The result that would have been produced by paying £1,500 damages at the date of the breach can today be produced only by paying £5,500 damages, with *d* in each case the return of the deposit. On facts such as these, the general rule of assessing damages as at the date of the breach seems to defeat the general principle, rather than carry it out. In the ordinary case of a buyer of goods which the seller fails to deliver, the buyer can at once spend his money in purchasing equivalent goods from another, as was pointed out in *Gainsford v Carroll*[1], and so the rule works well enough; but that is a very different case. It therefore seems to me that on the *e* facts of this case there are strong reasons for applying the principle rather than the rule. The question is whether it is proper to do so.

    I do not think that I need enquire whether such an award could be made at common law. It may be that it could. The rule requiring damages to be ascertained as at the date of the breach does not seem to be inflexible, and in any case the rule may be one which, though normally carrying out the principle, does on occasion fail to do so; *f* and on those occasions the rule may have to be modified so as to accord with the principle. However, as I have said, I do not think I need explore that; for it seems to me that this case, in which there is a proper claim for specific performance, falls within the Chancery Amendment Act 1858 (better known as Lord Cairns' Act), and that damages assessed under that Act are to be ascertained in accordance with that Act on a basis which is not identical with that of the common law. That Act provides, *g* by s 2, that:

    'In all cases in which the Court of Chancery has jurisdiction to entertain an application for an injunction against a breach of any covenant, contract, or agreement, or against the commission or continuance of any wrongful act, or for the specific performance of any covenant, contract, or agreement, it shall be *h* lawful for the same court, if it shall think fit, to award damages to the party injured, either in addition to or in substitution for such injunction or specific performance, and such damages may be assessed in such manner as the court shall direct.'

The 1858 Act itself has been repealed, but in *Leeds Industrial Co-operative Society Ltd v Slack*[2] the House of Lords established that statute has maintained in force the *j* jurisdiction conferred by s 2. I should say that Fry's *Specific Performance*[3] states:

    'It is apprehended that where damages are awarded under this Act in substitution for specific performance, the measure of damages would be the same as in

---

1 (1824) 2 B & C 624
2 [1924] AC 851, [1924] All ER Rep 259
3 6th Edn (1921), p 602

an action at Common Law for breach of the contract. So, where the damages
at Common Law would be nominal, they would also, it is submitted, be nominal
under the statute.'

That, however, was written before the *Leeds* case[1] had been decided, though there
were other authorities on the point which perhaps had not been borne in mind.

In the case before me, the *Leeds* case[1] is both relevant and important. It shows that
Lord Cairns' Act extended the field of damages. In the *Leeds* case[1] the House of
Lords, by a majority, held that the Act allowed damages to be awarded quia timet.
An injunction had been sought to restrain a threatened obstruction of ancient lights;
and although no actual obstruction had taken place, and so there could be no claim
for damages at common law, the Act was held to have empowered the court to award
damages for the whole of the threatened injury. That case, of course, was concerned
with the award of damages under the 1858 Act which could not be awarded at common law, and not with the quantum of damages in a case where damages could be
claimed at common law. The same may be said of *Eastwood v Lever*[2]. That case
suggests that damages could be awarded under the 1858 Act when the right infringed
was a purely equitable right and the remedy of an injunction had been lost by acquiescence or delay. Yet in a sense the contention that there is jurisdiction to award
damages on a scale different from that applicable at law is a fortiori the established
jurisdiction to award damages when no claim at all lies at law.

On the wording of the section, the power 'to award damages to the party injured . . .
in substitution for such . . . specific performance' at least envisages that the damages
awarded will in fact constitute a true substitute for specific performance. Furthermore, the section is speaking of the time when the court is making its decision to
award damages in substitution for specific performance, so that it is at that moment
that the damages must be a substitute. The fact that a different amount of damages
would have been a substitute if the order had been made at the time of the breach
must surely be irrelevant. In the case before me, I cannot see how £1,500 damages
would constitute any true substitute for a decree of specific performance of the
contract to convey land which at the time of the decree is worth £5,500 more than
the contract price. A choice between the inadequate and the equivalent seems to me
to be no real choice at all. It may seem strange that nearly 115 years should have
elapsed before this aspect of Lord Cairns' Act should have emerged; but the economic
conditions which reveal its significance have not been with us long.

There are dicta in the *Leeds* case[1] which support this view, or are at least consistent
with it. In a speech with which the Earl of Birkenhead expressed his agreement,
Viscount Finlay said[3]:

> '. . . the power to give damages in lieu of an injunction must in all reason im-
> port the power to give an equivalent for what is lost by the refusal of the injunc-
> tion; for this purpose compensation only for what has passed would be futile.'

He added[4]:

> 'It has been urged that the word "damages" must be used as denoting com-
> pensation for what has already happened. It is, of course, true that a Court of
> common law gives damages as compensation for past wrongs, but the word
> "damages" is perfectly apt to denote compensation for the damage which will
> be sustained if a building is allowed to proceed so as to obstruct ancient lights.
> If an injunction is granted the obstruction will never take place. If damages
> are given instead of the injunction, they must be in respect of an injury which
> is still in the future.'

---

1   [1924] AC 851, [1924] All ER Rep 259
2   (1863) 4 De GJ & Sm 114
3   [1924] AC at 859, [1924] All ER Rep at 263
4   [1924] AC at 859, 860, [1924] All ER Rep at 263, 264

a Lord Dunedin expressly concurred in Lord Finlay's speech; but he also said[1] that the
   words referring to damages in substitution for an injunction—

   'clearly point to a pecuniary payment equalling the loss to be occasioned by the
   act against which, but for the provision in question, an injunction would have
   been obtained . . .'

b I must, of course, have care in applying dicta uttered in a case where the problem
   before me was obviously not in view, even though s 2 of the Act lays down the same
   rule for injunctions and specific performance alike. Yet on principle I would say
   simply that damages 'in substitution' for specific performance must be a substitute,
   giving as nearly as may be what specific performance would have given. There are,
   moreover, certain other authorities which provide assistance. In *Fritz v Hobson*[2]
c it was held that damages awarded under the 1858 Act in substitution for an injunction
   were not confined to damages down to the issue of the writ, as at law, but included
   damages down to the hearing. Fry J said[3]:

   'Now it is manifest that damages cannot be an adequate substitute for an
   injunction unless they cover the whole area which would have been covered by
   the injunction . . .'

d
   In *Chapman, Morsons & Co v Guardians of Auckland Union*[4], the Court of Appeal
   approved the view taken by Fry J in *Fritz v Hobson*[2]. In *Dreyfus v Peruvian Guano Co*[5]
   Fry LJ said of Lord Cairns' Act:

   'I am clear that the statute often enables the Court, where a wrong has been
e done, to give damages upon a different scale from what was done by the Courts
   of Common Law, because it may give them in substitution for an injunction . . .'

   Cotton LJ, who had previously delivered the leading judgment, then said that he
   agreed with what Fry LJ had said about Lord Cairns' Act.
   I should say at once that these additional authorities were not discussed before me,
f but as they support the view which I took without their aid, it seems proper for me
   to cite them without incurring the costs and delay of restoring the case for further
   argument. There seems to me to be adequate authority for the view that damages
   under Lord Cairns' Act may be awarded in cases in which there is no claim at all
   at law, and also that the quantum of damages is not limited by the rules at law. No
   doubt in exercising the jurisdiction conferred by the 1858 Act a court with equitable
g jurisdiction will remember that equity follows the law, and will in general apply
   the common law rules for the assessment of damages; but this is subject to the
   overriding statutory requirement that damages shall be 'in substitution for' the
   injunction or specific performance. In the words of Cardozo CJ, 'Equity follows the
   law, but not slavishly nor always': see *Graf v Hope Building Corporation*[6]. Obedience
   to statute, whether in its precise words or in its spirit, is an excellent and compelling
h reason for not following the law.
   In my judgment, therefore, if under Lord Cairns' Act damages are awarded in
   substitution for specific performance, the court has jurisdiction to award such damages
   as will put the plaintiffs into as good a position as if the contract had been performed,
   even if to do so means awarding damages assessed by reference to a period subsequent
   to the date of the breach. This seems to me to be consonant with the nature of specific

j
   1 [1924] AC at 865, [1924] All ER Rep at 266
   2 (1880) 14 Ch D 542, [1874-80] All ER Rep 75
   3 (1880) 14 Ch D at 556, 557, [1874-80] All ER Rep at 82
   4 (1889) 23 QBD 294
   5 (1889) 23 Ch D 316 at 342
   6 (1930) 254 NY 1 at 9

performance, which is a continuing remedy, designed to secure, inter alia, that the
purchaser receives in fact what is his in equity as soon as the contract is made, subject a
to the vendor's right to the money, and so on. On the one hand, a decree may be
sought before any breach of contract has occurred, and so before any action lies for
common law damages; and on the other hand the right to a decree may continue
long after the breach has occurred. On the facts of this case, the damages that may be
awarded are not limited to the £1,500 that is appropriate to the date of the breach, b
but extend to the £5,500 that is appropriate at the present day, when they are being
awarded in substitution for specific performance. I should add that no contention has
been advanced (in my judgment, quite rightly) that the case does not fall within Lord
Cairns' Act.   The sale of a house is a case par excellence in which the court 'has
jurisdiction to entertain an application . . . for the specific performance' of a contract,
and the plaintiffs have done nothing to disentitle themselves to a decree. The undesirability of granting the decree if any suitable alternative exists springs from the c
position of the defendant and his wife.

That brings me to a subsidiary point which counsel for the defendant urged on me.
He contended that an award of damages of the order of £5,500 was precluded by the
operation of what is often called the 'second rule' in *Hadley v Baxendale*[1], relating to
what was in the contemplation of the parties. I was very properly referred to that case d
in the light of the discussion in later cases set out in McGregor on Damages[2]. It was
beyond question that a rise in the price of houses was in the contemplation of the
parties when the contract was made in this case. But counsel for the defendant took it
further. He contended that what a plaintiff must establish is not merely a contemplation of a particular head of damage, but also of the quantum under that head. Here,
the parties contemplated a rise in house prices, but not a rise of an amount approach- e
ing that which in fact took place. A rise which nearly doubled the market price of the
property was, as the evidence showed, outside the contemplation of the parties, and
so it could not be recovered. Thus ran the argument.

I do not think that this can be right. On principle, it seems to me to be quite wrong
to limit damages flowing from a contemplated state of affairs to the amount that the
parties can be shown to have had in contemplation, for to do this would require f
evidence of the calculation in advance of what is often incalculable until after
the event.   The function of the so-called 'second rule' in *Hadley v Baxendale*[1]
seems to me to be not so much to add to the damages recoverable as to exclude
from them any liability for any type or kind of loss which could not have been
foreseen when the contract was made.   No authority was put before me which
appeared to me to provide any support for the alleged requirement that the quantum g
should have been in contemplation. So far as it went, the language used in the authorities that were cited seems to me to have been directed to the heads of damage rather
than to quantum.   Thus one finds phrases such as 'special circumstances' and the
'type' or 'kind' of damage.   I would therefore on principle reject the defendant's
contention, and hold that a plaintiff invoking the so-called 'second rule' in *Hadley v
Baxendale*[1] need show only a contemplation of circumstances which embrace the h
head or type of damage in question, and need not demonstrate a contemplation
of the quantum of damages under that head or type. Accordingly, in my judgment,
this subsidiary contention of the defendant's fails, even if it is one that would apply,
either directly or by analogy, to damages under Lord Cairns' Act.

During the argument it seemed to me surprising that the point should not be covered
by authority; yet the only authority put before me that seemed to bear on the j
point was *Vacwell Engineering Co Ltd v B D H Chemicals Ltd*[3]. Counsel for the defendant

---

1   (1854) 9 Exch 341, [1843-60] All ER Rep 461
2   13th Edn (1972), principally at pp 124-132
3   [1969] 3 All ER 1681, [1971] 1 QB 88

a referred me to this case in performance of his duty of assisting the court, although it was against him. The point does not seem to have been argued there in terms, but it was held that where the parties to a contract could reasonably have foreseen that there might be a small or minor explosion, with some damage to property, if a proper warning was not given as to the precautions to be taken in handling the chemical sold, but could not reasonably have foreseen the major explosion which in

b fact occurred, killing a scientist and doing extensive damage to property, the vendors were nevertheless liable for the whole of the damage done. As Rees J said[1]:

> '. . . the explosion and the type of damage being foreseeable, it matters not in the law that the magnitude of the former and the extent of the latter were not.'

c An appeal was settled[2].

That case, however, does not stand alone. In *Great Lakes Steamship Co v Maple Leaf Milling Co Ltd*[3] the respondents, in breach of contract, had failed 'to lighter immediately' the appellants' vessel on its arrival at the respondents' wharf on Lake Erie. Three days later, before any lightering had taken place, the vessel settled on the bottom as a result of a fall in the level of the water in the lake that was within the

d contemplation of the parties. Unknown to either party, a large anchor was resting on the bottom at that point, projecting two feet above the rock floor which there formed the bottom. This anchor caused serious injuries to the hull, for which the appellants claimed over $40,000 damages. In delivering the advice of the Judicial Committee, Lord Carson said[4]:

e > 'There can be no doubt that it was from breach of the contract immediately to lighter that the vessel grounded by reason of the lowering of the water, the very thing which it was anticipated might occur and which rendered the immediate lightering so important, and it must, in their Lordships' opinion, be held that it was the breach of contract in not lightering the vessel which was the immediate cause of the damage, and the fact that such damage might not have occurred if
f > the anchor had not been sunk can make no difference. If grounding takes place in breach of contract, the precise nature of the damage incurred by grounding is immaterial.'

That case seems to me to provide strong support for the view that I take. In the present case, the argument is directed purely to quantum. The precise head of damage, a general rise in the price of houses, was admittedly in contemplation: all

g that could be said to be outside the contemplation was the full amount, or the higher stages of the rise from £6,000 to £11,500. In the *Great Lakes* case[3], what was in contemplation was the fact that delay in lightering might cause the vessel to rest on the bottom by the wharf, a bottom consisting of rock; nobody contemplated the anchor, yet the damages recoverable included those stemming from the anchor. On the

h authority of that case, the case before me seems a fortiori. I therefore find confirmation in that case of the view that at the hearing I took without its aid.

The conclusion that I have reached, therefore, is that as matters stand I ought to award damages to the plaintiffs of the order of £5,500, in substitution for decreeing specific performance, with all the doubts and difficulties and probably undesirable consequences that a decree in either form would produce. An award of damages on

j this scale, I accept, will bear hardly on the defendant. Although he is able in one way or another to raise £1,500 without selling his bungalow, £5,500 is another matter; in all probability he could not raise that sum without selling the bungalow with

---

1 [1969] 3 All ER at 1699, [1971] 1 QB at 110
2 See [1970] 3 All ER 553, [1971] 1 QB at 112
3 (1924) 41 TLR 21
4 (1924) 41 TLR at 23

vacant possession, and he has no power to do this. If, however, he becomes bankrupt,
then his trustee in bankruptcy can sell the bungalow free from the wife's rights, even *a*
though they are registered: see the 1967 Act, s 2 (5). With the money so raised, the
trustee in bankruptcy will then be able to pay the plaintiffs their damages, one hopes
in full; or it may be possible for the plaintiffs to take the bungalow in satisfaction of
their claim. This is a dismal prospect for the defendant, but if the plaintiffs obtain
neither a decree of specific performance nor £5,500 by way of damages, theirs also is *b*
a dismal prospect. Having made a binding contract to purchase for £6,000 a bungalow
now worth £11,500, they would recover neither the bungalow nor damages that would
enable them to purchase anything like its equivalent. It is the plaintiffs who are wholly
blameless. Nothing whatever can be said against them, or has been, save as to the
contention that delay barred them from a decree of specific performance; and that I
have rejected. Nor do I think that there was any delay on their part that could affect *c*
the measure of damages.

The ultimate truth as between the defendant and his wife I do not know. As the
evidence stands, his wife did nothing whatever to warn the plaintiffs that she was not
willing to leave the bungalow, but conducted herself so as to lead them to believe that
she concurred in the sale. So far as the defendant was concerned, his wife was very
cool about the move, and it may well be that the move was one which a strong-willed *d*
husband was in effect imposing on a reluctant yet secretive wife. Nevertheless, the
consequences of disputes between husband and wife, whether open or concealed,
ought not to be visited on innocent purchasers.

In these circumstances, I think that what I ought to do is to make no order today,
but, subject to what counsel may have to say, to adjourn the case until the first day
of next term. In ordinary circumstances, I would adjourn the case for only a week,
but unfortunately the impending vacation makes this impossible. During the adjourn- *e*
ment I hope that the defendant and his wife will take advice, separately or together.
When I resume the hearing, it may be that the defendant's wife will not have changed
her mind about her charge. In that case, I shall award the plaintiffs damages against
the defendant of the order of £5,500, even though the probable consequence will
be the bankruptcy of the defendant and the sale of the bungalow with vacant possession by his trustee in bankruptcy, free from the wife's rights. On the other hand, the *f*
defendant's wife may by then have changed her mind, and rather than force her
husband into bankruptcy without avoiding having to vacate the bungalow, she may
have taken effective steps to enable the defendant to convey the bungalow to the
plaintiffs free from her rights. In that case I shall decree specific performance of the
contract. In this way the plaintiffs will obtain either the bungalow that they bought
or else an amount of damages which will enable them to purchase its equivalent. I *g*
may add that of course I give each side liberty to apply in the meantime; and I
should say that I shall be available until 4.00 pm today. As I have indicated, I feel much
sympathy for the defendant as well as for the plaintiffs at being embroiled in this way.
Yet as between the two sides both the law and the merits seem to me to point to the
plaintiffs as being the parties who should be as little hurt as possible; and they have
already suffered considerably, not least in relation to their temporary accommodation *h*
pending these proceedings. Counsel will no doubt assist me with any submissions
that they may have on this proposed adjournment, which was not mooted during
the argument.

There are three other matters that I should mention. First, this case is a potent
illustration of the need for the 1967 Act and its operation to be given urgent reconsideration, whether by the Law Commission or otherwise. What has happened to the *j*
plaintiffs in this case might happen to any purchaser of any house from a married
man or woman. The Act can be used to involve purchasers in matrimonial disputes
about where the spouses shall live. The Act can be used by spouses who are not in
the smallest peril of being deprived of a matrimonial home. 'Spite' registrations may
easily be made. Despite the example of the years of litigation that were necessary

a   to clarify the nature of a statutory tenancy under the Rent Acts, litigation which was in large part conducted at the expense of those who could ill afford it, the legislature has created a new 'charge' with scant information as to the nature and effect of the charge. There is now a companion in obloquy for what in *Keeves v Dean, Nunn v Pellegrini*[1], Scrutton LJ stigmatised as 'monstrum horrendum informe ingens'[2]. Millions of spouses who need no protection at present, but may possibly need it in

b   the future, can secure that protection (and by some are encouraged to secure it) by cluttering up the Land Registry with millions of entries, most of which will never do anyone any good. As may be seen by comparing this case with *Miles v Bull*[3] and *Miles v Bull (No 2)*[4], the Act is one which sometimes does too much and sometimes does too little. For these and many other reasons that I need not specify it seems to me to be a matter of some urgency that the scope and operation of the 1967 Act be re-

c   considered so as to evolve some means of protecting those who need protection without the cumbersome uncertainties that the 1967 Act has produced, to the peril of all, and not least to those of modest means. One must not underestimate the difficulties; but something better than the 1967 Act—much better—must be possible. I have done my best to see how the Act could and should work, but after prolonged consideration and much assistance from counsel, many serious difficulties remain. The Act certainly changed the law; but not every change is reform.

d   Second, this case may serve as a warning to conveyancers to reconsider their practice. Although much has been discussed before me, much has not. Can conveyancers safely continue their practice of not registering a contract for the purchase of land as an estate contract (or by a notice on the Land Register) except in cases of suspicion or delayed completion? On the other hand, how far would such registration provide protection against rights under the Act? Is it, or ought it to be, the practice for abstracts of title

e   to abstract a spouse's statutory rights of occupation as being a charge? These questions, with many others, did not arise in this case, and so have not been explored. It may be that a purchaser of a house from an owner-occupier ought to be suspicious in every case in which the vendor is or may be married. Perhaps I exaggerate if I say that until questions such as these are answered, there should be displayed in every conveyancer's office the minatory legend Cave uxorem.

f   Third, for obvious reasons I very much regret the length of this judgment. It would have been even longer had I considered in detail all that was urged before me in argument. Counsel for the defendant and for the plaintiffs both obviously devoted time and skill to the preparation and argument of this case that went beyond the normal call of duty even in a profession which rightly demands high standards. I am indeed grateful to them for their great assistance. I would only add that their

g   authorities and contentions which do not appear at large in this judgment have not been overlooked.

h   11th January. The defendant's wife refusing to remove her notice, his Lordship ordered that the defendant pay damages to the plaintiffs to be quantified as at the date of judgment, i e 11th January. Counsel having agreed that as no increase in prices had taken place since the date of hearing, damages were assessed at £5,500.

Judgment accordingly.

Solicitors: *Boyes, Turner & Burrows*, Ashford, Surrey (for the plaintiffs); *Owen White & Catlin*, Ashford, Surrey (for the defendant).

j   Susan Corbett   Barrister.

---

1   [1924] 1 KB 685, 93 LJKB 203, [1923] All ER Rep 12
2   93 LJKB 203 at 207, [1923] All ER Rep at 17
3   [1968] 3 All ER 632, [1969] 1 QB 258
4   [1969] 3 All ER 1585

George and another v Pinnock and another   *a*

COURT OF APPEAL, CIVIL DIVISION
SACHS, BUCKLEY AND ORR LJJ
1st, 2nd, 8th NOVEMBER 1972

b

Damages – Personal injury – Amount of damages – Brain damage – Total mental and physical incapacity – Plaintiff aged 21 at time of accident – Needing help night and day in all activities – Inability to work or marry – Mother aged 48 giving up employment to devote herself to care of plaintiff – Need for nursing help – Possibility of plaintiff having to go into hospital – Plaintiff and mother moving to accommodation more suited to plaintiff's needs – Method of assessing nursing expenses – Cost of accommodation.

c

Damages – Personal injury – Assessment – Appeal – Appeal by plaintiff against quantum – Defendant seeking to uphold award on ground that total sum awarded reasonable, notwithstanding one element might be too low – Plaintiff suffering severe brain damage as result of accident – Defendant admitting liability for accident – Trial judge awarding plaintiff £48,682 and specifying how total made up – Plaintiff appealing against quantum – Right of parties *d* *to challenge any error in assessment.*

In June 1967 the plaintiff was injured in a road accident for which the defendant accepted full responsibility. She was at the time 21 years old, earning £900 a year and living with her mother, her grandmother and her brother in a council-acquired house in Bromley the rent of which was at 17s 9d a week. The mother, who was *e* aged 48, was earning £13 a week. The plaintiff's injuries included, besides a dislocated hip, head injuries involving severe brain stem damage. Three reports by a neuro-surgeon made in October 1969, June 1970 and September 1971 found little change in condition over that time. The first described her as being 'in a wheel-chair and physically unable to move from it . . . totally incapacitated both from the mental and physical point of view and requiring continuous help in every activity'. In the third *f* the neuro-surgeon put the plaintiff's expectation of life at ten to 15 years. From the reports it was clear that the plaintiff would never be able to work or marry and would have to be cared for by others for the rest of her life. Her mother gave up her employment to devote her whole life to the plaintiff's care. The plaintiff required day and night attention and should the mother be unable to cope at any time the plaintiff would have to go into hospital until the mother was able to resume. Between the last *g* two reports the plaintiff, her mother and her grandmother had gone to live in a bungalow in Dorset which was more suited to the needs of the plaintiff arising from the accident. It was bought in the plaintiff's name at a cost of £14,500 (provided by the defendant's insurers). The plaintiff brought an action against the defendant for damages. At the trial the neuro-surgeon stated that the plaintiff's expectation of life could well be extended, possibly to 20 years, if the plaintiff continued to receive the *h* present high level of attention and care but he doubted the mother's ability to continue for long without some trained help. The trial judge assessed the total damage at £48,682 which included: (i) for the plaintiff's loss of earnings £10,000, arrived at on the basis of an expectation of life of 13 years, by applying a multiplier of ten to an estimated income of £1,000 a year; (ii) for paid help £7,800, arrived at by applying the same multiplier of ten to £15 a week (the trial judge discounting a larger figure than *j* that to allow for the contingency of the plaintiff having at some stage to go into a hospital or institution); (iii) for the mother's loss of earnings, £6,760, arrived at by applying a multiplier of ten to estimated earnings of £13 a week; (iv) for other items of general damage, including loss of amenities and pain and suffering, £19,000. The plaintiff appealed against the quantum of damages. The defendant sought to uphold the trial judge's award, inter alia, on the ground that the total sum awarded was *a*   reasonable and adequate, even though it might be shown that one element in it was too low.

Held – (i) On the evidence the trial judge was fully justified in taking the plaintiff's expectation of life as 13 years and applying a multiplier of ten; accordingly the award of £10,000 for loss of earnings should stand (see p 932 b to d and p 933 j to p 934 a, post).

b   (ii) The sum awarded however for care of the plaintiff should be increased to £10,900; instead of adopting the method that he did to reach the £7,800 the trial judge should have estimated the cost of hired help the mother needed (which was £30 per week) and then applied a lower multiplier than ten to reflect the contingency of the plaintiff having to go into hospital; the appropriate multiplier was seven giving a figure of £10,900 (see p 932 e to g and p 933 j to p 934 a, post).

c   (iii) The award of £6,760 for the mother's loss of earnings would be affirmed; the proper multiplier was ten and should not be reduced to allow for the contingency of the plaintiff having to go permanently into hospital, for if that occurred it was unlikely that the mother would, at her age, be able to resume employment (see p 932 h and j and p 933 j to p 934 a, post).

d   (iv) The trial judge had included nothing in respect of the expenses incurred in or as a result of the acquisition of the bungalow in the £19,000 awarded for other items of general damages, and the plaintiff should be awarded additional damages for, although she could be awarded nothing in respect of the cost of the bungalow as she still had the capital in the form of the bungalow, she was entitled to be compensated to the extent that the loss of income or notional outlay by way of mortgage interest in providing the special accommodation needed exceeded what would have been her

e   expenses but for the accident; the plaintiff was entitled to an award of £3,000 under that head (see p 933 d to h and j to p 934 a, post).

(v) The £19,000 awarded for other elements of general damage, although near the lower end of the bracket applicable to such injuries, would be upheld as it was not so low as to justify interference by the court (see p 933 h and j to p 934 a, post).

(vi) In consequence the appeal would be allowed and the total damages awarded

f   to the plaintiff would be increased from £48,682 to £54,782 (see p 933 j to p 934 a, post).

Per Curiam. The modern practice in awarding damages is for the trial judge to state in his judgment what are the main components of his global figure, so as to enable the plaintiff and defendant alike to know what is the sum assessed for each relevant head of damage and to be able on appeal to challenge any error in the

g   assessments; a respondent should not, without giving a cross-notice, seek to uphold a quantum of damage judgment on the ground that even if one head of damage as awarded by the judge is held to be demonstrably too low, another is equally demonstrably too high (see p 934 b f g and j to p 935 a, post); *Jefford v Gee* [1970] 1 All ER 1202 applied; *Povey v W E & E Jackson (a firm)* [1970] 2 All ER 495 explained.

h   **Notes**

For damages for torts causing personal injury, see 11 Halsbury's Laws (3rd Edn) 255-257 and 258-261, paras 427, 428 and 430-432, and for cases on the subject, see 36 Digest (Repl) 199-201, *1050-1062*, 229-232, *1209-1234*, and Digest (Cont Vol A) 1190-1197, *1051a-1070d*, 17 Digest (Repl) 101, *164, 165*, 102, *167, 168*, and Digest (Cont Vol A) 464, 465, *155a-168a*.

j

Cases referred to in judgment

Jefford v Gee [1970] 1 All ER 1202, [1970] 2 QB 130, [1970] 2 WLR 702; sub nom *Jefford and Jefford v Gee* [1970] 1 Lloyd's Rep 107, CA, Digest (Cont Vol C) 709, *182a*.

Povey v W E & E Jackson (a firm) [1970] 2 All ER 495, [1970] 1 WLR 969, 8 KIR 942, CA, Digest (Cont Vol C) 293, *916b*.

Appeal

Judith Martin George, the first plaintiff in an action brought by her and her mother, Iris George, against the defendants, Leonard Charles Pinnock and Henry Charles Philpot, for damages in respect (i) of the personal injuries sustained by the first plaintiff in a road accident on 24th June 1967 caused by the admitted negligence of the first defendant and (ii) of the loss sustained by the second plaintiff in consequence of looking after the first plaintiff, appealed against an order of Thesiger J made on 3rd December 1971 awarding her £48,682 damages. At the hearing it had been agreed (i) that the damages claimed by the second plaintiff should be included in the damages awarded to the first plaintiff, and (ii) that the trial should proceed in relation to quantum of damage against the first defendant only and not against the second defendant, in whose taxi the first plaintiff was travelling at the time of the accident. The grounds of appeal were as follows: (i) the damages awarded by the judge were excessively low; (ii) the judge misdirected himself as to the evidence on the medical necessity for future nursing for the first plaintiff and relief for the second plaintiff in her capacity as a nurse to the first plaintiff; (iii) there was no evidence to support the judge's finding that £15 per week was an adequate sum to cover future nursing for the first plaintiff; (iv) the judge was wrong in law in finding that the probabilities were that the first plaintiff would go into an institution, in the face of unchallenged evidence that to do so would result in damage to her health and morale and would have no advantages over home care; (v) the judge failed to direct himself adequately as to the risk of the second plaintiff or her mother or both becoming unable to continue to nurse the first plaintiff full time or at all and to make adequate allowance in his award for that eventuality; (vi) the judge was wrong in law in failing to consider the evidence as to the cost of the provision of nursing and home help; (vii) the judge was wrong in law in failing to make any allowance under a separate head of damage for the provision of a bungalow for the first plaintiff at a cost of £14,500, with the result that the award for general damages for loss of amenity was largely consumed by the provision of the bungalow which was itself necessitated by the nature of the first plaintiff's injuries; (viii) the judge was wrong in his calculation of the first plaintiff's expectation of life and the multiplier calculated therefrom and it was not supported by the medical evidence.

The first defendant served a respondent's notice that he intended to contend that the judgment of Thesiger J should be affirmed and supported on the following grounds additional to those in his judgment: (i) the total sum awarded by way of damages was reasonable and adequate compensation to the plaintiff having regard to the totality of the evidence; (ii) the sum awarded in respect of the future cost of care of the first plaintiff was £14,560 and was more than sufficient having regard to the facts appearing in the evidence and in particular to the following facts: (a) that some assistance in the care of the first plaintiff was available without cost to the plaintiff from the local district nurse system; (b) that the probability was that assistance would be available from relatives and friends without cost to the first plaintiff in order to help her mother, who was to be paid for caring for her daughter, the cost thereof being included in the damages; (c) that the date at which any other expenditure on care for the first plaintiff would start was uncertain and would in all probability be postponed for some considerable time; (d) that the period during which the cost of care would be incurred in any year was uncertain, having regard to the fact that in certain circumstances which were likely to arise the first plaintiff would be admitted to a state hospital for treatment, without expense to herself; (e) that the length of the period of time during which any cost of care would arise was uncertain having regard to the fact that if the first plaintiff's mother became unable to care for the first plaintiff, she would in all probability be admitted to a state hospital without expense to herself; (f) that the cost of provision of full-time nursing services for the first plaintiff at her home would not in probability be incurred by or in behalf of the first plaintiff, and would, in any event be unreasonable expenditure; (iii) the judge

a was correct in making no allowance under a separate head of damage for the provision of a bungalow for the first plaintiff in that apart from the fact that such provision
did not in law constitute a separate head of damage no such claim was either pleaded
or advanced by the first plaintiff at the trial. The facts are set out in the judgment of
Orr LJ.

b *R G Rougier QC* and *T W Preston* for the first plaintiff.
Ralph Gibson QC and *J D Crowley* for the first defendant.

Cur adv vult

8th November. The following judgments were read.

c **ORR LJ** read the first judgment at the invitation of Sachs LJ. This is an appeal, on
the ground that it was too low, against an award of damages made by Thesiger J on
3rd December 1971 in respect of injuries arising out of a road accident. The first
plaintiff in the action is the appellant, Miss Judith George, whom I will call the
plaintiff, since in the event she was the only effective plaintiff; it being agreed at the
hearing that damages claimed by the second plaintiff, her mother, in respect of loss
d by her in consequence of her looking after her daughter since the accident should be
included in the damages awarded to the daughter.
   At the time of the accident, which took place on 24th June 1967, the plaintiff was
21 years of age; was employed as a punch operator in a data processing department
and earning some £900 a year, and was living with her mother, Mrs Iris George, then
aged 48, her grandmother, Mrs Martin, then in her late sixties, and a brother a little
e older than herself, at Bromley in a house acquired by the local authority and let
by them at the very low rent of 17s 9d a week. Her parents had lived apart for many
years and have subsequently been divorced, and the mother was in employment
from which it was common ground that she received an income of £13 a week, and
which it was also common ground that she gave up shortly after the accident in order
to look after her daughter, which she had done with devoted care ever since.
f   The circumstances of the accident were that on the morning of 24th June 1967
the plaintiff was being driven in a taxi towards Victoria Station when it was run into
by a motor car driven by the first defendant, Mr Pinnock, who has accepted his
responsibility for the collision. The result of the collision was that the plaintiff was
thrown forward against the glass partition behind the driver. She was admitted the
same morning, unconscious, to St George's Hospital, where she was found to be suffering from head injuries and from a dislocation of the left hip. The hip injury caused
g some pain, which the learned judge took into account in his award, but it is of small
importance in comparison with the head injuries, which were diagnosed as involving
severe brain stem damage, the effect of which is revealed by passages in successive
reports made by Mr Richardson, a neuro-surgeon, and quoted in the judgment
under appeal. In his first report, dated 10th October 1969, Mr Richardson said:

h   'She first came under my care on 3rd September, 1968, at which point the
       situation was that she was in a wheelchair and physically unable to move from it,
       and had evidence of marked mental blunting with severe impairment of memory,
       lack of initiative and intellectual blunting of quite a severe degree. In addition,
       she had marked difficulty in voice production and could only produce occasional
       words. She had, in essence, severe weakness of all her limbs and her state at this
j   point could best be described as totally incapacitated both from the mental and
       physical point of view and requiring continuous help in every activity.'

In a later report, dated 29th June 1970, Mr Richardson said:

       'Since my last report of October 1969 there has, unfortunately, been no
       improvement in the [plaintiff's] abilities and she is still confined to a wheelchair

and still requires considerable help in assuming the standing position. There is
no change in the degree of dependence which she showed in relation to personal
activities such as washing, dressing, toilet etc., all of which require the full assistance of two people. The mental blunting which I referred to in my previous report has changed little and the additional point which both parents made was
that she has recently been subject to recurrent attacks of bronchitis, which persist
for several weeks.'

In a passage headed 'On Examination', he adds:

'She was still confined to a wheelchair. Word production was severely limited
and was almost inaudible. She still showed severe weakness of both upper limbs
with poor control and grossly limited co-ordination. As before, the left arm was
more markedly affected than the right, but even in these circumstances the use
to which she could put her right hand was markedly limited. The lower limbs
remained unchanged with severe spastic weakness of both legs with impairment
of sensation below the knees, particularly on the left side. Her sitting balance was
poor and we were only able to stand her from the chair with great difficulty.'

In the interval between that report and Mr Richardson's final report the plaintiff,
with her mother and grandmother, had left Bromley and gone to live in a bungalow
at Broadstone, Dorset, which, with the furniture in it, was bought in the plaintiff's
name at a cost of £14,500 (being £12,000 for the bungalow and £2,500 for the furniture), which sum the first defendant's insurers paid to the plaintiff on account of the
award of damages which would in due course be made in her favour. This bungalow
had two main attractions; the first, that it provided a bathroom on the ground floor,
which was quite essential in view of the plaintiff's disability; and the second, that the
air of Dorset offered alleviation from the bronchitis referred to in the report of Mr
Richardson from which I have just quoted, of which after the accident the plaintiff
had suffered at Bromley, attacks lasting several weeks at a time, but on the evidence
she has been free from that trouble since the move was made.

In his third and last report, dated 8th September 1971, after this move was made,
Mr Richardson said:

'This move only has some relevance in relation to the ease with which the
[plaintiff] can be cared for as opposed to the previous arrangement where the
structure of the house increased the difficulties. In general it is fair to say that the
situation has changed very little in any significant way since the last report was
completed. Her mother felt that [the plaintiff] was a little more cheerful and
suggested that she tried to help a little more but this resolved itself into a somewhat increased ability to wash her face and clean her teeth and feed herself and
to apply cosmetics. There has, however, been no change in the patient's dependence for all the other essentials of life such as getting in and out of bed, dressing,
bathing, attention to menstrual hygiene and other personal details. Whilst
the mother suggested that [the plaintiff] was feeding herself, it was still clear
that food required to be cut up and presented in a very simple form so that the
patient could manage it easily with a fork and spoon.'

From these reports it is clear, and has not been in dispute, that the plaintiff will
never be able to work, will not marry, and will have to be cared for by others for
the rest of her life.

There were called as witnesses for the plaintiff at the hearing, Mr Richardson and
her present general practitioner, Dr Fleming, and also her mother and a friend of
the mother's, a Miss Dixon, who also lives at Broadstone. The mother's evidence
was that she had given up her employment to look after her daughter, and also the
prospect of remarriage: and it is, I think, true to say that she has since the accident
devoted her whole life to her daughter's care. She gave evidence that she had tried

a before leaving her former home to use the district nursing service, but that had been abandoned after an incident involving a dirty sheet. She had not tried the district nursing service at the new home, but was looking after the plaintiff with the help of her mother and Miss Dixon, who takes the daughter out in her car. She described her routine, which includes at night turning the plaintiff over in her bed and attending to her other needs, and in the morning, with the assistance of her mother, Mrs Martin,

b now 74, lifting the plaintiff out of bed; the necessity of supplying a suppository to facilitate the plaintiff's motions; a delay of half an hour or more before that takes effect; and then putting her back to bed again with the help of her mother. She does not feel able to leave the plaintiff for more than a short time because of the age gap between the plaintiff and her mother. She recognised that, if the time came when she could no longer cope, the plaintiff would have to go into hospital until she (the mother) was able to look after her again. She thought that for the time being she

c could cope, although she admitted that she was having to force herself to carry on as she had been doing. She had not so far tried to find any help, but said that the kind of help she would like would be someone to take the burden off her in the mornings. If, on the other hand, she had some nursing help at night, she thought she could manage the housework.

d Miss Dixon's evidence was that she could not see the mother being able to carry on without help, and that things were getting on top of her.

Mr Richardson gave evidence that the plaintiff would need indefinitely a high standard of intelligent care, and he would be surprised if the present care by the mother and grandmother could continue over the next year or two without a breakdown. He was surprised that the mother had managed as she had for so long. He could see only two possibilities: the first to import some help into the house, and the

e other to arrange for institutional care. He had had experience of the plaintiff in an institutional setting and it was not regarded as a success. In his view, the plaintiff made more effort and concentrated more at home with her mother. For this reason he thought it for her advantage that she should remain at home; and on this basis he thought that what she required was someone with the qualities of a state enrolled

f nurse to take over at night in turning the plaintiff in her bed and attending to her other needs. He accepted, however, that in the long run some help for the mother in the day-time would also be necessary.

The plaintiff's general practitioner, Dr Fleming, gave evidence that her mother needed relief from her 24 hour responsibility. He considered that she needed help at night, although not every night, and also for eight hours or so during the day. But he agreed that as respects the help of a qualified nurse, it would be better for her to

g come at times when help was needed rather than for eight-hour periods.

On the evidence which I have summarised the learned judge assessed the total damage, before allowing credit for the £14,500 paid on account, and before the addition of interest, at £48,682, made up as follows. (i) For loss of earnings of the plaintiff, £10,000, arrived at on the basis of an expectation of life of 13 years, by applying a multiplier of ten years to an estimated income of £1,000 a year. (ii) For care of the

h plaintiff, £14,560, made up as follows: (a) for earnings of which the mother would be deprived because of her decision to devote herself to the care of her daughter, £6,760, arrived at by applying the same multiplier to estimated earnings of £13 a week; (b) for paid help which the mother would require in caring for the plaintiff, £7,800, arrived at by applying the same multiplier to cost of hired help estimated at £15 a week. (iii) For the remaining elements of general damages, including loss of amenities

i and pain and suffering, £19,000. (iv) For the plaintiff's loss of expectation of life, £500. (v) For agreed special damage, £4,622. As to the last two of these items, the damages for loss of expectation of life and the agreed special damages, no issue arises on the appeal. As to the other items, the issues which arise are as follows.

As to the loss of earnings of the plaintiff, the estimated earnings of £1,000 a year are not in dispute, and the sole issue concerns the estimated expectation of life and the

multiplier of ten, it being claimed that the learned judge should have adopted a
higher expectation of life than 13 years, and should in consequence have adopted a
higher multiplier. Mr Richardson, in his last report from which I have quoted, put
the plaintiff's expectation of life at ten to 15 years. In his evidence he said that this
period could well be extended if she continued to receive the present high level of
attention and care; that he would not contest that on another opinion the expectation
could be ten to 20 years; and that if it were suggested that with the present level of
care she could live for 20 years, he would find that suggestion acceptable. No other
evidence was adduced in this respect.

It has been argued on behalf of the plaintiff that the learned judge should have
taken 15 years as the mean expectation of life and applied to it a higher multiplier
than ten. I am, however, unable to accept this argument. In my judgment, the
learned judge was entitled to have regard to two facts: first, that while Mr Richardson
accepted the possibility of a more optimistic view, his own estimate was ten to 15
years; and secondly that his acceptance of the possibility of her living for 20 years
was conditional on the continuance of the present high standard of care, of which
there could be no certainty. The learned judge, in adopting an expectation of 13
years, took a figure slightly in excess of the mean between ten and 15, and in my
judgment this conclusion was fully justified on the evidence, as also was the multiplier
of ten based on it. I can find no substance in this ground of appeal.

I turn next to the damages awarded for care of the plaintiff and will deal first under
that heading with the sum of £7,800 awarded in respect of hired help and calculated
by applying the same multiplier of ten to estimated expenses of £15 a week. It is
to be noted that this latter sum represents a little less than the cost (on the table of
charges before us, £15-£36 a week) of employing a state enrolled nurse to come in
for eight hours on four nights a week, but it seems to me clear that the learned judge
arrived at £15 by discounting a larger figure so as to allow for the very real contingency of the plaintiff having to go at some stage into a hospital or some other institution, in which event the expense here in question would come to an end; that contingency not having been reflected in the multiplier of ten which related to the
plaintiff's expectation of life. In my judgment, with great respect to a very experienced judge, the resulting figure is, in all the circumstances, too low. I prefer to
approach this matter by adopting an estimated cost of hired help and applying to it a
lower multiplier than ten so as to reflect the contingency to which I have referred.
Various permutations of help in the day-time and at night have been canvassed before
us, as to which I do not find it possible to say that any one is right and the others
wrong. In my judgment, however, the mother clearly needs help in the form of some
attendance daily and also for at least some nights of the week, and approaching the
matter on a broad basis, I would assess the resulting cost at £30 a week and apply it to
a multiplier of seven, giving a figure of £10,900 in place of the figure of £7,800
awarded by the learned judge.

As to the damages of £6,760 awarded for loss of earnings of the mother in caring for
the daughter, the figure of £13 a week for her loss of earnings has not been challenged,
and the multiplier of ten is in my judgment, for the reasons I have already given,
the proper multiplier in relation to the plaintiff's expectation of life. I would not
reduce this multiplier for the contingency of the plaintiff having to go permanently
into hospital, since if and when that contingency occurs it is in my judgment unlikely
that the mother, having regard to her age, would be able to resume employment.
She made her decision in 1967 to care for her daughter, and it is unreal in my judgment
to assume that at some uncertain future date she would be able to go back into
employment.

The next issue concerns a head of damage not separately dealt with by the learned
judge, namely, expenses incurred in or as a result of the acquisition of the bungalow
in Dorset. The case put for the plaintiff is that either the learned judge had included
these expenses in his figure of £19,000 for the remaining elements of general damages,

a in which case it was contended that that figure was manifestly too low, or alternatively he had wrongly failed to make a separate award under this heading. Nothing in the judgment suggests that any figure under this heading was included in the £19,000, or that indeed the learned judge appreciated that he was being asked to make an award under this heading. We were told that a note made by Mr Dow for the purpose of his opening the case at the trial indicated that he was putting forward these expenses as a separate head of damage, but I have not been satisfied

b that this was ever made clear to the learned judge. It has, however, been agreed that, rather than remit the case for a further hearing, we should deal with this issue on such material as is available to us. For the plaintiff it has been contended in the first place that she should receive as additional damages either the whole or some part of the capital cost of acquiring the bungalow, since it was acquired to meet the particular needs arising from the accident. But this argument, in my judgment, has

c no foundation. The plaintiff still has the capital in question in the form of the bungalow.

An alternative argument advanced was, however, that as a result of the particular needs arising from her injuries, the plaintiff has been involved in greater annual expenses of accommodation than she would have incurred if the accident had not happened. In my judgment, this argument is well founded, and I do not think it

d makes any difference for this purpose whether the matter is considered in terms of a loss of income from the capital expended on the bungalow or in terms of annual mortgage interest which would have been payable if capital to buy the bungalow had not been available. The plaintiff is, in my judgment, entitled to be compensated to the extent that this loss of income or notional outlay by way of mortgage interest exceeds what the cost of her accommodation would have been but for the accident.

e She would also, in my judgment, have been entitled to claim the expenses of a move to a new home imposed by her condition and the expense of any new items of furniture required because of that condition, but there was no evidence before the learned judge under either of those headings. As to the increased cost of accommodation, if any, it was, as I have said, agreed that we should make the best estimate we could

f on the available material, and the matter can only be approached on a broad basis.

I am not prepared to assume that the plaintiff, if the accident had not happened, would have been able to continue for more than a very short time living in accommodation rented at 17s 9d a week. If she had remained unmarried, I would have expected that she would contribute to realistic rent, and might well in a year or two have found accommodation of her own. If she had married, it is in my judgment more likely than not that she would have continued to work, not necessarily con-

g tinuously, and would have made substantial contributions to the matrimonial home. Taking into account, on the one side, the loss of income arising from the purchase of the bungalow, and, on the other, the expenses she would have been likely to incur apart from the accident, and allowing for tax in the calculation, I would assess the damages under this heading at £3,000, and I would award that sum as additional damages.

h The remaining item to be considered is the £19,000 awarded for the other elements of general damage. As already stated, I cannot accept that this figure includes anything for the cost of the bungalow. Even so, it is in my judgment near the lower end of the bracket which would be applicable today to injuries such as these, but I have not been satisfied that it is so low as to justify interference by this court. I

j would add that the total of the figures at which I have arrived is, in my judgment, not out of line with the figures of other awards to which we have been referred.

To the extent that I have indicated, I would allow this appeal, and I would increase the total awarded by the learned judge (before giving credit for the payment made on account, and before the addition of interest) from £48,682 to £54,782.

BUCKLEY LJ. I have prepared some notes of a judgment of my own to be delivered on this occasion, but having heard the judgment given by Orr LJ, I so entirely

agree with it that I think it would be a waste of time for me to attempt to restate   *a*
the same point of view in my own words.   Accordingly, I agree.

SACHS LJ.   I too agree that the appeal should be allowed to the extent stated by
Orr LJ, and for the reasons which he has given, with which I am in full accord, I
only wish to add some observations, with which Buckley and Orr LJJ authorise me
to say they agree, on one of the contentions pressed on behalf of the defendant.   *b*
On his behalf, counsel laid special stress, with the aid of *Povey v W E & E Jackson (a
firm)*[1], on the global figure awarded by the learned trial judge.   He sought, inter alia,
to persuade us to add the sum assessed at £19,000 for general damages to those
allocated in the judgment to attendance, and then to compare the total figure with
other combined figures in a number of cases which he cited to us.   That, however,
was an exercise the usefulness of which is obviously limited.   For instance, as counsel   *c*
very fairly conceded, one must bear in mind that reasonable expenditure on nursing
attendance must vary largely in different cases and if for one reason such expenditure
is above the average in a particular case, then acceptance of the defendant's contention could result in the award for general damages being whittled away to an unduly
small sum.   In the instant case, moreover, as has already been indicated by Orr LJ,
the £19,000 damages is at the bottom of today's bracket for similar cases, although   *d*
a couple of years ago it might merely have been in the lower half of such a bracket.
To reduce that £19,000 indirectly by failing to give this particular plaintiff an
appropriate award for attendance would definitely be wrong.
    As regards *Povey v W E & E Jackson*[1] (decided in March 1970), it is to be observed that
week in and week out this court has that case cited to it by respondents seeking to
uphold a quantum of damage judgment when the appellants have shown one element   *e*
to be definitely too low;   it is so cited, moreover, irrespective of whether a cross-
notice has been given impugning any other element in the global figure.   It is thus as
well to say that, whatever may have been the differing judicial views up to a few
years ago and, indeed, up to 1970, as to whether a judge should simply award a global
sum, or whether he should state in his judgment what are the main components of
that figure, the modern practice, since *Jefford v Gee*[2] (also decided in March 1970), is to   *f*
adopt the second course.   It is true that that adoption has to a considerable extent come
into being because of the differing rates of interest applicable to differing heads of
damage under the *Jefford v Gee*[2] decision.   On the other hand, it is also in part due to
the general adoption of that considerable body of judicial opinion which held the effect
that plaintiff and defendant alike are entitled to know what is the sum assessed for
each relevant head of damage and thus to be able on appeal to challenge any error   *g*
in the assessments.   In my judgment, this court should be slow to emasculate that
right of litigants.
    The *Povey* case[1] was one in which the court considered that of the two sums which
made up the total global figure one was appealably too low and the other appealably
too high—and by 'appealably' I mean, of course, that, as stated in the judgments,
each if it stood alone would have called for interference of the Court of Appeal.   *h*
It was also a case in which a notice of cross-appeal had been given.   That case should
not be cited without reference to these facts or to the fact that it was decided before
the effects of *Jefford v Gee*[2] came to be fully appreciated and incorporated into modern
practice.
    It is of course always open to a respondent to do something which was not done
here;   that is, to give a cross-notice that even if one head as awarded by the judge is   *j*
held to be demonstrably too low, some other head is demonstrably too high, and thus
to seek to produce what is sometimes called a swings and roundabouts position.   In

---

1   [1970] 2 All ER 495, [1970] 1 WLR 969
2   [1970] 1 All ER 1202, [1970] 2 QB 130

a other circumstances it seems to me that a court should normally be slow to deal with an appeal on such a basis.

Appeal allowed.   Total award of damages increased from £48,682 to £54,782.

Solicitors: *Bolton & Lowe* (for the first plaintiff); *Badham, Comins & Main* (for the
b first defendant).

F A Amies Esq Barrister.

R v Governor of Pentonville Prison, ex parte
c Tzu-Tsai Cheng

QUEEN'S BENCH DIVISION
LORD WIDGERY CJ, JAMES LJ AND EVELEIGH J
24th JANUARY 1973

d

*Extradition – Political offence – Offence of political character only as between offender and
state other than requesting state – Offence committed in United States – Offence committed
in course of dispute between governing regime of Taiwan and movement dedicated to its
overthrow – Offence committed in furtherance of purposes of movement – United States
requesting extradition of offender – Whether offence 'one of a political character' – Extradition*
e *Act 1870, s 3.*

The applicant was a member of a Formosan organisation in the United States of
America, which was dedicated to the overthrow of the existing regime in Taiwan.
The organisation planned a demonstration in the State of New York against the
visit of a prominent member of the regime.   The applicant was present when, in
f the course of the demonstration, a shot was fired.   The applicant was charged with,
and convicted of, the attempted murder of the Taiwanese visitor, contrary to the
New York State Penal Law.   He was granted bail pending sentence.   While on bail,
he fled to Sweden.   Sweden acceded to a request for his extradition and he was in
the process of being returned by air to the United States when he fell ill.   He was
landed at London airport and taken to a prison hospital where he was detained
g pursuant to the Aliens Order 1953[a].   A request was made by the United States for
his extradition.   He was brought before the chief metropolitan magistrate at Bow
Street, who ordered him to be detained in prison pending his extradition.   The
applicant applied for a writ of habeas corpus, contending that the offence in respect
of which his extradition was sought was 'one of a political character' within the
meaning of s 3[b] of the Extradition Act 1870.

h
Held – The application would be refused for (i) on the true construction of s 3 the
words 'offence . . . of a political character' referred only to an offence of a political
character as between the applicant and the state requesting his extradition, and did
not extend to an offence of a political character between him and any other state;
and (ii) on the evidence the applicant and the United States were not at odds on an
j issue connected with the political control or government of the United States (see
p 938 h to p 939 b and f g, post).
   Dictum of Viscount Radcliffe in *Schtraks v Government of Israel* [1962] 3 All ER at
540 applied.

----

a SI 1953 No 1671, as amended
b Section 3, so far as material, is set out at p 937 j to p 938 b, post

Notes

For restrictions under the Extradition Act 1870 on surrender of criminals, see 16 Halsbury's Laws (3rd Edn) 578, para 1198, and for cases on the subject, see 24 Digest (Repl) 993, 994, 36-38.

For the Extradition Act 1870, s 3, see 13 Halsbury's Statutes (3rd Edn) 252.

Cases referred to in judgment

Castioni, Re [1891] 1 QB 149, [1886-90] All ER Rep 640, 60 LJMC 22, 64 LT 344, 55 JP 328, 17 Cox CC 225, DC, 24 Digest (Repl) 993, 36.

Kolczynski, Re [1955] 1 All ER 31, sub nom *R v Brixton Prison Governor, ex parte Kolczynski* [1955] 1 QB 540, [1955] 2 WLR 116, 119 JP 68, DC, 24 Digest (Repl) 993, 37.

Meunier, Re [1894] 2 QB 415, 63 LJMC 198, 71 LT 403, 18 Cox CC 15, DC, 24 Digest (Repl) 994, 38.

Schtraks v Government of Israel [1962] 3 All ER 529, [1962] 3 WLR 1013, sub nom *R v Governor of Brixton Prison, ex parte Schtraks* [1964] AC 556, HL, Digest (Cont Vol A) 575, 4a.

Motion for writ of habeas corpus

This was an application by way of motion on behalf of Tzu-Tsai Cheng, who was detained in HM Prison Pentonville, for a writ of habeas corpus directed to the Governor of Pentonville Prison to bring the applicant before the Divisional Court of the Queen's Bench Division and quash a warrant of committal issued by the chief metropolitan magistrate (Sir Frank Milton) on 30th November 1972 at Bow Street Magistrates' Court, pending his return to the United States of America pursuant to the Extradition Act 1870. His extradition had been requested by the United States. He was a member of the organisation known as the World United Formosans for Independence and he had been tried in the Supreme Court of New York in May 1971 on the charge of the attempted murder of Chiang Ching-Kuo and convicted. The facts are set out in the judgment of James LJ.

Brian Capstick for the applicant.
Richard Du Cann for the respondent, the Governor of Pentonville Prison.

JAMES LJ delivered the first judgment at the request of Lord Widgery CJ. In these proceedings counsel moves, on behalf of Tzu-Tsai Cheng, the applicant, who is now detained in Her Majesty's Prison, Pentonville, for a writ of habeas corpus. The applicant is detained pursuant to the order of the chief metropolitan magistrate dated 30th November 1972 and is awaiting delivery to the United States of America.

The matter in respect of which the order was made is that on 17th May 1971, in the county of New York, the applicant was convicted of the offence of attempted murder (contrary to the New York State Penal Law). The applicant stood indicted with his brother-in-law, one Peter Huang, who pleaded guilty to that offence. On the conviction of the applicant, he was allowed bail pending appearance on the appointed day of 6th July for sentence. He failed to appear in answer to his bail of some $90,000, and fled the country, eventually arriving in Sweden. In the summer of 1972 a request was made to Sweden for his extradition to the United States; that was acceded to. In the course of the journey he fell ill and was landed at London airport on 4th September 1972. He was taken to a medical reception centre, and then to a prison hospital, and was detained pursuant to the Aliens Order 1953[1]. He was here without any authority, and eventually after several remands on requests from the United States for his extradition, a hearing took place at Bow Street on 23rd and 24th November; the magistrate gave his decision on 30th November.

The point that is in issue in these proceedings is a narrow one indeed. Counsel for the applicant formulated it in this way: whether an offence committed within the

---

1   SI 1953 No 1671, as amended

a   jurisdiction of the state requesting extradition can amount to an offence of a political character where (1) the offence was committed in the course of a dispute between the governing party of another state, not the requesting state, on the one hand, and a movement dedicated to its overthrow; and (2) that the offence was committed directly to further the purposes of that movement and for no other purpose, or for any other motive.

b   The facts of the offence of which the applicant was convicted in New York can be stated quite shortly. On 24th April 1970 the Vice-President of China, Chiang Ching-Kuo (the son of General Chiang Kai Shek), was visiting the State of New York and was to arrive at a hotel at about noon. It appears from the evidence that his intending visit was known to an organisation of Formosans calling themselves the World United Formosans for Independence. There had been discussions within the executive council of that organisation in the United States as to what should be *c*   done in relation to demonstration and protest against the visit of that person, who was a person holding high office in the regime in Taiwan to which they objected. In the course of those discussions, it was advocated that an attempt be made to assassinate the visitor. The discussion having taken place, the executive committee decided against any attempt to assassinate, on the basis that the time and place was not right. *d*   On 24th April a demonstration took place outside the hotel where Chiang Ching Kuo was visiting, and in the course of that demonstration Peter Huang drew a pistol; he was overpowered. In the course of overpowering him a shot was fired; no one was injured. At the same time the applicant was observed to be conducting a diversionary campaign, shouting and waving papers, at the far end of the crowd who were demonstrating, and he was also overpowered and arrested. The pistol *e*   that was drawn on that occasion was one that had been provided by another member of the organisation at the request and instigation of the applicant, who had shown it to Peter Huang and shown him how to operate it. The applicant, as I have indicated, pleaded not guilty; he was in fact convicted and the matter now comes before this court by way of an application for habeas corpus.

  The defence put forward by the applicant to the request of the respondent for his *f*   delivery up is that his offence was one of a political character within the meaning of s 3 of the Extradition Act 1870. It is convenient to refer first to the opening words of s 2 of that Act, which are:

    'Where an arrangement has been made with any foreign state with respect to the surrender to such state of any fugitive criminals, Her Majesty may, by Order in Council, direct that this Act shall apply in the case of such foreign *g*   state.'

  There is a treaty between this country and the United States of America; it is a treaty entitled United States of America (Extradition) Order in Council 1935[1], and it is not without interest to observe that in recitals of that treaty it is said that—

    'His Majesty the King of Great Britain . . . And the President of the United *h*   States of America: Desiring to make more adequate provision for the reciprocal extradition of criminals . . .'

Section 3 of the 1870 Act reads:

    'The following restriction shall be observed with respect to the surrender of fugitive criminals:
j   '(1.) A fugitive criminal shall not be surrendered if the offence in respect of which his surrender is demanded is one of a political character, or if he prove to the satisfaction of the police magistrate or the court before whom he is brought on habeas corpus, or to the Secretary of State, that the requisition for his surrender

---

1 SR & O 1935 No 574

has in fact been made with a view to try or punish him for an offence of a political
character:　*a*

'(2.) A fugitive criminal shall not be surrendered to a foreign state unless provision
is made by the law of that state, or by arrangement, that the fugitive criminal
shall not, until he has been restored or had an opportunity of returning to Her
Majesty's dominions, be detained or tried in that foreign state for any offence
committed prior to his surrender other than the extradition crime proved by the
facts on which the surrender is grounded . . .'　*b*

Those provisions have come before the courts on a number of occasions for consideration. But we are told that this is the first occasion on which this precise point has
arisen, namely, whether the character of the place where the offence was committed
has any relevance to the political character of the offence. We have been helpfully
referred to *Re Castioni*[1] but there is nothing in that case at all which touches on the　*c*
fine point involved in this decision. Also we have been referred to the words of
Cave J in *Re Meunier*[2] where he expressed the view that there must be two or more
parties in the state for there to be a political character involved in the offence. In
Re Kolczynski[3], the Polish seaman's case, one gets away from the idea of two parties
competing for control of power within a state as a necessary background to an offence
of a political character, and one gets away from the concept referred to in earlier　*d*
cases of 'political disturbance'. In this case one has a central feature of individuals
seeking to escape from a regime with which they were strongly at odds as a basis
for the argument that their offence was one of a political character. But, as I see it,
one can go for assistance in the problem that faces the court immediately to *Schtraks
v Government of Israel*[4]. It is said by counsel for the applicant in his formulation of
the point that arises in this case that the questions there posed would be answered　*e*
in the affirmative if one reads the speech of Lord Reid, but would be answered in
the negative if one reads the speech of Viscount Radcliffe. It is suggested that there
is a conflict of view as expressed between Lord Reid and Lord Radcliffe in that case,
that case being one in which the three party situation did not arise, and therefore it
was not a case in which either of their Lordships was directing his mind particularly to the narrow problem in this case. But if one does look at the speeches in　*f*
that case, one finds the following passage in the speech of Lord Reid[5]:

'It appears to me that the provisions of s. 3 of the Act of 1870 are clearly intended to give effect to the principle that there should in this country be asylum
for political refugees, and I do not think that it is possible, or that the Act evinces
any intention, to define the circumstances in which an offence can properly be
held to be of a political character.'　*g*

In those words, Lord Reid as I see it is expressing very much the same views as were
expressed by Lord Radcliffe, but for my part I find the greatest help and guidance
from the following words of Lord Radcliffe[6]:

'In my opinion the idea that lies behind the phrase "offence of a political charac-　*h*
ter" is that the fugitive is at odds with the state that applies for his extradition
on some issue connected with the political control or government of the country.
The analogy of "political" in this context is with "political" in such phrases as
"political refugee", "political asylum" or "political prisoner". It does indicate,

j

1　[1891] 1 QB 149, [1886-90] All ER Rep 640
2　[1894] 2 QB 415 at 419
3　[1955] 1 All ER 31, [1955] 1 QB 540
4　[1962] 3 All ER 529, [1964] AC 556
5　[1962] 3 All ER at 535, [1964] AC at 584
6　[1962] 3 All ER at 540, [1964] AC at 591

a

I think, that the requesting state is after him for reasons other than the enforcement of the criminal law in its ordinary, what I may call its common or international, aspect.'

Counsel for the respondent submits, and for my part I think rightly submits, that looking at the speech of Lord Hodson in particular, one gets again impliedly, if not expressly, an expression of the view that one looks to the requesting state in order to

b

determine whether this is an offence of a political character or not, and it is not concerned with political character in relation to any other state than the requesting state. Applying that reasoning to the facts of this case, one finds that it is not really contended that the applicant was at odds with the state of the United States of America or that the United States of America was after him for any offence other than an offence against its ordinary criminal law. In my view the ambit of the

c

Extradition Act 1870 is limited, in respect of s 3, to offences of a political character as between the applicant and the requesting state, that is all. It is not a case of having to add words to the section in order to obtain that meaning.

Counsel for the respondent submits, and again for my part I consider rightly submits, that the meaning is clearly there already in the words, and one is not grafting on any limitation. In my judgment the applicant here fails, and his application should

d

be dismissed.

EVELEIGH J. I agree. I will only add that to limit the section to the political affairs of the requesting state is wholly consistent with the object of s 3 (1), as I see it, that is (a) political asylum; (b) to avoid this country becoming involved in another country's political affairs, or both. Insofar as political asylum is concerned, this

e

involves protection from maltreatment of the offender motivated by political considerations. There is no possible ground for thinking such protection is called for here. Insofar as political involvement is concerned, there is no possible ground for thinking that American political affairs are affected, and if it is to be said that the affairs of Taiwan are concerned, then in my view the answer to that is that no involve-

f

ment can arise when the court's decision is expressly on the basis that the politics of Taiwan are irrelevant.

LORD WIDGERY CJ. I agree with both judgments and have nothing to add.

Application for habeas corpus refused.   Leave to appeal granted.

g

Solicitors: *B M Birnberg & Co* (for the applicant); *Director of Public Prosecutions.*

N P Metcalfe Esq Barrister.

Director of Public Prosecutions v Doot and others

HOUSE OF LORDS

LORD WILBERFORCE, VISCOUNT DILHORNE, LORD PEARSON, LORD KILBRANDON AND LORD SALMON

4th, 5th, 6th DECEMBER 1972, 21st MARCH 1973

Criminal law – Jurisdiction – Conspiracy – Agreement made by parties abroad – Agreement to perform acts in England – Acts unlawful under English law – Acts performed in England in pursuance of agreement – Whether English court having jurisdiction to try charge of conspiracy.

The five respondents, all American citizens, were parties to an agreement made either in Belgium or Morocco to import cannabis resin into England with the object of re-exporting it from there to the United States. No part of the agreement was made in England. By s 2[a] of the Dangerous Drugs Act 1965 it was unlawful to import cannabis resin into the United Kingdom without a licence. The respondents had no licence. They concealed the cannabis resin in three separate vans which were then shipped to England. The cannabis was discovered by customs officers in one of the vans when it arrived at Southampton; the other vans were subsequently traced and the cannabis found in them. The respondents were convicted, inter alia, of conspiracy to import dangerous drugs, the particulars of the offence alleging that between certain dates 'in Hampshire and elsewhere' they had conspired together 'fraudulently to evade the prohibition imposed by the Dangerous Drugs Act, 1965, on the importation of a dangerous drug, namely cannabis resin, into the United Kingdom'. On appeal against conviction on the conspiracy count the Court of Appeal[b] quashed the conviction holding that the English courts had no jurisdiction to try the offence charged since the essence of the offence was the agreement between the respondents to do the unlawful act, the offence was complete when the agreement had been made, and the agreement had been made abroad. The Crown appealed.

Held – The appeal would be allowed and the conviction restored. An agreement made outside the jurisdiction of the English courts to commit an unlawful act within the jurisdiction was a conspiracy which could be tried in England if the agreement was subsequently performed, wholly or in part, in England. Although the crime of conspiracy was complete once the agreement had been made, nevertheless, the con-spiratorial agreement remained in being until terminated by completion of its per-formance or by abandonment; accordingly where acts were committed in England in performance of the agreement that would suffice to show the existence of a con-spiracy within the jurisdiction triable by the English courts. It followed that the crime of conspiracy had been committed by the respondents in England (see p 942 g, p 943 j, p 947 f and j to p 948 b, p 949 a e and f, p 951 c to h, p 954 a and p 958 c to e, post). In any event (per Lord Salmon), having regard to the special nature of the offence, a conspiracy to commit a crime in England was an offence against the common law even when entered into abroad, at least when acts in furtherance of the conspiracy were done in England; a conspiracy was equally a threat to the Queen's peace whether hatched in England or abroad (see p 956 c and f to h and p 957 j to p 958 a, post).

R v Brisac (1803) 4 East 164 applied.

Decision of the Court of Appeal, Criminal Division, sub nom *R v Doot* [1972] 2 All ER 1046 reversed.

---

a Section 2 is set out at p 954 c, post
b [1972] 2 All ER 1046

Notes

a For the limits of criminal jurisdiction, see 10 Halsbury's Laws (3rd Edn) 316-319, paras 577-581, and for cases on the subject, see 14 Digest (Repl) 145-149, 1074-1123.

For the meaning of conspiracy, see 10 Halsbury's Laws (3rd Edn) 310, 311, para 569, and for cases on the subject, see 14 Digest (Repl) 121-126, 851-877.

Cases referred to in opinions

b *Board of Trade v Owen* [1957] 1 All ER 411, [1957] AC 602, [1957] 2 WLR 351, 121 JP 177, 41 Cr App Rep 11, HL, Digest (Cont Vol A) 341, 1100a.

Ford v United States (1927) 273 US 593.

Hyde and Schneider v United States (1912) 225 US 347.

Macleod v Attorney-General for New South Wales [1891] AC 455, 60 LJPC 55, 65 LT 321, 17 Cox CC 341, PC, 14 Digest (Repl) 145, 1075.

c *Mulcahy v R* (1868) LR 3 HL 306, HL, 14 Digest (Repl) 123, 856.

People, The v Mather (1830) 4 Wend 230.

Poulterers' Case (1610) 9 Co Rep 55b, 77 ER 813, sub nom *Stone v Walter* Moore KB 813, 14 Digest (Repl) 124, 861.

R v Aspinall (1876) 2 QBD 48, 46 LJMC 145, 36 LT 297, 42 JP 52, 13 Cox CC 563, CA, 14 Digest (Repl) 121, 853.

d *R v Best* (1705) 1 Salk 174, 2 Ld Raym 1167, Holt KB 151, 6 Mod Rep 137, 91 ER 160, 14 Digest (Repl) 126, 873.

R v Bowes (30th May 1787) unreported, cited in 4 East 171, 102 ER 795, 6 Term Rep 527, 14 Digest (Repl) 161, 1248.

R v Brisac (1803) 4 East 164, 102 ER 792, 14 Digest (Repl) 149, 1122.

R v Burdett (1820) 3 B & Ald 717, 106 ER 823; *subsequent proceedings* (1820) 4 B & *e* Ald 95, [1814-23] All ER Rep 80, 1 State Tr NS 1, 106 ER 873, 14 Digest (Repl) 156, 1188.

R v Hardy (1794) 24 State Tr 199, 14 Digest (Repl) 135, 987.

R v Meany (1867) 10 Cox CC 506, 15 Digest (Repl) 775, *4861.

R v Murphy (1837) 8 C & P 297, 173 ER 502, 14 Digest (Repl) 127, 890.

R v Stone (1796) 6 Term Rep 527, 25 State Tr 1155, 101 ER 684, 14 Digest (Repl) 135, 986.

Treacy v Director of Public Prosecutions [1971] 1 All ER 110, [1971] AC 537, [1971] 2 *f* WLR 112, 135 JP 112, 55 Cr App Rep 113, HL.

Appeal

On 8th December 1971 at Winchester Assizes before Lawson J and a jury the respondent Jeffrey Richard Loving pleaded guilty on count 2 of an indictment to importing prohibited drugs, the respondents James Wesley Watts and Michael Augustus Fay pleaded guilty to a similar offence (count 3), and on 13th December 1971 the respon- *g* dent Robert Leroy Doot pleaded guilty to a similar offence (count 4). On the direction of Lawson J, the jury returned verdicts of guilty on those counts. On 14th December 1971 the respondents Doot, Loving, Watts and Fay pleaded guilty (after Lawson J had ruled that the court had jurisdiction to try the count) to count 1 of the indictment, which charged conspiracy to import dangerous drugs, and the jury returned ver- *h* dicts of guilty. On 15th December 1971 the respondent Thomas Shanahan was found guilty of conspiracy to import dangerous drugs on count 1 and of importing prohibited drugs on count 4. On 15th December 1971 the respondents were sentenced as follows: Doot to 30 months' imprisonment on count 1, and three months' imprisonment consecutive on count 4 (33 months in all); Loving to 12 months' imprisonment on count 1 and nine months' imprisonment concurrent on count 2; Watts to 18 months' imprisonment on count 1 and to nine months' imprisonment concurrent on count 3; *j* Fay to be fined £250 on count 1 and £50 on count 3 (£300 in all, or three months' imprisonment in default); and Shanahan to two years' imprisonment on count 1 and to three months' imprisonment consecutive on count 4 (27 months in all). All the respondents (as United States citizens) were recommended for deportation. In addition the respondents Doot and Loving were respectively ordered to pay £300 and £250 towards their legal aid costs. The respondent Fay paid his fine and was released

on bail on 20th December 1971 with a condition that he would return to the USA on *a*
22nd December 1971.

The respondents appealed against conviction on count 1 of the indictment pursuant
to a certificate of Lawson J under s 1 (2) of the Criminal Appeal Act 1968: 'Whether,
upon the facts proved by the prosecution, there was any offence of conspiracy within
the jurisdiction of the court of trial'. On 5th May 1972 the Court of Appeal, Criminal
Division[1] (Stephenson LJ, Cusack and Forbes JJ) allowed the appeals and quashed *b*
the conviction in each case. The Director of Public Prosecutions appealed against
that decision with the leave of the Court of Appeal, the court having certified that a
point of law of general public importance was involved. The facts are set out in the
opinion of Viscount Dilhorne.

Sir Joseph Molony QC and *Martin Tucker* for the Crown.
I S Hill QC and *I A Kennedy* for the respondents.   *c*

Their Lordships took time for consideration.

21st March. The following opinions were delivered.

LORD WILBERFORCE. My Lords, the question of law which has been certified, *d*
under s 33 (2) of the Criminal Appeal Act 1968, as fit for consideration by this House
is as follows:

> 'Whether an agreement made outside the jurisdiction of the English Courts to
> import a dangerous drug into England and carried out by importing it into
> England is a conspiracy which can be tried in England.'

The question so stated is precise, and necessarily so. For it was on the basis of a ruling *e*
by the learned judge who tried the case, answering this question in the affirmative,
that four of the respondents pleaded guilty to, and the fifth was convicted on, count 1
of the indictment which embodied the conspiracy charge. It was equally this question
which the Court of Appeal (Criminal Division)[1] answered in the negative, and consequently quashed the convictions on count 1. This House is not called on, or entitled,
to consider what the position would have been had a different view of the evidence, *f*
or admitted facts, been presented at the trial. We must deal with the question—the
only question before us—as it is stated, with one addition inherent, though not
expressed, namely, that to import a dangerous drug is a statutory offence under
English law (Dangerous Drugs Act 1965, s 2, Customs and Excise Act 1952, ss 45 and
304).

I have had the benefit of reading in advance the opinion of my noble and learned *g*
friend, Lord Pearson. I agree with it, and with his examination of the authorities
which it contains. I desire only to add some brief observations.

The basis of the Court of Appeal's judgment[1], the starting point of legal discussion
in this case, is the proposition that all crime is territorial. In following this principle
derived from the Digest and modernised by Huber, common law jurisdictions have
been consistent—more so, I believe, than systems of the civil law. It has been applied *h*
both as a principle for the construction of statutes (eg *Macleod v Attorney-General
for New South Wales*[2]) and as a principle determining the reach of the common law.
It has also a reflection in disputes between states, where international law is concerned.
The present case involves international elements—the accused are aliens and the
conspiracy was initiated abroad—but there can be no question here of any breach
of any rules of international law if they are prosecuted in this country. Under the *j*
objective territorial principle (I use the terminology of the Harvard Research in
International Law) or the principle of universality (for the prevention of the trade in

---

1   [1972] 2 All ER 1046, [1972] 3 WLR 33
2   [1891] AC 455

a narcotics falls within this description) or both, the courts of this country have a clear right, if not a duty, to prosecute in accordance with our municipal law. The position as it is under international law is not, however, determinative of the question whether, under our municipal law, the acts committed amount to a crime. That has to be decided on different principles. If conspiracy to import drugs were a statutory offence, the question whether foreign conspiracies were included would be decided on the

b terms of the statute. Since it is (if at all) a common law offence, this question must be decided on principle and authority.

In the search for a principle, the requirement of territoriality does not, in itself, provide an answer. To many simple situations, where all relevant elements occur in this country, or, conversely, occur abroad, it may do so. But there are many 'crimes' (I use the word without prejudice at this stage) the elements

c of which cannot be so simply located. They may originate in one country, be continued in another, produce effects in a third. Some constituent fact, the posting or receipt of a letter, the firing of a shot, the falsification of a document, may take place in one country, the other necessary elements in another. There is no mechanical answer, either through the Latin maxim or by quotation of Lord Halsbury LC's words in *Macleod's* case[1] or otherwise, which can solve these. The present is such a case.

d In my opinion, the key to a decision for or against the offence charged, can be found in an answer to the question why the common law treats certain actions as crimes. And one answer must certainly be because the actions in question are a threat to the Queen's peace, or as we would now perhaps say, to society. Judged by this test, there is every reason for, and none that I can see against, the prosecution. Conspiracies are intended to be carried into effect; and one reason why, in addition to individual

e prosecution of each participant, conspiracy charges are brought, is because criminal action organised, and executed, in concert, is more dangerous than an individual breach of the law. Why, then, refrain from prosecution, where the relevant concert was, initially, formed outside the United Kingdom?

Often in conspiracy cases the implementing action is itself the only evidence of the conspiracy—this is the doctrine of overt acts. Could it be said, with any plausibility,

f that if the conclusion or a possible conclusion to be drawn from overt acts in England was that there was a conspiracy, entered into abroad, a charge of conspiracy would not lie? Surely not; yet, if it could, what difference should it make if the conspiracy is directly proved or is admitted to have been made abroad? The truth is that, in the normal case of a conspiracy carried out, or partly carried out, in this country, the location of the formation of the agreement is irrelevant; the attack on the laws of

g this country is identical wherever the conspirators happened to meet; the 'conspiracy' is a complex, formed indeed, but not severally completed, at the first meeting of the plotters.

A legal principle which would enable concerting law breakers to escape a conspiracy charge by crossing the Channel before making their agreement or to bring forward arguments, which we know can be subtle enough, as to the location of agree-

h ments or, conversely, which would encourage the prosecution into allegation or fiction of a renewed agreement in this country, all this with no compensating merit, is not one which I could endorse.

In addition to these considerations, there is substantial authority, both English and American, that jurisdiction exists to try in our courts conspiracies entered into abroad but implemented here. My noble and learned friend, Lord Pearson, has quoted the

j English and some of the United States cases—there are others there which could be cited. I adopt and do not repeat his analysis. It establishes, in my opinion, that under existing principles of common law, supported by authority, the offence charged was triable in England.

I would add that the further question whether a conspiracy formed abroad to do

---

1 [1891] AC at 458

an illegal act in England, but not actually implemented here, could be tried in the courts of this country, is not before us and I express no opinion on it.

The appeal must be allowed, the question submitted answered in the affirmative and the convictions on count 1 restored. I do not feel able or entitled to comment on the sentences imposed as to which we were not supplied with argument or background information. They were, of course, not the subject of appeal.

VISCOUNT DILHORNE. My Lords, the five respondents, all Americans, were, according to the statement made by four of them, all parties to a conspiracy to import cannabis resin into the United States of America. In pursuance of that conspiracy Volkswagen vans were bought in Europe, taken to Belgium and there fitted out with beds in which hashish could be concealed. The vans were then driven to Morocco by different routes. There hashish was bought and loaded into two of the vans and concealed in the beds. Two vans, one driven by the respondent Loving and the other by the respondents Watts and Fay, were shipped on the 'Eagle' to Southampton. A third van in the charge of the respondents Doot and Shanahan was driven to Ostend and brought to Dover, the intention being that the vans carrying the cannabis resin should be driven to Liverpool and shipped across the Atlantic.

Section 2 of the Dangerous Drugs Act 1965 makes it unlawful to import into this country, inter alia, cannabis resin, and s 3 of that Act makes it illegal to export it, in each case without a licence. So the conspiracy to import cannabis resin into the United States through the United Kingdom comprehended a conspiracy to import into and also a conspiracy to export from the United Kingdom.

On 5th August 1971 the two vans shipped on the 'Eagle' arrived at Southampton. Watts and Fay got their van through customs and drove to Liverpool. On 6th August customs officers at Southampton found 64 kilogrammes of cannabis resin in the bed in the van driven by Loving. Watts's and Fay's van was traced to Liverpool from where it was to be shipped on 10th August and in the bed in it were found 65 kilogrammes of cannabis resin. Doot and Shanahan arrived with their van at Dover on 13th August. They were seen in London and when their van was examined it was found that there was no cannabis resin in the bed but 138 grammes of cannabis resin and 247 grammes of cannabis were found in a polythene bag, a tobacco pouch and a carrier bag in the van.

The five respondents were charged at Winchester Assizes on an indictment which contained four counts. The first charged them with conspiracy to import dangerous drugs, the particulars of offence alleging that between 1st January and 15th August 1971, 'in Hampshire and elsewhere' they had conspired together 'fraudulently to evade the prohibition imposed by the Dangerous Drugs Act, 1965, on the importation of a dangerous drug, namely cannabis resin, into the United Kingdom'. The second count charged Loving with importing prohibited goods, contrary to s 304 of the Customs and Excise Act 1952, the particulars of offence alleging that in relation to 64 kilogrammes of cannabis resin he was knowingly concerned in a fraudulent evasion of the prohibition on importation imposed by the Dangerous Drugs Act 1965. The third count charged Watts and Fay with a similar offence in relation to 65 kilogrammes of cannabis resin and the fourth count charged Doot and Shanahan with a similar offence in relation to 138 grammes of cannabis resin and 247 grammes of cannabis.

Section 304 of the Customs and Excise Act 1952 is in the following terms:

'Without prejudice to any other provision of this Act, if any person—(a) knowingly and with intent . . . to evade any prohibition or restriction for the time being in force under or by virtue of any enactment with respect thereto, acquires possession of, or is in any way concerned in carrying, removing, depositing, harbouring, keeping or concealing or in any manner dealing with any goods which have been unlawfully removed from a warehouse or Queen's warehouse . . . or with respect to the importation or exportation of which any prohibition *a* or restriction is for the time being in force as aforesaid . . . he may be detained and, save where, in the case of an offence in connection with a prohibition or restriction, a penalty is expressly provided for that offence by the enactment or other instrument imposing the prohibition or restriction, shall be liable to a penalty of three times the value of the goods . . . or to imprisonment for a term not exceeding two years[1], or to both.'

b In the first count the statement of offence alleges a conspiracy to import dangerous drugs, which can be read as alleging a conspiracy to commit an offence against s 2 of the Dangerous Drugs Act 1965. The language of the particulars of offence to this count is culled from s 304 of the Customs and Excise Act 1952 and, it could be argued, alleges a different conspiracy, one to commit the offence created by that section. Rule 4 (4) of Sch 1 to the Indictments Act 1915 provides that: 'After the statement of the *c* offence, particulars of such offence shall be set out in ordinary language . . .' So the particulars given should have been of the conspiracy to import and not a conspiracy fraudulently to evade the prohibition imposed by the Dangerous Drugs Act 1965. They should not allege the commission of any other offence than that stated in the statement of offence. No point was taken by the respondents as to this and the Court of Appeal[2], as did Lawson J, treated this count as alleging a conspiracy to import danger-*d* ous drugs into England in breach of the Dangerous Drugs Act 1965. The inclusion of words from s 304 in this count and the preferment in the other count of charges of offences against s 304 and not charges under s 45 of the Customs and Excise Act 1952 were apparently made in the belief that their inclusion would facilitate the task of the prosecution.

To count 1 all the respondents pleaded not guilty. It was submitted that the offence *e* of conspiracy alleged had not been committed within the jurisdiction of the courts of this country. Lawson J rejected this submission made on behalf of the first four respondents, saying that he was satisfied that there was an agreement between the accused—

'to import dangerous drugs into England in breach of the Dangerous Drugs Act, and that the English element in that agreement consisted in conduct on the part *f* of one or more of these accused who were party to the agreement, of conduct in England which was conduct in furtherance or implementation of the agreement to import illegally into England.'

All the respondents other than Shanahan then changed their pleas to count 1 to pleas of guilty on the basis that it was open to them on appeal to contend that the court *g* had no jurisdiction with regard to count 1. Shanahan, who pleaded not guilty to both charges against him, was found guilty on both, Lawson J directing the jury on court 1 in accordance with his ruling on the submission made on behalf of the other respondents. The others charged in counts 2, 3, and 4 pleaded guilty. Doot who was regarded by Lawson J as 'the chief man in this conspiracy' was sentenced to 30 months imprisonment on count 1 and three months consecutive on count 4. Loving, the *h* driver of one of the two vans, each containing £30,000 worth of cannabis resin received a sentence of 12 months' imprisonment on count 1 and nine months concurrent on count 2. Watts, one of the drivers of the second van containing cannabis resin, received a sentence of 18 months' imprisonment on count 1 and nine months concurrent on count 3. Fay, the other driver of that van, was fined £250 on count 1 and £50 on count 3. Shannahan was sentenced to two years' imprisonment on count *j* 1 and three months consecutive on count 4. All were recommended for deportation.

1 In relation to offences in connection with a prohibition or restriction imposed by ss 2, 7 or 10 of the Dangerous Drugs Act 1965, the words 'imprisonment for a term not exceeding ten years' were substituted for 'imprisonment for a term not exceeding two years' by s 7 of the Dangerous Drugs Act 1967
2 [1972] 2 All ER 1046, [1972] 3 WLR 33

No question arose in this appeal as to the propriety of the sentences imposed by the learned judge and I, therefore, do not think it right to comment on them. The determination of the proper sentence to impose is often a most difficult task and without going fully into the respondents' circumstances and antecedents which was not done on the hearing of this appeal, I would not think it right to criticise. But, I think I can, without impropriety, repeat what I have said before, that in my opinion it would be a very desirable change in the law if the Court of Appeal, Criminal Division, was given power on the hearing of an appeal, whether against conviction or sentence, to review the sentence passed at the trial and, if thought right, to increase it. Now they can only reduce it. Such a power would not only lead to greater uniformity in sentences but also might be a deterrent against frivolous appeals.

The Court of Appeal, Criminal Division[1], allowed the respondents' appeal, holding that there was no jurisdiction to try the conspiracy charged in count 1. Stephenson LJ, delivering the judgment of the court, after referring to Lawson J's ruling, said[2]:

'We think that this ruling assumes that conspiracy is a continuing offence and that this particular conspiracy was not completed as long as anything remained to be done in furtherance or implementation of it. But, in our judgment, the ruling ignores the peculiar nature of the offence of conspiracy and the distinction between two kinds of conspiratorial agreement to which we shall refer, and confuses the offence itself and its essential elements with overt acts in furtherance of it and with acts which are merely evidence of its existence. The essence of the offence is the agreement to do the unlawful act. The offence is completed when the agreement is made. It matters not that it is never carried out. Acts in performance of it go to prove the offence but are not constituent or essential parts of it. They may be substantive offences committed in England and so triable in England; but they do not make the agreement to commit them itself triable in England. The agreement does, of course, continue until ended and the conspiracy remains in existence and may be joined by others or be varied, or lose some of its participants, as long as it continues to exist. If the conspirators come within the jurisdiction while their agreement still exists and then do acts in furtherance of it there is much to be said for the English courts having jurisdiction to try them for the conspiracy, as the judge held. Perhaps that ought to be the law, but in our view, it is not the law and if it is to be the law Parliament or the House of Lords, not this court, must declare it to be so.'

The court certified that the following question involved a point of law of general public importance and granted leave to appeal to this House:

'Whether an agreement made outside the jurisdiction of the English Courts to import a dangerous drug into England and carried out by importing it into England is a conspiracy which can be tried in England.'

If the law be as the Court of Appeal[1] held it was, that law can only be changed by Parliament. This House in its judicial capacity cannot alter the law so as to bring offences not triable in the courts of this country within the jurisdiction. If an offence committed out of this country and not now triable in this country is to be made triable in this country that must be done by statute.

It has long been settled law that the agreement of two or more to do an unlawful act constitutes a conspiracy. It matters not, as Stephenson LJ said, that the agreement is never carried out. To establish the guilt of an accused all that is necessary is to prove that he was a party to such an agreement.

If it be the case that it is the country in which the agreement is made which is the country having jurisdiction to try the charge of conspiracy, it would not be easy in

---

1   [1972] 2 All ER 1046, [1972] 3 WLR 33
2   [1972] 2 All ER at 1051, [1972] 3 WLR at 37, 38

a this case to determine in which country the agreement was initially made. According to Doot's statement the plan to import hashish in Volkswagens was initially made between him and a man called Evans in the United States. Doot then flew to Canada and enlisted Watts. Next he approached Shanahan in New York, who later telephoned him when he was in Luxemburg. Fay later joined Doot and Watts in Frankfurt and from Frankfurt Doot telephoned to Loving in Miami and enlisted him. No part of the agreement to import the cannabis resin was made in England and if it be the *b* law that the offence of conspiracy is only triable in the country in which the agreement to do the unlawful act is made, this history of the sequence of events in this case indicates the difficulties which the prosecution may encounter.

A conspiracy is usually proved by proving acts on the part of the accused which lead to the inference that they were acting in concert in pursuance of an agreement to do an unlawful act. Here the acts of the respondents in bringing into this country *c* three Volkswagen vans fitted with beds constructed for the concealment of hashish and with two of the vans containing substantial quantities of it gave rise to a very strong inference that they were acting in concert and in pursuance of an agreement which involved the importation of cannabis resin into this country.

In *R v Aspinall*[1] Brett JA said:

d   'In order to apply these rules to the present case it is necessary next to determine what are the essential facts to be alleged in order to support a charge of conspiracy. Now, first, the crime of conspiracy is completely committed, if it is committed at all, the moment two or more have agreed that they will do, at once or at some future time, certain things. It is not necessary in order to complete the offence that any one thing should be done beyond the agreement. The conspirators *e* may repent and stop, or may have no opportunity, or may be prevented, or may fail. Nevertheless the crime is complete; it was completed when they agreed.'

I see no reason to criticise this passage unless it be interpreted to mean that the crime, though completed by the agreement, ends when the agreement is made. When *f* there is agreement between two or more to commit an unlawful act all the ingredients of the offence are there and in that sense the crime is complete. But a conspiracy does not end with the making of the agreement. It will continue so long as there are two or more parties to it intending to carry out the design. It would be highly unreal to say that the conspiracy to carry out the gunpowder plot was completed when the conspirators met and agreed to the plot at Catesby.

g In *R v Murphy*[2] Coleridge J said in the course of his direction to the jury:

     'It is not necessary that it should be proved that these defendants met to concoct this scheme, nor is it necessary that they should have originated it. If a conspiracy be already formed, and a person joins it afterwards, he is equally guilty. You are to say whether, from the acts that have been proved, you are *h* satisfied that these defendants were acting in concert in this matter.'

This statement of Coleridge J has not been questioned and I take it to be well established that it is a correct statement of the law. If it is, it is not easy to reconcile it with the view expressed by the Court of Appeal[3], for the man who joins a conspiracy after it has been formed was not a party to the conspiracy when it was 'completed'. The *j* fact that a man who later joins a conspiracy may be convicted of it shows that although the offence is complete in one sense when the conspiracy is made, it is nevertheless a continuing offence.

---

1 (1876) 2 QBD 48 at 58, 59
2 (1837) 8 C & P 297 at 311
3 [1972] 2 All ER 1046, [1972] 3 WLR 33

If it is, as in my opinion it is, a continuing offence then the courts of England, in my view, have jurisdiction to try the offence if, and only if, the evidence suffices to show that the conspiracy whenever or wherever it was formed was in existence when the accused were in England. Here the acts of the respondents in England, to which I have referred, suffice to show that they were acting in concert in pursuance of an existing agreement to import cannabis, and that there was then within the jurisdiction a conspiracy to import cannabis resin to which they were parties.

In *R v Brisac*[1], where the captain and purser of a man-of-war were charged with conspiracy to cheat the Crown by the use of false vouchers, the planning and fabrication of the vouchers was done on the high seas. Brisac was found guilty at Middlesex and when he was brought up for judgment it was objected that as the conspiracy was committed on the high seas it was only triable under the Offences at Sea Act 1799[2]. It was contended that it made no difference that[3]—

'the ultimate object and completion of the conspiracy was to operate on shore, as all the acts of the defendants which constituted the offence of conspiracy were commited out of the jurisdiction of the common law.'

Grose J, delivering the opinion of the court, said[3]:

'. . . it would be to be recollected that conspiracy is a matter of inference, deduced from certain criminal acts of the parties accused, done in pursuance of an apparent criminal purpose in common between them, and which hardly ever are confined to one place; and that from analogy, there seems no reason why the crime of conspiracy . . . may not be tried wherever one distinct overt act of conspiracy is in fact committed, as well as the crime of high treason in compassing and imagining the King's death, or in conspiring to levy war.'

He then referred to the unreported case of *R v Bowes*[4]. There, he said[3]:

'. . . no proof of actual conspiracy embracing all the several conspirators was attempted to be given in Middlesex, where the trial took place, and where the individual actings of some of the conspirators were wholly confined to other counties than Middlesex: but still the conspiracy as against all having been proved from the community of criminal purpose, and by their joint co-operation in forwarding the objects of it, in different places and counties, the locality required for the purpose of trial was holden to be satisfied by overt acts done by some of them in prosecution of the conspiracy in the county where the trial was had.'

Grose J[5] went on to say that the delivery of the false vouchers and of the bills of exchange was in Middlesex and held that the act of delivery was the act of the defendants 'for the persons who innocently delivered the vouchers were mere instruments in their hands for that purpose'.

In Russell on Crime[6] this decision is cited and it is then stated:

'It would therefore seem that if there was a conspiracy on land abroad, a jury might try it in any place in England where an overt act in pursuance of it was done.'

Why, one may ask, if the offence of conspiracy is completed, when the agreement to do the unlawful act is made, should the conspiracy made abroad or on the high seas

---

1   (1803) 4 East 164
2   39 Geo 3, c 37
3   4 East at 171
4   30th May 1787
5   4 East at 172
6   12th Edn (1964), vol 1, p 613

a be triable at common law in any place where an overt act takes place? This, in my view, can only be on the basis that the overt act, coupled, it may be, with evidence of overt acts in other parts of England, shows that there was at the time of the overt act a conspiracy in England, no matter when or where it was formed.

In the United States of America it appears to be recognised that conspiracy may be a continuous offence for in *Ford v United States*[1] Taft CJ delivering the opinion of the b court said: 'The petitioners and fifty-five others were indicted in November, 1924, for carrying on a continuous conspiracy . . .' And[2]: 'The charge is unitary in relating to one continuous conspiracy . . .' And[3]: 'The conspiracy was continuously in operation . . .' And[4]:

> 'Generally the cases show that jurisdiction exists to try one who is a conspirator whenever the conspiracy is in whole or in part carried on in the country whose c laws are conspired against.'

In *R v Best*[5], a case which was very briefly reported, it is stated that 'The *venue* must be where the conspiracy was, not where the result of the conspiracy is put in execution'. I cannot reconcile this statement with the decision in *R v Brisac*[6] or with the observations of Grose J in relation to *R v Bowes*[7] and I do not think in the light of the decision d in *R v Brisac*[6] it is accurate to say that this is the first time this question has come before the courts of this country. Further I do not think that if this House relies on the decision in that case, it can be said that it is extending the application of the criminal law.

The conclusion to which I have come after consideration of these authorities and of many others to which the House was referred but to which I do not think it is necessary to refer is that though the offence of conspiracy is complete when the e agreement to do the unlawful act is made and it is not necessary for the prosecution to do more than prove the making of such an agreement, a conspiracy does not end with the making of the agreement. It continues so long as the parties to the agreement intend to carry it out. It may be joined by others, some may leave it. Proof of acts done by the accused in this country may suffice to prove there was at the time of those acts a conspiracy in existence in this country to which they were parties and f if that is proved, then the charge of conspiracy is within the jurisdiction of the English courts, even though the initial agreement was made outside the jurisdiction.

For the reasons I have stated, in my opinion this appeal should be allowed and the convictions of the respondents on count 1 restored.

LORD PEARSON. My Lords, at some place on land outside England—in Belgium g or Morocco—six American citizens agreed that they would secretly import cannabis from Morocco to England and transport it across England and over to Canada and into the United States. That was an agreement to break the law of England by illegal importation of dangerous drugs, and therefore it was, if and insofar as English law applied to it, a conspiracy. I will refer to the six American citizens who were parties to it as 'the conspirators'. The conspirators had Volkswagen vans fitted with h wooden sleeping beds containing secret compartments in which the cannabis could be hidden. The secret compartments of three of these vans were loaded with substantial quantities of cannabis—for instance, 64 kilogrammes in one and 65 kilogrammes in another. The loading was done in Morocco, and then the vans were taken by car ferry from Morocco to Southampton. The first of the three vans was taken by a conspirator named Evans. He was not detected and he succeeded in importing the

---

j 1   (1927) 273 US 593 at 601
2   273 US at 602
3   273 US at 620
4   273 US at 621, 622
5   (1705) 1 Salk 174
6   (1803) 4 East 164
7   (30th May 1787) unreported

cannabis and transporting it across and out of England. A second van, with its secret load of cannabis, was taken by another conspirator named Loving. He achieved the importation but afterwards the cannabis was found and he was arrested in England. Similarly the third van, with its secret load of cannabis, was taken by two other conspirators, named Watts and Fay, and they achieved the importation but were afterwards detected and arrested. The two remaining conspirators, Doot and Shanahan, also had a van but there was no cannabis loaded in its secret compartment, and they did not take the car ferry from Morocco to Southampton. They had in the van only a small quantity of cannabis, said by Doot to be for his own use, and they travelled from Ostend to Dover and drove the van to London.

The five conspirators who did not escape were prosecuted in England. In the first count of the indictment all five were charged with conspiracy to import dangerous drugs. In the second, third and fourth counts respectively Loving, Watts and Fay, and Doot and Shannahan were charged with importing prohibited goods, contrary to s 304 of the Customs and Excise Act 1952. Loving, Watts, Fay and Doot pleaded guilty to the counts which concerned them, but did so without prejudice to their contention that the English court had no jurisdiction to try the count of conspiracy. Shannahan pleaded not guilty and was tried and convicted on the count of conspiracy as well as on the fourth count.

After hearing argument on the question of jurisdiction the trial judge, Lawson J, gave his ruling. He said:

'My ruling is this: that I reject the submissions of the [respondents] that this court has no jurisdiction to try the offence charged in count 1 which is a conspiracy to import dangerous drugs in breach of the prohibition imposed by the Dangerous Drugs Act 1965 . . . The grounds, briefly, on which I so ruled are, first of all, that I am satisfied on the evidence adduced by the prosecution that there was an agreement between these accused and others (I will deal with the case of Shanahan separately in a moment) to import dangerous drugs into England in breach of the Dangerous Drugs Act, and that the English element in that agreement consisted in conduct on the part of one or more of these accused who were party to the agreement, of conduct in England which was conduct in furtherance or implementation of the agreement to import illegally into England. For those reasons, therefore, I hold that I have jurisdiction to try count 1.'

This ruling was reversed by the Court of Appeal, who said[1]:

'We think that this ruling assumes that conspiracy is a continuing offence and that this particular conspiracy was not completed as long as anything remained to be done in furtherance or implementation of it. But, in our judgment, the ruling ignores the peculiar nature of the offence of conspiracy and the distinction between two kinds of conspiratorial agreement to which we shall refer, and confuses the offence itself and its essential elements with overt acts in furtherance of it and with acts which are merely evidence of its existence. The essence of the offence is the agreement to do the unlawful act. The offence is completed when the agreement is made. It matters not that it is never carried out. Acts in performance of it go to prove the offence but are not constituent or essential parts of it. They may be substantive offences committed in England and so triable in England; but they do not make the agreement to commit them itself triable in England. The agreement does, of course, continue until ended and the conspiracy remains in existence and may be joined by others or be varied, or lose some of its participants, as long as it continues to exist. If the conspirators come within the jurisdiction while their agreement still exists and then do acts in furtherance of it there is much to be said for the English courts having jurisdiction to try them

---

1 [1972] 2 All ER 1046 at 1051, [1972] 3 WLR 33 at 37, 38

a   for the conspiracy, as the judge held. Perhaps that ought to be the law, but in our view, it is not the law and if it is to be the law Parliament or the House of Lords, not this court, must declare it to be so.'

The Court of Appeal[1] certified that a point of law of general importance was involved in their decision to quash the respondents' convictions on the first count, namely:

b   'Whether an agreement made outside the jurisdiction of the English Courts to import a dangerous drug into England and carried out by importing it into England is a conspiracy which can be tried in England.'

The Court of Appeal[1] held that the point appeared to be one which might be considered in your Lordships' House and they granted leave to appeal.

c   In my opinion, the ruling of the learned judge that he had jurisdiction to try the count of conspiracy was correct, and the Court of Appeal's reversal of his ruling was erroneous. With respect I am unable to agree with the Court of Appeal's view as to what the existing law is.

A conspiracy involves an agreement expressed or implied. A conspiratorial agreement is not a contract, not legally binding, because it is unlawful. But as an agreement

d   it has its three stages, namely (1) making or formation (2) performance or implementation (3) discharge or termination. When the conspiratorial agreement has been made, the offence of conspiracy is complete, it has been committed, and the conspirators can be prosecuted even though no performance has taken place: *R v Aspinall*[2] per Brett JA. But the fact that the offence of conspiracy is complete at that stage does not mean that the conspiratorial agreement is finished with. It is not dead. If it is being performed, it is very much alive. So long as the performance continues, it is

e   operating, it is being carried out by the conspirators, and it is governing or at any rate influencing their conduct. The conspiratorial agreement continues in operation and therefore in existence until it is discharged (terminated) by completion of its performance or by abandonment or frustration or however it may be.

On principle, apart from authority, I think (and it would seem the Court of Appeal

f   also thought) a conspiracy to commit in England an offence against English law ought to be triable in England if it has been wholly or partly performed in England. In such a case the conspiracy has been carried on in England with the consent and authority of all the conspirators. It is not necessary that they should all be present in England. One of them, acting on his own behalf and as agent for the others, has been performing their agreement, with their consent and authority, in England. In such a case the

g   conspiracy has been committed by all of them in England. Be it granted that 'All crime is local' and 'The jurisdiction over the crime belongs to the country where the crime is committed' (per Lord Halsbury LC in *Macleod v Attorney-General for New South Wales*[3]). The crime of conspiracy in the present case was committed in England, personally or through an agent or agents, by all the conspirators.

The balance of authority is in favour of the view that the English courts have juris-

h   diction in a case such as this. There is indeed an early authority which tends the other way. That is *R v Best*[4] where:

j   'It was agreed by the Court, 1st, That several people may lawfully meet and consult to prosecute a guilty person; otherwise if to charge one that is innocent, right or wrong, for that is indictable. That so it is here, that the conspiracy is the gist of the indictment, and that though nothing be done in prosecution of it, it is a complete and consummate offence of itself; and whether the conspiracy be to charge a temporal or ecclesiastical offence on an innocent person, it is the same

---

1   [1972] 2 All ER 1046, [1972] 3 WLR 33
2   (1876) 2 QBD 48 at 58, 59
3   [1891] AC 455 at 458
4   (1705) 1 Salk 174

thing . . . The *venue* must be where the conspiracy was, not where the result
of the conspiracy is put in execution: And confederacies are one of the articles
in the commission of oyer and terminer, to be inquired of.'

But the prevalent authorities are *R v Brisac*[1] and *R v Bowes*[2]. In *R v Brisac*[3] Grose
J delivering the opinion of the court said:

'If it were necessary on this occasion to consider how far every count in this
information has been established by the evidence adduced, so as to bring every
one of them within the jurisdiction of this Court, it would be to be recollected
that conspiracy is a matter of inference, deduced from certain criminal acts of the
parties accused, done in pursuance of an apparent criminal purpose in common
between them, and which hardly ever are confined to one place; and that from
analogy, there seems no reason why the crime of conspiracy, amounting only to
a misdemeanor, may not be tried wherever one distinct overt act of conspiracy
is in fact committed, as well as the crime of high treason in compassing and
imagining the King's death, or in conspiring to levy war. In *The King* v. *Bowes and
Others*[2] the trial proceeded upon this principle; where no proof of actual conspiracy embracing all the several conspirators was attempted to be given in
Middlesex, where the trial took place, and where the individual actings of some of
the conspirators were wholly confined to other counties than Middlesex: but still
the conspiracy as against all having been proved from the community of criminal
purpose, and by their joint co-operation in forwarding the objects of it, in different
places and counties, the locality required for the purpose of trial was holden to
be satisfied by overt acts done by some of them in prosecution of the conspiracy
in the county where the trial was had. But upon this occasion it is not necessary
to go at large into this point . . .'

He went on to say[4] in effect that both defendants had caused false vouchers to be
delivered in Middlesex through innocent agents, and on that ground they could be
held to have committed offences in Middlesex.   There seems to be no report of
R v Bowes[2] but there is a reference to it in *R v Stone*[5].   The Attorney-General in
argument said[6]:

'. . . as the overt act charged was a conspiracy of which proof was before the
Court, the act of each conspirator in the prosecution of such conspiracy was
evidence against all: that it had been so determined by Buller J. in the case of
The King v. *Bowes and Others*[2], 30th May, 1787, who were convicted for a conspiracy
to carry away Lady Strathmore; and that the same principle had been also settled
in *The King* v. *Hardy*[7], and *The King* v. *Tooke*[7], at the Old Bailey in 1794'.

The trial of Hardy and Tooke is referred to in East's Pleas of the Crown.
In *R v Burdett*[8] there was cited in argument a passage from Starkie's Treatise on
Criminal Pleading[9] referring to *R v Brisac*[1] and *R v Bowes*[2] and in the same case

1 (1803) 4 East 164
2 (30th May 1787) unreported
3 (1803) 4 East at 171
4 4 East at 172
5 (1796) 6 Term Rep 527
6 (1796) 6 Term Rep at 528
7 (1794) 24 State Tr 199
8 (1820) 3 B & Ald 717 at 736, 737
9 (1828), pp 27, 28

a   Abbott CJ[1] in his judgment cited the passage in the judgment of Grose J in *R v Brisac*[2]
    from 'there seems no reason ...' to '... where the trial was had'. In Starkie's Treatise
    on Criminal Pleading[3] it is said:

> 'An indictment for a conspiracy may be tried in any county, in which an overt
b   > act has been committed in pursuance of the original illegal combination and
    > design; so that when several conspired upon the high seas, to fabricate false
    > vouchers to defraud certain commissioners in Middlesex, and in consequence
    > those vouchers were delivered by innocent persons, their agents in Middlesex,
    > the court intimated an opinion, that the offence had been properly tried in
    > Middlesex, in analogy to the case of treason, which offence may be tried in any
    > county in which an overt act has been committed. So several defendants were
c   > holden to have been properly convicted upon an indictment for a conspiracy,
    > though no joint conspiracy had been proved in the county where they were tried,
    > but only overt acts done in consequence of a general conspiracy, evidenced
    > by various acts in other counties.'

    This paragraph was evidently based on *R v Brisac*[4] and *R v Bowes*[5].
       In *R v Meany*[6] in the Irish Court for Crown Cases Reserved there was a difference
d   of opinion, but the view of the majority was that a member of the Fenian brother-
    hood who had acted in pursuance of the conspiracy in America could be tried in
    Ireland for treason-felony under the Treason Felony Act 1848 because fellow-conspira-
    tors had committed in Ireland overt acts in pursuance of the conspiracy. The statute,
    however, required an overt act to be proved. Some of the judgments refer to *R v
    Brisac*[4] and *R v Bowes*[5].
e   Also in the majority opinion of the Supreme Court of the United States in *Hyde
    and Schneider v United States*[7], after citation of a passage referring to *R v Brisac*[4] and
    R v Bowes[5], approval was given to this statement by Marcy J in *The People v Mather*[8]
    as to the position at common law:

> 'If conspirators enter into the illegal agreement in one county, the crime is
f   > perpetrated there, and they may be immediately prosecuted; but the proceed-
    > ings against them must be in that county. If they go into another county to
    > execute their plans of mischief, and there commit an overt act, they may be
    > punished in the latter county without any evidence of an express renewal of
    > their agreement. The law considers that wherever they act there they renew,
    > or perhaps, to speak more properly they continue, their agreement, and this
g   > agreement is renewed or continued as to all whenever any one of them does an
    > act in furtherance of their common design.'

    Having regard to the balance of authority as well as to considerations of principle,
    I would allow the appeal and restore the convictions on the first count.
       On the question of prosecuting policy, whether it was appropriate to include the
h   count of conspiracy in addition to the charges of specific offences, I would say it was
    appropriate because it provided for each conspirator being held responsible, as morally
    and legally he was responsible, for each of the illegal importations effected in
    pursuance of the conspiracy.

---

1   (1820) 4 B & Ald 95 at 178, 179, [1814-23] All ER Rep 80 at 98
j   2   (1803) 4 East at 171
    3   (1828), pp 27, 28
    4   (1803) 4 East 164
    5   (30th May 1787) unreported
    6   (1867) 10 Cox CC 506
    7   (1912) 225 US 347 at 365
    8   (1830) 4 Wend 230 at 261

LORD KILBRANDON. My Lords, it is not, I believe, necessary that I should do
more than express my concurrence with the opinion, that the question of law put
by the Court of Appeal[1] should be answered in the affirmative. I limit my observations to this the more readily, since I understand that the criminal law of conspiracy
is at this time under review by the Law Commission. Such review is much to be
desired.

LORD SALMON. My Lords, I will not repeat the facts which are fully set out in
the speeches of my noble and learned friends, Viscount Dilhorne and Lord Pearson.
Section 2 of the Dangerous Drugs Act 1965 enacts that:

> 'It shall not be lawful for a person to import into the United Kingdom a drug
> to which [Part I] of this Act applies except under a licence granted by the Secretary
> of State.'

Section 3 contains a similar provision in respect of exportation. The 1965 Act does
not, however, create an offence in respect of any breach of s 2 or s 3. These sections
constitute statutory prohibitions or restrictions within the meaning of ss 45, 56 and
304 of the Customs and Excise Act 1952. Section 45 makes it an offence punishable
amongst other things with imprisonment for not more than two years to import or to
be concerned in importing any goods contrary to any prohibition or restriction for
the time being in force. Section 56 creates a similar offence in respect of exportation.
Section 304 enacts that:

> 'Without prejudice to any other provision of this Act, if any person—(a) know-
> ingly and with intent . . . to evade any prohibition or restriction for the time
> being in force under . . . any enactment with respect thereto . . is in any way
> concerned in carrying, . . . keeping or concealing or in any manner dealing with
> any goods . . . with respect to the importation or exportation of which any pro-
> hibition or restriction is. . . in force'

he shall be liable to the same term of imprisonment as that specified in ss 45 and 56.
This term was increased to ten years by s 7 of the Dangerous Drugs Act 1967. Section
304 is obviously a long stop for ss 45 and 56 to catch anyone against whom actual importing, exporting or being concerned in actual importing or exporting cannot be
proved although no doubt it is wide enough to cover importing and exporting also.
In the present case the evidence established importing and being concerned in importing or nothing. Indeed, in all the counts save the conspiracy count, the respondents were charged with 'importing prohibited goods'. I do not understand why they
were not charged under s 45 which deals directly with importation rather than under
the more complicated s 304 which deals only obliquely with it. The evidence of
importing was overwhelming. Indeed, all the respondents save Shanahan pleaded
guilty to it. The respondent Doot admitted that he had planned and directed the
whole smuggling operation and the evidence established that Shanahan was his
chief lieutenant. These two were actively concerned in concealing and dealing with
all the goods and participating in their unlawful importations and therefore guilty
of offences under ss 45 and 304. The doctrine of qui facit per alium facit per se applies
no less in criminal than in civil cases. The respondent Loving unlawfully imported
64 kilogrammes of cannabis resin. The respondents Watts and Fay unlawfully
imported 65 kilogrammes of cannabis resin. The total value of these consignments was
not less than £60,000. This was not a case of merely being in possession of a small
quantity of dangerous drugs for one's own use or that of one's friends. It was a case
of trading on a vast scale in dangerous drugs for gain. The minimum sentence normally imposed for unlawfully importing £30,000 worth of cannabis alone is certainly

---

1   [1972] 2 All ER 1046, [1972] 3 WLR 33

a not less than four years' imprisonment for a defendant with a clean record. Indeed, I have known the Court of Appeal on more than one occasion to refuse leave to appeal against a sentence of six years for such an offence. These were carefully planned crimes involving in all at least £60,000 worth of cannabis. Doot and Shanahan had also participated in the unlawful importation of a further £30,000 load of cannabis by Evans. Loving and Watts were sentenced respectively to 12 months' and 18

b months' imprisonment on the conspiracy count and concurrently to nine months' imprisonment each on the counts for unlawfully importing the vast quantities of cannabis to which I have referred. Doot, who master-minded the whole operation, was sentenced to 33 months' imprisonment in all and Shanahan, his chief lieutenant, to 27 months in all.   So far as I am concerned these sentences pass all understanding. No factor mentioned when the sentences were pronounced in any way explains them.

c It is surely no mitigation that the respondents intended to commit further crimes by exporting the prohibited drugs from this country. There is unfortunately a ready market in this country for these dangerous drugs. I do not doubt that if the respondents had received an acceptable offer for them here, it would have been accepted. However this may be, it hardly seems in accordance with the rules of international comity that our courts should treat the respondents with special leniency because their crimes were more likely to ruin young lives in the United States of America than in

d this country. In these circumstances, I think it right and indeed necessary to take the exceptional course of commenting on these sentences lest silence might lead courts, in the future, into the belief that such sentences could be appropriate for crimes of this extreme gravity.

I will now consider whether there was jurisdiction to try the conspiracy count since the conspiracy was entered into abroad. The learned trial judge ruled that such

e jurisdiction existed. Stephenson LJ in delivering the powerful judgment of the Court of Appeal[1] referred to the absence of direct authority on the point. Indeed, this was the first time that the point has ever come before the court for decision. He came to the conclusion that since there was no authority which recognised that our courts have jurisdiction over a conspiracy entered into abroad to commit a crime in this

f country even if any act had been done here in furtherance of the conspiracy, such jurisdiction ought not to be assumed by our courts until Parliament or the House of Lords declared otherwise.

I recognise that if your Lordships were to hold that our courts are invested with jurisdiction in circumstances such as the present your Lordships would in a sense be extending the application of the criminal law since such a case as the present has never yet been decided in our courts. I bear in mind and respectfully endorse what Sir

g William Holdsworth said in his History of English Law[2]:

'Moreover, at all periods of our history it has always been far more difficult to extend the criminal law by a process of judicial decision than any other branch of the law.   There has always been a wholesome dread of enlarging its boundaries by anything short of an Act of the legislature.'

h There may, however, be most exceptional cases, and I think that this is one of them, in which a new point falls to be decided and accordingly a development of the law in accordance with principle becomes permissible and indeed necessary. The crime of conspiracy is the creation of the common law and peculiar to it. In essence it consists of an agreement between two or more persons to do an unlawful act or a lawful act

j by unlawful means: *Mulcahy v R*[3]. The offence is complete as soon as the agreement is made. This is so because the law recognises that once people go so far as to agree to act unlawfully there is a serious risk that they will carry out their agreement. The

1   [1972] 2 All ER 1046, [1972] 3 WLR 33
2   Vol 3, p 277
3   (1868) LR 3 HL 306

agreement is in itself made an offence in order to preserve the Queen's peace by preventing the offence which the conspirators have agreed to perpetrate before it reaches
even the stage of an attempt. This has been the basis of the law of conspiracy since
the earliest times[1].

> '... the usual commission of *oyer* and *terminer* gives power to the commis-
> sioners to enquire, &c. *de omnibus coadunationibus, confœderationibus, et falsis
> alligantiis* ... in these cases before the unlawful act executed the law punishes
> the coadunation, confederacy or false alliance, to the end to prevent the unlaw-
> ful act ... and in these cases the common law is a law of mercy, for it prevents
> the malignant from doing mischief, and the innocent from suffering it.'

It is obvious that a conspiracy to carry out a bank robbery in London is equally a
threat to the Queen's peace whether it is hatched, say, in Birmingham or in Brussels.
Accordingly, having regard to the special nature of the offence a conspiracy to commit
a crime in England is, in my opinion, an offence against the common law even when
entered into abroad, certainly if acts in furtherance of the conspiracy are done in this
country. There can in such circumstances be no doubt that the conspiracy is in fact
as well as in theory a real threat to the Queen's peace.

I recognise that the proposition that a conspiracy entered into abroad to commit a
crime in England may be an offence under our law appears perhaps to be an exception
to the well established general rule that 'all crime is local' and that our criminal law
does not, as a rule, extend to acts done abroad: *Macleod v Attorney-General for New
South Wales*[2]. Such acts may or may not be criminal under the law of the state in
which they are committed. If they are not criminal under that law and do no harm
here nor amount to a conspiracy to commit a crime here it would be contrary to
the rules of international comity to punish a foreigner and pointless to punish a
British subject who had committed such an act abroad and then come to this country.
The criminal law of England exists to protect this realm and all those within it, eg an
agreement made in England to commit an unlawful act constitutes the crime of
conspiracy only if the act is unlawful by the laws of England. It is not enough that it
is unlawful only by the law of the country in which it is to be committed: *Board of
Trade v Owen*[3].

If a conspiracy is entered into abroad to commit a crime in England, exactly the
same public mischief is produced by it as if it had been entered into here. It is unnecessary for me to consider what the position might be if the conspirators came to England
for an entirely innocent purpose unconnected with the conspiracy. If, however, the
conspirators come here and do acts in furtherance of the conspiracy, eg by preparing
to commit the planned crime, it cannot, in my view, be considered contrary to the
rules of international comity for the forces of law and order in England to protect
the Queen's peace by arresting them and putting them on trial for conspiracy whether
they are British subjects or foreigners and whether or not conspiracy is a crime
under the law of the country in which the conspiracy was born. It was unusual until
recently to have any direct evidence of conspiracy. Conspiracy was usually proved
by what are called overt acts, being acts from which an antecedent conspiracy is to
be inferred. Where and when the conspiracy occurs is often unknown and seldom
relevant. Today, however, it is possible to have direct evidence such as tape recordings
of oral agreements. Suppose a case in which evidence existed of a conspiracy hatched
abroad by bank robbers to raid a bank in London, or by terrorists to carry out some
violent crime at an English airport, or by drug pedlars to smuggle large quantities of
dangerous drugs on some stretch of the English coast. Suppose the conspirators
came to England for the purpose of carrying out the crime and were detected by the

1 See *The Poulterer's Case* (1610) 9 Co Rep at 56b, 57a
2 [1891] AC 455
3 [1957] 1 All ER 411, [1957] AC 602

a police reconnoitring the place where they proposed to commit it, but doing nothing which by itself would be illegal, it would surely be absurd if the police could not arrest them then and there but had to take the risk of waiting and hoping to be able to catch them as they were actually committing or attempting to commit the crime. Yet that is precisely what the police would have to do if a conspiracy entered into abroad to commit a crime here were not in the circumstances postulated recognised by our law as a criminal offence which our courts had any jurisdiction to try.

b   I do not believe that any civilised country, even assuming that its own laws do not recognise conspiracy as a criminal offence, could today have any reasonable objection to its nationals being arrested, tried and convicted by English courts in the circumstances to which I have referred. Today, crime is an international problem—perhaps not least, crimes connected with the illicit drug traffic—and there is a great deal of co-operation between the nations to bring criminals to justice. Great care also is taken by most countries to do nothing which might help their own nationals to commit what would be crimes in other countries, see eg s 3 (2) of the Dangerous Drugs Act 1965.

c   I am not impressed by the argument that certain statutory enactments would have been unnecessary if the view I have propounded is correct, eg the Statute of Treason and the Explosive Substances Act 1883, s 3, which latter statute makes it a crime for any British subject abroad to conspire to cause an explosion in the United Kingdom. The purpose of these Acts may well have been to underline the heinousness of crimes which at the time it was considered particularly important publicly to discourage. In any event, the rules of international comity are not static and I do not believe that in the modern world nations are nearly as sensitive about exclusive jurisdiction over crime as they may have been formerly. I do not derive much assistance from *R v Brisac*[1] and *R v Best*[2] nor from any of the other old cases which were concerned with what are now obsolete questions of venue. Nor do I think that much help can be derived in the present case from the learned judgments in the American authorities to which this House has been referred. There are some passages in the judgments which appear to help the Crown and others which seem to favour the respondents.

f   The most important and relevant of these cases is *Hyde and Schneider v United States*[3] in which the Supreme Court divided 5:4. The decision seems to have turned chiefly on the point that since s 5440 of the Revised Statutes made an overt act an essential ingredient in the crime of conspiracy, the conspirator could be tried in the state in which the overt act was committed even although the agreement had been made in a different state. It seems to me that these American cases were concerned like the old English cases with questions of venue and also with the constitutional rights of the citizen relating to the state in which he could be brought to trial. They had nothing to do with the rules of international comity with which, in my view, the present appeal is largely concerned.

g   I agree with and adopt what my noble and learned friend, Lord Diplock, said in *Treacy v Director of Public Prosecutions*[4]:

h   '. . . the rules of international comity, in my view, do not call for more than that each sovereign State should refrain from punishing persons for their conduct within the territory of another sovereign State, where that conduct has had no harmful consequences within the territory of the State which imposes the punishment.'

i   There can be no doubt but that the respondents' conduct in conspiring in Belgium or Morocco to commit crimes in England caused harm in this country because the

---

1   (1803) 4 East 164
2   (1705) 1 Salk 174
3   (1912) 225 US 347
4   [1971] 1 All ER 110 at 124, [1971] AC 537 at 564

respondents carried out those very crimes in furtherance of that conspiracy. No one *a* suggests that to charge the respondents with those crimes in our courts could violate the rules of international comity; nor do I think that anyone could suppose that the inclusion of a charge in respect of the conspiracy could offend those rules whatever other criticisms might be made of it.

It is, unfortunately, by no means unlikely that cases may arise in the future in which there will be conclusive evidence of persons having conspired abroad to commit *b* serious crimes in England and then having done acts here in furtherance of the conspiracy and in preparation for the commission of those crimes yet none of these acts will in itself be unlawful. Although such a case would be very different from the present, if the reasoning on which I have based this opinion is sound, it follows that such persons could properly be arrested and tried for conspiracy in our courts.

My Lords, even if I am wrong in thinking that a conspiracy hatched abroad to *c* commit a crime in this country may be a common law offence because it endangers the Queen's peace, I agree that the convictions for conspiracy against these respondents can be supported on another ground, namely, that they conspired together in this country notwithstanding the fact that they were abroad when they entered into the agreement which was the essence of the conspiracy. That agreement was and remained a continuing agreement and they continued to conspire until the offence *d* they were conspiring to commit was in fact committed. Accordingly, when Watts, Loving and Fay sailed into English territorial waters they were still agreeing and conspiring to import into this country the dangerous drugs which a little later they smuggled ashore. Moreover, they were agreeing, not only on their own behalf, but also on behalf and with the authority of Doot and Shanahan. Therefore, they were, all five of them, guilty of conspiring in England. It is irrelevant for this purpose *e* that they had originally entered into the conspiracy abroad and that an offence of conspiracy is committed at the moment when the agreement to commit a crime is first made.

If, however, a conspiracy is entered into abroad by a number of conspirators to commit a series of crimes in England and only one conspirator comes to this country and commits one of the planned crimes, it would, I think, be unrealistic to regard *f* him as agreeing with himself, whilst here, on behalf of each of the other conspirators. It is true that he would be committing an act in furtherance of the conspiracy, indeed one of the very crimes which, whilst abroad, all the conspirators had conspired to commit. The act, however, would not be an ingredient of the crime of conspiracy, but only evidence of the existence of the conspiracy entered into abroad. If another of the conspirators who had perhaps master-minded the whole conspiracy later *g* came here to obtain information useful to enable the other planned crimes to be committed, he would be immune from a charge of conspiracy however overwhelming the evidence of conspiracy might be, if conspiracy abroad to commit a crime in England cannot be a common law offence: neither he nor anyone on his behalf would have conspired in England. This is why I have taken up time in explaining why, on principle, conspiracy abroad to commit a crime in England may, in my view, be a *h* common law offence certainly when acts in furtherance of it are committed in this country.

My Lords, for the reasons I have indicated, I would allow the appeal.

Appeal allowed. Question answered in the affirmative. Convictions on count 1 restored.

Solicitors: *Director of Public Prosecutions*; *J E Baring & Co* (for the respondents).   *j*

S A Hatteea Esq   Barrister.

a

Davies v Taylor (No 2)

HOUSE OF LORDS

LORD REID, LORD MORRIS OF BORTH-Y-GEST, VISCOUNT DILHORNE, LORD SIMON OF
GLAISDALE AND LORD CROSS OF CHELSEA

19th FEBRUARY, 21st MARCH 1973

b

*Legal aid – Costs – Unassisted person's costs out of legal aid fund – Costs incurred by un-
assisted party – Incurred by – Agreement by insurance company to pay unassisted person's
costs – No agreement by unassisted party's solicitors not to look to him for payment of costs–
Whether costs 'incurred by' unassisted party – Legal Aid Act 1964, s 1 (1).*

Legal aid – Costs – Unassisted person's costs out of legal aid fund – Just and equitable –
c *Order for payment if (and only if) court satisfied that it is just and equitable in all the circumstances – Discretion – Scope of discretion – Circumstances justifying order – Whether
fact that unassisted party successful alone sufficient to justify an order – Legal Aid Act 1964,
s 1 (2).*

The costs of a successful unassisted party in the appeal proceedings are 'costs incurred
by him in those proceedings', within s 1 (1)[a] of the Legal Aid Act 1964, even though,
d under the terms of an insurance policy, his insurance company has agreed to pay
the costs, unless there is an agreement between the party and his solicitors or between
the solicitors and his insurance company that the solicitors will not look to the
unassisted party for costs; *Adams v London Improved Motor Coach Builders Ltd* [1920]
All ER Rep 340 and *Gundry v Sainsbury* [1910] 1 KB 645 applied. Furthermore, the
mere fact that the order will enure for the benefit of the insurance company does
e not necessarily prevent it from being 'just and equitable', within s 1 (2) of the 1964
Act, to make it (see p 960 h and j, p 962 c and d, p 964 e and p 965 e f and g, post).

Section 1 (2) of the 1964 Act confers a very wide discretion to do what is just and
equitable in all the circumstances; the fact that the unassisted party has been successful in the appeal is an important circumstance and may alone be sufficient to justify
f an order under s 1 (1) in his favour (see p 960 h and j, p 962 f, p 963 d, p 964 e, p 965
h and j and p 966 a and b, post); dictum of Sachs LJ in *Clifford v Walker* [1972] 2 All
ER at 809 disapproved.

Per Viscount Dilhorne. (i) Ordinarily the court should not give any reasons for
granting or refusing an application for costs under the 1964 Act (see p 963 e and f, post).

(ii) An unassisted party who wants to apply to the House of Lords for an order
g under the 1964 Act should give notice of the intended application to the Law Society,
preferably before judgment is given (see p 964 b to d, post).

Notes

For the award of costs to an unassisted party out of the legal aid fund, see Supplement
to 30 Halsbury's Laws (3rd Edn) para 933A.

For the Legal Aid Act 1964, s 1, see 25 Halsbury's Statutes (3rd Edn) 789.

h ───
a Section 1, so far as material, provides:
   '(1) Where a party receives legal aid in connection with any proceedings between him
   and a party not receiving legal aid (in this Act referred to as "the unassisted party") and those
   proceedings are finally decided in favour of the unassisted party, the court by which the
   proceedings are so decided may, subject to the provisions of this section, make an order for
   the payment to the unassisted party out of the legal aid fund of the whole or any part of
j the costs incurred by him in those proceedings.
   '(2) An order may be made under this section in respect of any costs if (and only if) the
   court is satisfied that it is just and equitable in all the circumstances that provision for
   those costs should be made out of public funds; and before making such an order the
   court shall in every case (whether or not application is made in that behalf) consider
   what orders should be made for costs against the party receiving legal aid and for
   determining his liability in respect of such costs . . .'

Cases referred to in opinions

Adams v London Improved Motor Coach Builders Ltd [1921] 1 KB 495, [1920] All ER Rep *a*
    340, 90 LJKB 685, 124 LT 587, CA, 51 Digest (Repl) 994, 5320.
Clifford v Walker [1972] 2 All ER 806, [1972] 1 WLR 724, CA.
Davies v Taylor [1972] 3 All ER 836, [1972] 3 WLR 801, HL; affg [1971] 3 All ER 1259,
    [1972] 1 QB 286, [1971] 3 WLR 515, CA.
Gundry v Sainsbury [1910] 1 KB 645, 79 LJKB 713, 102 LT 440, CA, 43 Digest (Repl) *b*
    137, 1240.
Lewis v Averay (No 2) (1973) The Times, 15th February, CA.
Povey v Povey [1970] 3 All ER 612, [1972] Fam 40, [1971] 2 WLR 381, DC.
Saunders v Anglia Building Society (No 2) [1971] 1 All ER 243, [1971] AC 1039, [1971] 2
    WLR 349, HL.

c
Application
The appellant, Jean Elizabeth Davies, suing as administratrix of the estate of her
deceased husband, Kenneth Stanley Davies, brought an action against the respondent,
Clarence Leopold Taylor, in respect of the deceased's death in a motor accident
caused by the negligent driving of the respondent. The appellant claimed damages
(i) under the Fatal Accidents Acts 1846-1959 for the benefit of herself as a dependant *d*
of the deceased, and (ii) under the Law Reform (Miscellaneous Provisions) Act 1934
for the benefit of the deceased's estate for loss of expectation of life and consequential
loss. On 16th October 1970 Bridge J, at Shrewsbury Assizes, gave judgment for the
appellant on her claim under the 1934 Act for £500 plus funeral expenses amounting to £56 6s 4d, but dismissed her claim under the Fatal Accidents Acts. The
appellant appealed against the dismissal of the Fatal Accidents Acts claim and was *e*
granted legal aid for the purpose of prosecuting the appeal. On 25th May 1971 the
Court of Appeal[1] (Davies and Megaw LJJ, Cairns LJ dissenting) dismissed the appeal
and ordered the appellant pay to the respondent the costs of the appeal which were
assessed at £50. With the leave of the appeal committee the appellant appealed to
the House of Lords and was granted legal aid for the purposes of that appeal. On
25th October the House[2] dismissed the appeal and the respondent applied for an *f*
order under s 1 (1) of the Legal Aid Act 1964 that the costs incurred by him in the
proceedings on the appeal be paid to him out of the legal aid fund. The application
was adjourned for the Law Society to be represented.

R H Tucker QC for the respondent.
D M Thomas for the appellant.
Jack Hames QC and D J Ritchie for the Law Society. *g*

Their Lordships took time for consideration.

21st March. The following opinions were delivered.

LORD REID. My Lords, for the reasons given by my noble and learned friend, *h*
Lord Cross of Chelsea, I am of opinion that an order shall be made as he proposes.

LORD MORRIS OF BORTH-Y-GEST. My Lords, for the reasons given by my
noble and learned friends, Viscount Dilhorne and Lord Cross of Chelsea, I am of
opinion that an order should be made as proposed.

j

VISCOUNT DILHORNE. My Lords, at the trial of this action the appellant,
Mrs Davies, who was not then legally aided, had an order for costs made against

---

1 [1971] 3 All ER 1259
2 [1972] 3 All ER 836

a her as the amount for which she obtained judgment was less than the sum paid into court. She appealed with legal aid to the Court of Appeal[1] against the learned judge's decision that she was not entitled to damages on her claim under the Fatal Accidents Act 1846 in respect of the death of her husband in a motor car accident. Her appeal was dismissed and she was ordered to pay £50 costs. She then obtained legal aid to appeal to this House and when her appeal was dismissed by the

b unanimous decision of this House[2], counsel for the respondent, Mr Taylor, asked that an order should be made under the Legal Aid Act 1964 for the payment of his costs out of the legal aid fund. The matter was then adjourned in order to enable the Law Society to be heard if it so wished.

Counsel for the Law Society at the adjourned hearing advanced a number of arguments in opposition to the making of such an order. His main argument was

c that as the respondent was insured and the insurance company were bound to pay the cost of defending the action brought against him he had himself incurred no costs in those proceedings. Section 1 (1) of the Legal Aid Act 1964 provides that an order may be made for a payment out of the legal aid fund to the unassisted party 'of the costs incurred by him in those proceedings'.

Insurance against liability in respect of motor accidents was as common in 1964

d as it is now and if counsel for the Law Society's contention is well founded, it means that in every case where a motorist is insured and the insurance company undertakes, as under the policy it is usually entitled to do, the conduct of the defence of an action brought against him and incurs liability for the costs thereof, no order can properly be made for the costs of a successful defence to be paid by the plaintiff.

In support of this contention counsel for the Law Society relied on *Gundry v Sains-*

e *bury*[3] where there had been an agreement between a plaintiff in a county court action and his solicitor that he, the plaintiff, should not pay the solicitor any costs, and it was held that the plaintiff could not recover more costs than he was liable to pay his solicitor. In this case counsel for the Law Society was not able to establish any such agreement. All he could do was to seek to rely on a letter from the respondent's solicitors in which it was stated that the terms of the respondent's policy of

f insurance were such that the insurance company concerned would not in any circumstances have looked to the respondent for payment of costs.

In *Adams v London Improved Motor Coach Builders Ltd*[4] a somewhat similar question arose for consideration. There a trade union gave legal aid to one of its members and instructed a firm of solicitors to act for him. The plaintiff gave no written retainer to the solicitors, but, having succeeded in the action, was held entitled to judgment with costs. Bankes LJ said[5]:

g

'When once it is established that the solicitors were acting for the plaintiff with his knowledge and assent, it seems to me that he became liable to the solicitors for costs, and that liability would not be excluded merely because the Union also undertook to pay the costs. It is necessary to go a step further and prove that there was a bargain, either between the Union and the solicitors,

h or between the plaintiff and the solicitors, that under no circumstances was the plaintiff to be liable for costs.'

And Atkin LJ said[6]:

'It appears to me therefore that the learned judge was perfectly correct in saying that the solicitors were in fact acting as solicitors for the plaintiff. If they

j

---

1 [1971] 3 All ER 1259, [1972] 1 QB 286
2 [1972] 3 All ER 836, [1972] 3 WLR 801
3 [1910] 1 KB 645
4 [1921] 1 KB 495, [1920] All ER Rep 340
5 [1921] 1 KB at 501, cf [1920] All ER Rep at 343
6 [1921] 1 KB at 502, 503, cf [1920] All ER Rep at 344

were so acting, they did so upon the ordinary terms applicable to a person who *a*
employs a professional man to do professional work on his behalf—namely,
that he shall remunerate him. That is the prima facie obligation which at once
emerges when the employment is proved. It is perfectly possible for the agreement of employment to contain a term by which the agent agrees that he will
not claim remuneration from his employer, but will either do the work for nothing or claim remuneration from some third party. But in the absence of such *b*
a term—which would have to be proved by the party setting it up—the ordinary
deduction from the employment of a professional man accepted in this way is
that the person accepting the agent's services is bound to remunerate the agent.'

In this case the solicitors, no doubt first instructed by the insurance company,
were the solicitors on the record as solicitors for the respondent. They acted for him
and, in the absence of proof of an agreement between him and them or between *c*
them and the insurance company that he would not pay their costs, they could look
to him for payment for the work done and his liability would not be excluded by
the fact that the insurance company had itself agreed to pay their costs. In my opinion,
the costs incurred were incurred by the respondent in the sense in which those words
are used in the Legal Aid Act 1964. They were the successful unassisted litigant's costs
and, in my opinion, this contention advanced by counsel for the Law Society should *d*
be rejected.

Counsel for the Law Society, who conceded that in this case if the respondent stood
alone it would have been just and equitable to make the order asked for, drew
attention to the reported cases in which observations have been made with regard
to the award of costs under this Act. He asked that guidance should be given to
the Law Society to ease their task in deciding whether or not to oppose a particular *e*
application. While recognising that guidance would assist the Law Society, I am not
in favour of any gloss or limitation being put on the words of the Act. They confer
on the courts a very wide discretion to do what is just and equitable in all the circumstances. The courts are entitled to have regard to any relevant circumstances.
In some cases the conduct of the applicant may be relevant. In this case the respondent acted reasonably throughout. In some, and perhaps the majority, of cases the *f*
conduct of the legally aided litigant is also relevant. In this case there were two
appeals by the appellant when legally aided, both of which were unsuccessful.
Where a second appeal is brought with legal aid after a first appeal with legal aid
has failed, ordinarily, and in the absence of special circumstances, in my opinion it
would be just and reasonable to make an order that costs of the second appeal should
be paid out of the legal aid fund. *g*

In *Saunders v Anglia Building Society (No 2)*[1] the House was unanimous in its decision
that an order should be made for the payment of the costs incurred in this House
by the successful respondents, the building society, out of the fund, and also
unanimous in its decision that no such order should be made in relation to the
respondents' costs in the Court of Appeal. In the course of my speech in that case
I ventured to say[2]:   'No such order should be made unless it is patently clear that *h*
it would be unjust and inequitable not to do so', words which I see were criticised
in *Clifford v Walker*[3], and which counsel for the Law Society in that case said he did
not seek to support. Phillimore LJ said[4] it was—

> 'putting the matter very much wider than it is put in the section of the Act
> of Parliament, and indeed it is difficult to see how, if that were the right test, *j*
> any order would ever be made at all.'

1   [1971] 1 All ER 243, [1971] AC 1039
2   [1971] 1 All ER at 250, [1971] AC at 1051
3   [1972] 2 All ER 806, [1972] 1 WLR 724
4   [1972] 2 All ER at 810, 811, [1972] 1 WLR at 729

a   If it is patently unjust and inequitable not to make an order under the Act, then, to
my mind, it clearly follows that it is just and equitable to make one and I regret that
I do not follow why it was said that my statement of the position would make it
difficult to make any order at all. In *Saunders v Anglia Building Society (No 2)*[1] it would
have been patently unfair and inequitable if the successful respondents had not had
an order made in their favour and if they had been left to pay the costs that they were
b   forced to incur. In this case, too, it would, in my opinion, be patently unfair and
inequitable to decline to make an order. I did not think that my sentence was capable
of being so interpreted. In that case I emphasised the wide discretion entrusted by
Parliament to the courts and it was not my intention to fetter that discretion at all.
    In *Clifford v Walker* Sachs LJ said[2]:

c   '... it is not sufficient merely to put into the scales, when the costs of an appeal
        fall to be considered, the fact that the unassisted party seeking the order
        succeeded.'

    I do not myself think that there is any such rule or that *Saunders v Anglia Building
Society (No 2)*[1] decided that. For an application under the Act to be made the unassisted
litigant must have succeeded. That is a sine qua non. In some cases it may be that that
d   alone suffices to render it just and equitable to make an order, or, to put it as I did
in *Saunders v Anglia Building Society (No 2)*[1] in the converse way, unjust and inequitable not to do so. It would, in my view, be wrong to limit the exercise of the
court's discretion by laying down the general rule, for which counsel for the Law
Society sought the authority of this House, that success alone can never suffice.
    Reasons are being given in this case as they have been in other cases for the making
e   of an order under the Act. Ordinarily the courts do not give their reasons for making
or refusing to make an order for costs and I hope that, unless there are particular
grounds for doing so, reasons will not in future ordinarily be given for granting
or refusing an application under the 1964 Act for costs; for if reasons are given in
every case, a body of law will be built up with the consequence that when an application is made there may be the citation of many cases and considerable argument
f   when all that has to be decided is whether or not in all the circumstances of that
particular case an order should be made.
    I do not ignore the requirement of the Act that before making any such order the
court must consider what orders for costs should be made against the party receiving
legal aid. In this case it is clear that no order should be made.
    There is one other matter to which I desire to refer. In relation to this application
g   the Law Society have treated the provisions of the Legal Aid (Costs of Successful
Unassisted Parties) Regulations 1964[3], and in particular reg 15 (2), as applying to
applications under the Act to this House. The Legal Aid and Advice Act 1949, by
s 1, made provision for the grant of legal aid 'in connection with proceedings before
courts and tribunals in England and Wales', unless and until regulations otherwise
provided, of a description mentioned in Part I of Sch 1 to the Act. That part is headed
h   'DESCRIPTION OF PROCEEDINGS' and para 1 thereof reads, as far as material, as follows:

        'Proceedings in any of the following courts—(a) the House of Lords in the
        exercise of its jurisdiction in relation to appeals from courts in England or
        Northern Ireland ...'

    So in the 1949 Act the House was treated as a court.
j   Pursuant to s 12 (2) of the 1949 Act a statutory instrument was made, the Legal
Aid and Advice Act 1949 (Commencement) Order 1950[4], bringing ss 1 to 6, except

---

1   [1971] 1 All ER 243, [1971] AC 1039
2   [1972] 2 All ER at 809, [1972] 1 WLR at 727
3   SI 1964 No 1276
4   SI 1950 No 1357

s 5, and the schedules to the Act into force in relation to certain courts but not bring-   *a*
ing them into operation in relation to appeals to this House. It was not until 1st
December 1960 that the provisions of Part I of the 1949 Act were brought into operation by the Legal Aid and Advice Act 1949 (Commencement No 9) Order 1960¹,
dated 10th November 1960, in relation to appeals to this House.

It was against this background that the Legal Aid Act 1964 was passed and the
Legal Aid (Costs of Successful Unassisted Parties) Regulations 1964 were made.   *b*
Paragraph 15 of the regulations deals with applications to an appellate court, but
the regulations do not define what is meant by 'appellate proceedings' or 'appellate
court' in the regulations. In these circumstances it may be open to doubt whether
the regulations were intended to apply to this House, but whether or not they do so
nevertheless an unassisted party who wishes to apply to the House for an order
under the 1964 Act should give notice of the intended application to the Law Society   *c*
and preferably before judgment is given. In some cases it may be possible for the
Law Society to decide whether or not they should oppose such an application, if the
unassisted litigant is successful, before judgment is given and, if they can do that,
then the question can be dealt with on the same day as the giving of judgment, in
which case the further substantial costs necessarily consequent on an adjournment
for consideration of the question will be avoided.   *d*

In my opinion, an order should be made that the respondent's costs incurred in
the appeal to this House, including the costs of the adjourned hearing in relation to
the application for an order under the 1964 Act, should be paid out of the legal aid
fund.

LORD SIMON OF GLAISDALE. My Lords, I have had the advantage of   *e*
reading in draft the speeches prepared by my noble and learned friends, Viscount
Dilhorne and Lord Cross of Chelsea. I agree with them; and, for the reasons they
give, I concur in the orders which they propose.

I wish to give my particular assent to the proposition of my noble and learned
friend, Viscount Dilhorne, that, in determining whether it is 'just and equitable' to
make an order under the 1964 Act, it is undesirable to put any limitation on the   *f*
words of the Act. For this reason I prefer the views of the majority of the Divisional
Court of the Probate, Divorce and Admiralty Division in *Povey v Povey*² to those
expressed on the point in the Court of Appeal in *Lewis v Averay (No 2)*³, although
I respectfully agree with the actual decision in that case (which is very close to the
instant one). On the other hand, the affirmative reasons which, in the other cases
cited to your Lordships, led various courts to consider that an order under the 1964   *g*
Act would be just and equitable all seem to me to be relevant to the question.

LORD CROSS OF CHELSEA. My Lords, in this appeal the appellant, Mrs
Davies, was legally aided but the respondent, Mr Taylor, was not. The appeal has
been dismissed and your Lordships have now to consider an application by the respondent for an order under the Legal Aid Act 1964 that the costs incurred by him   *h*
in resisting the appeal be paid out of the legal aid fund.

The appellant's husband had been killed as a result of the negligent driving of
the respondent and the appellant, suing as his widow and the administratrix of his
estate, brought this action against the respondent claiming damages (a) for herself
as a dependant under the Fatal Accidents Acts 1846-1959, and (b) for the benefit of
the estate under the Law Reform (Miscellaneous Provisions) Act 1934. In the court   *j*
of first instance—where neither party was legally aided—the second claim succeeded
but the first failed, and as the respondent had paid into court a sum in excess of

1   SI 1960 No 2056
2   [1970] 3 All ER 612, [1972] Fam 40
3   (1973) The Times, 15th February

a the damages awarded to the appellant on the second claim, an order was made for
payment by her of his costs as from the date of the payment in. The appellant was
granted legal aid to prosecute an appeal to the Court of Appeal against the dismissal
of her first claim. The appeal was dismissed[1] and the court made an order in favour
of the respondent, who was not legally aided, that the appellant should pay him
£50 towards his costs. The appellant then obtained legal aid again in order to pro-
b secute an appeal to this House which has, in its turn, been dismissed[2]. Her financial
position is such that no order could properly be made for payment of any part of
the respondent's costs by her personally. In these circumstances we have power
under s 1 (1) and (2) of the Legal Aid Act 1964 to make an order for payment out of
the legal aid fund of 'the costs incurred' by the respondent 'if (and only if)' we are
'satisfied that it is just and equitable in all the circumstances' to make such an order.
c Counsel for the Law Society, which has been joined as a respondent to the application in order to protect the fund, submits that such an order ought not to be made in
this case for two reasons.

He relies, in the first place, on the fact that the respondent is insured, inter alia,
in respect of any costs which he may have to pay in defending this action and that,
accordingly, any order which we might make would in reality be an order in favour
d of the insurance company. He conceded that the fact that the insurance company
is not in financial need is irrelevant, since in appellate proceedings, unlike proceedings
at first instance, it is not necessary for the unassisted person to show that he would
suffer financial hardship if no order was made; but he submitted that the costs in
question were not 'costs incurred by' the respondent within the meaning of s 1 (1)
and that, even if they were, the fact that in the end the respondent would gain
e nothing personally by the order prevents us from saying that it is 'just and equitable'
to make it. I cannot accept either of those submissions. No doubt if it were shown
that the respondent's solicitor had agreed with him that in no circumstances would
he hold him liable to pay any part of them then the costs, although incurred by the
solicitor in defending the case, would not be costs 'incurred' by the respondent, but
it was not suggested that any such agreement (which would be most unusual) was
f made in this case. If there was no such agreement then the fact that the insurance
company had undertaken to indemnify the respondent against his liability for
these costs would not mean that they were not costs 'incurred' by him (see *Adams
v London Improved Motor Coach Builders Ltd*[3]). Further, I do not think that the fact
that the benefit of the order will enure to the insurance company necessarily prevents
it from being 'just and equitable' to make it. Parliament, when it passed this Act,
must have been well aware that in many cases the liability of successful litigants for
g their own costs would be covered by policies under which the insurance companies
would acquire by subrogation the rights of the insured and if it had intended that
orders should never be made in such cases it would surely have said so.

The second ground on which counsel argued that the order sought should not be
made in this case was that although no criticism of any sort could be levelled against
the respondent's conduct in the proceedings there was nothing which could be said
h to tell positively in his favour beyond the mere fact that he had succeeded. Success
in the appeal was—so the argument ran—a condition precedent to the right to make
an application and so could not alone make it 'just and equitable' for an order to
be made. He conceded that if the respondent had not been insured in respect of
his costs he could not have resisted the making of the order sought; but that—he
j said—was because the respondent would have had in his favour not simply the fact
of success but also the fact of financial hardship. I cannot accept this submission
either. As my noble and learned friend, Lord Reid, said in *Saunders v Anglia Building*

1   [1971] 3 All ER 1259, [1972] 1 QB 286
2   [1972] 3 All ER 836, [1972] 3 WLR 801
3   [1921] 1 KB 495, [1920] All ER Rep 340

Society (No 2)[1], the Act directs the court to consider all the circumstances and decide
on broad lines. One circumstance—and a very important circumstance—is the fact
that the appeal has resulted in success for the unassisted litigant. In any given case
there may be many other relevant circumstances—some telling in favour of the
unassisted party and some against him—which the court has to take into account
and weigh against each other; but I do not think that one can deduce from the
wording of the Act a hard and fast rule such as was contended for by counsel that,
even though there is nothing to be said against the applicant, the fact of his success
alone can never entitle him to an order. On the facts of this case where the legal
aid authorities have financed two wholly unsuccessful appeals, I am clearly of opinion
that it is 'just and equitable' that the order asked for should be made.

*Costs of the respondent in the appeal to the House of Lords including the costs of this
application to be paid out of the legal aid fund.*

Solicitors: *Sharpe, Pritchard & Co*, agents for *Thomas Cooksey & Co*, Wolverhampton
(for the respondent); *Peacock & Goddard*, agents for *J C H Bowdler & Sons*, Shrewsbury
(for the appellant); *the Law Society*.

S A Hatteea Esq Barrister.

Shiloh Spinners Ltd v Harding (No 2)

HOUSE OF LORDS
LORD WILBERFORCE, VISCOUNT DILHORNE, LORD PEARSON, LORD SIMON OF GLAISDALE AND
LORD KILBRANDON
19th FEBRUARY, 21st MARCH 1973

*Legal aid – Costs – Unassisted person's costs out of legal aid fund – Costs incurred by unassis-
ted party – Costs incurred in proceedings between him and party receiving legal aid – Proceedings – Appeal – Order by appellate court – Whether 'proceedings' including proceedings
in court below – Whether appellate court entitled to order payment of costs incurred in
connection with proceedings in court below – Legal Aid Act 1964, s 1 (1).*

Where an appellate court determines an appeal in favour of an unassisted party, the
other party being legally aided in respect of the proceedings in the court below and
on appeal, the court may make an order under s 1 (1)[a] of the Legal Aid Act 1964 for
payment to the unassisted party out of the legal aid fund of the costs incurred by
him not only in the proceedings before the appellate court but also in the proceedings
in the court below (see p 967 g, p 968 d h and j and p 969 b, post).

Notes
For the award of costs to an unassisted person out of the legal aid fund, see Supplement
to 30 Halsbury's Laws (3rd Edn) para 933A.
For the Legal Aid Act 1964, s 1, see 25 Halsbury's Statutes (3rd Edn) 789.

Case referred to in opinion
Shiloh Spinners Ltd v Harding p 90, ante, [1973] 2 WLR 28, HL; *rvsg* [1971] 2 All ER
307, [1972] Ch 326, [1971] 3 WLR 34, CA.

1 [1971] 1 All ER 243 at 247, [1971] AC 1039 at 1048
a Section 1 (1), so far as material, is set out at p 967 f, post

Application

On 13th December 1972 the House of Lords[1] allowed an appeal by Shiloh Spinners Ltd, against a decision of the Court of Appeal[2] (Russell, Sachs and Buckley LJJ) dated 10th February 1971, allowing an appeal by the respondent, James Joseph Harding, against a decision of Burgess V-C dated 9th February 1970 in the Chancery of the County Palatine of Lancaster. The respondent was granted legal aid in respect of the proceedings in the Court of Appeal and the House of Lords. Following the decision of the House of Lords the appellants applied for an order under s 1 (1) of the Legal Aid Act 1964 that the costs incurred by them in the proceedings in the Court of Appeal and the House of Lords be paid to them out of the legal aid fund. The proceedings were adjourned for the Law Society to be represented.

John Vinelott QC and *Andrew Morritt* for the appellants.
P B Keenan for the respondent.
Jack Hames QC and *D J Ritchie* for the Law Society.

LORD WILBERFORCE. My Lords, I have had the benefit of reading the opinion of my noble and learned friend, Viscount Dilhorne. I agree with the order he proposes.

VISCOUNT DILHORNE. My Lords, in this application for costs, the Law Society does not dispute that an order should be made under the Legal Aid Act 1964, that the appellants' costs in this House should be paid out of the legal aid fund but they resist the application that such an order should be made in respect of the appellants' costs in the Court of Appeal. The Society contends that this House has no jurisdiction to make that order.

Section 1 (1) of the 1964 Act provides:

'Where a party receives legal aid in connection with any proceedings between him and a party not receiving legal aid . . . and those proceedings are finally decided in favour of the unassisted party, the court by which the proceedings are so decided may . . . make an order for the payment to the unassisted party out of the legal aid fund of . . . the costs incurred by him in those proceedings.'

Prima facie 'proceedings' in this section include the proceedings in the same piece of litigation in which a party has received legal aid before the proceedings in an appellate court are finally decided. Indeed, if it were otherwise, reg 15 (1) of the Legal Aid (Costs of Successful Unassisted Parties) Regulations 1964[3] would appear to be ultra vires for it provides for an application to an appellate court for an order for the payment of the unassisted litigant's costs incurred in proceedings at first instance, whereas, if the Law Society's contention is well-founded, the appellate court has no power to do so.

Section 2 (1) of the 1964 Act gives power to make regulations under the Legal Aid and Advice Act 1949 'for determining the proceedings which are or are not to be treated as separate proceedings for the purposes of this Act' and by reg 2 of the Legal Aid (Costs of Successful Unassisted Parties) Regulations 1964, made under the 1949 and the 1964 Acts, it is provided as follows:

'Any proceedings in respect of which a separate civil aid certificate could properly be issued under the General Regulations to a person receiving legal aid shall be treated as separate proceedings for the purposes of the Act.'

Regulation 6 of the Legal Aid (General) Regulations 1971[4] provides:

---

1   Page 90, ante
2   [1971] 2 All ER 307
3   SI 1964 No 1276
4   SI 1971 No 62

'(1) A certificate may be issued in respect of—(a) . . . (b) the whole or part of— (i) proceedings in a court of first instance, or (ii) proceedings in an appellate court; but no certificate shall relate to proceedings (other than interlocutory appeals) both in a court of first instance and in an appellate court or to proceedings in more than one appellate court.'

It follows that a separate civil aid certificate must have been issued in relation to the appeal to this House and a separate certificate for the appeal to the Court of Appeal. It was consequently contended by the Law Society that the proceedings of this House were the only proceedings in respect of which this House could make an order under the 1964 Act; and it follows that, if the contention is well founded, by the issue of certificates for different parts of the proceedings in this House, the Law Society could restrict the liability of the legal aid fund for costs to the costs in relation to the part in which a final decision was made.

Why it was thought necessary to include in the 1964 Act power to make regulations to determine what proceedings are to be treated as separate proceedings, I do not know. The Act, itself, does not require the determination of separate proceedings. The distinction it draws is between proceedings at first instance and proceedings in the appellate courts. I see no reason to read s 1 (1) of the Act so as to limit the powers of an appellate court only to 'separate proceedings' as defined by the regulations under the Act, when there is no reference to 'separate proceedings' in that subsection of the Act. I, therefore, reject this contention.

Having considered whether an order should be made for costs against the respondent, and it being clear that no such order should be made, the final question for determination is whether it is just and equitable in all the circumstances to make the order sought. In my opinion, it is. The conduct of the respondent was such that the appellants really had no alternative but to institute proceedings against him. They were successful at first instance and obtained an order for costs which has not been satisfied. They were taken to the Court of Appeal[1] on a point of law not related to the merits when, it may be, the respondent, if not legally aided, would not have appealed, bearing in mind the possibility that, if he appealed unsuccessfully, he might be ordered to pay the costs of the appeal. This House[2] has found in the appellants' favour and it has been conceded that an order for payment of their costs in this House would be just and equitable.

In these circumstances, in my opinion it would be unjust and inequitable if the appellants were left to bear the costs they were compelled to incur in the Court of Appeal, costs which, it is apparent, there is no possibility of their recovering from the respondent, and it is just and equitable that an order should be made for the payment of the appellants' costs in the Court of Appeal and in this House, including the costs of this application, out of the legal aid fund.

LORD PEARSON. My Lords, I also agree with the order proposed by my noble and learned friend, Viscount Dilhorne, and with the reasons he gives.

LORD SIMON OF GLAISDALE. My Lords, I have had the advantage of reading in draft the speech prepared by my noble and learned friend, Viscount Dilhorne. I agree with his construction of the Act and regulations; and although on the facts I would myself have concluded on narrow balance that the appellants had failed to discharge the onus of proving that it was just and equitable that their costs in the Court of Appeal should be paid out of the legal aid fund, I am not prepared to oppose the order which commends itself to the majority of your Lordships who

---

1 [1971] 2 All ER 307, [1972] Ch 326
2 Page 90, ante, [1973] 2 WLR 28

a   think otherwise, nor to presume on your Lordships' patience by setting out the reasons which led me narrowly to the contrary conclusion.

I should like to add, however, that the practice adopted by the appellants seems to me to be a most useful one. They tendered in advance a written statement of their submissions as to costs, with the relevant documents annexed and a list of the Acts, regulations and authorities on which they intended to rely.

b

LORD KILBRANDON. My Lords, I also agree with the order proposed by my noble and learned friend, Viscount Dilhorne, and with the reasons he gives.

Costs of appellants in the Court of Appeal and the House of Lords, including the costs of the application, to be paid out of the legal aid fund.

c

Solicitors: *Gregory, Rowcliffe & Co*, agents for *John Taylor & Co*, Manchester (for the appellants); *Collyer-Bristow & Co*, agents for *Frederick Howarth, Son & Maitland*, Bury (for the respondent); *the Law Society*.

S A Hatteea Esq   Barrister.

d

Note
O'Brien and another v Robinson (No 2)

e   HOUSE OF LORDS
LORD REID, LORD MORRIS OF BORTH-Y-GEST, LORD DIPLOCK, LORD SIMON OF GLAISDALE AND LORD CROSS OF CHELSEA
19th FEBRUARY, 21St MARCH 1973

Legal aid – Costs – Unassisted person's costs out of legal aid fund – Just and equitable – Leapfrog
f *appeal – Appeal direct to House of Lords from High Court on point of law of general public importance – Legal aid granted to appellant in connection with appeal – Appeal dismissed – Costs incurred by respondent – Whether just and equitable that order for payment of costs out of legal aid fund be made – Legal Aid Act 1964, s 1 (1), (2).*

Notes

For the award of costs to an unassisted party out of the legal aid fund, see Supplement
g to 30 Halsbury's Laws (3rd Edn) para 933A.

For the Legal Aid Act 1964, s 1, see 25 Halsbury's Statutes (3rd Edn) 789.

Cases referred to in opinion

Davies v Taylor [1972] 3 All ER 836, [1972] 2 WLR 801, HL; *affg* [1971] 3 All ER 1259,
[1972] 1 QB 286, [1971] 3 WLR 515, CA.
h *O'Brien v Robinson* p 583, ante, [1973] 2 WLR 393, HL.

Application

On 6th March 1972 Bristow J dismissed a claim by the appellants, Lawrence Joseph O'Brien and Doris Muriel O'Brien, against the respondent, Martin C Robinson, for damages for personal injuries. Bristow J certified, however, pursuant to s 12 of the
j Administration of Justice Act 1969, that the decision involved a point of law of general public importance and that that point of law was one in respect of which he was bound by a decision of the House of Lords in previous proceedings and was fully considered in the judgments given by the House of Lords in those previous proceedings, and granted the appellants' application for a certificate for leave to present a petition of appeal to the House of Lords. On 12th April 1972 the appellants were granted legal aid in

connection with the proceedings on the appeal direct to the House of Lords. On 26th
April 1972 the appeal committee of the House of Lords gave leave to the appellants
to present a petition of appeal to the House. On 19th February 1973 the House of
Lords[1] dismissed the appeal. The respondent applied for an order under s 1 (1)
of the Legal Aid Act 1964 that the costs incurred by him in the proceedings on the
appeal be paid to him out of the legal aid fund.

Michael Turner for the respondent.
Barbara Calvert for the appellants.
Jack Hames QC and *D J Ritchie* for the Law Society.

Their Lordships took time for consideration.

21st March. The following opinions were delivered.

LORD REID. My Lords, for the reasons given by my noble and learned friend,
Lord Diplock, I would allow the respondent to recover his costs from the legal aid
fund.

LORD MORRIS OF BORTH-Y-GEST. My Lords, I am of the opinion, for the
reasons given by my noble and learned friend, Lord Diplock, that the respondent
should recover from the legal aid fund the costs incurred by him in resisting this
appeal.

LORD DIPLOCK. My Lords, this appeal[1] came direct from the High Court to
your Lordships' House pursuant to s 12 of the Administration of Justice Act 1969, on
a certificate of the judge that a point of law of general public importance was involved
and that that point of law was one in which the judge was bound by a decision of the
House of Lords in previous proceedings and was fully considered in the judgments
given by the House of Lords in those previous proceedings.

In the High Court none of the parties was legally aided and the plaintiffs' action was
dismissed with costs. For the proceedings on the direct appeal to this House the plain-
tiffs/appellants were granted legal aid. The defendant/respondent was not. His
liability for the costs incurred by him to his own solicitors in successfully resisting the
appeal was covered by insurance.

The financial position of the unsuccessful appellants is such that no order for payment of costs could properly be made against either of them personally. Application
has accordingly been made by the respondent for an order under s 1 (1) and (2) of
the Legal Aid Act 1964, that the costs incurred by him in the appeal should be paid
out of the legal aid fund.

The application was resisted by the Law Society on the same grounds as those
advanced in a similar application in *Davies v Taylor*[2] where the successful respondent
was also covered by insurance in respect of his costs. I would adopt, without repeating,
the reasons for rejecting the submissions of the Law Society which are to be found
in the speech of my noble and learned friend, Lord Cross of Chelsea[3], in that appeal.
So we are left with the broad question whether we are 'satisfied that it is just and
equitable in all the circumstances' to make the order.

The only relevant circumstances which distinguish the present appeal from that in
Davies v Taylor is that in the latter the unsuccessful plaintiff in the action had appealed
successively to the Court of Appeal[4] and to this House[5]; each time unsuccessfully,

1   Page 583, ante
2   Page 959, ante
3   Pages 965, 966, ante
4   [1971] 3 All ER 1259, [1972] 1 QB 286
5   [1972] 3 All ER 836, [1972] 3 WLR 801

a whereas in the present appeal there was but one appeal direct from the High Court to this House.

My Lords, as the judge had certified and as this House has held[1], the law was well settled adversely to the appellants' claim by a decision of the Court of Appeal which had been approved by your Lordships' House. Neither the respondent himself nor his insurers, as a company engaged in the business of insuring property owners against liability to third parties, had any business interest in altering it. They were

b content with the law as it had previously been laid down and as it would remain unless your Lordships could be persuaded to hold that the reasoning of a previous decision of this House was wrong.

The point of law involved was one of general public importance. The judge had so certified before a legal aid certificate was granted to the appellants. No criticism can be made of the legal aid authorities for granting it. But in the result the respond-

c ent's insurers have been put to the expense of successfully resisting an attempt to alter the law as previously laid down by your Lordships' House. In these circumstances, I am satisfied that it is just and equitable that they should recover their costs of doing so from the legal aid fund.

d **LORD SIMON OF GLAISDALE.** My Lords, I have had the advantage of reading in draft the speech prepared by my noble and learned friend, Lord Diplock. I agree with it and with the order which he in consequence proposes.

LORD CROSS OF CHELSEA. My Lords, for the reasons given by my noble and learned friend, Lord Diplock, I am of opinion that the respondent should recover

e from the legal aid fund the costs incurred by him in resisting this appeal.

Respondent to recover his costs from the legal aid fund.

Solicitors: *B M Birnberg & Co* (for the appellants); *Herbert Smith & Co* (for the respondent); *the Law Society.*

f
                                                    S A Hatteea Esq   Barrister·

g   # Practice Direction

SUPREME COURT TAXING OFFICE

Costs – Taxation – Value added tax – Crown Court – Bills lodged for taxation which include charge for work done or services rendered.

h

Value added tax ('VAT') was introduced by the Finance Act 1972 and is chargeable from 1st April 1973. Every taxable person as defined by the Act must be registered and in general terms (and subject to the exceptions set out in the Act) whenever a taxable person supplies goods or services in the United Kingdom in the course

j of business a liability to tax arises. Responsibility for making a charge for VAT in a proper case and for accounting to Customs and Excise for the proper amount of VAT is solely that of the registered person concerned. The following directions will apply to all bills lodged for taxation which include any charge for work done or services rendered on or after 1st April 1973, namely:

---

1 Page 583, ante

1. REGISTERED NUMBER

The registered number allocated by Customs and Excise to every person registered under the Act must appear in a prominent place at the head of every bill of costs, fee note, account or voucher on which VAT is claimed or chargeable.

2. ACTION BEFORE TAXATION

(a) If there is a possibility of a dispute arising whether any person claiming costs is a taxable person or whether any service in respect of which a charge is proposed to be made in the bill is zero-rated or exempt, reference should be made to Customs and Excise, and wherever possible a statement produced on taxation.

(b) Where VAT is claimed by a person who is engaged in business and the costs of the proceedings to be submitted for taxation are chargeable as an expense of that business, then (unless the taxing officer or the party paying costs is able to agree the basis on which VAT is claimed) a certificate must be produced to the taxing officer that the receiving party is not entitled to recover, or is only entitled to recover a stated proportion of, the VAT claimed on such costs as input tax in his VAT account with Customs and Excise. A form of certificate to be given by the solicitor or accountant for the party receiving costs is set out in the schedule hereto.

3. FORM OF FEE NOTE OR BILL OF COSTS

In whatever form counsel submits his fee note or a solicitor submits his bill of costs it must take account of the following:

(a) *Apportionment*

The fee note or bill must be divided into separate parts so as to show the work done before and from 1st April 1973. In a solicitor's bill the totals of the profit costs and disbursements in each part must be carried separately to the summary.

(b) *Disbursements*

(i) VAT attributable to taxable disbursements must be shown stating if it has been paid. This will consist of the VAT which has been paid at the time when the bill is drawn, and an amount in respect of any unpaid disbursement. These amounts may be indicated in a separate VAT column inserted in the fee note or bill of costs. As an alternative the VAT may be shown immediately below the disbursement to which it relates.

(ii) Petty (or general) disbursements such as postages, fares etc, which are normally treated as part of a solicitor's overheads and included in his profit costs, should be charged with VAT even though they bear no tax when the solicitor incurs them. It is otherwise where the disbursement is normally charged as a specific disbursement to the client, e g the cost of travel by public transport on a specific journey for a particular client.

(c) *Summary*

Where a summary at the end of the bill is necessary it must also include a column for VAT so that the VAT can be cast separately. The VAT on the total of the profit costs as allowed on taxation should also be inserted in this VAT column. Specimen forms of bill with summary may be inspected on application to the taxing officer.

4. TAX INVOICE

(a) In respect of a taxation of costs payable by one party to another the tax invoice will be the bill rendered by the solicitor to his own client on conclusion of the work to which his retainer relates.

(b) Where costs, including legal aid costs, are payable out of central funds pursuant to any authority the tax invoice in the case of counsel will consist of his fee note and in the case of a solicitor his bill of costs as taxed and in either case if none is lodged, the statement supplied by the court as to the fees or costs allowed on taxation.

a
5. VOUCHERS
Where receipted accounts for disbursements are retained as tax invoices a photostat copy of any such receipted account may be produced and will be accepted as sufficient evidence of payment when disbursements are vouched.

6. RATE OF VAT
b The rate of VAT which will be applied on taxation will be the rate at that date, save in respect of disbursements which have been paid when the rate will be the rate at the date of payment. Should there be a change in the rate applied on taxation between the date of taxation and the signing of the certificate of taxation, any interested party may apply for the taxation to be varied so as to take account of any increase or reduction in the amount of tax payable. Once the certificate of taxation has been signed no variation will be possible.
c

7. EVIDENCE OF RESULT OF TAXATION
Both counsel and solicitors will be given a statement showing details of the amount of fees or costs and disbursements arrived at exclusive of VAT and of the sum added to each for VAT.

d
8. VARIATION ON APPEAL
Where the fees or costs as taxed are varied on appeal the VAT charged will be amended as appropriate by the taxing officer.

SCHEDULE
Form of Certificate

e To: The Chief Clerk   Address:
       Crown Court at

Date:

Regina v A

With reference to the pending taxation of the [prosecutor's] [defendants'] costs and disbursements herein which are payable by [the defendant] [the prosecutor]
f [central funds], we the undersigned, as [solicitors to] [the auditors of] the [prosecutor] [defendant], hereby certify that he on the basis of his last completed VAT return would [not be entitled to recover] [be entitled to recover only . . . per cent of the] value added tax on such costs and disbursements, as input tax pursuant to s 3 of the Finance Act 1972.

[Signed]
g [Solicitor to] [Auditor of] . . . [Prosecutor] [Defendant]
Registered no. . .

GRAHAM GRAHAM-GREEN
12th March 1973   Chief Master

Practice Direction

SUPREME COURT TAXING OFFICE

Costs – Taxation – Value added tax – Civil proceedings and non-contentious business – Bills lodged for taxation which include charge for work done or services rendered.

Value added tax ('VAT') was introduced by the Finance Act 1972 and is chargeable from 1st April 1973. Every taxable person as defined by the Act must be registered and in general terms (and subject to the exceptions set out in the Act) whenever a taxable person supplies goods or services in the United Kingdom in the course of business a liability to tax arises. Responsibility for making a charge for VAT in a proper case and for accounting to Customs and Excise for the proper amount of VAT is solely that of the registered person concerned. The following directions will apply to all bills lodged for taxation which include any charge for work done or services rendered on or after 1st April 1973, namely:

1. REGISTERED NUMBER
   The registered number allocated by Customs and Excise to every person registered under the Act must appear in a prominent place at the head of every bill of costs, account or voucher on which VAT is claimed or chargeable.

2. ACTION BEFORE TAXATION
   (a) If there is a possibility of a dispute arising whether any person claiming costs is a taxable person or whether any service in respect of which a charge is proposed to be made in the bill is zero-rated or exempt, reference should be made to Customs and Excise, and wherever possible a statement produced on taxation.
   (b) Where VAT is claimed by a person who is engaged in business and the costs of the proceedings to be submitted for taxation are chargeable as an expense of that business, then (unless the paying party agrees the basis on which VAT is claimed) a certificate must be produced on taxation that the receiving party is not entitled to recover, or is only entitled to recover a stated proportion of, the VAT claimed on such costs as input tax in his VAT account with Customs and Excise. A form of certificate to be given by the solicitor or accountant for the party receiving costs is set out in the schedule hereto.

3. FORM OF BILL OF COSTS
   The form of bill of costs in practice will require amendment as follows:

(a) *Apportionment*
   The bill must be divided into separate parts so as to show the work done on a day-to-day basis before and from 1st April 1973. Wherever a lump sum charge has been made for work, only part of which was performed by 31st March 1973, the lump sum must also be apportioned. The totals of the profit costs and disbursements in each part must be carried separately to the summary.

(b) *Disbursements*
   (i) VAT attributable to any disbursement must be shown stating if it has been paid. This will consist of the VAT which has been paid at the time when the bill is drawn, and an amount in respect of any unpaid disbursement. These amounts may be indicated in a separate VAT column inserted to the left of the normal disbursement column. As an alternative the VAT may be shown in the disbursement column immediately below the disbursement to which it relates.
   (ii) Petty (or general) disbursements such as postages, fares etc, which are normally treated as part of a solicitor's overheads and included in his profit costs, should be charged with VAT even though they bear no tax when the solicitor incurs them. It is otherwise where the disbursement is normally charged as a specific disburse-

ment to the client, e g the cost of travel by public transport on a specific journey
a for a particular client.

(c) *Summary*

The summary at the end of the bill must also include an additional column for
VAT so that the VAT can be cast separately. The VAT on the total of the profit
costs as allowed on taxation should also be inserted in this VAT column. The taxing
b fee will be calculated on the total of profit costs and disbursements as taxed and
the VAT thereon.

(d) *Legal aid summary*

In legal aid cases the legal aid summary must be drawn so as to show the total
VAT on counsel's fees as a separate item from the VAT on profit costs and other
disbursements and must take account of the fact that VAT will only be payable
c on 90 per cent of the solicitor's profit costs and counsel's fees, (see para 7, infra).
Specimen summaries may be inspected on application to the chambers concerned.

4. TAX INVOICE

The taxed bill lodged for certificate is always retained in chambers so that where a
solicitor waives his solicitor and own client costs and accepts the taxed costs payable
d by the unsuccessful party in settlement, it will be necessary for a short statement as
to the amount of the taxed costs and the VAT thereon to be prepared for use as the
tax invoice.

5. VOUCHERS

Where receipted accounts for disbursements made by the solicitor or his client
are retained as tax invoices a photostat copy of any such receipted account may be
e produced and will be accepted as sufficient evidence of payment when disbursements
are vouched.

6. RATE OF VAT

The rate of VAT which will be applied on taxation will be the rate at that date,
save in respect of disbursements which have been paid when the rate will be the
f rate at the date of payment. Should there be a change in the rate applied on taxation
between the date of taxation and the signing of the certificate of taxation, any
interested party may apply for the taxation to be varied so as to take account of any
increase or reduction in the amount of tax payable. Once the certificate of taxation
has been signed no variation will be possible.

7. CALCULATION OF VAT RECOVERABLE BY A LEGALLY AIDED PARTY

g VAT will not be recoverable on the 10 per cent of the solicitor's costs and counsel's
fees which is retained by the legal aid fund. Accordingly, the recoverable VAT
must be calculated on 90 per cent of the solicitor's profit costs and 90 per cent of
counsel's fees. This will not apply to other disbursements, which are paid in full by
the legal aid fund.

h 8. CERTIFICATE OR ALLOCATUR

In non-legal aid cases the total VAT allowed will be shown as a separate item.
In legal aid cases the VAT on counsel's fees will be shown separately from the
remaining VAT.

SCHEDULE

Form of Certificate

j

Address:

Date:

To: The [Master] [Registrar]
Address:

A v B C Ltd

With reference to the pending taxation of the defendant's [*or as the case may be*] costs and disbursements herein which are payable by the plaintiff [*or as the case may be*], we the undersigned, as [solicitors to] [the auditors of] the above-named defendant [*or as the case may be*] company, hereby certify that the defendant [*or as the case may be*] company on the basis of its last completed VAT return would [not be entitled to recover] [be entitled to recover only . . . per cent of the] value added tax on such costs and disbursements, as input tax pursuant to s 3 of the Finance Act 1972.

[Signed]
[Solicitor to] [Auditor of] [defendant]
Registered no. . .

This Direction is issued with the concurrence of the Senior Registrar of the Family Division to the intent that it should be followed in that Division.

GRAHAM GRAHAM-GREEN
9th March 1973   Chief Master

Practice Direction

PATENTS APPEAL TRIBUNAL

Patent – Appeal to Court of Appeal – Application for leave to appeal – Procedure – Time for application – Time for service of notice of appeal if leave granted by tribunal – Ex parte application to Court of Appeal if leave refused – Patents Act 1949, s 87 (1) (aa), (c) – RSC Ord 59, rr 14, 18.

Appeals to the Court of Appeal from decisions of the Patents Appeal Tribunal are regulated by s 87 (1)[1] of the Patents Act 1949 (as amended by s 46[2] of the Courts Act 1971).

Appeals to the Court of Appeal under s 87 (1) (*aa*) and s 87 (1) (*c*) require the leave of the tribunal which, if given, will cause the provisions of RSC Ord 59, r 18, to apply, whereunder the notice of appeal is required to be served within six weeks from the date of the decision or within such further time as the tribunal may allow.

Applications to the tribunal for leave to appeal to the Court of Appeal under s 87 (1) (*aa*) or s 87 (1) (*c*) should be made on notice to the parties entitled to notice of the appeal proper within 14 days of the date of the tribunal decision or within such further time as the tribunal may allow.

Where an application to the tribunal for leave to appeal to the Court of Appeal is refused, an application for a similar purpose may be made to the Court of Appeal ex parte within seven days after the date of the refusal. The provisions of RSC Ord 59, r 14, shall apply to such applications.

The Practice Direction[3] dated 6th May 1969 with regard to appeals to the Court of Appeal is hereby cancelled.

By direction of Mr Justice Graham.

C L DALLEY
21st February 1973   Registrar

---

1 See 24 Halsbury's Statutes (3rd Edn) 634
2 See 41 Halsbury's Statutes (3rd Edn) 1061
3 [1969] 2 All ER 544, [1969] 1 WLR 1259

a   # Clinch v Inland Revenue Commissioners

QUEEN'S BENCH DIVISION
ACKNER J
29th, 30th, 31st JANUARY, 1st, 13th FEBRUARY 1973

b *Income tax – Avoidance – Transfer of assets abroad – Information – Power of commissioners by notice to require information – Power to require such information as commissioners think necessary for specified purposes – Commissioners not entitled to have regard to irrelevant considerations or to act unreasonably – Information as to introduction of customers to bank with view to carrying out specified transactions – Information as to advice given to customer resulting in carrying out transactions – Plaintiff London representative of bank incorporated*
c *in Bermuda – Bank providing facilities for and advice in relation to transfer of money to Bermuda – Commissioners serving notice on plaintiff requiring particulars of customers and transactions or operations – Validity of notice – Income and Corporation Taxes Act 1970, s 481 (1), (2).*

Between November 1964 to November 1970 the plaintiff acted as the London repre-
d sentative of a banking company ('the bank') incorporated under the laws of Bermuda. Since November 1970 he had been the managing director of a wholly-owned sub-sidiary of the bank ('the London bank') formed mainly to take over the office of the London representative. It was the function of the plaintiff (a) to provide general advice to potential customers who came direct to the London bank enquiring about the advantages of transferring money to Bermuda and the various options open to
e them for that purpose such as using the medium of companies, partnerships and settlements and (b) to provide general information to customers, referred to him by their solicitors and/or accountants, about Bermuda and the services which the bank could offer in relation to the incorporation of companies, the setting up of partnerships and their management in Bermuda, and the services of the bank as trustee of settlements, etc. On 31st January 1972 the defendants, the Commis-
f sioners of Inland Revenue, issued a notice pursuant to s 481 (1)[a] of the Income and Corporation Taxes Act 1970 requiring the plaintiff, as a former London representative of the bank, to furnish them, in any case where he had, since 5th April 1965, acted for a United Kingdom customer in or in connection with any transactions or opera-tions involving (1) the formation or management of a foreign company, (2) the forma-tion or management of a foreign partnership, (3) the creation, or the execution of
g the trusts of, a foreign settlement, (4) the transfer of assets to any foreign company, foreign partnership or foreign settlement and (5) the acquisition (by purchase or otherwise) of any interest (or option to acquire an interest) in the share capital or loan capital of any foreign company or in or under any foreign partnership or foreign settlement, (a) the name and address of the customer (or where that was not known, the name and address of any agent who had dealt with him on the customer's behalf);
h (b) particulars in respect of the above transactions or operations so far as within the plaintiff's knowledge; and (c) the name and address of any other person to whom the plaintiff introduced the customer for the purpose of completing or carrying out any of the above transactions or operations. At all material times the plaintiff was aware of the powers of the defendants to serve notice on him pursuant to s 414 of the Income Tax Act 1952 (subsequently s 481 (1) of the 1970 Act). Nevertheless he had not kept
j a special s 414 file so as to be able quickly and conveniently to supply the information which the defendants might seek. The plaintiff sought a declaration that the notice was invalid contending (a) that s 481 of the 1970 Act did not permit questions to be asked of an intermediary relating to unidentified transactions on behalf of unidentified

---

a   Section 481, so far as material, is set out at p 984 **a** to **c**, post

principals; and (b) that the defendants, in exercising their powers under the
section, had acted unreasonably in that the requirements of the notice were unduly
burdensome and oppressive.

Held – (i) Section 481 (1) of the 1970 Act, on its true construction, was wide enough
in its terms to justify the commissioners in asking for the information set out in the
notice.   The breadth of that subsection was not cut down by s 481 (2) which in any
event obliged an intermediary to specify what part, if any, he had taken in any
transaction of a description specified in the notice and also, if asked, to give particulars
of the transaction; the introduction of a customer to a bank or to any other person
with a view to carrying out a transaction specified was within the scope of the section
and so was the giving of advice to a customer which resulted in a specified transaction
or operation being carried out (see p 985 g and p 986 h to p 987 a, post).
     (ii) The defendants' statutory authority under s 481 (1) to require 'such particulars
as they think necessary' enabled them to obtain detailed information relating to the
transfer of assets abroad in order to decide whether or not in their opinion tax had
been evaded.   They were not, however, entitled to have regard to irrelevant considerations or to act quite unreasonably.   Therefore if the particulars sought went
substantially beyond that which was required for that purpose they could properly
be described as unduly oppressive or burdensome, entitling the court to intervene.
The particulars required in the defendants' notice did not, however, go substantially
beyond what was required; furthermore, on the evidence, the plaintiff had failed
to establish that the time and expense involved in providing the information required
by the defendants imposed on him an unduly heavy burden and he could not for that
purpose pray in aid his own failure to have the necessary material reasonably available.
Accordingly the plaintiff was not entitled to the declaration asked for (see p 989 d
to g and p 991 c to f, post).

Notes
For the power of the Board of Inland Revenue to require information in relation to
the transfer of assets abroad, see 20 Halsbury's Laws (3rd Edn) 593, para 1163.
     For the Income and Corporation Taxes Act 1970, s 481, see 33 Halsbury's Statutes
(3rd Edn) 620.

Cases referred to in judgment
Associated Provincial Picture Houses Ltd v Wednesbury Corpn [1947] 2 All ER 680, [1948]
     1 KB 223, [1948] LJR 190, 177 LT 641, 112 JP 55, 45 LGR 635, CA, 45 Digest (Repl)
     215, 189.
Ayrshire Pullman Motor Services and Ritchie v Inland Revenue Comrs (1929) 14 Tax Cas
     754, 28 (2) Digest (Reissue) 392, *1122.
Cape Brandy Syndicate v Inland Revenue Comrs [1921] 1 KB 64, 12 Tax Cas 358, 90 LJKB
     113, 125 LT 108; *affd* [1921] 2 KB 403, 90 LJKB 461, CA, 28 (1) Digest (Reissue)
     586, 2172.
Entick v Carrington (1765) 19 State Tr 1029, [1558-1774] All ER Rep 41, 2 Wils 257,
     1 Digest (Repl) 318, 45.
Fawcett Properties Ltd v Buckinghamshire County Council [1960] 3 All ER 503, [1961]
     AC 636, [1960] 3 WLR 831, 125 JP 8, 59 LGR 69, 12 P & CR 1, HL, 45 Digest (Repl)
     342, 60.
Hall & Co Ltd v Shoreham-by-Sea Urban District Council [1964] 1 All ER 1, [1964] 1 WLR
     240, 128 JP 120, 62 LGR 206, 15 P & CR 119, CA, 45 Digest (Repl) 342, 61.
Inland Revenue Comrs v Duke of Westminster [1936] AC 1, [1935] All ER Rep 259, 104
     LJKB 383, 153 LT 223; sub nom *Duke of Westminster v Inland Revenue Comrs* 19 Tax
     Cas 490, HL, 28 (1) Digest (Reissue) 507, 1845.
Roberts v Hopwood [1925] AC 578, [1925] All ER Rep 24, 94 LJKB 542, 133 LT 289,
     89 JP 105, 23 LGR 337, HL, 33 Digest (Repl) 23, 107.

a   *Royal Bank of Canada v Inland Revenue Comrs* [1972] 1 All ER 225, [1972] Ch 665, [1972] 2 WLR 106.

Smith v East Elloe Rural District Council [1956] 1 All ER 855, [1956] AC 736, [1956] 2 WLR 888, 120 JP 263, 54 LGR 233, HL, 26 Digest (Repl) 703, *135.*

Williams v Summerfield [1972] 2 All ER 1334, [1972] 2 QB 512, [1972] 3 WLR 131, DC.

b   **Action**

By a writ issued on 20th March 1972 the plaintiff, Geoffrey Bertram Clinch, brought an action against the defendants, the Commissioners of Inland Revenue. By paras 1-4 of his statement of claim the plaintiff alleged that he was, and since November 1970 had been, a managing director of N T Butterfield & Son (Bermuda) Ltd ('the London bank') and from November 1964 to November 1970 had been the London

c   representative of the bank of N T Butterfield & Son Ltd ('the bank'), a banking company incorporated under the laws of Bermuda. At all material times the function of the plaintiff was to interest people in the banking and allied services offered by the bank and generally to represent the bank in the United Kingdom. In pursuance of that function the plaintiff kept records of actual and prospective customers of the bank and of those interested or potentially interested in dealing with the bank.

d   Those records comprised over 500 files, 4,000 index cards and 15 boxes of office memoranda. The files, index cards and boxes were the property of the bank or of the London bank. Paragraphs 5-8 of the statement of claim were in the following terms:

'5. On the 2nd day of February 1972 the Plaintiff received a Notice from the Defendants dated the 31st day of January 1972 ... The said Notice purported to be a Notice under Section 481 (1) of the Income and Corporation Taxes Act

e   1970 and the Plaintiff will refer thereto for its full terms and effect.

'6. In order to comply with the terms of the said Notice the Plaintiff would have to conduct a detailed analysis of the said files index cards and memoranda a task which would occupy the Plaintiff full time for a period estimated to be not less than two months. On the basis that the Plaintiff continued to carry out

f   the duties for which he is employed and paid such task would occupy his spare time for many months.

'7. The Plaintiff will contend that upon the true construction of the said Section 481 (1) and the said purported Notice the said Notice is not a valid Notice within the meaning of the said Section in that *inter alia* it is a fishing notice and gives no details whatever of the persons in whose transactions the Defendants are interested or other sufficient details.

g   '8. Further if the said Notice is not of itself as a matter of construction invalid it is invalid as being burdensome and oppressive having regard to the work required in order to comply with its terms.'

The plaintiff claimed: (1) a declaration that on a true construction of s 481 of the 1970 Act and the defendants' notice, the notice was invalid; (2) a declaration that the plain-

h   tiff was not compelled or obliged to furnish the defendants with the information requested in the notice, and (3) costs.

The notice served on the plaintiff was in the following terms:

'1. The [defendants] in exercise of their powers under Section 481 (1) of the Income and Corporation Taxes Act 1970 hereby require you as former London

j   Representative of the Bank of N. T. Butterfield & Son Ltd. to furnish to them on or before the 7th day of April, 1972, at the address given above, the information indicated in paragraph 3 below.

'*Interpretation*

'2. For the purposes of this notice—(i) "the Bank" means the Bank of N. T. Butterfield & Son Ltd. at its head office or branches in Bermuda; (ii) references

to things done by you are to things done by you, or by any staff employed under
you, in your former capacity as London Representative of the bank of N. T.   *a*
Butterfield & Son Ltd. and references to matters within your knowledge are to
matters coming within your knowledge in that capacity or in your subsequent
capacity as director of [the London bank], or recorded in any records maintained
by you in either capacity, or maintained by [the London bank]; (iii) references
to your "acting in or in connection with" a specified transaction or operation   *b*
include—(a) the giving of advice to a customer, if but only if, a specified transaction or operation has within your knowledge been carried out as a result of the
advice, and (b) the introducing of a customer to the bank or to any other person
with a view to the carrying out of a specified transaction or operation; (iv)
"customer" includes any person (whether or not a customer of the bank for
other purposes) for whom you have acted in or in connection with any specified   *c*
transaction or operation; and "United Kingdom customer" means any customer
with whom you dealt, not being a customer who is known to you to have had
at all times during your dealings with him since 5th April 1965 a permanent
address outside the United Kingdom but no permanent address in the United
Kingdom; (v) "foreign company" means any company incorporated in a
specified territory, and any other company which within your knowledge was,   *d*
or was intended at any time in the future to be, so managed and controlled that
it qualified or would qualify for purposes of United Kingdom income tax as
resident in a specified territory, but does not include a company, or the subsidiary of a company, of which the ordinary shares have at all times since 5th
April 1965 (or, if later, since the first anniversary of the company's incorporation)
been quoted on a stock exchange; (vi) "foreign partnership" means any partnership constituted under the laws of a specified territory and any other partnership   *e*
which within your knowledge was, or was intended at any time in the future to
be, so managed and controlled that it qualified or would qualify for purposes
of United Kingdom income tax as resident in a specified territory; (vii) "foreign
settlement" means any settlement or trust expressed to be governed by the law of
a specified territory, and any other settlement or trust which within your knowledge was, or was intended at any time in the future to be, so constituted that   *f*
income arising under the settlement or trust qualified or would qualify for
purposes of United Kingdom income tax as the income of a person resident in a
specified territory; (viii) "specified territory" means any of the following territories: Bahama Islands, Barbados, Bermuda, British Virgin Islands, Cayman
Islands, Channel Islands, Isle of Man, Netherlands Antilles; (ix) "specified
transaction or operation" means a transaction or operation of any kind mentioned   *g*
in the first column in paragraph 3 below.

'*Information required*
    '3.   In any case where you have since 5th April 1965 acted for a United Kingdom
customer in or in connection with any transaction or operation of a kind mentioned in the first column below you are hereby required subject to paragraph   *h*
4 below to give—(a) the name and address of the customer (or, where that is
not known, the name and address of any agent who has dealt with you on the
customer's behalf); (b) the respective particulars specified in the second column
below so far as within your knowledge; and (c) the name and address of any
other person to whom you introduced the customer for the purpose of completing
or carrying out the transaction or operation.   *j*

'*Transaction or operation*	*Particulars*
'(1) The formation or management of a foreign company.	The name of the company; the date and place of its incorporation; its registered or other known address.

'(2) The formation or management of a foreign partnership.

The name and address of the partnership; the country in which it is constituted; the names and addresses of the partners; the date of any deed or other document regulating the partnership.

'(3) The creation, or the execution of the trusts of, a foreign settlement.

The name and address of the settlor; the date and nature of any document or other act constituting or regulating the settlement; the names and addresses of the trustees.

'(4) The transfer of assets to any foreign company, foreign partnership or foreign settlement.

Description of the assets transferred; particulars relating to the company, partnership or settlement as required under (1), (2) or (3) above.

'(5) The acquisition (by purchase or otherwise) of any interest (or option to acquire an interest) in the share capital or loan capital of any foreign company, or in or under any foreign partnership or foreign settlement. (In the case of a company having no share capital the reference to any interest in share capital shall be taken as a reference to any corresponding interest in the company.)

Description of the interest acquired; particulars relating to the company, partnership or settlement as required under (1), (2) or (3) above.

'4. You are not obliged by reason of this notice to furnish any particulars of any ordinary banking transactions between you (or the bank) and a customer carried out in the ordinary course of banking business, unless you (or the bank) acted on behalf of the customer as mentioned in Section 481 (4) of the Income and Corporation Taxes Act 1970.'

Sir Elwyn Jones QC and *P G Whiteman* for the plaintiff.
D C Potter QC, Patrick Medd and *P L Gibson* for the defendants.

Cur adv vult

13th February. **ACKNER J** read the following judgment. Bermuda has throughout this case been described as a tax haven. Perhaps a tax refuge is a more accurate word, since there is apparently no taxation on profits, no income tax, no capital gains tax and no estate duty. Understandably, in those circumstances there are no tax treaties between Bermuda and any other country, and accordingly no mutual agreements covering the exchange of fiscal information.

The plaintiff was from November 1964 to November 1970 the London representative of N T Butterfield & Son Ltd ('the bank'), a banking company incorporated under the laws of Bermuda. Since November 1970 the plaintiff has been the managing director of N T Butterfield & Son (Bermuda) Ltd ('the London bank'). The London bank is a wholly owned subsidiary of the bank.

Only a very small amount of the London bank's business is concerned with deposit and other accounts. It specialises, as is apparent from the various advertisements in the Times, Financial Times, Economist and other papers and journals put before me, in the—

'management and trusteeship of international funds, the incorporation of Bermuda-based companies and partnerships, trusteeship of settlements and comprehensive advice on investment portfolios.'

The majority of the London bank's customers were, at the material time, persons *a*
of considerable wealth who wanted to transfer their money to Bermuda either to
avoid paying tax in the United Kingdom and/or in order to have part of their
capital outside this country. The plaintiff's function was essentially twofold: (1)
Potential customers might come direct to the London bank enquiring about the
advantages of transferring money to Bermuda and the various options open, for
example via the medium of companies, partnerships and settlements, in which case *b*
the plaintiff would give them general advice and refer them, as far as the technicalities
were concerned, to their own solicitors and accountants, if they had such advisers,
or alternatively recommend a firm or firms which he knew to be expert in this field.
(2) Customers would be referred to him by their solicitors and/or accountants
for general information about Bermuda and the services which the bank could offer
in relation to the incorporation of companies, the setting up of partnerships and *c*
their management in Bermuda, the services which the bank could offer as trustee
of settlements, etc. In his own words, the service of his office was co-opted to give
the customer an assurance about the stability of Bermuda, and the respectability
and expertise of the bank in relation to the services which it provided in Bermuda.

Chapter IV of Part XVIII of the Income Tax Act 1952 is entitled 'Transactions Resulting in Transfer of Income to Persons Abroad'. The marginal note to s 412 refers to *d*
the sections in this chapter, and is entitled 'Provisions for preventing avoidance of
income tax by transactions resulting in the transfer of income to persons abroad'.
It is a highly complicated section, but happily it is sufficient for the purposes of this
action for me to recite but a small portion of it as amended in one short aspect by the
Finance Act 1969. Surprisingly, it starts with its own preamble:

'For the purpose of preventing the avoiding by individuals ordinarily resident *e*
in the United Kingdom of liability to income tax by means of transfers of assets
by virtue or in consequence whereof, either alone or in conjunction with associated operations, income becomes payable to persons resident or domiciled out of
the United Kingdom, it is hereby enacted as follows:—

'(1) Where by virtue or in consequence of any such transfer, either alone or in
conjunction with associated operations, such an individual has, within the mean- *f*
ing of this section, power to enjoy, whether forthwith or in the future, any income
of a person resident or domiciled out of the United Kingdom which, if it were
income of that individual received by him in the United Kingdom, would be
chargeable to income tax by deduction or otherwise, that income shall, whether it
would or would not have been chargeable to income tax apart from the provisions of this section, be deemed to be income of that individual for all the *g*
purposes of this Act.

'(2) Where, whether before or after any such transfer, such an individual
receives or is entitled to receive any capital sum the payment whereof is in any
way connected with the transfer or any associated operation, any income which,
by virtue or in consequence of the transfer, either alone or in conjunction with
associated operations, has become the income of a person resident or domiciled *h*
out of the United Kingdom shall, whether it would or would not have been
chargeable to income tax apart from the provisions of this section, be deemed
to be the income of that individual for all the purposes of the Income this Act...'

At all material times this section was well known to the plaintiff, as was s 414,
which gave power to the Commissioners of Income Tax to serve notices requiring such
particulars as the commissioners 'think necessary for the purpose of this Chapter'. *j*
He agreed that he was well aware that every customer might be the subject of a s 412
enquiry and that the enquiry might be made of him as representing the London bank.
He accepted that it must have occurred to him that the Revenue might serve on him
notice under s 414. However, it did not occur to him to keep a special s 414 file so
as to be able quickly and conveniently to supply the information which the Revenue

a   might seek. It did not occur to him to take advice on the subject, taking the view that he was no more than an adviser on the facilities that the bank could supply. He further accepted that had he kept records to enable him to answer any s 414 notice, there would now be no problem in providing the information required. He accepted that he knew that the London bank was dealing in a field that was attractive because it had tax and exchange control advantages or potential advantages. It was, moreover, a field in which there was no double taxation agreement, because tax was not paid in Bermuda and therefore no agreement or arrangement existed between the United Kingdom and Bermuda for the latter to provide information on fiscal matters.

b

Sections 412 to 414 of the Income Tax Act 1952 have been re-enacted in virtually identical terms in ss 478 to 481 of the Income and Corporation Taxes Act 1970. On 26th July 1971, the plaintiff received a letter written on behalf of the defendants in these terms:

c

> 'SECTIONS 478-481 INCOME AND CORPORATION TAXES ACT 1970
> I understand that in 1964 you were appointed London Representative of the Bank of N T Butterfield & Son Ltd of Bermuda and that recently you became Managing Director of the Bank's newly created London subsidiary company, N T Butter-field & Son (Bermuda) Ltd, which presumably took over the functions of the London Representative Office. With reference to the above-mentioned statutory provisions, and in particular to Section 481, I enclose a formal notice under subsection (1) of the latter Section which, as you will see, requires you as former London Representative to supply the information indicated therein by 30 September 1971 . . .'

d

e   After an exchange of correspondence between the plaintiff and his solicitors and the defendants, during which the original notice was criticised, discussed, ultimately withdrawn and re-drafted, the defendants, on 31st January 1972, sent the plaintiff a fresh notice dated 31st January 1972 requiring on or before 7th April 1972 the information specified in that notice. On 20th March 1972 the plaintiff issued a writ claiming a declaration that the notice was invalid.

f   Counsel for the plaintiff made a vigorous and sustained attack on the notice—a two-pronged attack as he described it—contending that the notice was invalid since: (1) there was no statutory authority entitling the defendants to issue a notice in the form issued and to require the information specified in such a notice; (2) the defendants had failed to exercise their statutory powers reasonably in that the requirements of the notice were unduly burdensome and oppressive. Counsel ex-pressly accepted that, however unreasonably the commissioners might have behaved, viewed objectively, he was not suggesting that they did not think that the notice was other than necessary for preventing the avoidance of income tax by transactions resulting in the transfer of income to persons abroad. I will seek to deal with each of the two submissions separately in the order in which I have set them out above.

g

h   (1) *Is the notice ultra vires?*

It is contended on behalf of the plaintiff that s 481 does not permit questions to be asked of an intermediary about unidentified transactions on behalf of an unidentified principal. Moreover, it was contended that the plaintiff, on the evidence which he gave, established that he played no positive role in any transaction. He merely advised as to the facilities which the bank could offer and gave assurances about the reliability and expertise of the bank. While he may have mentioned some of the red lights which shone forth with varying degrees of brightness or dimness from s 478, he left all advice on that subject to lawyers and accountants. He was thus not 'acting' in any 'transaction'.

j

I think it is convenient at this stage to set out the terms of the first two subsections of s 481. They provide:

'(1) The Board or, for the purpose of charging tax at the standard rate, an
inspector may by notice in writing require any person to furnish them within
such time as they may direct (not being less than twenty-eight days) with *such
particulars as they think necessary* for the purposes of this Chapter.

'(2) The particulars which a person must furnish under this section, if he is
required by such a notice so to do, *include* particulars—(a) as to transactions with
respect to which he is or was acting on behalf of others, and (b) as to transactions
which in the opinion of the Board or, for the purpose of charging tax at the
standard rate, an inspector it is proper that they should investigate for the
purposes of this Chapter notwithstanding that, in the opinion of the person to
whom the notice is given, no liability to tax arises under this Chapter, and (c)
as to whether the person to whom the notice is given has taken or is taking
any, and if so what, part in any, and if so what, transactions of a description
specified in the notice.'

The notice. I do not think it is necessary to set out the full terms of the notice, but
there are certain parts to which I should make specific reference.

The notice contains, wisely, an interpretation section. As to the plaintiff's capacity
and his knowledge, the following important definition is provided:

'For the purposes of this notice . . . references to things done by you are to things
done by you, or by any staff employed under you, in your former capacity as
London Representative of the Bank of N. T. Butterfield & Son Ltd. and references
to matters within your knowledge are to matters coming within your knowledge
in that capacity or in your subsequent capacity as director of N. T. Butterfield &
Son (Bermuda) Ltd, or recorded in any records maintained by you in either
capacity, or maintained by the last-named company . . .'

Further, it is stated that for the purposes of the notice references to the plaintiff
'acting in or in connection with' a specified transaction or operation include:

'(a) the giving of advice to a customer, if but only if, a specified transaction or
operation has within your knowledge been carried out as a result of the advice,
and (b) the introducing of a customer to the bank or to any other person with a
view to the carrying out of a specified transaction or operation.'

The words 'customer', 'United Kingdom customer', 'foreign company', 'foreign
partnership', 'foreign settlement' and 'specified territory' are all defined.

The information required was as follows:

'In any case where you have since 5th April 1965 acted for a United Kingdom
customer in or in connection with any transaction or operation of a kind mentioned in the first column below you are hereby required subject to paragraph 4
below to give—(a) the name and address of the customer (or, where that is not
known, the name and address of any agent who has dealt with you on the customer's behalf); (b) the respective particulars specified in the second column
below so far as within your knowledge; and (c) the name and address of any other
person to whom you introduced the customer for the purpose of completing or
carrying out the transaction or operation.'

The transactions and operations specified were (1) the formation or management of
a foreign company, in which case the particulars sought were the name of the company, the date and place of its incorporation, its registered or other known address;
(2) the formation or management of a foreign partnership, in which case the name
and address of the partnership, the country in which it was constituted, the name and
address of the partners and the date of any deed or other document regulating the
partnership were required; (3) the creation or execution of the trusts of a foreign
settlement, in which case the name and address of the settlor, the date and nature of

a any document or other act constituting or regulating the settlement, the names and addresses of the trustees, were required; (4) the transfer of assets to any foreign company, foreign partnership or foreign settlement, in which case the particulars sought were a description of the assets transferred and particulars relating to the company, partnership or settlement as required under (1), (2) and (3) above; and finally (5) the acquisition of any interest in the share capital or loan capital of any foreign

b company or in or under any foreign partnership or foreign settlement, in which case the description of the interest acquired and the particulars relating to the company partnership or settlement under (1), (2) and (3) above were also sought.

Counsel for the plaintiff drew my attention to many authorities from the well-known case of *Entick v Carrington*[1], where a publisher's house and papers were ransacked by King's messengers sent by the Secretary of State, to the very recent case of

c *Williams v Summerfield*[2], which concerned an application by a police officer for an order under s 7 of the Bankers Book Evidence Act 1879. These cases were but illustrations of a common theme, that the clearest authority must exist to justify any invasion of private rights or any interference with the liberty of the subject. I must, so it was submitted, in approaching this statute, construe it strictly, it being a taxing statute and one where a failure to comply with the section involves penal consequences.

d While having all this in mind, I must also have regard to the words of Rowlatt J in *Cape Brandy Syndicate v Inland Revenue Comrs*[3], where he said:

'It is urged by Sir William Finlay that in a taxing Act clear words are necessary in order to tax the subject. Too wide and fanciful a construction is often sought to be given to that maxim, which does not mean that words are to be unduly restricted against the Crown, or that there is to be any discrimination against the

e Crown in those Acts. It simply means that in a taxing Act one has to look merely at what is clearly said. There is no room for any intendment. There is no equity about a tax. There is no presumption as to a tax. Nothing is to be read in, nothing is to be implied. One can only look fairly at the language used.'

f As I have previously stated, the provisions of s 481 are not novel. They are to be found in s 414 of the Income Tax Act 1952. This was a consolidating Act and the section owed its origins to the Finance Act 1936.

In *Royal Bank of Canada v Inland Revenue Comrs*[4], where a notice under s 414 of the Income Tax Act 1952 came under heavy attack, Megarry J[5], in commenting on the words of s 414 (1) (now s 481 (1)), considered that the phrase 'such particulars as they think necessary for the purposes of preventing the avoiding of liability to tax by means

g of transfer of assets abroad' was an expression that is wide in its meaning both in itself and in its context. In dealing with the word 'include' in sub-s (2), he held that this was not defining or restricting the breadth of sub-s (1), but either enlarging its meaning or referring, for the avoidance of doubt, to specific particulars which the board were entitled to require. I respectfully agree.

Counsel for the plaintiff castigated the notice as being a 'fishing' notice and thus,

h since it is supported by penal sanctions, an intolerable interference with the liberty of the subject and a gross invasion of privacy. As 'fishing' is a forensic term of art normally associated with interrogatories which do not 'relate to any matter in question in the cause or matter', as required by RSC Ord 26, r 1, it was replaced or added to by the word 'snooping'. Counsel for the defendants while doubting the value of emotive language as an aid to construction, contended that the legislature had given

j

---

1   (1765) 19 State Tr 1029, [1558-1774] All ER Rep 41
2   [1972] 2 All ER 1334, [1972] 2 QB 512
3   [1921] 1 KB 64 at 71, 12 Tax Cas 358 at 366
4   [1972] 1 All ER 225, [1972] Ch 665
5   [1972] 1 All ER at 232, 233, [1972] Ch at 676

the Revenue very extensive powers to require and obtain information in the field of
tax avoidance. The words of s 478 are of extremely wide ambit and in many respects
of uncertain meaning, which have been the subject of considerable litigation. Different
views from that of the Revenue might well be taken of the meaning and effect of some
of its terms and provisions. No criticism was being made of the bona fides of the
plaintiff or the London bank or its customers, but counsel contended that they could
well have taken, on certain matters, the view that they were not caught by its provisions and therefore had not made the appropriate disclosures, which view the
defendants might wish to challenge.

The position, he submitted, is similar in relation to sales by an individual of income
derived from his personal activities (the 'Constellation' type scheme), and artificial
transactions in land, covered by ss 487 and 488 respectively, also sections of considerable width and obscurity. Hence s 490, which gives the board the same powers
as those contained in s 481. The Taxes Management Act 1970, s 13, related to persons
in receipt of taxable income belonging to others. Subsequent sections obliged individuals to give returns of lodgers, employees, fees and commissions, interest paid or
credited with and without deduction of income tax etc. In order to deal with capital
gains, the Revenue can require from issuing houses, stockbrokers and auctioneers,
etc, extensive returns of information relating to transactions effected by them—see
s 25 of the same Act. All these were examples of the Revenue's extensive powers of
making roving enquiries.

The so-called 'right of silence', currently alleged with such emphasis and fervour
by many lawyers as going to the very root of British notions of justice, seems to find
no place in the field of tax avoidance—a fortiori where tax *evasion* is concerned. Counsel tells me that in the field of value added tax the inquisitorial powers of the
Commissioners of Customs and Excise far exceed those of his clients.

If it is an essential part of our principles of jurisprudence that silence should be
sanctified, I pause only to wonder why, when it comes to the detection of deceptions
practised on the Commissioners of Inland Revenue and Customs and Excise, those
principles have no application. Indeed, so far from being entitled to remain silent,
the individual is subject to penal sanctions if he refuses to supply the very information
that may lead to his conviction.

Had such powers been reserved for use in the detection of the most serious offences
in the criminal calendar, doubtless there would have been, not acclamation, but a
public outcry, judged by the emotion that has been generated by the recent suggestion of a very learned law reform committee that a judge should be allowed to suggest
to a jury that silence could, if *they* thought fit, be considered by them as some evidence
of the accused's guilt. When one explores this aspect of legal philosophy, there seems
to be much that is irrational. I therefore hasten to return to the words of the statute
to see whether the statutory authority alleged is clearly set out in the words used in
the relevant section.

In my judgment, s 481 (1) of the Income and Corporation Taxes Act 1970, on its
true construction, is wide enough in its terms to justify the commissioners in asking
for the particulars set out in this notice. As I have already stated, the breadth of this
subsection is not cut down by sub-s (2). Moreover, the express terms of sub-s (2)
make it perfectly clear that an intermediary can be required to specify what part, if
any, he has taken in any transaction of a description specified in the notice which
could be relevant to this Chapter. He is also obliged, if so asked, both by sub-s (2)
(a) and (c), which overlap, to give particulars of the transaction. It may be that the
part played by the intermediary is a minor one, but the introduction of a customer
to a bank or to any other person with a view to carrying out a specified transaction,
would, in my judgment, be covered, as would the giving of advice to a customer.
Of course, if that advice did not result in a specified transaction or operation being
carried out, there would not be, to the knowledge of the intermediary, any information of the kind required by the commissioners. Hence the sensible, though in no way

a generous, dispensation, to be found in the interpretation section of the notice, of the phrase 'acting in or in connection with' set out above.
   I return now to counsel for the plaintiff's second ground of attack.

(2) *Has the plaintiff established that the commissioners have exercised their discretion unreasonably?*

b One of the few matters on which the parties were in agreement was that the onus lay on the plaintiff to establish the unreasonable exercise of the discretion. What had to be established to entitle the court to interfere with an act of executive authority was, however, strongly contested.

The power of the court to interfere

c It is quite clear from the words of s 481 (1) that the legislature has entrusted a wide discretion and power to the board, who may by written notice require 'such particulars as they think necessary for the purposes of this Chapter'. Counsel for the defendants maintains that this section is virtually 'judge-proof', in the sense that unless bad faith is shown on the part of the board, the court cannot interfere, however unreasonable may be the requirements of the notice. He of course contends, in the alternative, that the notice can only be attacked for unreasonableness, if the degree
d of unreasonableness is such that no reasonable person could consider the notice necessary for the purposes of the Act. Such 'unreasonableness' he categorises as 'overwhelming'.
   Counsel for the plaintiff contends that the courts are entitled to interfere if it can be shown that, viewed objectively, the authority was acting unreasonably, albeit that they were acting within the four corners of the authority conferred on them.
e The case on which he placed the greatest reliance was *Roberts v Hopwood*[1]. The facts are worth recounting. In 1922 a metropolitan borough council, purporting to act under s 62 of the Metropolis Management Act 1855, which entitled them to employ such servants as may be necessary and to 'allow to such . . . servants . . . such . . . wages as the [council] may think fit', paid to its lowest grade of workers, whether men or women, a minimum wage of £4 per week notwithstanding that the cost of living had
f fallen during that year from 176 per cent to 82 per cent above the pre-war level. The borough council were of the opinion that £4 was the least wage which a local authority ought, as a model employer, to pay adult labour. By s 247 (7) of the Public Health Act 1875, as applied to the accounts of metropolitan borough councils, a district auditor 'shall disallow every item of account contrary to law, and surcharge the same on the person making or authorising the making of the illegal payment . . .' The dis-
g trict auditor found that these payments were not wages but gratuities to the employees, and were contrary to law, and disallowed the excess over the sum he thought was the right sum. The House of Lords reversed the decision of the Court of Appeal and held that the disallowance and surcharge were rightly made. Lord Wrenbury in his speech stated[2]:

h   'A person in whom is vested a discretion must exercise his discretion upon reasonable grounds. A discretion does not empower a man to do what he likes merely because he is minded to do so—he must in the exercise of his discretion do not what he likes but what he ought. In other words, he must, by use of his reason, ascertain and follow the course which reason directs. He must act reasonably . . . The words "as they think fit" do not mean "as they choose."
j   The measure is not the volition of the person vested with the discretion, it is the suitability or adequacy or fitness of the amount in the reasonable judgment of the person vested with the discretion.'

1 [1925] AC 578, [1925] All ER Rep 24
2 [1925] AC at 613, [1925] All ER Rep at 42

Counsel for the defendants relies essentially on the well-known case of *Associated* *a* *Provincial Picture Houses Ltd v Wednesbury Corpn*[1], where a local authority, acting under the Sunday Entertainments Act 1932, giving it power to allow a licensed place to be open and used for Sundays 'subject to such conditions as the authority think fit to impose', granted the plaintiffs leave for Sunday performances subject to the condition that no children under 15 years of age should be admitted to Sunday performances with or without an adult. Lord Greene MR stated that when an executive discretion *b* is entrusted by Parliament to a body such as the local authority, what appears to be an exercise of that discretion can only be challenged in a strictly limited class of case. The discretion must be exercised reasonably. In answering the question, 'what does that mean?' he said[2]:

'Lawyers familiar with the phraseology commonly used in relation to the exercise of statutory discretions often use the word "unreasonable" in a rather *c* comprehensive sense. It is frequently used as a general description of the things that must not be done. For instance, a person entrusted with a discretion must direct himself properly in law. He must call his own attention to the matters which he is bound to consider. He must exclude from his consideration matters which are irrelevant to the matter that he has to consider. If he does not obey those rules, he may truly be said, and often is said, to be acting "unreasonably" *d* ... the court is entitled to investigate the action of the local authority with a view to seeing whether it has taken into account matters which it ought not to take into account, or, conversely, has refused to take into account or neglected to take into account matters which it ought to take into account. Once that question is answered in favour of the local authority, it may still be possible to say that the local authority, nevertheless, have come to a conclusion so unreasonable *e* that no reasonable authority could ever have come to it. In such a case, again, I think the court can interfere. The power of the court to interfere in each case is not that of an appellate authority to override a decision of the local authority, but is that of a judicial authority which is concerned, and concerned only, to see whether the local authority have contravened the law by acting in excess of the powers which Parliament has confided in it.' *f*

The judgment of Lord Greene MR has been frequently referred to with approval, for example in *Hall & Co Ltd v Shoreham-by-Sea Urban District Council*[3], *Fawcett Properties Ltd v Buckinghamshire County Council*[4], and by Lord Reid in *Smith v East Elloe Rural District Council*[5].

I do not consider that there is any conflict in the principles so clearly enunciated *g* by Lord Greene MR and the basis of the decision in *Roberts v Hopwood*[6]. It seems clear from the quotations I give below that the local authority had taken into account matters which the House of Lords considered they ought not to have taken into account, or conversely had refused to take into account or neglected to take into account matters which they ought to have taken into account. Lord Sumner said[7]:

'... I can find nothing in the Acts empowering bodies, to which the Metropolis *h* Management Act, 1855, applies, which authorizes them to be guided by their personal opinions on political, economic or social questions in administering the funds which they derive from levying rates ... To my mind a council acts for a collateral purpose, if it fixes by standards of its own on social grounds a minimum

1   [1947] 2 All ER 680, [1948] 1 KB 223   *j*
2   [1947] 2 All ER at 682, 683, 685, [1948] 1 KB at 229, 233, 234
3   [1964] 1 All ER 1, [1964] 1 WLR 240
4   [1960] 3 All ER 503, [1961] AC 636
5   [1956] 1 All ER 855 at 867, [1956] AC 736 at 763
6   [1925] AC 578, [1925] All ER Rep 24
7   [1925] AC at 606, [1925] All ER Rep at 38, 39

a   wage for all adults, and is not in so doing acting for the benefit of the whole
     community.'

Lord Atkinson said[1]:

         'Nobody has contended that the council should be bound by any of these
     things [by 'these things' he was referring to trade union rates, the cost of living
b   and so on in fixing wages], but it is only what justice and common sense demand
     that, when dealing with funds contributed by the whole body of the ratepayers,
     they should take each and every one of these enumerated things into considera-
     tion in order to help them to determine what was a fair, just and reasonable wage
     to pay their employees for the services the latter rendered. The council would,
     in my view, fail in their duty if, in administering funds which did not belong to
c   their members alone, they put aside all these aids to the ascertainment of what
     was just and reasonable remuneration to give for the services rendered to them,
     and allowed themselves to be guided in preference by some eccentric principles
     of socialistic philanthropy . . .'

         I am accordingly satisfied that the plaintiff does not have to go to the extent of
d   establishing bad faith against the commissioners. The commissioners may have had
     regard to quite irrelevant considerations or may have acted quite unreasonably in the
     sense defined by Lord Greene MR, but yet be entirely innocent of dishonesty or
     malice.
         The statutory authority in this case is in effect to ask questions—to require such
     particulars as the commissioners think necessary—for the purpose of the Chapter
e   dealing with the transfer of assets abroad. The particulars are sought of the intermedi-
     ary in order that he may be used as a stepping-stone towards obtaining the more
     detailed information required by the commissioners to enable them to decide whether
     or not, in their opinion, tax has been unlawfully avoided. The information which
     they require is such as to give them a shrewd idea of the relationship between a tax-
     payer and a foreign company, partnership, trust or settlement.
f   Accordingly, if the particulars sought went substantially beyond that which was
     required for this purpose, so that they could be properly described as unduly oppres-
     sive or burdensome, I have no doubt that a court would be entitled to intervene, and
     declare the notice invalid. One of the vital functions of the courts is to protect the
     individual from any abuse of power by the executive, a function which nowadays
     grows more and more important as governmental interference increases.

g
     Has the plaintiff established that the notice is inordinately burdensome or oppressive?
         The plaintiff gave evidence to the effect that in respect of every customer to whom
     more than mere advice was given, there is a separate file. There were some 600 to
     650 such files. In addition, there were 6,500 index cards, since such a card was created
     in respect of every customer. In addition, there were some 17 miscellaneous custo-
h   mers' files and 15 files containing office memoranda. The plaintiff has had a number
     of trial runs in relation to both the card indices and the files and he estimated that it
     would take some five months working full time, with the assistance of a secretary
     also working full time, for him to comply with the notice. This would involve,
     if the London bank is to continue in operation, someone being seconded as his assistant
     and for another secretary to be provided. The salary of such an assistant would be
j   approximately £3,000 a year and of a secretary about half this sum. In addition to
     that there would be lawyers' and accountants' fees to pay. The defendants have made
     it tolerably clear that they have no present or future intention of making any
     contribution to those expenses.

     _____

     1   [1925] AC at 594, [1925] All ER Rep at 33

I think an unnecessarily pessimistic view has been taken by the plaintiff of the time
it would take to comply with the notice. In making this calculation he has taken into *a*
account two matters: (1) that in regard to matters in which he has given advice, but
where he is doubtful whether any specified transaction or operation has been carried
out as a result of the advice, he would have to make enquiries as to what the position
was. In my judgment, the notice imposes no such obligation. The notice does not
require him to carry out any researches in order to obtain knowledge which he never
had. He must examine the records maintained by him or maintained by the London *b*
company and he must seek to *refresh* his knowledge from any sources which he considers are capable of providing such refreshment. He is not obliged to acquire new
knowledge which he has never possessed. (2) He feels that the London bank is under
a duty to its customers to inform them of the information that it gives to the defendants. This may well be a matter of ordinary banking courtesy—I know not—but
it is not strictly part of the compliance with the notice. *c*

Moreover, from what I have been told about the nature of the files, I would not
have thought it would have taken the plaintiff, who is clearly a most able person, long
to go through each file to pick out the relevant information and to dictate this on to a
tape in order that it might be included in the appropriate schedule. The estimate of
half an hour per file, I consider to be excessive.

As regards the cards, a trial run disclosed that out of 100 cards eight required further *d*
investigation. The plaintiff was kind enough, at my suggestion, to produce some
five typical, but quite fictitious cards, designed to show the variations in the information which would be found on the cards kept by the London bank. Having heard his
evidence with regard to them, I am again quite satisfied that his estimate that it would
take half an hour for each card which required further examination, i e approximately
500 cards, is an excessive estimate. An intelligent assistant to whom an adequate *e*
explanation had been given as to the information required, in respect of customers
who had no files with the London bank, could dictate quite speedily the relevant
information contained on the files within a fraction of the time suggested by the
plaintiff. I would be surprised if it would take as long as a week. It certainly would
not take the six weeks' work estimated. The other two categories of documents,
miscellaneous customers' files and contacts' files, were very minor matters compared *f*
with the customers' files and customers' cards, and if, as I am satisfied is the fact, the
plaintiff has been over-pessimistic in his estimates on those latter documents, the
time which would be spent on miscellaneous customers' files and contacts' files is
also likely to have been overestimated.

Even if I had been satisfied that the plaintiff's estimates were correct and that it
would take some five months to provide the information required by the defendants, *g*
I consider there is substance in the point made by counsel for the defendants that the
plaintiff cannot pray in aid his own failure to have this material reasonably available.
The London office was, and the London bank is, the tax avoidance office of the bank.
I use the expression in no pejorative sense, since every man is entitled, if he can, to
order his affairs so that the tax attaching under the appropriate Acts is less than it
otherwise would be. If he succeeds in ordering them so as to secure this result, then, *h*
however unappreciative the Commissioners of Inland Revenue or his fellow taxpayers
may be of his ingenuity, he cannot be compelled to pay an increased tax (per Lord
Tomlin in *Inland Revenue Comrs v Duke of Westminster*[1]).

'No man in this country is under the smallest obligation, moral or other,
so to arrange his legal relations to his business or to his property as to enable the *j*
Revenue to put the largest possible shovel into his stores. The Revenue is not
slow—and quite rightly—to take every advantage which is open to it under the
taxing statutes for the purpose of depleting the taxpayer's pocket. And, the

---

1   [1936] AC 1 at 19, [1935] All ER Rep 259 at 267, 19 Tax Cas 490 at 520

a taxpayer is, in like manner, entitled to be astute to prevent, so far as he honestly can, the depletion of his means by the Revenue.'

(Per Lord Clyde in *Ayrshire Pullman Motor Services and Ritchie v Inland Revenue Comrs*[1]). The plaintiff was well aware of the existence and general effect of ss 478-481 and its predecessors and of the possibility of a notice being served requiring information similar to that which is now sought. His task would now be a relatively light one *b* if he had taken any steps to anticipate being required to give this information. He did not contend for one moment that the time, which he estimates as a day a month, spent in his office on PAYE documents, was unduly burdensome or oppressive, and yet over the six years this had resulted in some three months' work. If he had not caused those records to be compiled and the necessary information to be provided in an orderly fashion and had had to provide it now, some six years later, it would *c* doubtless have taken double the time that has in fact been spent. Any complaint that to be asked now to provide that information places an unduly oppressive burden on him, would be met with the obvious answer: you have been the author of your own misfortune.

So much for the time element in complying with the notice. Counsel for the plaintiff further contends that the notice is unduly burdensome and oppressive because *d* the plaintiff would have to have a lawyer and an accountant at his elbow, constantly advising him as to how to comply with it, due to its obscurities and ambiguities. I would accept in principle that a notice could well be inordinately burdensome or oppressive and therefore invalid if it had the consequences described by counsel. But this is not the case here. The interpretation clause of the notice removes many problems that otherwise might have arisen. Although it may well be necessary for *e* the plaintiff to refer, on occasions, to his legal advisers or to his accountants for advice, this is by no means an unusual situation where information is sought by the Revenue. I am not satisfied that there is any substantial degree of ambiguity or obscurity in the notice the subject-matter of these proceedings, whatever may have been the criticisms that could have been levelled at the previous notice which had been served.

Apart from the time factor and the alleged obscurity of the notice, no attack was *f* made on the notice on the basis that it went well beyond what could reasonably be required for the purpose of the relevant chapter of the Act.

For the reasons which I have stated at perhaps undue length, the plaintiff is not entitled to the declarations which he claims, and there must be judgment for the defendants. I should like to record my gratitude to counsel for the very great assistance which they have given, and I hope I shall be forgiven for not having referred to each *g* and every authority to which my attention was directed.

Declaration refused.

Solicitors: *Lovell, White & King* (for the plaintiff); *Solicitor of Inland Revenue.*

h
                                        Rengan Krishnan Esq   Barrister.

---

1 (1929) 14 Tax Cas 754 at 763, 764

Evans Marshall & Co Ltd v Bertola SA and another
Evans Marshall & Co Ltd v Bertola SA

a

COURT OF APPEAL, CIVIL DIVISION   *b*
SACHS, EDMUND DAVIES AND CAIRNS LJJ
11th, 12th, 13th, 14th, 18th, 19th, 20th DECEMBER 1972

Practice – Service – Service out of the jurisdiction – Foreign jurisdiction clause – Circumstances justifying service out of jurisdiction despite clause – Distributorship agreement – Plaintiffs having sole agency rights for distribution of first defendants' products in United Kingdom – First defendants a Spanish company – Agreement providing for 'law claims' to be submitted to Barcelona court – First defendants terminating agreement and appointing second defendants as agents – Second defendants an English company – Plaintiffs claiming injunctions and damages against both defendants for breach of contract, interference with contract and conspiracy – First defendants a proper and necessary party to proceedings against second defendants – RSC Ord 11, r 1.

c

d

Injunction – Interlocutory – Principle governing grant – Preservation of status quo – Prospect of obtaining permanent injunction at trial – Failure to show strong or at least reasonable prospect not a factor precluding grant of interlocutory injunction – Factor weighing against grant.

e

The plaintiffs, an English company, were wholesale wine merchants. In 1951 the plaintiffs entered into an agreement with the first defendants ('Bertola'), a company incorporated in Spain, whereby Bertola granted the plaintiffs sole agency and dis-tribution rights for their products in the United Kingdom and certain Commonwealth territories, specifically agreeing not to sell them there except through the plaintiffs. *f* By cl 13 Bertola were entitled to determine the agreement if the plaintiffs did not fulfil their duties. Clause 15 provided: 'If any law claim arises between the two parties it will be submitted to the Barcelona Court of Justice.' In 1954 the agreement, originally for five years, was extended to 20 years from 26th September 1953. In 1961 it was extended until 30th September 1986. The arrangements between the parties worked satisfactorily until June 1972. Bertola had been anxious to market *g* a sweet sherry and sales had steadily expanded during that period. No demand had been made by Bertola to market medium or dry sherries and so Bertola had become a name associated with sweet sherry. In June 1972 Bertola became a wholly owned subsidiary of Rumasa, a public company incorporated in Spain, which operated through subsidiaries in many different spheres including the wine trade. Rumasa had close links with the second defendants ('ISI'), an English company, who acted *h* on behalf of Rumasa as agents for another brand of sherry. ISI were well aware of the terms of the distributorship agreement between Bertola and the plaintiffs. The new management of Bertola was clearly dissatisfied with the terms of that agree-ment. At meetings in June and July 1972 Bertola announced decisions which involved important changes in the way in which the agreement had hitherto been operated, including an unspecified increase in the fob price per case, a demand that the plain- *j* tiffs forthwith give an order for 50,000 cases, and the marketing of medium and dry sherries under the Bertola name. In subsequent negotiations with the plaintiffs, ISI acted as the mouthpiece for Bertola. The plaintiffs took time to consider the implica-tions of the changes announced by Bertola. Bertola became impatient and, in October, gave notice that they were terminating the distributorship agreement, complaining of 'lack of performance on your part and your obstructive conduct *a*   towards adaptation to the commercial policy established . . .' On 30th October Bertola appointed ISI to be their distributing agency in the United Kingdom. On 10th November the plaintiffs issued a writ against Bertola and ISI which, as subsequently amended, claimed injunctions against both defendants and, against ISI damages for interference with the plaintiffs' contracts and conspiracy. By a further writ against Bertola they claimed damages for breach of contract and conspiracy.

b   On 30th November Kerr J refused Bertola's application to discharge an ex parte order granting leave under RSC Ord 11, r 1^a, to serve notice of the first writ on them out of the jurisdiction and gave leave for service of notice of the second writ. He refused, however, the plaintiffs' application for interlocutory injunctions, (a) taking into account an offer made by Rumasa and announced at the hearing to hold themselves responsible up to £500,000 for any damages awarded against Bertola in the actions and (b) holding that, since he was not satisfied that the plaintiffs had at least

c   a reasonable, if not a strong, prospect of obtaining a permanent injunction at the trial, he had no choice but to refuse an interlocutory injunction. The plaintiffs appealed against that refusal and Bertola cross-appealed against the orders granting leave to serve notice of the writs out of the jurisdiction.

d   **Held** – (i) On the assumption that cl 15 of the agreement was to be treated as an exclusive jurisdiction clause, leave should nevertheless be given to serve the writs on Bertola out of the jurisdiction under RSC Ord 11 since there were exceptional circumstances justifying such a course: (a) the substance of the case concerned the marketing of sherry in the United Kingdom; (b) all the essential witnesses were within the jurisdiction; (c) Bertola were a proper and necessary party, within RSC Ord 11, r 1 (*j*)^a,

e   to the plaintiffs' proceedings against ISI, which had nothing to do with the Barcelona court, a state of affairs which had been brought about by Bertola's own actions in purporting to terminate the agency agreement and to appoint ISI instead; (d) the evidence disclosed that the relevant Spanish law did not differ from English law to any substantial extent. Accordingly it would, in all the circumstances, be unjust to allow Bertola to terminate the plaintiffs' agency in the United Kingdom and at the

f   same time avoid the jurisdiction of the English courts. It followed that Bertola's cross-appeals would be dismissed (see p 1001 g to p 1002 g, p 1009 f and p 1010 f and g, post); dicta of Diplock LJ in *Mackender v Feldia AG* [1966] 3 All ER at 853 and of Lord Denning MR in *The Fehmarn* [1958] 1 All ER at 335 applied.

(ii) The plaintiffs' appeal, however, would be allowed and interlocutory injunctions granted for the following reasons—

g   (a) Although the failure of a plaintiff to show that he had a reasonable prospect of obtaining a permanent injunction at the trial was a factor which would normally weigh heavily against the grant of an interlocutory injunction, it was not a factor which, as a matter of law, precluded its grant; there were special cases in which it was proper to maintain a status quo irrespective of whether the relief granted at trial

---

h   *a*   Rule 1, so far as material, provides: '(1) . . . service of a writ, or notice of a writ, out of the jurisdiction is permissible with the leave of the Court in the following cases, that is to say . . . (*g*) if the action begun by the writ is brought against a defendant not domiciled or ordinarily resident in Scotland or Northern Ireland, in respect of a breach committed within the jurisdiction of a contract made within or out of the jurisdiction, and irrespective of the fact, if such be the case, that the breach was preceded or accompanied by a breach committed out of the jurisdiction that rendered impossible the performance of so much of

j   the contract as ought to have been performed within the jurisdiction; (*h*) if the action begun by the writ is founded on a tort committed within the jurisdiction; (*i*) if in the action begun by the writ an injunction is sought ordering the defendant to do or refrain from doing anything within the jurisdiction (whether or not damages are also claimed in respect of a failure to do or the doing of that thing); (*j*) if the action begun by the writ being properly brought against a person duly served within the jurisdiction, a person out of the jurisdiction is a necessary or proper party thereto . . .'

would include an injunction. On the evidence before the court the plaintiffs had *a* established a reasonable prima facie case which could lead to success; if they were right the disruption caused by the defendants' action was unjustified and so great that damages would not be an adequate remedy. Accordingly the plaintiffs' appeal would be allowed and an interlocutory injunction granted (see p 1004 a and d, p 1005 f, p 1007 c d and g, p 1008 e and p 1010 e and j to p 1011 a and c, post); *Warner Brothers Pictures Inc v Nelson* [1936] 3 All ER 160, *Decro-Wall International SA v Practitioners in Marketing Ltd* [1971] 2 All ER 216, *Hill v C A Parsons & Co Ltd* [1971] 3 All ER 1345 and *b* dictum of Lord Denning MR in *Hubbard v Vosper* [1972] 1 All ER at 1029 applied.

(b) The offer by Rumasa to guarantee damages up to £500,000 was not to be taken into account since it had emerged at a late stage of the proceedings, it had been made by somebody who was not a party, it lacked particularity, there was no information whether the foreign exchange control system would enable Rumasa to remit the sum guaranteed and (per Sachs LJ) the offer only related to securing payment *c* of damages which anyway were not an adequate remedy (see p 1006 h, p 1009 h and p 1010 c and e, post).

Notes

For the principles on which court acts in granting interlocutory injunctions, see 21 Halsbury's Laws (3rd Edn) 364-366, paras 763-766, and for cases on the subject, see *d* 28 (2) Digest (Reissue) 966-980, 60-161.

For the exercise of discretion to grant leave to serve notice of writ out of the jurisdiction, see 30 Halsbury's Laws (3rd Edn) 326, para 589, and for cases on the subject, see 50 Digest (Repl) 336-338, 652-663.

Cases referred to in judgments

e

Alfonal Ltd v Stratenport Ltd (20th May 1969) unreported, [1969] Bar Library transcript 197, CA.

Decro-Wall International SA v Practitioners in Marketing Ltd [1971] 2 All ER 216, [1971] 1 WLR 361, CA.

Doherty v Allman (1878) 3 App Cas 709, 39 LT 129, 42 JP 788, HL, 28 (2) Digest (Reissue) 958, 14.

Eleftheria, The, Owners of Cargo lately laden on board ship or vessel, Eleftheria v Owners of *f* *ship or vessel Eleftheria* [1969] 2 All ER 641, [1970] P 94, [1969] 2 WLR 1073, [1969] 1 Lloyd's Rep 237, Digest (Cont Vol C) 156, 1511b.

Fehmarn, The [1958] 1 All ER 333, [1958] 1 WLR 159, [1957] 2 Lloyd's Rep 551, CA; *affg* [1957] 2 All ER 707, [1957] 1 WLR 815, [1957] 1 Loyd's Rep 511, Digest (Cont Vol A) 256, 1511a.

Hill v C A Parsons & Co Ltd [1971] 3 All ER 1345, [1972] Ch 305, [1971] 3 WLR 995, CA. *g*

Hubbard v Vosper [1972] 1 All ER 1023, [1972] 2 QB 84, [1972] 2 WLR 389, CA.

Mackender v Feldia AG [1966] 3 All ER 847, [1967] 2 QB 590, [1967] 2 WLR 119, CA, 50 Digest (Repl) 341, 689.

Strathcona (Lord) Steamship Co Ltd v Dominion Coal Co Ltd [1926] AC 108, [1925] All ER Rep 87, 95 LJPC 71, 134 LT 227, 16 Asp MLC 585, 31 Com Cas 80, PC, 28 (2) *h* Digest (Reissue) 1060, 767.

Vine v National Dock Labour Board [1956] 3 All ER 939, [1957] AC 488, [1957] 2 WLR 106, [1956] 2 Lloyd's Rep 567, HL; *rvsg* [1956] 1 All ER 1, [1956] 1 QB 658, [1956] 2 WLR 311, [1955] 2 Lloyd's Rep 531, CA, Digest (Cont Vol A) 475, 58a.

Warner Brothers Pictures Inc v Nelson [1936] 3 All ER 160, [1937] 1 KB 209, 106 LJKB 97, 155 LT 538, 28 (2) Digest (Reissue) 1049, 701.

YTC Universal Ltd (in Liquidation) v Trans Europa Compania de Aviacion SA (1968) 112 *j* Sol Jo 842, [1968] Bar Library transcript 366, CA.

Cases also cited

Metropolitan Electric Supply Co Ltd v Ginder [1901] 2 Ch 799.

Page One Records Ltd v Britton [1967] 3 All ER 822, [1968] 1 WLR 157.

Texaco Ltd v Mulberry Filling Station Ltd [1972] 1 All ER 513, [1972] 1 WLR 814.

Interlocutory appeals

a By a writ issued on 10th November 1972, and re-issued as re-amended by order of Kerr J on 17th November, the plaintiffs, Evans Marshall & Co Ltd, claimed against the defendants, Bertola SA ('Bertola') and Independent Sherry Importers Ltd ('ISI'): (1) an injunction restraining the defendants and each of them whether by themselves their servants or agents or any of them from selling and distributing in England or Wales Bertola's Spanish sherry wine and Spanish brandy other than through the *b* agency of the plaintiffs; (2) an injunction restraining the defendants and each of them whether by themselves their servants or agents or any of them from appointing or holding out in England or Wales anyone else in the United Kingdom other than the plaintiffs as Bertola's agents or sub-agents in respect of that sherry or brandy; (3) an injunction restraining the defendants and each of them whether by themselves their servants or agent or any of them in combination or otherwise howsoever from *c* doing the following acts or any of them: (a) wrongfully informing in England or Wales third parties in the United Kingdom that the sole agency distribution agreement between the plaintiffs and Bertola dated 26th September 1951 had been terminated, (b) making alternative arrangements in England or Wales in respect of the distribution of Bertola's sherry in the United Kingdom; and they further claimed against ISI: (4) *d* damages for wrongful interference with contracts to which the plaintiffs were parties or would be parties when those contracts were made in accordance with the plaintiffs' regular course of dealings; (5) damages for interference with the plaintiffs' trade by unlawful means; (6) damages for unlawful conspiracy to injure. By an order of Kerr J dated 17th November the plaintiffs were given leave to issue a concurrent writ against Bertola and to serve notice of that writ on Bertola in Spain. On 30th November *e* Kerr J dismissed an application by the plaintiffs for interlocutory injunctions against both defendants in the terms of those claimed in the writ of 10th November, and dismissed applications by Bertola to discharge the order of 17th November and any order that the judge might make giving the plaintiffs leave to issue a writ claming damages against Bertola and to serve notice of the writ on Bertola out of the jurisdiction. Pursuant to leave given by Kerr J on 30th November the plaintiffs, on *f* 1st December, issued a writ against Bertola claiming (1) damages for breach of the sole distribution agreement dated 26th September 1951; (2) a declaration that the agreement was valid and subsisting and (3) damages for unlawful conspiracy to injure. The plaintiffs appealed against that part of the judgment of Kerr J whereby he refused to grant the plaintiffs interlocutory injunctions and Bertola appealed against so much of Kerr J's judgment as (1) refused to discharge the order of 17th November and to set aside the writ issued pursuant thereto and all subsequent *g* proceedings against Bertola, and (2) refused to discharge the order made on 30th November granting leave to the plaintiffs to issue a writ claiming damages against Bertola, notice of which might be served outside the jurisdiction. The facts are set out in the judgment of Sachs LJ.

C W G Ross-Munro QC, Anthony Lester and *D T Donaldson* for the plaintiffs.
h *R J Parker QC, Robert Alexander* and *Nicholas Phillips* for the defendants.

SACHS LJ. In the proceedings before this court the plaintiffs are Evans Marshall & Co Ltd, wholesale wine merchants, with a registered office in London; they are, and have since 1961 been, a wholly owned subsidiary of Bass, Charrington (Vintners) Ltd. They have issued two writs in the Queen's Bench Division (Commercial Court), one *i* dated 10th November 1972 and one dated 1st December 1972. There are two defendants: the first Bertola SA, incorporated in Spain (whom I will refer to as 'Bertola'), sherry merchants, a wholly owned subsidiary of another Spanish company, Rumasa SA ('Rumasa'); the second, Independent Sherry Importers Ltd ('ISI'), whose registered office in London is 293 Regent Street, which is also the registered office of Rumasa (UK) Ltd, another subsidiary of Rumasa SA.

The relief claimed in each writ relates to the same set of events, the division of the
claims for relief being due to concern, when the matter first came before the Com- *a*
mercial Court judge, not to prejudice Bertola on certain points which arose under
the provisions of RSC Ord 11—reasons which need not now be recited. In view of
the course thus adopted, whilst both Bertola and ISI are defendants in the first action,
Bertola are the only defendants in the second.

The claims in both actions arise out of the purported unilateral termination by *b*
Bertola of a sole distributor and agency agreement with the plaintiffs that had, at
the date that termination was intended to operate, 30th October 1972, still some 14
years to run—unless, of course, there was good cause for its termination. The claims
against ISI arise from the fact that they were, as from that date, 30th October, granted
the distributor rights previously held by the plaintiffs, having been privy to the
purported termination of the latter's agreement with Bertola.

On 24th November four applications came before Kerr J. One was by Bertola to *c*
discharge an order made ex parte on 16th November giving leave to serve on them
in Spain the concurrent writ in relation to the first action, which as against them
claims only an injunction; one was an application by the plaintiffs for leave to serve
on Bertola in Spain the second writ claiming against them damages and further
relief; and the third and fourth were by the plaintiffs for interlocutory injunctions *d*
designed to restrain Bertola from selling or distributing sherry in the United Kingdom
otherwise than through the agency of the plaintiffs and to restrain ISI from
distributing or selling Bertola sherry in this country.

After a hearing which occupied some 2½ days Kerr J delivered, on 30th November,
a considered judgment refusing Bertola's application to discharge the order for
service on them of the first concurrent writ; granting leave for service of the second
concurrent writ; and refusing to grant an interlocutory injunction—taking into *e*
account, in regard to this refusal, an offer made by Rumasa to hold themselves
responsible for any damages up to £500,000 which might be awarded against Bertola
to the plaintiffs in the actions. Bertola now appeal against the first two orders, and
the plaintiffs appeal against the refusal to grant interlocutory injunctions.

Looking at the two actions together, the claims made in them, as originally set out
in the 10th November writ, can be summarised as follows. As against both defend- *f*
dants there are claims for damages for unlawful conspiracy to injure, for the above-
mentioned injunctions to restrain them from selling or distributing Bertola sherry
in this country except through the plaintiffs, and for ancillary injunctions aimed at
preventing the appointment of other agents or the making of statements to the effect
that the distributorship agreement had been terminated. As against Bertola there
are claims for a declaration that this agreement was valid and subsisting, and also a *g*
claim for damages for its breach; as against ISI damages for wrongful interference
with contracts to which the plaintiffs are a party, and also damages for interference
with their trade by unlawful means.

The facts with which these proceedings are concerned have been the subject of
affidavits extending to more than 80 pages, accompanied by exhibits with a matching
number of pages. These have been fully analysed with great care in the judgment *h*
of Kerr J. It is accordingly sufficient in this court to summarise in narrative form the
salient features of the series of events which preceded the issue of the writs. Naturally
here, as at first instance, it must be remembered that anything said as to those facts
simply relates to such evidence as has been made available on affidavit and must in
no way be taken as prejudging such findings as may become necessary at trial.

j

Contractual relationship: September 1951 to June 1972
The contractual relationship between the plaintiffs and Bertola commenced with an
agreement dated 26th September 1951. At that time both parties to it were independent companies: Bertola had not previously marketed their sherry in the United
Kingdom, the British Empire (except Nigeria), or the Commonwealth. The plaintiffs,

a for their part, had apparently not previously been concerned with the marketing of Spanish sherrry. The agreement was to extend over a period of five years, and then for a further period of five, unless one of the parties had given notice to terminate it at the end of the first five years.

By the provisions of the agreement, Bertola granted to the plaintiffs sole agency and distribution rights for their products in the territories already mentioned, specifi-

b cally agreeing not to sell them there except through the plaintiffs. The plaintiffs, on their side, bound themselves to sell and distribute the relevant products in those territories and not there to sell any that were similar. The prices to be charged by Bertola were to be subject to market fluctuations, and they were in effect to be fixed by Bertola, subject to being in conformity with the practice of the Association of Sherry Shippers. There was no clause binding the plaintiffs to adhere to any particular wholesale or retail prices or to any specific margin of profit. Advertising in the

c relevant territories was to be done by the plaintiffs at their own expense, save insofar as Bertola might direct any additional advertising, which would then be at their expense. By cl 13 Bertola were entitled to determine the agreement if the plaintiffs did not execute their duties.

Two further clauses were also of importance. Clause 14 gave the plaintiffs the

d right to nominate as many sub-agents as they desired in the above territories. Clause 15 provided that: 'If any law claim arises between the two parties it will be submitted to the Barcelona Court of Justice.' (Disputes as to quality were to go to an official body at Jerez.)

The 1951 agreement was varied on 9th April 1954 by providing that it should extend 20 years from 26th September 1953; this longer period being 'substituted for the first period of five years' in the old agreement. Save that Bertola were to

e transfer to the plaintiffs certain shares in an English company (Bertola & Co Ltd), there was in substance no change in the subsisting arrangements apart from that relating to the duration of the agreement.

In 1961 the plaintiffs became a wholly owned subsidiary of Bass, Charrington Vintners Ltd, and in due course had the same marketing director (Mr Holloway) as that company, and a chairman (Mr Williams) who was the latter's managing

f director. After that had happened, a fresh agreement was negotiated between the plaintiffs and Bertola and concluded on 19th February 1962, under which the duration of the 1951 agreement was again varied. This time it was extended until 30th September 1986. Subject to that extension all the other terms and provisions of the older agreement were confirmed.

According to the uncontradicted evidence of Mr Williams, the managing director

g of the plaintiffs, the extensions to the original agreement resulted from a happy commercial relationship between the parties, and the arrangements between them again worked satisfactorily from June 1961 to June 1972. During those long periods of time, sales of Bertola sherry gradually increased. From a nil start the annual sales had reached 41,000 cases by 1958, and 102,000 cases by the end of 1971; the projection for 1972 was 112,000.

h Bertola had, during that period, been concerned to market a sweet sherry that would compete with Bristol Cream. Considerable advertising expenditure had been incurred by the plaintiffs in promoting sales. Over the period of years from 1959 to 1971 inclusive that expenditure had averaged about £40,000 a year, totalling £475,000, and Messrs J Walter Thompson were, at any rate during the latter part of that period, in charge of the relevant advertising schemes. The main success of

j Bertola had been in Scotland, where it had become a leading brand, marketed at a price appreciably below that of Bristol Cream. In the north of England there were also substantial sales, but there had not been equivalent progress in the south.

Over the whole 20 years there appears to have been no demand by Bertola that the plaintiffs should market medium or dry sherries, or that they should market Spanish brandy, which was also the subject of the agreement. Thus Bertola had become a

name associated with sweet sherry. The contractual relationship between the two *a*
parties having thus proceeded satisfactorily over two decades, a change occurred in
June 1972.

The events of June to October 1972
    In June 1972 Bertola became a wholly owned subsidiary of Rumasa, a public com-
pany incorporated in Spain in 1961 and operating through their numerous subsidiaries *b*
in many different spheres—including banking, property development, industry and
the wine trade. Insofar as the wine trade was concerned, the subsidiary companies
were in the main selling sherry. The chairman of Rumasa was Senor Ruiz-Mateos.
This gentleman was a close associate of a Mr Edward Butler, whose family owned a
bodega in Jerez. Mr Butler has since its formation been the chairman of ISI, which was
incorporated on 26th June 1970, whose present share capital is £5,000, and which is
closely linked with other wine trade companies whose shares are substantially owned *c*
by members of his family.
    ISI act on behalf of Rumasa as agents for Varela sherries and have, as already stated,
their registered office at 293 Regent Street, which is also the registered office of Rumasa
(UK) Ltd. Mr Butler is also the managing director of Rumasa (UK) Ltd. One employee
of ISI was, at all material times, a Mr John Laidlaw, who had been engaged in January
1972 to assist Mr Butler in the management of that company. From June 1972 *d*
onwards, Mr Butler was well aware of the terms of the sale and distributorship
agreement subsisting between the plaintiffs and Bertola, and so was Mr Laidlaw.
    It is manifest from the evidence filed in these proceedings that Rumasa, at the time
they took over Bertola, were not only aware of the latter's agreement with the plaintiffs but were thoroughly dissatisfied with its terms. The affidavit of a gentleman styled
Inspector General of the Rumasa Group, Senor Fernandez Garcia Figueras (herein- *e*
after referred to as 'Senor Fernandez'), who became a director of and secretary of
Bertola, so states in positive terms. This dissatisfaction related to such subjects as the
length of the agreement, the fact that the plaintiffs were part of the Bass, Charrington
group, the absence of specific requirements in the agreement for a percentage increase
of sales by the plaintiffs each year, and the fact that the plaintiffs were permitted to
fix their own price for Bertola sherry. *f*
    Their adverse view of the terms of the distributor agreement, although formed early
in June, does not appear to have been disclosed to the plaintiffs during the June to
October period now under consideration. Whether that view was disclosed to
Mr Butler or to Mr Laidlaw at some and what stage may become the subject of
examination at trial; here it can only be a matter for inference.
    What was disclosed to the plaintiffs early in that period was the determination of *g*
those controlling Rumasa to alter the operation of that agreement from the way
which had so long proved satisfactory. The channel of communication selected for
announcing changes was initially ISI, whose precise position and authority and
responsibility was at all material times far from clear. At first Mr Butler was ISI's
main mouthpiece, but a little later Mr Laidlaw took over that task. It may be an issue
at trial whether the commission given to those in ISI at some of the stages of the *h*
relevant period was to work and negotiate within the terms of the existing agreement
or was to act as hatchet-men preparing for, or with their eyes on, the termination of
that agreement one way or another. Suffice it at present to say that there were occasions when the latter attitude could be inferred from the way Mr Laidlaw conducted
matters.
    The sequence of events during this period commenced with meetings of 21st June *j*
and 13th July—on the latter occasion Senor Ruiz-Mateos and Senor Fernandez taking
part. At those meetings were announced a number of decisions of Bertola. They
included (i) that bottling should in future take place in Spain and not in this country;
(ii) that advertising should be withdrawn from the plaintiffs and taken over by Bertola
at the latter's expense; (iii) that the f o b price per case was to be increased—although to

a what level was not specified; (iv) that the plaintiffs must forthwith comply with a demand by Bertola to give an order for 50,000 cases; (v) that it was intended in future to have marketed in this country medium and dry sherry as well as sweet sherry under the Bertola name.

Although there is a conflict of evidence on many points between the parties, there does not seem to have been on the occasion of either of those two meetings a sugges-
b tion that the plaintiffs had in the past acted in any way in breach of the distributor agreement, although it was stated that Bertola were not content with the current sales results.

On the above announced changes no difficulty arose as regards the bottling (although consideration had to be given to the bottles and labels being such as to continue to attract existing customers); nor was any raised as to the changes in advertising procedure—although this was a variation of the contract terms which might adversely
c affect linkage with sales activities in this country, something which obviously needed careful consideration and working out.

The other three demands related to matters which obviously involved even more consideration from a practical angle. As regards price, a new trade price structure would have to be worked out, and it was not clear whether the increase might not be
d greater than was in conformity with the practice of the Association of Sherry Distribu-
tors. As regards the demand for an order for 50,000 cases—this was something which was contrary to the practice of the parties and had no warrant under the contract; moreover, the market for Bertola sherry plainly required re-assessment in the light of the effect of any raising of the price. As regards introducing medium and dry Bertola sherry—that again was something which required careful working out and there could be two views whether it was a wise merchanting step, having regard to Bertola's
e exclusive and valuable reputation in the sweet sherry market.

The new price for sherry was not stated by Bertola until 18th August—and then turned out to be £5·65 a case as against the previous £1·85, an increase far above the aggregate differences made by the advertising and bottling decisions. Moreover this date was uncomfortably close to early September, when the Christmas trade orders come in; and the great increase made a new price structure difficult to work out.
f In those circumstances the plaintiffs, without acting unreasonably (so far as the present evidence goes), took more time to think over matters and come to conclu-
sions than Bertola, represented by ISI, liked. In particular, Mr Laidlaw, who had taken over from Mr Butler ISI's dealings with the plaintiffs, appears to have become impatient and angry. On one occasion, 22nd September, he actually went so far as to insist on the telephone, at 10·53 a m, that a girl secretary convey a message to Mr
g Holloway, the plaintiffs' marketing director, that if the latter did not telephone to Mr Laidlaw before 11.00 a m with certain shipping instructions the distributor agree-
ment would be cancelled from that hour. For that extraordinary procedure, it is true, he subsequently apologised to the girl secretary, and in these proceedings he has stated on affidavit that he had no authority and was bluffing. There is, however, no evidence that the ultimatum was at that time withdrawn. There is, moreover, other evidence
h before the court as to the way in which Mr Laidlaw conducted matters which may require explanation at the trial.

Some six days after that ultimatum the plaintiffs, on 28th September, placed a firm order for 15,000 cases. This included 3,000 cases of 24 half bottles each—a material proportion of their trade having for many years been in half bottles. The price was not stated in this order, any more than it had been in previous orders passing between
j the parties. This order was accompanied by a letter of intent to order a further 30,000 cases in consignments of 10,000 each before Christmas. Bertola, however, have chosen not to deliver any cases at all—leaving the plaintiffs unable to supply orders previously given to them for the Christmas trade, or those which normally reached them shortly after that time of the year.

After this ultimatum, and the receipt of the above-named order and letter of intent,

Bertola, at a meeting on 2nd October, intimated their firm intention to discontinue
subsisting agreements and cabled confirmation next day. Formal notice was given on
26th October to take effect from the receipt of that letter, which occurred on 30th
October. In that letter Bertola complained of 'lack of performance on your part and
your obstructive conduct towards adaptation to the commercial policy established . . .'
On 30th October Bertola, by an agreement so dated, formally appointed ISI to
be their distributing agency in this country. I use the word 'formally' because, on
29th October, a sub-agent of ISI was already circulating the plaintiffs' customers to
obtain their orders in Scotland for Bertola sherry, providing them with a temporary
price list. Very considerable confusion thereupon ensued in relation to supplies for
orders given a long time ago to the plaintiffs and their sub-agents for Bertola sherry
for the Christmas trade, and also as between the plaintiffs and those sub-agents, at
any rate one of whom had still two years sub-agency to run. On 10th November,
as already indicated, the plaintiffs very promptly issued the first writ and these
proceedings ensued.

Bertola's defence

In support of the allegation that they were entitled to determine the distributor
agreement in the way they did on 26th October, Bertola allege a number of breaches
of that agreement, contending that these justified them in taking action under cl 13.
Prominent amongst those complaints are, first that no order was placed for 50,000
cases as demanded—although 15,000 cases were ordered on 28th September (after a
re-appraisal of the effect of raising prices) accompanied by the letter of intent to which
I have referred in regard to a further 30,000 cases. This order is described as 'derisory'.
Secondly, that the hand-over of advertising had not been sufficiently speedy. Thirdly,
that the plaintiffs had not responded appropriately to Bertola's desire to introduce
medium and dry sherry. In addition, there were complaints as to failure to provide
Bertola with the plaintiffs' market research data and as to inadequate performance in
the past.

These complaints were carefully examined in detail by Kerr J and rejected by him
as being unlikely to provide grounds entitling Bertola to determine the agreement.
With those views expressed in that judgment I respectfully concur, and would only
add that some of the complaints at present appear so ill-founded as to be consistent
with a firmly fixed intention to wreck the agreement without regard to whether
such a course was justified. Instances were the 'serious view' taken by Senor Fernandez
of the fact that the 28th September order included cases of 24 half bottles, and the so
far vague charge of making undue profits. I should perhaps add that in this court it
has been submitted that the plaintiffs were at fault also in not placing orders between
13th July and 18th August when they did not even know what the new price would
be.

Bertola have also raised in these proceedings the question whether the length of the
sole distributor agreement and the extent of the territories affected was reasonable
and as such void in restraint of trade. On this issue the judgment of 30th November
contains this statement:

'As regards the restraint of trade point which has been mentioned, I think that
the length and nature of this agreement are relevant to the question whether or
not a permanent injunction should be granted at the trial. But, as at present
advised, I would not regard this point as a sufficient threat to the plaintiffs'
prospects of success on liability to warrant a refusal of an injunction on this
ground.'

With that view I again express concurrence. The relevant issue can be ventilated at
trial, and anything I say should not be regarded as pre-judging it, but I would mention
two points which will need examination. First, no case has been cited in which the
doctrine of restraint of trade has been applied to agreements in any way parallel to

a   that under consideration. Secondly, it does not seem to be suggested that the
agreement or any part of it is void by the law of Spain which governs its validity.
   It should be recorded that, in the closing stages of his address in this court, counsel
for the defendants felt himself unable to rely on the restraint of trade point in resisting an interlocutory injunction, whilst reserving it for trial.

b   *Jurisdiction*
   I now turn to the first of the main points with which this appeal is concerned. The
question is whether the courts in this country should permit the continuance of these
proceedings against Bertola in view of cl 15 of the agreement, which provides for
'law claims' to be submitted to the Barcelona Court of Justice. It appears likely that at
trial there may be a contest whether or not that clause is an 'exclusive jurisdiction
clause': for the purposes of this appeal, however, it was conceded on behalf of the
c   plaintiffs that it should be so regarded, and that accordingly the burden lying on the
plaintiffs when asserting that they can successfully claim to continue proceedings here
is heavier than it would be if the jurisdiction given to the Barcelona court had not
been exclusive.
   The authorities relating to this aspect of the case were cited in the first instance
d   judgment. Thereupon the learned judge rightly decided to apply the most stringent
of the tests laid down in them. He referred to the judgment of Diplock LJ in *Mackender v Feldia AG*[1], where he said: 'I . . . should require very strong reasons to induce me
to permit one of them [i e the parties] to go back on his word'; and of Lord Denning
MR in *YTC Universal Ltd (in Liquidation) v Trans Europa Compania de Aviacion SA*[2] where
he said:

e   '. . . effect should usually be given to [the] agreement, though there may be
        exceptional cases where a case may be allowed to proceed in these courts despite
        such agreement . . .'

   Kerr J went on to say that, having taken all relevant matters into consideration, he
nevertheless concluded—

f   'without hesitation that for a number of reasons this is a proper case for the
        exercise of jurisdiction under RSC Ord 11 in relation to both writs, because of
        the special circumstances.'

   In my judgment, too, this is plainly a case in which jurisdiction under RSC Ord 11
should be exercised as regards both concurrent writs in favour of the plaintiffs. The
g   reasons for this course being adopted were fully set out in the judgment of Kerr J
and can be summarised as follows by quoting from the judgment. First:

        'This is a case of which the substance is exclusively concerned with this country.
        It is a battle about the proper marketing of sherry in the United Kingdom.'

   Secondly:

h   'Whatever may be the right view about all the relevant allegations, all the
        essential witnesses concerning these issues are here, and all these issues essentially
        relate to the marketing conditions of sherry in this country and nowhere else.'

   Thirdly:

j   'Having chosen to give battle about the plaintiffs' marketing achievements in
        this country, Bertola have not merely purported to terminate the agreement but
        also to appoint another distributor, ISI, in the place of [the plaintiffs]. In doing this

---

1   [1966] 3 All ER 847 at 853, [1967] 2 QB 590 at 604
2   [1968] Bar Library transcript 366 at p 3

they must have known that it would be likely, if not certain, as happened, to provoke a bitter conflict between [the plaintiffs] and ISI in the sherry market of *a* the United Kingdom over this brand of sherry. Predictably, [the plaintiffs] have then instituted proceedings against both ISI and Bertola to restrain them from continuing with this course and to claim damages. In these circumstances it seems to me that it does not lie in the mouth of Bertola to say that the conflict between [the plaintiffs] and Bertola should be separated from that between [the plaintiffs] and ISI. But [the plaintiffs'] claims against ISI, which were pro- *b* voked by the actions of Bertola, have nothing to do with the court at Barcelona. It follows that Bertola are therefore not only a proper and necessary party to [the plaintiffs'] proceedings against ISI, within RSC Ord 11, but that Bertola have brought this state of affairs about by their own actions in purporting to terminate the agreement and to appoint ISI instead. How then can Bertola be heard to say that [the plaintiffs] must fight one battle here and the other in Spain?' *c*

Fourthly:

'. . . it is clear from the evidence that Spanish law does not differ from English law in the relevant respects to any substantial extent.'

Kerr J had previously brought out the fact that insofar as Bertola seek to establish that *d* the agreement is void as being an unreasonable restraint of trade they rely on English law, which, I would add, involves difficult and controversial contentions. He accordingly expressed the view that:

'In all these circumstances I consider that it would be unjust if Bertola could on the one hand take the course which they have taken in relation to the agency in *e* this country, but at the same time avoid the jurisdiction of the courts of this country. I believe that the discretion which the English courts have, notwith-standing a foreign jurisdiction clause—exclusive or otherwise—is designed to avoid unjust results such as those.'

Despite the powerful argument advanced by counsel for the defendants as to the fact that the disputes in this country are of a kind which would be likely to have *f* been anticipated when the agreement was signed, and despite the point that the true issue in this case is whether, under Spanish law, the contract was properly terminated, I find myself in complete agreement with the view expressed by Kerr J and the above reasons as stated by him.

It does not seem necessary, in the circumstances, to examine in detail the suggestions of the plaintiffs (to which some weight was attached in his judgment) as to the poten- *g* tial disadvantages of proceedings in the Spanish courts in such a case as this. It is, however, worth mentioning that on behalf of the defendants two affidavits by Spanish lawyers were filed stating that interlocutory injunctions would not be granted in this type of case; also that it would have been unlikely that there could be matched there the rate of progress by which this case has now reached the stage of a Court of Appeal decision within six weeks of the issue of the writ—despite the fact that here and at first *h* instance an aggregate of nine working days has been occupied by submissions.

I would, moreover, refer to one further factor which in my judgment has consider-able weight. The conspiracy allegations, which we were told are definitely being pursued and are supported by evidence prima facie fit to be left to a jury, sound in tort and fall within head (*h*) of RSC Ord 11, r 1. It would seem odd indeed, even if such a tort exists, or alternatively is recognised, in Spain (as to which no evidence has been *j* put before us), were we, in all the circumstances, to adopt a course which necessitated separate trials of this cause of action in Spain and in England.

It will be observed that I have reached a conclusion firmly supporting the decision to allow service of concurrent writs under RSC Ord 11 without referring to the ques-tion of whether this is a case for an interlocutory injunction. Suffice it to say that if *a*   this is such a case that would, of itself, provide an additional and very cogent reason for allowing such service.

Should an interlocutory injunction be granted?
I now turn to the vexed question whether this is a case in which an interlocutory injunction should issue. Kerr J came to the following conclusions on four important preliminary issues. First, that the plaintiffs had a reasonable prospect of success at trial
b   on the issue whether Bertola were entitled to determine the distributorship agreement; in other words—

> 'of the court being satisfied at the trial that the failure of [the plaintiffs] to react to Bertola's requirements and suggestions as quickly and positively as Bertola wanted during this period of three months did not justify cancellation of an agree-
c   ment which had run apparently satisfactorily for 20 years and had 14 more years to run.'

Secondly, that he was 'not impressed with the allegations that for years [the plaintiffs] had failed to perform this agreement in accordance with its terms'. Thirdly, that he did not regard the restraint of trade point 'as a sufficient threat to the plaintiffs' prospects of success . . . to warrant a refusal of an injunction on this ground'. And
d   fourthly, that so far as the balance of convenience was concerned he could see nothing against the grant of an injunction. He then ended by stating that—

> 'on the merits of this case the plaintiffs have a strong case for an injunction against both defendants except for the one vital point, that I am not satisfied that they have shown—and I quote from Salmon LJ[1]—"a strong prima facie
e   case that the claim for an injunction will succeed at the trial".'

He had previously stated that point in parallel terms, i e:

> '. . . if the court is not satisfied, as I am not, that the plaintiffs have at least a reasonable, if not a strong, prospect of obtaining a permanent injunction at the trial, then the court . . . has no choice [but to refuse an interlocutory injunction].'
f

Accordingly with regret he refused that injunction but ordered a speedy trial.
The main grounds on which he considered that an injunction might well be refused at trial would appear to have been these. First, the length of the period sought being 14 years, no case having been cited where an injunction had been granted for a comparable time. Secondly, that the agreement between the parties was in the nature of a joint venture requiring co-operation and confidence between the parties.
g   Thirdly, that, particularly having regard to certain negotiations between the parties in the middle of October, the plaintiffs had failed to show that damages were not an adequate remedy: as regards their recoverability he stated his concern had been allayed by an undertaking offered by Rumasa SA to execute a deed to which I will refer later.
h   As regards the four preliminary conclusions, I find myself in full agreement with the learned judge. It does not seem necessary—especially in view of the fact that these conclusions are in no way binding when the trial takes place—to examine further the relevant facts beyond saying that they are to be found in his judgment and in what I have already stated in mine.
Accordingly it is now necessary to examine whether his final approach to the exer-
j   cise of his discretion was correct and, if not, how the relevant discretion should now be exercised.

Approach to the exercise of discretion
It is clear from what the learned judge said that he considered there was in effect

---

1 In *Alfonal Ltd v Stratenport Ltd* (20th May 1969) unreported

some strict rule of law which precluded the grant of an interlocutory injunction
unless there was sufficient prospect of a permanent injunction being obtained at trial. *a*
With all respect, he fell into the error of considering that a factor which may normally weigh heavily against granting an interlocutory injunction was a factor which,
as a matter of law, precluded its grant.

The line of approach to the exercise of the court's discretion whether or not an interlocutory injunction should be granted is that stated by Lord Denning MR in *Hubbard
v Vosper*[1]: *b*

'In considering whether to grant an interlocutory injunction, the right course
for a judge is to look at the whole case. He must have regard not only to the
strength of the claim but also to the strength of the defence, and then decide
what is best to be done. Sometimes it is best to grant an injunction so as to maintain the status quo until the trial. At other times it is best not to impose a restraint *c*
on the defendant but leave him free to go ahead ... The remedy by interlocutory
injunction is so useful that it should be kept flexible and discretionary. It must not
be made the subject of strict rules.'

It is true that this statement of Lord Denning MR was obiter, but it expresses in
felicitous language the view applied nine days earlier in his considered judgment and *d*
in mine in *Hill v C A Parsons & Co Ltd*[2]. There, too, when joining in rejecting a submission that a much-followed practice had become a rule of law[3], I held that flexibility
was an essential feature of the court's jurisdiction. That was a master and servant case.
There can always arise other special cases in which it is proper to maintain a status quo
irrespective of whether the relief granted at trial will include a permanent injunction.

The learned judge having thus erred in his approach, it is now for this court to come *e*
to its own conclusions as to how, in this case, the relevant discretion should be
exercised.

Length of injunction

On the question of length of injunction we had cited to us *Lord Strathcona Steamship
Co Ltd v Dominion Coal Co Ltd*[4]. There the Privy Council upheld a first instance injunction *f*
granted in 1922 restraining for ten years any dealing with The Lord Strathcona inconsistent with a 1914 charterparty granted by the previous owners of the vessel.
Moreover, we have properly been reminded of a much-cited passage in the speech of
Lord Cairns in *Doherty v Allman*[5]. This makes it plain that there can and, indeed, should
be taken into account as a cogent factor that the court is being asked to do more than
what the parties have previously freely agreed. It seems to me that the learned *g*
judge gave rather over-great weight to the potential length of the injunction sought
by the plaintiffs and may also have overlooked the possibility that at trial the court
might merely grant an injunction for a lesser term, for instance of sufficient length to
enable an orderly winding-up of the existing arrangements, or for the duration of the
plaintiffs' current agreements with sub-agents.

The nature of the agreement *h*

Next I turn to the weight to be given to the nature of the relations between the
parties which the learned judge likened to that of a joint venture where confidence
and co-operation between the parties is required. I am not at all sure that the analogy
is quite correct. This is a commercial agreement between trading companies that can
be implemented to the profit of both parties, if each conforms with its express and *j*

1   [1972] 1 All ER 1023 at 1029, [1972] 2 QB 84 at 96
2   [1971] 3 All ER 1345 at 1349, 1350, 1354, 1355, [1972] Ch 305 at 314, 320
3   See [1971] 3 All ER at 1351, 1352, [1972] Ch at 320, 321
4   [1926] AC 108, [1925] All ER Rep 87
5   (1878) 3 App Cas 709 at 720

a implied terms. As in a great many commercial contracts consultation between the parties as to implementation is desirable; but that does not necessarily turn them into joint ventures. But in any event, the fact that some degree of mutual co-operation or confidence is needed does not preclude the court from granting negative injunctions designed to encourage the party in breach to perform his part. Examples are to be found in *Warner Brothers Pictures Inc v Nelson*[1], a film producer and film artist case, and *b* *Decro-Wall International SA v Practitioners in Marketing Ltd*[2], which concerned a sole distributor agreement.

It is also worth observing that in the case of partnerships—where mutual confidence is normally of high importance—the codifying Partnership Act 1890 leans against a dissolution at the instance of the misconducting party. See, for example, the powers given to the court by s 35 to dissolve a partnership '(*d*) When a partner, *other than the partner suing* [I emphasise those words], wilfully or persistently commits a breach of *c* the partnership agreement . . .'

Here again, the learned judge appears to have given undue weight to the factor now under consideration.

Whether damages are an adequate remedy

d The standard question in relation to the grant of an injunction, are damages an adequate remedy? might perhaps, in the light of the authorities of recent years, be re-written: is it just, in all the circumstances, that a plaintiff should be confined to his remedy in damages?

ISI, by Mr Butler's affidavit, chose to emphasise the damage to their goodwill and trade reputation that they would suffer if the agency at will which they had held for *e* three weeks was unjustifiably disrupted: he emphasised the difficulty of assessing the resulting damage. These assertions appear a little naive when one looks in comparison at the loss of goodwill, the disruption in trade, and the litigation with sub-agents which would be inflicted on the plaintiffs by an unjustified abrupt termination of an agreement with 14 years to run—terminated with the aid of allegations of their having failed to carry out their obligations and of having made undue profits.

f In my judgment damages would not be an adequate remedy in this case, any more than they were held to be in any of the three cases already cited, *Warner's* case[1], the *Decro-Wall* case[2] and *Hill v C A Parsons & Co Ltd*[3]. The courts have repeatedly recognised that there can be claims under contracts in which, as here, it is unjust to confine a plaintiff to his damages for their breach. Great difficulty in estimating these damages is one factor that can be and has been taken into account. Another factor is the *g* creation of certain areas of damage which cannot be taken into monetary account in a common law action for breach of contract: loss of goodwill and trade reputation are examples—see also, in another sphere, the judgment of Jenkins LJ in *Vine v National Dock Labour Board*[4] which, albeit a dissenting judgment, was unanimously adopted in toto in the House of Lords[5]. Generally, indeed, the grant of injunctions in contract cases stems from such factors.

h

The 13th October negotiations and the Rumasa offer

It is urged on behalf of the defendants that certain negotiations that took place on 13th October showed that damages were in fact an adequate remedy, or at least were so regarded by the plaintiffs—and that accordingly they should be so regarded by the court.
j
_____

1 [1936] 3 All ER 160, [1937] 1 KB 209
2 [1971] 2 All ER 216, [1971] 1 WLR 361
3 [1971] 3 All ER 1345, [1972] Ch 305
4 [1956] 1 All ER 1 at 10, [1956] 1 QB 658 at 676
5 [1956] 3 All ER 939, [1957] AC 488

What happened on 13th October must, however, be looked at against the back- *a*
ground that after Bertola had, on 2nd October, announced their intention of terminating the agreement at some unspecified date, the plaintiffs brought to the 13th October
interview and there presented at its outset a letter dated 11th October referring to
their rights under Spanish law both to damages and to specific performance of the
agreement.

Figures for compensation were then discussed on an 'if' basis—those figures ranging *b*
from £1,500,000 or more mentioned by the plaintiffs down to £250,000 suggested
by Bertola. Neither on that date nor on a further discussion on 18th October was
agreement reached—and those discussions do not seem to me to provide a basis
on which the defendants can now say that the plaintiffs' relief must now be confined to an inadequate remedy—damages less than those commercially suffered—
any more than that the defendants are disentitled to put forward defences which *c*
were never raised on those occasions. To hold that unsuccessful negotiations to
settle a dispute might be held to debar parties from subsequent enforcement remedies otherwise open to them would not encourage sensible businessmen to come
to settlements.

So far the question of adequacy of damages has been discussed on the footing that
if judgment was recovered the sum awarded would be paid. But whenever the *d*
adequacy of damages falls to be considered in this class of case, there arises the further
question—are the defendants good for the money? Also (if they are abroad), will
their government's exchange control permit the payment? In other words, will the
judgment be satisfied?

Bertola being a wholly owned subsidiary of unknown financial status in Spain, and
ISI a company with a £5,000 share capital, the chances of a judgment for sums such *e*
as have just been mentioned being satisfied by them cannot be rated as other than
questionable. So on that ground, too, damages would prima facie in this case not
be an adequate remedy.

It is, however, urged on behalf of Bertola that an offer made by their counsel in
his closing address at first instance should be treated as so altering the position with
regard to this last factor as to eliminate the chances that a judgment might not be *f*
satisfied.

That offer was in the form of an unconditional undertaking by Rumasa to execute
some sort of bond guaranteeing payment of damages up to £500,000. (Costs do
not appear to have been mentioned.) The day before yesterday, this offer was here
said to be still open for the plaintiffs to accept, and it was also stated that it would
so remain whatever be the judgments in this appeal. The plaintiffs, however, had *g*
made it plain to the Court of Appeal within 24 hours of Kerr J's judgment that,
having regard inter alia to the potential exchange control difficulties in Spain, they
did not regard the offer as useful. Nothing was done after that to implement the
offer, or to remove those difficulties, except that, at the very last hour of yesterday's
address, it was expanded into an offer to provide security to the satisfaction of a master
for damages up to £500,000.

Strictly, there is no need to discuss these offers, designed to affect the court's de- *h*
cision on the question of an interlocutory injunction—as that offer only relates to
securing payment of damages which are anyway not an adequate remedy. It is,
however, as well to observe that offers of guarantee by a third party not before the
court are indeed a novelty; and if designed to stave off an injunction must be looked
at with considerable caution.

  j

Conclusions

Having thus examined separately and in turn those factors which led Kerr J to
refuse an interlocutory injunction, and which have been so powerfully canvassed in
this court by counsel for the defendants, it is now right to step back and look at the
matter as a whole.

a   In essence, the plaintiffs' case is that the men who took over the management of
Bertola in June 1972 formed an instant dislike for the terms of the distributorship
agreement, sought at once to impose new trading arrangements without any regard
either to the content of the agreement or to reasonable considerations affecting its
implementation and, when they did not get an instant compliance on points which
obviously required time for consideration, deliberately proceeded to adopt a course
b   calculated to end that agreement; and that ISI collaborated with them in that
objective. Bertola, it is said, then determined the agreement with no just cause
and handed over the profitable distributorship to ISI as planned. The plaintiffs
assert that the purported determination of that agreement was unlawful.
       The defendants contend that the termination was justified because of the lack of
sufficiently speedy compliance with their demands and on account of pre-June 1972
failures by the plaintiffs to carry out the terms of the agreement—throwing in, for
c   good measure, an allegation that the relevant terms of that agreement are void.
       On the evidence so far before the court the plaintiffs seem to have a reasonable
prima facie case which could lead to success, whilst the defences, as so far raised,
cannot be said to be impressive. If the plaintiffs are right, the disruption caused by
the defendants' action is unjustified, and so great that damages are not an adequate
d   remedy.
       It is true to say that specific performance of such an agreement will not be ordered,
but it is no less plain that the court will grant negative injunctions to encourage a
party in breach to keep to his contract. As Salmon LJ put it in the Decro-Wall case[1],
in relation to an undertaking given in lieu of an injunction:

e   'If the plaintiffs were released from it, they and the concessionaires they
           appointed in breach of their contract with the defendants would be left free to
           take advantage of this breach and enjoy the fruits of the time, effort and money
           which the defendants have expended during the last three years in creating and
           building up a thriving market for the plaintiffs' goods in the United Kingdom.
           Damages in such a case are very difficult to prove and I do not believe that they
           would by themselves be an adequate remedy.'

f   In the instant case, as in that case, an attempt is being made which, if unjustified
would deprive the plaintiffs of the benefit of having built up a name for Bertola
sherry with the aid of expending the best part of half a million pounds for that
purpose in a dozen years.
       In my judgment, this is accordingly a case where there is everything to be said for
g   maintaining the status quo up to trial—which ought, if the parties use proper efforts,
to commence in not more than four months from now. Whatever its result as
regards liability, there is nothing to be said at this stage in favour of abrupt and
disruptive changes in trading methods and policy.
       It is urged that Senor Fernandez has threatened not to resume trading with the
plaintiffs despite any injunction granted. Again to quote from the judgment of
h   Salmon LJ[2] (when referring to an undertaking given in lieu of an injunction):

           'The undertaking however ensures that they could obtain no advantage from
           adopting such a course. Indeed if they did so they would probably lose the
           benefit of the market built up for them by the defendants in the United Kingdom
           and increase the damages which are to be assessed ...'

j   It has been suggested that the court, if it did grant an injunction, should confine its
operation to some part of England and to one product only—cream sherry. In my
judgment, however, such a course would be wrong—not only would it provide

---

1   [1971] 2 All ER at 225, [1971] 1 WLR at 371, 372
2   [1971] 2 All ER at 225, [1971] 1 WLR at 372

confusion but it would adopt a basis that some breaches should be permitted although others are not.

I would accordingly favour granting the injunction until trial or further order in the terms of the two applications heard by Kerr J on 24th November, save that as regards Bertola the injunctions will be limited to England and Wales. This, of course, results in Bertola being free, if they so wish, to advertise medium and dry sherry, and the plaintiffs being under an obligation to take reasonable steps to market such sherry. Incentives for the plaintiffs to make a success of such an operation are not lacking.

The grant of these injunctions would be in conformity with the trend of recent decisions that the court, in using its discretion, is disposed to set its face against those who seek abruptly to break contracts in circumstances such as obtain in this case. That trend works in the interests of justice and also in the interests of the proper conduct of commercial relations.

The usual cross-undertakings must, of course, be given by the plaintiffs. Having regard to the relatively short period over which the injunctions would operate, and the size of the plaintiffs' previous trading operations, there is no need to make provision for any financial backing of that further undertaking.

It follows that I would dismiss the two appeals by Bertola and would allow that of the plaintiffs.

EDMUND DAVIES LJ. I am in respectful agreement with what, unfortunately for his colleagues, falls to be described as the terminal judgment of Sachs LJ. Its quality and breadth are such that I simply desire to add two marginal comments.

(A) The first relates to RSC Ord 11, r 1, and to cl 15 of the original agreement of 26th September 1951 made between the plaintiffs and the first defendants, Bertola, an agreement which, like its successors, it is common ground is governed by Spanish law. This 'exclusive jurisdiction' clause (as the trial judge held it to be) is in two parts: (a) 'If any law claim arises between the two parties it will be submitted to the Barcelona Court of Justice'; (b) if the plaintiffs made a claim relating to the quality of the wines supplied it was to be referred to a controlling body at Jerez, whose decision 'must be accepted without appeal'.

In the light of this clause counsel for the defendants referred with considerable frequency to the plaintiffs as being in breach of their contract in seeking in English courts any contractual relief against the first defendants. It is therefore said that they should not be permitted to bring Bertola within the jurisdiction of our courts, and particular reliance was placed on the judgment of Brandon J in *The Eleftheria*[1]. That case was before Kerr J, as well as the authorities therein reviewed by Brandon J. These included *The Fehmarn*[2], where a bill of lading provided that all claims thereunder should be judged in the Union of Soviet Socialist Republics. The English company who held the bill of lading sued the owners of the German vessel in which a cargo of turpentine was carried, on the ground that it had arrived here in a contaminated condition. Willmer J[3] refused to stay the action, and the Court of Appeal declined to interfere with that decision, Lord Denning MR saying[4]:

'... is this dispute a matter which properly belongs to the courts of this country? Here are English importers ... who, when they take delivery of the goods in England, find them contaminated ... It has been said ... that this contract is governed by Russian law and should be judged by the Russian courts,

---

1 [1969] 2 All ER 641, [1970] P 94
2 [1958] 1 All ER 333, [1958] 1 WLR 159
3 [1957] 2 All ER 707, [1957] 1 WLR 815
4 [1958] 1 All ER at 335, [1958] 1 WLR at 162

a who know that law . . . I do not regard the choice of law in the contract as decisive. I prefer to look to see with what country the dispute is most closely concerned.'

Counsel for the defendants pointed out that *The Fehmarn*[1] dealt with an action in rem, and I gathered that he regarded this as a feature which diminished the relevance of what was there said to the facts of the present case. As to this, it is sufficient to
b say that *The Eleftheria*[2], on which counsel himself strongly relied, was also an action in rem. In my judgment both decisions may properly be here adverted to, and Kerr J was entitled to apply, as he did, the test enunciated by Lord Denning MR[3] in the former.

Kerr J furthermore properly directed himself:

c '[(a)] in RSC Ord 11 cases there is a heavier burden on the plaintiff who wants to bring the defendant within the jurisdiction than in cases of applications for staying actions properly instituted here [(b)] to bring a defendant before the English courts in the face of a foreign jurisdiction clause clearly goes further than merely allowing an action against a defendant properly served here to proceed.'

He nevertheless concluded 'without hesitation . . . that this is a proper case for the
d exercise of jurisdiction under RSC Ord 11 [for] both writs'. This conclusion was based on a wide and helpful survey of the relevant circumstances adduced both for and against the courts of this country assuming jurisdiction. No point would be served by again reviewing the matters covered in that careful summary, which Sachs LJ has quoted only in part. While counsel for the defendants submitted that the learned judge had arrived at the wrong conclusion, he did not suggest that he had taken into
e consideration irrelevant matters or failed to have regard to those which were relevant. His criticism was of a different kind, namely, that insufficient *weight* had been given to those features which should have led to the judge refusing to exercise his discretion in favour of English jurisdiction. For my part I do not regard that criticism as well-founded. On the contrary, I consider that Kerr J was fully entitled to deal with this discretionary matter as he did.

f (B) I want secondly to deal shortly with what Kerr J described as—

'an unconditional undertaking offered by Rumasa SA to execute a deed, or to take equivalent steps, to guarantee the payment of any damages . . . up to the sum of £500,000.'

He made it clear that he regarded this offer as of considerable importance, and that
g he took it into consideration in declining interlocutory injunctions, for he stressed that 'there is nothing to show on the evidence that Bertola, let alone ISI, would have the means of meeting such a claim'. Should it have affected the trial judge's mind? In my respectful view it should have been ignored. It is no reflection on Rumasa to describe the undertaking as a novelty which the plaintiffs were entitled to regard with suspicion when it was suddenly proffered. It emerged at a late stage in the
h proceedings, it was made on behalf of somebody who was not a party, it lacked particularity, and there was no information whether the foreign exchange control system would enable Rumasa to remit what on any view must be a large sum in the event of the plaintiffs succeeding in their claim.

The judgment having been delivered on 30th November, it is to be observed that the plaintiffs' notice of appeal delivered the following day specifically alleged that
j Kerr J had misdirected himself in having regard to the undertaking. Being thus forewarned, one would have thought that the defendants would have taken the steps

---

1 [1958] 1 All ER 333, [1958] 1 WLR 159
2 [1969] 2 All ER 641, [1970] P 94
3 [1958] 1 All ER at 335, [1958] 1 WLR at 162

necessary to place a concrete proposition before this court, dealing in proper detail not only with the form of the undertaking but also with the safeguards offered to the *a* plaintiffs in order to secure its fulfilment, including, of course, clarification of the important matter of exchange control. But no such steps have been taken, and in reply to a direct question from a member of this court as to the position regarding exchange control, all that counsel for the defendants was able to say, at the twenty-third hour, was that 'the offer is still unconditionally open' and that security satisfactory to a master would be forthcoming. He must allow me to say, for my part, that I *b* think this deplorably lax approach to a matter to which the defendants ask this court to attach importance is nothing like good enough, even though (for all we know to the contrary) the financial stability of Rumasa may be as impregnable as a rock. Nevertheless, the repeated offer through the mouth of learned counsel of the undertaking inevitably lacks the formality, precision and assurance that it could lawfully be implemented which the plaintiffs are entitled to expect and which it should possess *c* if this court is to have regard to it. These features the undertaking lacks even now, and I therefore take the view that it should be left wholly out of account.

I desire to say no more than that I concur in the order proposed by Sachs LJ.

CAIRNS LJ. I concur cordially in the observations made by Edmund Davies LJ *d* in the first few words of his judgment, and I agree that the appeals against the orders for service of the writs on Bertola should be dismissed and that the appeal against the refusal of injunctions should be allowed for the reasons given by Sachs LJ. I add only a few observations of my own.

With regard to the orders for service, counsel for the defendants laid great stress on the fact that by suing in this country the plaintiffs are (on the assumption that cl 15 *e* of the agreement is an exclusive jurisdiction clause) in breach of their agreement that any law claim between the parties should be submitted to the Barcelona Court of Justice. That is a consideration of substance, but the passage already quoted from the judgment of Diplock LJ in *Mackender v Feldia AG*[1] and of Lord Denning MR in *YTC Universal Ltd v Trans Europa Compania de Aviacion SA*[2] make it clear that there are exceptional cases when it is right to allow a party to sue in England *f* notwithstanding such an agreement.

In my opinion this is one of those exceptional cases. I base that view on all the grounds set out in the judgment of Kerr J, but particularly on the ground that the plaintiffs have claims against both ISI and Bertola, and there can be no question but that the action against ISI is properly brought in England. Counsel for the *g* defendants suggested that the plaintiffs should first proceed in Spain against Bertola to establish their contractual rights, and then, if they succeeded, bring or continue this action against ISI here. Not only would this involve duplication of proceedings, but it would greatly delay the enforcement of any claim the plaintiffs have against ISI and inhibit the obtaining of an interlocutory injunction against them.

I am also impressed by the fact that two Spanish lawyers have deposed in affidavits *h* filed on behalf of the defendants that Spanish courts will in no circumstances grant injunctions such as are sought here. As I understand it, these opinions are expressed in relation to both interlocutory and final injunctions. I am therefore of opinion that Kerr J rightly exercised his discretion in giving leave for service of the writs on Bertola and in refusing to set aside such leave.

On the matter of the injunction, I agree that if Kerr J thought there was a rule of *j* law preventing him from granting an interlocutory injunction in the absence of 'a strong prima facie case that the claim for an injunction will succeed at the trial',

1 [1966] 3 All ER 847 at 853, [1967] 2 QB 590 at 604
2 (1968) 112 Sol Jo 842

a   this was a wrong view. I do not think Salmon LJ can have intended in *Alfonal Ltd v Stratenport Ltd*[1] to lay down a proposition of law to that effect. For instance, there may be cases where the contract has only a few months to run and will probably terminate before the trial, but where an interlocutory injunction is nevertheless appropriate. Further, there may be cases where the case for an injunction at the trial is not a very strong one but there is *some* prospect of its being granted provided the status quo is maintained, whereas if breaches were allowed to continue it would be impossible

b   or useless to grant an injunction at the trial. In such circumstances I would consider it right that an interlocutory injunction should be made.

After considering the facts so far as they appear from the affidavits here, and the authorities, particularly that of *Decro-Wall*[2] and that of *Warner Brothers Pictures Inc v Nelson*[3], I am of opinion that, in all the circumstances of this case, there is a reasonable prospect of the trial court granting an injunction and that that is sufficient to justify

c   the granting of an interlocutory injunction now.

I therefore agree with the orders proposed by Sachs LJ.

Appeal allowed; cross-appeals dismissed.

d   Solicitors: *Herbert Smith & Co* (for the plaintiffs); *Stephenson, Harwood & Tatham* (for the defendants).

Ilyas Khan Esq   Barrister.

e
R v Epping and Harlow Justices, ex parte Massaro

QUEEN'S BENCH DIVISION
LORD WIDGERY CJ, ASHWORTH AND WILLIS JJ
f   15th DECEMBER 1972

Criminal law – Committal – Preliminary hearing before justices – Prima facie case – Evidence – Witnesses – Crown not calling principal witness for prosecution – Whether committal invalid.

g   The function of committal proceedings is to ensure that no one shall stand trial unless a prima facie case has been made out. If the prosecution believe that it is possible to make out a prima facie case without calling a particular witness, even though the principal witness, that is a matter within their discretion and they cannot be compelled to call the witness at the committal proceedings (see p 1012 j to p 1013 a, post).

h
Notes
For committal for trial by justices, see 10 Halsbury's Laws (3rd Edn) 365, 366, para 666, and for cases on the subject, see 14 Digest (Repl) 224, 225, *1870-1877*.

Motion for certiorari
j   This was an application by Raffaele Massaro for an order of certiorari to bring up and quash an order of the Epping and Harlow justices dated 16th October 1972 committing

---

1   (20th May 1969) unreported
2   [1971] 2 All ER 216, [1971] 1 WLR 361
3   [1936] 3 All ER 160, [1937] 1 KB 209

him for trial in the Crown Court on a charge of indecent assault on a young girl, *a*
contrary to s 14 (1) of the Sexual Offences Act 1956, on the grounds that he had been
deprived of the opportunity of hearing the evidence of the girl, who was the principal
witness for the Crown, and of being able to cross-examine her, and that in all the
circumstances of the case the committal was contrary to natural justice. The facts
are set out in the judgment.

Michael Beckman for the applicant.   *b*
Suzanne Norwood for the Crown.

LORD WIDGERY CJ. In these proceedings counsel moves on behalf of one
Raffaele Massaro for leave to apply for an order of certiorari to bring up to this court
with a view to its being quashed a committal for trial by the justices of the petty   *c*
sessional division of Epping and Harlow effected on 16th October 1972, whereby the
applicant was committed to stand his trial at the Chelmsford Crown Court for an
offence contrary to s 14 (1) of the Sexual Offences Act 1956.

A good deal of evidence has been put before the court as to precisely what happened
in the course of the committal proceedings, but I find it quite unnecessary to refer to   *d*
that evidence, because this can most conveniently be dealt with as a short point of
general application and importance. What happened in essence at the committal
proceedings was that the prosecution indicated that they were not anxious to call
the little girl who was alleged to have been the victim of the sexual assault at the
preliminary hearing as well as at the trial in the Crown Court. It was anticipated
that the matter would go to trial, and it was anticipated that the girl would have to
give her evidence then. The prosecution were unwilling to subject her to this   *e*
experience on more than one occasion. However, at the committal proceedings
counsel was instructed to represent the applicant, and no doubt was left in the mind
of anybody that he wanted to cross-examine the girl there and then. One need not
take up time in order to explain why he thought it would be to the advantage of his
client to have the girl cross-examined at that stage and not merely at the trial.

The question which is posed for us, and the only question on which leave to move   *f*
was given, is simply this: when committal proceedings are being undertaken in a
case such as this, is it open to the prosecution, if they wish, to support the application
for committal by calling other supporting evidence and not calling the child at all?
That was a course very much in the mind of counsel for the prosecution in this case,
because there was other supporting evidence, and he was of the opinion that it would
be possible to show a prima facie case and have the man committed, without the   *g*
necessity for calling the girl, the complainant, herself.

For the purposes of this judgment I would assume that he decided so to do contrary
to the request of the defence, who wanted the girl called. Thus stated, this as a point
is a very short one: what is the function of the committal proceedings for this purpose? Is it, as the prosecution might contend, simply a safeguard for the citizen to
ensure that he cannot be made to stand his trial without a prima facie case being   *h*
shown; or is it, as counsel for the applicant would contend, a rehearsal proceeding
so that the defence may try out their cross-examination on the prosecution witnesses
with a view to using the results to their advantage in the Crown Court at a later
stage?

This matter has never been raised to be the subject of authority, and this was
another reason why leave was given in the present case. For my part I think it is   *j*
clear that the function of committal proceedings is to ensure that no one shall stand
his trial unless a prima facie case has been made out. The prosecution have the duty
of making out a prima facie case, and if they wish for reasons such as the present not
to call one particular witness, even though a very important witness, at the committal proceedings, that in my judgment is a matter within their discretion, and their

a failure to do so cannot on any basis be said to be a breach of the rules of natural justice. I would refuse the application

ASHWORTH J. I agree.

WILLIS J. I agree.

b *Application refused. The court certified the following to be a point of law of public general importance, namely, whether in committal proceedings where the defendant has given notice that he requires any particular prosecution witness to be present in order to give oral evidence the prosecution is bound to call such witness to give oral evidence, but refused leave to appeal to the House of Lords.*

c Solicitors: *Marks, Shavin & Co,* Barnet (for the applicant); *Solicitor, Metropolitan Police.*

N P Metcalfe Esq Barrister.

---

d # Rothermere and others v Times Newspapers Ltd and others

COURT OF APPEAL, CIVIL DIVISION
LORD DENNING MR, CAIRNS AND LAWTON LJJ
e 24th, 25th JANUARY, 13th FEBRUARY 1973

Jury – Trial by jury – Libel – Trial of action requiring prolonged examination of documents – Discretion of court to order trial by judge alone – Exercise of discretion – Circumstances in which proper to order trial by jury although trial requiring prolonged examination of documents – Importance of case to party's reputation and honour – Action raising issues of
f *national importance – Party entitled to trial by jury if he desires it – Administration of Justice (Miscellaneous Provisions) Act 1933, s 6 (1).*

The first and second defendants were respectively the proprietors and editor of the Times newspaper. The third defendant wrote an article which was published in the Times, headed 'Profit and dishonour in Fleet St'. The article attacked the
g plaintiffs, who were the proprietors of the Daily Mail and, before its closure, of the Daily Sketch. The plaintiffs brought an action for libel against the defendants in respect of the article, alleging that it meant, and was understood to mean, that the plaintiffs' group of companies was an ill-run group which had shamefully shut down a great newspaper, ie the Daily Sketch, for bogus reasons of economy, while the true reason was to make unconscionable additional profits; and that they had closed it down in
h a brutal manner causing acute hardship to their loyal staff. The defendants pleaded justification and fair comment on a matter of public interest. In reply the plaintiffs alleged that the defendants were actuated by express malice. The particulars of defence covered 58 pages of foolscap, the plaintiffs' list of documents covered 77 pages, containing 2,033 items, many of them files with numerous pages. The defendants' list of documents covered four pages containing 108 items. The defendants
j asked for trial by jury on the grounds, inter alia, that the case was of special importance to them and to the public. The judge however held that the case would require 'prolonged examination of documents' and, in the exercise of his discretion under s 6 (1)[a] of the Administration of Justice (Miscellaneous Provisions) Act 1933, ordered that the action be tried by judge alone. The defendants appealed.

---

a Section 6 (1), so far as material, is set out at p 1015 f, post

Held (Cairns LJ dissenting) – The appeal would be allowed and trial by jury ordered for the following reasons—

(i) (per Lord Denning MR) it was not the length or complication of the case which took away the right to trial by jury under s 6 (1) but the 'prolonged examination of documents'; the plaintiffs had failed to show that the case would require prolonged examination of documents since it was likely that the imputations and allegations made by the respective parties would be resolved on a broad picture rather than on small details (see p 1016 b to d, post);

(ii) even if the case would require prolonged examination of documents it did not follow that s 6 (1) gave the court an absolute discretion; there were cases in which one party might have a prior claim to trial by jury, e g where his honour or reputation was at stake; the judge had failed to give sufficient weight to the national importance of the subject-matter of the action, to the gravity of the charges made against the defendants and to their legitimate desire to have them tried by jury (see p 1016 e and f, p 1017 h, p 1018 b and c and p 1021 j to p 1022 a and e to h, post).

Notes

For the right to trial by jury, see 30 Halsbury's Laws (3rd Edn) 376, para 700, and for cases on the subject, see 51 Digest (Repl) 648-651, 2564-2582.

For the Administration of Justice (Miscellaneous Provisions) Act 1933, s 6, see 25 Halsbury's Statutes (3rd Edn) 749.

Cases referred to in judgment

Barnes v Hill [1967] 1 All ER 347, [1967] 1 QB 579, [1967] 2 WLR 632, Digest (Cont Vol C) 597, 496a.

Broome v Cassell & Co Ltd [1972] 1 All ER 801, [1972] AC 1027, [1972] 2 WLR 645, HL.

Capital and Counties Bank v Henty (1882) 7 App Cas 741, 52 LJQB 232, 47 LT 662, 47 JP 214, HL, 32 Digest (Repl) 23, 135.

Dunlop Rubber Co Ltd v Dunlop [1921] 1 AC 367, [1920] All ER Rep 745, 90 LJPC 140, 124 LT 584, HL, 51 Digest (Repl) 652, 2593.

Nevill v Fine Art and General Insurance Co Ltd [1897] AC 68, [1895-99] All ER Rep 164, 66 LJQB 195, 75 LT 606, 61 JP 500, HL, 51 Digest (Repl) 858, 4094.

R v Murray (22nd July 1960) unreported, CCC.

R v Shipley (1784) 4 Doug KB 73, State Tr 847, 99 ER 774, 32 Digest (Repl) 82, 1049.

Seven Bishops' Case (1688) 3 Mod Rep 212, 12 State Tr 183, 87 ER 136, 15 Digest (Repl) 780, 7316.

Ward v James [1965] 1 All ER 563, [1966] 1 QB 273, [1965] 2 WLR 455, [1965] 1 Lloyd's Rep 145, CA, Digest (Cont Vol B) 129, 783a.

Cases and authority also cited

Broadway Approvals Ltd v Odhams Press Ltd [1965] 2 All ER 523, [1965] 1 WLR 805, CA.

Hodges v Harland & Wolff Ltd [1965] 1 All ER 1086, [1965] 1 WLR 523, CA.

Osenton (Charles) & Co v Johnston [1941] 2 All ER 245, [1942] AC 130, HL.

Truth (New Zealand) Ltd v Avery [1959] NZLR 274.

Gatley on Libel and Slander (6th Edn, 1967), p 794.

Interlocutory appeal

This was an appeal by the defendants, Times Newspapers Ltd, William Rees-Mogg and Bernard Levin, against the order of Ackner J made on 21st December 1971 allowing an appeal by the plaintiffs, the Right Hon Esmond Cecil Viscount Rothermere, the Hon Vere Harold Esmond Harmsworth and Associated Newspapers Ltd, against the order of Master Lubbock dated 29th July 1971 and ordering that the plaintiffs' action against the defendants be tried by a judge alone. The facts are set out in the judgment of Lord Denning MR.

a J P Comyn QC and Peter Bowsher for the first and third defendants.
The second defendant appeared in person.
David Hirst QC and Thomas Bingham QC for the plaintiffs.

Cur adv vult

b 13th February. The following judgments were read.

LORD DENNING MR. On 19th March 1971 the Times published an article by Mr Bernard Levin headed 'Profit and dishonour in Fleet St'. It referred to Lord Rothermere and his colleagues. It commented on the closing down of the Daily Sketch and the continuance of the Daily Mail. I will not read it at large, but I will take the 'sting' of it as formulated by counsel for the plaintiffs. He said that the *c* article meant, and was understood to mean, that the Rothermere group was an ill-run group of companies which shamefully shut down a great newspaper for bogus reasons of economy—while the true reason was to make unconscionable additional profits—and that they closed it down in a brutal manner causing acute hardship to their loyal staff.

Lord Rothermere and his colleagues took exception to this article. They at once *d* issued a writ for libel. They sued the Times Newspapers Ltd, the editor of the Times, Mr Rees-Mogg, and the writer, Mr Bernard Levin, for libel. By way of defence the defendants pleaded justification, and fair comment on a matter of public interest. In reply the plaintiffs alleged that the defendants were actuated by express malice.

The question is, how should the action be tried? The defendants want trial by *e* jury. The plaintiffs want trial by judge alone. The relevant statutory provision is s 6 (1) of the Administration of Justice (Miscellaneous Provisions) Act 1933. It says that:

'... if, on the application of any party ... the Court or a judge is satisfied that—
(a) a charge of fraud against that party; or (b) a claim in respect of libel, slander,
f malicious prosecution, false imprisonment [or] seduction, is in issue, the action shall be ordered to be tried with a jury unless the Court or judge is of opinion that the trial thereof requires any prolonged examination of documents or accounts or any scientific or local investigation which cannot conveniently be made with a jury ...'

The defendants say that this case falls within these first words 'a claim in respect *g* of libel ... is in issue', and that they are entitled to have it tried by a jury. The plaintiffs say that the case falls within the exception 'the trial thereof requires ... prolonged examination of documents or accounts ... which cannot conveniently be made with a jury', and so it should be tried by a judge alone.

In support of their contention, the plaintiffs point to the particulars of defence. These cover 58 pages of foolscap. The plaintiffs' list of documents covers 77 pages *h* containing 2,033 items, many of which are files with numerous pages. The defendants' list of documents covers four pages containing 108 items. The plaintiffs assert that there will be a massive number of documents which will have to be copied and made available for the trial; and that the trial will require prolonged examination of them.

j *Prolonged examination of documents*
The first point is whether the trial will require the prolonged examination of documents which cannot conveniently be tried with a jury. The figures given by the plaintiffs make things look very alarming. But, I do not think they are nearly so bad as they appear. Many of the pages of particulars of defence contain long extracts from statements made by the chairman of the plaintiff company; or extracts from

their records, as to which there can be little controversy. In the plaintiffs' list of   a
documents there are many redundancy files which are, no doubt, very much of a
pattern.   I think this assertion of 'prolonged examination of documents' may well
turn out to be a bogey which, in capable hands, can be cut down to size.   I have tried
cases with masses of documents on many occasions.   It is remarkable how often
they can be reduced to manageable proportions.   One very useful thing is to get
accountants and experts to go through the documents and to state the general result   b
of them, without going into details.   Another useful thing is for counsel to make a
wise selection out of the available material, using some instances as typical of others.
    It must be remembered, too, that the imputations contained in the article are
made with a wide sweeping brush—as also are the allegations of malice alleged in
the reply.   Such imputations and such allegations will fall to be determined on a
broad picture.   They will not be resolved on small details.
    No doubt the trial will be long and complicated, but length and complication of   c
themselves are no bar to a jury.   Many of the important libel cases in recent years
were long and complicated, but they were tried with juries.   It is not the length and
complication but the 'prolonged examination of documents' which takes away the
right to a jury.   I am not myself satisfied that this case will require such 'prolonged
examination' and, for that reason alone, I would grant the defendants' request for trial   d
by jury.   But I may well be wrong about this.   So I turn to the next point: should
the court, in its discretion, order trial by jury?

Should the case be tried with a jury?
    Counsel for the plaintiffs submitted that once through the gateway of the exception,
the court had an absolute discretion, and the sole question was: which mode of trial
will best achieve justice for *both* sides?   I am not sure that this is altogether correct.   e
There are some cases in which *one* side may have a prior claim to a jury.   Thus,
where a man's honour or reputation is at stake, it may be of special importance to
him to have a jury.   Take *Broome v Cassell & Co Ltd*[1].   A distinguished naval officer
was accused of cowardice in the face of the enemy.   The case might be said
to involve prolonged examination of documents.   His right to a jury was not   f
disputed but, if it had been, surely he would have been given a jury.   Take this
very present case.   Lord Rothermere and his colleagues have been accused of shame-
ful conduct in the management of great newspapers.   If they had themselves asked
for a jury, surely they would have been given one.   The defendants would not have
been able to deprive them of a jury by saying: 'We have pleaded such lengthy
particulars and quoted so many documents that you cannot have a jury.'   So I
would not accept counsel's test.   I prefer to follow the words of Lord Devlin in his   g
little book on 'Trial by Jury'[2]:

    '. . . I think it will be found that the cases in which trial by jury is ordered—
    whether the order is made under a claim of right or in accordance with the
    general principles by which the discretion is exercised—are those in which for
    one reason or another *it is specially important to one or other of the parties* that he   h
    should have a judgment that fits the merits of his particular case.'

    The defendants here say that it is of special importance to them that they should
have a judgment that fits the merits; and this on two grounds: (1) on the defence of
fair comment; (2) on express malice.

Fair comment   j
    It is one of the essential freedoms that the newspapers should be able to make
fair comment on matters of public interest.   So long as they get their facts correct,
they are entitled to speak out.   The editor of the Times sees this case as a challenge

1   [1972] 1 All ER 801, [1972] AC 1027
2   (1956), p 158

a to this freedom. He asks that this challenge should be tried by a jury. He himself came before us. He reminded us of the right given by our constitution to a defendant who is charged with libel, either in criminal or in civil proceedings. Every defendant has a constitutional right to have his guilt or innocence determined by a jury. This right is of the highest importance, especially when the defendant has ventured to criticise the government of the day, or those who hold authority or power in the

b state. At one time there were those who would take away this right. There were judges who claimed that it was for them to declare whether a paper was a libel or not. On the trial of the seven bishops in 1688[1], Wright CJ, who is described by Lord Campbell[2] as 'the lowest wretch that had ever appeared on the bench in England', told the jury that the question whether the petition presented by the bishops was a libel was a question of law, and that in his opinion it was a libel[3]. Nearly 100 years

c later—in 1784—Lord Mansfield, one of the greatest ornaments of his day, repeated the error. He held on several occasions that the question of libel or no libel was for the judge. But his views were disputed by Willes J, who held that the jury have 'a constitutional right, if they think fit, to examine the innocence or criminality of the paper': see R v Shipley[4]. Eight years later, in 1792, the legislature, at the instance of Charles James Fox, adopted the view of Willes J. It gave every defendant on a

d libel charge the right to have his guilt or innocence determined by a jury: see the Libel Act 1729[5] and Lord Stanhope's celebrated broadside on the rights of juries[6]. Fox's Libel Act[5] was in terms confined to criminal proceedings, but it has been universally accepted that the same right applies to civil proceedings also: see Capital and Counties Bank v Henty[7] per Lord Blackburn, Nevill v Fine Art and General Insurance Co Ltd[8] per Lord Halsbury LC and Dunlop Rubber Co Ltd v Dunlop[9] per

e Lord Birkenhead LC.

I can understand the concern of the editor to reserve this right of a defendant to trial by jury. He regards it as the duty of his newspaper to bring to the notice of the people those matters which are of public interest and concern, and to point out those things which in his view are wrong, no matter how high and mighty the partici-pators may be. If he should overstep the mark, he would rather have his guilt or

f innocence decided by a jury of his fellow men than by a judge. So he asks for a jury here.

Likewise Mr Bernard Levin. He says that he has often in the past criticised the judiciary, and that is one of the reasons why he would wish to be tried by a jury. If he means by this that he thinks the judges, or any one of them, would be prejudiced against him, he would be entirely wrong. Every single one of them would be

g most scrupulous to be fair to him. No judge whom he had criticised would dream of sitting on the case. But I would not let him have any disquiet on this score. One of the advantages of trial by jury—as proclaimed by Blackstone[10]—is in case the judges should cease to be impartial. So Mr Levin too asks for a jury here.

I find these reasons compelling. Looking back on our history, I hold that, if a newspaper has criticised in its columns the great and the powerful on a matter of

h large public interest—and is then charged with libel—then its guilt or innocence should be tried with a jury, if the newspaper asks for it, even though it requires the prolonged examination of documents.

1   Seven Bishops' Case (1688) 3 Mod Rep 212, 87 ER 136
2   The Lives of the Chief Justices of England, vol II, p 104
3   See ibid p 109 and 12 State Tr 183 at 425, 426
j   4   (1784) 4 Doug KB 73 at 171
5   32 Geo III c 60
6   The Rights of Juries defended; together with authorities of law in support of those rights, and the objections to Mr Fox's Libel Bill refuted (1792)
7   (1882) 7 App Cas 741 at 775
8   [1897] AC 68 at 72, [1895-99] All ER Rep 164 at 165
9   [1921] 1 AC 367 at 373, [1920] All ER Rep 745 at 748
10   Commentaries (8th Edn, 1778), bk III, p 380, bk IV, p 349

Malice

In their reply the plaintiffs charged the Times with actual malice. They alleged *a* that the Times had published the words: 'when they knew the same to be false and/or had no adequate reason to believe them to be true and/or were reckless whether they were true or false'. In their particulars they alleged that the Times, by their managing director, Mr M J Hussey, knew them to be false. This is a most serious allegation to make. It is a charge that the Times made false accusations *b* against the plaintiffs knowing them to be false. It is almost like a charge of fraud. Faced with such a charge, I think the Times are entitled to ask that their guilt or innocence should be tried by a jury.

Generally

The judge ordered trial by judge alone. It is said that it is a matter for his discretion. But it is open to this court to interfere if he has given no weight, or no *c* sufficient weight, to those considerations which ought to have weighed with him: see *Ward v James*[1]. In my opinion, the judge has failed to give sufficient weight to the national importance of the subject-matter, to the gravity of the charges made against the defendants, and to their legitimate desire to have them tried by a jury.

It is true that trial by judge alone would have many advantages. In particular, *d* a judge could deal better with the mass of documents; and he would give reasons which could be reviewed by a Court of Appeal. But the result is not always better justice. As Lord Devlin points out in his little book[2]:

'The malady that sooner or later affects most men of a profession is that they tend to construct a mystique that cuts them off from the common man.'

e

In no department is this mystique more pronounced than the law of libel. But a jury look at a case more broadly. They give weight to factors which impress the lay mind more strongly than the legal. To achieve a just result, I do not think they should be set an examination paper containing many questions to answer. Only three or four at the most. But it must always be remembered that they have an absolute right to give a general verdict; that is to say, whether they find for the *f* plaintiff or the defendant; and, if for the plaintiff, how much damages. And once they have given a general verdict, that is the end of the matter: see *Barnes v Hill*[3].

So I would be in favour of trial by jury. I would allow the appeal, accordingly.

CAIRNS LJ. In my opinion Ackner J's direction for this action to be tried by judge alone should stand. He made no error of law, he took account of all relevant factors *g* and none that was irrelevant. So far from being satisfied that his decision was wrong, I am satisfied that it was right.

This action is of great importance to all the parties to it. In my view it is not of any exceptional importance to the public. I do not believe that future public confidence in the Times on the one hand or the Daily Mail on the other is going to depend on the result of this libel action. The case has nothing to do with extending or limiting *h* the freedom of the Press. No fresh development of the law relating to justification, fair comment or malice is likely to result from it. If all the statements in the article are found to be true or if the statements as to facts are found to be true and the comments fair and free from malice, then the defendants will win; if not they will lose and have to pay damages. It is in the highest degree unlikely that the case will afford any guidance in future cases as to what constitutes truth or fair comment or *j* malice. And if it were tried by a jury the verdict of the jury could not form any precedent for other cases.

---

1 [1966] 1 All ER 563, [1966] 1 QB 273
2 Trial by Jury (1956), p 159
3 [1967] 1 All ER 347, [1967] 1 QB 579

a   Nor do I regard our decision on this interlocutory issue as involving any question of constitutional importance. Parliament has laid down that libel actions in general are to be tried by jury if any party so desires. It has provided exceptions to the general rule, the relevant one of which is that if the court or judge is of opinion that the trial requires a prolonged examination of documents which cannot conveniently be made with a jury the court or judge may order trial by judge alone. Thus it is clear law (1) that in a libel action if one party asks for a jury he is entitled to it unless *b* (a) the master, or on appeal from him, the judge in chambers, is of opinion that a prolonged examination of documents will be involved at the trial and (b) he is of opinion that such an examination cannot conveniently be made with a jury; (2) that if these matters are established there is a discretion to order either trial by judge and jury or trial by judge alone; (3) that in exercising that discretion all relevant circumstances should be taken into account. These circumstances must, I think, include *c* among other things the gravity of the allegations made in the pleadings on each side and, in relation to the documents, the bulk of them and the degree of complexity of their contents. There is no question of the court's whittling away an Englishman's fundamental right to a jury. It is Parliament that has recognised that jury trial is not always the best mode of trial. It is true that since 1933, in cases other than those of fraud, libel, etc, the courts have tended increasingly towards exercising their dis-*d* cretion in favour of judge alone rather than judge and jury. Not only has Parliament found no occasion to check this tendency but it is the experience of all practitioners that litigants themselves nowadays more often than not prefer trial by judge alone even in those cases where it would be open to them to demand a jury.

    It is certainly not the policy of the law that whenever reputation is at stake trial by jury should be available. Allegations of the gravest character may be made in *e* divorce suits, probate actions, actions for breach of trust and many other types of proceedings in the Chancery and Family Divisions. In the Queen's Bench Division itself allegations, say in a personal injuries case, may amount to conduct of a serious criminal character, yet a jury cannot be obtained as of right. The fact that reputation is at stake does not therefore constitute any overriding reason for ordering *f* a jury.

    However, the first questions to be considered here are whether prolonged examination of documents or accounts will be necessary and whether this would make trial by jury inconvenient. The defendants have pleaded particulars of defence which run to 59 pages and refer directly to scores of documents, many of which are by way of accounts. This has led to the disclosure by the plaintiffs of some 10,000 documents altogether. No doubt only a fraction of these will be read at the trial but inevitably a *g* considerable number of them will have to be read and understood. I have no doubt that prolonged examination of them will be necessary. Nor have I any doubt that this would be highly inconvenient with a jury. There will be many separate files and the sheer bulk of them will be enormous. Moreover, the financial complications are such that a great deal of time will have to be taken up in explaining them to the jury. I am therefore satisfied that the conditions are fulfilled which give rise to the discretion. *h* In considering the exercise of discretion I would put on one side of the scale the fact that very serious charges are made against the defendants and that they wish for trial by jury, but I put on the other side the fact that at least equally serious (I would say more serious) charges are made against the plaintiffs and they wish for trial by judge alone. Then I take into account at this stage that the documents are not only numerous but some of them would be difficult for jurymen to understand at all *j* and injustice might result from their failure to understand them. One disadvantage of a trial by jury is that if they reach a wrong result through misunderstanding there is (unless their verdict can be seen to be perverse) no way of correcting it. The fact that a judge has to give reasons for his decision is to my mind a point in favour of trial by judge alone. The plaintiffs say that they would welcome a decision which not merely awards them damages or dismisses their claim, but also tells them and

the public why they have won or lost. In a case of this kind this seems to me a
thoroughly sensible attitude. Further, if a judge goes wrong it can be seen why he
has gone wrong and it is far easier to put things right on appeal than it is to upset the
verdict of a jury. As to damages I am by no means satisfied that a jury is more likely
than a judge to reach a correct result. Now that it is accepted that a jury's assessment of damages is not always final and binding there is much to be said for a system
under which the tribunal's reasons for a high or low award can be seen instead of
merely guessed at, and where a substantially excessive or insufficient award can be
corrected on appeal without the need for a new trial or for a decision that the damages
awarded are such as no reasonable people could have arrived at.

There remains here the special factor that Mr Levin has been critical of the judiciary
in the past in a way which might cause a judge to feel some resentment against him.
I do not think there is any substance in this suggestion. In any case where a well-
known writer or other public figure is involved a judge may have private feelings,
favourable or unfavourable, towards him. If the judge had been the subject of some
individual criticism or had had some private disagreement with the litigant he obviously would not hear the case, although even in those circumstances I think the risk
of prejudice would be more apparent than real. Every judge by his training is used
to putting out of his mind any knowledge or feelings that he has had about a party
before he came into court. If a judge could not do that, not only would he not be
fit to try the case alone, he would not be fit to direct the jury.

At the end of it all the question to be asked is which mode of trial is most conducive
to justice? Justice of course means justice to both sides. I see no good reason for
supposing that one mode of trial rather than the other is likely to result in success
for one side rather than the other. I am convinced that trial by judge alone is more
likely to achieve a just result. I would therefore dismiss the appeal.

LAWTON LJ. In my judgment two questions arise for consideration in this appeal:
first, what is the construction of s 6 (1) of the Administration of Justice (Miscellaneous
Provisions) Act 1933; and secondly, how should that construction be applied to this
case.

Section 6 effected a great change in the way actions at common law were tried. The
right which litigants had enjoyed for centuries of having their cases tried by a jury
if they so wished was extinguished save in a few cases. The discretion of the court or
judge was put in its place. Why did Parliament make special provision for cases in
which there was a charge of fraud against a party or there was a claim in respect of
libel, slander, malicious prosecution, false imprisonment and the now obsolete claims
in respect of seduction or breach of promise of marriage? All these cases have a
common characteristic, namely, that the trial is likely to end with the honour,
integrity and reputation of either the plaintiff or the defendant being tarnished or even
destroyed. Parliament must have thought that in common law claims in which issues
of this kind arose it would be wrong to get rid of a mode of trial which had become
identified in the minds of many with constitutional rights and liberties. In my
judgment this factor must be considered whenever the court, on being satisfied that
the trial will require prolonged examination of documents or accounts, comes to exercise its discretion. The strength of this factor will vary from case to case: for example,
it would not be so strong in an action for slander arising out of a stormy shareholders'
meeting during which the company's auditors had been accused of negligence in the
preparation of the company's accounts as in an action for libel arising from the fact
that a national newspaper had accused a firm of accountants of corruptly and fraudulently falsifying accounts. Both actions might require a prolonged examination of
accounts but in the second it might be more appropriate and just for the court to
order trial by jury.

Another facet of the same factor is the importance to the public of the honour,
integrity and reputation of the parties in a libel action. The wiping out of a litigant's

a   reputation may be of no consequence to anybody save himself, his family and his friends; but the wiping out of another's, for example, a Cabinet Minister's, may have consequences for the whole nation. When the public is likely to be affected by the result of an action for defamation it may be advisable to bring the public into the administration of justice by ordering trial by jury, even though the trial may be long, the issues complex and the documentary evidence massive and formidable.

b   What is the result in this case of weighing these factors against the near certainty that at the trial the jury will have to consider a very large number of documents. In my experience, jury trials in which many documents have to be considered, can be divided into three main categories. First the cases in which the documents have to be looked at to find out what happened. This category can be very difficult for juries if what happened produced a complex legal situation of a kind which was unfamiliar to the jury or to most of them. An example is provided by R v Murray[1], which was

c   tried at the Central Criminal Court in 1960. In that case the jury had to examine a large number of documents and books of account in order to decide whether many complex property deals had been effected in breach of s 54 of the Companies Act 1948, the defence being that the transactions under attack were lawful and in their real nature nothing more than the arranging of bridging finance by one company for the benefit of another. The second category is comprised of those cases in which the jury

d   are asked to say whether money proved to have been received has been dealt with honestly or dishonestly. Such cases often involve the long and tedious tracing of sums from one book of account to another. It has been my experience that once juries have grasped what they are expected to do, they become interested in their task and have no difficulty in performing it. The third category is that in which the issues in the case turn on who is to be believed and both parties use documents to test the credibility of

e   the witnesses. Having had the benefit of counsel for the plaintiffs' analysis of the issues in this case on which most of the documentary evidence will be relevant I have no doubt that in the end the jury will have to decide who is to be believed. Juries tend to have less difficulty with this category of case than with the first. In my judgment the jury will probably not have as much difficulty with the documents as the plaintiffs at present envisage. One of the benefits of trial by jury is that both the judge and counsel

f   have to keep the issues few and clear.

The defendants have submitted a number of reasons why there should be trial by jury in this case. In my judgment two of them have no substance. On behalf of the newspaper and Mr Levin it was said that his well-known and trenchantly expressed antipathy towards certain aspects of judicial behaviour and his past criticisms of certain judges, both living and recently dead, makes trial by jury necessary so as to main-

g   tain the appearance of justice. I do not agree. I am sure that the public have enough confidence in the integrity and independence of the Bench not to pay any attention to this factor. No doubt any judge who had been criticised by Mr Levin and who would be embarrassed by being asked to try this case would say so.

Mr Rees-Mogg eloquently argued that this case is of great importance to the Press and that for years to come editors will look to it as a guide through the thicket of the

h   law of defamation as it affects newspapers. This, he submitted, was a good enough reason for having the case tried by a jury. I can see nothing in either the issues or the subject-matter of this case which is likely to make it a leading one in the law of defamation.

The two principal reasons urged for ordering trial by jury were the importance of the case first to the defendants and secondly to the public. This case is clearly an

j   important one for all the parties. The plaintiffs, who have large newspaper interests, have been accused of dishonourable and heartless conduct in winding up a national newspaper, the Daily Sketch. The defendants are alleged to have been guilty of most irresponsible behaviour in the editorial management of another national newspaper;

---

1   (22nd July 1960) unreported

and both the personal defendants are alleged in the reply to have been reckless, which can only mean that they foresaw the grave consequences of any false state- *a* ments in Mr Levin's article but were indifferent whether the contents were true or false. In addition Mr Levin has been accused of being spiteful towards the plaintiffs because in June 1970 he left their employment in circumstances which were not to his liking. Serious though the accusations are on both sides, judges sitting without juries in civil actions from time to time have to consider even graver allegations. The judges in the Chancery Division sometimes have to say whether there has been a *b* breach of trust and their decisions may mean that defendants have been guilty of criminal offences. In the Commercial Court charges of fraud are sometimes made which, if established, could result in the guilty party being prosecuted and, if con- victed, sentenced to a long term of imprisonment. There is nothing to suggest that either litigants or the public generally are disturbed that such weighty issues should be tried by a judge sitting alone. Indeed the recent history of the City of London special *c* jury provides some evidence that litigants and the public prefer such cases to be tried by a judge rather than by a jury. The Juries Act 1949 abolished the special jury but retained the City of London special jury for trials in the commercial list if the com- mercial judge in his discretion ordered such a mode of trial: see ss 18 and 19. Between 1948 and 1971 very, very few commercial cases were tried with a City of London special *d* jury. The recollection of Roskill LJ, whom I have consulted on this point, is that in only three cases was trial by jury ordered, and that in only two of them did the jury return a verdict. Such was the lack of interest and perhaps confidence in such a mode of trial that s 40 of the Courts Act 1971 abolished the City of London special jury. The defendants have not satisfied me that a judge sitting alone could not deal adequately and fairly with issues involving their professional competence and integrity, but the fact that they want trial by jury rather than by a judge sitting alone cannot, and should *e* not, be overlooked for the reasons given earlier in this judgment.

There remains the question whether the issues in this case are likely to affect the public to such an extent that through a jury they should be involved. This factor does not seem to have been considered by Ackner J. Stripped of all the detail the charges come to this. The plaintiffs are alleged by the defendants to have put profits before *f* people. If the facts on which they have based this allegation are true, the court may have to decide whether the imputation of dishonour was one which the defen- dants could fairly make against the plaintiffs. Jobs for men or profits for shareholders is the Morton's fork of our times. I have no doubt that many judges would welcome the help of a jury on a problem of this kind. The opinions of 12 jurors may reflect the public's view more accurately than the assessment of any judge.

The public, through the jury, would be concerned in yet another way. If the *g* defendants lose their action and heavy damages are awarded against them, the newspaper scene in this country may never be the same again. The reputation which the Times has enjoyed for so long around the whole world for responsible journalism will be badly dented, if not destroyed. The destruction of itsi reputation would be the destruction of a national institution. In my judgment a tr al which could have this result should not be the responsibility of one man. *h*

I would allow the appeal and order trial by jury.

Appeal allowed. Trial by jury ordered. Leave to appeal to the House of Lords refused.

9th April. Settlement of the action was announced in court before Eveleigh J and the record was, by leave, withdrawn. *j*

Solicitors: *Charles Russell & Co* (for the first and third defendants); *Swepstone, Walsh & Son* (for the plaintiffs).

L J Kovats Esq   Barrister.

Seabrook v Gascoignes (Reading) Ltd and another

CHANCERY DIVISION
MEGARRY J
21st DECEMBER 1972

Legal aid – Costs – Taxation – Duty of Master on taxation – Duty to consider each item – Solicitors agreeing quantum of profit costs in bill – Master allowing profit costs as agreed – Master taxing counsel's fees – Master disallowing item representing counsel's fee for conference on basis that no evidence conference had taken place – Solicitors' profit costs as allowed containing item for same conference – Master on disallowing one item bound to consider effect on other items in bill of costs.

An action between the plaintiff and defendants was compromised by a Tomlin order which directed a taxation on a common fund basis of the costs to which the Legal Aid Acts 1949 to 1964 applied which had been incurred on behalf of the plaintiff. The schedule to the order provided that the defendants should pay to the plaintiff such sum as should represent the net liability of the legal aid fund in respect of the plaintiff's costs to be taxed pursuant to the order. Before the Master, solicitors for the plaintiff and defendants informed him that agreement had been reached in regard to the quantum of the solicitors' profit costs included in the bill and that he was required to tax only counsel's fees. The Master allowed the profit costs as agreed and taxed counsel's fees, disallowing an item of £4·70 representing counsel's fee for a conference on the ground that no evidence had been proffered that any such conference had taken place. In the column of the bill for profit costs, however, there was an item of £3·50 for the plaintiff's solicitors attending the same conference and that item had been left standing in the bill. The Master stated that, since the overall figure for solicitors' profit costs was consistent with his tentative conclusions after considering each item, he had allowed it without argument; however he had heard argument and adjudicated on each of the fees sought by counsel. On a review of the taxation at the instance of counsel,

Held – The item of £4·70 should be restored since, on the footing accepted by the solicitors and the Master, there was no ground for disallowing the conference fee. On a legal aid taxation the Master was bound to apply his mind to every item; although that process was normally carried out by consideration of the bill before formal taxation began, the process did not end there and if on the taxation any items were reduced or taxed off the Master was bound to consider any effect that that might have on any other items in the bill (see p 1026 c to f, post).

Notes
For legal aid taxation, see 30 Halsbury's Laws (3rd Edn) 526, 527, para 997, and for cases on the subject, see 50 Digest (Repl) 495-500, 1755-1779.

Authority cited
Matthews and Oulton on Legal Aid and Advice (1971), p 331.

Summons to review taxation
This was a summons to review a legal aid taxation by Master Berkeley. The hearing took place in chambers but judgment was delivered in open court. The facts are set out in the judgment.

P M H Mottershead for the plaintiff, on behalf of counsel.
Mr T A Salmons, solicitor, for the first defendants.   *a*
Mr J D Haslam, solicitor, appointed by the Lord Chancellor to intervene.
Rupert Evans for Dutton, Gregory & Williams, the plaintiff's solicitors.
The second defendant did not appear and was not represented.

MEGARRY J. This is a review of a legal aid taxation by Master Berkeley. It is   *b*
made at the instance of counsel, certain of whose fees had been reduced or disallowed.
There are four items in dispute. Three of these I have already disposed of in chambers,
and it is the remaining item alone which I have adjourned into court for judgment.
The other items are larger and this one is small; but questions of principle arise.
    The action in question was compromised by a Tomlin order in the Chancery
Division. The curial part of the order directed a taxation on the common fund   *c*
basis of the costs to which the Legal Aid Acts 1949 to 1964 applied which were incurred on behalf of the plaintiff. The schedule to the order provides that the first
defendants, a limited company (to which I shall refer as 'the defendants'), should pay
to the plaintiff such sum as should represent the net liability of the legal aid fund
in respect of the plaintiff's costs to be taxed pursuant to the order. On the taxation
before the Master the solicitors for the plaintiff and defendants informed the Master   *d*
(and I quote from the Master's answers set forth in an undated document) 'that
agreement had been reached between them in regard to the quantum of the
Solicitors profit costs included in the bill and that I was required to tax only Counsels
fees'. The taxation then proceeded on this footing, and the item in question, a fee
of £4·70 for counsel for a conference on 23rd June 1965, was wholly disallowed by
the Master. The Master's endorsement at the end of the bill of costs was 'Profit   *e*
costs agreed at £2,100·85 and Solicitors disbursements as asked in bill. Counsels
fees as taxed.' There were then lodged objections to the taxation which included
an objection to the disallowance of this conference fee, and the Master overruled that
objection on the ground that 'no oral or written evidence was proffered that any
Conference took place on the 23rd June 1965' and that 'no reason was put forward to
support the necessity for or the likelihood of a Conference at that particular stage of   *f*
the proceedings'. It is that item alone that is now before me on the summons to
review the taxation.
    The curious feature of the case is that in the column of the bill for profit costs there
is an item of £3·50 for this particular conference for the plaintiff's solicitors 'Attending
appointing conference with Counsel and attending thereon'; and that item has been
left standing in the bill. In other words, the Master, directed to carry out a legal aid   *g*
taxation, has disallowed (and on objection has refused to restore) counsel's fee for
this conference on the ground that there is nothing to show that it ever took place,
and yet he has left standing as part of the bill that he certifies that he has taxed the
solicitors' charge of £3·50 for this self-same conference. In those circumstances, when
the case first came before me I caused the Master to be invited to add to his answers
on the point, drawing his attention to this particular pair of items; and I adjourned   *h*
the summons for this purpose.
    The Master's further answer on the point, set out in another undated document,
is as follows:

> 'In the event that agreement was reached inter partes as to the overall figure
> of profit costs as endorsed by me at the foot of the bill no separate consideration   *j*
> was given to any item of profit costs. The agreement of the parties to an in-
> clusive figure of £2,100·85 profit costs was not intended to be affected by the
> allowance or disallowance of a single conference or any other specific item.'

In answer to a further question as to how far the Master had considered all the
items in the bill, the Master added:

a
'As I have stated in my answer to 1 above, I considered each item in the bill before the taxation and formed a tentative conclusion about the profit costs which should be allowed to the solicitor and the fees which should be allowed to Counsel. The overall figure for solicitors profit costs which I was asked to approve was consistent with my tentative conclusions and I accordingly allowed it without argument. I would confirm that on the taxation I did hear argument and adjudicate upon each of the fees sought by Counsel.'

b
Now, of course, in the normal course of events no liability for the plaintiff's costs will fall on the legal aid fund, for the defendants will pay them all. Nevertheless, until they are paid there is always the possibility (no doubt remote in this case) that the defendants might refuse to honour their agreement or might fall into insolvency, in which case the bill would no doubt be presented to the legal aid authorities for
c payment, supported by the Master's certificate. That certificate, dated 6th March 1972, refers to the Tomlin order and then certifies that the Master has—

'taxed the costs of the Plaintiff thereby directed to be taxed on the Common Fund basis in accordance with the provisions of the Third Schedule to the Legal Aid and Advice Act 1949';
d
and it then sets out the various amounts.

Accordingly, two questions seem to me to arise. First, where a bill of costs is referred to a Master to be taxed on a legal aid taxation, is it a sufficient compliance with that order for the Master to deal with the matter on the basis that this matter has been dealt with? Second, in particular, is it right that counsel's fee for a conference should
e be disallowed on the ground that the conference never took place when all concerned were agreed that the solicitors should have their profit costs of £3·50 for the same conference?

I shall answer the second question first, and in so doing I shall in effect also deal with the first. Even on the footing that there is no evidence that the conference ever took place, there remains the fact that the defendants' solicitors agreed that
f the plaintiff's solicitors should be paid their profit costs for this conference, and the Master has allowed that figure to remain in the bill that he has certified that he has taxed. In those circumstances, I do not see how it can be open to the defendants' solicitors to object to counsel's fees for that conference. It seems to me to be wholly inconsistent for them to say: 'We accept the assertion of the plaintiff's solicitors that the conference took place and that they should be paid the costs of that confer-
g ence, but we object to counsel having his fee for that conference, because we say that it never took place.' Furthermore, I find it difficult to see how the Master can be said to have duly taxed a bill of costs in accordance with the order as regards an item for a conference in respect of which he certifies that nothing is to be paid to counsel for the conference because it did not occur, but that the solicitors' costs of £3·50 are nevertheless to be paid to them for arranging and attending the confer-
h ence that never was. The Master's further answer, when the point had been drawn to his attention, saying that 'the agreement of the parties to an inclusive figure of £2,100·85 profit costs was not intended to be affected by the allowance or disallowance of a single conference or any other specific item', seems to me to be no answer at all. The direction to him was to tax the bill, and not to find out what was intended by any agreement between the parties. Once the Master has dis-
j allowed counsel's fees for a conference because it was not held he must, it seems to me, of necessity either disallow the costs of the solicitors for that conference as well, or else restore counsel's fees for it. This he did not do. Nor do I see how the solicitors' costs for the non-existent conference could be justified on any footing such as that the global sum was about right, and that even if the £3·50 had been struck out for the conference, it could be restored by some silent and unrevealed process of allowing a bit extra for one or more of the other items. I cannot regard

either the process of taxation or the Master's reasons as being satisfactory in respect of this sum.

Nobody, of course, has made any suggestion that on a taxation every single item must be specifically mentioned and disposed of, or that on a party and party taxation the solicitors may not properly agree any or all of the items of costs. But it is quite different when the order is for a legal aid taxation and the Master certifies that such a taxation has taken place; and I do not see how this can be affected by an agreement between the parties which in all probability will preserve the legal aid fund from having to bear any of the costs. An order of the court that there shall be a taxation on a legal aid basis is an order that can be complied with only by truly carrying out a taxation on that basis; and the Master's certificate that he has taxed the costs on that basis must be one that can be relied upon as establishing that this is what in fact he has done. Even where, as here, there is an agreement that will indemnify the legal aid fund, at least two minds should normally be applied to each item in the bill. First, there is the party on whom the burden of the costs will fall, apart from the legal aid fund, and, second, there is the Master. The party paying the costs may naturally, if he wishes, give no attention to any of the items; but the Master must still apply his mind to every item. This process, of course, is normally carried out by the consideration that the Master's clerk and the Master give to the bill before the formal taxation begins; and that is what happened here, as the Master's further answers show. But the process of taxation should not end there, ignoring what happens on the taxation itself. Taxation is to this extent a continuing process, and if on the taxation any items are reduced or taxed off, the Master must consider any effect that this may have on any other items in the bill.

The question, then is what should be done in the present case. The solicitors' costs are not before me for review: only counsel's fees are. For the reasons that I have given, I do not see how the defendants' solicitors can validly contend that despite their agreement, fortified by the Master's certificate, that the solicitors' costs should be paid for the disputed conference, there was in fact no such conference and counsel's fees for it should therefore be disallowed. Accordingly, on the footing accepted by the solicitors and by the Master, I can see no grounds for disallowing counsel's fee for the conference, and I therefore restore that item of £4·70. My hesitations about the position of the legal aid fund are dispelled by the fact that in this particular case it is agreed on all hands that the risk of the legal aid fund not being in effect indemnified by the defendants is negligible; and in this particular instance I think I can with reasonable safety act on that footing.

I should add that from first to last there has been no suggestion whatever of any impropriety on the part of any of the solicitors and counsel involved. In particular, although comment might be made that the agreement as to the solicitors' costs and the objection to counsel's fees, when taken together, have overtones of discrimination against the Bar, I do not for one moment think that there was any conscious process of this kind. I am, however, concerned to see that if possible the problems that have arisen in this case will not arise in the future, and that the legal aid fund will have the protection which an order for legal aid taxation is intended to give it. It is for that reason that I have adjourned this part of the summons into open court for judgment.

The question of costs has been disposed of.

Determination accordingly.

Solicitors: *Waterhouse & Co*, agents for *Dutton, Gregory & Williams*, Winchester (for the plaintiff); *Kingsley, Napley & Co* (for the first defendants); *Joynson-Hicks & Co* (appointed by the Lord Chancellor to intervene); *Dutton, Gregory & Williams*, Winchester.

Susan Corbett Barrister.

Surrey County Council v S and others

QUEEN'S BENCH DIVISION
LORD WIDGERY CJ, EVELEIGH AND MAY JJ
2nd FEBRUARY 1973

Children and young persons – Care – Proceedings in juvenile court – Conditions to be satisfied before making order – Neglect or ill-treatment of child or young person – Probability of neglect etc having regard to fact that 'the court or another court' has found neglect or ill-treatment of another child or young person belonging to same household – Meaning of 'the court' – Whether necessary that finding of neglect or ill-treatment in relation to other child should have been made by the court in earlier proceedings – Whether open to court hearing proceedings to make finding in relation to other child – Children and Young Persons Act 1969, s 1 (2) (a), (b).

The council, as the local authority, made an application to the justices for a care order under s 1ᵃ of the Children and Young Persons Act 1969 in respect of a child. At the hearing of the application they sought to fulfil the condition laid down by s 1 (2) (b) of the 1969 Act ('condition (b)') by adducing evidence that the child's sister had been ill-treated by the child's parents, and that, therefore, the condition contained in s 1 (2) (a) of the 1969 Act ('condition (a)') had been or would be satisfied in respect of the child, i e that her proper development would be avoidably prevented or neglected or her health would be avoidably impaired or neglected or she would be ill-treated. The sister had been a member of the household to which the child belonged and had died in December 1971. However at no time prior to the hearing before the justices had the justices, or any other court in any other proceedings, found that condition (a) had been or was satisfied in respect of the sister. The justices held that they were not competent to make a finding in relation to the sister in the proceedings before them and in consequence, there being no other evidence, they made no order. The council appealed.

Held (Lord Widgery CJ dissenting) – The appeal would be allowed and the case remitted to the justices with a direction to hear the evidence in relation to the sister. Although, in order to satisfy condition (b) in an application relating to child A, it was necessary to have regard to the fact that 'the court or another court has found that [condition (a)] is or was satisfied' in the case of another child ('child B'), who was a member of the same household, the words 'the court' meant the court currently hearing the application in relation to child A. Accordingly it was not necessary to establish that the court, or another court, had found in earlier proceedings that condition (a) had been satisfied in relation to child B; it was open to the court hearing the application in relation to child A to make that finding and then, having regard to that finding, to determine that it was probable that condition (a) would be satisfied in the case of child A (see p 1030 e h and j and p 1031 b to d, post).

Notes

For power to make orders in care proceedings in juvenile courts, see Supplement to 21 Halsbury's Laws (3rd Edn) para 554A, 3.

For the Children and Young Persons Act 1969, s 1, see 40 Halsbury's Statutes (3rd Edn) 849.

Case stated

This was an appeal by way of case stated by justices for the county of Surrey acting

---

a Section 1, so far as material, is set out at p 1029 g to h, post

in and for the petty sessional division of Esher and Walton in respect of their
adjudication as a juvenile court sitting at Walton-on-Thames on 28th July 1972.   *a*

By notice dated 5th January 1972, on 28th July 1972 the appellants, the county
council of the administrative county of Surrey ('the council') as the local authority
for the purposes of the Children and Young Persons Act 1969, reasonably believing
that there were grounds for making an order under s 1 of the 1969 Act in respect
of a minor ('the child') who was born on 29th October 1971, the daughter of the
first and second respondents ('the parents'), brought the child before the justices   *b*
for the Esher and Walton division of the county of Surrey, sitting as a juvenile court.
The council alleged that the following condition contained in s 1 (2) of the Act
would be satisfied in respect of the child, namely, that it was probable that her proper
development would be avoidably prevented or neglected or her health would be
avoidably impaired or neglected or she would be ill-treated having regard to the
fact that the court or another court might find that such condition was or had been   *c*
satisfied in the case of another child who had been a member of the household to
which the child belonged. The notice dated 5th January 1972 stated more specifically:

> 'It is alleged that the following condition will be satisfied with respect to the
> [child], that is to say, it is probable that the condition set out in [s 1 (2) (*a*)] of
> the [1969] Act will be satisfied in her case, having regard to the fact that another   *d*
> Court may find that the condition was satisfied in the case of another child
> who was a member of the household to which she belongs.'

At the hearing on 28th July 1972 the council amended the grounds on which they
brought the child before the court by substituting the words 'the Court may find'
for the words 'another Court may find'.

At the hearing on 28th July 1972 the council sought to adduce evidence that the   *e*
sister of the child had been ill-treated and therefore that the condition contained
in s 1 (2) (*b*) of the Act had been or would be satisfied in respect of the child. It was
admitted on behalf of the parents that the sister had been a member of the household to which the child belonged and that the sister had died on 19th December
1971. It was admitted on behalf of the council that at no time prior to the hearing
had the justices or any other court in any other proceedings found that the   *f*
condition in s 1 (2) (*a*) of the Act was or had been satisfied in respect of the sister.

After hearing submissions on the true construction of s 1 (2) of the Act made on
behalf of the council, the child and the parents respectively, the justices held
that they would expect the council to adduce evidence that a court had found that
the condition in s 2 (1) (*a*) was satisfied in relation to the sister and further that they
were not competent to make such a finding in relation to her in the proceedings   *g*
then before them. The case for the council depended solely on evidence in relation
to alleged ill-treatment of the sister and in the premises the council offered no
evidence and the justices made no order.

It was contended on behalf both of the council and of the child: (i) that notwithstanding that neither the justices nor any other court had found in other proceedings
that the sister had been ill-treated within the meaning of s 1 (2) (*a*) it was nevertheless   *h*
their duty to hear evidence to establish that the condition had been satisfied in respect
of the sister; (ii) that if they then determined that that condition had in fact been
so satisfied in respect of the sister they should then proceed to hear evidence for the
purpose of establishing that it was probable, within the meaning of s 1 (2) (*b*), that
that condition would be satisfied in respect of the child and make an order under
s 1 accordingly.   *j*

It was contended on behalf of the parents: (i) that since neither the justices nor any
other court had previously found in other proceedings that any of the conditions
contained in s 1 (2) (*a*) had been satisfied in respect of the sister no evidence was
admissible before the justices to establish that that condition had been satisfied in
respect of the sister and hence no evidence could be admitted to establish that it

a was probable that that condition would be satisfied in respect of the child; (ii) that in any event the justices had no power to make an order under s 1 (2) of the Act in relation to the child in the circumstances of the present case unless they were satisfied that the court or another court had found that the condition contained in para (a) thereof had been satisfied in relation to the sister prior to the hearing.

The justices upheld the submissions made on behalf of the parents and gave reasons for their determination in the following terms:

b
'We are unable to find any authority as to how we should interpret the wording of this Act, and accordingly we have decided to interpret the Act on the strict wording of the sub-section we are dealing with. It follows, therefore, that we would expect the [council] to provide evidence that a Court had found that [the] condition [in s 1 (2) (a)] has been satisfied with regard to a child who is
c or was a member of the same household. We are of the opinion that this Court is not competent to make a finding in these proceedings.'

The question of law for the opinion of the High Court was whether notwithstanding that neither the court before whom the relevant child was brought under s 1 of the Act nor any other court had previously found that any of the conditions contained
d in s 1 (2) (a) had been satisfied in respect of another child who was or had been a member of the household to which the relevant child belonged, the court before whom the relevant child was brought was nevertheless empowered in the proceedings in which the relevant child was brought before that court to consider evidence in respect of such other child and if on such evidence it determined that the conditions contained in s 1 (2) (a) were or had been satisfied in respect of such other child
e it might then proceed to consider evidence whether it was probable that such conditions or any of them would be satisfied in respect of the relevant child.

S L Newcombe for the council.
A W Stevenson for the parents.
A Garfitt for the child.

f

EVELEIGH J delivered the first judgment at the request of Lord Widgery CJ. This is a case stated by justices for the county of Surrey acting in and for the petty sessional division of Esher and Walton. The council, being the local authority, made an application for a care order under s 1 of the Children and Young Persons Act 1969 in respect of a child. The council relied on s 1 (2) (b) which refers back to
g s 1 (2) (a); those provisions read as follows:

'(1) If the court before which a child or young person is brought under this section is of opinion that any of the following conditions is satisfied with respect to him, that is to say—(a) his proper development is being avoidably prevented or neglected or his health is being avoidably impaired or neglected or he is being
h ill-treated; or (b) it is probable that the condition set out in the preceding paragraph will be satisfied in his case, having regard to the fact that the court or another court has found that that condition is or was satisfied in the case of another child or young person who is or was a member of the household to which he belongs . . .'

There then follow other conditions which may be satisfied, but they are not relevant
j for the present purposes. At the hearing before the justices, the council sought to adduce evidence that the sister of the child had been ill-treated and therefore the condition contained in s 1 (2) (b) of the 1969 Act had been or would be satisfied in respect of the child. It was admitted on behalf of the parents that the sister had been a member of the household to which the child belonged, and that the sister had died on 19th December 1971. It was admitted on behalf of the council that at no time prior

to the hearing before the justices had those justices, or any other court in any other
proceedings, found that the condition in s 1 (2) (a) had been or was satisfied in respect   *a*
of the sister.

After hearing submissions on the construction of the subsection, the justices held
that they were not competent to make a finding in relation to the sister in the proceedings before them, and as the case for the council then depended solely on their
evidence in relation to the alleged ill-treatment of the sister, the council offered no
evidence and the justices made no order. The matter thus comes before the court   *b*
to decide in effect whether the finding referred to in s 1 (2) (b) is one that had to be
made on a previous occasion.

Reading the whole of s 1, one observes that three different expressions are used in
relation to the justices. We have 'a court'; we have 'the court', and we have 'another
court'. Section 1 (2) begins:

c

'If the court before which a child or young person is brought under this section
is of opinion that any of the following conditions is satisfied with respect to him,
that is to say . . .'

and then follow the conditions. We have again in sub-s (2) (b), which I have already
read, 'the court' and 'another court'. Section 1 (2) concludes 'subject to the following   *d*
provisions of this section and sections 2 and 3 of this Act, the court may if it thinks
fit make such an order'.

I am therefore of the opinion that 'the court' means the court currently deciding
whether or not to make an order under s 1. The other court could only have made
its finding at a time previous to the moment when the justices had to arrive at their
decision, in other words at a moment previous to the current deliberations of the   *e*
bench trying the case. That other court could therefore only have found if the condition under s 1 (2) (a) was then satisfied, that is to say whether that condition was
satisfied at the time that the previous court was making its deliberations.

It is in my opinion impossible grammatically to say that someone has found that
a condition is satisfied if that someone did his finding yesterday; and if one has
oneself no independent knowledge of the matter found. I appreciate that it is quite   *f*
possible for someone to say that such and such an explorer found that the earth is
round. That is because I, as the speaker, am associating myself with the veracity of the
finding; when it is to depend on the finding of some other person, it is quite impossible
in indirect speech to use other than the past tense, and consequently it seems to
me that 'is' must be a verb in this clause that relates to the finding of the court
actually trying the matter. If the sentence had read 'A court has found', I could   *g*
see a possible difficulty, but the expression is 'the court' or 'another court'. That in
my view permits a choice between the court currently trying the application and
a court that has dealt with it on another occasion. Read in that way it seems to me
that a useful result is achieved, for it means that the court considering whether or not
a care order should be made is entitled to say on the one hand: another child is
currently in danger, that matter is proved before us; we think that the child with   *h*
whom we are dealing will also be in danger, although at the moment it is not suffering. Then, on the other hand, it permits the court trying the matter to say: we
hear that another child was in danger; that child is now dead but as that child was
in danger we think it will probably be that the child whose position we are considering will also be in danger, and consequently we are in a position, the other
requirements being satisfied of course, to make the order. In my view the justices   *j*
erred in law here, and I would allow the appeal.

MAY J. I agree. I think it is necessary at the outset to bear in mind that under s 1 (2)
of the 1969 Act a care order can only be made if, first, one of the conditions set out
in sub-paras (a) to (f) inclusive is found to obtain, and secondly that the child is in

a need of care or control. There are these two stages in the examination and adjudication. Secondly, this being a matter of pure construction, I think it is necessary to notice clearly that the draftsman has used the words 'the court or another court' instead of 'a court' or 'any court', and in my opinion 'the court' in s 1 (2) (b) refers back to the opening words of s 1 (2) 'If the court before which a child or young person is brought under this section . . . ', that is to say not the Walton-on-Thames court

b generally, but the actual court as constituted at the time that the application in respect of the particular child is being heard. If one bears that in mind, and if that is the correct meaning of the words 'the court' in s 1 (2) (b), remembering the dual nature of the examination before the court to which I have already referred, then s 1 (2) (b) involves, as I understand it, that the court before which the child or young person is at the moment should find that the condition in s 1 (2) (a) is or was satisfied in relation to another child who is or was a member of the household, and should

c then go on in relation to the relevant child, the first child, to consider whether or not that child is in need of care or control.

If 'the court' in s 1 (2) (b) is the court before which a child or young person is brought under s 1 (2), then in my opinion the only view that one can take of the proper construction of the sub-paragraph is that that court at that time is entitled as part of its investigation into the circumstances of child A to consider the circumstances

d in relation to child B, and if satisfied that in relation to child B the conditions set out in (a) are satisfied, then to proceed under (b) in respect of the first child. It was contended that choosing this construction of this sub-paragraph may involve findings being made in respect of a second child unrepresented before the court. In my judgment that is not a valid argument against this construction, because nothing is being found against that second child. All that is being found is that somebody else acted in an

e improper or neglectful fashion in relation to that particular child, and the fact that that child is not actually represented before the court does not affect my view of the proper construction of this subsection. For those reasons and for the reasons which have been set out by Eveleigh J, I agree that this appeal should succeed.

f **LORD WIDGERY CJ.** On this nicely balanced point I have the misfortune to take the opposite view. I think one must look at sub-s (2) (a) and sub-s (2) (b) of s 1 of the 1969 Act together, and I think it quite clear that sub-s (2) (a) contains what one might call the basic provision whereby care proceedings can be taken in respect of a child who is suffering in his development or is being neglected or ill-treated, because to proceed under s 1 (2) (a) involves establishing to the satisfaction of the court that

g that condition applies in relation to that child.

Subsection (2) (b) as it seems to me is a supplement to sub-s (2) (a) in the sense that it is a concession; it is making provision for a care order without proving the actual danger to the child in question, and I think it means that without proving actual danger to the child in question under s 1 (2) (a) a care order can be justified if it is probable that the provisions of s 1 (2) (a) will be satisfied in the case having regard

h to the fact that a previous decision of a competent court has been made that the condition was satisfied in respect of another child in the household.

I agree with the justices that looking at the language of the section, and giving it its ordinary meaning, the impression conveyed to me, at any rate, is that the decision in relation to the other child is something which should antedate the seeking of an order under s 1 (2) (b). I also think the expression 'the court or another court has

j found' is significant to this extent, that the phrase 'has found' would clearly have applied to a finding made by a competent court in the exercise of its ordinary jurisdiction. There is on the face of it no jurisdiction for the court hearing the present application to hear an application in respect of another child who is not before it. Again it seems to me very difficult to operate this statute except on the footing that the finding of 'the court' or 'another court' is something which has already happened when the proceedings are begun. Section 1 of the Act requires a local authority, a constable or another person to bring proceedings if he reasonably believes that grounds exist under s 1 (2). The conception that he can reasonably believe that grounds exist under s 1 (2) (b) is one that I find very difficult to accept, except on the basis that the relevant order in respect of the other child is already an existing fact. For those reasons, if the matter were left to me alone, I would dismiss the appeal and support the justices' findings, but in the event the appeal will be allowed.

Appeal allowed. Case remitted to the justices with a direction to hear the evidence relating to the sister.

Solicitors: *Crofts & Ingram and Wyatt & Co*, agents for *W W Ruff*, Kingston-upon-Thames (for the council); *Cree, Godfrey & Co*, agents for *Thomas K Dobson & Co*, Walton-on-Thames (for the parents); *Allan Jay & Co*, agents for *Timcke, Carter & Co*, Walton-on-Thames (for the child).

N P Metcalfe Esq   Barrister.

Sole v W J Hallt Ltd

QUEEN'S BENCH DIVISION
SWANWICK J
6th, 7th, 8th, 9th JUNE 1972

Occupier – Negligence – Common duty of care – Liability in contract – Option to claim in contract or tort for breach of duty – Building occupied by building contractors – Building in course of erection – Plaintiff engaged as independent sub-contractor to work on building – Building contractors in breach of common duty of care – Plaintiff injured – Breach a cause of injury – Plaintiff guilty of contributory negligence – Contributory negligence precluding claim in contract – Whether plaintiff entitled to claim in tort for breach of duty to him as visitor – Occupiers' Liability Act 1957, ss 2 (1), 5 (1).

The defendants were building contractors. They owned an estate on which they were building houses. The plaintiff, an experienced and competent tradesman, was engaged by the defendants on the basis of a labour-only sub-contract to tack and nail plaster board sheets into position to form ceilings in one of the houses. When the plaintiff started work on the first floor of the house there was only one internal wall; otherwise the working area consisted of a flat space covered by floorboards except for the well of the staircase. The plaintiff supplied his own trestles and worked from a scaffold board supplied by the defendants supported on the trestles. The staircase had not been boxed in and the staircase well was open and unguarded. Before starting work the plaintiff found a single board outside the house; there were no other boards in the house which could be used to cover the staircase well, although unknown to the plaintiff there was a supply of boards in a nearby house. Having fixed a number of sheets in position the plaintiff stepped down from the board and took one or two steps backwards looking at the ceiling. In doing so he fell into the unguarded well. He brought an action against the defendants in respect of injuries which he had suffered in consequence of the fall.

Held – (i) The defendants were in breach of their common duty of care under s 2 (1)[a] of the Occupiers' Liability Act 1957 to provide for the plaintiff boards either over the well or readily available to cover it. On the evidence the plaintiff would have

---

a   Section 2 (1) provides: 'An occupier of premises owes the same duty, the "common duty of care", to all his visitors, except in so far as he is free to and does extend, restrict, modify or exclude his duty to any visitor or visitors by agreement or otherwise.'

a used the boards for that purpose if they had been available. Accordingly the defendants' breach of duty was, subject to contributory negligence, a cause of the accident (see p 1039 c g and j to p 1040 c, post).

(ii) Since the plaintiff had entered into the house by virtue of a right conferred on him by his contract with the plaintiffs the common duty of care owed by the defendants to the plaintiff was imposed on them by a term of the contract implied by s 5

b (1)*b* of the 1957 Act. It did not follow however that the plaintiff was confined to claiming under that implied term; he had the option of claiming in tort under s 2 (1) as a visitor. The plaintiff had been guilty of negligence in walking backwards in the direction of the unguarded stair-well and, if his claim had had to be pleaded in contract, his contributory negligence would have constituted a break in the chain of causation, and a defence to the claim. Since it was open to him, however, to found his claim in tort, he was entitled to recover damages subject to a deduction in

c respect of his own contributory negligence (see p 1035 h and j and p 1040 d and e, post); *Quinn v Burch Brothers (Builders) Ltd* [1966] 2 All ER 283 distinguished.

Notes

For an occupier's statutory duty of care to visitors, see 28 Halsbury's Laws (3rd Edn)
d 40-47, paras 35-42, and for cases on the subject, see Digest (Cont Vol A) 1150, 254Aa, Digest (Cont Vol B) 556, 557, 245Ab-245Ae, and Digest (Cont Vol C) 731-733, 245Af-245Ak.

For the Occupiers' Liability Act 1957, ss 2, 5, see 23 Halsbury's Statutes (3rd Edn) 793, 798.

Cases referred to in judgment
e *Bonnington Castings Ltd v Wardlaw* [1956] 1 All ER 615, [1956] AC 613, [1956] 2 WLR 707, 54 LGR 153, 1956 SC (HL) 26, 1956 SLT 135, HL, Digest (Cont Vol A) 596, 325c.
Quinn v Burch Brothers (Builders) Ltd [1966] 2 All ER 283, [1966] 2 QB 370, [1966] 2 WLR 1017, CA; *affg* [1965] 3 All ER 801, [1966] 2 WLR 430, Digest (Cont Vol B) 565, 996a.
Woollens v British Celanese Ltd (1966) 1 KIR 438, CA.

f **Action**
By a writ issued on 13th January 1970 the plaintiff, Arthur John Sole, brought an action against the defendants, W J Hallt Ltd, claiming damages for personal injuries suffered by the plaintiff on 27th November 1967 while working under a contract with the defendants on the first floor of a partially constructed house occupied by the defendants. The plaintiff alleged that the defendants were in breach of contract

g and, in particular, in breach of a term implied by s 5 (1) of the Occupiers' Liability Act 1957 whereby they owed him a common duty of care; further and alternatively he alleged negligence and breach of the common duty of care under s 2 (1) of the 1957 Act. The facts are set out in the judgment.

h S A Hockman for the plaintiff.
J F A Archer for the defendants.

j **SWANWICK J.** The accident giving rise to this claim took place on 27th November 1967 when the plaintiff fell from the first floor of a house on the Mole Abbey Estate, at Hampton Court, which was being constructed by the defendants, as building contractors, the plaintiff being Mr Arthur John Sole, and the defendants W J Hallt Ltd. The plaintiff, as I find, fell into the deep end of the well of an unguarded staircase leading up from the ground floor. Fortunately, he fell so as to wedge himself in the corner of the opening of the well, hanging in effect from his right elbow. As

---

b Section 5 (1), so far as material, is set out at p 1035 f, post a result of the fall, the plaintiff suffered a comminuted fracture of the head and neck of the right humerus. He now brings this action claiming damages for breach of contract and negligence on the part of the defendants.

At the conclusion of the case I allowed certain amendments to the statement of claim and defence as representing the case as explored in evidence and argument. I refused another proposed amendment to the defence designed to raise a plea of volenti non fit injuria since the plaintiff had not had an opportunity to deal in evidence with this allegation. In its final form, the statement of claim pleads an express agreement between the plaintiff and the defendant company, by their director, Peter Hallt, in a series of telephone conversations beginning on 19th November, and in an oral conversation at the site on the day of the accident, the express term being that the defendant company would provide and install guardrails round the staircase well. It is further pleaded that it was a term of such agreement implied by a custom of the trade that the defendant company would provide and install such guards, or would take other suitable precautions to prevent the plaintiff from falling into the well. In further and better particulars the alternative precaution alleged is the laying of floorboards over the well, leaving a gap with spare boards for the plaintiff to complete the closure. This particular allegation was made after, and, I suspect, inspired by an allegation of contributory negligence contained in the defence.

The statement of claim alternatively alleges negligence in failing to provide guard-rails or such alternative precautions as I have indicated, the duty being founded on knowledge of the danger, coupled with alleged frequent requests by the plaintiff to Peter Hallt, and promises by the latter made on previous occasions. The plaintiff also relies on the Occupiers' Liability Act 1957 as imposing similar duties on the defendant company, both as an implied term of the contract and as an allegation of negligence.

The defence, as amended, denies that there was any such express or implied term, or custom, or negligence, and pleads contributory negligence on the part of the plaintiff in failing to board over the hole with scaffold boards or to look for or ask for such boards, if not provided, and in stepping off the scaffold without looking, and in failing to keep a proper look-out or maintain his balance.

Those being the pleadings, I turn to the facts. At the accident the plaintiff was aged about 66. He had been in the trade of lathing and plastering since the age of 14, and he was a highly experienced and competent tradesman. In more than 50 years he had never had an accident, which he rightly claims vouches for his general careful-ness. Since 1960 he had worked as an independent sub-contractor, and for the past three years prior to the accident his son had been his partner. Sometimes the firm engaged one or two assistants, according to the volume of work, these working also as independent sub-sub-contractors. For nearly 20 years, the plaintiff had done work in this capacity at one time or another for the defendant company.

Until almost exactly one year before the accident, the principal member of the defendant company was the gentleman who has been referred to as 'old Mr William Hallt'. When he died, his son, Peter Hallt, took over the running of the business with William Hallt's brother, Bert Hallt, who is not being called as a witness, he apparently, on the second day of the trial having gone on a holiday to Italy, which he had apparently booked in advance.

I cannot accept the plaintiff's evidence that Peter Hallt had no experience of the building business. On the contrary, I accept the evidence of Peter Hallt as to that, that ever since 1960 he had been actively engaged in the defendant company's busi-ness, and with his uncle had been in effect in charge of the construction side, about which I am satisfied he was pretty knowledgable, having had six or seven years' experience of organising and supervising that side of the business.

The defendant company owned the Mole Abbey Estate, on which they were in the course of erecting about 25 houses in all at the rate of about six a year. About maybe ten or 12 of these houses had been built before William Hallt died, and about

a six more were built in the year between his death and the accident. For the whole of the relevant period, and particularly with regard to these houses, the plaintiff and his firm worked for the defendant company on the basis of a series of individual labour-only oral contracts. By those contracts, as I find, the plaintiff's firm was to supply labour for the work of tacking and nailing the plasterboard sheets into position to form ceilings, and also to supply two trestles, and the defendant company were to supply all plant and materials, which they knew the plaintiff would reason-
b ably want, or which he reasonably requested, for the proper performance of his work. I use the words 'want' and 'request' advisedly, because this was a contractual relationship and not one of master and servant, and it devolved primarily on the plaintiff to decide what he wanted for his work, as distinct of course from the defendant company's duty to him as a visitor to their premises. In that respect the defen-
c dant company, as occupiers of the partly constructed house, would of course owe to the plaintiff, as a visitor, the duty of common care under the Occupiers' Liability Act 1957. It is to be observed that by s 1 (1) of that Act, this duty extends to 'dangers due to the state of the premises or to things done or omitted to be done on them'. By s 2 (3) (*b*) the duty is modified to this extent. I read the relevant part of the subsection:

d   'The circumstances relevant for the present purpose include the degree of care, and of want of care, which would ordinarily be looked for in such a visitor, so that (for example) in proper cases—... (*b*) an occupier may expect that a person, in the exercise of his calling, will appreciate and guard against any special risks ordinarily incident to it, so far as the occupier leaves him free to do so.'

e As I understand the law, this means that the occupier is not liable in respect of what would not be dangerous to the ordinary visitor but is dangerous to a particular visitor simply by reason of his special occupation: see *Woollens v British Celanese Ltd*[1]. Finally, s 5 (1) provides:

f   'Where persons enter or use ... any premises in exercise of a right conferred by contract with a person occupying or having control of the premises, the duty he owes them in respect of dangers due to the state of the premises or to things done, or omitted to be done on them, in so far as the duty depends on a term to be implied in the contract by reason of its conferring that right, shall be the common duty of care.'

g There is no authority that I can find or that counsel have been able to quote to me whether this means that a person who enters premises, being under a contractual relationship with the occupier as to what he is to do on those premises, is confined to claiming under this implied term or can also claim in tort as a visitor under s 2 (1), and this may be highly material when considering the effects of contributory negligence, which vary according to whether the plaintiff is claiming in contract or in tort. As I understand the purpose of this section, it is designed to reduce what
h was at common law the higher duty of an occupier owed to such persons entering by right of contract and to equate them in this respect with other visitors. It would, I am sure be an unintended effect if they were now to be at a disadvantage compared with such other visitors in the respect that I have indicated. And I hold that they, and in particular the plaintiff in this case, can sue in tort or contract at their option— in other words, they have rights both in tort and in contract—unless there are
j particular circumstances which drive them to rely on an implied term alone.
To return to the facts as I find them, the plaintiff's firm's work on each house would take about a day—that is to say, that the firm would only be working a few days each year for the defendant company: and of course, the plaintiff's firm work

---

1 (1966) 1 KIR 438

for other builders also. The defendant company's practice was to call in the plain- *a*
tiff's firm at the stage when the staircase and floors of each two-storey house had
been put in. The plaintiff's firm's job was then to fix to the ceiling joists, which of
course were already in position and running from back to front of the house, sheets
of plaster-board measuring eight foot by four foot and butted up against one another
and nailed to the joists.

The plan produced by the defendants shows the layout of a typical house on this *b*
estate, and is agreed as such, and has been taken throughout this case as representing
the house in question in this action. This plan, together with the evidence of the
plaintiff, shows that the staircase would eventually be boxed in by studded partition
walls reaching the ceiling, and that partitions, either studded or made of breeze
blocks would be ultimately erected to form, on the first floor, four bedrooms and a
bathroom, with wash basin and wc.

However, when the plaintiff came to work on, at any rate, the house in question, *c*
the staircase was in position, but there were no internal walls at all on the first floor,
other than one brick wall separating bedrooms one and two and going up to support
the roof—that is to say, except for this wall, and the well of the staircase, the plaintiff
and his son were presented with a flat space covered with floorboards. Above this,
their job was to erect and fix a ceiling formed of these eight foot by four foot plaster- *d*
board sheets. For this purpose they would use their own two trestles, two feet six
inches high, and a single unlined scaffold board to be supplied by the defendants,
being some 12 feet long by nine inches wide by 1¼ inches thick, which they would lay
across the trestles with a span of six feet to seven feet or thereabouts, and use as a
working platform.

The plaintiff and his son varied in their evidence with regard to the exact order in
which they tackled this particular job. Where they differ, I prefer the evidence of *e*
the son. They would start at one of the corners furthest from the stairway, fitting and
nailing to the ceiling joists rows of plaster-board sheets side by side, and, as I say,
butted up against each other, their length running north and south on the plan, some
with half-sheets, as sketched for me by the plaintiff's son. They would work thus
gradually towards the south or front end of the house. With each sheet, the plaintiff *f*
and his son would be each at one end of the sheet, usually back-to-back. When
they were satisfied that the sheet had been properly fitted, each would secure his
end with a few nails and then one of them would normally get down to fetch and, if
necessary, cut the next sheet, while the other would finish nailing up the sheet erected.
Fifty nails about had to be put into each sheet. The only impediment to smooth
working over the whole ceiling would be the one brick wall separating bedrooms
one and two, and the well of the staircase. *g*

Prior to the day of the accident the plaintiff had been told by Peter Hallt on the
telephone in an advance telephone call probably made on 19th November, and another telephone call a day or two before the accident, that another house would be,
and was, ready for his work. In those conversations I am satisfied that there had been
no mention of guardrails.

On 27th November the plaintiff, with his son and his two trestles, duly arrived at *h*
the house at 7.30 a m. The plaintiff told me that he was not surprised to find no
guard rails. The plaintiff took the trestles up, whilst, as I accept, the son went round
outside and found a single scaffold board of the standard dimensions which I have
already given. He brought it back, they wiped the frost off it, they turned it over,
and they used the dry side on which to stand, and started work. At that time there
was no one else on the site. Soon after 8.00 a m first Bert Hallt and then, at about *j*
8.10 a m, Peter Hallt arrived. The plaintiff says that he told Peter Hallt that there
were still no guardrails round the well hole, and that Peter Hallt said he would see
to it, but that he did not.

At the time of the accident, which occurred round about 9.00 a m, the plaintiff and
his son had completed bedrooms three and four, and were working in bedroom two.

a As I find the facts, they had fixed a four inch strip along the east wall of that room, and were working from south to north on the first proper row of sheets with the son on the south end of the scaffold board facing south, and the plaintiff four feet or five feet behind him, probably facing north—that is to say, back-to-back. The sheet was duly fitted and the first few nails put in, and the plaintiff stepped down to walk to the west wall, where south of the stairway the sheets were stacked in order to prepare the next board. The plaintiff, as I find, stepped off the scaffold board, took one or

b two steps backward looking up at the ceiling and put his foot into the unguarded well hole and fell in the position I have described.

I do not accept the suggestion made on behalf of the defence, that the plaintiff slipped off the board. This suggestion was, I consider, founded on a misunderstanding of what the plaintiff said to Peter Hallt when the latter was sent for and came from his house, which was nearby, very shortly after the son had rescued the plaintiff.

c The plaintiff probably said he had come off the board and fallen down the hole, and this could be taken in two ways. I am satisfied that the accident happened as I have said it occurred, and that this is what the plaintiff meant to say to Peter Hallt.

As I say, prior to this accident, the plaintiff and his son had worked on this estate on and off for about two years. Both on this site, up to the death of William Hallt, and everywhere else that he had worked, the plaintiff's evidence was that it was a

d universal practice to have guardrails fixed round the well of the staircase for the safety of men such as himself working near it. With a staircase of the type shown on the plan, the plaintiff said that it would be a simple matter to fix a guardrail and would take a carpenter no more than 15 minutes to erect it, and workers some five to ten minutes to dismantle and re-erect it for the passage of materials etc. The method, said the plaintiff, would be that there would already be in position a four

e inches by four inches newel post to take the weight of the stairs; other posts would be fixed to trimmers—that is to say, beams—about six inches by three inches, or seven inches by three inches, into which floor joists were slotted. One such post would be at the head of the stairs, as I understood it, and another at what, on the plan, is the south-east corner of the well, and a batten would be fixed on the wall and then ropes or boards would be fixed to these posts and this batten would form a guardrail

f three feet six inches to four feet high. The plaintiff marked on the plan how he would have placed the trestles to span the well in order to fix the sheets on the ceiling, above the hole itself, with a safe span of some six feet to seven feet between the trestles.

With this method of guarding the well, it would mean that for this part of the operation the plaintiff and his son would be working on this single unlined scaffold board, probably back-to-back, over the well hole, with the rope of the guardrail

g running across it at shin or ankle height. The plaintiff said that he had done this thousands of times without accident, presumably indicating that he was sure-footed from experience, and because he said he could feel the rope against his legs and he said that the danger for which he wanted a guardrail was that of walking backwards into the well hole.

The plaintiff went on to say that following the death of William Hallt no guardrails

h had been provided by the defendant company; that he had pointed this out each time to Peter Hallt, and that each time Peter Hallt had said it would be seen to but had done nothing about it. Therefore, said the plaintiff, when he was sent for to come and work in this particular house, he did not expect to find guardrails erected and they were not, but that, as I have said, on the day of the accident he and his son had been working for upwards of half an hour on the ceiling, when first Bert Hallt and

j then Peter Hallt arrived. He said that he again asked Peter Hallt for guardrails, and Peter Hallt said he would see to it, but none were fixed before the accident.

This evidence of the plaintiff with regard to the usual practice, both generally and in the days of William Hallt, with regard to the defendant company, and the plaintiff's request to Peter Hallt, was not supported by his son when he came to give evidence. The son said, indeed, that he had not seen guardrails in any houses

built by the defendant company before the accident, in some, at least, of which he   a
had worked.   Although he had been the plaintiff's partner since 1964, he said nothing
about any request on the day of the accident and there was certainly no evidence
to show that he was not present at the time that Peter Hallt arrived and had any
relevant conversation with the plaintiff.   He did say that the defendants fitted
guardrails after the accident, nine out of ten times, but added that they were a
thorough nuisance.   b
   Peter Hallt, on the other hand, said in evidence that it had never been the usual
practice of the defendant company before or after his father's death to tell their
carpenters to fix guardrails before the tackers had finished their work.   'Tackers'
I may say, if I have not said so before, is a convenient phrase to describe the plaintiff
and his son, as people fixing these ceiling boards.   He said, moreover, that the
plaintiff had never requested this before or on the day of the accident.   He agreed   c
that he did go to see if the plaintiff had arrived and was all right, but said, 'And
nothing was then said about guardrails at all'.   He said that if the plaintiff had
asked for guardrails, he would have had them erected, because he was anxious to
please everybody if he could.   But he himself did not believe in erecting them for the
tackers because they would be ankle height, and therefore useless.   Indeed they
would be positively dangerous when working on the scaffold board either over the   d
well or adjacent to such guardrails, as well as being in the way of getting the plaster-
boards up the stairs.   He said that guardrails would be put up after the tackers had
finished their work if there was any delay in boxing in the staircase, which would be
the next operation, or if the plans involved an open staircase, which was not the case
in this house.   This would be done, if it was, for the protection of clients visiting the
house, either to make an intended purchase, or to see the progress of the work, and   e
in the case of an open staircase for the benefit of the plasterers, who would then come
on the scene.   He said that sometimes the plaintiff would no doubt have come across
guardrails in the lifetime of William Hallt but that would be when the carpenters
had erected them without instructions and to save themselves the trouble of coming
back.   In such cases, however, he said the rails were invariably knocked down by
the tackers and he added that this had indeed happened in the last two houses that   f
the defendants had built since the accident, when the plaintiff's sub-sub-contractors
had knocked down the guardrails thus erected.   He said that there had been no
change in the practice since the accident.
   I have carefully considered all the evidence and observed the witnesses, and weighed
up the probabilities.   On this aspect of the case I prefer the evidence of Peter Hallt
to that of the plaintiff, especially in view of the lack of support of the plaintiff's
evidence displayed in that of his son.   I do not find that in the contract for the work   g
of this house there was any express term as pleaded, that the defendant company
would provide and install guardrails for the plaintiff's work.   Indeed, on the plaintiff's evidence—if I accepted it, which I do not—no such express term is disclosed.
He does not say there was any mention of guardrails for this contract either in the
telephone conversations or until after the contract work had been started on 27th
November.   Nor do I accept the plaintiff's evidence as against that of Peter Hallt   h
with regard to the alleged conversation between them, an alleged conversation
between them on the way home from hospital after the accident, when the plaintiff
said that he did blame Peter Hallt, saying in effect, 'If you had fixed guardrails I
would not have been like this, would I?' and adding that Peter Hallt made no comment.   Peter Hallt denied any such conversation and, as I say, I accept his evidence
on this matter.   Nor, in my judgment, was there any such term implied either by   j
the course of dealing between the parties, as to which I accept Peter Hallt's evidence
in preference to the plaintiff's, or as being necessary to give business efficacy to
the contract, or as resulting from an application of the officious bystander test, or as
deriving from any such custom as is pleaded.   Indeed, I find that no such custom is
established.   My judgment on the last three possible bases of implication is fortified

by the evidence of the defendant company's expert, Mr Rimmer, who said, in effect,
a what seems to me to be good sense, that he had never seen a guardrail erected so
that it would cross a trestle scaffold at ankle height, as described by the plaintiff.
He further said that while guardrails round the staircase wells were quite common
and might well be found by tackers to have been already erected, tackers would
virtually only need guardrails when working over or adjacent to the well, and that
on those occasions such a guardrail would be a danger rather than a protection
b because the rail would be at ankle height. I accept this view. He further said, and
again this seems to be good sense, that a simpler and safer method would be to use
spare scaffold boards to place across the well hole. It would need about four full
boards and two short pieces to cover the hole completely, although the plaintiff
said that two long and two short boards would provide sufficient cover for safety.

In my judgment, the common duty of care under the Occupiers' Liability Act
c 1957 did require the defendants in the circumstances to provide for the plaintiff
boards, not necessarily over the hole but readily available, which in the circumstances
would, in my judgment, mean in a place handy near the foot or head of the stairs and
being obviously available to cover the well. If they had done this, in my judgment,
they would have been entitled to leave it to the plaintiff and his son to use such
boards to cover the hole for the period necessary for their protection. But I would
d add that, if Peter Hallt had then arrived and seen the plaintiff and his son not using
the boards, his duty would, in my judgment, have extended at least to pointing out
that such boards were available for their protection.

The first question, then, is: 'Did the defendants provide boards readily available?'
And the second question is: 'If not, would the plaintiff have used them if provided?'
[His Lordship then considered the evidence in relation to the question whether
e boards were readily available and continued:] The position therefore, as I find it,
was this. There were no spare boards in the house and certainly not near the head
or the foot of the stairs. There were ample boards in another house, but that fact
was not communicated to the plaintiff. When he arrived on the site he only knew
that there were boards in a scaffold already erected round the house that was under
construction, but there was no one else then on the site, and it would have been
f wrong and dangerous to the bricklayers to raid these boards without permission.

I do not consider that the defendant company's duty of common care was complied
with, either by having a supply of boards in another house, perhaps not very far
away, but unknown to the plaintiff, particularly when there was no one else on the
site when the plaintiff arrived, or by Peter Hallt merely coming to see the plaintiff
an hour later to check up if he was there and was contented. Nor, in my judgment,
g was it negligence on the part of the plaintiff not to search the estate for boards, or
to ask Peter Hallt for them. It was, as I see it, the duty of the defendant company
to make the boards readily available for the plaintiff and, in my judgment, they were
in breach of that duty.

Would the plaintiff have used the boards if available in the house? The authorities
(and I refer particularly to *Bonnington Castings Ltd v Wardlaw*[1]) show that the burden
h is on the plaintiff to prove this as part of the chain of causation. I have given this
aspect of the case much anxious thought. The plaintiff's evidence was that if he and
his son had found boards over the well, they would have removed them—to get
their materials on to the first floor, and then replaced the boards, and when necessary
have placed trestles on them or near them. So doing, of course, they would have
been perfectly safe. I accept their evidence about this. While it does not necessarily
j follow that if the boards had been left in the house, not over the hole, but near to
either the head or foot of the stairs, the plaintiff would have used them, and while
there is no evidence that either he or his son had ever used this method, on the whole
I have come to the conclusion that they probably would have used boards if left

---

1 [1956] 1 All ER 615, [1956] AC 613

in the position that I have described, and if they had not it would, as I say, further
have been the duty of Peter Hallt, when he visited the plaintiff about 8.10 a m, to call *a*
the plaintiff's attention to the fact that such boards were available for this purpose,
in which event, I am sure, that they would have been used.

It is true that the plaintiff said that he was not interested in scaffold boards. He
gave two reasons for this: first, that what he wanted was a guardrail. I have rejected
this. But he also said that he knew that there were no boards because his son had
been looking round, and that, therefore, there was no point in asking for them. If, *b*
as I find, he did not ask for a guardrail, I do not think he would have asked for boards,
but it does not follow that he would not have used them if they were to hand and
obviously left for this purpose, or if his attention was called to them. He was, as
I judged him, a competent and generally careful workman, as his hitherto accident-
free record shows.

I, therefore, find that the defendant company were in breach of their duty of *c*
common care and that subject to contributory negligence this was a cause of the
accident.

The next issue is that of contributory negligence. My finding is that it was negligent of the plaintiff to walk backwards in the direction of what he knew, if he thought
about it, was an unguarded stair-well, and while looking at the ceiling. If his claim had
had to be pleaded in contract, I would have felt compelled by the authority of *d*
Quinn v Burch Brothers (Builders) Ltd[1] to hold that his contributory negligence was such
as to amount to a novus actus interveniens and a break in the chain of causation,
particularly as it occurred after the defendant company's negligent act in breach
of their contract. But holding as I do that it is open to him to found his claim in
tort under the Occupiers' Liability Act 1957, I find that he was one-third to blame.
He is, therefore, entitled to recover two-thirds of his total damages. *e*

This brings me to the question of damages. [His Lordship then considered the
medical evidence and the effect of his injuries and concluded:] The agreed special
damages are £500, and there is no running or foreseeable loss of wages in the coming
year, so far as one can tell. I would add to this, for the pain and suffering that he
has sustained in the past, and his loss of amenity, both at work and at home, in the
future, the sum of £1,250. That makes a total of £1,750, of which the plaintiff is *f*
entitled to two-thirds, and taking it to the nearest pound I make that, and subject to
counsel's correction, £1,167, and for that sum I would give judgment to the plaintiff.

Judgment for the plaintiff for £1,167 with interest.

Solicitors: *W H Matthews & Co*, Sutton (for the plaintiff); *L Bingham & Co* (for the *g*
defendants).

Janet Harding   Barrister.

---

1   [1966] 2 All ER 283, [1966] 2 QB 370, *affg* [1965] 3 All ER 801   *h*

End of Volume One